HANDBOOKS IN OPERATIONS RESEARCH
AND MANAGEMENT SCIENCE
VOLUME 1

Handbooks in Operations Research and Management Science

Editors

G.L. Nemhauser
Georgia Institute of Technology

A.H.G. Rinnooy Kan
Erasmus University Rotterdam

Volume 1

ELSEVIER
AMSTERDAM - LAUSANNE - NEW YORK - OXFORD - SHANNON - SINGAPORE - TOKYO

Optimization

Edited by

G.L. Nemhauser
Georgia Institute of Technology

A.H.G. Rinnooy Kan
Erasmus University Rotterdam

M.J. Todd
Cornell Univerisity

ELSEVIER
AMSTERDAM - LAUSANNE - NEW YORK - OXFORD - SHANNON - SINGAPORE - TOKYO

ELSEVIER SCIENCE B.V.
S. Burgerhartstraat 25
P.O. Box 211, 1000 AE Amsterdam
The Netherlands

Library of Congress Cataloging-in-Publication Data

Optimization / edited by G.L. Nemhauser, A.H.G. Rinnooy Kan, M.J. Todd.
      p.   cm. – (Handbooks in operations research and management
science; v. 1)
   Bibliography: p.
   Includes index.
   ISBN 0-444-87284-1 (U.S.)
   1. Programming (Mathematics) 2. Mathematical optimization.
I. Nemhauser, George L. II. Rinnooy Kan, A. H. G., 1949-
III. Todd, M. J. IV. Series.
T57.7.O67 1989
519.7. – dc20   89-11916
                        CIP

First edition: 1989
Second impression: 1994
Third impression: 1998

ISBN 0-444-87284-1

Preface

Not surprisingly, the first volume in this series of handbooks is devoted to the topic of *Optimization*. No other class of techniques is so central to operations research and management science, both as a solution tool and as a modeling device. To translate a problem into a mathematical optimization model is characteristic of the discipline, located as it is at the crossroads of economics, mathematics and engineering.

Optimization deals with problems of minimizing or maximizing a function of several variables usually subject to equality and/or inequality constraints. This book collects together ten state-of-the-art expository articles on the most important topics in optimization, written by leading experts in the field. It therefore provides a primary reference for those performing research in some area of optimization or for those who have some basic knowledge of optimization techniques but wish to learn the most up-to-date and efficient algorithms for particular classes or problems. Each chapter starts at an introductory level suitable for master's level graduate students, but includes discussion of the references to the latest developments in the area.

Optimization has undergone very rapid development in recent years; articles in the book describe for instance the polynomial-time linear programming algorithms of Khachian and Karmarkar, the strongly-polynomial network flow algorithms of Tardos, Orlin, and others, and the techniques used to solve combinatorial and integer programming problems an order of magnitude larger than was possible just a few years ago.

The book includes chapters on unconstrained optimization, linear programming, constrained nonlinear programming, network flows, combinatorial optimization, integer programming, nondifferentiable optimization, stochastic programming, global optimization, and multicriterion optimization, thus providing broad coverage of finite-dimensional optimization theory and methods.

The first chapter, by Dennis and Schnabel, discusses the most basic optimization problems, those without constraints. A fundamental role is played by first-or second order Taylor approximations to the nonlinear functions involved, which can be viewed as model functions. This viewpoint leads to Newton's method for nonlinear equations or for nonlinear minimization. In order to avoid the calculation of matrices of derivatives at every iteration, methods using approximate derivative information are next considered, including quasi-Newton and finite-difference approximations; the latter can be very effective for large sparse problems. To obtain globally convergent algorithms, these methods must be modified to recognize the fact that only local information is used. Some control of the step size, either by a line search or by using trust regions, is necessary. The latter methods have become popular recently due to their excellent convergence properties. Dennis and Schnabel next discuss two methods that are not based on Taylor series; the Nelder–Mead simplex method can be very effective in low dimensions, and conjugate gradient approaches are attractive in high dimensions where matrices of derivatives cannot be stored. The final section discusses recent research on large-scale problems, data-fitting applications, secant updates, singular problems, and the exciting new area of parallel computation.

The second chapter, by Goldfarb and Todd, covers linear programming. After a discussion of typical linear programming formulations, a section on the structure of convex polyhedra leads into a geometrical treatment of Dantzig's simplex method and a description of efficient schemes to maintain and update representations of the basis inverse matrix. The key duality results and their use in sensitivity analysis are next presented. The ability to exploit special structure is essential in solving large-scale linear programming problems, and Goldfarb and Todd describe how to streamline the computations for problems with various upper bounding constraints and for network flow problems. Column generation techniques and the Dantzig–Wolfe decomposition principle are presented, and then the focus changes to discussion of the complexity of linear programming and recent results on the expected behavior of the simplex method. The final sections provide detailed descriptions of two polynomial algorithms – the ellipsoid method and Karmarkar's new projective algorithm for linear programming. While the former has attractive theoretical properties that have important consequences in combinatorial optimization (see Chapter 5), it seems to have no computational significance for linear programming. By contrast, the recent interior methods have considerable potential in practical computation.

Chapter 3, by Gill, Murray, Saunders and Wright, discusses constrained nonlinear programming. The first part covers the easier case of equality constraints. The optimality conditions lead to a system of linear equations in the fundamental case of quadratic programming, and the authors describe several numerical methods to solve these for both the optimal solution and the associated multiplier vector. Several classes of algorithms are presented for the general nonlinear case. Penalty methods reduce constrained to unconstrained problems, although either the penalty parameter must become infinite or a nonsmooth problem must be solved. Other methods involve solving a sequence of quadratic programming (one reason for the importance of such problems) or linearly constrained subproblems (e.g., the well-known MINOS code of Murtagh and Saunders). Finally, augmented Lagrangian methods are discussed. The second part considers inequality constraints, again first presenting the optimality conditions and the important special case of quadratic programming. The authors show how to extend sequential quadratic programming, sequential linearly-constrained and augmented Langrangian methods to the case of inequality constraints. Finally, barrier-function methods are discussed in detail. While unpopular for many years, these have received enormous attention recently because of their close relationship with the new polynomial approaches to linear programming arising from the work of Karmarkar.

Chapter 4, by Ahuja, Magnanti and Orlin, treats network optimization, concentrating on network flow problems and, in particular, the design of efficient algorithms. Network flow problems have provided: (1) a fertile domain for operations research applications, (2) significant theoretical developments, which, among other things, yielded the historical bridge between linear programming and combinatorial optimization and (3) a rich collection of efficient algorithms that, in part, has arisen from a synergism between optimization and computer science. The chapter begins with a section on applications and some key ideas from computer science that underlie the design of many algorithms. This is followed by a section that gives basic properties of network flow problems including the characterization of the structure of optimal solutions. The three fundamental problems of network flows, namely, the shortest path problem, the maximum flow problem and the minimum cost flow problem are presented in the subsequent sections. For each of these problems, the chapter gives an up-to-date account of recent algorithmic developments, especially from the perspective of computational complexity.

Polyhedral combinatorics is the subject of Chapter 5 by Pulleyblank. The goal of polyhedral combinatorics is to represent the feasible region of a discrete optimization problem by a polyhedron and thus reduce the problem to a linear program. The chapter systematically develops the techniques of polyhedral combinatorics with emphasis placed on min–max or dual relationships between pairs of problems, e.g. the famous max-flow min-cut theorem of network flow theory. The first two sections illustrate min–max relations and their connection to decision problems with 'good characterizations'. This is followed by two sections giving algebraic and geometric results on the description of polyhedra and the connection between linear systems and combinatorial optimization problems. Subsequent sections develop the techniques of separation and polarity and show how to obtain strengthened min–max relations by identifying essential inequalities and dual integrality. There are also sections on the dimension and adjacency relations of polyhedra, and the use of extended formulations and projection. The chapter closes with an appendix on computational complexity which provides prerequisite material for several other chapters as well.

Chapter 6 on integer programming, by Nemhauser and Wolsey, continues the development of discrete optimization to encompass more general and computationally difficult problems for which polyhedral results are, at best, incomplete. The chapter begins with model formulation with emphasis placed on representations that are 'good' with respect to the efficiency of solving them. The following sections present some theoretical aspects of integer programs, including complexity, relaxation and duality. They lay the foundation for the algorithms that are presented in the remainder of the chapter in sections on cutting plane, branch-and-bound and approximation algorithms.

Nondifferentiable optimization is the subject of Chapter 7, by Lemaréchal. Several examples of nonsmooth problems are discussed; they arise in minimax problems, for instance in data-fitting or exact penalty functions, and in various decomposition schemes, in particular in obtaining good bounds in integer programming via Langrangian relaxation. The reasons that smooth methods fail are then discussed, to motivate how successful algorithms can be designed. First special methods for composite optimization problems are described, which are close to classical smooth (constrained) nonlinear approaches. Then the general problem is considered, and the two main classes of algorithms, subgradient and bundle methods, are discussed in detail. Subgradient methods include algorithms employing the acceleration techniques of Shor, and in particular the ellipsoid method of Judin and Nemirovski (developed well before Khachian's use of it in linear programming); they also include cutting-plane methods, which leads to a discussion of notions of 'center', also fundamental in barrier-function methods and Karmarkar's algorithm and its extensions. Bundle methods, developed by Lemaréchal, Wolfe, Kiwiel and others, achieve a better approximation to a nonsmooth function by retaining a 'bundle' of useful previously-computed subgradients on which to base the current step. The final section describes recent work of Lemaréchal and his coworkers in attempting to build a 'second-order' model for nonsmooth optimization and raises a number of issues for future research.

Chapter 8, by Wets, is on the subject of stochastic programming, i.e. optimization models in which uncertainty about model parameters is represented by probabilistic tools. Mostly, one assumes that the true value of these parameters is only known (in the form of a realization of a random variable) after one or more initial decisions have been made. Hence, these decisions have to be based on a priori information about the random variables involved. In principle, the maximization or minimization of an expected objective function value is, of course, a deterministic problem, but its special structure warrants the development of a range of specialized techniques. Careful modelling of the prevailing uncertainty is always the first step towards a successful application. The chapter provides the mathematical basis for several of the better known solution methods, such as stochastic quasi-gradient methods, scenario aggregation (in which an attempt is made to focus on a subset of computationally relevant future scenarios), decomposition (e.g., Benders decomposition for linear stochastic programming, leading to the L-shaped algorithm, and the Lagrangean relaxation for the nonlinear case) and Monte Carlo methods. A final section deals with the important issues of stability and incomplete information.

Global optimization is the subject of Chapter 9, by Rinnooy Kan and Timmer. Here, the focus is on the seemingly impossibly difficult problem of finding the global optimum of an objective function which may have a large number of local optima. Additional assumptions on the objective function are obviously necessary to secure a deterministic guarantee of success, and several examples of such assumptions are given. E.g., if the objective function is Lipschitzian with known Lipschitz constant, then implicit enumeration techniques can be devised that solve the global problem in a finite amount of time. From a computational point of view, much better results have been obtained by dropping the requirement of a deterministic guarantee and substituting an asymptotic probabilistic guarantee, thus allowing the development of sampling-based techniques whose accuracy can only be guaranteed in the long run. The chapter pays special attention to a scheme that combines sampling with clustering techniques, through which prominent local optima are identified. But it also addresses a wide range of other, sometimes quite esoteric techniques, ranging from heuristics such as the method that tunnels through hills in search of better and better valleys, to more sophisticated approaches based on stochastic differential equations.

The final chapter, by Yu, reports on how to proceed in the (realistic) case of more than one objective function being present. Starting from a survey of useful results on binary relations, the chapter introduces a variety of approaches from multi-criterion decision making, including goal programming, maximum programming, interactive methods that elicit useful information from the decision maker, the construction of utility functions, the elimination of all but undominated feasible points, and special simplex methods to cover the linear programming subclass. A survey of this broad area cannot be exhaustive; however, the reader will find extensive references to the rest of the literature.

Overall, we hope that these articles provide a comprehensive yet lively and up-to-date discussion of the state-of-the-art in optimization. We believe that this book contains a coherent view of the important unifying ideas throughout the many facets of optimization and a guide to the most significant current areas of research.

G.L. Nemhauser
A.H.G. Rinnooy Kan
M.J. Todd

Contents

G.L. Nemhauser et al., Eds., *Handbooks in OR & MS, Vol. 1*
© Elsevier Science Publishers B.V. (North-Holland) 1989

Chapter I

A View of Unconstrained Optimization

J.E. Dennis Jr.

Department of Mathematical Sciences, Rice University, Houston, TX 77251, U.S.A.

Robert B. Schnabel

Department of Computer Science, Campus Box 430, University of Colorado, Boulder, CO 80309, U.S.A.

1. Preliminaries

1.1. Introduction

This chapter discusses the most basic nonlinear optimization problem in continuous variables, the *unconstrained optimization* problem. This is the problem of finding the minimizing point of a nonlinear function of n real variables, and it will be denoted

$$\text{given } f : \mathbb{R}^n \to \mathbb{R}, \quad \underset{x \in \mathbb{R}^n}{\text{minimize}} \ f(x) . \tag{1.1}$$

It will be assumed that $f(x)$ is at least twice continuously differentiable.

The basic methods for unconstrained optimization are most easily understood through their relation to the basic methods for a second nonlinear algebraic problem, the *nonlinear equations* problem. This is the problem of finding the simultaneous solution of n nonlinear equations in n unknowns, denoted

$$\text{given } F : \mathbb{R}^n \to \mathbb{R}^n , \quad \text{find } x_* \text{ for which } F(x_*) = 0 \tag{1.2}$$

where $F(x)$ is assumed to be at least once continuously differentiable. Therefore, this chapter also will discuss the nonlinear equations problem as necessary for understanding unconstrained optimization.

Unconstrained optimization problems arise in virtually all areas of science and engineering, and in many areas of the social sciences. In our experience, a

* Research supported by DOE DE-FG05-86ER25017, SDIO/IST/ARO DAAG-03-86-K-0113, and AFOSR 85-0243.
** Research supported by ARO contract DAAG 29-84-K-0140 and NSF grant CCR-8702403.

significant percentage of real-world unconstrained optimization problems are data fitting problems (see Section 6.2). The size of real-world unconstrained optimization problems is widely distributed, varying from small problems, say with n between 2 and 10, to large problems, say with n in the hundreds or thousands. In many cases, the objective function $f(x)$ is a computer routine that is expensive to evaluate, so that even small problems often are expensive and difficult to solve.

The user of an unconstrained optimization method is expected to provide the function $f(x)$ and a starting guess to the solution, x_0. The routine is expected to return an estimate of a *local minimizer* x_* of $f(x)$, the lowest point in some open subregion of $\mathbb{R}^n$. The user optionally may provide routines for evaluating the first and second partial derivatives of $f(x)$, but in most cases they are not provided and instead are approximated in various ways by the algorithm. Approximating these derivatives is one of the main challenges of creating unconstrained optimization methods. The other main challenge is to create methods that will converge to a local minimizer even if x_0 is far from any minimum point. This is referred to as the *global* phase of the method. The part of the method that converges quickly to x_*, once it is close to it, is referred to as the *local* phase of the method.

The emphasis of this chapter is on modern, efficient methods for solving unconstrained optimization problems, with particular attention given to the main areas of difficulty mentioned above. Since function evaluation so often is expensive, the primary measure of efficiency often is the number of function (and derivative) evaluations required. For problems with large numbers of variables, the number of arithmetic operations required by the method itself (aside from function evaluations) and the storage requirements of the method become increasingly important.

The remainder of the section reviews some basic mathematics underlying this area and the rest of continuous optimization. Section 2 discusses the basic local method for unconstrained optimization and nonlinear equations, Newton's method. Section 3 discusses various approaches to approximating derivatives when they aren't provided by the user. These include finite difference approximations of the derivatives, and secant approximations, less accurate but less expensive approximations that have proven to lead to more efficient algorithms for problems where function evaluation is expensive. We concentrate on the most successful secant method for unconstrained optimization, the 'BFGS' method, and as motivation we also cover the most successful secant method for nonlinear equations, Broyden's method. Sections 2 and 3 cover both small and large dimension problems, although the solution of small problems is better understood and therefore is discussed in more detail. Methods that are used when starting far from the solution, called global methods, are covered in Section 4. The two main approaches, line search methods and trust region methods, are both covered in some detail. In Section 5 we cover two important methods that do not fit conveniently in the Taylor series approach that underlies Sections 2 through 4. These are the Nelder–Mead simplex method, an important method for solving problems in very few variables, and conjugate gradient methods, one of the leading approaches to problems with very many variables. Section 6 briefly surveys a number of current research directions in unconstrained optimization. These include further approaches to solving problems in many variables, special methods for problems arising from data fitting, further issues in secant approximation of derivatives, the solution of problems where the Jacobian or Hessian matrix at the solution is singular, and the use of parallel computers in solving unconstrained optimization problems.

The scope of this chapter is limited in many important ways which are then addressed by other chapters of this book. We do not consider *constrained optimization* problems, where the domain of permissible solutions is limited to those variables *x* satisfying one or more equality or inequality constraints. Constrained optimization problems in continuous variables are discussed in Chapter 3; the techniques for solving these problems draw heavily upon the techniques for solving unconstrained problems. We do not consider problems where $f(x)$ is not differentiable; these are discussed in Chapter 9. We do not discuss methods that attempt to find the *global minimizer*, the lowest of the possibly multiple local minimizers of $f(x)$. Methods for finding the global minimizer, called *global optimization* methods, are discussed in Chapter 11. Finally, we do not consider problems where some or all of the variables are restricted to a discrete set of values, for example the integers; these problems must be solved by techniques such as those discussed in Chapters 2, 4, 5, and 6. It should be noted that in most nonlinear optimization problems solved today, the variables are continuous, $f(x)$ is differentiable, and a local minimizer provides a satisfactory solution. This probably reflects available software as well as the needs of practical applications.

A number of books give substantial attention to unconstrained optimization and are recommended to readers who desire additional information on this topic. These include Ortega and Rheinboldt (1970), Fletcher (1980), Gill, Murray, and Wright (1981), and Dennis and Schnabel (1983).

1.2. Taylor series models

Most methods for optimizing nonlinear differentiable functions of continuous variables rely heavily upon Taylor series expansions of these functions. This section briefly reviews the Taylor series expansions used in unconstrained (and constrained) optimization and in solving systems of nonlinear equations, and also reviews a few mathematical properties of these expansions. The material of this section is developed fully in Ortega and Rheinboldt (1970) or Dennis and Schnabel (1983).

The fundamental Taylor series approximation used in solving a system of nonlinear equations (1.2) is the first two terms of the Taylor series approximation to $F(x)$ around a current point x_c,

$$M_c^N(x) = F(x_c) + J(x_c)(x - x_c) .\qquad(1.3)$$

Here the notation M_c^N stands for the current Newton *model* because we will see in Section 2 that local methods for solving nonlinear equations are based on Taylor series models of the form (1.3), and Newton's method is based specifically on (1.3). $J(x_c)$ denotes the $n \times n$ *Jacobian* matrix of first partial derivatives of $F(x)$ at x_c; in general,

$$[J(x)]_{ij} = \frac{\partial F_i(x)}{\partial x_j} , \quad i = 1, \ldots, n , \quad j = 1, \ldots, n \tag{1.4}$$

where $F_i(x)$ denotes the i-th component function of $F(x)$.

The local convergence analysis of methods based upon (1.3) depends on the difference between $F(x)$ and $M_c^N(x)$. This and the next error bounds in this subsection, as well as most convergence results in continuous optimization, use the concept of Lipschitz continuity. A function G of the n-vector x is said to be Lipschitz continuous with constant γ in an open neighborhood $D \subset \mathbb{R}^n$, written $G \in \text{Lip}_\gamma(D)$, if for all $x, y \in D$,

$$|||G(x) - G(y)||| \leq \gamma \|x - y\| \tag{1.5}$$

where $\| \cdot \|$ and $||| \cdot |||$ are appropriate norms. Now if $J \in \text{Lip}_\gamma(D)$ in an open convex neighborhood $D \in \mathbb{R}^n$ containing x and x_c, using a vector norm $\| \cdot \|$ and the associated matrix norm, then it is a standard result that

$$\|M_c^N(x) - F(x)\| \leq \tfrac{1}{2}\gamma \|x - x_c\|^2 . \tag{1.6}$$

This result is similar to the familar Taylor series with remainder results for functions of one variable but requires no mention of higher derivatives of F.

The fundamental Taylor series expansion used in unconstrained optimization is the first three terms of the Taylor series of f around x_c,

$$m_c^N(x_c + d) = f(x_c) + g(x_c)^T d + \tfrac{1}{2} d^T H(x_c) d . \tag{1.7}$$

Here $g(x_c)$ denotes the n component *gradient* column vector of first partial derivatives of f evaluated at x_c; in general

$$[g(x)]_j = \frac{\partial f(x)}{\partial x_j} , \quad j = 1, \ldots, n . \tag{1.8}$$

Also, $H(x_c)$ denotes the $n \times n$ *Hessian* matrix of second partial derivatives of f evaluated at x_c; in general

$$[H(x)]_{ij} = \frac{\partial^2 f(x)}{\partial x_i \partial x_j} , \quad i = 1, \ldots, n , \quad j = 1, \ldots, n . \tag{1.9}$$

Note that $H(x)$ is symmetric if f is twice continuously differentiable.

If H is Lipschitz continuous with constant γ in an open convex neighborhood of $\mathbb{R}^n$ containing x and x_c, using the norm $\| \cdot \|$, then it is a standard result that

$$|m_c^N(x) - f(x)| \leq \tfrac{1}{6}\gamma \|x - x_c\|^3 . \tag{1.10}$$

This result is used in convergence analyses of unconstrained optimization methods.

The standard Taylor series with remainder results from the calculus of one variable also extend to real valued functions of multiple variables. For any direction $d \in \mathbb{R}^n$ there exist $t_1, t_2 \in (0, 1)$ for which

$$f(x + d) = f(x) + g(x + t_1 d)^{\mathrm{T}} d \tag{1.11}$$

and

$$f(x + d) = f(x) + g(x)^{\mathrm{T}} d + \tfrac{1}{2} d^{\mathrm{T}} H(x + t_2 d) d . \tag{1.12}$$

These results are the keys to the necessary and sufficient conditions for unconstrained minimization that we consider next.

1.3. Necessary and sufficient conditions for unconstrained optimization

Algorithms for solving the unconstrained minimization problem are based upon the first and second order conditions for a point x_* to be a local minimizer of f. These conditions are briefly reviewed in this section.

For x_* to be a local minimizer of f, it is necessary that $g(x_*) = 0$, where g denotes the gradient defined in (1.8).

Theorem 1.1. *Let $f : \mathbb{R}^n \to R$ be continuously differentiable, and let $y \in \mathbb{R}^n$. If $g(y) \neq 0$, then y is not a local minimizer of f.*

Proof. If $g(y) \neq 0$, then there exist directions $d \in \mathbb{R}^n$ for which $g(y)^{\mathrm{T}} d < 0$; an example is $d = -g(y)$. For any such direction d, we have from (1.11) that

$$f(y + td) - f(y) = t \cdot d^{\mathrm{T}} g(y + t_1 d) \tag{1.13}$$

for some $t_1 \in (0, t)$. Also by the continuity of g, there exists $\delta > 0$ such that $g(y + t_2 d)^{\mathrm{T}} d < 0$ for any $t_2 \in [0, \delta]$. Thus for any stepsize $t < \delta$,

$$f(y + td) < f(y) . \tag{1.14}$$

Therefore y cannot be a local minimizer of f.

Directions d for which $g(y)^{\mathrm{T}} d < 0$ are called descent directions for f at y. Descent directions play an important role in the global methods for unconstrained optimization discussed in Section 4.

The above argument with $d = g(x_*)$ also shows that $g(x_*) = 0$ is necessary for x_* to be a local maximizer of f. To distinguish between minimizers and maximizers it is necessary to consider the second derivative matrix $H(x_*)$ defined in (1.9). First we need the definition of a *positive definite* matrix.

Definition 1.1. Let $H \in \mathbb{R}^{n \times n}$ be symmetric. Then H is positive definite if $v^T H v > 0$ for all nonzero $v \in \mathbb{R}^n$.

There are several equivalent characterizations of positive definite matrices; another common one is that a symmetric matrix H is positive definite if and only if all of its eigenvalues are positive. If $v^T H v \geq 0$ for all v, H is said to be *positive semi-definite*. A negative definite or negative semi-definite matrix is one whose negative is positive definite or positive semi-definite.

Theorem 1.2. *Let $f : \mathbb{R}^n \to R$ be twice continuously differentiable, and let $x_* \in \mathbb{R}^n$. If $g(x_*) = 0$ and $H(x_*)$ is positive definite, then x_* is a local minimizer of f.*

Proof. By (1.12) for any $d \in \mathbb{R}^n$,

$$f(x_* + d) = f(x_*) + g(x_*)^T d + \tfrac{1}{2} d^T H(x_* + td) d \qquad (1.15)$$

for some $t \in (0, 1)$. By the continuity of H and the positive definiteness of $H(x_*)$, there exists $\delta > 0$ such that for any direction d with $\|d\| < \delta$ and any scalar t with $|t| \leq 1$, $H(x_* + td)$ is positive definite. Thus for any d with $\|d\| < \delta$, we have from (1.15) and $g(x_*) = 0$ that

$$f(x_* + d) > f(x_*) . \qquad (1.16)$$

Therefore x_* is a local minimizer of f.

By a similar argument it is easy to show that a necessary condition for x_* to be a local minimizer of a twice continuously differentiable f is that $g(x_*) = 0$ and $H(x_*)$ is positive semi-definite; if $H(x_*)$ is positive semi-definite but not positive definite, it is necessary to examine higher order derivatives to determine whether x_* is a local minimizer. If $g(x_*) = 0$ and $H(x_*)$ is negative definite, then the above argument shows that x_* is a local maximizer of f. If $g(x_*) = 0$ and $H(x_*)$ has both positive and negative eigenvalues, then x_* is said to be a *saddle point* of f. A saddle point is a local minimizer of some cross-section of f and a local maximizer of some other cross-section.

1.4. Rates of convergence

Most algorithms for nonlinear optimization problems in continuous variables are iterative. They generate iterates $x_k \in \mathbb{R}^n$, $k = 0, 1, 2, \ldots$, which are meant to converge to a solution x_*. In this case, the rate of convergence is of interest.

This subsection reviews the rates of convergence that are important in continuous optimization.

Definition 1.2. Let $x_k \in \mathbb{R}^n$, $k = 0, 1, \dots$. Then the sequence $\{x_k\}$ is said to converge to a point $x_* \in \mathbb{R}^n$ if for every i, the i-th component $(x_k - x_*)_i$ satisfies

$$\lim_{k \to \infty} (x_k - x_*)_i = 0 . \tag{1.17}$$

If, for some vector norm $\| \cdot \|$, there exist $K \geqslant 0$ and $\alpha \in [0, 1)$ such that for all $k \geqslant K$,

$$\|x_{k+1} - x_*\| \leqslant \alpha \|x_k - x_*\| , \tag{1.18}$$

then $\{x_k\}$ is said to converge *q-linearly* to x_* in the norm $\| \cdot \|$. If for some sequence of scalars $\{\alpha_k\}$ that converge to 0

$$\|x_{k+1} - x_*\| \leqslant \alpha_k \|x_k - x_*\| , \tag{1.19}$$

then $\{x_k\}$ is said to converge *q-superlinearly* to x_*. If $\{x_k\}$ converges to x_* and there exist $K \geqslant 0$, $p > 0$, and $\alpha \geqslant 0$ such that for all $k \geqslant K$,

$$\|x_{k+1} - x_*\| \leqslant \alpha \|x_k - x_*\|^p , \tag{1.20}$$

$\{x_k\}$ is said to converge to x_* with *q-order at least p*. If $p = 2$, then the convergence is called *q-quadratic*.

Note that q-order 1 is not the same as q-linear convergence and that a sequence may be linearly convergent in one norm but not another, but that superlinear and q-order $p > 1$ convergence are independent of the choice of norm on $\mathbb{R}^n$.

Most methods for continuously differentiable optimization problems are *locally q-superlinearly* or *locally q-quadratically convergent*, meaning that they converge to the solution x_* with a superlinear or quadratic rate if they are started sufficiently close to x_*. In practice, local quadratic convergence is quite fast as it implies that the number of significant digits in x_k as an approximation to x_* roughly doubles at each iteration once x_k is near x_*. Locally superlinearly convergent methods that occur in optimization also are often quickly convergent in practice. Linear convergence, however, can be quite slow, especially if the constant α depends upon the problem as it usually does. Thus linearly convergent methods are avoided wherever possible in optimization unless it is known that α is acceptably small. It is easy to define rates of convergence higher than quadratic, e.g. cubic, but they play virtually no role in practical algorithms for multi-variable optimization problems.

The prefix q preceding the words linear, superlinear, or quadratic stands for

'quotient' rates of convergence. This notation, commonly used in the optimization literature, is used to contrast with r ('root') rates of convergence, which
are a weaker form of convergence. A sequence is *r-linearly* convergent, for
example, if the errors $\|x_k - x_*\|$ are bonded by a sequence of scalars $\{b_k\}$
which converge q-linearly to 0. The bisection algorithm for solving scalar
nonlinear equations is a perfect example of an r-linear method since the
midpoints of the intervals containing a root can be taken as the iterates and
half the lengths of the intervals are a sequence of error bounds that converge
q-linearly to zero. Similar definitions apply to other r-rates of convergence; for
further detail see Ortega and Rheinboldt (1970). Thoughout this book if no
prefix precedes the words linear, superlinear, or quadratic, q-order convergence is assumed.

2. Newton's method

Among nonlinear optimization researchers, there is a strong suspicion that if
any iterative method for any problem in any field is exceptionally effective,
then it is Newton's method in some appropriate context. This is not to say that
Newton's method is always practical.

In this section we derive the Newton iteration for nonlinear equations
through the affine or linear Taylor series model (1.3) in Subsection 2.1, and the
Newton iteration for unconstrained optimization through the corresponding
quadratic model (1.7) in Subsection 2.2. We give a rigorous, but intuitive,
analysis of the local convergence of the corresponding iterative method, called
the Newton or Newton–Raphson method, and set the stage for a discussion of
some clever and effective modifications. The first of these modifications is
controlled inaccuracies in the solutions of the model problems. The resulting
inexact Newton method is the topic of Subsection 2.3, and it can greatly reduce
the expense of computing Newton steps far from the solution. This is especially
important for large problems, since then the Newton step itself is likely to be
computed by an iterative method. Some additional modifications are discussed
Section 3.

2.1. Newton's method for nonlinear equations

The underlying principle in most of continuous optimization is to build, at
each iteration, a local model of the problem which is valid near the current
solution estimate. The next, improved, solution estimate is gotten at least in
part from solving this local model problem.

For nonlinear equations, the local model is the Taylor series model (1.3).
The basic Newton iteration can be written as the root of this model,

$$x_+ = x_c - J(x_c)^{-1} F(x_c) .$$

But in keeping with the local model point of view, we prefer to think of it as:

$$\text{Solve} \quad J(x_c)s_c^N = -F(x_c)$$
$$\text{and set} \quad x_+ = x_c + s_c^N, \tag{2.1.1}$$

where s_c^N denotes the current Newton step, because this results directly from

$$0 = F(x_c) + J(x_c)(x - x_c). \tag{2.1.2}$$

Notice that we could also have solved directly for x_+ from (2.1.2), giving

$$J(x_c)x_+ = -F(x_c) + J(x_c)x_c. \tag{2.1.3}$$

In exact arithmetic, these formulations are equivalent as long as the columns of $J(x_c)$ span $\mathbb{R}^n$. In computer arithmetic, (2.1.1) generally is preferable. The reason is that in practice, we expect the magnitude of the relative error in solving a linear system $Az = b$ by a matrix factorization and backsolve technique to be estimated by

$$\frac{\|\hat{z} - z\|}{\|z\|} \approx \mu \|A\| \cdot \|A^{-1}\| \equiv \mu\kappa(A),$$

where $\hat{z}$ is the computed solution, the components of A and b are machine numbers, and μ is the quantity known as 'machine epsilon' or 'unit rounding error', i.e., the smallest positive number such that the computed sum of $1 + \mu$ is different from 1. Since we generally expect s_c^N to be smaller than x_+, we expect $\|\hat{s}_c^N - s_c^N\|$ in (2.1.1) to be smaller than $\|\hat{x}_+ - x_+\|$ in (2.1.3). Of course, we commit an error of magnitude $\mu\|x_c\|$ when we add $\hat{s}_c^N$ to x_c to get $\hat{x}_c$ in (2.1.1), but this does not involve $\kappa(J(x_c))$. Thus, we will think always of (2.1.1) as Newton's method with the linear system solved using an appropriate matrix factorization. This discussion is relevant for all the methods based on Taylor series type models. For a discussion of the computer solution of linear equations, see Stewart (1973) or Golub and Van Loan (1983).

The main theorem of this section is given below. We use the notation $N(x, \delta)$ to denote the open neighborhood about x of radius δ.

Theorem 2.1.1. *Let $F:\mathbb{R}^n \to \mathbb{R}^n$ be continuously differentiable in an open convex set $D \subset \mathbb{R}^n$. If there exists $x_* \in D$ and $r, \beta > 0$ such that $J \in \text{Lip}_\gamma(N(x_*, r))$, $F(x_*) = 0$, and $\|J(x_*)^{-1}\| \leq \beta$, then there exists $\varepsilon > 0$ such that for every $x_0 \in N(x_*, \varepsilon)$ the sequence $\{x_k\}$ generated by*

$$x_{k+1} = x_k - J(x_k)^{-1}F(x_k), \quad k = 0, 1, \dots,$$

is well defined, converges to x_*, *and satisfies*

$$\|x_{k+1} - x_*\| \leq \beta\gamma\|x_k - x_*\|^2 .$$

Proof. Since Lipschitz continuity implies continuity, and since the determinant is a continuous function of the entries of a matrix, it is easy to see that we can assume without loss of generality that $J(x)$ is invertible, and that $\|J(x)^{-1}\| \leq 2\beta$, for $x \in N(x_*, r)$.

Thus, if $x_k \in N(x_*, \varepsilon)$ for $\varepsilon \leq \min\{r, (2\beta\gamma)^{-1}\}$, x_{k+1} exists and

$$x_{k+1} - x_* = x_k - J(x_k)^{-1}F(x_k) - x_* + J(x_k)^{-1}F(x_*)$$
$$= J(x_k)^{-1}[F(x_*) - F(x_k) - J(x_k)(x_* - x_k)] .$$

Using (1.6), this gives

$$\|x_{k+1} - x_*\| \leq \|J(x_k)^{-1}\| \cdot \|F(x_*) - F(x_k) - J(x_k)(x_* - x_k)\|$$
$$\leq 2\beta \frac{\gamma}{2} \|x_k - x_*\|^2 \leq \beta\gamma\|x_k - x_*\|^2$$
$$\leq \beta\gamma\varepsilon\|x_k - x_*\| \leq \tfrac{1}{2}\|x_k - x_*\| ,$$

which establishes both convergence and the quadratic rate of convergence, and completes the proof.

Notice that we could apply Newton's method to $G(x) = J(x_*)^{-1}F(x)$, for which $G(x_*) = 0$, $J_G(x_*) \equiv G'(x_*) = I$, and $J_G \in \mathrm{Lip}_{\beta\gamma}N(x_*, r)$, and the identical sequence of iterates and convergence analysis would result. This emphasizes one of the major advantages of Newton's method; it is invariant under any affine scaling of the independent variable. Furthermore, note that the Lipschitz constant of J_G, $\beta\gamma$, is a relative measure of the nonlinearity of F as given by the change in J scaled by $J(x_*)^{-1}$. This is satisfying since we would like to believe that F is no more or less nonlinear if we change our basis.

In Section 3.3, we give an example of the application of Newton's method to a specific problem. It is compared there to Broyden's method which is superlinearly rather than quadratically convergent, but which does not share two major disadvantages of Newton's method. Broyden's method does not require the expensive and error-prone computation of $J(x)$ or the finite difference approximation discussed in section 3.2, and it reduces the work to solve the linear system (2.1.1) for the Newton step from $O(n^3)$ to $O(n^2)$ operations. Broyden's method shares the third major disadvantage of Newton's method in that both require a good initial guess x_0 to guarantee success. Because of this, they are referred to as *local methods*, and must be augmented by the techniques discussed in Section 4 to be successful from poor starting points.

2.2. Newton's method for unconstrained optimization

In this section, we look at Newton's method for the unconstrained minimization problem (1.1). It can be derived by applying the basic iteration (2.1.1) to the first order necessary condition $g(x) = 0$ for unconstrained optimization given by Theorem 1.1. This gives the basic Newton iteration

$$H(x_c)s_c^N = -g(x_c),$$

$$x_+ = x_c + s_c^N.$$

(2.2.1)

The Newton iteration (2.2.1) is equivalent to solving for a zero of the gradient of the Taylor series quadratic model $m_c^N(x_c + s)$ given by (1.7). If $H(x_c)$ is positive definite, then x_+ is a local minimizer of m_c^N by Theorem 1.2. In fact, it is the global minimizer of the model m_c^N since x_* is the only zero of ∇m_c^N. This leads to a very satisfying interpretation of Newton's method for (1.2) when $H(x_c)$ is positive definite. We construct a uniformly convex quadratic model m_c^N of f by matching function, gradient, and curvature to f at x_c, and then step to the global minimum of the model. Furthermore, since $H(x_c)$ is positive definite, then the Cholesky factorization can be used to solve for s_c^N in (2.2.1). We will see another advantage in Section 4.1. If $H(x_c)$ is not positive definite, however, then we have no reason to believe that (2.2.1) may not lead towards a saddle point or even a maximizer.

Newton's method has all the same disadvantages for unconstrained minimization that it had for nonlinear equations. That is, it is not necessarily globally convergent, and it requires $O(n^3)$ operations per iteration. In addition, we need $H(x_c)$ to be positive definite rather than just nonsingular. Furthermore, both first and second partial derivatives are required. We will address these issues in Sections 3 and 4.

We finish the subsection by stating a convergence theorem for (2.2.1) that follows directly from Theorems 1.2 and 2.1.1.

Theorem 2.2.1. *Let $f : \mathbb{R}^n \to \mathbb{R}$ be twice continuously differentiable in an open convex set $D \subset \mathbb{R}^n$. Assume there exists $x_* \in D$ and $r, \beta > 0$ such that $g(x_*) = 0$, $H(x_*)$ is positive definite, $\|H(x_*)^{-1}\| \le \beta$, and $H \in \mathrm{Lip}_\gamma N(x_*, r)$. Then, there exists $\varepsilon > 0$ such that for every $x_0 \in N(x_*, \varepsilon)$, the sequence $\{x_k\}$ generated by*

$$x_{k+1} = x_k - H(x_k)^{-1}g(x_k)$$

is well defined, converges to the local minimizer x_* of f, and satisfies

$$\|x_{k+1} - x_*\| \le \beta\gamma\|x_k - x_*\|^2.$$

2.3. The inexact Newton method

This section deals with a topic of importance in the use of Newton's method, particularly for large dimensional problems. In such cases, iterative methods like the Gauss–Seidel or conjugate direction methods are often the only practical way to solve the linear system (2.1.1) or (2.2.1) for the Newton step. The natural question is "how does the inaccuracy in the solution of (2.1.1) for the Newton step affect the rate of convergence in the exact Newton method".

An analysis by Dembo, Eisenstat and Steihaug (1982) leads to the following result.

Theorem 2.3.1. *Let the hypotheses of Theorem 2.1.1 hold, and let $\{\eta_k\}$ be a sequence of real numbers satisfying $0 \leq \eta_k \leq \eta < 1$. Then for some $\varepsilon > 0$, and any $x_0 \in N(x_*, \varepsilon)$, the inexact Newton method corresponding to any $\{x_k\}$ defined by*

$$J(x_k)s_k = -F(x_k) + r_k , \quad \text{where} \quad \frac{\|r_k\|}{\|F(x_k)\|} \leq \eta_k , \tag{2.3.1}$$

$$x_{k+1} = x_k + s_k ,$$

is well defined and converges at least q-linearly to x_*, with

$$\|x_{k+1} - x_*\| \leq \eta \|x_k - x_*\| .$$

If $\{\eta_k\}$ converges to 0, then $\{x_k\}$ converges superlinearly to x_*. If $\{\eta_k\}$ is $O(\{\|F(x_k)\|^p\}$ for $0 \leq p \leq 1$, then $\{x_k\}$ converges to x_* with q-order $1 + p$.

For example, this result guarantees quadratic convergence if at each iteration the approximate Newton step s_k satisfies

$$\frac{\|F(x_k) + J(x_k)s_k\|}{\|F(x_k)\|} < \min\{1, \|F(x_k)\|\} . \tag{2.3.2}$$

The quantity on the left of (2.3.2), sometimes called the relative residual, is usually monitored in practice when solving a linear system by iteration. Thus, the analysis gives a convenient stopping rule for the linear, or inner, iteration for solving the linear problem (2.1.1) which is embedded in the outer iteration for solving the nonlinear problem (1.2). All these results also apply to the unconstrained optimization problem.

Notice that here we are considering Theorem 2.3.1 as applied to an algorithm of the form (2.3.1) in which every $J(x_k)$ and $F(x_k)$ can be computed exactly but the linear systems in (2.1.1) can be solved only inexactly. In the next section, we will consider the effects of using approximations to the Taylor series model. There are strong connections between the analysis of those approaches and the inexact Newton method. In particular, for unconstrained optimization, (2.3.1) is equivalent to a statement about the inaccuracy in an approximation to the gradient $\nabla f(x_k)$.

3. Derivative approximations

In Section 2, we developed the local theory for Newton's method based on the appropriate Taylor series model. In practice, users prefer routines the approximate the required derivatives either by finite differences or by some of the clever and effective multi-dimensional secant methods. In this section, we will consider several instances of these approximations. They all involve using local models of the form

$$M_c(x_c + d) = F(x_c) + B_c d \tag{3.1}$$

to solve (1.2) or of the form

$$m_c(x_c + d) = f(x_c) + g(x_c)^T d + \tfrac{1}{2} d^T B_c d \tag{3.2}$$

to solve (1.1). We call these quasi-Newton models.

In Section 3.1, we will see the surprisingly simple local convergence analysis for any quasi-Newton iterative method

$$B_c s^{qN} = -F(x_c) \quad \text{or} \quad B_c s^{qN} = -g(x_c),$$
$$x_+ = x_c + s^{qN} \tag{3.3}$$

based on these local models. Section 3.2 will present the finite-difference Newton method.

Sections 3.3 and 3.4 will be devoted to some popular multi-dimensional secant methods for choosing B_c. We will concentrate on Broyden's method for nonlinear equations and the BFGS method for unconstrained optimization. Finally, in Section 3.5, we will consider the incorporation of sparsity into the approaches for approximating derivatives, including some techniques to save significantly on the cost of obtaining B_c by finite differences when $J(x_c)$ has a known sparsity structure.

Since we will deal with sparsity later in this section, it seems appropriate to introduce this important practical property here. In general, we say that a matrix is sparse if few of its entries, say less than 15%, are nonzero. For nonlinear systems of equations, $J(x)$ is sparse if most of the component equations F_i involve very few of the unknowns x_j. For unconstrained minimization, $H(x)$ is sparse if most variables do not interact in the sense that most of the cross partial derivatives are zero.

In practice, the sparsity of $J(x)$ or $H(x)$ is independent of the value of x, and this allows for some important savings at every iteration in solving for the Newton step in (2.1.1). Naturally, we wish to incorporate such a useful property into B_c in order to have the same savings in (3.3). Furthermore, it seems intuitive that we should be able to more efficiently approximate $J(x)$ or $H(x)$ if we know that most of its entries are zero.

To some extent, this is true. However, sparsity is entirely a property of the basis used to represent x, and so we may make our approximation methods more dependent than before on the specific representation of the problem. This can lead to practical difficulties of the sort that are usually called 'bad scaling'.

3.1. General convergence theory

In this section, we will consider general local models of the forms (3.1) and (3.2), and we will compare them to the appropriate Taylor series or Newton model to obtain one-step local convergence estimates for the associated iterative methods (3.3).

Lemma 3.1.1. *Let F satisfy the hypotheses of Theorem* 2.1.1 *and let* $M_c(x_c + d)$ *be given by* (3.1). *Then for any d,*

$$\|F(x_c + d) - M_c(x_c + d)\| \leq \tfrac{1}{2}\gamma\|d\|^2 + \|[B_c - J(x_c)]d\| . \qquad (3.1.1)$$

In addition, if B_c^{-1} *exists and* $e_c = x_* - x_c,\ e_+ = x_* - x_+$ *for* x_+ *defined by* (3.3), *then*

$$\|e_+\| \leq \|B_c^{-1}\| \left[\frac{\gamma}{2}\|e_c\| + \frac{\|[B_c - J(x_c)]e_c\|}{\|e_c\|} \right]\|e_c\|$$

$$\leq \|B_c^{-1}\|[\tfrac{1}{2}\gamma\|e_c\| + \|B_c - J(x_c)\|]\|e_c\| . \qquad (3.1.2)$$

Proof. First, we add and subtract the Newton model (1.3) to obtain

$$\|F(x_c + d) - M_c(x_c + d)\|$$
$$= \|F(x_c + d) - M_c^N(x_c + d) + M_c^N(x_c + d) - M_c(x_c + d)\|$$
$$\leq \|F(x_c + d) - M_c^N(x_c + d)\| + \|F(x_c) + J(x_c)d - M_c(x_c + d)\| .$$

This says that the error in the model (3.1) is bounded by the sum of the error in the Newton model and the difference between the Newton and quasi-Newton models. Now we apply (1.6) to the first term and simplify the second term to obtain (3.1.1).

To obtain (3.1.2), we use $F(x_*) = 0$ and (3.3) to write

$$x_+ - x_* = x_c - x_* - B_c^{-1}[F(x_c) - F(x_*)]$$
$$= B_c^{-1}[F(x_c + e_c) - (F(x_c) + B_c e_c)] ,$$

so

$$\|e_+\| \leq \|B_c^{-1}\| \cdot \|F(x_c + e_c) - M_c(x_c + e_c)\|$$

and (3.12) follows from (3.1.1).

The convergence theorems of Section 2 for Newton's method follow very simply from (3.1.2) with $B_c = J(x_c)$. Indeed, we have reduced the analysis of any quasi-Newton method (3.3) to an analysis of the corresponding Jacobian or Hessian approximation rule. There are three especially important properties to consider.

First, sometimes the error in B_c as an approximation to $J(x_c)$ is controlled by a parameter θ in the approximation rule; we will see that the finite difference Newton method fits this mold. In such rules, it is sometimes the case that if the sequence of iterates $\{x_k\}$ is well defined and converges to x_*, then $\{B_k\}$ converges to $J(x_*)$. Such rules are said to provide *consistent* Jacobian or Hessian approximations. (See Ortega and Rheinboldt (1970).) The reader will immediately see from (3.1.2) that consistent methods are at least q-superlinear. Of course, Newton's method is consistent and q-quadratic, if $J(x)$ is Lipschitz continuous.

Second, Dennis and Moré (1974) prove that a quasi-Newton method that is convergent with sufficient speed that $\Sigma_{k=1}^{\infty} \|e_k\| < \infty$ (r-linear is sufficient), will be q-superlinear if and only if the approximations are *directionally consistent* in the sense that

$$\lim_{k \to \infty} [B_k - J(x_k)] \frac{e_k}{\|e_k\|} = 0 . \qquad (3.1.3)$$

The sufficiency of (3.1.3) for superlinearity is obvious from (3.1.2). The proof of necessity is a bit harder.

These two consistency properties are useful especially for analyzing rates of convergence after convergence of $\{x_k\}$ has been established. It is clear that convergence can be established with much less. In particular, we see from (3.1.2) that if we could ensure that for every k such that $x_0, \ldots, x_k$ is defined, that B_k would be defined and

$$\|B_k^{-1}\| \leq \bar{\beta} , \quad \|B_k - J(x_k)\| \leq \bar{\delta} , \text{ and } \bar{\beta}\bar{\delta} < 1 , \qquad (3.1.4)$$

then we could get convergence by starting so close that

$$\alpha \equiv \bar{\beta}[\tfrac{1}{2}\gamma\|e_0\| + \bar{\delta}] < 1 .$$

This would ensure that $\|e_1\| \leq \alpha\|e_0\| < \|e_0\|$ and local q-linear convergence would follow by induction.

A useful property of the Jacobian or Hessian approximation rule in obtaining (3.1.4) is called *bounded deterioration*. There are various useful forms, but the one needed to analyze the Broyden, PSB, Schubert, and DFP secant methods is from Dennis and Walker (1981), p. 981, where the reader can find a proof of the next two theorems. It might be useful on first reading for the reader to think of the l_2 vector norm as the vector norm, its induced operator norm as the operator norm, and the Frobenius norm as the more general matrix norm. In fact, these choices are the ones needed for the Broyden, PSB, and Schubert methods.

Theorem 3.1.2. *Let F satisfy the hypotheses of Theorem 2.1.1, and let $B_* \in \mathbb{R}^{n \times n}$ have the property that B_*^{-1} exists and for some vector norm and the induced operator norm $|\cdot|$,*

$$|I - B_*^{-1} J(x^*)| \le r_* < 1 .$$

Let $U : \mathbb{R}^n \times \mathbb{R}^{n \times n} \to 2^{\mathbb{R}^{n \times n}}$ be defined in a neighborhood $N = N_1 \times N_2$ of (x_*, B_*) where $N_1 \subset \Omega$ and N_2 contains only nonsingular matrices. Assume that there is a norm $\|\cdot\|$ and that there are nonnegative constants α_1 and α_2 such that for each $(x, B) \in N$, and for $x_+ = x - B^{-1} F(x)$, every $B_+ \in U(x, B)$ satisfies

$$\|B_+ - B_*\| \le [1 + \alpha_1 \sigma(x, x_+)^p] \cdot \|B - B_*\| + \alpha_2 \sigma(x, x_+)^p$$

for $\sigma(x, x_+) = \max\{|x - x_*|, |x_+ - x_*|\}$.

Under these hypotheses, for any $r \in (r_*, 1)$, there exist constants ε_r, δ_r such that if $|x_0 - x_*| < \varepsilon_r$ and $|B_0 - B_*| < \delta_r$, then any iteration sequence $\{x_k\}$ defined by

$$x_{k+1} = x_k - B_k^{-1} F(x_k) , \quad B_{k+1} \in U(x_k B_k) ,$$

$k = 0, 1, \ldots$, exists, converges q-linearly to x_* with

$$|x_{k+1} - x_*| \le r \cdot |x_k - x_*| ,$$

and has the property that $\{|B_k|\}$ and $\{|B_k^{-1}|\}$ are uniformly bounded.

There are some important ways in which bounded deterioration may be weaker than consistency. In particular, the essence of the method might be to make B_k not be too much like $J(x_k)$, but to be more convenient to use in (3.3). For example, in the nonlinear Jacobi iteration, B_k is taken to be the diagonal of $J(x_k)$ so that s_k^{qN} defined by (3.3) only costs n divisions. Of course, the Jacobi iteration will not converge unless the partial derivatives on the diagonal dominate the rest of $J(x_k)$. A standard sufficient condition for this which implies (3.1.4) in the l_∞ norm is called strict diagonal dominance. See Ortega and Rheinboldt (1970). This brings up another point; the key to a convergence analysis for a specific method is often in choosing the proper norm.

Finally, some methods, like the BFGS secant method, are more readily analyzed by thinking of them as directly generating approximations to the inverse. The following theorem from Dennis and Walker (1981), p. 982, gives an inverse form of the bounded deterioration principle.

Theorem 3.1.3. *Let F satisfy the hypotheses of Theorem 2.1.1, and let K_* be an invertible matrix with $|I - K_* J(x_*)| \le r_* < 1$.*

Let $U: \mathbb{R}^n \times \mathbb{R}^{n \times n} \to 2^{\mathbb{R}^{n \times n}}$ be defined in a neighborhood $N = N_1 \times N_2$ of (x_*, K_*), where $N_1 \subset \Omega$. Assume that there are nonnegative constants α_1, α_2 such that for each (x, K) in N, and for $x_+ = x - KF(x)$, the function U satisfies

$$\|K_+ - K_*\| \leq [1 + \alpha_1 \sigma(x, x_+)^p] \|K - K_*\| + \alpha_2 \sigma(x, x_+)^p$$

for each $K_+ \in U(x, K)$. Then for each $r \in (r_*, 1)$ there exist positive constants ε_r, δ_r such that for $|x_0 - x_*| < \varepsilon_r$ and $|K_0 - K_*| < \delta_r$, any sequence $\{x_k\}$ defined by

$$x_{k+1} = x_k - K_k F(x_k), \quad K_{k+1} \in U(x_k, K_k),$$

$k = 0, 1, \ldots$, exists, converges q-linearly to x_* with $|x_{k+1} - x_*| \leq r|x_k - x_*|$, and has the property that $\{|K_k|\}$ and $\{|K_k^{-1}|\}$ are uniformly bounded.

3.2. Finite-difference derivatives

In Section 2 we saw that the local models furnished by the appropriate partial Taylor series are very useful in solving continuous optimization problems. Sometimes, the appropriate partial derivatives are not available analytically, and other times the user is not willing to be bothered providing them. Thus, most good optimization packages provide routines for estimating partial derivatives by finite differences. These routines may (and should) even be used to check for errors in any derivatives the user does provide.

In this section, we will discuss briefly the surprisingly rich topic of how to compute finite-difference approximations to first and second partial derivatives. We will discuss aspects of mathematical accuracy, numerical roundoff, convergence, and efficiency. We begin with accuracy.

We know from elementary calculus that

$$\lim_{h \to 0} \frac{F_i(x + he_j) - F_i(x)}{h} = \frac{\partial F_i(x)}{\partial x_j}$$

where e_j is the j-th column of the $n \times n$ identity matrix. This is called the *forward difference* approximation and it suggests approximating the j-th column of $J(x_c)$ by

$$\Delta_j F(x_c, h) = \frac{1}{h_j} [F(x_c + h_j e_j) - F(x_c)] \tag{3.2.1}$$

for an appropriately chosen vector h of finite-difference steps. We will use the notation $\Delta F(x_c, h)$ for the Jacobian approximation whose j-th column is given by (3.2.1).

Lemma 3.2.1. *Let $\|\cdot\|$ be a norm for which $\|e_j\| = 1$ and let $F \in \text{Lip}_\gamma(D)$ with $x_c, x_c + h_j e_j, j = 1, \ldots, n$, all contained in D. Then*

$$\|\Delta_j F(x_c, h) - J(x_c)e_j\| \leq \tfrac{1}{2}\gamma|h_j|. \tag{3.2.2}$$

Furthermore, if $\|\cdot\|$ is the l_1 vector norm $\|\cdot\|_1$ defined by $\|v\|_1 = \Sigma_{j=1}^{n} |v_j|$, then in the l_1 operator norm,

$$\|A\|_1 \equiv \max_{1\leq j\leq n} \sum_{i=1}^{n} |a_{ij}| ,$$

it follows that

$$\|\Delta F(x_c, h) - J(x_c)\|_1 \leq \tfrac{1}{2}\gamma\|h\|_\infty \tag{3.2.3}$$

where $\|h\|_\infty \equiv \max_{i\leq j\leq n} |h_j|$ is the l_∞ vector norm.

Proof. The proof follows easily from the Taylor series remainder (1.6), since

$$\|\Delta_j F(x_c, h) - J(x_c)e_j\| = |h_j|^{-1} \cdot \|F(x_c + h_je_j) - F(x_c) - J(x_c)h_je_j\|$$
$$= |h_j|^{-1} \cdot \|F(x_c + h_je_j) - M_c^N(x_c + h_je_j)\|$$
$$\leq |h_j|^{-1} \cdot \tfrac{1}{2}\gamma\|h_je_j\|^2 = \tfrac{1}{2}\gamma|h_j| .$$

We get (3.2.3) directly from (3.2.2) since $\|e_j\|_1 = 1$ and so

$$\|\Delta F(x_c, h) - J(x_c)\|_1 \equiv \max_{1\leq j\leq n} \|\Delta_j F(x_c, h) - J(x_c)e_j\|_1$$
$$\leq \max_{1\leq j\leq n} \tfrac{1}{2}\gamma|h_j| = \tfrac{1}{2}\gamma\|h\|_\infty .$$

Equation (3.2.1) also is used to approximate the gradient by the forward difference approximation

$$\delta_i f(x_c, h) = \frac{f(x_c + h_ie_i) - f(x_c)}{h_i} , \quad i = 1, \ldots, n . \tag{3.2.4}$$

Although this forward difference approximation is generally accurate enough, sometimes *central differences* are useful because of roundoff consideration we will discuss later. Since central differences are most often used for gradient approximations, we define them in that context.

$$\delta_i f(x_c, h) = \frac{f(x_c + h_ie_i) - f(x_c - h_ie_i)}{2h_i} \tag{3.2.5}$$

and

$$\delta f(x_c, h) = (\delta_1 f(x_c, h), \ldots, \delta_n f(x_c, h))^{\mathsf{T}} .$$

Lemma 3.2.2. *Let $\|\cdot\|$ be a norm such that $\|e_j\| = 1$, and let $H \in \mathrm{Lip}_\gamma(D)$, with $x_c, x_c + h_ie_i, i = 1, \ldots, n$, all contained in D. Then $\delta_i f(x_c, h)$ given by (3.2.5) obeys*

$$|\delta_i f(x_c, h) - \frac{\partial f}{\partial x_i}(x_c)| \leq \frac{1}{6}\gamma|h_i|^2 \tag{3.2.6}$$

and

$$\|\delta f(x_c, h) - g(x_c)\|_\infty \leq \frac{1}{6}\gamma\|h\|_\infty^2 .$$

Proof. Note that from (1.7), (1.8) we get

$$[f(x_c + h_i e_i) - m_c^N(x_c + h_i e_i)] - [f(x_c - h_i e_i) - m_c^N - h_i e_i)]$$

$$= f(x_c + h_i e_i) - f(x_c - h_i e_i) - 2h_i \frac{\partial f}{\partial x_i}(x_c) .$$

Thus, from (1.10) and the triangle inequality,

$$|f(x_c + h_i e_i) - f(x_c - h_i e_i) - 2h_i \frac{\partial f}{\partial x_i}(x_c)| = \frac{1}{3}\gamma|h_i|^3$$

from which (3.2.6) follows directly.

Note that the central difference gradient is more accurate than the forward difference gradient, but that it requires $2n$ rather than n evaluations of $f(x)$ if we assume that $f(x_c)$ is already available.

If the gradient is obtained analytically, but the Hessian is to be approximated by finite differences, then it can be approximated by applying (3.2.1) to $g(x)$, obtaining the approximation $\Delta g(x_c, h)$. However the matrix $\Delta g(x_c, h)$ would not be symmetric although $H(x_c)$ would be. In this case, a sensible strategy would be to use $B_c = \frac{1}{2}[\Delta g(x_c) + \Delta g(x_c)^T]$ as the Hessian approximation. Some theoretical justification for this comes from noting that B_c is the Frobenius norm projection of $\Delta g(x_c)$ into the subspace of all symmetric matrices. Thus, from the Pythagorean Theorem,

$$\|H(x_c) - B_c\|_F \leq \|H_c - \Delta g(x_c, h)\|_F$$

where

$$\|A\|_F \equiv \left(\sum_{i,j}|a_{ij}|^2\right)^{1/2} \tag{3.2.7}$$

is the Frobenius norm. This norm will be useful later when we again want an inner product structure on the vector space of real matrices.

It is also possible to obtain an approximate Hessian using $\frac{1}{2}(n^2 + 3n)$ evaluations of $f(x)$. By expanding the Taylor series through third order terms, a stronger version of (3.2.9–10) can be proven in which the $|h_i|^2/|h_j|$ and $|h_j|^2/|h_i|$ terms are removed, and the constant is different.

Lemma 3.2.3. *Let* $\| \cdot \|$ *be a norm such that* $\|e_i\| = 1$ *and let* $H \in \mathrm{Lip}_\gamma(D)$ *with* $x_c, x_c + h_i e_i, x_c + h_j e_j,$ *and* $x_c + h_i e_i + h_j e_j, i, j = 1, \ldots, n,$ *all contained in D. Let*

$$[H_c]_{ij} \equiv \frac{f(x_c + h_i e_i + h_j e_j) - f(x_c + h_i e_i) - f(x_c + h_j e_j) + f(x_c)}{h_i h_j} .$$

(3.2.8)

Then,

$$|[H_c]_{ij} - [H(x_c)]_{ij}| \leq \frac{\gamma}{6} \left(2 \frac{|h_i|^2}{|h_j|} + 3|h_i| + 3|h_j| + 2 \frac{|h_j|^2}{|h_i|} \right) .$$

(3.2.9)

If the $l_1, l_\infty,$ *or Frobenius norm is used, then*

$$\|H_c - H(x_c)\| \leq \frac{n\gamma}{6} \max_{i,j} \left(2 \frac{|h_i|^2}{|h_j|} + 3|h_i| + 3|h_j| + 2 \frac{|h_j|^2}{|h_i|} \right) .$$

(3.2.10)

Proof. The argument is very much like that used in the previous proof. Let $s_i = h_i e_i, s_j = h_j e_j$ and $s_{ij} = s_i + s_j,$ then

$$[f(x_c + s_{ij}) - m_c^N(x_c + s_{ij})] - [f(x_c + s_i) - m_c^N(x_c + s_i)]$$
$$- [f(x_c + s_j) - m_c^N(x_c + s_j)]$$
$$= f(x_c + s_{ij}) - f(x_c + s_i) - f(x_c + s_j) + f(x_c) - h_i h_j [H(x_c)]_{ij} .$$

From the triangle inequality and (1.10), we get

$$|h_i h_j [H_c] - h_i h_j [H(x_c)]_{ij}| \leq \tfrac{1}{6} \gamma [\|s_{ij}\|^3 + \|s_i\|^3 + \|s_j\|^3]$$
$$\leq \tfrac{1}{6} \gamma [(\|s_i\| + \|s_j\|)^3 + \|s_i\|^3 + \|s_j\|^3]$$
$$\leq \tfrac{1}{6} \gamma [(|h_i| + |h_j|)^3 + |h_i|^3 + |h_j|^3]$$

from which (3.2.9) and (3.2.10) follow.

Now we have seen some useful rules for approximating derivatives by differences of function values, and we have analyzed the accuracy of these approximations. So far, it seems as though the obvious thing to do is to choose the vector h to be very small in order to make the approximate derivatives more accurate. The difficulty is that these approximation rules are certain to lose more accuracy due to finite-precision cancellation errors as h becomes smaller.

In Section 2.1, we introduced *machine epsilon* μ as the smallest positive quantity for which the floating-point sum $1 + \mu$ would be different from the floating point representation of 1. Thus, even if we ignore the fact that all functions are to be evaluated in finite-precision, we see that $|h_j|$ must be large enough that $x_c + h_j e_j$ is not the same as x_c in finite precision arithmetic, or else the numerator in the forward difference would be zero. This means that $|h_j| \geqslant \mu |[x_c]_j|$.

If we remember that function values are computed in finite precision with t digits then we can believe that if we obtain a value of say $F_i(x_c) = (0.d_1 \ldots d_t)10^e$, it is reasonable that d_t or d_{t-1} are much less likely to be correct than d_1 or d_2. This can lead to real problems when coupled with the fact that $F_i(x_c + h_j e_j) = (0.d_1' \ldots d_t')10^{e'}$ will probably have $e' = e$, and $d_k' = d_k$ for $k = 1, 2, \ldots, \bar{t} < t$, with $\bar{t}$ closer to t the smaller $|h_j|$ is. In other words, the smaller we take $|h_j|$, the more of the most accurate leading digits of $F(x)$ are canceled out by the subtraction $F_i(x_c + h_j e_j) - F_i(x_c)$ in the numerator of the forward-difference formula (3.2.1). This means that the difference will have at most $t - \bar{t}$ meaningful digits, which are computed using the less trustworthy trailing digits of $F(x)$. Thus, $|h_j|$ must at least be large enough so that $F_i(x_c)$ and $F_i(x_c + h_j e_j)$ differ in some trustworthy digits.

The standard rule to use in setting the entire vector h for (3.2.1) or (3.2.4) is

$$h_c = \mu_F^{1/2} x_c , \tag{3.2.11}$$

where μ_F is the relative accuracy in the subroutine used to evaluate F or f. In other words, if the routine is accurate to $t_F < t$ digits, then $\mu_F = 10^{-t_F}$ while if it is accurate in all its digits we take $\mu_F = \mu$. If some component $[x]_i = 0$, then we take $h_i = \mu_F^{1/2}$ for lack of a better choice. This rule attempts to balance the mathematical and numerical error in (3.2.1); see e.g. Dennis and Schnabel (1983).

The reader will see that all these numerical difficulties clearly are compounded in the Hessian approximation (3.2.8), which calls for a larger relative magnitude of h since the inaccuracies in the numerator are divided by h^2. We also see that the bound in (3.2.9) points toward choosing all the components of h to be about the same magnitude. Thus, we recommended that x_c be scaled as well as possible, and an analysis suggests that

$$h_c = \mu_F^{1/3} x_c . \tag{3.2.12}$$

This rule is also suggested for use in (3.2.5).

Next we state a theorem on the theoretical rate of convergence of finite-difference methods. The reader can easily furnish a proof by combining Lemma 3.2.1 with Lemma 3.1.1.

Theorem 3.2.4. *Let F and x_* obey the hypotheses of Theorem 2.1.1 in the l_1 norm. There exists $\varepsilon, \eta > 0$ such that if $\{h_k\}$ is a sequence in $\mathbb{R}^n$ with $0 \leqslant \|h_k\|_\infty \leqslant \eta$, and $x_0 \in N(x_*, \varepsilon)$, then the sequence $\{x_k\}$ generated by*

$$B_k e_j = \begin{cases} \dfrac{F(x_k + (h_k)_j e_j) - F(x_k)}{(h_k)_j} \,, & (h_k)_j \neq 0 \,, \\[2ex] J(x_k) e_j \,, & (h_k)_j = 0 \,, \end{cases}$$

$$x_{k+1} = x_k - B_k^{-1} F(x_k) \,, \quad k = 0, 1, \dots \,,$$

is well defined and converges q-linearly to x_*. If $\lim_{k \to \infty} \|h_k\|_\infty = 0$, then the convergence is q-superlinear. If there exists some constant C_1 such that $\|h_k\|_\infty \leq C_1 \|x_k - x_*\|_1$, or equivalently, a constant C_2 such that $\|h_k\|_\infty \leq C_2 \|F(x_k)\|_1$, then the convergence is q-quadratic.

Even though Theorem 3.2.4 does not consider the finite precision effects discussed above, it reflects the practical experience with finite difference approximations: if the stepsizes are properly selected, then finite difference methods give similar performance to the same methods using analytic derivatives. The main disadvantage of using these approximations is their cost. The forward difference approximations (3.2.1) to $J(x)$ or (3.2.4) to $g(x)$ require n additional evaluations of $F(x)$ or $f(x)$, respectively, while the central difference approximation (3.2.5) to $g(x)$ requires $2n$ additional evaluations of $f(x)$. The approximations to $H(x)$ require either n additional evaluations of $g(x)$ for (3.2.1) or, for (3.2.8), $\frac{1}{2}(n^2 + 3n)$ evaluations of $f(x)$. These costs can be considerable for problems where function evaluation is expensive. In the remainder of this section we discuss cheaper approximations to $J(x)$ and $H(x)$ that may be used instead.

It turns out that if $g(x)$ is not available analytically, it is almost always approximated by finite differences, because an accurate gradient is crucial to the progress and termination of quasi-Newton methods, and the secant approximations that we discuss next are not accurate enough for this purpose. In Section 5.1 we discuss a class of methods that does not require gradients.

3.3. Broyden's method

In one dimension, the secant method is an effective local method for solving nonlinear equations. It can be viewed as a forward-difference method in which the step size h_+ used in constructing the new iterate from x_+ is taken to be $x_c - x_+$, so that the local model derivative B_+ is $[F(x_+ + (x_c - x_+)) - F(x_+)]/[x_c - x_+]$. Thus, no extra F values are needed to determine B_+ and build the new local model since $F(x_+ + h_+) = F(x_c)$.

From the local model point of view, the scant method follows from assuming that we will determine the approximate derivative B_+ in the new model of $F(x_+ + d)$, $M_+(x_+ + d) = F(x_+) + B_+ d$, by requiring $M_+(x_c)$ to match $F(x_c)$. This means that

$$F(x_c) = M_+(x_+ + (x_c - x_+)) = F(x_+) + B_+(x_c - x_+)$$

is used to determine B_+. This results in the system of linear equations

$$B_+ s_c = y_c \tag{3.3.1}$$

where $s_c = x_+ - x_c$ and $y_c = F(x_+) - F(x_c)$.

For $n = 1$, (3.3.1) uniquely determines B_+. For $n > 1$, there is an $n \times (n - 1)$ dimensional linear manifold in $\mathbb{R}^{n \times n}$ of solutions B to (3.3.1). The most commonly used secant method for systems of nonlinear equations, Broyden's method, makes a specific selection of B_+ from this manifold which costs only a small multiple of n^2 to compute and is a rank-one correction to B_c. It also has a very elegant geometric interpretation given by the following lemma from Dennis and Moré (1977).

Lemma 3.3.1. *Let* $B_c \in \mathbb{R}^{n \times n}$, s_c, $y_c \in \mathbb{R}^n$, $s \neq 0$. *Then Broyden's update*

$$B_+ = B_c + \frac{(y_c - B_c s_c) s_c^T}{s_c^T s_c} \tag{3.3.2}$$

is the unique solution to

$$\min \|B - B_c\|_F \quad \text{subject to } B s_c = y_c .$$

Proof. If $B s_c = y_c$, then $B_+ - B_c = [B - B_c] s_c s_c^T / s_c^T s_c$ and so

$$\|B_+ - B_c\|_F \leq \|B - B_c\|_F \cdot \left\| \frac{s_c s_c^T}{s_c^T s_c} \right\|_2 = \|B - B_c\|_F .$$

Thus, Broyden's method generalizes the one-dimensional secant method by changing the current derivative approximation as little as possible in the Frobenius norm consistent with satisfying the secant or quasi-Newton equation (3.3.1). For this reason it is called a *least-change secant update*. Of course, this leaves the problem of finding B_0 to start the process. Generally B_0 is obtained by finite differences.

Broyden, Dennis and Moré (1973) proved that Broyden's method is locally q-superlinearly convergent. The proof is in two parts, and it is typical of all the least-change secant method proofs. First, one establishes local q-linear convergence by proving bounded deterioration and applying Theorem 3.1.2. Then, one gets q-superlinearity by establishing (3.1.5).

Lemma 3.3.2. *Let* $D \subset \mathbb{R}^n$ *be a convex domain containing* x_c, x_+, *and* x_*. *Let* $J \in \text{Lip}_\gamma(D)$, $B_c \in \mathbb{R}^{n \times n}$, *and let* B_+ *be given by Broyden's update* (3.3.2). *Then,*

$$\|B_+ - J(x_*)\|_F \leq \|B_c - J(x_*)\|_F + \gamma \sigma(x_c, x_+) . \tag{3.3.3}$$

Proof. Remember that $\sigma(x_c, x_+) \equiv \max\{\|x_c - x_*\|_2, \|x_+ - x_*\|_2\}$.

$$B_+ - J(x_*) = B_c - J(x_*) + \frac{(y_c - J(x_*)s_c + J(x_*)s_c - B_c s_c)s_c^T}{s_c^T s_c}$$

$$= [B_c - J(x_*)]\left[I - \frac{s_c s_c^T}{s_c^T s_c}\right] + \frac{(y_c - J(x_*)s_c)s_c^T}{s_c^T s_c}$$

$$= [B_c - J(x_*)]\left[I - \frac{s_c s_c^T}{s_c^T s_c}\right]$$

$$+ \int_0^1 [(J(x_c + ts_c) - J(x_*)]\, dt\, \frac{s_c s_c^T}{s_c^T s_c}.$$

It is then straightforward to obtain

$$\|B_+ - J(x_*)\|_F \leq \|B_c - J(x_*)\|_F \cdot \left\|I - \frac{s_c s_c^T}{s_c^T s_c}\right\|_2$$

$$+ \gamma \int_0^1 \|x_c + ts_c - x_*\|_2\, dt \cdot \left\|\frac{s_c s_c^T}{s_c^T s_c}\right\|_2$$

$$\leq \|B_c - J(x_*)\|_F + \gamma\sigma(x_+, x_c),$$

since $I - s_c s_c^T/s_c^T s_c$ and $s_c s_c^T/s_c^T s_c$ are l_2 projection matrices and so they have unit norm.

This completes the proof, but we can't resist some comments about the geometry of the proof and its relation to the more general derivation of least-change secant methods. Notice that

$$B_+ - J(x_*) = [B_+ - J(x_*)]\left[I - \frac{s_c s_c^T}{s_c^T s_c}\right] + [B_+ - J(x_*)]\left[\frac{s_c s_c^T}{s_c^T s_c}\right].$$

In $\mathbb{R}^{n \times n}$ with the Frobenius norm inner product, this is just the orthogonal decomposition of $B_+ - J(x_*)$ into its projection into the subspace of matrices that annihilate s_c and the orthogonal complement of the annihilators of s_c. But the essence of Broyden's method is that B_+ has the same projection as B_c into the annihilators of s_c. Thus,

$$B_+ - J(x_*) = [B_c - J(x_*)]\left[I - \frac{s_c s_c^T}{s_c^T s_c}\right] + [B_+ - J(x_*)]\frac{s_c s_c^T}{s_c^T s_c}. \qquad (3.3.4)$$

Now the norm of the first term on the right hand side of (3.3.4) will be smaller than $\|B_c - J(x_*)\|$, while the magnitude of the second term is totally dependent on the sagacity of our choice of $y_c = B_+ s_c$ as an approximation to $J(x_*)s_c$.

In general, the idea of a least-change secant method is to adopt an inner product structure on matrix space and a secant condition (3.3.1). In addition, one may require B_c and B_+ to be in some closed linear manifold A of matrices defined by another desirable property like symmetry or sparsity. One then obtains B_+ by orthogonally projecting B_c into the generalized intersection of A with the matrices that satisfy (3.3.1), using the chosen inner product. By generalized intersection, we mean the intersection of the set of secant matrices with A if this intersection is nonempty, and the projection of the set of secant matrices into A otherwise.

The next subsection contains another application of this approach. Dennis and Schnabel (1979) derive many more interesting updates based on this approach. Dennis and Walker (1981) give conditions on the secant equations and the inner products used at each iteration so that the resulting quasi-Newton method has the same local q-linear convergence rate as the method that uses $B_k \equiv B_*$. Schnabel (1983) considers multiple secant equations. Dennis and Walker (1985) consider the case when an appropriate secant condition is imperfectly known. Grzegorski (1985) and Flachs (1986) relax the conditions on A to convexity.

Now we return to the consideration of Broyden's method. In order to complete the proof of superlinear convergence, we need to show that (3.1.3) holds. In fact, it is not hard to show that

$$\lim_{k \to \infty} \frac{\|[B_k - J(x_*)]s_k\|}{\|s_k\|} = 0 \qquad (3.3.5)$$

is also equivalent to superlinear convergence under the same hypotheses. Notice that

$$\frac{\|[B_k - J(x_*)]s_k\|_2}{\|s_k\|_2} = \left\| \frac{[B_k - J(x_*)]s_k s_k^T}{s_k^T s_k} \right\|_F \qquad (3.3.6)$$

and so (3.3.5) seems a reasonable condition to try for in light of our previous discussion. For completeness, we state the theorem. For an elementary complete proof, see page 177 of Dennis and Schnabel (1983).

Theorem 3.3.3. *Let F satisfy the hypotheses of Theorem 2.1.1. There exist positive constants ε, δ such that if $\|x_0 - x_*\|_2 < \varepsilon$ and $\|B_0 - J(x_0)\| < \delta$, then the sequence $\{x_k\}$ generated by Broyden's method*

$$x_{k+1} = x_k - B_k^{-1} F(x_k) \,,$$

$$B_{k+1} = B_k + \frac{(y_k - B_k s_k)s_k^T}{s_k^T s_k} \,, \quad k = 0, 1, \ldots \,,$$

$$y_k = F(x_{k+1}) - F(x_k) \,, \quad s_k = x_{k+1} - x_k \,,$$

is well defined and converges q-superlinearly to x_*.

Proof. We will sketch the proof. First, notice that Lemma 3.3.2 shows that the hypotheses of the bounded deterioration result, Theorem 3.1.2, holds with $B_* = J(x_*)$. Thus the method is at least q-linearly convergent. Let $E_k = B_k - J(x_*)$.

In order to show (3.3.5), we need a technical lemma. From the Pythagorean Theorem in $\mathbb{R}^{n \times n}$, we have

$$\left\| E_k \left(I - \frac{s_k s_k^T}{s_k^T s_k} \right) \right\|_F = \left(\|E_k\|_F^2 - \left\| \frac{E_k s_k s_k^T}{s_k^T s_k} \right\|_F^2 \right)^{1/2}$$

$$\leq \|E_k\|_F - \frac{1}{2\|E_k\|_F} \left\| \frac{E_k s_k s_k^T}{s_k^T s_k} \right\|_2^2 , \tag{3.3.7}$$

where the inequality follows from: $\alpha \geq |\beta| \geq 0$ implies $(\alpha^2 - \beta^2)^{1/2} \leq \alpha - \beta^2/2\alpha$.

By (3.3.4), (3.3.6), and (3.3.7),

$$\|E_{k+1}\|_F \leq \left\| E_k \left(I - \frac{s_k s_k^T}{s_k^T s_k} \right) \right\|_F + \left\| E_{k+1} \frac{s_k s_k^T}{s_k^T s_k} \right\|_F$$

$$\leq \|E_k\|_F - \frac{1}{2\|E_k\|_F} \left(\frac{\|E_k s_k\|_2}{\|s_k\|_2} \right)^2 + \frac{\|E_{k+1} s_k\|_2}{\|s_k\|_2} .$$

Thus, from some manipulation and the proof of Lemma 3.3.2,

$$\left(\frac{\|E_k s_k\|_2}{\|s_k\|_2} \right)^2 \leq 2\|E_k\|_F (\|E_k\|_F - \|E_{k+1}\|_F + \gamma \sigma(x_{k+1}, x_k)) .$$

Now, since Lemma 3.3.2 shows that $\{\|B_k\|_F\}$ is uniformly bounded and $\|x_k - x_*\|_2$ converges to zero at least q-linearly, $\{\|E_k\|_F\}$ is uniformly bounded by some b and $\sum_{j=0}^{\infty} \sigma(x_{j+1}, x_j) < \infty$. This gives that

$$\sum_{j=0}^{k} \left(\frac{\|E_j s_j\|_2}{\|s_j\|_2} \right)^2 \leq 2b \left(\|E_0\|_F - \|E_{k+1}\|_F + \gamma \sum_{j=0}^{k} \sigma(x_{k+1}, x_k) \right) < \infty ,$$

and (3.3.5) follows.

A natural question is whether $\{B_k\}$ always converges to $J(x_*)$. The answer is that it does not and that the final approximation may be arbitrarily far from $J(x_*)$, cf. p. 185 of Dennis and Schnabel (1983). On the same page is the following example which provides a comparison with Newton's method.

Let

$$F(x) = \left(\begin{array}{c} x_1^2 + x_2^2 - 2 \\ e^{x_1 - 1} + x_2^3 - 2 \end{array} \right) ,$$

Table 3.3.1

Broyden's method			Newton's method	
1.5	2.0	x_0	1.5	2.0
0.8060692	1.457948	x_1	0.8060692	1.457948
0.7410741	1.277067	x_2	0.8901193	1.145571
0.8022786	1.159900	x_3	0.9915891	1.021054
0.9294701	1.070406	x_4	0.9997085	1.000535
1.004003	1.009609	x_5	0.999999828	1.000000357
1.003084	0.9992213	x_6	0.99999999999992	1.0000000000002
1.000543	0.9996855	x_7	1.0	1.0
0.99999818	1.00000000389	x_8		
0.9999999885	0.999999999544	x_9		
0.99999999999474	0.99999999999998	x_{10}		
1.0	1.0	x_{11}		

which has a root $x_* = (1, 1)^{\mathrm{T}}$. The sequences of points generated by Broyden's method and Newton's method from $x_0 = (1.5, 2)^{\mathrm{T}}$ with $B_0 = J(x_0)$ for Broyden's method, are shown in Table 3.3.1.

The final approximation to the Jacobian generated by Broyden's method is

$$B_{10} \approx \begin{bmatrix} 1.999137 & 2.021829 \\ 0.9995643 & 3.011004 \end{bmatrix}, \quad \text{whereas} \quad J(x_*) = \begin{bmatrix} 2 & 2 \\ 1 & 3 \end{bmatrix}.$$

We proved superlinear convergence by proving that

$$\sum_{k=0}^{\infty} \left(\frac{\|E_k s_k\|}{\|s_k\|} \right)^2 < \infty .$$

It is easy to see that if $\Sigma_{k=0}^{\infty} (\|E_k s_k\| / \|s_k\|) < \infty$, then $\{B_k\}$ converges, because

$$B_{k+1} - B_k = \frac{(y_k - B_k s_k) s_k}{s_k^{\mathrm{T}} s_k} = -\frac{E_k s_k s_k^{\mathrm{T}}}{s_k^{\mathrm{T}} s_k} + \mathrm{O}(\sigma(x_{k+1}, x_k)) .$$

Furthermore, if we just knew how fast $\|E_k s_k\| / \|s_k\|$ goes to zero, we could say more about the rate of convergence of $\{x_k\}$ to x_*. The only related result we know about is due to Gay (1979). He proves that $x_{2n+1} \equiv x_*$ if $J(x)$ is constant for all x, i.e., F is affine. This allows him to prove the $2n$-step q-quadratic convergence of $\{x_k\}$ to x_*, and that in turn implies r-order at least $2^{1/2n}$.

Broyden's method is very popular in practice, for two main reasons. First, it generally requires fewer function evaluations than a finite difference Newton's method. Second, it can be implemented in ways that require only $\mathrm{O}(n^2)$ arithmetic operations per iteration. We conclude this section by mentioning three basic ways to do this.

If n is small enough to allow storage of a full $n \times n$ Jacobian approximation and use of a QR factorization to solve (3.3), then we recommend a scheme due to Gill, Golub, Murray, and Saunders (1974). In this scheme, one has

$B_c = Q_c R_c$ but wants $B_+ = Q_+ R_+$ and, since

$$B_+ = B_c + \frac{(y_c - B_c s_c) s_c^T}{s_c^T s_c} \equiv B_c + uv^T \, ,$$

it follows that

$$B_+ = Q_c [R_c + (Q_c^T u) v^T] \equiv Q_c [R_c + wv^T] \, .$$

Now a low multiple of n^2 operations is sufficient to get a QR factorization of a rank-one update to an upper triangular matrix and so

$$B_+ = Q_+ R_+ \quad \text{where} \quad R_c + wv^T = \tilde{Q} R_+ \text{ and } Q_+ = Q_c \tilde{Q} \, .$$

The second and third ways of implementing the update are both based on the Sherman–Morrison–Woodbury formula (cf. Dennis and Schnabel (1983), p. 188). It is easy to see that if B is nonsingular and $u, v \in \mathbb{R}^n$, then $B + uv^T$ is nonsingular if and only if $1 + v^T B^{-1} u \equiv \omega \neq 0$. Then,

$$(B + uv^T)^{-1} = B^{-1} - \frac{1}{\omega} (B^{-1} u) v^T B^{-1} \tag{3.3.8}$$

$$= \left[I - \frac{1}{\omega} (B^{-1} u) v^T \right] B^{-1} \, . \tag{3.3.9}$$

Broyden (1965) suggests updating the sequence of approximate inverse Jacobians using (3.3.8), i.e.,

$$(B^{-1})_+ = (B^{-1})_c + \frac{(s_c - (B^{-1})_c y_c) s_c^T (B^{-1})_c}{s_c^T (B^{-1})_c y_c} \, .$$

This is only feasible for about the same class of dense problems as the QR updating scheme. The QR scheme is more trouble to implement, but it has the advantage that the condition number of the current Jacobian approximation can always be monitored by using standard techniques to estimate the condition number of an upper triangular matrix. Approaches based on (3.3.8) may become of increased importance on parallel computers.

The final way of implementing Broyden's method is very useful for large problems, and it is based on (3.3.9). The idea can be found in Matthies and Strang (1979). At the k-th step, we assume that we have some way of solving $B_0 x = b$ for any b; for example, we might have a sparse factorization of B_0. We also assume we have storage available for a small number of additional vectors. This allows us to recursively solve

$$B_{k+1} s_{k+1} = -F(x_{k+1})$$

by using (3.3.9) and solving

$$B_k w_k = \frac{1}{\|s_k\|_2} (y_k - B_k s_k),$$

computing

$$\omega_k = 1 + \frac{s_k^{\mathrm{T}}}{\|s_k\|} w_k,$$

solving

$$B_k \bar{s}_{k+1} = -F(x_{k+1}),$$

and computing

$$s_{k+1} = \bar{s}_{k+1} - \frac{1}{\omega_k} w_k \frac{s_k^{\mathrm{T}} \bar{s}_{k+1}}{\|s_k\|_2}.$$

This scheme must be restarted whenever the number of vectors allocated to store the update vectors is filled.

3.4. BFGS method for unconstrained minimization

Now we discuss the selection of a secant approximation B_c to the Hessian matrix in the model (3.3.1). We could simply apply Broyden's method to find a root of $g(x) = 0$. This is not done because more effective alternatives exist based on using more of the structure of the Hessian matrix which we are trying to approximate. In this section we will try to acquaint the reader with the high points of this rich material. For more information, see Dennis and Moré (1977), Dennis and Schnabel (1979), Fletcher (1980), or Dennis and Schnabel (1983).

The analog of (3.3.1) for solving $g(x) = 0$ is the same except for the definition of y_c:

$$Bs_c = y_c = g(x_+) - g(x_c), \qquad (3.4.1)$$

where B is meant to approximate $H(x_+)$. Equation (3.4.1) causes the quadratic model

$$m(x_+ + d) = f(x_+) + g(x_+)^{\mathrm{T}} d + \tfrac{1}{2} d^{\mathrm{T}} B_+ d$$

to interpolate $f(x_+)$, $g(x_+)$, and $g(x_c)$. However $H(x_+)$ is symmetric, while the Broyden update B_+ of B_c generally will not be. Also

$$\left\| \tfrac{1}{2} [B_+ + B_+^{\mathrm{T}}] - H(x_+) \right\|_{\mathrm{F}} \leqslant \|B_+ - H(x_+)\|_{\mathrm{F}}$$

indicates that we can approximate $H(x_+)$ more closely with a symmetric B_+.

Thus, it is natural to use the least change ideas of the last section to select B_+ as the projection of B_c onto the intersection of the matrices obeying (3.4.1) with the subspace A of symmetric matrices in $\mathbb{R}^{n \times n}$. Then we obtain the PSB or Powell symmetric Broyden update

$$B_+ = B_c + \frac{(y_c - B_c s_c)s_c^T + s_c(y_c - B_c s_c)^T}{s_c^T s_c} - \frac{s_c^T(y_c - B_c s_c)s_c s_c^T}{(s_c^T s_c)^2}.$$

$$(3.4.2)$$

Note that B_+ will inherit symmetry from B_c. This update can be quite effective, and we will meet it again in the next section. It is not generally used in practice for two reasons. First, it can have difficulty with poorly scaled problems. Second, we will see in Section 4 that it is desirable that each B_+ be positive definite, but B_+ will only inherit positive definiteness from B_c under some conditions more restrictive than those required from (3.4.1) to have a symmetric positive definite solution B.

An obviously necessary condition for (3.4.1) to have a positive definite solution B is that

$$s_c^T y_c = s_c^T B s_c > 0 .$$

$$(3.4.3)$$

We will now prove by construction that (3.4.3) is also sufficient for the existence of a symmetric and positive definite solution B to (3.4.1), by constructing the BFGS method due to Broyden (1969), Fletcher (1970), Goldfarb (1970) and Shanno (1970).

If we assume that B_c is symmetric and positive definite, then it can be written in terms of its Cholesky factors

$$B_c = L_c L_c^T , \quad L_c \text{ lower triangular} .$$

In fact, L_c will probably be available as a by-product of solving (3.3). We want B_+ to be a symmetric positive definite secant matrix which is equivalent to the existence of a nonsingular J_+ for which

$$B_+ = J_+ J_+^T \quad \text{and} \quad J_+ J_+^T s_c = y_c .$$

Let $v_c = J_+^T s_c$, so that $J_+ v_c = y_c$ and $v_c^T v_c = y_c^T s_c$ if J_+ exists. If we knew v_c, then it would seem reasonable to take

$$J_+ = L_c + \frac{(y_c - L_c v_c)v_c^T}{v_c^T v_c}$$

$$(3.4.4a)$$

in view of the success of Broyden's method. Transposing (3.4.4a), multiplying both sides by s_c, and using $J_+^T s_c = v_c$ and $v_c^T v_c = y_c^T s_c$ gives

$$v_c = J_+^T s_c = L_c^T s_c + v_c \left(1 - \frac{v_c^T L_c^T s_c}{y_c^T s_c} \right)$$

which simplifies to

$$v_c = \left(\frac{y_c^T s_c}{s_c^T B_c s_c} \right)^{1/2} L_c^T s_c \tag{3.4.4b}$$

and which exists if $y_c^T s_c > 0$.

Equations (3.4.4a,b) define J_+ such that $J_+ J_+^T = B_+$ is the BFGS update. It is customary to write the BFGS update as

$$B_+ = B_c + \frac{y_c y_c^T}{y_c^T s_c} - \frac{B_c s_c s_c^T B_c}{s_c^T B_c s_c} \tag{3.4.5}$$

but it is not efficient to actually calculate and factor such a matrix at each iteration. Instead Goldfarb (1976) recommends updating the Cholesky factorization $L_c L_c^T$ of B_c by applying the QR update scheme of Subsection 3.3.3 to

$$J_+^T = L_c^T + v_c w_c^T$$

to get $J_+^T = Q_+ L_+^T$ in $O(n^2)$ operations. In fact, we don't need to form Q_+ since we only care about

$$B_+ = J_+ J_+^T = L_+ Q_+^T Q_+ L_+^T = L_+ L_+^T .$$

This Cholesky update form is the recommended way to implement the BFGS method if a full Cholesky factor can be stored. For large problems, updates can be saved and the Sherman–Morrison–Woodbury formula applied in the manner of Subsection 3.3.3. It is also possible to obtain the direct update to the inverse,

$$(B^{-1})_+ = (B^{-1})_c + \frac{(s_c - (B^{-1})_c y_c)s_c^T + s_c(s_c - (B^{-1})_c y_c)^T}{y_c^T s_c}$$

$$- \frac{y_c^T(s_c - (B^{-1})_c y_c)^T s_c s_c^T}{(y_c^T s_c)^2} . \tag{3.4.6}$$

The BFGS method can also be derived as the least-change symmetric secant update to $(B^{-1})_c$ in *any* inner product norm of the form $|||(\cdot)||| = \|M_+(\cdot)M_+^T\|_F$ where $M_+ M_+^T s_c = y_c$. In other words, the BFGS method is the result of projecting $(B_c)^{-1}$ into the symmetric matrices that satisfy $B^{-1} y_c = s_c$, and the projection is independent of which choice is made from a large class of inner-product norms.

If instead we project B_c into the symmetric matrices for which $B_c s_c = y_c$, in any norm of the form $\|M_+^{-1}(\cdot)M_+^{-T}\|_F \equiv \||(\cdot)\||$ where $M_+M_+^T s_c = y_c$, the result is the update formula

$$B_+ = B_c + \frac{(y_c - B_c s_c)y_c^T + y_c(y_c - B_c s_c)^T}{y_c^T s_c} - \frac{s_c^T(y_c - B_c s_c)y_c y_c^T}{(y_c^T s_c)^2} .$$

$$(3.4.7)$$

Equation (3.2.7) is called the DFP update for Davidon (1959), Fletcher and Powell (1963), and it also passes positive definiteness from B_c to B_+ whenever $y_c^T s_c > 0$.

Theorem 3.4.1 is a local superlinear convergence result for all three methods we have discussed in this subsection. This is a combination of three theorems from Broyden, Dennis and Moré (1973). The proofs follow the same outline as the proof for Broyden's method.

Theorem 3.4.1. *Let f satisfy the hypothesis of Theorem 2.2.1. Then, there exist $\varepsilon > 0$, $\delta > 0$ such that the sequences generated respectively by the BFGS, DEP, or PSB methods exist and converge q-superlinearly to x_* from any x_0, B_0 for which $\|x_* - x_0\| \leq \varepsilon$ and $\|B_0 - H(x_*)\| \leq \delta$. Furthermore, the PSB method converges if $H(x_*)$ is nonsingular but not positive definite.*

The BFGS method seems to work especially well in practice. Generally it requires more iterations to solve a given problem than a finite-difference Newton method would, but fewer function and gradient evaluations. Most experts feel that a property which contributes to the success of the DFP and BFGS methods is that the iteration sequences are invariant with respect to linear basis changes under reasonable hypotheses. This property is not shared by the PSB method. The superiority of the BFGS to the DFP is still an interesting research topic and is discussed briefly in Section 6.3.

A final issue is how to choose the initial Hessian approximation B_0 in a BFGS method. Scale invariance of the iteration depends on scale invariance of B_0. Thus, in analogy to Section 3.3 we could choose B_0 to be a finite difference approximation to $\nabla^2 f(x_0)$, but besides being expensive, an initial Hessian often is indefinite and then may be perturbed anyhow as we will see in Section 4. Instead, the common practice is to set $B_0 = I$ so that B_0 is positive definite and the first step is in the steepest descent direction. This choice may not correctly reflect the scale of the Hessian, and so a one-time scaling correction often is applied during the first iteration; see Shanno and Phua (1978a) or Dennis and Schnabel (1983).

3.5. Sparse finite-difference and secant methods

In this section, we will consider briefly the incorporation of sparsity into the methods of the previous three subsections. We will see that there are important opportunities for efficiency in finite-difference Jacobian and Hessian approximations. The development of effective sparse secant methods will be seen to be more problematical.

Medium size dense problems are usually solvable by library subroutines based on local models we have already considered. When a problem is large enough to make sparsity an important consideration, it often is useful to develop methods specifically suited to the class of problems under consideration. In Section 6.1 we will discuss some promising approaches to this end. Here we discuss general purpose approaches.

We begin with a discussion of special finite-difference methods for sparse problems.

Curtis, Powell and Reid (1974) began one of the most elegant and useful lines of research on sparse nonlinear problems. They noticed that if the sparsity structure of $J(x)$ is such that some subset C_J of the column indices has the property that there is at most one nonzero in any row of the submatrix composed of these columns, then all the nonzero element in this submatrix of $\Delta F(x_c, h)$ could be calculated from the single function difference

$$F\left(x_c + \sum_{j \in C_J} h_j e_j\right) - F(x_c)$$

by assigning the rows of this difference to the nonzeros elements of the rows of the submatrix of $J(x)$ determined by C_J. In order to illustrate the enormous savings possible in finite-difference methods, notice that if $J(x)$ is tridiagonal, then only three extra values of $F(x)$ are needed for any n to build $\Delta F(x_c, h)$. They are

$$F(x_c + h_1 e_1 + h_4 e_4 + h_7 e_7 + \cdots) \equiv F(x_c + d_1) \,,$$
$$F(x_c + h_2 e_2 + h_5 e_5 + h_8 e_8 + \cdots) \equiv F(x_c + d_2) \,,$$
$$F(x_c + h_3 e_3 + h_6 e_6 + h_9 e_9 + \cdots) \equiv F(x_c + d_3) \,.$$

The submatrix consisting of the first, fourth, seventh, tenth, . . . columns of $\Delta F(x_c, h)$ is then determined from the function difference $F(x_c + d_1) - F(x_c)$. The other two submatrices are determined in the same way from $F(x_c + d_2) - F(x_c)$ and $F(x_c + d_3) - F(x_c)$.

Curtis, Powell, and Reid suggested some effective heuristics to keep the number of submatrices, and hence the number of function evaluations, small. Coleman and Moré (1983) and Coleman, Garbow, and Moré (1984) exploited the connection between a subclass of graph coloring problems and the problem of determining how to partition the columns of $J(x)$ to save further on function evaluations. Although they proved that the problem of minimizing the number of submatrices is NP-complete, they developed some very useful heuristics.

Li (1986) noticed that if no component of $s_- = x_c - x_-$ is zero, where x_- is the past iterate, then the function value $F(x_-)$ can be used to reduce the number of extra function evaluations in either of these approaches by one.

In the tridiagonal case, this reduces to using $h = s$ and $F(x_c) - F(x_c - d_1)$, $F(x_c - d_1) - F(x_c - d_1 - d_2)$, and $F(x_c - d_1 - d_2) - F(x_-)$ respectively to calculate the three submatrices. He suggests leaving the j-th column unchanged if $(s_c)_j = 0$. His analytical and computational results support this approach.

This approach can also be applied to approximate a sparse Hessian from gradient values. Powell and Toint (1979) developed methods to further reduce the number of gradient evaluations required in this case. To illustrate their main idea, assume that $H(x)$ is diagonal except for a full last row and column. We can then approximate the last column by $[g(x_c + h_n e_n) - g(x_c)] \cdot h_n^{-1}$ and the last row by its transpose. The first $n - 1$ components of $g(x_c + \Sigma_{j=1}^{n-1} h_j e_j) - g(x_c)$ suffice to obtain an approximation to the rest of $H(x_c)$. Thus two extra gradient evaluations suffice while n would be required for the same sparsity pattern without symmetry. Powell and Toint also suggest a more complex indirect approximation method. Coleman and Moré (1984) and Coleman, Garbow, and Moré (1985) showed that the problem of minimizing the number of extra gradient evaluations also is related to graph coloring, and again developed useful heuristics although this problem is also NP-complete. Goldfarb and Toint (1984) show the connection between the finite-difference approximation and tiling the plane when the nonlinear problem arises from numerically solving a partial differential equation.

Now we consider sparse secant methods. Schubert (1970) and Broyden (1971) independently suggested a sparse form of Broyden's method. Reid (1973) showed that their update is the Frobenius norm least change secant update to B_c with A taken to be the set of matrices with the sparsity of $J(x)$.

In order to state the algorithm, let us define P_i to be the l_2 projection of $\mathbb{R}^n$ onto the subspace z_i of $\mathbb{R}^n$ consisting of all vectors with zeros in every row position for which the corresponding column position of the i-th row of $J(x)$ is always zero. That is, $P_i v$ zeroes the elements of v corresponding to the zero elements of row i of $J(x)$ and leaves the others unchanged. We also need the pseudoinverse notation a^+ to denote 0 when the real scalar is $a = 0$ and a^{-1} otherwise. Then the sparse Broyden or Schubert method is:

> Given B_c sparse, and x_c
> solve $B_c s_c = -F(x_c)$.
> Set $x_+ = x_c + s_c$ and

$$B_+ = B_c + \sum_{i=1}^{n} [(P_i(s_c))^T (P_i(s_c))]^+ e_i^T (y_c - B_c s_c) e_i (P_i(s_c))^T.$$
(3.5.1)

Note that (3.5.1) reduces to Broyden's method if $J(x)$ has no nonzeroes.

Marwil (1979) gave the first complete proof that (3.5.1) is locally q-superlinearly convergent under the hypothesis of Theorem 3.3.3. In practice, this method is cheaper than the Broyden update, but the savings are small because there is no reduction over the cost of Newton's method in solving for the quasi-Newton step. An important practical use of this method is to update a submatrix of an approximate Jacobian, the other columns of which might be generated by finite differences as suggested above. Dennis and Li (1988) test and analyze a strategy based on using heuristics of Coleman and Moré to pick out subsets of columns that can be very efficiently approximated by finite differences. The remaining columns are then updated by (3.5.1). The results are very good, and there are indications that similar approaches are useful in engineering applications.

For unconstrained optimization, Marwil (1978) and Toint (1977) constructed a sparse analog of the PSB update (3.4.2). Toint analyzed the method under some safeguarding, and Dennis and Walker (1981) give a complete proof of local q-superlinear convergence. An example by Sorensen (1981), however, raises doubts about the utility of the method. We will not dwell on this topic because the update seems to share the shortcomings of the PSB, and in addition, it requires the solution of an extra $n \times n$ positive definite linear system with the same sparsity as $H(x)$ for the update of B_c to B_+. Thus this method has not had a major practical impact.

Professor Angelo Lucia of Clarkson reports good results using the cheap and simple expedient of projecting B_+ defined by (3.5.1) into the subspace of symmetric matrices, i.e., he uses the approximate Hessian defined by $\frac{1}{2}[B_+ + B_+^T]$. Steihaug (1980) had shown this method to be locally q-superlinearly convergent.

Unfortunately, extending the BFGS and DFP algorithms to sparse problems seems at a dead end. One problem is that a sparse positive definite approximation may not exist in some cases where $y_c^T s_c > 0$. A more pervasive problem is that sparsity is not invariant under general linear basis changes, while the essence of these secant methods is their invariance to any linear basis changes. We will comment in Section 6.1 on some work that uses more fundamental problem structure to get around the problems of the straightforward approach to least change secant methods for sparse unconstrained minimization.

4. Globally convergent methods

The methods for unconstrained optimization discussed in Sections 2 and 3 are *locally convergent* methods, meaning that they will converge to a minimizer if they are started sufficiently close to one. In this section we discuss the modifications that are made to these methods so that they will converge to a local minimizer from a poor starting point x_0. Methods with this property are called *globally convergent*.

Two main approaches have emerged for making the methods of Sections 2 and 3 more globally convergent while retaining their excellent local convergence properties. They are *line search* methods and *trust region* methods. Both are used in successful software packages, and neither has been shown clearly superior to the other. Furthermore, both approaches certainly will play important roles in future research and development of optimization methods.

Therefore we cover both approaches, in Sections 4.2 and 4.3 respectively. We briefly compare these approaches in Section 4.4.

The basic idea of both line search and trust region methods, is that they use the quickly convergent local methods of Sections 2 and 3 when they are close to a minimizer, and that when these methods are not sufficient, they use some reliable approach that gets them closer to the region where local methods will work. The basic concept behind this global phase is that of a *descent direction*, a direction in which $f(x)$ initially decreases from the current iterate x_c. Descent directions and their relation to local methods are discussed in Section 4.1. Included in Section 4.1 is a discussion of the well-known, but slow, *method of steepest descent*.

Global strategies for solving systems of nonlinear equations are obtained from global strategies for unconstrained optimization, for example by applying the methods of this section to $f(x) = \|F(x)\|^2$. For a discussion of this topic, see e.g. Dennis and Schnabel (1983), Section 6.5.

4.1. Descent directions

The basic strategy of most globally convergent methods for unconstrained optimization is to decrease $f(x)$ at each iteration. Fundamental to this is the idea of a *descent direction* from x_c, a direction d from x_c in which $f(x)$ initially decreases.

The proof of Theorem 1.1 (the necessary condition for unconstrained optimization) showed that if $g(x_c) \neq 0$, d is a descent direction from x_c if and only if

$$g(x_c)^T d < 0 ,$$

i.e., the directional derivative in the direction d is negative. In this case, for all sufficiently small $\varepsilon > 0$, $f(x_c + \varepsilon d) < f(x_c)$. Thus given a descent direction d, one can always choose a new iterate $x_+ = x_c + \varepsilon d$ so that $f(x_+) < f(x_c)$. This property is the basis of globally convergent methods.

A natural question to ask is whether the local methods for unconstrained optimization discussed in Sections 2 and 3 yield steps in descent directions. These methods were derived by considering the local quadratic model of $f(x)$ around x_c, which in general had the form

$$m_c(x_c + d) = f(x_c) + g(x_c)^T d + \tfrac{1}{2} d^T H_c d . \tag{4.1.1}$$

They then chose $d = -H_c^{-1} g(x_c)$ causing $x_+ = x_c + d$ to be the critical point of (4.1.1).

If H_c is positive definite, x_+ is the unique minimizer of the model; furthermore

$$g(x_c)^T d = -g(x_c)^T H_c^{-1} g(x_c) < 0$$

so that d is a descent direction. On the other hand, if H_c is not positive definite, then not only doesn't the model have a minimizer, but also d may not be a descent direction.

In implementations of the leading secant methods for unconstrained minimization such as the BFGS method, H_c always is positive definite. Thus the steps generated by these methods always are in descent directions.

When $H_c = H(x_c) \equiv \nabla^2 f(x_c)$, however, it may not be positive definite when x_c is far from a local minimizer. Thus the Newton step $d = -H(x_c)^{-1}g(x_c)$ is not necessarily in a descent direction. We will see that line search and trust region methods deal with indefinite Hessian matrices in different ways.

The idea of choosing x_+ to be a step from x_c in a descent direction d also leads naturally to the idea of taking steps in the 'steepest' descent direction. By this one means the direction d for which the initial rate of decrease from x_c in the direction d is greatest. For this definition to make sense, the direction d must be normalized; then we can define the 'steepest' descent direction as the solution to

$$\min_{d \in R^n} g(x_c)^T d \quad \text{subject to } \|d\| = 1 . \tag{4.1.2}$$

The solution to (4.1.2) depends on the choice of norm; for the Euclidean norm it is $d = -g(x_c)/\|g(x_c)\|_2$, which is generally known as the *steepest descent direction*.

One classic minimization algorithm is based solely on the steepest descent direction. It is to choose each new iterate x_{k+1} to be the minimizer of $f(x)$ in this direction, i.e.

$$\text{choose } t_k \text{ to solve:} \quad \underset{t>0}{\text{minimize }} f(x_k - tg(x_k))$$

$$x_{k+1} = x_k - t_k g(x_k) . \tag{4.1.3}$$

This is known as the *method of steepest descent*.

The method of steepest descent is an example of a globally convergent method. By this we mean that if a sequence of iterates $\{x_k\}$ is generated by (4.1.3), for a continuously differentiable $f(x)$ that is bounded below, then $\lim_{k \to \infty} g(x_k) = 0$. However the method has several important practical drawbacks. Most importantly, it usually is slow. If the method converges to x_*, then it can be shown that

$$\limsup_{k \to \infty} \frac{\|M(x_{k+1} - x_*)\|}{\|M(x_k - x_*)\|} \leqslant c \tag{4.1.4}$$

where $M^2 = H(x_*)$, and $c = (\lambda_1 - \lambda_n)/(\lambda_1 + \lambda_n)$ for (λ_1, λ_n) the largest and smallest eigenvalues of $H(x_*)$. Furthermore, for any $f(x)$, (4.1.4) can be shown to be an equality for some starting x_0. Thus the method is only linearly convergent and may be very slowly convergent for problems with even slightly poorly conditioned $H(x_*)$. Secondly, as written (4.1.3) requires the solution of an exact one-variable minimization problem at each iteration. The steepest descent method may be implemented with an inexact minimization and still retain (4.1.4) but the work per iteration may still be large. Thirdly, the method is very sensitive to transformations of the variable space. If the variable space is changed to $\hat{x} = T \cdot x$, the Hessian matrix in this new variable space becomes $T^{-T}H(x)T^{-1}$, so that by the above discussion the rate of convergence may be significantly altered. Indeed, the effectiveness of even a single steepest descent iteration in reducing $f(x)$ may depend significantly upon the units used in defining the variables. In contrast, the performance of the Newton method is unaffected by linear transformations of the variable space, and the BFGS method is affected only through the scale dependence of B_0.

For these reasons, the method of steepest descent is not recommended as a general purpose optimization method. We will see, however, that steepest descent steps play a role in the trust region methods discussed in Section 4.2 and in the conjugate gradient methods of Section 5.2. Furthermore, versions of the method of steepest descent continue to be used successfully in some practical applications, for example problems where x_0 is close to x_* and the cost of computing $H(x)$ is prohibitive, even though conjugate gradient or BFGS methods may be more efficient for such problems.

4.2. Line search methods

The general idea of a *line search method* is to choose a descent direction from x_c at each iteration, and select the next iterate x_+ to be a point in this direction that decreases $f(x)$. That is,

choose d_c for which $g(x_c)^T d_c < 0$,

choose $x_+ = x_c + t_c d_c, t_c > 0$, so that $f(x_+) < f(x_c)$.

Note that the method of steepest descent fits this framework.

Modern line search methods differ from the method of steepest descent in three important ways: (1) d_c usually is chosen to be the Newton or secant direction; (2) t_c is chosen by a procedure that requires much less work than an exact minimization; and (3) $t_c = 1$ is used whenever possible, so that the line search method reduces to Newton's method or a secant method close to a local minimizer. In this section we summarize the convergence properties of such methods, the selection of the search direction d_c, and practical procedures for calculating t_c.

Starting with the work of Armijo (1966) and Goldstein (1967), it has been shown that line search methods will be globally convergent if each step satisfies two simple conditions. The first is that the decrease in $f(x)$ is sufficient in relation to the length of the step $s_c = t_c d_c$; the relation

$$f(x_+) < f(x_c) + \alpha g(x_c)^T s_c \qquad (4.2.1)$$

usually is chosen to implement this condition where $\alpha \in (0, 1)$ is some constant. Note that for any sufficiently small step in a descent direction d_c, (4.2.1) is satisfied for any $\alpha < 1$. The second condition is that the step is not too short. The equation

$$g(x_+)^T s_c \geq \beta g(x_c)^T s_c \qquad (4.2.2)$$

is most commonly chosen to implement this condition, where $\beta \in (\alpha, 1)$; it says that the step must be long enough so that the directional derivative increases by some fixed fraction of its original magnitude.

The main value of equations (4.2.1) and (4.2.2) is that incorporating them into a line search algorithm leads to a practical and globally convergent method. Theorem 4.2.1 says that given any descent direction d_c and $0 < \alpha < \beta < 1$, it is always possible to choose $t_c > 0$ so that $x_+ = x_c + t_c d_c$ satisfies (4.2.1) and (4.2.2) simultaneously. Theorem 4.2.2 says that if every iterate is chosen in this way and the directions d_c are selected reasonably, the method will be globally convergent. For proofs of these theorems, see Wolfe (1969, 1971) or Dennis and Schnabel (1983).

Theorem 4.2.1. *Let* $f : \mathbb{R}^n \to \mathbb{R}$ *be continuously differentiable and bounded below. Let* $x_k \in \mathbb{R}^n$, $d_k \in \mathbb{R}^n$ *satisfy* $g(x_k)^T d_k < 0$. *Then if* $0 < \alpha < \beta < 1$, *there exist* $0 < t_1 < t_2$ *such that for any* $t_k \in [t_1, t_2]$, $x_{k+1} = x_k + t_k d_k = x_k + s_k$ *satisfies*

$$f(x_{k+1}) < f(x_k) + \alpha g(x_k)^T s_k \qquad (4.2.3)$$

and

$$g(x_{k+1})^T s_k \geq \beta g(x_k)^T s_k . \qquad (4.2.4)$$

Theorem 4.2.2. *Let* $f : \mathbb{R}^n \to \mathbb{R}$ *be continuously differentiable and bounded below, and assume g is Lipschitz continuous in* $\mathbb{R}^n$. *Given* $x_0 \in \mathbb{R}^n$, *suppose the sequence* $\{x_k\}$ *is defined by* $x_{k+1} = x_k + d_k$, $k = 0, 1, \ldots$, *and that there exists* $\sigma > 0$ *such that for each* $k > 0$,

$$g(x_k)^T s_k < -\sigma \| g(x_k) \|_2 \| s_k \|_2 \qquad (4.2.5)$$

and (4.2.3), (4.2.4) *are satisfied. Then either* $g(x_k) = 0$ *for some* k, *or* $\lim_{k \to \infty} g(x_k) = 0$.

The only restriction in Theorem 4.2.2 that we have not yet discussed is inequality (4.2.5). This simply says that each step direction must be a descent direction where in addition, the angle between s_c and the negative gradient is less than some fixed angle less than $90°$. For example, if $s_k = -H_k^{-1} g(x^k)$ where H_k is $H(x_k)$ or any approximation to it, then (4.2.5) is satisfied if the condition numbers of H_k are uniformly bounded above. This is not a big restriction in practice although not all methods can be shown to enforce it in theory.

Other conditions can be substituted for (4.2.2) and still allow Theorem 4.2.1 and 4.2.2 to hold. A common substitution for (4.2.2) is

$$|g(x_+)^{\mathrm{T}} s_c| \le \beta |g(x_c)^{\mathrm{T}} s_c| \qquad (4.2.6)$$

again with $\beta \in (\alpha, 1)$; as $\beta \to 0$, (4.2.6) causes x_+ to approach a minimizer of $f(x)$ along the line in the direction d_c from x_c. Another substitution for (4.2.2) which causes our theorems to remain true is

$$f(x_+) \ge f(x_c) + \gamma g(x_c)^{\mathrm{T}} s_c$$

for some $\gamma \in (0, \alpha)$.

Note that (4.2.2) (or (4.2.6)) and $g(x_c)^{\mathrm{T}} d_c < 0$ imply

$$(g(x_+) - g(x_c))^{\mathrm{T}} s_c \ge (\beta - 1) g(x_c)^{\mathrm{T}} s_c > 0$$

which is the condition (3.4.3) that we saw is necessary and sufficient for the existence of symmetric and positive definite secant updates. Thus by enforcing (4.2.2) or (4.2.6) in a BFGS method, we also ensure that it is possible to make a positive definite update at each iteration.

Two practical issues remain in applying Theorems 4.2.1 and 4.2.2 to obtain a practical line search algorithm: the choices of the step direction d_c, and the efficient calculation of the step length t_c to satisfy (4.2.1) and (4.2.2). In addition, we need to show how we retain the fast local convergence of the methods discussed in Sections 2 and 3.

Our methods are based upon the quadratic model (4.1.1) where $H_c = H(x_c)$ or an approximation to it. When H_c is a BFGS approximation, then it is positive definite and line search methods use $d_c = -H_c^{-1} g(x_c)$. We saw in Section 4.1 that this d_c is always a descent direction. Generally BFGS based line search methods do not explicitly enforce (4.2.5); it can be shown to be true in theory under certain assumptions (see e.g. Broyden, Dennis and Moré (1973), Powell (1976)).

When $H_c = H(x_c)$ or a finite difference approximation to it, then H_c may or may not be positive definite. The standard practice, due to Gill and Murray (1974), is to attempt the Cholesky factorization of H_c in such a way that the result is the factorization $L_c L_c^{\mathrm{T}}$ (or $L_c D_c L_c^{\mathrm{T}}$) of $(H_c + E_c)$. Here L_c is lower triangular, D_c is positive diagonal, and E_c is a non-negative diagonal matrix which is zero if H_c is positive definite and not too badly conditioned. Then d_c is obtained by solving $L_c L_c^{\mathrm{T}} d_c = -g(x_c)$, so that $d_c = -(H_c + E_c)^{-1} g(x_c)$. Thus d_c is the Newton direction if H_c is safely positive definite, as it will be near a strong local minimizer and usually at most other iterations as well. Otherwise d_c is some descent direction related to the Newton direction. In all cases, the cost of the factorization is only $O(n^2)$ operations more than a normal Cholesky factorization, d_c obeys (4.2.5), and the size of E_c is bounded in terms of the size of H_c.

Thus any line search method, whether it chooses H_c to be the Hessian or a BFGS approximation to it, will use $d_c = -H_c^{-1}g(x_c)$ as the search direction in the neighborhood of a minimizer x_* where $H(x_*)$ is positive definite. If the steplength $t_c = 1$ is permissible, this means that the global convergence results of this section are consistent with the fast local convergence of Sections 2.2 and 3.4. Theorem 4.2.3, due to Dennis and Moré (1974), shows that this is the case as long as $\alpha < \frac{1}{2}$ in (4.2.1).

Theorem 4.2.3. *Let* $f:\mathbb{R}^n \to \mathbb{R}$ *have a Lipschitz continuous Hessian in an open convex set D. Consider a sequence* $\{x_k\}$ *generated by* $x_{k+1} = x_k + t_k d_k$*, where* $g(x_k)^T d_k < 0$ *for all k and* t_k *is chosen to satisfy (4.2.1) with* $\alpha < \frac{1}{2}$*, and (4.2.2). If* $\{x_k\}$ *converges to a point* $x_* \in D$ *at which* $H(x_k)$ *is positive definite, and if*

$$\lim_{k \to \infty} \frac{\| g(x_k) + H(x_k)d_k \|}{\|d_k\|} = 0 , \tag{4.2.7}$$

then there is an index $k_0 \geqslant 0$ *such that for all* $k \geqslant k_0$*,* $t_k = 1$ *is admissible. Furthermore,* $g(x_*) = 0$*, and if* $t_k = 1$ *for all* $k \geqslant k_0$*, then* $\{x_k\}$ *converges q-superlinearly to* x_**.*

If exact Hessians are used, d_k will be $-H(x_k)^{-1}g(x_k)$ for all x_k sufficiently close to x^*, so that (4.2.7) is trivially true and quadratic convergence is achieved by using $t_k = 1$. In a BFGS method, the analysis of Broyden, Dennis, and Moré (1973) or Powell (1976) shows that (4.2.7) is true so that q-superlinear convergence can be retained. Powell's result is especially interesting because the use of a line search to prevent divergence allows him to dispense with the need to begin with a good Hessian approximation.

From Theorem 4.2.3, we see that to combine fast local convergence with global convergence, a practical procedure for selecting the steplength t_c should always try $t_c = 1$ first (at least near a minimizer) and use it if it is admissible. Beyond this, experience has shown that a practical procedure for choosing t_c to satisfy (4.2.1) and (4.2.2) should aim to be as efficient as possible, in that it chooses α and β so that there is a wide range of points satisfying (4.2.1) and (4.2.2), and uses the first point that it finds in this range rather than trying to closely approximate the minimizer of $f(x)$ along the line $x_c + td_c$. Many strategies for accomplishing these goals efficiently have been proposed, and probably every line search that is coded is unique in some way. Algorithm 4.2.1 indicates the structure of a representative line search.

There are four possible stages in this line search. If $t_c = 1$ satisfies both (4.2.1) and (4.2.2), then $x_+ = x_c + d_c$, and no further line search calculations are performed. If $t_c = 1$ is not admissible because it fails (4.2.1), then t_c will be decreased. This is most often done by safeguarded quadratic interpolation. In this procedure the minimizer t_m of the one-dimensional quadratic approxima-

Algorithm 4.2.1
Line search structure

Given $f(x):\mathbb{R}^n\to\mathbb{R}$, x_c, $f(x_c)$, $g(x_c)$, descent direction d_c
$tlow := 0$, $tup := \infty$, $done := false$, $t_c := 1$
Repeat
  evaluate $f(x_c + t_c d_c)$
  If $x_c + t_c d_c$ satisfies (4.2.1) then
    evaluate $g(x_c + t_c d_c)$
    If $x_c + t_c d_c$ satisfies (4.2.2) then
      done := true
    Else
      $tlow := t_c$
      If $tup = \infty$ then
        $t_c :=$ Init-Increase(t_c)
      Else $t_c :=$ Refine$(t_c, tlow, tup)$
  Else
    $tup := t_c$
    If $tlow = 0$ then
      $t_c :=$ Init-Decrease(t_c)
    Else $t_c :=$ Refine$(t_c, tlow, tup)$
Until *done* = true

---

tion $q(t)$ to $f(x_c + td_c)$ that interpolates $f(x_c)$, $g(x_c)^T d_c$, and $f(x_c + t_c d_c)$ is calculated by

$$t_m = \frac{-t_c^2 g(x_c)^T d_c}{2[f(x_c + t_c d_c) - f(x_c) - t_c g(x_c)^T d_c]}, \tag{4.2.8}$$

and the next stepsize is then set to $\max\{t_m, c_1 t_c\}$, where typically $c_1 = 0.1$. (It can be shown that $t_m > t_c/2(1 - \alpha)$.) This Init-Decrease stage may be repeated one or more times if the new $x_c + t_c d_c$ continues to fail (4.2.1). Sometimes a form of safeguarded cubic interpolation is used instead in this stage, see e.g. Dennis and Schnabel (1983).

    Alternately, if $t_c = 1$ satisfies (4.2.1) but not (4.2.2), t_c will be increased. Generally a simple rule like $t_c = 2t_c$ is used although more sophisticated strategies are possible. This Init-Increase stage also may be repeated if $x_c + t_c d_c$ continues to satisfy (4.2.1) and fail (4.2.2).

    After one or more repetitions of either the Init-Increase or Init-Decrease phase, either an admissible $x_c + t_c d_c$ is found, or it must be the case that the last two values of t_c that have been tried bracket an acceptable value of t. That is, the one with the lower value of t_c, $tlow$ must satisfy (4.2.1) but not (4.2.2), while the one with the higher value of t_c, tup, must fail (4.2.1). In this case an admissible t_c must be in $(tlow, tup)$, and it is identified by the final, Refine, phase of the line search. Let $\delta = tup - tlow$. A typical Refine phase would calculate

$$t_m = tlow - \frac{\delta^2 g(tlow)^{\mathrm{T}} d_c}{2[f(tup) - f(tlow) - \delta g(tlow)^{\mathrm{T}} d_c]}$$

the minimizer of the one dimensional quadratic interpolating $f(tlow)$, $g(tlow)^{\mathrm{T}} d_c$, and $f(tup)$, and then set $t_c = \min\{\max\{t_m, tlow + c_2\delta\}, tup - c_2\delta\}$ where typically $c_2 = 0.2$. This phase may also be repeated one or more times.

In theory it can be shown that our line search terminates in a finite number of iterations. In practice, very little work usually is necessary. Experience has shown that line search algorithms with relatively loose tolerances generally produce algorithms that require fewer total number of function and derivative evaluations to reach the minimizer than algorithms with tight tolerances. Typical line search algorithms set $\alpha = 10^{-4}$ in (4.2.1), so that virtually any decrease in $f(x)$ is acceptable, and β between 0.7 and 0.9 in (4.2.2), so that only a small decrease in the magnitude of the directional derivative is required. Due to these tolerances, $t_c = 1$ is admissible much of the time, and when it is not, generally one or at most two more values of t_c must be attempted. Thus the three procedures described above, Init-Decrease, Init-Increase, and especially Refine, are used only infrequently.

The above line search is related to the ones described by Shanno and Phua (1978b), Fletcher (1980), Dennis and Schnabel (1983), and many other authors. Many line searches have been proposed, especially variants that deal differently with the case when the Hessian is indefinite; see e.g. McCormick (1977), Moré and Sorensen (1979). Some line searchers only allow $t_c \leq 1$ and only enforce (4.2.1); in this case Algorithm 4.2.1 is much simpler as the Init-Increase and Refine stages and the check for (4.2.2) are eliminated. The techniques of Shultz, Schnabel, and Byrd (1985) show that such a line search still leads to a globally convergent algorithm, but satisfaction of the condition (3.4.3) for positive definite secant updates is not guaranteed. Finally, some line search algorithms do not start with $t_c = 1$ if the previous step was very short; good strategies for doing this are closely related to the trust region approach that we discuss next.

4.3. Trust region methods

Trust region methods are the other main group of methods for ensuring global convergence while retaining fast local convergence in optimization algorithms. The fundamental difference between line search and trust region methods is how they combine the use of the quadratic model with the choice of the step length. We saw in Section 4.2 that in a line search method, the quadratic model $m_c(x_c + d)$ given by (4.1.1) is used to obtain a search direction $d_c = -H_c^{-1} g_c$ (or $-(H_c + E_c)^{-1} g_c$ if H_c is not positive definite), and then a steplength is chosen. The procedure for choosing the steplength does not make further use of the Hessian (approximation) H_c.

A trust region method takes the different philosophy that one *first* chooses a trial step length Δ_c, and then uses the quadratic model to select the best step of (at most) this length for the quadratic model by solving

$$\underset{s \in \mathbb{R}^n}{\text{minimize }} m_c(x_c + s) = f(x_c) + g(x_c)^T s + \tfrac{1}{2} s^T H_c s$$

$$\text{subject to } \|s_c\| \le \Delta_c .$$

(4.3.1)

The trial step length Δ_c is considered an estimate of how far we *trust* the quadratic model, hence it is called a *trust radius* and the resultant method is called a *trust region* method. We will see below that Δ_c is closely related to the length of the successful step at the previous iteration, and may be adjusted as the current iteration proceeds. First we describe the solution to (4.3.1) in Theorem 4.3.1. An early proof of much of Theorem 4.3.1 is given in Goldfeldt, Quandt, and Trotter (1966); other seminal references include Gay (1981) and Sorensen (1982).

Theorem 4.3.1. *Let* $g_c = g(x_c) \in \mathbb{R}^n$, $H_c \in \mathbb{R}^{n \times n}$ *symmetric,* $\Delta_c > 0$. *Let* $\lambda_1 \in \mathbb{R}$ *denote the smallest eigenvalue of* H_c *and let* $v_1 \in \mathbb{R}^n$ *denote the corresponding eigenvector. Then if* H_c *is positive definite and* $\|H_c^{-1} g_c\| \le \Delta_c$, $s_c = -H_c^{-1} g_c$ *is the unique solution to (4.3.1). Otherwise the solution to (4.3.1) satisfies* $\|s_c\| = \Delta_c$ *and*

$$(H_c + \mu_c I) s_c = -g_c$$

for some $\mu_c \ge 0$ *where* $H_c + \mu_c I$ *is at least positive semi-definite. Furthermore either* $H_c + \mu_c i$ *is positive definite and*

$$s_c = -(H_c + \mu_c I)^{-1} g_c$$

(4.3.2)

for the unique $\mu_c > \max\{0, -\lambda_1\}$ *for which* $\|s_c\| = \Delta_c$, *or* $\mu_c = -\lambda_1$ *and*

$$s_c = -(H_c - \lambda_1 I)^+ g_c + \omega v_1 ,$$

(4.3.3)

where $+$ *denotes the Moore–Penrose pseudoinverse, and* $\omega \in \mathbb{R}$ *is chosen so that* $\|s_c\| = \Delta_c$. *If* H_c *is positive definite, the solution must be given by (4.3.2); the case (4.3.3) only occurs if* H_c *is indefinite and* $\|(H_c + \mu_c I)^{-1} g_c\| < \Delta_c$ *for all* $\mu_c > -\lambda_1$.

Theorem 4.3.1 indicates several differences between the step taken in line search and trust region methods. From (4.3.2) we see that, even if H_c is positive definite, the trust region step is not always in the Newton direction $-H_c^{-1} g(x_c)$. In fact, it is straightforward to show that for all $\mu \ge \max\{0, -\lambda_1\}$, $\|(H_c + \mu I)^{-1} g(x_c)\|$ is a monotonically decreasing function of μ. Thus as $\Delta_c \to 0$, $\mu \to \infty$, and $-(H_c + \mu I)^{-1} g(x_c) \to -g(x_c)/\mu$. Therefore for small Δ_c,

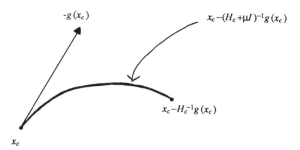

Fig. 4.3.1. The trust region curve.

the trust region step is nearly in the steepest descent direction, while as Δ_c increases, the trust region step approaches and ultimately becomes the Newton step $-H_c^{-1}g(x_c)$ as long as H_c is positive definite. This is depicted in Figure 4.3.1.

A second difference between line search and trust region methods is how they deal with the case when H_c is not positive definite. Since the minimization of an indefinite or negative definite quadratic model is not mathematically well-posed, a line search method must perturb a non-positive definite Hessian to be positive definite, as was seen in Section 4.2. On the other hand, the minimization of such a model within some closed region is well defined and reasonable, and this is what the trust region method does. Indeed, even if x_c is a maximum or saddle point, (4.3.1) is well-defined with a solution given by (4.3.3).

The above discussion indicates two attractive properties of trust region methods. First, small steps are in the steepest descent direction, the best direction for sufficiently small steps, while the Newton step is used when it is within the trust region and H_c is positive definite, thereby hopefully preserving fast local convergence. We will see that the property is retained by all the practical approximations to the ideal trust region step that are discussed later in this section. Second, the trust region method deals naturally with indefinite Hessian matrices. This will be seen to lead to stronger convergence results than were possible for the line search methods of Section 4.2.

On the other hand, the ideal trust region step described in Theorem 4.3.1 is difficult to calculate. The main difficulty is that there is no closed formula that gives the unique $\mu_c \geqslant \max\{0, -\lambda_1\}$ for which $\|(H_c + \mu_c I)^{-1}g(x_c)\| = \Delta_c$. Instead, this μ_c must be calculated by an iterative process with each iteration requiring the Cholesky factorization of a matrix of the form $H_c + \mu I$. In contrast, the line search methods of Section 4.2 require only one matrix factorization per iteration. Furthermore, it is possible that the step (4.3.3) will be required which necessitates an eigenvalue–eigenvector calculation. This case is rare, especially in finite precision arithmetic, but in cases that are close to this the calculation of (4.3.2) becomes more difficult.

For these reasons, efficient computational implementations of trust region

methods solve (4.3.1) approximately. Before we present these approximate
solution methods, we discuss the overall schema of a trust region method
including the adjustment of the trust radius Δ_c, and the convergence properties
of a method that uses this schema while solving (4.3.1) exactly. This theorem
will help justify our continued interest in these methods. We will then see that
these convergence properties are retained when using various efficient, approximate trust region steps in place of the exact solution to (4.3.1).

After the trust region s_c is calculated, a trust region method must evaluate
$f(x_c + s_c)$ to see whether $x_c + s_c$ is a satisfactory next iterate. It may not be if
the quadratic model does not accurately reflect $f(x)$ within the trust region. In
this case the trust radius is decreased and the trust region step recalculated.
Otherwise, $x_c + s_c$ becomes the next iterate and the new trust radius must be
calculated. Such an approach is outlined in Algorithm 4.3.1.

The reader will recognize the step acceptance condition

$$\text{actual-reduction} \leq \alpha_1(\text{predicted-reduction}) \tag{4.3.4}$$

as being very similar to the sufficient decrease condition (4.2.1) used in line
search algorithms. The only difference is that the second order term $\frac{1}{2}s_c^T H_c s_c$ is
included on the right hand side of (4.3.4). Again, $\alpha_1 = 10^{-4}$ is typical. No
analog to condition (4.2.2) is needed by trust region methods because the
strategy for adjusting the trust radius prevents the step from being too short.

If (4.3.4) is failed, the current iteration is repeated with a smaller trust
radius. The procedure for decreasing Δ_c is similar or identical to the procedure

Algorithm 4.3.1
Trust region iteration

Given $f:\mathbb{R}^n \to \mathbb{R}$, x_c, $f(x_c)$, $g(x_c)$, Hessian (approximation) H_c,
  trust radius $\Delta_c > 0$, $0 < \alpha_1 < \alpha_2 < 1$, $0 < \eta_1 < \eta_2 < 1 < \eta_3 < \eta_4$
done := false
Repeat
  s_c := exact or approximate solution to (4.3.1)
  evaluate $f(x_c + s_c)$
  actual-reduction := $f(x_c + s_c) - f(x_c)$
  predicted-reduction := $g(x_c)^T s_c + \frac{1}{2}s_c^T H_c s_c$
  If actual-reduction $\leq \alpha_1$ predicted-reduction then
    done := true
    $x_+ := x_c + s_c$
    If actual-reduction $\leq \alpha_2$ predicted-reduction then
      $\Delta_+ :=$ Increase-$\Delta(\Delta_c)$ $(*\Delta_+ \in [\eta_3, \eta_4]\Delta_c *)$
    Else $\Delta_+ := \Delta_c$ $(*\text{ or } \Delta_+ \in [\eta_1, 1]\Delta_c *)$
  Else $\Delta_c :=$ Decrease-$\Delta(\Delta_c)$ $(*\text{new } \Delta_c \in [\eta_1, \eta_2]\text{old } \Delta_c *)$
Until *done* = true

Init-Decrease for decreasing t_c in a line search. Typically, quadratic interpolation (equation (4.2.8)) with a safeguard such as new $\Delta_c \in [0.1, 0.5]$ old Δ_c is
used.

If (4.3.4) is satisfied, $x_c + s_c$ is acceptable as the next iterate x_+ and the new
trust radius Δ_+ must be determined. Algorithm 4.3.1 increases Δ_+ over Δ_c if the
quadratic model and function have agreed quite well; the condition actual-
reduction $\leq \alpha_2$(predicted-reduction) tests this with $\alpha_2 = 0.75$ typical. Some
methods instead allow the *current* iteration to be continued with this larger
trust radius in this case, which complicates the description considerably and
doesn't affect the theoretical properties. This may help in practice by saving
gradient evaluations. In either case, the Increase-Δ procedure usually doubles
Δ_c analogous to the Init-Increase portion of the line search. Otherwise, $\Delta_+ = \Delta_c$
in Algorithm 4.3.1. Some methods may set the new $\Delta_+ < \Delta_c$ if agreement
between the actual function and the model was rather poor, for example if
(4.3.4) was failed with $\alpha = 0.1$. This also does not affect the method's
convergence properties.

Theorem 4.3.2 gives the main global and local convergence properties of a
method based on the trust region iteration of Algorithm 4.3.1, in the case
where (4.3.1) is solved exactly. Similar results may be found in many references including Fletcher (1980), Gay (1981), and Sorensen (1982).

Theorem 4.3.2. *Let $f : \mathbb{R}^n \to \mathbb{R}$ be twice continuously differentiable and bounded
below. Also, for $x_0 \in \mathbb{R}^n$ and some $\beta_1, \beta_2 > 0$, let $H(x)$ be uniformly continuous
and satisfy $\|H(x)\| \leq \beta_1$ for all x with $f(x) \leq f(x_0)$. Let $\{x_k\}$ be the sequence
produced by iterating Algorithm 4.3.1 starting from x_0, and using $H_c = H(x_c)$ or
any symmetric approximation with $\|H_c\| \leq \beta_2$ at each iteration, and the exact
solution to (4.3.1) to calculate d_c. Then $\lim_{k \to \infty} \|g(x_k)\| = 0$. If in addition each
$H_c = H(x_c)$, then for any limit point x_* of the sequence $\{x_k\}$, $g(x_*) = 0$ and
$H(x_*)$ is at least positive semi-definite. Furthermore if each $H_c = H(x_c)$, then if
$\{x_k\}$ converges to x_*, $H(x_*)$ is positive definite, and $H(x)$ is Lipschitz continuous around x_*, then the rate of convergence is q-quadratic.*

Theorem 4.3.2 shows that a trust region method that solves the trust region
problem exactly has attractive convergence properties. The same first order
result is established as for line search methods, and no assumption about the
condition number of H_c is needed. In addition, if exact second derivatives are
used, then the second order necessary conditions for a minimum are satisfied
by any limit point, which means that saddle points and maxima are avoided.
The analysis also shows that near a local minimum with $H(x_*)$ positive definite,
asymptotically the trust region constraint becomes inactive so that only Newton
steps are taken and local quadratic convergence is retained.

These nice convergence properties help motivate the interest in trust region
methods which follow the general schema of Algorithm 4.3.1, but where the
step is calculated by a considerably more efficient procedure than that required
for the exact solution of problem (4.3.1). There are two obvious relaxations to

problem (4.3.1) that may make it easier to solve: the trust region constraint may be satisfied only approximately, and/or the quadratic model may be minimized only approximately. We will see that both may be relaxed substantially without weakening the theoretical properties of the method.

In fact, two general classes of efficient methods for approximately solving (4.3.1) have arisen, corresponding to these two possible relaxations of (4.3.1). In the first, *approximate optimal step methods*, mainly the trust region constraint is relaxed; the step generally is still of the form $-(H_c + \mu I)^{-1} g(x_c)$ for some positive definite $H_c + \mu I$. These methods are summarized below. In the second, *dogleg methods*, the minimization of the quadratic model is relaxed; we defer the consideration of these methods until later in this section.

Hebden (1973) and Moré (1978) were the first to construct efficient approximate optimal step methods. They developed an efficient procedure for finding a $\mu > 0$ for which

$$\|(H_c + \mu I)^{-1} g(x_c)\| \approx \Delta_c \qquad\qquad (4.3.5)$$

in the case when H_c is positive definite and $\|H_c^{-1} g(x_c)\| > \Delta_c$. Their algorithms are based on applying Newton's method in μ to

$$\frac{1}{\|(H_c + \mu I)^{-1} g(x_c)\|} - \frac{1}{\Delta_c} = 0 , \qquad\qquad (4.3.6)$$

following the observation that (4.3.6) is more nearly linear in μ near the desired solution than in (4.3.5). This results in the μ-iteration

$$\mu_+ = \mu - \frac{\|s_c\|^2 (\|s_c\| - \Delta_c)}{\Delta_c (s_c^T (H_c + \mu I)^{-1} s_c)} \qquad\qquad (4.3.7)$$

where $s_c = -(H_c + \mu I)^{-1} g(x_c)$, which requires our factorization of a matrix of the form $H_c + \mu I$ for each μ-iteration. Typically the trust region constraint is relaxed to $\|s_c\| \in [0.9, 1.1]\Delta_c$; then usually only one or two iterations of (4.3.7), and the same number of matrix factorizations, are required for each iteration of the optimization algorithm.

Several authors, including Gay (1981), Sorensen (1982), and Moré and Sorensen (1983), have investigated generalizations of these approximate optimal step methods that extend to the case when H_c is indefinite. Moré and Sorensen present an efficient algorithm that guarantees that their approximate solution to (4.3.1) reduces the quadratic model $m_c(x_c + s)$ by at least γ times the amount that the exact solution to (4.3.1) would, for any fixed $\gamma < 1$. Their algorithm combines the Hebden–Moré procedure mentioned above with a use of the LINPACK condition number estimator to obtain a satisfactory solution when the exact solution is in or near the 'hard case' (4.3.3). No eigenvalue/eigenvector calculations are required. They show that their method still generally requires only 1-2 matrix factorizations per iteration, and that it retains the convergence properties of Theorem 4.3.2.

The analyses of these approximate optimal step methods are subsumed by Theorem 4.3.3 below, due to Shultz, Schnabel, and Byrd (1985). Similar first order results are proven by Powell (1970, 1975) and Thomas (1975). Details of the interpretations that are given following Theorem 4.3.3 are also found in Shultz, Schnabel, and Byrd (1985).

Theorem 4.3.3. *Let the assumptions in the first two sentences of Theorem* 4.3.2 *hold. Let* $\{x_k\}$ *be the sequence produced by iterating Algorithm* 4.3.1 *starting from* x_0, *using* $H_c = H(x_c)$ *or any symmetric approximation with* $\|H_c\| \leq \beta_2$ *at each iteration. If there exist* $\eta_1, \eta_2 > 0$ *such that each* s_c *satisfies*

$$g(x_c)^\mathrm{T} s_c + \tfrac{1}{2} s_c^\mathrm{T} H_c s_c \leq -\eta_1 \|g(x_c)\| \min\left\{\Delta_c, \frac{c_2\|g(x_c)\|}{\|H_c\|}\right\}, \qquad (4.3.8)$$

then $\lim_{k\to\infty} \|g(x_k)\| = 0$. *If in addition each* $H_c = H(x_c)$ *and there exists* $\eta_3 > 0$ *such that each* d_c *satisfies*

$$g(x_c)^\mathrm{T} s_c + \tfrac{1}{2} s_c^\mathrm{T} H_c s_c \leq -\eta_3(-\lambda_1(H_c))\Delta_c^2 \qquad (4.3.9)$$

where $\lambda_1(H_c)$ *denotes the smallest eigenvalue of* H_c, *then for any limit point* x_* *of* $\{x_k\}$, $g(x_*) = 0$ *and* $H(x_*)$ *is at least positive semi-definite. Also, if each* $H_c = H(x_c)$, *each* s_c *satisfies* (4.3.8), *and there exists* $\eta_4 \in (0, 1]$ *such that* $s_c = -H_c^{-1} g(x_c)$ *whenever* H_c *is positive definite and* $\|H_c^{-1} g(x_c)\| \leq \eta_4\Delta_c$, *then if* $\{x_k\}$ *converges to* x_* *with* $H(x_*)$ *positive definite and* $H(x)$ *Lipschitz continuous around* x_*, *then the rate of convergence is* q*-quadratic.*

Theorem 4.3.3 contains two equations, (4.3.8) and (4.3.9), that say what conditions a trust region step needs to satisfy in order to be globally convergent to points satisfying the first and second order necessary conditions for minimization, respectively. Equation (4.3.8) gives a condition on the sufficient use of descent directions in order to assure first order global convergence. With $\eta_1 = \tfrac{1}{2}$ and $\eta_2 = 1$, it implies that the step s_c provides at least as much decrease in the quadratic model as the best permissible step in the steepest descent direction. (Here 'permissible' means 'obeying the trust region constraint'.) This interpretation forms part of the motivation for the dogleg methods for approximating (4.3.1) that are discussed below. By using smaller η_1 and η_2 in (4.3.8), condition (4.3.8) says that each s_c provides at least a fixed fraction of the decrease in the quadratic model that would be obtained by the best permissible step in some direction p_c of 'bounded' descent (i.e. the angle between p_c and $g(x_c)$ is uniformly bounded above by a constant $<90°$). This is all that is needed to assure $\lim_{k\to\infty}\{g(x_k)\} = 0$. Thus Theorem 4.3.3 also applies to a line search method where the trust region bound Δ_c is used to determine the steplength.

Equation (4.3.9) gives a condition on the sufficient use of negative curvature directions that, in conjunction with (4.3.8), assures global convergence to a point satisfying second order necessary conditions for minimization. Equation (4.3.9) can be interpreted as saying that, whenever H_c is indefinite, s_c provides at least a fixed fraction of the reduction in the quadratic model that would be obtained by the best permissible step in some direction v_c of 'bounded' negative curvature (i.e. $(v_c^T H_c v_c)/(\lambda_1 v_c^T v_c)$ is uniformly bounded below by a fixed positive constant). This constitutes a considerable relaxation of the 'hard case' (4.3.3) in the exact solution of (4.3.1).

Thus any trust region method that uses the schema of Algorithm 4.3.1 and chooses its steps to satisfy conditions (4.3.8–9) has strong global convergence properties. It is straightforward to show that (4.3.8–9) implies the condition on a trust region step used by Moré and Sorensen (1983), that the reduction in the quadratic model by s_c be at least a fixed fraction of the reduction from solving (4.3.1) exactly. The converse is only true under stronger assumptions on H_c (see Byrd, Schnabel, and Shultz (1986)). Now we return to the second class of methods for approximately solving (4.3.1), dogleg methods, which are now easily seen as another way to satisfy conditions (4.3.8–9).

The earliest trust region method, of Powell (1970), is the original dogleg method. Given a quadratic model $m_c(x_c + s)$ with H_c positive definite, and $\Delta_c > 0$, it selects $x_c + s_c$ to be the Newton point $x_N = x_c - H_c^{-1} g(x_c)$ if it is inside the trust region. Otherwise it selects $x_c + s_c$ to be the point on the piecewise linear curve connecting x_c, x_{Cp}, and x_N which is distance Δ_c from x_c. (See Fig. 4.3.2.) Here x_{Cp} is the *Cauchy point*, the minimum of the quadratic model in the steepest descent direction $-g(x_c)$ from x_c. (It is straightforward to show that $\|x_{Cp} - x_c\| \leq \|x_N - x_c\|$, and that the intersection of the dogleg curve with the trust radius is unique.) Dennis and Mei (1979) constructed a generalization, the *double dogleg method*, which selects $x_c + s_c$ to be the unique point on the piecewise linear curve connecting x_c, x_{Cp}, γx_N, and x_N which is distance Δ_c from x_c, or $x_c + s_c = x_N$ if x_N is inside the trust region, for a particular $\gamma < 1$. For either method, it can be shown that as one moves along the piecewise linear curve from x_c to x_N, the distance from x_c increases and the value of the quadratic method decreases.

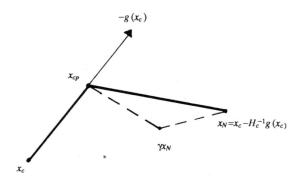

Fig. 4.3.2. The dogleg curve (dotted part is double dogleg modification).

Thus these dogleg methods take small steps in the steepest descent direction when the trust radius is small, take Newton steps when the trust radius is sufficiently large, and take steps in a linear combination of the steepest descent and Newton directions otherwise. Due to the use of steepest descent steps when $\Delta_c \leq \|x_{Cp} - x_c\|$ and to the monotonic decrease of the quadratic model along the entire dogleg curve, they always obtain at least as much descent on the quadratic model as the best steepest descent step of length at most Δ_c. Thus they obey (4.3.8) and by Theorem 4.3.3 are globally convergent in the sense that the sequence of gradients of the iterates converges to zero.

An attraction of these dogleg methods, in comparison to the approximate optimal step methods discussed above, is that they only require one matrix factorization (of H_c) per iteration. All the remaining calculations are easily seen to require at most $O(n^2)$ operations, and no additional factorizations are required if the trust region must be decreased during the current iteration. On the other hand, neither version described above makes explicit use of an indefinite H_c or satisfies (4.3.9). Thus no second order global convergence results can be proven for them.

These dogleg methods are closely related to minimizing the quadratic model $m_c(x_c + s_c)$ over the two dimensional subspace spanned by the steepest descent and Newton directions, subject to the trust region constraint. This two dimensional trust region problem also is easy to solve using only the factorization of H_c, and the inclusion of the steepest descent direction assures satisfaction of (4.3.8) and hence first order global convergence. Shultz, Schnabel, and Byrd (1985) propose an algorithm along these lines where, if H_c is indefinite, the two dimensional subspace is changed to the one spanned by $-g(x_c)$ and some direction of bounded negative curvature which is fairly efficient to compute. Thus the algorithm obeys (4.3.9) as well and has the same theoretical convergence properties as an approximate optimal step method. Byrd, Schnabel, and Shultz (1986) show that an optimization algorithm based on this approach is very competitive with a modern approximate optimal step method in robustness and efficiency.

In practice both approximate optimal step methods and various dogleg methods are used in solving unconstained optimization problems and in other contexts. Some additional comments on their relative merits are contained in Section 4.4.

4.4. Comparison of line search and trust region methods

Sections 4.2 and 4.3 have presented two classes of methods, line searches and trust regions, for obtaining globally convergent unconstrained optimization methods while also retaining fast local convergence. The reasons for presenting both approaches are that neither appears to be consistently superior to the other in practice, that both are used in modern software, and that both can be expected to play important roles in the future development of optimization methods. This section elaborates briefly on these remarks.

Gay (1983) and Schnabel, Koontz, and Weiss (1985) have conducted comparisons of line search and trust region codes on a standard set of test problems from Moré, Garbow, and Hillstrom (1981). Gay compared a BFGS method utilizing a line search with a BFGS method using a double-dogleg trust region step. Schnabel, Koontz, and Weiss tested methods using finite difference Hessians and methods using BFGS approximations, in both cases comparing line search, double-dogleg, and approximate optimal trust region steps. Both studies showed that while there can be considerable differences between the performance of line search, dogleg, and optimal step methods on individual problems, no one method is consistently more efficient or robust than any other. Indeed, the average differences in efficiency between the line search and trust region methods tested were quite small, and they had similar success rates.

In modern numerical software libraries, one finds both line searches and trust regions used in conjunction with both (finite difference) Hessians or BFGS approximations. Philosophically, some people prefer to use line searches in conjunction with BFGS methods because the necessary condition (3.4.3) for positive definite updates can be guaranteed to be satisfied at each iteration; in trust region methods no such guarantee is possible and occasionally (3.4.3) is not satisfied and the update must be skipped. Similarly, some people advocate using trust region methods in codes where the (finite difference) Hessian is used, because a 'natural' treatment of indefiniteness is possible and it can be guaranteed that saddle points and local maxima are avoided. But as the previous paragraph has indicated, neither of these theoretical arguments has been shown to correspond to any significant computational advantage.

Algorithm developers in areas such as constrained optimization, least squares data fitting, and large scale optimization often need to choose between using line searches or trust regions in developing new codes. Some trade-offs are fairly consistent. Line searches often are a little simpler to code, but sometimes it is not clear how to deal with indefiniteness, rank deficiency, or other factors that may cause the line search direction to be in an unacceptable direction. Trust region methods often offer a mathematical solution to these problems, but usually require some additional linear algebra cost. In addition it sometimes is challenging to construct efficient, approximate solution algorithms for the appropriate trust region problem. The result is that both approaches are used; for example there currently is considerable research activity in both line search and trust region methods for nonlinear constrained optimization. The two-dimensional trust region technique mentioned at the end of Section 4.3 seems to offer a good compromise in cases where the trust region approach seems desirable to assure acceptable step directions, but an (approximate) optimal solution to the exact trust region problem is very difficult or expensive to find.

One case where there appears to be a discernible difference between line search and trust region methods is in Gauss–Newton methods for nonlinear least squares (see Section 6.2). In this case the underlying local method is at best linearly convergent on most problems. For such algorithms, trust region algorithms, which may be viewed as combining two linearly convergent directions, the standard Gauss–Newton direction and the steepest descent direction, appear generally to be more robust and efficient than line search algorithms which only use the Gauss–Newton direction. For a detailed discussion of such algorithms, see Dennis and Schnabel (1983), Ch. 10.

5. Non-Taylor series methods

This section presents two fundamentally different algorithmic approaches that have proven themselves useful for unconstrained minimization. First, we will describe the Nelder–Mead simplex algorithm (Nelder and Mead (1965)), an effective pattern search technique for problems of very low dimension which is beloved of users but generally ignored by optimization researchers. Then, we will provide a unifying framework for the proliferation of conjugate direction algorithms that have been devised for solving problems with large numbers of variables.

5.1. The Nelder–Mead simplex algorithm

The Nelder–Mead algorithm moves a simplex through the domain space with the goal of getting the function minimizer x_* in the interior of the simplex. Once ad hoc tests indicate that the minimizer has been surrounded, the algorithm shrinks the simplex toward the vertex corresponding to the lowest function value and returns to the process of trying to get x_* into the interior of the (smaller) simplex.

We will confine ourselves here to a description of the four basic moves of the algorithm. Each iteration begins with a set of $n + 1$ current points $x_c^1, \ldots, x_c^{n+1}$ in general position, i.e., the convex hull S_c of $\{x_c^1, \ldots, x_c^{n+1}\}$ is an n-dimensional simplex. Furthermore, these vertices are assumed to be sorted on their objective function values so that $f(x_c^i) \leqslant f(x_c^{i+1})$, $i = 1, \ldots, n$. The first goal of each iteration is to replace the worst vertex x_c^{n+1} with a better one by moving the simplex away from x_c^{n+1}. If this fails, we tacitly assume that we are close enough to the minimizer to need smaller moves for improvement. Thus, we keep the best vertex and shrink the simplex along each edge by replacing each of the other vertices by its average with the old best vertex. We then evaluate f at the n new vertices and sort and label them to obtain $S_+ = \langle x_+^1, \ldots, x_+^{n+1} \rangle$. The convention we use is that the older vertex is numbered lower when two vertices have equal function values.

We have described the *shrinkage step* through which the algorithm tries to close in on x_*; now we describe the moves aimed at getting the larger simplex close by moving away from the worst vertex.

The first trial step in each iteration is to consider the *reflection* $x_c^r =$

$2\bar{x}_c - x_c^{n+1}$ of x_c^{n+1} through the centroid $\bar{x}_c = n^{-1} \Sigma_{i=1}^n x_c^i$ of the best n-face of S_c. If success is so great that $f(x_c^r) < f(x_c^1)$, then we try expanding the simplex in the same direction by testing $f(x_c^e) < f(x_c^1)$, where $x_c^e = 2x_c^r - x_c^{n+1}$. If the expansion is successful, we drop x_c^{n+1} in favor of x_c^e, otherwise we drop x_c^{n+1} in favor of x_c^r, and sort the vertices to obtain S_+. There are two things to note about a successful *expansion* step. The first is that we do not continue in the same vein even if $f(x_c^e) < f(x_c^r) < f(x_c^1)$. This is because we want to avoid a simplex that gets elongated enough that its vertices are not numerically in general position. The second point is that we accept the expansion vertex even if it is not as good as the reflection vertex. Thus, the best approximate minimizer we have found so far might not be retained as a vertex. This is in keeping with our view of trying to move the simplex over the minimizer before we start to close in on it.

The reflection vertex is taken without an expansion attempt if $f(x_c^1) \leqslant f(x_c^r) < f(x_c^n)$. In this case, x_c^n will become x_c^{n+1} after sorting. If $f(x_c^r) \geqslant f(x_c^{n+1})$, then we try to contract the simplex internally along the reflection direction by testing $f(x_c^c) < f(x_c^{n+1})$, where the contraction vertex is $x_c^c = \frac{1}{2}[\bar{x}_c + x_c^{n+1}]$. If the *contraction* fails, then we shrink the simplex as explained above. If it succeeds, then we replace x_c^{n+1} by x_c^c and sort to prepare for the next iteration.

There is one more possibility to consider for the trial of a reflection step. If $f(x_c^n) \leqslant f(x_c^r) < f(x_c^{n+1})$, then we can see immediately that if we replace x_c^{n+1} by x_c^r, the outcome would be that x_+^{n+1} would be x_c^r and that the subsequent reflection step would be rejected, because $x_+^r = x_c^{n+1}$, in favor of a trial contraction. Thus, we pass over this 'shadow' iteration and compute the indicated shadow contraction directly from the current vertices as $x_c^{sc} = \frac{1}{2}(x_c^r + \bar{x}_c)$. We finish the iteration exactly as we did for a regular contraction.

Many users have suggested minor modifications of this algorithm. The best known modifications and the history of the algorithm are collected in Woods (1985). Woods also gives a novel application of one of the three major advantages of the algorithm. He applies the algorithm to multicriteria optimization by exploiting the fact that we only use the objective function f to decide which is the 'better' of two vertices. In common use, this indicates that the algorithm should be robust with respect to noise or inaccuracies in the values of f. For example, we have experience with an engineer who was able to use it to resolve parameters to 0.5% after only reaching 5% resolution with a standard finite-difference Newton code.

The three main strengths of the Nelder–Mead simplex method are its tolerance of function noise, its nonreliance on any gradient approximations, and the extreme simplicity of its implementation. It takes less than 100 statements to implement in any high level language, and this is an important factor in its popularity with users who still distrust black boxes.

The major weaknesses of the algorithm are that it can be very slow for more than about 5 variables, and that it can converge to a nonminimizer. Furthermore, there is no satisfying convergence analysis.

5.2. Conjugate direction methods

The second class of methods that we discuss in this section consists of the conjugate direction algorithms. It is not entirely accurate to say that they are not based on quadratic models, but there is never a need to store a full Hessian. Therefore, these methods are especially suited for large dimensional problems where $f(x)$ and $g(x)$ are available but n is too large to store or factor an $n \times n$ matrix at each iteration.

Conjugate direction algorithms are usually presented as they would be programmed. This demonstrates their most important property, computational simplicity and little storage, but it obscures the geometric elegance that better helps the novice gain an overview of the whole class of methods.

Conjugate direction methods are most simply presented as methods for minimizing strictly convex quadratic functions. We will follow the point of view taken in Dennis and Turner (1987) where the reader can find all the proofs of results claimed here. We will adopt the standard convenience of taking $x_0 = 0$.

Assume that we are at the k-th iterate and that we have a scheme for generating a descent direction d_k for $q(x) = \frac{1}{2}x^{\mathrm{T}}Hx - h^{\mathrm{T}}x$, H symmetric and positive definite, from x_k. Suppose that x_k minimizes $q(x)$ on a k-dimensional subspace spanned by the previous iteration steps. Choose x_{k+1} to be the unique minimizer of $q(x)$ on the $(k + 1)$-dimensional subspace formed by adding d_k to the previous spanning set. These two sentences characterize the conjugate direction algorithms. It is interesting to note that this point of view is identical to the definition given by Cantrell (1969), Cragg and Levy (1969), and Miele and Cantrell (1969) of a 'memory gradient' method. It is completely developed in Dennis and Turner (1986). Nazareth (1986) gives a corresponding algorithm for general minimization problems.

It is easy to show that if we define at each iteration $p_j = x_{j+1} - x_j$, then $p_j^{\mathrm{T}}Hp_i = 0$ for $0 \leqslant j < i \leqslant k - 1$ and $p_j^{\mathrm{T}}\nabla q(x_k) = 0$ for $0 \leqslant j \leqslant k - 1$. Thus, solving the $k + 1$ dimensional minimization problem on span$\{p_0, \ldots, p_{k-1}, d_k\}$ for x_{k+1} requires the solution of a $(k + 1)$-dimensional symmetric positive definite linear system which is diagonal except for a full last row and column. This system can be solved explicitly, but the expense of saving all the previous p_i's is too high for large problems.

If one can arrange to have $d_k^{\mathrm{T}}Hp_i = 0$ for the oldest p_i's, then those p_i do not have to be saved because they are not needed explicitly in solving for x_{k+1}. It turns out that $d_k = -\nabla q(x_k) = h - Hx_k$ accomplishes this purpose for $0 \leqslant i \leqslant k - 2$ so that p_k is a linear combination of p_{k-1} and d_k. This fortunate circumstance follows from a more general result.

Let B be an arbitrary matrix and select each $d_j \in \mathrm{span}\{d_0, Bp_0, \ldots, Bp_{j-1}\}$. Then, it is easy to show x_k minimizes $q(x)$ on span$\{d_0, Bd_0, \ldots, B^{k-1}d_0\} \equiv K(d_0, B, k - 1)$, and that $-\nabla q(x_k)^{\mathrm{T}}Bp_j = 0$ for $j = 0, \ldots, k - 2$. Thus, if we choose any B and generate d_k so that $d_k^{\mathrm{T}}H = -\nabla q(x_k)^{\mathrm{T}}B$, then we only need x_k, p_{k-1} and d_k to generate

$$p_k = d_k + \beta_k \cdot p_{k-1}, \quad \beta_k = -\frac{d_k^T H p_{k-1}}{p_{k-1}^T H p_{k-1}}, \tag{5.2.1}$$

and

$$x_{k+1} = x_k + \alpha_k \cdot p_k, \quad \alpha_k = \frac{-d_k^T \nabla q(x_k)}{d_k^T H p_k}. \tag{5.2.2}$$

In this case, the p_k's are to be thought of as directions rather than iterative steps as they were defined above, but there is no difficulty introduced into the discussion above by doing so. Of course $\pm d_k$ must also be a descent direction for q from x_k, i.e., $d_k^T \nabla q(x_k) \neq 0$. The choice $B = H$ gives rise to $d_k = -\nabla q(x_k)$ mentioned above. This is called the *conjugate gradient* algorithm. The subspace $K(d_0, B, k-1)$ is called the k-dimensional Krylov subspace generated from d_0 by B.

If M is any symmetric positive definite matrix for which $d_k = -M^{-1}\nabla q(x_k)$ is easy to compute, then d_k is a descent direction and corresponds to $B = M^{-1}H$. The resultant method is called the *preconditioned conjugate gradient algorithm* and M is called the *preconditioner*. The use of a preconditioner can significantly improve the conjugate gradient algorithm. Let us now discuss briefly some factors in choosing M.

Intuitively, there are two things we might want to accomplish in our choice of M and hence B. We can try for a big reduction in q by choosing M^{-1} to be a good approximation to H^{-1}. In other words, we can try to make our new directions d_k approximate the Newton direction for q. This is the point of most iterative methods, like SOR or Gauss–Seidel for example, and it is common to exploit such methods as preconditioners for problems where they were once used alone. In such preconditioners, one never needs to work explicitly with M since $M^{-1}\nabla q(x_k)$ is the iterative step. It is worth noting that SOR does not correspond to a symmetric positive definite preconditioner M and so SSOR, which involves a forward and then backward sweep, is generally used because it does correspond to a symmetric positive definite M. See Golub and Van Loan (1983).

This way of choosing an iterative method as a preconditioner for a conjugate direction algorithm lends itself to two popular points of view: an optimizer would feel that the iterative method is being used to accelerate the conjugate direction algorithm, but the numerical partial differential equations solver would be more likely to feel that conjugate directions is being used to accelerate the basic iterative method being used as a preconditioner.

From a purely matrix algebra point of view, the first way of choosing M, which we have been discussing, corresponds to making the condition number of $M^{-1/2}HM^{-1/2}$ small, since this is the Hessian and $M^{-1}\nabla q(x_k)$ is the steepest descent direction for q at x_k in the transformed variables $x' = M^{1/2}x$. It is worth pointing out the result that the DFP or BFGS method applied to minimize $q(x)$ with exact line searches and initial Hessian approximation M generates exactly the same points in exact arithmetic as the conjugate gradient algorithm preconditioned by M.

The second point of view in choosing M, and hence $M^{-1}H = B$, is to try to make $K(M^{-1}h, B, n-1)$ have the smallest possible dimension, say $k \ll n$. The reason is that in this case the algorithm solves the problem in k steps. This can be seen from the fact that $\nabla q(x_k)$ is orthogonal to $K(M^{-1}h, B, k-1)$. Thus, $M^{-1}\nabla q(x_k)$ cannot lie in $K(M^{-1}h, B, k-1)$ unless it is zero. Then it must be zero since $M^{-1}\nabla q(x_k) \in K(M^{-1}h, B, k)$ and the Krylov subspaces have stopped increasing their dimension so $K(M^{-1}h, B, k) = K(M^{-1}h, B, k-1)$.

If we ignore the influence of the initial direction on the dimension of $K(M^{-1}h, B, n-1)$, then an upper bound on that dimension is the degree of the minimal polynomial of B. This is easy to see since if $m(B) = \Sigma_{i=0}^{k} \alpha_i B^i = 0$ is the minimal polynomial for B, then $0 = m(B)M^{-1}h$ is a nonzero linear combination of the $k+1$ generators for $K(M^{-1}h, B, k)$ whose dimension must be less than $k+1$. Since B is similar to a symmetric matrix, k is the number of distinct eigenvalues of $B = M^{-1}H$. See Hoffman and Kunze (1971).

It is not unusual for strictly convex quadratics arising from discretized partial differential equations to be solved with $k \sim n/10^3$. Such spectacularly successful preconditionings nearly always come from deep insight into the problem and not from matrix theoretic considerations. They often come from discretizing and solving a simplified problem.

The choice of preconditioners for optimization problems is not nearly so well understood. This may be because most of our effort has been directed toward algorithms and software for general library use, and effective preconditioners are problem specific.

We have generally used conjugate direction methods only for nonquadratic problems, and then only for problems so large that we have no other choice (see Section 6.1). For nonquadratics, the conjugate gradient formulas are generally given by

$$p_k = -g(x_k) + \beta_k \cdot p_{k-1}, \quad \beta_k = \frac{g(x_k)^T g(x_k)}{g(x_{k-1})^T g(x_{k-1})}, \quad (5.2.3)$$

and

$$x_{k+1} = x_k + \alpha_k \cdot p_k, \quad \alpha_k \text{ minimizes } f \text{ along } p_k. \quad (5.2.4)$$

If $f(x)$ is quadratic, (5.2.3–4) are equivalent to (5.2.1–2), but no matrix is required by (5.2.3–4). In general, the line search is not done exactly but it has to be done fairly accurately; see Gill, Murray, and Wright (1981).

Of course, the conjugate directions do not remain conjugate in finite precision implementations, and there is no clear sense in which they should be conjugate for nonquadratics. The standard way to handle this is to save some past vectors and make sure d_k is made conjugate with respect to these few vectors (see Vinsome (1976), Young and Jea (1981)), or to restart the method, perhaps by taking d_k periodically to be a linear combination of some restart vector and the d_k that would have been chosen if a restart were not due. See Beale (1972) or Powell (1977).

6. Some current research directions

In this section we will give brief summaries of some interesting area of ongoing activity. We will discuss large problems, data fitting, secant updates, singular problems, and parallel computation.

6.1. Large problems

There are three different scenarios we wish to consider here:
 (i) A quadratic model can be formed and the model Hessian can be factored if sparsity is taken into account.
 (ii) A quadratic model can be formed but linear iterative methods must be used to solve the model problem in place of matrix factorizations.
 (iii) The problem is too large for any explicit use of a model Hessian.

It is important to note that the number of variables alone does not determine which class fits a particular problem. If a big problem has a nice enough sparsity structure in the Hessian it fits in class (i); if the sparsity structure is not so nice it fits in (ii); and if it isn't sparse enough for (ii) it fits in (iii).

For problems in class (i), our first choice would be to use a Newton or finite difference Newton model as outlined in Section 3.5. If we wish to use a secant method, then we should use a so-called 'limited memory' method in the spirit of the last implementation in Section 3.3. Probably, these methods fit better with a linesearch rather than a trust region. Buckley and Lenir (1983) is a limited memory method which has been highly recommended to us by users.

For problems of class (ii), there is an elegant generalization of the dogleg algorithm (Steihaug (1980), Toint (1981)) which has shown its mettle in dealing with seismic inversion. This algorithm can be viewed as a trust region implementation of the conjugate direction inexact Newton method. The idea is simple. Given a quadratic model and a trust radius, perform conjugate direction iterations to compute the Newton step until either the Newton step is computed inside the trust region and taken as the trial step, or until some conjugate direction iterate lands outside the trust region. When the latter happens, the trial step is taken to be at the intersection of the trust region and the last conjugate direction step, or a direction of negative curvature for the quadratic model is generated at some conjugate direction iterate inside the trust region, and the trial step is taken where this negative curvature direction strikes the boundary of the trust region. If a preconditioner is used, it can be thought of as defining the shape of the trust region.

As computer storage has become less expensive, fewer problems must be related to class (iii). Generally, these problems are solved using the non-matrix form of conjugate direction methods mentioned at the end of Section 5.2.

Finally, Griewank and Toint (1982a,b) have suggested and analyzed an interesting approach to obtaining Hessian approximations for problems where the objective function can be written as the sum of objective functions that each involves its own subset of the variables. Generally speaking, the summand functions should have small dense Hessians which are positive semidefinite at the point formed by selecting the relevant subset of the components of the minimizer of the problem. This allows an approximate Hessian of the sum to be assembled from (for example) BFGS updates of the summand Hessians. The reader familiar with research on sparse matrices will recognize the connection with so-called clique or finite-element storage. See Duff, Erisman, and Reid (1986).

6.2. Data fitting

One of the most common sources of optimization problems is in parameter estimation arising from fitting mathematical models to data. Typically, data

$$(t_i, y_i), \quad i = 1, \dots, m, \tag{6.2.1}$$

has been collected, and one wants to select the free parameters $x \in \mathbb{R}^n$ in the model $m(t, x)$ so that

$$m(t_i, x) \cong y_i, \quad i = 1, \dots, m. \tag{6.2.2}$$

Such problems arise in almost all areas of science, engineering, and social science. A more common notation in these applications is (x_i, y_i), $i = 1, \dots, n$, for the data, and $f(x, \theta)$, $\theta \in \mathbb{R}^p$, for the model (θ may be replaced by β or other symbols), but we will use (6.2.1–2) to be consistent with the remainder of the book. Generally, there are far more data points than parameters, that is $m \gg n$ in (6.2.2).

Usually it is assumed that each t_i is known exactly in (6.2.1) but that y_i is measured with some error. In that case it makes sense to achieve (6.2.2) by making each *residual*

$$r_i(x) = m(t_i, x) - y_i$$

as small as possible. Let

$$R(x) = (r_1(x), \dots, r_m(x))^{\mathrm{T}}.$$

Then we wish to choose x so that the vector $R(x)$ is as small as possible, in some sense.

If we choose x to

$$\underset{x \in \mathbb{R}^n}{\text{minimize}} \|R(x)\|_1 \quad \text{or} \quad \underset{x \in \mathbb{R}^n}{\text{minimize}} \|R(x)\|_\infty \tag{6.2.3}$$

then we have a non-differentiable unconstrained optimization problem. There has been considerable research into methods for solving (6.2.3), see e.g. Gill, Murray, and Wright (1981), Murray and Overton (1980, 1981), Bartels and Conn (1981) and Conn (1985). Research is continuing into producing algorithms and software for such problems.

It is much more common to use the l_2 norm instead of (6.2.3), i.e.

$$\underset{x \in \mathbb{R}^n}{\text{minimize}} \ f(x) = \frac{1}{2} \sum_{i=1}^m r_i(x)^2 = \frac{1}{2} R(x)^T R(x) . \tag{6.2.4}$$

If each $y_i = m(t_i, \hat{x}) + e_i$ for some true parameter value $\hat{x}$ and some random error e_i, and if the m random errors arise from independent and identical normal distribution with mean 0, then (6.2.3) produces the maximum likelihood estimator of $\hat{x}$. In any case, (6.2.4) generally is easier to solve than (6.2.3).

If $R(x)$ is linear in x then (6.2.4) is a *linear least squares* problem and it can be solved in $O(mn^2)$ operations; see Stewart (1973), Lawson and Hanson (1974), or Golub and Van Loan (1983). Otherwise it is a *nonlinear least squares* problem. The nonlinear least squares problem is a particular case of unconstrained optimization and can be solved by the techniques of the preceding sections. But many special purpose methods have arisen that take advantage of the special form of the derivatives of $f(x)$,

$$g(x) = \sum_{i=1}^m \nabla r_i(x) r_i(x) \equiv J(x)^T R(x)$$

where $J(x) \in \mathbb{R}^{m \times n}$ denotes the Jacobian matrix of $R(x)$, and

$$H(x) = \sum_{i=1}^m (\nabla r_i(x) \nabla r_i(x)^T + \nabla^2 r_i(x) r_i(x)) \equiv J(x)^T J(x) + S(x) \tag{6.2.5}$$

where $S(x) \in \mathbb{R}^{n \times n}$ is the part of $H(x)$ that is a function of second derivatives of $R(x)$.

If both first and second derivatives of $R(x)$ are available (and n is not too large) then the nonlinear least squares problem should probably just be solved by standard unconstrained optimization methods. Otherwise the goal of most special purpose nonlinear least squares methods is to produce efficient methods that require only analytic or finite difference first derivatives of $R(x)$. This supplies $g(x)$ and the first part of $H(x)$, but not the second order part $S(x)$. Many strategies for using this special structure exist, and we summarize them very briefly. For more detail see Dennis and Schnabel (1983).

Gauss–Newton and Levenberg–Marquardt methods simply omit $S(x)$ and base their step on the model

$$m(x_c + d) = f(x_c) + g(x_c)^T d + \tfrac{1}{2} d^T J(x_c)^T J(x_c) d . \tag{6.2.6}$$

This is very reasonable if the data (6.2.1) is fit well by the optimal model $m(t_i, x_*)$ since in this case $R(x_*)$ and hence $S(x_*)$ will be nearly zero, and omitting $S(x)$ will cause little harm. Methods that use a line search in conjunction with (6.2.6) are generally called Gauss–Newton methods, while the use of a trust region leads to Moré's (1978) derivation of the Levenberg–Marquardt method. This method is implemented in MINPACK (Moré, Garbow, and Hillstrom (1980)) and has been quite effective in practice. Note that (6.2.6) is equivalent to

$$m(x_c + d) = \tfrac{1}{2}\|R(x_c) + J(x_c)d\|_2^2$$

and so these methods can be derived from the linear Taylor series model of $R(x)$.

Alternatively, secant methods for nonlinear least squares construct approximations to $H(x)$ given by (6.2.5). Some codes have used the methods of Section 3.4 to approximate all of $H(x)$, but more successful methods have arisen by approximating $H(x_c)$ by

$$J(x_c)^T J(x_c) + A_c$$

where A_c approximates $S(x_c)$. That is, the available part of the Hessian is used and only the unavailable part is approximated. Dennis, Gay and Walsch (1981a,b) constructed a very effective method along these lines. In general, such quasi-Newton methods are more effective than modern Levenberg–Marquardt methods on problems where $R(x_*)$, and hence $S(x_*)$ is large, and of comparable effectiveness otherwise.

Research is continuing on various aspects of nonlinear least squares calculations, including large residual problems (Salane (1987)), large dimensional problems (Toint (1987)), secant approximation (Al Baali and Fletcher (1983)), and application of the tensor methods mentioned in Section 6.5 (Hanson and Krogh (1987), Bouaricha and Schnabel (1988)).

An interesting variant of the data fitting problem occurs when there is experimental error in both t_i and y_i. In this case it becomes appropriate to measure the distance between the data point (t_i, y_i) and the fitting function $m(t, x)$ by the (weighted) Euclidean distance from the point to the curve. Boggs, Byrd, and Schnabel (1987) show that minimizing the sum of the squares of these distances leads to the problem

$$\underset{x\in\mathbb{R}^n,\delta\in\mathbb{R}^m}{\text{minimize}} \sum_{i=1}^{m} ((m(t_i + \delta_i, x) - y_i)^2 + w_i^2 \delta_i^2) \tag{6.2.7}$$

for appropriate weights w_i. Problem (6.2.7) is a nonlinear least squares problems in $m + n$ variables, but Schwetlick and Tiller (1985) and Boggs, Byrd, and Schnabel (1987) show how to solve it efficiently using essentially the same work per iteration as for the standard nonlinear least squares problem

(6.2.4). Boggs, Byrd, Donaldson, and Schnabel (1987) provide a software package for (6.2.7). The case when $m(t, x)$ is linear in both t and x is addressed in Golub and Van Loan (1980).

Finally, there is an increasing amount of cross-fertilization between the optimization and statistical communities in the study of data fitting problems. Areas of interest include the application of modern optimization techniques to specialized data fitting problems (see e.g. Bates and Watts (1987), Bunch (1987)), and the statistical analysis of parameter estimates obtained by non-linear least squares (see e.g. Bates and Watts (1980), Cook and Witmer (1985), Donaldson and Schnabel (1987)).

6.3. Secant updates

The investigation of alternative secant methods for unconstrained optimization is enjoying a recent revival. This was a very active area in the 1960's and 70's, starting with the discovery of the first secant update, the DFP update (3.4.7), and continuing with the discovery of the BFGS update (3.4.5). Much interest was focused on the Broyden family of updates (Broyden (1970))

$$B_+(\theta) = \theta B_+^{\mathrm{DFP}} + (1 - \theta) B_+^{\mathrm{BFGS}} \tag{6.3.1}$$

which differ from each other only by multiples of a rank-one matrix; this topic is discussed extensively in Fletcher (1980). Several convergence results for any choice of $\theta \in [0, 1]$ have been proven; see e.g. Griewank and Toint (1982b) and Stachurski (1981). But the consensus for over 10 years has been that the BFGS is best in practice. One hint is a powerful convergence result of Powell (1976) for the BFGS that has never been extended to the DFP.

Some recent research has attempted to explain theoretically the superiority of the BFGS. Powell (1986) uses a simple example to show that the DFP can be very much slower than the BFGS. Byrd, Nocedal, and Yuan (1987) extend Powell's 1976 convergence result to any $\theta \in [0, 1)$, i.e. any convex combination of the DFP and the BFGS except the DFP, and in doing so show that the DFP lacks a self-correcting term in its update formula. Dennis, Martinez, and Tapia (1987) show that the BFGS has an optimal bounded deterioration property in the convex class.

Other recent research has resumed computational and theoretical investigation of choices other than the BFGS ($\theta = 0$) in (6.3.1). Zhang and Tewarson (1986) consider using $\theta < 0$; they extend Powell's convergence result to their strategy and their computational results show that it may produce better results than the BFGS in practice. Conn, Gould, and Toint (1981) revisit the symmetric-rank-one update,

$$B_+ = B_c + \frac{(y_c - B_c s_c)(y_c - B_c s_c)^{\mathrm{T}}}{(y_c - B_c s_c)^{\mathrm{T}} s_c}$$

the choice $\theta = (y_c^{\mathrm{T}} s_c)/(y_c - B_c s_c)^{\mathrm{T}} s_c$ in (6.3.1), which may have a zero denominator, and show that it may be competitive with the BFGS when used in conjunction with a trust region method and safeguarding of the denominator.

Dennis and Walker (1985) and Vu (1984) have studied the problem of dealing with noise in y for the least change Frobenius norm updates, but the more important analysis for the BFGS update is not so well understood.

A very important practical problem in secant updating comes from constrained optimization. We want to extend the BFGS method to maintain an approximation to the Hessian of the Lagrangian with respect to the primal variables. The most commonly used method is due to Powell (1978), but he shows in Powell (1985) that it can lead to ill-conditioning in the approximate Hessians. Tapia (1984) suggests and analyzes a promising procedure.

Some very elegant work on secant methods for *nonlinear* problems that come from discretization of infinite dimensional problems has been done by Griewank (1983) and Kelley and Sachs (1985). They give a new derivation of the method for nonlinear two points boundary value problems suggested in Hart and Soul (1973). The idea behind this work is to consider the operator equation in its natural function space setting. Roughly speaking, one defines a least-change secant method for the operator equation using the norm in which Newton's method could be shown to have its familiar convergence properties. This gives a point-wise quasi-Newton method equivalent to a local affine model which one discretizes and solves. In other words, linearization precedes discretization instead of the standard approaches in which one discretizes the operator equation and then iteratively linearizes it.

Finally, the advent of parallel computers is leading to revived interest in *multiple secant updates*. These are methods that attempt to satisfy more than one secant equation at each iteration in order to interpolate more than one previous value of $g(x)$ for optimization, or of $F(x)$ for nonlinear equations. They were first mentioned by Barnes (1965) for nonlinear equations and shown by Gay and Schnabel (1978) and Schnabel and Frank (1987) to lead to small gains over Broyden's method for nonlinear equations. The application of this approach to unconstrained optimization has fundamental limitations, see Schnabel (1983). But these methods now seem naturally suited to parallel computation where multiple values of $g(x)$ or $F(x)$ may be calculated at one iteration; see e.g. Byrd, Schnabel, and Shultz (1987).

6.4. Singular problems

There are a number of practical problems for which $J(x_*)$ (for nonlinear equations) or $H(x_*)$ (for optimization) are singular or nearly singular. We call these *singular problems*. None of the convergence results of Sections 2-3 apply to singular problems, and by considering one variable problems we can see that slow convergence is to be expected. For example, applying Newton's method for nonlinear equations to solve $x^2 = 0$ produces linear convergence with constant $\frac{1}{2}$, while applying Newton's method for optimization to minimize x^4 gives linear convergence with constant $\frac{2}{3}$. Clearly the standard linear and quadratic models are less helpful in these cases since all the derivatives used in the standard models approach zero as x converges to x_*.

There has been a considerable amount of recent research analyzing the behavior of standard methods on singular problems, and suggesting improved methods. Most of this research has been for nonlinear equations problems and is summarized excellently in Griewank (1985). We will give a very brief indication of this work.

Many researchers have analyzed the convergence of Newton's method for solving singular systems of nonlinear equations. For 'regular' singularities, results such as those in Decker and Kelley (1980a,b) or Griewank (1980) show that one can still expect linear convergence with the constant converging to $\frac{1}{2}$. Decker and Kelley (1985) show that Broyden's method, like the one-dimensional secant method, is linearly convergent on singular problems with constant converging to $(\sqrt{5} - 1)/2 \cong 0.62$, from certain starting points.

Various acceleration schemes for solving singular systems of equations have been proposed, and they are surveyed in Greiwank (1985). Many authors have suggested methods related to the one variable idea of doubling the Newton step that are intended solely for singular problems. One difficulty in applying these techniques is that one may not know a priori whether the problem is singular. Some methods from curve following are also applicable to singular systems of equations (see e.g. Moore and Spense (1980)). Griewank (1985) and Schnabel and Frank (1984, 1987) have proposed methods that are applicable to both singular and nonsingular problems. These methods append a simple low rank quadratic term to the standard linear model, in a way that doesn't significantly increase the costs of forming, storing, or solving the model. Schnabel and Frank report that their 'tensor' methods lead to significant improvements on both singular and nonsingular test problems.

The solution of singular unconstrained optimization problems is more complex. This is related to the fact that for one variable problems, if $f^{ii}(x_*) = 0$, then we must also have $f^{iii}(x_*) = 0$ and $f^{iv}(x_*) \geq 0$. Similarly, Griewank and Osborne (1983) show that if $H(x_*)v = 0$ at a minimizer x_*, then we must have $\nabla^3 f(x_*)vvv = 0$, $\nabla^4 f(x_*)vvvv \geq 0$, and $\nabla^3 f(x)vv$ not too large. These conditions imply that the singularity is 'irregular' and invalidate most of the approaches mentioned above. Schnabel and Chow (1988) introduce a 'tensor' method that appends low rank third and fourth order terms to the standard quadratic model, without requiring any additional function or derivative evaluations and without appreciably increasing the cost of forming, storing, or solving the model. They report that their approach leads to a substantial reduction in the cost of solving both singular and nonsingular test problems.

6.5. Parallel computation

An important recent development in computing is the commercial availability of *parallel computers*, computers that can perform multiple operations concurrently. These include *MIMD* (Multiple Instruction Multiple Data) *com-*

puters that allow different instruction streams to be executed concurrently, *processor arrays* that apply the same instruction stream to multiple data streams concurrently, and *vector computers* that use data pipelining to rapidly perform pairwise addition or multiplication of vectors. Since it appears that many of the significant future gains in computer speed will come from effectively utilizing such machines, it is becoming important to design optimization methods that utilize them efficiently. Virtually all the research in this area is quite recent, and we will simply indicate some of the approaches that are emerging. These are primarily oriented towards MIMD computers, which seem to be the class of parallel computers best suited towards parallel optimization because they support concurrency at a coarse-grain algorithmic level.

One approach towards parallel optimization is to design general purpose parallel variants of the Newton or quasi-Newton methods discussed in Sections 2–4. These types of methods have two potentially significant costs that must be considered in constructing parallel versions. They are the evaluations of functions and derivatives, and the linear algebra costs in solving linear systems or updating secant approximations. Both can be adapted to parallel computers.

The most obvious way to use a parallel computer effectively during the evaluation of functions or derivatives is to perform the multiple function evaluations of a finite difference gradient or Hessian calculation concurrently (Dixon (1981), Patel (1982), Lootsma (1984)). Schnabel (1987) introduces the idea of performing a *speculative* finite difference gradient evaluation concurrently with the evaluation of $f(x)$ at a trial point, before it is known whether this point will be accepted as the next iterate. Since the acceptance rate for trial points usually is at least 70%, this gradient value will usually be needed, so this simple strategy will utilize $n + 1$ or fewer processors quite efficiently if function evaluation is the dominant cost. Byrd, Schnabel, and Shultz (1987) investigate the more difficult question of effectively utilizing more than $n + 1$ (but fewer than $\frac{1}{2}n^2$) processors; this leads to new optimization methods that usually require significantly fewer iterations than the BFGS method. An alternative (see e.g. Patel (1982)) is to evaluate $f(x)$ at many trial points simultaneously, but this appears unlikely to produce as much increase in speed.

As n becomes large it is also important to perform the linear algebra calculations in parallel. For methods that use the Hessian, parallel matrix factorizations and backsolves are required and many effective algorithms have been produced (see e.g. Heller (1978), Geist and Heath (1986)). For parallel BFGS methods, Han (1986) has proposed an implementation that sequences a factorization ZZ^T of the inverse of the Hessian approximation. An alternative is to utilize the unfactored inverse update (3.4.6), which appears to parallelize as well and require fewer arithmetic operations. Traditionally there has been some concern over the numerical stability of these approaches (see e.g. Powell (1987)); this issue is now being reexamined since they seem better suited to parallel computation than the Cholesky factorization update (3.4.4).

It will also be increasingly important to develop specific parallel optimization methods for particular classes of expensive optimization problems. Some early examples include Dixon, Ducksbury, and Singh (1982), and Dixon and Spedicato (1985). There has also been work on parallel methods related to other optimization methods we have discussed; for example see Housos and Wing (1980) for a parallel conjugate direction method, and Lescrenier (1986) for a parallel approach to partially separable optimization.

References

Al-Baali, and Fletcher (1983), Variational methods for nonlinear least squares, Department of Mathematical Sciences Report NA/71, University of Dundee, Dundee, Scotland.

Armijo, L. (1966), Minimization of function having Lipschitz-continuous first partial derivatives, *Pacific Journal of Mathematics* **16**, 1–3.

Barnes, J. (1965), An algorithm for solving nonlinear equations based on the secant method, *Computer Journal* **8**, 66–72.

Bartels, R.H. and A.R. Conn (1982), An approach to nonlinear l_1 data fitting in: J.P. Hennert (ed.), *Proceedings of the Third IIMAS Workshop, Lecture Notes in Mathematics*, No. 909 (Springer Verlag, Berlin) 48–58.

Bates, D.M. and D.G. Watts (1980), Relative curvature measures of nonlinearity, *Journal of the Royal Statistical Society Ser. B* **42**, 1–25.

Bates, D.M. and D.G. Watts (1987), A generalized Gauss–Newton procedure for multi-response parameter estimation, *SIAM Journal on Scientific and Statistical Computing* **8**, 49–55.

Beale, E.M.L. (1972), A derivation of conjugate gradients, in: F.A. Lootsma, (ed.), *Numerical Methods for Nonlinear Optimization* (Academic Press, London) 39–43.

Boggs, P.T., R.H. Byrd, and R.B. Schnabel (1987), A stable and efficient algorithm for orthogonal distance regression, *SIAM Journal on Scientific and Statistical Computing* **8**, 1052–1078.

Boggs, P.T., R.H. Byrd, J.R. Donaldson and R.B. Schnabel (1987), ORDPACK – Software for weighted orthogonal distance regression, Department of Computer Science, Report CU-CS-360-87, University of Colorado, Boulder, CO.

Bouaricha, A. and R.B. Schnabel (1989), A software package for tensor methods for nonlinear equations and nonlinear least squares, in preparation.

Broyden, C.G. (1965), A class of methods for solving nonlinear simultaneous equations, *Mathematics of Computation* **19**, 577–593.

Broyden, C.G. (1969), A new double-rank minimization algorithm, *Notices of the American Mathematical Society* **16**, 670.

Broyden, C.G. (1970), The convergence of a class of double-rank minimization algorithms, Parts I and II, *Journal of the Institute of Mathematics and its Applications* **6**, 76–90, 222–236.

Broyden, C.G. (1971), The convergence of an algorithm for solving sparse nonlinear systems, *Mathematics of Computation* **25**, 285–294.

Broyden, C.G., J.E. Dennis Jr. and J.J. Moré (1973), On the local and superlinear convergence of quasi-Newton methods, *IMA Journal of Applied Mathematics* **12**, 223–246.

Buckley, A. and A. Lenir (1983), QN-like variable storage conjugate gradients, *Mathematical Programming* **27**, 155–175.

Bunch, D.S. (1987), Maximum likelihood estimation of probabilistic choice models, *SIAM Journal on Scientific and Statistical Computing* **8**, 56–70.

Byrd, R.H., J. Nocedal and Y. Yuan (1987), Global convergence of a class of quasi-Newton methods on convex problems. *SIAM Journal on Numerical Analysis* **24**, 1171–1189.

Byrd, R.H., R.B. Schnabel and G.A. Shultz (1988), Approximate solution of the trust regions problem by minimization over two-dimensional subspaces, *Mathematical Programming* **40**, 247–263.

Cantrell, J.W. (1969), Relation between the memory gradient method and the minimization of functions, *Journal of Optimization Theory and its Applications* **4**, 67–71.

Coleman, T.F., B. Garbow and J.J. Moré (1984), Software for estimating sparse Jacobian matrices, *ACM Transactions on Mathematical Software* **10**, 329–347.

Coleman, T.F., J.J. Garbow and J.J. Moré (1985), Software for estimating sparse Hessian matrices, *ACM Transactions on Mathematical Software* **11**, 363–378.

Coleman, T.F. and J.J. Moré (1983), Estimation of sparse Jacobian matrices and graph coloring problems, *SIAM Journal on Numerical Analysis* **20**, 187–209.

Coleman, T.F. and J.J. Moré (1984), Estimation of sparse Hessian matrices and graph coloring problems, *SIAM Journal on Numerical Analysis* **28**, 243–270.

Conn, A.R. (1985), Nonlinear programming, exact penalty functions and projection techniques for non-smooth functions, in: P.T. Boggs, R.H. Byrd, and R.B. Schnabel, (eds.), *Numerical Optimization 1984* (SIAM, Philadelphia, PA) 3–25.

Cook, R.D. and J.A. Witmer (1985), A note on parameter-effects curvature, *Journal of the American Statistical Association* **80**, 872–878.

Cragg, E.E. and A.V. Levy (1969), Study on a supermemory gradient method for the minimization of functions, *Journal of Optimization Theory and its Applications* **4**, 191–205.

Curtis, A., M.J.D. Powell and J.K. Reid (1974), On the estimation of sparse Jacobian matrices, *IMA Journal of Applied Mathematics* **13**, 117–120.

Davidon, W.C. (1959), Variable metric methods for minimization, Argonne National Labs Report ANL-5990.

Decker, D.W. and C.T. Kelley (1980a), Newton's method at singular points I, *SIAM Journal on Numerical Analysis* **17**, 66–70.

Decker, D.W. and C.T. Kelley (1980b), Newton's method at singular points II, *SIAM Journal on Numerical Analysis* **17**, 465–471.

Decker, D.W. and C.T. Kelley (1985), Broyden's method for a class of problems having singular Jacobian at the root, *SIAM Journal on Numerical Analysis* **22**, 566–574.

Dembo, R.S., S.C. Eisenstat and T. Steihaug (1982), Inexact Newton methods, *SIAM Journal on Numerical Analysis* **19**, 400–408.

Dennis, J.E. Jr., D.M. Gay and R.E. Welsch (1981), An adaptive nonlinear least-squares algorithm, *ACM Transactions on Mathematical Software* **7**, 348–368.

Dennis, J.E. Jr. and G. Li (1988), A hybrid algorithm for solving sparse nonlinear systems of equations, *Mathematics of Computation* **50**, 155–166.

Dennis, J.E. Jr., H.J. Martinez and R.A. Tapia (1987), A convergence theory for the structured BFGS secant method with an application to nonlinear least squares, TR87-15, Department of Mathematical Sciences, Rice University, Houston, TX.

Dennis, J.E. Jr. and H.H. Mei (1979), Two new unconstrained optimization algorithms which use function and gradient values, *Journal of Optimization Theory and its Applications* **28**, 453–482.

Dennis, J.E. Jr. and J.J. Moré (1974), A characterization of superlinear convergence and its application to quasi-Newton methods, *Mathematics of Computation* **28**, 549–560.

Dennis, J.E. Jr. and J.J. Moré (1977), Quasi-Newton methods, motivation and theory, *SIAM Review* **19**, 46–89.

Dennis, J.E. Jr. and R.B. Schnabel (1979), Least change secant updates for quasi-Newton methods, *SIAM Review* **21**, 443–459.

Dennis, J.E. Jr. and R.B. Schnabel (1981), A new derivation of symmetric positive definite secant updates, in: O.L. Mangasarian, R.R. Meyer, and S.M. Robinson (eds.), *Nonlinear Programming* 4 (Academic Press, New York).

Dennis, J.E. Jr. and R.B. Schnabel (1983), *Numerical Methods for Unconstrained Optimization and Nonlinear Equations* (Prentice-Hall, Englewood Cliffs, NJ).

Dennis, J.E. Jr. and K. Turner (1986), Generalized Conjugate Directions, *Journal for Linear Algebra and Applications* **88/89**, 187–209.

Dennis, J.E. Jr. and H.F. Walker (1981), Convergence theorems for least-change secant update methods, *SIAM Journal on Numerical Analysis* **18**, 949–987.

Dennis, J.E. Jr. and H.F. Walker (1985), Least-change sparse secant update methods with inaccurate secant conditions, *SIAM Journal on Numerical Analysis* **22**, 760–778.

Dennis, J.E. Jr. and D.J. Woods (1987), Optimization on microcomputers: The Nelder-Mead simplex algorithm, in: A. Wouk (ed.), *New Computing Environments: Microcomputers in Large-Scale Computing*, (SIAM, Philadelphia, PA) 116–122.

Dixon, L.C.W. (1981), The place of parallel computation in numerical optimization I, the local problem, Technical Report No. 118, Numerical Optimisation Centre, The Hatfield Polytechnic.

Dixon, L.C.W., P.G. Ducksbury and P. Singh (1982), A parallel version of the conjugate gradient algorithm for finite element problems, Technical Report No. 132, Numerical Optimisation Centre, The Hatfield Polytechnic.

Dixon, L.C.W. and E. Spedicato (1985), Software developments for numerical on-line parallel optimisation of engine fuel consumption, Technical Report No. 172, Numerical Optimisation Centre, The Hatfield Polytechnic.

Donaldson, J.R. and R.B. Schnabel (1987), Computational experience with confidence regions and confidence intervals for nonlinear least squares, *Technometrics* **29**, 67–82.

Duff, I.S., A.M. Erisman and J.K. Reid (1986), *Direct Methods for Sparse Matrices* (Clarendon Press, Oxford).

Flachs, J. (1986), On the generation of updates for quasi-Newton method, *Journal of Optimization Theory and its Applications* **48**, 379–418.

Fletcher, R. (1970), A new approach to variable metric methods, *Computer Journal* **13**, 317–322.

Fletcher, R. (1980), *Practical Methods of Optimization, vol. 1, Unconstrained Optimization* (John Wiley and Sons, New York).

Fletcher, R. and M.J.D. Powell (1963), A rapidly convergent descent method for minimization, *Computer Journal* **6**, 163–168.

Fletcher, R. and C.M. Reeves (1964), Function minimization by conjugate gradients, *Computer Journal* **7**, 149–154.

Gay, D.M. (1979), Some convergence properties of Broyden's method, *SIAM Journal on Numerical Analysis* **16**, 623–630.

Gay, D.M. (1981), Computing optimal locally constrained steps, *SIAM Journal on Scientific and Statistical Computing* **2**, 186–197.

Gay, D.M. (1983), Subroutines for unconstrained minimization using a model/trust-region approach, *ACM Transactions on Mathematical Software* **9**, 503–524.

Gay, D.M. and R.B. Schnabel (1978), Solving systems of nonlinear equations by Broyden's method with projected updates, in: L. Mangasarian, R.R. Meyer, and S.M. Robinson (eds.), *Nonlinear Programming 3* (Academic Press, New York) 245–281.

Geist, G.A. and M.T. Heath (1986), Matrix computation on distributed memory multiprocessors, in: M.T. Heath (ed.), *Hypercube Multiprocessors 1986* (SIAM, Philadelphia, PA) 161–180.

Gill, P.E., G.H. Golub, W. Murray and M.A. Saunders (1974), Methods for modifying matrix factorizations, *Mathematics of Computation* **28**, 505–535.

Gill, P.E. and W. Murray (1974), Newton-type methods for unconstrained and linearly constrained optimization, *Mathematical Programming* **28**, 311–350.

Gill, P.E., W. Murray and M.H. Wright (1981), *Practical Optimization* (Academic Press, London–New York).

Goldfarb, D. (1970), A family of variable metric methods derived by variational means, *Mathematics of Computation* **24**, 23–26.

Goldfarb, D. (1976), Factorized variable metric methods for unconstrained optimization, *Mathematics of Computation* **30**, 796–811.

Goldfarb, D. and Ph.L. Toint (1984), Optimal estimation of Jacobian and Hessian matrices that arise in finite difference calculations, *Mathematics of Computation* **43**, 69–88.

Goldfeldt, S.M., R.E. Quandt, and H.F. Trotter (1966), Maximization by quadratic hill-climbing, *Econometrica* **34**, 541–551.

Goldstein, A.A. (1967), *Constructive Real Analysis* (Harper & Row, New York).

Golub, G.H. and C.F. Van Loan (1983), *Matrix Computations* (Johns Hopkins University Press, Baltimore, MD).

Golub, G.H. and C.F. Van Loan (1980), An analysis of the total least squares problem, *SIAM Journal on Numerical Analysis* **17**, 883–893.

Griewank, A.O. (1980a), Analysis and modification of Newton's method at singularities, Ph.D. thesis, Australian National University.

Griewank, A.O. (1980b), Starlike domains of convergence for Newton's method at singularities, *Numerische Mathematik* **35**, 95–111.

Griewank, A.O. (1983), Note on the weighting of Schubert's update for discretizations of ordinary differential equations, Technical Report, Department of Mathematics, Southern Methodist University.

Griewank, A.O. (1985), On solving nonlinear equations with simple singularities or nearly singular solutions, *SIAM Review* **27**, 537–564.

Griewank, A.O. and Ph.L. Toint (1982a), Partitioned variable metric updates for large sparse optimization problems, *Numerische Mathematik* **39**, 119–137.

Griewank, A.O. and Ph.L. Toint (1982b), Local convergence analysis for partitioned quasi-Newton updates, *Numerische Mathematik* **39**, 429–448.

Grzegorski, S.M. (1985), Orthogonal projections on convex sets for Newton-like methods, *SIAM Journal on Numerical Analysis* **22**, 1208–1219.

Hart, W.E. and S.O.W. Soul (1973), Quasi-Newton methods for discretized nonlinear boundary value problems, *IMA Journal of Applied Mathematics* **11**, 351–359.

Han, S.P. (1986), Optimization by updated conjugate subspaces, in: D.F. Griffiths and G.A. Watson (eds.), *Numerical Analysis: Pitman Research Notes in Mathematics Series 140* (Longman Scientific and Technical Press, Burnt Mill, England) 82–97.

Hanson, R.J. and F.T. Krogh (1987), A new algorithm for constrained nonlinear least squares problems, Manuscript.

Hebden, M.D. (1973), An algorithm for minimization using exact second derivatives, Technical report TP515, Atomic Energy Research Establishment, Harwell, England.

Heller, D. (1978), A survey of parallel algorithms in numerical linear algebra, *SIAM Review* **20**, 740–777.

Hoffman, K. and R. Kunze (1971), *Linear Algebra* (Prentice-Hall, Englewood Cliffs, NJ).

Housos, E.C. and O. Wing (1980), Parallel nonlinear minimization by conjugate directions, *Proceedings of the 1980 International Conference on Parallel Processing*, 157–158.

Kelley, C.T. and E.W. Sachs (1985), A new quasi-Newton method for some differential equations, Technical Report, Department of Mathematics, North Carolina State University.

Lescrenier, M. (1986), Partially separable optimization and parallel computing, Report No. 86/5, Department of Mathematics, Facultés Universitaires ND de la Paix, Namur, Belgium.

Lawson, C.L. and R.J. Hanson (1974), *Solving Least Squares Problems* (Prentice Hall, Englewood Cliffs, NJ).

Levenberg, K. (1944), A method for the solution of certian problems in least squares, *Quarterly of Applied Mathematics* **2**, 164–168.

Li, G. (1986), Algorithms for solving sparse nonlinear systems of equations, TR86-6, Department of Mathematical Sciences, Ph.D. Thesis, Rice University.

Lootsma, F.A. (1984), Parallel unconstrained optimization methods, Report 84-30, Department of Mathematics and Informatics, Delft University of Technology.

Marquardt, D. (1963), An algorithm for least-squares estimation of nonlinear parameters, *SIAM Journal on Applied Mathematics* **11**, 431–441.

Marwil, E.S. (1978), Exploiting sparsity in Newton-type methods, Ph.D. Thesis, Applied Mathematics, Cornell University.

Marwil, E.S. (1979), Convergence results for Schubert's method for solving sparse nonlinear equations, *SIAM Journal on Numerical Analysis* **16**, 588–604.

Matthies, H. and G. Strang (1979), The solution of nonlinear finite element equations, *International Journal on Numerical Methods in Engineering* **14**, 1613–1626.

McCormick, G.P. (1977), A modification of Armijo's step-size rule for negative curvature, *Mathematical Programming* **13**, 111–115.

Miele, A. and J.W. Cantrell (1969), Study on a memory gradient method for the minimization of functions, *Journal of Optimization Theory and its Applications* **3**, 459–470.

Moore, G. and A. Spence (1980), The calculation of turning points of nonlinear equations, *SIAM Journal on Numerical Analysis* **17**, 567–576.

Moré, J.J. (1978), The Levenberg-Marquardt algorithm: implementation and theory, in: G.A. Watson (ed.), *Numerical Analysis, Dundee 1977. Lecture Notes in Mathematics 630* (Springer-Verlag, Berlin) 105–116.

Moré, J.J., B.S. Garbow, and K.E. Hillstrom (1980), User guide for MINPACK-1, Argonne National Laboratory Report ANL-80-74.

Moré, J.J., B.S. Garbow and K.E. Hillstrom (1981), Fortran subroutines for testing unconstrained optimization software, *ACM Transactions on Mathematical Software* **7**, 136–140.

Moré, J.J. and D.C. Sorensen (1979), On the use of directions of negative curvature in a modified Newton method, *Mathematical Programming* **16**, 1–20.

Moré, J.J. and D.C. Sorensen (1983), Computing a trust region step, *SIAM Journal on Scientific and Statistical Computing* **4**, 553–572.

Moré, J.J. and D.C. Sorensen (1984), Newton's method, in: G.H. Golub (ed.), *Studies in Numerical Analysis* (The Mathematical Association of America, Washington, DC) 29–82.

Murray, W. and M.L. Overton (1980), A projected Lagrangian algorithm for nonlinear minimax optimization, *SIAM Journal on Scientific and Statistical Computing* **1**, 345–370.

Murray, W. and M.L. Overton (1981), A projected Lagrangian algorithm for nonlinear l_1 optimization, *SIAM Journal on Scientific and Statistical Computing* **2**, 207–224.

Nazareth, J.L. (1986), The method of successive affine reduction for nonlinear minimization *Mathematical Programming* **35**, 97–109.

Nelder, J.A. and R. Mead (1965), A simplex method for function minimization, *Computer Journal* **7**, 308–313.

Ortega, J.M. and W.C. Rheinboldt (1970), *Iterative Solution of Nonlinear Equations in Several Variables* (Academic Press, New York).

Patel, K.D. (1982), Implementation of a parallel (SIMD) modified Newton algorithm on the ICL DAP, Technical Report 131, The Hatfield Polytechnic Numerical Optimisation Centre.

Powell, M.J.D. (1970a), A hybrid method for nonlinear equations, in: P. Rabinowitz (ed.), *Numerical Methods for Nonlinear Algebraic Equations* (Gordon and Breach, London) 87–114.

Powell, M.J.D. (1970b), A new algorithm for unconstrained optimization, in: J.B. Rosen, O.L. Mangasarian and K. Ritter (eds.), *Nonlinear Programming* (Academic Press, New York) 31–65.

Powell, M.J.D. (1975), Convergence properties of a class of minimization algorithms, in: O.L. Mangasarian, R.R. Meyer, S.M. Robinson (eds.), *Nonlinear Programming* 2 (Academic Press, New York) 1–27.

Powell, M.J.D. (1976), Some global convergence properties of a variable metric algorithm without exact line searches, in: R. Cottle and C. Lemke (eds.), *Nonlinear Programming* (AMS, Providence, RI) 53–72.

Powell, M.J.D. (1977), Restart procedures for the conjugate-gradient method, *Mathematical Programming* **12**, 241–254.

Powell, M.J.D. (1978), The convergence of variable metric methods for nonlinearly constrained optimization problems, in: O.L. Mangasarian, R. Meyer, S. Robinson (eds.), *Nonlinear Programming* 3 (Academic Press, New York) 27–63.

Powell, M.J.D. (1984), On the global convergence of trust region algorithms for unconstrained minimization, *Mathematical Programming* **29**, 297–303.

Powell, M.J.D. (1985), The performance of two subroutines for constrained optimization on some difficult test problems, in: P.T. Boggs, R.H. Byrd, R.B. Schnabel (eds.), *Numerical Optimization 1984* (SIAM, Philadelphia, PA) 160–177.

Powell, M.J.D. (1986), How bad are the BFGS and DFP methods when the objective function is quadratic?, *Mathematical Programming* **34**, 34–47.

Powell, M.J.D. (1987), Updating conjugate directions by the BFGS formula, *Mathematical Programming* **38**, 29–46.

Powell, M.J.D. and Ph.L. Toint (1979), On the estimation of sparse Hessian matrices, *SIAM Journal on Numerical Analysis* **16**, 1060–1074.

Reid, J.K. (1973), Least squares solution of sparse systems of non-linear equations by a modified Marquardt algorithm, in: *Proceedings of the NATO Conf. at Combridge*, July 1972 (North-Holland, Amsterdam) 437–445.

Reinsch, C. (1971), Smoothing by spline functions II, *Numerische Mathematik* **16**, 451–454.

Salane, D.E. (1987), A continuation approach for solving large-residual nonlinear least squares problems, *SIAM Journal on Scientific and Statistical Computing* **8**, 655–671.

Schnabel, R.B. (1983), Quasi-Newton methods using multiple secant equations, Technical Report CU-CS-247-83, Department of Computer Science, University of Colorado at Boulder.

Schnabel, R.B. (1987), Concurrent function evaluations in local and global optimization, *Computer Methods in Applied Mechanics and Engineering* **64**, 537–552.

Schnabel, R.B. and T. Chow (1989), Tensor methods for unconstrained optimization, In preparation.

Schnabel, R.B. and P.D. Frank (1984), Tensor methods for nonlinear equations, *SIAM Journal on Numerical Analysis* **21**(5), 815–843.

Schnabel, R.B. and P.D. Frank (1987), Solving systems of nonlinear equations by tensor methods, in: A. Iserles and M.J.D. Powell (eds.), *The State of the Art in Numerical Analysis* (Clarendon Press, Oxford) 245–271.

Schnabel, R.B., J.E. Koontz and B.E. Weiss (1985), A modular system of algorithms of unconstrained minimization, *ACM Transactions on Mathematical Software* **11**, 419–440.

Schubert, L.K. (1970), Modification of a quasi-Newton method for nonlinear equations with a sparse Jacobian, *Mathematics of Computation* **24**, 27–30.

Schwetlick, H. and V. Tiller (1985), Numerical methods for estimating parameters in nonlinear models with errors in the variables, *Technometrics* **27**, 17–24.

Shanno, D.F. (1970), Conditioning of quasi-Newton methods for function minimization, *Mathematics of Computation* **24**, 647–657.

Shanno, D.F. and K.H. Phua (1978a), Matrix conditioning and nonlinear optimization, *Mathematical Programming* **14**, 145–160.

Shanno, D.F. and K.H. Phua (1978b), Numerical comparison of several variable metric algorithms, *Journal of Optimization Theory and its Applications* **25**, 507–518.

Shultz, G.A., R.B. Schnabel and R.H. Byrd (1985), A family of trust-region-based algorithms for unconstrained minimization with strong global convegence properties, *SIAM Journal on Numerical Analysis* **22**, 47–67.

Sorensen, D.C. (1981), An example concerning quasi-Newton estimation of a sparse Hessian, *ACM SIGNUM Newsletter* **16**(2), 8–10.

Sorensen, D.C. (1982), Newton's method with a model trust region modification, *SIAM Journal on Numerical Analysis* **19**, 409–426.

Stachurski, A. (1981), Superlinear convergence of Broyden's bounded Θ-class of methods, *Mathematical Programming* **20**, 196–212.

Stewart, G.W. III (1973), *Introduction to Matrix Computations* (Academic Press, New York).

Steihaug, T. (1980), Quasi-Newton methods for large scale nonlinear programs, Ph.D Dissertation, SOM Technical Report #49, Yale University.

Steihaug, T. (1981), The conjugate gradient method and trust regions in large scale optimization, *SIAM Journal on Numerical Analysis* **20**, 626–637.

Tapia, R.A. (1984), On secant updates for use in general constrained optimization, TR84-3, Department of Mathematical Sciences, Rice University, Houston, TX. Revised January 1987. To appear in *Mathematics of Computation*.

Thomas, S.W. (1975), Sequential estimation techniques for quasi-Newton algorithms, Technical Report TR75-227, Department of Computer Science, Cornell University.

Toint, Ph.L. (1977), On sparse and symmetric matrix updating subject to a linear equation, *Mathematics of Computation* **31**, 954–961.

Toint, Ph.L. (1978), Some numerical results using a sparse matrix updating formula in unconstrained optimization, *Mathematics of Computation* **32**, 839–851.

Toint, Ph.L. (1981), Towards an efficient sparsity exploiting Newton method for minimization, in: I.S. Duff (ed.), *Sparse Matrices and their Uses* (Academic Press, London) 57–88.

Toint, Ph.L. (1987), On a large scale nonlinear least squares calculation, *SIAM Journal on Scientific and Statistical Computing* **8**, 416–435.

Vinsome, P.K.W. (1976), Orthomin, an iterative method for solving sparse sets of simultaneous linear equations, in Society of Petroleum Engineers of AIME, *Proceedings of the Fourth Symposium on Reservoir Simulation*.

Vu, P.A. (1984), Symmetric secant updates with inaccurate secant conditions. Ph.D. Thesis, University of Houston.

Wolfe, P. (1969), Convergence conditions for ascent methods, *SIAM Review* **11**, 226–235.

Wolfe, P. (1971), Convergence conditions for ascent methods II: some corrections, *SIAM Review* **13**, 185–188.

Woods, D.J. (1985), An interactive approach for solving multi-objective optimization problems, Ph.D. Thesis, Rice University; available as Math. Science TR85-5.

Young, D.M. and K.C. Jea (1980), Generalized conjugate gradient acceleration of iterative methods, *Linear Algebra and its Applications* **34**, 159–194.

Zhang, Y. and R.P. Tewarson (1986), On the development of algorithms superior to the BFGS method in Broyden's family of updates, Department of Applied Mathematics and Statics Report AMS 86-69, State University of New York, Stony Brook, NY.

G.L. Nemhauser et al., Eds., *Handbooks in OR & MS, Vol. 1*

Chapter II

Linear Programming

*Donald Goldfarb**

Department of Industrial Engineering and Operations Research, Columbia University, New York, NY 10027, U.S.A.

*Michael J. Todd***

School of Operations Research and Industrial Engineering, Cornell University, Ithaca, NY 14853, U.S.A.

1. Introduction

Although the origin of linear programming as a mathematical discipline is quite recent, linear programming is now well established as an important and very active branch of applied mathematics. The wide applicability of linear programming models and the rich mathematical theory underlying these models and the methods developed to solve them have been the driving forces behind the rapid and continuing evolution of the subject.

Linear programming problems involve the optimization of a linear function, called the objective function, subject to linear constraints, which may be either equalities or inequalities, in the unknowns. The recognition of the importance of linear programming models, especially in the areas of economic analysis and planning, coincided with the development of both an effective method, the 'simplex method' of G.B. Dantzig, for solving linear programming problems, (Dantzig 1951) and a means, the digital computer, for doing so. A major part of the foundation of linear programming was laid in an amazingly short period of intense research and development between 1947 and 1949, as the above three key factors converged.

Prior to 1947 mathematicians had studied systems of linear inequalities, starting with Fourier (1826), and optimality conditions for systems with inequality constraints within the classical theory of the calculus of variations (Bolza 1914; Valentine 1937). For the finite dimensional case, the first general result of the latter type appeared in a master's thesis by Karush (1939). (See also (John 1948).) Also, as early as 1939, L.V. Kantorovich had proposed linear

* This work was partially supported by NSF Grant DMS-85-12277 and ONR Contract N00014-87-K-0214.
** This work was partially supported by NSF Grant ECS-8602534 and ONR Contract N00014-87-K-0212.

programming models for production planning and a rudimentary algorithm for their solution (Kantorovich 1939). However, Kantorovich's work was ignored in the U.S.S.R. and remained unknown in the West until long after linear programming had been well established. For a thorough historical survey of linear programming see (Dantzig 1963) and (Schrijver 1986).

In the last decade, linear programming has again become a major focus of attention and an area of heightened activity. This is a result of two developments, both of which are concerned with linear programming algorithms which differ radically from the simplex method. The first was a proof by Khachian (1979) that the so-called ellipsoid method of Shor (1970) and Yudin and Nemiroviskii (1976) for convex, not necessarily differentiable, programming could solve linear programming problems quickly in a theoretical sense. The second was the development by Karmarkar (1984a, b) of a projective interior-point algorithm which appears to have enormous potential for efficiently solving very large problems.

In this chapter, we present and analyze these new methods for solving linear programs (i.e., linear programming problems) as well as providing a thorough development of the simplex method and the basic theory of linear programming. Our point-of-view is both algorithmic and geometric, and we discuss practical, computational issues and give economic interpretations of several aspects of linear programming. We cover most of the standard topics found in textbooks on linear programming. We do not, however, treat specialized applications of linear programming such as game theory, or extensions of it such as integer or quadratic programming. The latter two subjects are discussed in Chapters 6 and 3.

In the remainder of this section we present three standard examples of linear programming problems and introduce several canonical forms for linear programs. Section 2 presents the geometry of linear programming models and algebraically characterizes relevant geometrical concepts. Basic results concerning the fundamental role played by the vertices of the polyhedron of feasible solutions of a linear program are given. In Section 3 we develop the simplex method from a geometric point of view. This development produces, as a by-product, various basic theorems concerning conditions for optimality and unboundedness, and leads in a natural way to the so-called *revised* (i.e., matrix) version of the simplex method. Degeneracy and cycling are briefly considered as are various approaches for implementing the simplex method. These include the standard 'tableau' approach as well as factorizations for the basis matrix in the revised version of the simplex method. This section concludes with a discussion of the use of artificial variables and the so-called phase I problem for obtaining an initial feasible (vertex) solution for the simplex method.

Duality theory and sensitivity analysis are treated in Section 4. In addition to showing that the 'dual' of a linear program arises naturally from the optimality conditions for the latter problem, we show that the dual and its constraints and variables can be given an economic interpretation. The duals of two of the linear programming examples considered in Section 1 are presented, and an important variant of the simplex method, the dual simplex algorithm, is derived. We conclude Section 4 with a discussion of sensitivity (or postoptimality) analysis.

Sections 5 and 6 consider efficient application of the revised simplex method to large and structured problems. Section 5 describes the approach of using a compact (partitioned) inverse which is useful when there are special constraints such as generalized or variable upper bounds, and illustrates the method in the case of simple upper bounds. Efficient implementation of the simplex method for solving network flow problems is also discussed. Section 6 addresses column generation and the use of the decomposition principle to reduce very large problems to ones that are of manageable size. The former technique, which allows columns (of which there may be an astronomical number) to be generated as needed, is illustrated on the classic cutting-stock problem.

The final three sections discuss the complexity of linear programming (Section 7), and two new methods, the ellipsoid method (Section 8) and Karmarkar's projective method (Section 9), which are distinguished from the simplex method in that they have the desirable theoretical property of polynomial-time boundedness. For each of these methods, we describe the basic idea of the method, provide a precise statement of the algorithm, give a sketch of the proof that the algorithm requires only polynomial time to solve linear programming problems and discuss some extensions and the theoretical and computational significance of the method.

1.1. Examples of linear programming problems

Very many problems of practical interest can be formulated as linear programs. In this section we present several well-known examples of such problems.

Example 1 (The transportation problem). A company needs to ship a product from m locations (origins) to n destinations. Suppose that a_i units of the product are available at the i-th origin, $i = 1, 2, \ldots, m$, and b_j units are required at the j-th destination, $j = 1, 2, \ldots, n$. Further suppose that the total amount available at the origins equals the total amount required at the destinations, i.e.,

$$\sum_{i=1}^{m} a_i = \sum_{j=1}^{n} b_j .$$

If the cost of shipping one unit of product from origin i to destination j is c_{ij}, $i = 1, 2, \ldots, m; j = 1, 2, \ldots, n$, how many units of product should be shipped between each origin-destination pair so as to minimize the total transportation cost?

Defining x_{ij} to be the number of units of product shipped from origin i to destination j, we can formulate this problem as the linear program:

$$\text{minimize} \quad \sum_{i=1}^{m} \sum_{j=1}^{n} c_{ij} x_{ij}$$

$$\text{subject to} \quad \sum_{j=1}^{n} x_{ij} = a_i , \quad i = 1, 2, \ldots, m , \tag{1.1}$$

$$\sum_{i=1}^{m} x_{ij} = b_j , \quad j = 1, 2, \ldots, n , \tag{1.2}$$

$$x_{ij} \geq 0 , \quad i = 1, 2, \ldots, m , \quad j = 1, 2, \ldots, n .$$

The objective function that is being minimized is clearly equal to the total shipping cost. Each of the quality constraints (1.1) represents the requirement that the total amount of product shipped from origin i to all destinations is equal to the amount available at the origin. Similarly the constraints (1.2) express the requirement that the demand b_j at destination j is exactly satisfied by the amounts shipped there from all origins. Notice that the nonnegativity restrictions on the amounts shipped are crucial since otherwise one could save money by shipping negative quantities along some routes.

The transportation problem is a linear programming problem with a rather special structure; all coefficients of the decision variables in the equality constraints (1.1) and (1.2) are either zero or one. As we shall see later, the transportation problem is a special case of a network flow problem. It also illustrates why linear programs that are solved in practice often tend to be quite large. For example, if both m and n are 100, then the above problem contains 200 equations in 10 000 nonnegative variables. Because of their special structure, very large transportation problems can be solved in a reasonable amount of computer time; in fact, the solution of a problem with 63 million variables was reported several years ago.

Example 2 (The diet problem). Consider the problem of determining the most economical diet that satisfies certain minimum daily requirements for calories and such nutrients as proteins, calcium, iron and vitamins. Suppose there are n different foods available and our diet must satisfy m minimum nutritional requirements. We can also have maximum requirements on certain nutrients such as fats and carbohydrates, but we will ignore these in our example. Let c_j be the unit cost of the j-th food, b_i be the minimum daily requirement of the i-th nutrient, and a_{ij} be the amount of nutrient i provided by a unit of food j.

If we let x_j be the number of units of food j included in our diet then a minimum cost diet can be found by solving the linear programming problem:

$$\text{minimize} \quad \sum_{j=1}^{n} c_j x_j$$

$$\text{subject to} \quad \sum_{j=1}^{n} a_{ij} x_j \geq b_i , \quad i = 1, 2, \ldots, m ,$$

$$x_j \geq 0 , \quad j = 1, 2, \ldots, n .$$

Example 3 (Product mix problem). A manufacturer is capable of producing n different products using m different limited resources. These may be hours of labor or operation times for various machines per week, or material availabilities. Let c_j be the profit (revenue minus cost) obtainable from each unit of product j manufactured, b_i be the amount of resource i available and a_{ij} the amount of resource i used in the production of one unit of product j. The problem facing the manufacturer is one of determining the product mix (i.e., production plan) that maximizes total profit.

If we let x_j be the number of units of product j manufactured, then this linear programming problem can be formulated as:

$$\text{maximize} \quad \sum_{j=1}^{n} c_j x_j$$

$$\text{subject to} \quad \sum_{j=1}^{n} a_{ij} x_j \leq b_i , \quad i = 1, 2, \ldots, m ,$$

$$x_j \geq 0 , \quad j = 1, 2, \ldots, n .$$

1.2. Canonical forms

Linear programs are usually expressed in either of two forms (however, see Section 8 for an exception). These are the *inequality form*

$$\begin{aligned} \text{minimize} \quad & z = c^T x \\ \text{subject to} \quad & Ax \leq b , \\ & x \geq 0 , \end{aligned}$$

and the *standard form*

$$\begin{aligned} \text{minimize} \quad & z = c^T x \\ \text{subject to} \quad & Ax = b , \\ & x \geq 0 , \end{aligned}$$

where A in both cases denotes an $(m \times n)$ matrix, $c \in \mathbb{R}^n$, $b \in \mathbb{R}^m$ and $x \in \mathbb{R}^n$ is the n-vector of variables. These forms are completely equivalent and any linear program can be put into either form using the following simple transformations.

A *free*, or unrestricted variable x_j can be replaced by a pair of non-negative variables, $x_j' \geq 0$, $x_j'' \geq 0$ by writing

$$x_j = x_j' - x_j'' .$$

The sense of an inequality can be reversed by multiplying both sides of it by minus one. Further, an inequality

$$\sum_{j=1}^{n} a_{ij} x_j \leq b_i$$

can be converted to an equality by the addition of a nonnegative *slack* variable

$$x_{n+i} = b_i - \sum_{j=1}^{n} a_{ij}x_j \, ,$$

and an equality

$$\sum_{j=1}^{n} a_{ij}x_j = b_i$$

can be replaced by two inequalities

$$\sum_{j=1}^{n} a_{ij}x_j \lessgtr b_i \, .$$

Finally, maximizing the linear function $c^{\mathrm{T}}x$ is equivalent to minimizing $-c^{\mathrm{T}}x$.

Observe that the first example of Section 1.1, the transportation problem, is in standard form, while the other examples, the diet and product mix problems are essentially in inequality form.

Slack variables can usually be given some economic or physical interpretation. For example, if we add a slack variable x_{n+i} to the i-th inequality in the product mix example to make it an equality then x_{n+i} is the amount of resource .i not used in the production of the product mix.

2. Geometric interpretation

In order to understand the theory underlying linear programming and the methods used to solve linear programming problems, it is essential to have a geometric understanding of these problems and be able to algebraically characterize relevant geometrical concepts. With this in mind we now give several definitions.

2.1. Definitions

Definition 2.1. A set $C \subseteq \mathbb{R}^n$ is *convex* if for any two points $x', x'' \in C$, all points of the form $x(\lambda) = \lambda x' + (1 - \lambda)x''$, where $0 \leq \lambda \leq 1$, are in C.

That is, for any two points in the set, the line segment between these points must lie in the set for it to be convex (see Figure 2.1).

Definition 2.2. x is a *convex combination* of points $x_1, \ldots, x_N$ if

$$x = \sum_{i=1}^{N} \lambda_i x_i \, , \quad \lambda_i \geq 0 \, , \text{ all } i \quad \text{and} \quad \sum_{i=1}^{N} \lambda_i = 1 \, .$$

convex set   nonconvex set   set of all convex combinations

Fig. 2.1.

Definition 2.3. A set $C \subseteq \mathbb{R}^n$ is a *cone* if for any point $x \in C$ and any nonnegative scalar λ, the point λx is in C. The set $\{x \in \mathbb{R}^n : x = A\alpha, \alpha \geq 0\}$ is a *convex cone generated by the columns of $A \in \mathbb{R}^{n \times m}$.* (Here, $\alpha \in \mathbb{R}^m$.)

Definition 2.4. An *extreme point* of a convex set C is a point $x \in C$ which cannot be expressed as a convex combination of (two) other points in C.

Definition 2.5. The set $H = \{x \in \mathbb{R}^n : a^{\mathrm{T}} x = \beta\}$ where $a \in \mathbb{R}^n$, $a \neq 0$, and $\beta \in \mathbb{R}$ is a *hyperplane. The set* $\bar{H} = \{x \in \mathbb{R}^n : a^{\mathrm{T}} x \leq \beta\}$ is a *closed half-space.* The hyperplane H associated with the half-space $\bar{H}$ is referred to as the *bounding hyperplane* for that half-space.

The vector a in the above definition is orthogonal to the hyperplane H and is called its *normal*, and it is directed towards the exterior of $\bar{H}$. To see this let y, $z \in H$ and $w \in \bar{H}$. Then

$$a^{\mathrm{T}}(y - z) = a^{\mathrm{T}} y - a^{\mathrm{T}} z = \beta - \beta = 0 ,$$

i.e., a is orthogonal to all vectors parallel to H, and

$$a^{\mathrm{T}}(w - z) = a^{\mathrm{T}} w - a^{\mathrm{T}} z \leq \beta - \beta = 0 ,$$

i.e., a makes an obtuse angle with any vector which points towards the interior of $\bar{H}$. A hyperplane in $\mathbb{R}^n$ is just an $(n-1)$-dimensional *affine set* (or *affine subspace*) of $\mathbb{R}^n$ which is defined as:

Definition 2.6. A set $S_a \subseteq \mathbb{R}^n$ is an *affine set* if for any two points $x', x'' \in S_a$, all points of the form $x(\lambda) = \lambda x' + (1 - \lambda)x''$ where $-\infty < \lambda < \infty$, are in S_a.

Note that in contrast with the definition of a convex set, given any two points in an affine set we have that the entire line passing through them lies in that set rather than just the line segment between them. We also note that an affine set S_a is simply a linear subspace S translated by a vector y; i.e., $S_a = \{y + x : x \in S\}$. We say S_a is *parallel* to S.

Definition 2.7. A *convex polyhedron* is a set formed by the intersection of a finite number of closed half-spaces (and hyperplanes). If it is non-empty and bounded it is called *convex polytope*, or simply a *polytope*.

It is easy to show that hyperplanes and closed half-spaces are convex and that the intersection of convex sets is convex; hence, a *convex polyhedron* as defined above is convex. Clearly, the set of feasible solutions of a linear programming problem, $P = \{x \in \mathbb{R}^n : Ax \leq b, x \geq 0\}$ (or $\bar{P} = \{x \in \mathbb{R}^n : Ax = b, x \geq 0\}$) is a convex polyhedron since it is the intersection of the half-spaces defined by the inequalities

$$a_1^T x \leq b_1, \ldots, a_m^T x \leq b_m$$

and   (2.1)

$$e_1^T x \geq 0, \ldots, e_n^T x \geq 0$$

where a_i^T is the i-th row of A and e_i^T is the i-th row of the $n \times n$ identity matrix.

Before we can define certain important features of convex polyhedra we need the following two definitions.

Definition 2.8. The *dimension* of a subspace S, and any affine subspace S_a parallel to it, is equal to the maximum number of linearly independent vectors in S. The *dimension* of any subset of $D \subseteq R^n$ is the smallest dimension of any affine subspace which contains D.

Definition 2.9. A *supporting hyperplane* of a convex set C is a hyperplane H such that $H \cap C \neq \emptyset$ and $C \subseteq \bar{H}$, one of the two closed half-spaces associated with H.

Definition 2.10. Let P be a convex polyhedron and H be any supporting hyperplane of P. The intersection $F = P \cap H$ defines a *face* of P.

There are three special kinds of faces.

Definition 2.11. A *vertex*, *edge*, and *facet* are faces of a d-dimensional convex polyhedron of dimension zero, one, and $d - 1$, respectively. ·

If $P = \{x \in \mathbb{R}^n : Ax \leq b, x \geq 0\}$ then it is fairly obvious that every facet of P corresponds to the intersection of P with a half-space defined by one of the inequalities (2.1). However, not all such intersections necessarily define facets since some of the inequalities may be *redundant*; i.e., deleting them from the definition of P does not change P.

Vertices of a convex polyhedron P are obviously extreme points of P and we shall henceforth use these terms interchangeably. A rigorous proof of this equivalence is left to the reader. Edges are either line segments which connect *neighboring* (or *adjacent*) vertices or are semi-infinite lines emanating from a vertex.

2.2. *Extreme points and basic feasible solutions*

It is easy to see that if a linear programming problem in two or three variables has a finite optimal solution then it occurs at a vertex (i.e., extreme point) of the polyhedron P of feasible solutions. As we shall prove in the next section, this statement holds in higher dimension as well. For this reason, we now algebraically characterize the vertices of P. For the remainder of this section we shall use P to denote the polyhedron $\{x \in \mathbb{R}^n: Ax = b, x \geqslant 0\}$.

Theorem 2.1. *A point* $x \in P = \{x \in \mathbb{R}^n: Ax = b, x \geqslant 0\}$ *is a vertex of P if and only if the columns of A corresponding to positive components of x are linearly independent.*

Proof. Without loss of generality, let us assume that the first p components of x are positive and the last $n - p$ components of x are zero. If we partition x so that $x = \binom{\bar{x}}{0}$, $\bar{x} > 0$, and we denote the first p columns of A by $\bar{A}$, then $Ax = \bar{A}\bar{x} = b$.

Suppose that the columns of $\bar{A}$ are *not* linearly independent. Then, there exists a vector $\bar{w} \neq 0$ such that $\bar{A}\bar{w} = 0$. Therefore, $\bar{A}(\bar{x} \pm \varepsilon \bar{w}) = \bar{A}\bar{x} = b$ and for small enough ε, $(\bar{x} \pm \varepsilon \bar{w}) \geqslant 0$. Consequently the points

$$y' = \begin{pmatrix} \bar{x} + \varepsilon \bar{w} \\ 0 \end{pmatrix} \quad \text{and} \quad y'' = \begin{pmatrix} \bar{x} - \varepsilon \bar{w} \\ 0 \end{pmatrix}$$

are both in P. Further, since $x = \frac{1}{2}(y' + y'')$, x cannot be a vertex (extreme point) of P. Thus, if x is a vertex, then the columns of $\bar{A}$ are linearly independent.

Now suppose that x is not a vertex. This means that $x = \lambda y' + (1 - \lambda)y''$ where $y', y'' \in P$, $y' \neq y''$ and $0 < \lambda < 1$. Since both x and y' are in P, $A(x - y') = Ax - Ay' = b - b = 0$. Further, since both λ and $1 - \lambda$ are strictly positive, the last $n - p$ components of y', and hence $x - y'$, must be zero, since those components of x are zero. Therefore, it follows that the columns of $\bar{A}$ are linearly dependent. Thus, if the columns of $\bar{A}$ are linearly independent, then x is a vertex.

When A has full row rank, an equivalent characterization of the vertices of P involves the concept of a *basic solution*.

Definition 2.12. Let B be any nonsingular $m \times m$ matrix composed of m (linearly independent) columns of A. If all components of x not associated with the columns of B, called *nonbasic variables*, are set equal to zero and the set of linear equations $Ax = b$ is solved for the remaining components of x, called *basic variables*, then the resulting x is said to be a *basic solution* with respect to the *basis* (matrix) B. We shall also use the term *basis* to refer both to the set of basic variables and the set of indices of those variables.

Notice that if we set the nonbasic variables equal to zero, we are left with a system of m equations in m unknowns.

$$Bx_B = b ,$$

which is uniquely solvable for the basic variables x_B. The reason for the above terminology is that the columns of B form a basis for the column space of A and $Ax = b$ can be thought of as expressing b as a linear combination of the columns of A.

When A does not have full row rank, either the system of linear equations $Ax = b$ has no solution and P is the empty set, or some of the equations in the system are *redundant*. In the latter case, redundant constraints can be removed one by one to give a reduced system of equations and a constraint matrix of full row rank.

If a basic solution x with respect to a basis B is nonnegative then it is called a *basic feasible solution*, and the following corollary to Theorem 2.1 is an immediate consequence of the above definitions.

Corollary 2.1. *A point $x \in P$ is a vertex of P if and only if x is a basic feasible solution corresponding to some basis B.*

Corollary 2.2. *The polyhedron P has only a finite number of vertices.*

Proof. This follows from the previous corollary and the fact that there are only a finite number of ways to choose m linearly independent 'basis' columns from the n columns of A. Clearly an upper bound on the number of vertices of P is $n!/(m!(n-m)!)$.

If the polyhedron P is bounded – i.e., P is a polytope – then any point in P can be represented as a convex combination of the vertices of P. (See Corollary 2.6 below.) When P is unbounded the representation of any point in P is slightly more complicated and requires the following definition.

Definition 2.13. A *direction* of P is a nonzero vector $d \in \mathbb{R}^n$, such that for any point $x_0 \in P$ the ray $\{x \in \mathbb{R}^n : x = x_0 + \lambda d, \lambda \geq 0\}$ lies entirely in P.

Obviously P is unbounded if and only if P has a direction. It is also easily proved that $d \neq 0$ is a direction of P if and only if

$$Ad = 0 \quad \text{and} \quad d \geq 0 .$$

We can now state the following representation theorem.

Theorem 2.2 (Representation theorem). *Any point $x \in P$ can be represented as*

$$x = \sum_{i \in I} \lambda_i v_i + d ,$$

where $\{v_i : i \in I\}$ *is the set of vertices of P,*

$$\sum_{i \in I} \lambda_i = 1, \quad \lambda_i \geq 0 \quad \text{for all } i \in I,$$

and either d is a direction of P or d = 0.

Proof. We prove this theorem by induction on p, the number of positive components of x. It is obviously true for $p = 0$ (x is a vertex). Now assume that it is true for points with fewer than p positive components, and that x has p positive components.

If x is a vertex, then the theorem is obviously true since $x = v_i$ for some $i \in I$. Therefore suppose that x is not a vertex. Then there is a vector $w \neq 0$ with $w_i = 0$ if $x_i = 0$ such that $Aw = 0$. There are three cases to consider.

Case (a): w has components of both signs.

Consider points $x(\theta) = x + \theta w$ on the line through x determined by w, and let θ' and θ'' be, respectively, the smallest positive, and (algebraically) largest negative values of θ at which $x(\theta)$ has at least one more zero component than x. Clearly the points $x' = x(\theta')$ and $x'' = x(\theta'')$ lie in P and can be represented as in the statement of the theorem by the induction hypothesis. Consequently, we can represent x, which lies on the line between x' and x'', as

$$x = \mu x' + (1 - \mu)x''$$
$$= \mu\left(\sum_{i \in I} \lambda_i' v_i + d'\right) + (1 - \mu)\left(\sum_{i \in I} \lambda_i'' v_i + d''\right)$$
$$= \sum_{i \in I} (\mu\lambda_i' + (1 - \mu)\lambda_i'')v_i + \mu d' + (1 - \mu)d'',$$

where $\mu = -\theta''/(\theta' - \theta'')$.

Since $0 < \mu < 1$,

$$\lambda_i' \geq 0 \text{ and } \lambda_i'' \geq 0 \quad \text{for all } i \in I, \qquad \sum_{i \in I} \lambda_i' = \sum_{i \in I} \lambda_i'' = 1,$$
$$Ad' = Ad'' = 0, \qquad d' \geq 0 \quad \text{and} \quad d'' \geq 0,$$

it follows that

$$\lambda_i \equiv \mu\lambda_i' + (1 - \mu)\lambda_i'' \geq 0 \quad \text{for all } i \in I, \qquad \sum_{i \in I} \lambda_i = 1,$$
$$d \equiv \mu d' + (1 - \mu)d'' \geq 0 \quad \text{and} \quad Ad = 0,$$

and we have proved that x has the desired form.

Case (b): $w \leq 0$.

Define x' as in Case (a). Now x can be written as

$$x = x' + \theta'(-w) \quad \text{where} \quad \theta' > 0.$$

Since x' can be represented in the desired form by induction, and $(-w)$ is a direction of P, x clearly has the desired form.

   Case (c): $w \geq 0$.

   The proof for this case is identical to case (b) with x', θ', and $-w$ replaced by x'', $-\theta''$, and w, respectively.

Hence we obtain:

Corollary 2.3. *If P is bounded (i.e., a polytope) then any $x \in P$ can be represented as a convex combination of its vertices.*

2.3. Fundamental theorems of linear programming

In this section we prove two theorems that are of fundamental importance to the development of algorithms (and in particular the simplex algorithm) for solving linear programs. Specifically, these theorems identify the special importance of the vertices of P – i.e., basic feasible solutions – for such methods.

Theorem 2.3. *If P is nonempty, then it has at least one vertex.*

Proof. This follows immediately from Theorem 2.2 and its proof.

Theorem 2.4. *If P is nonempty, then the minimum value of $z = c^T x$ for $x \in P$ is attained at a vertex of P or z has no lower bound on P.*

Proof. There are two cases to consider:

   Case (a): P has a direction d such that $c^T d < 0$. In this case P is unbounded and the value of $z \to -\infty$ along the direction d.

   Case (b): P has no direction d such that $c^T d < 0$. In this case we need only consider points that can be expressed as convex combination of the vertices v_i of P, since even if P is unbounded any point of the form $x = \hat{x} + d$, where

$$\hat{x} = \sum_{i \in I} \lambda_i v_i , \qquad \sum_{i \in I} \lambda_i = 1 , \quad \text{and} \quad \lambda_i \geq 0 \text{ for all } i \in I ,$$

has an objective value that is bounded below by $c^T \hat{x}$. But

$$c^T \hat{x} = c^T \left[\sum_{i \in I} \lambda_i v_i \right] = \sum_{i \in I} \lambda_i c^T v_i \geq \min_{i \in I} \{ c^T v_i \} .$$

Hence, the minimum of z is attained at a vertex.

   This theorem is fundamental to solving linear programming problems. It shows that we need only consider vertices of P, i.e., basic feasible solutions, as candidates for the optimal solution. Also it shows that we must be on the lookout for directions along which $z \to -\infty$.

3. The simplex method

We saw in Section 2 that to solve the linear programming problem,

$$\begin{aligned} \text{minimize} \quad & z = c^{\mathrm{T}}x \\ \text{subject to} \quad & Ax = b\,, \\ & x \geqslant 0\,, \end{aligned} \qquad (3.1)$$

we need only consider the vertices of the polyhedron $P = \{x\colon Ax = b, x \geqslant 0\}$ of feasible solutions as candidates for the optimal solution, assuming for the moment that (3.1) has a finite optimal solution. For large m and n, determining all of the vertices of P is impractical; P can have as many as $\binom{n}{m} = n!/m!(n-m)!$ basic solutions. Clearly a more systematic approach such as the *simplex method* developed by George Dantzig in 1947 is required. In fact, the simplex method has been so successful that it has become one of the best known and, in terms of computer time, one of the most used methods in numerical computing.

3.1. Geometric motivation

The idea of the simplex method is really quite simple. First a vertex of P is found. Then the method proceeds from vertex to vertex along edges of P that are 'downhill' with respect to the objective function $z = c^{\mathrm{T}}x$, generating a sequence of vertices with strictly decreasing objective values. Consequently, once the method leaves a vertex the method can never return to that vertex. Thus, in a finite number of steps, a vertex will be reached which is optimal, or an edge will be chosen which goes off to infinity and along which z goes to $-\infty$.

Our task here is to convert the above geometric description of the simplex method into an algebraic and, hence, computational form. We will consider first, the so-called *second phase* (*phase II*) of the simplex method which assumes that a vertex of P is given, for as we shall see later, the algorithm for this second phase can itself by used to solve the *phase I* problem of finding a vertex of P if P is nonempty. Also, we shall assume that the rows of A are linearly independent, i.e., the rank of A is m, and that $m < n$, so that our problem is not trivial. If the rank of A is less than m, then either the equality constraints are inconsistent or some of them are redundant and can be removed. Our assumptions ensure that there is at least one basic solution and that a basis matrix B can be formed from the columns of A.

For simplicity in describing a step of the simplex method, let us assume that the components of the current vertex x are ordered so that the first m are *basic*. That is, the vertex x of P corresponds to the basic feasible solution

$$x = \begin{bmatrix} x_B \\ x_N \end{bmatrix} = \begin{bmatrix} B^{-1}b \\ 0 \end{bmatrix} \qquad (3.2)$$

where A is partitioned as $A = [B \,|\, N]$. We also partition c^{T} as $c^{\mathrm{T}} = [c_B^{\mathrm{T}} \ c_N^{\mathrm{T}}]$ to conform to the above partition of x into basic and nonbasic parts.

Definition 3.1. If one or more basic variables are zero then such a basic solution is called *degenerate*; otherwise, it is called *nondegenerate*.

If the basic feasible solution (3.2) is nondegenerate then it lies in the intersection in $\mathbb{R}^n$ of the m hyperplanes corresponding to the equality constraints $Ax = b$ and the $n - m$ hyperplanes corresponding to requirement that the $n - m$ nonbasic variables equal zero, i.e., $x_N = 0$. Consider the matrix

$$M = \begin{bmatrix} B & N \\ 0 & I \end{bmatrix} \tag{3.3}$$

whose rows are just the normals to these n hyperplanes. Since B is non-singular, the rows of M are linearly independent, and hence M is non-singular. Thus the vertex (3.2) is determined by the intersection of n linearly independent hyperplanes.

If a basic feasible solution is degenerate, then some of the basic variables x_B are also equal to zero. Consequently, more than $n - m$ of the nonnegativity constraints $x_j \geq 0$ are satisfied as equalities and the point x satisfies more than n equations.

A conceptual illustration of degeneracy is given in Figure 3.1. It might appear from this illustration that there are always redundant constraints at a degenerate vertex. However, this is only the case when $n - m \leq 2$.

When a basic feasible solution x is degenerate, there can be an enormous number of bases associated with the vertex x. In fact, if x has $p < m$ positive components, there may be as many as

$$\binom{n - p}{n - m} = \frac{(n - p)!}{(n - m)!(m - p)!}$$

'different' basic feasible solutions corresponding to x. The point x is the same in each, but the sets of variables that we label basic and nonbasic are different.

An extreme example of degeneracy is exhibited by the so-called 'assignment' problem. It can be shown that the polytope

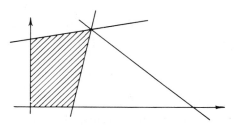

Fig. 3.1. An illustration of degeneracy.

$$P_k = \left\{ x_{ij}, 1 \le i, j \le k: \sum_{j=1}^{k} x_{ij} = 1, 1 \le i \le k; \right.$$

$$\left. \sum_{i=1}^{k} x_{ij} = 1, 1 \le j \le k; \quad 0 \le x_{ij}, 1 \le i, j \le k \right\}$$

of this rather special 'capacitated transportation' problem has $k!$ vertices, and that there are $2^{k-1}k^{k-2}$ bases corresponding to each of these vertices. Thus, for $k = 8$, each of the 40 320 vertices of P_8 has 33 554 432 different bases associated with it (Balinski and Russakoff 1972).

Let us assume for simplicity that the basic feasible solution (3.2) is non-degenerate. This ensures that there are exactly $n - m$ edges (i.e., one-dimensional faces) of P emanating from the vertex. The directions of these edges are given by the last $n - m$ columns of the inverse of the matrix of active constraint normals M in (3.3). It is easily verified that

$$M^{-1} = \begin{bmatrix} B^{-1} & -B^{-1}N \\ 0 & I \end{bmatrix}. \tag{3.4}$$

Each edge direction corresponds to increasing one of the nonbasic variables while keeping all of the remaining nonbasic variables fixed at zero. To verify the above statements we observe that the q-th column of M^{-1}, $q > m$, is orthogonal to all rows of M other than the q-th, and hence, it is orthogonal to the normals of all of the hyperplanes that intersect at x except the one corresponding to $x_q = 0$. This means that this vector $\eta_q = M^{-1}e_q$ (where e_q is again the q-th column of the $n \times n$ identity matrix) is parallel to the intersection of the $n - 1$ linearly independent hyperplanes corresponding to $Ax = b$ and $x_k = 0$, $k > m$, $k \ne q$. Also the edge direction η_q is a feasible direction because, for small enough $\theta > 0$, points of the form

$$x(\theta) = x + \theta\eta_q \tag{3.5}$$

are feasible. In fact $x_k(\theta) = 0$, $k > m$, $k \ne q$, $x_q(\theta) = \theta > 0$, and

$$x_B(\theta) = x_B - \theta B^{-1}a_q \ge 0 \tag{3.6}$$

for θ small enough, where a_q denotes the q-th column of A.

Now, the first task in an iteration of the simplex method is to find a 'downhill' edge. This involves computing the so-called *reduced* or *relative costs*

$$\bar{c}_j = c^T\eta_j = c_j - c_B^T B^{-1}a_j, \quad j > m.$$

If $\bar{c}_j < 0$, then the gradient c of the objective function $z = c^Tx$ makes an obtuse angle with the edge direction η_j and z decreases as one moves along that direction, i.e., as θ is increased. The terminology reduced cost comes from the fact that $\bar{c}_j$ represents the change in the objective function z per unit change in the nonbasic variable x_j, keeping all other nonbasic variable fixed, since from (3.5) with $q = j$, it follows that

$$z(x(\theta)) = c^T x(\theta) = c^T x + \theta c^T \eta_j = z(x) + \theta \bar{c}_j .$$

Clearly the reduced cost $\bar{c}_j$ is the directional derivative of $z = c^T x$ with respect to the edge direction η_j.

Although any downhill edge will do for the simplex method, the usual rule used in textbooks is to choose the edge corresponding to the most negative reduced cost. (This is not the 'steepest-edge' with respect to the objective function z. Such a choice η_q, corresponds to

$$\frac{c^T \eta_q}{\|\eta_q\|} = \underset{j>m}{\mathrm{Min}} \left\{ \frac{c^T \eta_j}{\|\eta_j\|} \right\} .$$

That is, the steepest edge is the one which makes the most obtuse angle ϕ_q with c, where

$$\phi_q = \cos^{-1} \left(\frac{c^T \eta_q}{\|c\| \cdot \|\eta_q\|} \right) .$$

This pivot rule can be implemented in a practicable manner for large problems if the quantities $\|\eta_j\|^2 = \eta_j^T \eta_j$ for all of the nonbasic variables are stored and updated from one iteration to the next. (See (Goldfarb and Reid 1977).))

Note that the reduced costs corresponding to basic variables are zero and that those corresponding to nonbasic variables can be obtained by first computing the vector of *simplex multipliers* $\pi^T = c_B^T B^{-1}$ followed by 'pricing-out' all nonbasic columns, i.e.,

$$\bar{c}_j = c_j - \pi^T a_j , \quad j > m .$$

The terminology used above is derived from the interpretation of the components of π both as Lagrange multipliers and as equilibrium prices at optimality.

We now show that every point $y \in P$ lies within the convex polyhedral cone generated by a given basic feasible solution x and the 'edge directions' η_j emanating from x determined by the basis. In the nondegenerate case these directions are true edge directions. In the degenerate case some of them are infeasible.

Lemma 3.1. *Given the basic feasible solution x in (3.2), every point $y \in P$ can be expressed as*

$$y = x + \sum_{j=m+1}^{n} y_j \eta_j , \quad y_j \geqslant 0 , \quad j = m+1, \ldots, n$$

where η_j is the j-th column of M^{-1} in (3.4).

Proof. Since $y \in P$, $Ay = b$ and $y = \binom{y_B}{y_N} \geq 0$. Moreover, since $Ax = b$ and $x_N = 0$, it follows that

$$\dot{M}(y - x) = \begin{bmatrix} B & N \\ 0 & I \end{bmatrix} (y - x) = \binom{0}{y_N},$$

and hence that

$$(y - x) = M^{-1} \binom{0}{y_N} = \begin{bmatrix} -B^{-1}N \\ I \end{bmatrix} y_N$$

where $y_N \geq 0$.

From this lemma we have that

$$z(y) - z(x) = c^{\mathrm{T}}(y - x) = \sum_{j=m+1}^{n} (c^{\mathrm{T}}\eta_j)y_j = \sum_{j=m+1}^{n} \bar{c}_j y_j \qquad (3.7)$$

for all $y \in P$. Since y is nonnegative, if the reduced costs $\bar{c}_j$ are nonnegative, it follows that $z(y) \geq z(x)$ for all $y \in P$. Thus we have proved:

Theorem 3.1. *A basic feasible solution is an optimal solution to the linear programming problem* (3.1) *if all* reduced costs (*relative to the given basis*) *are nonnegative.*

In the nondegenerate case the converse of this theorem is true. However a degenerate basic feasible solution can be optimal even if some reduced costs are negative, since the corresponding downhill edge directions may not be feasible. A direction is infeasible at a point x where $x_j = 0$ if its j-th component is negative. The following corollaries are also immediate consequences of (3.7).

Corollary 3.1. *A basic feasible solution x is the unique optimal solution to* (3.1) *if all nonbasic reduced costs are strictly positive.*

Corollary 3.2. *If x given by* (3.2) *is an optimal basic feasible solution, with nonbasic reduced costs $\bar{c}_{j_1} = \bar{c}_{j_2} \cdots = \bar{c}_{j_k} = 0$, then any point $y \in P$ of the form*

$$y = x + \sum_{i=1}^{k} y_{j_i}\eta_{j_i} \qquad (3.8)$$

is also optimal.

If an optimal basic feasible solution is degenerate and the reduced costs corresponding to some of the nonbasic variables are zero, it does not follow from Corollary 3.2 that the optimal solution is nonunique. This is because in the degenerate case x may be the only point of the form (3.8) that is actually in P, due to the infeasibility of the edge directions η_{j_i} in (3.8).

Once a downhill edge η_q has been chosen the next task in an iteration of the simplex method involves moving along that edge to the vertex adjacent to x. This is accomplished by increasing the nonbasic variable x_q – i.e., increasing θ in (3.5) – until one of the basic variables becomes zero.

Letting

$$w = B^{-1}a_q \tag{3.9}$$

it follows from (3.5) and (3.6) that $x(\theta) \geq 0$ if and only if $x_B - \theta w \geq 0$ and $\theta \geq 0$. Hence we obtain:

Theorem 3.2. *If $\bar{c}_q$ is negative and w in (3.9) is nonpositive, then the linear programming problem (3.1) is unbounded; $x(\theta)$ is feasible for all $\theta \geq 0$ and $z(x(\theta)) \to -\infty$ as $\theta \to \infty$. In this case, $d = \eta_q$ is a direction with $c^T d = \bar{c}_q < 0$.*

If w has a positive component, the largest step θ that we can take while still keeping $x(\theta) \geq 0$, and the basic variable, say x_p, which first becomes zero as we increase θ are determined by the so-called 'minimum ratio test'

$$\theta = \bar{x}_q = \min\left\{ \frac{x_i}{w_i} : w_i > 0, 1 \leq i \leq m \right\} = \frac{x_p}{w_p}. \tag{3.10}$$

We have used an overbar to indicate that $\bar{x}_q$ is the value of the q-th variable at the new vertex. All that remains to be done in a simplex iteration is to change the basis, making the q-th variable basic and the p-th variable nonbasic. As far as the basis matrix B is concerned, one of its columns, a_p, is replaced by the column a_q, i.e.

$$\bar{B} = B + (a_q - a_p)e_p^T.$$

From (3.5)–(3.10) it follows that

$$\bar{x}_q = x_p/w_p,$$
$$\bar{x}_i = x_i - w_i\bar{x}_q, \quad i = 1, \ldots, m.$$

Summarizing the above we obtain:

Theorem 3.3. *If $\bar{c}_q$ is negative and w in (3.9) has a positive component, then $\bar{x}$ given above is another basic feasible solution with $c^T\bar{x} = c^Tx - \theta\bar{c}_q$ strictly less than c^Tx if θ in (3.10) is positive, i.e., if the basic feasible solution x is nondegenerate.*

3.2. The revised simplex method

We are now ready to formally state the simplex method in algorithmic form.

Simplex method

(0) Let the basic feasible solution, x_B, to the linear program (3.1), corresponding to the basis matrix $B = [a_{j_1}, \ldots, a_{j_m}]$, be given. Let $B = \{j_1, \ldots, j_m\}$ denote the index set of basic variables; hence x_{j_i} denotes the i-th basic variable.

(1) Compute *simplex multipliers* by solving

$$B^T\pi = c_B$$

for π, and compute the *reduced costs*

$$\bar{c}_j = c_j - \pi^T a_j, \quad \text{for all } j \notin B .$$

(2) Check for optimality: If $\bar{c}_j \geq 0$, for all $j \notin B$, STOP; the current solution is optimal.

(3) Determine the nonbasic variable x_q to enter the basis; i.e., find a downhill edge: Choose

$$q \in V \equiv \{j \notin B : \bar{c}_j < 0\} .$$

(4) Check for an unbounded ray: Compute w by solving

$$Bw = a_q .$$

If $w \leq 0$, STOP; there is a feasible ray of solutions along which $z \to -\infty$.

(5) Determine the basic variable x_{j_p} to leave the basis: Compute

$$\frac{x_{j_p}}{w_p} = \min_{1 \leq i \leq m} \left\{ \frac{x_{j_i}}{w_i} : w_i > 0 \right\} .$$

(6) Update the solution and the basis matrix B: Set

$$x_q \leftarrow \theta = x_{j_p}/w_p ,$$

$$x_{j_i} \leftarrow x_{j_i} - \theta w_i , \quad 1 \leq i \leq m ,$$

$$B \leftarrow B + (a_q + a_{j_p})e_p^T ,$$

$$B \leftarrow B \cup \{q\}\backslash\{j_p\} ,$$

$$j_p \leftarrow q ,$$

and go to step (1).

The above form of the simplex method is usually referred to as the *revised simplex method*.

3.3. Degeneracy and cycling

Although we assumed earlier that x was nondegenerate, degeneracy does not usually cause any real difficulty for the above algorithm. All that may happen is

that in step (5) $x_{j_p} = 0$, which results in a step being taken without any actual
change in x. This occurs because the 'edge direction' η_q immediately runs into
the constraint $x_{j_p} \geq 0$. Although x does not change the basis does. Because x
and hence, z, do not change it is theoretically possible for the simplex method
to 'cycle' indefinitely through a sequence of bases and corresponding basic
feasible solutions, all associated with the same vertex. In practice this is not a
problem and there are pivot rules (i.e., rules for choosing the entering and
leaving basic variable) which prevent cycling. For example, if one always
chooses the entering and leaving basic variables when there is more than one
candidate as the one with the smallest subscript, then it can be shown that the
simplex method terminates in a finite number of iterations (Bland 1977). No
matter what pivot rule is used, if every pivot is nondegenerate – i.e., θ in step
(6) is strictly positive – then z decreases on each iteration; consequently, the
simplex method must terminate in a finite number of iterations since there are
only a finite number of basic feasible solutions to problem (3.1).

3.4. *Implementations*

For large m it is just not practicable to solve the $m \times m$ systems of equations
$B^T \pi = c_B$ and $Bw = a_q$ to compute Π and w at each simplex step. In most
textbooks the simplex method is described by a set of procedures for man-
ipulating a tableau of the form (actually a column permutation of the form):

$$
\begin{array}{|c|c|c|c|}
\hline
1 & 0 & \bar{c}_N^T & -z_0 \\
\hline
0 & I & B^{-1}N & B^{-1}b \\
\hline
\end{array}
\tag{3.11}
$$

where $\bar{c}_N^T = c_N^T - c_B^T B^{-1} N$ and $z_0 = c_B^T B^{-1} b$.

If T is the matrix of numbers in tableau (3.11) then this tableau actually
represents the system

$$
T \begin{bmatrix} -z \\ x_B \\ x_N \\ -1 \end{bmatrix} = 0
$$

of $m + 1$ linear equations in $n + 1$ unknowns x and z.

To implement the tableau version of the simplex method one follows the
simplex algorithm presented above except that the computation of Π and $\bar{c}_N$ in
step (1) and w in step (4) are eliminated and step (6) is replaced by a 'pivot
operation'. If we assume that the entering and leaving basic variable on a
simplex pivot step are q and p, respectively, and that the rows and columns of
the current tableau T given by (3.11) are numbered starting from zero, this
pivot operation

(i) divides the p-th row of T by $t_{p,q}$, the (p, q)-th element of T, and

(ii) for $0 \leqslant i \leqslant m$, $i \neq p$, subtracts t_{iq} times this new p-th row from row i to zero out the element in column q of that row.

This operation maintains the form of (3.11) with respect to the new basis. Moreover, the reduced costs, $\bar{c}_N$, basic components of the edge direction η_q, $- B^{-1}a_q$, and the vector of basic variables, $B^{-1}b$, required by the simplex method are all available directly from the tableau.

The tableau version of the simplex method is often referred to simply as the simplex method since it was the form in which the method was originally described. Although this approach is acceptable for small 'textbook' problems, it is not suitable for solving the large and typically sparse problems that arise in practice. This is because pivoting in the tableau usually destroys any sparsity that is present in A, and hence in the 'initial' tableau

1	c_B^T	c_N^T	0
0	B	N	b

Furthermore, it generates all columns of $B^{-1}N$ on each iteration when only $B^{-1}a_j$ is needed.

In the revised simplex method given in the previous section only the information required on each iteration is generated directly from the original data. The initial implementations of the revised simplex method maintained an 'explicit inverse', B^{-1}, of the basis matrix, updating it after each pivot (i.e., basis change). The required update can be expressed as

$$\bar{B}^{-1} = EB^{-1}$$

where

$$E = I - \frac{(w - e_p)e_p^T}{w_p} = \begin{bmatrix} 1 & & & -w_1/w_p & & \\ & \ddots & & \vdots & & \\ & & 1 & -w_{p-1}/w_p & & \\ & & & 1/w_p & & \\ & & & -w_{p+1}/w_p & 1 & \\ & & & \vdots & & \ddots \\ & & & -w_m/w_p & & 1 \end{bmatrix} \qquad (3.12)$$

$$\uparrow$$
$$\text{column } p$$

and $w = B^{-1}a_q$.

This follows from the fact that

$$\bar{B} = BE^{-1} ,$$

where

$$E^{-1} = \begin{bmatrix} 1 & & & w_1 & & & \\ & \ddots & & \vdots & & & \\ & & 1 & w_{p-1} & & & \\ & & & w_p & & & \\ & & & w_{p+1} & 1 & & \\ & & & \vdots & & \ddots & \\ & & & w_m & & & 1 \end{bmatrix}$$

is the inverse of the matrix E in (3.12). Notice that postmultiplication of B by E^{-1} leaves all columns of B unchanged except for the p-th, which is transformed into $Bw = a_q$, as required.

Since B itself can be formed by replacing the columns of I, one at a time, by the appropriate columns of B, it follows that we can express any inverse basis matrix in *product form* as

$$B^{-1} = E_k E_{k-1} \cdots E_1 \tag{3.13}$$

where each E_i has the form (3.12). Clearly only the column of E_i that differs from a column of the identity matrix, and its place in E_i, need to be stored. Every now and then it is also advisable to refactorize B^{-1} to reduce a very long string of elementary elimination matrices, E_i, to one of only m matrices. This saves computational time on subsequent iterations, saves storage, and reduces the effects of roundoff errors.

When B is refactorized it is usually worthwhile to permute its rows and columns so that the resulting factorization is as sparse as possible. Several schemes for doing this have been proposed, the most popular of these being the 'preassigned pivot procedures' P^3 and P^4 of Hellerman and Rarick (1971, 1972) and those which use the Markowitz criterion (see Section 9). The procedures P^3 and P^4 permute B into a block lower triangular matrix with nonzeros above the diagonal confined to a relatively small number of spikes within each diagonal block when B is sparse. The advantage of doing this is that when Gauss–Jordan elimination is applied to B to produce the product form representation (3.13) or the LU factors of B (see below), fill-in occurs only in spike columns.

Recently, the product form representation for B^{-1} has been replaced in large-scale linear programming codes by a numerically stable LU *factorization* of B. In this approach L^{-1} is stored as a sequence of elementary elimination matrices which differ from the identity by just one nonzero below the diagonal, and permutation matrices (for numerical stability). U is stored as a permuted upper triangular matrix. Bartels and Golub (1969) first showed how such a factorization could be efficiently and stably updated when a column of B was replaced by a new column. Variants of their algorithm and the product form algorithm which take advantage of sparsity, make it practicable today to solve truly large linear programming problems. (For example, see (Forrest and Tomlin 1972), (Saunders 1976) and (Reid 1982).)

3.5. *Artificial variables and Phase I*

One nice feature of the simplex method is that it can be used to find a basic feasible solution to problem (3.1). The application of the simplex method to this feasibility problem is called phase I, while its application to finding the optimal solution to (3.1) is called phase II. The feasibility problem for (3.1) can be defined as the (artificial) minimization problem

$$\text{Minimize} \quad \sum_{i=1}^{m} y_i$$

$$\text{subject to} \quad Ax + y = b \quad (b \geq 0),$$
$$x \geq 0, \quad y \geq 0.$$

As this problem has the obvious basic feasible solution $x = 0$, $y = b$, with basis I, the simplex method can be immediately applied to it. The y_i, $i = 1, \ldots, m$, are called *artificial variables* and the purpose of the above minimization problem is to drive them to zero. If the original problem has a feasible solution, then this will be possible. In such a case the simplex method will terminate with a basic feasible solution with all $y_i = 0$. If this solution is degenerate, any artificial variables remaining in the basis can be either exchanged for nonbasic x variables or eliminated along with *redundant* equations so that a basic feasible solution involving only x variables is available for the start of phase II. Specifically, if $y_i = 0$ is the k-th basic variable and $e_k^T B^{-1} a_j \neq 0$, y_i can be replaced by the nonbasic variable x_j. If $e_k^T B^{-1} a_j = 0$ for all $j \notin B$, the original system of equations $Ax = b$ is *redundant*, and the k-th row and column can be removed from B and the k-th row eliminated from A. If the original problem has no feasible solutions, then phase I will terminate with a positive artificial objective function value.

Another approach is to combine phases I and II into one phase by minimizing the objective function

$$z = \sum_{j=1}^{n} c_j x_j + M \sum_{i=1}^{m} y_i$$

where M is chosen so large that eventually all of the artificial variables will be driven to zero if the original problem has a feasible solution.

4. Duality and sensitivity analysis

In this section we introduce the very important and powerful concept of duality. In particular we show that every linear program has associated with it another linear program called the dual that is intimately related to optimality conditions for the original problem. We provide an economic interpretation for the variables of the dual and give several illustrations of how the entire dual problem can be interpreted. We also develop a variant of the simplex method known as the dual simplex method and discuss how to deal with changes that are made to a linear program after it has been solved.

4.1. Duality and optimality

If a basic feasible solution x is nondegenerate then the conditions given in Theorem 3.1 (i.e., all $\bar{c}_j \geq 0$) for x to be an optimal solution are both necessary and sufficient, as mentioned below the statement of that theorem. This follows from the fact that the simplex method can be used in this case to compute another basic feasible solution with a lower value of z if and only if some relative cost $\bar{c}_j$ is <0. When x is a nondegenerate basic feasible solution, we can also state necessary and sufficient conditions for x to be optimal in a different way.

Theorem 4.1. *The basic nondegenerate feasible solution*

$$x = \begin{bmatrix} x_B \\ x_N \end{bmatrix} = \begin{bmatrix} B^{-1}b \\ 0 \end{bmatrix} \tag{4.1}$$

to the linear programming problem

$$\begin{aligned} minimize \quad & z = c^T x \\ subject\ to \quad & Ax = b, \quad x \geq 0, \end{aligned} \tag{4.2}$$

is optimal if, and only if,

$$c^T = (y^T, \bar{w}^T)\begin{bmatrix} B & N \\ 0 & I \end{bmatrix}, \tag{4.3}$$

where $\bar{w} \geq 0$.

Proof. Recall that the rows of

$$M = \begin{bmatrix} B & N \\ 0 & I \end{bmatrix}$$

are linearly independent. Hence they form a basis for $\mathbb{R}^n$, implying that there is a unique vector $(y^T, \bar{w}^T)$ that satisfies (4.3). To complete the proof we need only observe that $\bar{w}$ is the vector of nonbasic reduced costs, $\bar{c}_N$, since from (4.3) we have

$$\begin{aligned} (y^T, \bar{w}^T) &= c^T M^{-1} = (c_B^T, c_N^T)\begin{bmatrix} B^{-1} & -B^{-1}N \\ 0 & I \end{bmatrix} \\ &= (c_B^T B^{-1}, c_N^T - c_B^T B^{-1}N). \end{aligned}$$

Note that y is the vector of simplex multipliers π computed by the revised simplex method at optimality, and that the 'if' part of this theorem is true even if the basic feasible solution (4.1) is degenerate.

Geometrically, this theorem states that at an optimal nondegenerate vertex x, the gradient of the objective function can be expressed as a linear combination of the normals to all equality constraints plus a nonnegative linear combination of the inward normals to all nonnegativity constraints satisfied as equalities at x.

Let us now consider a linear programming problem which is related in very important ways to the linear program (4.2):

$$\text{maximize} \quad v = b^{\mathrm{T}}y$$
$$\text{subject to} \quad A^{\mathrm{T}}y \leq c. \tag{4.4}$$

This problem is called the *dual* of problem (4.2), which is now referred to as the *primal*. Note that the dual problem makes use of the same data, A, b, and c, as the primal, and that the dual is, in a sense, a transposed version of the primal, with minimization replaced by maximization. Further, by putting (4.4) into standard form using the techniques of Section 1.2, we can easily prove the following.

Lemma 4.1. *The dual of the dual problem* (4.4) *is the primal problem* (4.2).

We now show that the dual problem (4.4) arises quite naturally from the optimality conditions of Theorem 4.1. Observe that these conditions can be written as $c^{\mathrm{T}} = y^{\mathrm{T}}A + w^{\mathrm{T}}$, where $w^{\mathrm{T}} \equiv (0, \bar{w}^{\mathrm{T}}) \geq 0$. Relaxing the requirement that the first m components of w equal zero yields

$$A^{\mathrm{T}}y + w = c, \quad w \geq 0, \tag{4.5}$$

which are just the constraints of the dual problem (4.4) put into equality form by the introduction of nonnegative slack variables $w \geq 0$. Moreover we have:

Lemma 4.2 (Weak duality). *If x is primal feasible and y is dual feasible, then $b^{\mathrm{T}}y \leq c^{\mathrm{T}}x$.*

Proof. Since $Ax = b$, $y^{\mathrm{T}}Ax = y^{\mathrm{T}}b$ for any $y \in \mathbb{R}^m$, and since $A^{\mathrm{T}}y \leq c$ and $x \geq 0$, $y^{\mathrm{T}}Ax \leq c^{\mathrm{T}}x$. Combining these results concludes the proof.

This lemma states that the objective value corresponding to a primal (dual) feasible solution provides an upper (a lower) bound for the objective value for any feasible solution including an optimal solution for the other problem. An immediate consequence of this lemma is:

Corollary 4.1. *If x is primal feasible and y is dual feasible and $c^{\mathrm{T}}x = b^{\mathrm{T}}y$, then x and y are optimal solutions.*

But are there feasible solutions x and y that satisfy the hypotheses of this corollary? The answer to this question is provided by:

Theorem 4.2 (Duality theorem of linear programming). (a) *If either the* primal *problem or the* dual *problem has a finite optimal solution, then so does the other and* min $c^{\mathrm{T}}x = $ max $b^{\mathrm{T}}y$.

(b) *If either problem has an unbounded objective function value then the other has no feasible solution.*

Proof. Because of Lemma 4.1 and Corollary 4.1, to prove part (a) we need only exhibit a (finite) primal optimal solution x and a dual feasible solution y that satisfy $c^{\mathrm{T}}x = b^{\mathrm{T}}y$. Let x be an optimal basic feasible solution, say (4.1), obtained by the simplex method and let y be the corresponding vector of simplex multipliers $\pi = B^{-\mathrm{T}}c_B$. Now y is dual feasible, since

$$c - A^{\mathrm{T}}y = \begin{bmatrix} c_B \\ c_N \end{bmatrix} - \begin{bmatrix} B^{\mathrm{T}} \\ N^{\mathrm{T}} \end{bmatrix} \pi = \begin{bmatrix} 0 \\ \bar{c}_N \end{bmatrix} \geq 0$$

and

$$c^{\mathrm{T}}x = c_B^{\mathrm{T}}B^{-1}b = y^{\mathrm{T}}b \, ,$$

which concludes the proof of part (a).

Part (b) of the theorem follows directly from weak duality (Lemma 4.2).

The proof shows that the vector of simplex multipliers corresponding to the primal optimal solution x is a dual optimal solution y. Indeed, at any iteration of the simplex method, the simplex multipliers form a vector y with $c^{\mathrm{T}}x = b^{\mathrm{T}}y$, but unless all reduced costs are nonnegative, y is not dual feasible. So the algorithm maintains primal feasibility and $c^{\mathrm{T}}x = b^{\mathrm{T}}y$, while trying to attain dual feasibility.

We note that the converse of part (b) is not necessarily true. That is, if either the primal or dual is infeasible then it does *not* follow that the other problem is unbounded; both can be infeasible.

The following well-known and useful *alternative* theorem for systems of equalities and inequalities is easily derived from part (b) of the Duality theorem.

Theorem 4.3 (Farkas' Lemma). *The system*

(I) $Ax = b \, , \quad x \geq 0 \, ,$

is unsolvable if and only if the system

(II) $y^{\mathrm{T}}A \leq 0 \, , \quad b^{\mathrm{T}}y > 0 \, ,$

is solvable.

Proof. Consider the primal–dual pair of linear programs

(P)   minimize $0^{\mathrm{T}}x$ (D)   maximize $b^{\mathrm{T}}y$
         subject to $Ax = b$,   subject to $y^{\mathrm{T}}A \leqslant 0$.
                $x \geqslant 0$,

Since (D) is feasible ($y = 0$ is a solution), it follows from Theorem 4.2 that (P) is infeasible, or equivalently, (I) is unsolvable, if and only if (D) is unbounded. But clearly (D) is unbounded if and only if (II) is solvable, completing the proof.

Farkas' Lemma (1902) predates the development of linear programming and is often used to prove the Duality theorem rather than the other way round. Geometrically it states that exactly one of the following is true: (I) b is in the convex cone C generated by the columns of A; or (II) there is a vector y that makes an acute angle with b but not with any vector in C.

Before presenting other consequences of the Duality theorem, we note that corresponding to any linear program, there is a dual linear program, and that the Weak duality lemma, its corollary, and the Duality theorem apply to such primal–dual pairs. For example, the linear programs

(P)   minimize $c^{\mathrm{T}}x$ (D)   maximize $b^{\mathrm{T}}y$
         subject to $Ax \geqslant b$,   subject to $A^{\mathrm{T}}y \leqslant c$,   (4.6)
                $x \geqslant 0$, $y \geqslant 0$,

are a primal–dual pair. The dual (D) in (4.6) above can be derived by first converting (P) into standard form, then writing down the latter problem's dual and simplifying. The above primal–dual pair is often referred to when discussing duality, since the pair is nicely 'symmetric', in that both problems involve inequalities in nonnegative variables with the inequalities being '$\geqslant$' in the minimization problem and '$\leqslant$' in the maximization problem. We now state two more theorems that characterize the optimal solutions of this primal–dual pair of problems.

Theorem 4.4 (Complementary slackness). *Let x and y be primal and dual feasible solutions, respectively, of the primal–dual pair* (4.6). *Necessary and sufficient conditions that they be optimal solutions for their respective problems are*

$$(c^{\mathrm{T}} - y^{\mathrm{T}}A)x = 0 \tag{4.7}$$

and

$$y^{\mathrm{T}}(Ax - b) = 0 . \tag{4.8}$$

Proof. For primal feasible x and dual feasible y we have

$$s \equiv Ax - b \geqslant 0 , \quad x \geqslant 0 , \text{ and } w^{\mathrm{T}} \equiv c^{\mathrm{T}} - y^{\mathrm{T}}A \geqslant 0 , \quad y \geqslant 0 , \tag{4.9}$$

and hence

$$c^{\mathrm{T}}x \geqslant y^{\mathrm{T}}Ax \geqslant y^{\mathrm{T}}b .\tag{4.10}$$

If the conditions (4.7) and (4.8) hold then equality holds throughout (4.10), and the optimality of x and y follows from Corollary 4.1. Conversely, by the Duality theorem if x and y are optimal then $c^{\mathrm{T}}x = y^{\mathrm{T}}b$, which implies that equality holds throughout (4.10) and hence that conditions (4.7) and (4.8) are satisfied.

For the primal–dual pair of linear programs (4.2) and (4.4) only condition (4.7) is meaningful, as (4.8) is true for all primal feasible x. Because of the nonnegativity of the primal and dual variables x and y and slack vectors s and w (see (4.9)) conditions (4.7) and (4.8) can be stated in the following more useful form.

Complementary slackness conditions

$$w_j \equiv (c - A^{\mathrm{T}}y)_j = 0 \text{ or } x_j = 0 , \quad \text{for all } j = 1, \ldots , n ,$$
$$s_i \equiv (Ax - b)_i = 0 \text{ or } y_i = 0 , \quad \text{for all } i = 1, \ldots , m .\tag{4.11}$$

Using these conditions Theorem 4.4 states that feasible solutions to the primal and dual problems (4.6) are optimal if and only if (i) a variable is zero in one of the problems whenever the corresponding slack variable is strictly positive (i.e., the corresponding inequality constraint is strictly satisfied) in the other problem, and (ii) a slack variable is zero (i.e., the corresponding inequality constraint is satisfied as an equality) in one of the problems whenever the corresponding variable is positive in the other problem.

The so-called Kuhn–Tucker necessary conditions (Kuhn and Tucker 1951) (developed independently by Karush (1939) and John (1948)) for a solution to be optimal to a nonlinear programming problem are easily derived from Theorem 4.4 for the special case of linear programming. Here they are also sufficient conditions. We state them now for the standard form linear program (4.2).

Theorem 4.5 (Kuhn–Tucker conditions). *x is an optimal solution to the linear program* (4.2) *if and only if there exist vectors y and w such that*
   (i) $Ax = b, x \geqslant 0$,
   (ii) $A^{\mathrm{T}}y + w = c, w \geqslant 0$, *and*
   (iii) $w^{\mathrm{T}}x = 0$.

A proof based upon Theorem 4.4 is obvious since condition (i) is primal feasibility, (ii) is dual feasibility, and (iii) is complementary slackness. The standard development of the Kuhn–Tucker conditions for nonlinear programs extends the use of the so-called Lagrangian function of classical equality-constrained nonlinear optimization to the inequality constrained case. In the case of Theorem 4.5 the dual variables y are classical Lagrange multipliers. The dual slacks w are also Lagrange multipliers; however they are not classical as they correspond to inequality constraints and consequently are restricted to be nonnegative. Moreover, the complementary slackness condition (iii) in Theorem 4.5 requires those multipliers that correspond to inactive constraints (inequalities satisfied strictly) to be zero, which makes sense since inactive constraints should not play any part is deciding the optimality of a point.

4.2. Economic interpretation of duality

In the previous section we showed that the dual of a linear program arises naturally from the optimality conditions for the primal problem. In this section we shall show that, typically, if the primal problem has an economic interpretation, so does its dual and the optimal values of the dual variables can be interpreted as prices.

To demonstrate the latter, suppose that

$$x^* = \begin{pmatrix} x_B^* \\ 0 \end{pmatrix} = \begin{pmatrix} B^{-1}b \\ 0 \end{pmatrix}$$

is a nondegenerate optimal basic feasible solution to the standard form linear program (4.2). Since, by assumption $x_B^* > 0$, making a small change Δb to b will not cause the optimal basis B to change. Hence, if b is replaced by $b + \Delta b$, the new optimal solution becomes

$$\hat{x}^* = \begin{pmatrix} \hat{x}_B^* \\ 0 \end{pmatrix} = \begin{bmatrix} B^{-1}(b + \Delta b) \\ 0 \end{bmatrix}$$

and the optimal value of the objective function changes by

$$\Delta z = c_B^T B^{-1} \Delta b = \pi^{*T} \Delta b ,$$

where $\pi^* = B^{-T} c_B$ is the vector of simplex multipliers for the primal problem (4.2) at optimality. As shown in the proof of Theorem 4.2, π^* is the optimal solution to the dual problem (4.4). Clearly, π_i^* can be viewed as the *marginal price* (or *value*) of the i-th resource (i.e., right hand side b_i) in (4.2), since it gives the change in the optimal objective value per unit increase in that resource. This economic interpretation can be very useful since it indicates the maximum amount that one should be willing to pay to increase the amount of the i-th resource. Note that the complementary slackness conditions (4.11) imply that the marginal price for a resource is zero if that resource is not fully utilized at optimality. Other names for these 'prices at optimality' are *shadow prices* and *equilibrium prices*.

These shadow or marginal prices are also useful in determining whether or not to engage in a new activity. For example in the diet problem of Section 1.1 suppose that a previously unavailable food can be purchased. Having obtained a minimal cost diet without this food, should we consider adding it to our diet? To answer this question let the amount of nutrient i provided by the new food be a_{ik} and let the unit cost of the food be c_k. Since the optimal value y_i of the i-th dual variable can be interpreted as the marginal price of a unit of the i-th nutrient, the nutrients provided by the new food have a value of $\sum_{i=1}^{m} y_i a_{ik}$. Consequently if c_k is less than this value, the new food is worth purchasing and should be considered for inclusion in the optimal diet (y is not feasible in the new constraint); otherwise, the current optimal diet remains optimal (y remains feasible). In the former case, if the simplex method is invoked to reoptimize, the activity of purchasing the new food is immediately selected to enter the basis. The above operation corresponds to the computation of the reduced cost of an activity in the revised simplex method. The economic interpretation given above accounts for the terminology 'pricing-out' used to describe the operation.

Let us consider the first two linear programming examples presented in Section 1.1. We now show that their duals can be given economic interpretations.

Example 1 (The transportation problem). The dual of the transportation problem is:

$$\text{maximize} \quad \sum_{i=1}^{m} a_i u_i + \sum_{j=1}^{n} b_j v_j \tag{4.12}$$

$$\text{subject to} \quad u_i + v_j \leq c_{ij}, \quad i = 1, \ldots, m; \; j = 1, \ldots, n. \tag{4.13}$$

According to the discussion above, the dual variables u_i and v_j correspond to the marginal value of increasing the supply at the i-th origin and increasing the demand at the j-th destination by one unit, respectively. This interpretation makes sense from the point of view of the company that is trying to determine an optimal shipping schedule. An interpretation which gives economic meaning to the dual problem, and not just the variables of that problem, is the following:

Suppose that a 'shipping' company proposes to the producer (i.e., the company facing the primal problem) to remove a unit of product from origin i for a price of u_i per unit and to deliver a unit of product at destination j for a price of v_j per unit. By imposing the inequality constants (4.13) of the dual, the shipping company ensures that its prices are 'competitive' since the producer will always do better to have its product removed and delivered by the shipping company than to ship it directly. Assuming that the amounts, a_i and b_j, of a product available at origin i and required at destination j, respectively, are known to the shipping company, its problem is to set the prices $u_1, \ldots, u_m$ and $v_1, \ldots, v_n$ so as to satisfy (4.13) and maximize its total return (4.12).

Because of the Duality theorem, the producer will not save money by using the shipping company instead of shipping directly. However, by having someone else formulate and solve the dual problem, the producer is saved the task of solving the primal problem.

Example 2 (The diet problem). The diet problem has the form of the primal (P) in (4.6). Consequently, its dual has the form of the dual (D) in (4.6). As in the transportation problem let us interpret the dual of the diet problem as one which is faced by a competitor of the solver of the primal problem. Let this competitor be a pill salesman who sells pure nutrient pills – e.g., pills containing only iron, or only protein. In order to sell such pills to the dietician of the primal problem, this salesman must price these pills competitively. This requires that the nonnegative prices $y_1, \ldots, y_m$ satisfy

$$\sum_{i=1}^{m} y_i a_{ij} \leq c_j, \quad j = 1, \ldots, n .$$

Recall that a_{ij} is the amount of nutrient i provided by a unit of food j and c_j is the unit cost of food j. Since the minimum daily requirement of nutrient i is b_i, the pill salesman will attempt to maximize $\sum_{i=1}^{m} b_i y_i$; i.e., solve the dual problem (D) in (4.6).

The dual of the product mix problem (Example 3 in Section 1.1) can also be given an economic interpretation as an optimization problem faced by a competitor of the manufacturer that wishes to solve the primal problem. For this and other examples of the use of linear programming, and duality theory in particular, in economic analysis, the reader is referred to (Gale 1960) and (Dorfman, Samuelson, and Solow 1958).

4.3. The dual simplex algorithm

Suppose that one has an infeasible basic solution to a linear programming problem which prices out optimally; i.e., whose simplex multipliers are dual feasible. Such a situation arises, for example, when an inequality constraint is added to a linear programming problem after that problem has already been solved. If the new inequality is satisfied by the current optimal solution, nothing needs to be done. If the inequality is not satisfied, it can be converted to an equality by the addition of a nonnegative slack variable and added to the constraints of the linear program. Clearly, the optimal basis for the original problem and the new slack variable provide a basis for the expanded problem. This basis prices out optimally but is infeasible because the value of the new basic slack variable equals the negative of the amount by which the current solution fails to satisfy the new inequality.

The dual simplex method (Lemke 1954; Beale 1954) is designed to deal with just such a situation. As in the (primal) simplex method, the method proceeds from basic solution to neighboring basic solution. However, instead of maintaining primal feasibility at each step, dual feasibility is maintained. When a dual feasible basis is obtained that is also primal feasible, the algorithm terminates with the optimal solution of the linear program. In this section, we will abuse nomenclature somewhat by calling a basic (not necessarily feasible) solution of (4.2) 'optimal' if its basis is dual feasible.

To derive the method, let us assume that we are solving the linear program (4.2), and that the current basis consists of the first m variables. Hence, $x_B = B^{-1}b$, $\pi^T = c_B^T B$, and $\bar{c}_N^T = c_N^T - \pi^T N \geqslant 0$. If $x_B \not> 0$, the point $x^T = (x_B^T, 0)$ corresponds to an optimal but infeasible vertex of the polyhedron of feasible solutions of (4.2); i.e., x would be an optimal vertex if we could ignore the nonnegativity constraints to the basic variables that are negative in the current solution.

Suppose that $x_p < 0$. Clearly, it makes sense to move to a neighboring basic solution (feasible or infeasible vertex) that has $x_p = 0$, by replacing x_p in the basis by a nonbasic variable x_q. The selection of x_q is governed by the requirement that dual feasibility be maintained. To determine which of the $n - m$ neighboring vertices of the current vertex are optimal (i.e., dual feasible) we shall make use of the following:

Lemma 4.3 (Sherman–Morrison–Woodbury modification formula). (a) *If M is an $n \times n$ nonsingular matrix and u and v are any two vectors in $\mathbb{R}^n$ then $M + uv^T$ is nonsingular if and only $w \equiv 1 + v^T M^{-1} u \neq 0$.*
  (b) *Moreover, in this case, $(M + uv^T)^{-1} = M^{-1} - (1/w)M^{-1}uv^T M^{-1}$.*

Proof. Since $M + uv = (I + uv^T M^{-1})M$, (a) follows from the fact that $I + uv^T M^{-1}$ has $n - 1$ eigenvalues equal to one and one eigenvalue equal to $1 + v^T M^{-1} u$. The updating formula (b) is easily verified by multiplication by $M + uv^T$.

From the proof of Theorem 4.1, we see that the simplex multipliers and nonbasic reduced costs can be computed as

$$(\pi^T, \bar{c}_N^T) = c^T M^{-1} ,$$

where M is the matrix of active constraint normals (3.3), and M^{-1} is given by (3.4). If on a simplex pivot the p-th basic variable (i.e., x_p) is replaced by x_q, this is equivalent to replacing the q-th row of M (currently e_q^T) by e_p^T; i.e., M becomes $\bar{M} = M + e_q(e_p - e_q)^T$. Now using Lemma 4.3 and the fact that $e_q^T M^{-1} = e_q^T$ we have that

$$\bar{M}^{-1} = M^{-1} - \frac{M^{-1}e_q(e_p^T M^{-1} - e_q^T)}{e_p^T M^{-1} e_q} .$$

Premultiplying both sides of this expression by c^T we obtain the following formulas for computing the updated simplex multipliers $\bar{\bar{\pi}}$ and reduced costs $\bar{\bar{c}}_N$:

$$\bar{\bar{\pi}} = \pi + \gamma u ,$$

$$\bar{\bar{c}}_j = \bar{c}_j - \gamma \alpha_j , \quad j > m , \ j \neq q ,$$

and

$$\bar{\bar{c}}_p = -\gamma ,$$

where

$$u^{\mathrm{T}} = e_p^{\mathrm{T}} B^{-1} , \quad \alpha_j = u^{\mathrm{T}} a_j , \quad \text{and} \quad \gamma = \bar{c}_q / \alpha_q .$$

Note that u^{T} is the p-th row of B^{-1} and α_q is the so-called pivot element w_p in the primal simplex algorithm presented in Section 3. It follows from the recurrence relations for the reduced costs, that in order for $\bar{c}$, the reduced cost vector at the new basic solution, to be nonnegative we must choose q so that

$$0 \leqslant -\gamma = -\bar{c}_q / \alpha_q \leqslant -\bar{c}_j / \alpha_j , \quad \text{for all } \alpha_j < 0, \ j > m .$$

If $\alpha_j \geqslant 0$ for all nonbasic j, then $u^{\mathrm{T}} A$ is a nonnegative vector; hence $u^{\mathrm{T}} Ax = u^{\mathrm{T}} b$ cannot have a nonnegative solution since $u^{\mathrm{T}} b = x_p < 0$. This implies that the linear program (4.2) is infeasible. We can now give a 'revised' version of the dual simplex method.

Dual simplex method

(0) Let the dual feasible basic solution x_B to the linear program (4.2), corresponding to the basis matrix $B = [a_{j_1}, \ldots, a_{j_m}]$, be given. Let $B = \{j_1, \ldots, j_m\}$ denote the index set of basic variables. Compute an initial vector of feasible dual variables (simplex multipliers) by solving $B^{\mathrm{T}} \pi = c_B$, and compute $\bar{c}_j = c_j - \Pi^{\mathrm{T}} a_j$, for all $j \notin B$.

(1) Check for primal feasibility: If $x_B \geqslant 0$, STOP; the current solution is feasible, and hence, optimal. Otherwise, continue.

(2) Determine the basic variable x_{j_p} to leave the basis: Choose

$$j_p \in V \equiv \{ j_i \in B : x_{j_i} < 0 \} .$$

(3) Check for infeasibility: Compute u by solving $B^{\mathrm{T}} u = e_p$ for u and compute $\alpha_j = u^{\mathrm{T}} a_j$, for all $j \notin B$. If $\alpha_j \geqslant 0$ for all $j \notin B$, STOP; the problem is infeasible.

(4) Determine the nonbasic variable x_q to enter the basis: Choose

$$-\bar{c}_q / \alpha_q = \min \{ -\bar{c}_j / \alpha_j : \alpha_j < 0, \ j \notin B \} = -\gamma .$$

(5) Update the reduced costs: Set

$$\bar{c}_j \leftarrow \bar{c}_j - \gamma \alpha_j , \quad j \notin B , \ j \neq q ,$$
$$\bar{c}_p \leftarrow -\gamma .$$

(6) Update the solution and the basis matrix B: Compute w by solving

$$Bw = a_q .$$

Set

$$x_q \leftarrow \theta = x_{j_p}/\alpha_q \,,$$

$$x_{j_i} \leftarrow x_{j_i} - \theta w_i \,, \quad \text{for } 1 \leq i \leq m \,, \ i \neq p$$

$$B \leftarrow B + (a_q - a_{j_p})e_p^{\mathrm{T}} \,,$$

$$\boldsymbol{B} \leftarrow \boldsymbol{B} \cup \{q\}\backslash\{j_p\} \,,$$

$$j_p \leftarrow q \,,$$

and go to step (1).

By updating the reduced costs at each iteration, the above version of the dual simplex method requires essentially the same amount of work per iteration as a similarly implemented revised version of the primal simplex method. The principal effort in both cases comes from one B^{-1} and one B^{-T} operation, the computation of inner products of a vector with all nonbasic columns of A, and the updating of the representation of B^{-1}. If we update π instead of $\bar{c}_N$, additional inner products are required to compute $\bar{c}_j$ for all $j \not\in \boldsymbol{B}$ such that $\alpha_j < 0$. We can also compute π directly at each iteration but this requires an extra B^{-T} operation. One practical disadvantage of the dual simplex method is that all of the $n - m$ inner products $\alpha_j = u^{\mathrm{T}}a_j, j \not\in \boldsymbol{B}$, must be performed, while in the primal method, one need only compute inner products $\pi^{\mathrm{T}}a_j$ until some specified number of columns price out negatively or all columns have been priced out. This strategy is called *partial pricing* and is commonly used in practice.

Solving the linear program (4.2) by the dual simplex method is mathematically equivalent to solving the dual of that problem by the primal simplex method. This is not surprising since both approaches generate basic feasible solutions to the dual problem and maintain complementary slackness. Applying the simplex method directly to the dual involves working with an $n \times n$ basis matrix $\hat{B}$, in contrast with the $m \times m$ basis matrix B used by the dual simplex method. This seems to indicate that the methods are different. However, it is easy to see that $\hat{B}$ equals M^{T}, where M is the matrix (3.3). For simplicity we are assuming that we are using a variant of the primal simplex method that keeps all free variables in the basis at every iteration. Because of the special form of M and M^{-1} (see (3.4)), we only need a representation of B^{-1} to implement this method, and it is easily verified that such an implementation is essentially equivalent to the dual simplex method. This corresponds to a 'compact inverse' implementation of the simplex method as described in Section 5 using the 'working basis' B.

Before ending our discussion of the dual simplex method we should point out that it is extensively used in solving integer and mixed integer linear programs using either branch-and-bound or cutting-plane approaches. (See Chapter 6.)

4.4. Sensitivity analysis

In the previous two sections we showed how to obtain the optimal solution of a linear program after the addition of new activities and new constraints, given the optimal solution of the original problem, without resolving the resulting modified problems from scratch. We also explained, in Section 4.2, that the optimal simplex multipliers (i.e., dual variables) give the changes in the optimal objective value for small changes in the right hand sides of the constraints, in the case of a nondegenerate optimal basic feasible solution.

We shall now investigate how more general changes in the right hand sides or in the objective function coefficients effect a previously obtained optimal solution. Such studies are referred to as *sensitivity* or *post-optimality analyses*.

Let us first consider changes in the objective function. In particular, consider the one-parameter family of linear programs

$$\text{minimize} \quad z(\theta) = (c + \theta d)^{\mathrm{T}} x$$
$$\text{subject to} \quad Ax = b, \quad x \geq 0. \tag{4.14}$$

Suppose that we have an optimal basic feasible solution for $\theta = \theta_0$, and we wish to determine the interval $\underline{\theta} \leq \theta \leq \bar{\theta}$ for the parameter θ for which the current basis remains optimal. Let this basis be B and let c and d be partitioned into basic and nonbasic parts c_B, d_B and c_N and d_N, respectively. B will be optimal as long as the nonbasic reduced costs remain nonnegative; i.e., $(c_N + \theta d_N)^{\mathrm{T}} - (c_B + \theta d_B)^{\mathrm{T}} B^{-1} N \geq 0$. Defining reduced costs $\bar{c}_N^{\mathrm{T}} = c_N^{\mathrm{T}} - c_B^{\mathrm{T}} B^{-1} N$ and $\bar{d}_N^{\mathrm{T}} = d_N^{\mathrm{T}} - d_B^{\mathrm{T}} B^{-1} N$, in terms of c and d alone, the above condition becomes $\theta \bar{d}_N^{\mathrm{T}} \geq -\bar{c}_N^{\mathrm{T}}$. Consequently, the range is

$$\underline{\theta} = \max\{\max\{-\bar{c}_j/\bar{d}_j : \bar{d}_j > 0, \ j \notin B\}, -\infty\} \leq \theta$$
$$\leq \min\{\min\{-\bar{c}_j/\bar{d}_j : \bar{d}_j < 0, \ j \notin B\}, \infty\} = \bar{\theta}. \tag{4.15}$$

And, for $\underline{\theta} \leq \theta \leq \bar{\theta}$, the optimal objective value is a linear function of θ; i.e.,

$$z^*(\theta) = (c_B^{\mathrm{T}} + \theta d_B^{\mathrm{T}}) B^{-1} b = z^*(\theta_0) + (\theta - \theta_0) d_B^{\mathrm{T}} x_B.$$

If $\theta_0 = 0$ and we choose $d = e_j$, then $[c_j + \underline{\theta}, c_j + \bar{\theta}]$ gives the *range* for the j-th cost coefficient for which the optimal solution, corresponding to $\theta = 0$, remains optimal as long as all other problem data remain fixed.

The optimal solution of the parametric linear program (4.14) can be determined for all values of the parameter θ. Given a range $[\underline{\theta}, \bar{\theta}]$ of θ for a particular optimal basic feasible solution, either there is a neighboring basic feasible solution that is optimal for values of θ in an interval $[\underline{\theta}, \underline{\theta}]$, with $-\infty < \underline{\theta}$, or $z^*(\theta)$ is unbounded below for all θ in $(-\infty, \underline{\theta})$. This new solution and basis is obtained by performing a simplex pivot which introduces into the basis the variable x_j that yields $\underline{\theta} = -\bar{c}_j/\bar{d}_j$ in (4.15), and $\underline{\theta}$ is determined using the new basis. If an unbounded ray is detected while trying to execute a simplex pivot, $z^*(\theta)$ is unbounded below for all $\theta < \underline{\theta}$. An analogous procedure gives a neighboring optimal basic feasible solution, if one exists, and range $[\bar{\theta}, \bar{\bar{\theta}}]$ for $\theta \ge \bar{\theta}$.

As in the simplex method, degenerate pivots can occur; however, the number of nontrivial ranges is clearly finite, and it can be easily shown that $z^*(\theta)$ is a piecewise linear and concave function of θ. Although the number of ranges can be as large as 2^n in pathological cases (Murty 1980), the probabilistic analysis of variants of the simplex method based upon solving (4.14) has yielded bounds on the expected number of iterations which are quadratic in the problem size (see Section 7).

Consider now the right hand side parametric linear program

$$\text{minimize} \quad z(\theta) = c^{\mathrm{T}} x$$
$$\text{subject to} \quad Ax = b + \theta d, \quad x \ge 0.$$

If B is an optimal basis for some value of $\theta = \theta_0$, then the interval $[\underline{\theta}, \bar{\theta}]$ for which this basis remains feasible, and hence yields an optimal solution $x^{\mathrm{T}} = (x_B^{\mathrm{T}}, x_N^{\mathrm{T}}) = (\bar{b}^{\mathrm{T}} + \theta \bar{d}^{\mathrm{T}}, 0)$ where $\bar{b} = B^{-1} b$ and $\bar{d} = B^{-1} d$, is clearly given by

$$\underline{\theta} = \max\{ \max_{1 \le i \le m} \{-\bar{b}_i / \bar{d}_i : \bar{d}_i > 0\}, -\infty\} \le \theta$$

$$\le \min\{ \min_{1 \le i \le m} \{-\bar{b}_i / \bar{d}_i : \bar{d}_i < 0\}, \infty\} = \bar{\theta}.$$

In this interval, although the optimal primal solution varies linearly with θ, the basis and optimal dual solution remain fixed. Neighboring bases and ranges are determined by dual simplex pivots if infeasibility is not detected in contrast with the case of cost function parametrics, which involves primal simplex pivots or the detection of unboundedness.

5. Exploiting structure

The computation required by each iteration of the revised simplex method (Section 3.2) is usually dominated by the solution of the linear systems $B^{\mathrm{T}} \pi = c_B$ and $Bw = a_q$ and the update of the basis inverse representation (in product form or using an LU factorization – see Section 3.3). Since B is an $m \times m$ nonsingular matrix, and large problems may have m of the order of 10^4, it is imperative to exploit any structure in the coefficient matrix A to decrease the computational work. In this section we discuss two kinds of special structure: upper bounds and network constraints. The next section considers other approaches to handling very large structured problems efficiently.

5.1. Upper bounds and compact (partitioned) inverse methods

Modifying the revised simplex method to handle upper-bounded variables efficiently can be motivated directly as in Section 3. However, we will treat a more general case to give a flavor of the power of 'compact inverse' methods and refer to the upper-bounded case as a simple illustration.

The methods we discuss here exploit the simple idea that if B has special structure, we may be able to solve systems with coefficient matrix B by solving systems of smaller dimension. More precisely, we will partition B of order m into smaller matrices of order $k \times k$, $k \times l$, $l \times k$ and $l \times l$ such that solving a system with coefficient matrix B is reduced to solving two (trivial) systems of order l and one system of order k involving a smaller matrix called the *working basis*.

This idea has appeared before, in Section 3: the key matrix there was M in (3.3), whose inverse was given in terms of B^{-1} in (3.4). In that context, M was the 'basis', I the coefficient matrix in the 'trivial' system, and B the 'working basis'. Thus the revised simplex method automatically exploits the special structure of the nonnegativities to deal with the $m \times m$ matrix B instead of the $n \times n$ matrix M. We can often decrease the dimension further by exploiting structure within B.

Consider the linear programming problem in standard form:

(P)   minimize $c^{\mathrm{T}}x$

subject to $\begin{pmatrix} A \\ R \end{pmatrix} x \equiv \hat{A}x = \hat{b} \equiv \begin{pmatrix} b \\ r \end{pmatrix}$,

$x \geqslant 0$,

where we assume that $\hat{A}$ has full row rank m, and that the constraints have been partitioned into 'general' constraints $Ax = b$ and 'special' constraints $Rx = r$, where A and b have k rows, R and r have l rows, and $k + l = m$.

Example 5.1. The upper bounded problem

minimize $\tilde{c}^{\mathrm{T}}\tilde{x}$

subject to $\tilde{A}\tilde{x} = \tilde{b}$,

$0 \leqslant \tilde{x} \leqslant \tilde{r}$,

where $\tilde{A}$ has full row rank and $\tilde{r} > 0$, is an instance of (P) if we set

$x^{\mathrm{T}} = (\tilde{x}^{\mathrm{T}}, \tilde{y}^{\mathrm{T}})$

$A = [\tilde{A}, 0]$, $b = \tilde{b}$,

$R = [I, I]$, $r = \tilde{r}$,   and

$c^{\mathrm{T}} = [\tilde{c}^{\mathrm{T}}, 0]$

so that $\tilde{y}$ is the vector of slack variables for the upper bounds.

Suppose we have a basic feasible solution of (P) whose first $m = k + l$ components are basic, and partition the cost vector and coefficient matrices as follows:

$$
\begin{bmatrix} c^T \\ A \\ R \end{bmatrix} = \begin{bmatrix} c_B^T & c_C^T & c_D^T \\ B & C & D \\ S & T & H \end{bmatrix} \begin{matrix} 1 \\ k \\ l \end{matrix} .
$$
$$
\quad\quad k \quad l \quad n-m
$$

(5.1)

The usual basis matrix is then

$$
\hat{B} = \begin{bmatrix} B & C \\ S & T \end{bmatrix}.
$$

(5.2)

Since $[S, T]$ is of full rank l it contains a nonsingular $l \times l$ submatrix. Assume the variables have been ordered so that T is nonsingular. We wish to express $\hat{B}^{-1}$ in terms of smaller inverses.

These involve the matrix T (here 'T' stands for trivial: linear systems involving T are assumed very easy to solve) and the matrix

$$
W = B - CT^{-1}S
$$

(the working basis). Indeed, if we make row operations to eliminate block C, we find

$$
\hat{B} = \begin{bmatrix} I & CT^{-1} \\ 0 & I \end{bmatrix} \begin{bmatrix} W & 0 \\ S & T \end{bmatrix},
$$

so that

$$
\begin{aligned}
\hat{B}^{-1} &= \begin{bmatrix} W^{-1} & 0 \\ -T^{-1}SW^{-1} & T^{-1} \end{bmatrix} \begin{bmatrix} I & -CT^{-1} \\ 0 & I \end{bmatrix} \\
&= \begin{bmatrix} W^{-1} & -W^{-1}CT^{-1} \\ -T^{-1}SW^{-1} & T^{-1} + T^{-1}SW^{-1}CT^{-1} \end{bmatrix}.
\end{aligned}
$$

(5.3)

Henceforth we assume that we have W^{-1} and T^{-1} explicitly or in product form, or LU factorizations of W and T.

Example 5.1 (continued). Since the $(k+j)$-th row of $\hat{A}$ only has nonzeroes in the columns corresponding to $\tilde{x}_j$ and $\tilde{y}_j$, at least one of these variables must be basic at any basic solution, else $\hat{B}$ would have a zero row. If $\tilde{y}_j$ is basic, call it the j-th *key* variable; otherwise, call $\tilde{x}_j$ the j-th key variable. Now order the basic variables so that the key variables, in order, come last. Then T will be the identity matrix. For instance, if $k=1$ and $l=3$, so that $n=2l=6$, we have

$$
\hat{A} = \begin{bmatrix} a_1 & a_2 & a_3 & 0 & 0 & 0 \\ 1 & 0 & 0 & 1 & 0 & 0 \\ 0 & 1 & 0 & 0 & 1 & 0 \\ 0 & 0 & 1 & 0 & 0 & 1 \end{bmatrix}
$$

where a_j is the j-th column of A (or of $\tilde{A}$). If $\tilde{x}_1, \tilde{x}_2, \tilde{y}_2$ and $\tilde{y}_3$ are basic, then $\tilde{x}_1, \tilde{y}_2$ and $\tilde{y}_3$ are the key variables, and

$$\hat{B} = \begin{bmatrix} a_2 & a_1 & 0 & 0 \\ 0 & 1 & 0 & 0 \\ 1 & 0 & 1 & 0 \\ 0 & 0 & 0 & 1 \end{bmatrix} = \begin{bmatrix} B & C \\ S & T \end{bmatrix}. \tag{5.4}$$

Thus T is the 3×3 identity matrix, and $W = B - CT^{-1}S = B - CS = B$ is the 1×1 matrix a_2. Indeed we have:

Lemma 5.1. *In the upper-bound case, we always have $W = B$.*

Proof. Our choice of key variables guarantees that $T = I$, so that $W = B - CT^{-1}S = B - CS$. Moreover, if the i-th column of S is the j-th unit vector, then the i-th basic variable is $\tilde{x}_j$ which is not key, so the j-th key variable is $\tilde{y}_j$. But then the j-th column of C corresponds to a slack variable and is therefore 0. Thus each column of CS is the zero vector, whence $W = B$.

Note that B consists of the columns of $\tilde{A}$ corresponding to basic variables $\tilde{x}_j$ whose slacks $\tilde{y}_j$ are also basic. In the nondegenerate case, therefore, the working basis consists of columns of $\tilde{A}$ corresponding to variables that are strictly between their lower and upper bounds.

We now return to the general case, and consider first the computation of the simplex multipliers $\hat{\pi}^{T} = (\pi^{T}, \rho^{T})$, where π is a k-vector and ρ an l-vector. Thus

$$(\pi^{T}, \rho^{T}) = (c_B^{T}, c_C^{T})\hat{B}^{-1}$$

$$= (c_B^{T}, c_C^{T})\begin{bmatrix} W^{-1} & 0 \\ -T^{-1}SW^{-1} & T^{-1} \end{bmatrix}\begin{bmatrix} I & -CT^{-1} \\ 0 & I \end{bmatrix}$$

from (5.3). Hence if

$$(\alpha^{T}, \beta^{T}) = (c_B^{T}, c_C^{T})\begin{bmatrix} W^{-1} & 0 \\ -T^{-1}SW^{-1} & T^{-1} \end{bmatrix}$$

we find $\pi^{T} = \alpha^{T}$ and $\rho^{T} = -\alpha^{T}CT^{-1} + \beta^{T}$. Therefore we calculate

$$\beta^{T} = c_C^{T}T^{-1},$$
$$\pi^{T} = (c_B^{T} - \beta^{T}S)W^{-1}, \quad \text{and} \tag{5.5}$$
$$\rho^{T} = \beta^{T} - \pi^{T}CT^{-1},$$

to get $\hat{\pi}^{T} = (\pi^{T}, \rho^{T})$. Note that we have organized the calculations so that T^{-1} appears twice (in the expressions for β^{T} and ρ^{T}) and W^{-1} once (in that for π^{T}).

We use $\hat{\pi}^{T}$ to price out nonbasic columns; thus if such a column is denoted $\hat{a}_j = \binom{d_j}{h_j}$, with cost c_j, we find the reduced cost

$$\bar{c}_j = c_j - \hat{\pi}^{\mathrm{T}}\hat{a}_j = c_j - \pi^{\mathrm{T}}d_j - \rho^{\mathrm{T}}h_j \, . \tag{5.6}$$

If all $\bar{c}_j$'s are nonnegative, the current solution is optimal; otherwise we choose q with $\bar{c}_q < 0$.

Example 5.1 (continued). In the case of upper bounds, T is the identity so that $\beta^{\mathrm{T}} = c_C^{\mathrm{T}}$. It is also easy to check as in the proof of Lemma 5.1 that $\beta^{\mathrm{T}} S = 0$, so that

$$\pi^{\mathrm{T}} = c_B^{\mathrm{T}} W^{-1} = c_B^{\mathrm{T}} B^{-1} \, . \tag{5.7}$$

Using the fact that T is the identity again and the form of β^{T} and C, we find that

$$\rho_j = \begin{cases} c_j - c_B^{\mathrm{T}} B^{-1} a_j & \text{if the } j\text{-th key variable is } \tilde{x}_j \, , \\ 0 & \text{if the } j\text{-th key variable is } \tilde{y}_j \, . \end{cases} \tag{5.8}$$

Now consider pricing out the nonbasic columns. If $x_j = \tilde{x}_j$ is nonbasic, then $\tilde{y}_j$ is the j-th key variable and the reduced cost is

$$\bar{c}_j = c_j - \pi^{\mathrm{T}} a_j - \rho^{\mathrm{T}} e_j = c_j - c_B^{\mathrm{T}} B^{-1} a_j \tag{5.9}$$

using (5.6)–(5.8), since ρ_j is zero. On the other hand, if $x_j = \tilde{y}_j$ is nonbasic, then $\tilde{x}_j$ is the j-th key variable and the reduced cost is

$$\bar{c}_j = 0 - \pi^{\mathrm{T}} 0 - \rho^{\mathrm{T}} e_j = -\rho_j = -(c_j - c_B^{\mathrm{T}} B^{-1} a_j) \, . \tag{5.10}$$

Hence the rule for entering variables is simple and intuitive: if $\tilde{x}_j$ is nonbasic at its lower bound 0, then it is eligible to enter the basis of its 'usual' reduced cost as in (5.9) is negative. On the other hand, if $\tilde{x}_j$ is at its upper bound $\tilde{r}_j$ (so that the slack variable $\tilde{y}_j$ is nonbasic), then $\tilde{y}_j$ is eligible to enter the basis (and hence $\tilde{x}_j$ to decrease from its upper bound) if $\bar{c}_j$ in (5.10) is negative, so that the 'usual' reduced cost $c_j - c_B^{\mathrm{T}} B^{-1} a_j$ is positive.

Having determined an entering variable x_q, we need to calculate the updated column w, which we partition into $u \in R^k$ and $v \in R^l$:

$$w = \begin{pmatrix} u \\ v \end{pmatrix} = \hat{B}^{-1} \begin{pmatrix} d_q \\ h_q \end{pmatrix}$$

$$= \begin{bmatrix} W^{-1} & 0 \\ -T^{-1} S W^{-1} & T^{-1} \end{bmatrix} \begin{bmatrix} I & -C T^{-1} \\ 0 & I \end{bmatrix} \begin{pmatrix} d_q \\ h_q \end{pmatrix} \, . \tag{5.11}$$

Thus we compute

$$t = T^{-1}h_q ,$$

$$u = W^{-1}(d_q - Ct), \quad \text{and} \tag{5.12}$$

$$v = t - T^{-1}Su .$$

Again, T^{-1} occurs twice above and W^{-1} once.

If $w = \binom{u}{v}$ is nonpositive, we conclude that (P) is unbounded; otherwise we use w in a minimum ratio test to determine the leaving basic variable and to update the values of the basic variables.

The final step of the iteration is to obtain (representations of) the inverses of the new matrices W and T. This can be the most complicated part of the iteration. We will now describe a special case which reduces to a standard basis inverse update, but the procedure to be followed in general depends very much on the particular structure in the matrix R.

The special case is when the leaving column is in the first part of the basis matrix $\hat{B}$. In that case, C and T remain unchanged while the new column, say $\binom{d_q}{h_q}$, replaces the column $\binom{b_p}{s_p}$ of $\hat{B}$. Notice that $W = B - CT^{-1}S$ has columns

$$We_j = b_j - CT^{-1}s_j \tag{5.13}$$

corresponding directly to the columns of $\begin{bmatrix} B \\ S \end{bmatrix}$. Thus W becomes $\bar{W}$ where $d_q - CT^{-1}h_q$ replaces the old column We_p; moreover, $d_q - CT^{-1}h_q = d_q - Ct$ has already been computed in (5.12). Hence in this case our representation of T^{-1} is unchanged, while that for W^{-1} is updated as in a standard column exchange, as discussed in Section 3.4.

Example 5.1 (concluded). We assume that $\tilde{y}_j$ is entering the basis; the case for $\tilde{x}_j$ is similar. Then $d_q = 0$ and $h_q = e_j$. Moreover, $\tilde{x}_j$ is then the j-th key variable, and thus the j-th column of C is a_j and $\tilde{x}_j$ is currently at its upper bound $\tilde{r}_j$. Using (5.12) we find

$$t = T^{-1}h_q = h_q = e_j ,$$

$$u = W^{-1}(d_q - Ct) = W^{-1}(0 - Ce_j) \tag{5.14}$$

$$= W^{-1}(-a_j) = -B^{-1}a_j , \quad \text{and}$$

$$v = t - T^{-1}Su = e_j + SB^{-1}a_j .$$

Note that the j-th row of S is zero since $\tilde{x}_j$ is key and $\tilde{y}_j$ nonbasic; thus $v_j = 1 > 0$, so that we cannot get an indication of unboundedness (which would be most unexpected in a problem with all the variables bounded). Moreover, apart from $v_j = 1$, each component of $w = \binom{u}{v}$ is either zero, or a component of $-B^{-1}a_j$ or of $+B^{-1}a_j$, since each row of S is zero or a unit vector. The entry one corresponds to $\tilde{x}_j$, which decreases by one for each unit $\tilde{y}_j$ is increased, while the entries 0 correspond to variables $\tilde{x}_j$ or $\tilde{y}_j$ which are at their upper bounds and do not change as $\tilde{y}_j$ is increased. The other entries, components of $\pm B^{-1}a_j$, indicate the necessary changes in components $\tilde{x}_i$ and $\tilde{y}_i$ between their bounds as $\tilde{y}_j$ increases; the different signs occur since if $\tilde{x}_i$ increases, $\tilde{y}_i$ must decrease and vice-versa.

The different minimum ratios that might occur correspond to such a $\tilde{x}_i$ or $\tilde{y}_i$ becoming zero; if the minimum ratio occurs in row $k + j$, corresponding to $v_j = 1$, it indicates that $\tilde{x}_j$ has become nonbasic, i.e. it has travelled from its upper to its lower bound. In this last case, $\tilde{y}_j$ replaces $\tilde{x}_j$ as the j-th key variable, T remains the identity, and $W = B$ remains unchanged! However, the values of the basic variables do change and the j-th column of C changes from a_j to 0.

We have indicated above the easy case where $\tilde{y}_j$ replaces $\tilde{x}_j$; in addition, if $\tilde{y}_j$ replaces a variable that is not key, then T is unchanged and $W = B$ suffers a column exchange as described for the general case. Let us address the final case, where $\tilde{y}_j$ replaces a key variable other than $\tilde{x}_j$. Since each basis must contain either $\tilde{x}_i$ or $\tilde{y}_i$ for each i, the replaced variable must be a $\tilde{y}_i$ with $\tilde{x}_i$ also basic. Thus $\tilde{x}_i$ must become the new i-th key variable, $\tilde{x}_j$ must fill its place in the non-key basic variables, and $\tilde{y}_j$ must replace $\tilde{x}_j$ as the j-th key variable. (For example, consider the basis of (5.4), and suppose $\tilde{y}_1$ enters the basis and replaces $\tilde{y}_2$, so that $j = 1$ and $i = 2$. Then the new key variables will be $\tilde{y}_1, \tilde{x}_2$ and $\tilde{y}_3$, with $\tilde{x}_1$ the new non-key basic variable.) T remains the identity, and $W = B$, the matrix of columns associated with variables strictly between their bounds (assuming nondegeneracy) suffers a column exchange: a_j replaces a_i. Finally, a_i and 0 replace the i-th and j-th columns of C respectively, and e_j replaces the column of S that had been e_i. (In the example above, $\hat{B}$ becomes

$$\begin{bmatrix} a_1 & 0 & a_2 & 0 \\ 1 & 1 & 0 & 0 \\ 0 & 0 & 1 & 0 \\ 0 & 0 & 0 & 1 \end{bmatrix},$$

and it is easy to check in general that these are precisely the required changes.) Hence, after updating the representation of the inverse of W (which is either unchanged or undergoes a column exchange), we are ready for the next iteration.

The compact inverse idea has been applied to other forms of special constraints: generalized upper bounds (Dantzig and Van Slyke 1967), variable upper bounds (Schrage 1975), (Todd 1982), and network constraints, e.g. (Klingman and Russell 1975). An elementary treatment of generalized upper bounds can be found for example in (Chvátal 1983) and a geometric view of compact inverse methods is presented by Todd (1983). Our aim here has been to describe the basic ideas of the approach and illustrate them on a particularly simple problem, which is treated directly in most linear programming texts.

5.2. Network problems

Here we will outline how the simplex method can be efficiently implemented when the problem is to find a minimum cost network flow subject to capacity and flow conservation constraints.

Let $G = (V, E)$ be a directed graph. Thus V is a finite set of *nodes*, and E a finite set of ordered pairs of distinct nodes called *arcs*. If $e = (i, j) \in E$, we say e *joins* its *tail* $i = t(e)$ to its *head* $j = h(e)$. A *path* P is an alternating sequence $(i_0, e_1, i_1, \ldots, e_l, i_l)$ of distinct nodes and distinct arcs with $e_k = (i_{k-1}, i_k)$ (a *forward* arc) or $e_k = (i_k, i_{k-1})$ (a *reverse* arc) for $1 \leqslant k \leqslant l$. It is *from* i_0 *to* i_l and of *length* l. A sequence satisfying all these requirements except that $i_0 = i_l$ is a *cycle*. A graph is *connected* if there is a path from any node to any other node, and *acyclic* if it contains no cycle. A graph $H = (W, F)$ is a *subgraph of G* if $W \subseteq V$ and $F \subseteq E$; it is a *spanning* subgraph if $W = V$.

Suppose $G = (V, E)$ is a connected directed graph, $\hat{b} = (b_i)_{i \in V}$ is a vector of net supplies satisfying $\Sigma_{i \in V} \, b_i = 0$, and $c = (c_e)_{e \in E}$ is a vector of costs. Then the *transshipment problem*

(P) minimize $\displaystyle\sum_{e \in E} c_e x_e$

subject to $\displaystyle\sum_{e \,:\, t(e) = i} x_e - \sum_{e \,:\, h(e) = i} x_e = b_i \, , \quad i \in V \, ,$

$$x_e \geqslant 0 \, , \quad e \in E \, ,$$

is that of shipping a good at minimum cost to satisfy given demands (at nodes i with $b_i < 0$) from given supplies (at nodes i with $b_i > 0$). The minimum cost network flow problem adds upper bounds (capacities) on the flows x_e, but since such problems can be solved by easy extensions of methods for transshipment problems (corresponding to extensions of the simplex method for handling upper bounds), we will keep the discussion simple by ignoring capacities.

Let us denote by $\hat{A}$ the node–arc incidence matrix of G. Thus $\hat{A}$ has a row for each node and a column for each arc with

$$\hat{a}_{ie} = \begin{cases} +1 & \text{if } t(e) = i \, , \\ -1 & \text{if } h(e) = i \, , \\ 0 & \text{otherwise.} \end{cases}$$

Then we can write (P) as

minimize $c^{\mathrm{T}} x$
subject to $\hat{A} x = \hat{b} \, ,$
$x \geqslant 0 \, .$

The reason for the carets is that this representation violates our usual assumption that the constraint matrix has full row rank. Indeed it is clear that each column contains one $+1$ and one -1 so that the sum of the rows of $\hat{A}$ is the zero vector. (This is why we required that the sum of the components of $\hat{b}$ be zero, i.e. that the total net supply be zero.) We shall now show that omitting any row from $\hat{A}$ and $\hat{b}$ remedies this difficulty.

Let r be an arbitrary node of G, which we call the root. Let A and b be $\hat{A}$ and $\hat{b}$ with the row corresponding to r deleted; then (P) is equivalent to the standard form problem

$$\text{minimize} \quad c^{\mathrm{T}}x$$

$$\text{subject to} \quad Ax = b,$$

$$x \geqslant 0.$$

We will show that A has rank $n - 1$, where $n = |V|$. At the same time we will characterize the bases or nonsingular submatrices of A of order $n - 1$. We require the notion of a *spanning tree*.

Lemma 5.2. *Let $H = (V, F)$ be a subgraph of the connected directed graph $G = (V, E)$ where $|V| = n$. Then the following are equivalent:*
   (i) *$|F| = n - 1$ and H is connected;*
   (ii) *$|F| = n - 1$ and H is acyclic;*
   (iii) *H is connected and acyclic;*
   (iv) *H is minimally connected – the removal of any arc disconnects it; and*
   (v) *H is maximally acyclic – the addition of any arc creates a cycle.*

We omit the proof of this standard result in graph theory. If any of these equivalent conditions hold, we say H (or just F) is a spanning tree of G, and we will often omit the adjective spanning.

We can now prove:

Theorem 5.1. *Let $G = (V, E)$ be a connected directed graph with $|V| = n$, let $\hat{A}$ be its node–arc incidence matrix, let $r \in V$ be arbitrary, and let A be $\hat{A}$ with the row indexed by r deleted. Then A has full row rank $n - 1$, and if B is a square submatrix of A of order $n - 1$, then B is nonsingular iff its columns are indexed by the arcs of a spanning tree of G.*

Proof. We first note that any connected graph has a spanning tree by Lemma 5.2(iv): just keep removing arcs until the resulting subgraph is minimally connected.

Next we show that the columns of A indexing the arcs of a cycle of G are linearly dependent. Indeed, if $P(Q)$ indexes the forward (reverse) arcs of the cycle, then it is easy to see that

$$\sum_{e \in P} a_e - \sum_{e \in Q} a_e = 0.$$

It therefore suffices to show that any submatrix B of A whose columns index the arcs of a spanning tree is nonsingular. This follows from:

Lemma 5.3. *Let* $H = (V, F)$ *be a spanning tree of* G, *and let* B *be the corresponding submatrix of* A. *Then there is an ordering of the rows and columns of* B *that makes it upper triangular with nonzero diagonal entries.*

Proof. By induction on n. For $n = 1$, B is the null matrix of order 0, which trivially satisfies the conclusions. (If the reader objects to null matrices, the case $n = 2$ is just as easy: B is the 1×1 matrix whose entry is ± 1.) Suppose the lemma is true for $n < k$, and consider the case $n = k$. Since $2n - 2 = 2|F|$ equals the sum of the degrees of the nodes in H (i.e., the sum over $i \in V$ of the number of arcs e of H with $h(e)$ or $t(e)$ equal to i), and each node has degree at least 1 (H is connected), we deduce that there are at least two nodes of degree 1 (these are called *leaves*). Pick a leaf $i \in V$ other than r and let $e \in F$ be its incident arc. Consider the graph $H' = (V \backslash \{i\}, F \backslash \{e\})$. By Lemma 5.2(ii) it is a spanning tree of $G' = (V \backslash \{i\}, E \backslash \{e\})$, and by the inductive hypothesis we can therefore order the nodes and arcs of H' so that the corresponding matrix, B', is upper triangular with nonzero diagonal entries. Now add node i as the last row and arc e as the last column, to find

$$B = \begin{pmatrix} B' & u \\ 0 & \pm 1 \end{pmatrix}$$

for some vector u. Hence B has been ordered to have the desired form, proving the inductive step.

Lemma 5.3 shows that every submatrix of A of order $n - 1$ has determinant 0, $+1$, or -1 (since the determinant of a triangular matrix is the product of its diagonal entries). In fact, the proof of the lemma can be easily extended to show that every square submatrix of A has determinant in $\{0, +1, -1\}$, i.e. A is *totally unimodular*. Such matrices are of great interest in combinatorial optimization, since the inverse of any nonsingular square submatrix is integer-valued. Hence for any integer-valued b, the basic solutions of $Ax = b$, $x \geq 0$, are integer-valued. We record this formally in:

Corollary 5.1. *The transshipment problem* (P) *has the integrality property that if the net supplies* b_i *are all integer, every basic solution is integer-valued. Moreover, every basic solution* x *has* x_e *nonzero only for* $e \in F$ *for some spanning tree* $F \subseteq E$ *of* G.

We now discuss the implementation of the primal simplex algorithm for problem (P). We ignore problems of getting an initial basic feasible solution and resolving degeneracy, for both of which there are special network techniques available – see for instance Chapter 19 of Chvátal (1983). The key idea is to represent the basis B or the corresponding tree $H = (V, F)$ to allow the efficient solution of the linear systems $B^T \pi = c_B$ and $Bw = a_e$. Since B can be reordered to make it triangular, these systems can be solved very fast.

Let $e = (u, v) \in E \backslash F$. Our proof of Theorem 5.1 shows that the solution to

$Bw = a_e$ can be obtained by finding the path from u to v in H. If P denotes the set of forward and Q the reverse arcs in this path, then $w_f = +1$ if $f \in P$, -1 if $f \in Q$, and 0 otherwise. To quickly determine such a path we store the *predecessor* $p(i)$ of i for each $i \in V$ other than the root r, i.e. the next node to i in the unique path from i to r, as well as the *depth* $d(i)$ of i, the length of this path. We can also use signs on $p(i)$ to indicate whether the arc joining i and $p(i)$ is a forward or reverse arc of this path.

The system $B^T \pi = c_B$ can be written as

$$\pi_j - \pi_i = c_f \quad \text{for } f = (i, j) \in F,$$

where $\pi_r \equiv 0$. We can solve for the π's successively by traversing the nodes of the tree starting from the root r so that $p(i)$ is always visited before i. Such an order is called a *preorder* of the tree; we let $s(i)$ denote the successor of i in this order.

To illustrate these ideas, consider the following:

Example 5.2. Let $V = \{1, 2, \ldots, 9\}$ with $r = 1$, where H is the tree shown in Figure 5.1. Let $x_{35} = x_{94} = 1$, $x_{37} = x_{18} = 2$, $x_{23} = x_{48} = 3$, and $x_{31} = x_{64} = 4$. The tree is represented by the three vectors p, d and s of length $|V|$ as in Table 5.1.

The steps of each iteration are then performed efficiently as follows:

(1) Solve $B^T \pi = c_B$, or $\pi_j - \pi_i = c_f$ for $f = (i, j) \in F$, where $\pi_r \equiv 0$. To do this, we calculate the π's in preorder so that $\pi_{|p(i)|}$ is available when we compute π_i. In our example, we calculate $\pi_3, \pi_5, \pi_2, \pi_7, \pi_8, \pi_4, \pi_9$ and then π_6. (As we shall see, it is cheaper to update π.)

(2) Check whether $\pi_j - \pi_i \leq c_e$ for all $e = (i, j) \in E$. This is a search as in the revised simplex method, except that we need only look up $i = h(e)$ and $j = t(e)$ instead of the column a_e. If all inequalities are satisfied, the current solution is optimal and we stop.

(3) Otherwise, choose some $e = (u, v) \in E \backslash F$ with $\bar{c}_e = c_e + \pi_u - \pi_v < 0$.

(4) Solve $Bw = a_e$ and check for unboundedness. We must find the path from u to v in H, using p and d. If the path has no forward arcs, there is an unbounded ray. In our example, suppose $u = 7$, $v = 9$. Since $d(9) > d(7)$, we find $p(9) = +4$; thus $(9, 4)$ is a reverse arc of the path. Now $d(7) = d(4)$, but $7 \neq 4$. So we find $p(7) = -3$, $p(4) = +8$, and $(3, 7)$ and $(4, 8)$ are reverse arcs of

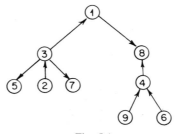

Fig. 5.1.

Table 5.1

i	1	2	3	4	5	6	7	8	9
$p(i)$	–	+3	+1	+8	−3	+4	−3	−1	+4
$d(i)$	0	2	1	2	2	3	2	1	3
$s(i)$	3	7	5	9	2	–	8	4	6

the path. Since $3 \neq 8$, we find $p(3) = +1$, $p(8) = -1$, so $(3, 1)$ and $(1, 8)$ are forward arcs of the path, and since the two subpaths from u and v have now coalesced, we have found the complete path from u to v.

(5) Find the leaving arc f; this is the forward arc in the path ($w_f = +1$) with minimum flow. We calculate f as we determine the path in step 4 by comparing the flow on each forward arc found with the current minimum flow for such arcs. In our example, $f = (1, 8)$.

(6) Update:

$$F \leftarrow (F \cup \{e\}) \backslash \{f\} \ .$$

Update x:

$$x_e \leftarrow x_f \ ,$$

$$x_g \leftarrow \begin{cases} x_g - x_e & g \text{ forward arc of path} , \\ x_g + x_e & g \text{ reverse arc of path} , \\ x_g & \text{otherwise} , \end{cases}$$

In our example, $x_{79} \leftarrow 2$, $x_{37} \leftarrow 4$, $x_{31} \leftarrow 2$, $x_{18} \leftarrow 0$, $x_{48} \leftarrow 5$ and $x_{94} \leftarrow 3$, with others unchanged.

Update π: let $f = (i, j)$, and assume $d(i) < d(j)$ – analogous rules hold if $d(i) > d(j)$.

$$\pi_j \leftarrow \pi_j + \bar{c}_e \ , \quad k \leftarrow s(j)$$

While $d(k) > d(j)$,

$$\pi_k \leftarrow \pi_k + \bar{c}_e \ ,$$
$$k \leftarrow s(k) \ .$$

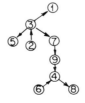

Fig. 5.2.

Table 5.2

i	1	2	3	4	5	6	7	8	9
$p(i)$	–	+3	+1	−9	−3	+4	−3	−4	−7
$d(i)$	0	2	1	4	2	5	2	5	3
$s(i)$	3	7	5	6	2	8	9	–	4

In our example, we add $\bar{c}_e$ to π_8, then to π_4, π_9 and π_6. (It is easy to see that $\bar{c}_g$ remains zero for arcs in the subtree hanging from node j. Also, π_v increases by $\bar{c}_e$ so that $\bar{c}_e$ becomes zero as required for tree arcs.)

Finally, we must update our representation of the tree, i.e., p, d, and s. While this can be done efficiently, the rules are somewhat complicated and we refer the reader to, e.g., Chvátal (1983). Basically, if $d(i) < d(j)$, the subtree below j now hangs down from the arc (u, v); a crucial role is played by the path from v to j, called the *backpath*.

In our example, the result is the tree shown in Figure 5.2, with representation given in Table 5.2.

The specialization of the primal simplex algorithm for network problems as above is called the network simplex algorithm. While there are examples of problems for which a very large (exponential in n) number of iterations are required using standard choices of entering arc (see (Zadeh 1973)), the method is usually very efficient in practice. For this special class of linear programming problems, there are combinatorial algorithms available which are guaranteed to terminate in a polynomial number of steps – see Chapter 4. Comparisons of different algorithms can be found in the papers in (Gallo and Sandi, 1986).

6. Column generation and the decomposition principle

In this section we continue to consider the efficient application of the revised simplex method to large-scale problems. The first problem we address is the standard form problem

$$
\begin{array}{ll}
\text{minimize} & z = c^{\mathrm{T}}x \\
\text{subject to} & Ax = b, \\
& x \geqslant 0,
\end{array}
\tag{6.1}
$$

where A is $m \times n$ and the columns of A are only known implicity (there may be an astronomical number of them). However, the *form* of such columns is known, and they can be generated as needed during the course of the algorithm – hence the name column generation. We will discuss a classic example of such a problem, the cutting-stock problem analyzed by Gilmore and Gomory (1961, 1963) in the first subsection.

Next, suppose we wish to solve the linear programming problem

$$\text{minimize} \quad z = c^{\mathrm{T}}x$$

$$\text{subject to} \quad A_0 x = b_0, \tag{6.2}$$
$$A_1 x = b_1,$$
$$x \geq 0,$$

where the constraints have been partitioned into 'general' constraints $A_0 x = b_0$ and 'special' constraints $A_1 x = b_1$, $x \geq 0$. For example, the special constraints could define a network problem, or could separate into several groups of constraints involving disjoint sets of variables. We wish to solve (6.2) efficiently, using the fact that linear programming problems involving only the special constraints can be solved much more easily. We shall see that this leads again to the column generation idea; the resulting method is known as the decomposition principle of Dantzig and Wolfe (1960). We discuss this in Subsection 6.2 – note that we are reversing chronological order for expository reasons.

6.1. *The cutting-stock problem*

Suppose that a paper company has a supply of large rolls of paper of width W. However, customer demand is for smaller widths of paper; suppose b_i rolls of width w_i, $i = 1, 2, \ldots, m$, need to be produced. We obtain smaller rolls by slicing a large roll using a particular *pattern*; for example, a large roll of width $w = 70''$ can be cut into three rolls of width $w_1 = 17''$ and one roll of width $w_2 = 15''$, with a waste of $4''$. We can (conceptually at least) consider all such patterns and thus form a matrix A, with a_{ij} indicating how many rolls of width w_i are produced by the j-th pattern, $i = 1, 2, \ldots, m$; $j = 1, 2, \ldots, n$. For example, the pattern described above yields a column $(3, 1, 0, \ldots, 0)^{\mathrm{T}}$ of A. If we let c_j equal 1 for all j, then (6.1) is the problem of determining the minimum number of large rolls $(z = \Sigma_j x_j)$ to cut to satisfy the demand for b_i rolls of width w_i for all i. Actually, we would like to solve the corresponding integer programming problem (see Chapter 6) where x_j, the number of large rolls cut according to pattern j, is also restricted to be integer-valued; however, a solution to the linear programming problem (6.1) often provides a sufficiently accurate solution by rounding and ad hoc procedures, at least if the demands b_i are reasonably large.

Solving (6.1) itself is already a considerable computational task; even if m is comparatively small the number of possible patterns n can be huge, so that just forming the coefficient matrix A in full is impractical. However, as shown by (Gilmore and Gomory 1961, 1963), the problem can be solved efficiently by the revised simplex method, by generating columns of A as required rather than in advance.

Finding an initial basic feasible solution is easy. Indeed, by letting pattern i consist of $[W/w_i]$ rolls of width w_i and none of any other width ($[\lambda]$ denotes the largest integer not exceeding λ), the first m columns of A yield a feasible and diagonal basis matrix. Suppose therefore that at some iteration we have a basic feasible solution and we wish to continue the revised simplex algorithm.

We compute the simplex multipliers π by solving $B^T\pi = e$ as usual. (Here e denotes a vector of all ones of appropriate dimension. Recall that all c_j's are one, so $c_B = e$.) The next step is to compute the reduced costs

$$\bar{c}_j = 1 - \pi^T a_j \tag{6.3}$$

for all j, in order to either determine that we are currently optimal or choose a nonbasic variable x_q, with $\bar{c}_q < 0$, to enter the basis. This appears difficult, since we do not know all columns a_j of A. However, because of the structure of the problem, we can perform this step implicitly.

A vector $a = (\alpha_1, \alpha_2, \ldots, \alpha_m)^T \in Z_+^m$ (each α_i is a nonnegative integer) will be a column of A if it corresponds to a feasible pattern, i.e. if $w^T a \leq W$, where $w = (w_1, w_2, \ldots, w_m)^T$. We wish to know whether the reduced cost $1 - \pi^T a$ is nonnegative for all such a, and, if not, find a feasible vector a with $1 - \pi^T a$ negative. Hence we solve the subproblem

$$\begin{aligned} \text{maximize} \quad & \pi^T a \\ \text{subject to} \quad & w^T a \leq W, \\ & a \in Z_+^m. \end{aligned} \tag{6.4}$$

This is an instance of the so-called *knapsack* problem. (Think of π_i as the value and w_i the weight of the i-th item; we seek the most valuable knapsack of weight at most W.) If the optimal value of (6.4) is at most 1, then all reduced costs are nonnegative and our current basic feasible solution is optimal. Otherwise, an optimal solution to (6.4) provides the column $a_q = a$ for a nonbasic variable to enter the basis, and the iteration proceeds as usual.

We have therefore demonstrated how the revised simplex method can be applied to the cutting-stock problem (6.1) without knowing all the columns of A in advance, by generating them as needed from the subproblem (6.4). We indicate briefly how (6.4) can be solved using a dynamic programming recursion when, as is reasonable, W and all w_i's are integers. Let $f(v)$ denote the optimal value of (6.4) when the right-hand side W is replaced by v. Then $f(v) = 0$ for $0 \leq v < w_{\min}$, where $w_{\min} = \min w_i$. We obtain $f(W)$ by using the recursion

$$f(v) = \max_{\substack{1 \leq i \leq m \\ w_i \leq v}} \{ f(v - w_i) + \pi_i \}$$

for $v = w_{\min}, \ldots, W$. The optimal solution yielding $f(W)$ can easily be obtained by backtracking if a record is kept of a maximizing index at each step.

Similar column generation methods, with more complicated subproblems to be solved at each iteration, can be used for generalized problems, for instance in 2-dimensional cutting-stock problems or where there is a limit on the number of knives (and hence on the number of nonzero components in a column) in a 1-dimensional problem.

6.2. Dantzig–Wolfe decomposition

We now turn to (6.2), which we rewrite as

$$\text{minimize} \quad z = c^{\mathrm{T}}x$$
$$\text{subject to} \quad A_0 x = b_0 , \tag{6.5}$$
$$x \in X ,$$

where

$$X = \{ x \in \mathbb{R}^n \colon A_1 x = b_1, x \geq 0 \} . \tag{6.6}$$

We suppose A_0 is $m_0 \times n$ and A_1 is $m_1 \times n$, with the vectors c, x, b_0 and b_1 of conforming dimensions. For example, (6.5) could represent a large-scale production-distribution model, where $A_0 x = b_0$ includes the scarce resource constraints from the production side while $A_1 x = b_1$ involves network constraints from the distribution system. A classical example also arises from multi-divisional problems, as we now briefly outline.

Suppose a corporation consists of k divisions, indexed 1 through k; we will also refer to the corporation itself as division 0. Each division j has a vector x_j of decision variables (so that x_0 refers to corporate variables, for example corresponding to ways of financing debt); it also has a vector b_j of amounts of resources available to it. Let c_j denote the vector of costs corresponding to x_j, and let A_{ij} be the matrix representing the use of resources of division i by the variables of division j. We typically assume that $A_{ij} = 0$ if $i \neq j$ and $i > 0$; thus division j uses the resources of the corporation and its own resources, but not those of any other division. The resulting problem is

$$\text{minimize} \quad c_0^{\mathrm{T}}x_0 + c_1^{\mathrm{T}}x_1 + \cdots + c_k^{\mathrm{T}}x_k$$
$$\text{subject to} \quad A_{00}x_0 + A_{01}x_1 + \cdots + A_{0k}x_k = b_0 ,$$
$$A_{11}x_1 \qquad\qquad\qquad = b_1 , \tag{6.7}$$
$$\ddots \qquad \vdots$$
$$A_{kk}x_k = b_k ,$$
$$x_0, x_1, \ldots, x_k \geq 0 ,$$

whose structure is said to be primal block-angular. Similarly, the problem is called dual block-angular if $A_{ij} = 0$ for $i \neq j$ and $j > 0$ (so the division j does not use the corporate resources, but the corporate variables x_0 may impinge on each division since A_{i0} can be nonzero). In this case, we say x_0 is a vector of linking variables, while the first constraints in (6.7) are called linking constraints. Finally, we can allow both linking variables and linking constraints.

Clearly, problem (6.7) can be viewed as an instance of the general form (6.5), by setting $c^{\mathrm{T}} = (c_0^{\mathrm{T}}, c_1^{\mathrm{T}}, \ldots, c_k^{\mathrm{T}})$ and $A_0 = [A_{00}, A_{01}, \ldots, A_{0k}]$, and

$$X = \{ x = (x_0^{\mathrm{T}}, x_1^{\mathrm{T}}, \ldots, x_k^{\mathrm{T}})^{\mathrm{T}} \colon x_0 \geq 0, A_{jj}x_j = b_j, x_j \geq 0,$$
$$j = 1, \ldots, k \} .$$

We will discuss (6.7) later, but for now it will be simpler to assume that there are no corporate variables. Then the problem becomes

$$
\begin{aligned}
\text{minimize} \quad & c_1^{\mathrm{T}} x_1 + \cdots + c_k^{\mathrm{T}} x_k \\
\text{subject to} \quad & A_{01} x_1 + \cdots + A_{0k} x_k = b_0 , \\
& A_{11} x_1 = b_1 , \\
& \phantom{A_{11}x_1\cdots} \ddots \vdots \\
& \phantom{A_{kk}} A_{kk} x_k = b_k , \\
& x_1, \ldots, x_k \geq 0 .
\end{aligned}
\tag{6.8}
$$

Again, it is easy to put (6.8) into the form (6.5), with

$$
X = \{ x = (x_1^{\mathrm{T}}, \ldots, x_k^{\mathrm{T}})^{\mathrm{T}} : A_{jj} x_j = b_j,\, x_j \geq 0,\, j = 1, \ldots, k \} .
$$

Alternatively, we can consider each division separately and write (6.8) as

$$
\begin{aligned}
\text{minimize} \quad & c_1^{\mathrm{T}} x_1 + \cdots + c_k^{\mathrm{T}} x_k \\
\text{subject to} \quad & A_{01} x_1 + \cdots + A_{0k}^{\mathrm{T}} x_k = b_0 , \\
& x_1 \in X_1, \ldots, x_k \in X_k ,
\end{aligned}
\tag{6.9}
$$

with $X_j = \{ x_j : A_{jj} x_j = b_j,\, x_j \geq 0 \}$.

There are several ways to motivate the decomposition idea. One which has a strong economic interpretation is to consider the corporation as trying to decentralize its decision-making by announcing prices for the corporate resources. If no limitations are placed on division j's use of corporate resources, but it must buy them at prices given by the vector $-\pi_0$, then division j will seek to solve the subproblem

$$
\mathrm{SP}_j(\pi_0) \quad
\begin{aligned}
\text{minimize} \quad & (c_j^{\mathrm{T}} - \pi_0^{\mathrm{T}} A_{0j}) x_j \\
\text{subject to} \quad & x_j \in X_j .
\end{aligned}
\tag{6.10}
$$

Of course, the corporation would like to set the prices $-\pi_0$ so that, when each division solves its corresponding subproblem $\mathrm{SP}_j(\pi_0)$ to get an optimal solution $\bar{x}_j$, $\sum_j A_{0j} \bar{x}_j = b_0$. This is akin to a classical economic scenario: we wish to choose prices so that the resulting demands (of the independently utility-maximizing agents) sum to the total supply. We will call $(\bar{\pi}_0, \bar{x}_1, \ldots, \bar{x}_k)$ an *equilibrium* if $\bar{x}_j$ solves $\mathrm{SP}_j(\bar{\pi}_0)$ for each j and $\sum_j A_{0j} \bar{x}_j = b_0$.

A major problem in economic theory is to determine conditions under which an equilibrium exists. Here it is easy and nicely illustrates linear programming duality:

Theorem 6.1. *If $(\bar{x}_1, \ldots, \bar{x}_k)$ and $(\bar{\pi}_0, \bar{\pi}_1, \ldots, \bar{\pi}_k)$ are optimal primal and dual solutions to (6.8), then $(\bar{\pi}_0, \bar{x}_1, \ldots, \bar{x}_k)$ is an equilibrium. Conversely, if $(\bar{\pi}_0, \bar{x}_1, \ldots, \bar{x}_k)$ is an equilibrium, then $(\bar{x}_1, \ldots, \bar{x}_k)$ is an optimal primal (and $\bar{\pi}_0$ part of an optimal dual) solution to (6.8).*

Proof. Consider the first part. Clearly $\Sigma_j A_{0j}\bar{x}_j = b_0$, so we only need to establish that $\bar{x}_j$ is optimal in $\mathrm{SP}_j(\bar{\pi}_0)$. It is obviously feasible. Now dual feasibility and complementary slackness in (6.8) show that

$$A_{0j}^{\mathrm{T}}\bar{\pi}_0 + A_{jj}^{\mathrm{T}}\bar{\pi}_j \leqslant c_j , \qquad (A_{0j}^{\mathrm{T}}\bar{\pi}_0 + A_{jj}^{\mathrm{T}}\bar{\pi}_j - c_j)^{\mathrm{T}}\bar{x}_j = 0 . \qquad (6.11a)$$

But then

$$A_{jj}^{\mathrm{T}}\bar{\pi}_j \leqslant (c_j - A_{0j}^{\mathrm{T}}\bar{\pi}_0) , \qquad (A_{jj}^{\mathrm{T}}\bar{\pi}_j - (c_j - A_{0j}^{\mathrm{T}}\bar{\pi}_0))^{\mathrm{T}}\bar{x}_j = 0 , \qquad (6.11b)$$

which shows again by duality that $\bar{x}_j$ is primal optimal (and $\bar{\pi}_j$ dual optimal) in $\mathrm{SP}_j(\bar{\pi}_0)$. For the converse, let $\bar{\pi}_j$ be an optimal dual solution to $\mathrm{SP}_j(\bar{\pi}_0)$. By duality, we have (6.11b), and hence (6.11a), which implies that $(\bar{x}_1, \ldots, \bar{x}_k)$ and $(\bar{\pi}_0, \bar{\pi}_1, \ldots, \bar{\pi}_k)$ are optimal primal and dual solutions to (6.8). $\blacksquare$

As well as establishing the existence of equilibrium (if (6.8) has a solution), Theorem 6.1 offers the possibility of efficient computation. If we only knew the appropriate prices $-\bar{\pi}_0$, then it appears that we could solve (6.8) by solving k small linear programming problems (the $\mathrm{SP}_j(\bar{\pi}_0)$) instead of one large one.

Unfortunately, two difficulties now arise. First, it is far from clear how a suitable vector $\bar{\pi}_0$ can be found. Second, even if an appropriate $\bar{\pi}_0$ were known, obtaining $\bar{x}_1, \ldots, \bar{x}_k$ would not be easy. Indeed, given nondegeneracy, an optimal solution to (6.8) will have $m_0 + \Sigma_{j\geqslant 1}m_j$ positive variables, where b_j is an m_j-vector for each j. On the other hand, a basic optimal solution to $\mathrm{SP}_j(\bar{\pi}_0)$ will have only m_j positive variables, so that putting these together will yield only $\Sigma_{j\geqslant 1} m_j$ positive variables. The conclusion is that any equilibrium $\bar{\pi}_0$ will make at least one of the subproblems have alternate optimal solutions, and that these may have to be chosen suitably to clear the market of the corporate resources.

These difficulties are eliminated by taking another viewpoint. We will construct a new linear programming problem so that applying the revised simplex method will automatically generate a (finite) sequence of trial vectors π_0: and we will explicitly consider convex combinations of the vertices of X_j for the subproblems.

For notational simplicity we return now to the general problem (6.5) with a single polyhedron X; we will consider the case of several X_j's, as in (6.9), later. The key step is to present the polyhedron X in (6.6) in terms of its vertices and (certain of its) directions, as in Theorem 2.4. We need a slight extension:

Definition 6.1. A direction d of X is *extreme* if it cannot be written as a nonnegative combination of two different (i.e., not proportional) directions. That is

$$d = \mu_1 d_1 + \mu_2 d_2 , \quad \mu_1 \geqslant 0, \mu_2 \geqslant 0 ,$$

with d_1 and d_2 also directions of X, implies $d_1 = \alpha_1 d$ and $d_2 = \alpha_2 d$ for some α_1, $\alpha_2 \geq 0$.

Theorem 6.2. *Any point $x \in X$ can be presented as*

$$x = \sum_{i \in I} \lambda_i v_i + \sum_{j \in J} \mu_j d_j$$

where $\{v_i : i \in I\}$ is the set of vertices, and $\{d_j : j \in J\}$ is the set of extreme directions, of X, and $\sum_{i \in I} \lambda_i = 1$, $\lambda_i \geq 0$ for all $i \in I$, $\mu_j \geq 0$ for all $j \in J$. Conversely, any such x lies in X. Moreover, X has only finitely many extreme directions.

We will not prove this result; its proof is similar to that of Theorem 2.4. An important consequence is:

Corollary 6.1. *Let the columns of V and D be all vertices and extreme directions, respectively, of X. Then*

$$X = \{V\lambda + D\mu : e^{\mathrm{T}}\lambda = 1, \lambda \geq 0, \mu \geq 0\} .$$

(Recall that e denotes a vector of ones of appropriate dimension.)

By substituting for x using this representation, we see that our original problem (6.5) is equivalent to the so-called *master problem*

$$\begin{aligned}
\text{minimize} \quad & (c^{\mathrm{T}}V)\lambda + (c^{\mathrm{T}}D)\mu \\
\text{subject to} \quad & (A_0 V)\lambda + (A_0 D)\mu = b_0 , \\
& e^{\mathrm{T}}\lambda \qquad\qquad\quad = 1 , \\
& \lambda \geq 0 , \quad \mu \geq 0 .
\end{aligned} \qquad (6.12)$$

The decomposition principle of Dantzig and Wolfe is to apply the revised simplex method to the master problem (6.12). Note that, in contrast to (6.2), (6.12) has only $m_0 + 1$ constraints; to compensate, it has an astronomical number of columns, one for each vertex and each extreme direction of X, and those are known only implicitly. Thus we will use a column generation technique as in Subsection 6.1.

Suppose that we have a basic feasible solution to (6.12), $(\bar{\lambda}, \bar{\mu})$, with associated simplex multipliers $\bar{\pi}_0$ (for the first m_0 constraints) and $\bar{\sigma}$. Here $\bar{\lambda}_i > 0$ implies that we know the corresponding vertex v_i of X, and similarly for $\bar{\mu}_j$ and the extreme direction d_j. However, the set of all vertices and extreme directions is unknown to us, so that we shall have to generate them (and the associated columns in (6.12)) as needed.

An iteration of the revised simplex method demands that we first seek a vertex v_i with reduced cost

$$c^{\mathrm{T}}v_i - \bar{\pi}_0^{\mathrm{T}}A_0v_i - \bar{\sigma} < 0 \tag{6.13}$$

or an extreme direction d_j with reduced cost

$$c^{\mathrm{T}}d_j - \bar{\pi}_0^{\mathrm{T}}A_0d_j < 0. \tag{6.14}$$

If there are none, we can conclude that the current solution $(\bar{\lambda}, \bar{\mu})$ is optimal in (6.12), and hence $\bar{x} = V\bar{\lambda} + D\bar{\mu}$ optimal in (6.5).

Consider first (6.13). We wish to find a vertex v_i of X so that the linear function $(c^{\mathrm{T}} - \bar{\pi}_0^{\mathrm{T}}A_0)v_i$ is smaller than $\bar{\sigma}$. Since a linear function is minimized over a polyhedron at a vertex (if it is not unbounded below), it is natural to consider the subproblem

$$\mathrm{SP}(\bar{\pi}_0) \qquad \min\{(c^{\mathrm{T}} - \bar{\pi}_0^{\mathrm{T}}A_0)x : x \in X\} \tag{6.15}$$

(cf. (6.10)).

Let us discuss each possible outcome of solving $\mathrm{SP}(\bar{\pi}_0)$. First, if it is infeasible, then X is empty and our original problem (6.5) is also infeasible; in this case, we could not have a current basic feasible solution to (6.12).

Second, $\mathrm{SP}(\bar{\pi}_0)$ may be unbounded. In this case, application of the revised simplex algorithm will generate an edge vector η_q from some vertex v of X with $v + \theta\eta_q$ in X for all $\theta \geq 0$ and $(c^{\mathrm{T}} - \bar{\pi}_0^{\mathrm{T}}A_0)\eta_q < 0$. In fact η_q is of the form

$$\eta_q = \begin{pmatrix} -w \\ e_{q-m_1} \end{pmatrix}, \quad \text{where } w = B_1^{-1}a_{1q},$$

if the current basis matrix B_1 consists of the first m_1 columns of A_1 and a_{1q} is the entering q-th column of A_1. (See Sections 2 and 3.) It is not too hard to see that η_q is an extreme direction of X, so that setting $d_j = \eta_q$ yields (6.14). Of course η_q is not necessarily a direction of the polyhedron of feasible solutions to (6.2), since we have ignored the constraints $A_0x = b_0$.

Finally, $\mathrm{SP}(\bar{\pi}_0)$ may have a finite optimal solution $\bar{x}$. Then, by the fundamental theorems of linear programming (see in particular Theorem 2.7 and its proof), $(c^{\mathrm{T}} - \bar{\pi}_0^{\mathrm{T}}A_0)d \geq 0$ for all directions d and $\bar{x}$ can be taken to be a vertex of X (and the revised simplex method finds such a vertex). Hence (6.14) fails for all j; no column arising from an extreme direction is a candidate for entering the basis. If $(c^{\mathrm{T}} - \bar{\pi}_0^{\mathrm{T}}A_0)\bar{x} \geq \sigma$ then, since we minimized over all X and hence all its vertices, (6.13) fails for each i, thus no column arising from a vertex is a candidate for entering the basis, and we conclude that $(\bar{\lambda}, \bar{\mu})$ is optimal in (6.12) and $x^* = V\bar{\lambda} + D\bar{\mu}$ optimal in (6.5). On the other hand, if $(c^{\mathrm{T}} - \bar{\pi}_0A_0)\bar{x} < \sigma$, then setting $v_i = \bar{x}$ we have (6.13).

Thus in any case, we either prove optimality or generate a column for (6.12) to introduce into the basis, in which case the iteration of the revised simplex method can continue as usual. Summarizing, we have:

Theorem 6.3. (a) *If* SP($\bar{\pi}_0$) *is unbounded, the revised simplex method applied to it yields an extreme direction d_j satisfying* (6.14), *so that the column*

$$\begin{pmatrix} A_0 d_j \\ 0 \end{pmatrix} \quad \text{with cost } c^T d_j$$

is eligible to enter the current basis for the master problem (6.12).

(b) *If* SP($\bar{\pi}_0$) *has optimal solution v_i with optimal value less than $\bar{\sigma}$, then the column*

$$\begin{pmatrix} A_0 v_i \\ 1 \end{pmatrix} \quad \text{with cost } c^T v_i$$

is eligible to enter the current basis for the master problem (6.12).

(c) *Finally, if* SP($\bar{\pi}_0$) *has optimal value at least $\bar{\sigma}$, with optimal dual solution $\bar{\pi}_1$, then the current basic feasible solution $(\bar{\lambda}, \bar{\mu})$ is optimal in* (6.12) *with optimal dual solution $(\bar{\pi}_0, \bar{\sigma})$, and $x^* = V\bar{\lambda} + D\bar{\mu}$ is optimal in* (6.2), *with optimal dual solution $(\bar{\pi}_0, \bar{\pi}_1)$.*

Proof. We only need to show the last part. Clearly, since (6.13) and (6.14) fail for all $i \in I$, $j \in J$, $(\bar{\pi}_0, \bar{\sigma})$ is feasible in the dual of (6.12), and hence $(\bar{\lambda}, \bar{\mu})$ and $(\bar{\pi}_0, \bar{\sigma})$ are respectively primal and dual optimal so that $c^T V\bar{\lambda} + c^T D\bar{\mu} = \bar{\pi}_0^T b_0 + \bar{\sigma}$. Now x^* is feasible in (6.2), since it satisfies $A_0 x^* = b_0$ and lies in X by Theorem 6.2. It has value $c^T x^* = c^T V\bar{\lambda} + c^T D\bar{\mu}$, the optimal value of (6.12). Now since $\bar{\pi}_1$ is dual optimal in SP($\bar{\pi}_0$), it is dual feasible:

$$\bar{\pi}_1^T A_1 \leqslant c^T - \bar{\pi}_0^T A_0 \tag{6.16}$$

and has value

$$\begin{aligned} \bar{\pi}_1^T b_1 \geqslant \bar{\sigma} &= (\bar{\pi}_0^T b_0 + \bar{\sigma}) - \bar{\pi}_0^T b_0 \\ &= (c^T V\bar{\lambda} + c^T D\bar{\mu}) - \bar{\pi}_0^T b_0 \\ &= c^T x^* - \bar{\pi}_0^T b_0 . \end{aligned} \tag{6.17}$$

Hence $(\bar{\pi}_0, \bar{\pi}_1)$ is feasible in the dual of (6.2) by (6.16) and has value at least that of x^* in the primal. Thus weak duality implies that x^* is primal and $(\bar{\pi}_0, \bar{\pi}_1)$ dual optimal in (6.2) as desired.

The theorem shows that we can solve (6.5) by solving instead the master problem (6.12); finite convergence is assured since we are applying the revised simplex method to a finite problem, even though its coefficients are not all known in advance. The algorithm terminates either with an optimal solution of (6.12), and hence one for (6.2), or with an indication of unboundedness; in the latter case, it is easy to see that (6.2) is also unbounded. The proof also shows that, when the algorithm terminates with an optimal solution, the optimal value of SP($\bar{\pi}_0$) is precisely $\bar{\sigma}$, and, by complementary slackness, all v_i with $\bar{\lambda}_i$

positive will be alternate optimal solutions to $\mathrm{SP}(\bar{\pi}_0)$. Hence we have resolved the two difficulties discussed below Theorem 6.1. Applying the revised simplex method to the master problem automatically generates a sequence of vectors $-\bar{\pi}_0$ which converges to an 'equilibrium price vector' $-\pi_0^*$; and the master problem explicitly considers how to combine the optimal solutions to $\mathrm{SP}(\pi_0^*)$ to get an optimal solution to (6.5), which is likely not to be a vertex of X. Dantzig (1963) includes a discussion that motivates from an economic viewpoint the proposed equilibrium price vectors $-\bar{\pi}_0$ that are generated in this way.

A natural question concerns the computational behavior of the decomposition algorithm; we may hope that only a small multiple of m_0 iterations are required in (6.12) (see the next section), even though this problem has a huge number of columns. We defer discussion of this point until we have addressed a number of issues we have skirted so far.

First, suppose there are variables that occur only in the 'general' constraints $A_0 x = b_0$, but not in the 'special' constraints $A_1 x = b_1$, like the corporate variables x_0 in (6.7). It is then more natural to omit these variables from X and carry them over unchanged into the master problem (6.12). To apply the revised simplex algorithm to (6.12), we first check at each iteration whether any of these x-variables is a candidate to enter the basis, and, if so, perform the pivot. Only if no such x-variable is eligible do we form the subproblem $\mathrm{SP}(\bar{\pi}_0)$ and proceed as above. The analysis follows the argument we have already made.

Second, we need to describe how an initial basic feasible solution to (6.12) is found. We first find a vertex v_1 of X by any method – if we discover X is empty, (6.5) is infeasible and we stop. Then we introduce m_0 artificial variables into (6.12) so that λ_1 together with these variables gives a basic feasible solution to the modified (6.12). We now apply a phase I revised simplex method to this problem to minimize the sum of the artificial variables, using again the decomposition idea. If all artificial variables are eliminated, we have a basic feasible solution to (6.12) from which we initiate phase II. We can view this phase I procedure as applying the decomposition algorithm to a phase I version of (6.2), where the artificial variables (in the constraints $A_0 x = b_0$ only) are carried over into the master problem as in the previous paragraph.

Third, let us reconsider the multi-divisional problem (6.7). We known now that we can treat the variables x_0 separately, but can we separate the variables $x_1, x_2, \ldots, x_k$ as in (6.9) rather than considering them together? The answer is yes; we must apply the same idea to each polyhedron X_j. Thus the master problem is

$$
\begin{aligned}
\text{minimize} \quad & c_0^{\mathrm{T}} x_0 + (c_1^{\mathrm{T}} V_1)\lambda_1 + (c_1^{\mathrm{T}} D_1)\mu_1 + \cdots + (c_k^{\mathrm{T}} V_k)\lambda_k + (c_k^{\mathrm{T}} D_k)\mu_k \\
\text{subject to} \quad & A_{00} x_0 + (A_{01} V_1)\lambda_1 + (A_{01} D_1)\mu_1 + \cdots + (A_{0k} V_k)\lambda_k + (A_{0k} D_k)\mu_k = b, \\
& e^{\mathrm{T}}\lambda_1 \ldots\ldots\ldots\ldots\ldots\ldots\ldots\ldots\ldots\ldots = 1, \\
& \qquad\qquad\qquad\qquad\ldots\ldots\ldots e^{\mathrm{T}}\lambda_k = 1, \\
& x_0, \lambda_1, \mu_1, \ldots, \lambda_k, \mu_k \geq 0, \qquad\qquad\qquad\qquad (6.18)
\end{aligned}
$$

where the columns of V_j and D_j are the vertices and extreme directions, respectively, of X_j, and the components of the vectors λ_j and μ_j give the corresponding weights. Note that (6.18) has $m_0 + k$ rows, rather than $m_0 + 1$; but this is still a great reduction from the number in (6.7). At any iteration, we will have simplex multipliers $\bar{\pi}_0, \bar{\sigma}_1, \ldots, \bar{\sigma}_k$. If any x_0-variable is eligible to enter the basis, we make the appropriate pivot. Otherwise, we solve $\mathrm{SP}_j(\bar{\pi}_0)$ (see (6.10)) for each j. If any such problem is unbounded, the extreme direction generated yields an eligible column for (6.18). If not, and if the optimal value of some $\mathrm{SP}_j(\bar{\pi}_0)$ is less than $\bar{\sigma}_j$, then the optimal vertex v_{ji} again yields an eligible column. Finally, if all optimal values are equal to the corresponding $\bar{\sigma}_j$, then we have the optimal solution to (6.18), and $x_0^* = \bar{x}_0$, $x_j^* = V_j \bar{\lambda}_j + D_j \bar{\mu}_j$, $j = 1, 2, \ldots, k$, is an optimal solution to (6.7).

This idea of having several subproblems (rather than just one) is also appropriate in multicommodity flow problems; for a discussion of these and various solution strategies, including primal and dual decomposition methods, see Kennington (1978). Another important special case is where A has a staircase structure, which arises in multiperiod models. In this case, nested decomposition approaches may be attractive (Ho and Manne 1974). More recent developments are discussed in Ho (1987), who also includes a summary of computational experience.

Papers and textbooks of the 60's and 70's generally cite poor computational results for the decomposition approach compared to applying a sophisticated revised simplex code directly to (6.2). The folklore suggests that slow final convergence is typical. However, there is some indication (see (Ho 1987) and the papers cited therein) that 'long tails' are the fault more of numerical accuracy difficulties than of the algorithmic approach. Here it is worth pointing out that, at any iteration where $\mathrm{SP}(\bar{\pi}_0)$ (or all $\mathrm{SP}_j(\bar{\pi}_0)$'s) has an optimal solution, one can obtain a feasible dual solution to the master problem, with a duality gap equal to the difference between $\bar{\sigma}$ and the optimal value of $\mathrm{SP}(\bar{\pi}_0)$. Hence one can terminate early with a feasible solution which is guaranteed to be close to optimal. With such early termination, large-scale dynamic problems have been solved faster by sophisticated implementations of decomposition approaches than using IBM's MPSX simplex code – see again (Ho 1987). For problems of more moderate size, however, say up to 5000 rows, it seems generally preferable to use a good revised simplex code on the original problem, ignoring its structure.

7. The complexity of linear programming

The previous sections have described in some detail the solution of linear programming problems by the simplex method. The next sections will discuss two new methods, which enjoy the desirable property of polynomial-time boundedness. Here we wish to motivate briefly these new developments by outlining what is known about the complexity of the simplex method. Quite complete surveys are provided by Shamir (1987) and Megiddo (1987).

A vast amount of practical experience in solving real-world linear programming problems has confirmed that the number of iterations required grows roughly linearly with m, the number of rows of the constraint matrix, and sublinearly with n, the number of columns. Since, in most problems, n is a small multiple of m, usually at most $10m$, the folklore claims that the typical number of iterations for both Phase I and Phase II is between m and $4m$. Qualitatively similar results have been obtained by several authors using Monte Carlo experimentation. For details, see (Shamir 1987).

In contrast to its excellent empirical performance, the simplex method can be exceedingly slow on specially-constructed examples. This was first demonstrated by Klee and Minty (1972), who gave a class of $d \times 2d$ examples for which the simplex variant employing the most negative reduced cost rule required $2^d - 1$ iterations, visiting every vertex of the feasible region. Similar behavior was shown by others for several different simplex variants and for network problems.

Thus there is a large gap between practical experience and theoretical (worst-case) bounds. The main distinction here is between a polynomially growing number of iterations and an exponentially growing number. Actually, real problems seem to require only $O(m)$ iterations, but each might require up to $O(mn)$ arithmetic operations. (We write $O(f(n))$ for a function that is bounded by some constant times $f(n)$ as n tends to infinity.) A major open question is whether there is a simplex variant requiring only a polynomial (in m and n) number of iterations for any $m \times n$ linear programming problem.

The next sections describe two radically new methods for solving linear programming problems, the ellipsoid method and Karmarkar's projective method, which require only a polynomial amount of time (in terms of m, n and the number of bits L necessary to define the problem). Of course, it is natural that L should occur in the number of bit operations required, since it determines the precision necessary to state the optimal solutions exactly. However, the algorithms to be described require, in theory, a multiple of L iterations, even if exact arithmetic is allowed. The question thus arises as to whether a *strongly polynomial* algorithm exists for linear programming, one which requires a number of elementary arithmetic operations that is polynomial in m and n only and which, when applied to problems with rational data of length L, generates numbers whose sizes (numbers of bits) are bounded by polynomials in m, n and L. While this question remains open, Tardos (1986) has shown how to use polynomial linear programming algorithms to generate strongly polynomial algorithms for those classes of problems where the input length of the constraint matrix A is bounded by a polynomial in m and n. (Note that no restriction is placed on the input length of b and c.) Roughly speaking, to solve

(P) $\min\{c^{\mathrm{T}}x: Ax = b, x \geqslant 0\}$

Tardos uses a subroutine to solve a related problem

$(\hat{\mathrm{P}})$ $\min\{\hat{c}^{\mathrm{T}}x: Ax = b, x \geqslant 0\}$,

where each component of $\hat{c}$ is a rational whose size is bunded by a polynomial
in m and n. If $\hat{c}$ is appropriately defined, then any index j for which $\hat{c}_j - a_j^T \hat{y}$ is
sufficiently large has the property that x_j must be zero in any optimal solution
to (P) (here $\hat{y}$ is an optimal dual solution to ($\hat{P}$)). In this way, variables are
eliminated recursively. When no further eliminations are possible all feasible
solutions to the current ($\hat{P}$) are optimal, and a feasible solution is found using
similar ideas. If the components of b are 'large', then the subroutine works by
dualizing ($\hat{P}$) and proceeding as above, first approximating b by some $\hat{b}$, etc.
Details may be found in (Tardos 1986).

Tardos' algorithm clearly applies to network flow problems, and in fact was
originally developed in that setting. Many strongly polynomial algorithms have
been derived for special network flow problems such as the assignment,
shortest path and maximum flow problem. See Chapter 4.

Megiddo (1984) has given an algorithm for linear programming problems
whose time-complexity is linear in the number of constraints when the dimension d is fixed; however the complexity grows faster than exponentially with d.
See (Megiddo 1987) for a description of this method and later developments.

To conclude this section we describe work done to explain the large gap
between practice and theory for the simplex method using probabilistic analysis. A deterministic simplex variant is chosen, along with a probability distribution (or class of distributions satisfying certain properties) on problem instances. Then it is shown that the average number of iterations required by the
chosen variant on problems generated randomly from the chosen distribution
grows slowly with m or n or both. Currently the best bound of this nature,
$O(\min\{m^2, n^2\})$, has been obtained independently by Adler, Karp and Shamir
(1983), Adler and Megiddo (1985) and Todd (1986), for a lexicographic
variant of Dantzig's self-dual parametric algorithm (Dantzig 1963). The probabilistic model assumes that the problem instances $\max\{c^Tx: Ax \leq b, x \geq 0\}$
are generated according to some distribution that satisfies certain nondegeneracy conditions as well as the sign-invariance property that if S and T are
diagonal matrices with diagonal entries ± 1, then (SAT, Sb, Tc) has the same
distribution as (A, b, c). Notice that setting the i-th diagonal entry of $S(T)$ to
-1 is equivalent to reversing the sense of the i-th inequality of $Ax \leq b$ $(x \geq 0)$.

Significant work on the problem has also been done by Borgwardt, Smale
and Haimovich. Borgwardt was the first to obtain a polynomial expected
number of steps – see (Borgwardt 1987). The method that he analyzes is a
special variable-dimension phase I method together with a parametric objective
algorithm for phase II. The problem instances are of the form $\max\{c^Tx: Ax \leq e\}$
where e is a vector of ones and the vector c and the rows of A are
generated independently from a rotationally-symmetric distribution. If A is
$m \times n$, the expected number of iterations is $O(m^4 n^{1/(m-1)})$.

Both probability distributions have some rather unsatisfactory features, not
typical of real-world instances. The sign-invariant model generates problem
instances which are almost always infeasible or unbounded, while Borgwardt's
model generates problem instances which all have the origin as an obvious

feasible solution. However, the results obtained provide a significant theoretical justification to the good behavior of the simplex method observed in practice. For further details on this work and earlier developments in the subject we refer to (Shamir 1987), (Megiddo 1987) and (Borgwardt 1987).

8. The ellipsoid method

There have been many alternatives to the simplex algorithm proposed for solving linear programming problems. In this section and the next, we discuss two such methods that are distinguished from previous proposals by their property of polynomial-time boundedness. Under the assumption that all the data of a linear programming problem are integers, these methods require a number of elementary operations that is bounded by a polynomial function of the length of an encoding of the input. For a linear programming problem in standard form, this length can be estimated by

$$L = \sum_{i=0}^{m} \sum_{j=0}^{n} \lceil \log(|a_{ij}| + 1) + 1 \rceil \tag{8.1}$$

where $a_{i0} \equiv b_i$ and $a_{0j} \equiv c_j$. An elementary operation is the addition, subtraction, multiplication or comparison of two bits; for the purpose of polynomial algorithms, we can equivalently allow elementary arithmetic operations on real numbers where the number of digits before and after the decimal point is bounded by a polynomial in the length of the input.

The concept of polynomial-time algorithms and the related notion of computational complexity have proved extraordinarily fruitful in the study of combinatorial optimization problems – we refer to Chapters 5 and 6 for more details. In the context of linear programming the significance of polynomial-time boundedness (especially in view of the notoriously bad practical performance of the ellipsoid method) seems less compelling; we will discuss this further below.

This section is divided into four parts. In 8.1 we introduce the basic idea of the algorithm. The precise statement of the algorithm and its volume-reduction properties are given in 8.2, along with some extensions to the basic method. In 8.3 we give a sketch of the proof that this algorithm requires only polynomial time to solve linear programming problems, and we conclude in 8.4 by discussing its theoretical and computational significance.

8.1. The idea of the ellipsoid algorithm

Let us note first that the ellipsoid method was not devised by Khachian in 1979; it is an outgrowth of the method of central sections of Levin (1965) and Newman (1965) and the method of generalized gradient descent with space dilation of Shor (1970) and was developed by Yudin and Nemirovskii (1976) for convex, not necessarily differentiable, programming. Further remarks on its antecedents can be found in Bland, Goldfarb and Todd (1981). The contribution of Khachian (1979 and 1980) was to demonstrate that this method could be used to provide a polynomial algorithm for linear programming.

The ellipsoid method can be applied most directly to problems in inequality form. Thus we will assume that we wish to solve

$$\text{minimize} \quad a_0^\mathrm{T} y, \quad \text{subject to } y \in Y, \tag{8.2}$$

where

$$Y = \{ y \in \mathbb{R}^m : a_j^\mathrm{T} y \leq c_j \text{ for } j = 1, 2, \dots, n \}. \tag{8.3}$$

Note that the dual of a problem in standard form is of this type. For the moment, we assume that the components of the vectors $a_j \in \mathbb{R}^m$ and the scalars c_j are arbitrary real numbers. We also suppose for simplicity that we only require a *feasible* point $\bar{y} \in Y$. For the optimization problem, we can proceed in either of two ways. We can consider the feasibility problem for a sequence of polyhedra

$$Y(c_0) = \{ y \in \mathbb{R}^m : a_j^\mathrm{T} y \leq c_j \text{ for } j = 0, 1, \dots, n \}, \tag{8.4}$$

depending on a decreasing sequence $\{c_0\}$ of upper bounds on the optimal value of (8.2). An alternative approach is to combine primal and dual feasibility and equality of objective function values into a large system of inequalities – see Section 8.3.

The algorithm to find a point in Y (if one exists) operates by generating a sequence $\{E_k\}$ of ellipsoids with centers $\{y_k\}$. At each step y is contained in E_k, and either $y_k \in Y$ (in which case the algorithm terminates) or a new ellipsoid E_{k+1} is constructed with $Y \subseteq E_{k+1}$ and the volume of E_{k+1} smaller than that of E_k by some fixed factor Φ depending only on m. See Figure 8.1.

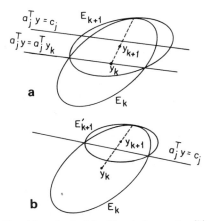

Fig. 8.1. The ellipsoid method: (a) without deep cuts, (b) with deep cuts.

In order to start the method and provide a guarantee of its terminating, we assume for now:

(A1) For some known $y_0 \in \mathbb{R}^m$ and $R > 0$, the polyhedron Y is contained in the ball $S(y_0, R) = \{y \in \mathbb{R}^m : \|y - y_0\| \leq R\}$; and

(A2) There is a known $\rho > 0$ such that, if Y is nonempty, it contains a ball $S(y^*, \rho)$ of radius ρ.

Assumption (A1) allows us to choose $E_0 = S(y_0, R)$. If $\mathrm{vol}(E_{k+1}) \leq \Phi \, \mathrm{vol}(E_k)$ for all k, then for $K > \lceil m \log(\rho/R)/\log \Phi \rceil$, the volume of E_K is smaller than that of a sphere of radius ρ, so that if no feasible y_k has been generated in K iterations, (A2) allows us to conclude that Y is empty.

8.2. Statement of the algorithm

We will represent each ellipsoid E_k by means of its center y_k and a symmetric positive definite $m \times m$ matrix B_k:

$$E_k = \{y \in \mathbb{R}^m : (y - y_k)^T B_k^{-1}(y - y_k) \leq 1\} . \tag{8.5}$$

Note that, if $B_k = J_k J_k^T$, then $E_k = \{y_k + J_k z : \|z\| \leq 1\}$, the image of the unit ball under the affine transformation $z \to y_k + J_k z$. It follows that the volume of E_k is

$$\mathrm{vol} \, E_k = (\det B_k)^{1/2} \mathrm{vol}(S(0, 1)) . \tag{8.6}$$

From assumption (A1), we can choose $B_0 = R^2 I$ to ensure that $Y \subseteq E_0$.

At each iteration k, we assume we have E_k as in (8.5) with $Y \subseteq E_k$, and we check whether $y_k \in Y$. If so, we stop; otherwise, we choose j with $a_j^T y_k > c_j$. In this case, we know that Y is contained in

$$\tfrac{1}{2} E_k \equiv \{y \in E_k : a_j^T y \leq a_j^T y_k\} , \tag{8.7}$$

which is half the ellipsoid E_k cut off by a hyperplane through its center. We now construct the ellipsoid E_{k+1} of minimum volume containing $\tfrac{1}{2} E_k$. See Figure 8.1(a).

Let $\tau = 1/(m+1)$, $\delta = m^2/(m^2 - 1)$ and $\sigma = 2/(m+1)$, and set

$$y_{k+1} = y_k - \tau B_k a_j /(a_j^T B_k a_j)^{1/2} , \tag{8.8}$$

$$B_{k+1} = \delta \left(B_k - \sigma \frac{B_k a_j a_j^T B_k}{a_j^T B_k a_j} \right) . \tag{8.9}$$

Theorem 8.1 (see, e.g., Bland, Goldfarb, and Todd (1981)). *The ellipsoid E_{k+1}, given as in (8.5) from y_{k+1} and B_{k+1} in (8.8–8.9), is the minimum* *volume ellipsoid containing* $\frac{1}{2}E_k$. *We have*

$$\frac{\text{vol } E_{k+1}}{\text{vol } E_k} = \left(\frac{m^2}{m^2 - 1}\right)^{(m-1)/2} \frac{m}{m+1} < \exp\left(-\frac{1}{2(m+1)}\right). \qquad (8.10)$$

Let us now state the algorithm concisely:

Algorithm 8.1.
Input: $m \times n$ matrix $A = [a_1, \ldots, a_n]$, *n*-vector $c = [c_1, \ldots, c_n]^{\text{T}}$ and $y_0 \in \mathbb{R}^m$ such that Y defined by (8.3) satisfies (A1)–(A2).
Output: *m*-vector $y \in Y$ or determination that $Y = \emptyset$.
Initialization: Set $B_0 = R^2 I$, $K = \lceil 2m(m+1) \ln(R/\rho) \rceil + 1$.
For $k = 0, 1, \ldots, K - 1$ do
Iteration k: If $y_k \in Y$, STOP: result is $y = y_k$. Otherwise, choose j with $a_j^{\text{T}} y_k > c_j$. Update y_k and B_k using (8.8)–(8.9).
STOP: result is "$Y = \emptyset$".

From Theorem 8.1 and the discussion at the end of the last section we can conclude that this algorithm is correct.

In Section 8.3 we will sketch how a modification of Algorithm 8.1 can be used to provide a polynomial time algorithm for linear programming. To conclude this section we discuss some of the extensions and improvements that have been proposed for this basic method.

The most obvious change, suggested by a number of authors (see (Bland, Goldfarb and Todd 1981)), is to replace the semi-ellipsoid $\frac{1}{2}E_k$ in (8.7) with the smaller set

$$\{y \in E_k : a_j^{\text{T}} y \leq c_j\}. \qquad (8.11)$$

Thus we use so-called 'deep' cuts. See Figure 8.1(b). If we define

$$\alpha = (a_j^{\text{T}} y_k - c_j)/(a_j^{\text{T}} B_k a_j)^{1/2}, \qquad (8.12)$$

then $\alpha \geq 0$ by our choice of j, and the set (8.11) is nonempty iff $\alpha \leq 1$. For $\alpha \in [0, 1]$, the minimum volume ellipsoid E_{k+1} containing (8.11) is given as in (8.5), with y_{k+1} and B_{k+1} defined by (8.8)–(8.9) with revised parameters

$$\tau = \frac{1 + m\alpha}{m+1}, \qquad \delta = (1 - \alpha^2)\frac{m^2}{m^2 - 1}, \qquad \sigma = \frac{2(1 + m\alpha)}{(1 + \alpha)(m+1)}. \qquad (8.13)$$

The corresponding ratio of the volumes of successive ellipsoids is

$$\frac{\text{vol } E_{k+1}}{\text{vol } E_k} = \left(\frac{m^2(1 - \alpha^2)}{m^2 - 1}\right)^{(m-1)/2} \frac{m(1 - \alpha)}{m+1}. \qquad (8.14)$$

Further reductions in the volume ratio can be achieved using surrogate cuts and parallel cuts (see Bland, Goldfarb, and Todd (1981)).

Finally, we note that a completely different way to represent the ellipsoid E_k has been proposed by Burrell and Todd (1985). Since (A1) provides a bound on each component of y in Y, it is easy to find $l^0 \in \mathbb{R}^n$ such that

$$Y = \{ y \in \mathbb{R}^m : l^0 \leq A^T y \leq c \} .$$

At iteration k, suppose we have a vector $l^k = (l^k_j)$ of lower bounds on $A^T y$ for $y \in Y$, so that

$$Y = \{ y \in \mathbb{R}^m : l^k \leq A^T y \leq c \} . \tag{8.15}$$

Suppose we also have a diagonal $n \times n$ matrix D_k with nonnegative diagonal entries, such that $AD_k A^T$ is positive definite. It then follows immediately from (8.15) that Y is contained in the ellipsoid E_k given by

$$E_k = \{ y \in \mathbb{R}^m : (A^T y - l^k)^T D_k (A^T y - c) \leq 0 \} . \tag{8.16}$$

This can also be written in the form (8.5), with B_k a scalar multiple of $(AD_k A^T)^{-1}$, and center y_k the solution of the linear equations

$$(AD_k A^T) y = AD_k r^k \tag{8.17}$$

with $r^k = \frac{1}{2}(l^k + c)$.

If y_k is in Y, the algorithm terminates. Otherwise, we choose an index j with $a_j^T y_k > c_j$. If l^k_j is greater than $\lambda_j = \min\{a_j^T y : y \in E_k\}$ then $l^{k+1} = l^k$; otherwise we can update just this component of l^k so that l^{k+1}_j is at least λ_j. Indeed, Burrell and Todd show how to obtain the new j-th component of l^{k+1} as the value of a dual feasible solution of $\min\{a_j^T y : A^T y \leq c\}$, and how this dual solution can be obtained using the representation (8.16). Having updated l^k to l^{k+1}, we increase the j-th diagonal entry of D_k suitably to get D_{k+1}, and then the resulting ellipsoid E_{k+1} is exactly the minimum volume ellipsoid containing

$$\{ y \in E_k : l^{k+1}_j \leq a_j^T y \leq c_j \} .$$

(In fact, this is a slight simplification of the true situation; if E_k already depends on l^k_j – the j-th diagonal entry of D_k is nonzero – and l^k_j is increased to l^{k+1}_j, then we must compensate for the effect of the changed lower bound on E_k before updating the lower bounds and the ellipsoid.)

There are many advantages to the representation (8.16). First, Y is contained in E_k regardless of round-off errors as long as $D_k \geq 0$ and l^k is a vector of valid lower bounds. Second, these lower bounds are certified by maintaining dual solutions for the linear programming problems $\min\{a_j^T y : A^T y \leq c\}$. Third, if in fact Y is empty, and α in (8.12) exceeds one at some iteration k, then the representation can be used to produce a vector x with $Ax = 0$ and $c^T x < 0$, demonstrating $Y = \emptyset$ by Farkas' lemma. Details may be found in (Burrell and Todd 1985). Here we merely wish to point out that the equations (8.17) for determining the center y_k of the ellipsoid E_k are the normal equations for the (weighted) least-squares problem

$$\min_{y \in \mathbb{R}^m} \| D_k^{1/2} (A^T y - r^k) \| \,, \tag{8.18}$$

where the weighting matrix $D_k^{1/2}$ is a diagonal matrix with diagonal entries equal to the square roots of those of D_k. Moreover, as we proceed from one iteration to the next, the linear system (8.17) changes in just two respects: the j-th component of l^k (and hence of r^k) may increase, and the j-th diagonal of D_k increases, where j indexes a violated constraint at y_k.

8.3. Polynomial-time solvability

First we suppose we wish to find a feasible point in

$$Y = \{ y \in \mathbb{R}^m : A^T y \leq c \} \tag{8.19}$$

in time polynomial in the length of input of the system,

$$L = \sum_{i=0}^{m} \sum_{j=1}^{n} (\log(|a_{ij}| + 1) + 1) + 1 \,. \tag{8.20}$$

Here A is an $m \times n$ integer matrix, c is an integer n-vector, and $a_{0j} \equiv c_j$.

We wish to use the argument in Section 7.1, which relied on assumptions (A1) and (A2). Unfortunately, these assumptions may fail to hold, but the argument can be salvaged using perturbations. let $c' = c + 2^{-L} e$ where e is an n-vector of ones, and

$$Y' = \{ y \in \mathbb{R}^m : A^T y \leq c' \} \,. \tag{8.21}$$

Then one can prove (see, e.g., Khachian (1980) or Gács and Lovász (1981)):

Lemma 8.1. *If Y is nonempty, then so is $Y \cap S(0, 2^L)$; moreover, there is some y_* with $S(y_*, 2^{-2L}) \subseteq Y' \cap S(0, 2^L)$. If Y is empty, so is Y'.*

Thus the argument of Section 8.1 can be applied to $Y' \cap S(0, 2^L)$ *with* $R = 2^L$, $\rho = 2^{-2L}$. Moreover, the algorithm is precisely algorithm 7.1 with the stopping rule $y_k \in Y'$ replacing $y_k \in Y$. Lemma 8.1 shows that Y' being nonempty implies the same for Y. Thus we can determine feasibility of the system $A^T y \leq c$ in $O(m^2 \ln(R/\rho)) = O(m^2 L)$ steps, assuming exact arithmetic. Finally, it is not hard to use an algorithm for determining feasibility recursively to actually obtain a solution for a feasible system of inequalities. Alternatively, one can use a rounding method (see (Grötschel, Lovasz, and Schrijver 1981)) to obtain a feasible point in Y from one in Y'.

The simplest way to solve the optimization problem

$$\min\{a_0^T y\colon y \in Y\} \tag{8.22}$$

with Y given as in (8.19) is to recast it as the feasibility problem:

$$
\begin{aligned}
A^T y &\le c\,, \\
Ax &\le -a_0\,, \\
-Ax &\le a_0\,, \\
-x &\le 0\,, \\
c^T x + a_0^T y &\le 0\,.
\end{aligned}
\tag{8.23}
$$

Then the algorithm as described can be applied; the length of input of (8.23) is polynomial in the length of input

$$L = \sum_{i=0}^{m} \sum_{j=0}^{n} (\log(|a_{ij}| + 1) + 1) \tag{8.24}$$

of (8.22), where $a_{0j} \equiv c_j$ and $a_0 = (a_{i0})$.

Alternatively, one can use a sliding-objective method (see (Bland, Goldfarb, and Todd 1981) and (Grötschel, Lovász and Schrijver 1981)), as follows. First, a feasible point $\bar{y}$ to Y (or Y') is found; then the constraint $a_0^T y \le c_0 = a_0^T \bar{y}$ is added and the iterations continued, starting by choosing the 0th constraint as 'violated'. Thus at the k-th iteration we work with the polyhedron

$$\{y \in \mathbb{R}^m\colon a_i^T y \le c_i \text{ for } i = 0, 1, \ldots, n\}$$

where $c_0 = \min\{a_0^T y_l\colon A^T y_l \le c,\ 0 \le l \le k\}$ is revised and a_j chosen as a_0 whenever a feasible iterate is generated. The polynomiality of this version can be established by considering the volumes of sections of the cone with vertex an optimal solution of (8.22) and base a small ball of radius 2^{-2L} in Y or Y'.

To conclude the section we note that the analysis above assumes that the iterates y_k and B_k are computed exactly. For a polynomial algorithm, however, we can only use finite precision. Because the resulting rounding may cause the fundamental inclusion $Y \subseteq E_k$ to fail, we must slightly enlarge the ellipsoid E_k by increasing δ in (8.9) slightly. See, e.g., (Khachian 1980) or (Grötschel, Lovász and Schrijver 1981). Then y_k and B_k can be updated and rounded to $O(L)$ bits before and after the decimal point. In so doing, the number of iterations is increased only by a constant factor. Hence we finally have:

Theorem 8.2. *The ellipsoid method can be adapted to find a feasible solution to (8.19) or an optimal solution to (8.22), if one exists, in time bounded by a polynomial in the length of its input, given by (8.20) or (8.24) respectively.*

The number of bit operations to determine feasibility of (8.19) is bounded (see (Khachian 1980)) by

$$O(n^4 L^2) .$$
(8.25)

Note that this contrasts with the earlier estimate $O(n^6 L^2)$ given in Khachian (1979) and quoted by Karmarkar (1984a,b).

8.4. Theoretical and computational significance

The discovery of a polynomial-time algorithm for linear programming resolved an important question concerning the computational complexity of this problem. For many years, linear programming had been thought to be much easier than the so-called NP-complete problems (see Chapter 5), which include for example the notorious travelling salesman and graph coloring problems; yet no polynomial algorithm was known. Khachian's result thus settled a significant theoretical question. As we shall see, its theoretical implications are much broader than this result indicates.

For practical computation, however, the ellipsoid method seems at present to be of little use. Even with considerable enhancements, as described in (Bland, Goldfarb and Todd 1981) and outlined above, convergence appears to be very slow on problems of even moderate dimension; the volume reduction achieved at each iteration is not much better than that given by (8.10). While the worst-case complexity of several variants of the simplex method is exponential, its practical performance is far better than that of the ellipsoid method. We must point out, however, that good results have been reported by Ecker and Kupferschmidt (1985) for certain nonlinear programming problems of small to medium dimension. In addition, Shor (1985) quotes successful experience on nonsmooth optimization problems using various space dilation methods, which differ from the ellipsoid method is using different constants τ, δ, σ than those in (8.13) – see Chapter 7.

Finally we return to the broader theoretical significance of the ellipsoid method. This stems from the way in which the algorithm uses the constraints of a linear programming problem. Indeed, the discussion above shows that it is enough to recognize whether a given $\bar{y}$ is feasible, and, if not, to generate some constraint $a_j^T y \leq c_j$ that is violated by $\bar{y}$. Hence no a priori listing of the constraints is necessary as long as they can be obtained in this way as needed. This permits the application of the ellipsoid method to a host of combinatorial optimization problems where the constraints are only known implicitly and may be exponential (in the dimension of the problem) in number. This potentiality was noted by Grötschel, Lovàsz and Schrijver (1981), Karp and Papadimitriou (1980) and Padberg and Rao (1980), and is developed extensively in Grötschel, Lovàsz and Schrijver (1986). An elementary discussion is contained in Chapter 5.

In summary, the ellipsoid method is of little significance for practical computation in linear programming, but its theoretical significance in linear, nonlinear and combinatorial optimization is profound.

9. Karmarkar's projective scaling algorithm

In 1984, a new polynomial-time algorithm for linear programming was developed by N.K. Karmarkar of AT&T Bell Laboratories (Karmarkar 1984a,b). In constrast to the ellipsoid method, this new algorithm seems to have the potential to rival the simplex method for practical computation. It is still too early to make a definitive comparison, and claims and counter-claims on the efficiency of the new method have been put forward at a sequence of conferences. At the moment, it can certainly be asserted that Karmarkar's algorithm has considerable promise, and some outstanding results for very large sparse problems have been obtained (e.g. (Karmarkar and Sinha 1985) (Karmarkar and Ramakrishnan 1988)); on the other hand, codes developed outside Bell Laboratories ((Adler, Karmarkar, Resende and Veiga 1986), (Gill, Murray, Saunders, Tomlin and Wright 1986), (McShane, Monma and Shanno 1988) and (Monma and Morton 1987)) report times from five or more times faster to five times slower than the widely-used MINOS code (Murtagh and Saunders 1977) which implements the simplex method when the objective function is linear.

In this section we will describe the new algorithm and the ideas (coming from nonlinear programming and projective geometry) on which it is based. Our discussion is divided into seven parts: we describe the idea of the algorithm in 9.1, state it precisely in 9.2, and sketch the proof of polynomiality in 9.3. Section 9.4 reviews extensions and variants, while Section 9.5 describes related approaches, including the so-called 'affine scaling' method, which turns out to have been proposed by the Soviet mathematician I.I. Dikin as long ago as 1967, and the recent path-following methods. Section 9.6 discusses implementation of the algorithms, and we conclude in 9.7 by commenting on their theoretical and computational significance. We remark here that these comments stand in sharp contrast to our conclusions for the ellipsoid method; while for computation Karmarkar's algorithm has potentially very high significance, its theoretical consequences appear far more limited than those of the earlier method.

9.1. The idea of the projective scaling algorithm

As with the ellipsoid method, Karmarkar's algorithm has a preferred form for linear programming problems; in this case the canonical form is

$$
\begin{aligned}
\text{minimize} \quad & c^{\mathrm{T}}x \\
\text{subject to} \quad & Ax = 0, \\
& x \in \Delta,
\end{aligned}
\tag{9.1}
$$

where Δ is the standard simplex in $\mathbb{R}^n$,

$$
\Delta = \{x \in \mathbb{R}^n : e^{\mathrm{T}}x = 1, x \geq 0\}
\tag{9.2}
$$

and e is the n-vector of ones. We also assume that

(Ai) A is an $m \times n$ matrix of rank m;

(Aii) $Ae = 0$, so that $x^0 = e/n$ is feasible; and

(Aiii) the optimal value v of (9.1) is zero.

We will see later how to convert a general programming problem into one in this form, satisfying the assumptions above.

Now that the dual of problem (9.1) is to find $y \in \mathbb{R}^m$ and $z \in \mathbb{R}$ to

$$\begin{aligned} &\text{maximize} \quad z \\ &\text{subject to} \quad A^T y + ze \le c \,. \end{aligned} \tag{9.3}$$

There are two interesting properties of this dual problem. First, it is clearly feasible; indeed, for any given $\bar{y} \in \mathbb{R}^m$ it is easy to choose z to make $(\bar{y}, z)$ feasible – the best such z is $\min_j (c - A^T \bar{y})_j$. Second, our assumption that the optimal value of (9.1) and hence of (9.3) is zero means that we are really seeking $\bar{y} \in \mathbb{R}^m$ with $A^T \bar{y} \le c$, and this feasibility problem is exactly what the ellipsoid method of Section 8 is designed for.

It will be convenient to call a feasible solution x to (9.1) strictly feasible if each component of x is positive. Karmarkar's algorithm generates a sequence $\{x^k\}$ of strictly feasible solutions, starting with $x^0 = e/n$, that satisfy

$$c^T x^k \le \exp(-k/5n) c^T x^0 \tag{9.4}$$

for all k. This performance guarantee suffices to provide a polynomial algorithm as follows. If the length of input of the integer data A, c is

$$L = \sum_{i=0}^{m} \sum_{j=1}^{n} \lceil \log(|a_{ij}| + 1) \rceil + 1 \,, \tag{9.5}$$

where $a_{0j} \equiv c_j$, then from a strictly feasible solution x^k with $c^T x^k \le 2^{-2L} c^T x^0$ an exact solution can be found by moving to a vertex with objective function value no greater. Hence $O(nL)$ iterations are enough to obtain an optimal solution. (In practice, several variants of Karmarkar's algorithm appear to require only 20–50 iterations even for very large problems.)

The basic idea of an iteration is as follows. Suppose we are given a strictly feasible solution $x^k \in \Delta$. We then make a *projective transformation* (or projective scaling) of the simplex Δ that carries Δ into itself and x^k into the center of the simplex e/n. Indeed, the vertices of Δ are fixed under this transformation, and this would force a linear or affine transformation to be the identity; the extra freedom of a projective transformation allows us to deform the interior of Δ to map x^k into e/n. The advantage of such a transformation is that the current iterate in the transformed space is far from all the inequality constraints $x \ge 0$. While forcing a certain subset of these to be equalities forms the foundation of the simplex method, the projective scaling method seeks to avoid the combinatorial complexities of switching among an exponential number of such active sets.

Following the transformation, we ignore the inequality constraints and make a move in the direction of the negative of the gradient of the transformed objective function, projected onto the transformed equality constraints. A suitable step size in this direction leads to a new strictly feasible point in the transformed space. An application of the inverse projective transformation then yields the next iterate x^{k+1}.

Obtaining the crucial inequality (9.4) requires a more complicated analysis, since the linear objective function of (9.1) becomes nonlinear under the projective transformation. Karmarkar introduces the potential function

$$f(x) = n \ln c^T x - \sum_j \ln x_j = \sum_j \ln(c^T x / x_j) \qquad (9.6)$$

to measure progress towards the solution. This important function is invariant under the projective transformations used, and can be reduced by a constant at each iteration. This reduction then implies (9.4) – details are given later.

9.2. Statement of the algorithm

First we describe the projective transformation. We suppose given a strictly feasible solution $x^k \in \Delta$. To simplify the notation, we suppress the index k and write $\bar{x}$ for x^k.

Define the diagonal matrix $\bar{X}$ to have as its diagonal entries the components of $\bar{x}$, so that $\bar{X}e = \bar{x}$. Then the projective transformation is defined by

$$x \rightarrow \hat{x} = \frac{\bar{X}^{-1}x}{e^T \bar{X}^{-1}x} \qquad (9.7a)$$

with inverse

$$\hat{x} \rightarrow x = \frac{\bar{X}\hat{x}}{e^T \bar{X}\hat{x}} . \qquad (9.7b)$$

Note that $\bar{x}$ is indeed transformed into $\hat{x} = e/n$.

We illustrate this transformation in the case $n = 3$, $m = 1$, with $A = [-7, 2, 5]$. Then the feasible region is the line segment joining $(2/9, 7/9, 0)^T$ and $(5/12, 0, 7/12)^T$, and $e/n = (1/3, 1/3, 1/3)^T$ is indeed feasible. We let $\bar{x} = (1/4, 2/3, 1/12)^T$. See Figure 9.1(a).

To aid in understanding the projective transformation, we carry it out in two steps. The first is just a diagonal scaling taking x to $\tilde{x} = n^{-1}\bar{X}^{-1}x$. Thus $\bar{x}$ is taken into e/n, but the simplex Δ is distorted. In our example, $\bar{x}$ is transformed to $(1/3, 1/3, 1/3)^T$, and Δ is taken into the triangle with vertices $(4/3)e_1$, $(1/2)e_2$, and $4e_3$, where e_1, e_2 and e_3 are the unit vectors in $\mathbb{R}^3$. The feasible region is transformed into the intersection of this distorted triangle with the null-space of $\hat{A} = A\bar{X} = [-7/4, 4/3, 5/12]$, which is the line segment joining $(8/27, 7/18, 0)^T$ and $(5/9, 0, 7/3)^T$. See Figure 9.1(b).

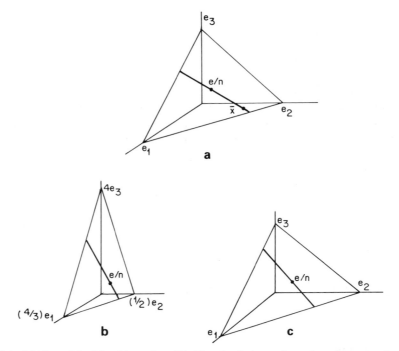

Fig. 9.1. (a) The original feasible region. (b) After the first transformation, $\bar{x}$ goes to e/n. (c) After the second transformation.

Finally we transform the distorted simplex into Δ by performing a radial projection taking $\tilde{x}$ to $\hat{x} = \tilde{x}/e^T\tilde{x}$. Both e/n and the subspace $\{\tilde{x}: \hat{A}\tilde{x} = 0\}$ are invariant under this transformation, but e/n becomes the center of the new undistorted simplex. In our example, the feasible region becomes the line segment joining $(16/37, 21/37, 0)^T$ and $(5/26, 0, 21/26)^T$. See Figure 9.1(c).

Now we return to the general case. Using (9.7b) to substitute for x in (9.1), we obtain the equivalent problem:

$$\text{minimize} \quad \frac{c^T \bar{X}\hat{x}}{e^T \bar{X}\hat{x}}$$

$$\text{subject to} \quad A\bar{X}\hat{x} = 0, \tag{9.8}$$

$$\hat{x} \in \Delta,$$

with a linear fractional objective function. However, assumption (Aiii) implies that it is sufficient to obtain a solution with objective value zero, and for this it is enough if the numerator is zero. Hence, defining

$$\hat{A} = A\bar{X}, \qquad \hat{c} = \bar{X}c, \tag{9.9}$$

we are led to

$$\text{minimize} \quad \hat{c}^{\mathrm{T}}\hat{x}$$

$$\text{subject to} \quad \hat{A}\hat{x} = 0 , \tag{9.10}$$

$$\hat{x} \in \Delta .$$

This has the identical form to our original problem (9.1). Moreover, in this transformed space, our current solution is in the center of Δ, $\hat{x} = e/n$.

In order to improve this solution, we replace the constraint $\hat{x} \in \Delta$ with its n inequalities by a stronger but smoother constraint. Let

$$S'(e/n, \rho) = \{x \in \mathbb{R}^n : e^{\mathrm{T}}x = 1, \|x - e/n\| \leq \rho\} \tag{9.11}$$

denote the ball of radius ρ around e/n in the affine space $\{x \in \mathbb{R}^n : e^{\mathrm{T}}x = 1\}$. It is easy to check that

$$S'(e/n, r) \subseteq \Delta \subseteq S'(e/n, R) \tag{9.12}$$

where

$$r = (n(n-1))^{-1/2} , \qquad R = ((n-1)/n)^{1/2} . \tag{9.13}$$

Then, for any $\rho > 0$, the solution to

$$\text{minimize} \quad \hat{c}^{\mathrm{T}}\hat{x}$$

$$\text{subject to} \quad \hat{A}\hat{x} = 0 , \tag{9.14}$$

$$\hat{x} \in S'(e/n, \rho) ,$$

is given by

$$\hat{x}(\rho) = e/n + \rho\hat{d}/\|\hat{d}\| , \tag{9.15}$$

where $\hat{d}$ is the negative of the orthogonal projection of $\hat{c}$ onto the null space of

$$B = \begin{bmatrix} \hat{A} \\ e^{\mathrm{T}} \end{bmatrix} . \tag{9.16}$$

Thus

$$\hat{d} = -(I - B^{\mathrm{T}}(BB^{\mathrm{T}})^{-1}B)\hat{c} . \tag{9.17}$$

The algorithm chooses $\rho = \alpha/n < \alpha r$, where $0 < \alpha < 1$ is chosen so that $\hat{x}(\rho)$ is feasible and so that the potential function defined below is sufficiently reduced. Setting $\alpha = \frac{1}{3}$ at each iteration suffices, although other choices are preferable in practice. We thus have:

Algorithm 9.1 (projective scaling).
  Input: $m \times n$ matrix A, n vector c such that (Ai)–(Aiii) are satisfied.

Output: n-vector x feasible in (9.1) with $c^T x \leq 2^{-q} c^T e/n$.
Initialization: Set $x^0 = e/n$.
For $k = 0, 1, \ldots, 5nq$ do
Iteration k: If $c^T x^k \leq 2^{-q} c^T e/n$, STOP: result is $x = x^k$. Otherwise, let $X_k = \text{diag}(x^k)$. Define $\hat{c} = X_k c$, $\hat{A} = A X_k$. Compute $\hat{d}$ from (9.16) and (9.17), and hence $\|\hat{d}\|$ and $\hat{x} = e/n + \alpha_k \hat{d}/n\|\hat{d}\|$, where $\alpha_k = \frac{1}{3}$.
Set $x^{k+1} = X_k \hat{x}/e^T X_k \hat{x}$.

In the next subsection we show why this algorithm will indeed stop in the required $5nq$ iterations.

9.3. Polynomial-time solvability

In this section we briefly describe how Algorithm 9.1 can be used to solve arbitrary linear programming problems with integer data in polynomial time. We first show that the algorithm does indeed provide the desired accuracy.

Let us recall the potential function

$$f(x) \equiv f(x; c) \equiv \sum_j \ln(c^T x/x_j) \tag{9.18}$$

where we have explicitly shown the dependence on the cost vector c. We write

$$\hat{f}(\hat{x}) \equiv f(\hat{x}; \hat{c}) .$$

The first result demonstrates the value of this function in dealing with the projective transformation used in the algorithm:

Lemma 9.1. *If x and $\hat{x}$ are related as in* (9.7), *then*

$$\hat{f}(\hat{x}) = f(x) + \ln \det \bar{X} . \tag{9.19}$$

The proof is straightforward from the definitions. Thus if we can reduce $\hat{f}$ by a constant from its value at e/n we can reduce f by the same amount using the corresponding step in the untransformed space.

Next we show:

Lemma 9.2. *Let $\hat{x} = e/n + \alpha \hat{d}/n\|\hat{d}\|$, where $\hat{d} = -(I - B^T(BB^T)^{-1}B)\hat{c}$. Then*

$$n \ln \hat{c}^T \hat{x} \leq n \ln(\hat{c}^T e/n) - \alpha . \tag{9.20}$$

Proof. We note that $\hat{c}^T \hat{x}(\rho) = \hat{c}^T e/n - \rho\|\hat{d}\|$, since $\hat{c}^T \hat{d} = -\hat{d}^T \hat{d} = -\|\hat{d}\|^2$. Also, with $\rho = R$, problem (9.14) is a relaxation of (9.10), so that its optimal value is nonpositive. Hence $\hat{c}^T \hat{x}(R) \leq 0$ by (Aiii), implying $-\|\hat{d}\| \leq -(1/R)\hat{c}^T e/n$. Therefore

$$\hat{c}^T \hat{x} = \hat{c}^T e/n - (\alpha/n)\|\hat{d}\| \leq (1 - \alpha/nR)\hat{c}^T e/n < (1 - \alpha/n)\hat{c}^T e/n$$

since $R < 1$. Taking logarithms and using $\ln(1 - \alpha/n) \leq -\alpha/n$ gives the result.

The following lemma bounds the barrier function part $-\Sigma_j \ln \hat{x}_j$ in the potention function. A slightly sharper version is quoted in (Karmarkar 1984b), which can be proved using power series.

Lemma 9.3. *If* $\hat{x} \in S'(e/n, \alpha/n)$, *then*

$$-\sum_j \ln \hat{x}_j \leq -\sum_j \ln(1/n) + \alpha^2/2(1-\alpha)^2 . \tag{9.21}$$

Proof. For each j, using the Taylor series expansion of $\ln(1 + (n\hat{x}_j - 1))$ there is a ξ_j between 1 and $n\hat{x}_j$ such that

$$\ln(n\hat{x}_j) = \ln 1 + (n\hat{x}_j - 1) - \frac{1}{2\xi_j^2}(n\hat{x}_j - 1)^2 .$$

Now $\hat{x} \in S'(e/n, \alpha/n)$ implies that $n\hat{x}_j \geq 1 - \alpha$, so $\xi_j \geq 1 - \alpha$ and hence

$$\ln(n\hat{x}_j) \geq n\hat{x}_j - 1 - \frac{1}{2(1-\alpha)^2}(n\hat{x}_j - 1)^2 .$$

Thus, since $\Sigma_j n\hat{x}_j = n$ and $\Sigma_j(n\hat{x}_j - 1)^2 = \|n\hat{x} - e\|^2 = n^2\|\hat{x} - e/n\|^2 \leq \alpha^2$, we obtain

$$\sum_j \ln(n\hat{x}_j) \geq -\alpha^2/2(1-\alpha)^2 ,$$

from which (9.21) is immediate.

From Lemmas 9.1 to 9.3 we conclude:

Theorem 9.1. *If the sequence* $\{x^k\}$ *is defined by Algorithm 9.1 then*

$$f(x^k) \leq f(x^0) - \tfrac{1}{5}k . \tag{9.22}$$

Proof. By Lemmas 9.2 and 9.3, at each iteration we have

$$\hat{f}(\hat{x}) \leq \hat{f}(e/n) - \alpha_k + \alpha_k^2/2(1-\alpha_k)^2 ;$$

with $\alpha_k = \tfrac{1}{3}$ we find $\hat{f}(\hat{x}) \leq \hat{f}(e/n) - \tfrac{1}{5}$. Now using Lemma 9.1 gives

$$f(x^{k+1}) \leq f(x^k) - \tfrac{1}{5}$$

whence (9.22) follows.

Corollary 9.1. *With* $\{x^k\}$ *as above,* (9.4) *holds:*

$$c^T x^k \leq \exp(-k/5n)c^T x^0 .$$

Proof. From (9.22),

$$n \ln c^{\mathrm{T}} x^k - \sum_j \ln x_j^k \le n \ln c^{\mathrm{T}} x^0 - \sum_j \ln x_j^0 - \tfrac{1}{5} k \,.$$

But $\Sigma_j \ln x_j$, for $x \in \Delta$, is maximized by $x = x^0$; hence

$$n \ln c^{\mathrm{T}} x^k \le n \ln c^{\mathrm{T}} x^0 - \tfrac{1}{5} k \,,$$

and (9.4) follows by dividing by n and exponentiating.

By the remarks earlier in the section we now have a polynomial-time algorithm for problems of the form (9.1).

To handle a general linear programming problem, we first convert it to a feasibility system

$$Mz \le u \tag{9.23}$$

as in Section 8.3, taking care to bound the primal and dual variables so that there is no non-trivial solution to $Mz \le 0$. Then consider the linear programming problem

$$
\begin{aligned}
\text{minimize} \quad & \lambda \\
\text{subject to} \quad & Mz + Is - ut + (u - Me - e)\lambda = 0 \,, \\
& e^{\mathrm{T}} z + e^{\mathrm{T}} s + t + \qquad\qquad \lambda = 1 \,, \\
& z, s, t, \lambda \ge 0 \,,
\end{aligned}
\tag{9.24}
$$

(where e represents a vector of ones of appropriate dimension throughout). If $Mz \le u$, then a scaling of $(z, u - Mz, 1, 0)$ is an optimal solution to this problem with value 0. Conversely, given such an optimal solution, the precaution taken above ensures that $t > 0$, and hence by scaling we find a feasible solution to (9.23). If the algorithm fails to achieve the promised reduction in the potential function at any iteration, then (9.23) is infeasible, and we can proceed in a similar way to determine the feasibility of the primal and dual constraints.

The complexity of each iteration is dominated by the work necessary to compute $\hat{d}$. For this, we must solve $BB^{\mathrm{T}} w = B\hat{c}$. Using the fact that $A\bar{X}e = A\bar{x} = 0$, and writing $w^{\mathrm{T}} = (\bar{y}^{\mathrm{T}}, \tilde{z})$, we find that $\bar{y}$ and $\tilde{z}$ satisfy

$$(A\bar{X}^2 A^{\mathrm{T}})\bar{y} = A\bar{X}^2 c \,, \tag{9.25}$$

$$(e^{\mathrm{T}} e)\tilde{z} = c^{\mathrm{T}} \bar{x} \,. \tag{9.26}$$

Hence $\tilde{z} = c^{\mathrm{T}} \bar{x}/n$. Note that (9.25) are the normal equations for the weighted least-squares problem

$$\min_{\bar{y} \in \mathbb{R}^m} \| \bar{X}(A^{\mathrm{T}} \bar{y} - c) \| \,; \tag{9.27}$$

compare with (8.17)–(8.18). Having obtained $\bar{y}$, we calculated $\hat{d}$ from

$$\hat{d} = -\bar{X}(c - A^{\mathrm{T}}\bar{y}) + (c^{\mathrm{T}}\bar{x}/n)e \ . \tag{9.28}$$

Finally, all computations can be carried out with $O(L)$ precision, so that each iteration requires about $O(n^3L)$ bit operations. Since at most $O(nL)$ iterations are required to obtain the necessary accuracy in the objective function, we have:

Theorem 9.2. *Karmarkar's algorithm can be adapted to solve a general linear programming problem with m constraints and p variables in about* $O(n^4L^2)$ *bit operations, where* $n = m + p$.

We note that the complexity is of the same order as that for the ellipsoid method, given in (8.25). Karmarkar described a modification of his algorithm that removed a factor $n^{1/2}$; we will comment on this in the next subsection, which describes extensions and further research related to the projective method.

9.4. Extensions and variants

We first point out that the analysis of the decrease of the potential function given in Lemmas 9.2 and 9.3 can be improved, as has been shown by Blair (1986), Padberg (1985) and others. This leads to a best value for α_k of $n(n-1)r/(2n-3)$ in Algorithm 9.1 and a resulting decrease in f of $(1 - \ln 2) \approx 0.3$ at each iteration. While this is of interest in the theoretical analysis, in practice it is advisable to perform a line search in the direction $\hat{d}$; typically far larger reductions in the potential function can be achieved.

One of the severest limitations of the canonical form (9.1) is the requirement (Aiii) that its optimal value be zero. Of course, if the optimal value is known to be z^*, then replacing c by $c - z^*e$ gives a problem with the same optimal solution but value 0. In Karmarkar (1984a) this idea was developed with z^* an estimate of the optimal value, bounds on which were updated as the algorithm progressed. More satisfactory solutions were proposed in Todd and Burrell (1986) and Anstreicher (1986) where lower bounds $\underline{z}$ on z^* based on duality and geometry, respectively, were used. We now show how the duality bounds, which are the stronger of the two, are derived. Note that equations (9.25)–(9.26) with c replaced by $c - ze$ can be written

$$(A\bar{X}^2A^{\mathrm{T}})\bar{y} = A\bar{X}^2(c - ze) \ , \tag{9.29}$$

$$(e^{\mathrm{T}}e)\tilde{z} = (c - ze)^{\mathrm{T}}\bar{x} \ . \tag{9.30}$$

Let us write $\bar{y} = \bar{y}(z)$ to denote the dependence on z. Corresponding to $\bar{y}$ is the value

$$\bar{z} = \bar{z}(z) = \min_{j}(c - A^{\mathrm{T}}\bar{y}(z))_j \tag{9.31}$$

so that $(\bar{y}, \bar{z})$ is feasible in (9.3) and $\bar{z}$ is a lower bound on v, the value of (9.1).

Todd and Burrell show that if $\bar{z}(\underline{z}) \leqslant \underline{z}$ then, even though $\underline{z}$ may be less than v, the potential function

$$f(\,\cdot\,; c - \underline{z}e) \tag{9.32}$$

is decreased by a constant amount. If $\bar{z}(\underline{z}) > \underline{z}$, so that a better lower bound is found, a search is made for an improved bound $\underline{z}'$ with $\bar{z}(\underline{z}') = \underline{z}'$; such a value can be found by a minimum ratio test. Then $\underline{z}'$ replaces $\underline{z}$, and again the potential function (9.32) can be reduced by a constant amount. In this way an algorithm is developed for problems in the form (9.1) satisfying (Ai) and (Aii) but not necessarily (Aiii); this algorithm generates strictly feasible primal solutions x^k and feasible solutions (y^k, z^k) which satisfy

$$(c^{\mathrm{T}}x^k - z^k) \leqslant \exp(-k/5n)(c^{\mathrm{T}}x^0 - z^0)\,, \tag{9.33}$$

so that the duality gap converges linearly to zero.

Several authors (Anstreicher (1986), Gay (1987), Gonzaga (1989a), Jensen and Steger, see Steger (1985), and Ye and Kojima (1987)) have developed an extension that permits a simple treatment of standard form problems. Suppose we have a strictly feasible solution $\bar{x}$ to

$$
\begin{array}{ll}
\text{minimize} & c^{\mathrm{T}}x \\
\text{subject to} & Ax = 0\,, \\
& g^{\mathrm{T}}x = 1\,, \\
& x \geqslant 0\,,
\end{array}
\tag{9.34}
$$

where $g \geqslant 0$. Then a scalar multiple of $\bar{x}$ is feasible in

$$
\begin{array}{ll}
\text{minimize} & (c - zg)^{\mathrm{T}}x \\
\text{subject to} & Ax = 0\,, \\
& e^{\mathrm{T}}x = 1\,, \\
& x \geqslant 0\,;
\end{array}
\tag{9.35}
$$

moreover, if z is the optimal value of (9.34), then a scalar multiple of its optimal solution is optimal in (9.35). Thus we can apply the ideas above to (9.35) and hence reduce $f(\,\cdot\,; c - zg)$ for a suitable z. At each iteration, z is a lower bound on the optimal value of (9.34) corresponding to a dual feasible solution, and these bounds are updated when possible. In this way, a polynomial algorithm can be derived for (9.34) assuming its feasible region is bounded. Details may be found in the cited papers. Note that the standard form problem

$$
\begin{array}{ll}
\text{minimize} & c^{\mathrm{T}}x \\
\text{subject to} & Ax = b\,, \\
& x \geqslant 0\,,
\end{array}
$$

can be rewritten as

$$\text{minimize} \quad (c^{\mathrm{T}}, 0)\begin{pmatrix} x \\ \xi \end{pmatrix}$$

$$\text{subject to} \quad (A, -b)\begin{pmatrix} x \\ \xi \end{pmatrix} = 0,$$

$$(0, 1)\begin{pmatrix} x \\ \xi \end{pmatrix} = 1,$$

$$x \geq 0, \quad \xi \geq 0,$$

which is of the required form with $g^{\mathrm{T}} = (0, 1)$. In addition, Anstreicher shows that fractional linear programming problems can also be handled in this way. A related method was proposed by de Ghellinck and Vial (1986).

The bulk of the work at each iteration consists of obtaining the projection of the gradient in the transformed space, or equivalently solving the linear system (9.25) or (9.29). Thus there is considerable interest in using an approximate projection; such a projection however is unlikely to preserve feasibility if computed in the way described above. An alternative method uses a representation of the null space of $\hat{A}$. Suppose $\hat{Z}$ satisfies $\hat{A}\hat{Z} = 0$ and $[\hat{A}^{\mathrm{T}}, \hat{Z}]$ is square and nonsingular. Then

$$-(I - \hat{A}^{\mathrm{T}}(\hat{A}\hat{A}^{\mathrm{T}})^{-1}\hat{A}) = -\hat{Z}(\hat{Z}^{\mathrm{T}}\hat{Z})^{-1}\hat{Z}^{\mathrm{T}}$$

and this permits the determination of the direction $\hat{d}$ by solving

$$(\hat{Z}^{\mathrm{T}}\hat{Z})w = \hat{Z}^{\mathrm{T}}\hat{c} \tag{9.36}$$

and setting $\hat{d} = -\hat{Z}w$. The important point is that $\hat{d}$ is in the null space of $\hat{A}$ even if w is an inexact solution of (9.36). Moreover, if Z is an appropriate null-space matrix for A, then $\hat{Z} = \bar{X}^{-1}Z$ is suitable for $\hat{A} = A\bar{X}$; thus, except to take care of numerical problems, the null-space matrix need not be recomputed at every iteration. Computing the search direction thus was proposed by Shanno and Marsten (1985), who also consider a reduced gradient version, and by Goldfarb and Mehrotra (1988a), who show how accurate $\hat{d}$ needs to be to preserve polynomiality. Goldfarb and Mehrotra (1988b) also show how to combine their inexact projection approach with the ideas in (Todd and Burrell 1986) for improving a lower bound $\underline{z}$ for problems with unknown optimal value. These authors all use the technology of the simplex method and basis matrices to derive a null-space matrix for A or $\hat{A}$.

In (Goldfarb and Mehrotra 1988c) an algorithm is proposed that does not even preserve feasibility; this method must operate on a primal–dual system similar to (9.24). However, when an iterative method is used, the dimensionality of the corresponding system is less important than its structure, and Goldfarb and Mehrotra have shown how to exploit the primal–dual structure efficiently. Another algorithm that does not require feasibility is that of de Ghellinck and Vial (1986). While this paper requires exact projection, Vial (1989) shows how to preserve polynomiality with inexact projections. Finally, applying Karmarkar's projective method to the dual problem, as proposed by Gay (1987), allows projections to be done inexactly because of the flexibility afforded by the inequality constraints of the dual.

In fact, the first papers to suggest inexact projections were (Karmarkar 1984a,b). The idea was to approximate the diagonal matrix $\bar{X}$ so that, apart from a multiplicative factor, it differed from the diagonal matrix used in the previous iteration in only a few entries. Thus $A\bar{X}^2A^T$ and its inverse differ from (a multiple of) the corresponding matrices at the previous iteration by a matrix of low rank. Karmarkar showed that each entry of the diagonal matrix could be kept within a constant factor of the appropriate component of x while performing only an average of $O(\sqrt{n})$ rank-one updates per iteration; this led to a reduction of $O(\sqrt{n})$ in the worst-case bound. Recently, Shanno (1988) has investigated this idea further and given encouraging computational results; Shanno notes that approximating $\bar{X}$ can avoid some numerical difficulties when on degenerate problems $A\bar{X}^2A^T$ approaches singularity. An alternative algorithm which updates an approximate $\bar{X}$ using a quasi-Newton method, has been proposed by Dennis, Morshedi and Turner (1987).

Relationships between Karmarkar's algorithm and the ellipsoid method have been investigated by Todd (1988b) and Ye (1986), who show that Karmarkar's algorithm generates a sequence of shrinking ellipsoids containing all dual optimal solutions. In fact, Ye shows that, when viewed in the space of dual slack vectors, the logarithm of the volume of the containing ellipsoid is exactly Karmarkar's potential function.

Finally, Kapoor and Vaidya (1986) have shown how to extend Karmarkar's method to convex quadratic programming. This extension is complicated by the fact that a projective transformation maps the convex quadratic objective into a nonconvex conic function. The next section discusses approaches related to Karmarkar's method which are more easily extended to this case.

9.5. Related methods

Among the drawbacks of Karmarkar's algorithm are the complications that result from its use of projective transformations. One way to avoid these complications is to use affine rather than projective transformations at each iteration. This gives rise to the so-called 'affine scaling' algorithm which was proposed by several researchers, including Barnes (1986) and Vanderbei, Meketon and Freedman (1986), who give convergence analyses. Indeed, this method was developed before Karmarkar's method by Dikin (1967, 1974), who also provided convergence results. In contrast to Karmarkar's, this method operates directly on problems given in standard form and does not require knowledge of the optimal value. Unfortunately, however, no polynomial bound is known for this algorithm.

Let $\bar{x}$ be a strictly feasible solution (i.e., $\bar{x} > 0$) of the standard form problem

$$\begin{aligned}
\text{minimize} \quad & c^{\mathrm{T}}x \\
\text{subject to} \quad & Ax = b , \\
& x \geq 0 ,
\end{aligned} \tag{9.37}$$

and consider the affine transformation defined by

$$x \rightarrow \hat{x} = \bar{X}^{-1}x , \qquad \hat{x} \rightarrow x = \bar{X}\hat{x} ,$$

which takes $\bar{x}$ into the interior point e, which is equidistant from all inequality constraints. The linear programming problem in the transformed space is

$$\begin{aligned}
\text{minimize} \quad & \hat{c}^{\mathrm{T}}\hat{x} \\
\text{subject to} \quad & \hat{A}\hat{x} = b , \\
& \hat{x} \geq 0 ,
\end{aligned}$$

with $\hat{A} = A\bar{X}$, $\hat{c} = \bar{X}c$ as before. We then take a step in the negative projected gradient direction

$$\hat{d} = -(I - \hat{A}^{\mathrm{T}}(\hat{A}\hat{A}^{\mathrm{T}})^{-1}\hat{A})\hat{c} ,$$

cf. (9.17). In the original space, this direction is the negative of the (scaled) reduced cost vector:

$$\bar{d} = -\bar{X}^2(c - A^{\mathrm{T}}\bar{y}) \tag{9.38}$$

where

$$(A\bar{X}^2A^{\mathrm{T}})\bar{y} = A\bar{X}^2c ; \tag{9.39}$$

note the similarity to (9.25) and (9.28). Then $\bar{x}$ is replaced by $\bar{x} + \bar{\alpha}\bar{d}$ for a suitable $\bar{\alpha} > 0$. Here $\bar{\alpha}$ is typically chosen to be a large fraction (say 0.95) of $\alpha_{\max}$, where $\alpha_{\max} = \max\{\alpha : \bar{x} + \alpha\bar{d} \geq 0\}$.
  More formally, we have:

Algorithm 9.2 (primal affine scaling).
  Given a strictly feasible solution x^0 to (9.37), choose $0 < \gamma < 1$.
  For $k = 0, 1, \ldots$, do
  Iteration k: Let $X_k = \mathrm{diag}(x^k)$. Compute the solution $\bar{y}^k$ to

$$(AX_k^2A^{\mathrm{T}})y = AX_k^2c , \tag{9.40}$$

and let $\hat{d} = -X_k(c - A^{\mathrm{T}}\bar{y}^k)$, $d^k = X_k\hat{d}$. If $d^k > 0$, STOP: problem is unbounded. Otherwise, let $\alpha = -\gamma/\min_j\hat{d}_j$ and set $x^{k+1} = x^k + \alpha d^k$. Test for convergence.

We have not been specific about the convergence test, since without lower bounds it is not clear when x^k is sufficiently accurate. Note that, if $\hat{d} \le 0$ at any iteration, then y^k is dual feasible so that $b^T y^k$ yields a valid lower bound. Usually, the algorithm is terminated when the improvement obtained is small, i.e.

$$\frac{c^T x^k - c^T x^{k+1}}{\max\{1, |c^T x^k|\}} \le \epsilon . \tag{9.41}$$

Observe that

$$c^T x^k - c^T x^{k+1} = \alpha c^T X_k (I - X_k A^T (A X_k^2 A^T)^{-1} A X_k) X_k c = \alpha \|\hat{d}\|^2 > 0 ,$$

so that the algorithm is a descent method, in contrast to Karmarkar's.

The choice of α above corresponds to moving a proportion γ of the way to the boundary. Alternatively, one could set $\alpha = \gamma / \|\hat{d}\|$, so that the step moves a proportion γ of the way to the boundary of the inscribed ball to the nonnegative orthant centered at $\hat{x} = e$ in the transformed space. This version is analyzed by Barnes (1986) and Dikin (1974).

A popular way of using the affine scaling method is to apply it to the dual of problem (9.37):

$$\begin{aligned} \text{maximize} \quad & b^T y \\ \text{subject to} \quad & A^T y \le c . \end{aligned} \tag{9.42}$$

The advantage, as with the projective scaling method, is that the direction can be computed inexactly without losing feasibility. By introducing slack variables $s = c - A^T y$, eliminating the unrestricted variables y, and applying the affine scaling method to the resulting problem in standard form, one is led to the dual affine scaling method of Adler, Karmarkar, Resende and Veiga (1986). We state this as:

Algorithm 9.3 (dual affine scaling).

Given an interior feasible solution y^0 to (9.42), choose $0 < \gamma < 1$.

For $k = 0, 1, \ldots,$ do:

Iteration k. Let $s^k = c - A^T y^k > 0$ and $S_k = \text{diag}(s^k)$. Compute the solution d^k to

$$(A S_k^{-2} A^T) d = b \tag{9.43}$$

and let $u^k = -A^T d^k$, $\hat{u} = S_k^{-1} u^k$, and $x^k = -S_k^{-2} u^k$. If $u^k \ge 0$, STOP: problem (9.42) is unbounded and hence (9.37) is infeasible. Otherwise, let $\alpha = -\gamma / \min_j \hat{u}_j$ and set $y^{k+1} = y^k + \alpha d^k$ (so that $s^{k+1} = s^k + \alpha u^k$). Test for convergence.

Note that $A x^k = b$, and if $u^k \le 0$, then x^k is a feasible solution to (9.37), yielding an upper bound $c^T x^k$ to the optimal value of (9.42). Usually, a termination criterion analagous to (9.41) is used; now it is easy to see that $b^T y^k$ is increasing.

There appears to be no suitable potential function for these affine scaling algorithms, and a polynomial bound is thought to be unlikely. Nevertheless, they perform well in practice – see Vanderbei, Meketon and Freedman (1986) and Adler, Karmarkar, Resende and Veiga (1986). Convergence has been established under various nondegeneracy conditions – see, e.g., Dikin (1974), Barnes (1986), Vanderbei, Meketon and Freedman (1986) and Vanderbei and Lagarias (1988). Assuming suitable nondegeneracy conditions one can also show that the vectors y^k defined in Algorithm 9.2 converge to the optimal dual solution and the vectors x^k defined in Algorithm 9.3 converge to the optimal primal solution.

Recently Gonzaga (1988) and Ye (1988) have described methods using the same affine transformation as in the primal affine scaling method, but where the direction in the transformed space is the negative projected gradient of a potential function instead of the cost vector. The potential function has the form

$$f(x, \underline{z}) = q \ln(c^T x - \underline{z}) - \sum_j \ln x_j$$

where $q = n + \sqrt{n}$ and $\underline{z}$ is a lower bound. These methods are polynomial, and Ye's algorithm in fact only requires $O(\sqrt{n}L)$ iterations, as in the path-following algorithms to be discussed below. Ye's method generates sequences of both primal and dual feasible solutions, and whenever the dual solution is changed, he shows that his primal and dual solutions lie close to the central paths to be defined below. Hence his algorithm combines ideas from the projective scaling (potential functions), affine scaling (affine transformations) and path-following (central paths) methods, and achieves what is currently the best complexity bound on the number of iterations.

Potential functions can be thought of as barrier functions. If the optimal value z^* is known, there is no parameter required, so that they can be considered 'exact' barrier functions, similar to the exact penalty functions used in nonlinear programming. On the other hand, the relationship of Karmarkar's algorithm to classical logarithmic barrier methods is explored by Gill, Murray, Saunders, Tomlin and Wright (1986). In particular, it is shown that Karmarkar's algorithm takes a step in the same direction as a projected Newton barrier method with a certain value of the penalty parameter. Gill et al. also describe an implementation of the barrier method and provide extensive computational results.

The ideal of approximately following the path of minimizers of a parametrized family of logarithmic barrier problems gives rise to a class of methods which are referred to as 'path-following'. The logarithmic barrier function method was first proposed by Frisch (1955) for solving convex programming problems and its properties in the context of nonlinear programming have been carefully studied by Fiacco and McCormick (1968). For linear programming problems this path of minimizers is called the 'central path'. It has been thoroughly studied by Megiddo (1989) and by Bayer and Lagarias (1987a) who also show that it is the locus of 'analytic centers' of a family of polyhedra determined by the constraints of the linear program together with a parametrized objective value constraint $c^{\mathrm{T}}x \leqslant \mu$ (or $c^{\mathrm{T}}x = \mu$).

If the polyhedron $P \equiv \{x \in \mathbb{R}^n : a_i^{\mathrm{T}}x \leqslant \beta_i,\ i = 1, \ldots, m\}$ has a nonempty interior $\mathrm{Int}(P)$, and we let

$$f(x) = \ln \prod_{i=1}^{m} (\beta_i - a_i^{\mathrm{T}}x), \quad x \in \mathrm{Int}(P),$$

then ξ is said to be an analytic center of (the linear system of inequalities defining) P if $f(\xi) \geqslant f(x)$ for all $x \in \mathrm{Int}(P)$. Huard's (1967) 'method of centers' for solving (nonlinear) convex programming problems was the first method to use the approach of approximately following a path of centers. In the linear programming case the notion of 'analytic center' is explored in Sonnevend (1986, 1987) and Bayer and Lagarias (1987a) and is the basis for Renegar's (1988) algorithm. That algorithm was the first path-following algorithm proposed for linear programming and, like the algorithms described below, it approximately follows the central path by using Newton's method and terminates in at most $O(\sqrt{n}L)$ iterations. A modified version requiring at most $O(n^3L)$ arithmetic operations has been developed by Vaidya (1987).

To solve the standard form linear program (9.37), the logarithmic barrier function method considers the family of problems

$$\mathrm{P}(\mu) \qquad \text{minimize} \quad f(x; \mu) \equiv c^{\mathrm{T}}x - \mu \sum_{j=1}^{n} \ln x_j$$
$$\text{subject to} \quad Ax = b, \quad x > 0,$$

where the barrier parameter μ is positive. Assume that (9.37) has a strictly positive feasible solution and that the set of its optimal solutions is nonempty and bounded – or equivalently, that the dual problem (9.42) has a solution with strictly positive slacks $s = c - A^{\mathrm{T}}y$. Then $\mathrm{P}(\mu)$ has a unique global minimizer $x(\mu)$ for all $\mu > 0$ and $x(\mu)$ converges to an optimal solution of (9.37) as $\mu \to 0$. For each μ, the minimizer $x(\mu)$ satisfies the Karush–Kuhn–Tucker necessary conditions

$$SXe - \mu e = 0, \tag{9.44a}$$

$$Ax - b = 0, \quad x > 0, \tag{9.44b}$$

$$A^{\mathrm{T}}y + s - c = 0. \tag{9.44c}$$

Since $\mu > 0$ and $x > 0$, (9.44a) implies that the vector of dual slacks s is strictly positive. Hence y is feasible in the dual problem (9.42) and in fact solves the corresponding dual barrier problem

D(μ)   maximize $b^\mathrm{T}y + \mu \sum_{j=1}^{n} \ln s_j$,

subject to $A^\mathrm{T}y + s = c$,

$s > 0$.

Kojima et al. (1989) were the first to propose an algorithm for following the path of solutions $\Gamma \equiv \{x(\mu), y(\mu), s(\mu): \mu > 0\}$ to (9.44) as $\mu \to 0$. Their algorithm, which converges in at most $O(nL)$ steps, and a similar but faster $O(\sqrt{n}L)$ algorithm developed independently by Kojima et al. (1987) and Monteiro and Adler (1987a), both apply a single step of Newton's method to (9.44) to obtain an approximation $(\bar{x}, \bar{y}, \bar{s})$ to $(x(\bar{\mu}), y(\bar{\mu}), s(\bar{\mu}))$, given an approximation (x, y, s) to $(x(\mu), y(\mu), s(\mu))$ where $\bar{\mu}$ is slightly smaller than μ.

One alternate way to follow the central path $\{x(\mu): \mu > 0\}$, or equivalently Γ, was proposed by Gonzaga (1989b). Given x, Gonzaga's method computes $\bar{x}$ by taking a single projected Newton step h for problem P($\bar{\mu}$). That is, it computes h by solving the equality constrained quadratic program

QP($\bar{\mu}$)   minimize $\frac{1}{2}\bar{\mu}h^\mathrm{T}X^{-2}h + (c - \bar{\mu}X^{-1}e)^\mathrm{T}h$

subject to $Ah = 0$,

obtained by approximating $f(x; \bar{\mu})$ in P($\bar{\mu}$) by its second order Taylor series expansion about the feasible point x. Notice that if h solves QP($\bar{\mu}$) then there exists a vector $\bar{y} \in \mathbb{R}^m$ such that

$$\bar{\mu}X^{-2}h + c - \bar{\mu}X^{-1}e - A^\mathrm{T}\bar{y} = 0 . \tag{9.45}$$

Since $Ah = 0$ we obtain from (9.45) that

$$h = \frac{1}{\mu} X^2(c - \bar{\mu}X^{-1}e - A^\mathrm{T}\bar{y})$$

where

$$(AX^2A^\mathrm{T})\bar{y} = AX^2(c - \bar{\mu}X^{-1}e) . \tag{9.46}$$

We can now formally state:

Algorithm 9.4 (primal path following).
   Choose a strictly feasible solution $x^0 > 0$ to (9.37) and constants $\mu_1 > 0$, $\tau > 0$, and $\sigma > 0$.
   For $k = 0, 1, \ldots$, do
   Iteration k: Let $X_k = \mathrm{diag}(x^k)$. Compute the solution y^{k+1} to

$$(AX_k^2A^\mathrm{T})y^{k+1} = AX_k^2(c - \mu_{k+1}X_k^{-1}e)$$

and let

$$s^{k+1} = c - A^T y^{k+1}, \qquad h^k = -(1/\mu_{k+1}) X_k^2 (s^{k+1} - \mu_{k+1} X_k^{-1} e)$$

and $x^{k+1} = x^k + h^k$. If $x^{k+1^T} s^{k+1} < \tau$, STOP: x^{k+1} is a near-optimal solution. Otherwise, set $\mu_{k+2} = (1 - \sigma/\sqrt{n}) \mu_{k+1}$.

We shall now prove that by properly choosing the initial point x^0, the barrier parameter's initial value μ_1 and its reduction factor σ, and the termination criterion τ, Algorithm 9.4 will obtain a solution x^k such that $c^T x^k - c^T x^* \le 2^{-L}$ in $O(\sqrt{n}L)$ iterations. Our proof depends upon three lemmas which show, respectively, that

(i) if the norm of the scaled step $X_k^{-1} h^k$ is small then (y^{k+1}, s^{k+1}) is dual feasible and the duality gap

$$s^{k+1^T} x^{k+1} = (c - A^T y^{k+1})^T x^{k+1} = c^T x^{k+1} - b^T y^{k+1}$$

is a small multiple of μ_{k+1};

(ii) if $\|X_k^{-1} h^k\|$ is small, then $\|X_{k+1}^{-1} h^{k+1}\|$ is also small; and

(iii) if x^0 is chosen to be the analytic center of the feasible region of (9.37) and μ_1 is chosen suitably large then $\|X_0^{-1} h^0\|$ is small.

Note that, if $\|X_k^{-1} h^k\|$ is small, then the norm of the left hand side of (9.44a) is a small multiple of μ, where $s = s^{k+1}$, $x = x^k$, and $\mu = \mu_{k+1}$. Hence x^k is close to the central path.

Lemma 9.4. *If* $\|X_k^{-1} h^k\| \le \delta \le 1$, *then* (y^{k+1}, s^{k+1}) *is dual feasible and*

$$0 \le (s^{k+1})^T x^{k+1} \le \mu_{k+1} (\delta + \sqrt{n})^2 .$$

Proof. Observe that on iteration k, (9.45) is equivalent to

$$s^{k+1} - \mu_{k+1} X_k^{-1} w^k = 0 , \tag{9.47a}$$

where

$$s^{k+1} = c - A^T y^{k+1} \tag{9.47b}$$

and

$$w^k = e - X_k^{-1} h^k . \tag{9.47c}$$

Since $\|X_k^{-1} h^k\| \le \delta \le 1$, $w^k \ge 0$ from (9.47c) and $s^{k+1} \ge 0$ from (9.47a). Consequently (y^{k+1}, s^{k+1}) is dual feasible and the duality gap is

$$(x^{k+1})^T s^{k+1} = \mu_{k+1} (x^{k+1})^T X_k^{-1} w^k \le \mu_{k+1} \|X_k^{-1} x^{k+1}\| \cdot \|w^k\|$$

$$\le \mu_{k+1} (\delta + \sqrt{n})^2$$

since

$$\|X_k^{-1}x^{k+1}\| \leqslant \|X_k^{-1}x^{k+1} - e\| + \|e\| = \|X_k^{-1}h^k\| + \|e\|$$

and $\|w^k\| \leqslant \|e\| + \|X_k^{-1}h^k\|$.

Lemma 9.5. *Let* $0 < \delta < 1$ *and* $0 < \sigma \leqslant \bar{\sigma} \equiv (\delta - \delta^2)/(1 + \delta/\sqrt{n})$. *If* $\|X_k^{-1}h^k\| \leqslant \delta$ *then* $\|X_{k+1}^{-1}h^{k+1}\| \leqslant \delta$.

Proof. Since $Ah^{k+1} = 0$, it follows from (9.47b) for iterations k and $k + 1$ that $(h^{k+1})^T s^{k+1} = (h^{k+1})^T c = (h^{k+1})^T s^{k+2}$. Hence from (9.47a) we have that

$$\mu_{k+1}(h^{k+1})^T X_k^{-1} w^k = \mu_{k+2}(h^{k+1})^T X_{k+1}^{-1} w^{k+1}.$$

Substituting for w^k and w^{k+1} using (9.47c) and rearranging terms yields

$$\mu_{k+2}(h^{k+1})^T X_{k+1}^{-2} h^{k+1} = \mu_{k+1}(h^{k+1})^T X_k^{-2} h^k + \mu_{k+2}(h^{k+1})^T X_{k+1}^{-1} e$$
$$- \mu_{k+1}(h^{k+1})^T X_k^{-1} e.$$

Now using $\mu_{k+2} = (1 - \sigma/\sqrt{n})\mu_{k+1}$ and the identity

$$X_{k+1}^{-1} e - X_k^{-1} e = -X_{k+1}^{-1} X_k^{-1} h^k$$

yields

$$\|X_{k+1}^{-1}h^{k+1}\|^2 = (h^{k+1})^T X_{k+1}^{-2} h^{k+1}$$
$$= \frac{1}{1 - \sigma/\sqrt{n}} (h^{k+1})^T X_{k+1}^{-1} \left[(X_{k+1}X_k^{-1} - I)X_k^{-1}h^k - \frac{\sigma}{\sqrt{n}} e \right].$$

It then immediately follows that

$$\|X_{k+1}^{-1}h^{k+1}\| \leqslant \frac{\delta^2 + \sigma}{1 - \sigma/\sqrt{n}} \equiv \theta$$

since

$$\|X_{k+1}X_k^{-1} - I\| = \max_j \left\{ \frac{x_j^{k+1}}{x_j} - 1 \right\} = \max_j \{ h_j^k/x_j^k \} \leqslant \delta.$$

Finally, if $\sigma \leqslant \bar{\sigma}$ then $\theta \leqslant \delta$. Moreover $\delta = \frac{1}{2}$ and $\sigma = \frac{1}{6}$ satisfy the conditions imposed on δ and σ.

Lemma 9.6. *If $x^0 > 0$ is feasible to (9.37) and*

$$X_0^{-1}e = A^T v, \quad \text{for some } v \in \mathbb{R}^m , \tag{9.48a}$$

and

$$\|X_0 c\| \leq \mu_1 \delta , \tag{9.48b}$$

then

$$\|X_0^{-1}h^0\| \leq \delta. \tag{9.49}$$

Proof. On the initial iteration, we have from (9.45) and (9.48a) that

$$\mu_1 X_0^{-2} h^0 + c - \mu_1 A^T v - A^T y^1 = 0 \quad \text{for some } v \text{ and } y_1 \in \mathbb{R}^m .$$

Since $Ah^0 = 0$, premultiplying by $(h^0)^T$ yields

$$\|X_0^{-1}h^0\|^2 = -\frac{1}{\mu_1} h_0^T c = -\frac{1}{\mu_1} (h^0)^T X_0^{-1} X_0 c \leq \frac{1}{\mu_1} \|X_0^{-1}h^0\|\|X_0 c\| .$$

whence (9.49) follows from (9.48b).

The condition (9.48a) requires that x^0 be an analytic center for (the linear system defining) the feasible region of (9.37), since it and the requirements that x^0 be strictly positive and feasible are Karush–Kuhn–Tucker conditions for the point x^0 to maximize $\Sigma_{j=1}^n \ln x_j$ subject to $Ax = b$, $x > 0$.

One way to satisfy (9.48a) is to scale the variables in (9.37) so that each is bounded by one and add an artificial variable and column to the problem (i.e., a 'big-M' approach) so that the point e is feasible. This results in the linear program

$$\text{minimize} \quad c^T \tilde{x} + M \tilde{x}_{k-1}$$

$$\text{subject to} \quad A\tilde{x} + (b/\rho - Ae)\tilde{x}_{k-1} = b/\rho ,$$

$$\tilde{x} + \tilde{x}_{k-1} + \tilde{x}_k = k ,$$

$$\tilde{x} \geq 0, \quad \tilde{x}_{k-1} \geq 0, \quad \tilde{x}_k \geq 0 ,$$

where $k = n + 2$ and $\tilde{x} = x/\rho$. Moreover, it suffices to take $\ln M$ and $\ln \rho$ to be $O(L)$ (e.g., see (Kojima et al. 1989) and (Monteiro and Alder 1987a,b)). Hence we can take $\mu_1 = 2^{O(L)}$ in Algorithm 9.4.

From Lemmas 9.4–9.6 and the above remarks we immediately obtain:

Theorem 9.3. *Let $\ln \mu_1 = O(L)$ and $\ln \tau = -O(L)$ and let the initial feasible point x^0 and constants δ and σ satisfy the conditions of Lemmas 9.4 and 9.5. Then for all $k \geq 1$, x^k is feasible to (9.37), (y^k, s^k) is dual feasible,*

$$\|X_k^{-1}h^k\| \leq \delta \, ,$$

and

$$s^{k^{\mathrm{T}}}x^k \leq \mu_k(\delta + \sqrt{n})^2 \, ,$$

and Algorithm 9.4 *terminates in at most* $\mathrm{O}(\sqrt{n}L)$ *iterations.*

This theorem shows that the path following algorithms have a worst case complexity bound on the number of iterations that is better than the bound for Karmarkar's algorithm and its variants by a factor of $n^{1/2}$. In (Gonzaga 1987) it is shown how to apply to the path following algorithms the modification introduced by Karmarkar, which allows each iteration to be performed in $\mathrm{O}(n^{2.5})$ arithmetic operations amortized over all iterations. Consequently these algorithms have a complexity bound of $\mathrm{O}(n^3L)$ arithmetic operations – the best bound yet achieved.

One of the nice things about path following algorithms is that they can be extended in a straightforward way to solve convex quadratic programs (Monteiro and Adler 1987b; Goldfarb and Liu 1988; Mehrotra and Sun 1987), linear complementarity problems (Kojima et al. 1987), quadratically constrained convex programs (Jarre 1988; Mehrotra and Sun 1988) and general convex programs (Monteiro and Adler 1987c; Mehrotra and Sun 1988b). On the negative side, the nice theoretical complexity bounds for these algorithms depend crucially on closely following the central path and hence require that very small steps be taken. In contrast the projective methods and the recently introduced potential function methods of Gonzaga (1988) and Ye (1988) allow large steps to be taken without destroying their theoretical properties.

9.6. Implementation

All variants of Karmarkar's algorithm and related methods described in the previous section require the solution of a sequence of symmetric positive definite systems of linear equations of the form

$$B_k y = r \tag{9.50}$$

where $B_k = AD_k^2A^{\mathrm{T}}$ and D_k is a positive diagonal matrix; e.g., see (9.25), (9.39) and (9.46). There are two basic approaches for solving such systems – direct methods and iterative methods – although as we shall see, sophisticated methods often combine both approaches.

Direct methods usually involve computing either the LU factorization

$$B_k = LU \tag{9.51}$$

using Gaussian elimination or the Cholesky factorization

$$B_k = \tilde{L}\tilde{L}^{\mathrm{T}} \, , \tag{9.52}$$

where L, U^T and $\tilde{L}$ are all $m \times m$ lower triangular matrices. All have positive diagonal elements, with those of L identically equal to one. Because of symmetry

$$L = D_u^{-1} U^T = D_u^{-1/2} \tilde{L} \, ,$$

where D_u is a diagonal matrix formed by setting all off-diagonal elements of U to zero. After B_k has been factorized, say into LU, the solution of (9.50) is easily obtained by successively solving the triangular systems

$$Lw = r \quad \text{and} \quad Uy = w$$

for w and y, respectively.

Because B_k is positive definite the factorizations (9.51) and (9.52) are numerically stable without any need for pivoting. If B_k is sparse, this means that we can try to find a symmetric permutation, PB_kP^T, of the rows and columns of B_k – here P is a permutation matrix – to give as sparse a factorization, or equivalently, to produce as little 'fill-in', as possible. Although finding such a permutation is NP-hard (Yannakakis 1981), there are several efficient ordering heuristics which usually yield good results. These include the 'minimum degree' ordering heuristic (Rose 1970; Tinney and Walker 1967) and the 'minimum local fill-in' ordering heuristic (Markowitz, 1957; Tinney and Walker 1967). The former is a symmetrized version of the so-called Markowitz criterion (Markowitz 1957) which was proposed for unsymmetric matrices. That criterion selects a pivot so as to minimize the product of the number of nonzeros in the pivotal row in columns that have not been pivotal and the number of nonzeros in the pivotal column in rows that have not been pivotal, excluding the pivot element itself in each case. Clearly, this product is an upper bound on the actual amount of fill-in produced by the prospective pivot. The 'minimum local fill-in' heuristic minimizes the number of non-zeros actually created on a single pivot and is far more expensive to execute than the 'minimum degree ordering' heuristic.

Since the matrix B_k has the same sparsity structure on every iteration k, 'symbolic' factorization of B_k – i.e., determination of the pivot sequence (symmetric permutation) and fill-in pattern from the non-zero pattern of AA^T and formation of the data structure for U, including fill-in entries – needs to be done only once at the start. Consequently, the extra effort required to execute the 'minimum local fill-in' heuristic does not necessarily rule out its use in favor of the 'minimum degree' heuristic.

When the matrix A contains several dense columns, B_k will be dense even if the overall density of A is very low. One way to deal with this situation, so that advantage can be taken of the sparsity in the non-dense columns of A, is to use the Sherman–Morrison–Woodbury (SMW) modification formula to effectively compute projections. Specifically, if A is a partitioned into sparse columns $\bar{A}$ and dense columns $\bar{\bar{A}}$ and the rows and columns of D_k are partitioned conformally, then

$$B_k = \bar{A}\bar{D}_k^2\bar{A}^{\mathrm{T}} + \bar{\bar{A}}\bar{\bar{D}}_k^2\bar{\bar{A}}^{\mathrm{T}}$$

and the SMW formula yields

$$B_k^{-1} = \bar{B}_k^{-1} - \bar{B}_k^{-1}\bar{\bar{A}}\bar{\bar{D}}_k^2(I - \bar{\bar{A}}^{\mathrm{T}}\bar{B}_k^{-1}\bar{\bar{A}}\bar{\bar{D}}_k^2)\bar{\bar{A}}^{\mathrm{T}}\bar{B}_k^{-1} ,$$

where $\bar{B}_k = \bar{A}\bar{D}_k\bar{A}^{\mathrm{T}}$ (see Lemma 4.3 for the rank-one case).

An alternate approach described in (Adler et al., 1986, 1987) is to compute the Cholesky factorization of $\bar{B}_k$, i.e.,

$$\bar{B}_k = \bar{L}_k\bar{L}_k^{\mathrm{T}}$$

and solve (9.50) by the 'preconditioned conjugate gradient' method using $\bar{L}_k$ as a preconditioner (e.g., see (Golub and Van Loan, 1983)). This is equivalent to solving

$$\bar{L}_k^{-1}B_k\bar{L}_k^{-\mathrm{T}}u = \bar{L}_k^{-1}r$$

by the conjugate gradient method and then setting $y = \bar{L}_k^{-\mathrm{T}}u$. The conjugate gradient method has been used with other or no preconditioners in several variants of Karmarkar's method to compute approximate projections. For example, see (Gill et al. 1986; Goldfarb and Mehrotra 1988a; Karmarkar and Ramakrishnan 1988; and Shanno and Marsten 1985).

During symbolic factorization all memory addresses needed to perform all subsequent numerical factorizations can be computed. This makes it possible for the symbolic factorization step to automatically generate loop-free code – i.e., a loop-free sequence of machine or FORTRAN instructions (the latter uses subscripts in place of memory addresses) for performing the numerical factorization – specific to the matrix at hand. See (Duff, Erisman and Reid 1986) and (Gay 1988) for details. However, the storage requirements of such an approach grow very rapidly with problem size. An alternate approach is to generate an 'operations list' – i.e., an array of pointers to the locations of the elements that are arithmetically combined in each line of standard loop-free FORTRAN code in the numerical factorization step. This approach since it requires less memory than automatic generation of loop-free code can be used for moderately sized problems (e.g., see (Adler et al. 1987)) but its enormous storage demands make it prohibitive for large problems.

Although the factorization of B_k is the most time consuming task in Karmarkar's algorithm, the time required just to form B_k is also significant. (A similar statement applies more generally to the normal equations for solving a linear least squares problem.) Since B_k can be expressed as a sum of symmetric rank-one outer products

$$B_k = \sum_{j=1}^{m} D_k^2(j, j)(Ae_j)(Ae_j)^{\mathrm{T}} ,$$

and only D_k changes from iteration to iteration, computational effort can be saved by computing all outer-products $(Ae_j)(Ae_j)^{\mathrm{T}}$, $j = 1, \ldots, m$, at the start of the algorithm, storing their upper-diagonal elements for later use. Additional savings are effected if inexact projections, as first suggested by Karmarkar (1984a, b), are used. In this scheme an approximate scaling matrix $\tilde{D}_k$ is used and $\tilde{D}_k(j, j)$ is kept the same as $\tilde{D}_{k-1}(j, j)$ unless the relative difference $|D_k(j, j) - \tilde{D}_{k-1}(j, j)|/|\tilde{D}_{k-1}(j, j)|$ is not small, in which case $\tilde{D}_k(j, j)$ is set to the exact value $D_k(j, j)$, and B_k is computed as

$$B_k = B_{k-1} + \sum_{j=1}^{m} (\tilde{D}_k^2(j, j) - \tilde{D}_{k-1}^2(j, j))(Ae_j)(Ae_j)^{\mathrm{T}} .$$

9.7. Theoretical and computational significance

It is far too early to make a definitive statement on the comparative computational performance of Karmarkar's algorithm and the simplex method. There are many variants of both algorithms, and more importantly, differences in implementation lead to vastly different behaviors on large sparse problems. Both methods are very sensitive to the structure of the problem; simplex methods perform very poorly on time-staged formulations, whereas the projective method prefers such 'low-bandwidth' problems; on the other hand, the reverse situation is likely to hold if each basis matrix B is relatively sparse with BB^{T} relatively dense. However, a number of computational investigations with great variability in variant used, sophistication of implementation, and classes of problems attacked, have all confirmed a highly significant finding; the new methods typically require only 20–50 iterations to provide highly accurate solutions even to very large problems, and the number of iterations grows very slowly if at all with the problem dimension. This result contrasts strongly with the worst-case bound, which indicates at least linear growth with n.

On the other hand, the time taken per iteration with any straightforward implementation renders the complete algorithm uncompetitive with modern simplex codes, and it is necessary to take great care in handling the large sparse least-squares subproblems that arise. When this is done, the result can be a computer code that appears at least comparable to the simplex implementations, and at least on some large-scale problems superior – see (Adler, Karmarkar, Resende and Veiga 1986; Gill, Murray, Saunders, Tomlin and Wright 1986; and Karmarkar and Ramakrishnan 1988).

In contrast to our cautiously optimistic view of the new algorithm's computational significance, it appears that its theoretical implications are far more limited than those of the ellipsoid method. Indeed, Karmarkar's algorithm requires the linear programming problem to be given explicitly with all its constraints and variables listed, and does not appear directly susceptible to column or constraint generation. Thus it cannot be used to provide polynomial algorithms for several combinatorial optimization problems that have been successfully analyzed by the ellipsoid method. Similarly, it seems hard to develop in this framework the many useful post-optimality techniques for handling the addition of new variables or constraints to a given linear programming problem that has already been solved. Doubtless much research will be devoted to providing such flexibility for Karmarkar's algorithm and methods related to it in the coming years.

This striking contrast between the ellipsoid method and the projective algorithm with respect to their computational and theoretical significance prompts us to conclude by remarking on the close similarity between the fundamental subproblems to be solved at each iteration of the two methods. In the ellipsoid method, the center $\bar{y}$ of the current ellipsoid is the solution to the weighted least-squares problem

$$\min_{y \in \mathbb{R}^m} \| D^{1/2}(A^{\mathrm{T}} \bar{y} - r) \|$$

as in (8.18), while in Karmarkar's algorithm the dual solution $\bar{y}$ which leads to the search direction $\hat{d}$ used in the primal solves the weighted least-squares problem

$$\min_{y \in \mathbb{R}^m} \| \bar{X}(A^{\mathrm{T}} \bar{y} - c) \|$$

as in (9.27). The difference lies in the way the weighting matrix $D^{1/2}$ or $\bar{X}$ changes at each iteration. In the ellipsoid method, as we have indicated, only one diagonal entry of D changes; this leads to a simple update of $\bar{y}$, but a very large number of iterations. In projective algorithms all diagonal entries of $\bar{X}$ change, in a sophisticated way; this means a fresh least-squares subproblem must be solved at each iteration, but the number of iterations required appears very low.

References

Adler, I., Karmarkar, N., Resende, M.G.C., and Veiga, G. (1986), An implementation of Karmarkar's algorithm for linear programming, Working Paper, Operations Research Center, University of California, Berkeley, CA.

Adler, I., Karmarkar, N., Resende, M.G.C., and Veiga, G. (1987), Data structures and programming techniques for the implementation of Karmarkar's algorithm, Working Paper, Operations Research Center, University of California, Berkeley, CA.

Alder, I., Karp, R.M., and Shamir, R. (1983), A simplex variant solving an $m \times d$ linear program in $O(\min(m^2, d^2))$ expected number of pivot steps, Report UCB/CSD83/158, Computer Science Division, University of California, Berkeley, CA.

Adler, I. and Megiddo, N. (1984), A simplex algorithm whose average number of steps is bounded between two quadratic functions of the smaller dimension, *Journal of the Association for Computing Machinery* **32**, 871–895.

Anstreicher, K.M. (1986), A monotonic projective algorithm for fractional linear programming, *Algorithmica* **1**, 483–498.

Balinski, M.L. and Russakoff, A. (1972), On the assignment polytope, *Mathematical Programming* **3**, 257–258.

Barnes, E.R. (1986), A variation on Karmarkar's algorithm for solving linear programming problems, *Mathematical Programming* **36**, 174–182.

Bartels, R.H. (1971), A stabilization of the simplex method, *Numerische Mathematik* **16**, 414–434.

Bartels, R.H. and Golub, G.H. (1969), The simplex method for linear programming using LU decomposition, *Communications of the ACM* **12**, 266–268.

Bayer, D. and Lagarias, J.C. (1987a), The nonlinear geometry of linear programming, I. Affine and projective scaling trajectories, to appear in *Transactions of the American Mathematical Society*, 1989.

Bayer, D. and Lagarias, J.C. (1987b), The nonlinear geometry of linear programming, II. Legendre transform coordinates and central trajectories, to appear in *Transactions of the American Mathematical Society*, 1989.

Beale, E.M.L. (1954), An alternative method for linear programming, *Proceedings of the Cambridge Philosophical Society* **50**, 513–523.

Blair, C.E. (1986), The iterative step in the linear programming algorithm of N. Karmarkar, *Algorithmica* **1**, 537–539.

Bland, R.G., Goldfarb, D., and Todd, M.J. (1981), The ellipsoid method: a survey, *Operations Research* **29**, 1039–1091.

Bolza, O. (1914), Über variations probleme mit Ungleichungen als Nebenbedingungen, *Mathematische Abhandlungen* (H.A. Schwartz, ed.), 1–18.

Borgwardt, K.H. (1987), *The Simplex Method: A Probabilistic Analysis* (Springer-Verlag, Berlin).

Burrell, B.P. and Todd, M.J. (1985), The ellipsoid method generates dual variables, *Mathematics of Operations Research* **10**, 688–700.

Chvátal, V. (1983), *Linear Programming* (Freeman, New York).

Dantzig, G.B. (1951), Maximization of a linear function of variables subject to linear inequalities, in: Tj. C. Koopmans (ed.), *Activity Analysis of Production and Allocation* (Wiley, New York) 339–347.

Dantzig, G.B. (1963), *Linear Programming and Extensions* (Princeton University Press, Princeton, NJ).

Dantzig, G.B. and Van Slyke, R.M. (1967), Generalized upper bounding techniques, *Journal of Computer System Sciences* **1**, 213–226.

Dantzig, G.B. and Wolfe, Ph. (1960), Decomposition principle for linear programs, *Operations Research* **8**, 101–111.

de Ghellinck, G. and Vial, J.-Ph. (1986), A polynomial Newton method for linear programming, *Algorithmica* **1**, 425–453.

Dennis, J.E., Jr., Morshedi, A.M., and Turner, K. (1987), A variable-metric variant of the Karmarkar algorithm for linear programming, *Mathematical Programming* **39**, 1–20.

Dikin, I.I. (1967), Iterative solution of problems of linear and quadratic programming, *Doklady Akademiia Nauk SSSR* **174**, 747–748 [English translation: *Soviet Mathematics Doklady* **8**, 674–675].

Dikin, I.I. (1974), On the convergence of an iterative process, *Upravlyaemye Sistemi* **12**, 54–60 (in Russian).

Dorfman, R., Samuelson, P.A., and Solow, R.M. (1958), *Linear Programming and Economic Analysis* (McGraw-Hill, New York).

Duff, I.S., Erisman, A.M., and Reid, J.K. (1986), *Direct Methods for Sparse Matrices* (Clarendon Press, Oxford).

Ecker, J.G. and Kupferschmidt, M. (1985), A computational comparison of the ellipsoid algorithm with several nonlinear programming algorithms, *SIAM Journal on Control and Optimization* **23**, 657–674.

Farkas, J. (1902), Theorie der einfachen Ungleichungen, *Journal für die reine und angewandte Mathematik* **124**, 1–27.

Fiacco, A.V. and McCormick, G.P. (1968), *Nonlinear Programming: Sequential Unconstrained Minimization Techniques* (Wiley, New York).

Forrest, J.J.H. and Tomlin, J.A. (1972), Updating triangular factors of the basis to maintain sparsity in the product form of the simplex method, *Mathematical Programming* **2**, 263–278.

Fourier, J.B.J. (1826), Solution d'une question particulière du calcul des inégalités, *Nouveau Bulletin des Sciences par la Société Philomathique de Paris*, 99–100.

Frisch, K.R. (1955), The logarithmic potential method of convex programming, Memorandum, University Institute of Economics, Oslo, Norway,

Gács, P. and Lovász, L. (1981), Khachiyan's algorithm for linear programming, *Mathematical Programming Study* **14**, 61–68.

Gale, D. (1960), *The Theory of Linear Economic Models* (McGraw-Hill, New York).

Gallo, G. and Sandi, C. (1986), Netflow at Pisa, *Mathematical Programming Study* **26**.

Gay, D. (1987), A variant of Karmarkar's linear programming algorithm for problems in standard form, *Mathematical Programming* **37**, 81–90.

Gay, D.M. (1988), Massive memory buys little speed for complete, in-core sparse Cholesky factorizations, Manuscript, AT&T Bell Laboratories, Murray, Hill, NJ.

Gill, P.E., Murray, W., Saunders, M.A., Tomlin, J.A., and Wright, M.H. (1986), On projected Newton barrier methods for linear programming and an equivalance to Karmarkar's projective method, *Mathematical Programming* **36**, 183–209.

Gilmore, P.C. and Gomory, R.E. (1961), A linear programming approach to the cutting-stock problem, *Operations Research* **9**, 849–859.

Gilmore, P.C. and Gomory, R.E. (1963), A linear programming approach to the cutting-stock problem–Part II, *Operations Research* **11**, 863–888.

Goldfarb, D. and Liu, S. (1988), An $O(n^3L)$ primal interior point algorithm for convex quadratic programming, Manuscript, Department of Industrial Engineering and Operations Research, Columbia University, New York.

Goldfarb, D. and Mehrotra, S. (1988a), A relaxed version of Karmarkar's method, *Mathematical Programming* **40**, 289–315.

Goldfarb, D. and Mehrotra, S. (1988b), Relaxed variants of Karmarkar's algorithm for linear programs with unknown optimal objective value, *Mathematical Programming* **40**, 183–195.

Goldfarb, D. and Mehrotra, S. (1988c), A self-correcting version of Karmarkar's algorithm, Manuscript, Department of Industrial Engineering and Operations Research, Columbia University, New York; to appear in *SIAM Journal on Numerical Analysis* **26** (1989).

Goldfarb, D. and Reid, J.K. (1977), A practicable steepest-edge simplex algorithm, *Mathematical Programming* **12**, 361–371.

Golub, G.H. and Van Loan, C.F. (1983), *Matrix Computations* (Johns Hopkins University Press, Baltimore, MD).

Gonzaga, C. (1988), Polynomial affine algorithms for linear programming, Report ES-139/88, Universidade Federal do Rio de Janeiro, Brazil.

Gonzaga, C. (1989a), A conical projection algorithm for linear programming, *Mathematical Programming* **43**, 151–173.

Gonzaga, C. (1989b), An algorithm for solving linear programming in $O(n^3L)$ operations, in: N. Meggido (ed.), *Progress in Mathematical Programming* (Springer-Verlag, New York) 1–28.

Grötschel, M., Lovász, L., and Schrijver, A. (1981), The ellipsoid method and its consequences in combinatorial optimization, *Combinatorica* **1**, 169–197.

Grötschel, M., Lovász, L., and Schrijver, A. (1988), *The Ellipsoid Method and Combinatorial Optimization* (Springer-Verlag, Heidelberg).

Hellerman, E. and Rarick, D. (1971), Reinversion with the preassigned pivot procedure, *Mathematical Programming* **1**, 195–216.

Hellerman, E. and Rarick, D. (1972), The partitioned preassigned pivot procedure (P^4), in: D.J. Rose and R.A. Willoughby (eds.), *Sparse Matrices and their Applications* (Plenum Press, New York) 67–76.

Ho, J.K. (1987), Recent advances in decomposition, *Mathematical Programming Study* **31**, 119–128.

Huard, P. (1967), Resolution of mathematical programming with nonlinear constraints by the method of centers, in: J. Abadie (ed.), *Nonlinear Programming* (North-Holland, Amsterdam).

Jarre, F. (1987), On the convergence of the method of analytic centers when applied to convex quadratic programs, Manuscript, Institut für Angewandte Mathematik und Statistik, Universität Wurzburg, Wurzburg.

John, F. (1948), Extremum problems with inequalities as subsidary conditions, *Studies and Essays* (Interscience, New York) 187–204.

Kantorovich, L.V. (1939), *Mathematical Methods of Organizing and Planning Production* (in Russian) (Publication House of the Leningrad State University, Leningrad); English translation: *Management Science* **6** (1959–60), 366–422.

Kapoor, S. and Vaidya, P.M. (1986), Fast algorithms for convex quadratic programming and multicommodity flows, *Proceedings of the 18th ACM Symposium on Theory of Computing*, 147–159.

Karmarkar, N. (1984a), A new polynomial time algorithm for linear programming, *Proceedings of the 16th Annual ACM Symposium on the Theory of Computing*, 302–311.

Karmarkar, N. (1984b), A new polynomial time algorithm for linear programming, *Combinatorica* **4**, 373–395.

Karmarkar, N. and Ramakrishnan, K.G. (1988), Implementation and computational results of the Karmarkar algorithm for linear programming, using an iterative method for computing projections, Extended abstract. AT&T Bell Laboratories, Murray Hill, NJ, presented at the XIII International Symposium on Mathematical Programming, Tokyo.

Karmarkar, N. and Sinha, L.P. (1985), Application of Karmarkar's algorithm to overseas telecommunications facilities planning, Paper presented at XII International Symposium on Mathematical Programming, Boston, MA.

Karp, R.M. and Papadimitriou, C.H. (1982), On linear characterizations of combinatorial optimization problems, *SIAM Journal on Computing* **11**, 620–632.

Karush, W. (1939), Minima of Functions of Several Variables with Inequalities as Side Constraints, M.Sc. Dissertation, Department of Mathematics, University of Chicago, Chicago, IL.

Kennington, J.L. (1978), A survey of linear cost multicommodity network flows, *Operations Research* **26**, 209–236.

Khachian, L.G. (1979), A polynomial algorithm in linear programming (in Russian), *Doklady Akademiia Nauk SSSR* **244**, 1093–1096; English translation: *Soviet Mathematics Doklady* **20**, 191–194.

Khachian, L.G. (1980), Polynomial algorithms in linear programming (in Russian), *Zhurnal Vychisditel'noi Matematiki i Matematicheskoi Fiziki* **20**, 51–68; English translation: *USSR Computational Mathematics and Mathematical Physics* **20**, 53–72.

Klee, V. and Minty, G.J. (1972), How good is the simplex algorithm?, in: O. Shisha (ed.), *Inequalities III* (Academic Press, New York) 159–175.

Klingman, D. and Russell, R. (1975), Solving constrained transportation problems, *Operations Research* **23**, 91–106.

Kojima, M., Mizuno, S. and Yoshise, A. (1987), A polynomial-time algorithm for a class of linear complementarity problems, Research Report No. B–193, Department of Information Sciences, Tokyo Institute of Technology, Tokyo, Japan; to appear in *Mathematical Programming* **44** (1989).

Kojima, M., Mizuno, S., and Yoshise, A. (1989), A primal-dual interior point method for linear programming, in: N. Meggido (ed.), *Progress in Mathematical Programming* (Springer-Verlag, New York) 29–47.

Kuhn, H.W. and Tucker, A.W. (1951), Nonlinear programming, in: *Proceedings of the Second Berkeley Symposium on Mathematical Statistics and Probability* (University of California Press, Berkeley, CA) 481–492.

Lemke, C.E. (1954), The dual method of solving the linear programming problem, *Naval Research Logistics Quarterly* **1**, 36–47.

Levin, A. Yu. (1965), On an algorithm for the minimization of convex functions (in Russian), *Doklady Akademiia Nauk SSR* **160**, 1244–1247; English translation: *Soviet Mathematics Doklady* **6**, 286–290.

Markowitz, H.M. (1957), The elimination form of the inverse and its application to linear programming, *Management Science* **3**, 255–269.

McShane, K.A., Monma, C.L., and Shanno, D. (1988), An implementation of a primal-dual interior point method for linear programming, Rutcor Research Report, Rutgers University, New Brunswick, NJ.

Megiddo, N. (1984), Linear programming in linear time when the dimension is fixed, *Journal of the Association for Computing Machinery* **31**, 114–127.

Megiddo, N. (1987), On the complexity of linear programming, in: T. Bewley (ed.), *Advances in Economic Theory* (Cambridge University Press, Cambridge) 225–268.

Megiddo, N. (1989), Pathways to the optimal set in linear programming, in: N. Meggido (ed.), *Progress in Mathematical Programming* (Springer-Verlag, New York) 131–158.

Megiddo, N. and Shub, M. (1989), Boundary behavior of interior point algorithms in linear programming, *Mathematics of Operations Research* **14**, 97–146.

Mehrotra, S. and Sun, J. (1987), An algorithm for convex quadratic programming that requires $O(n^{3.5}L)$ arithmetic operations, Manuscript, Department of Industrial Engineering and Management Science, Northwestern University, Evanston, IL.

Mehrotra, S. and Sun, J. (1988a), A method of analytic centers for quadratically constrained convex quadratic programs, Manuscript, Department of Industrial Engineering and Management Sciences, Northwestern University, Evanston, IL.

Mehrotra, S. and Sun, J. (1988b), An interior point algorithm for solving smooth convex programs based on Newton's method, Manuscript, Department of Industrial Engineering and Management Sciences, Northwestern University, Evanston, IL.

Monma, C.L. and Morton, A.J. (1987), Computational experience with a dual affine variant of Karmarkar's method for linear programming, *Operations Research Letters* **6**, 261–267.

Monteiro, R.C. and Adler, I. (1987a), An $O(n^3L)$ primal–dual interior point algorithm for linear programming, Manuscript, Department of Industrial Engineering and Operations Research, University of California, Berkeley, CA, to appear in *Mathematical Programming* **44** (1989).

Monteiro, R.C. and Adler, I. (1987b), An $O(n^3L)$ interior point algorithm for convex quadratic programming, Manuscript, Department of Industrial Engineering and Operations Research, University of California, Berkeley, CA; to appear in *Mathematical Programming* **44** (1989).

Monteiro, R.C. and Adler, I. (1987c), An extension of Karmarkar type algorithm to a class of convex separable programming problems with global linear rate of convergence, Manuscript, Department of Industrial Engineering and Operations Research, University of California, Berkeley, CA.

Murtagh, B.A. and Saunders, M.A. (1978), Large-scale linearly constrained optimization, *Mathematical Programming* **14**, 41–72.

Murty, K.G. (1980), Computational complexity of parametric linear programming, *Mathematical Programming* **19**, 213–219.

Murty, K.G. (1983), *Linear Programming* (John Wiley, New York).

Newman, D.J. (1965), Location of the maximum on unimodal surfaces, *Journal of the Association for Computing Machinery* **12**, 395–398.

Padberg, M.W. (1985), A different convergence proof of the projective method for linear programming, Report, New York University, New York.

Padberg, M.W. and Rao, M.R. (1980), The Russian method and integer programming, GBA Working Paper, New York University, New York.

Reid, J.K. (1982), A sparsity-exploiting variant of the Bartels–Golub decomposition for linear programming bases, *Mathematical Programming* **24**, 55–69.

Renegar, J. (1988), A polynomial-time algorithm based on Newton's method for linear programming, *Mathematical Programming* **40**, 59–93.

Rose, D.J. (1970), Symmetric elimination on sparse positive definite sysems and potential flow network problem, Ph.D. Thesis, Harvard University, Cambridge, MA.

Saunders, M.A. (1976), A fast stable implementation of the simplex method using Bartels–Golub updating, in: J.R. Bunch and D.J. Rose (eds.), *Sparse Matrix Computations* (Academic Press, New York) 213–226.

Schrage, L. (1975), Implicit representation of variable upper bounds in linear programming, *Mathematical Programming Study* **4**, 118–132.

Schrijver, A. (1986), *Theory of Linear and Integer Programming* (John Wiley, Chichester–New York).

Shamir, R. (1987), The efficiency of the simplex method: a survey, *Management Science* **33**, 301–334.

Shanno, D.F. (1988), Computing Karmarkar projections quickly, *Mathematical Programming* **41**, 61–71.

Shanno, D.F. and Marsten, R.E. (1985), On implementing Karmarkar's algorithm, Working Paper, Graduate School of Administration, University of California, Davis, CA.

Shor, N.Z. (1970), Utilization of the operation of space dilatation in the minimization of convex functions (in Russian), *Kibernetika* **1**, 6–12; English translation: *Cybernetics* **6**, 7–15.

Shor, N.Z. (1985), *Minimization Methods for Non-Differentiable Functions* (Springer-Verlag, Berlin).

Sonnevend, G. (1986), An analytical centre for polyhedrons and new classes of global algorithms for linear (smooth, convex) programming, *System Modelling and Optimization*, Budapest; *Lecture Notes in Control and Information Sciences* No. 84 (Springer-Verlag, Berlin) 866–875.

Sonnevend, G. (1987), A new method for solving a set of linear (convex) inequalities and its application for identification and optimization, *Dynamic Modelling and Control of National Economies* (Pergamon, Oxford–New York).

Steger, A. (1985), An extension of Karmarkar's Algorithm for Bounded Linear Programming Problems, M.S. Thesis, SUNY at Stony Brook, NY.

Tardos, E. (1986), A strongly polynomial algorithm to solve combinatorial linear programs, *Operations Research* **35**, 250–256.

Tinney, W.F. and Walker, J.W. (1967), Direct solutions of sparse network equations by optimally ordered triangular factorization, *Proceedings of the IEEE* **55**, 1801–1809.

Todd, M.J. (1982), An implementation of the simplex method for linear programming problems with variable upper bounds, *Mathematical Programming* **23**, 34–49.

Todd, M.J. (1983), Large-scale linear programming: geometry, working bases and factorization, *Mathematical Programming* **26**, 1–20.

Todd, M.J. (1986), Polynomial expected behavior of a pivoting algorithm for linear complementarity and linear programming problems, *Mathematical Programming* **35**, 173–192.

Todd, M.J. (1988a), Polynomial algorithms for linear programming, in: H.A. Eiselt and G. Pederzoli (eds.), *Advances in Optimization and Control* (Springer-Verlag, Berlin) 49–66.

Todd, M.J. (1988b), Improved bounds and containing ellipsoids in Karmarkar's linear programming algorithm, *Mathematics of Operations Research* **13**, 650–659.

Todd, M.J. and Burrell, B.P. (1986), An extension of Karmarkar's algorithm for linear programming using dual variables, *Algorithmica* **1**, 409–424.

Vaidya, P.M. (1987), An algorithm for linear programming which requires $O(((m + n)n^2 + (m + n)^{1.5}n)L)$ arithmetic operations, Preprint, AT&T Bell Laboratories, Murray Hill, NJ.

Valentine, F.A. (1937), The problem of Lagrange with differential inequalities as added side conditions, *Contributions to the Calculus of Variations 1933–37* (University of Chicago Press, Chicago, IL).

Vanderbei, R.J. and Lagarias, J.C. (1988), I.I. Dikin's convergence result for the affine–scaling algorithm, Manuscript, AT&T Bell Laboratories, Murray Hill, NJ.

Vanderbei, R.J., Meketon, M.S., and Freedman, B.A. (1986), A modification of Karmarkar's linear programming algorithm, *Algorithmica* **1**, 395–407.

Vial, J.-Ph. (1989), Approximate projections in a projective method for the linear feasibility problem, in: N. Meggido (ed.), *Progress in Mathematical Programming* (Springer-Verlag, New York) 65–78.

Yannakakis, M. (1981), Computing the minimum fill-in is NP-complete, *SIAM Journal on Algebraic and Discrete Methods* **2**, 77–79.

Ye, Y. (1987), Karmarkar's algorithm and the ellipsoid method, *Operations Research Letters* **4**, 177–182.

Ye, Y. (1988), An $O(n^3 L)$ potential reduction algorithm for linear programming, Manuscript, Department of Management Sciences, The University of Iowa, Iowa City, IA; to appear in *Mathematical Programming*.

Ye, Y. and Kojima, M. (1987), Recovering optimal dual solutions in Karmarkar's polynomial algorithm for linear programming, *Mathematical Programming* **39**, 305–317.

Yudin, D.B. and Nemirovskii, A.S. (1976), Informational complexity and efficient methods for the solution of convex extremal problems (in Russian), *Ékonomika i Mathematicheskie Metody* **12**, 357–369; English translation: *Matekon* **13**(2), 3–25.

Zadeh, N. (1973), A bad network problem for the simplex method and other minimum cost flow algorithms, *Mathematical Programming* **5**, 255–266.

G.L. Nemhauser et al., Eds., *Handbooks in OR & MS, Vol. 1*
© Elsevier Science Publishers B.V. (North-Holland) 1989

Chapter III

Constrained Nonlinear Programming

Philip E. Gill, Walter Murray,
Michael A. Saunders and Margaret H. Wright

Systems Optimization Laboratory, Department of Operations Research, Stanford University,
Stanford, CA 94305-4022, U.S.A.

1. Equality constraints

Broadly speaking, the constrained nonlinear programming problem involves minimization of a smooth nonlinear function subject to smooth constraints on a finite set of continuous variables. This problem can be stated in several forms whose appropriateness varies with the context. We shall sometimes distinguish constraint types in order to emphasize different algorithmic approaches.

To simplify the exposition, we first consider algorithms for a problem in which all constraints are *equalities*:

$$\text{NEP} \qquad \underset{x \in \mathbb{R}^n}{\text{minimize}} \quad f(x)$$
$$\text{subject to} \quad c(x) = 0 , \tag{1.1}$$

where $c(x)$ is an m-vector of nonlinear functions with i-th component $c_i(x)$, $i = 1, \ldots, m$, and f and $\{c_i\}$ are twice-continuously differentiable. Let $g(x)$ denote the gradient vector of $f(x)$, $a_i(x)$ the gradient vector of $c_i(x)$, and $A(x)$ the $m \times n$ Jacobian matrix of $c(x)$. A solution of NEP will be denoted by x^*.

The most powerful algorithms for solving NEP are based on seeking a point satisfying conditions that hold at the solution. The key role of optimality conditions in algorithm design has already been discussed in the context of *unconstrained* problems, in which the gradient of the objective function must vanish at the solution, and the Hessian matrix must be positive semidefinite. We seek analogous conditions for constrained problems.

Definition 1.1. A point $\hat{x} \in \mathbb{R}^n$ is *feasible* with respect to the constraint $c_i(x) = 0$ if $c_i(\hat{x}) = 0$ (in which case we say that the constraint is satisfied at $\hat{x}$).

The material contained in this paper is based upon research supported by the Air Force Office of Scientific Research Grant 87-01962; the U.S. Department of Energy Grant DE-FG03-87ER25030; National Science Foundation Grant CCR-8413211; and the Office of Naval Research Contract N00014-87-K-0142.

Otherwise, $\hat{x}$ is *infeasible*, and we say that the constraint is violated at $\hat{x}$. A point $\hat{x}$ is feasible with respect to the set of constraints $c(x) = 0$ if it is feasible with respect to every constraint.

Definition 1.2. The point x^* is a *local minimizer* (or local solution) of NEP if:
    (i) x^* is feasible with respect to all the constraints;
    (ii) there exists a neighborhood $N(x^*)$ such that

$$f(x^*) \leq f(x) \quad \text{for all feasible } x \in N(x^*). \tag{1.2}$$

If inequality (1.2) is strict for all feasible $x \in N(x^*)$, $x \neq x^*$, then x^* is said to be a *strong* or *strict* local minimizer. Otherwise, x^* is called a *weak* local minimizer.

In order to verify that Definition 1.2 applies at a feasible point, a characterization is needed of neighboring feasible points. In general, feasibility can be retained with respect to nonlinear equality constraints only by movement along a *nonlinear* path in $\mathbb{R}^n$, which is called a *feasible arc*. For example, the nonlinear constraint $x_1^2 + x_2^2 = 1$ defines a unit circle in $\mathbb{R}^2$, centered at the origin, whose curved boundary is a feasible arc. In general, a *feasible arc* is a directed differentiable curve $x(\alpha)$ emanating from a feasible point x, parameterized by the scalar α such that $x(0) = x$ and

$$c(x(\alpha)) = 0 \,,$$

for all α satisfying $0 \leq \alpha \leq \bar{\alpha}$, where $\bar{\alpha} > 0$, and $dx(0)/d\alpha \neq 0$.

If a feasible arc exists at the feasible point x, then every neighborhood of x contains feasible points. To test optimality, a condition is needed that indicates whether a feasible arc exists. The Taylor series expansion of c along any direction p is

$$c(x + \varepsilon p) = c(x) + \varepsilon A(x)p + O(\varepsilon^2 \| p \|^2) \,, \tag{1.3}$$

where ε is any scalar. The points along a path from x to a neighboring feasible point will be feasible only if the direction of movement from x is *tangent* to a feasible arc. The relationship (1.3) implies that p will be tangent to a feasible arc only if

$$A(x)p = 0 \,. \tag{1.4}$$

(If (1.4) does not hold, even an infinitesimal move along any path tangent to p will lead to a constraint violation.) Unfortunately, the nonlinearity of $c(x)$ means that condition (1.4) is not *sufficient* to ensure that p is tangent to a feasible arc. Requirements that $c(x)$ must satisfy in order to permit analysis of feasible arcs are called *constraint qualifications*, and have been widely studied. We consider only one constraint qualification for equality constraints. (For further discussion, see, e.g., Kuhn and Tucker (1951), Fiacco and McCormick (1968).)

Definition 1.3 (Constraint qualification for equality constraints). The constraint qualification with respect to the equality constraints $c(x) = 0$ holds at the feasible point x if every nonzero vector p satisfying (1.4) is tangent to a twice-differentiable feasible arc emanating from x.

When the constraints are *linear*, the constraint qualification always holds. For nonlinear constraints, however, Definition 1.3 has the unsatisfactory feature that it cannot easily be checked. In contrast, the following result provides a computationally practical test for verifying satisfaction of the constraint qualification when the constraints are nonlinear. (See Fiacco and McCormick (1968) for a proof.)

Theorem 1.1 (Regular point for equality constraints). *If x is feasible and $A(x)$ has full rank, the constraint qualification holds at x, and x is said to be a regular point.* □

At a regular point, (1.4) provides a complete characterization of tangents to feasible arcs. Relation (1.4) states that p lies in the *null space* of the matrix $A(x)$. Given a point x, let $Z(x)$ denote a (non-unique) matrix whose columns form a basis for the null space of $A(x)$, so that

$$A(x)Z(x) = 0 . \tag{1.5}$$

The relationship (1.5) is crucial in all subsequent analysis. (We shall henceforth use Z as a generic notation for a basis for the null space, where the relevant point x and matrix A should always be clear from context. Note that a basis for the null space exists even when $A(x)$ is rank-deficient.) By definition of a basis, every vector p such that $Ap = 0$ may be written as a linear combination of the columns of Z, so that

$$Ap = 0 \quad \text{if and only if} \quad p = Zp_Z$$

for some vector p_Z.

We now state the well known *first-order Karush–Kuhn–Tucker* conditions for a solution of NEP.

Theorem 1.2 (First-order necessary optimality conditions). *If the constraint qualification holds at x^*, a necessary condition for x^* to be a local minimizer of NEP is that*

$$g(x^*) = A(x^*)^T\lambda^* = \sum_{i=1}^{m} \lambda_i^* a_i(x^*) , \tag{1.6}$$

for some λ^*. Equivalently, if $Z(x)$ denotes a null-space basis for $A(x)$, then

$$Z(x^*)^T g(x^*) = 0 . \tag{1.7}$$

174 P.E. Gill et al.

Proof. Assume that x^* is a local minimizer of NEP, and consider all nonzero vectors p such that

$$A(x^*)p = 0 . \tag{1.8}$$

(If there are none, then (1.6) must hold, since the columns of $A(x^*)$ span all of $\mathbb{R}^n$.)

By hypothesis, the constraint qualification holds at x^*, and hence any vector p satisfying (1.8) is tangent to a feasible arc emanating from x^*. From Definition 1.2, x^* can be a local minimizer only if f does not strictly decrease along any such arc, which implies that $g(x^*)^\mathrm{T}p = 0$. It follows from standard linear algebra that if $g(x^*)^\mathrm{T}p = 0$ for *every* p satisfying (1.8), then $g(x^*)$ must lie entirely in the range space of $A(x^*)$, which gives the desired result (1.6). □

We emphasize the key role of the constraint qualification in proving this theorem. Without it, relationship (1.8) does not imply that p is tangent to a feasible arc, and hence there can exist directions satisfying (1.8) along which no feasible points exist. For example, the origin is the *only* feasible point in $\mathbb{R}^1$ with respect to the nonlinear constraint $x_1^2 = 0$, and hence no feasible arcs exist. Nonetheless, (1.8) is satisfied for every nonzero p because the Jacobian matrix vanishes at the origin.

The m-vector λ^* such that $g(x^*) = A(x^*)^\mathrm{T}\lambda^*$ is called the *Lagrange multiplier vector*, and the vector $Z(x^*)^\mathrm{T}g(x^*)$ of (1.7) is called the *reduced gradient*. Condition (1.6) can also be written as

$$g(x^*) - A(x^*)^\mathrm{T}\lambda^* = 0 ,$$

which can be interpreted as a statement that x^* is a *stationary point* (with respect to x) of the *Lagrangian function*

$$L(x, \lambda) \equiv f(x) - \lambda^\mathrm{T}c(x) \tag{1.9}$$

when $\lambda = \lambda^*$. Note that λ^* is a stationary point of $L(x, \lambda)$ (with respect to λ) at any feasible point x.

We emphasize that in general the solution x^* of NEP is *not* an unconstrained minimizer of the Lagrangian function. For example, consider the one-variable problem

$$\begin{aligned} &\underset{x \in \mathbb{R}^1}{\text{minimize}} && x^3 \\ &\text{subject to} && x + 1 = 0 , \end{aligned} \tag{1.10}$$

whose (unique) solution is obviously $x^* = -1$, with Lagrange multiplier $\lambda^* = 3$. However, x^* is an unconstrained *maximizer* of the associated Lagrangian function $L(x, \lambda^*) = x^3 - 3(x + 1)$.

To derive second-order optimality conditions, we examine the behavior of f along feasible arcs from an alleged solution of NEP.

Theorem 1.3 (Second-order necessary optimality conditions). *If the constraint qualification holds at x^*, necessary conditions for x^* to be a minimizer of NEP are*:
(i) $g(x^*) = A(x^*)^T\lambda^*$ *for some* λ^*; *and*
(ii) $p^T\nabla^2 L(x^*, \lambda^*)p \geqslant 0$ *for any nonzero vector p satisfying $A(x^*)p = 0$ and for any λ^* satisfying* (i).

Proof. Assume that x^* is a local minimizer of NEP. Part (i) holds by Theorem 1.2. Now consider a nonzero vector p satisfying (1.8). (If none exists, the theorem holds vacuously.) Let $x(\alpha)$ be the twice-differentiable arc whose existence is guaranteed by the constraint qualification, where $x(0) = x^*$ and $dx(0)/d\alpha = p$. Let v denote $d^2x(0)/d\alpha^2$, and assume henceforth that all vector and matrix functions are evaluated at x^* unless otherwise specified. Since each constraint function c_i is identically zero along $x(\alpha)$, we have

$$\frac{d^2}{d\alpha^2} c_i(x(0)) = a_i^T \frac{d^2}{d\alpha^2} x(0) + \frac{d}{d\alpha}(a_i^T) \frac{d}{d\alpha} x(0)$$

$$= a_i^T v + p^T\nabla^2 c_i p = 0 . \tag{1.11}$$

Further, using (1.6) and (1.8),

$$\frac{d}{d\alpha} f(x(0)) = g^T \frac{d}{d\alpha} x(0) = g^T p$$

$$= \lambda^{*T}Ap = 0 . \tag{1.12}$$

Condition (i) implies that x^* is a stationary point of f along the feasible arc. In order for x^* to be a local minimizer, the *curvature* of f along any feasible arc must be nonnegative, i.e., it must hold that

$$\frac{d^2}{d\alpha^2} f(x(0)) \geqslant 0 . \tag{1.13}$$

Using (1.12), the definition of v, and (1.6), we write (1.13) as

$$\frac{d^2}{d\alpha^2} f(x(0)) = \frac{d}{d\alpha}\left(g^T \frac{d}{d\alpha} x(0)\right)$$

$$= g^T \frac{d^2}{d\alpha^2} x(0) + p^T\nabla^2 fp$$

$$= \lambda^{*T}Av + p^T\nabla^2 fp \geqslant 0 . \tag{1.14}$$

Rewriting (1.11) as $a_i^T v = -p^T \nabla^2 c_i p$ and substituting this expression into (1.14), we obtain

$$\frac{d^2}{d\alpha^2} f(x(0)) = -p^T\left(\sum_{i=1}^{m} \lambda_i^* \nabla^2 c_i\right)p + p^T \nabla^2 fp$$

$$= p^T \nabla^2 L(x^*, \lambda^*)p \geqslant 0,$$

which is the desired result. □

A compact statement of condition (ii) of this theorem is that the $(n - m) \times (n - m)$ matrix $Z(x^*)^T \nabla^2 L(x^*, \lambda^*) Z(x^*)$ must be positive semi-definite. (This matrix is called the *reduced Hessian of the Lagrangian function*.)

Sufficient conditions for x^* to be a local minimizer of NEP can be similarly derived, and the following theorem will be stated without proof.

Theorem 1.4 (Sufficient conditions for optimality). *A feasible point x^* is a strong local minimizer of NEP if there exists a vector λ^* such that*
  (i) $g(x^*) = A(x^*)^T \lambda^*$; *and*
  (ii) $Z(x^*)' \nabla^2 L(x^*, \lambda^*) Z(x^*)$ *is positive definite*. □

Before treating methods for general nonlinear constraints, we consider the special problem category of *quadratic programming*, in which $f(x)$ is quadratic and $c(x)$ is linear.

2. Equality-constrained quadratic programming

The *quadratic programming* (QP) problem involves minimizing a quadratic function subject to linear constraints. Quadratic programming is of great interest in its own right, and also plays a fundamental role in methods for general nonlinear problems. Our discussion will only hint at the myriad of interesting topics in quadratic programming. (For further information, the interested reader should consult the overviews and references given in, for example, Fletcher (1981), Gill, Murray and Wright (1981).)

A quadratic program with equality constraints may be stated as follows:

EQP $\underset{x \in \mathbb{R}^n}{\text{minimize}} \quad d^T x + \frac{1}{2} x^T H x$

                subject to $Ax = b$,   (2.1)

where H is symmetric and A has m rows. Let $q(x)$ denote the quadratic objective function of EQP, so that

$$q(x) = d^T x + \tfrac{1}{2} x^T H x, \quad \nabla q(x) = d + Hx \quad \text{and} \quad \nabla^2 q(x) = H.$$

Problems of the form EQP occur as subproblems within many active-set methods for inequality-constrained quadratic programs (Section 10) as well as in sequential quadratic programming methods (Section 6).

Since the constraint qualification always holds for linear constraints, Theorem 1.2 implies that a solution x^* of EQP must satisfy

$$\nabla q(x^*) = d + Hx^* = A^T\mu^* . \tag{2.2}$$

(We shall usually denote the multiplier vector of a quadratic program by μ.) Using Theorem 1.3, the properties of a minimizer of EQP are summarized in the following lemma for the case when A has full rank.

Lemma 2.1. *Let A be an $m \times n$ matrix of rank m and let Z denote a basis for the null space of A. Then: (i) EQP has a strong local minimizer at a point x^* satisfying (2.2) if and only if Z^THZ is positive definite; (ii) EQP has an infinite number of weak solutions if the overdetermined system (2.2) is compatible and if Z^THZ is positive semidefinite and singular; (iii) EQP has no finite solution otherwise (if (2.2) is incompatible or Z^THZ is indefinite).* □

(Note that a local minimizer of EQP is also a global minimizer.)

Using (2.2), the feasibility and optimality conditions for EQP may be written as two linear relations:

$$d + Hx^* = A^T\mu^* , \tag{2.3a}$$

$$Ax^* = b . \tag{2.3b}$$

Rearranging (2.3), we see that x^* and μ^* solve the following $(n + m)$-dimensional linear system:

$$K\begin{pmatrix} x^* \\ -\mu^* \end{pmatrix} = \begin{pmatrix} -d \\ b \end{pmatrix} \quad \text{where } K = \begin{pmatrix} H & A^T \\ A & \end{pmatrix}. \tag{2.4}$$

When A has full rank and Z^THZ is positive definite, K is nonsingular. The matrix K is often called the *Karush–Kuhn–Tucker* (or just *KKT*) *matrix*.

Given any point x, the linear relation (2.4) allows a convenient representation of the step p from x to x^*. Writing $x + p = x^*$, (2.3b) becomes

$$Ap = -c \quad \text{where } c = Ax - b . \tag{2.5}$$

Similarly, (2.3a) can be rewritten as

$$g + Hp = A^T\mu^* \quad \text{with } g = d + Hx . \tag{2.6}$$

Combining (2.5) and (2.6), we have the following equation for p and μ^*:

$$K\begin{pmatrix} -p \\ \mu^* \end{pmatrix} = \begin{pmatrix} g \\ c \end{pmatrix}. \tag{2.7}$$

In order to *compute* the solution of EQP, a variety of numerical methods are available, depending on the size and representation of the problem. For example, since K is symmetric but *indefinite*, (2.7) may be solved directly using a symmetric indefinite factorization (e.g., the Bunch–Parlett factorization; see Dongarra et al. (1979)), which may be especially appropriate for sparse problems (see Duff and Reid (1983), Gill, Murray, Saunders and Wright (1984), Gill et al. (1987)).

Assume that A has full rank. Alternative representations of the solution are typically based on transforming (2.7) to a more convenient form. In particular, it is sometimes useful to think of p (the step from x to x^*) as a combination of two orthogonal vectors:

$$p = Yp_Y + Zp_Z = (Y \quad Z)\binom{p_Y}{p_Z}, \tag{2.8}$$

where Y is a basis for the range space of A^T and Z is a basis for the null space of A. The m-vector p_Y is determined solely by the *constraints* of EQP, since

$$Ap = A(Yp_Y + Zp_Z) = AYp_Y = -c, \tag{2.9}$$

and AY must be nonsingular by definition of Y as a basis. We emphasize that the matrices Y and Z in (2.8) are not unique.

Popular choices for Y and Z are based on the QR factorization of A^T:

$$A^T = Q\binom{R}{0}, \tag{2.10}$$

where Q is an $n \times n$ orthogonal matrix and R is an $m \times m$ nonsingular upper triangle (see Gill and Murray (1974)). (The nonsingularity of R follows from the full rank of A.) When the columns of Q from (2.10) are partitioned as

$$Q = (Y \quad Z), \tag{2.11}$$

where Y has m columns, the columns of Y form an orthonormal basis for the range space of A^T, and the columns of Z form an orthonormal basis for the null space of A. Further, it follows from (2.10) and (2.11) that $Y^TA^T = R$.

Equation (2.9) thus becomes

$$R^Tp_Y = -c, \tag{2.12}$$

and p_Y is easily determined from a forward substitution. Given p_Y, relation (2.6) can be written as

$$g + HYp_Y + HZp_Z = A^T\mu^*.$$

Multiplying by Z^T and rearranging, we obtain

$$Z^THZp_Z = -Z^Tg - Z^THYp_Y, \tag{2.13}$$

from which p_Z may be determined by computing the Cholesky factorization of the positive-definite symmetric matrix $Z^T H Z$. The vector p is then computed from (2.8), and μ^* from the compatible overdetermined system (2.6). The QR factors (2.10) give μ^* as the solution of the upper-triangular system

$$R\mu^* = Y^T(g + Hp) .$$

An important special case occurs when x is feasible, so that $Ax = b$ and $c = 0$. Since R is nonsingular, (2.12) shows that $p_Y = 0$, and p lies entirely in the null space of A. Equation (2.13) simplifies to

$$Z^T H Z p_Z = -Z^T g ,$$

which is often called the *null-space equation*, and is a reduced analogue of the equations for the Newton search direction in the unconstrained case.

One alternative choice of Y and Z can be derived when H is positive definite, since a nonsingular matrix V exists such that

$$V^T A^T = \begin{pmatrix} R \\ 0 \end{pmatrix} \quad \text{and} \quad V^T H V = I . \tag{2.14}$$

(The matrix V in (2.14) is *not* in general orthogonal.) Partitioning V as $(Y \ Z)$, the vector p_Y is again defined by (2.12). Because of the second relation in (2.14), the equations for p_Z and μ^* simplify to

$$p_Z = -Z^T g ,$$
$$R\mu^* = p_Y + Y^T g .$$

If U denotes the upper-triangular Cholesky factor of H, a suitable V is given by $U^{-1}Q$, where Q is the orthogonal QR factor of $(AU^{-1})^T$. Variations on this method for defining p have been suggested by a number of authors – for example, see Murray (1971a), Bunch and Kaufman (1980), Goldfarb and Idnani (1983), and Gill, Gould, Murray, Saunders and Wright (1984).

The final representation to be mentioned can be defined when H is nonsingular but not necessarily positive definite, and $Z^T H Z$ is positive definite. Multiplying (2.6) by $A H^{-1}$ and using (2.5), we obtain

$$A H^{-1} A^T \mu^* = A H^{-1} g - c , \tag{2.15a}$$
$$Hp = A^T \mu^* - g , \tag{2.15b}$$

where (2.15b) is a trivial rearrangement of (2.6). Equations (2.15) are sometimes called the *range–space equations*.

We emphasize that the above formulations are all *equivalent* mathematically under certain conditions (for example, when H is positive definite). However, their relative merits for computational purposes depend on the size and properties of A and H. For example, calculation of a dense QR factorization (2.10) of A^T with an explicit matrix Q may be too expensive in time or storage for sparse problems.

3. Overview of methods

Before considering different classes of methods for solving NEP (1.1), we present an overview of the motivation that underlies many seemingly different algorithms. The basic principle invoked in solving NEP is that of *replacing a difficult problem by an easier problem*. Application of this principle leads to methods that formulate and solve a *sequence of subproblems*, where each subproblem is related in a known way to the original problem. In some of the methods to be discussed, the subproblem involves the *unconstrained* minimization of a model function; in other instances, the subproblem includes bounds and/or linear constraints derived from constraints of the original problem.

The most common source of the (simpler) model functions in the subproblems is the Taylor series expansion of a general nonlinear (but smooth) function, which is widely used throughout numerical analysis. For example, Newton's method for zero-finding is based on successively finding the zero of the local linear approximation obtained by including only the first-order term of the Taylor series. When *minimizing*, a linear model is usually inappropriate, since a general linear function is unbounded below. Therefore, minimization is most frequently based on developing a *quadratic* model of the function to be minimized. For example, suppose that the problem is to minimize the unconstrained function $f(x)$, and that x_k is the current iterate. A local quadratic model is obtained by truncating the usual Taylor expansion of f about x_k:

$$f(x_k + p) \approx f(x_k) + g(x_k)^T p + \tfrac{1}{2} p^T H(x_k)p , \qquad (3.1)$$

where $H(x)$ denotes the (symmetric) Hessian matrix $\nabla^2 f(x)$. If $H(x_k)$ is positive definite, the quadratic model (3.1) has a proper minimizer at $x_k + p_k$, where p_k solves the following system of linear equations:

$$H(x_k)p_k = -g(x_k) . \qquad (3.2)$$

Based on this analysis, Newton-based linesearch methods for unconstrained optimization typically define the next iterate as

$$x_{k+1} = x_k + \alpha_k p_k ,$$

where α_k is a positive steplength, and the search direction p_k is defined by (3.2). The value of α_k is chosen to ensure a decrease in a quantity that measures progress toward the solution. For details, see, e.g., Ortega and Rheinboldt (1970) or Dennis and Schnabel (1983).

Because models derived from the Taylor series necessarily neglect higher-order terms, their validity is assured only in a neighborhood (of unknown size) of the current point. Therefore, a standard technique for restricting the region in which the model applies is to add constraints that prevent iterates from moving too far from the current point. For example, the step p_k from x_k to x_{k+1} might be chosen not as the unconstrained minimizer of (3.1), but as the minimizer of (3.1) subject to a restriction on the size of $\|p\|$. Trust-region methods are based on *explicitly* restricting the domain in which a model function is considered reliable, and vary depending on the measure and form of the domain restriction. (For an overview of trust-region methods for unconstrained optimization, see, e.g., Chapter 1 (unconstrained optimization), Fletcher (1981), or Dennis and Schnabel (1983).)

For constrained problems, the same general principle applies of creating subproblems based on local models of the objective and constraint functions. Approaches to solving NEP vary in the form of the subproblem to be solved at each iteration, and in the definition of any model functions. Further variation is induced by the use of different numerical methods for solving mathematically equivalent problems.

4. The quadratic penalty function

4.1. Background

Although penalty functions in their original form are not widely used today, a thorough understanding of their properties is important background for more recent methods. For more detailed discussions of penalty-function methods, see, e.g., Fiacco and McCormick (1968), Fletcher (1981), Gill, Murray and Wright (1981) and Luenberger (1984). Penalty functions have a long history, occur in many forms, and are often called by special names in different applications. Their motivation is always to ensure that the iterates do not deviate "too far" from the constraints.

In general, an unconstrained minimizer of f will occur at an infeasible point, or f may be unbounded below. Therefore, any algorithm for NEP must consider not only the minimization of f, but also the enforcement of feasibility. In solving NEP, a "natural" strategy is to devise a *composite function* whose *unconstrained* minimizer is either x^* itself, or is related to x^* in a known way. The original problem can then be solved by formulating a sequence of unconstrained subproblems (or possibly a single unconstrained subproblem). Intuitively, this can be achieved by minimizing a function that combines f and a term that "penalizes" constraint violations.

A "classical" penalty term (usually attributed to Courant (1943)) is the squared Euclidean norm of the constraint violations, which leads to the well known *quadratic penalty function*

$$P_Q(x, \rho) \equiv f(x) + \tfrac{1}{2}\rho c(x)^{\mathrm{T}}c(x) = f(x) + \tfrac{1}{2}\rho\|c(x)\|_2^2 , \qquad (4.1)$$

where the nonnegative scalar ρ is called the *penalty parameter*. Let $x^*(\rho)$ denote an unconstrained minimizer of $P_Q(x, \rho)$. The following theorem, which is proved in Fiacco and McCormick (1968), shows that, under reasonably general conditions,

$$\lim_{\rho \to \infty} x^*(\rho) = x^* \,.$$

Theorem 4.1 (Convergence of the quadratic penalty method). *Let $\{\rho_k\}$ be a strictly increasing unbounded positive sequence. Assume that there exists a nonempty, isolated compact set Ω of local solutions of NEP with the same optimal function value. Then there exists a compact set S such that $\Omega \subset S$, and for sufficiently large ρ_k, there exist unconstrained minimizers of $P_Q(x, \rho_k)$ in the interior of S. Further, every limit of any subsequence of the minimizing points is in Ω.* □

In effect, this result ensures that applying the quadratic penalty-function transformation creates a set of *local minimizers* of the penalty function. For ρ sufficiently large, and within a bounded region including x^*, the sequence of local minimizers of $P_Q(x, \rho)$ will converge to x^*. It may nonetheless happen that the unconstrained algorithm used to minimize $P_Q(x, p)$ will fail to converge to the desired local minimizer. This limitation is illustrated in an example given by Powell (1972):

$$\text{minimize}_{x \in \mathbb{R}^1} \quad x^3$$

$$\text{subject to} \quad x - 1 = 0 \,,$$

whose solution is trivially $x^* = 1$. The associated penalty function is

$$P_Q(x, \rho) = x^3 + \tfrac{1}{2}\rho(x - 1)^2 \,, \tag{4.2}$$

and has a local minimizer at

$$x^*(\rho) = \frac{-\rho + \sqrt{\rho^2 + 12\rho}}{6} \quad \text{with} \lim_{\rho \to \infty} x^*(\rho) = x^* = 1 \,.$$

The function (4.2) is unbounded below for any finite ρ, and hence there is no guarantee that an unconstrained algorithm will converge to the minimizer from an arbitrary starting point.

4.2. Properties of the quadratic penalty function

The solutions of intermediate unconstrained subproblems have several interesting features. Given a strictly increasing positive unbounded sequence $\{\rho_k\}$, assume that k is large enough so that the result of Theorem 4.1 holds, and let $\{x_k^*\}$ denote the local unconstrained minimizer of $P(x, \rho_k)$ nearest to x^*. Let c_k

denote $c(x_k^*)$ and f_k denote $f(x_k^*)$. Then the following properties hold:
   (i) the sequence $\{P(x_k^*, \rho_k)\}$ is nondecreasing;
   (ii) $\{f_k\}$ is nondecreasing;
   (iii) $\{\|c_k\|_2\}$ is nonincreasing.
Thus, in general, each successive x_k^* displays a decreasing measure of infeasibility and an increasing value of the objective function. Further, each x_k^* is a point at which no descent direction exists with respect to both f and $\|c\|_2$.

Since P_Q is a smooth function, its gradient must vanish at the unconstrained minimizer $x^*(\rho)$, so that the following condition holds:

$$g(x^*(\rho)) = -\rho A(x^*(\rho))^\mathrm{T} c(x^*(\rho)) . \tag{4.3}$$

Condition (4.3) states that the gradient of the objective function at $x^*(\rho)$ is a linear combination of the constraint gradients, and hence has the same form as the first-order necessary condition for optimality when x^* satisfies the constraint qualification (Theorem 1.2), namely

$$g(x^*) = A(x^*)^\mathrm{T} \lambda^* . \tag{4.4}$$

Comparing (4.3) and (4.4), we see that the quantity $\lambda_i(\rho) = -\rho c_i(x^*(\rho))$, $i = 1, \ldots, m$, is analogous to the i-th Lagrange multiplier at x^*. When $A(x^*)$ has full rank and the sufficient conditions of Theorem 1.4 hold at x^*, the convergence of $x^*(\rho)$ to x^* and the uniqueness of the Lagrange multipliers imply that

$$\lim_{\rho \to \infty} \lambda_i(\rho) = \lambda_i^* . \tag{4.5}$$

Under suitable assumptions, the set of unconstrained minimizers of the penalty function can be regarded as a function of an independent variable, tracing out a smooth *trajectory* of points converging to x^*. The following result is proved in Fiacco and McCormick (1968).

Theorem 4.2 (Smooth trajectory of the quadratic penalty function). *Assume that $A(x^*)$ has full rank, and that the sufficient conditions of Theorem* 1.4 *hold at x^*. Then for ρ sufficiently large, there exist continuously differentiable functions $x(\rho)$ and $\lambda(\rho)$, such that*

$$\lim_{\rho \to \infty} x(\rho) = x^* \quad \text{and} \quad \lim_{\rho \to \infty} \lambda(\rho) = \lambda^* .$$

Furthermore, $x(\rho)$ is an unconstrained local minimizer of $P(x, \rho)$ for any finite ρ. □

The trajectory of minimizers of the quadratic penalty function has several interesting properties. In order to discuss conditions at the limit point, we introduce the variable $r = 1/\rho$, use the notation $x(r) \equiv x(\rho)$, and take limits as r

approaches zero. Since Theorem 4.2 implies the existence of a smooth function $x(r)$, we expand about $r = 0$:

$$x(r) = x^* + ry + O(r^2),$$

where

$$y \equiv \lim_{r \to 0} \frac{x(r) - x^*}{r} = x'(0) = \frac{dx(r)}{dr}\bigg|_{r=0}.$$

Because $x(r)$ is an unconstrained minimizer of the quadratic penalty function, for $r > 0$ we have the identity

$$r\nabla P(x(r), r) \equiv rg(r) + A(r)^T c(r) = 0, \tag{4.6}$$

where the notation "(r)" denotes evaluation at $x(r)$. Differentiating (4.6) with respect to r at $x(r)$ and using the chain rule, we obtain

$$\frac{d}{dr}(rg + A^T c) = g + rHx'(r) + A^T A x'(r) + \sum_{i=1}^{m} c_i H_i x'(r) = 0, \tag{4.7}$$

where H denotes $\nabla^2 f$, H_i denotes $\nabla^2 c_i$, and all functions are evaluated at $x(r)$. As $r \to 0$, we know that $c_i \to 0$, and hence, using (4.4), (4.7) becomes in the limit

$$g(x^*) + A(x^*)^T A(x^*) y = A(x^*)^T \lambda^* + A(x^*)^T A(x^*) y = 0. \tag{4.8}$$

Equation (4.8) implies that $A(x^*)^T (\lambda^* + A(x^*) y) = 0$ and since $A(x^*)$ has full row rank, we may assert that

$$A(x^*) y = -\lambda^*. \tag{4.9}$$

If $\lambda_i^* \neq 0$, (4.9) implies that the trajectory of minimizers of the quadratic penalty function generates a *nontangential* approach to x^*.

4.3. Practical issues

Based on the theory developed thus far, it might appear that the solution to NEP could be found simply by setting ρ to a very large value and using a standard unconstrained method. Unfortunately, the quadratic penalty function has the property that the Hessian matrices $\nabla^2 P(x^*(\rho), \rho)$ become increasingly ill-conditioned as ρ increases (see Murray (1969) and Lootsma (1969)). To see why, observe that the Hessian of P_Q at an arbitrary point x is given by

$$\nabla^2 P_Q(x, \rho) = H + \sum_{i=1}^{m} \rho c_i H_i + \rho A^T A. \tag{4.10}$$

At $x^*(\rho)$, for large ρ, it follows from (4.5) that the first two terms in (4.10) form an approximation to the bounded matrix $\nabla^2 L(x^*, \lambda^*)$. Thus, if $m < n$, the matrix (4.10) evaluated at $x^*(\rho)$ is dominated by the unbounded rank-deficient matrix $\rho A^T A$.

Analysis of the eigenvalues and eigenvectors of $\nabla^2 P(x^*(\rho), \rho)$ as $\rho \to \infty$ (see Murray (1971b)) reveals that $(n - m)$ eigenvalues are bounded, with associated eigenvectors that in the limit lie in the null space of $A(x^*)$. However, the remaining m eigenvalues are of order ρ, i.e., unbounded in the limit, and the corresponding eigenvectors lie in the range of $A(x^*)^T$. Thus, application of a *general* unconstrained method to minimize $P_Q(x, \rho)$ (i.e., a method that simply solves equations involving $\nabla^2 P$ without taking account of the special structure) is unsatisfactory because the near-singularity of the Hessian matrices will impede local convergence. To overcome this drawback, the search direction can be computed by solving an augmented system similar to (2.7) that reflects the very special structure of $\nabla^2 P$ (see Gould (1986)). This approach is closely related to sequential quadratic programming methods (see Section 6).

5. The l_1 penalty function

With the quadratic penalty function, the penalty parameter ρ must become infinite in order to achieve convergence to x^*. In contrast, we can devise a *non-differentiable* penalty function of which x^* is the unconstrained minimizer. (Such a function is called an *exact* penalty function.)

The most widely used exact penalty function is the l_1 *penalty function*, or *absolute-value penalty function*:

$$P_1(x, \rho) \equiv f(x) + \rho \sum_{i=1}^{m} |c_i| = f(x) + \rho \|c(x)\|_1 , \qquad (5.1)$$

where $\rho \geq 0$. The l_1 penalty function has been used for many years (under different names) in structural and mechanical design problems.

The function $P_1(x, \rho)$ has discontinuous derivatives at any point where a constraint function vanishes, and hence x^* will be a point of discontinuity in the gradient of P_1. An important difference between P_1 and P_Q (4.1) is that, under mild conditions, ρ in (5.1) need not become arbitrarily large in order for x^* to be an unconstrained minimizer of P_1. Rather, there is a threshold value $\bar\rho$ such that x^* is an unconstrained minimizer of P_1 for *any* $\rho > \bar\rho$. Thus, whenever ρ is (5.1) is "sufficiently large", an unconstrained minimizer of P_1 will be a solution of the original problem NEP.

For example, consider the problem

$$\underset{x \in \mathbb{R}^1}{\text{minimize}} \quad x^2$$

$$\text{subject to} \quad x - 1 = 0 ,$$

with solution $x^* = 1$ and multiplier $\lambda^* = 2$. The associated l_1 penalty function is

$$P_1(x, \rho) = x^2 + \rho|x - 1|,$$

of which x^* is an unconstrained minimizer if $\rho > 2$.

Methods based on non-differentiable penalty functions avoid the ill-conditioning associated with P_Q, since the penalty parameter can remain finite. Unfortunately, the crucial value $\bar{\rho}$ depends on quantities evaluated at x^* (which is, of course, unknown), and therefore the value of ρ may need to be adjusted as the algorithm proceeds. Difficulties can arise if an unsuitable value of the penalty parameter is chosen. If ρ is too small, the penalty function may be unbounded below. On the other hand, the unconstrained subproblem will be ill-conditioned if ρ is too large, and special techniques are then required to obtain an accurate solution.

Since P_1 is non-differentiable even at the solution, standard unconstrained methods designed for smooth problems cannot be applied directly. However, special algorithms (see, e.g., Coleman and Conn (1982a,b)) have been designed for minimizing (5.1) that utilize information about the original nonlinearly constrained problem. These methods will be discussed in Section 6.5.

6. Sequential quadratic programming methods

6.1. Motivation

Penalty function methods are based on the idea of combining a weighted measure of the constraint violations with the objective function. In contrast, we now turn to methods based directly on the optimality conditions for problem NEP. The idea of a *quadratic model* is a major ingredient in the most successful methods for unconstrained optimization. However, some care is needed for the nonlinearly constrained case, since we have clearly seen in the derivation of optimality conditions for NEP (Section 1) that the important curvature is that of the *Lagrangian function* $L(x, \lambda) = f(x) - \lambda^T c(x)$ (see equation (1.9)), and not merely that of f itself. This suggests that our quadratic model should be of the *Lagrangian function*. However, such a model would not be a complete representation of the properties of problem NEP.

Recall from Section 1 that x^* is (in general) only a *stationary point* of the Lagrangian function, and *not* an unconstrained minimizer. Even when the sufficient conditions of Theorem 1.4 hold, x^* is a minimizer of the Lagrangian function only within the subspace of vectors satisfying $A(x^*)p = 0$. Such a restriction to a subspace suggests that *linear constraints* should be imposed on a quadratic model of the Lagrangian function.

With this in mind, we consider the development of an algorithm of the form

$$x_{k+1} = x_k + \alpha_k p_k, \tag{6.1}$$

where p_k is a search direction and α_k is a nonnegative steplength. As in the QP methods of Section 2, p_k is intended to be an estimate of the step from the current iterate x_k to x^*, and thus the optimality conditions at x^* should guide the definition of p_k.

The most obvious property of x^* is that it is *feasible*, i.e., $c(x^*) = 0$. Expanding c in a Taylor series about x_k along a general vector p, we have

$$c(x_k + p) = c_k + A_k p + O(\|p\|^2) , \tag{6.2}$$

where c_k and A_k denote $c(x_k)$ and $A(x_k)$. Ignoring the quadratic and higher-order terms in (6.2), the desired search direction p_k will be the step to a zero of a local *linear* approximation to c if

$$c_k + A_k p_k = 0 \quad \text{or} \quad A_k p_k = -c_k . \tag{6.3}$$

The relationship (6.3) defines a set of *linear equality constraints* to be satisfied by p_k.

We know from the discussion in Section 2 that the constraints (6.3) uniquely determine the portion of p_k in the *range* of A_k^T. Note that (6.3) is analogous to the definition of a Newton step to the solution of the (underdetermined) nonlinear equations $c(x) = 0$. If A_k has linearly independent rows, the constraints (6.3) are always consistent. However, if the rows of A_k are linearly dependent, (6.3) may have no solution.

An important aspect of such methods is that, although to first order the search direction is a step to a zero of the constraints, the right-hand side of (6.3) generally becomes zero only in the limit. This property contrasts with the widely used feasible-point methods for *linear* constraints, and arises because of the extreme difficulty of remaining feasible with respect to even a single nonlinear constraint. In fact, the enforced maintenance of feasibility (or even near-feasibility) at every iterate tends almost without exception to produce inefficiency when the constraints display a significant degree of nonlinearity. The effort to remain feasible is thus "wasted" at points that are far from optimal. (In effect, enforcement of feasibility at every iterate means that the algorithm takes very small steps along the curved surface defined by the constraints.)

6.2. Formulation of a quadratic programming subproblem

Beyond satisfying the linear constraints (6.3), the search direction p_k in (6.1) should be defined by minimization of a quadratic model of the Lagrangian function. By analogy with the EQP subproblem (2.1), p_k is taken as the solution of the following equality-constrained quadratic program:

$$\underset{p \in \mathbb{R}^n}{\text{minimize}} \quad g_k^T p + \tfrac{1}{2} p^T B_k p \tag{6.4a}$$

$$\text{subject to} \quad A_k p = -c_k , \tag{6.4b}$$

where g_k is $g(x_k)$, the gradient of f at x_k, and the matrix B_k is intended to represent the *Hessian of the Lagrangian function*. For simplicity, we assume that A_k has full rank.

Let Z_k denote a matrix whose columns form a basis for the null space of A_k, i.e., such that $A_k Z_k = 0$. If $Z_k^T B_k Z_k$ is positive definite, the subproblem (6.4) has a unique minimizer p_k (see Lemma 2.1). The vector p_k can be expressed conveniently in terms of Z_k and a complementary matrix Y_k, whose columns form a basis for the range space of A_k^T, as

$$p_k = Y_k p_Y + Z_k p_Z , \tag{6.5}$$

where $Y_k p_Y$ and $Z_k p_Z$ will be called the *range-space* and *null-space* components of p_k.

The constraints (6.4b) completely determine the range-space portion of p_k. Substituting from (6.5) into (6.4b) gives

$$A_k p_k = A_k(Y_k p_Y + Z_k p_Z) = A_k Y_k p_Y = -c_k ,$$

by definition of Y_k and Z_k (since $A_k Y_k$ is nonsingular and $A_k Z_k = 0$).

The null-space portion of p_k is determined by minimization of the quadratic objective function within the appropriate null space, after moving in the range space to satisfy the constraints (6.4b). The vector p_Z satisfies the following nonsingular linear system (cf. (2.13)):

$$Z_k^T B_k Z_k p_Z = - Z_k^T g_k - Z_k^T B_k Y_k p_Y . \tag{6.6}$$

The Lagrange multiplier μ_k of (6.4) satisfies the (compatible) overdetermined system

$$g_k + B_k p_k = A_k^T \mu_k . \tag{6.7}$$

The subproblem (6.4) has several interesting properties. First, observe that the linear term of the quadratic objective function (6.4a) is simply g_k, rather than the gradient of the Lagrangian function. This does not alter the solution p_k of (6.4), since multiplication by Z_k^T in (6.6) annihilates all vectors in the range of A_k^T. However, taking the linear term as g_k produces the desirable feature that, as $p_k \to 0$, the Lagrange multipliers of the subproblem (6.4) will become the Lagrange multipliers of the original nonlinearly constrained problem. Observe that, when x_k is "close" to x^* and $\|p_k\|$ is "small", (6.7) becomes arbitrarily close to the first-order optimality condition

$$g(x^*) = A(x^*)^T \lambda^* .$$

The solution p_k and multiplier vector μ_k can be interpreted as the result of a "Newton-like" iteration applied to the set of $n + m$ nonlinear equations that hold at the solution of NEP, namely

$$g(x^*) - A(x^*)^{\mathrm{T}}\lambda^* = 0 , \tag{6.8}$$

$$c(x^*) = 0 . \tag{6.9}$$

The constraints $A_k p = -c_k$ define the (underdetermined) Newton step to a point that satisfies (6.9). When $B_k = \nabla^2 L(x_k, \lambda_k)$, equation (6.7) defines a Newton step in *both* x and λ to a point (x^*, λ^*) that satisfies (6.8).

6.3. Definition of the Hessian

An obviously important element in formulating the subproblem (6.4) is the choice of the matrix B_k, which is intended to approximate the Hessian of the Lagrangian function. (Note that the linear constraints of (6.4) do not involve the Lagrangian function.) The "best" choice of B_k is still an open question, particularly in the quasi-Newton case (as we shall mention below), and is the subject of much active research today.

When *exact* second derivatives of f and c are available, an "ideal" choice for B_k near the solution would be $\nabla^2 L(x_k, \lambda_k)$, where x_k and λ_k are the current approximations to x^* and λ^*. With this choice, the "pure" SQP method defined by (6.1) with $\alpha_k = 1$ should produce quadratic local convergence in both x and λ. (See, e.g., Goodman (1985).) However, with $B_k = \nabla^2 L(x_k, \lambda_k)$, the reduced Hessian $Z_k^{\mathrm{T}} B_k Z_k$ may be indefinite, in which case the QP subproblem (6.4) has an unbounded solution (see Lemma 2.1). Research is actively being carried out on strategies to resolve this situation.

When second derivatives are not available, an obvious approach is to let B_k be a *quasi-Newton* approximation to the Hessian of the Lagrangian function. In this case, the solution of the subproblem (6.4) is not a Newton step in both the range and null space. Although the constraints (6.4b) (and hence the range-space component of p_k) are independent of B_k, the null-space component of p_k will be based on *approximate* second-derivative information. Because of this disparity in the quality of information, *the constraints tend to converge to zero faster than the reduced gradient*. During the final iterations, the behavior of quasi-Newton SQP methods is typically characterized by the relationship

$$\frac{\|p_Y\|}{\|p_Z\|} \to 0 ,$$

i.e., the final search directions lie almost wholly in the null space of $A(x^*)$.

In defining B_k as a quasi-Newton approximation, the BFGS formula (see Chapter 1) seems a logical choice for updating an approximation to the Hessian of the Lagrangian function. However, certain complications arise because x^* is *not* necessarily an unconstrained minimizer of the Lagrangian function (see Section 1). Consider a BFGS-like update of the form

$$\bar{B} = B - \frac{Bss^TB}{s^TBs} + \frac{vv^T}{v^Ts} , \tag{6.10}$$

where a barred quantity is "new", $s = \bar{x} - x$, and v is a vector to be chosen. Since B is intended to approximate the Hessian of the Lagrangian function, a "natural" choice for v in (6.10) would be y_L, the change in gradient of the Lagrangian function, i.e.

$$y_L = \bar{g} - g - (\bar{A}^T - A^T)\lambda , \tag{6.11}$$

with λ the best available multiplier estimate. However, it may be impossible, with any linesearch, to find a steplength α_k in (6.1) such that y_L^Ts is positive (see Section 6.4, below). Since the updated matrix $\bar{B}$ will be positive definite only if $v^Ts > 0$, performing the update with $v = y_L$ as in (6.11) would lead to an indefinite Hessian approximation.

The question thus arises of what to do under these circumstances. If the update is *skipped* when $y_L^Ts < 0$, *no new information* about curvature of the Lagrangian function will be gained from this iteration (or possibly from *any* iteration), and favorable local convergence properties of the quasi-Newton method are unlikely to apply. Therefore, a popular method for dealing with this difficulty is to use $v = y_L$ to perform the update (6.10) when y_L^Ts is sufficiently positive; otherwise, v is taken as a perturbed vector $\bar{y}_L$ such that $\bar{y}_L^Ts > 0$. (Such a strategy was first suggested by Powell (1978).) For constrained problems, a necessary condition for superlinear convergence (Boggs, Tolle and Wang (1982)) is that the approximate Hessian matrices must satisfy

$$\lim_{k \to \infty} \frac{\|Z_kZ_k^T(B_k - \nabla^2L(x^*, \lambda^*))Z_kZ_k^Tp_k\|}{\|p_k\|} = 0 . \tag{6.12}$$

The definition of $\bar{y}_L$ should ensure that (6.12) is satisfied as the solution is approached, so that superlinear convergence is not inhibited by the update.

6.4. *Choice of the steplength; merit functions*

A steplength α_k is included in the definition (6.1) of the SQP iteration in order to ensure "progress" at every iteration, since the current approximation of the Lagrangian function and/or the constraints may be inaccurate when the current iterate is far from x^*. In linesearch methods for unconstrained and linearly constrained optimization, the value of the objective function f alone provides a "natural" measure to guide the choice of α_k. Not too surprisingly, matters are much more complicated when solving a nonlinearly constrained problem. Except in a few special cases, it is impossible to generate a feasible sequence of iterates with decreasing values of the objective function.

The most common approach is to choose α_k in (6.1) to yield a "sufficient decrease" (in the sense of Ortega and Rheinboldt (1970)) in a *merit function M* that measures progress toward the solution of NEP. Typically, a merit function is a combination of the objective and constraint functions. An "ideal" merit function should have certain properties, some more important than others. An *essential* property is that it should always be possible to achieve a sufficient decrease in M when the search direction is defined by the QP subproblem (6.4). A desirable feature is that the merit function should not restrict the "natural" rate of convergence of the SQP method, e.g., if $B_k = \nabla^2 L(x_k, \lambda_k)$, then $\alpha_k = 1$ should be accepted at all iterations "near" the solution, in order to achieve quadratic convergence (see Section 6.2). An intuitively appealing feature is that x^* should be an unconstrained minimizer of M. A feature with great practical importance is that calculation of M should not be "too expensive" in terms of evaluations of the objective and constraint functions and/or their gradients.

A commonly used merit function is the l_1 *penalty function* (see Section 5):

$$M_1(x, \rho) = f(x) + \rho \|c(x)\|_1 , \qquad (6.13)$$

where ρ is a nonnegative penalty parameter. (Han (1977) first suggested use of this function as a means of "globalizing" an SQP method.) This merit function has the property that, for ρ sufficiently large, x^* is an unconstrained minimizer of $M_1(x, \rho)$. In addition, ρ can always be chosen so that the SQP search direction p_k is a descent direction for $M_1(x, \rho)$. However, requiring a decrease in M_1 at every iteration can lead to the inhibition of superlinear convergence (the "Maratos effect"; see Maratos (1978)), and various strategies have been devised to overcome this drawback (see, e.g., Chamberlain et al. (1982)). In practice, the choice of penalty parameter in (6.13) can have a substantial effect on efficiency.

An increasingly popular alternative is the *augmented Lagrangian function*:

$$M_A(x, \lambda, \rho) \equiv f(x) - \lambda^{\mathrm{T}} c(x) + \tfrac{1}{2} \rho c(x)^{\mathrm{T}} c(x) , \qquad (6.14)$$

where λ is a multiplier estimate and ρ is a nonnegative penalty parameter (see Sections 4 and 8). Use of (6.14) as a merit function was suggested by Wright (1976) and Schittkowski (1981). If λ in (6.14) is the optimal multiplier vector λ^*, then x^* is a stationary point (with respect to x) of M_A (see Section 1). As with M_1 (6.13), it can be shown that there exists a *finite* $\bar{\rho}$ such that x^* is an *unconstrained minimizer* of $M_A(x, \lambda^*, \rho)$ for all $\rho > \bar{\rho}$. With suitable choice of λ, (6.14) does not impede superlinear convergence.

Many subtle points need to be studied in using (6.14) as a merit function – in particular, extreme care must be exercised in defining the multiplier estimate λ. If λ is taken simply as the "latest" multiplier estimate (i.e., the multiplier vector of the most recent QP subproblem (6.4)), the merit function changes *discontinuously* at every iteration, and difficulties consequently arise in proving global convergence. To avoid this situation, the vector λ can be treated as an *additional unknown*, which is then included in the linesearch. Typically, the QP multipliers μ_k are used to define a multiplier "search direction" ξ_k, so that

$\xi_k = \mu_k - \lambda$. (See, e.g., Tapia (1977), Schittkowski (1981), Gill, Muray, Saunders and Wright (1986).)

The most successful implementations of SQP methods for problems in which only first derivatives are available typically use a modified BFGS update to define B_k (see (6.10)), and either M_1 (6.13) or M_A (6.14) as a merit function.

6.5. Related methods

It is often difficult to classify methods because the chosen hierarchical structure tends to be subjective. (Other authors may consider that SQP methods are subsumed under a category defined by the methods of this section!) We take the general view that an "SQP method" includes a subproblem derived from the optimality conditions of Theorem 1.3, with linearized versions of the nonlinear constraints, and a quadratic objective function whose Hessian reflects the curvature of the Lagrangian function. The methods to be discussed are considered as "related" to SQP methods because they are derived in one sense or another from the optimality conditions. However, the subproblem may not have the precise form stated above. In some cases, the subproblem may be *equivalent* to a quadratic program, but with modified objective function or constraints.

Two obvious deficiencies of any SQP method defined by (6.4) are that the constraints (6.4b) may be inconsistent if A_k does not have full row rank, and that the search direction may "blow up" in size if the rows of A_k are "nearly" linearly dependent. Several modifications to the basic SQP structure are designed to correct these difficulties.

Fletcher (1981, 1985) has suggested a class of methods called "Sl_1QP methods" in which the search direction p_k is the solution of the following subproblem:

$$\underset{p\in\mathbb{R}^n}{\text{minimize}} \quad g_k^T p + \tfrac{1}{2}p^T H p + \rho\|A_k p + c_k\|_1$$
$$\text{subject to} \quad \|p\|_\infty \leq \beta, \tag{6.15}$$

where ρ is a penalty parameter and β is a positive number. The benefit of this formulation is that a solution to (6.15) always exists, even when the linearized constraints (6.4b) are inconsistent. Further, the l_1 penalty term in the objective and the explicit bound ("trust-region") constraints on each component of p ensure that the search direction and multiplier vector are bounded.

We characterize this approach as "SQP-related" because subproblem (6.15) is equivalent to the following quadratic program with inequality constraints:

$$\underset{p\in\mathbb{R}^n}{\text{minimize}} \quad g_k^T p + \tfrac{1}{2}p^T H p + \rho e^T(u+v)$$
$$\text{subject to} \quad -\beta e \leq p \leq \beta e, \tag{6.16}$$
$$A_k p + c_k = u - v, \quad u \geq 0, \quad v \geq 0,$$

where e denotes the vector $(1,1,\ldots,1)^T$ of appropriate dimension. Methods for solving quadratic programs with inequality constraints such as (6.16) will be discussed in Section 10.

Other approaches have been suggested that are closely related to SQP methods, although derived from a different perspective. For example, Coleman and Conn (1982a,b) suggest a method based on unconstrained minimization of the l_1 penalty function of Section 6. The similarity to an SQP method arises because the search is computed as two orthogonal components that lie in the range space of A_k^T and null space of A_k, with the range-space component based on linearization of the nonlinear constraints.

SQP and SQP-related methods are widely considered the most effective general methods today for solving NEP. Several have been implemented in highly reliable software, and perform extremely well in practice, even on test problems formerly regarded as difficult.

7. Sequential linearly constrained methods

The methods to be discussed in this section — *reduced Lagrangian or sequential linearly constrained (SLC)* methods — were originally devised by Robinson (1972) and Rosen and Kreuser (1972). They have tended to be most widely used for *large-scale* optimization problems (e.g., in the well known MINOS code; see Murtagh and Saunders (1982, 1983)). The motivation for an SLC method is the same as that of an SQP method: to minimize the *Lagrangian function* subject to linearizations of the original nonlinear constraints. In contrast to an SQP method, which develops a quadratic model of the Lagrangian function, an SLC method solves a linearly constrained subproblem in which the objective function is a *general* approximation to the Lagrangian function.

A typical subproblem in an SLC method applied to a problem with equality constraints has the form

$$\begin{array}{ll} \underset{x \in \mathbb{R}^n}{\text{minimize}} & \mathcal{F}_k(x) \\ \\ \text{subject to} & A_k(x - x_k) = -c_k , \end{array} \tag{7.1}$$

where $\mathcal{F}_k(x)$ is a general approximation to the Lagrangian function at x_k, based on a current multiplier estimate λ_k. Let x_{k+1} be the solution of the subproblem (7.1).

Ideally, an SLC method would choose $\mathcal{F}_k(x)$ in (7.1) as

$$\mathcal{F}_k(x) = f(x) - \lambda_k^T \bar{c}_k(x) , \tag{7.2}$$

where λ_k is the "latest" multiplier estimate, and

$$\bar{c}_k(x) = c(x) - c_k - A_k(x - x_k) . \tag{7.3}$$

(The function $\bar{c}_k(x)$ in (7.3) is the difference between $c(x)$ and its linearization at x_k.) With this choice of $\mathcal{F}_k$, the multiplier vector of (7.1) will converge to λ^* if x_k converges to x^*. For this reason, λ_k in (7.2) is typically taken as the multiplier vector from the previous subproblem (7.1).

The SLC method defined by (7.1) and (7.2) has extremely favorable local convergence properties. (For details, see Robinson (1972).) If x_0 and λ_0 are "sufficiently close" to x^* and λ^*, and each subproblem (7.1) is solved exactly, the sequence of solutions (x_k, λ_k) converges *quadratically* to (x^*, λ^*). Unfortunately, this convergence result is *purely local*, and the iterates may diverge outside a small neighborhood of x^*. For this reason, various strategies have been proposed to improve the reliability of SLC methods, such as executing a few iterations of a penalty function method (Section 4) to determine a "good" initial point Rosen (1978). Alternatively, Murtagh and Saunders (1982) give an algorithm in which $\mathcal{F}_k(x)$ in (7.1) is taken as the following close relative of an *augmented* Lagrangian function:

$$\mathcal{F}_k(x) = f(x) - \lambda_k^T \bar{c}_k(x) + \tfrac{1}{2}\rho \bar{c}_k(x)^T \bar{c}_k(x) ,$$

where $\bar{c}_k$ is defined by (7.3), and the *penalty parameter* ρ is a nonnegative scalar (cf. (6.14)). The penalty parameter can be adjusted to attain the ideal quadratic convergence rate.

Subproblem (7.1) involves the minimization of a general nonlinear function subject to linear equality constraints. The choice of solution method for a given problem will depend on the information available about the problem functions (i.e., the level and cost of derivative information), and on the problem size. Because several iterations may be required to solve the subproblem, SLC methods have a "two-level" structure of *major* and *minor* iterations. Each major iteration involves formulation of a new subproblem, using the current values of x_k and λ_k; the minor iterations are then those of the method used to solve the particular subproblem.

In general, an SLC method tends to require more evaluations of the problem functions than an SQP method to solve the same nonlinearly constrained problem. However, the solution is typically found by an SLC method in fewer *major* iterations, where a major iteration in an SQP method simply involves solving the QP subproblem (6.4). The reason that SLC methods are so widely used for large-scale problems is that, somewhat surprisingly, general-purpose techniques for solving large-scale linearly constrained problems are better developed today than general methods for large-scale quadratic programming. However, this situation is likely to change during the next few years. Even in the most advanced SLC methods today, unresolved issues remain concerning proofs of global convergence, the use of a merit function, the definition of $\mathcal{F}_k$, and strategies for early termination of unpromising subproblems.

A source of inefficiency in an SLC method is that the effort required to solve (7.1) accurately may be excessive with respect to the improvement gained in the current iterate. If x_k is far from optimal and/or λ_k is a poor estimate of λ^*, overall efficiency may be improved by terminating the minor iterations before (7.1) has been solved. Such strategies remain an open research question, since they include a delicate balance between possible gains in speed and loss of theoretical convergence properties.

8. Augmented Lagrangian methods

The class of *augmented Lagrangian methods* can be derived from several different viewpoints. In all cases, a fundamental aim is to use the optimality conditions to devise a well-behaved *unconstrained* subproblem of which x^* is the solution. Augmented Lagrangian methods became extremely popular in the early 1970's, largely because of the great success of methods for unconstrained optimization. This approach to nonlinear programming was suggested independently by Hestenes (1969) and Powell (1969).

Assume that the sufficient conditions for optimality (Theorem 1.4) hold at x^*. Then x^* is a *stationary point* of the Lagrangian function $L(x, \lambda) = f(x) - \lambda^T c(x)$, when $\lambda = \lambda^*$ (see Section 1). Because x^* is not necessarily a *minimizer* of the Lagrangian function, the Lagrangian function itself is not a suitable choice for the objective function of the subproblem, even if λ^* were known.

Since the *reduced* Hessian of the Lagrangian function is positive definite, x^* is a minimizer of the Lagrangian function within the subspace of vectors orthogonal to $A(x^*)$. (This observation was the primary motivation for SQP and SLC methods; see Sections 6 and 7.) Positive-definiteness of the *reduced* Hessian of the Lagrangian function indicates that the Lagrangian function can display negative curvature at x^* *only along directions in the range space* of $A(x^*)^T$. This suggests that a suitable function for an unconstrained subproblem might be obtained by *augmenting* the Lagrangian function through addition of a term than retains the stationary properties of x^*, but alters the Hessian in the range space of $A(x^*)^T$.

The most popular such *augmented Lagrangian function* is obtained by adding a quadratic penalty term, which gives

$$L_A(x, \lambda, \rho) \equiv f(x) - \lambda^T c(x) + \tfrac{1}{2}\rho c(x)^T c(x) , \qquad (8.1)$$

where ρ is a nonnegative penalty parameter. Both the quadratic penalty term of (8.1) and its gradient vanish at x^*. Thus, if $\lambda = \lambda^*$, x^* is a stationary point (with respect to x) of (8.1). The Hessian matrix of the augmented Lagrangian function is

$$\nabla^2 L_A(x, \lambda, \rho) = \nabla^2 f(x) - \sum_{i=1}^{m} (\lambda_i - \rho c_i(x)) \nabla^2 c_i(x) + \rho A(x)^T A(x) .$$

Since $c(x^*) = 0$, the Hessian of the penalty term at x^* is simply

$\rho A(x^*)^{\mathrm{T}} A(x^*)$, which is a positive semi-definite matrix with strictly positive eigenvalues corresponding to eigenvectors in the range of $A(x^*)^{\mathrm{T}}$. Thus, the presence of the penalty term in L_A has the effect of increasing the (possibly negative) eigenvalues of $\nabla^2 L(x^*, \lambda^*)$ corresponding to eigenvectors in the range space of $A(x^*)^{\mathrm{T}}$, but leaving the other eigenvalues unchanged. Using this property, under mild conditions there exists a finite $\bar{\rho}$ such that x^* is an unconstrained minimizer of $L_A(x, \lambda^*, \rho)$ for all $\rho > \bar{\rho}$. In example (1.10), the crucial value is $\bar{\rho} = 6$, since $x^* = -1$ is a (local) unconstrained minimizer of $L_A(x, \lambda^*, \rho) = x^3 - 3(x + 1) + \frac{1}{2}\rho(x + 1)^2$ if $\rho > 6$.

In a typical augmented Lagrangian method, x_k is taken as the unconstrained minimizer of L_A in (8.1), where λ is taken as λ_k, the latest multiplier estimate. Strategies must therefore be developed for choosing both λ_k and ρ.

Although the penalty parameter in (8.1) need not become infinite, this restriction is of little practical value in actually choosing a specific value of ρ. Obviously, ρ must be large enough so that x^* is a local minimizer of L_A. However, there are difficulties with either a too-large or a too-small value of ρ. The phenomenon of an ill-conditioned subproblem occurs if ρ becomes too large, as with the quadratic penalty function (Section 4). However, if the current ρ is too small, the augmented function may be unbounded, or the Hessian matrix of L_A may be ill-conditioned because ρ is too close to the critical value $\bar{\rho}$ at which the Hessian of L_A is singular.

Since x^* is not a stationary point of L_A except when $\lambda = \lambda^*$, an augmented Lagrangian method will converge to x^* only if the associated multiplier estimates converge to λ^*. Furthermore, when x_k is defined by minimizing (8.1), the rate of convergence of x_k to x^* is restricted to the rate of convergence of λ_k to λ^* (see, e.g., Fletcher (1974)). This result is quite significant, since it implies that even a quadratically convergent technique applied to determine the unconstrained minimizer of (8.1) will not converge quadratically to x^* unless λ_k also converges quadratically to λ^*. (In contrast, the rate of convergence of x_k is not restricted in this fashion in SQP and SLC methods; see Sections 6 and 7.)

As with an SLC method, it could be argued that the effort required to solve a general unconstrained subproblem to full accuracy may be unjustified if the penalty parameter is wildly out of range, or the Lagrange multiplier estimate is significantly in error. Hence, various strategies have been developed for prematurely terminating the solution of an unpromising subproblem.

9. Inequality constraints

We now derive optimality conditions for a problem in which all constraints are assumed to be *inequalities*:

NIP$\qquad$ $\displaystyle\operatorname*{minimize}_{x \in \mathbb{R}^n}$ $\quad f(x)$

$\qquad\qquad$ subject to $\quad c(x) \geq 0$, $\hfill$ (9.1) where $c(x)$ has m_N components $c_i(x)$, and f and $\{c_i(x)\}$ are twice-continuously differentiable. The matrix $\mathscr{A}(x)$ will denote the Jacobian matrix of the constraint vector $c(x)$, and a solution of NIP will be denoted by x^*.

The derivation of optimality conditions for inequality constraints is more complicated than for equalities for two reasons: first, in general only a subset of the constraints are involved in some of the optimality conditions; and second, the set of feasible perturbations is much larger. The following definitions indicate the increase complexity of terminology.

Definition 9.1. The point $\hat{x}$ is said to be *feasible* with respect to the inequality constraint $c_i(x) \geq 0$ if $c_i(\hat{x}) \geq 0$. (Equivalently, the constraint is *satisfied* at $\hat{x}$.) The constraint $c_i(x) \geq 0$ is said to be *active* at $\hat{x}$ if $c_i(\hat{x}) = 0$ and *inactive* if $c_i(\hat{x}) > 0$. If $c_i(\hat{x}) < 0$, $\hat{x}$ is *infeasible*, and the constraint is said to be *violated* at $\hat{x}$.

The definition of a local solution of problem NIP is identical to that for problem NEP (Definition 1.2), using the appropriate definition of feasibility. For problem NIP, the active constraints at an alleged solution have special importance because they restrict feasible perturbations. If a constraint is inactive at the point x, then it will remain inactive for *any* perturbation in a sufficiently small neighborhood. However, an *active* constraint may be violated by certain perturbations. As in the equality-constraint case, we now consider conditions under which it is possible to characterize feasible perturbations, and accordingly define two constraint qualifications (see Fiacco and McCormick (1968)). Let $\hat{c}(x)$ denote the subset of constraints that are *active* at x, and $A(x)$ the Jacobian of $\hat{c}$. We emphasize that $A(x)$ includes only the gradients of the *active* constraints, whereas $\mathscr{A}(x)$ is the full Jacobian of all the constraints. We shall use the notation $a_i(x)$ for the gradient of an active or inactive constraint, where the meaning should always be clear from the context.

Definition 9.2 (First-order constraint qualification for inequality constraints). The first-order constraint qualification with respect to the set of inequality constraints $c(x) \geq 0$ holds at the feasible point x if, for any nonzero vector p such that $A(x)p \geq 0$, p is tangent to a differentiable feasible arc emanating from x and contained in the feasible region.

Definition 9.3 (Second-order constraint qualification for inequality constraints). The second-order constraint qualification with respect to the inequalities $c(x) \geq 0$ holds at the feasible point x if, for any nonzero vector p such that $A(x)p = 0$, p is tangent to a twice-differentiable arc along which $\hat{c}$ is identically zero.

In contrast to the single constraint qualification for equality constraints, these conditions are distinct, and neither implies the other. A condition that ensures satisfaction of both constraint qualifications is given in the following theorem. (See Fiacco and McCormick (1968) for a proof.)

Theorem 9.1 (Regular point for inequality constraints). *The first- and second-order constraint qualifications for inequalities hold at the feasible point x if $A(x)$ has full rank, i.e., if the gradients of the active constraints are linearly independent.* $\square$

We now consider deriving optimality conditions for problem NIP. First, observe from the Taylor expansion (1.3) that if $c_i(x) = 0$, i.e., if the i-th constraint is active at x, the constraint becomes *inactive* along a perturbation p such that $a_i^T p > 0$. The optimality theorems utilize the following well known result. (For further discussion and details, see, e.g., Fletcher (1981).)

Lemma 9.1 (Farkas' Lemma). *Given an $m \times n$ matrix C, a given n-vector b can be expressed as a nonnegative linear combination of the rows of C if and only if, for each vector y such that $Cy \geq 0$, it also holds that $b^T y \geq 0$, i.e.,*

$$b = C^T\lambda, \quad \lambda \geq 0 \quad \text{if and only if} \quad Cy \geq 0 \Rightarrow b^T y \geq 0. \quad \square$$

An alternative statement of this result is that a vector z exists such that $b^T z < 0$ and $Cz \geq 0$ if and only if there exists no nonnegative vector λ such that $b = C^T\lambda$. Farkas' Lemma can then be used to prove the following theorem.

Theorem 9.2 (First-order necessary optimality conditions). *If the first-order constraint qualification for inequalities holds at x^*, a necessary condition for x^* to be a minimizer of NIP is that there exists a vector λ^* such that*

$$g(x^*) = A(x^*)^T\lambda^* \quad \text{with} \quad \lambda^* \geq 0. \tag{9.2}$$

Proof. Assume that x^* is a solution of NIP, and consider any nonzero vector p satisfying

$$A(x^*)p \geq 0. \tag{9.3}$$

The first-order constraint qualification implies that p is tangent to a feasible arc emanating from x^* and contained in the feasible region. If $g(x^*)^T p \geq 0$, then Farkas' Lemma immediately implies the existence of $\lambda^* \geq 0$ satisfying (9.2). Therefore, we now suppose that there exists a nonzero p satisfying (9.3), but such that

$$g(x^*)^T p < 0. \tag{9.4}$$

The rate of change of f along the associated feasible arc is $g(x^*)^T p$, so that (9.4) implies that f is strictly less than $f(x^*)$ at feasible points in every neighborhood of x^*, thereby contradicting the assumption that x^* is a local minimizer. Thus, there can be no vector p satisfying (9.3) and (9.4), and Farkas' Lemma implies that (9.2) holds. $\square$

The crucial difference from the analogous theorem for equality constraints is that *the Lagrange multipliers corresponding to active inequality constraints must be nonnegative.*

In some circumstances, it is useful to define a Lagrange multiplier for *every* constraint, with the convention that the multiplier corresponding to an inactive constraint is zero. Let l^* denote the "extended" multiplier vector. The necessary condition (9.2) then becomes

$$g(x^*) = \mathcal{A}(x^*)^T l^* , \quad l^* \geq 0 , \tag{9.5a}$$

where

$$l_i^* c_i(x^*) = 0 , \quad i = 1, 2, \ldots, m . \tag{9.5b}$$

(Condition (9.5b) is often called a *complementarity* condition.)

As in the equality case, condition (9.5a) implies that x^* is a *stationary point* (with respect to x) of the Lagrangian function, which can be expressed either in terms of the active constraints or all the constraints. We shall use the same notation for both Lagrangian functions—i.e.,

$$L(x, \lambda) \equiv f(x) - \lambda^T \hat{c}(x) \quad \text{and} \quad L(x, l) \equiv f(x) - l^T c(x) .$$

The second-order necessary condition for inequality constraints analogous to Theorem 1.3 involves both constraint qualifications.

Theorem 9.3 (Second-order necessary conditions for optimality). *If the first- and second-order constraint qualifications hold at x^*, a necessary condition for x^* to be a local minimizer of NIP is that, for every nonzero vector p satisfying*

$$A(x^*)p = 0 , \tag{9.6}$$

it holds that $p^T \nabla^2 L(x^*, \lambda^*)p \geq 0$ for all λ^* satisfying (9.2).

Proof. Assume that x^* is a minimizer of NIP. Since the first-order constraint qualification holds at x^*, the existence of Lagrange multipliers satisfying (9.2) is implied by Theorem 9.2. Now consider any nonzero vector p satisfying (9.6). Because of the second-order constraint qualification, p is tangent to a feasible arc along which the constraints active at x^* remain identically zero. Exactly as in the proof of Theorem 1.3, analysis of the curvature of f along the arc implies the desired result. $\square$

Sufficient conditions for x^* to be a local minimizer of NIP are given in the following theorem (see, e.g., Fiacco and McCormick (1968)):

Theorem 9.4 (Sufficient optimality conditions). *The feasible point x^* is a strong* *local minimizer of NIP if there exists a vector λ^* such that*

(i) $g(x^*) = A(x^*)^{\mathrm{T}}\lambda^*$;

(ii) $\lambda^* > 0$;

(iii) $Z(x^*)^{\mathrm{T}}\nabla^2 L(x^*, \lambda^*)Z(x^*)$ *is positive definite, where $Z(x^*)$ is a basis for the null space of $A(x^*)$.* $\square$

Condition (ii) of Theorem 9.4 – that the Lagrange multipliers corresponding to active constraints are strictly positive – is usually termed *strict complementarity*. If any multiplier corresponding to an active constraint is zero, the optimality conditions become more complicated. (For details, see, e.g., Fiacco and McCormick (1968).)

Before considering methods for the general problem NIP, we turn to the special case of quadratic programming.

10. Inequality-constrained quadratic programming

The inequality-constrained quadratic programming problem is that of minimizing a quadratic function subject to a set of linear inequality constraints:

$$\text{IQP} \qquad \underset{x \in \mathbb{R}^n}{\text{minimize}} \quad d^{\mathrm{T}}x + \tfrac{1}{2}x^{\mathrm{T}}Hx$$
$$\text{subject to} \quad \mathcal{A}x \geqslant b . \tag{10.1}$$

For overviews of quadratic programming, see, e.g., Fletcher (1981), Gill, Murray and Wright (1981) and Fletcher (1986). Let $g(x)$ denote $d + Hx$, the gradient of the quadratic objective function.

Using the results of Section 9, the following conditions must hold if x^* is a minimizer of (10.1), where μ^* includes a multiplier for every constraint:

$$\mathcal{A}x^* \geqslant b ,$$
$$g(x^*) = d + Hx^* = \mathcal{A}^{\mathrm{T}}\mu^* , \tag{10.2}$$
$$\mu^* \geqslant 0 ,$$
$$\mu_i^*(a_i^{\mathrm{T}}x^* - b_i) = 0 .$$

Let A denote the matrix of constraints active at x^*, and let Z denote a matrix whose columns span the null space of A, i.e., such that $AZ = 0$; then $Z^{\mathrm{T}}HZ$ must be positive semi-definite.

The most popular approach to solving IQP is to use a so-called *active-set strategy*, which is based on the following idea. If a feasible point and the correct active set A were known, the solution could be computed directly as described above in the discussion of EQP. Since these are unknown, we develop a *prediction* of the active set—called the *working set*—that is used to compute the search direction, and then change the working set as the iterations proceed.

We shall illustrate the steps of a QP method for a *primal-feasible active-set method*. An initial feasible (non-optimal) point x is required such that $\mathcal{A}x \geq b$. Let A_W (the *working set*) denote a linearly independent set of constraints that are satisfied exactly at the current iterate, and b_W the corresponding components of b, so that $A_W x = b_W$. Let Z_W denote a basis for the null space of A_W, and assume that $Z_W^T H Z_W$ is positive definite. (The treatment of the indefinite and semidefinite cases is complicated, and will not be discussed here.)

A *search direction* p is computed by solving (2.7) with $A = A_W$, after which two situations are possible. The point $x + p$ may *violate* a constraint (or several constraints) not currently in the working set. (In this case, A_W is not the correct active set.) In order to remain feasible, a nonnegative step $\bar{\alpha} < 1$ is determined such that $\bar{\alpha}$ is the largest step that retains feasibility. A constraint that becomes satisfied exactly at $x + \bar{\alpha}p$ is then "added" to the working set (i.e., A_W includes a new row), and a new search direction is computed with the modified working set.

Otherwise, the feasible point $x + p$ is the minimizer of the quadratic objective function with the working set treated as a set of equality constraints. Let $\bar{x} = x + p$, and note that $Z_W^T g(\bar{x}) = 0$, which implies that $g(\bar{x}) = A_W^T \mu_W$ for some vector μ_W. If μ_W is nonnegative, then $\bar{x}$ is the solution of IQP, since conditions (10.2) are satisfied and $Z_W^T H Z_W$ is positive definite by assumption. Otherwise, there is at least one strictly negative component of μ_W (say, the i-th), and hence there exists a feasible descent direction p, such that $g(\bar{x})^T p < 0$ and $A_W p = e_i$, where e_i is the i-th column of the identity matrix. Movement along p causes the i-th constraint in the working set to become strictly satisfied, and hence effectively "deletes" the constraint from the working set.

Methods of this general structure will converge to a local solution of IQP in a finite number of iterations if at every iteration the active set has full rank, $Z_W^T H Z_W$ is positive definite, and $\mu_W \neq 0$. For details concerning methods that treat more complex situations, see the references given at the beginning of this section.

11. Penalty-function methods for inequalities

In applying a penalty-function approach to problem NIP, the motivation is identical to that in the equality-constrained case, namely to add a weighted penalty for infeasibility. Thus, the quadratic or absolute value penalty function may be used as in Section 3 and 4, but only the *violated* constraints are included in the penalty term. The quadratic and absolute value penalty functions for NIP may be written as

$$P_Q(x, \rho) = f(x) + \tfrac{1}{2}\rho \|\hat{c}(x)\|_2^2 \quad \text{and} \quad P_1(x, \rho) = f(x) + \rho \|\hat{c}(x)\|_1 ,$$

where $\hat{c}(x)$ is the vector of constraints *violated* at x.

The convergence of the quadratic and absolute value penalty function methods applied to NIP can be proved as for the equality-constrained problem.

(See Sections 4 and 5.) In an implementation of a penalty-function method, a small tolerance is usually included in the definition of "violated" to avoid discontinuities in the second derivatives of P_Q at x^*, so that, for example:

$$\hat{c}(x) = \{c_i(x) | c_i(x) \le \varepsilon\} , \tag{11.1}$$

where ε $(\varepsilon > 0)$ is "small".

For P_Q, the existence of a trajectory $x^*(\rho)$, with a multiplier function $\lambda(\rho)$, can be demonstrated as in the equality case, subject to the assumption of strict complementarity (see Sections 4 and 9). An important property of penalty-function methods can be derived from the behavior of the Lagrange multiplier estimates obtainable at $x^*(\rho)$. (See (4.5).) Since

$$-\rho c_i(x^*(\rho)) \to \lambda_i^* \quad \text{and} \quad \lambda_i^* \ge 0 ,$$

it is clear that a constraint active at x^* with a positive multiplier will be strictly violated at $x^*(\rho)$ for sufficiently large ρ. This relationship explains why the violated set of constraints (11.1) is often taken as a prediction of the active set when using a quadratic penalty function method.

12. Sequential quadratic programming methods

The *general* motivation given in Section 6 for sequential quadratic programming (SQP) methods is unaffected by the change from equality to inequality constraints. Because the optimal point x^* for NIP is a minimizer of the Lagrangian function within the subspace defined by the active constraint gradients (Theorem 9.3), the ideas of developing a quadratic model of the Lagrangian function and of linearizing the nonlinear constraints carry over directly. However, this approach will succeed only if we are somehow able to *identify the correct active set*, which is essential in defining the Lagrangian function.

An obvious strategy is to formulate a quadratic programming subproblem like (6.4), but with the linear constraints generalized to *inequalities*, to reflect the nature of the nonlinear constraints. Accordingly, the most common SQP method for NIP retains the standard form (6.1) for each iteration. The search direction p_k is taken as the solution of the following *inequality-constrained* quadratic program:

$$\underset{p \in \mathbb{R}^n}{\text{minimize}} \quad g_k^{\mathsf{T}} p + \tfrac{1}{2} p^{\mathsf{T}} B_k p \tag{12.1a}$$

$$\text{subject to} \quad \mathcal{A}_k p \ge -c_k , \tag{12.1b}$$

where g_k is $g(x_k)$, the gradient of f at x_k, and the matrix B_k is intended to represent the Hessian of the Lagrangian function. The crucial difference from the equality constrained case is that the linear constraints of (12.1) are *inequalities* involving all the constraints of the original problem.

At the solution of the QP (12.1), a subset of the constraints (12.1b) will be active. Let A_k denote the subset of active constraints at the solution of (12.1), and $\hat{c}_k$ the corresponding constraint values, so that

$$A_k p_k = -\hat{c}_k .$$

We know from the optimality conditions for (12.1) that its Lagrange multiplier vector μ_k must satisfy the following two conditions:

$$g_k + B_k p_k = A_k^T \mu_k , \tag{12.2a}$$

$$\mu_k \geq 0 . \tag{12.2b}$$

Comparing the conditions of Theorem 9.4 and (12.2), we see that as $p_k \to 0$, the Lagrange multipliers of the subproblem (12.1) approach the Lagrange multipliers λ^* of NIP. In fact, it can be shown that if $A(x^*)$ has full rank and x^* satisfies the sufficient conditions of Theorem 9.4, then the QP subproblem (12.1) *will identify the correct active set* if x_k is "sufficiently close" to x^* (see Robinson (1974)). This favorable result suggests that the active set of the QP subproblem can be taken as a prediction of the active set of NIP. (However, the working set is "implicit", in the sense that it is obtained as the solution of a subproblem.) Enormous algorithmic advantage can be taken of this property if the subproblem (12.1) is solved using a QP method that permits a "warm start" (i.e., that can exploit a prediction of the active set to enhance efficiency).

The treatment of inequality constraints in the definition of a merit function for SQP methods has been approached in several ways, of which we mention two. The l_1 penalty function for inequalities has been the most common choice (see Han (1976), Powell (1978)), because of the desirable properties mentioned in Section 6.4. However, recent work suggests that an augmented Lagrangian merit function can also be extended to inequality constraints. Schittkowski (1981) and Gill, Murray, Saunders and Wright (1986) have proved global convergence of an SQP method based on an augmented Lagrangian function. The latter algorithm performs a linesearch not only with respect to x and λ (as in Section 6.4), but also with respect to a set of nonnegative *slack variables*. The slack variables are introduced *purely during the linesearch* to convert the inequality constraint $c_i(x) \geq 0$ to an equality constraint:

$$c_i(x) \geq 0 \quad \text{if and only if} \quad c_i(x) - s_i = 0, \ s_i \geq 0 .$$

The merit function then has the form

$$M_A(x, \mu, s, \rho) \equiv f(x) - \mu^T(c(x) - s) + \tfrac{1}{2}\rho(c(x) - s)^T(c(x) - s) ,$$

where μ is an estimate of the multiplier vector (see (9.5)).

13. Sequential linearly constrained methods

Exactly as in extending an SQP method to treat inequality constraints, the obvious strategy in an SLC method (see Section 7) is to formulate the subproblem with linearized *inequality* constraints. A typical subproblem in an SLC method will thus have the form:

$$\underset{x\in\mathbb{R}^n}{\text{minimize}} \quad \mathscr{F}_k(x)$$

$$\text{subject to} \quad \mathscr{A}_k(x - x_k) \geq -c_k ,$$

where $\mathscr{F}_k(x)$ is (as before) a general approximation to the Lagrangian function at x_k, based on a current multiplier estimate λ_k.

For this SLC method, it can be shown (Robinson (1972)) that the subproblem will identify the correct active set in a sufficiently small neighborhood of the solution, and that the favorable local convergence rate is therefore maintained (see Section 7). An SLC method (the code MINOS; Murtagh and Saunders (1983)) is widely viewed as the most effective algorithm for solving *large-scale* problems of the form NIP.

When $\mathscr{F}_k(x)$ is defined as an augmented Lagrangian function (see (8.1)), some decision must be made about which constraints are to be treated as active. Any strategies designed to permit early termination of unpromising subproblems must exercise special caution to ensure that the multiplier estimates have the properties needed to achieve global convergence.

14. Augmented Lagrangian methods

The application of augmented Lagrangian methods to problems with inequalities is much less straightforward than for SQP and SLC methods (in which the constraints in the subproblem become inequalities), or for penalty function methods (in which the penalty term includes the violated inequality constraints). Augmented Lagrangian methods do *not* include constraints in the associated subproblem, and furthermore do not approach x^* via a sequence of points where the active constraints are violated. Hence, some other strategy must be devised to identify the active constraints.

Once a "working set" $\hat{c}(x)$ of constraints has been identified, an augmented Lagrangian function can be defined that includes only the working set:

$$L_A(x, \lambda, \rho) = f(x) - \lambda^T \hat{c}(x) + \tfrac{1}{2}\rho \hat{c}(x)^T \hat{c}(x) .$$

However, tests must be made at every stage to ensure that the working set is correct, and great difficulties have been encountered in developing a general set of guidelines for this purpose. Other approaches are based on enforcing sign restrictions on the Lagrange multiplier estimates (see, e.g., Rockafellar (1973)).

15. Barrier-function methods

In this final section, we turn to a class of methods with a different flavor from any suggested previously for solving NIP. *Barrier-function methods* can be applied only to inequality constraints for which a strictly feasible initial point exists. Thereafter, a barrier-function method generates a sequence of strictly feasible iterates. These methods have received enormous attention recently because of their close relationship with the "new" polynomial approaches to linear programming (see Chapter 2 (linear programming), Karmarkar (1984), and Gill, Murray, Saunders, Tomlin and Wright (1986)).

15.1. Motivation

In many physical and engineering applications, the constraint functions not only characterize the desired properties of the solution, but also define a region in which the problem statement is meaningful (for example, $f(x)$ or some of the constraint functions may be undefined outside the feasible region). An artificial convention for extending the problem statement outside the feasible region would not lend itself to the design of a computationally reasonable algorithm, and might introduce complications not present in the original problem.

Barrier-function methods require strict satisfaction of all constraints at the starting point and subsequent iterates. The continued enforcement of feasibility is the "opposite" of a penalty function method for inequalities (Section 11), where the constrained solution is approached through a sequence of strictly *infeasible* points with respect to the active constraints.

As in the penalty case, a barrier-function method creates a sequence of modified functions whose successive unconstrained minimizers should converge in the limit to the constrained solution. In general, the unconstrained minimizer of f will be infeasible, or f may be unbounded below. In order to guarantee that successive iterates are feasible, the modified objective function includes a term to keep iterates "inside" the feasible region. If a "barrier" is created at the boundary of the feasible region by constructing a continuous function with a positive singularity, any unconstrained minimizer of the modified function must lie strictly inside the feasible region. If the weight assigned to the barrier term is decreased toward zero, the sequence of unconstrained minimizers should generate a strictly feasible approach to the constrained minimizer.

The two most popular barrier functions are the *logarithmic* barrier function, usually attributed to Frisch (1955):

$$B(x, r) = f(x) - r \sum_{i=1}^{m_N} \ln(c_i(x)) , \qquad (15.1)$$

and the inverse barrier function (Carroll (1961)):

$$B(x, r) = f(x) + r \sum_{i=1}^{m_N} \frac{1}{c_i(x)} . \qquad (15.2)$$

The positive weight r in (15.1) and (15.2) is called the *barrier parameter*.

We henceforth consider only the logarithmic barrier function (15.1). Fiacco and McCormick (1968) present a convergence proof that, under quite general conditions of f and $\{c_i\}$, there exists a compact set containing x^* within which the sequence $\{x^*(r)\}$, the minimizers of successive $B(x, r)$, converges to x^* as $r \to 0$. As in the analogous proof for penalty function methods, the conditions for convergence do not require satisfaction of the constraint qualification at the limit point, so that barrier-function methods will converge to minimizers not satisfying the Karush–Kuhn–Tucker conditions. However, the proof of convergence requires that x^* must lie in the closure of the interior of the feasible region, and consequently x^* is not permitted to be isolated from strictly feasible points.

Because convergence of $x^*(r)$ to x^* is guaranteed only within a compact set including x^*, it is possible for the logarithmic barrier function to be unbounded below, as in an example given by Powell (1972):

$$\text{minimize}_{x \in \mathbb{R}^1} \quad -\frac{1}{x^2 + 1}$$

$$\text{subject to} \quad x \geqslant 1.$$

The solution is $x^* = 1$, but the logarithmic barrier function is given by

$$B(x, r) = -\frac{1}{x^2 + 1} - r \ln(x - 1),$$

which is unbounded below for any $r > 0$. However, unboundedness is much less likely to happen than with penalty functions, because the feasible region is often compact.

15.2. Properties

Let $\{r_k\}$ be a strictly decreasing positive sequence, with $\lim_{k \to \infty} r_k = 0$. The minimizers of successive barrier functions exhibit the following properties, where B_k denotes $B(x^*(r_k))$, f_k denotes $f(x^*(r_k))$ and c_k denotes $c(x^*(r_k))$:
   (i) $\{B_k\}$ is strictly decreasing for sufficiently small r_k and bounded c_k;
   (ii) $\{f_k\}$ is nonincreasing;
   (iii) $-\Sigma_{i=1}^{m_N} \ln c_i(x^*(r_k))$ is nondecreasing.
Property (iii) does *not* imply that the constraint values decrease at successive $x^*(r_k)$. A reduction in the barrier parameter allows the constraints to approach the boundary of the feasible region, but does not enforce a decrease.

By definition of an unconstrained minimizer, the following relation holds at $x^*(r)$:

$$\nabla B = g - r \sum_{i=1}^{m_N} \frac{1}{c_i} a_i = g - \mathcal{A}^T \begin{pmatrix} r/c_1 \\ \vdots \\ r/c_{m_N} \end{pmatrix} = 0. \tag{15.3}$$

Since $r > 0$ and $c_i > 0$ for all i, (15.3) shows that the gradient of f at $x^*(r)$ is a *nonnegative linear combination* of *all* the constraint gradients, where the coefficient of a_i is r/c_i. As r approaches zero, the quantity $r/c_i(x^*(r))$ will converge to zero if c_i is not active at x^*, since c_i is strictly bounded away from zero in a neighborhood of x^*. Assume that m constraints are active at x^*. Then for sufficiently small r, the relation holding at $x^*(r)$ can be written:

$$g = A^T \left\{ \begin{matrix} r/\hat{c}_1 \\ \vdots \\ r/\hat{c}_m \end{matrix} \right\} + O(r) , \qquad (15.4)$$

where $\hat{c}_i$ denotes the i-th active constraint, and A denotes the $m \times n$ matrix of active constraint gradients.

It follows from (15.4) that the quantity

$$\lambda_i(r) \equiv \frac{r}{\hat{c}_i(x^*(r))} , \qquad (15.5)$$

defined only for the active constraints, satisfies a relationship with g and A analogous to the multiplier relation that must hold at x^* if $A(x^*)$ has full rank. The vector $\lambda(r)$ satisfies $\lambda(r) = \lambda^* + O(r)$, where λ^* is the vector of Lagrange multipliers at x^*.

As with the quadratic penalty function (Section 4), the barrier parameter can be considered as an independent variable defining a trajectory of values $x(r)$. The following result is proved in Fiacco and McCormick (1968).

Theorem 15.1. *If $A(x^*)$ has full rank, and the sufficient conditions of Theorem 9.4 hold at x^*, then for sufficiently small r, there exists a continuously differentiable trajectory $x(r)$ such that*

$$\lim_{r \to 0} x(r) = x^* ,$$

and for any $r > 0$, $x(r)$ is a local minimizer of $B(x, r)$. □

The trajectory $x(r)$ has several interesting properties. Expanding about $r = 0$ gives the following expression:

$$x(r) = x^* + ry + O(r^2) ,$$

where

$$y = \lim_{r \to 0} \frac{x(r) - x^*}{r} = \frac{dx(r)}{dr} \bigg|_{r=0} . \qquad (15.6)$$

Differentiating the identity (15.3) and using (15.6), we obtain the following expression (cf. (4.9) for the penalty case):

$$Ay = \left\{ \begin{matrix} 1/\lambda_1^* \\ \vdots \\ 1/\lambda_m^* \end{matrix} \right\}. \tag{15.7}$$

The relationship (15.7) implies that the minimizers of successive barrier functions do not approach x^* tangentially to any constraint for which $0 < \lambda_i^* < \infty$.

Barrier-function methods are not well suited to application of general-purpose unconstrained minimization techniques, primarily because of ill-conditioning of the Hessian matrices at $x^*(r)$ if $0 < m < n$. The ill-conditioning of the Hessian matrices of barrier functions does not result from the influence of the barrier parameter, but rather from the singularities caused by the active constraints. The Hessian of $B(x^*(r), r)$ is given by:

$$H - \sum_{i=1}^{m_N} \frac{r}{c_i} H_i + \mathcal{A}^T \left\{ \begin{matrix} r/c_{1.}^2 \\ \ddots \\ \qquad r/c_{m_N}^2 \end{matrix} \right\} \mathcal{A} , \tag{15.8}$$

where all quantities are evaluated at $x^*(r)$. For inactive constraints, c_i is bounded away from zero, and thus the quantities r/c_i and r/c_i^2 go to zero as $x^*(r)$ approaches x^*. For the active constraints, we know from (15.5) that $r/c_i(x^*(r))$ approaches the corresponding (bounded) Lagrange multiplier. For a nonzero Lagrange multiplier, the ratio $r/c_i(x^*(r))^2$ is thus unbounded as $c_i \to 0$. The first two terms of (15.8) constitute an increasingly accurate approximation to $\nabla^2 L(x^*, \lambda^*)$, the Hessian of the Lagrangian function at the solution. However, if $0 < m < n$, or $m = n$ and A has some dependent rows, the dominant rank-deficient matrix causes the condition number of (15.8) to become unbounded. In particular, $\nabla^2 B(x^*(r), r)$ has m unbounded eigenvalues as $r \to 0$, with corresponding eigenvectors in the range of $A(x^*)^T$. The remaining $(n - m)$ eigenvalues are bounded and their eigenvectors lie in the null space of $A(x^*)$. (See Murray (1971b) for details.)

References

P.T. Boggs, J.W. Tolle and P. Wang (1982), On the local convergence of quasi-Newton methods for constrained optimization, *SIAM J. on Control and Optimization* **20**, 161–171.

J.R. Bunch and L.C. Kaufman (1980), A computational method for the indefinite quadratic programming problem, *Linear Algebra and its Applications* **34**, 341–370.

C.W. Carroll (1961), The created response surface technique for optimizing nonlinear restrained systems, *Operations Research* **9**, 169–184.

R.W. Chamberlain, C. Lemaréchal, H. Pedersen and M.J.D. Powell (1982), The watchdog technique for forcing convergence in algorithms for constrained optimization, *Mathematical Programming Study* **16**, 1–17.

T.F. Coleman and A.R. Conn (1982a), Nonlinear programming via an exact penalty function: Asymptotic analysis, *Mathematical Programming* **24**, 123–136.

T.F. Coleman and A.R. Conn (1982b), Nonlinear programming via an exact penalty function: Global analysis, *Mathematical Programming* **24**, 137–161.

R. Courant (1943), Variational methods for the solution of problems of equilibrium and vibrations, *Bulletin of the American Mathematical Society* **49**, 1–23.

J.E. Dennis Jr. and R.B. Schnabel (1983), *Numerical Methods for Unconstrained Optimization and Nonlinear Equations* (Prentice-Hall, Englewood Cliffs, NJ).

J.J. Dongarra, J.R. Bunch, C.B. Moler and G.W. Stewart (1979), *LINPACK Users Guide* (SIAM Publications, Philadelphia, PA).

I.S. Duff and J.K. Reid (1983), The multifrontal solution of indefinite sparse symmetric linear equations, *ACM Transactions on Mathematical Software* **9**, 302–325.

A.V. Fiacco and G.P. McCormick (1968), *Nonlinear Programming: Sequential Unconstrained Minimization Techniques* (John Wiley and Sons, New York and Toronto).

R. Fletcher (1974), Methods related to Lagrangian functions, in: P.E. Gill and W. Murray (eds.), *Numerical Methods for Constrained Optimization* (Academic Press, London and New York) 219–240.

R. Fletcher (1981), *Practical Methods of Optimization, Volume 2, Constrained Optimization* (John Wiley and Sons, New York and Toronto).

R. Fletcher (1985), An l_1 penalty method for nonlinear constraints, in: P.T. Boggs, R.H. Byrd and R.B. Schnabel (eds.), *Numerical Optimization 1984* (SIAM, Philadelphia, PA) 26–40.

R. Fletcher (1986), Recent developments in linear and quadratic programming, Report NA94, Department of Mathematical Sciences, University of Dundee, Scotland.

K.R. Frisch (1955), The logarithmic potential method of convex programming, Memorandum of May 13, 1955, University Institute of Economics, Oslo, Norway.

P.E. Gill, N.I.M. Gould, W. Murray, M.A. Saunders and M.H. Wright (1984), A weighted Gram–Schmidt method for convex quadratic programming, *Mathematical Programming* **30**, 176–195.

P.E. Gill and W. Murray (1974), Newton-type methods for unconstrained and linearly constrained optimization, *Mathematical Programming* **28**, 311–350.

P.E. Gill, W. Murray, M.A. Saunders, J.A. Tomlin and M.H. Wright (1986), On projected Newton barrier methods for linear programming and an equivalence to Karmarkar's projective method, *Mathematical Programming* **36**, 183–209.

P.E. Gill, W. Murray, M.A. Saunders and M.H. Wright (1984), Sparse matrix methods in optimization, *SIAM J. on Scientific and Statistical Computing* **5**, 562–589.

P.E. Gill, W. Murray, M.A. Saunders and M.H. Wright (1986), Some theoretical properties of an augmented Lagrangian merit function, Report SOL 86-6, Department of Operations Research, Stanford University.

P.E. Gill, W. Murray, M.A. Saunders and M.H. Wright (1987), A Schur-complement method for sparse quadratic programming, Report SOL 87-12, Department of Operations Research, Stanford University.

P.E. Gill, W. Murray and M.H. Wright (1981), *Practical Optimization* (Academic Press, London and New York).

D. Goldfarb and A. Idnani (1983), A numerically stable dual method for solving strictly convex quadratic programs, *Mathematical Programming* **27**, 1–33.

J. Goodman (1985), Newton's method for constrained optimization, *Mathematical Programming* **33**, 162–171.

N.I.M. Gould (1986), On the accurate determination of search directions for simple differentiable penalty functions, *IMA J. on Numerical Analysis* **6**, 357–372.

S.-P. Han (1976), Superlinearly convergent variable metric algorithms for general nonlinear programming problems, *Mathematical Programming* **11**, 263–282.

S.-P. Han (1977), A globally convergent method for nonlinear programming, *J. Optimization Theory and Applications* **22**, 297–310.

M.R. Hestenes (1969), Multiplier and gradient methods, *J. Optimization Theory and Applications* **4**, 303–320.

N. Karmarkar (1984), A new polynomial-time algorithm for linear programming, *Combinatorica* **4**, 373–395.

H.W. Kuhn and A.W. Tucker (1951), Nonlinear programming, in: J. Neyman (ed.), *Proceedings of the Second Berkeley Symposium on Mathematical Statistics and Probability* (University of California Press, Berkeley, CA) 481–492.

F.A. Lootsma (1969), Hessian matrices of penalty functions for solving constrained optimization problems, *Philips Res. Repts* **24**, 322–331.

D.G. Luenberger (1984), *Introduction to Linear and Nonlinear Programming* (Addison-Wesley, Menlo Park, CA).

N. Maratos (1978), Exact Penalty Function Algorithms for Finite-Dimensional and Control Optimization Problems, Ph.D. Thesis, University of London.

W. Murray (1969), An algorithm for constrained minimization, in: R. Fletcher (ed.), *Optimization* (Academic Press, London and New York) 247–258.

W. Murray (1971a), An algorithm for finding a local minimum of an indefinite quadratic program, Report NAC 1, National Physical Laboratory, England.

W. Murray (1971b), Analytical expressions for the eigenvalues and eigenvectors of the Hessian matrices of barrier and penalty functions, *J. Optimization Theory and Applications* **7**, 189–196.

B.A. Murtagh and M.A. Saunders (1982), A projected Lagrangian algorithm and its implementation for sparse nonlinear constraints, *Mathematical Programming Study* **16**, 84–117.

B.A. Murtagh and M.A. Saunders (1983), MINOS 5.0 User's Guide, Report SOL 83-20, Department of Operations Research, Stanford University.

J.M. Ortega and W.C. Rheinboldt (1970), *Iterative Solution of Nonlinear Equations in Several Variables*, Academic Press, London and New York.

M.J.D. Powell (1969), A method for nonlinear constraints in minimization problems, in: R. Fletcher (ed.), *Optimization* (Academic Press, London and New York) 283–298.

M.J.D. Powell (1972), Problems relating to unconstrained optimization, in: W. Murray (ed.), *Numerical Methods for Unconstrained Optimization* (Academic Press, London and New York) 29–55.

M.J.D. Powell (1978), The convergence of variable metric methods for nonlinearly constrained optimization calculations, in: O.L. Mangasarian, R.R. Meyer, and S.M. Robinson (eds.), *Nonlinear Programming 3* (Academic Press, London and New York) 27–63.

S.M. Robinson (1972), A quadratically convergent algorithm for general nonlinear programming problems, *Mathematical Programming* **3**, 145–156.

S.M. Robinson (1974), Perturbed Kuhn–Tucker points and rates of convergence for a class of nonlinear programming algorithms, *Mathematical Programming* **7**, 1–16.

R.T. Rockafellar (1973), The multiplier method of Hestenes and Powell applied to convex programming, *J. Optimization Theory and Applications* **12**, 555–562.

J.B. Rosen (1978), Two-phase algorithm for nonlinear constraint problems, in: O.L. Mangasarian, R.R. Meyer, and S.M. Robinson (eds.), *Nonlinear Programming 3* (Academic Press, London and New York) 97–124.

J.B. Rosen and J. Kreuser (1972), A gradient projection algorithm for nonlinear constraints, in: F.A. Lootsma (ed.), *Numerical Methods for Non-Linear Optimization* (Academic Press, London and New York) 297–300.

K. Schittkowski (1981), The nonlinear programming method of Wilson, Han and Powell with an augmented Lagrangian type line search function, *Numerische Mathematik* **38**, 83–114.

R.A. Tapia (1977), Diagonalized multiplier methods and quasi-Newton methods for constrained optimization, *J. Optimization Theory and Applications* **22**, 135–194.

M.H. Wright (1976), Numerical Methods for Nonlinearly Constrained Optimization, Ph.D. Thesis, Stanford University, CA.

G.L. Nemhauser et al., Eds., *Handbooks in OR & MS, Vol. 1*
© Elsevier Science Publishers B.V. (North-Holland) 1989

Chapter IV

Network Flows

Ravindra K. Ahuja*, Thomas L. Magnanti, and James B. Orlin

Sloan School of Management, Massachusetts Institute of Technology, Cambridge, MA 02139, U.S.A.

1. Introduction

Perhaps no subfield of mathematical programming is more alluring than network optimization. Highway, rail, electrical, communication and many other physical networks pervade our everyday lives. As a consequence, even non-specialists recognize the practical importance and the wide ranging applicability of networks. Moreover, because the physical operating characteristics of networks (e.g., flows on arcs and mass balance at nodes) have natural mathematical representations, practitioners and non-specialists can readily understand the mathematical descriptions of network optimization problems and the basic nature of techniques used to solve these problems. This combination of widespread applicability and ease of assimilation has undoubtedly been instrumental in the evolution of network planning models as one of the most widely used modeling techniques in all of operations research and applied mathematics.

Network optimization is also alluring to methodologists. Networks provide a concrete setting for testing and devising new theories. Indeed, network optimization has inspired many of the most fundamental results in all of optimization. For example, price-directive decomposition algorithms for both linear programming and combinatorial optimization had their origins in network optimization. So did cutting plane methods and branch and bound procedures of integer programming, primal–dual methods of linear and nonlinear programming, and polyhedral methods of combinatorial optimization. In addition, networks have served as the major prototype for several theoretical domains (for example, the field of matroids) and as the core model for a wide variety of min/max duality results in discrete mathematics.

Moreover, network optimization has served as a fertile meeting ground for

---

* Now at Indian Institute of Technology, Kanpur − 208016, India.

ideas for optimization and computer science. Many results in network optimization are routinely used to design and evaluate computer systems, and ideas
from computer science concerning data structures and efficient data manipulation have had a major impact on the design and implementation of many
network optimization algorithms.

The aim of this paper is to summarize many of the fundamental ideas of
network optimization. In particular, we concentrate on network flow problems
and highlight a number of recent theoretical and algorithmic advances. We
have divided the discussion into the following broad major topics:

- Applications.
- Basic properties of network flows.
- Shortest path problems.
- Maximum flow problems.
- Minimum cost flow problems.
- Assignment problems.

Much of our discussion focuses on the design of provably good (i.e.,
polynomial-time) algorithms. Among good algorithms, we have presented
those that are simple and are likely to be efficient in practice. We have
attempted to structure our discussion so that it not only provides a survey of
the field for the specialists, but also serves as an introduction and summary to
the non-specialists who have a basic working knowledge of the rudiments of
optimization, particularly linear programming.

In this chapter, we limit our discussions to the problems listed above. Some
important generalizations of these problems such as (i) the generalized network flows, (ii) the multicommodity flows, and (iii) the network design, will
not be covered in our survey. We do, however, briefly describe these problems
in Section 6.6 and provide some important references.

As a prelude to the remainder of our discussion, in this section we present
several important preliminaries. We discuss (i) different ways to measure the
performance of algorithms; (ii) graph notation and various ways to represent
networks quantitively; (iii) a few basic ideas from computer science that
underlie the design of many algorithms; and (iv) two generic proof techniques
that have proven to be useful in designing polynomial-time algorithms.

1.1. Applications

Networks arise in numerous application settings and in a variety of guises. In
this section, we briefly describe a few prototypical applications. Our discussion
is intended to illustrate a range of applications and to be suggestive of how
network flow problems arise in practice; a more extensive survey would take us
far beyond the scope of our discussion. To illustrate the breadth of network
applications, we consider some models requiring solution techniques that we
will not describe in this chapter.

For the purposes of this discussion, we will consider four different types of
networks arising in practice:

• Physical networks (streets, railbeds, pipelines, wires).
• Route networks.
• Space-time networks (scheduling networks).
• Derived networks (through problem transformations).

These four categories are not exhaustive and overlap in coverage. Nevertheless, they provide a useful taxonomy for summarizing a variety of applications. Network flow models are also used for several purposes:

• Descriptive modeling (answering "what is?" questions).
• Predictive modeling (answering "what will be?" questions).
• Normative modeling (answering "what should be?" questions, that is, performing optimization).

We will illustrate models in each of these categories. We first introduce the basic underlying network flow model and some useful notation.

The network flow model

Let $G = (N, A)$ be a directed network with a cost c_{ij}, a lower bound l_{ij}, and a capacity u_{ij} associated with every arc $(i, j) \in A$. We associate with each node $i \in N$ an integer number $b(i)$ representing its supply or demand. If $b(i) > 0$, then node i is a *supply* node; if $b(i) < 0$, then node i is a *demand* node; and if $b(i) = 0$, then node i is a *transhipment* node. Let $n = |N|$ and $m = |A|$. The minimum cost network flow problem can be formulated as follows:

$$\text{minimize} \quad \sum_{(i,j) \in A} c_{ij} x_{ij} \tag{1.1a}$$

subject to

$$\sum_{\{j:(i,j) \in A\}} x_{ij} - \sum_{\{j:(j,i) \in A\}} x_{ji} = b(i), \quad \text{for all } i \in N, \tag{1.1b}$$

$$l_{ij} \leq x_{ij} \leq u_{ij}, \quad \text{for all } (i, j) \in A. \tag{1.1c}$$

We refer to the vector $x = (x_{ij})$ as the *flow* in the network. Each constraint (1.1b) implies that the total flow out of a node minus the total flow into that node must equal the net supply/demand of the node. We henceforth refer to these constraints as the *mass balance constraints*. The flow must also satisfy the lower bound and capacity constraints (1.1c) which we refer to as the *flow bound constraints*. The flow bounds might model physical capacities, contractual obligations or simply operating ranges of interest. Frequently, the given lower bounds l_{ij} are all zero; we show later that they can be made zero without any loss of generality.

In matrix notation, we represent the minimum cost flow problem

$$\text{minimize}\{cx : Nx = b \text{ and } l \leq x \leq u\}, \tag{1.2}$$

in terms of a *node–arc incidence matrix* N. The matrix N has one row for each node of the network and one column for each arc. We let N_{ij} represent the column of N corresponding to arc (i, j), and let e_j denote the *j-th unit vector* which is a column vector of size n whose entries are all zeros except for the j-th entry which is a 1. Note that each flow variable x_{ij} appears in two mass balance equations, as an outflow from node i with a $+1$ coefficient and as an inflow to node j with a -1 coefficient. Therefore the column corresponding to arc (i, j) is $N_{ij} = e_i - e_j$.

The matrix N has very special structure: only $2m$ out of its nm entries are nonzero, all of its nonzero entries are $+1$ or -1, and each column has exactly one $+1$ and one -1. Figure 1.1 gives an example of the node–arc incidence matrix. Later in Sections 2.2 and 2.3, we consider some of the consequences of this special structure. For now, we make two observations.

(i) Summing all the mass balance constraints eliminates all the flow variables and gives

$$\sum_{i \in N} b(i) = 0, \quad \text{or} \quad \sum_{\{i \in N: b(i) > 0\}} b(i) = \sum_{\{i \in N: b(i) < 0\}} - b(i).$$

Consequently, total supply must equal total demand if the mass balance constraints are to have any feasible solution.

(ii) If the total supply does equal the total demand, then summing all the mass balance equations gives the zero equation $0x = 0$, or equivalently, any equation is equal to minus the sum of all other equations, and hence is redundant.

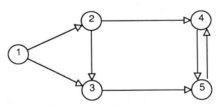

(a) An example network.

	(1, 2)	(1, 3)	(2, 3)	(2, 4)	(3, 5)	(4, 5)	(5, 4)
1	1	1	0	0	0	0	0
2	−1	0	1	1	0	0	0
3	0	−1	−1	0	1	0	0
4	0	0	0	−1	0	1	−1
5	0	0	0	0	−1	−1	1

(b) The node–arc incidence matrix of the example network.

Fig. 1.1. An example of the matrix N.

The following special cases of the minimum cost flow problem play central roles in the theory and applications of network flows.

The shortest path problem. The shortest path problem is to determine directed paths of smallest cost from a given node 1 to all other nodes. If we choose the data in the minimum cost flow problem as $b(1) = (n - 1)$, $b(i) = -1$ for all other nodes, c_{ij} = length of arc (i, j), and $l_{ij} = 0$ and $u_{ij} = n$ for all arcs, then the optimum solution sends unit flow from node 1 to every other node along a shortest path.

The maximum flow problem. The maximum flow problem is to send the maximum possible flow in a network from a specified *source* node s to a specified *sink* node t. In the minimum cost flow problem, if we add an additional arc (t, s) with $c_{ts} = -1$ and $u_{ts} = \infty$, set the supply/demand of all nodes and costs of all other arcs to zero, then the minimum cost solution maximizes the flow on arc (t, s), which equals the maximum possible flow from the source node to the sink node.

The assignment problem. The data of the assignment problem consist of a set N_1, say of persons, and a set N_2, say of objects, satisfying $|N_1| = |N_2|$, a collection of node pairs $A \subseteq N_1 \times N_2$ representing possible person-to-object assignments, and a cost c_{ij} associated with each element (i, j) in A. The objective is to assign each person to exactly one object in a way that minimizes the cost of the assignment. The assignment problem is a minimum cost flow problem on a network $G = (N_1 \cup N_2, A)$ with $b(i) = 1$ for all $i \in N_1$ and $b(i) = -1$ for all $i \in N_2$ (we set $l_{ij} = 0$ and $u_{ij} = 1$ for all $(i, j) \in A$).

Physical networks

The familiar city street map is perhaps the prototypical physical network, and the one that most readily comes to mind when we envision a network. Many network planning problems arise in this problem context. As one illustration, consider the problem of managing, or designing, a street network to decide upon such issues as speed limits, one way street assignments, or whether or not to construct a new road or bridge. In order to make these decisions intelligently, we need a descriptive model that tells us how to model traffic flows and measure the performance of any design as well as a predictive model for measuring the effect of any change in the system. We can then use these models to answer a variety of 'what if' planning questions.

The following type of equilibrium network flow model permits us to answer these types of questions. Each link of the network has an associated delay function that specifies how long it takes to traverse the link. The time to do so depends upon traffic conditions; the more traffic that flows on the link, the longer is the travel time to traverse it. Now also suppose that each user of the system has a point of origin (e.g., his or her home) and a point of destination (e.g., his or her workplace in the central business district). Each of these users must choose a route through the network. Note, however, that these route choices affect each other; if two users traverse the same link, they add to each other's travel time because of the added congestion on the link. Now let us make the behavioral assumption that each user wishes to travel between his or her origin and destination as quickly as possible, that is, along a shortest travel time path. This situation leads to the following equilibrium problem with an embedded set of network optimization problems (shortest path problems): Is there a flow pattern in the network with the property that no user can unilaterally change his (or her) choice of origin to destination path (that is, all other users continue to use their specified paths in the equilibrium solution) to reduce his (or her) travel time? Operations researchers have developed a set of sophisticated models for this problem setting, as well as related theory (concerning, for example, existence and uniqueness of equilibrium solutions) and algorithms for computing equilibrium solutions. Used in the mode of 'what if' scenario analysis, these models permit analysts to answer the type of questions we posed previously. These models are actively used in practice. Indeed, the Urban Mass Transit Authority in the United States requires that communities perform a network equilibrium impact analysis as part of the process for obtaining federal funds for highway construction or improvement.

Similar types of models arise in many other problem contexts. For example, a network equilibrium model forms the heart of the Project Independence Energy Systems (PIES) model developed by the U.S. Department of Energy as an analysis tool for guiding public policy on energy. The basic equilibrium model of electrical networks is another example. In this setting, Ohm's Law serves as the analog of the congestion function for the traffic equilibrium problem, and Kirchoff's Law represents the network mass balance equations.

Another type of physical network is a very large-scale integrated circuit (VLSI circuit). In this setting the nodes of the network correspond to electrical components and the links correspond to wires that connect these links. Numerous network planning problems arise in this problem context. For example, how can we lay out, or design, the smallest possible integrated circuit to make the necessary connections between its components and maintain necessary separations between the wires (to avoid electrical interference).

Route networks

Route networks, which are one level of abstraction removed from physical networks, are familiar to most students of operations research and management science. The traditional operations research transportation problem is illustrative. A shipper with supplies at its plants must ship to geographically dispersed retail centers, each with a given customer demand. Each arc connecting a supply point to a retail center incurs costs based upon some physical network, in this case the transportation network. Rather than solving the problem directly on the physical network, we preprocess the data and construct transportation routes. Consequently, an arc connecting a supply point and retail center might correspond to a complex four leg distribution channel with legs (i) from a plant (by truck) to a rail station, (ii) from the rail station to a rail head elsewhere in the system, (iii) from the railhead (by truck) to a distribution center, and (iv) from the distribution center (on a local delivery truck) to the final customer. If we assign the arc with the composite distribution cost of all the intermediary legs, as well as with the distribution capacity for this route, this problem becomes a classic network transportation model: find the flows from plants to customers that minimizes overall costs. This type of model is used in numerous applications. As but one illustration, a prize winning practice paper written several years ago described an application of such network planning system by the Cahill May Roberts Pharmaceutical Company (of Ireland) to reduce overall distribution costs by 20%, while improving customer service as well.

Many related problems arise in this type of problem setting, for instance, the design issue of deciding upon the location of the distribution centers. It is possible to address this type of decision problem using integer programming methodology for choosing the distribution sites and network flows to cost out (or optimize flows) for any given choice of sites; using this approach, a noted study conducted several years ago permitted Hunt Wesson Foods Corporation to save over $1 million annually.

One special case of the transportation problem merits note – the assignment problem that we introduced previously in this section. The problem has numerous applications, particularly in problem contexts such as machine scheduling. In this application context, we would identify the supply points with jobs to be performed, the demand points with available machines, and the cost associated with arc (i, j) as the cost of completing job i on machine j. The solution to the problem specifies the minimum cost assignment of the jobs to the machines, assuming that each machine has the capacity to perform only one job.

Space–time networks

Frequently in practice, we wish to schedule some production or service activity over time. In these instances it is often convenient to formulate a network flow problem on a 'space–time network' with several nodes representing a particular facility (a machine, a warehouse, an airport) but at different points in time.

Figure 1.2, which represents a core planning model in production planning, *the economic lot size problem*, is an important example. In this problem context, we wish to meet prescribed demands d_t for a product in each of the T time periods. In each period, we can produce at level x_t and/or we can meet the demand by drawing upon inventory I_t from the previous period. The network representing this problem has $T + 1$ nodes: one node $t = 1, 2, \ldots, T$ represents each of the planning periods, and one node 0 represents the 'source' of all production. The flow on arc $(0, t)$ prescribes the production level x_t in period t, and the flow on arc $(t, t + 1)$ represents the inventory level I_t to be carried from period t to period $t + 1$. The mass balance equation for each period t models the basic accounting equation: incoming inventory plus production in that period must equal demand plus final inventory. The mass balance equation for node 0 indicates that all demand (assuming zero beginning and

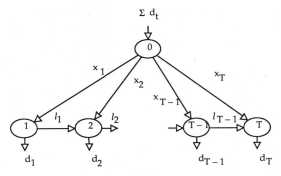

Fig. 1.2. Network flow model of the economic lot size problem.

zero final inventory over the entire planning period) must be produced in some period $t = 1, 2, \ldots, T$. Whenever the production and holding costs are linear, this problem is easily solved as a shortest path problem (for each demand period, we must find the minimum cost path of production and inventory arcs from node 0 to that demand point). If we impose capacities on production or inventory, the problem becomes a minimum cost network flow problem.

One extension of this economic lot sizing problem arises frequently in practice. Assume that production x_t in any period incurs a fixed cost: that is, whenever we produce in period t (i.e., $x_t > 0$), no matter how much or how little, we incur a fixed cost F_t. In addition, we may incur a per unit production cost c_t in period t and a per unit inventory cost h_t for carrying any unit of inventory from period t to period $t + 1$. Hence, the cost on each arc for this problem is either linear (for inventory carrying arcs) or linear plus a fixed cost (for production arcs). Consequently, the objective function for the problem is concave. As we indicate in Section 2.2, any such concave cost network flow problem always has a special type of optimum solution known as a spanning tree solution. This problem's spanning tree solution decomposes into disjoint directed paths; the first arc on each path is a production arc (of the form $(0, t)$) and each other arc is an inventory carrying arc. This observation implies the following *production property*: in the solution, each time we produce, we produce enough to meet the demand for an integral number of contiguous periods. Moreover, in no period do we both carry inventory from the previous period and produce.

The production property permits us to solve the problem very efficiently as a shortest path problem on an auxiliary network G' defined as follows. The network G' consists of nodes 1 to $T + 1$, and for every pair of nodes i and j with $i < j$, it contains an arc (i, j). The length of arc (i, j) is equal to the production and inventory cost of satisfying the demand of the periods from i to $j - 1$. Observe that for every production schedule satisfying the production property, G' contains a directed path from node 1 to node $T + 1$ with the same objective function value and vice-versa. Hence we can obtain the optimum production schedule by solving a shortest path problem.

Many enhancements of the model are possible, for example (i) the production facility might have limited production capacity or limited storage for inventory, or (ii) the production facility might be producing several products that are linked by common production costs or by changeover costs (for example, we may need to change dies in an automobile stamping plant when making different types of fenders), or that share common limited production facilities. In most cases, the enchanced models are quite difficult to solve (they are NP-complete), though the embedded network structure often proves to be useful in designing either approximation or optimization methods.

Another classical network flow scheduling problem is the *airline scheduling problem* used to design a flight schedule for an airline. In this application setting, each node represents both a geographical location (e.g., an airport) and a point in time (e.g., New York at 10 A.M.). The arcs are of two types: (i) service arcs connecting two airports, for example New York at 10 A.M. to Boston at 11 A.M.; (ii) layover arcs that permit a plane to stay at New York from 10 A.M. until 11 A.M. to wait for a later flight, or to wait overnight at New York from 11 P.M. until 6 A.M. the next morning. If we identify revenues with each service leg, a flow in this network (with no external supply or demand) will specify a set of flight plans (circulation of airplanes through the network). A flow that maximizes revenue will prescribe a schedule for an airline's fleet of planes. The same type of network representation arises in many other dynamic scheduling applications.

Derived networks

This category is a 'grab bag' of specialized applications and illustrates that sometimes network flow problems arise in surprising ways from problems that on the surface might not appear to involve networks. The following examples illustrate this point.

Single duty crew scheduling. Table 1.1 illustrates a number of possible duties for the drivers of a bus company.

For example, the first duty (the first column in the table) represents a schedule in which a driver works from 9 A.M. to 10 A.M.; the second duty

Table. 1.1
Available duties for a single duty scheduling problem

Time Period	Duty Number										
	1	2	3	4	5	6	7	8	9	10	11
9–10 A.M.	1	0	0	0	1	0	1	0	0	0	0
10–11 A.M.	0	0	0	0	1	0	1	0	0	0	0
11–Noon	0	0	1	0	0	0	0	0	1	0	0
12–1 P.M.	0	0	1	0	0	0	0	0	1	0	0
1–2 P.M.	0	0	1	0	0	1	0	0	0	0	1
2–3 P.M.	0	1	0	0	0	1	0	1	0	0	1
3–4 P.M.	0	1	0	0	0	0	0	1	0	1	0
4–5 P.M.	0	0	0	1	0	0	0	0	0	1	0

specifies that a driver works from 2 P.M. to 4 P.M. Suppose each duty j has an associated cost c_j. If we wish to ensure that a driver is on duty for each hour of the planning period (9 A.M. to 5 P.M. in the example), and the cost of scheduling is minimum, then the problem is an integer program:

$$\text{minimize} \quad cx \tag{1.3a}$$

$$\text{subject to} \quad Ax = b , \tag{1.3b}$$

$$x_j = 0 \text{ or } 1 \quad \text{for all } j . \tag{1.3c}$$

In this formulation the binary variable x_j indicates whether ($x_j = 1$) or not ($x_j = 0$) we select the j-th duty; the matrix A represents the matrix of duties and b is a column vector whose components are all 1's. Observe that the ones in each column of A occur in consecutive rows because each driver's duty contains a single work shift (no split shifts or work breaks). We show that this problem is a shortest path problem. To make this identification, we perform the following operations: In (1.3b) subtract each equation from the equation below it. This transformation does not change the solution to the system. Now add a redundant equation equal to minus the sums of all the equations in the revised system. Because of the structure of A, each column j in the revised system will have a single $+1$ (corresponding to the first hour of the duty in the j-th column of A) and a single -1 (corresponding to the row in A, or the added row, that lies just below the last $+1$ in the j-th column of A). Moreover, the revised right hand side vector of the problem will have a $+1$ in row 1 and a -1 in the last (the appended) row. Therefore, the problem is to ship one unit of flow from node 1 to node 9 at minimum cost in the network given in Figure 1.3, which is an instance of the shortest path problem.

If instead of requiring a single driver to be on duty in each period, we specify a number to be on duty in each period, the same transformation would produce a network flow problem, but in this case the right hand side coefficients (supply and demands) could be arbitrary. Therefore, the transformed problem would be a general minimum cost network flow problem, rather than a shortest path problem.

Critical path scheduling and networks derived from precedence conditions
In construction and many other project planning applications, workers need to complete a variety of tasks that are related by precedence conditions; for

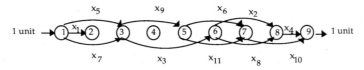

Fig. 1.3. Shortest path formulation of the single duty scheduling problem.

example, in constructing a house, a builder must pour the foundation before framing the house and complete the framing before beginning to install either electrical or plumbing fixtures. This type of application can be formulated mathematically as follows. Suppose we need to complete J jobs and that job j ($j = 1, 2, \ldots, J$) requires t_j days to complete. We are to choose the start time s_j of each job j so that we honor a set of specified precedence constraints and complete the overall project as quickly as possible. If we represent the jobs by nodes, then the precedence constraints can be represented by arcs, thereby giving us a network. The precedence constraints imply that for each arc (i, j) in the network, job j cannot start until job i has been completed. For convenience of notation, we add two dummy jobs, both with zero processing time: a 'start' job 0 to be completed before any other job can begin and a 'completion' job $J + 1$ that cannot be initiated until we have completed all other jobs. Let $G = (N, A)$ represent the network corresponding to this augmented project. Then we wish to solve the following optimization problem:

$$\text{minimize} \quad s_{J+1} - s_0 \,,$$

$$\text{subject to} \quad s_j \geq s_i + t_i \,, \quad \text{for each arc } (i, j) \in A \,.$$

On the surface, this problem, which is a linear program in the variables s_j, seems to bear no resemblance to network optimization. Note, however, that if we move the variable s_i to the left hand side of the constraint, then each constraint contains exactly two variables, one with a plus one coefficient and one with a minus one coefficient. The linear programming dual of this problem has a familiar structure. If we associate a dual variable x_{ij} with each arc (i, j), then the dual of this problem is

$$\text{maximize} \quad \sum_{(i,j) \in A} t_i x_{ij} \,,$$

subject to

$$- \sum_{\{j:(i,j) \in A\}} x_{ij} + \sum_{\{j:(j,i) \in A\}} x_{ji} = \begin{cases} -1 & \text{if } i = 0 \,, \\ 0 & \text{otherwise, for all } i \in N \,, \\ 1 & \text{if } i = J + 1 \,, \end{cases}$$

$$x_{ij} \geq 0 \,, \quad \text{for all } (i, j) \in A \,.$$

This problem requires us to determine the longest path in the network G from node 0 to node $J + 1$ with t_i as the arc length of arc (i, j). This longest path has the following interpretation. It is the longest sequence of jobs needed to fulfill the specified precedence conditions. Since delaying any job in this sequence must necessarily delay the completion of the overall project, this path has become known as the *critical path* and the problem is now known as the *critical path problem*. This model has become a principal tool in project management, particularly for managing large-scale construction projects. The critical path itself is important because it identifies those jobs that require managerial attention in order to complete the project as quickly as possible.

Researchers and practitioners have enhanced this basic model in several ways. For example, if resources are available for expediting individual jobs, we could consider the most efficient use of these resources to complete the overall project as quickly as possible. Certain versions of this problem can be formulated as minimum cost flow problems.

The *open pit mining* problem is another network flow problem that arises from precedence conditions. Consider the open pit mine shown in Figure 1.4. As shown in this figure, we have divided the region to be mined into blocks. The provisions of any given mining technology, and perhaps the geography of the mine, impose restrictions on how we can remove the blocks: for example, we can never remove a block until we have removed any block that lies immediately above it; restrictions on the 'angle' of mining blocks might impose similar precedence conditions. Suppose now that each block j has an associated revenue r_j (e.g., the value of the ore in the block minus the cost for extracting the block) and we wish to extract blocks to maximize overall revenue. If we let y_j be a zero–one variable indicating whether ($y_i = 1$) or not ($y_j = 0$) we extract block j, the problem will contain (i) a constraint $y_j \leq y_i$ (or, $y_j - y_i \leq 0$) whenever we need to mine block j before block i, and (ii) an objective function specifying that we wish to maximize total revenue $r_j y_j$, summed over all blocks j. The dual linear program (obtained from the linear programming version of the problem with the constraints $0 \leq y_j \leq 1$, rather than $y_j = 0$ or 1) will be a network flow problem with a node for each block, a variable for each precedence constraint, and the revenue r_j as the demand at node j. This network will also have a dummy 'collection node' 0 with demand equal to minus the sum of the r_j's, and an arc connecting it to node j (that is, block j); this arc corresponds to the upper bound constraint $y_j \leq 1$ in the original linear program. The dual problem is one of finding a network flow that minimizes the sum of flows on the arcs incident to node 0.

The critical path scheduling problem and open pit mining problem illustrate one way that network flow problems arise indirectly. Whenever two variables

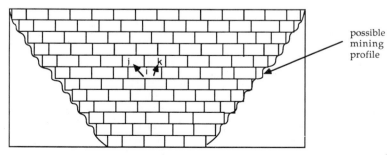

Fig. 1.4. Open pit Mine; we must extract blocks j and k before block i.

in a linear program are related by a precedence conditions, the variable corresponding to this precedence constraint in the dual linear program will have a network flow structure. If the only constraints in the problem are precedence constraints, the dual linear program will be a network flow problem.

Matrix rounding of census information

The U.S. Census Bureau uses census information to construct millions of tables for a wide variety of purposes. By law, the Bureau has an obligation to protect the source of its information and not disclose statistics that can be attributed to any particular individual. It can attempt to do so by rounding the census information contained in any table. Consider, for example, the data shown in Table 1.2(a). Since the upper leftmost entry in this table is a 1, the tabulated information might disclose information about a particular individual. We might disguise the information in this table as follows; round each entry in the table, including the row and column sums, either up or down to a multiple of three, say, so that the entries in the table continue to add to the (rounded) row and column sums, and the overall sum of the entries in the new table adds to a rounded version of the overall sum in the original table. Table 1.2(b) shows a rounded version of the data that meets this criterion. The problem can be cast as finding a feasible flow in a network and can be solved by an application of the maximum flow algorithm. The network contains a node for each row in the table and a node for each column. It contains an arc connecting node i (corresponding to row i) and node j (corresponding to column j): the flow on this arc should be the ij-th entry in the prescribed table, rounded either up or down. In addition, we add a supersource s to the network connected to each row node i: the flow on this arc must be the i-th row sum, rounded up or down. Similarly, we add a supersink t with an arc connecting each column node j to this node; the flow on this arc must be the j-th column sum, rounded up or down. We also add an arc connecting node t and node s; the flow on this arc must be the sum of all entries in the original table rounded up or down. Figure 1.5 illustrates the network flow problem corresponding to the census data

Table 1.2
Rounding census table

Income	(a) Raw data Time in service (years)				(b) Rounded data Time in service (years)			
	<1	1–5	>5	Row Total	<1	1–5	>5	Row Total
less than $10 000	1	5	1	7	3	3	0	6
$10 000–$30 000	0	2	2	4	0	3	3	6
$30 000–$50 000	0	2	1	3	0	3	0	3
more than $50 000	0	1	4	5	0	0	6	6
Column Total	1	10	8	19	3	9	9	21

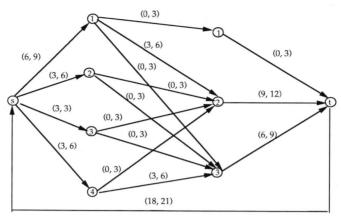

Fig. 1.5. Network flow problem for census rounding: the network shows lower and upper bounds for arc flows.

specified in Table 1.2. If we rescale all the flows, measuring them in integral units of the rounding base (multiples of 3 in our example), then the flow on each arc must be integral at one of two consecutive integral values. The formulation of a more general version of this problem, corresponding to tables with more than two dimensions, will not be a network flow problem. Nevertheless, these problems have an imbedded network structure (corresponding to 2-dimensional 'cuts' in the table) that we can exploit in devising algorithms to find rounded versions of the tables.

1.2. Complexity analysis

There are three basic approaches for measuring the performance of an algorithm: empirical analysis, worst-case analysis, and average-case analysis. *Empirical analysis* typically measures the computational time of an algorithm using statistical sampling on a distribution (or several distributions) of problem instances. The major objective of empirical analysis is to estimate how algorithms behave in practice. *Worst-case analysis* aims to provide upper bounds on the number of steps that a given algorithm can take on *any* problem instance. Therefore, this type of analysis provides *performance guarantees*. The objective of *average-case analysis* is to estimate the expected number of steps taken by an algorithm. Average-case analysis differs from empirical analysis because it provides rigorous mathematical proofs of average-case performance, rather than statistical estimates.

Each of these three performance measures has its relative merits, and is appropriate for certain purposes. Nevertheless, this chapter will focus primarily on worst-case analysis, and only secondarily on empirical behavior. Researchers have designed many of the algorithms described in this chapter specifically to improve worst-case complexity while simultaneously maintaining good empirical behavior. Thus, for the algorithms we present, worst-case analysis is the primary measure of performance.

Worst-case analysis

For worst-case analysis, we bound the running time of network algorithms in terms of several basic problem parameters: the number of nodes (n), the number of arcs (m), and upper bounds C and U on the cost coefficients and the arc capacities. Whenever C (or U) appears in the complexity analysis, we assume that each cost (or capacity) is integer valued. As an example of a worst-case result within this chapter, we will prove that the number of steps for the label correcting algorithm to solve the shortest path problem is less than pnm steps for some sufficiently large constant p.

To avoid the need to compute or mention the constant p, researchers typically use a 'big O' notation, replacing the expressions: "the label correcting algorithm requires pmn steps for some constant p" with the equivalent expression "the running time of the label correcting algorithm is $O(nm)$." The $O(\ )$ notation avoids the need to state a specific constant; also, this notation indicates only the *dominant* terms of the running time. By dominant, we mean the term that would dominate all other terms for *sufficiently* large values of n and m. Therefore, the time bounds are called *asymptotic* running times. For example, if the actual running time is $10nm^2 + 2^{100}n^2m$, then we would state that the running time is $O(nm^2)$, assuming that $m \geqslant n$. Observe that the running time indicates that the $10nm^2$ term is dominant even though for most practical values of n and m, the $2^{100}n^2m$ term would dominate. Although ignoring the constant terms may have this undesirable feature, researchers have widely adopted the $O(\ )$ notation for several reasons:

1. Ignoring the constants greatly simplifies the analysis. Consequently, the use of $O(\ )$ notation typically has permitted analysts to avoid the prohibitively difficult analysis required to compute the leading constants, which, in turn, has led to a flourishing of research on the worst-case performance of algorithms.

2. Estimating the constants correctly is fundamentally difficult. The least value of the constants is not determined solely by the algorithm; it is also highly sensitive to the choice of the computer language, and even to the choice of the computer.

3. For all of the algorithms that we present, the constant terms are relatively small integers for all the terms in the complexity bound.

4. For large practical problems, the constant factors do not contribute nearly as much to the running time as do the factors involving n, m, C or U.

Counting steps

The running time of a network algorithm is determined by counting the number of steps it performs. The counting of steps relies on a number of assumptions, most of which are quite appropriate for most of today's computers.

A1.1. The computer carries out instructions sequentially, with at most one instruction being executed at a time.

A1.2. Each comparison and basic arithmetic operation counts as one step.

By envoking A1.1, we are adhering to a sequential model of computation; we will not discuss parallel implementations of network flow algorithms.

Assumption A1.2 implicitly assumes that the only operations to be counted are comparisons and arithmetic operations. In fact, even by counting all other computer operations, on today's computers we would obtain the same asymptotic worst-case results for the algorithms that we present. Our assumption that each operation, be it an addition or division, takes equal time, is justified in part by the fact that O( ) notation ignores differences in running times of at most a constant factor, which is the time difference between an addition and a multiplication on essentially all modern computers.

On the other hand, the assumption that each arithmetic operation takes one step may lead us to underestimate the asymptotic running time of arithmetic operations involving very large numbers on real computers since, in practice, a computer must store large numbers in several words of its memory. Therefore, to perform each operation on very large numbers, a computer must access a number of words of data and thus takes more than a constant number of steps. To avoid this systematic underestimation of the running time, in comparing two running times, we will typically assume that both C and U are polynomially bounded in n, i.e., $C = O(n^k)$ and $U = O(n^k)$, for some constant k. This assumption, known as the *similarity assumption*, is quite reasonable in practice. For example, if we were to restrict costs to be less than $100n^3$, we would allow costs to be as large as $100\,000\,000\,000$ for networks with 1000 nodes.

Polynomial-time algorithms

An algorithm is said to be a *polynomial-time* algorithm if its running time is bounded by a polynomial function of the input length. The *input length* of a problem is the number of bits needed to represent that problem. For a network problem, the input length is a low order polynomial function of n, m, $\log C$ and $\log U$ (e.g., it is $O((n + m)(\log n + \log C + \log U))$. Consequently, researchers refer to a network algorithm as a polynomial-time algorithm if its running time is bounded by a polynomial function in n, m, $\log C$ and $\log U$. (In this chapter, $\log x$ denotes $\log_2 x$.) For example, the running time of one of the polynomial-time maximum flow algorithms we consider is $O(nm + n^2 \log U)$. Other instances of polynomial-time bounds are $O(n^2 m)$ and $O(n \log n)$. A polynomial-time algorithm is said to be a *strongly polynomial-time* algorithm if its running time is bounded by a polynomial function in only n and m, and does not involve $\log C$ or $\log U$. The maximum flow algorithm alluded to, therefore, is not a strongly polynomial-time algorithm. The interest in strongly polynomial-time algorithms is primarily theoretical. In particular, if we envoke the similarity assumption, all polynomial-time algorithms are strongly polynomial-time because $\log C = O(\log n)$ and $\log U = O(\log n)$.

An algorithm is said to be an *exponential-time* algorithm if its running time grows as a function that can not be polynomially bounded. Some examples of exponential time bounds are $O(nC)$, $O(2^n)$, $O(n!)$ and $O(n^{\log n})$. (Observe that nC cannot be bounded by a polynomial function of n and $\log C$.) We say that an algorithm is *pseudopolynomial-time* if its running time is polynomially bounded in n, m, C and U. The class of pseudopolynomial-time algorithms is an important subclass of exponential-time algorithms. Some instances of pseudopolynomial-time bounds are $O(m + nC)$ and $O(mC)$. For problems that satisfy the similarity assumption, pseudopolynomial-time algorithms become polynomial-time algorithms, but the algorithms will not be attractive if C and U are high degree polynomials in n.

There are two major reasons for preferring polynomial-time algorithms to exponential-time algorithms. First, any polynomial-time algorithm is asymptotically superior to any exponential-time algorithm. Even in extreme cases this is true. For example, n^{1000} is smaller than $n^{0.1 \log n}$ if n is sufficiently large. (In this case, n must be larger than $2^{10\,000}$.) Table 1.3 illustrates the asymptotic superiority of polynomial-time algorithms. The second reason is more pragmatic. Much practical experience has shown that, as a rule, polynomial-time algorithms perform better than exponential time algorithms. Moreover, the polynomials in practice are typically of a small degree.

In computational complexity theory, the basic objective is to obtain polynomial-time algorithms, preferably ones with the lowest possible degree. For example, $O(\log n)$ is preferable to $O(n^k)$ for any $k > 0$, and $O(n^2)$ is preferable to $O(n^3)$. However, running times involving more than one parameter, such as $O(nm \log n)$ and $O(n^3)$, may not be comparable. If $m < n^2/\log n$ then $O(nm \log n)$ is superior; otherwise $O(n^3)$ is superior.

Related to the $O(\ )$ notation is the $\Omega(\ )$, or 'big omega', notation. Just as $O(\ )$ specifies an upper bound on the computational time of an algorithm, to within a constant factor, $\Omega(\ )$ specifies a lower bound on the computational time of an algorithm, again to within a constant factor. We say that an algorithm runs in $\Omega(f(n, m))$ time if for some example the algorithm can indeed take $qf(n, m)$ time for some constant q. For example, it is possible to show that the label correcting algorithm that we consider in Section 3.4 for the shortest path problem can take qnm time. Therefore, we write the equivalent statement, "the running time of the label correcting algorithm is $\Omega(nm)$".

Table 1.3
The growth of polynomial and exponential functions

					Approximate values		
n	$\log n$	$n^{0.5}$	n^2	n^3	$n^{\log n}$	2^n	$n!$
10	3.32	3.16	10^2	10^3	2.10×10^3	10^3	3.6×10^6
100	6.64	10.00	10^4	10^6	1.94×10^{13}	1.27×10^{30}	9.33×10^{157}
1000	9.97	31.62	10^6	10^9	7.90×10^{29}	1.07×10^{301}	$4.02 \times 10^{2,567}$
10 000	13.29	100.00	10^8	10^{12}	1.42×10^{53}	$0.99 \times 10^{3,010}$	$2.85 \times 10^{35,659}$

1.3. Notation and definitions

For convenience, in this section we collect together several basic definitions and describe some basic notation. We also state without proof some elementary properties of graphs.

We consider a *directed graph* $G = (N, A)$ consisting of a set, N, of nodes, and a set, A, of arcs whose elements are ordered pairs of distinct nodes. A *directed network* is a directed graph with numerical values attached to its nodes and/or arcs. As before, we let $n = |N|$ and $m = |A|$. We associate with each arc $(i, j) \in A$ a cost c_{ij} and a capacity u_{ij}. We assume throughout that $u_{ij} \geq 0$ for each $(i, j) \in A$. Frequently, we distinguish two special nodes in a graph: the *source* s and *sink* t.

An arc (i, j) has two *end points*, i and j. The arc (i, j) is *incident to* nodes i and j. We refer to node i as the *tail* and node j as the *head* of arc (i, j), and say that the arc (i, j) *emanates from* node i. The arc (i, j) is an *outgoing* arc of node i and an *incoming* arc of node j. The *arc adjacency list* of node i, $A(i)$, is defined as the set of arcs emanating from node i, i.e., $A(i) = \{(i, j) \in A : j \in N\}$. The degree of a node is the number of incoming and outgoing arcs incident to that node.

A *directed path* in $G = (N, A)$ is a sequence of distinct nodes and arcs i_1, (i_1, i_2), i_2, (i_2, i_3), $i_3, \ldots, (i_{r-1}, i_r)$, i_r satisfying the property that $(i_k, i_{k+1}) \in A$ for each $k = 1, \ldots, r - 1$. An *undirected path* is defined similarly except that for any two consecutive nodes i_k and i_{k+1} on the path, the path contains either arc (i_k, i_{k+1}) or arc (i_{k+1}, i_k). We refer to the nodes $i_2, i_3, \ldots, i_{r-1}$ as the *internal* nodes of the path. A *directed cycle* is a directed path together with the arc (i_r, i_1) and an undirected cycle is an undirected path together with the arc (i_r, i_1) or (i_1, i_r).

We shall often use the terminology *path* to designate either a directed or an undirected path, whichever is appropriate from context. If any ambiguity might arise, we shall explicitly state directed or undirected path. For simplicity of notation, we shall often refer to a path as a sequence of nodes $i_1 - i_2 - \cdots - i_k$ when its arcs are apparent from the problem context. Alternatively, we shall sometimes refer to a path as a set of (sequence of) arcs without any mention of the nodes. We shall use similar conventions for representing cycles.

A graph $G = (N, A)$ is called a *bipartite graph* if its node set N can be partitioned into two subsets N_1 and N_2 so that for each arc (i, j) in A, $i \in N_1$ and $j \in N_2$.

A graph $G' = (N', A')$ is a *subgraph* of $G = (N, A)$ if $N' \subseteq N$ and $A' \subseteq A$. A graph $G' = (N', A')$ is a *spanning subgraph* of $G = (N, A)$ if $N' = N$ and $A' \subseteq A$.

Two nodes i and j are said to be *connected* if the graph contains at least one undirected path from i to j. A graph is said to be *connected* if all pairs of its nodes are connected; otherwise, it is *disconnected*. In this chapter, we always assume that the graph G is connected and hence $m \geq n - 1$. We refer to any set

$Q \subseteq A$ with the property that the graph $G' = (N, A - Q)$ is disconnected, and no subset of Q has this property, as a *cutset* of G. A cutset partitions the graph into two sets of nodes, X and $N - X$. We shall alternatively represent the cutset Q as the node partition $(X, N - X)$.

A graph is *acyclic* if it contains no cycle. A *tree* is a connected acyclic graph. A *subtree* of a tree T is a connected subgraph of T. A tree T is said to be a *spanning tree* of G if T is a spanning subgraph of G. Arcs belonging to a spanning tree T are called *tree arcs*, and arcs not belonging to T are called *nontree arcs*. A spanning tree of $G = (N, A)$ has exactly $n - 1$ tree arcs. A node in a tree with degree equal to one is called a *leaf* node. Each tree has at least two leaf nodes.

A spanning tree contains a unique path between any two nodes. The addition of any nontree arc to a spanning tree creates exactly one cycle. Removing any arc in this cycle again creates a spanning tree. Removing any tree-arc from a spanning tree creates two subtrees. Arcs whose end points belong to the two different subtrees constitute a cutset. If any arc belonging to this cutset is added to the subtrees, the resulting graph is again a spanning tree.

1.4. Network representations

The complexity of a network algorithm depends not only on the algorithm, but also upon the manner used to represent the network within a computer and the storage scheme used for maintaining and updating the intermediate results. The running time of an algorithm (either worst-case or empirical) can often be improved by representing the network more cleverly and by using improved data structures. In this section, we discuss some popular ways of representing a network.

In Section 1.1, we have already described the node–arc incidence matrix representation of a network. This scheme requires nm words to store a directed (or undirected) network, of which only $2m$ words have nonzero values. Clearly, this network representation is not space efficient. Another popular way to represent a network is the *node–node adjacency matrix representation*. This representation stores an $n \times n$ matrix I with the property that the element $I_{ij} = 1$ if arc $(i, j) \in A$, and $I_{ij} = 0$ otherwise. The arc costs and capacities are also stored in $n \times n$ matrices. This representation is adequate for very dense networks, but is not attractive for storing a sparse network.

The *forward star* and *reverse star representations* are probably the most popular ways to represent networks, both sparse and dense. (These representations are also known as *incidence list representations* in the computer science literature.) The forward star representation numbers the arcs in a certain order: we first number the arcs emanating from node 1, then the arcs emanating from node 2, and so on. Arcs emanating from the same node can be numbered arbitrarily. We then sequentially store the (tail, head) and the cost of arcs in this order. We also maintain a pointer with each node i, denoted by *point(i)*, that indicates the smallest number in the arc list of an arc emanating from node i. Hence the outgoing arcs of node i are stored at positions point(i) to (point$(i+1)-1$) in the arc list. If point$(i)>$point$(i+1)-1$, then node i has no outgoing arc. For consistency, we set point$(1)=1$ and point$(n+1)=m+1$. Figure 1.6(b) specifies the forward star representation of the network given in Figure 1.6(a).

The forward star representation allows us to determine efficiently the set of outgoing arcs at any node. To determine, simultaneously, the set of incoming arcs at any node efficiently, we need an additional data structure known as the *reverse star representation*. Starting from a forward star representation, we can create a reverse star representation as follows. We examine the nodes $j=1$ to n in order and sequentially store the (tail, head) and the cost of incoming arcs of

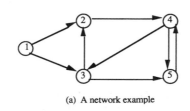

(a) A network example

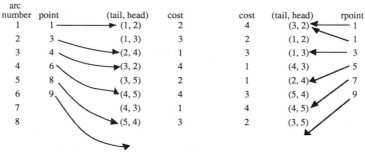

(b) The forward star representation.

(c) The reverse star representation.

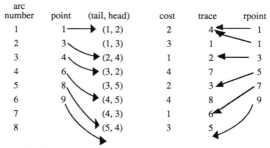

(d) The forward and reverse star representations.

Fig. 1.6. Example of forward and reverse star network representations.

node j. We also maintain a reverse pointer with each node i, denoted by *rpoint*(i) which denotes the first position in these arrays that contains information about an incoming arc at node i. For the sake of consistency, we set rpoint(1) = 1 and rpoint($n + 1$) = $m + 1$. As earlier, we store the incoming arcs at node i at positions rpoint(i) to (rpoint($i + 1$) $- 1$). This data structure gives us the representation shown in Figure 1.6(c).

Observe that by storing both the forward and reverse star representations, we will maintain a significant amount of duplicate information. We can avoid this duplication by storing arc numbers instead of the (tail, head) and the cost of the arcs. For example, arc $(3, 2)$ has arc number 4 in the forward star representation. The arc $(1, 2)$ has arc number 1. So instead of storing (tail, head) and cost of arcs, we can simply store the arc numbers and once we know the arc numbers, we can always retrieve the associated information from the forward star representation. We store arc numbers in an m-array *trace*. Figure 1.6(d) gives the complete trace array.

1.5 Search algorithms

Search algorithms are fundamental graph techniques; different variants of search lie at the heart of many network algorithms. In this section, we discuss two of the most commonly used search techniques: *breadth-first search* and *depth-first search*.

Search algorithms attempt to find all nodes in a network that satisfy a particular property. For purposes of illustration, let us suppose that we wish to find all the nodes in a graph $G = (N, A)$ that are reachable through directed paths from a distinguished node s, called the *source*. At every point in the search procedure, all nodes in the network are in one of two states: *marked* or *unmarked*. The marked nodes are known to be reachable from the source, and the status of unmarked nodes is yet to be determined. We call an arc (i, j) *admissible* if node i is marked and node j is unmarked, and *inadmissible* otherwise. Initially, only the source node is marked. Subsequently, by examining admissible arcs, the search algorithm will mark more nodes. Whenever the procedure marks a new node j by examining an admissible arc (i, j) we say that node i is a *predecessor* of node j, i.e., pred(j) = i. The algorithm terminates when the graph contains no admissible arcs. The following algorithm summarizes the basic iterative steps.

algorithm SEARCH;
begin
    unmark all nodes in N;
    mark node s;
    LIST := $\{s\}$;
    while LIST $\neq \emptyset$ **do**
    begin
        select a node i in LIST;

    if node i is incident to an admissible arc (i, j) **then**
    begin
       mark node j;
       pred(j) := i;
       add node j to LIST;
    end;
    else delete node i from LIST;
  end;
end;

When this algorithm terminates, it has marked all nodes in G that are reachable from s via a directed path. The predecessor indices define a tree consisting of marked nodes.

We use the following data structure to identify admissible arcs. The same data structure is also used in the maximum flow and minimum cost flow algorithms discussed in later sections. We maintain with each node i the list $A(i)$ of arcs emanating from it. Arcs in each list can be arranged arbitrarily. Each node has a *current arc* (i, j), which is the current candidate for being examined next. Initially, the current arc of node i is the first arc in $A(i)$. The search algorithm examines this list sequentially and whenever the current arc is inadmissible, it makes the next arc in the arc list the current arc. When the algorithm reaches the end of the arc list, it declares that the node has no admissible arc.

It is easy to show that the search algorithm runs in $O(m + n) = O(m)$ time. Each iteration of the **while** loop either finds an admissible arc or does not. In the former case, the algorithm marks a new node and adds it to LIST, and in the latter case it deletes a marked node from LIST. Since the algorithm marks any node at most once, it executes the **while** loop at most $2n$ times. Now consider the effort spent in identifying the admissible arcs. For each node i, we scan the arcs in $A(i)$ at most once. Therefore, the search algorithm examines a total of $\sum_{i \in N} |A(i)| = m$ arcs, and thus terminates in $O(m)$ time.

The algorithm, as described, does not specify the order for examining and adding nodes to LIST. Different rules give rise to different search techniques. If the set LIST is maintained as a *queue*, i.e., nodes are always selected from the front and added to the rear, then the search algorithm selects the marked nodes in the first-in, first-out order. This kind of search amounts to visiting the nodes in order of increasing distance from s; therefore, this version of search is called a *breadth-first search*. It marks nodes in the nondecreasing order of their distance from s, with the distance from s to i measured as the minimum number of arcs in a directed path from s to i.

Another popular method is to maintain the set LIST as a *stack*, i.e., nodes are always selected from the front and added to the front; in this instance, the search algorithm selects the marked nodes in the last-in, first-out order. This algorithm performs a deep probe, creating a path as long as possible, and backs up one node to initiate a new probe when it can mark no new nodes from the tip of the path. Hence, this version of search is called a *depth-first search*.

1.6. Developing polynomial-time algorithms

Researchers frequently employ two important approaches to obtain polynomial algorithms for network flow problems: the *geometric improvement* (or linear convergence) approach, and the *scaling* approach. In this section, we briefly outline the basic ideas underlying these two approaches. We will assume, as usual, that all data are integral and that algorithms maintain integer solutions at intermediate stages of computations.

Geometric improvement approach

The geometric improvement approach shows that an algorithm runs in polynomial time if at every iteration it makes an improvement proportional to the difference between the objective function values of the current and optimum solutions. Let H be an upper bound on the difference in objective function values between any two feasible solutions. For most network problems, H is a function of n, m, C, and U. For instance, in the maximum flow problem $H = mU$, and in the minimum cost flow problem $H = mCU$.

Lemma 1.1. *Suppose z^k is the objective function value of a minimization problem of some solution at the k-th iteration of an algorithm and z^* is the minimum objective function value. Further, suppose that the algorithm guarantees that*

$$(z^k - z^{k+1}) \geq \alpha(z^k - z^*) \tag{1.4}$$

(i.e., the improvement at iteration $k + 1$ is at least α times the total possible improvement) for some constant α with $0 < \alpha < 1$. Then the algorithm terminates in $O((\log H)/\alpha)$ iterations.

Proof. The quantity $z^k - z^*$ represents the total possible improvement in the objective function value after the k-th iteration. Consider a sequence of $2/\alpha$ consecutive iterations starting from iteration k. If in each iteration, the algorithm improves the objective function value by at least $\alpha(z^k - z^*)/2$ units, then the algorithm would determine an optimum solution within these $2/\alpha$ iterations. On the other hand, if at some iteration q, the algorithm improves the objective function value by no more than $\alpha(z^k - z^*)/2$ units, then (1.4) implies that

$$\alpha(z^k - z^*)/2 \geq z^q - z^{q+1} \geq \alpha(z^q - z^*),$$

and, therefore, the algorithm must have reduced the possible improvement $z^k - z^*$ by a factor of 2 within these $2/\alpha$ iterations. Since H is the maximum

possible improvement and every objective function value is an integer, the
algorithm must terminate within $O((\log H)/\alpha)$ iterations. $\square$

We have stated this result for minimization versions of optimization problems. A similar result applies to maximization versions of optimization
problems.

The geometric improvement approach might be summarized by the statement "network algorithms that have a geometric convergence rate are polynomial time algorithms". In order to develop polynomial time algorithms using
this approach, we can look for local improvement techniques that lead to large
(i.e., fixed percentage) improvements in the objective function. The maximum
augmenting path algorithm for the maximum flow problem and the maximum
improvement algorithm for the minimum cost flow problem are two examples
of this approach. (See Sections 4.2 and 5.3.)

Scaling approach

Researchers have extensively used an approach called *scaling* to derive
polynomial-time algorithms for a wide variety of network and combinatorial
optimization problems. In this discussion, we describe the simplest form of
scaling which we call *bit-scaling*. Section 5.11 presents an example of a
bit-scaling algorithm for the assignment problem. Sections 4 and 5, using more
refined versions of scaling, describe polynomial-time algorithms for the maximum flow and minimum cost flow problems.

Using the bit-scaling technique, we solve a problem P parametrically as a
sequence of problems $P_1, P_2, P_3, \ldots, P_K$: the problem P_1 approximates data
to the first *bit*, the problem P_2 approximates data to the second bit, and each
successive problem is a better approximation until $P_K = P$. Further, for each
$k = 2, \ldots, K$, the optimum solution of problem P_{k-1} serves as the starting
solution for problem P_k. The scaling technique is useful whenever reoptimization from a good starting solution is more efficient than solving the problem
from scratch.

For example, consider a network flow problem whose largest arc capacity
has value U. Let $K = \lceil \log U \rceil$ and suppose that we represent each arc capacity
as a K bit binary number, adding leading zeros if necessary to make each
capacity K bits long. Then the problem P_k would consider the capacity of each
arc as the k leading bits in its binary representation. Figure 1.7 illustrates an
example of this type of scaling.

The manner of defining arc capacities easily implies the following observation.

Observation. *The capacity of an arc in P_k is twice that in P_{k-1} plus 0 or 1.*

The following algorithm encodes a generic version of the bit-scaling technique.

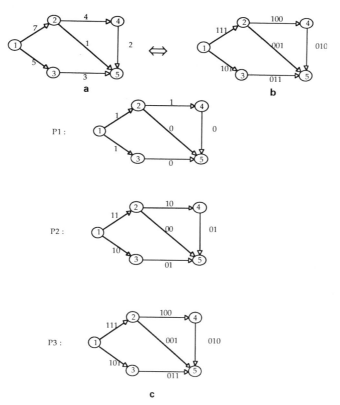

Fig. 1.7. Example of a bit-scaling technique. (a) Network with arc capacities. (b) Network with binary expansion of arc capacities. (c) The problems P_1, P_2, and P_3.

algorithm BIT-SCALING;
begin
    obtain an optimum solution of P_1;
    for $k := 2$ to K **do**
    begin
        reoptimize using the optimum solution of P_{k-1} to
            obtain an optimum solution of P_k;
    end;
end;

This approach is very robust; variants of it have led to improved algorithms for both the maximum flow and minimum cost flow problems. This approach works well for these applications, in part, because of the following reasons. (i) The problem P_1 is generally easy to solve. (ii) The optimal solution of problem P_{k-1} is an excellent starting solution for problem P_k, since P_{k-1} and P_k are quite similar. Hence, the optimum solution of P_{k-1} can be easily transformed to obtain an optimum solution of P_k. (iii) For problems that satisfy the similarity assumption, the number of problems solved is $O(\log n)$. Thus for this approach to work, reoptimization needs to be only a little more efficient (i.e., by a factor of $\log n$) than optimization.

Consider, for example, the maximum flow problem. Let v_k denote the maximum flow value for problem P_k and x_k denote an arc flow corresponding to v_k. In the problem P_k, the capacity of an arc is twice its capacity in P_{k-1} plus 0 or 1. If we multiply the optimum flow x_{k-1} for P_{k-1} by 2, we obtain a feasible flow for P_k. Moreover, $v_k - 2v_{k-1} \leq m$ because multiplying the flow x_{k-1} by 2 takes care of the doubling of the capacities and the additional 1's can increase the maximum flow value by at most m units (if we add 1 to the capacity of any arc, then we increase the maximum flow from source to sink by at most 1). In general, it is easier to reoptimize such a maximum flow problem. For example, the classical labeling algorithm as discussed in Section 4.1 would perform the reoptimization in at most m augmentations, taking $O(m^2)$ time. Therefore, the scaling version of the labeling algorithm runs in $O(m^2 \log U)$ time, whereas the non-scaling version runs in $O(nmU)$ time. The former time bound is polynomial and the latter bound is only pseudopolynomial. Thus this simple scaling algorithm improves the running time dramatically.

2. Basic properties of network flows

As a prelude to the rest of this chapter, in this section we describe several basic properties of network flows. We begin by showing how network flow problems can be modeled in either of two equivalent ways: as flows on arcs as in our formulation in Section 1.1 or as flows on paths and cycles. Then we partially characterize optimal solutions to network flow problems and demonstrate that these problems always have certain types of optimal solutions (so-called cycle free and spanning tree solutions). Consequently, in designing algorithms, we need only consider these special types of solutions. We next establish several important connections between network flows and linear and integer programming. Finally, we discuss a few useful transformations of network flow problems.

2.1. Flow decomposition properties and optimality conditions

It is natural to view network flow problems in either of two ways: as flows on arcs or as flows on paths and cycles. In the context of developing underlying theory, models, or algorithms, each view has its own advantages. Therefore, as the first step in our discussion, we will find it worthwhile to develop several connections between these alternate formulations.

In the arc formulation (1.1), the basic decision variables are flows x_{ij} on arcs (i, j). The path and cycle formulation starts with an enumeration of the paths

P and cycles *Q* of the network. Its decision variables are $h(p)$, the flow on path p, and $f(q)$, the flow on cycle q, which are defined for every directed path p in *P* and every directed cycle q in *Q*.

Notice that every set of path and cycle flows uniquely determines arc flows in a natural way: the flow x_{ij} on arc (i, j) equals the sum of the flows $h(p)$ and $f(q)$ for all paths p and cycles q that contain this arc. We formalize this observation by defining some new notation: $\delta_{ij}(p)$ equals 1 if arc (i, j) is contained in path p and 0 otherwise; similarly, $\delta_{ij}(q)$ equals 1 if arc (i, j) is contained in cycle q and is 0 otherwise. Then

$$x_{ij} = \sum_{p \in P} \delta_{ij}(p)h(p) + \sum_{q \in Q} \delta_{ij}(q)f(q) .$$

If the flow vector x is expressed in this way, we say that the flow is represented as path flows and cycle flows and that the path flow vector h and cycle flow vector f constitute a path and cycle flow representation of the flow.

Can we reverse this process? That is, can we decompose any arc flow into (i.e., represent it as) path and cycle flows? The following result provides an affirmative answer to this question.

Theorem 2.1. Flow decomposition property (directed case). *Every directed path and cycle flow has a unique representation as nonnegative arc flows. Conversely, every nonnegative arc flow x can be represented as a directed path and cycle flow (though not necessarily uniquely) with the following two properties*:

C2.1. *Every path with positive flow connects a supply node of x to a demand node of x.*

C2.2. *At most $n + m$ paths and cycles have nonzero flow; out of these, at most m cycles have nonzero flow.*

Proof. In the light of our previous observations, we need to establish only the converse assertions. We give an algorithmic proof to show that any feasible arc flow x can be decomposed into path and cycle flows. Suppose i_0 is a supply node. Then some arc (i_0, i_1) carries a positive flow. If i_1 is a demand node then we stop; otherwise the mass balance constraint (1.1b) of node i_1 implies that some other arc (i_1, i_2) carries positive flow. We repeat this argument until either we encounter a demand node or we revisit a previously examined node. Note that one of these cases will occur within n steps. In the former case we obtain a directed path p from the supply node i_0 to some demand node i_k consisting solely of arcs with positive flow, and in the latter case we obtain a directed cycle q. If we obtain a directed path, we let $h(p) = \min[b(i_0), -b(i_k), \min\{x_{ij}: (i, j) \in p\}]$, and redefine $b(i_0) = b(i_0) - h(p)$, $b(i_k) = b(i_k) + h(p)$ and $x_{ij} = x_{ij} - h(p)$ for each arc (i, j) in p. If we obtain a cycle q, we let $f(q) = \min\{x_{ij}: (i, j) \in q\}$ and redefine $x_{ij} = x_{ij} - f(q)$ for each arc (i, j) in q.

We repeat this process with the redefined problem until the network contains no supply node (and hence no demand node). Then we select a transhipment node with at least one outgoing arc with positive flow as the starting node, and repeat the procedure, which in this case must find a cycle. We terminate when for the redefined problem $x = 0$. Clearly, the original flow is the sum of flows on the paths and cycles identified by the procedure. Now observe that each time we identify a path, we reduce the supply/demand of some node or the flow on some arc to zero; and each time we identify a cycle, we reduce the flow on some arc to zero. Consequently, the path and cycle representation of the given flow x contains at most $n + m$ total paths and cycles, of which there are at most m cycles.   □

It is possible to state the decomposition property in a somewhat more general form that permits arc flows x_{ij} to be negative. In this case, even though the underlying network is directed, the paths and cycles can be undirected, and can contain arcs with negative flows. Each undirected path p, which has an orientation from its initial to its final node, has *forward arcs* and *backward arcs* which are defined as arcs along and opposite to the path's orientation. A *path flow* will be defined on p as a flow with value $h(p)$ on each forward arc and $-h(p)$ on each backward arc. We define a *cycle flow* in the same way. In this more general setting, our representation using the notation $\delta_{ij}(p)$ and $\delta_{ij}(q)$ is still valid with the following provision: we now define $\delta_{ij}(p)$ and $\delta_{ij}(q)$ to be -1 if arc (i, j) is a backward arc of the path or cycle.

Theorem 2.2. Flow decomposition property (undirected case). *Every path and cycle flow has a unique representation as arc flows. Conversely, every arc flow x can be represented as an (undirected) path and cycle flow (though not necessarily uniquely) with the following three properties*:
   C2.3. *Every path with positive flow connects a source node of x to a sink node of x.*
   C2.4. *For every path and cycle, any arc with positive flow occurs as a forward arc and any arc with negative flow occurs as a backward arc.*
   C2.5. *At most $n + m$ paths and cycles have nonzero flow; out of these, at most m cycles have nonzero flow.*

Proof. This proof is similar to that of Theorem 2.1. The major modification is that we extend the path at some node i_{k-1} by adding an arc (i_{k-1}, i_k) with positive flow or an arc (i_k, i_{k-1}) with negative flow. The other steps can be modified accordingly.   □

The flow decomposition property has a number of important consequences. As one example, it enables us to compare any two solutions of a network flow problem in a particularly convenient way and to show how we can *build* one solution from another by a sequence of simple operations.
   We need the concept of augmenting cycles with respect to a flow x. A cycle q with flow $f(q) > 0$ is called an *augmenting cycle* with respect to a flow x if

$$0 \leq x_{ij} + \delta_{ij}(q)f(q) \leq u_{ij}, \quad \text{for each arc } (i, j) \in q.$$

In other words, the flow remains feasible if some positive amount of flow (namely $f(q)$) is *augmented* around the cycle q. We define the cost of an augmenting cycle as $c(q) = \sum_{(i,j) \in A} c_{ij} \delta_{ij}(q)$. The cost of an augmenting cycle represents the change in cost of a feasible solution if we augment along the cycle with one unit of flow. The change in flow cost for augmenting around cycle q with flow $f(q)$ is $c(q)f(q)$.

Suppose that x and y are any two solutions to a network flow problem, i.e., $Nx = b$, $0 \leq x \leq u$ and $Ny = b$, $0 \leq y \leq u$. Then the difference vector $z = y - x$ satisfies the homogeneous equations $Nz = Ny - Nx = 0$. Consequently, flow decomposition implies that z can be represented as cycle flows, i.e., we can find at most $r \leq m$ cycle flows $f(q_1), f(q_2), \ldots, f(q_r)$ satisfying the property that for each arc (i, j) of A,

$$z_{ij} = \delta_{ij}(q_1)f(q_1) + \delta_{ij}(q_2)f(q_2) + \cdots + \delta_{ij}(q_r)f(q_r) \, .$$

Since $y = x + z$, for any arc (i, j) we have

$$0 \leq y_{ij} = x_{ij} + \delta_{ij}(q_1)f(q_1) + \delta_{ij}(q_2)f(q_2) + \cdots + \delta_{ij}(q_r)f(q_r) \leq u_{ij} \, .$$

Now by condition C2.4 of the flow decomposition property, arc (i, j) is either a forward arc on each cycle $q_1, q_2, \ldots, q_m$ that contains it or a backward arc on each cycle $q_1, q_2, \ldots, q_m$ that contains it. Therefore, each term between x_{ij} and the rightmost inequality in this expression has the same sign; moreover, $0 \leq x_{ij} \leq u_{ij}$. Consequently, for each cycle q_k, $0 \leq x_{ij} + \delta_{ij}(q_k)f(q_k) \leq u_{ij}$ for each arc $(i, j) \in q_k$. That is, if we add any of these cycle flows q_k to x, the resulting solution remains feasible on each arc (i, j). Hence, each cycle $q_1, q_2, \ldots, q_r$ is an augmenting cycle with respect to the flow x. Further, note that

$$\sum_{(i,j) \in A} c_{ij} y_{ij} = \sum_{(i,j) \in A} c_{ij} x_{ij} + \sum_{(i,j) \in A} c_{ij} z_{ij}$$

$$= \sum_{(i,j) \in A} c_{ij} x_{ij} + \sum_{(i,j) \in A} c_{ij} \left(\sum_{k=1}^{r} \delta_{ij}(q_k)f(q_k) \right)$$

$$= \sum_{(i,j) \in A} c_{ij} x_{ij} + \sum_{k=1}^{r} c(q_k)f(q_k) \, .$$

We have thus established the following important result.

Theorem 2.3. Augmenting cycle property. *Let x and y be any two feasible solutions of a network flow problem. Then y equals x plus the flow on at most m augmenting cycles with respect to x. Further, the cost of y equals the cost of x plus the cost of flow on these augmenting cycles.* $\square$

The augmenting cycle property permits us to formulate optimality conditions for characterizing the optimum solution of the minimum cost flow problem.

Suppose that x is any feasible solution, that x^* is an optimum solution of the minimum cost flow problem, and that $x \neq x^*$. The augmenting cycle property implies that the difference vector $x^* - x$ can be decomposed into at most m augmenting cycles and the sum of the costs of these cycles equals $cx^* - cx$. If $cx^* < cx$ then one of these cycles must have a negative cost. Further, if every augmenting cycle in the decomposition of $x^* - x$ has a nonnegative cost, then $cx^* - cx \geq 0$. Since x^* is an optimum flow, $cx^* = cx$ and x is also an optimum flow. We have thus obtained the following result.

Theorem 2.4. Optimality conditions. *A feasible flow x is an optimum flow if and only if it admits no negative cost augmenting cycle.* □

2.2. Cycle free and spanning tree solutions

We start by assuming that x is a feasible solution to the network flow problem

$$\text{minimize}\{cx: Nx = b \text{ and } l \leq x \leq u\}$$

and that $l = 0$. Much of the underlying theory of network flows stems from a simple observation concerning the example in Figure 2.1. In the example, arc flows and costs are given besides each arc.

Let us assume for the time being that all arcs are uncapacitated. The network in this figure contains flow around an undirected cycle. Note that adding a given amount of flow θ to all the arcs pointing in a clockwise direction and subtracting this flow from all arcs pointing in the counterclockwise direction preserves the mass balance at each node. Also, note that the per unit incremental cost for this flow change is the sum of the cost of the clockwise arcs minus the sum of the cost of counterclockwise arcs, i.e.,

$$\text{Per unit change in cost} = \Delta = \$2 + \$1 + \$3 - \$4 - \$3 = \$ -1 .$$

Let us refer to this incremental cost Δ as the *cycle cost* and say that the cycle is a *negative*, *positive* or *zero cost* cycle depending upon the sign of Δ. Consequently, to minimize cost in our example, we set θ as large as possible while preserving nonnegativity of all arc flows, i.e., $3 - \theta \geq 0$ and $4 - \theta \geq 0$, or

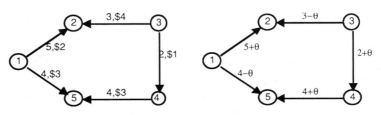

Fig. 2.1. Improving flow around a cycle.

$\theta \leqslant 3$; that is, we set $\theta = 3$. Note that in the new solution (at $\theta = 3$), we no longer have positive flow on all arcs in the cycle.

Similarly, if the cycle cost were positive (i.e., we were to change c_{12} from 2 to 4), then we would decrease θ as much as possible (i.e., $5 + \theta \geqslant 0$, $2 + \theta \geqslant 0$, and $4 + \theta \geqslant 0$, or $\theta \geqslant -2$) and again find a lower cost solution with the flow on at least one arc in the cycle at value zero. We can restate this observation in another way: to preserve nonnegativity of all flows, we must select θ in the interval $-2 \leqslant \theta \leqslant 3$. Since the objective function depends linearly in θ, we optimize it by selecting $\theta = 3$ or $\theta = -2$ at which point one arc in the cycle has a flow value of zero.

We can extend this observation in several ways:

(i) If the per unit cycle cost $\Delta = 0$, we are indifferent to all solutions in the interval $-2 \leqslant \theta \leqslant 3$ and therefore can again choose a solution as good as the original one but with the flow of at least one arc in the cycle at value zero.

(ii) If we impose upper bounds on the flow, e.g., such as 6 units on all arcs, then the range of flows that preserves feasibility (i.e., mass balances, lower and upper bounds on flows) is again an interval, in this case $-2 \leqslant \theta \leqslant 1$, and we can find a solution as good as the original one by choosing $\theta = -2$ or $\theta = 1$. At these values of θ, the solution is cycle free, that is, for some arc on the cycle, either the flow is zero (the lower bound) or is at its upper bound ($x_{12} = 6$ at $\theta = 1$).

Some additional notation will be helpful in encapsulating and summarizing our observations up to this point. Let us say that an arc (i, j) is a *free arc* with respect to a given feasible flow x if x_{ij} lies strictly between the lower and upper bounds imposed upon it. We will also say that arc (i, j) is *restricted* if its flow x_{ij} equals either its lower or upper bound. In this terminology, a solution x has the 'cycle free property' if the network contains no cycle made up entirely of free arcs.

In general, our prior observations apply to *any* cycle in a network. Therefore, given any initial flow we can apply our previous argument repeatedly, one cycle at a time, and establish the following fundamental result:

Theorem 2.5. Cycle free property. *If the objective function value of the network optimization problem*

$$minimize \quad \{cx: Nx = b, \ l \leqslant x \leqslant u\}$$

is bounded from below on the feasible region and the problem has a feasible solution, then at least one cycle free solution solves the problem. □

Note that the lower bound assumption imposed upon the objective value is necessary to rule out situations in which the flow change variable θ in our prior argument can be made arbitrarily large in a negative cost cycle, or arbitrarily small (negative) in a positive cost cycle; for example, this condition rules out any negative cost directed cycle with no upper bounds on its arc flows.

It is useful to interpret the cycle free property in another way. Suppose that the network is connected (i.e., there is an undirected path connecting every pair of nodes). Then, either the free arcs of a given cycle free solution x connect the nodes of G or we can add to the free arcs some restricted arcs so that the resulting set S of arcs has the following three properties:

(i) S contains all the free arcs in the current solution,

(ii) S contains no undirected cycles, and

(iii) no superset of S satisfies properties (i) and (ii).

We will refer to any set S of arcs satisfying (i) through (iii) as a *spanning tree* of the network and any feasible solution x for the network together with a spanning tree S that contains all free arcs as a *spanning tree solution*. (At times we will also refer to a given cycle free solution x as a spanning tree solution, with the understanding that restricted arcs may be needed to form the spanning tree S).

Figure 2.2 illustrates a spanning tree corresponding to a cycle free solution. Note that it may be possible (and often is) to complete the set of free arcs into a spanning tree in several ways (e.g., replace arc $(2, 4)$ with arc $(3, 5)$ in Figure 2.2(c)); therefore, a given cycle free solution can correspond to several spanning trees S. We will say that a spanning tree solution x is *nondegenerate* if the set of free arcs forms a spanning tree. In this case, the spanning tree S corresponding to the flow x is unique. If the free arcs do not span (i.e., do not connect) all the nodes, then any spanning tree corresponding to this solution will contain at least one arc whose flow equals the arc's lower or upper bound. In this case, we will say that the spanning tree is *degenerate*.

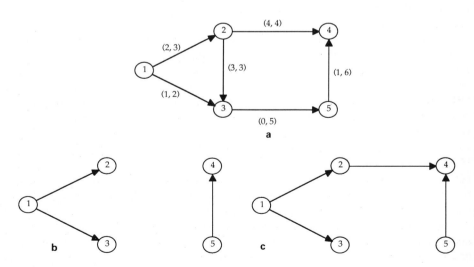

Fig. 2.2. Converting a cycle free solution to a spanning tree solution. (a) An example network with arc flows and capacities represented as (x_{ij}, u_{ij}). (b) Free arcs. (c) A spanning tree solution.

When restated in the terminology of spanning trees, the cycle free property becomes another fundamental result in network flow theory.

Theorem 2.6. Spanning tree property. *If the objective function value of the network optimization problem*

$$minimize \quad \{cx: Nx = b, l \leq x \leq u\}$$

is bounded from below on the feasible region and the problem has a feasible solution then at least one spanning tree solution solves the problem. □

We might note that the spanning tree property is valid for concave cost versions of the flow problem as well, i.e., those versions where the objective function is a concave function of the flow vector x. This extended version of the spanning tree property is valid because if the incremental cost of a cycle is negative at some point, then the incremental cost remains negative (by concavity) as we augment a positive amount of flow around the cycle. Hence, we can increase flow in a negative cost cycle until at least one arc reaches its lower or upper bound.

2.3. *Networks, linear and integer programming*

The cycle free property and spanning tree property have many other important consequences. In particular, these two properties imply that network flow theory lies at the cusp between two large and important subfields of optimization – linear and integer programming. This positioning may, to a large extent, account for the emergence of network flow theory as a cornerstone of mathematical programming.

Triangularity property

Before establishing our first results relating network flows to linear and integer programming, we first make a few observations. Note that any spanning tree S has at least one (actually at least two) leaf nodes, that is, a node that is incident to only one arc in the spanning tree. Consequently, if we rearrange the rows and columns of the node–arc incidence matrix of S so that the leaf node is row 1 and its incident arc is column 1, then row 1 has only a single nonzero entry, a $+1$ or a -1, which lies on the diagonal of the node–arc incidence matrix. If we now remove this leaf node and its incident arc from S, the resulting network is a spanning tree on the remaining nodes. Consequently, by rearranging all but row and column 1 of the node–arc incidence matrix for the spanning tree, we can now assume that row 2 has $+1$ or -1 element on the diagonal and zeros to the right of the diagonal. Continuing in this way permits us to rearrange the node–arc incidence matrix of the spanning tree so that its first $n-1$ rows are lower triangular. Figure 2.3 shows the resulting lower triangular form (actually, one of several possiblities) for the spanning tree in Figure 2.2(c).

$$
L = \begin{array}{c}
\text{nodes} \\
5 \\
4 \\
3 \\
2 \\
1
\end{array}
\begin{array}{cccc}
(5,4) & (2,4) & (1,3) & (1,2) \\
\left[\begin{array}{c} 1 \\ -1 \\ 0 \\ 0 \\ 0 \end{array}\right. &
\begin{array}{c} 0 \\ -1 \\ 0 \\ 1 \\ 0 \end{array} &
\begin{array}{c} 0 \\ 0 \\ -1 \\ 0 \\ 1 \end{array} &
\left.\begin{array}{c} 0 \\ 0 \\ 0 \\ -1 \\ 1 \end{array}\right]
\end{array}
$$

Fig. 2.3. The lower triangular form corresponding to a basis.

The node–arc incidence matrix of any spanning tree contains one more row than it has columns (it has n rows and $n - 1$ columns). Therefore, after we have rearranged the matrix so that the first $n - 1$ rows are in triangular form, the node–arc incidence matrix contains one additional row. We will, however, adopt the convention of still referring to it as lower triangular. (As we have noted previously, since each column of any node–arc incidence matrix contains exactly one $+1$ and one -1, the rows always sum to zero – equivalently, the last row equals -1 times the sum of the other rows and, therefore, is redundant.)

Theorem 2.7. Triangularity property. *The rows and columns of the node–arc incidence matrix of any spanning tree can be rearranged to be lower triangular.* $\square$

Integrality of optimal solutions

The triangularity property has several important consequences. First, let us evaluate the flows on arcs in a spanning tree solution x. By rearranging rows and columns, we partition the node–arc incident matrix N of the network as $N = [L, M]$, where L is a lower triangular matrix corresponding to a spanning tree. Suppose that $x = (x^1, x^2)$ is partitioned compatibly. Then

$$
Nx = Lx^1 + Mx^2 = b , \quad \text{or} \quad Lx^1 = b - Mx^2 . \tag{2.1}
$$

Now further suppose that the supply/demand vector b and lower and upper bound vectors l and u have all integer components. Then since every component of x^2 equals an arc lower or upper bound and M has integer components (each equal to 0, $+1$, or -1), the right hand side $b - Mx^2$ is an integer vector. But this observation implies that the components of x^1 are integral as well: since the first diagonal element of L equals $+1$ or -1, the first equation in (2.1) implies that x_1^1 is integral; now if we move x_1^1 to the right of the equality in (2.1), the right hand side remains integral and we can solve for x_2^1 from the second equation; continuing this forward substitution by successively solving for one variable at a time shows that x^1 is integral.

This argument shows that for problems with integral data, every spanning tree solution is integral. Since the spanning tree property ensures that network flow problems always have spanning tree solutions, we have established the following fundamental result.

Theorem 2.8. Integrality property. *If the objective value of the network optimization problem*

$$\text{minimize} \quad \{cx: Nx = b, \, l \leqslant x \leqslant u\}$$

is bounded from below on the feasible region, the problem has a feasible solution, and the vectors b, l, and u are integer, then the problem has at least one integer optimum solution. $\square$

Our observation at the end of Section 2.2 shows that this integrality property is also valid in the more general situation in which the objective function is concave.

Relationship to linear programming

The network flow problem with the objective function cx is a linear program which, as the last result shows, always has an integer solution. Network flow problems are distinguished as the most important large class of problems with this property.

Linear programs, or generalizations with concave cost objective functions, also satisfy another well-known property: they always have, in the parlance of convex analysis, *extreme point solutions*; that is, solutions x with the property that x cannot be expressed as a weighted combination of two other feasible solutions y and z, i.e., as $x = \alpha y + (1 - \alpha)z$ for some weight $0 < \alpha < 1$. Since, as we have seen, network flow problems always have cycle free solutions, we might expect to discover that extreme point solutions and cycle free solutions are closely related, and indeed they are as shown by the next result.

Theorem 2.9. Extreme point property. *For network flow problems, every cycle free solution is an extreme point and, conversely, every extreme point is a cycle free solution. Consequently, if the objective value of the network optimization problem*

$$\text{minimize} \quad \{cx: Nx = b, \, l \leqslant x \leqslant u\}$$

is bounded from below on the feasible region and the problem has a feasible solution, then the problem has an extreme point solution.

Proof. With the background developed already, this result is easy to establish. First, if x is not a cycle free solution, then it cannot be an extreme point, since by perturbing the flow by a small amount θ and by a small amount $-\theta$ around a cycle with free arcs, as in our discussion of Figure 2.1, we define two feasible solutions y and z with the property that $x = \frac{1}{2}y + \frac{1}{2}z$. Conversely, suppose that x is not an extreme point and is represented as $x = \alpha y + (1 - \alpha)z$ with $0 < \alpha < 1$. Let x^1, y^1 and z^1 be the components of these vectors for which y and z differ, i.e., $l_{ij} \leqslant y_{ij} < x_{ij} < z_{ij} \leqslant u_{ij}$ or $l_{ij} \leqslant z_{ij} < x_{ij} < y_{ij} \leqslant u_{ij}$, and let N_1 denote the submatrix of N corresponding to these arcs (i, j). Then $N_1(z^1 -$

$y^1) = 0$, which implies, by flow decomposition, that the network contains an undirected cycle with y_{ij} not equal to z_{ij} for any arc on the cycle. But by definition of the components x^1, y^1, and z^1, this cycle contains only free arcs in the solution x. Therefore, if x is not an extreme point solution, then it is not a cycle free solution. $\square$

In linear programming, extreme points are usually represented algebraically as *basic solutions*; for these special solutions, the columns B of the constraint matrix of a linear program corresponding to variables strictly between their lower and upper bounds are linearly independent. We can extend B to a basis of the constraint matrix by adding a maximal number of linearly independent columns. Just as cycle free solutions for network flow problems correspond to extreme points, spanning tree solutions correspond to basic solutions.

Theorem 2.10. Basis property. *Every spanning tree solution to a network flow problem is a basic solution and, conversely, every basic solution is a spanning tree solution.* $\square$

Let us now make one final connection between networks and linear and integer programming – namely, between bases and the integrality property. Consider a linear program of the form $Nx = b$ and suppose that $N = [B, M]$ for some basis B and that $x = (x^1, x^2)$ is a compatible partitioning of x. Also suppose that we eliminate any redundant rows so that B is a nonsingular matrix. Then

$$Bx^1 = b - Mx^2, \quad \text{or} \quad x^1 = B^{-1}(b - Mx^2).$$

Also, by Cramer's rule from linear algebra, it is possible to find each component of x^1 as sums and multiples of components of $b' = b - Mx^2$ and B, divided by $\det(B)$, the determinant of B. Therefore, if the determinant of B equals $+1$ or -1, then x^1 is an integer vector whenever x^2, b, and M are composed of all integers. In particular, if the partitioning of A corresponds to a basic feasible solution x and the problem data A, b, l and u are all integers, then x^2 and consequently x^1 is an integer. Let us call a matrix A *unimodular* if all of its bases have determinants either $+1$ or -1, and call it *totally unimodular* if all of its square submatrices have determinant equal to either 0, $+1$, or -1.

How are these notions related to network flows and the integrality property? Since bases of N correspond to spanning trees, the triangularity property shows that the determinant of any basis (excluding the redundant row now), equals the product of the diagonal elements in the triangular representation of the basis, and therefore equals $+1$ or -1. Consequently, a node–arc incident matrix is unimodular. Even more, it is totally unimodular. For let S be any square submatrix of N. If S is singular, it has determinant 0. Otherwise, it must correspond to a cycle free solution, which is a spanning tree on each of its connected components. But, then, it is easy to see that the determinant of S is the product of the determinants of the spanning trees and, therefore, it must be equal to $+1$ or -1. (An induction argument, using an expansion of determinants by minors, provides an alternate proof of the total unimodularity property.)

Theorem 2.11. Total unimodularity property. *The constraint matrix of a minimum cost network flow problem is totally unimodular.* $\square$

2.4. Network transformations

Frequently, analysts use network transformations to simplify a network problem, to show equivalences of different network problems, or to put a network problem into a standard form required by a computer code. In this subsection, we describe some of these important transformations.

T1. *Removing nonzero lower bounds.* If an arc (i, j) has a positive lower bound l_{ij}, then we can replace x_{ij} by $x'_{ij} + l_{ij}$ in the problem formulation. As measured by the new variable x'_{ij}, the flow on arc (i, j) will have a lower bound of 0. This transformation has a simple network interpretation (Figure 2.4): we begin by sending l_{ij} units of flow on the arc and then measure incremental flow above l_{ij}.

T2. *Removing capacities.* If an arc (i, j) has a positive capacity u_{ij}, then we can remove the capacity, making the arc uncapacitated, using the following ideas. The capacity constraint (i, j) can be written as $x_{ij} + s_{ij} = u_{ij}$, if we introduce a slack variable $s_{ij} \geq 0$. Multiplying both sides by -1, we obtain

$$-x_{ij} - s_{ij} = -u_{ij} . \tag{2.2}$$

This transformation is tantamount to turning the slack variable into an additional node k with equation (2.2) as the mass balance constraint for that node. Observe that the variable x_{ij} now appears in three mass balance constraints and s_{ij} in only one. By subtracting (2.2) from the mass balance constraint of node j, we assure that each of x_{ij} and s_{ij} appears in exactly two constraints – in one with a positive sign and in the other with a negative sign. These algebraic manipulations correspond to the network transformation shown in Figure 2.5.

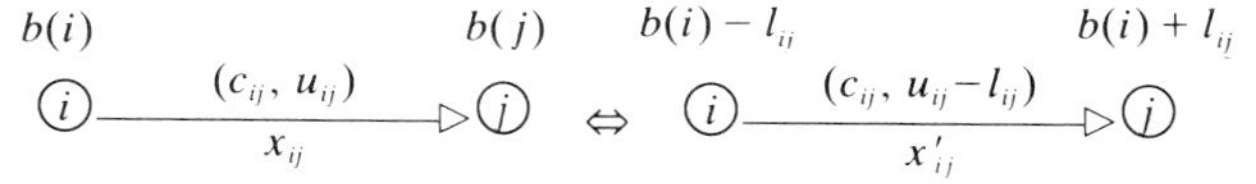

Fig. 2.4. Transforming a positive lower bound to zero.

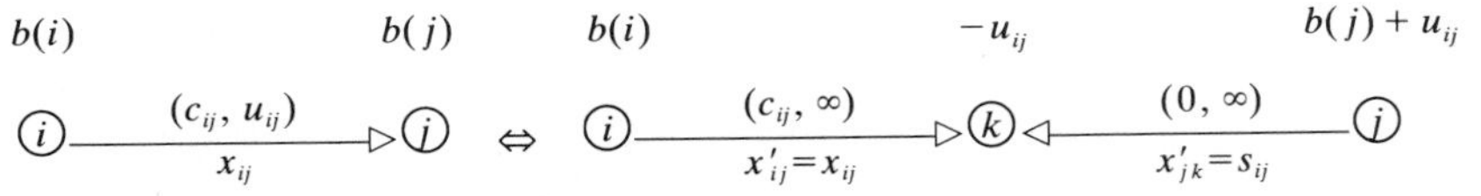

$b(i)$ $b(j)$ $b(i)$ $-u_{ij}$ $b(j)+u_{ij}$

$$(i)\xrightarrow[\ x_{ij}\ ]{(c_{ij},\,u_{ij})}\!\!\triangleright(j)\quad\Leftrightarrow\quad (i)\xrightarrow[\ x'_{ij}=x_{ij}\ ]{(c_{ij},\,\infty)}\!\!\triangleright(k)\triangleleft\!\!\xleftarrow[\ x'_{jk}=s_{ij}\ ]{(0,\,\infty)}(j)$$

Fig. 2.5. Removing arc capacities.

In the network context, this transformation implies the following. If x_{ij} is a flow on arc (i, j) in the original network, the corresponding flow in the transformed network is $x'_{ik} = x_{ij}$ and $x'_{jk} = u_{ij} - x_{ij}$; both the flows x and x' have the same cost. Likewise, a flow x_{ij}, x_{jk} in the transformed network yields a flow of $x_{ij} = x'_{jk}$ of the same cost in the original network. Further, since $x'_{ik} + x'_{jk} = u_{ij}$ and x'_{ik} and x'_{jk} are both nonnegative, $x_{ij} = x'_{ik} \leq u_{ij}$. Consequently, this transformation is valid.

T3. *Arc reversal.* Let u_{ij} represent the capacity of the arc (i, j) or an upper bound on the arc flow if it is uncapacitated. This transformation is a change in variable: replace x_{ij} by $u_{ij} - x'_{ji}$ in the problem formulation. Doing so replaces arc (i, j) with its associated cost c_{ij} by the arc (j, i) with a cost $-c_{ij}$. Therefore, this transformation permits us to remove arcs with negative costs. This transformation has the following network interpretation (Figure 2.6): send u_{ij} units of flow on the arc and then replace arc (i, j) by arc (j, i) with cost $-c_{ij}$. The new flow x'_{ji} measures the amount of flow we "remove" from the 'full capacity' flow of u_{ij}.

T4. *Node splitting.* This transformation splits each node i into two nodes i and i' and replaces each original arc (k, i) by an arc (k, i') of the same cost and capacity. We also add arcs (i', i) of cost zero for each i. Figure 2.7 illustrates the resulting network when we carry out the node splitting transformation for all the nodes of a network.

We shall see the usefulness of this transformation in Section 5.11 when we use it to reduce a shortest path problem with arbitrary arc lengths to an assignment problem. This transformation is also used in practice for representing node activities and node data in the standard 'arc flow' form of the network flow problem: we simply associate the cost or capacity for the throughput of node i with the new throughput arc (i', i).

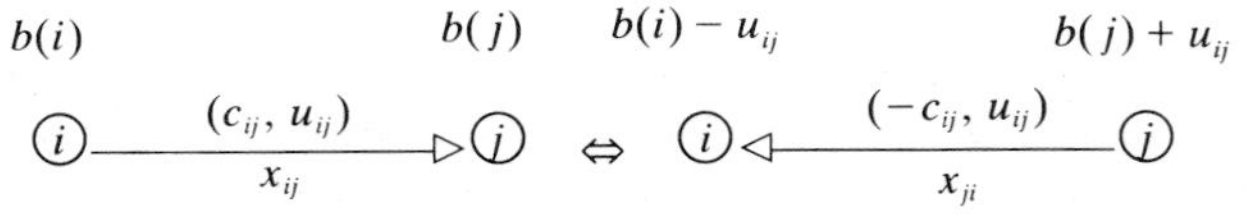

$b(i)$ $b(j)$ $b(i)-u_{ij}$ $b(j)+u_{ij}$

$$(i)\xrightarrow[\ x_{ij}\ ]{(c_{ij},\,u_{ij})}\!\!\triangleright(j)\quad\Leftrightarrow\quad (i)\triangleleft\!\!\xleftarrow[\ x_{ji}\ ]{(-c_{ij},\,u_{ij})}(j)$$

Fig. 2.6. An example of arc reversal.

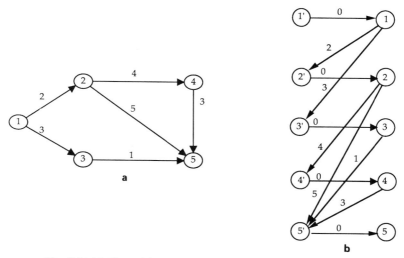

Fig. 2.7. (a) The original network. (b) The transformed network.

3. Shortest paths

Shortest path problems are the most fundamental and also the most commonly encountered problems in the study of transportation and communication networks. The shortest path problem arises when trying to determine the shortest, cheapest, or most reliable path between one or many pairs of nodes in a network. More importantly, algorithms for a wide variety of combinatorial optimization problems such as vehicle routing and network design often call for the solution of a large number of shortest path problems as subroutines. Consequently, designing and testing efficient algorithms for the shortest path problem has been a major area of research in network optimization.

Researchers have studied several different (directed) shortest path models. The major types of shortest path problems, in increasing order of solution difficulty, are (i) finding shortest paths from one node to all other nodes when arc lengths are nonnegative; (ii) finding shortest paths from one node to all other nodes for networks with arbitrary arc lengths; (iii) finding shortest paths from every node to every other node; and (iv) finding various types of constrained shortest paths between nodes (e.g., shortest paths with turn penalties, shortest paths visiting specified nodes, the k-th shortest path).

In this section, we discuss problems types (i), (ii) and (iii). The algorithmic approaches for solving problem types (i) and (ii) can be classified into two groups – *label setting* and *label correcting*. The label setting methods are applicable to networks with nonnegative arc lengths, whereas label correcting methods apply to networks with negative arc lengths as well. Each approach assigns tentative distance labels (shortest path distances) to nodes at each step. Label setting methods designate one or more labels as permanent (optimum) at each iteration. Label correcting methods consider all labels as temporary until the final step when they all become permanent. We will show that label setting methods have the most attractive worst-case performance; nevertheless, practical experience has shown the label correcting methods to be modestly more efficient.

Dijkstra's algorithm is the most popular label setting method. In this section, we first discuss a simple implementation of this algorithm that achieves a time bound of $O(n^2)$. We then describe two more sophisticated implementations that achieve improved running times in practice and in theory. Next, we consider a generic version of the label correcting method, outlining one special implementation of this general approach that runs in polynomial time and another implementation that performs very well in practice. Finally, we discuss a method to solve the all pairs shortest path problem.

3.1. Dijkstra's algorithm

We consider a network $G = (N, A)$ with an arc length c_{ij} associated with each arc $(i, j) \in A$. Let $A(i)$ represent the set of arcs emanating from node $i \in N$, and let $C = \max\{c_{ij} : (i, j) \in A\}$. In this section, we assume that arc lengths are integer numbers, and in this section as well as in Sections 3.2 and 3.3, we further assume that arc lengths are nonnegative. We suppose that node s is a specially designated node, and assume without any loss of generality that the network G contains a directed path from s to every other node. We can ensure this condition by adding an artificial arc (s, j), with a suitably large arc length, for each node j. We invoke this connectivity assumption throughout this section.

Dijkstra's algorithm finds shortest paths from the source node s to all other nodes. The basic idea of the algorithm is to fan out from node s and label nodes in order of their distances from s. Each node i has a label, denoted by $d(i)$; the label is *permanent* once we know that it represents the shortest distance from s to i; otherwise it is *temporary*. Initially, we give node s a permanent label of zero, and each other node j a temporary label equal to c_{sj} if $(s, j) \in A$, and ∞ otherwise. At each iteration, the label of a node i is its shortest distance from the source node along a path whose internal nodes are all permanently labeled. The algorithm selects a node i with the minimum temporary label, makes it permanent, and scans arcs in $A(i)$ to update the distance labels of adjacent nodes. The algorithm terminates when it has designated all nodes as permanently labeled. The correctness of the algorithm relies on the key observation (which we prove later) that it is always possible to designate the node with the minimum temporary label as permanent. The following algorithmic representation is a basic implementation of Dijkstra's algorithm.

algorithm DIJKSTRA;
begin
    $P := \{s\};\ T := N - \{s\};$

$d(s):=0$ and pred(s) $:=0$;
$d(j):=c_{sj}$ and pred(j) $:= s$ if $(s, j) \in A$, and $d(j):=\infty$ otherwise;
while $P \neq N$ **do**
begin
(*node selection*) let $i \in T$ be a node for which $d(i) = \min\{d(j): j \in T\}$;
  $P := P \cup \{i\}$; $T := T - \{i\}$;
(*distance update*) **for** each $(i, j) \in A(i)$ **do**
  if $d(j) > d(i) + c_{ij}$ **then** $d(j) := d(i) + c_{ij}$ and pred(j) $:= i$;
end;
end;

The algorithm associates a predecessor index, denoted by pred(i), with each node $i \in N$. The algorithm updates these indices to ensure that pred(i) is the last node prior to i on the (tentative) shortest path from node s to *node i*. At termination, these indices allow us to trace back along a shortest path from each node to the source.

To establish the validity of Dijkstra's algorithm, we use an inductive argument. At each point in the algorithm, the nodes are partitioned into two sets, P and T. Assume that the label of each node in P is the length of a shortest path from the source, whereas the label of each node j in T is the length of a shortest path subject to the restriction that each node in the path (except j) belongs to P. Then it is possible to transfer the node i in T with the smallest label $d(i)$ to P for the following reason: any path P from the source to node i must contain a first node k that is in T. However, node k must be at least as far away from the source as node i since its label is at least that of node i; furthermore, the segment of the path P between node k and node i has a nonnegative length because arc lengths are nonnegative. This observation shows that the length of path P is at least $d(i)$ and hence it is valid to permanently label node i. After the algorithm has permanently labeled node i, the temporary labels of some nodes in $T - \{i\}$ might decrease, because node i could become an internal node in the tentative shortest paths to these nodes. We must thus scan all of the arcs (i, j) in $A(i)$; if $d(j) > d(i) + c_{ij}$, then setting $d(j) = d(i) + c_{ij}$ updates the labels of nodes in $T - \{i\}$.

The computational time for this algorithm can be split into the time required by its two basic operations – selecting nodes and updating distances. In an iteration, the algorithm requires O(n) time to identify the node i with minimum temporary label and takes O($|A(i)|$)) time to update the distance labels of adjacent nodes. Thus, overall, the algorithm requires O(n^2) time for selecting nodes and O($\Sigma_{i \in N}|A(i)|$) = O(m) time for updating distances. *This implementation of Dijkstra's algorithm thus runs in* O(n^2) *time*.

Dijkstra's algorithm has been a subject of much research. Researchers have attempted to reduce the node selection time without substantially increasing the time for updating distances. Consequently, they have, using clever data structures, suggested several implementations of the algorithm. These implementations have either dramatically reduced the running time of the algorithm in practice or improved its worst case complexity. In the following discussion, we describe Dial's algorithm, which is currently comparable to the best label setting algorithm in practice. Subsequently we describe an implementation using R-heaps, which is nearly the best known implementation of Dijkstra's algorithm from the perspective of worst-case analysis. (A more complex version of R-heaps gives the best worst-case performance for almost all choices of the parameters n, m, and C).

3.2. Dial's implementation

The bottleneck operation in Dijkstra's algorithm is node selection. To improve the algorithm's performance, we must ask the following question. Instead of scanning all temporarily labeled nodes at each iteration to find the one with the minimum distance label, can we reduce the computation time by maintaining distances in a sorted fashion? Dial's algorithm tries to accomplish this objective, and reduces the algorithm's computation time in practice, using the following fact:

Fact 3.1. *The distance labels that Dijkstra's algorithm designates as permanent are nondecreasing.*

This fact follows from the observation that the algorithm permanently labels a node i with smallest temporary label $d(i)$, and while scanning arcs in $A(i)$ during the distance update step, never decreases the distance label of any permanently labeled node since arc lengths are nonnegative. Fact 3.1 suggests the following scheme for node selection. We maintain $nC + 1$ *buckets* numbered $0, 1, 2, \ldots, nC$. Bucket k stores each node whose temporary distance label is k. Recall that C represents the largest arc length in the network and, hence, nC is an upper bound on the distance labels of all the nodes. In the node selection step, we scan the buckets in increasing order until we identify the first nonempty bucket. The distance label of each node in this bucket is minimum. One by one, we delete these nodes from the bucket, making them permanent and scanning their arc lists to update distance labels of adjacent nodes. We then resume the scanning of higher numbered buckets in increasing order to select the next nonempty bucket.

By storing the content of these buckets carefully, it is possible to add, delete, and select the next element of any bucket very efficiently; in fact, in O(1) time, i.e., a time bounded by some constant. One implementation uses a data structure known as a *doubly linked list*. In this data structure, we order the content of each bucket arbitrarily, storing two pointers for each entry: one pointer to its immediate predecessor and one to its immediate successor. Doing so permits us, by rearranging the pointers, to select easily the topmost node from the list, add a bottommost node, or delete a node. Now, as we relabel nodes and decrease any node's temporary distance label, we move it from a higher index bucket to a lower index bucket; this transfer requires O(1) time.

Consequently, this algorithm runs in $O(m + nC)$ time and uses $nC + 1$ buckets. The following fact allows us to reduce the number of buckets to $C + 1$.

Fact 3.2. *If $d(i)$ is the distance label that the algorithm designates as permanent at the beginning of an iteration, then at the end of that iteration $d(j) \leqslant d(i) + C$ for each finitely labeled node j in T.*

This fact follows by noting that (i) $d(k) \leqslant d(i)$ for each $k \in P$ (by Fact 3.1), and (ii) for each finitely labeled node j in T, $d(j) = d(k) + c_{kj}$ for some $k \in P$ (by the property of distance updates). Hence, $d(j) \leqslant d(i) + c_{kj} \leqslant d(i) + C$. In other words, all finite temporary labels are bracketed from below by $d(i)$ and from above by $d(i) + C$. Consequently, $C + 1$ buckets suffice to store nodes with finite temporary distance labels. We need not store the nodes with infinite temporary distance labels in any of the buckets – we can add them to a bucket when they first receive a finite distance label.

Dial's algorithm uses $C + 1$ buckets numbered $0, 1, 2, \ldots, C$, which can be viewed as arranged in a circle as in Figure 3.1. This implementation stores a temporarily labeled node j with distance label $d(j)$ in the bucket $d(j)$ $\text{mod}(C + 1)$. Consequently, during the entire execution of the algorithm, bucket k stores nodes with temporary distance labels k, $k + (C + 1)$, $k + 2(C + 1)$, and so forth; however, because of Fact 3.2, at any point in time this bucket will hold only nodes with the same distance labels. This storage scheme also implies that if bucket k contains a node with minimum distance label, then buckets $k + 1$, $k + 2, \ldots$, C, 0, 1, $2, \ldots$, $k - 1$, store nodes in increasing values of the distance labels.

Dial's algorithm examines the buckets sequentially, in a wrap-around fashion, to identify the first nonempty bucket. In the next iteration, it reexamines the buckets starting at the place where it left off earlier. A potential disadvantage of this scheme, as compared to the $O(n^2)$ implementation of Dijkstra's algorithm, is that C may be very large, necessitating large storage and increased computational time. In addition, the algorithm may wrap around as many as $n - 1$ times, resulting in a large computation time. The algorithm, however, typically does not encounter these difficulties in practice. For most applications, C is not very large, and the number of passes through all of the

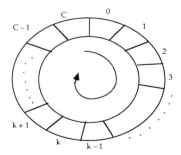

Fig. 3.1. Bucket arrangement in Dial's algorithm.

buckets is much less than n. Dial's algorithm, however, is not attractive theoretically. The algorithm runs in $O(m + nC)$ time, which is not even polynomial time. Rather, it is pseudopolynomial time. For example, if $C = n^4$, then the algorithm runs in $O(n^5)$ time, and if $C = 2^n$ the algorithm takes exponential time in the worst case.

The search for the theoretically fastest implementations of Dijkstra's algorithm has led researchers to develop several new data structures for sparse networks. In the next section, we consider an implementation using a data structure called a *redistributive heap* (R-heap) that runs in $O(m + n \log nC)$ time. The discussion of this implementation is of a more advanced nature than the previous sections and the reader can skip it without any loss of continuity.

3.3. R-heap implementation

Our first $O(n^2)$ implementation of Dijkstra's algorithm and then Dial's implementation represent two extremes. The first implementation considers all the temporarily labeled nodes together (in one large bucket, so to speak) and searches for a node with the smallest label. Dial's algorithm separates nodes by storing any two nodes with different labels in different buckets. Could we improve upon these methods by adopting an intermediate approach, perhaps by storing many, but not all, labels in a bucket? For example, instead of storing only nodes with a temporary label of k in the k-th bucket, we could store temporary labels from $100k$ to $100k + 99$ in bucket k. The different temporary labels that can be stored in a bucket make up the *range* of the bucket; the cardinality of the range is called its *width*. For the preceding example, the range of bucket k is $[100k, \ldots, 100k + 99]$ and its width is 100.

Using widths of size k permits us to reduce the number of buckets needed by a factor of k. But in order to find the smallest distance label, we need to search all of the elements in the smallest index nonempty bucket. Indeed, if k is arbitrarily large, we need only one bucket, and the resulting algorithm reduces to Dijkstra's original implementation.

Using a width of 100, say, for each bucket reduces the number of buckets, but still requires us to search through the lowest numbered bucket to find the node with minimum temporary label. If we could devise a variable width scheme, with a width of one for the lowest numbered bucket, we could conceivably retain the advantages of both the wide and narrow bucket approaches. The R-heap algorithm we consider next uses variable widths and changes the ranges dynamically. In the version of redistributive heaps that we present, the widths of the buckets are 1, 1, 2, 4, 8, 16, ..., so that the number of buckets needed is only $O(\log nC)$. Moreover, we dynamically modify the ranges of numbers stored in each bucket and we reallocate nodes with temporary distance labels in a way that stores the minimum distance label in a bucket whose width is 1. In this way, as in the previous algorithm, we avoid the need to search the entire bucket to find the minimum. In fact, the running time of this version of the R-heap algorithm is $O(m + n \log nC)$.

We now describe an *R*-heap in more detail. For a given shortest path problem, the *R*-heap consists of $1 + \lceil \log nC \rceil$ buckets. The buckets are numbered as $0, 1, 2, \ldots, K = \lceil \log nC \rceil$. We represent the range of bucket k by range(k) which is a (possibly empty) closed interval of integers. We store a temporary node i in bucket k if $d(i) \in$ range(k). We do not store permanent nodes. The nodes in bucket k are denoted by the set CONTENT(k). The algorithm will change the ranges of the buckets dynamically, and each time it changes the ranges, it redistributes the nodes in the buckets.

Initially, the buckets have the following ranges:

range(0) = [0];
range(1) = [1];
range(2) = [2, 3];
range(3) = [4, ... , 7];
range(4) = [8, ... , 15];
.
.
.
range(K) = $[2^{K-1}, \ldots, 2^K - 1]$.

These ranges will change dynamically; however, the widths of the buckets will not increase beyond their initial widths. Suppose for example that the initial minimum distance label is determined to be in the range $[8, \ldots, 15]$. We could verify this fact quickly by verifying that buckets 0 through 3 are empty and bucket 4 is nonempty. At this point, we can not identify the minimum distance label without searching all nodes in bucket 4. The following observation is helpful. Since the minimum index nonempty bucket is the bucket whose range is $[8, \ldots, 15]$, we know that no temporary label will ever again be less than 8, and hence buckets 0 to 3 will never be needed again. Rather than leaving these buckets idle, we can redistribute the range of bucket 4 (whose width is 8) to the previous buckets (whose combined width is 8) resulting in the ranges [8], [9], [10, ... , 11], and [12, ... , 15]. We then set the range of bucket 4 to $\emptyset$, and we shift (or redistribute) its temporarily labeled nodes into the appropriate buckets (0, 1, 2, and 3). Thus, each of the elements of bucket 4 moves to a lower indexed bucket.

Essentially, we have replaced the node selection step (i.e., finding a node with smallest temporary distance label) by a sequence of redistribution steps in which we constantly shift nodes to lower indexed buckets. Roughly speaking, the redistribution time is $O(n \log nC)$ time in total, since each node can be shifted at most $K = 1 + \lceil \log nC \rceil$ times. Eventually, the minimum temporary label is in a bucket with width one, and the algorithm selects it in an additional $O(1)$ time.

Actually, we would carry out these operations a bit differently. Since we will be scanning all of the elements of bucket 4 in the redistribute step, it makes sense to first find the minimum temporary label in the bucket. Suppose for

example that the minimum label is 11. Then rather than redistributing the
range [8, . . . , 15], we need only redistribute the subrange [11, . . . , 15]. In this
case the resulting ranges of buckets 0 to 4 would be [11], [12], [13, 14], [15], ∅.
Moreover, at the end of this redistribution, we are guaranteed that the
minimum temporary label is stored in bucket 0, whose width is 1.

To reiterate, we do not carry out the actual node selection step until the
minimum nonempty bucket has width one. If the minimum nonempty bucket is
bucket k, whose width is greater than 1, we redistribute the range of bucket k
into buckets 0 to $k - 1$, and then we reassign the content of bucket k to buckets
0 to $k - 1$. The redistribution time is $O(n \log nC)$ and the running time of the
algorithm is $O(m + n \log nC)$.

We now illustrate R-heaps on the shortest path example given in Figure 3.2.
In the figure, the number beside each arc indicates its length.

For this problem, $C = 20$ and $K = \lceil \log 120 \rceil = 7$. Table 3.1 specifies the
starting solution of Dijkstra's algorithm and the initial heap.

To select the node with the smallest distance label, we scan the buckets 0, 1,
2, . . . , K to find the first nonempty bucket. In our example, bucket 0 is
nonempty. Since bucket 0 has width 1, every node in this bucket has the same
(minimum) distance label. So the algorithm designates node 3 as permanent,
deletes node 3 from the R-heap, and scans the arc (3, 5) to change the distance
label of node 5 from 20 to 9. We check whether the new distance label of node
5 is contained in the range of its present bucket, which is bucket 5. It isn't.
Since its distance label has decreased, node 5 should move to a lower index
bucket. So we sequentially scan the buckets from right to left, starting at
bucket 5, to identify the first bucket whose range contains the number 9, which
is bucket 4. Node 5 moves from bucket 5 to bucket 4. Table 3.2 shows the new
R-heap.

We again look for the node with smallest distance label. Scanning the
buckets sequentially, we find that bucket $k = 4$ is the first nonempty bucket.
Since the range of this bucket contains more than one integer, the first node in
the bucket need not have the minimum distance label. Since the algorithm will
never use the ranges range(0), . . . , range($k - 1$) for storing temporary distance labels, we can redistribute the range of bucket k into the buckets
0, 1, . . . , $k - 1$ and reinsert its nodes into the lower indexed buckets. In our

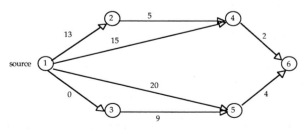

Fig. 3.2. The shortest path example.

Table 3.1
The initial R-heap

Node i	1	2	3	4	5	6	
Label $d(i)$	0	13	0	15	20	$nC = 120$	

Buckets	0	1	2	3	4	5	6	7
Ranges	[0]	[1]	[2, 3]	[4, . . . , 7]	[8, . . . , 15]	[16, . . . , 31]	[32, ... 63]	[64, . . . , 127]
CONTENT	{3}	Ø	Ø	Ø	{2, 4}	{5}	Ø	{6}

Table 3.2
The R-heap at the end of Iteration 1

Node i	2	4	5	6				
Label $d(i)$	13	15	9	120				

Buckets	0	1	2	3	4	5	6	7
Ranges	[0]	[1]	[2, 3]	[4, . . . , 7]	[8, . . . , 15]	[16, . . . , 31]	[32, . . . , 63]	[64, . . . , 127]
CONTENT	Ø	Ø	Ø	Ø	{2, 4, 5}	Ø	Ø	{6}

example, the range of bucket 4 is [8, . . . , 15], but the smallest distance label in this bucket is 9. We therefore redistribute the range [9, . . . ,15] over the lower indexed buckets in the following manner:

$$\text{range}(0) = [9];$$
$$\text{range}(1) = [10];$$
$$\text{range}(2) = [11, 12];$$
$$\text{range}(3) = [13, . . . , 15];$$
$$\text{range}(4) = \emptyset.$$

Other ranges do not change. The range of bucket 4 is now empty, and we must reassign the contents of bucket 4 to buckets 0 through 3. We do so by successively selecting nodes in bucket 4, sequentially scanning the buckets 3, 2, . . . , 0 and inserting the node in the appropriate bucket. The resulting buckets have the following contents:

$$\text{CONTENT}(0) = \{5\};$$
$$\text{CONTENT}(1) = \emptyset;$$
$$\text{CONTENT}(2) = \emptyset;$$
$$\text{CONTENT}(3) = \{2, 4\};$$
$$\text{CONTENT}(4) = \emptyset.$$

This redistribution necessarily empties bucket 4, and moves the node with the smallest distance label to bucket 0.

We are now in a position to outline the general algorithm and analyze its complexity. Suppose that $j \in \text{CONTENT}(k)$ and that $d(j)$ decreases. If the modified $d(j) \not\in \text{range}(k)$, then we sequentially scan lower numbered buckets from right to left and add the node to the appropriate bucket. Overall, this operation takes $O(m + nK)$ time. The term m reflects the number of distance updates, and the term nK arises because every time a node moves, it moves to a lower indexed bucket; since there are $K + 1$ buckets, a node can move at most K times. Therefore, $O(nK)$ is a bound on the total number of node movements.

Next we consider the node selection step. Node selection begins by scanning the buckets from left to right to identify the first nonempty bucket, say bucket k. This operation takes $O(K)$ time per iteration and $O(nK)$ time in total. If $k = 0$ or $k = 1$, then any node in the selected bucket has the minimum distance label. If $k \leq 2$, then we redistribute the 'useful' range of bucket k into the buckets $0, 1, \ldots, k - 1$ and reinsert its contents to those buckets. If the range of bucket k is $[l, \ldots, u]$ and the smallest distance label of a node in the bucket is $d_{\min}$, then the useful range of the bucket is $[d_{\min}, \ldots, u]$.

The algorithm redistributes the useful range in the following manner: we assign the first integer to bucket 0, the next integer to bucket 1, the next two integers to bucket 2, the next four integers to bucket 3, and so on. Since bucket k has width $\leq 2^{k-1}$ and since the widths of the first k buckets can be as large as $1, 1, 2, \ldots, 2^{k-2}$ for a total potential width of 2^{k-1}, we can redistribute the useful range of bucket k over the buckets $0, 1, \ldots, k - 1$ in the manner described. This redistribution of ranges and the subsequent reinsertions of nodes empties bucket k and moves the nodes with the smallest distance labels to bucket 0. Whenever we examine a node in the nonempty bucket k with the smallest index, we move it to a lower indexed bucket; each node can move at most K times, so all the nodes can move a total of at most nK times. Thus, the node selection steps take $O(nK)$ total time. Since $K = \lceil \log nC \rceil$, the algorithm runs in $O(m + n \log nC)$ time. We now summarize our discussion.

Theorem 3.1. *The R-heap implementation of Dijkstra's algorithm solves the shortest path problem in* $O(m + n \log nC)$ *time.* $\square$

This algorithm requires $1 + \lceil \log nC \rceil$ buckets. Fact 3.2 permits us to reduce the number of buckets to $1 + \lceil \log C \rceil$. This refined implementation of the algorithm runs in $O(m + n \log C)$ time. For problem that satisfy the similarity assumption (see Section 1.2), this bound becomes $O(m + n \log n)$. Using substantially more sophisticated data structures, it is possible to reduce this bound further to $O(m + n\sqrt{\log n})$, which is a linear time algorithm for all but the sparsest classes of shortest path problems.

3.4. Label correcting algorithms

Label correcting algorithms, as the name implies, maintain tentative distance labels for nodes and correct the labels at every iteration. Unlike label setting algorithms, these algorithms maintain all distance labels as temporary until the end, when they all become permanent simultaneously. The label correcting algorithms are conceptually more general than the label setting algorithms and are applicable to more general situations, for example, to networks containing negative length arcs. To produce shortest paths, these algorithms typically require that the network does not contain any negative directed cycle, i.e., a directed cycle whose arc lengths sum to a negative value. Most label correcting algorithms have the capability to detect the presence of negative cycles.

Label correcting algorithms can be viewed as a procedure for solving the following recursive equations:

$$d(s) = 0; \tag{3.1}$$

$$d(j) = \min\{d(i) + c_{ij} : (i, j) \in A\}, \text{ for each } j \in N - \{s\}. \tag{3.2}$$

As usual, $d(j)$ denotes the length of a shortest path from the source node to node j. These equations are known as *Bellman's equations* and represent necessary conditions for optimality of the shortest path problem. These conditions are also sufficient if every cycle in the network has a positive length. We will prove an alternate version of these conditions which is more suitable from the viewpoint of label correcting algorithms.

Theorem 3.2. *Let $d(i)$ for $i \in N$ be a set of labels. If $d(s) = 0$ and if in addition the labels satisfy the following conditions, then they represent the shortest path lengths from the source node:*
  C3.1. *$d(i)$ is the length of some path from the source node to node i; and*
  C3.2. *$d(j) \leq d(i) + c_{ij}$ for all $(i, j) \in A$.*

Proof. Since $d(i)$ is the length of some path from the source to node i, it is an upper bound on the shortest path length. We show that if the labels $d(i)$ satisfy C3.2, then they are also lower bounds on the shortest path lengths, which implies the conclusion of the theorem. Consider any directed path P from the source to node j. Let P consist of nodes $s = i_1 - i_2 - i_3 - \cdots - i_k = j$. Condition C3.2 implies that $d(i_2) \leq d(i_1) + c_{i_1 i_2} = c_{i_1 i_2}$, $d(i_3) \leq d(i_2) + c_{i_2 i_3}, \ldots, d(i_k) \leq d(i_{k-1}) + c_{i_{k-1} i_k}$. Adding these inequalities yields $d(j) = d(i_k) \leq \Sigma_{(i,j) \in P} c_{ij}$. Therefore $d(j)$ is a lower bound on the length of any directed path from the source to node j, including a shortest path from s to j. $\square$

We note that if the network contains a negative cycle then no set of labels $d(i)$ satisfies C3.2. Suppose that the network did contain a negative cycle W and some labels $d(i)$ satisfy C3.2. Consequently, $d(i) - d(j) + c_{ij} \geq 0$ for each $(i, j) \in W$. These inequalities imply that

$$\sum_{(i,j) \in W} (d(i) - d(j) + c_{ij}) = \sum_{(i,j) \in W} c_{ij} \geq 0,$$

since the labels $d(i)$ cancel out in the summation. This conclusion contradicts our assumption that W is a negative cycle.

Conditions C3.1 in Theorem 3.2 correspond to primal feasibility for the linear programming formulation of the shortest path problem. Conditions C3.2 correspond to dual feasibility. From this perspective, we might view label correcting algorithms as methods that always maintain primal feasibility and try to achieve dual feasibility. The generic label correcting algorithm that we consider first is a general procedure for successively updating distance labels $d(i)$ until they satisfy the condition C3.2. At any point in the algorithm, the label $d(i)$ is either ∞ indicating that we have yet to discover any path from the source to node i, or it is the length of some path from the source to node i. The algorithm is based upon the simple observation that whenever $d(j) > d(i) + c_{ij}$, the current path from the source to node i, of length $d(i)$, together with the arc (i, j) is a shorter path to node j than the current path of length $d(j)$.

algorithm LABEL CORRECTING;
begin
    $d(s) := 0$ and $\mathrm{pred}(s) := 0$;
    $d(j) := \infty$ for each $j \in N - \{s\}$;
    while some arc (i, j) satisfies $d(j) > d(i) + c_{ij}$ **do**
    begin
        $d(j) := d(i) + c_{ij}$;
        $\mathrm{pred}(j) := i$;
    end;
end;

The correctness of the label correcting algorithm follows from Theorem 3.2. At termination, the labels $d(i)$ satisfy $d(j) \leq d(i) + c_{ij}$ for all $(i, j) \in A$, and hence represent the shortest path lengths. We now note that this algorithm is finite if there are no negative cost cycles and if the data are integral. Since $d(j)$ is bounded from above by nC and below by $-nC$, the algorithm updates $d(j)$ at most $2nC$ times. Thus when all data are integral, the number of distance updates is $O(n^2 C)$, and hence the algorithm runs in pseudopolynomial time.

A nice feature of this label correcting algorithm is its flexibility: we can select the arcs that do not satisfy conditions C3.2 in any order and still assure finite convergence. One drawback of the method, however, is that without a further restriction on the choice of arcs, the label correcting algorithm does not necessarily run in polynomial time. Indeed, if we start with a pathological instance of the problem and make a poor choice of arcs at every iteration, then the number of steps can grow exponentially with n. (Since the algorithm is pseudopolynomial time, these instances do have exponentially large values of C.) To obtain a polynomial time bound for the algorithm, we can organize the computations carefully in the following manner. Arrange the arcs in A in some (possibly arbitrary) order. Now make passes through A. In each pass, scan arcs in A in order and check the condition $d(j) > d(i) + c_{ij}$; if the arc satisfies this condition, then update $d(j) = d(i) + c_{ij}$. Terminate the algorithm if no distance label changes during an entire pass. We call this algorithm the *modified label correcting algorithm*.

Theorem 3.3. *When applied to a network containing no negative cycles, the modified label correcting algorithm requires* O(nm) *time to determine shortest paths from the source to every other node.*

Proof. We show that the algorithm performs at most $n - 1$ passes through the arc list. Since each pass requires O(1) computations for each arc, this conclusion implies the O(nm) bound. Let $d^r(j)$ denote the length of the shortest path from the source to node j consisting of r or fewer arcs. Further, let $D^r(j)$ represent the distance label of node j after r passes through the arc list. We claim, inductively, that $D^r(j) \le d^r(j)$ for each $j \in N$, and for each $r = 1, \ldots, n - 1$. We perform induction on the value of r. Suppose $D^{r-1}(j) \le d^{r-1}(j)$ for each $j \in N$. The provisions of the modified labeling algorithm imply that

$$D^r(j) \le \min\{D^{r-1}(j), \min_{i \ne j}\{D^{r-1}(i) + c_{ij}\}\} \ .$$

Next note that the shortest path to node j containing no more than r arcs either (i) has no more than $r - 1$ arcs, or (ii) it contains exactly r arcs. In case (i), $d^r(j) = d^{r-1}(j)$, and in case (ii), $d^r(j) = \min_{i \ne j}\{d^{r-1}(i) + c_{ij}\}$. Consequently,

$$d^r(j) = \min\{d^{r-1}(j), \min_{i \ne j}\{d^{r-1}(i) + c_{ij}\}\}$$

$$\ge \min\{D^{r-1}(j), \min_{i \ne j}\{D^{r-1}(i) + c_{ij}\}\};$$

the inequality follows from the induction hypothesis. Hence, $D^r(j) \le d^r(j)$ for all $j \in N$. Finally, we note that the shortest path from the source to any node consists of at most $n - 1$ arcs. Therefore, after at most $n - 1$ passes, the algorithm terminates with the shortest path lengths. □

The modified label correcting algorithm is also capable of detecting the presence of negative cycles in the network. If the algorithm does not update any distance label during an entire pass, up to the $(n - 1)$-th pass, then it has a set of labels $d(j)$ satisfying C3.2. In this case, the algorithm terminates with the shortest path distances and the network does not contain any negative cycle. On the other hand, when the algorithm modifies distance labels in all the $n - 1$ passes, we make one more pass. If the distance label of some node i changes in the n-th pass, then the network contains a directed *walk* (a path together with a cycle that have one or more nodes in common) from node 1 to i of length greater than $n - 1$ arcs that has smaller distance than all paths from the source node to i. This situation cannot occur unless the network contains a negative cost cycle.

Practical improvements

As stated so far, the modified label correcting algorithm considers every arc of the network during every pass through the arc list. It need not do so.

Suppose we order the arcs in the arc list by their tail nodes so that all arcs with the same tail node appear consecutively on the list. Thus, while scanning the arcs, we consider one node i at a time, scanning arcs in $A(i)$ and testing the optimality conditions. Now suppose that during one pass through the arc list, the algorithm does not change the distance label of a node i. Then, during the next pass $d(j) \leq d(i) + c_{ij}$ for every $(i, j) \in A(i)$, and the algorithm need not test these conditions. To achieve these savings, the algorithm can maintain a list of nodes whose distance labels have changed since it last examined them. It scans this list in the first-in, first-out order to assure that it performs passes through the arc list A and, consequently, terminates in $O(nm)$ time. The following procedure is a formal description of this further modification of the modified label correcting method.

algorithm MODIFIED LABEL CORRECTING;
begin
   $d(s) := 0$ and $\text{pred}(s) := 0$;
   $d(j) := \infty$ for each $j \in N - \{s\}$;
   LIST $:= \{s\}$;
   while LIST $\neq \emptyset$ **do**
   begin
      select the first element i of LIST;
      delete i from LIST;
      for each $(i, j) \in A(i)$ **do**
        if $d(j) > d(i) + c_{ij}$ **then**
        begin
           $d(j) := d(i) + c_{ij}$;
           $\text{pred}(j) := i$;
           if $j \notin$ LIST **then** add j to the end of LIST;
        end;
   end;
end;

Another modification of this algorithm sacrifices its polynomial time behavior in the worst case, but greatly improves its running time in practice. The modification alters the manner in which the algorithm adds nodes to LIST. While adding a node i to LIST, we check to see whether it has already appeared in the LIST. If yes, then we add i to the *beginning* of LIST, otherwise we add it to the *end* of LIST. This heuristic rule has the following plausible justification. If the node i has previously appeared on the LIST, then some nodes may have i as a predecessor. It is advantageous to update the distances for these nodes immediately, rather than update them from other nodes and then update them again when we consider node i. Empirical studies indicate that with this change alone, the algorithm is several times faster for many reasonable problem classes. Though this change makes the algorithm very attractive in practice, the worst-case running time of the algorithm is exponential. Indeed, this version of the label correcting algorithm is the fastest algorithm in practice for finding the shortest path from a single source to all nodes in non-dense networks. (For the problem of finding a shortest path from a single source node to a single sink, certain variants of the label setting algorithm are more efficient in practice.)

3.5. All pairs shortest path algorithm

In certain applications of the shortest path problem, we need to determine shortest path distances between all pairs of nodes. In this section we describe two algorithms to solve this problem. The first algorithm is well suited for sparse graphs. It combines the modified label correcting algorithm and Dijkstra's algorithm. The second algorithm is better suited for dense graphs. It is based on dynamic programming.

If the network has nonnegative arc lengths, then we can solve all pairs shortest path problem by applying Dijkstra's algorithm n times, considering each node as the source node once. If the network contains arcs with negative arc lengths, then we can first transform the network to one with nonnegative arc lengths as follows. Let s be a node from which all nodes in the network are reachable, i.e., connected by directed paths. We use the modified label correcting algorithm to compute shortest path distances from s to all other nodes. The algorithm either terminates with the shortest path distances $d(j)$ or indicates the presence of a negative cycle. In the former case, we define the new length of the arc (i, j) as $\bar{c}_{ij} = c_{ij} + d(i) - d(j)$ for each $(i, j) \in A$. Condition C3.2 implies that $\bar{c}_{ij} \geqslant 0$ for all $(i, j) \in A$. Further, note that for any path P from node k to node l,

$$\sum_{(i,j) \in P} \bar{c}_{ij} = \sum_{(i,j) \in P} c_{ij} + d(k) - d(l)$$

since the intermediate labels $d(j)$ cancel out in the summation. This transformation thus changes the length of all paths between a pair of nodes by a constant amount (depending on the pair) and consequently preserves shortest paths. Since arc lengths become nonnegative after the transformation, we can apply Dijkstra's algorithm $n - 1$ additional times to determine the shortest path distances between all pairs of nodes in the transformed network. We then obtain the shortest path distance from node k to node l in the original network by adding $d(l) - d(k)$ to the corresponding shortest path distance in the transformed network. This approach requires $O(nm)$ time to solve the first shortest path problem, and if the network contains no negative cost cycle, the method takes an extra $O(nS(n, m, C))$ time to compute the remaining shortest path distances. The expression $S(n, m, C)$ is the time needed to solve a shortest path problem with nonnegative arc lengths. For the R-heap implementations of Dijkstra's algorithm we considered previously, $S(n, m, C) = m + n \log nC$.

Another way to solve the all pairs shortest path problem is by dynamic programming. The approach we present is known as Floyd's algorithm. We define the variables $d^r(i, j)$ as follows:

$d^r(i, j)$ = the length of a shortest path from node i to node j subject to the condition that the path uses only the nodes $1, 2, \ldots, r-1$ as internal nodes.

Let $d(i, j)$ denote the actual shortest path distance. To compute $d^{r+1}(i, j)$, we first observe that a shortest path from node i to node j that passes through the nodes $1, 2, \ldots, r$ either (i) does not pass through the node r, in which case $d^{r+1}(i, j) = d^r(i, j)$, or (ii) does pass through the node r, in which case $d^{r+1}(i, j) = d^r(i, r) + d^r(r, j)$. Thus we have

$$d^1(i, j) = c_{ij} ,$$

and

$$d^{r+1}(i, j) = \min\{d^r(i, j), d^r(i, r) + d^r(r, j)\} .$$

We assume that $c_{ij} = \infty$ for all node pairs $(i, j) \notin A$. It is possible to solve the previous equations recursively for increasing values of r, and by varying the node pairs over $N \times N$ for a fixed value of r. The following procedure is a formal description of this algorithm.

algorithm ALL PAIRS SHORTEST PATHS;
begin
    for all node pairs $(i, j) \in N \times N$ **do** $d(i, j) := \infty$ and $\text{pred}(i, j) := 0$;
    for each $(i, j) \in A$ **do** $d(i, j) := c_{ij}$ and $\text{pred}(i, j) := i$;
    for each $r := 1$ to n **do**
      for each $(i, j) \in N \times N$ **do**
        if $d(i, j) > d(i, r) + d(r, j)$ **then**
        begin
          $d(i, j) := d(i, r) + d(r, j)$;
          if $i = j$ and $d(i, i) < 0$ **then** the network contains a negative cycle,
            STOP;
          $\text{pred}(i, j) := \text{pred}(r, j)$;
        end;
end;

Floyd's algorithm uses predecessor indices, $\text{pred}(i, j)$, for each node pair (i, j). The index $\text{pred}(i, j)$ denotes the last node prior to node j in the tentative shortest path from node i to node j. The algorithm maintains the property that for each finite $d(i, j)$, the network contains a path from node i to node j of length $d(i, j)$. This path can be obtained by tracing the predecessor indices.

This algorithm performs n iterations, and in each iteration it performs O(1) computations for each node pair. Consequently, it runs in O(n^3) time. The algorithm either terminates with the shortest path distances or stops when $d(i, i) < 0$ for some node i. In the latter case, for some node $r \neq i$, $d(i, r) + d(r, i) < 0$. Hence, the union of the tentative shortest paths from node i to node r and from node r to node i contains a negative cycle. This cycle can be obtained by using the predecessor indices.

Floyd's algorithm is in many respects similar to the modified label correcting algorithm. This relationship becomes more transparent from the following theorem.

Theorem 3.4. *If $d(i, j)$ for $(i, j) \in N \times N$ satisfy the following conditions, then they represent the shortest path distances:*
  (i) $d(i, i) = 0$ *for all i;*
  (ii) $d(i, j)$ *is the length of some path from node i to node j;*
  (iii) $d(i, j) \leq d(i, r) + c_{rj}$ *for all i, r, and j.*

Proof. For fixed i, this theorem is a consequence of Theorem 3.2. □

4. Maximum flows

An important characteristic of a network is its capacity to carry flow. What, given capacities on the arcs, is the maximum flow that can be sent between any two nodes? The resolution of this question determines the 'best' use of arc capacities and establishes a reference point against which to compare other ways of using the network. Moreover, the solution of the maximum flow problem with capacity data chosen judiciously establishes other performance measures for a network. For example, what is the minimum number of nodes whose removal from the network destroys all paths joining a particular pair of nodes? Or, what is the maximum number of node disjoint paths that join this pair of nodes? These and similar reliability measures indicate the robustness of the network to failure of its components.

In this section, we discuss several algorithms for computing the maximum flow between two nodes in a network. We begin by introducing a basic labeling algorithm for solving the maximum flow problem. The validity of these algorithms rests upon the celebrated *max-flow min-cut theorem* of network flows. This remarkable theorem has a number of surprising implications in machine and vehicle scheduling, communication systems planning, and several other application domains. We then consider improved versions of the basic labeling algorithm with better theoretical performance guarantees. In particular, we describe *preflow–push* algorithms that have recently emerged as the most powerful techniques for solving the maximum flow problem, both theoretically and empirically.

We consider a capacitated network $G = (N, A)$ with a *nonnegative integer* capacity u_{ij} for any arc $(i, j) \in A$. The source s and sink t are two distinguished nodes of the network. We assume that for every arc (i, j) in A, (j, i) is also in A. There is no loss of generality in making this assumption since we allow zero capacity arcs. We also assume, without any loss of generality, that all arc capacities are finite (since we can set the capacity of any uncapacitated arc equal to the sum of the capacities of all capacitated arcs). Let $U = \max\{u_{ij} : (i, j) \in A\}$. As earlier, the arc adjacency list defined as $A(i) = \{(i, k) : (i, k) \in A\}$ designates the arcs emanating from node i. In the maximum flow problem, we wish to find the maximum flow from the source node s to the sink node t that satisfies the arc capacities. Formally, the problem is to

$$\text{maximize} \quad v \tag{4.1a}$$

subject to

$$\sum_{\{j : (i,j) \in A\}} x_{ij} - \sum_{\{j : (j,i) \in A\}} x_{ji} = \begin{cases} v & \text{if } i = s, \\ 0 & \text{if } i \neq s, t, \text{ for all } i \in N, \\ -v & \text{if } i = t, \end{cases} \tag{4.1b}$$

$$0 \leq x_{ij} \leq u_{ij}, \quad \text{for each } (i, j) \in A. \tag{4.1c}$$

It is possible to relax the integrality assumption on arc capacities for some algorithms, though this assumption is necessary for others. Algorithms whose complexity bounds involve U assume integrality of data. Note, however, that rational arc capacities can always be transformed to integer arc capacities by appropriately scaling the data. Thus, the integrality of data is not a restrictive assumption in practice.

The concept of *residual network* is crucial to the algorithms we consider. Given a flow x, the *residual capacity*, r_{ij}, of any arc $(i, j) \in A$ represents the maximum additional flow that can be sent from node i to node j using the arcs (i, j) and (j, i). The residual capacity has two components: (i) $u_{ij} - x_{ij}$, the unused capacity of arc (i, j), and (ii) the current flow x_{ji} on arc (j, i) which can be cancelled to increase flow to node j. Consequently, $r_{ij} = u_{ij} - x_{ij} + x_{ji}$. We call the network consisting of the arcs with positive residual capacities the *residual network* (with respect to the flow x), and represent it as $G(x)$. Figure 4.1 illustrates an example of a residual network.

4.1. Labeling algorithm and the max-flow min-cut theorem

One of the simplest and most intuitive algorithms for solving the maximum flow problem is the *augmenting path algorithm* due to Ford and Fulkerson. The algorithm proceeds by identifying directed paths from the source to the sink in the residual network and augmenting flows on these paths, until the residual network contains no such path. The following high-level (and flexible) descrip-

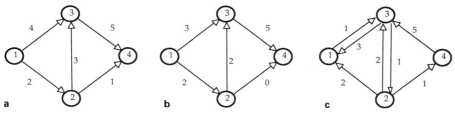

Fig. 4.1. Example of a residual network. (a) Network with arc capacities. Node 1 is the source and node 4 is the sink. (Arcs not shown have zero capacities.) (b) Network with a flow x. (c) The residual network with residual arc capacities.

tion of the algorithm summarizes the basic iterative steps, without specifying any particular algorithmic strategy for how to determine augmenting paths.

algorithm AUGMENTING PATH;
begin
    $x := 0$;
    while there is a path P from s to t in $G(x)$ **do**
    begin
        $\Delta := min\{r_{ij}: (i, j) \in P\}$;
        augment Δ units of flow along P and update $G(x)$;
    end;
end;

For each $(i, j) \in P$, augmenting Δ units of flow along P decreases r_{ij} by Δ and increases r_{ji} by Δ. We now discuss this algorithm in more detail. First, we need a method to identify a directed path from the source to the sink in the residual network or to show that the network contains no such path. Second, we need to show that the algorithm terminates finitely. Finally, we must establish that the algorithm terminates with a maximum flow. The last result follows from the proof of the *max-flow min-cut theorem*.

A directed path from the source to the sink in the residual network is also called an *augmenting path*. The residual capacity of an augmenting path is the minimum residual capacity of any arc on the path. The definition of the residual capacity implies that an additional flow of Δ in arc (i, j) of the residual network corresponds to (i) an increase in x_{ij} by Δ in the original network, or (ii) a decrease in x_{ji} by Δ in the original network, or (iii) a convex combination of (i) and (ii). For our purposes, it is easier to work directly with residual capacities and to compute the flows only when the algorithm terminates.

The labeling algorithm performs a search of the residual network to find a directed path from s to t. It does so by *fanning out* from the source node s to find a directed tree containing nodes that are reachable from the source along a directed path in the residual network. At any step, we refer to the nodes in the tree as *labeled* and those not in the tree as *unlabeled*. The algorithm selects a labeled node and scans its arc adjacency list (in the residual network) to label more unlabeled nodes. Eventually, the sink becomes labeled and the algorithm sends the maximum possible flow on the path from s to t. It then erases the labels and repeats this process. The algorithm terminates when it has scanned all labeled nodes and the sink remains unlabeled. The following algorithmic description specifies the steps of the labeling algorithm in detail. The algorithm maintains a predecessor index, pred(i), for each labeled node i indicating the node that caused node i to be labeled. The predecessor indices allow us to trace back along the path from a node to the source.

algorithm LABELING;
begin
  loop
    pred(j) := 0 for each $j \in N$;
    $L := \{s\}$;
    while $L \neq \emptyset$ and t is unlabeled **do**
    begin
      select a node $i \in L$;
      for each $(i, j) \in A(i)$ **do**
        if j is unlabeled and $r_{ij} > 0$ **then**
        begin
          pred(j) := i;
          mark j as labeled and add this node to L;
        end;
      delete node i from L;
    end;

    if t is labeled **then**
    begin
      use the predecessor labels to track back to obtain the augmenting path P
      from s to t;
      $\Delta := \min\{r_{ij}: (i, j) \in P\}$;
      augment Δ units of flow along P;
      erase all labels and go to loop;
    end;
    else quit the loop;
  end; {loop}
end;

The final residual capacities r can be used to obtain the arc flows as follows. Since $r_{ij} = u_{ij} - x_{ij} + x_{ji}$, the arc flows satisfy $x_{ij} - x_{ji} = u_{ij} - r_{ij}$. Hence, if $u_{ij} > r_{ij}$ we can set $x_{ij} = u_{ij} - r_{ij}$ and $x_{ji} = 0$; otherwise we set $x_{ij} = 0$ and $x_{ji} = r_{ij} - u_{ij}$.

In order to show that the algorithm obtains a maximum flow, we introduce some new definitions and notation. Recall from Section 1.3 that a set $Q \subseteq A$ is a *cutset* if the subnetwork $G' = (N, A - Q)$ is disconnected and no subset of Q has this property. A cutset partitions the set N into two subsets. A cutset is called an *s–t cutset* if the source and the sink nodes are contained in different subsets of nodes, S and $\bar{S} = N - S$: S is the set of nodes connected to s. Conversely, any partition of the node set as S and $\bar{S}$ with $s \in S$ and $t \in \bar{S}$ defines an *s–t* cutset. Consequently, we alternatively denote an *s–t* cutset as $(S, \bar{S})$. An arc (i, j) with $i \in S$ and $j \in \bar{S}$ is called a *forward arc*, and an arc (i, j) with $i \in \bar{S}$ and $j \in S$ is called a *backward arc* in the cutset $(S, \bar{S})$.

Let x be a flow vector satisfying the flow conservation and capacity constraints of (4.1). For this flow vector x, let v be the amount of flow leaving the source. We refer to v as the *value* of the flow. The flow x determines the net flow across an *s–t* cutset $(S, \bar{S})$ as

$$F_x(S, \bar{S}) = \sum_{i \in S} \sum_{j \in \bar{S}} x_{ij} - \sum_{i \in \bar{S}} \sum_{j \in S} x_{ij} \, . \tag{4.2}$$

The capacity $C(S, \bar{S})$ of an *s–t* cutset $(S, \bar{S})$ is defined as

$$C(S, \bar{S}) = \sum_{i \in S} \sum_{j \in \bar{S}} u_{ij} \, . \tag{4.3}$$

We claim that the flow across any *s–t* cutset equals the value of the flow and does not exceed the cutset capacity. Adding the mass balance constraints (4.1b) for nodes in S and noting that when nodes i and j both belong to S, x_{ij} in the equation for node j cancels $-x_{ij}$ in the equation for node i, we obtain

$$v = \sum_{i \in S} \sum_{j \in \bar{S}} x_{ij} - \sum_{i \in \bar{S}} \sum_{j \in S} x_{ij} \equiv F_x(S, \bar{S}) \, . \tag{4.4}$$

Substituting $x_{ij} \le u_{ij}$ in the first summation and $x_{ij} \ge 0$ in the second summation shows that

$$F_x(S, \bar{S}) \le \sum_{i \in S} \sum_{j \in \bar{S}} u_{ij} \equiv C(S, \bar{S}) \, . \tag{4.5}$$

This result is the weak duality property of the maximum flow problem when viewed as a linear program. Like most weak duality results, it is the 'easy' half of the duality theory. The more substantive strong duality property asserts that (4, 5) holds as an equality for some choice of x and some choice of an *s–t* cutset $(S, \bar{S})$. This strong duality property is the max-flow min-cut theorem.

Theorem 4.1. (Max-flow min-cut theorem). *The maximum value of flow from s to t equals the minimum capacity of all s–t cutsets.*

Proof. Let x denote a maximum flow vector and v denote the maximum flow value. (Linear programming theory, or our subsequent algorithmic developments, guarantee that the problem always has a maximum flow as long as some cutset has finite capacity.) Define S to be the set of labeled nodes in the residual network $G(x)$ when we apply the labeling algorithm starting from the flow x. Let $\bar{S} = N - S$. Clearly, since x is a maximum flow, $s \in S$ and $t \in \bar{S}$. Adding the flow conservation equations for nodes in S, we obtain (4.4). Note that nodes in $\bar{S}$ cannot be labeled from the nodes in S, hence $r_{ij} = 0$ for each forward arc (i, j) in the cutset $(S, \bar{S})$. Since $r_{ij} = u_{ij} - x_{ij} + x_{ji}$, the conditions $x_{ij} \leq u_{ij}$ and $x_{ji} \geq 0$ imply that $x_{ij} = u_{ij}$ for each forward arc in the cutset $(S, \bar{S})$ and $x_{ij} = 0$ for each backward arc in the cutset. Making these substitutions in (4.4) yields

$$v = F_x(S, \bar{S}) = \sum_{i \in S} \sum_{j \in \bar{S}} u_{ij} = C(S, \bar{S}) . \qquad (4.6)$$

But we have observed earlier that v is a lower bound on the capacity of any $s-t$ cutset. Consequently, the cutset $(S, \bar{S})$ is a minimum capacity $s-t$ cutset and its capacity equals the maximum flow value v. We thus have established the theorem. $\square$

The proof of this theorem not only establishes the max-flow min-cut property, but the same argument shows that when the labeling algorithm terminates, it has at hand both the maximum flow value (and a maximum flow vector) and a minimum capacity $s-t$ cutset. But does it terminate finitely? Each labeling iteration of the algorithm scans any node at most once, inspecting each arc in $A(i)$. Consequently, the labeling iteration scans each arc at most once and requires $O(m)$ computations. If all arc capacities are integral and bounded by a finite number U, then the capacity of the cutset $(s, N - \{s\})$ is at most nU. Since the labeling algorithm increases the flow value by at least one unit in any iteration, it terminates within nU iterations. This bound on the number of iterations is not entirely satisfactory for large values of U; if $U = 2^n$, the bound is exponential in the number of nodes. Moreover, the algorithm can indeed perform that many iterations. In addition, if the capacities are irrational, the algorithm may not terminate: although the successive flow values converge, they may not converge to the maximum flow value. Thus if the method is to be effective, we must select the augmenting paths carefully. Several refinements of the algorithm, including those we consider in Section 4.2–4.4, overcome this difficulty and obtain an optimum flow even if the capacities are irrational; moreover, the max-flow min-cut theorem (and our proof of Theorem 4.1) is true even if the data are irrational.

A second drawback of the labeling algorithm is its 'forgetfulness'. At each iteration, the algorithm generates node labels that contain information about augmenting paths from the source to other nodes. The implementation we have described erases the labels when it proceeds from one iteration to the next, even though much of this information may be valid in the next residual network. Erasing the labels therefore destroys potentially useful information. Ideally, we should retain a label when it can be used profitably in later computations.

4.2. Decreasing the number of augmentations

The bound of nU on the number of augmentations in the labeling algorithm is not satisfactory from a theoretical perspective. Furthermore, without further modifications, the augmenting path algorithm may take $\Omega(nU)$ augmentations, as the example given in Figure 4.2 illustrates.

Flow decomposition shows that, in principle, augmenting path algorithms should be able to find a maximum flow in no more than m augmentations. For suppose x is an optimum flow and y is any initial flow (possibly zero). By the flow decomposition property, it is possible to obtain x from y by a sequence of at most m augmentations on augmenting paths from s to t plus flows around augmenting cycles. If we define x' as the flow vector obtained from y by applying only the augmenting paths, then x' also is a maximum flow (flows around cycles do not change flow value). This result shows that it is, in theory, possible to find a maximum flow using at most m augmentations. Unfortunately, to apply this flow decomposition argument, we need to know a maximum flow. No algorithm developed in the literature achieves this theoretical bound. Nevertheless, it is possible to improve considerably on the bound of $O(nU)$ augmentations of the basic labeling algorithm.

One natural specialization of the augmenting path algorithm is to augment flow along a 'shortest path' from the source to the sink, defined as a path consisting of the fewest number of arcs. If we augment flow along a shortest path, then the length of any shortest augmenting path either stays the same or increases. Moreover, after m augmentations, the length of the shortest augmenting path is guaranteed to increase. (We will prove these results in the next section.) Since no path contains more than $n-1$ arcs, this rule guarantees that the number of augmentations is at most $(n-1)m$.

An alternative is to augment flow along a path of maximum residual capacity. This specialization also leads to improved complexity. Let v be any flow value and v^* be the maximum flow value. By flow decomposition, the network contains at most m augmenting paths whose residual capacities sum to

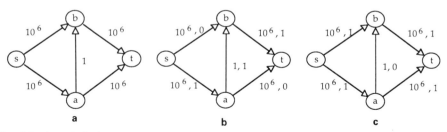

Fig. 4.2. A pathological example for the labeling algorithm. (a) The input network with arc capacities. (b) After augmenting along the path $s-a-b-t$. Arc flow is indicated beside the arc capacity. (c) After augmenting along the path $s-b-a-t$. After 2×10^6 augmentations, alternately along $s-a-b-t$ and $s-b-a-t$, the flow is maximum.

$v^* - v$. Thus the maximum capacity augmenting path has residual capacity at least $(v^* - v)/m$. Now consider a sequence of $2m$ consecutive maximum capacity augmentations, starting with flow v. At least one of these augmentations must augment the flow by an amount $(v^* - v)/2m$ or less, for otherwise we will have a maximum flow. Thus after $2m$ or fewer augmentations, the algorithm would reduce the capacity of a maximum capacity augmenting path by a factor of at least two. Since this capacity is initially at most U and the capacity must be at least 1 until the flow is maximum, after $O(m \log U)$ maximum capacity augmentations, the flow must be maximum. (Note that we are essentially repeating the argument used to establish the geometric improvement approach discussed in Section 1.6.)

In the following section, we consider another algorithm for reducing the number of augmentations.

4.3. Shortest augmenting path algorithm

The natural approach of augmenting along shortest paths would successively look for shortest paths by performing a breadth first search in the residual network. If the labeling algorithm maintains the set L of labeled nodes as a queue, then by examining the labeled nodes in a first-in, first-out order, it would obtain a shortest path in the residual network. Each of these iterations would take $O(m)$ steps both in the worst case and in practice, and (by our subsequent observations) the resulting computation time would be $O(nm^2)$. Unfortunately, this computation time is excessive. We can improve this running time by exploiting the fact that the minimum distance from any node i to the sink node t is monotonically nondecreasing over all augmentations. By fully exploiting this property, we can reduce the average time per augmentation to $O(n)$.

The algorithm

The concept of distance labels will prove to be an important construct in the maximum flow algorithms that we discuss in this section and in Sections 4.4 and 4.5. A *distance function* $d: N \rightarrow Z^+$ with respect to the residual capacities r_{ij} is a function from the set of nodes to the nonnegative integers. We say that a distance function is *valid* if it satisfies the following two conditions:

C4.1. $d(t) = 0$;

C4.2. $d(i) \le d(j) + 1$ for every arc $(i, j) \in A$ with $r_{ij} > 0$.

We refer to $d(i)$ as the *distance label* of node i and condition C4.2 as the *validity condition*. It is easy to demonstrate that $d(i)$ is a lower bound on the length of the shortest directed path from i to t in the residual network. Let $i = i_1 - i_2 - i_3 - \cdots - i_k - t$ be any path of length k in the residual network from node i to t. Then, from C4.2 we have $d(i) = d(i_1) \le d(i_2) + 1$, $d(i_2) \le d(i_3) + 1, \ldots, d(i_k) \le d(t) + 1 = 1$. These inequalities imply that $d(i) \le k$ for *any* path of length k in the residual network and, hence, any shortest path from node i to t contains at least $d(i)$ arcs. If for each node i, the distance label $d(i)$ equals the length of the shortest path from i to t in the residual network, then we call the distance labels *exact*. For example, in Figure 4.1(c), $d = (0, 0, 0, 0)$ is a valid distance label, though $d = (3, 1, 2, 0)$ represents the exact distance label.

We now define some additional notation. An arc (i, j) in the residual network is *admissible* if it satisfies $d(i) = d(j) + 1$. Other arcs are *inadmissible*. A path from s to t consisting entirely of admissible arcs is an *admissible path*. The algorithm we describe next repeatedly augments flow along admissible paths. For any admissible path of length k, $d(s) = k$. Since $d(s)$ is a lower bound on the length of any path from the source to the sink, the algorithm augments flows along shortest paths in the residual network. Thus, we refer to the algorithm as the shortest augmenting path algorithm.

Whenever we augment along a path, each of the distance labels for nodes in the path is exact. However, for other nodes in the network it is not necessary to maintain exact distances; it suffices to have valid distances, which are lower bounds on the exact distances. There is no particular urgency to compute these distances exactly. By allowing the distance label of node i to be less than the distance from i to t, we maintain flexibility in the algorithm, without incurring any significant cost.

We can compute the initial distance labels by performing a backward breadth first search of the residual network, starting at the sink node. The algorithm generates an admissible path by adding admissible arcs, one at a time, as follows. It maintains a path from the source node to some node i^*, called the *current node*, consisting entirely of admissible arcs. We call this path a *partial admissible path* and store it using *predecessor* indices, i.e., pred(j) = i for each arc (i, j) on the path. The algorithm performs one of the two steps at the current node: *advance* or *retreat*. The advance step identifies some admissible arc (i^*, j^*) emanating from node i^*, adds it to the partial admissible path, and designates j^* as the new current node. If no admissible arc emanates from node i^*, then the algorithm performs the retreat step. This step increases the distance label of node i^* so that at least one admissible arc emanates from it (we refer to this step as a *relabel* operation). Increasing $d(i^*)$ makes the arc $(\text{pred}(i^*), i^*)$ inadmissible (assuming $i^* \ne s$). Consequently, we delete $(\text{pred}(i^*), i^*)$ from the partial admissible path and node pred(i^*) becomes the new current node. Whenever the partial admissible path becomes an admissible path (i.e., contains node t), the algorithm makes a maximum possible augmentation on this path and begins again with the source as the current node. The algorithm terminates when $d(s) \ge n$, indicating that the network contains no augmenting path from the source to the sink. We next describe the algorithm formally.

algorithm SHORTEST AUGMENTING PATH;
begin
   $x := 0$;
   perform backward breadth first search of the residual network
      from node t to obtain the distance labels $d(i)$;
   if there is no path from i to t **then** $d(i) = n$;
   $i^* := s$;
   while $d(s) < n$ **do**
   begin
      if i^* has an admissible arc **then** ADVANCE(i^*)
      else RETREAT(i^*);
      if $i^* = t$ **then** AUGMENT and set $i^* := s$;
   end;
end;

procedure ADVANCE(i^*);
begin
   let (i^*, j^*) be an admissible arc in $A(i^*)$;
   pred(j^*) := i^* and $i^* := j^*$;
end;

procedure RETREAT/RELABEL(i^*);
begin
   $d(i^*) := \min\{d(j) + 1: (i^*, j) \in A(i^*)$ and $r_{i^*j} > 0\}$;
   if $i^* \neq s$ **then** $i^* := \mathrm{pred}(i^*)$;
end;

procedure AUGMENT;
begin
   using predecessor indices identify an augmenting path P from the source to
      the sink;
   $\Delta := \min\{r_{ij}: (i, j) \in P\}$;
   augment Δ units of flow along path P;
end;

We use the following data structure to select an admissible arc emanating from a node. We maintain the list $A(i)$ of arcs emanating from each node i. Arcs in each list can be arranged arbitrarily, but the order, once decided, remains unchanged throughout the algorithm. Each node i has a *current-arc* (i, j) which is the current candidate for the next advance step. Initially, the current-arc of node i is the first arc in its arc list. The algorithm examines this list sequentially and whenever the current arc is inadmissible, it makes the next arc in the arc list the current arc. When the algorithm has examined all arcs in $A(i)$, it updates the distance label of node i and the current arc once again becomes the first arc in its arc list. In our subsequent discussion we shall always implicitly assume that algorithms select admissible arcs using this technique.

Correctness of the algorithm

We first show that the shortest augmenting path algorithm correctly solves the maximum flow problem.

Lemma 4.1. *The shortest augmenting path algorithm maintains valid distance labels at each step. Moreover, each relabel step strictly increases the distance label of a node.*

Proof. We show that the algorithm maintains valid distance labels at every step by performing induction on the number of augment and relabel steps. Initially, the algorithm constructs valid distance labels. Assume, inductively, that the distance function is valid prior to a step, i.e., satisfies the validity condition C4.2. We need to check whether these conditions remain valid (i) after an augment step (when the residual graph changes), and (ii) after a relabel step.

(i) A flow augmentation on arc (i, j) might delete this arc from the residual network, but this modification to the residual network does not affect the validity of the distance function of this arc. Augmentation on arc (i, j) might, however, create an additional arc (j, i) with $r_{ji} > 0$ and, therefore, also create an additional condition $d(j) \leq d(i) + 1$ that needs to be satisfied. The distance labels satisfy this validity condition, though, since $d(i) = d(j) + 1$ by the admissibility property of the augmenting path.

(ii) The algorithm performs a relabel step at node i when the current arc reaches the end of arc list $A(i)$. Observe that if an arc (i, j) is inadmissible at some stage, then it remains inadmissible until $d(i)$ increases because of our inductive hypothesis that distance labels are nondecreasing. Thus, when the current arc reaches the end of the arc list $A(i)$, then no arc $(i, j) \in A(i)$ satisfies $d(i) = d(j) + 1$ and $r_{ij} > 0$. Hence, $d(i) < \min\{d(j) + 1 : (i, j) \in A(i)$ and $r_{ij} > 0\} = d'(i)$, thereby establishing the second part of the lemma.

Finally, the choice for changing $d(i)$ ensures that the condition $d(i) \leq d(j) + 1$ remains valid for all (i, j) in the residual network; in addition, since $d(i)$ increases, the conditions $d(k) \leq d(i) + 1$ remain valid for all arcs (k, i) in the residual network. $\square$

Theorem 4.2. *The shortest augmenting path algorithm correctly computes a maximum flow.*

Proof. The algorithm terminates when $d(s) \geq n$. Since $d(s)$ is a lower bound on the length of the shortest augmenting path from s to t, this condition implies that the network contains no augmenting path from the source to the sink, which is the termination criterion for the generic augmenting path algorithm. $\square$

At termination of the algorithm, we can obtain a minimum s–t cutset as follows. For $0 \leq k \leq n$, let α_k denote the number of nodes with distance label equal to k. Note that α_{k^*} must be zero for some $k^* \leq n - 1$ since $\sum_{k=0}^{n-1} \alpha_k \leq n - 1$. (Recall that $d(s) \geq n$.) Let $S = \{i \in N : d(i) > k^*\}$ and $\bar{S} = N - S$. When

$d(s) \geq n$ and the algorithm terminates, $s \in S$ and $t \in \bar{S}$, and both the sets S and $\bar{S}$ are nonempty. Consider the $s–t$ cutset $(S, \bar{S})$. By construction, $d(i) > d(j) + 1$ for all $(i, j) \in (S, \bar{S})$. The validity condition C4.2 implies that $r_{ij} = 0$ for each $(i, j) \in (S, \bar{S})$. Hence, $(S, \bar{S})$ is a minimum $s–t$ cutset and the current flow is maximum.

Complexity of the algorithm
We next show that the algorithm computes a maximum flow in $O(n^2 m)$ time.

Lemma 4.2. (a) *Each distance label increases at most n times. Consequently, the total number of relabel steps is at most n^2.* (b) *The number of augment steps is at most $\frac{1}{2} nm$.*

Proof. Each relabel step at node i increases $d(i)$ by at least one. After the algorithm has relabeled node i at most n times, $d(i) \geq n$. From this point on, the algorithm never selects node i again during an advance step since for every node k in the current path, $d(k) < d(s) < n$. Thus the algorithm relabels a node at most n times and the total number of relabel steps is bounded by n^2.

Each augment step saturates at least one arc, i.e., decreases its residual capacity to zero. Suppose that the arc (i, j) becomes saturated at some iteration (at which $d(i) = d(j) + 1$). Then no more flow can be sent on (i, j) until flow is sent back from j to i (at which point $d'(j) = d'(i) + 1 \geq d(i) + 1 = d(j) + 2$). Hence, between two consecutive saturations of arc (i, j), $d(j)$ increases by at least 2 units. Consequently, any arc (i, j) can become saturated at most $\frac{1}{2} n$ times and the total number of arc saturations is no more than $\frac{1}{2} nm$. □

Theorem 4.3. *The shortest augmenting path algorithm runs in $O(n^2 m)$ time.*

Proof. The algorithm performs $O(nm)$ flow augmentations and each augmentation takes $O(n)$ time, resulting in $O(n^2 m)$ total effort in the augmentation steps. Each advance step increases the length of the partial admissible path by one, and each retreat step decreases its length by one; since each partial admissible path has length at most n, the algorithm requires at most $O(n^2 + n^2 m)$ advance steps. The first term comes from the number of retreat (relabel) steps, and the second term from the number of augmentations, which are bounded by $\frac{1}{2} nm$ by the previous lemma.

For each node i, the algorithm performs the relabel operation $O(n)$ times, each execution requiring $O(|A(i)|)$ time. The total time spent in all relabel operation is $\Sigma_{i \in N} O(n |A(i)|) = O(nm)$. Finally, we consider the time spent in identifying admissible arcs. The time taken to identify the admissible arc of node i is $O(1)$ plus the time spent in scanning arcs in $A(i)$. After having performed $|A(i)|$ such scannings, the algorithm reaches the end of the arc list and relabels node i. Thus the total time spent in all scannings is

$O(\Sigma_{i \in N} n|A(i)|) = O(nm)$. The combination of these time bounds establishes the theorem. □

The proof of Theorem 4.3 also suggests an alternative termination condition for the shortest augmenting path algorithm. The termination criterion of $d(s) \geq n$ is satisfactory for a worst-case analysis, but may not be efficient in practice. Researchers have observed empirically that the algorithm spends too much time in relabeling, a major portion of which is done *after* it has already found the maximum flow. The algorithm can be improved by detecting the presence of a minimum cutset prior to performing these relabeling operations. We can do so by maintaining the number of nodes α_k with distance label equal to k, for $0 \leq k \leq n$. The algorithm updates this array after every relabel operation and terminates whenever it first finds a *gap* in the α array, i.e., $\alpha_k^* = 0$ for some $k^* < d(s)$. As we have seen earlier, if $S = \{i: d(i) > k^*\}$, then $(S, \bar{S})$ denotes a minimum cutset.

The idea of augmenting flows along shortest paths is intuitively appealing and easy to implement in practice. The resulting algorithms identify at most $O(nm)$ augmenting paths and this bound is tight, i.e., on particular examples these algorithms perform $\Omega(nm)$ augmentations. The only way to improve the running time of the shortest augmenting path algorithm is to perform fewer computations per augmentation. The use of a sophisticated data structure, called *dynamic trees*, reduces the average time for each augmentation from $O(n)$ to $O(\log n)$. This implementation of the maximum flow algorithm runs in $O(nm \log n)$ time and obtaining further improvements appears quite difficult except in very dense networks. These implementations with sophisticated data structures appear to be primarily of theoretical interest, however, because maintaining the data structures requires substantial overhead that tends to increase rather than reduce the computational times in practice. A detailed discussion of dynamic trees is beyond the scope of this chapter.

Potential functions and an alternate proof of Lemma 4.2(b)

A powerful method for proving computational time bounds is to use *potential functions*. Potential function techniques are general purpose techniques for proving the complexity of an algorithm by analyzing the effects of different steps on an appropriately defined function. The use of potential functions enables us to define an 'accounting' relationship between the occurrences of various steps of an algorithm that can be used to obtain a bound on the steps that might be difficult to obtain using other arguments. Rather than formally introducing potential functions, we illustrate the technique by showing that the number of augmentations in the shortest augmenting path algorithm is $O(nm)$.

Suppose in the shortest augmenting path algorithm we kept track of the number of admissible arcs in the residual network. Let $F(k)$ denote the number of admissible arcs at the end of the k-th step; for the purpose of this argument, we count a step either as an augmentation or as a relabel operation. Let the algorithm perform K steps before it terminates. Clearly, $F(0) \le m$ and $F(K) \ge 0$. Each augmentation decreases the residual capacity of at least one arc to zero and hence reduces F by at least one unit. Each relabeling of node i creates as many as $|A(i)|$ new admissible arcs, and increases F by the same amount. This increase in F is at most nm over all relabelings, since the algorithm relabels any node at most n times (as a consequence of Lemma 4.1) and $\Sigma_{i \in N} n|A(i)| = nm$. Since the initial value of F is at most m more than its terminal value, the total decrease in F due to all augmentations is at most $m + nm$. Thus the number of augmentations is at most $m + nm = O(nm)$.

This argument is fairly representative of the potential function argument. Our objective was to bound the number of augmentations. We did so by defining a potential function that decreases whenever the algorithm performs an augmentation. The potential increases only when the algorithm relabels distances, and thus we can bound the number of augmentations using bounds on the number of relabels. In general, we bound the number of steps of one type in terms of known bounds on the number of steps of other types.

4.4. Preflow–push algorithms

Augmenting path algorithms send flow by augmenting along a path. This basic step further decomposes into the more elementary operation of sending flow along an arc. Thus sending a flow of Δ units along a path of k arcs decomposes into k basic operations of sending a flow of Δ units along an arc of the path. We shall refer to each of these basic operations as a *push*.

A path augmentation has one advantage over a single push: it maintains conservation of flow at all nodes. In fact, the push-based algorithms such as those we develop in this and the following sections necessarily violate conservation of flow. Rather, these algorithms permit the flow into a node to exceed the flow out of this node. We will refer to any such flows as *preflows*. The two basic operations of the generic preflow–push methods are (i) pushing the flow on an admissible arc, and (ii) updating a distance label, as in the augmenting path algorithm described in the last section. (We define the distance labels and admissible arcs as in the previous section.)

Preflow–push algorithms have several advantages over augmentation based algorithms. First, they are more general and more flexible. Second, they can push flow closer to the sink before identifying augmenting paths. Third, they are better suited for distributed or parallel computation. Fourth, the best preflow–push algorithms currently outperform the best augmenting path algorithms in theory as well as in practice.

The generic algorithm

A *preflow* x is a function $x : A \to R^+$ that satisfies (4.1c) and the following relaxation of (4.1b):

$$\sum_{\{j: (j,i) \in A\}} x_{ji} - \sum_{\{j: (i,j) \in A\}} x_{ij} \ge 0 , \quad \text{for all } i \in N - \{s, t\} .$$

The preflow–push algorithms maintain a preflow at each intermediate stage. For a given preflow x, we define the *excess* for each node $i \in N - \{s, t\}$ as

$$e(i) = \sum_{\{j:\, (j,i) \in A\}} x_{ji} - \sum_{\{j:\, (i,\, j) \in A\}} x_{ij}.$$

We refer to a node with positive excess as an *active* node. We adopt the convention that the source and sink nodes are never active. The preflow–push algorithms perform all operations using only local information. At each iteration of the algorithm (except its initialization and its termination), the network contains at least one active node, i.e., a node $i \in N - \{s, t\}$ with $e(i) > 0$. The goal of each iterative step is to choose some active node and to send its excess *closer* to the sink, closeness being measured with respect to the current distance labels. As in the shortest augmenting path algorithm, we send flow only on admissible arcs. If the method cannot send excess from this node to nodes with smaller distance labels, then it increases the distance label of the node so that it creates at least one new admissible arc. The algorithm terminates when the network contains no active nodes. The preflow–push algorithm uses the following subroutines:

procedure PREPROCESS;
begin
    $x := 0$;
    perform a backward breadth-first search of the residual network, starting at
        node t, to determine initial distance labels $d(i)$;
    $x_{sj} := u_{sj}$ for each arc $(s, j) \in A(s)$ and $d(s) := n$;
end;

procedure PUSH/RELABEL(i);
begin
    if the network contains an admissible arc (i, j) **then**
        push $\delta := \min\{e(i), r_{ij}\}$ units of flow from node i to node j;
    else replace $d(i)$ by $\min\{d(j) + 1 : (i, j) \in A(i)$ and $r_{ij} > 0\}$;
end;

A push of δ units from node i to node j decreases both $e(i)$ and r_{ij} by δ units and increases both $e(j)$ and r_{ji} by δ units. We say that a push of δ units of flow on arc (i, j) is *saturating* if $\delta = r_{ij}$ and *nonsaturating* otherwise. We refer to the process of increasing the distance label of a node as a *relabel* operation. The purpose of the relabel operation is to create at least one admissible arc on which the algorithm can perform further pushes.

The following generic version of the preflow–push algorithm combines the subroutines just described.

algorithm PREFLOW–PUSH;
begin
    PREPROCESS;

```
    while the network contains an active node do
    begin
        select an active node i;
        PUSH/RELABEL(i);
    end;
end;
```

It might be instructive to visualize the generic preflow–push algorithm in terms of a physical network: arcs represent flexible water pipes, nodes represent joints, and the distance function measures how far nodes are above the ground; and in the network, we wish to send water from the source to the sink. In addition, we visualize flow in an admissible arc as water flowing downhill. Initially, we move the source node upward, and water flows to its neighbors. In general, water flows downhill towards the sink; however, occasionally flow becomes trapped locally at a node that has no downhill neighbors. At this point, we move the node upward, and again water flows downhill towards the sink. Eventually, no flow can reach the sink. As we continue to move nodes upwards, the remaining excess flow eventually flows back towards the source. The algorithm terminates when all the water flows either into the sink or into the source.

Figure 4.3 illustrates the push/relabel steps applied to the example given in Figure 4.1(a). Figure 4.3(a) specifies the preflow determined by the preprocess step. Suppose the select step examines node 2. Since arc $(2,4)$ has residual capacity $r_{24} = 1$ and $d(2) = d(4) + 1$, the algorithm performs a (saturating) push of value $\delta = \min\{2, 1\}$ units. The push reduces the excess of node 2 to 1. Arc $(2,4)$ is deleted from the residual network and arc $(4,2)$ is added to the residual network. Since node 2 is still an active node, it can be selected again for further pushes. The arcs $(2,3)$ and $(2,1)$ have positive residual capacities, but they do not satisfy the distance condition. Hence, the algorithm performs a relabel operation and gives node 2 a new distance $d'(2) = \min\{d(3) + 1, d(1) + 1\} = \min\{2, 5\} = 2$.

The preprocessing step accomplishes several important tasks. First, it gives each node adjacent to node s a positive excess, so that the algorithm can begin by selecting some node with positive excess. Second, since the preprocessing step saturates all arcs incident to node s, none of these arcs is admissible and setting $d(s) = n$ will satisfy the validity condition C4.2. Third, since $d(s) = n$ is a lower bound on the length of any shortest path from s to t, the residual network contains no path from s to t. Since distances in d are nondecreasing, we are also guaranteed that in subsequent iterations the residual network will never contain a directed path from s to t, and so there never will be any need to push flow from s again.

In the push/relabel(i) step, we identify an admissible arc in $A(i)$ using the same data structure we used in the shortest augmenting path algorithm. We maintain with each node i a *current arc* (i, j) which is the current candidate for the push operation. We choose the current arc by sequentially scanning the arc

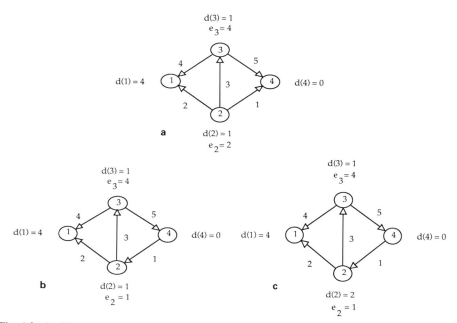

Fig. 4.3. An illustration of push and relabel steps. (a) The residual network after the preprocessing step. (b) After the execution of step PUSH(2). (c) After the execution of step RELABEL(2).

list. We have seen earlier that scanning the arc lists takes $O(nm)$ total time, if the algorithm relabels each node $O(n)$ times.

Assuming that the generic preflow–push algorithm terminates, we can easily show that it finds a maximum flow. The algorithm terminates when the excess resides either at the source or at the sink implying that the current preflow is a flow. Since $d(s) = n$, the residual network contains no path from the source to the sink. This condition is the termination criterion of the augmenting path algorithm, and thus the total flow on arcs directed into the sink is the maximum flow value.

Complexity of the algorithm

We now analyze the complexity of the algorithm. We begin by establishing one important result: that distance labels are always valid and do not increase too many times. The first of these conclusions follows from Lemma 4.1, because as in the shortest augmenting path algorithm, the preflow–push algorithm pushes flow only on admissible arcs and relabels a node only when no admissible arc emanates from it. The second conclusion follows from the following lemma.

Lemma 4.3. *At any stage of the preflow–push algorithm, each node i with positive excess is connected to node s by a directed path from i to s in the residual network.*

Proof. By the flow decomposition theory, any preflow x can be decomposed with respect to the original network G into nonnegative flows along (i) paths from the source s to t, (ii) paths from s to active nodes, and (iii) flows around directed cycles. Let i be an active node relative to the preflow x in G. Then there must be a path P from s to i in the flow decomposition of x, since paths from s to t and flows around cycles do not contribute to the excess at node i. Then the residual network contains the reversal of P (P with the orientation of each arc reversed), and hence a directed path from i to s. □

This lemma implies that during a relabel step, the algorithm does not minimize over an empty set.

Lemma 4.4. *For each node $i \in N$, $d(i) < 2n$.*

Proof. The last time the algorithm relabeled node i, it had a positive excess, and hence the residual network contained a path of length at most $n - 1$ from node i to node s. The fact that $d(s) = n$ and condition C4.2 imply that $d(i) \le d(s) + n - 1 < 2n$. □

Lemma 4.5. (a) *Each distance label increases at most $2n$ times. Consequently, the total number of relabel steps is at most $2n^2$.* (b) *The number of saturating pushes is at most nm.*

Proof. The proof is very much similar to that of Lemma 4.2. □

Lemma 4.6. *The number of nonsaturating pushes is $O(n^2 m)$.*

Proof. We prove the lemma using an argument based on potential functions. Let I denote the set of active nodes. Consider the potential function $F = \Sigma_{i \in I} d(i)$. Since $|I| \le n$, and $d(i) \le 2n$ for all $i \in I$, the initial value of F (after the preprocessing step) is at most $2n^2$. At termination, F is zero. During the push/relabel(i) step, one of the following two cases must apply:

Case 1. The algorithm is unable to find an admissible arc along which it can push flow. In this case the distance label of node i increases by $\varepsilon \ge 1$ units. This operation increases F by ε units. Since the total increase in $d(i)$ throughout the running time of the algorithm for each node i is bounded by $2n$, the total increase in F due to increases in distance labels is bounded by $2n^2$.

Case 2. The algorithm is able to identify an arc on which it can push flow, and so it performs a saturating or a nonsaturating push. A saturating push on arc (i, j) might create a new excess at node j, thereby increasing the number of active nodes by 1, and increasing F by $d(j)$, which may be as much as $2n$ per saturating push, and hence $2n^2 m$ over all saturating pushes. Next note that a nonsaturating push on arc (i, j) does not increase $|I|$. The nonsaturating push will decrease F by $d(i)$ since i becomes inactive, but it simultaneously increases F by $d(j) = d(i) - 1$ if the push causes node j to become active. If node j was active before the push, then F decreases by an amount $d(i)$. The net decrease in F is at least 1 unit per nonsaturating push.

We summarize these facts. The initial value of F is at most $2n^2$ and the maximum possible increase in F is $2n^2 + 2n^2m$. Each nonsaturating push decreases F by one unit and F always remains nonnegative. Hence, the nonsaturating pushes can occur at most $2n^2 + 2n^2 + 2n^2m = O(n^2m)$ times, proving the lemma. □

Finally, we indicate how the algorithm keeps track of active nodes for the push/relabel steps. The algorithm maintains a set I of active nodes. It adds to I nodes that become active following a push and are not already in I, and deletes from I nodes that become inactive following a nonsaturating push. Several data structures (for example, doubly linked lists) are available for storing I so that the algorithm can add, delete, or select elements from it in $O(1)$ time. Consequently, it is easy to implement the preflow–push algorithm in $O(n^2m)$ time. We have thus established the following theorem:

Theorem 4.4. *The generic preflow–push algorithm runs in $O(n^2m)$ time.* □

A specialization of the generic algorithm

The running time of the generic preflow–push algorithm is comparable to the bound of the shortest augmenting path algorithm. However, the preflow–push algorithm has several nice features; in particular, its flexibility and its potential for further improvements. By specifying different rules for selecting nodes for push/relabel operations, we can derive many different algorithms from the generic version. For example, suppose that we always select an active node with the highest distance label for push/relabel step. Let $h^* = \max\{d(i): e(i) > 0, i \in N\}$ at some point of the algorithm. Then nodes with distance h^* push flow to nodes with distance $h^* - 1$, and these nodes, in turn, push flow to nodes with distance $h^* - 2$, and so on. If a node is relabeled then excess moves up and then gradually comes down. Note that if the algorithm relabels no node during n consecutive node examinations, then all excess reaches the sink node and the algorithm terminates. Since the algorithm requires $O(n^2)$ relabel operations, we immediately obtain a bound of $O(n^3)$ on the number of node examinations. Each node examination entails at most one nonsaturating push. Consequently, this algorithm performs $O(n^3)$ nonsaturating pushes.

We use the following technique to select a node with the highest distance label efficiently. We maintain a set of nodes $\text{LIST}(k) = \{i \in N: d(i) = k\}$ for every $k = 1, 2, \ldots, 2n - 1$. The set $\text{LIST}(k)$ stores the set of nodes with distance label equal to k. We also maintain a variable *level* which is an upper bound on the highest index r for which $\text{LIST}(r)$ is nonempty. We can store these lists as doubly linked lists so that adding, deleting, or selecting an element takes $O(1)$ time. We identify the highest indexed nonempty list starting at $\text{LIST}(level)$ and sequentially scanning the lower indexed lists. We leave it as an exercise to show that the overall effort needed to scan the lists is bounded by n plus the total increase in the distance labels, which is $O(n^2)$. The following theorem is now evident.

R.K. Ahuja et al.

Theorem 4.5. *The version of preflow–push algorithm that always pushes flow from an active node with the highest distance label runs in* $O(n^3)$ *time.* □

The $O(n^3)$ bound for the highest label preflow push algorithm is straightforward, and can be improved. Researchers have shown using more clever analysis that the highest label preflow push algorithm in fact runs in $O(n^2\sqrt{m})$ time. We will next describe another implementation of the generic preflow–push algorithm that dramatically reduces the number of nonsaturating pushes, from $O(n^2m)$ to $O(n^2 \log U)$. Recall that U represents the largest arc capacity in the network. We refer to this algorithm as the *excess-scaling algorithm* since it is based on scaling the node excesses.

4.5. Excess-scaling algorithm

The generic preflow–push algorithm allows flows at each intermediate step to violate mass balance equations. By pushing flows from active nodes, the algorithm attempts to satisfy the mass balance equations. The function $e_{\max} = \max\{e(i): i$ is an active node$\}$ is one measure of the infeasibility of a preflow. Note, though, that during the execution of the generic algorithm, we would observe no particular pattern in $e_{\max}$, except that $e_{\max}$ eventually decreases to the value 0. In this section, we develop an *excess-scaling technique* that systematically reduces $e_{\max}$ to 0.

The excess-scaling algorithm is based on the following ideas. Let Δ denote an upper bound on $e_{\max}$. We refer to this bound as the *excess-dominator*. The excess-scaling algorithm pushes flow from nodes whose excess is at least $\frac{1}{2}\Delta \geq \frac{1}{2}e_{\max}$. This choice assures that during nonsaturating pushes the algorithm sends relatively large excess closer to the sink. Pushes carrying small amounts of flow are of little benefit and can cause bottlenecks that retard the algorithm's progress.

The algorithm also does not allow the maximum excess to increase beyond Δ. This algorithmic strategy may prove to be useful for the following reason. Suppose several nodes send flow to a single node j, creating a very large excess. It is likely that node j cannot send the accumulated flow closer to the sink, and thus the algorithm will need to increase its distance and return much of its excess back toward the source. Thus, pushing too much flow to any node is likely to be a wasted effort.

The excess-scaling algorithm has the following algorithmic description.

algorithm EXCESS-SCALING;
begin
    PREPROCESS;
    $K := 2^{\lceil \log U \rceil}$;

for $k := K$ **down to** 0 **do**
begin (Δ-scaling phase)
$\quad \Delta := 2^k$;
$\quad$ **while** the network contains a node i with $e(i) > \Delta/2$ **do**
$\qquad$ perform push/relabel(i) while ensuring that no node excess exceeds Δ;
end;
end;

The algorithm performs a number of scaling phases with the value of the excess-dominator Δ decreasing from phase to phase. We refer to a specific scaling phase with a certain value of Δ as the Δ-*scaling phase*. Initially, $\Delta = 2^{\lceil \log U \rceil}$ when the logarithm has base 2. Thus, $U \leqslant \Delta \leqslant 2U$. During the Δ-scaling phase, $\frac{1}{2}\Delta < e_{max} \leqslant \Delta$, and e_{max} may vary up and down during the phase. When $e_{max} \leqslant \frac{1}{2}\Delta$, a new scaling phase begins. After the algorithm has performed $\lceil \log U \rceil + 1$ scaling phases, e_{max} decreases to the value 0 and we obtain the maximum flow.

The excess-scaling algorithm uses the same push/relabel(i) step as in the generic preflow–push algorithm, but with one slight difference: instead of pushing $\delta = \min\{e(i), r_{ij}\}$ units of flow, it pushes $\delta = \min\{e(i), r_{ij}, \Delta - e(j)\}$ units. This change will ensure that the algorithm permits no excess to exceed Δ. The algorithm uses the following node selection rule to guarantee that the flow in each nonsaturating push is at least $\frac{1}{2}\Delta$.

Selection rule. Among all nodes with excess of more than $\frac{1}{2}\Delta$, select a node with minimum distance label.

Lemma 4.7. *The algorithm satisfies the following two conditions*:
$\quad$ C4.3. *Each nonsaturating push sends at least $\frac{1}{2}\Delta$ units of flow.*
$\quad$ C4.4. *No excess ever exceeds Δ.*

Proof. For every push on arc (i, j), we have $e(i) > \frac{1}{2}\Delta$ and $e(j) \leqslant \frac{1}{2}\Delta$, since node i is a node with smallest distance label among nodes whose excess is more than $\frac{1}{2}\Delta$, and $d(j) = d(i) - 1 < d(i)$ since arc (i, j) is admissible. Hence, by sending $\min\{e(i), r_{ij}, \Delta - e(j)\} \geqslant \min\{\frac{1}{2}\Delta, r_{ij}\}$ units of flow, we ensure that in a nonsaturating push the algorithm sends at least $\frac{1}{2}\Delta$ units of flow. Further, the push operation increases only $e(j)$. Let $e'(j)$ be the excess at node j after the push. Then $e'(j) = e(j) + \min\{e(i), r_{ij}, \Delta - e(j)\} \leqslant e(j) + \Delta - e(j) \leqslant \Delta$. All node excesses thus remain less than or equal to Δ. $\square$

Lemma 4.8. *The excess-scaling algorithm performs $O(n^2)$ nonsaturating pushes per scaling phase and $O(n^2 \log U)$ pushes in total.*

Proof. Consider the potential function $F = \Sigma_{i \in N} e(i)d(i)/\Delta$. Using this potential function we will establish the first assertion of the lemma. Since the algorithm has $O(\log U)$ scaling phases, the second assertion is a consequence of the first. The initial value of F at the beginning of the Δ-scaling phase is bounded by $2n^2$ because $e(i)$ is bounded by Δ and $d(i)$ is bounded by $2n$. During the push/relabel(i) step, one of the following two cases must apply:

Case 1. The algorithm is unable to find an admissible arc along which it can push flow. In this case the distance label of node i increases by $\varepsilon \geq 1$ units. This relabeling operation increases F by at most ε units because $e(i) \leq \Delta$. Since for each i, the total increase in $d(i)$ throughout the running of the algorithm is bounded by $2n$ (by Lemma 4.4), the total increase in F due to the relabels of nodes is bounded by $2n^2$ in the Δ-scaling phase (actually, the increase in F due to node relabels is at most $2n^2$ over *all* scaling phases).

Case 2. The algorithm is able to identify an arc on which it can push flow and so it performs either a saturating or a nonsaturating push. In either case, F decreases. A nonsaturating push on arc (i, j) sends at least $\frac{1}{2}\Delta$ units of flow from node i to node j. Since $d(j) = d(i) - 1$, after this operation F decreases by at least $\frac{1}{2}$ units. Since the initial value of F at the beginning of a Δ-scaling phase is at most $2n^2$ and the increases in F during this scaling phase sum to at most $2n^2$ (from Case 1), the number of nonsaturating pushes is bounded by $8n^2$. □

This lemma implies a bound of $O(nm + n^2 \log U)$ for the excess-scaling algorithm since we have already seen that all other operations – such as saturating pushes, relabel operations and finding admissible arcs – require $O(nm)$ time. Up to this point, we have ignored the method needed to identify a node with the minimum distance label among nodes with excess more than $\frac{1}{2}\Delta$. Making this identification is easy if we use a scheme similar to the one used in the preflow–push method in Section 4.4 to find a node with the highest distance label. We maintain the lists $\text{LIST}(r) = \{i \in N: e(i) > \frac{1}{2}\Delta \text{ and } d(i) = r\}$, and a variable *level* which is a lower bound on the smallest index r for which $\text{LIST}(r)$ is nonempty. We identify the lowest indexed nonempty list starting at $\text{LIST}(level)$ and if it is empty sequentially scan higher indexed lists. We leave as an exercise to show that the overall effort needed to scan the lists is bounded by the number of pushes performed by the algorithm plus $O(n \log U)$ and, hence, is not a bottleneck operation. With this observation, we can summarize our discussion by the following result.

Theorem 4.6. *The preflow–push algorithm with excess-scaling runs in* $O(nm + n^2 \log U)$ *time.* □

Networks with lower bounds on flows

To conclude this section, we show how to solve maximum flow problems with nonnegative lower bounds on flows. Let $l_{ij} \geq 0$ denote the lower bound for flow on any arc $(i, j) \in A$. Although the maximum flow problem with zero lower bounds always has a feasible solution, the problem with nonnegative lower bounds could be infeasible. We can, however, determine the feasibility of this problem by solving a maximum flow problem with zero lower bounds as follows. We set $x_{ij} = l_{ij}$ for each arc $(i, j) \in A$. This choice gives us a pseudo-flow with $e(i)$ representing the excess or deficit of any node $i \in N$. (We refer the reader to Section 5.4 for the definition of a pseudoflow with both excesses and deficits.) We introduce a *super source*, node s^*, and a *super sink*, node t^*. For each node i with $e(i) > 0$, we add an arc (s^*, i) with capacity $e(i)$, and for each node i with $e(i) < 0$, we add an arc (i, t^*) with capacity $-e(i)$. We then solve a maximum flow problem from s^* to t^*. Let x^* denote the maximum flow and v^* denote the maximum flow value in the transformed network. If $v^* = \Sigma_{\{i:\, e(i) > 0\}} e(i)$, then the original problem is feasible and choosing the flow on each arc (i, j) as $x_{ij}^* + l_{ij}$ is a feasible flow; otherwise, the problem is infeasible.

Once we have found a feasible flow, we apply any of the maximum flow algorithms with only one change: initially define the residual capacity of an arc (i, j) as $r_{ij} = (u_{ij} - x_{ij}) + (x_{ji} - l_{ji})$. The first and second terms in this expression denote, respectively, the residual capacity for increasing flow on arc (i, j) and for decreasing flow on arc (j, i). It is possible to establish the optimality of the solution generated by the algorithm by generalizing the max-flow min-cut theorem to accomodate situations with lower bounds. These observations show that it is possible to solve the maximum flow problem with nonnegative lower bounds by two applications of the maximum flow algorithms we have already discussed.

5. Minimum cost flows

In this section, we consider algorithmic approaches for the minimum cost flow problem. We consider the following node–arc formulation of the problem:

$$\text{minimize} \quad \sum_{(i,j) \in A} c_{ij} x_{ij} \tag{5.1a}$$

subject to

$$\sum_{\{j:\, (i,j) \in A\}} x_{ij} - \sum_{\{j:\, (j,i) \in A\}} x_{ji} = b(i), \quad \text{for all } i \in N, \tag{5.1b}$$

$$0 \le x_{ij} \le u_{ij}, \quad \text{for each } (i, j) \in A. \tag{5.1c}$$

We assume that the lower bounds l_{ij} on arc flows are all zero and that arc costs are nonnegative. Let

$$C = \max\{c_{ij}: (i, j) \in A\}$$

and

$$U = \max[\max\{|b(i)|: i \in N\}, \max\{u_{ij}: (i, j) \in A \text{ and } u_{ij} < \infty\}].$$

The transformations T1 and T3 in Section 2.4 imply that these assumptions do not impose any loss of generality. We remind the reader of our blanket assumption that all data (cost, supply/demand and capacity) are integral. We also assume that the minimum cost flow problem satisfies the following two conditions.

A5.1. *Feasibility assumption.* We assume that $\Sigma_{i \in N} b(i) = 0$ and that the minimum cost flow problem has a feasible solution.

We can ascertain the feasibility of the minimum cost flow problem by solving a maximum flow problem as follows. Introduce a *super source* node s^*, and a *super sink* node t^*. For each node i with $b(i) > 0$, add an arc (s^*, i) with capacity $b(i)$, and for each node i with $b(i) < 0$, add an arc (i, t^*) with capacity $-b(i)$. Now solve a maximum flow problem for s^* to t^*. If the maximum flow value equals $\Sigma_{\{i: b(i) > 0\}} b(i)$ then the minimum cost flow problem is feasible; otherwise, it is infeasible.

A5.2. *Connectedness assumption.* We assume that the network G contains an uncapacitated directed path (i.e., each arc in the path has infinite capacity) between every pair of nodes.

We impose this condition, if necessary, by adding *artificial* arcs $(1, j)$ and $(j, 1)$ for each $j \in N$ and assigning a large cost and infinite capacity to each of these arcs. No such arc would appear in a minimum cost solution unless the problem contains no feasible solution without artificial arcs.

Our algorithms rely on the concept of residual networks. The residual network $G(x)$ corresponding to a flow x is defined as follows: We replace each arc $(i, j) \in A$ by two arcs (i, j) and (j, i). The arc (i, j) has cost c_{ij} and *residual capacity* $r_{ij} = u_{ij} - x_{ij}$, and the arc (j, i) has cost $-c_{ij}$ and residual capacity $r_{ji} = x_{ij}$. The residual network consists *only* of arcs with positive residual capacity.

The concept of residual networks poses some notational difficulties. For example, if the original network contains both the arcs (i, j) and (j, i), then the residual network may contain two arcs from node i to node j and/or two arcs from node j to node i with possibly different costs. Our notation for arcs assumes that at most one arc joins one node to any other node. By using more complex notation, we can easily treat this more general case. However, rather than changing our notation, we will assume that parallel arcs never arise (or, by inserting extra nodes on parallel arcs, we can produce a network without any parallel arcs).

Observe that any directed cycle in the residual network $G(x)$ is an augmenting cycle with respect to the flow x and vice-versa (see Section 2.1 for the definition of augmenting cycle). This equivalence implies the following alternate statement of Theorem 2.4.

Theorem 5.1. *A feasible flow x is an optimum flow if and only if the residual network $G(x)$ contains no negative cost directed cycle.* $\square$

5.1. Duality and optimality conditions

As we have seen in Section 1.2, due to its special structure, the minimum cost flow problem has a number of important theoretical properties. The linear programming dual of this problem inherits many of these properties. Moreover, the minimum cost flow problem and its dual have, from a linear programming point of view, rather simple complementary slackness conditions. In this section, we formally state the linear programming dual problem and derive the complementary slackness conditions.

We consider the minimum cost flow problem (5.1) assuming that $u_{ij} > 0$ for each arc $(i, j) \in A$. It is possible to show that this assumption imposes no loss of generality. We associate a dual variable $\pi(i)$ with the mass balance constraint of node i in (5.1b). Since one of the constraints in (5.1b) is redundant, we can set one of these dual variables to an arbitrary value. We therefore assume that $\pi(1) = 0$. Further, we associate a dual variable δ_{ij} with the upper bound constraint of arc (i, j) in (5.1c). The dual problem to (5.1) is:

$$\text{maximize} \quad \sum_{i \in N} b(i)\pi(i) - \sum_{(i,j) \in A} u_{ij}\delta_{ij} \tag{5.2a}$$

subject to

$$\pi(i) - \pi(j) - \delta_{ij} \leq c_{ij} \quad \text{for all } (i, j) \in A, \tag{5.2b}$$

$$\delta_{ij} \geq 0, \quad \text{for all } (i, j) \in A, \tag{5.2c}$$

and

$$\pi(i) \text{ are unrestricted}.$$

The complementary slackness conditions for this primal–dual pair are:

$$x_{ij} > 0 \implies \pi(i) - \pi(j) - \delta_{ij} = c_{ij}, \tag{5.3}$$

$$\delta_{ij} > 0 \implies x_{ij} = u_{ij}. \tag{5.4}$$

These conditions are equivalent to the following optimality conditions:

$$x_{ij} = 0 \implies \pi(i) - \pi(j) \leq c_{ij}, \tag{5.5}$$

$$0 < x_{ij} < u_{ij} \implies \pi(i) - \pi(j) = c_{ij}, \tag{5.6}$$

$$x_{ij} = u_{ij} \implies \pi(i) - \pi(j) \geq c_{ij}. \tag{5.7}$$

To see that (5.3) and (5.4) imply (5.5)–(5.7), suppose that $0 < x_{ij} < u_{ij}$ for some arc (i, j). The condition (5.3) implies that

$$\pi(i) - \pi(j) - \delta_{ij} = c_{ij} . \tag{5.8}$$

Since $x_{ij} < u_{ij}$, (5.4) implies that $\delta_{ij} = 0$; substituting this result in (5.8) yields (5.6). Whenever $x_{ij} = u_{ij} > 0$ for some arc (i, j), (5.3) implies that $\pi(i) - \pi(j) - \delta_{ij} = c_{ij}$. Substituting $\delta_{ij} \geq 0$ in this equation gives (5.7). Finally, if $x_{ij} = 0 < u_{ij}$ for some arc (i, j) then (5.4) implies that $\delta_{ij} = 0$ and substituting this result in (5.2b) gives (5.5).

We define the *reduced cost* of an arc (i, j) as $\bar{c}_{ij} = c_{ij} - \pi(i) + \pi(j)$. The conditions (5.5)–(5.7) imply that a pair x, π of flows and node potentials is optimal if it satisfies the following conditions:

C5.1. x is feasible.

C5.2. If $\bar{c}_{ij} > 0$, then $x_{ij} = 0$.

C5.3. If $\bar{c}_{ij} = 0$, then $0 \leq x_{ij} \leq u_{ij}$.

C5.4. *If $\bar{c}_{ij} < 0$, then $x_{ij} = u_{ij}$.*

Observe that the condition C5.3 follows from the conditions C5.1, C5.2 and C5.4; however, we retain it for the sake of completeness. These conditions, when stated in terms of the residual network, simplify to:

C5.5. (Primal feasibility). x is feasible.

C5.6. (Dual feasibility). $\bar{c}_{ij} \geq 0$ for each arc (i, j) in the residual network $G(x)$.

Note that the condition C5.6 subsumes C5.2, C5.3, and C5.4. To see this result, note that if $\bar{c}_{ij} > 0$ and $x_{ij} > 0$ for some arc (i, j) in the original network, then the residual network would contain arc (j, i) with $\bar{c}_{ji} = -\bar{c}_{ij}$. But then $\bar{c}_{ji} < 0$, contradicting C5.6. A similar contradiction arises if $\bar{c}_{ij} < 0$ and $x_{ij} < u_{ij}$ for some (i, j) in A.

It is easy to establish the equivalence between these optimality conditions and the condition stated in Theorem 5.1. Consider any pair x, π of flows and node potentials satisfying C5.5 and C5.6. Let W be any directed cycle in the residual network. Condition C5.6 implies that $\sum_{(i,j) \in W} \bar{c}_{ij} \geq 0$. Further,

$$0 \leq \sum_{(i,j) \in W} \bar{c}_{ij} = \sum_{(i,j) \in W} c_{ij} + \sum_{(i,j) \in W} (-\pi(i) + \pi(j)) = \sum_{(i,j) \in W} c_{ij} .$$

Hence, the residual network contains no negative cost cycle.

To see the converse, suppose that x is feasible and $G(x)$ does not contain a negative cycle. Then in the residual network the shortest distances from node 1, with respect to the arc lengths c_{ij}, are well defined. Let $d(i)$ denote the shortest distance from node 1 to node i. The shortest path optimality condition

C3.2 implies that $d(j) \leq d(i) + c_{ij}$ for all (i, j) in $G(x)$. Let $\pi = -d$. Then $0 \leq c_{ij} + d(i) - d(j) = c_{ij} - \pi(i) + \pi(j) = \bar{c}_{ij}$ for all (i, j) in $G(x)$. Hence, the pair x, π satisfies C5.5 and C5.6.

5.2. Relationship to shortest path and maximum flow problems

The minimum cost flow problem generalizes both the shortest path and maximum flow problems. The shortest path problem from node s to all other nodes can be formulated as a minimum cost flow problem by setting $b(s) = n - 1$, $b(i) = -1$ for all $i \neq s$, and $u_{ij} = \infty$ for each $(i, j) \in A$ and setting c_{ij} as the length of arc (i, j) for each (i, j) in A. (In fact, setting u_{ij} equal to any integer greater than $n - 1$ will suffice if we wish to maintain finite capacities.) Similarly, the maximum flow problem from node s to node t can be transformed to the minimum cost flow problem by introducing an additional arc (t, s) with $c_{ts} = -1$ and $u_{ts} = \infty$ (in fact, $u_{ts} = m \cdot \max\{u_{ij} : (i, j) \in A\}$ would suffice), and setting $c_{ij} = 0$ for each arc $(i, j) \in A$. Thus, algorithms for the minimum cost flow problem solve both the shortest path and maximum flow problems as special cases.

Conversely, algorithms for the shortest path and maximum flow problems are of great use in solving the minimum cost flow problem. Indeed, many of the algorithms for the minimum cost flow problem either explicitly or implicitly use shortest path and/or maximum flow algorithms as subroutines. Consequently, improved algorithms for these two problems have led to improved algorithms for the minimum cost flow problem. This relationship will be more transparent when we discuss algorithms for the minimum cost flow problem. We have already shown in Section 5.1 how to obtain an optimum dual solution from an optimum primal solution by solving a single shortest path problem. We now show how to obtain an optimal primal solution from an optimal dual solution by solving a single maximum flow problem.

Suppose that π is an optimal dual solution and $\bar{c}$ is the vector of reduced costs. We define the *cost-residual network* $G^* = (N, A^*)$ as follows. The nodes in G^* have the same supply/demand as the nodes in G. Any arc $(i, j) \in A^*$ has an upper bound u_{ij}^* as well as a lower bound l_{ij}^*, defined as follows:

(i) For each (i, j) in A with $\bar{c}_{ij} > 0$, A^* contains an arc (i, j) with $u_{ij}^* = l_{ij}^* = 0$.

(ii) For each (i, j) in A with $\bar{c}_{ij} < 0$, A^* contains an arc (i, j) with $u_{ij}^* = l_{ij}^* = u_{ij}$.

(iii) For each (i, j) in A with $\bar{c}_{ij} = 0$, A^* contains an arc (i, j) with $u_{ij}^* = u_{ij}$ and $l_{ij}^* = 0$.

The lower and upper bounds on arcs in the cost-residual network G^* are defined so that any flow in G^* satisfies the optimality conditions C5.2–C5.4. If $\bar{c}_{ij} > 0$ for some $(i, j) \in A$, then condition C5.2 dictates that $x_{ij} = 0$ in the optimum flow. Similarly, if $\bar{c}_{ij} < 0$ for some $(i, j) \in A$, then C5.4 implies the flow on arc (i, j) must be at the arc's upper bound in the optimum flow. If $\bar{c}_{ij} = 0$, then any flow value will satisfy the condition C5.3.

Now the problem is reduced to finding a feasible flow in the cost-residual network that satisfies the lower and upper bound restrictions of arcs and, at the same time, meets the supply/demand constraints of the nodes. We first eliminate the lower bounds of arcs as described in Section 2.4 and then transform this problem to a maximum flow problem as described after assumption A5.1. Let x^* denote the maximum flow in the transformed network. Then $x^* + l^*$ is an optimum solution of the minimum cost flow problem in G.

5.3. Negative cycle algorithm

Operations researchers, computer scientists, electrical engineers and many others have extensively studied the minimum cost flow problem and have proposed a number of different algorithms to solve this problem. Notable examples are the negative cycle, successive shortest path, primal-dual, out-of-kilter, primal simplex and scaling-based algorithms. In this and the following sections, we discuss most of these important algorithms for the minimum cost flow problem and point out relationships between them. We first consider the negative cycle algorithm.

The negative cycle algorithm maintains a primal feasible solution x and strives to attain dual feasibility. It does so by identifying negative cost directed cycles in the residual network $G(x)$ and augmenting flows on these cycles. The algorithm terminates when the residual network contains no negative cost cycles. Theorem 5.1 implies that when the algorithm terminates, it has found a minimum cost flow.

algorithm NEGATIVE CYCLE;
begin
    establish a feasible flow x in the network;
    while $G(x)$ contains a negative cycle **do**
    begin
        use some algorithm to identify a negative cycle W;
        $\delta := \min\{r_{ij}: (i, j) \in W\}$;
        augment δ units of flow in the cycle W and update $G(x)$;
    end;
end;

A feasible flow in the network can be found by solving a maximum flow problem as explained just after assumption A5.1. One algorithm for identifying a negative cost cycle is the label correcting algorithm for the shortest path problem, described in Section 3.4, which requires $O(nm)$ time to identify a negative cycle. Every iteration reduces the flow cost by at least one unit. Since mCU is an upper bound on an initial flow cost and zero is a lower bound on the optimum flow cost, the algorithm terminates after at most $O(mCU)$ iterations and requires $O(nm^2CU)$ time in total.

This algorithm can be improved in at least three ways (which we briefly summarize).

(i) Identifying a negative cost cycle in effort much less than $O(nm)$ time. The simplex algorithm (to be discussed later) nearly achieves this objective. It maintains a tree solution and node potentials that enable it to identify a negative cost cycle in $O(m)$ effort. However, due to degeneracy, the simplex algorithm cannot necessarily send a positive amount of flow along this cycle.

(ii) Identifying a negative cost cycle with maximum improvement in the objective function value. The improvement in the objective function due to the augmentation along a cycle W is $(-\Sigma_{(i,j)\in W} c_{ij})(\min\{r_{ij}:(i,j)\in W\})$. Let x be some flow and x^* be an optimum flow. The augmenting cycle theorem (Theorem 2.3) implies that x^* equals x plus the flow on at most m augmenting cycles with respect to x. Further, improvements in cost due to flow augmentations on these augmentating cycles sum to $cx - cx^*$. Consequently, at least one augmenting cycle with respect to x must decrease the objective function by at least $(cx - cx^*)/m$. Hence, if the algorithm always augments flow along a cycle with maximum improvement, then Lemma 1.1 implies that the method would obtain an optimum flow within $O(m \log mCU)$ iterations. Finding a maximum improvement cycle is a difficult problem, but a modest variation of this approach yields a polynomial time algorithm for the minimum cost flow problem.

(iii) Identifying a negative cost cycle with minimum mean cost. We define the *mean cost* of a cycle as its cost divided by the number of arcs it contains. A *minimum mean cycle* is a cycle whose mean cost is as small as possible. It is possible to identify a minimum mean cycle in $O(nm)$ or $O(\sqrt{n}m \log nC)$ time. Recently, researchers have shown that if the negative cycle algorithm always augments the flow along a minimum mean cycle, then from one iteration to the next, the minimum mean cycle value is nondecreasing; moreover, its absolute value decreases by a factor of $1 - (1/n)$ within m iterations. Since the mean cost of the minimum mean (negative) cycle is bounded from below by $-C$ and bounded from above by $-1/n$, lemma 1.1 implies that this algorithm will terminate in $O(nm \log nC)$ iterations.

5.4. Successive shortest path algorithm

The negative cycle algorithm maintains primal feasibility of the solution at every step and attempts to achieve dual feasibility. In contrast, the successive shortest path algorithm maintains dual feasibility of the solution at every step and strives to attain primal feasibility. It maintains a solution x that satisfies the nonnegativity and capacity constraints, but violates the supply/demand constraints of the nodes. At each step, the algorithm selects a node i with extra supply and a node j with unfulfilled demand and sends flow from i to j along a shortest path in the residual network. The algorithm terminates when the current solution satisfies all the supply/demand constraints.

A *pseudoflow* is a function $x: A \to R^+$ satisfying only the capacity and nonnegativity constraints. For any pseudoflow x, we define the *imbalance* of node i as

$$e(i) = b(i) + \sum_{\{j:\,(j,i)\in A\}} x_{ji} - \sum_{\{j:\,(i,\,j)\in A\}} x_{ij}\,, \quad \text{for all } i \in N\,.$$

If $e(i) > 0$ for some node i, then $e(i)$ is called the *excess* of node i, if $e(i) < 0$, then $-e(i)$ is called the *deficit*. A node i with $e(i) = 0$ is called *balanced*. Let S and T denote the sets of excess and deficit nodes respectively. The residual network corresponding to a pseudoflow is defined in the same way that we define the residual network for a flow.

The successive shortest path algorithm successively augments flow along shortest paths computed with respect to the reduced costs $\bar{c}_{ij}$. Observe that for any directed path P from a node k to a node l,

$$\sum_{(i,j)\in P} \bar{c}_{ij} = \sum_{(i,j)\in P} c_{ij} + \pi(l) - \pi(k)\,.$$

Hence, the node potentials change all path lengths between a specific pair of nodes by a constant amount, and the shortest path with respect to c_{ij} is the same as the shortest path with respect to $\bar{c}_{ij}$. The correctness of the successive shortest path algorithm rests on the following result.

Lemma 5.1. *Suppose a pseudoflow x satisfies the dual feasibility condition C5.6 with respect to the node potential π. Furthermore, suppose that x' is obtained from x by sending flow along a shortest path from a node k to a node l in $G(x)$. Then x' also satisfies the dual feasibility conditions with respect to some node potentials.*

Proof. Since x satisfies the dual feasibility conditions with respect to the node potentials π, we have $\bar{c}_{ij} \geq 0$ for all (i, j) in $G(x)$. Let $d(v)$ denote the shortest path distances from node k to any node v in $G(x)$ with respect to the arc lengths $\bar{c}_{ij}$. We claim that x also satisfies the dual feasibility conditions with respect to the potentials $\pi' = \pi - d$. The shortest path optimality conditions (i.e., C3.2) imply that

$$d(j) \leq d(i) + \bar{c}_{ij}\,, \quad \text{for all } (i, j) \text{ in } G(x)\,.$$

Substituting $\bar{c}_{ij} = c_{ij} - \pi(i) + \pi(j)$ in these conditions and using $\pi'(i) = \pi(i) - d(i)$ yields

$$\bar{c}'_{ij} = c_{ij} - \pi'(i) + \pi'(j) \geq 0\,, \quad \text{for all } (i, j) \text{ in } G(x)\,.$$

Hence, x satisfies C5.6 with respect to the node potentials π'. Next note that $\bar{c}'_{ij} = 0$ for every arc (i, j) on the shortest path P from node k to node l, since $d(j) = d(i) + \bar{c}_{ij}$ for every arc $(i, j) \in P$ and $\bar{c}_{ij} = c_{ij} - \pi(i) + \pi(j)$.

We are now in a position to prove the lemma. Augmenting flow along any arc in P maintains the dual feasibility condition C5.6 for this arc. Augmenting flow on an arc (i, j) may add its reversal (j, i) to the residual network. But since $\bar{c}_{ij} = 0$ for each arc $(i, j) \in P$, $\bar{c}_{ji} = 0$, and so arc (j, i) also satisfies C5.6. $\square$

The node potentials play a very important role in this algorithm. Besides using them to prove the correctness of the algorithm, we use them to ensure that the arc lengths are nonnegative, thus enabling us to solve the shortest path subproblems more efficiently. The following formal statement of the successive shortest path algorithm summarizes the steps of this method.

algorithm SUCCESSIVE SHORTEST PATH;
begin
  $x := 0$ and $\pi := 0$;
  compute imbalances $e(i)$ and initialize the sets S and T;
  while $S \neq \emptyset$ **do**
  begin
    select a node $k \in S$ and a node $l \in T$;
    determine shortest path distances $d(j)$ from node k to all
      other nodes in $G(x)$ with respect to the reduced costs $\bar{c}_{ij}$.
    let P denote a shortest path from k to l;
    update $\pi := \pi - d$;
    $\delta := \min[e(k), -e(l), \min\{r_{ij}: (i, j) \in P\}]$;
    augment δ units of flow along the path P;
    update x, S and T;
  end;
end;

To initialize the algorithm, we set $x = 0$, which is a feasible pseudoflow and satisfies C5.6 with respect to the node potentials $\pi = 0$ since, by assumption, all arc lengths are nonnegative. Also, if $S \neq \emptyset$, then $T \neq \emptyset$ because the sum of excesses always equals the sum of deficits. Further, the connectedness assumption implies that the residual network $G(x)$ contains a directed path from node k to node l. Each iteration of this algorithm solves a shortest path problem with nonnegative arc lengths and reduces the supply of some node by at least one unit. Consequently, if U is an upper bound on the largest supply of any node, the algorithm terminates in at most nU iterations. Since the arc lengths $\bar{c}_{ij}$ are nonnegative, the shortest path problem at each iteration can be solved using Dijkstra's algorithm. So the overall complexity of this algorithm is $O(nU \cdot S(n, m, C))$, where $S(n, m, C)$ is the time taken by Dijkstra's algorithm. Currently, the best strongly polynomial-time bound for an implementation of Dijkstra's algorithm is $O(m + n \log n)$ and the best (weakly) polynomial time bound is $O(\min\{m \log \log C, m + n\sqrt{\log C}\})$. The successive shortest path algorithm takes pseudopolynomial time since it is polynomial in n, m and the largest supply U. The algorithm is, however, polynomial time for the assignment problem, a special case of the minimum cost flow problem for which $U = 1$. In Section 5.7, we will develop a polynomial time algorithm for the minimum cost flow problem using the successive shortest path algorithm in conjunction with scaling.

5.5. Primal–dual and out-of-kilter algorithms

The *primal–dual algorithm* is very similar to the successive shortest path algorithm, except that instead of sending flow on only one path during an iteration, it might send flow along many paths. To explain the primal–dual algorithm, we transform the minimum cost flow problem into a single-source and single-sink problem (possibly by adding nodes and arcs as in the assumption A5.1). At every iteration, the primal–dual algorithm solves a shortest path problem from the source to update the node potentials (i.e., as before, each $\pi(j)$ becomes $\pi(j) - d(j)$) and then solves a maximum flow problem to send the maximum possible flow from the source to the sink *using only arcs with zero reduced cost*. The algorithm guarantees that the excess of some node strictly decreases at each iteration, and also assures that the node potential of the sink strictly decreases. The latter observation follows from the fact that after we have solved the maximum flow problem, the network contains no path from the source to the sink in the residual network consisting entirely of arcs with zero reduced costs; consequently in the next iteration $d(t) \geqslant 1$. These observations give a bound of $\min\{nU, nC\}$ on the number of iterations since the magnitude of each node potential is bounded by nC. This bound is better than that of the successive shortest path algorithm, but, of course, the algorithm incurs the additional expense of solving a maximum flow problem at each iteration. Thus, the algorithm has an overall complexity of O(min-$(nU\,S(n, m, C), nC\,M(n, m, U))$, where $S(n, m, C)$ and $M(n, m, U)$ respectively denote the solution times of shortest path and maximum flow algorithms.

The successive shortest path and primal–dual algorithms maintain a solution that satisfies the dual feasibility conditions and the flow bound constraints, but that violates the mass balance constraints. These algorithms iteratively modify the flow and potentials so that the flow at each step comes closer to satisfying the mass balance constraints. However, we could just as well have violated other constraints at intermediate steps. The *out-of-kilter algorithm* satisfies only the mass balance constraints and may violate the dual feasibility conditions and the flow bound restrictions. The basic idea is to drive the flow on an arc (i, j) to u_{ij} if $\bar{c}_{ij} < 0$, drive the flow to zero if $\bar{c}_{ij} > 0$, and to permit any flow between 0 and u_{ij} if $\bar{c}_{ij} = 0$. The *kilter number*, represented by k_{ij}, of an arc (i, j) is defined as the minimum increase or decrease in the flow necessary so that the arc satisfies its flow bound constraint and dual feasibility condition. For example, for an arc (i, j) with $\bar{c}_{ij} > 0$, $k_{ij} = |x_{ij}|$, and for an arc (i, j) with $\bar{c}_{ij} < 0$, $k_{ij} = |u_{ij} - x_{ij}|$. An arc with $k_{ij} = 0$ is said to be *in-kilter*; other arcs are said to be out-of-kilter. At each iteration, the out-of-kilter algorithm reduces the kilter number of at least one arc; it terminates when all arcs are in-kilter. Suppose the kilter number of an arc (i, j) would decrease by increasing flow on the arc. Then the algorithm would obtain a shortest path P from node j to node

i in the residual network and augment at least one unit of flow in the cycle $P \cup \{(i, j)\}$. The proof of the correctness of this algorithm is similar to, but more detailed than, that of the successive shortest path algorithm.

5.6. *Network simplex algorithm*

The network simplex algorithm for the minimum cost flow problem is a specialization of the bounded variable primal simplex algorithm for linear programming. The special structure of the minimum cost flow problem offers several benefits, particularly, streamlining of the simplex computations and eliminating the need to explicitly maintain the simplex tableau. The tree structure of the basis (see Section 2.3) permits the algorithm to achieve these efficiencies. The advances made in the last two decades for maintaining and updating the tree structure efficiently have substantially improved the speed of the algorithm. Through extensive empirical testing, researchers have also improved the performance of the simplex algorithm by developing various heuristic rules for identifying entering variables. Though no version of the primal network simplex algorithm is known to run in polynomial time, its best implementations are empirically comparable to or better than other minimum cost flow algorithms.

In this section, we describe the network simplex algorithm in detail. We first define the concept of a *basis structure* and describe a data structure to store and to manipulate the basis, which is a spanning tree. We then show how to compute arc flows and node potentials for any basis structure. We next discuss how to perform various simplex operations such as the selection of entering arcs, leaving arcs and pivots using the tree data structure. Finally, we show how to guarantee the finiteness of the network simplex algorithm.

The network simplex algorithm maintains a primal basic feasible solution at each stage. A basic solution of the minimum cost flow problem is defined by a triple (B, L, U); B, L and U partition the arc set A. The set B denotes the set of *basic arcs*, i.e., arcs of a spanning tree, and L and U respectively denote the sets of *nonbasic arcs* at their lower and upper bounds. We refer to the triple (B, L, U) as a *basis structure*. A basis structure (B, L, U) is called *feasible* if by setting $x_{ij} = 0$ for each $(i, j) \in L$, and setting $x_{ij} = u_{ij}$ for each $(i, j) \in U$, the problem has a feasible solution satisfying (5.1b) and (5.1c). A feasible basis structure (B, L, U) is called an *optimum* basis structure if it is possible to obtain a set of node potentials π so that the reduced costs defined by $\bar{c}_{ij} = c_{ij} - \pi(i) + \pi(j)$ satisfy the following optimality conditions:

$$\bar{c}_{ij} = 0 , \quad \text{for each } (i, j) \in B , \tag{5.9}$$

$$\bar{c}_{ij} \geq 0 , \quad \text{for each } (i, j) \in L , \tag{5.10}$$

$$\bar{c}_{ij} \leq 0 , \quad \text{for each } (i, j) \in U . \tag{5.11}$$

These optimality conditions have a nice economic interpretation. We shall see a little later that if $\pi(1) = 0$, then equations (5.9) imply that $-\pi(j)$ denotes the length of the tree path in B from node 1 to node j. Then, $\bar{c}_{ij} = c_{ij} - \pi(i) + \pi(j)$ for a nonbasic arc (i, j) in L denotes the change in the cost of flow achieved by sending one unit of flow through the tree path from node 1 to node i, through the arc (i, j), and then returning the flow along the tree path from node j to node 1. The condition (5.10) implies that this circulation of flow is not profitable for any nonbasic arc in L. The condition (5.11) has a similar interpretation.

The network simplex algorithm maintains a feasible basis structure at each iteration and successively improves the basis structure until it becomes an optimum basis structure. The following algorithmic description specifies the essential steps of the procedure.

algorithm NETWORK SIMPLEX;
begin
    determine an initial basic feasible flow x and the corresponding
      basis structure (B, L, U);
    compute node potentials for this basis structure;
    while some arc violates the optimality conditions **do**
    begin
        select an entering arc (k, l) violating the optimality conditions;
        add arc (k, l) to the spanning tree corresponding to the basis forming a
        cycle and augment the maximum possible flow in this cycle;
        determine the leaving arc (p, q);
        perform a basis exchange and update node potentials;
    end;
end;

In the following discussion, we describe the various steps performed by the network simplex algorithm in greater detail.

Obtaining an initial basis structure

Our connectedness assumption A5.2 provides one way of obtaining an initial basic feasible solution. We have assumed that for every node $j \in N - \{1\}$, the network contains arcs $(1, j)$ and $(j, 1)$ with sufficiently large costs and capacities. The initial basis B includes the arc $(1, j)$ with flow $-b(j)$ if $b(j) \leq 0$ and arc $(j, 1)$ with flow $b(j)$ if $b(j) > 0$. The set L consists of the remaining arcs, and the set U is empty. The node potentials for this basis are easily computed using (5.9), as we will see later.

Maintaining the tree structure

The specialized network simplex algorithm is possible because of the spanning tree property of the basis. The algorithm requires the tree to be represented so that the simplex algorithm can perform operations efficiently and update the representation quickly when the basis changes. We next describe one such tree representation.

We consider the tree as 'hanging' from a specially designated node, called the *root*. We assume that node 1 is the root node. See Figure 5.1 for an example of the tree. We associate three indices with each node i in the tree: a *predecessor* index, pred(i); a *depth* index, depth(i); and a *thread* index, thread(i). Each node i has a unique path connecting it to the root. The predecessor index stores the first node in that path (other than node i) and the depth index stores the number of arcs in the path. For the root node these indices are zero. The Figure 5.1 shows an example of these indices. Note that by iteratively using the predecessor indices, we can enumerate the path from any node to the root node. We say that pred(i) is the *predecessor* of node i and i is a *successor* of node pred(i). The *descendants* of a node i consist of the node i itself, its successors, successors of its successors, and so on. For example, the node set $\{5, 6, 7, 8, 9\}$ contains the descendents of node 5 in Figure 5.1. A

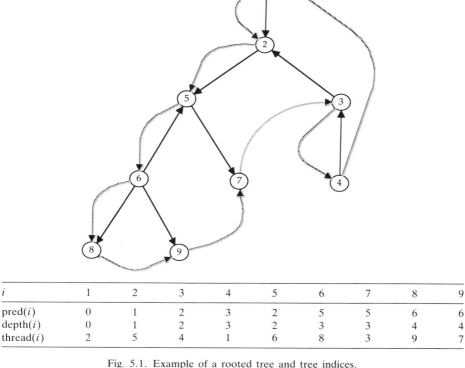

i	1	2	3	4	5	6	7	8	9
pred(i)	0	1	2	3	2	5	5	6	6
depth(i)	0	1	2	3	2	3	3	4	4
thread(i)	2	5	4	1	6	8	3	9	7

Fig. 5.1. Example of a rooted tree and tree indices.

node with no successors is called a *leaf* node. In Figure 5.1, nodes 4, 7, 8, and 9 are leaf nodes.

The thread indices define a *traversal* of a tree, a sequence of nodes that walks or threads its way through the nodes of the tree, starting at the root and visiting nodes in a 'top to bottom' and 'left to right' order, and then finally returning to the root. The thread indices can be formed by performing a depth first search of the tree as described in Section 1.5 and setting the thread of a node to be the node encountered after the node itself in this depth first search. For our example, this sequence would read 1-2-5-6-8-9-7-3-4-1 (see the shaded lines in Figure 5.1). For each node i, thread(i) specifies the next node in the traversal visited after node i. This traversal satisfies the following two properties: (i) the predecessor of each node appears in the sequence before the node itself; and (ii) the descendants of any node are consecutive elements in the traversal. The thread indices provide a particularly convenient means for visiting (or finding) all descendants of a node i: We simply follow the thread from node i, recording the nodes visited, until the depth of the visited node becomes at least as large as node i. For example, starting at node 5, we visit nodes 6, 8, 9, and 7 in order, which are the descendants of node 5, and then visit node 3. Since node 3's depth equals that of node 5, we know that we have left the 'descendant tree' lying below node 5. As we will see, finding the descendant tree of a node efficiently adds significantly to the efficiency of the simplex method.

The simplex method has two basic steps: (i) determining the node potentials of a given basis structure; and (ii) computing the arc flows for a given basis structure. We now describe how to perform these steps efficiently using the tree indices.

Computing node potentials and flows from a given basis structure

We first consider the problem of computing node potentials π for a given basis structure (B, L, U). We assume that $\pi(1) = 0$. Note that the value of one node potential can be set arbitrarily since one constraint in (5.1b) is redundant. We compute the remaining node potentials using the conditions that $\bar{c}_{ij} = 0$ for each arc (i, j) in B. These conditions can alternatively be stated as

$$\pi(j) = \pi(i) - c_{ij}, \quad \text{for every arc } (i, j) \in B . \tag{5.12}$$

The basic idea is to start at node 1 and fan out along the tree arcs using the thread indices to compute other node potentials. The traversal assures that whenever this fanning out procedure visits node j, it has already evaluated the potential of its predecessor, say node i; hence, the procedure can compute $\pi(j)$ using (5.12). The thread indices allow us to compute all node potentials in $O(n)$ time using the following method.

procedure COMPUTE POTENTIALS;
begin
   $\pi(1) := 0$;

```
  j := thread(1);
  while j ≠ 1 do
  begin
     i := pred(j);
     if (i, j) ∈ A then π(j) := π(i) - c_ij;
     if (j, i) ∈ A then π(j) := π(i) + c_ji;
     j := thread(j);
  end;
end;
```

A similar procedure will permit us to compute flows on basic arcs for a given basis structure (B, L, U). We proceed, however, in the reverse order: Start at a leaf node and move in toward the root using the predecessor indices, while computing flows on arcs encountered along the way. The following procedure accomplishes this task.

```
procedure COMPUTE FLOWS;
begin
  e(i) := b(i) for all i ∈ N;
  let T be the basis tree;
  for each (i, j) ∈ U do
     set x_ij := u_ij, subtract u_ij from e(i) and add u_ij to e(j);
  while T ≠ {1} do
  begin
     select a leaf node j in the subtree T;
     i := pred(j);
     if (i, j) ∈ T then x_ij := -e(j);
     else x_ji := e(j);
     add e(j) to e(i);
     delete node j and the arc incident to it from T;
  end;
end;
```

One way of identifying leaf nodes in T is to select nodes in the reverse order of the thread indices. A simple procedure completes this task in $O(n)$ time: Push all the nodes into a stack in order of their appearance on the thread, and then take them out from the top one at a time. Note that in the thread traversal, each node appears prior to its descendants. Hence, the reverse thread traversal examines each node after examining its decendants.

Now consider the steps of the method. The arcs in the set U must carry flow equal to their capacity. Thus, we set $x_{ij} = u_{ij}$ for these arcs. This assignment creates an additional demand of u_{ij} units at node i and makes the same amount available at node j. This effect of setting $x_{ij} = u_{ij}$ explains the initial adjustments in the supply/demand of nodes. The manner of updating $e(j)$ implies that each $e(j)$ represents the sum of the adjusted supply/demand of nodes in the subtree hanging from node j. Since this subtree is connected to the rest of the tree only by the arc (i, j) (or (j, i)), this arc must carry $-e(j)$ (or $e(j)$) units of flow to satisfy the adjusted supply/demand of nodes in the subtree.

The procedure COMPUTE FLOWS essentially solves the system of equations $Bx = b$, in which B represents the columns in the node–arc incidence matrix N corresponding to the spanning tree T. Since B is a lower triangular matrix (see Theorem 2.6 in Section 2.3), it is possible to solve these equations by forward substitution, which is precisely what the algorithm does. Similarly, the procedure COMPUTE POTENTIALS solves the system of equations $\pi B = c$ by back substitution.

Entering arc

Two types of arcs are eligible to enter the basis: any nonbasic arc at its lower bound with a negative reduced cost or any nonbasic arc at its upper bound with a positive reduced cost. These arcs violate condition (5.10) or (5.11). The method used for selecting an entering arc among these eligible arcs has a major effect on the performance of the simplex algorithm. An implementation that selects an arc that violates the optimality condition the most, i.e., has the largest value of $|\bar{c}_{ij}|$ among such arcs, might require the fewest number of iterations in practice, but must examine each arc at each iteration, which is very time-consuming. On the other hand, examining the arc list cyclically and selecting the *first* arc that violates the optimality condition would quickly find the entering arc, but might require a relatively large number of iterations due to the poor arc choice. One of the most successful implementations uses a *candidate list* approach that strikes an effective compromise between these two strategies. This approach also offers sufficient flexibility for fine tuning to special problem classes.

The algorithm maintains a candidate list of arcs violating the optimality conditions, selecting arcs in a two-phase procedure consisting of *major* iterations and *minor* iterations. In a major iteration, we construct the candidate list. We examine arcs emanating from nodes, one node at a time, adding to the candidate list the arcs emanating from node i (if any) that violate the optimality condition. We repeat this selection process for nodes $i + 1, i + 2, \ldots$ until either we have examined all nodes or the list has reached its maximum allowable size. The next major iteration begins with the node where the previous major iteration ended. In other words, the algorithm examines nodes cyclically as it adds arcs emanating from them to the candidate list.

Once the algorithm has formed the candidate list in a major iteration, it performs minor iterations, scanning all candidate arcs and choosing a nonbasic arc from this list that violates the optimality condition the most to enter the basis. As we scan the arcs, we update the candidate list by removing those arcs that no longer violate the optimality conditions. Once the list becomes empty or we have reached a specified limit on the number of minor iterations to be performed at each major iteration, we rebuild the list with another major iteration.

Leaving arc

Suppose we select the arc (k, l) as the entering arc. The addition of this arc to the basis B forms exactly one (undirected) cycle W, which is sometimes referred to as the *pivot cycle*. We define the orientation of W as the same as that of (k, l) if $(k, l) \in L$, and opposite to the orientation of (k, l) if $(k, l) \in U$. Let $\overline{W}$ and $\underline{W}$, respectively, denote the sets of arcs in W along and opposite to the cycle's orientation. Sending additional flow around the pivot cycle W in the direction of its orientation strictly decreases the cost of the current solution. We change the flow as much as possible until one of the arcs in the cycle W reaches its lower or upper bound; this arc leaves the basis. The maximum flow change δ_{ij} on an arc $(i, j) \in W$ that satisfies the flow bound constraints is

$$\delta_{ij} = \begin{cases} u_{ij} - x_{ij} & \text{if } (i, j) \in \overline{W}, \\ x_{ij} & \text{if } (i, j) \in \underline{W}. \end{cases}$$

We send $\delta = \min\{\delta_{ij} : (i, j) \in W\}$ units of flow around W, and select an arc (p, q) with $\delta_{pq} = \delta$ as the leaving arc. The crucial operation in this step is to identify the cycle W. If $P(i)$ denotes the unique path in the basis from any node i to the root node, then this cycle consists of the arcs $\{((k, l) \cup P(k) \cup P(l)) - (P(k) \cap P(l))\}$. In other words, W consists of the arc (k, l) and the disjoint portions of $P(k)$ and $P(l)$. Using predecessor indices alone permits us to identify the cycle W as follows. Start at node k and using predecessor indices trace the path from this node to the root and label all the nodes in this path. Repeat the same operation for node l until we encounter a node already labeled, say node w. Node w, which we might refer to as the *apex*, is the first common ancestor of nodes k and l. The cycle W contains the portions of the path $P(k)$ and $P(l)$ up to node w, along with the arc (k, l). This method is efficient, but it can be improved. It has the drawback of backtracking along some arcs that are not in W, namely, those in the portion of the path $P(k)$ lying between the apex w and the root. The simultaneous use of depth and predecessor indices, as indicated in the following procedure, eliminates this extra work.

procedure IDENTIFY CYCLE;
begin
    $i := k$ and $j := l$;
    while $i \neq j$ **do**
    begin
      if depth$(i) >$ depth(j) **then** $i := \text{pred}(i)$
      else if depth$(j) >$ depth(i) **then** $j := \text{pred}(j)$
        else $i := \text{pred}(i)$ and $j := \text{pred}(j)$;
    end;
    $w := i$;
end;

A simple modification of this procedure permits it to determine the flow δ that can be augmented along W as it determines the first common ancestor w of nodes k and l. Using predecessor indices to again traverse the cycle W, the algorithm can then update flows on arcs. The entire flow change operation takes $O(n)$ time in the worst-case, but typically examines only a small subset of the nodes.

Basis exchange

In the terminology of the simplex method, a basis exchange is a pivot operation. If $\delta = 0$, then the pivot is said to be *degenerate*; otherwise it is *nondegenerate*. A basis is called *degenerate* if the flow on some basic arc equals its lower or upper bound, and *nondegenerate* otherwise. Observe that a degenerate pivot occurs only in a degenerate basis.

Each time the method exchanges an entering arc (k, l) for a leaving arc (p, q), it must update the basis structure. If the leaving arc is the same as the entering arc, which would happen when $\delta = u_{kl}$, the basis does not change. In this instance, the arc (k, l) merely moves from the set L to the set U, or vice versa. If the leaving arc differs from the entering arc, then more extensive changes are needed. In this instance, the arc (p, q) becomes a nonbasic arc at its lower or upper bound depending upon whether $x_{pq} = 0$ or $x_{pq} = u_{pq}$. Adding (k, l) to and deleting (p, q) from the previous basis yields a new basis that is again a spanning tree. The node potentials also change and can be updated as follows. The deletion of the arc (p, q) from the previous basis partitions the set of nodes into two subtrees – one, T_1, containing the root node, and the other, T_2, not containing the root node. Note that the subtree T_2 hangs from node p or node q. The arc (k, l) has one endpoint in T_1 and the other in T_2. As is easy to verify, the conditions $\pi(1) = 0$ and $c_{ij} - \pi(i) + \pi(j) = 0$ for all arcs in the new basis imply that the potentials of nodes in the subtree T_1 remain unchanged, and the potentials of nodes in the subtree T_2 change by a constant amount. If $k \in T_1$ and $l \in T_2$, then all the node potentials in T_2 change by $-\bar{c}_{kl}$; if $l \in T_1$ and $k \in T_2$, they change by the amount $\bar{c}_{kl}$. The following method, using the thread and depth indices, updates the node potentials quickly.

procedure UPDATE POTENTIALS;
begin
  if $q \in T_2$ **then** $y := q$ **else** $y := p$;
  if $k \in T_1$ **then** change $:= -\bar{c}_{kl}$ **else** change $:= \bar{c}_{kl}$;
  $\pi(y) := \pi(y) +$ change;
  $z := \text{thread}(y)$;
  while depth$(z) <$ depth(y) **do**
  begin
    $\pi(z) := \pi(z) +$ change;
    $z := \text{thread}(z)$;
  end;
end;

The final step in the basis exchange is to update various indices. This step is rather involved and we refer the reader to the reference material cited in Section 6.4 for the details. We do note, however, that it is possible to update the tree indices in $O(n)$ time.

Termination

The network simplex algorithm, as just described, moves from one basis structure to another until it obtains a basis structure that satisfies the optimality conditions (5.9)–(5.11). It is easy to show that the algorithm terminates in a finite number of steps if each pivot operation is nondegenerate. Recall that $|\bar{c}_{kl}|$ represents the net decrease in the cost per unit flow sent around the cycle W. During a nondegenerate pivot (in which $\delta > 0$), the new basis structure has a cost that is $\delta|\bar{c}_{kl}|$ units lower than the previous basis structure. Since there are a finite number of basis structures and every basis structure has a unique associated cost, the network simplex algorithm will terminate finitely assuming nondegeneracy. Degenerate pivots, however, pose theoretical difficulties that we address next.

Strongly feasible bases

The network simplex algorithm does not necessarily terminate in a finite number of iterations unless we impose an additional restriction on the choice of entering and leaving arcs. Researchers have constructed very small network examples for which poor choices lead to *cycling*, i.e., an infinite repetitive sequence of degenerate pivots. Degeneracy in network problems is not only a theoretical issue, but also a practical one. Computational studies have shown that as many as 90% of the pivot operations in common networks can be degenerate. As we show next, by maintaining a special type of basis, called a *strongly feasible basis*, the simplex algorithm terminates finitely; moreover, it runs faster in practice as well.

Let (B, L, U) be a basis structure of the minimum cost flow problem with integral data. As earlier, we conceive of a basis tree as a tree hanging from the root node. The tree arcs either are *upward pointing* (towards the root) or are *downward pointing* (away from the root). We say that a basis structure (B, L, U) is *strongly feasible* if we can send a positive amount of flow from any node in the tree to the root along arcs in the tree without violating any of the flow bounds. See Figure 5.2 for an example of a strongly feasible basis. Observe that this definition implies that no upward pointing arc can be at its upper bound and no downward pointing arc can be at it lower bound.

The *perturbation technique* is a well-known method for avoiding cycling in the simplex algorithm for linear programming. This technique slightly perturbs the right-hand-side vector so that every feasible basis is nondegenerate and so that it is easy to convert an optimum solution of the perturbed problem to an optimum solution of the original problem. We show that a particular perturbation technique for the network simplex method is equivalent to the combinatorial rule known as the *strongly feasible basis technique*.

The minimum cost flow problem can be perturbed by changing the supply/ demand vector b to $b + \varepsilon$. We say that $\varepsilon = (\varepsilon_1, \varepsilon_2, \ldots, \varepsilon_n)$ is a feasible perturbation if it satisfies the following conditions:

(i) $\varepsilon_i > 0$ for all $i = 2, 3, \ldots, n$;

(ii) $\Sigma_{i=2}^n \varepsilon_i < 1$; and

(iii) $\varepsilon_1 = -\Sigma_{i=2}^n \varepsilon_i$.

One possible choice for a feasible perturbation is $\varepsilon_i = 1/n$ for $i = 2, \ldots, n$ (and thus $\varepsilon_1 = -(n-1)/n$). Another choice is $\varepsilon_i = \alpha^i$ for $i = 2, \ldots, n$, with α chosen as a very small positive number. The perturbation changes the flow on basic arcs. The justification we gave for the procedure COMPUTE FLOWS, earlier in this section, implies that perturbation of b by ε changes the flow on basic arcs in the following manner:

1. If (i, j) is a downward pointing arc of tree B and $D(j)$ is the set of descendants of node j, then the perturbation decreases the flow in arc (i, j) by $\Sigma_{k \in D(j)} \varepsilon_k$. Since $0 < \Sigma_{k \in D(j)} \varepsilon_k < 1$, the resulting flow is nonintegral and thus nonzero.

2. If (i, j) is an upward pointing arc of tree B and $D(i)$ is the set of descendants of node i, then the perturbation increases the flow in arc (i, j) by $\Sigma_{k \in D(i)} \varepsilon_k$. Since $0 < \Sigma_{k \in D(i)} \varepsilon_k < 1$, the resulting flow is nonintegral and thus nonzero.

Theorem 5.2. *For any feasible basis structure (B, L, U) of the minimum cost flow problem, the following statements are equivalent:*

(i) *(B, L, U) is strongly feasible.*

(ii) *No upward pointing arc of the basis is at its upper bound and no downward pointing arc of the basis is at its lower bound.*

(iii) *(B, L, U) is feasible if we replace b by $b + \varepsilon$, for any feasible perturbation ε.*

(iv) *(B, L, U) is feasible if we replace b by $b + \varepsilon$, for the perturbation $\varepsilon = (-(n-1)/n, 1/n, 1/n, \ldots, 1/n)$.*

Proof. (i) $\Rightarrow$ (ii). Suppose an upward pointing arc (i, j) is at its upper bound. Then node i cannot send any flow to the root, violating the definition of a strongly feasible basis. For the same reason, no downward pointing arc can be at its lower bound.

(ii) $\Rightarrow$ (iii). Suppose that (ii) is true. As noted earlier, the perturbation increases the flow on an upward pointing arc by an amount strictly between 0 and 1. Since the flow on an upward pointing arc is integral and strictly less than its (integral) upper bound, the perturbed solution remains feasible. Similar reasoning shows that after we have perturbed the problem, downward pointing arcs also remain feasible.

(iii) $\Rightarrow$ (iv). Follows directly because $\varepsilon = (-(n-1)/n, 1/n, 1/n, \ldots, 1/n)$ is a feasible perturbation.

(iv) $\Rightarrow$ (i). Consider the feasible basis structure (B, L, U) of the perturbed problem. Each arc in the basis B has a positive nonintegral flow. Consider the same basis tree for the original problem. If we remove the perturbation (i.e., replace $b + \varepsilon$ by b), flows on the downward pointing arcs increase, flows on the upward pointing arcs decrease, and the resulting flows are integral. Consequently, $x_{ij} > 0$ for downward pointing arcs, $x_{ij} < u_{ij}$ for upward pointing arcs, and (B, L, U) is strongly feasible for the original problem. □

This theorem shows that maintaining a strongly feasible basis is equivalent to applying the ordinary simplex algorithm to the perturbed problem. This result implies that both approaches obtain exactly the same sequence of basis structures if they use the same rule to select the entering arcs. As a corollary, this equivalence shows that any implementation of the simplex algorithm that maintains a strongly feasible basis performs at most $nmCU$ pivots. To establish this result, consider the perturbed problem with the perturbation $\varepsilon = ((n-1)/n, 1/n\ 1/n, \ldots, 1/n)$. With this perturbation, the flow on every arc is a multiple of $1/n$. Consequently, every pivot operation augments at least $1/n$ units of flow and therefore decreases the objective function value by at least $1/n$ units. Since mCU is an upper bound on the objective function value of the starting solution and zero is a lower bound on the minimum objective function value, the algorithm will terminate in at most $nmCU$ iterations. Therefore, any implementation of the simplex algorithm that maintains a strongly feasible basis runs in pseudopolynomial time.

We can thus maintain strong feasibility by perturbing b by a suitable perturbation ε. However, there is no need to actually perform the perturbation. Instead, we can maintain strong feasibility using a 'combinatorial rule' that is equivalent to applying the original simplex method after we have imposed the perturbation. Even though this rule permits degenerate pivots, it is guaranteed to converge. Figure 5.2 will illustrate our discussion of this method.

Combinatorial version of perturbation

The network simplex algorithm starts with a strongly feasible basis. The method described earlier to construct the initial basis always gives such a basis. The algorithm selects the leaving arc in a degenerate pivot carefully so that the next basis is also feasible. Suppose that the entering arc (k, l) is at its lower bound and the apex w is the first common ancestor of nodes k and l. Let W be the cycle formed by adding arc (k, l) to the basis tree. We define the orientation of the cycle as the same as that of arc (k, l). After updating the flow, the algorithm identifies the *blocking arcs*, i.e., those arcs (i, j) in the cycle W that satisfy $\delta_{ij} = \delta$. If the blocking arc is unique, then it leaves the basis. If the cycle contains more than one blocking arc, then the next basis will be degenerate; i.e., some basic arcs will be at their lower or upper bounds. In this case, the algorithm selects the leaving arc in accordance with the following rule:

Combinatorial pivot rule. When introducing an arc into the basis for the network simplex method, select the leaving arc as the last blocking arc, say arc (p, q), encountered in traversing the pivot cycle W along its orientation, starting at the apex w.

We next show that this rule guarantees that the next basis is strongly feasible. To do so, we show that in this basis every node in the cycle W can send positive flow to the root node. Notice that since the previous basis was strongly feasible, every node could send positive flow to the root node. Let W_1 be the segment of the cycle W between the apex w and arc (p, q), when we traverse the cycle along its orientation. Further, let $W_2 = W - W_1 - \{(p, q)\}$. Define the orientation of segments W_1 and W_2 to be compatible with the orientation of W. See Figure 5.2 for an illustration of the segments W_1 and W_2 for our example. Since arc (p, q) is the last blocking arc in W, no arc in W_2 is blocking and every node contained in the segment W_2 can send positive flow to the root along the orientation of W_2 and via node w. Now consider nodes contained in the segment W_1. We distinguish two cases. If the current pivot was a *nondegenerate* pivot, then the pivot augmented a positive amount of flow along the arcs in W_1; hence, every node in the segment W_1 can augment flow back to the root opposite to the orientation of W_1 and via node w. If the current pivot was a *degenerate* pivot, then W_1 must be contained in the segment of W between node w and node k, because by the property of strong feasibility, every node on the path from node l to node w can send a positive amount of flow to the root before the pivot and, thus, no arc on this path can be a

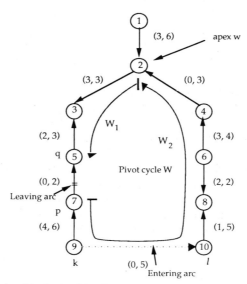

Fig. 5.2. A strongly feasible basis. The figure shows the flows and capacities represented as (x_{ij}, u_{ij}). The entering arc is $(9, 10)$; the blocking arcs are $(2, 3)$ and $(7, 5)$; and the leaving arc is $(7, 5)$. This pivot is a degenerate pivot. The segments W_1 and W_2 are as shown.

blocking arc in a degenerate pivot. Now observe that before the pivot, every node in W_1 could send positive flow to the root and, therefore, since the pivot does not change flow values, every node in W_1 must be able to send positive flow to the root after the pivot as well. This conclusion completes the proof that the next basis is strongly feasible.

We now study the effect of the basis change on node potentials during a degenerate pivot. Since arc (k, l) enters the basis at its lower bound, $\bar{c}_{kl} < 0$. The leaving arc belongs to the path from node k to node w. Hence, node k lies in the subtree T_2 and the potentials of all nodes in T_2 change by the amount $-\bar{c}_{kl} > 0$. Consequently, this degenerate pivot strictly increases the sum of all node potentials (which by our prior assumptions is integral). Since the sum of all node potentials is bounded from above, the number of successive degenerate pivots is finite.

So far we have assumed that the entering arc is at its lower bound. If the entering arc (k, l) is at its upper bound, then we define the orientation of the cycle W as opposite to the orientation of arc (k, l). The criteria to select the leaving arc remains unchanged – the leaving arc is the last blocking arc encountered in traversing W along its orientation starting at node w. In this case, node l is contained in the subtree T_2 and, thus, after the pivot all nodes in T_2 again increase by the amount $-\bar{c}_{kl}$; consequently, the pivot again increases the sum of the node potentials.

Complexity results

The strongly feasible basis technique implies some nice theoretical results about the network simplex algorithm implemented using Dantzig's pivot rule, i.e., pivoting in the arc that most violates the optimality conditions (that is, the arc (k, l) with the largest value of $|\bar{c}_{kl}|$ among all arcs that violate the optimality conditions). This technique also yields polynomial time simplex algorithms for the shortest path and assignment problems.

We have already shown that any version of the network simplex algorithm that maintains a strongly feasible basis performs $O(nmCU)$ pivots. Using Dantzig's pivot rule and geometric improvement arguments, we can reduce the number of pivots to $O(nmU \log H)$, with H defined as $H = mCU$. As earlier, we consider the perturbed problem with perturbation $\varepsilon = (-(n-1)/n, 1/n, 1/n, \ldots, 1/n)$. Let z^k denote the objective function value of the perturbed minimum cost flow problem at the k-th iteration of the simplex algorithm, x denote the current flow, and (B, L, U) denote the current basis structure. Let $\Delta > 0$ denote the maximum violation of the optimality condition of any nonbasic arc. If the algorithm next pivots in a nonbasic arc corresponding to the maximum violation, then the objective function value decreases by at least Δ/n units. Hence,

$$z^k - z^{k+1} \geq \Delta/n . \tag{5.13}$$

We now need an upper bound on the total possible improvement in the objective function after the k-th iteration. It is easy to show that

$$\sum_{(i,j)\in A} \bar{c}_{ij}x_{ij} = \sum_{(i,j)\in A} c_{ij}x_{ij} - \sum_{i\in N} \pi(i)b(i) .$$

Since the rightmost term in this expression is a constant for fixed values of the node potentials, the total improvement with respect to the objective function $\sum_{(i,j)\in A} c_{ij}x_{ij}$ is equal to the total improvement with respect to the objective function $\sum_{(i,j)\in A} \bar{c}_{ij}x_{ij}$. Further, the total improvement in the objective function $\sum_{(i,j)\in A} \bar{c}_{ij}x_{ij}$ is bounded by the total improvement in the following relaxed problem:

$$\text{minimize} \quad \sum_{(i,j)\in A} \bar{c}_{ij}x_{ij} , \tag{5.14a}$$

subject to

$$0 \le x_{ij} \le u_{ij} , \quad \text{for all } (i, j) \in A . \tag{5.14b}$$

For a given basis structure (B, L, U), we construct an optimum solution of (5.14) by setting $x_{ij} = u_{ij}$ for all arcs $(i, j) \in L$ with $\bar{c}_{ij} < 0$, by setting $x_{ij} = 0$ for all arcs $(i, j) \in U$ with $\bar{c}_{ij} > 0$, and by leaving the flow on the basic arcs unchanged. This readjustment of flow decreases the objective function by at most $m\Delta U$. We have thus shown that

$$z^k - z^* \le m\Delta U . \tag{5.15}$$

Combining (5.13) and (5.15) we obtain

$$z^k - z^{k+1} \ge \frac{1}{nmU} (z^k - z^*) .$$

By Lemma 1.1, if $H = mCU$, the network simplex algorithm terminates in $O(nmU \log H)$ iterations. We summarize our discussion as follows.

Theorem 5.3. *The network simplex algorithm that maintains a strongly feasible basis and uses Dantzig's pivot rule performs* $O(nmU \log H)$ *pivots.* $\square$

This result gives polynomial time bounds for the shortest path and assignment problems since both can be formulated as minimum cost flow problems with $U = n$ and $U = 1$ respectively. In fact, it is possible to modify the algorithm and use the previous arguments to show that the simplex algorithm solves these problems in $O(n^2 \log C)$ pivots and runs in $O(nm \log C)$ total time. These results can be found in the references cited in Section 6.4.

5.7. Right-hand-side scaling algorithm

Scaling techniques are among the most effective algorithmic strategies for designing polynomial time algorithms for the minimum cost flow problem. In this section, we describe an algorithm based on a right-hand-side scaling (RHS-scaling) technique. The next two sections present polynomial time algorithms based upon cost scaling and upon simultaneous right-hand-side and cost scaling.

The RHS-scaling algorithm is an improved version of the successive shortest path algorithm. The inherent drawback in the successive shortest path algorithm is that augmentations may carry relatively small amounts of flow, resulting in a fairly large number of augmentations in the worst case. The RHS-scaling algorithm guarantees that each augmentation carries *sufficiently large* flow and thereby reduces the number of augmentations substantially. We shall illustrate RHS-scaling on the uncapacitated minimum cost flow problem, i.e., a problem with $u_{ij} = \infty$ for each $(i, j) \in A$. This algorithm can be applied to the capacitated minimum cost flow problem after it has been converted into an uncapacitated problem (as described in Section 2.4).

The algorithm uses the pseudoflow x and the imbalances $e(i)$ as defined in Section 5.4. It performs a number of scaling phases. Much as we did in the excess scaling algorithm for the maximum flow problem, we let Δ be the least power of 2 satisfying either (i) $e(i) < 2\Delta$ for all i, or (ii) $e(i) > -2\Delta$ for all i, but not necessarily both. Initially, $\Delta = 2^{\lceil \log U \rceil}$. This definition implies that the sum of excesses (whose magnitude is equal to the sum of deficits) is bounded by $2n\Delta$. Let $S(\Delta) = \{i: e(i) \geq \Delta\}$ and let $T(\Delta) = \{j: e(j) \leq -\Delta\}$. Then at the beginning of the Δ-scaling phase, either $S(2\Delta) = \emptyset$ or $T(2\Delta) = \emptyset$. In the given Δ-scaling phase, we perform a number of augmentations, each from a node $i \in S(\Delta)$ to a node $j \in T(\Delta)$, and each of these augmentations carries Δ units of flow. The definition of Δ implies that within n augmentations the algorithm will decrease Δ by a factor of at least 2. At this point, we begin a new scaling phase. Hence, within $O(\log U)$ scaling phase, $\Delta < 1$. By the integrality of data, all imbalances are now zero and the algorithm has found an optimum flow.

The driving force behind this scaling technique is an invariant property (which we will prove later) that each arc flow in the Δ-scaling phase is a multiple of Δ. This flow invariant property and the connectedness assumption (A5.2) ensure that we can always send Δ units of flow from a node in $S(\Delta)$ to a node in $T(\Delta)$. The following algorithmic description is a formal statement of the RHS-scaling algorithm.

algorithm RHS-SCALING;
begin
    $x := 0$, $e := b$;
    let π be the shortest path distances in $G(0)$;
    $\Delta := 2^{\lceil \log U \rceil}$;
    while the network contains a node with nonzero imbalance **do**
    begin
        $S(\Delta) := \{i \in N: e(i) \geq \Delta\}$;
        $T(\Delta) := \{i \in N: e(i) \leq -\Delta\}$;
        while $S(\Delta) \neq \emptyset$ and $T(\Delta) \neq \emptyset$ **do**

begin
   select a node $k \in S(\Delta)$ and a node $l \in T(\Delta)$;
   determine shortest path distances d from node k to all other nodes
      in the residual network $G(x)$ with respect to the reduced cost $\bar{c}_{ij}$;
   let P denote the shortest path from node k to node l;
   update $\pi := \pi - d$;
   augment Δ units of flow along the path P;
   update x, $S(\Delta)$ and $T(\Delta)$);
   end;
   $\Delta := \Delta/2$;
 end;
end;

The RHS-scaling algorithm correctly solves the problem because during the Δ-scaling phase, it is able to send Δ units of flow on the shortest path from a node $k \in S(\Delta)$ to a node $l \in T(\Delta)$. This fact follows from the following result.

Lemma 5.2. *The residual capacities of arcs in the residual network are always integer multiples of Δ.*

Proof. We use induction on the number of augmentations and scaling phases. The initial residual capacities are a multiple of Δ because they are either 0 or ∞. Each augmentation changes the residual capacities by 0 or Δ units and preserves the inductive hypothesis. A decrease in the scale factor by a factor of 2 also preserves the inductive hypothesis. This result implies the conclusion of the lemma. $\square$

Let $S(n, m, C)$ denote the time to solve a shortest path problem on a network with nonnegative arc lengths.

Theorem 5.4. *The RHS-scaling algorithm correctly computes a minimum cost flow and performs $O(n \log U)$ augmentations and consequently solves the minimum cost flow problem in $O(n \log U\, S(n, m, C))$ time.*

Proof. The RHS-scaling algorithm is a special case of the successive shortest path algorithm and thus terminates with a minimum cost flow. We show that the algorithm performs at most n augmentations per scaling phase. Since the algorithm requires $1 + \lceil \log U \rceil$ scaling phases, this fact would imply the conclusion of the theorem. At the beginning of the Δ-scaling phase, either $S(2\Delta) = \emptyset$ or $T(2\Delta) = \emptyset$. We consider the case when $S(2\Delta) = \emptyset$. A similar proof applies when $T(2\Delta) = \emptyset$. At the beginning of the scaling phase, $|S(\Delta)| \leq n$. Observe that $\Delta \leq e(i) < 2\Delta$ for each node $i \in S(\Delta)$. Each augmentation starts at a node in $S(\Delta)$, ends at a node with a deficit, and carries Δ units of flow; therefore, it decreases $|S(\Delta)|$ by one. Consequently, each scaling phase can perform at most n augmentations. $\square$

Applying the scaling algorithm directly to the capacitated minimum cost flow problem introduces some subtlety, because Lemma 5.2 does not apply for this situation. The inductive hypothesis fails to be true initially since the residual capacities are 0 or u_{ij}. As we noted previously, one method of solving the capacitated minimum cost flow problem is to first transform the capacitated problem to an uncapacitated one using the technique described in Section 2.4. We then apply the RHS-scaling algorithm on the transformed network. The transformed network contains $n + m$ nodes, and each scaling phase performs at most $n + m$ augmentations. The shortest path problem on the transformed problem can be solved (using some clever techniques) in $S(n, m, C)$ time. Consequently, the RHS-scaling algorithm solves the capacitated minimum cost flow problem in $O(m \log U\, S(n, m, C))$ time. A recently developed modest variation of the RHS-scaling algorithm solves the capacitated minimum cost flow problem in $O(m \log n\ (m + n \log n))$ time. This method is currently the best *strongly* polynomial-time algorithm for solving the minimum cost flow problem.

5.8. Cost scaling algorithm

We now describe a cost scaling algorithm for the minimum cost flow problem. This algorithm can be viewed as a generalization of the preflow–push algorithm for the maximum flow problem.

This algorithm relies on the concept of *approximate optimality*. A flow x is said to be ε-*optimal* for some $\varepsilon > 0$ if x together with some node potentials π satisfy the following conditions.

C5.7 (Primal feasibility). x is feasible.
C5.8 (ε-Dual feasibility). $\bar{c}_{ij} \geq -\varepsilon$ for each arc (i, j) in the residual network $G(x)$.

We refer to these conditions as the ε-*optimality* conditions. These conditions are a relaxation of the optimality conditions and reduce to C5.5 and C5.6 when ε is 0. The ε-optimality conditions permit $-\varepsilon \leq \bar{c}_{ij} < 0$ for any arc (i, j) at its lower bound and $\varepsilon \geq \bar{c}_{ij} > 0$ for an arc (i, j) at its upper bound, which is a relaxation of the usual optimality conditions. The following facts are useful for analyzing the cost scaling algorithm.

Lemma 5.3. *Any feasible flow is ε-optimal for $\varepsilon \geq C$. Any ε-optimal feasible flow for $\varepsilon < 1/n$ is an optimum flow.*

Proof. Clearly, any feasible flow with zero node potentials satisfies C5.8 for $\varepsilon \geq C$. Now consider an ε-optimal flow with $\varepsilon < 1/n$. The ε-dual feasibility conditions imply that for any directed cycle W in the residual network, $\sum_{(i,j)\in W} c_{ij} = \sum_{(i,j)\in W} \bar{c}_{ij} \geq -n\varepsilon > -1$. Since all arc costs are integral, this result implies that $\sum_{(i,j)\in W} c_{ij} \geq 0$. Hence, the residual network contains no negative cost cycle and from Theorem 5.1 the flow is optimum. $\square$

The cost scaling algorithm treats ε as a parameter and iteratively obtains ε-optimal flows for successively smaller values of ε. Initially $\varepsilon = C$, and finally $\varepsilon < 1/n$. The algorithm performs cost scaling phases by repeatedly applying an IMPROVE-APPROXIMATION procedure that transforms an ε-optimal flow into a $\frac{1}{2}\varepsilon$-optimal flow. After $1 + \lceil \log nC \rceil$ cost scaling phases, $\varepsilon < 1/n$ and the algorithm terminates with an optimum flow. More formally, we can state the algorithm as follows.

algorithm COST SCALING;
begin
    $\pi := 0$ and $\varepsilon := C$;
    let x be any feasible flow;
    while $\varepsilon \geq 1/n$ **do**
    begin
        IMPROVE-APPROXIMATION(ε, x, π);
        $\varepsilon := \varepsilon/2$;
    end;
    x is an optimum flow for the minimum cost flow problem;
end;

The IMPROVE-APPROXIMATION procedure transforms an ε-optimal flow into a $\frac{1}{2}\varepsilon$-optimal flow. It does so by (i) first converting an ε-optimal flow into a 0-optimal pseudoflow (a pseudoflow x is called ε-optimal if it satisfies the ε-dual feasibility conditions C5.8), and then (ii) gradually converting the pseudoflow into a flow while always maintaining the $\frac{1}{2}\varepsilon$-dual feasibility conditions. We call a node i with $e(i) > 0$ *active* and call an arc (i, j) in the residual network *admissible* if $-\frac{1}{2}\varepsilon \leq \bar{c}_{ij} < 0$. The basic operations are selecting active nodes and pushing flows on admissible arcs. We shall see later that pushing flows on admissible arcs preserves the $\frac{1}{2}\varepsilon$-dual feasibility conditions. The IMPROVE-APPROXIMATION procedure uses the following subroutine.

procedure PUSH/RELABEL(i);
begin
    if $G(x)$ contains an admissible arc (i, j) **then**
        push $\delta := \min\{e(i), r_{ij}\}$ units of flow from node i to node j;
    else $\pi(i) := \pi(i) + \varepsilon/2 + \min\{\bar{c}_{ij}: (i, j) \in A(i) \text{ and } r_{ij} > 0\}$;
end;

Recall that r_{ij} denotes the residual capacity of an arc (i, j) in $G(x)$. As in our earlier discussion of preflow–push algorithms for the maximum flow problem, if $\delta = r_{ij}$, then we refer to the push as *saturating*; otherwise it is *nonsaturating*. We also refer to the updating of the potential of a node as a *relabel* operation. The purpose of a relabel operation is to create new admissible arcs. Moreover, we use the same data structure as used in the maximum flow algorithms to identify admissible arcs. For each node i, we maintain a *current arc* (i, j) which is the current candidate for pushing flow out of node i. The current arc is found by sequentially scanning the arc list $A(i)$.

The following generic version of the IMPROVE-APPROXIMATION procedure summarizes its essential operations.

procedure IMPROVE-APPROXIMATION(ε, x, π);
begin
    if $\bar{c}_{ij} > 0$ **then** $x_{ij} := 0$;
    else if $\bar{c}_{ij} < 0$ **then** $x_{ij} := u_{ij}$;
    compute node imbalances;
    while the network contains an active node **do**
    begin
        select an active node i;
        PUSH / RELABEL(i);
    end;
end;

The correctness of this procedure rests on the following result.

Lemma 5.4. *The* IMPROVE-APPROXIMATION *procedure always maintains* $\frac{1}{2}\varepsilon$-*optimality of the pseudoflow, and at termination yields a* $\frac{1}{2}\varepsilon$-*optimal flow.*

Proof. This proof is similar to that of Lemma 4.1. At the beginning of the procedure, the algorithm adjusts the flows on arcs to obtain an $\frac{1}{2}\varepsilon$-pseudoflow (in fact, it is a 0-optimal pseudoflow). We use induction on the number of push/relabel steps to show that the algorithm preserves $\frac{1}{2}\varepsilon$-optimality of the pseudoflow. Pushing flow on arc (i, j) might add its reversal (j, i) to the residual network. But since $-\frac{1}{2}\varepsilon \le \bar{c}_{ij} < 0$ (by the criteria of admissibility), $\bar{c}_{ji} > 0$ and the condition C5.8 is satisfied for any value of $\varepsilon > 0$. The algorithm relabels node i when $\bar{c}_{ij} \ge 0$ for every arc (i, j) in the residual network. By our rule for increasing potentials, after we increase $\pi(i)$ by $\frac{1}{2}\varepsilon + \min\{\bar{c}_{ij}: (i, j) \in A(i)$ and $r_{ij} > 0\}$ units, the reduced cost of every arc (i, j) with $r_{ij} > 0$ still satisfies $\bar{c}_{ij} \ge -\frac{1}{2}\varepsilon$. In addition, increasing $\pi(i)$ maintains the condition $\bar{c}_{ki} \ge -\frac{1}{2}\varepsilon$ for all arcs (k, i) in the residual network. Therefore, the procedure preserves $\frac{1}{2}\varepsilon$-optimality of the pseudoflow throughout and, at termination, yields a $\frac{1}{2}\varepsilon$-optimal flow. $\square$

We next analyze the complexity of the IMPROVE-APPROXIMATION procedure. We will show that the complexity of the generic version is $O(n^2 m)$ and then describe a specialized version running in time $O(n^3)$. These time bounds are comparable to those of the preflow–push algorithms for the maximum flow problem.

Lemma 5.5. *No node potential increases more than 3n times during an execution of the* IMPROVE-APPROXIMATION *procedure.*

Proof. Let x be the current $\frac{1}{2}\varepsilon$-optimal pseudoflow and x' be the ε-optimal flow at the end of the previous cost scaling phase. Let π and π' be the node potentials corresponding to the pseudoflow x and the flow x' respectively. It is possible to show, using a variation of the flow decomposition properties discussed in Section 2.1, that for every node v with positive imbalance in x there exists a node w with negative imbalance in x and a path P satisfying the properties that (i) P is an augmenting path with respect to x, and (ii) its reversal $\bar{P}$ is an augmenting path with respect to x'. This fact in terms of the residual network implies that there exists a sequence of nodes $v = v_0, v_1, \ldots,$ $v_l = w$ with the property that $P = v_0 = v_1 - \cdots - v_l$ is a path in $G(x)$ and its reversal $\bar{P} = v_l - v_{l-1} - \cdots - v_1$ is a path in $G(x')$. Applying the $\frac{1}{2}\varepsilon$-optimality conditions to arcs on the path P in $G(x)$, we obtain $\sum_{(i,j)\in P} \bar{c}_{ij} \geq -l(\frac{1}{2}\varepsilon)$. Alternatively,

$$\pi(v) \leq \pi(w) + l(\tfrac{1}{2}\varepsilon) + \sum_{(i,j)\in P} c_{ij} . \tag{5.16}$$

Applying the ε-optimality conditions to arcs on the path $\bar{P}$ in $G(x')$, we obtain

$$\pi'(w) \leq \pi'(v) + l\varepsilon + \sum_{(j,i)\in \bar{P}} c_{ji} = \pi'(v) + l\varepsilon - \sum_{(i,j)\in P} c_{ij} . \tag{5.17}$$

Combining (5.16) and (5.17) gives

$$\pi(v) \leq \pi'(v) + (\pi(w) - \pi'(w)) + \tfrac{3}{2}l\varepsilon .$$

Now we use the facts that (i) $\pi(w) = \pi'(w)$ (the potential of a node with a negative imbalance does not change because the algorithm never selects it for push/relabel), (ii) $l \leq n$, and (iii) each increase in potential increases $\pi(v)$ by at least $\frac{1}{2}\varepsilon$ units. The lemma is now immediate. $\square$

Lemma 5.6. *The* IMPROVE-APPROXIMATION *procedure performs* $O(nm)$ *saturating pushes.*

Proof. This proof is similar to that of Lemma 4.5 and essentially amounts to showing that between two consecutive saturations of an arc (i, j), the potentials of both the nodes i and j increase at least once. Since any node potential increases $O(n)$ times, the algorithm also saturates any arc $O(n)$ times, resulting in $O(nm)$ total saturating pushes. $\square$

To bound the number of nonsaturating pushes, we need one more result. We define the *admissible network* as the network consisting solely of admissible arcs. The following result is crucial to analyzing the complexity of the cost scaling algorithms.

Lemma 5.7. *The admissible network is acyclic throughout the cost scaling algorithm.*

Proof. We establish this result by an induction argument applied to the number of pushes and relabels. The result is true at the beginning of each cost scaling phase because the pseudoflow is 0-optimal and the network contains no admissible arc. We always push flow on an arc (i, j) with $\bar{c}_{ij} < 0$; hence, if the algorithm adds its reversal (j, i) to the residual network, then $\bar{c}_{ji} > 0$. Thus pushes do not create new admissible arcs and preserve the inductive hypothesis. A relabel operation at node i may create new admissible arcs (i, j), but it also deletes all admissible arcs (k, i). The latter result is true because for any arc (k, i), $\bar{c}_{ki} \geqslant -\frac{1}{2}\varepsilon$ before a relabel operation, and $\bar{c}_{ki} \geqslant 0$ after the relabel operation, since the relabel operation increases $\pi(i)$ by at least $\frac{1}{2}\varepsilon$ units. Therefore the algorithm can create no directed cycles. $\square$

Lemma 5.8. *The* IMPROVE-APPROXIMATION *procedure performs* $O(n^2m)$ *non-saturating pushes.*

Proof (Sketch). Let $g(i)$ be the number of nodes that are reachable from node i in the admissible network and let the potential function $F = \Sigma_{i \text{ active}} \, g(i)$. The proof amounts to showing that a relabel operation or a saturating push can increase F by at most n units and each nonsaturating push decreases F by at least 1 unit. Since the algorithm performs at most $3n^2$ relabel operations and $O(nm)$ saturating pushes, by Lemmas 5.5 and 5.6, these observations yield a bound of $O(n^2m)$ on the number of nonsaturating pushes. $\square$

As in the maximum flow algorithm, the bottleneck operation in the IMPROVE-APPROXIMATION procedure is the nonsaturating pushes, which takes $O(n^2m)$ time. The algorithm takes $O(nm)$ time to perform saturating pushes, and the same time to scan arcs while identifying admissible arcs. Since the cost scaling algorithm calls IMPROVE-APPROXIMATION $1 + \lceil \log nC \rceil$ times, we obtain the following result.

Theorem 5.5. *The generic cost scaling algorithm runs in* $O(n^2m \log nC)$ *time.* $\square$

The cost scaling algorithm illustrates an important connection between the maximum flow and the minimum cost flow problems. Solving an IMPROVE-APPROXIMATION problem is very similar to solving a maximum flow problem. Just as in the generic preflow–push algorithm for the maximum flow problem, the bottleneck operation is the number of nonsaturating pushes. Researchers have suggested improvements based on examining nodes in some specific order, or using clever data structures. We describe one such improvement, called the *wave algorithm*.

The wave algorithm is the same as the IMPROVE-APPROXIMATION procedure, but it selects active nodes for the push/relabel step in a specific order. The algorithm uses the acyclicity of the admissible network. As is well known, nodes of an acyclic network can be ordered so that for each arc (i, j) in the network, $i < j$. It is possible to determine this ordering, called a *topological ordering* of nodes, in $O(m)$ time. Observe that pushes do not change the admissible network since they do not create new admissible arcs. The relabel operations, however, may create new admissible arcs and consequently may affect the topological ordering of nodes.

The wave algorithm examines each node in the topological order and if the node is active, then it performs a push/relabel step. When examined in this order, active nodes push flow to higher numbered nodes, which in turn push flow to even higher numbered nodes, and so on. A relabel operation changes the numbering of nodes and the topological order, and thus the method again starts to examine the nodes according to the topological order. However, if within n consecutive node examinations, the algorithm performs no relabel operation, then all active nodes have discharged their excesses and the algorithm obtains a flow. Since the algorithm requires $O(n^2)$ relabel operations, we immediately obtain a bound of $O(n^3)$ on the number of node examinations. Each node examination entails at most one nonsaturating push. Consequently, the wave algorithm performs $O(n^3)$ nonsaturating pushes per IMPROVE-APROXIMATION.

We now describe a procedure for obtaining a topological order of nodes after each relabel operation. An initial topological ordering is determined using an $O(m)$ algorithm. Suppose that while examining node i, the algorithm relabels it. Note that after the relabel operation at node i, the network contains no incoming admissible arc at node i (see the proof of Lemma 5.7). We then move node i from its present position in the topological order to the first position. Notice that this altered ordering is a topological ordering of the new admissible network. This result follows from the fact (i) node i has no incoming admissible arc; (ii) for each outgoing admissible arc (i, j), node i precedes node j in the order; and (iii) the rest of the admissible network does not change and so the previous order is still valid. Thus the algorithm maintains an ordered set of nodes (possibly as a doubly linked list) and examines nodes in this order. Whenever it relabels a node i, the algorithm moves it to the first place in the order and again examines nodes in the order starting at node i.

We have established the following result.

Theorem 5.6. *The cost scaling approach using the wave algorithm as a subroutine solves the minimum cost flow problem in* $O(n^3 \log nC)$ *time.* $\square$

5.9. Double scaling algorithm

The double scaling approach combines ideas from both the RHS-scaling and cost scaling algorithms and obtains an improvement not obtained by either algorithm alone. For the sake of simplicity, we shall describe the double scaling algorithm on the uncapacitated transportation network $G = (N_1 \cup N_2, A)$, with N_1 and N_2 as the sets of supply and demand nodes respectively. A capacitated minimum cost flow problem can be solved by first transforming the problem into an uncapacitated transportation problem (as described in Section 2.4) and then applying the double scaling algorithm.

The double scaling algorithm is the same as the cost scaling algorithm discussed in the previous section except that it uses a more efficient version of the Improve-Approximation procedure. The IMPROVE-APPROXIMATION procedure in the previous section relied on a 'pseudoflow-push' method. A natural alternative would be to try an augmenting path based method. This approach would send flow from a node with excess to a node with deficit over an *admissible path*, i.e., a path in which each arc is admissible. A natural implementation of this approach would result in $O(nm)$ augmentations since each augmentation would saturate at least one arc and, by Lemma 5.6, the algorithm requires $O(nm)$ arc saturations. Thus, this approach does not seem to improve the $O(n^2m)$ bound of the generic IMPROVE-APPROXIMATION procedure.

We can, however, use ideas from the RHS-scaling algorithm to reduce the number of augmentations to $O(n \log U)$ for an uncapacitated problem by ensuring that each augmentation carries *sufficiently large* flow. This approach gives us an algorithm that does cost scaling in the outer loop and within each cost scaling phase performs a number of RHS-scaling phases; hence, this algorithm is called the *double scaling algorithm*. The advantage of the double scaling algorithm, contrasted with solving a shortest path problem in the RHS-scaling algorithm, is that the double scaling algorithm identifies an augmenting path in $O(n)$ time on average over a sequence of n augmentations. In fact, the double scaling algorithm appears to be similar to the shortest augmenting path algorithm for the maximum flow problem; this algorithm also requires $O(n)$ time on average to find each augmenting path. The double scaling algorithm uses the following IMPROVE-APPROXIMATION procedure.

procedure IMPROVE-APPROXIMATION-II(ε, x, π);
begin
    set $x := 0$ and compute node imbalances;
    $\pi(j) := \pi(j) + \varepsilon$, for all $j \in N_2$;
    $\Delta := 2^{\lceil \log U \rceil}$;
    while the network contains an active node **do**
    begin
        $S(\Delta) := \{i \in N_1 \cup N_2 : e(i) \geq \Delta\}$;
        while $S(\Delta) \neq \emptyset$ **do**
        begin (RHS-scaling phase)
            select a node k in $S(\Delta)$ and delete it from $S(\Delta)$;
            determine an admissible path P from node k to some node l
                with $e(l) < 0$;
            augment Δ units of flow on P and update x;
        end;
        $\Delta := \Delta/2$;
    end;
end;

We shall describe a method to determine admissible paths after first commenting on the correctness of this procedure. First, observe that $\bar{c}_{ij} \geq -\varepsilon$ for all $(i, j) \in A$ at the beginning of the procedure and, by adding ε to $\pi(j)$ for each $j \in N_2$, we obtain an $\frac{1}{2}\varepsilon$-optimal (in fact, a 0-optimal) pseudoflow. The procedure always augments flow on admissible arcs and, from Lemma 5.4, this choice preserves the $\frac{1}{2}\varepsilon$-optimality of the pseudoflow. Thus, at the termination of the procedure, we obtain an $\frac{1}{2}$-optimal flow. Further, as in the RHS-scaling algorithm, the procedure maintains the invariant property that all residual capacities are integer multiples of Δ and thus each augmentation can carry Δ units of flow.

The algorithm identifies an admissible path by gradually building the path. We maintain a *partial* admissible path P using a *predecessor index*, i.e., if $(u, v) \in P$ then $\mathrm{pred}(v) = u$. At any point in the algorithm, we perform one of the following two steps, whichever is applicable, at the last node of P, say node i, terminating when the last node has a deficit.

advance(i). If the residual network contains an admissible arc (i, j), then add (i, j) to P. If $e(j) < 0$, then stop.

retreat(i). If the residual network does not contain an admissible arc (i, j), then update $\pi(i)$ to $\pi(i) + \frac{1}{2}\varepsilon + \min\{\bar{c}_{ij} : (i, j) \in A(i)$ and $r_{ij} > 0\}$. If P has at least one arc, then delete $(\mathrm{pred}(i), i)$ from P.

The retreat step relabels (increases the potential of) node i for the purpose of creating new admissible arcs emanating from this node; in the process, the arc $(\mathrm{pred}(i), i)$ becomes inadmissible. Hence, we delete this arc from P. The proof of Lemma 5.4 implies that increasing the node potential maintains $\frac{1}{2}\varepsilon$-optimality of the pseudoflow.

We next consider the complexity of this implementation of the IMPROVE-APPROXIMATION procedure. Each execution of the procedure performs $1 + \lceil \log U \rceil$ RHS-scaling phases. At the beginning of the Δ-scaling phase, $S(2\Delta) = \emptyset$, i.e., $\Delta \leq e(i) < 2\Delta$ for each node $i \in S(\Delta)$. During the scaling phase, the algorithm augments Δ units of flow from a node k in $S(\Delta)$ to a node l with $e(l) < 0$. This operation reduces the excess at node k to a value less than Δ and ensures that the excess at node l, if there is any, is less than Δ. Consequently, each augmentation deletes a node from $S(\Delta)$ and after at most n augmentations, the method begins a new scaling phase. The algorithm thus performs a total of $O(n \log U)$ augmentations.

We next count the number of advance steps. Each advance step adds an arc to the partial admissible path, and a retreat step deletes an arc from the partial admissible path. Thus, there are two types of advance steps: (i) those that add arcs to an admissible path on which the algorithm later performs an augmentation; and (ii) those that are later cancelled by a retreat step. Since the set of admissible arcs is acyclic (by Lemma 5.7), after at most n advance steps of the first type, the algorithm will discover an admissible path and will perform an augmentation. Since the algorithm requires a total of $O(n \log U)$ augmentations, the number of the first type of advance steps is at most $O(n^2 \log U)$. The algorithm performs at most $O(n^2)$ advance steps of the second type because each retreat step increases a node potential, and by Lemma 5.5, node potentials increase $O(n^2)$ times. The total number of advance steps, therefore, is $O(n^2 \log U)$.

The amount of time needed to identify admissible arcs is $O(\Sigma_{i=1}^{n} |A(i)| n) = O(nm)$, since between a potential increase of a node i, the algorithm will examine $|A(i)|$ arcs for testing admissibility. We have therefore established the following result.

Theorem 5.7. *The double scaling algorithm solves the uncapacitated transportation problem in* $O((nm + n^2 \log U) \log nC)$ *time.* □

To solve the capacitated minimum cost flow problem, we first transform it into an uncapacitated transportation problem and then apply the double scaling algorithm. We leave it as an exercise for the reader to show that how the transformation permits us to use the double scaling algorithm to solve the capacitated minimum cost flow problem in $O(nm \log U \log nC)$ time. The references describe further modest improvements of the algorithm. For problems that satisfy the similarity assumption, a variant of this algorithm using more sophisticated data structures is currently the fastest polynomial-time algorithm for most classes of the minimum cost flow problem.

5.10. Sensitivity analysis

The purpose of sensitivity analysis is to determine changes in the optimum solution of a minimum cost flow problem resulting from changes in the data (supply/demand vector, capacity or cost of any arc). Traditionally, researchers and practioners have conducted this sensitivity analysis using the primal simplex or dual simplex algorithms. There is, however, a conceptual drawback to this approach. The simplex based approach maintains a basis tree at every iteration and conducts sensitivity analysis by determining changes in the basis tree precipitated by changes in the data. The basis in the simplex algorithm is often degenerate, though, and consequently changes in the basis tree do not necessarily translate into the changes in the solution. Therefore, the simplex based approach does not give information about the changes in the solution as the data changes; instead, it tells us about the changes in the *basis tree*.

We present another approach for performing sensitivity analysis. This approach does not share the drawback we have just mentioned. For simplicity, we limit our discussion to a unit change of only a particular type. In a sense, however, this discussion is quite general: it is possible to reduce more complex changes to a sequence of the simple changes we consider. We show that the sensitivity analysis for the minimum cost flow problem essentially reduces to solving shortest path or maximum flow problems.

Let x^* denote an optimum solution of a minimum cost flow problem. Let π^* be the corresponding node potentials and $\bar{c}_{ij} = c_{ij} - \pi^*(i) + \pi^*(j)$ denote the reduced costs. Further, let $d(k, l)$ denote the shortest distance from node k to node l in the residual network with respect to the original arc lengths c_{ij}. Since for any directed path P from node k to node l, $\Sigma_{(i,j) \in P} \bar{c}_{ij} = \Sigma_{(i,j) \in P} c_{ij} - \pi(k) + \pi(l)$, $d(k, l)$ equals the shortest distance from node k to node l with respect to the arc lengths $\bar{c}_{ij}$ plus $\pi^*(k) - \pi^*(l)$. At optimality, the reduced costs $\bar{c}_{ij}$ of all arcs in the residual network are nonnegative. Hence, we can compute $d(k, l)$ for all pairs of nodes k and l by solving n single-source shortest path problems with nonnegative arc lengths.

Supply/demand sensitivity analysis

We first study the change in the supply/demand vector. Suppose that the supply/demand of a node k becomes $b(k) + 1$ and the supply/demand of another node l becomes $b(l) - 1$. (Recall from Section 1.1 that feasibility of the minimum cost flow problem dictates that $\Sigma_{i \in N} b(i) = 0$; hence, we must change the supply/demand values of two nodes by equal magnitudes, and must increase one value and decrease the other.) Then x^* is a pseudoflow for the modified problem; moreover, this vector satisfies the dual feasibility conditions C5.6. Augmenting one unit of flow from node k to node l along the shortest path in the residual network $G(x^*)$ converts this pseudoflow into a flow. This augmentation changes the objective function value by $d(k, l)$ units. Lemma 5.1 implies that this flow is optimum for the modified minimum cost flow problem.

Arc capacity sensitivity analysis

We next consider a change in an arc capacity. Suppose that the capacity of an arc (p, q) increases by one unit. The flow x^* is feasible for the modified problem. In addition, if $\bar{c}_{pq} \geq 0$, it satisfies the optimality conditions C5.2–C5.4; hence, it is an optimum flow for the modified problem. If $\bar{c}_{pq} < 0$, then condition C5.4 dictates that flow on the arc must equal its capacity. We satisfy this requirement by increasing the flow on the arc (p, q) by one unit, which produces a pseudoflow with an excess of one unit at node q and a deficit of one unit at node p. We convert the pseudoflow into a flow by augmenting one unit of flow from node q to node p along the shortest path in the residual network, which changes the objective function value by an amount $c_{pq} + d(q, p)$. This flow is optimum from our observations concerning supply/demand sensitivity analysis.

When the capacity of the arc (p, q) decreases by one unit and flow on the arc is strictly less than its capacity, then x^* remains feasible, and hence optimum, for the modified problem. However, if the flow on the arc is at its capacity, we decrease the flow by one unit and augment one unit of flow from node p to node q along the shortest path in the residual network. This augmentation changes the objective function value by an amount $-c_{pq} + d(p, q)$.

The preceding discussion shows how to determine changes in the optimum solution value due to unit changes of any two supply/demand values or a unit change in any arc capacity by solving n single-source shortest path problems. We can, however, obtain useful upper bounds on these changes by solving only two shortest path problems. This observation uses the fact that $d(k, l) \le d(k, 1) + d(1, l)$ for all pairs of nodes k and l. Consequently, we need to determine shortest path distances from node 1 to all other nodes, and from all other nodes to node 1 to compute upper bounds on all $d(k, l)$. Recent empirical studies have suggested that these upper bounds are very close to the actual values; often these upper bounds and the actual values are equal, and usually they are within 5% of each other.

Cost sensitivity analysis

Finally, we discuss changes in arc costs, which we assume are integral. Suppose that a cost of an arc (p, q) increases by one unit. This change increases the reduced cost of arc (p, q) by one unit as well. If $\bar{c}_{pq} < 0$ before the change, then after the change $\bar{c}'_{pq} \le 0$. Similarly, if $\bar{c}_{pq} > 0$, before the change, then $\bar{c}'_{pq} \ge 0$ after the change. In both cases, we preserve the optimality conditions. However, if $\bar{c}_{pq} = 0$ before the change and $x_{pq} > 0$, then after the change $\bar{c}_{pq} = 1 > 0$ and the solution violates the condition C5.2. To satisfy the optimality condition of the arc, we must either reduce the flow on arc (p, q) to zero, or change the potentials so that the reduced cost of arc (p, q) becomes zero.

We first try to reroute the flow x^*_{pq} from node p to node q without violating any of the optimality conditions. We do so by solving a maximum flow problem defined as follows: (i) the flow on the arc (p, q) is set to zero, thus creating an excess of x^*_{pq} at node p and a deficit of x^*_{pq} at node q; (ii) define node p as the source node and node q as the sink node; and (iii) send a maximum of x^*_{pq} units from the source to the sink. We permit the maximum flow algorithm, however, to change flows only on arcs with zero reduced costs, since otherwise it may generate a solution that violates C5.2 and C5.4. Let v° denote the flow sent from node p to node q and x° denote the resulting arc flow. If $v^\circ = x^*_{pq}$, then x° denotes a minimum cost flow of the modified problem. In this case, the optimal objective function values of the original and modified problems are the same.

On the other hand, if $v^\circ < x^*_{pq}$ then the maximum flow algorithm yields an s–t cutset $(X, N - X)$ with the properties that $p \in X$, $q \in N - X$, and every forward arc in the cutset with zero reduced cost is capacitated and every backward arc in the cutset with zero reduced cost has zero flow. We then decrease the node potential of every node in $N - X$ by one unit. It is easy to verify by case analysis that this change in node potentials maintains the optimality conditions and, futhermore, decreases the reduced cost of arc (p, q) to zero. Consequently, we can set the flow on arc (p, q) equal to $x^*_{pq} - v^\circ$ and obtain a feasible minimum cost flow. In this case, the objective function value of the modified problem is $x^*_{pq} - v^\circ$ units more than that of the original problem.

5.11. Assignment problem

The *assignment problem* is one of the best-known and most intensively studied special cases of the minimum cost network flow problem. As already indicated in Section 1.1, this problem is defined by a set N_1, say of persons, a set N_2, say of objects ($|N_1| = |N_2| = n$), a collection of node pairs $A \subseteq N_1 \times N_2$ representing possible person-to-object assignments, and a cost c_{ij} (possibly negative) associated with each element (i, j) in A. The objective is to assign each person to one object, choosing the assignment with minimum possible cost. The problem can be formulated as the following linear program:

$$\text{minimize} \quad \sum_{(i,j) \in A} c_{ij} x_{ij} \tag{5.18a}$$

subject to

$$\sum_{\{j: (i,j) \in A\}} x_{ij} = 1, \quad \text{for all } i \in N_1, \tag{5.18b}$$

$$\sum_{\{i: (i,j) \in A\}} x_{ij} = 1, \quad \text{for all } j \in N_2, \tag{5.18c}$$

$$x_{ij} \geq 0, \quad \text{for all } (i, j) \in A. \tag{5.18d}$$

The assignment problem is a minimum cost flow problem defined on a network G with node set $N = N_1 \cup N_2$, arc set A, arc costs c_{ij}, and supply/demand specified as $b(i) = 1$ if $i \in N_1$ and $b(i) = -1$ if $i \in N_2$. The network G has $2n$ nodes and $m = |A|$ arcs. The assignment problem is also known as the *weighted bipartite matching problem*.

We use the following notation. A 0–1 solution x of (5.18) is an *assignment*. If $x_{ij} = 1$, then i is *assigned to* j and j is *assigned to* i. A 0–1 solution x satisfying

$$\sum_{\{j: (i,j) \in A\}} x_{ij} \leq 1 \quad \text{for all } i \in N_1$$

and

$$\sum_{\{i: (i,j) \in A\}} x_{ij} \leq 1 \quad \text{for all } j \in N_2$$

is called a *partial assignment*. Associated with any partial assignment x is an index set X defined as $X = \{(i, j) \in A: x_{ij} = 1\}$. A node not assigned to any other node is *unassigned*.

Researchers have suggested numerous algorithms for solving the assignment problem. Several of these algorithms apply, either explicitly or implicitly, the successive shortest path algorithm for the minimum cost flow problem. These algorithms typically select the initial node potentials with the following values: $\pi(i) = 0$ for all $i \in N_1$ and $\pi(j) = \min\{c_{ij}: (i, j) \in A\}$ for all $j \in N_2$. All reduced costs defined by these node potentials are nonnegative. The successive shortest path algorithm solves the assignment problem as a sequence of n shortest path problems with nonnegative arc lengths, and consequently runs in $O(n\,S(n, m, C))$ time. (Note that $S(n, m, C)$ is the time required to solve a shortest path problem with nonnegative arc lengths.)

The relaxation approach is another popular approach, which is also closely related to the successive shortest path algorithm. The relaxation algorithm removes, or relaxes, the constraint (5.18c), thus allowing any object to be assigned to more than one person. This relaxed problem is easy to solve: assign each person i to an object j with the smallest c_{ij} value. As a result, some objects may be unassigned and other objects may be overassigned. The algorithm gradually builds a feasible assignment by identifying shortest paths from overassigned objects to unassigned objects and augmenting flows on these paths. The algorithm solves at most n shortest path problems. Because this approach always maintains the optimality conditions, it can solve the shortest path problem by implementations of Dijkstra's algorithm. Consequently, this algorithm also runs in $O(n\,S(n, m, C))$ time.

One well known solution procedure for the assignment problem, the *Hungarian method*, is essentially the primal–dual variant of the successive shortest path algorithm. The network simplex algorithm, with provisions for maintaining a strongly feasible basis, is another solution procedure for the assignment problem. This approach is fairly efficient in practice; moreover, some implementations of it provide polynomial time bounds. For problems that satisfy the similarity assumption, however, a cost scaling algorithm provides the best-known time bound for the assignment problem. Since these algorithms are special cases of other algorithms we have described earlier, we will not specify their details. Rather, in this section, we will discuss a different type of algorithm based upon the notion of an *auction*. Before doing so, we show another intimate connection between the assignment problem and the shortest path problem.

Assignments and shortest paths

We have seen that by solving a sequence of shortest path problems, we can solve any assignment problem. Interestingly, we can also use any algorithm for the assignment problem to solve the shortest path problem with arbitrary arc lengths. To do so, we apply the assignment algorithm twice. The first application determines if the network contains a negative cycle; and, if it doesn't, the second application identifies a shortest path. Both the applications use the node splitting transformation described in Section 2.4.

The node splitting transformation replaces each node i by two nodes i' and i'', replaces each arc (i, j) by an arc (i, j'), and adds an (artificial) zero cost arc (i', i). We first note that the transformed network always has a feasible solution with zero cost: namely, the assignment containing all artificial arcs (i', i). We next show that the optimal value of the assignment problem is negative if and only if the original network has a negative cost cycle.

First, suppose the original network contains a negative cost cycle, $j_1 - j_2 - j_3 - \cdots - j_k - j_1$. Then the assignment $\{(j_1, j_2'), (j_2, j_3'), \ldots, (j_k, j_1'), (j_{k+1}', j_{k+1}), \ldots, (j_n', j_n)\}$ has a negative cost. Therefore, the cost of the optimal assignment must be negative. Conversely, suppose the cost of an optimal assignment is negative. This solution must contain at least one arc of the form (i, j') with $i \neq j$. Consequently, the assignment must contain a set of arcs of the form $PA = \{(j_1, j_2'), (j_2, j_3'), \ldots, (j_k, j_1')\}$. The cost of this 'partial' assignment is nonpositive, because it can be no more expensive than the partial assignment $\{(j_1', j_1), (j_2', j_2), \ldots, (j_k', j_k)\}$. Since the optimal assignment cost is negative, some partial assignment PA must be negative. But then by construction of the transformed network, the cycle $j_1 - j_2 - \cdots - j_k - j_1$ is a negative cost cycle in the original network.

If the original network contains no negative cost cycle, then we can obtain a shortest path between a specific pair of nodes, say from node 1 to node n, as follows. We consider the transformed network as described earlier and delete the nodes $1'$ and n and the arcs incident to these nodes. See Figure 5.3 for an example of this transformation. Now observe that each path from node 1 to node n in the original network has a corresponding assignment of the same cost in the transformed network, and the converse is also true. For example, the path 1-2-5 in Figure 5.3(a) has the corresponding assignment $\{(1, 2'), (2, 5'), (3', 3), (4', 4)\}$ in Figure 5.3(b), and an assignment $\{(1, 2'), (2, 4'), (4, 5'), (3', 3)\}$ in Figure 5.3(b) has the corresponding path 1-2-4-5 in Figure 5.3(a). Consequently, an optimum assignment in the transformed network gives a shortest path in the original network.

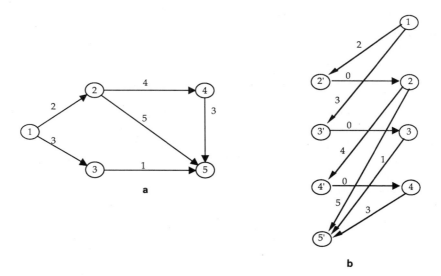

Fig. 5.3. (a) The original network. (b) The transformed network.

The auction algorithm

We now describe an algorithm for the assignment problem known as the *auction algorithm*. We first describe a pseudopolynomial time version of the algorithm and then incorporate scaling to make the algorithm polynomial time. This scaling algorithm is an instance of the bit-scaling algorithm described in Section 1.6. To describe the auction algorithm, we consider the maximization version of the assignment problem, since this version appears more natural for interpreting the algorithm.

Suppose n persons want to buy n cars that are to be sold by auction. Each person i is interested in a subset $A(i)$ of cars, and has a nonnegative utility u_{ij} for car j for each $(i, j) \in A(i)$. The objective is to find an assigment with maximum utility. We can set $c_{ij} = -u_{ij}$ to reduce this problem to (5.18). Let $C = \max\{|u_{ij}|: (i, j) \in A\}$. At each stage of the algorithm, there is an asking price for car j, represented by price(j). For a given set of asking prices, the *marginal utility of* person i for buying car j is $u_{ij} - $ price(j). At each iteration, an unassigned person bids on a car that has the highest marginal utility for that person. We assume that all utilities and prices are measured in dollars.

We associate with each person i a number value(i), which is an upper bound on that person's highest marginal utility, i.e., value(i) $\geqslant \max\{u_{ij} - $ price(j): $(i, j) \in A(i)\}$. We call a bid (i, j) *admissible* if value(i) $= u_{ij} - $ price(j) and *inadmissible* otherwise. The algorithm requires every bid in the auction to be admissible. If person i is next in turn to bid and has no admissible bid, then value(i) is too high and we decrease this value to $\max\{u_{ij} - $ price(j): $(i, j) \in A(i)\}$.

So the algorithm proceeds by persons bidding on cars. If a person i makes a bid on car j, then the price of car j goes up by \$1; therefore, subsequent bids are of higher value. Also, person i is assigned to car j. The person k who was the previous bidder for car j, if there was one, becomes unassigned. Subsequently, person k must bid on another car. As the auction proceeds, the prices of cars increase and hence the marginal values to the persons decrease. The auction stops when each person is assigned a car. We now describe this bidding procedure algorithmically. The procedure starts with some valid choices of value(i) and price(j). For example, we can set price(j) = 0 for each car j and value(i) = $\max\{u_{ij}: (i, j) \in A(i)\}$ for each person i. Although this initialization is sufficient for the pseudopolynomial time version, the polynomial time version requires a more clever initialization. At termination, the procedure yields an *almost* optimum assignment x°.

procedure BIDDING(u, x°, value, price);
begin
   let the initial assignment be a null assignment;
   while some person is unassigned **do**
   begin
      select an unassigned person i;
      if some bid (i, j) is admissible **then**

begin
    assign person i to car j;
    price(j) := price(j) + 1;
    if person k was already assigned to car j, **then**
        person k becomes unassigned;
  end
  else update value(i) := max$\{u_{ij} - $price($j$): $(i, j) \in A(i)\}$;
end;
  let x° be the current assignment;
end;

We now show that this procedure gives an assignment whose utility is within n of the optimum utility. Let x° denote a partial assignment at some point during the execution of the auction algorithm and x^* denote an optimum assignment. Recall that value(i) is always an upper bound on the highest marginal utility of person i, i.e., value(i) $\geq u_{ij} - $price($j$) for all $(i, j) \in A(i)$. Consequently,

$$\sum_{(i,j)\in x^*} u_{ij} \leq \sum_{i\in N_1} \text{value}(i) + \sum_{j\in N_2} \text{price}(j) . \tag{5.19}$$

The partial assignment x° also satisfies the condition

$$\text{value}(i) = u_{ij} - \text{price}(j) + 1 , \quad \text{for all } (i, j) \in x^\circ , \tag{5.20}$$

because at the time of bidding value $(i) = u_{ij} - $price($j$) and immediately after the bid, price(j) goes up by \$1. Let UB(x°) be defined as follows.

$$\text{UB}(x^\circ) = \sum_{(i,j)\in x^\circ} u_{ij} + \sum_{i\in N_1^\circ} \text{value}(i) , \tag{5.21}$$

with N_1° denoting the unassigned persons in N_1. Using (5.20) in (5.21) and observing that unassigned cars in N_2 have zero prices, we obtain

$$\text{UB}(x^\circ) \geq \sum_{i\in N_1} \text{value}(i) + \sum_{j\in N_2} \text{price}(j) - n . \tag{5.22}$$

Combining (5.19) and (5.22) yields

$$\text{UB}(x^\circ) \geq -n + \sum_{(i,j)\in x^*} u_{ij} . \tag{5.23}$$

As we show in our discussion to follow, the algorithm can change the node values and prices at most a finite number of times. Since the algorithm will either modify a node value or node price whenever x° is not an assignment, within a finite number of steps the method must terminate with a complete assignment x°. Then UB(x°) represents the utility of this assignment (since N_1^0

is empty). Hence, the utility of the assignment $x°$ is at most $\$n$ less than the maximum utility.

It is easy to modify the method, however, to obtain an optimum assignment. Suppose we multiply all utilities u_{ij} by $n + 1$ before applying the Bidding procedure. Since all utilities are now multiples of $n + 1$, two assignments with distinct total utility will differ by at least $n + 1$ units. The procedure yields an assignment that is within n units of the optimum value and, hence, must be optimal.

We next discuss the complexity of the Bidding procedure as applied to the assignment problem with all utilities multiplied by $n + 1$. In this modified problem the largest utility is $C' = (n + 1)C$. We first show that the value of any person decreases $O(nC')$ times. Since all utilities are nonnegative, (5.23) implies $\text{UB}(x°) \geq -n$. Substituting this inequality in (5.21) yields

$$\sum_{i \in N_1°} \text{value}(i) \geq -n(C' + 1) .$$

Since value(i) decreases by at least one unit each time it changes, this inequality shows that the value of any person decreases at most $O(nC')$ times. Since decreasing the value of a person i once takes $O(|A(i)|)$ time, the total time needed to update values of all persons is $O(\Sigma_{i \in N_1} n|A(i)|C') = O(nmC')$.

We next examine the number of iterations performed by the procedure. Each iteration either decreases the value of a person i or assigns the person to some car j. By our previous arguments, the values change $O(n^2C')$ times in total. Further, since value(i) $> u_{ij} - \text{price}(j)$ after person i has been assigned to car j and the price of car j increases by one unit, a person i can be assigned at most $|A(i)|$ times between two consecutive decreases in value(i). This observation gives us a bound of $O(nmC')$ on the total number of times all bidders become assigned. As can be shown, using the 'current arc' data structure permits us to locate admissible bids in $O(nmC')$ time. Since $C' = nC$, we have established the following result.

Theorem 5.8. *The auction algorithm solves the assignment problem in* $O(n^2mC)$ *time.* □

The auction algorithm is potentially very slow because it can increase prices (and thus decreases values) in small increments of $\$1$ and the final price can be as large as n^2C (the values as small as $-n^2C$). Using a scaling technique in the auction algorithm ensures that the prices and values do not change *too many* times. As in the *bit-scaling* technique described in Section 1.6, we decompose the original problem into a sequence of $O(\log nC)$ assignment problems and solve each problem by the auction algorithm. We use the optimum prices and values of a problem as a starting solution of the subsequent problem and show that the prices and values change only $O(n)$ times per scaling phase. Thus, we solve each problem in $O(nm)$ time and solve the original problem in $O(nm \log nC)$ time.

The scaling version of the auction algorithm first multiplies all utilities by $n + 1$ and then solves a sequence of $K = \lceil \log(n+1)C \rceil$ assignment problems $P_1, P_2, \ldots, P_K$. The problem P_k is an assignment problem in which the utility of arc (i, j) is the k leading bits in the binary representation of u_{ij}, assuming (by adding leading zeros if necessary) that each u_{ij} is K bits long. In other words, the problem P_k has the arc utilities $u_{ij}^k = \lfloor u_{ij}/2^{K-k} \rfloor$. Note that in the problem P_1, all utilities are 0 or 1, and subsequently $u_{ij}^{k+1} = 2u_{ij}^k + \{0 \text{ or } 1\}$, depending upon whether the newly added bit is 0 or 1. The scaling algorithm works as follows:

algorithm ASSIGNMENT;
begin
    multiply all u_{ij} by $(n + 1)$;
    $K := \lceil \log(n+1)C \rceil$;
    price(j) := 0 for each car j;
    value(i) := 0 for each person i;
    for $k := 1$ **to** K **do**
    begin
        let $u_{ij}^k := \lfloor u_{ij}/2^{K-k} \rfloor$ for each $(i, j) \in A$;
        price(j) := 2 price(j) for each car j;
        value(i) := 2 value(i) + 1 for each person i;
        BIDDING(u^k, x°, value, price);
    end;
end;

The assignment algorithm performs a number of cost scaling phases. In the k-th scaling phase, it obtains a near-optimum solution of the problem with the utilities u_{ij}^k. It is easy to verify that before the algorithm invokes the Bidding procedure, prices and values satisfy value(i) $\geq \max\{u_{ij} - \text{price}(j) : (i, j) \in A(i)\}$, for each person i. The Bidding procedure maintains these conditions throughout its execution. In the last scaling phase, the algorithm solves the assignment problem with the original utilities and obtains an optimum solution of the original problem. Observe that in each scaling phase, the algorithm starts with a null assignment; the purpose of each scaling phase is to obtain good prices and values for the subsequent scaling phase.

We next discuss the complexity of this assignment algorithm. The crucial result is that the prices and values change only $O(n)$ times during each execution of the Bidding procedure. We define the reduced utility of an arc (i, j) in the k-th scaling phase as

$$\bar{u}_{ij} = u_{ij}^k - \text{price}(j) - \text{value}(i) .$$

In this expression, price(j) and value(i) have the values computed just before calling the Bidding procedure. For any assignment x, we have

$$\sum_{(i,j)\in X} \bar{u}_{ij} = \sum_{(i,j)\in X} u_{ij}^{k} - \sum_{j\in N_2} \text{price}(j) - \sum_{i\in N_1} \text{value}(i) .$$

Consequently, for a given set of prices and values, the reduced utility of an assignment differs from the utility of that assignment by a constant amount. Therefore, an assignment that maximizes the reduced utility also maximizes the utility. Since $\text{value}(i) \geq u_{ij}^{k} - \text{price}(j)$ for each $(i, j) \in A$, we have

$$\bar{u}_{ij} \leq 0, \quad \text{for all } (i, j) \in A . \tag{5.24}$$

Now consider the reduced utilities of arcs in the assignment x^{k-1} (the final assignment at the end of the $(k-1)$-st scaling phase). The equality (5.20) implies that

$$u_{ij}^{k-1} - \text{price}'(j) - \text{value}'(i) = -1, \quad \text{for all } (i, j) \in x^{k-1}, \tag{5.25}$$

where $\text{price}'(j)$ and $\text{value}'(i)$ are the corresponding values at the end of the $(k-1)$-st scaling phase. Before calling the Bidding procedure, we set $\text{price}(j) = 2 \text{ price}'(j)$, $\text{value}(i) = 2 \text{ value}'(i) + 1$, and $u_{ij}^{k} = 2 u_{ij}^{k-1} + \{0 \text{ or } 1\}$. Substituting these relationships in (5.25), we find that the reduced utilities $\bar{u}_{ij}$ of arcs in x^{k-1} are either -2 or -3. Hence, the optimum reduced utility is at least $-3n$. If x° is some partial assignment in the k-th scaling phase, then (5.23) implies that $\text{UB}(x^{\circ}) \geq -4n$. Using this result and (5.24) in (5.21) yields

$$\sum_{i\in N_1^{\circ}} \text{value}(i) \geq -4n . \tag{5.26}$$

Hence, for any i, $\text{value}(i)$ decreases $O(n)$ times. Using this result in the proof of Theorem 5.7, we observe that the Bidding procedure would terminate in $O(nm)$ time. The assignment algorithm applies the Bidding procedure $O(\log nC)$ times and, consequently, runs in $O(nm \log nC)$ time. We summarize our discussion.

Theorem 5.9. *The scaling version of the auction algorithm solves the assignment problem in* $O(nm \log nC)$ *time.* $\square$

The scaling version of the auction algorithm can be further improved to run in $O(\sqrt{n}m \log nC)$ time. This improvement is based on the following implication of (5.26). If we prohibit person i from bidding if $\text{value}(i) \geq 4\sqrt{n}$, then by (5.26) the number of unassigned persons is at most $\sqrt{n}$. Hence, the algorithm takes $O(\sqrt{n}m)$ time to assign $n - \lceil\sqrt{n}\rceil$ persons and $O((n - \lceil\sqrt{n}\rceil)m)$ time to assign the remaining $\lceil\sqrt{n}\rceil$ persons. For example, if $n = 10\,000$, then the auction algorithm would assign the first 99% of the persons in 1% of the overall running time and would assign the remaining 1% of the persons in the remaining 99% of the time. We therefore terminate the execution of the auction algorithm when it has assigned all but $\lceil\sqrt{n}\rceil$ persons and use successive shortest path algorithms to assign these persons. It so happens that the shortest paths have length $O(n)$ and thus Dial's algorithm, as described in Section 3.2, will find these shortest paths in $O(m)$ time. This version of the auction algorithm solves a scaling phase in $O(\sqrt{n}m)$ time and its overall running time is $O(\sqrt{n}m \log nC)$. If we invoke the similarity assumption, then this version of the algorithm currently has the best known time bound for solving the assignment problem.

6. Reference notes

In this section, we present reference notes on topics covered in the text. This discussion has three objectives: (i) to review important theoretical contributions on each topic, (ii) to point out interrelationships among different algorithms, and (iii) to comment on the empirical aspects of the algorithms.

6.1. Introduction

The study of network flow models predates the development of linear programming techniques. The first studies in this problem domain, conducted by Kantorovich (1939), Hitchcock (1941), and Koopmans (1947), considered the transportation problem, a special case of the minimum cost flow problem. These studies provided some insight into the problem structure and yielded algorithmic approaches. Interest in network problems grew with the advent of the simplex algorithm by Dantzig in 1947. Dantzig (1951) specialized the simplex algorithm for the transportation problem. He noted the triangularity of the basis and integrality of the optimum solution. Orden (1956) generalized this work by specializing the simplex algorithm for the uncapacitated minimum cost flow problem. The network simplex algorithm for the capacitated minimum cost flow problem followed from the development of the bounded variable simplex method for linear programming by Dantzig (1955). The book by Dantzig (1962) contains a thorough description of these contributions along with historical perspectives.

During the 1950's, researchers began to exhibit increasing interest in the minimum cost flow problem as well as its special cases – the shortest path problem, the maximum flow problem and the assignment problem – mainly because of their important applications. Soon researchers developed special purpose algorithms to solve these problems. Dantzig, Ford and Fulkerson pioneered those efforts. Whereas Dantzig focused on the primal simplex based algorithms, Ford and Fulkerson developed primal–dual type combinatorial algorithms to solve these problems. Their book, Ford and Fulkerson (1962), presents a thorough discussion of the early research conducted by them and by others. It also covers the development of flow decomposition theory, which is credited to Ford and Fulkerson.

In the years following these groundbreaking works, network flow problems and their generalizations emerged as major research topics in operations research; this research is documented in thousands of papers and numerous text and reference books. In the following sections we shall be surveying many of these research papers. The following books summarize developments in the field and serve as a guide to the literature: Ford and Fulkerson (1962) (*Flows in Networks*), Berge and Ghouila-Houri (1962) (*Programming, Games and Transportation Networks*), Iri (1969) (*Network Flows, Transportation and Scheduling*), Hu (1969) (*Integer Programming and Network Flows*), Frank and Frisch (1971) (*Communication, Transmission and Transportation Networks*), Potts and Oliver (1972) (*Flows in Transportation Networks*), Christophides (1975) (*Graph Theory: An Algorithmic Approach*), Murty (1976) (*Linear and Combinatorial Programming*), Lawler (1976) (*Combinatorial Optimization: Networks and Matroids*), Bazaraa and Jarvis (1978) (*Linear Programming and Network Flows*), Minieka (1978) (*Optimization Algorithms for Networks and Graphs*), Kennington and Helgason (1980) (*Algorithms for Network Programming*), Jensen and Barnes (1980) (*Network Flow Programming*), Phillips and Garcia-Diaz (1981) (*Fundamentals of Network Analysis*), Swamy and Thulsiraman (1981) (*Graphs, Networks and Algorithms*), Papadimitriou and Steiglitz (1982) (*Combinatorial Optimization: Algorithms and Complexity*), Smith (1982) (*Network Optimization Practice*), Syslo, Deo, and Kowalik (1983) (*Discrete Optimization Algorithms*), Tarjan (1983) (*Data Structures and Network Algorithms*), Gondran and Minoux (1984) (*Graphs and Algorithms*), Rockafellar (1984) (*Network Flows and Monotropic Optimization*), and Derigs (1988) (*Programming in Networks and Graphs*). As an additional source of references, the reader might consult the bibliography on network optimization prepared by Golden and Magnanti (1977) and the extensive set of references on integer programming compiled by researchers at the University of Bonn (Kastning (1976), Hausman (1978), and Von Randow (1982, 1985)).

Since the applications of network flow models are so pervasive, no single source provides a comprehensive account of network flow models and their impact on practice. Several researchers have prepared general surveys of selected application areas. Notable among these is the paper by Glover and Klingman (1976) on the applications of minimum cost flow and generalized minimum cost flow problems. A number of books written in special problem domains also contain valuable insight about the range of applications of network flow models. Examples in this category are the paper by Bodin, Golden, Assad and Ball (1983) on vehicle routing and scheduling problems, books on communication networks by Bertsekas and Gallager (1987) and on transportation planning by Sheffi (1985), as well as a collection of survey articles on facility location edited by Francis and Mirchandani (1989). Golden (1988) has described the census rounding application given in Section 1.1.

General references on data structures serve as a useful backdrop for the algorithms presented in this chapter. The book by Aho, Hopcroft and Ullman (1974) is an excellent reference for simple data structures such as arrays, linked lists, doubly linked lists, queues, stacks, binary heaps and d-heaps. The book by Tarjan (1983) is another useful source of references for these topics as well as for more complex data structures such as dynamic trees.

We have mentioned the 'similarity assumption' throughout the chapter. Gabow (1985) coined this term in his paper on scaling algorithms for combinatorial optimization problems. This important paper, which presents scaling algorithms for several network problems, greatly helped in popularizing scaling techniques.

6.2. Shortest path problem

The shortest path problem and its generalizations have a voluminous research literature. As a guide to these results, we refer the reader to the extensive bibliographies compiled by Gallo, Pallattino, Ruggen and Starchi (1982) and Deo and Pang (1984). This section, which summarizes some of this literature, focuses on issues of computational complexity.

Label setting algorithms

The first label setting algorithm was suggested by Dijkstra (1959), and independently by Dantzig (1960) and Whiting and Hillier (1960). The original implementation of Dijkstra's algorithm runs in $O(n^2)$ time, which is the optimal running time for fully dense networks (those with $m = \Omega(n^2)$), since any algorithm must examine every arc. However, improved running times are possible for sparse networks. The Table 6.1 summarizes various implementations of Dijkstra's algorithm designed to improve the running time in the worst case or in practice. In the table, $d = \lceil 2 + m/n \rceil$ represents the average degree of a node in the network plus 2.

Computer scientists have tried to improve the worst-case complexity of Dijkstra's algorithm by using better data structures. When implemented with a

Table 6.1
Running times of label setting shortest path algorithms

#	Discoverers	Running time
1	Dijkstra (1959)	$O(n^2)$
2	Williams (1964)	$O(m \log n)$
3	Dial (1969), Wagner (1976)	$O(m + nC)$
4	Johnson (1977a)	$O(m \log_d n)$
5	Johnson (1977b)	$O((m + n \log C) \log \log C)$
6	Emde Boas, Kaas and Zijlstra (1977)	$O(nC + m \log \log nC)$
7	Denardo and Fox (1979)	$O(m \log \log C + n \log C)$
8	Johnson (1982)	$O(m \log \log C)$
9	Fredman and Tarjan (1984)	$O(m + n \log n)$
10	Gabow (1985)	$O(m \log_d C)$
11	Ahuja, Mehlhorn, Orlin and Tarjan (1988)	(a) $O(m + n \log C)$ (b) $O\left(m + \dfrac{n \log C}{\log \log C}\right)$ (c) $O(m + n\sqrt{\log C})$

binary heap data structure, Dijkstra's algorithm requires only $O(\log n)$ time for each node selection (and subsequent deletion) step and each distance update; consequently, this implementation runs in $O(m \log n)$ time. For sparse networks, this time is better than $O(n^2)$, but it is worse for dense networks. The *d-heap* data structure suggested by Johnson (1977a) takes $O(\log_d n)$ time for each node selection (and subsequent deletion) step and $O(\log_d n)$ for each distance update. For $d = \lceil 2 + m/n \rceil$, this approach leads to a time bound of $O(m \log_d n)$, which for very sparse networks (those with $m = O(n)$), reduces to $O(n \log n)$ and for very dense networks (those with $m = \Omega(n^2)$), becomes $O(n^2)$. For all other ranges of densities as well, the running time of this implementation is better than that of either the original implementation or the binary-heap implementation of Dijkstra's algorithm.

For problems that satisfy the similarity assumption, Gabow's (1985) scaling algorithm achieves the same time bound as Johnson (1977a). Gabow's approach decomposes the original problem into $\lceil \log_d C \rceil$ scaled problems and solves each problem in $O(m)$ time by Dial's algorithm, thus yielding an $O(m \log_d C)$ algorithm for the shortest path problem.

Emde Boas, Kaas and Zijlstra (1977) suggested a data structure whose analysis depends upon the largest key D stored in a heap. The initialization of this algorithm takes $O(D)$ time and each heap operation takes $O(\log \log D)$. When Dijkstra's algorithm is implemented using this data structure, it runs in $O(nC + m \log \log nC)$ time. Johnson (1982) suggested an improvement of this data structure and used it to implement Dijkstra's algorithm in $O(m \log \log C)$ time.

The best strongly polynomial-time algorithm to date is due to Fredman and Tarjan (1984) who use a *Fibonacci heap* data structure. The Fibonacci heap is an ingenious, but somewhat complex, data structure that takes an average of $O(\log n)$ time for each node selection (and subsequent deletion) step and an average of $O(1)$ time for each distance update. Consequently, this data structure implements Dijkstra's algorithm in $O(m + n \log n)$ time.

Dial (1969) suggested his implementation of Dijkstra's algorithm because of its encouraging empirical performance. This algorithm was independently discovered by Wagner (1976). Dial, Glover, Karney and Klingman (1979) proposed an improved version of Dial's algorithm that runs better in practice. Though Dial's algorithm is only pseudopolynomial-time, it has led to algorithms with better worst-case behavior. Denardo and Fox (1979) suggest several such improvements. Observe that if $w = \max[1, \min\{c_{ij} : (i, j) \in A\}]$, then using buckets of width w in Dial's algorithm reduces the number of buckets from $1 + C$ to $1 + (C/w)$. The correctness of this observation follows from the fact that if d^* is the current minimum temporary distance label, then the algorithm will modify no other temporary distance label in the range $[d^*, d^* + w - 1]$, since each arc has length at least $w - 1$. Using a multiple level bucket scheme, Denardo and Fox implemented the shortest path algorithm in $O(\max\{kC^{1/k}, m \log(k + 1), nk(1 + C^{1/k}/w)\})$ time for any choice of k; choosing $k = \log C$ yields a time bound of $O(m \log \log C + n \log C)$. Depending on

n, m and C, other choices might lead to a modestly better time bound.

Johnson (1977b) proposed a related bucket scheme with exponentially growing widths and obtained a running time of $O((m + n \log C)\log \log C)$. This data structure is the same as the R-heap data structure described in Section 3.3, except that it performs binary search over $O(\log C)$ buckets to insert nodes into buckets during the redistribution of ranges and the distance updates.

The R-heap implementation suggested by Ahuja, Mehlhorn, Orlin and Tarjan (1988) replaces the binary search by a sequential search and improves the running time by a factor of $O(\log \log C)$. The R-heap implementation described in Section 3.3 uses a single level bucket system. A two-level bucket system improves further on the R-heap implementation of Dijkstra's algorithm. The two-level data structure consists of K (big) buckets, each bucket being further subdivided into L (small) *subbuckets*. During redistribution, the two-level bucket system redistributes the range of a subbucket over all of its previous buckets. This approach permits the selection of much larger width of buckets, thus reducing the number of buckets. By using $K = L = 2 \log C/\log \log C$, this two-level bucket system version of Dijkstra's algorithm runs in $O(m + n \log C/\log \log C)$ time. Incorporating a generalization of the Fibonacci heap data structure in the two-level bucket system with appropriate choices of K and L further reduces the time bound to $O(m + n\sqrt{\log C})$. If we invoke the similarity assumption, this approach currently gives the fastest worst-case implementation of Dijkstra's algorithm for all classes of graphs except very sparse ones, for which the algorithm of Johnson (1982) appears more attractive. The Fibonacci heap version of the two-level R-heap is very complex, however, and is unlikely to perform well in practice.

Label correcting algorithms

Ford (1956) the first label correcting algorithm for the shortest path problem. Subsequently, several other researchers – Ford and Fulkerson (1962) and Moore (1957) – studied the theoretical properties of the algorithm. Bellman's (1958) algorithm can also be regarded as a label correcting algorithm. Though specific implementations of label correcting algorithms run in $O(nm)$ time, the most general form is nonpolynomial-time, as shown by Edmonds (1970).

Researchers have exploited the flexibility inherent in the generic label correcting algorithm to obtain algorithms that are very efficient in practice. A modification that adds a node to the LIST (see the description of the Modified Label Correcting Algorithm given in Section 3.4) at the front if the algorithm has previously examined the node earlier and at the end otherwise, is probably the most popular. This modification was conveyed to Pollack and Wiebenson (1960) by D'Esopo, and later refined and tested by Pape (1974). We shall refer to this algorithm as D'Esopo and Pape's algorithm. A FORTRAN listing of this algorithm can be found in Pape (1980). Though this modified label correcting algorithm has excellent computational behavior, in the worst case it runs in exponential time, as shown by Kershenbaum (1981).

Glover, Klingman and Phillips (1985) proposed a generalization of the FIFO label correcting algorithm, called the *partitioning shortest path* (*PSP*) *algorithm*. For general networks, the PSP algorithm runs in $O(nm)$ time, while for networks with nonnegative arc lengths it runs in $O(n^2)$ time and has excellent computational behavior. Other variants of the label correcting algorithms and their computational attributes can be found in Glover, Klingman, Phillips and Schneider (1985).

Researchers have been interested in developing polynomial-time primal simplex algorithms for the shortest path problem. Dial, Glover, Karney and Klingman (1979) and Zadeh (1979) showed that Dantzig's pivot rule (i.e., pivoting in the arc with largest violation of optimality condition) for the shortest path problem starting from an artificial basis leads to Dijkstra's algorithm. Thus the number of pivots is $O(n)$ if all arc lengths are nonnegative. Primal simplex algorithms for the shortest path problem with arbitrary arc lengths are not that efficient. Akgul (1985a) developed a simplex algorithm for the shortest path problem that performs $O(n^2)$ pivots. Using simple data structures, Akgül's algorithm runs in $O(n^3)$ time which can be reduced to $O(nm + n^2 \log n)$ using the Fibonacci heap data structure. Goldfarb, Hao and Kai (1986) described another simplex algorithm for the shortest path problem: the number of pivots and running time for this algorithm are comparable to those of Akgül's algorithm. Orlin (1985) showed that the simplex algorithm with Dantzig's pivot rule solves the shortest path problem in $O(n^2 \log nC)$ pivots. Ahuja and Orlin (1988) recently discovered a scaling variation of this approach that performs $O(n^2 \log C)$ pivots and runs in $O(nm \log C)$ time. This algorithm employs simple data structures, uses very natural pricing strategies, and also permits partial pricing.

All pair shortest path algorithms

Most algorithms that solve the all pair shortest path problem involve matrix manipulation. The first such algorithm appears to be a part of the folklore; Lawler (1976) describes it in his textbook. The complexity of this algorithm is $O(n^3 \log n)$, which can be improved slightly by using more sophisticated matrix multiplication procedures. The algorithm we have presented is due to Floyd (1962) and is based on a theorem by Warshall (1962). This algorithm runs in $O(n^3)$ time and is also capable of detecting the presence of negative length cycles. Dantzig (1967) devised another procedure requiring exactly the same order of calculations. The bibliography by Deo and Pang (1984) contains references for several other all pair shortest path algorithms.

From a worst-case complexity viewpoint, however, it might be desirable to solve the all pair shortest path problem as a sequence of single-source shortest path problems. As pointed out in the text, this approach takes $O(nm)$ time to construct an equivalent problem with nonnegative arc lengths and takes $O(n \, S(n, m, C))$ time to solve the n shortest path problems (recall that

$S(n, m, C)$ is the time needed to solve a shortest path problem with nonnegative arc lengths). For very dense networks, the algorithm by Fredman (1976) is faster than this approach in the worst case.

Computational results

Researchers have extensively tested shortest path algorithms on a variety of network classes. The studies due to Gilsinn and Witzgall (1973), Pape (1974), Kelton and Law (1978), Van Vliet (1978), Dial, Glover, Karney and Klingman (1979), Denardo and Fox (1979), Imai and Iri (1984), Glover, Klingman, Phillips and Schneider (1985), and Gallo and Pallottino (1988) are representative of these contributions.

Unlike the worst-case results, the computational performance of an algorithm depends upon many factors: for example, the manner in which the program is written; the language, compiler and computer used; and the distribution of networks on which the algorithm is tested. Hence, the results of computational studies are only suggestive, rather than conclusive. The results of these studies also depend greatly upon the density of the network. These studies generally suggest that Dial's algorithm is the best label setting algorithm for the shortest path problem. It is faster than the original $O(n^2)$ implementation, the binary heap, d-heap or the Fibonacci heap implementation of Dijkstra's algorithm for all network classes tested by these researchers. Denardo and Fox (1979) also find that Dial's algorithm is faster than their two-level bucket implementation for all of their test problems; however, extrapolating the results, they observe that their implementation would be faster for very large shortest path problems. Researchers have not yet tested the R-heap implementation and so at this moment no comparison with Dial's algorithm is available.

Among the label correcting algorithms, the algorithms by D'Esopo and Pape and by Glover, Klingman, Phillips and Schneider (1985) are the two fastest. The study by Glover et al. finds that their algorithm is superior to D'Esopo and Pape's algorithm. Other researchers have also compared label setting algorithms with label correcting algorithms. Studies generally suggest that, for very dense networks, label setting algorithms are superior and, for sparse networks, label correcting algorithms perform better.

Kelton and Law (1978) have conducted a computational study of several all pair shortest path algorithms. This study indicates that Dantzig's (1967) algorithm with a modification due to Tabourier (1973) is faster (up to two times) than the Floyd–Warshall algorithm described in Section 3.5. This study also finds that matrix manipulation algorithms are faster than a successive application of a single-source shortest path algorithm for very dense networks, but slower for sparse networks.

6.3. Maximum flow problem

The maximum flow problem is distinguished by the long succession of research contributions that have improved upon the worst-case complexity of algorithms; some, but not all, of these improvements have produced improvements in practice.

Several researchers – Dantzig and Fulkerson (1956), Ford and Fulkerson (1956) and Elias, Feinstein and Shannon (1956) – independently established the max-flow min-cut theorem. Fulkerson and Dantzig (1955) solved the maximum flow problem by specializing the primal simplex algorithm, whereas Ford and Fulkerson (1956) and Elias et al. (1956) solved it by augmenting path algorithms. Since then, researchers have developed a number of algorithms for this problem; Table 6.2 summarizes the running times of some of these algorithms. In the table, n is the number of nodes, m is the number of arcs, and U is an upper bound on the integral arc capacities. The algorithms whose time bounds involve U assume integral capacities; the bounds specified for the other algorithms apply to problems with arbitrary rational or real capacities.

Ford and Fulkerson (1956) observed that the labeling algorithm can perform as many as $O(nU)$ augmentations for networks with integer arc capacities. They also showed that for arbitrary irrational arc capacities, the labeling algorithm can perform an infinite sequence of augmentations and might converge to a value different from the maximum flow value. Edmonds and Karp (1972) suggested two specializations of the labeling algorithm, both with improved computational complexity. They showed that if the algorithm augments flow along a shortest path (i.e., one containing the smallest possible number of arcs) in the residual network, then the algorithm performs $O(nm)$

Table 6.2
Running times of maximum flow algorithms

#	Discoverers	Running time
1	Edmonds and Karp (1972)	$O(nm^2)$
2	Dinic (1970)	$O(n^2 m)$
3	Karzanov (1974)	$O(n^3)$
4	Cherkasky (1977)	$O(n^2\sqrt{m})$
5	Malhotra, Kumar and Maheshwari (1978)	$O(n^3)$
6	Galil (1980)	$O(n^{5/3} m^{2/3})$
7	Galil and Naamad (1980); Shiloach (1978)	$O(nm \log^2 n)$
8	Shiloach and Vishkin (1982)	$O(n^3)$
9	Sleator and Tarjan (1983)	$O(nm \log n)$
10	Tarjan (1984)	$O(n^3)$
11	Gabow (1985)	$O(nm \log U)$
12	Goldberg (1985)	$O(n^3)$
13	Goldberg and Tarjan (1986)	$O(nm \log(n^2/m))$
14	Bertsekas (1986)	$O(n^3)$
15	Cheriyan and Maheshwari (1987)	$O(n^2\sqrt{m})$
16	Ahuja and Orlin (1987)	$O(nm + n^2 \log U)$
17	Ahuja, Orlin and Tarjan (1988)	(a) $O\left(nm + \dfrac{n^2 \log U}{\log \log U}\right)$ (b) $O(nm + n^2\sqrt{\log U})$ (c) $O\left(nm \log\left(\dfrac{n\sqrt{\log U}}{m} + 2\right)\right)$

augmentations. A breadth first search of the network will determine a shortest augmenting path; consequently, this version of the labeling algorithm runs in $O(nm^2)$ time. Edmonds and Karp's second idea was to augment flow along a path with maximum residual capacity. They proved that this algorithm performs $O(m \log U)$ augmentations. Tarjan (1986) showed how to determine a path with maximum residual capacity in $O(m)$ time on average; hence, this version of the labeling algorithm runs in $O(m^2 \log U)$ time.

Dinic (1970) independently introduced the concept of shortest path networks, called *layered networks*, for solving the maximum flow problem. A layered network is a subgraph of the residual network that contains only those nodes and arcs that lie on at least one shortest path from the source to the sink. The nodes in a layered network can be partitioned into layers of nodes N_1, $N_2, \ldots$, so that every arc (i, j) in the layered network connects nodes in adjacent layers (i.e., $i \in N_k$ and $j \in N_{k+1}$ for some k). A *blocking flow* in a layered network $G' = (N', A')$ is a flow that blocks flow augmentations in the sense that G' contains no directed path with positive residual capacity from the source node to the sink node. Dinic showed how to construct a blocking flow in a layered network in $O(nm)$ time by performing at most m augmentations. His algorithm constructs layered networks and establishes blocking flows in these networks. He showed that after each blocking flow iteration, the length of the layered network increases and after at most n iterations, the source is disconnected from the sink in the residual network. Consequently, his algorithm runs in $O(n^2m)$ time.

The shortest augmenting path algorithm presented in Section 4.3 achieves the same time bound as Dinic's algorithm, but instead of constructing layered networks it maintains distance labels. Goldberg (1985) introduced distance labels in the context of his preflow push algorithm. Distance labels offer several advantages: they are simpler to understand and easier to manipulate than layered networks, and they have led to more efficient algorithms. Orlin and Ahuja (1987) developed the distance label based augmenting path algorithm given in Section 4.3. They also showed that this algorithm is equivalent both to Edmonds and Karp's algorithm and to Dinic's algorithm in the sense that all three algorithms enumerate the same augmenting paths in the same sequence. The algorithms differ only in the manner in which they obtain these augmenting paths.

Several researchers have contributed improvements to the computational complexity of maximum flow algorithms by developing more efficient algorithms to establish blocking flows in layered networks. Karzanov (1974) introduced the concept of preflows in a layered network. (See the technical report of Even (1976) for a comprehensive description of this algorithm and the paper by Tarjan (1984) for a simplified version.) By maintaining preflows and pushing flows from nodes with excesses, he constructs a blocking flow in $O(n^2)$ time. Malhotra, Kumar and Maheshwari (1978) present a conceptually simple maximum flow algorithm that runs in $O(n^3)$ time. Cherkasky (1977) and Galil (1980) presented further improvements of Karzanov's algorithm.

The search for more efficient maximum flow algorithms has stimulated researchers to develop new data structures for implementing Dinic's algorithm. The first such data structures were suggested independently by Shiloach (1978) and Galil and Naamad (1980). Dinic's algorithm (or the shortest augmenting path algorithm described in Section 4.3) takes $O(n)$ time on average to identify an augmenting path and, during the augmentation, it saturates some arcs in this path. If we delete the saturated arcs from this path, we obtain a set of *path fragments*. The basic idea is to store these path fragments using some data structure, for example, 2–3 trees (see Aho, Hopcroft and Ullman (1974) for a discussion of 2–3 trees) and use them later to identify augmenting paths quickly. Shiloach (1978) and Galil and Naamad (1980) showed how to augment flows through path fragments in a way that finds a blocking flow in $O(m(\log n)^2)$ time, so that their implementation of Dinic's algorithm runs in $O(nm(\log n)^2)$ time. Sleator and Tarjan (1983) improved this approach by using a data structure called *dynamic trees* to store and update path fragments. Their algorithm establishes a blocking flow in $O(m \log n)$ time and thereby yields an $O(nm \log n)$ time bound for Dinic's algorithm.

Gabow (1985) obtained a similar time bound by applying a bit scaling approach to the maximum flow problem. As outlined in Section 1.7, this approach solves a maximum flow problem at each scaling phase with one more bit of every arc's capacity. During a scaling phase, the initial flow value differs from the maximum flow value by at most m units and so the shortest augmenting path algorithm (and also Dinic's algorithm) performs at most m augmentations. Consequently, each scaling phase takes $O(nm)$ time and the algorithm runs in $O(nm \log C)$ time. If we invoke the similarity assumption, this time bound is comparable to that of Sleator and Tarjan's algorithm, but the scaling algorithm is much simpler to implement. Orlin and Ahuja (1987) presented a variation of Gabow's algorithm achieving the same time bound.

Goldberg and Tarjan (1986) developed the generic preflow–push algorithm and the highest-label preflow–push algorithm. Previously, Goldberg (1985) had shown that the FIFO version of the algorithm that pushes flow from active nodes in the first-in-first-out order runs in $O(n^3)$ time. (This algorithm maintains a *queue* of active nodes; at each iteration, it selects a node from the front of the queue, performs a push/relabel step at this node, and adds the newly active nodes to the rear of the queue.) Using a dynamic tree data structure, Goldberg and Tarjan (1986) improved the running time of the FIFO preflow–push algorithm to $O(nm \log(n^2/m))$. This algorithm currently gives the best strongly polynomial-time bound for solving the maximum flow problem.

Bertsekas (1986) obtained another maximum flow algorithm by specializing his minimum cost flow algorithm; this algorithm closely resembles Goldberg's FIFO preflow–push algorithm. Recently, Cheriyan and Maheshwari (1987) showed that Goldberg and Tarjan's highest-label preflow–push algorithm actually performs $O(n^2\sqrt{m})$ nonsaturating pushes and hence runs in $O(n^2\sqrt{m})$ time.

Ahuja and Orlin (1987) improved Goldberg and Tarjan's algorithm using the excess-scaling technique to obtain an $O(nm + n^2 \log U)$ time bound. If we invoke the similarity assumption, this algorithm improves Goldberg and Tarjan's $O(nm \log(n^2/m))$ algorithm by a factor of $\log n$ for networks that are both non-sparse and non-dense. Further, this algorithm does not use any complex data structures. Scaling excesses by a factor of $\log U/\log \log U$ and pushing flow from a large excess node with the highest distance label, Ahuja, Orlin and Tarjan (1988) reduced the number of nonsaturating pushes to $O(n^2 \log U/\log \log U)$. They also obtained another variation of the original excess scaling algorithm that further reduces the number of nonsaturating pushes to $O(n^2\sqrt{\log U})$.

The use of the dynamic tree data structure improves the running times of the excess-scaling algorithm and its variations, though the improvements are not as dramatic as they are for Dinic's and the FIFO preflow–push algorithms. For example, the $O(nm + n^2\sqrt{\log U})$ algorithm improves to $O(nm \log((n\sqrt{\log U}/m) + 2))$ by using dynamic trees, as shown in Ahuja, Orlin and Tarjan (1988). Tarjan (1987) conjectures that any preflow–push algorithm that performs p nonsaturating pushes can be implemented in $O(nm \log(2 + p/nm))$ time using dynamic trees. Although this conjecture is true for all known preflow–push algorithms, it is still open for the general case.

Until recently, developing a polynomial-time primal simplex algorithm for the maximum flow problem had long been an outstanding open problem. Goldfarb and Hao (1988) developed such an algorithm, which algorithm is essentially based on selecting pivot arcs so that flow is augmented along a shortest path from the source to the sink. As one would expect, this algorithm performs $O(nm)$ pivots and can be implemented in $O(n^2m)$ time. Goldberg, Grigoriadis and Tarjan (1988) showed how to implement this algorithm in $O(nm \log n)$ using dynamic trees.

Researchers have also investigated the maximum flow problem for the following special classes of networks: (i) unit capacity networks (i.e., $U = 1$); (ii) unit capacity simple networks (i.e., $U = 1$, and, every node in the network, except source and sink, has one incoming arc or one outgoing arc); (iii) bipartite networks; and (iv) planar networks. Observe that the maximum flow value for unit capacity networks is less than n, and so the shortest augmenting path algorithm will solve these problems in $O(nm)$ time. Clearly, these problems are easier to solve than those with large capacities. Even and Tarjan (1975) showed that Dinic's algorithm solves the maximum flow problem on unit capacity networks in $O(n^{2/3}m)$ time and on unit capacity simple networks in $O(n^{1/2}m)$ time. Orlin and Ahuja (1987) have achieved the same time bounds using a modification of the shortest augmenting path algorithm. Both of these algorithms rely on ideas from Hopcroft and Karp's (1973) algorithm for maximum bipartite matching. Fernandez-Baca and Martel (1987) generalized these ideas for networks with small integer capacities.

Versions of maximum flow algorithms can run considerably faster on a bipartite network $G = (N_1 \cup N_2, A)$ if $|N_1| \ll |N_2|$ (or $|N_2| \ll |N_1|$). Let $n_1 = |N_1|$, $n_2 = |N_2|$ and $n = n_1 + n_2$. Suppose that $n_1 \leq n_2$. Gusfield, Martel and

Fernandez-Baca (1985) obtained the first such results by showing how the running times of Karzanov's and Malhotra et al.'s algorithms reduce from $O(n^3)$ to $O(n_1^2 n_2)$ and $O(n_1^3 + nm)$, respectively. Ahuja, Orlin, Stein and Tarjan (1988) improved upon these ideas by showing that it is possible to substitute n_1 for n in the time bounds for all preflow–push algorithms to obtain new time bounds for bipartite networks. This result implies that the FIFO preflow push algorithm and the original excess scaling algorithm, respectively, solve the maximum flow problem on bipartite networks in $O(n_1 m + n_1^3)$ and $O(n_1 m + n_1^2 \log U)$ time.

It is possible to solve the maximum flow problem on planar networks much more efficiently than on general networks. (A network is called *planar* if it can be drawn in a two-dimensional plane so that arcs intersect one another only at the nodes.) Because a planar network has at most $6n$ arcs, the running times of the maximum flow algorithms on planar networks appear more attractive. Specialized solution techniques, that have even better running times, are quite different than those for the general networks. Some important references for planar maximum flow algorithms are Itai and Shiloach (1979), Johnson and Venkatesan (1982) and Hassin and Johnson (1985).

Researchers have also investigated whether the worst-case bounds of the maximum flow algorithms are *tight*, i.e., whether the algorithms achieve their worst-case bounds for some families of networks. Zadeh (1972) showed that the bound of Edmonds and Karp's algorithm is tight when $m = n^2$. Even and Tarjan (1975) noted that the same examples imply that the bound of Dinic's algorithm is tight when $m = n^2$. Baratz (1977) showed that the bound on Karzanov's algorithm is tight. Galil (1981) constructed an interesting class of examples and showed that the algorithms of Edmonds and Karp, Dinic, Karzanov, Cherkasky, Galil and Malhotra et al. achieve their worst-case bounds on those examples.

Other researchers have made some progress in constructing worst-case examples for preflow–push algorithms. Martel (1987) showed that the FIFO preflow push algorithm can take $\Omega(nm)$ time to solve a class of unit capacity networks. Cheriyan and Maheshwari (1987) showed that the bound of $O(n^2 \sqrt{m})$ for the highest-label preflow–push algorithm is tight. Cheriyan (1988) also constructed a family of examples to show that the bound $O(n^3)$ for FIFO preflow–push algorithm and the bound $O(n^2 m)$ for the generic preflow–push algorithm is tight. The research community has not established similar results for other preflow–push algorithms, in particular for the excess-scaling algorithms. It is worth mentioning, however, that these known worst-case examples are quite artificial and are not likely to arise in practice.

Several computational studies have assessed the empirical behavior of maximum flow algorithms. The studies performed by Hamacher (1979), Cheung (1980), Glover, Klingman, Mote and Whitman (1979, 1984), Imai (1983), and Goldfarb and Grigoriadis (1986) are noteworthy. These studies were conducted prior to the development of algorithms that use distance labels. These studies rank Edmonds and Karp, Dinic's and Karzanov's algorithms in increasing order of performance for most classes of networks. Dinic's algorithm is competitive with Karzanov's algorithm for sparse networks, but slower for dense networks. Imai (1983) noted that Galil and Naamad's (1980) implementation of Dinic's algorithm, using sophisticated data structures, is slower than the original Dinic's algorithm. Sleator and Tarjan (1983) reported a similar finding; they observed that their implementation of Dinic's algorithm using the dynamic tree data structure is slower than the original Dinic's algorithm by a constant factor. Hence, the sophisticated data structures improve only the worst-case performance of algorithms, but are not useful empirically. Researchers have also tested the Malhotra et al. algorithm and the primal simplex algorithm due to Fulkerson and Dantzig (1955) and found these algorithms to be slower than Dinic's algorithm for most classes of networks.

A number of researchers are currently evaluating the computational performance of preflow–push algorithms. Derigs and Meier (1988), Grigoriadis (1988), and Ahuja, Kodialam and Orlin (1988) have found that the preflow-push algorithms are substantially (often 2 to 10 times) faster than Dinic's and Karzanov's algorithms for most classes of networks. Among all nonscaling preflow push algorithms, the highest-label preflow push algorithm runs the fastest. The excess-scaling algorithm and its variations have not been tested thoroughly. We do not anticipate that dynamic tree implementations of preflow push algorithms would be useful in practice; in this case, as in others, their contribution has been to improve the worst-case performances of algorithms.

Finally, we discuss two important generalizations of the maximum flow problem: (i) the multi-terminal flow problem; and (ii) the maximum dynamic flow problem.

In the multi-terminal flow problem, we wish to determine the maximum flow value between every pair of nodes. Gomory and Hu (1961) showed how to solve the multi-terminal flow problem on undirected networks by solving $n - 1$ maximum flow problems. Recently, Gusfield (1987) has suggested a simpler multi-terminal flow algorithm. These results, however, do not apply to the multi-terminal maximum flow problem on directed networks.

In the simplest version of maximum dynamic flow problem, we associate with each arc (i, j) in the network a number t_{ij} denoting the time needed to traverse the arc. The objective is to send the maximum possible flow from the source node to the sink node within a given time period T. Ford and Fulkerson (1958) first showed that the maximum dynamic flow problem can be solved by solving a minimum cost flow problem. (Ford and Fulkerson (1962) give a nice treatment of this problem.) Orlin (1983) considered infinite horizon dynamic flow problems in which the objective is to minimize the average cost per period.

6.4. Minimum cost flow problem

The minimum cost flow problem has a rich history. The classical transportation problem, a simple case of the minimum cost flow problem, was posed and solved (though incompletely) by Kantorovich (1939), Hitchcock (1941), and Koopmans (1947). Dantzig (1951) developed the first complete solution procedure for the transportation problem by specializing his simplex algorithm for linear programming. He observed the spanning tree property of the basis and the integrality property of the optimum solution. Later, his development of the upper bounding technique for linear programming led to an efficient specialization of the simplex algorithm for the minimum cost flow problem. Dantzig's book (1962) discusses these topics.

Ford and Fulkerson (1956, 1957) suggested the first combinatorial algorithms for the uncapacitated and capacitated transportation problem; these algorithms are known as primal–dual algorithms. Ford and Fulkerson (1962) describe the primal–dual algorithm for the minimum cost flow problem. Jewell (1958), Iri (1960) and Busaker and Gowen (1961) independently discovered the successive shortest path algorithm. These researchers showed how to solve the minimum cost flow problem as a sequence of shortest path problems with arbitrary arc lengths. Tomizava (1971) and Edmonds and Karp (1972) independently observed that if the computations use node potentials, then these algorithms can be implemented so that the shortest path problems have nonnegative arc lengths.

Minty (1960) and Fulkerson (1961) independently discovered the out-of-kilter algorithm. The negative cycle algorithm is credited to Klein (1967). Helgason and Kennington (1977) and Armstrong, Klingman and Whitman (1980) describe the specialization of the linear programming dual simplex algorithm for the minimum cost flow problem (which is not discussed in this chapter). The number of iterations performed by each of these algorithms can (apparently) not be polynomially bounded. Zadeh (1973a) describes one example on which each of several algorithms – the primal simplex algorithm with Dantzig's pivot rule, the dual simplex algorithm, the negative cycle algorithm (which augments flow along a most negative cycle), the successive shortest path algorithm, the primal–dual algorithm, and the out-of-kilter algorithm – performs an exponential number of iterations. Zadeh (1973b) has also described other pathological examples for network algorithms.

The fact that one example is bad for many network algorithms suggests interrelationship among the algorithms. The insightful paper by Zadeh (1979) pointed out that each of the algorithms just mentioned are indeed equivalent in the sense that they perform the same sequence of augmentations, provided ties are broken using the same rule. All these algorithms essentially consist of identifying shortest paths betwen appropriately defined nodes and augmenting flow along these paths. Furthermore, these algorithms obtain shortest path using a method that can be regarded as an application of Dijkstra's algorithm.

The network simplex algorithm and its practical implementations have been most popular with operations researchers. Johnson (1966) suggested the first tree-manipulating data structure for implementing the simplex algorithm. The first implementations using these ideas, due to Srinivasan and Thompson (1973) and Glover, Karney, Klingman and Napier (1974), significantly reduced the running time of the simplex algorithm. Glover, Klingman and Stutz (1974),

Bradley, Brown and Graves (1977), and Barr, Glover, and Klingman (1979) subsequently discovered improved data structures. The book of Kennington and Helgason (1980) is an excellent source for references and background material concerning these developments.

Researchers have conducted extensive studies to determine the most effective pricing strategy, i.e., selection of the entering variable. These studies show that the choice of the pricing strategy has a significant effect on both the solution time and the number of pivots required to solve minimum cost flow problems. The candidate list strategy we described is due to Mulvey (1978a). Goldfarb and Reid (1977), Bradley, Brown and Graves (1978), Grigoriadis and Hsu (1979), Gibby, Glover, Klingman and Mead (1983) and Grigoriadis (1986) described other strategies that have been effective in practice. It appears that the best pricing strategy depends both upon the network structure and the network size.

Experience with solving large scale minimum cost flow problems has established that more than 90% of the pivoting steps in the simplex method can be degenerate (see Bradley, Brown and Graves (1978), Gavish, Schweitzer and Shlifer (1977) and Grigoriadis (1986)). Thus, degeneracy is a computational as well as a theoretical issue. The strongly feasible basis technique, proposed by Cunningham (1976) and independently by Barr, Glover and Klingman (1977a, 1977b, 1978) has contributed on both fronts. Computational experience has shown that maintaining a strongly feasible basis substantially reduces the number of degenerate pivots. On the theoretical front, the use of this technique led to a finitely converging primal simplex algorithm. Orlin (1985) showed, using a perturbation technique, that for integer data an implementation of the primal simplex algorithm that maintains a strongly feasible basis performs $O(nmCU)$ pivots when used with any arbitrary pricing strategy and $O(nmC \log(mCU))$ pivots when used with Dantzig's pricing strategy.

The strongly feasible basis technique prevents cycling during a sequence of consecutive degenerate pivots, but the number of consecutive degenerate pivots may be exponential. This phenomenon is known as *stalling*. Cunningham (1979) described an example of stalling and suggested several rules for selecting the entering variable to avoid stalling. One such rule is the LRC (Least Recently Considered) rule which orders the arcs in an arbitrary, but fixed, manner. The algorithm then examines the arcs in a wrap-around fashion, each iteration starting at the place where it left off earlier, and introduces the first eligible arc into the basis. Cunningham showed that this rule admits at most nm consecutive degenerate pivots. Goldfarb, Hao and Kai (1987) have described more anti-stalling pivot rules for the minimum cost flow problem.

Researchers have also been interested in developing polynomial-time simplex algorithms for the minimum cost flow problem or special cases of it. The only polynomial-time simplex algorithm for the minimum cost flow problem is a dual simplex algorithm due to Orlin (1984); this algorithm performs $O(n^3 \log n)$ pivots for the uncapacitated minimum cost flow problem. Developing a polynomial-time primal simplex algorithm for the minimum cost flow problem is still open. However, researchers have developed such algorithms for the shortest path problem, the maximum flow problem, and the assignment problem: Dial et al. (1979), Zadeh (1979), Orlin (1985), Akgul (1985a), Goldfarb, Hao and Kai (1986) and Ahuja and Orlin (1988) for the shortest path problem; Goldfarb and Hao (1988) for the maximum flow problem; and Roohy-Laleh (1980), Hung (1983), Orlin (1985), Akgül (1985b) and Ahuja and Orlin (1988) for the assignment problem.

The *relaxation algorithms* proposed by Bertsekas and his associates are other attractive algorithms for solving the minimum cost flow problem and its generalizations. For the minimum cost flow problem, this algorithm maintains a pseudoflow satisfying the optimality conditions. The algorithm proceeds by either (i) augmenting flow from an excess node to a deficit node along a path consisting of arcs with zero reduced cost, or (ii) changing the potentials of a subset of nodes. In the latter case, it resets flows on some arcs to their lower or upper bounds so as to satisfy the optimality conditions; however, this flow assignment might change the excesses and deficits at nodes. The algorithm operates so that each change in the node potentials increases the dual objective function value and when it finally determines the optimum dual objective function value, it has also obtained an optimum primal solution. This relaxation algorithm has exhibited nice empirical behavior. Bertsekas (1985) suggested the relaxation algorithm for the minimum cost flow problem (with integer data). Bertsekas and Tseng (1988b) extended this approach for the minimum cost flow problem with real data, and for the generalized minimum cost flow problem (see Section 6.6 for a definition of this problem).

A number of empirical studies have extensively tested minimum cost flow algorithms for wide variety of network structures, data distributions, and problem sizes. The most common problem generator is NETGEN, due to Klingman, Napier and Stutz (1974), which is capable of generating assignment, and capacitated or uncapacitated transportation and minimum cost flow problems. Glover, Karney and Klingman (1974) and Aashtiani and Magnanti (1976) have tested the primal–dual and out-of-kilter algorithms. Helgason and Kennington (1977) and Armstrong, Klingman and Whitman (1980) have reported on extensive studies of the dual simplex algorithm. The primal simplex algorithm has been a subject of more rigorous investigation; studies conducted by Glover, Karney, Klingman and Napier (1974), Glover, Karney and Klingman (1974), Bradley, Brown and Graves (1977), Mulvey (1978b), Grigoriadis and Hsu (1979) and Grigoriadis (1986) are noteworthy. Bertsekas and Tseng (1988b) presented computational results for the relaxation algorithm.

In view of Zadeh's (1979) result, we would expect that the successive shortest path algorithm, the primal–dual algorithm, the out-of-kilter algorithm, the dual simplex algorithm, and the primal simplex algorithm with Dantzig's pivot rule should have comparable running times. By using more effective pricing strategies that determine a good entering arc without examining all arcs, we would expect that the primal simplex algorithm should outperform

other algorithms. All the computational studies have verified this expectation
and until very recently the primal simplex algorithm has been a clear winner
for almost all classes of network problems. Bertsekas and Tseng (1988b) have
reported that their relaxation algorithm is substantially faster than the primal
simplex algorithm. However, Grigoriadis (1986) finds his new version of primal
simplex algorithm faster than the relaxation algorithm. At this time, it appears
that the relaxation algorithm of Bertsekas and Tseng, and the primal simplex
algorithm due to Grigoriadis are the two fastest algorithms for solving the
minimum cost flow problem in practice.

Computer codes for some minimum cost flow problems are available in the
public domain. These include the primal simplex codes RNET and NETFLOW
developed by Grigoradis and Hsu (1979) and Kennington and Helgason
(1980), respectively, and the relaxation code RELAX developed by Bertsekas
and Tseng (1988a).

Polynomial-time algorithms

In the recent past, researchers have actively pursued the design of fast
(weakly) polynomial and strongly polynomial-time algorithms for the minimum
cost flow problem. Recall that an algorithm is strongly polynomial-time if its
running time is polynomial in the number of nodes and arcs, and does not
involve terms containing logarithms of C or U. Table 6.3 summarizes these

Table 6.3
Polynomial-time algorithms for the minimum cost flow problem

#	Developers	Running time
Polynomial-time combinatorial algorithms		
1	Edmonds and Karp (1972)	$O((n + m') \log U\, S(n, m, C))$
2	Rock (1980)	$O((n + m') \log U\, S(n, m, C))$
3	Rock (1980)	$O(n \log C\, M(n, m, U))$
4	Bland and Jensen (1985)	$O(n \log C\, M(n, m, U))$
5	Goldberg and Tarjan (1988a)	$O(nm \log(n^2/m) \log nC)$
6	Bertsekas and Eckstein (1988)	$O(n^3 \log nC)$
7	Goldberg and Tarjan (1987)	$O(n^3 \log nC)$
7	Gabow and Tarjan (1987)	$O(nm \log n \log U \log nC)$
8	Goldberg and Tarjan (1987, 1988b)	$O(nm \log n \log nC)$
9	Ahuja, Goldberg, Orlin and Tarjan (1988)	$O(nm(\log U/\log \log U) \log nC)$ and $O(nm \log \log U \log nC)$
Strongly polynomial-time combinatorial algorithms		
1	Tardos (1985)	$O(m^4)$
2	Orlin (1984)	$O((n + m')^2 S(n, m))$
3	Fujishige (1986)	$O((n + m')^2 S(n, m))$
4	Galil and Tardos (1986)	$O(n^2 \log n\, S(n, m))$
5	Goldberg and Tarjan (1988a)	$O(nm^2 \log n \log(n^2/m))$
6	Goldberg and Tarjan (1988b)	$O(nm^2 \log^2 n)$
7	Orlin (1988)	$O((n + m') \log n\, S(n, m))$

theoretical developments in solving the minimum cost flow problem. The table reports running times for networks with n nodes and m arcs, m' of which are capacitated. It assumes that the integral cost coefficients are bounded in absolute value by C, and the integral capacities, supplies and demands are bounded in absolute value by U. The term $S(\cdot)$ is the running time for the shortest path problem and the term $M(\cdot)$ represents the corresponding running time to solve a maximum flow problem.

For the sake of comparing the polynomial and strongly polynomial-time algorithms, we invoke the similarity assumption. For problems that satisfy the similarity assumption, the best bounds for the shortest path and maximum flow problems are given in Table 6.4.

Using capacity and right-hand-side scaling, Edmonds and Karp (1972) developed the first (weakly) polynomial-time algorithm for the minimum cost flow problem. The RHS-scaling algorithm presented in Section 5.7, which is a variant of the Edmonds–Karp algorithm, was suggested by Orlin (1988). The scaling technique did not initially capture the interest of many researchers, since they regarded it as having little practical utility. However, researchers gradually recognized that the scaling technique has great theoretical value as well as potential practical significance. Rock (1980) developed two different bit-scaling algorithms for the minimum cost flow problem, one using capacity scaling and the other using cost scaling. This cost scaling algorithm reduces the minimum cost flow problem to a sequence of $O(n \log C)$ maximum flow problems. Bland and Jensen (1985) independently discovered a similar cost scaling algorithm.

The pseudoflow push algorithms for the minimum cost flow problem discussed in Section 5.8 use the concept of *approximate optimality*, introduced independently by Bertsekas (1979) and Tardos (1985). Bertsekas (1986) developed the first pseudoflow push algorithm. This algorithm was pseudo-polynomial-time. Goldberg and Tarjan (1987) used a scaling technique on a variant of this algorithm to obtain the generic pseudoflow push algorithm described in Section 5.8. Tarjan (1984) proposed a wave algorithm for the maximum flow problem. The wave algorithm for the minimum cost flow

Table 6.4

Polynomial-time bounds	Discoverers
$S(n, m, C) = \min\{m \log \log C, m + n\sqrt{\log C}\}$	Johnson (1982) and Ahuja, Mehlorn, Orlin and Tarjan (1988)
$M(n, m, C) = nm \log\left(\dfrac{n\sqrt{\log U}}{m} + 2\right)$	Ahuja, Orlin and Tarjan (1987)

Strongly polynomial-time bounds	Discoverers
$S(n, m) = m + n \log n$	Fredman and Tarjan (1984)
$M(n, m) = nm \log(n^2/m)$	Goldberg and Tarjan (1986)

problem described in Section 5.8, which was developed independently by
Goldberg and Tarjan (1987) and Bertsekas and Eckstein (1988), relies upon
similar ideas. Using a dynamic tree data structure in the generic pseudoflow
push algorithm, Goldberg and Tarjan (1987) obtained a computational time
bound of $O(nm \log n \log nC)$. They also showed that the minimum cost flow
problem can be solved using $O(n \log nC)$ blocking flow computations. (The
description of Dinic's algorithm in Section 6.3 contains the definition of a
blocking flow.) Using both *finger tree* (see Mehlhorn (1984)) and *dynamic tree*
data structures, Goldberg and Tarjan (1988a) obtained an $O(nm \log(n^2/m)$
$\cdot \log nC)$ bound for the wave algorithm.

These algorithms, except the wave algorithm, required sophisticated data
structures that impose a very high computational overhead. Although the wave
algorithm is very practical, its worst-case running time is not very attractive.
This situation has prompted researchers to investigate the possibility of improving the computational complexity of minimum cost flow algorithms without
using any complex data structures. The first success in this direction was due to
Gabow and Tarjan (1987), who developed a triple scaling algorithm running in
time $O(nm \log n \log U \log nC)$. The second success was due to Ahuja,
Goldberg, Orlin and Tarjan (1988), who developed a double scaling algorithm.
The double scaling algorithm, as described in Section 5.9, runs in $O(n$-
$m \log U \log nC)$ time. Scaling costs by an appropriately large factor improves
the algorithm to $O(nm(\log U/\log \log U) \log nC)$, and a dynamic tree implementation improves the bound further to $O(nm \log \log U \log nC)$. For
problems satisfying the similarity assumption, the double scaling algorithm is
faster than all other algorithms for all but very dense networks; in these
instances, algorithms by Goldberg and Tarjan appear more attractive.

Goldberg and Tarjan (1988b) and Barahona and Tardos (1987) have developed other polynomial-time algorithms. Both algorithms are based on the
negative cycle algorithm due to Klein (1967). Goldberg and Tarjan (1988b)
showed that if the negative cycle algorithm always augments flow along a
minimum-mean cycle (a cycle W for which $\Sigma_{(i,j) \in W} c_{ij}/|W|$ is minimum), then it
is strongly polynomialtime. Goldberg and Tarjan described an implementation
of this approach running in time $O(nm(\log n) \min\{\log nC, \ m \log n\})$.
Barahona and Tardos (1987), analyzing an algorithm suggested by Weintraub
(1974), showed that if the negative cycle algorithm augments flow along a cycle
with maximum improvement in the objective function, then it performs
$O(m \log mCU)$ iterations. Since identifying a cycle with maximum improvement is difficult (i.e., NP-hard), they describe a method (based upon solving
an auxiliary assignment problem) to determine a set of disjoint augmenting
cycles with the property that augmenting flows along these cycles improves the
flow cost by at least as much as augmenting flow along any single cycle. Their
algorithm runs in $O(m^2 \log(mCU)S(n, m, C))$ time.

Edmonds and Karp (1972) proposed the first polynomial-time algorithm for
the minimum cost flow problem, and also highlighted the desire to develop a
strongly polynomial-time algorithm. This desire was motivated primarily by

theoretical considerations. (Indeed, in practice, the terms $\log C$ and $\log U$ typically range from 1 to 20, and are sublinear in n.) Strongly polynomial-time algorithms are theoretically attractive for at least two reasons: (i) they might provide, in principle, network flow algorithms that can run on real valued data as well as integer valued data, and (ii) they might, at a more fundamental level, identify the source of the underlying complexity in solving a problem; i.e., are problems more difficult or equally difficult to solve as the values of the underlying data become increasingly larger?

The first strongly polynomial-time minimum cost flow algorithm is due to Tardos (1985). Several researchers including Orlin (1984), Fujishige (1986), Galil and Tardos (1986), and Orlin (1988) provided subsequent improvements in the running time. Goldberg and Tarjan (1988a) obtained another strongly polynomial time algorithm by slightly modifying their pseudoflow push algorithm. Goldberg and Tarjan (1988b) showed that their algorithm based on cancelling minimum mean cycles is also strongly polynomial time. Currently, the fastest strongly polynomial-time algorithm is due to Orlin (1988). This algorithm solves the minimum cost flow problem as a sequence of $O(\min(m \log U, m \log n))$ shortest path problems. For very sparse networks, the worst-case running time of this algorithm is nearly as low as the best weakly polynomial-time algorithm, even for problems that satisfy the similarity assumption.

Interior point linear programming algorithms are another source of polynomial-time algorithms for the minimum cost flow problem. Kapoor and Vaidya (1986) have shown that Karmarkar's (1984) algorithm, when applied to the minimum cost flow problem, performs $O(n^{2.5} mK)$ operations, where $K = \log n + \log C + \log U$. Vaidya (1986) suggested another algorithm for linear programming that solves the minimum cost flow problem in $O(n^{2.5}\sqrt{m}K)$ time. Asymptotically, these time bounds are worse than that of the double scaling algorithm.

At this time, the research community has yet to assess fully the computational worth of scaling and interior point linear programming algorithms for the minimum cost flow problem. According to the folklore, even though they might provide the best-worst case bounds on running times, the scaling algorithms are not as efficient as the non-scaling algorithms. Boyd and Orlin (1986) have obtained contradictory results. Testing the right-hand-side scaling algorithm for the minimum cost flow problem, they found the scaling algorithm to be competitive with the relaxation algorithm for some classes of problems. Bland and Jensen (1985) also reported encouraging results with their cost scaling algorithm. We believe that when implemented with appropriate speed-up techniques, scaling algorithms have the potential to compete with the best of the other algorithms.

6.5. *Assignment problem*

The assignment problem has been a popular research topic. The primary emphasis in the literature has been on the development of empirically efficient algorithms rather than the development of algorithms with improved worst-case complexity. Although the research community has developed several different algorithms for the assignment problem, many of these algorithms share common features. The successive shortest path algorithm, described in Section 5.4 for the minimum cost flow problem, appears to lie at the heart of many assignment algorithms. This algorithm is implicit in the first assignment algorithm due to Kuhn (1955), known as the *Hungarian method*, and is explicit in the papers by Tomizava (1971) and Edmonds and Karp (1972).

When applied to an assignment problem on the network $G = (N_1 \cup N_2, A)$, the successive shortest path algorithm operates as follows. To use this solution approach, we first transform the assignment problem into a minimum cost flow problem by adding a source node s and a sink node t, and introducing arcs (s, i) for all $i \in N_1$, and (j, t) for all $j \in N_2$; these arcs have zero cost and unit capacity. The algorithm successively obtains a shortest path from s to t with respect to the linear programming reduced costs, updates the node potentials, and augments one unit of flow along the shortest path. The algorithm solves the assignment problem by n applications of the shortest path algorithm for nonnegative arc lengths and runs in $O(nS(n, m, C))$ time, where $S(n, m, C)$ is the time needed to solve a shortest path problem. For a naive implementation of Dijkstra's algorithm, $S(n, m, C)$ is $O(n^2)$ and for a Fibonacci heap implementation it is $O(m + n \log n)$. For problems satisfying the similarity assumption, $S(n, m, C)$ is $\min\{m \log \log C, m + n\sqrt{\log C}\}$.

The fact that the assignment problem can be solved as a sequence of n shortest path problems with arbitrary arc lengths follows from the works of Jewell (1958), Iri (1960) and Busaker and Gowen (1961) on the minimum cost flow problem. However, Tomizava (1971) and Edmonds and Karp (1972) independently pointed out that working with reduced costs leads to shortest path problems with nonnegative arc lengths. Weintraub and Barahona (1979) worked out the details of the Edmonds–Karp algorithm for the assignment problem. The more recent *threshold assignment algorithm* by Glover, Glover and Klingman (1986) is also a successive shortest path algorithm, which integrates their threshold shortest path algorithm (see Glover, Glover and Klingman (1984)) with the flow augmentation process. Carraresi and Sodini (1986) also suggested a similar threshold assignment algorithm.

Hoffman and Markowitz (1963) pointed out the transformation of a shortest path problem to an assignment problem.

Kuhn's (1955) Hungarian method is the primal–dual version of the successive shortest path algorithm. After solving a shortest path problem and updating the node potentials, the Hungarian method solves a (particularly simple) maximum flow problem to send the maximum possible flow from the source node s to the sink node t using arcs with zero reduced cost. Whereas the successive shortest path problem augments flow along one path in an iteration, the Hungarian method augments flow along all the shortest paths from the source node to the sink node. If we use the labeling algorithm to solve the resulting maximum flow problems, then these applications take a total of

O(nm) time overall, since there are n augmentations and each augmentation takes O(m) time. Consequently, the Hungarian method, too, runs in O(nm + $nS(n, mC)$) = O($nS(n, m, C)$) time. (For some time after the development of the Hungarian method as described by Kuhn, the research community considered it to be an O(n^4) method. Lawler (1976) described an O(n^3) implementation of the method. Subsequently, many researchers realized that the Hungarian method in fact runs in O($nS(n, m, C)$) time.) Jonker and Volgenant (1986) suggested some practical improvements of the Hungarian method.

The relaxation approach for the minimum cost flow problem is due to Dinic and Kronrod (1969), Hung and Rom (1980) and Engquist (1982). This approach is closely related to the successive shortest path algorithm. Both approaches start with an infeasible assignment and gradually make it feasible. The major difference is in the nature of the infeasibility. The successive shortest path algorithm maintains a solution with unassigned persons and objects, and with no person or object overassigned. Throughout the relaxation algorithm, every person is assigned, but objects may be overassigned or unassigned. Both the algorithms maintain optimality of the intermediate solution and work toward feasibility by solving at most n shortest path problems with nonnegative arc lengths. The algorithms of Dinic and Kronrod (1969) and Engquist (1982) are essentially the same as the one we just described, except that the shortest path computations are somewhat disguised in the paper of Dinic and Kronrod (1969). The algorithm of Hung and Rom (1980) maintains a strongly feasible basis rooted at an overassigned node and, after each augmentation, reoptimizes over the previous basis to obtain another strongly feasible basis. All of these algorithms run in O($nS(n, m, C)$) time.

Another algorithm worth mentioning is due to Balinski and Gomory (1964). This algorithm is a primal algorithm that maintains a feasible assignment and gradually converts it into an optimum assignment by augmenting flows along negative cycles or by modifying node potentials. Derigs (1985) notes that the shortest path computations underlie this method, and that it runs in O($nS(n, m, C)$) time.

Researchers have also studied primal simplex algorithms for the assignment problem. The basis of the assignment problem is highly degenerate; of its $2n - 1$ variables, only n are nonzero. Probably because of this excessive degeneracy, the mathematical programming community did not conduct much research on the network simplex method for the assignment problem until Barr, Glover and Klingman (1977a) devised the strongly feasible basis technique. These authors developed an implementation of the network simplex algorithm that maintains a strongly feasible basis for the assignment problem; they also reported encouraging computational results. Subsequent research focused on developing polynomial-time simplex algorithms. Roohy-Laleh (1980) developed a simplex pivot rule requiring O(n^3) pivots. Hung (1983) describes a pivot rule that performs at most O(n^2) consecutive degenerate pivots and at most O($n \log nC$) nondegenerate pivots. Hence, his algorithm performs O($n^3 \log nC$) pivots. Akgül (1985b) suggested another primal simplex algorithm performing $O(n^2)$ pivots, which essentially solves n shortest path problems and runs in $O(nS(n, m, C))$ time

Orlin (1985) studied the theoretical properties of Dantzig's pivot rule for the network simplex algorithm and showed that for the assignment problem this rule requires $O(n^2 \log nC)$ pivots. A naive implementation of the algorithm runs in $O(n^2 m \log nC)$. Ahuja and Orlin (1988) described a scaling version of Dantzig's pivot rule that performs $O(n^2 \log C)$ pivots and can be implemented to run in $O(nm \log C)$ time using simple data structures. The algorithm essentially consists of pivoting in any arc with *sufficiently large* reduced cost. The algorithm defines the term 'sufficiently large' iteratively; initially, this threshold value equals C and within $O(n^2)$ pivots its value is halved.

Balinski (1985) developed the *signature method*, which is a dual simplex algorithm for the assignment problem. (Although his basic algorithm maintains a dual feasible basis, it is not a dual simplex algorithm in the traditional sense because it does not necessarily increase the dual objective at every iteration; some variants of this algorithm do have this property.) Balinski's algorithm performs $O(n^2)$ pivots and runs in $O(n^3)$ time. Goldfarb (1985) described some implementations of Balinski's algorithm that run in $O(n^3)$ time using simple data structures and in $O(nm + n^2 \log n)$ time using Fibonacci heaps.

The auction algorithm, due to Bertsekas, uses basic ideas originally suggested in Bertsekas (1979). Bertsekas and Eckstein (1988) described a more recent version of the auction algorithm. Our presentation of the auction algorithm and its analysis is somewhat different than the one given by Bertsekas and Eckstein (1988). For example, the algorithm we have presented increases the prices of the objects by one unit at a time, whereas their algorithm increases prices by the maximum amount that preserves ε-optimality of the solution. Bertsekas (1981) has presented another algorithm for the assignment problem that is in fact a specialization of this relaxation algorithm for the minimum cost flow problem (see Bertsekas (1985)).

Currently, the best strongly polynomial-time bound to solve the assignment problem is $O(nm + n^2 \log n)$ which is achieved by many assignment algorithms. Scaling algorithms can do better for problems that satisfy the similarity assumption. Gabow (1985), using bit-scaling of costs, developed the first scaling algorithm for the assignment problem. His algorithm performs $O(\log C)$ scaling phases and solves each phase in $O(n^{3/4} m)$ time, thereby achieving an $O(n^{3/4} m \log C)$ time bound. Using the concept of ε-optimality, Gabow and Tarjan (1987) developed another scaling algorithm running in time $O(n^{1/2} m \log nC)$. Observe that the generic pseudoflow push algorithm for the minimum cost flow problem described in Section 5.8 solves the assignment problem in $O(nm \log nC)$ since every push is a saturating push. Bertsekas and Eckstein (1988) showed that the scaling version of the auction algorithm runs in $O(nm \log nC)$. Section 5.11 presented a modified version of the algorithm found in Orlin and Ahuja (1988). They also improved the time bound of the auction algorithm to $O(n^{1/2} m \log nC)$. This time bound is comparable to that of Gabow and Tarjan's algorithm, but the two algorithms would probably have different computational attributes. For problems satisfying the similarity assumption, these two algorithms achieve the best time bound to solve the assignment problem without using any sophisticated data structure.

As mentioned previously, most of the research effort devoted to assignment algorithms has stressed the development of empirically faster algorithms. Over the years, many computational studies have compared one algorithm with a few other algorithms. Some representative computational studies are those conducted by Barr, Glover and Klingman (1977a) on the network simplex method, by McGinnis (1983) and Carpento, Martello and Toth (1988) on the primal–dual method, by Engquist (1982) on the relaxation methods, and by Glover et al. (1986) and Jonker and Volgenant (1987) on the successive shortest path methods. Since no paper has compared all of these algorithms, it is difficult to assess their relative computational merits. Nevertheless, results to date seem to justify the following observations. The primal simplex algorithm is slower than the primal–dual, relaxation and successive shortest path algorithms. Among the latter three approaches, the successive shortest path algorithms due to Glover et al. (1986) and Jonker and Volgenant (1987) appear to be the fastest. Bertsekas and Eckstein (1988) found that the scaling version of the auction algorithm is competitive with Jonker and Volgenant's algorithm. Carpento, Martello and Toth (1988) present several FORTRAN implementations of assignment algorithms for dense and sparse cases.

6.6. Other topics

Our discussion in this paper has featured single commodity network flow problems with linear costs. Several other generic topics in the broader problem domain of network optimization are of considerable theoretical and practical interest. In particular, four other topics deserve mention: (i) generalized network flows; (ii) convex cost flows; (iii) multicommodity flows; and (iv) network design. We shall now discuss these topics briefly.

Generalized network flows

The flow problems we have considered in this chapter assume that arcs conserve flows, i.e., the flow entering an arc equals the flow leaving the arc. In models of generalized network flows, arcs do not necessarily conserve flow. If x_{ij} units of flow enter an arc (i, j), then $r_{ij}x_{ij}$ units 'arrive' at node j; r_{ij} is a nonnegative flow multiplier associated with the arc. If $0 < r_{ij} < 1$, then the arc is *lossy*, and if $1 < r_{ij} < \infty$, then the arc is *gainy*. In the conventional flow networks, $r_{ij} = 1$ for all arcs. Generalized network flows arise in many application contexts. For example, the multiplier might model pressure losses in a water resource network or losses incurred in the transportation of perishable goods.

Researchers have studied several generalized network flow problems. An extension of the conventional maximum flow problem is the *generalized maximum flow problem* that either maximizes the flow out of a source node or maximizes the flow into a sink node (these two objectives are different!). The source version of the problem can be stated as the following linear program.

$$\text{maximize} \quad v_s \tag{6.1a}$$

subject to

$$\sum_{\{j:\,(i,j)\in A\}} x_{ij} - \sum_{\{j:\,(j,i)\in A\}} r_{ji} x_{ji} = \begin{cases} v_s & \text{if } i = s\,, \\ 0 & \text{if } i \neq s,\, t, \text{ for all } i \in N\,, \\ -v_t & \text{if } i = t\,, \end{cases} \tag{6.1b}$$

$$0 \leq x_{ij} \leq u_{ij}\,, \quad \text{for all } (i,\,j) \in A\,. \tag{6.1c}$$

Note that the capacity restrictions apply to the flows entering the arcs. Further, note that v_s is not necessarily equal to v_t, because of flow losses and gains within arcs.

The generalized maximum flow problem has many similarities with the minimum cost flow problem. Extended versions of the successive shortest path algorithm, the negative cycle algorithm, and the primal–dual algorithm for the minimum cost flow problem apply to the generalized maximum flow problem. The paper by Truemper (1977) surveys these approaches. These algorithms, however, are not pseudopolynomial-time, mainly because the optimal arc flows and node potentials might be fractional. The recent paper by Goldberg, Plotkin and Tardos (1988) describes the first polynomial-time combinatorial algorithms for the generalized maximum flow problem.

In the generalized minimum cost flow problem, which is an extension of the ordinary minimum cost flow problem, we wish to determine the minimum cost flow in a generalized network satisfying the specified supply/demand requirements of nodes. There are three main approaches to solve this problem. The first approach, due to Jewell (1962), is essentially a primal–dual algorithm. The second approach is the primal simplex algorithm studied by Elam, Glover and Klingman (1979), among others. Elam et al. find their implementation to be very efficient in practice; they find that it is about 2 to 3 times slower than their implementations for the ordinary minimum cost flow algorithm. The third approach, due to Bertsekas and Tseng (1988b), generalized their minimum cost flow relaxation algorithm.

Convex cost flows

We shall restrict this brief discussion to convex cost flow problems with *separable* cost functions, i.e., the objective function can be written in the form $\Sigma_{(i,j)\in A}\, C_{ij}(x_{ij})$. Problems containing nonconvex nonseparable cost terms such as $x_{12}x_{13}$ are substantially more difficult to solve and continue to pose a significant challenge for the mathematical programming community. Even problems with nonseparable but convex objective functions are more difficult

to solve; typically, analysts rely on the general nonlinear programming techniques to solve these problems. The separable convex cost flow problem has
the following formulation:

$$\text{minimize} \quad \sum_{(i,j)\in A} C_{ij}(x_{ij}) \tag{6.2a}$$

subject to

$$\sum_{\{j:\,(i,j)\in A\}} x_{ij} - \sum_{\{j:\,(j,i)\in A\}} x_{ij} = b(i), \quad \text{for all } i \in N, \tag{6.2b}$$

$$0 \leqslant x_{ij} \leqslant u_{ij}, \quad \text{for all } (i, j) \in A. \tag{6.2c}$$

In this formulation, $C_{ij}(x_{ij})$ for each $(i, j) \in A$ is a convex function. The
research community has focused on two classes of separable convex costs flow
problems: (i) each $C_{ij}(x_{ij})$ is a piecewise linear function; and (ii) each $C_{ij}(x_{ij})$ is
a continuously differentiable function. Solution techniques used to solve the
two classes of problems are quite different.

There is a well-known technique for transforming a separable convex
program with piecewise linear functions to a linear program (see, e.g., Bradley,
Hax and Magnanti (1977)). This transformation reduces the convex cost flow
problem to a standard minimum cost flow problem: it introduces one arc for
each linear segment in the cost function, thus increasing the problem size.
However, it is possible to carry out this transformation implicitly and therefore
modify many minimum cost flow algorithms such as the successive shortest
path algorithm, negative cycle algorithm, primal–dual, and out-of-kilter algorithms, to solve convex cost flow problems without increasing the problem
size. The paper by Ahuja, Batra, and Gupta (1984) illustrates this technique
and suggests a pseudopolynomial time algorithm.

Observe that it is possible to use a piecewise linear function, with linear
segments chosen (if necessary) with sufficiently small size, to approximate a
convex function of one variable to any desired degree of accuracy. More
elaborate alternatives are possible. For example, if we knew the optimal
solution to a separable convex problem a priori (which of course, we don't),
then we could solve the problem *exactly* using a linear approximation for any
arc (i, j) with only three breakpoints: at 0, u_{ij} and the optimal flow on the arc.
Any other breakpoint in the linear approximation would be irrelevant and
adding other points would be computationally wasteful. This observation has
prompted researchers to devise adaptive approximations that iteratively revise
the linear approximation based upon the solution to a previous, coarser,
approximation. (See Meyer (1979) for an example of this approach.) If we
were interested only in integer solutions, then we could choose the breakpoints
of the linear approximation at the set of integer values, and therefore solve the
problem in pseudopolynomial time.

Researchers have suggested other solution strategies, using ideas from nonlinear programming for solving this general separable convex cost flow problems. Some important references on this topic are Ali, Helgason and Kennington (1978), Kennington and Helgason (1980), Rockafellar (1984), Florian (1986), and Bertsekas, Hosein and Tseng (1987).

Some versions of the convex cost flow problem can be solved in polynomial time. Minoux (1984) has devised a polynomial-time algorithm for one special case, the minimum quadratic cost flow problem. Minoux (1986) has also developed a polynomial-time algorithm to obtain an *integer* optimum solution of the convex cost flow problem.

Multicommodity flows

Multicommodity flow problems arise when several commodities use the same underlying network, and share common arc capacities. In this section, we state a linear programming formulation of the multicommodity minimum cost flow problem and point the reader to contributions to this problem and its specializations.

Suppose that the problem contains r distinct commodities numbered 1 through r. Let b^k denote the supply/demand vector of commodity k. Then the multicommodity minimum cost flow problem can be formulated as follows:

$$\text{minimize} \quad \sum_{k=1}^{r} \sum_{(i,j)\in A} c_{ij}^k x_{ij}^k \tag{6.3a}$$

subject to

$$\sum_{\{j:\,(i,j)\in A\}} x_{ij}^k - \sum_{\{j:\,(i,j)\in A\}} x_{ji}^k = b_i^k, \quad \text{for all } i \text{ and } k, \tag{6.3b}$$

$$\sum_{k=1}^{r} x_{ij}^k \le u_{ij}, \text{ for all } (i,j), \tag{6.3c}$$

$$0 \le x_{ij}^k \le u_{ij}^k, \quad \text{for all } (i,j) \text{ and all } k. \tag{6.3d}$$

In this formulation, x_{ij}^k and c_{ij}^k represent the amount of flow and the unit cost of flow for commodity k on arc (i,j). As indicated by the 'bundle constraints' (6.3c), the total flow on any arc cannot exceed its capacity. Further, as captured by (6.3d), the model contains additional capacity restrictions on the flow of each commodity on each arc.

Observe that if the multicommodity flow problem does not contain bundle constraints, then it decomposes into r single commodity minimum cost flow problems, one for each commodity. With the presence of the bundle constraints (6.3c), the essential problem is to distribute the capacity of each arc to individual commodities in a way that minimizes overall flow costs.

We first consider some special cases. The *multicommodity maximum flow problem* is a special instance of (6.3). In this problem, every commodity k has a source node and a sink node, represented respectively by s^k and t^k. The objective is to maximize the sum of flows that can be sent from s^k to t^k for all k. Hu (1963) showed how to solve the two-commodity maximum flow problem on an undirected network in pseudopolynomial time by a labeling algorithm. Rothfarb, Shein and Frisch (1968) showed how to solve the multicommodity maximum flow problem with a common source or a common sink by a single application of any maximum flow algorithm. Ford and Fulkerson (1958) solved the general multicommodity maximum flow problem using a column generation algorithm. Dantzig and Wolfe (1960) subsequently generalized this decomposition approach to linear programming.

Researchers have proposed three basic approaches for solving the general multicommodity minimum cost flow problems: *price-directive decomposition*, *resource-directive decomposition* and *partitioning methods*. We refer the reader to the excellent surveys by Assad (1978) and Kennington (1978) for descriptions of these methods. The book by Kennington and Helgason (1980) describes the details of a primal simplex decomposition algorithm for the multicommodity minimum cost flow problem. Unfortunately, algorithmic developments on the multicommodity minimum cost flow problem have not progressed at nearly the pace as the progress made on the single commodity minimum cost flow problem. Although specialized primal simplex software can solve the single commodity problem 10 to 100 times faster than the general purpose linear programming systems, the algorithms developed for the multicommodity minimum cost flow problems generally solve these problems about 3 times faster than the general purpose software (see Ali et al. (1984)).

Network design

We have focused on solution methods for finding optimal routings in a network; that is, on analysis rather than synthesis. The design problem is of considerable importance in practice and has generated an extensive literature of its own. Many design problems can be stated as fixed cost network flow problems: (some) arcs have an associated fixed cost which is incurred whenever the arc carries *any* flow. These network design models contain 0–1 variables y_{ij} that indicate whether or not an arc is included in the network. Typically, these models involve multicommodity flows. The design decisions y_{ij} and routing decisions x^k_{ij} are related by 'forcing' constraints of the form

$$\sum_{k=1}^{r} x^k_{ij} \le u_{ij}y_{ij}, \quad \text{for all } (i, j),$$

which replace the bundle constraints of the form (6.3c) in the convex cost multicommodity flow problem (6.3). These constraints force the flow x^k_{ij} of each commodity k on arc (i, j) to be zero if the arc is not included in the network design; if the arc is included, the constraint on arc (i, j) restricts the total flow to be the arc's design capacity u_{ij}. Many modeling enhancements are possible; for example, some constraints may restrict the underlying network topology (for instance, in some applications, the network must be a tree; in other applications, the network might need alternate paths to ensure reliable operations). Also, many different objective functions arise in practice. One of the most popular is

$$\text{minimize} \quad \sum_{k=1}^{r} \sum_{(i,j) \in A} c_{ij}^{k} x_{ij}^{k} + \sum_{(i,j) \in A} F_{ij} y_{ij}$$

which models commodity-dependent per-unit routing costs c_{ij}^{k} (as well as fixed costs F_{ij} for the design arcs).

Usually, network design problems require solution techniques from integer programming and combinatorial optimization. These solution methods include dynamic programming, dual ascent procedures, optimization-based heuristics, and integer programming decomposition (Lagrangian relaxation, Benders decomposition) as well as emerging ideas from the field of polyhedral combinatorics. Magnanti and Wong (1984) and Minoux (1985, 1987) have described the broad range of applicability of network design models and summarize solution methods for these problems as well as many references from the network design literature. Nemhauser and Wolsey (1988) discuss many underlying methods from integer programming and combinatorial optimization.

Acknowledgments

We are grateful to Michel Goemans, Leslie Hall, Prakash Mirchandani, Hershel Safer, Laurence Wolsey, Richard Wong and Robert Tarjan for a careful reading of the manuscript and many useful suggestions. We are particularly grateful to William Cunningham for many valuable and detailed comments.

The research of the first and third authors was supported in part by the Presidential Young Investigator Grant 8451517-ECS of the National Science Foundation, by Grant AFOSR-88-0088 from the Air Force Office of Scientific Research, and by Grants from Analog Devices, Apple Computer, Inc., and Prime Computer.

References

Aashtiani, H.A., and T.L. Magnanti (1976), Implementing primal–dual network flow algorithms, Technical Report OR 055-76, Operations Research Center, M.I.T., Cambridge, MA.

Aho, A.V., J.E. Hopcroft, and J.D. Ullman (1974), *The Design and Analysis of Computer Algorithms* (Addison-Wesley, Reading, MA).

Ahuja, R.K., J.L. Batra, and S.K. Gupta (1984) A parametic algorithm for the convex cost network flow and related problems, *European J. of Oper. Res.* **16**, 222–235.

Ahuja, R.K., A.V. Goldberg, J.B. Orlin, and R.E. Tarjan (1988), Finding minimum-cost flows by double scaling, Working Paper No. 2047-88, Sloan School of Management, M.I.T., Cambridge, MA.

Ahuja, R.K., M. Kodialam, and J.B. Orlin (1988), Personal Communications.

Ahuja, R.K., K. Mehlhorn, J.B. Orlin, and R.E. Tarjan (1988), Faster algorithms for the shortest path problem, Technical Report No. 193, Operations Research Center, M.I.T., Cambridge, MA.

Ahuja, R.K., and J.B. Orlin (1987), A fast and simple algorithm for the maximum flow problem, Working Paper 1905-87, Sloan School of Management, M.I.T., Cambridge, MA, to appear in *Oper. Res.*

Ahuja, R.K., and J.B. Orlin (1988), Improved primal simplex algorithms for the shortest path, assignment and minimum cost flow problems, Working Paper 2090-88, Sloan School of Management, M.I.T., Cambridge, MA.

Ahuja, R.K., J.B. Orlin, C. Stein, and R.E. Tarjan (1988), Improved algorithms for bipartite network flow problems, to appear.

Ahuja, R.K., J.B. Orlin, and R.E. Tarjan (1988), Improved time bounds for the maximum flow problem, Working Paper 1966-87, Sloan School of Management, M.I.T., Cambridge, MA.

Akgül, M. (1985a), Shortest path and simplex method, Research Report, Department of Computer Science and Operations Research, North Carolina State University, Raleigh, NC.

Akgül, M. (1985b), A genuinely polynomial primal simplex algorithm for the assignment problem, Research Report, Department of Computer Science and Operations Research, North Carolina State University, Raleigh, NC.

Ali, I., D. Barnett, K. Farhangian, J. Kennington, B. Patty, B. Shetty, B. McCarl and P. Wong (1984), Multicommodity network problems: Applications and computations, *A.I.I.E. Trans.* **16**, 127–134.

Ali, A.I., R.V. Helgason, and J.L. Kennington (1978), The convex cost network flow problem: A state-of-the-art survey, Technical Report OREM 78001, Southern Methodist University, Dallas, TX.

Armstrong, R.D., D. Klingman, and D. Whitman (1980), Implementation and analysis of a variant of the dual method for the capacitated transshipment problem, *European J. Oper. Res.* **4**, 403–420.

Assad, A. (1978), Multicommodity network flows–A survey, *Networks* **8**, 37–91.

Balinski, M.L. (1985), Signature methods for the assignment problem, *Oper. Res.* **33**, 527–536.

Balinski, M.L., and R.E. Gomory (1964), A primal method for the assignment and transportation problems, *Man. Sci.* **10**, 578–593.

Barahona, F., and E. Tardos (1987), Note on Weintraub's minimum cost flow algorithm, Research Report, Dept. of Mathematics, M.I.T., Cambridge, MA.

Baratz, A.E. (1977), Construction and analysis of a network flow problem which forces Karzanov algorithm to $O(n^3)$ running time, Technical Report TM-83, Laboratory for Computer Science, MIT, Cambridge, MA.

Barr, R., F. Glover, and D. Klingman (1977a), The alternating path basis algorithm for the assignment problem, *Math. Prog.* **12**, 1–13.

Barr, R., F. Glover, and D. Klingman (1977b), A network augmenting path basis algorithm for transshipment problems, *Proceedings of the International Symposium on Extremal Methods and System Analysis*.

Barr, R., F. Glover, and D. Klingman (1978), Generalized alternating path algorithm for transportation problems, *European J. Oper. Res.* **2**, 137–144.

Barr, R., F. Glover, and D. Klingman (1979), Enhancement of spanning tree labeling procedures for network optimization, *INFOR* **17**, 16–34.

Bazaraa, M., and J.J. Jarvis (1978), *Linear Programming and Network Flows* (John Wiley & Sons, New York).

Bellman, R. (1958), On a routing problem, *Quart. Appl. Math.* **16**, 87–90.

Berge, C., and A. Ghouila-Houri (1962), *Programming, Games and Transportation Networks* (John Wiley & Sons, New York).

Bertsekas, D.P. (1979), A distributed algorithm for the assignment problem, Working Paper, Laboratory for Information and Decision Systems, M.I.T., Cambridge, MA; also in *Ann. of Oper. Res.* **14**, 105–123.

Bertsekas, D.P. (1981), A new algorithm for the assignment problem, *Math. Prog.* **21**, 152–171.

Bertsekas, D.P. (1985), A unified framework for primal–dual methods in minimum cost network flow problems, *Math. Prog.* **32**, 125–145.

Bertsekas, D.P. (1986), Distributed relaxation methods for linear network flow problems, *Proc. of 25th IEEE Conference on Decision and Control*, Athens, Greece.

Bertsekas, D.P. (1987), The auction algorithm: A distributed relaxation method for the assignment problem, Report LIDS-P-1653, Laboratory for Information Decision systems, M.I.T., Cambridge, MA; also in *Ann. of Oper. Res.* **14**, 105–123.

Bertsekas, D.P., and J. Eckstein (1988), Dual coordinate step methods for linear network flow problems, to appear in *Math. Prog. Ser. B*.

Bertsekas, D., and R. Gallager (1987), *Data Networks* (Prentice-Hall, Englewood Cliffs, NJ).

Bertsekas, D.P., P.A. Hosein, and P. Tseng (1987), Relaxation methods for network flow problems with convex arc costs, *SIAM J. Control and Optimization* **25**, 1219–1243.

Bertsekas, D.P., and P. Tseng (1988a), The relax codes for linear minimum cost network flow problems, in: B. Simeone, et al. (ed.), Fortran *Codes for Network Optimization*. As *Annals of Operations Research* **13**, 125–190.

Bertsekas, D.P., and P. Tseng (1988b), Relaxation methods for minimum cost ordinary and generalized network flow problems, *Oper. Res.* **36**, 93–114.

Bland, R.G., and D.L. Jensen (1985), On the computational behavior of a polynomial-time network flow algorithm, Technical Report 661, School of Operations Research and Industrial Engineering, Cornell University, Ithaca, N.Y.

Bodin, L.D., B.L. Golden, A.A. Assad, and M.O. Ball (1983), Routing and scheduling of vehicles and crews, *Comput. and Oper. Res.* **10**, 65–211.

Boyd, A., and J.B. Orlin (1986), Personal Communication.

Bradley, G., G. Brown, and G. Graves (1977), Design and implementation of large scale primal transshipment algorithms, *Man. Sci.* **21**, 1–38.

Bradley, S.P., A.C. Hax, and T.L. Magnanti (1977), *Applied Mathematical Programming* (Addison-Wesley, New York).

Busaker, R.G., and P.J. Gowen (1961), A procedure for determining a family of minimal-cost network flow patterns, O.R.O. Technical Report No. 15, Operational Research Office, Johns Hopkins University, Baltimore, MD.

Carpento, G., S. Martello, and P. Toth (1988), Algorithms and codes for the assignment problem, in: B. Simeone et al. (eds.), Fortran *Codes for Network Optimization*. As *Annals of Operations Research* **13**, 193–224.

Carraresi, P., and C. Sodini (1986), An efficient algorithm for the bipartite matching problem. *European J. Oper. Res.* **23**, 86–93.

Cheriyan, J. (1988), Parametrized worst case networks for preflow push algorithms. Technical Report, Computer Science Group, Tata Institute of Fundamental Research, Bombay, India.

Cheriyan, J., and S.N. Maheshwari (1987), Analysis of preflow push algorithm for maximum network flow, Technical Report, Dept. of Computer Science and Engineering, Indian Institute of Technology, New Delhi, India.

Cherkasky, R.V. (1977), Algorithm for construction of maximum flow in networks with complexity of $O(V^2\sqrt{E})$ operation, *Mathematical Methods of Solution of Economical Problems* **7**, 112–125 (in Russian).

Cheung, T. (1980), Computational comparison of eight methods for the maximum network flow problem, *ACM Trans. Math. Software* **6**, 1–16.

Christophides, N. (1975), *Graph Theory: An Algorithmic Approach* (Academic Press, New York).

Cunningham, W.H. (1976), A network simplex method, *Math. Prog.* **11**, 105–116.

Cunningham, W.H. (1979), Theoretical properties of the network simplex method, *Math. of Oper. Res.* **4**, 196–208.

Dantzig, G.B. (1951), Application of the simplex method to a transportation problem, in: T.C. Koopmans (ed.), *Activity Analysis of Production and Allocation* (John Wiley & Sons, New York) 359–373.

Dantzig, G.B. (1955), Upper bounds, secondary constraints, and block triangularity in linear programming, *Econometrica* **23**, 174–183.

Dantzig, G.B. (1960), On the shortest route through a network. *Man. Sci.* **6**, 187–190.

Dantzig, G.B. (1962), *Linear Programming and Extensions* (Princeton University Press, Princeton, NJ).

Dantzig, G.B. (1967), All shortest routes in a graph, in: P. Rosenthiel (ed.), *Theory of Graphs* (Gordon and Breach, New York) 91–92.

Dantzig, G.B., and D.R. Fulkerson (1956), On the max-flow min-cut theorem of networks, in: H.W. Kuhn and A.W. Tucker (ed.), *Linear Inequalities and Related Systems*, Annals of Mathematics Study 38 (Princeton University Press, Princeton, NJ) 215–221.

Dantzig, G.B., and P. Wolfe (1960), Decomposition principle for linear programs, *Oper. Res.* **8**, 101–111.

Dembo, R.S., and J.G. Klincewicz (1981), A scaled reduced gradient algorithm for network flow problems with convex separable costs, *Math. Prog. Study* **15**, 125–47.

Deo, N., and C. Pang (1984), Shortest path algorithms: Taxonomy and annotation, *Networks* **14**, 275–323.

Denardo, E.V., and B.L. Fox (1979), Shortest-route methods: 1. Reaching, pruning and buckets, *Oper. Res.* **27**, 161–186.

Derigs, U. (1985), The shortest augmenting path method for solving assignment problems: Motivation and computational experience, *Ann. of Oper. Res.* **4**, 57–102.

Derigs, U. (1988), *Programming in Networks and Graphs*, Lecture Notes in Economics and Mathematical Systems, Vol. 300 (Springer-Verlag, Berlin).

Derigs, U., and W. Meier (1988), Implementing Goldberg's max-flow algorithm: A computational investigation, Technical Report, University of Bayreuth, West Germany.

Dial, R. (1969), Algorithm 360: Shortest path forest with topological ordering, *Comm. ACM* **12**, 632–633.

Dial, R., F. Glover, D. Karney, and D. Klingman (1979), A computational analysis of alternative algorithms and labeling techniques for finding shortest path trees, *Networks* **9**, 215–248.

Dijkstra, E. (1959), A note on two problems in connexion with graphs, *Numerische Mathematik* **1**, 269–271

Dinic, E.A. (1970), Algorithm for solution of a problem of maximum flow in networks with power estimation, *Soviet Math. Dokl.* **11**, 1277–1280.

Dinic, E.A., and M.A. Kronrod (1969), An algorithm for solution of the assignment problem, *Soviet Math. Doklady* **10**, 1324–1326.

Edmonds, J. (1970), Exponential growth of the simplex method for the shortest path problem, Unpubished paper, University of Waterloo, Ontario, Canada.

Edmonds, J., and R.M. Karp (1972), Theoretical improvements in algorithmic efficiency of network flow problems, *J. ACM* **19**, 248–264.

Elam, J., F. Glover, and D. Klingman (1979), A strongly convergent primal simplex algorithm for generalized networks, *Math. of Oper. Res.* **4**, 39–59.

Emde Boas, P. van, R. Kaas, and E. Zijlstra (1977), Design and implementation of an efficient priority queue, *Math. Systems Theory* **10**, 99–127.

Elias, P., A. Feinstein, and C.E. Shannon (1956), Note on maximum flow through a network, *IRE Trans. on Inform. Theory* **2**, 117–119.

Engquist, M. (1982), A successive shortest path algorithm for the assignment problem, *INFOR* **20**, 370–384.

Even, S. (1976), The max-flow algorithm of Dinic and Karzanov: An exposition, Technical Report TM-80, Laboratory for Computer Science, M.I.T., Cambridge, MA.

Even, S. (1979), *Graph Algorithms* (Computer Science Press, Rockville, MD).

Even, S., and R.E. Tarjan (1975), Network flow and testing graph connectivity, *SIAM J. Comput.* **4**, 507–518.

Fernandez-Baca, D., and C.U. Martel (1987), On the efficiency of maximum flow algorithms on networks with small integer capacities, Research Report, Department of Computer Science, Iowa State University, Ames, IA; to appear in *Algorithmica*.

Florian, M. (1986), Nonlinear cost network models in transportation analysis, *Math. Prog. Study* **26**, 167–196.

Floyd, R.W. (1962), Algorithm 97: Shortest path, *Comm. ACM* **5**, 345.

Ford, L.R., Jr. (1956), Network flow theory, Report P-923, Rand Corp., Santa Monica, CA.

Ford, L.R., Jr., and D.R. Fulkerson (1956), Maximal flow through a network, *Canad. J. Math.* **8**, 399–404.

Ford, L.R., Jr., and D.R. Fulkerson (1956), Solving the transportation problem, *Man. Sci.* **3**, 24–32.

Ford, L.R., Jr., and D.R. Fulkerson (1957), A primal–dual algorithm for the capacitated Hitchcock problem, *Naval Res. Logist. Quart.* **4**, 47–54.

Ford, L.R., Jr., and D.R. Fulkerson (1958), Constructing maximal dynamic flows from static flows, *Oper. Res.* **6**, 419–433.

Ford, L.R., and D.R. Fulkerson (1958), A suggested computation for maximal multicommodity network flow, *Man. Sci.* **5**, 97–101.

Ford, L.R., Jr., and D.R. Fulkerson (1962), *Flows in Networks* (Princeton University Press, Princeton, NJ).

Francis, R., and P. Mirchandani (eds.) (1989), *Discrete Location Theory* (John Wiley & Sons, New York) to appear.

Frank, H., and I.T. Frisch. (1971), *Communication, Transmission, and Transportation Networks* (Addison-Wesley, New York).

Fredman, M.L. (1986), New bounds on the complexity of the shortest path problem, *SIAM J. of Computing* **5**, 83–89.

Fredman, M.L., and R.E. Tarjan (1984), Fibonacci heaps and their uses in improved network optimization algorithms, *25th Annual IEEE Symp. on Found. of Comp. Sci*, 338–346; also in *J. of ACM* **34**, (1987), 596–615.

Fujishige, S. (1986), An $O(m^3 \log n)$ capacity-rounding algorithm for the minimum cost circulation problem: A dual framework of Tardos' algorithm, *Math. Prog.* **35**, 298–309.

Fulkerson, D.R. (1961), An out-of-kilter method for minimal cost flow problems, *SIAM J. Appl. Math.* **9**, 18–27.

Fulkerson, D.R., and G.B. Dantzig (1955), Computation of maximum flow in networks, *Naval Res. Log. Quart.* **2**, 277–283.

Gabow, H.N. (1985), Scaling algorithms for network problems, *J. Comput. Systems Sci.* **31**, 148–168.

Gabow, H.N., and R.E. Tarjan (1987), Faster scaling algorithms for network problems, Manuscript.

Galil, Z. (1980), $O(V^{5/3}E^{2/3})$ algorithm for the maximum flow problem, *Acta Informatica* **14**, 221–242.

Galil, Z. (1981), On the theoretical efficiency of various network flow algorithms, *Theoretical Comp. Sci.* **14**, 103–111.

Galil, Z., and A. Naamad (1980), An $O(VE \log^2 V)$ algorithm for the maximum flow problem, *J. Comput. Systems Sci.* **21**, 203–217.

Galil, Z., and E. Tardos (1986), An $O(n^2(m + n \log n) \log n)$ min-cost flow algorithm, *Proc. 27th Annual Symp. on the Found. of Comp. Sci.*, 136–146.

Gallo, G., and S. Pallottino (1988), Shortest path algorithms, in: B. Simeone, P. Toth, G. Gallo, F. Maffioli, and S. Pallottino (eds.), *Fortran Codes for Network Optimization*. As *Annals of Operations Research* **13**, 3–79.

Gallo, G., S. Pallottino, C. Ruggen, and G. Starchi (1982), Shortest paths: A bibliography, Sofmat Document 81-P1-4-SOFMAT-27, Rome, Italy.

Gavish, B., P. Schweitzer, and E. Shlifer (1977), The zero pivot phenomenon in transportation problems and its computational implications, *Math. Prog.* **12**, 226–240.

Gibby, D., F. Glover, D. Klingman, and M. Mead (1983), A comparison of pivot selection rules for primal simplex based network codes, *Oper. Res. Letters* **2**, 199–202.

Gilsinn, J., and C. Witzgall (1973), A performance comparison of labeling algorithms for calculating shortest path trees, Technical Note 772, National Bureau of Standards, Washington, DC.

Glover, F., R. Glover, and D. Klingman (1984), The threshold shortest path algorithm, *Networks* **14** (1).

Glover, F., R. Glover, and D. Klingman (1986), Threshold assignment algorithm, *Math. Prog. Study* **26**, 12–37.

Glover, F., D. Karney, and D. Klingman (1974), Implementation and computational comparisons of primal, dual and primal–dual computer codes for minimum cost network flow problem, *Networks* **4**, 191–212.

Glover, F., D. Karney, D. Klingman, and A. Napier (1974), A computational study on start procedures, basis change criteria, and solution algorithms for transportation problem, *Man. Sci.* **20**, 793–813.

Glover, F., and D. Klingman (1976), Network applications in industry and government, *AIIE Transactions* **9**, 363–376.

Glover, F., D. Klingman, J. Mote, and D. Whitman (1979), Comprehensive computer evaluation and enhancement of maximum flow algorithms, *Applications of Management Science* **3**, 109–175.

Glover, F., D. Klingman, J. Mote, and D. Whitman (1984), A primal simplex variant for the maximum flow problem, *Naval Res. Logis. Quart.* **31**, 41–61.

Glover, F., D. Klingman, and N. Phillips (1985), A new polynomially bounded shortest path algorithm, *Oper. Res.* **33**, 65–73.

Glover, F., D. Klingman, N. Phillips, and R.F. Schneider (1985), New polynomial shortest path algorithms and their computational attributes, *Man. Sci.* **31**, 1106–1128.

Glover, F., D. Klingman, and J. Stutz (1974), Augmented threaded index method for network optimization, *INFOR* **12**, 293–298.

Goldberg, A.V. (1985), A new max-flow algorithm, Technical Report MIT/LCS/TM-291, Laboratory for Computer Science, M.I.T., Cambridge, MA.

Goldberg, A.V., M.D. Grigoriadis, and R.E. Tarjan (1988), Efficiency of the network simplex algorithm for the maximum flow problem. Manuscript.

Goldberg, A.V., S.A. Plotkin, and E. Tardos (1988), Combinatorial algorithms for the generalized circulation problem, Research Report, Laboratory for Computer Science, M.I.T., Cambridge, MA.

Goldberg, A.V., and R.E. Tarjan (1986), A new approach to the maximum flow problem, *Proc. 18th ACM Symp. on the Theory of Comput.*, 136–146.

Goldberg, A.V., and R.E. Tarjan (1987), Solving minimum cost flow problem by successive approximation, *Proc. 19th ACM Symp. on the Theory of Comput.*

Goldberg, A.V., and R.E. Tarjan (1988a), Solving minimum cost flow problem by successive approximation (A revision of Goldberg and Tarjan (1987)), to appear in *Math. Oper. Res.*

Goldberg, A.V., and R.E. Tarjan (1988b), Finding minimum-cost circulations by canceling negative cycles, *Proc. 20th ACM Symp. on the Theory of Comput.* 388–397.

Golden, B. (1988), Controlled rounding of tabular data for the census bureau: An application of LP and Networks, Seminar given at the Operations Research Center, M.I.T., Cambridge, MA.

Golden, B., and T.L. Magnanti (1977), Deterministic network optimization: A bibliography, *Networks* **7**, 149–183.

Goldfarb, D. (1985), Efficient dual simplex algorithms for the assignment problem, *Math. Prog.* **33**, 187–203.

Goldfarb, D., and M.D. Grigoriadis (1986), A computational comparison of the Dinic and network simplex methods for maximum flow, In: B. Simeone et al. (eds.), FORTRAN *Codes for Network Optimization.* As *Annals of Operations Research* **13**, 83–124.

Goldfarb, D., J. Hao, and S. Kai (1986), Efficient shortest path simplex algorithms, Research Report, Department of Operations Research and Industrial Engineering, Columbia University, New York, NY.

Goldfarb, D., J. Hao, and S. Kai (1987), Anti-stalling pivot rules for the network simplex algorithm, Research Report, Department of Operations Research and Industrial Engineering, Columbia University, New York, NY.

Goldfarb, D., and J. Hao (1988), A primal simplex algorithm that solves the maximum flow problem in at most nm pivots and $O(n^2m)$ time, Technical Report, Department of Operations Research and Industrial Engineering, Columbia University, New York, NY.

Goldfarb, D., and J.K. Reid (1977), A practicable steepest edge simplex algorithm, *Math. Prog.* **12**, 361–371.

Gomory, R.E., and T.C. Hu (1961), Multi-terminal network flows. *J. of SIAM* **9**, 551–570.

Gondran, M., and M. Minoux (1984), *Graphs and Algorithms* (Wiley-Interscience, New York).

Grigoriadis, M.D. (1986), An efficient implementation of the network simplex method, *Math. Prog. Study* **26**, 83–111.

Grigoriadis, M.D. (1988), Personal Communication.

Grigoriadis, M.D., and T. Hsu (1979), The Rutgers minimum cost network flow subroutines, *SIGMAP Bulletin of the ACM* **26**, 17–18.

Gusfield, D. (1987), Very simple algorithms and programs for all pairs network flow analysis, Research Report No. CSE-87-1, Dept. of Computer Science and Engineering., University of California, Davis, CA.

Gusfield, D., C. Martel, and D. Fernandez-Baca (1985), Fast algorithms for bipartite network flow, Technical Report No. YALEN/DCS/TR-356, Yale University, New Haven, CT.

Hamachar, H. (1979), Numerical investigations on the maximal flow algorithm of Karzanov, *Computing* **22**, 17–29.

Hassin, R., and D.B. Johnson (1985), An $O(n \log^2 n)$ algorithm for maximum flow in undirected planar networks, *SIAM J. Comput.* **14**, 612–624.

Hausman, D. (1978), *Integer Programming and Related Areas: A Classified Bibliography*, Lecture Notes in Economics and Mathematical Systems, Vol. 160 (Springer-Verlag, Berlin).

Helgason, R.V., and J.L. Kennington (1977), An efficient procedure for implementing a dual-simplex network flow algorithm, *AIIE Trans.* **9**, 63–68.

Hitchcock, F.L. (1941), The distribution of a product from several sources to numerous facilities, *J. Math. Phys.* **20**, 224–230.

Hoffman, A.J., and H.M. Markowitz (1963), A note on shortest path, assignment, and transportation problems, *Naval Res. Log. Quart.* **10**, 375–379.

Hopcroft, J.E., and R.M. Karp (1973), An $n^{5/2}$ algorithm for maximum matching in bipartite graphs, *SIAM J. of Comput.* **2**, 225–231.

Hu, T.C. (1963), Multicommodity network flows, *Oper. Res.* **11**, 344–360.

Hu, T.C. (1969), *Integer Programming and Network Flows* (Addison-Wesley, New York).

Hung, M.S. (1983), A polynomial simplex method for the assignment problem, *Oper. Res.* **31**, 595–600.

Hung, M.S., and W.O. Rom (1980), Solving the assignment problem by relaxation, *Oper. Res.* **28**, 969–982.

Imai, H. (1983), On the practical efficiency of various maximum flow algorithms, *J. Oper. Res. Soc. Japan* **26**, 61–82.

Imai, H., and M. Iri (1984), Practical efficiencies of existing shortest-path algorithms and a new bucket algorithm, *J. Oper. Res. Soc. Japan* **27**, 43–58.

Iri, M. (1960), A new method of solving transportation-network problems, *J. Oper. Res. Soc. Japan* **3**, 27–87.

Iri, M. (1969), *Network Flows, Transportation and Scheduling* (Academic Press, New York).

Itai, A., and Y. Shiloach (1979), Maximum flow in planar networks, *SIAM J. Comput.* **8**, 135–150.

Jensen, P.A., and W. Barnes (1980), *Network Flow Programming* (John Wiley & Sons, New York).

Jewell, W.S. (1958), Optimal flow through networks, Interim Technical Report No. 8, Operations Research Center, M.I.T., Cambridge, MA.

Jewell, W.S. (1962), Optimal flow through networks with gains, *Oper. Res.* **10**, 476–499.

Johnson, D.B. (1977a), Efficient algorithms for shortest paths in sparse networks, *J. ACM* **24**, 1–13.

Johnson, D.B. (1977b), Efficient special purpose priority queues, *Proc. 15th Annual Allerton Conference on Comm., Control and Computing*, 1–7.

Johnson, D.B. (1982), A priority queue in which initialization and queue operations take $O(\log \log D)$ time, *Math. Sys. Theory* **15**, 295–309.

Johnson, D.B., and S. Venkatesan (1982), Using divide and conquer to find flows in directed planar networks in $O(n^{3/2} \log n)$ time, in: *Proceedings of the 20th Annual Allerton Conference on Comm. Control, and Computing*, Univ. of Illinois, Urbana–Champaign, IL.

Johnson, E.L. (1966), Networks and basic solutions, *Oper. Res.* **14**, 619–624.

Jonker, R., and T. Volgenant (1986), Improving the Hungarian assignment algorithm, *Oper. Res. Letters* **5**, 171–175.

Jonker, R., and A. Volgenant (1987), A shortest augmenting path algorithm for dense and sparse linear assignment problems, *Computing* **38**, 325–340.

Kantorovich, L.V. (1939), Mathematical methods in the organization and planning of production, Publication House of the Leningrad University, 68 pp. Translated in *Man. Sci.* **6** (1960) 366–422.

Kapoor, S., and P. Vaidya (1986), Fast algorithms for convex quadratic programming and multicommodity flows, *Proc. of the 18th ACM Symp. on the Theory of Comp.*, 147–159.

Karmarkar, N. (1984), A new polynomial-time algorithm for linear programming, *Combinatorica* **4**, 373–395.

Karzanov, A.V. (1974), Determining the maximal flow in a network by the method of preflows, *Soviet Math. Doklady* **15**, 434–437.

Kastning, C. (1976), *Integer Programming and Related Areas: A Classified Bibliography*, Lecture Notes in Economics and Mathematical Systems. Vol. 128 (Springer-Verlag, Berlin).

Kelton, W.D., and A.M. Law (1978), A mean-time comparison of algorithms for the all-pairs shortest-path problem with arbitrary arc lengths, *Networks* **8**, 97–106.

Kennington, J.L. (1978), Survey of linear cost multicommodity network flows, *Oper. Res.* **26**, 209–236.

Kennington, J.L., and R.V. Helgason (1980), *Algorithms for Network Programming* (Wiley-Interscience, New York).

Kershenbaum, A. (1981), A note on finding shortest path trees, *Networks* **11**, 399–400.

Klein, M. (1967), A primal method for minimal cost flows, *Man. Sci.* **14**, 205–220.

Klincewicz, J.G. (1983), A Newton method for convex separable network flow problems, *Networks* **13**, 427–442.

Klingman, D., A. Napier, and J. Stutz (1974), NETGEN: A program for generating large scale capacitated assignment, transportation, and minimum cost flow network problems, *Man. Sci.* **20**, 814–821.

Koopmans, T.C. (1947), Optimum utilization of the transportation system, *Proceedings of the International Statistical Conference*, Washington, DC; also reprinted as supplement to *Econometrica* **17** (1949).

Kuhn, H.W. (1955), The Hungarian method for the assignment problem, *Naval Res. Log. Quart.* **2**, 83–97.

Lawler, E.L. (1976), *Combinatorial Optimization: Networks and Matroids* (Holt, Rinehart and Winston, New York).

Magnanti, T.L. (1981), Combinatorial optimization and vehicle fleet planning: Perspectives and prospects, *Networks* **11**, 179–214.

Magnanti, T.L., and R.T. Wong (1984), Network design and transportation planning: Models and algorithms, *Trans. Sci.* **18**, 1–56.

Malhotra, V.M., M.P. Kumar, and S.N. Maheshwari (1978), An $O(|V|^3)$ algorithm for finding maximum flows in networks, *Inform. Process. Lett.* **7**, 277–278.

Martel, C.V. (1978), A comparison of phase and non-phase network flow algorithms, Research Report, Dept. of Electrical and Computer Engineering, University of California, Davis, CA.

McGinnis, L.F. (1983), Implementation and testing of a primal–dual algorithm for the assignment problem, *Oper. Res.* **31**, 277–291.

Mehlhorn, K. (1984), *Data Structures and Algorithms* (Spinger-Verlag, Berlin).

Meyer, R.R. (1979), Two segment separable programming, *Man. Sci.* **25**, 285–295.

Meyer, R.R., and C.Y. Kao (1981), Secant approximation methods for convex optimization, *Math. Prog. Study* **14**, 143–162.

Minieka, E. (1978), *Optimization Algorithms for Networks and Graphs* (Marcel Dekker, New York).

Minoux, M. (1984), A polynomial algorithm for minimum quadratic cost flow problems, *European J. Oper. Res.* **18**, 377–387.

Minoux, M. (1985), Network synthesis and optimum network design problems: Models, solution methods and applications, Technical Report, Laboratoire MASI Universite Pierre et Marie Curie, Paris, France.

Minoux, M. (1986), Solving integer minimum cost flows with separable convex cost objective polynomially, *Math. Proc. Study* **26**, 237–239.

Minoux, M. (1987), Network synthesis and dynamic network optimization, *Ann. Discrete Math.* **31**, 283–324.

Minty, G.J. (1960), Monotone networks, *Proc. Roy. Soc. London Ser. A* **257**, 194–212.

Moore, E.F. (1957), The shortest path through a maze, in: *Proceedings of the International Symposium on the Theory of Switching Part II; The Annals of the Computation Laboratory of Harvard University* 30 (Harvard University Press, Boston, MA) 285–292.

Mulvey, J. (1978a), Pivot strategies for primal-simplex network codes, *J. ACM* **25**, 266–270.

Mulvey, J. (1978b), Testing a large-scale network optimization program, *Math. Prog.* **15**, 291–314.

Murty, K.G. (1976), *Linear and Combinatorial Programming* (John Wiley & Sons, New York).

Nemhauser, G.L., and L.A. Wolsey (1988), *Integer and Combinatorial Optimization* (John Wiley & Sons, New York).

Orden, A. (1956), The transshipment problem, *Man. Sci.* **2**, 276–285.

Orlin, J.B. (1983), Maximum-throughput dynamic network flows. *Math. Prog.* **27**, 214–231.

Orlin, J.B. (1984), Genuinely polynomial simplex and non-simplex algorithms for the minimum cost flow problem, Technical Report No. 1615-84, Sloan School of Management, M.I.T., Cambridge, MA.

Orlin, J.B. (1985), On the simplex algorithm for networks and generalized networks, *Math. Prog. Study* **24**, 166–178.

Orlin, J.B. (1988), A faster strongly polynomial minimum cost flow algorithm, *Proc. 20th ACM Symp. on the Theory of Comp.*, 377–387.

Orlin, J.B., and R.K. Ahuja. (1987), New distance-directed algorithms for maximum flow and parametric maximum flow problems, Working Paper 1908-87, Sloan School of Management, Massachusetts Institute of Technology, Cambridge, MA.

Orlin, J.B., and R.K. Ahuja (1988), New scaling algorithms for the assignment and minimum cycle mean problems, Working Paper No. OR 178-88, Operations Research Center, M.I.T., Cambridge, MA.

Papadimitriou, C.H., and K. Steiglitz. (1982), *Combinatorial Optimization: Algorithms and Complexity* (Prentice-Hall, Englewood Cliffs, NJ).

Pape, U. (1974), Implementation and Efficiency of Moore-algorithms for the shortest route problem, *Math. Prog.* **7**, 212–222.

Pape, U. (1980), Algorithm 562: Shortest path lengths, *ACM Trans. Math. Software* **6**, 450–455.

Phillips, D.T., and A. Garcia-Diaz (1981), *Fundamentals of Network Analysis* (Prentice-Hall, Englewood Cliffs, NJ).

Pollack, M., and W. Wiebenson (1960), Solutions of the shortest-route problem – A review, *Oper. Res.* **8**, 224–230.

Potts, R.B., and R.M. Oliver (1972), *Flows in Transportation Networks* (Academic Press, New York).

Rock, H. (1980), Scaling techniques for minimal cost network flows, in: V. Page (ed.), *Discrete Structures and Algorithms* (Carl Hansen, Munich) 101–191.

Rockafellar, R.T. (1984), *Network Flows and Monotropic Optimization* (Wiley-Interscience, New York).

Roohy-Laleh, E. (1980), *Improvements to the Theoretical Efficiency of the Network Simplex Method*, Unpublished Ph.D. Dissertation, Carleton University, Ottawa, Canada.

Rothfarb, B., N.P. Shein, and I.T. Frisch (1968), Common terminal multicommodity flow, *Oper. Res.* **16**, 202–205.

Sheffi, Y. (1985), *Urban Transportation Networks: Equilibrium Analysis with Mathematical Programming Methods* (Prentice-Hall, Englewood Cliffs, NJ).

Shiloach, Y., (1978), An $O(nI \log^2(I))$ maximum flow algorithm, Technical Report STAN-CS-78-702, Computer Science Dept., Stanford University, CA.

Shiloach, Y., and U. Vishkin (1982), An $O(n^2 \log n)$ parallel max-flow algorithm, *J. Algorithms* **3**, 128–146.

Sleator, D.D., and R.E. Tarjan (1983), A data structure for dynamic trees, *J. Comput. Systems Sci.* **24**, 362–391.

Smith, D.K. (1982), *Network Optimisation Practice: A Computational Guide* (John Wiley & Sons, New York).

Srinivasan, V., and G.L. Thompson (1973), Benefit-cost analysis of coding techniques for primal transportation algorithm, *J. ACM* **20**, 194–213.

Swamy, M.N.S., and K. Thulsiraman (1981), *Graphs, Networks, and Algorithms* (John Wiley & Sons, New York).

Syslo, M.M., N. Deo, and J.S. Kowalik (1983), *Discrete Optimization Algorithms* (Prentice-Hall, Englewood Cliffs, NJ).

Tabourier, Y. (1973), All shortest distances in a graph: An improvement to Dantzig's inductive algorithm, *Discrete Math.* **4**, 83–87.

Tardos, E. (1985), A strongly polynomial minimum cost circulation algorithm, *Combinatorica* **5**, 247–255.

Tarjan, R.E. (1983), *Data Structures and Network Algorithms* (SIAM, Philadelphia, PA).

Tarjan, R.E. (1984), A simple version of Karzanov's blocking flow algorithm, *Oper. Res. Letters* **2**, 265–268.

Tarjan, R.E. (1986), Algorithms for maximum network flow. *Math. Prog. Study* **26**, 1–11.

Tarjan, R.E. (1987), Personal Communication.

Tomizava N. (1972), On some techniques useful for solution of transportation network problems, *Networks* **1**, 173–194.

Truemper, K. (1977), On max flow with gains and pure min-cost flows, *SIAM J. Appl. Math.* **32**, 450–456.

Vaidya, P. (1987), An algorithm for linear programming which requires $O(((m + n)n^2 + (m + n)^{1.5}n)L)$ arithmetic operations, *Proc. of the 19th ACM Symp. on the Theory of Comp.*, 29–38.

Van Vliet, D. (1978), Improved shortest path algorithms for transport networks, *Transp. Res.* **12**, 7–20.

Von Randow, R. (1982), *Integer Programming and Related Areas: A Classified Bibliography 1978–1981*, Lecture Notes in Economics and Mathematical Systems, Vol. 197 (Springer-Verlag, Berlin).

Von Randow, R. (1985), *Integer Programming and Related Areas: A Classified Bibliography 1981–1984*, Lecture Notes in Economics and Mathematical Systems, Vol. 243 (Springer-Verlag, Berlin).

Wagner, R.A. (1976), A shortest path algorithm for edge-sparse graphs, *J. ACM* **23**, 50–57.

Warshall, S. (1962), A theorem on Boolean matrices, *J. ACM* **9**, 11–12.

Weintraub, A. (1974), A primal algorithm to solve network flow problems with convex costs, *Man. Sci.* **21**, 87–97.

Weintraub, A., and F. Barahona (1979), A dual algorithm for the assignment problem, Departmente de Industrias Report No. 2, Universidad de Chile-Sede Occidente, Chile.

Whiting, P.D., and J.A. Hillier (1960), A method for finding the shortest route through a road network, *Oper. Res. Quart.* **11**, 37–40.

Williams, J.W.J. (1964), Algorithm 232: Heapsort, *Comm. ACM* **7**, 347–348.

Zadeh, N. (1972), Theoretical efficiency of the Edmonds–Karp algorithm for computing maximal flows, *J. ACM* **19**, 184–192.

Zadeh, N. (1973a), A bad network problem for the simplex method and other minimum cost flow algorithms, *Math. Proc.* **5**, 255–266.

Zadeh, N. (1973b), More pathological examples for network flow problems, *Math. Prog.* **5**, 217–224.

Zadeh, N. (1979), Near equivalence of network flow algorithms, Technical Report No. 26, Dept. of Operations Research, Stanford University, CA.

G.L. Nemhauser et al., Eds., *Handbooks in OR & MS, Vol. 1*
© Elsevier Science Publishers B.V. (North-Holland) 1989

Chapter V

Polyhedral Combinatorics

W.R. Pulleyblank

*Department of Combinatorics and Optimization, University of Waterloo,
Waterloo, Ontario, Canada N2L 3G1*

1. Min–max relations, NP and co-NP

Polyhedral combinatorics deals with the interactions between linear algebra, Euclidean geometry, linear programming and combinatorial optimization. A problem of combinatorial optimization generally has the following characteristics. We have a finite groundset E, a family $\mathcal{F}$ of 'feasible' subsets of E and a weight w_e associated with each element e of E. We wish to find a feasible set $S \in \mathcal{F}$, for which $\Sigma\,(w_e \colon e \in S)$ is maximized, over all members of $\mathcal{F}$.

One of the main contributions of polyhedral combinatorics to this type of problem is that it provides min–max theorems. These often form an essential part of optimization algorithms, in ways which are discussed later. Another is that it provides so called adjacency criteria. These are methods of moving from one feasible member of $\mathcal{F}$ to another, in such a way that the change is 'simple' and the value of the objective function improves.

Most of this chapter deals with the role of polyhedral combinatorics in obtaining min–max relationships. This is introduced in the next section and the major methods and tools are presented in Sections 4 and 5. In Sections 7 and 8 we discuss two important ways of strengthening these relationships: facet characterizations and dual integrality.

Section 6 is devoted to polarity and blocking and antiblocking relations. This general theory provides methods for reversing the roles of objects in min–max relations. In Section 9 we discuss another useful polyhedral property, dimension, and explain some of its uses. In Section 10 we discuss adjacency, and describe several recent results, including a recent proof by D. Naddef that the famous Hirsch conjecture holds for all polyhedra having 0–1 vertices, which includes most of polyhedral combinatorics.

Section 3 is a basic section which presents all the relevant definitions and theorems (with proofs) of polyhedral theory. It should be viewed as a background section, and may be skimmed, then referred back to as necessary.

Section 11 discusses some recent approaches to obtaining polyhedral min–

max theorems using extra variables, as well as ways of eliminating such extra variables.

The following is an example which we will use throughout.

A *matching* in a graph $G = (V, E)$ is a set of edges which meet each node at most once. The *maximum matching problem* is to find a matching which contains as many edges as possible.

A *node cover* in a graph is a subset W of the nodes such that each edge is incident with at least one member of W. The *minimum node cover problem* is to find a node cover W in G such that $|W|$ is minimized. If M is any matching and W is any node cover, then W includes at least one end of each edge in M, and so $|W| \geq |M|$. This is a prototype of a combinatorial min–max relationship: For any graph $G = (V, E)$, the size of a maximum matching is always less than or equal to the size of a minimum node cover. The following are the sorts of questions we ask:

(1) For which graphs does this hold with equality?

(2) If it does not hold with equality for a class of graphs, can we find a different such relationship which does?

(3) How does this relationship extend to weighted problems?

The complete answer to (1) is surprisingly complicated. (See Lovász and Plummer (1986) or Bourjolly and Pulleyblank (1987).) The following is a classic theorem of König, which we prove in Section 2.

Theorem 1.1 (König (1916)). *If G is bipartite, then a maximum matching and a minimum node cover have the same cardinality.*

The triangle (see Figure 1.1(a)) shows that there are nonbipartite graphs for which we do not have equality, but the graph of Figure 1.1(b) shows that there are other nonbipartite graphs for which we do have equality.

Concerning question (2), Edmonds (1965) showed that we could obtain a similar relationship which would apply to general graphs, if we permitted covering not just with nodes but with odd cardinality subsets of the nodes according to the following rules:

Let S be an odd cardinality subset of the nodes. If $|S| = 1$, the S 'covers' all incident edges. If $|S| \geq 3$, then S 'covers' all edges with both ends in S.

In order to obtain a min–max relationship, we define the following 'weight' function. If $|S| = 1$, then the weight of S, denoted by w_S, is 1. If $|S| = 2k + 1$,

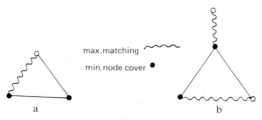

Fig. 1.1.

for $k \geq 1$, then $w_s = k$. An *odd set cover* is a family $\mathscr{C}$ of odd subsets of V such that each edge is covered by at least one member of $\mathscr{C}$. The weight $w(\mathscr{C})$ of $\mathscr{C}$ is the sum of the w_s for $S \in \mathscr{C}$. Again it is easy to see that $|M| \leq w(\mathscr{C})$ for any matching M and odd set cover $\mathscr{C}$.

Theorem 1.2 (Edmonds (1965)). *For any graph $G = (V, E)$, the maximum size of a matching equals the minimum weight of an odd set cover.*

These theorems of König and Edmonds illustrate a common theme in polyhedral combinatorics. Edmonds generalized König's theorem to a min–max equality which held for all graphs by adding extra objects with suitable weights to the relationship. However this resulted in a theorem which was not as strong as that of König for bipartite graphs, because of all these extra objects. Two fundamental problems of polyhedral combinatorics are finding valid min–max inequalities and finding 'minimal' such inequalities.

We could just as well ask for a min–max equation which gave the size of a minimum node cover in general graphs. Just as we had to enlarge our concept of a cover to obtain such a relationship for matchings, so too we would have to enlarge our concept of a matching to obtain such a relationship. However at present no such relationship is known and, indeed, since the problem of finding a minimum node cover in a general graph is NP-hard, it is generally believed that no general, tractable such relationship exists. We discuss the importance of computational complexity to polyhedral combinatorics later in this section.

Now we turn to the third question, the answer to which is a fundamental result of polyhedral combinatorics. Let us suppose that each edge e of our graph has a real weight c_e assigned to it and we wish to find a matching M for which $c(M) = \Sigma_{e \in M} c_e$ is maximized. This question is certainly more general – the maximum matching problem is obtained by letting $c_e = 1$ for all $e \in E$. In order to obtain a min–max relationship, we define a generalized cover: Assign to each node v a nonnegative value y_v such that for each edge e, if e joins nodes u and v, then $y_u + y_v \geq c_e$. Note that if $c_e = 1$ for all $e \in E$, and W is a node cover, then if we define

$$y_v = \begin{cases} 1 & \text{for } v \in W, \\ 0 & \text{for } v \in V \setminus W, \end{cases}$$

it follows that y is a generalized cover. Again, note that if M is any matching and y is any cover, then for each edge $e = uv \in M$, $y_u + y_v \geq c_e$ and so $c(M) \leq y(V) = \Sigma_{v \in V} y_v$. Thus once again we have a min–max inequality and we can ask for which graphs it holds and what to do when it does not.

Egerváry (1931) proved that if G is bipartite, then we have equality for any vector c of edge weights. He also showed that if c is integer valued, then an optimal y can be found which is also integer valued. This we show in the next section. Note that this result implies the König result – if $c_e = 1$ for all $e \in E$, then there exists an optimal cover $\hat{y}$ which is integral, and since $\hat{y}(V)$ is minimized subject to $\hat{y} \geq 0$, $\hat{y}_u + \hat{y}_v \geq c_e = 1$ for each edge $e = uv$, we automatically have $\hat{y}_v \in \{0, 1\}$ for all $v \in V$ and so y is the incidence vector of a cover W as described above.

If G is nonbipartite, and hence contains an odd cardinality cycle of cardinality $2k + 1$, we can let $c_e = 1$ for the edges of this cycle and $c_e = 0$ otherwise and the maximum weight of any matching will be k, whereas the minimum weight of any general cover y will be $k + \frac{1}{2}$, so we do not have equality.

This is a prototypical result of polyhedral combinatorics. Exactly why will become clear in the next section. It involves a weighted *linear* min–max relationship (i.e., we maximize the sum of the weights of the edges in the matching, not some nonlinear function of these weights) and we want a result which holds for all c. (Although, later we will see that this requirement is sometimes relaxed.)

There exists a weighted min–max theorem which applies to nonbipartite graphs, also due to Jack Edmonds. This is described in a later section, and remains one of the most important theorems of polyhedral combinatorics.

At this point we mention several other standard (unweighted) combinatorial optimization problems:

Spanning forest. Given a graph $G = (V, E)$, find a maximum cardinality subset of the edges which contains no cycle.

This is trivial – such a maximum spanning forest always contains $|V| - \kappa(G)$ elements, where $\kappa(G)$ is the number of components of G.

Node packing (or stable set). Given a graph $G = (V, E)$, a *node packing* or stable set is a set $S \subseteq V$ such that no edge joins two members of S. We wish to find a maximum cardinality node packing.

Since S is a node packing if and only if $W = V \setminus S$ is a node cover, this is equivalent to the minimum node cover problem.

Smallest cycle. Given a graph $G = (V, E)$ find a smallest cycle in G, i.e., a cycle having the minimum possible number of edges.

The size of a smallest cycle is called the *girth* of G, and this can be determined in polynomial time.

Longest cycle. Given a graph $G = (V, E)$, find a longest simple cycle in G, i.e., a simple cycle with the maximum possible number of edges.

This includes testing whether G is Hamiltonian, and so is NP-hard.

Disjoint paths. Given a directed graph $G = (V, A)$ and two designated nodes s and t, find a maximum number of pairwise arc disjoint paths from s to t.

The appendix contains a summary of the ideas from the field of computational complexity which are important to polyhedral combinatorics. A reader unfamiliar with these topics would be well-advised to read it at this time.

Finally, we address the question: Why are min–max relations useful? Entirely apart from any aesthetic considerations, these relationships are essential when it comes to developing algorithms. First, they provide a means for an algorithm to determine that it has obtained an optimal solution. This is a bigger problem than it may seem at first. In many cases, a branch and bound algorithm of a heuristic may chance upon a good or indeed optimal solution very quickly, but then spend enormous amounts of time trying to determine or verify optimality.

Even when we do not have a min–max equality, but just an inequality, we are often able to obtain very good bounds on the quality of a solution, which may make the solution quite acceptable for practical purposes. For example, examination scheduling problems are sometimes modelled as graph coloring problems in the following way: a node is constructed for each exam to be written and two nodes are joined if those examinations cannot be written concurrently. It is desired to 'color' the nodes with the smallest possible number of colors, in such a way that no two nodes receiving the same color are adjacent. Then the exams corresponding to the set of nodes of each color can be held concurrently, and so by minimizing the number of colors, we minimize the number of required periods.

Suppose we have 1000 examinations and have found a way to schedule them in 19 periods. Obviously if we can show that this is best possible, our work is done, but even if we could show that it was impossible to schedule them in fewer than 17 periods, we might be quite content to proceed with the 19 period schedule at hand.

It will turn out for hard problems, that the relationships obtained via polyhedral combinatorics are ideal for this sort of approximate bounding.

However, some caution is in order here. Not all min–max type relations and characterizations are equally useful. Consider as examples König's Theorem (Theorem 1.1) and the following result due to Berge. A node v is *unsaturated* by a matching M if M contains no edge incident with v. An *augmenting path* in a graph $G = (V, E)$ with respect to a matching M is a simple path joining two unsaturated nodes whose edges are alternately in $E \setminus M$ and M.

Theorem 1.3 (Berge (1957)). *A matching M in a graph is of maximum cardinality if and only if there is no augmenting path.*

Both provide correct and nontrivial characterizations of maximum matchings. However the first characterization enables us to give a short proof that a matching is of maximum cardinality. We simply exhibit a node cover of the same cardinality. The second enables us to give a short proof that a matching is *not* of maximum cardinality. We simply exhibit an augmenting path. But note that we already had a trivial means of showing this. All we had to do was display a larger matching.

Let us reformulate the maximum matching problem as a decision problem. Given G and a positive integer k, does there exist a matching of size (at least) k? Trivially the problem is in NP. The first theorem establishes that it is in co-NP. The second does not.

The min–max relations obtained via polyhedral combinatorics are generally of the former type. They provide 'good' characterizations of optimal solutions in that they provide a means to verify optimality in polynomial time. (This use of 'good' was initiated by Edmonds (1965).) Moreover, adjacency relationships of combinatorial polyhedra also often provide theorems of the augmenting path type, which gives us a method of improving a suboptimal solution.

In closing this section, we briefly discuss the previously mentioned (un-weighted) problems from the point of view of min–max relationships. We have seen that theorems of König and Edmonds give min–max relationships for maximum matching in bipartite and general graphs respectively. A min–max theorem for the size of a largest spanning tree is trivial. The node packing and node covering problems and the longest cycle problem are NP-hard, and no general min–max equations are known.

The size of a smallest cycle in a graph can however be computed polyno-mially – just delete each edge in turn, and find a shortest path joining its endpoints in the resulting graph. Thus the decision form of the problem is in P, hence NP and co-NP. However no 'natural' min–max relationship is known.

Finally, consider the disjoint paths problem. A subset C of A is called an s–t-cut in G if there exists a subset S of the nodes such that $s \in S$, $t \in V \setminus S$, and C consists of precisely all those arcs with tail in S and head in $V \setminus S$. Then if P is any set of arc disjoint s–t-paths and C is any s–t-cut, each path uses up at least one arc of C, so $|P| \leq |C|$. A fundamental theorem of Ford and Fulkerson (1956) and Elias et al. (1956) is that this relationship holds as a min–max equality – the maximum number of arc disjoint s–t-paths is equal to the minimum size of an s–t-cut.

Again, this is an example of a good characterization. We can prove that k disjoint s–t-paths exist by exhibiting them. We can show that there do not exist $k + 1$ such paths by exhibiting an s–t-cut of cardinality k.

In the next section we introduce weighted versions of these problems and min–max characterizations, and thereby the main ideas of polyhedral com-binatorics.

We conclude this introductory section by summarizing our graph theoretical notation and conventions. All graphs considered are finite. The graph $G = (V, E)$ has nodeset V and edgeset E. Unless we state otherwise, each edge has two distinct ends, belonging to V. If there is a unique edge with ends u, v, then we may denote it by uv. A *loop* is an edge with two identical ends. If the graph is directed, then each edge has one end designated as the *head* and the other as the *tail*. In this case we call the edges *arcs*.

For any graph $G = (V, E)$, $\kappa(G)$ denotes the number of connected compo-nents. For any $S \subseteq V$, we let $\delta(S)$ denote the set of edges with exactly one end in S, and call such a set of edges a *cut*. We abbreviate $\delta(\{v\})$ by $\delta(v)$. We let

$E(S)$ denote the set of edges with both ends in S and let $G[S] = (S, E(S))$ denote the subgraph induced by S. For any $J \subseteq E$, we let $G(J)$ denote the subgraph induced by J. That is, the nodeset of $G(J)$ consists of all nodes incident with edges in J, and the edgeset is J.

For any $S \subseteq V$, we let $G - S$ denote the graph obtained by deleting all nodes of S and incident edges. I.e., $G - S = G[V \backslash S]$. Similarly, for $J \subseteq E$, $G - J$ is the graph obtained by deleting the edges in J, i.e., $G - J = (V, E \backslash J)$. For singletons, we omit the brackets, i.e., we write $G - v$ for $G - \{v\}$ and $G - j$ for $G - \{j\}$, for $v \in V$ and $j \in E$.

A graph is *bipartite* if its nodeset can be partitioned into two sets U and V such that every edge joins a node of U to a node of V. A graph is bipartite if and only if every cycle contains an even number of edges (or nodes).

2. Weighted min–max relations and polyhedra

Let $G = (V, E)$ be a graph and let $c = (c_e : e \in E)$ be a vector of real edge weights. A *perfect matching* is a matching which meets, or saturates, every node. Suppose we wish to find a perfect matching M for which the sum of the weights of the edges is maximized. This has a natural formulation as a mathematical programming problem. For each edge e we define a variable x_e which will be permitted to take the value 0 or 1. We can then represent $J \subseteq E$ by its incidence vector x^J, where

$$x_e^J = \begin{cases} 0 & \text{if } e \notin J, \\ 1 & \text{if } e \in J. \end{cases}$$

We let $\mathbb{R}^E$ denote the set of all real valued vectors indexed by E. For any $J \subseteq E$ and $x \in \mathbb{R}^E$, we let $x(J)$ denote $\Sigma(x_j : j \in J)$. Now, let $\mathcal{M} = \{x^M \in \mathbb{R}^E : M$ is a perfect matching in $G\}$. Then $\mathcal{M}$ is a finite set of 0–1 valued vectors, and the convex hull of these vectors is a polytope, in $\mathbb{R}^E$, called the *perfect matching polytope* PM(G). Moreover, finding a perfect matching M for which $c(M)$ is maximized is almost the same as solving the problem: maximize cx, subject to $x \in$ PM(G). (We say 'almost', because there will in some cases exist a member of PM(G) which maximizes cx, but which is not the incidence vector of a perfect matching, rather it it is a convex combination of the incidence vectors of a set of perfect matchings, all of which maximize cx. See Section 3.)

A fundamental theorem of polyhedral theory, due to Weyl (1935), is that every polytope is the solution set of a finite system of linear inequalities and equations. Our objective now is to find such a system for PM(G). For if we are successful, we will then be able to use linear programming duality to obtain a weighted min–max theorem of the type we desire.

Theorem 2.1. *For any bipartite graph $G = (V, E)$, the perfect matching polytope* PM(G) *is the set of all $x \in \mathbb{R}^E$ satisfying*

$$x \geqslant 0 , \tag{2.1}$$

$$x(\delta(v)) = 1 \quad \text{for all } v \in V . \tag{2.2}$$

(Note that, by our notational conventions, $x(\delta(v))$ is the sum of the values x_e over all edges e incident with v.)

Proof. Let P be the solution set to (2.1) and (2.2). Since the incidence vector x^M of any perfect matching M satisfies (2.1) and (2.2), $\mathcal{M} \subseteq P$ and so $PM(G) \subseteq P$. Moreover, any integer valued solution to (2.1) and (2.2) can easily seen to be a member of $\mathcal{M}$. What we must show is that $P = PM(G)$, i.e., that every member of P is expressible as a convex combination of members of $\mathcal{M}$. Suppose there existed $\tilde{x} \in P$ which was not so expressible, and suppose we choose such an $\tilde{x}$ such that $F = \{e \in E : 0 < \tilde{x}_e < 1\}$ is minimal. As we remarked, $F \neq \emptyset$. Since $\tilde{x}$ satisfies (2.2), no node can be incident with just one member of F, so F contains the edgeset of some cycle C of G. Since G is bipartite, this cycle has an even number of edges. Let $d \in \mathbb{R}^E$ be a vector which is zero for all edges j not in C, and alternately 1 and -1 for the edges of C. Note that for any $\Delta \in \mathbb{R}$, the vector $\tilde{x} + \Delta \cdot d$ will satisfy $(\tilde{x} + \Delta \cdot d)(\delta(v)) = \tilde{x}(\delta(v)) = 1$. However if $|\Delta|$ is too large, we will not have $\tilde{x} + \Delta \cdot d \geqslant 0$. Choose Δ_1 and Δ_2 as large as possible such that $x^1 = \tilde{x} + \Delta_1 d \geqslant 0$ and $x^2 = \tilde{x} - \Delta_2 d \geqslant 0$. Then $x^1, x^2 \in P$ and each has strictly fewer fractional components than $\tilde{x}$ so each is in $PM(G)$. But $\tilde{x} = (\Delta_2 x^1 + \Delta_1 x^2)/(\Delta_1 + \Delta_2)$ and so $\tilde{x}$ is a convex combination of members of $PM(G)$, a contradiction. $\square$

Before discussing the weighted min–max relations we can obtain, we wish to give an (almost) equivalent form of this theorem. A matrix is called *doubly stochastic* if all entries are non-negative and the sum of the entries in each row and column is exactly one. A *permutation matrix* is a square matrix of 0's and 1's such that each row and each column contains exactly one 1. (That is, a permutation matrix is an integral doubly stochastic matrix.)

Theorem 2.2 (Birkhoff (1946), von Neumann (1953)). *A doubly stochastic matrix is a convex combination of permutation matrices.*

This is an immediate consequence of Theorem 2.1. For if A is an $n \times n$ doubly stochastic matrix, then we construct a bipartite graph $G = (V, E)$ with a node for each row and each column and an edge for each element a_{ij} joining the nodes corresponding to row i and column j. The conditions for A to be doubly stochastic are just (2.1) and (2.2). Moreover, M is a perfect matching in G if and only if the incidence vector corresponds to a permutation matrix.

Theorem 2.1 is slightly more general than Theorem 2.2, in that the latter theorem restricts its attention to complete bipartite graphs. However, it is an elementary result of polyhedral theory that Theorem 2.1 is implied by Theorem 2.2. This is discussed in the next section. See Proposition 3.12.

Notice too, that Theorem 2.1 is not exactly a weighted generalization of König's theorem concerning the size of a largest matching, in that it is restricted to perfect matchings. However this is easily remedied. Let $\mathcal{M} = \{x^M \in \mathbb{R}^E: M$ is a matching in $G\}$ and let $M(G)$ be the convex hull of the members of $\mathcal{M}$. The polytope $M(G)$ is called the *matching polytope* of G.

Theorem 2.3. *For any bipartite graph $G = (V, E)$, the matching polytope $M(G)$ is the set of all $x \in \mathbb{R}^E$ satisfying*

$$x \geq 0 \quad and \quad x(\delta(v)) \leq 1 \quad for \ all \ v \in V. \tag{2.3}$$

Proof. Construct a new bipartite graph G' by taking two disjoint copies $G^1 = (V^1, E^1)$ and $G^2 = (V^2, E^2)$ of G, and joining each node $v^1 \in V^1$ to the corresponding node $v^2 \in V^2$. Now let $\tilde{x}$ satisfy (2.1), (2.3) for G. Define a vector x' by letting $x'_{j_1} = x'_{j_2} = \tilde{x}_j$, for all $j \in E$, where j_1 and j_2 are the edges in E^1 and E^2 coresponding to j, and let $x'_j = 1 - \tilde{x}(\delta(v))$ if j joins the nodes $v^1 \in V^1$ and $v^2 \in V^2$ which correspond to $v \in V$. Then x' satisfies (2.1) and (2.2) so by Theorem 2.1, x' is a convex combination of the incidence vectors of perfect matchings of G'. But for each such perfect matching of G', the edges in E^1 correspond to a matching in G, so $\tilde{x}$ is the same convex combination of matchings in G, i.e., $\tilde{x} \in M(G)$. $\square$

Now we can apply linear programming duality (see Theorem 3.3) to obtain an equivalent min–max theorem:

Theorem 2.4. *Let $G = (V, E)$ be a bipartite graph and let $c = (c_e: e \in E)$ be a vector of edge weights. Then*

$$\max\{c(M): M \ is \ a \ matching \ in \ G\}$$

$$= \min\left\{\sum_{v \in V} y_v: y \geq 0 \ and \ y_u + y_v \geq c_{uv} \ for \ every \ uv \in E\right\}.$$

In order to give this theorem a more combinatorial flavor, we wish to impose some integrality constraints on the dual solution. In particular, we wish to show that if we restrict ourselves to integer edge weights, then there will always exist an integer optimal solution y. This is a common activity – attempting to show that, for certain objective functions, optimal solutions can be found which satisfy integrality conditions. The dual problem to the linear program of maximizing cx subject to (2.3) is minimize $y(V)$

subject to $y \geqslant 0$,   (2.4)

$y_u + y_v \geqslant c_{uv}$ for every $uv \in E$.

Theorem 2.5. *If c is integer valued, and G is bipartite, then* (2.4) *has an integer optimal solution.*

Proof. For any feasible solution y to (2.4), let $W(y) = \{v \in V: y_v = 0\}$ and let $J(y) = \{uv \in E: y_u + y_v = c_{uv}\}$. Since $y \geqslant 0$, the linear program (2.4) always has an optimal solution. Let $\hat{y}$ be an optimal solution for which $W(\hat{y}) \cup J(\hat{y})$ is maximal. Let G' be the subgraph of G induced by $J(\hat{y})$. Suppose some component K of G' contains no node of $W(\hat{y})$. Since K is bipartite, we can add a suitable $\Delta > 0$ to the value of $\hat{y}_v$ for all nodes belonging to the smaller part of K and subtract the same value from $\hat{y}_v$ for all nodes belonging to the other part, and obtain a new optimal solution y^* which contradicts the maximality of $W(\hat{y}) \cup J(\hat{y})$. Therefore every component contains a node having $\hat{y}_v = 0$, and so since $\hat{c}$ is integral, $\hat{y}$ is integral. $\square$

If we combine Theorems 2.4 and 2.5, we obtain the weighted generalization of König's theorem, due to Egerváry (1931):

Theorem 2.6. *Let $G = (V, E)$ be a bipartite graph and let $c = (c_e: e \in E)$ be a vector of integral weights. Then*

$$\max\{c(M): M \text{ is a matching of } G\}$$

$$= \min\left\{ \sum_{v \in V} y_v: y \geqslant 0, \text{ integer, and } y_u + y_v \geqslant c_{uv} \right.$$

$$\left. \text{ for every edge } uv \in E \right\}.$$

Now we make some important remarks: First, notice that König's theorem follows immediately from Theorem 2.6. Just let $c_j = 1$ for all $j \in E$. Since clearly $y_u^* \leqslant \max\{c_j: j \in E\}$ for all $u \in V$, for any optimal solution y^*, there must exist a 0–1 valued optimal solution which is the incidence vector of a node cover, as required. However, it is not nearly as easy to deduce König's theorem from Theorem 2.4, in which we do not have the integrality condition on the dual solution.

Second, we did not in fact need to prove Theorem 2.3. It is an immediate consequence of Theorem 2.5, plus a general theorem concerning *Total Dual Integrality*. Specifically, suppose we can obtain an integral linear system such that for every integral objective function for which the optimal value is bounded, there exists an integral optimal dual solution. Then it is true that all vertices of the corresponding polyhedron are integral valued. See Section 8.

Third, suppose that G is the triangle K_3, and we define all edge weights to be one. Then the maximum weight of a matching is 1, the maximum of $x(E)$, subject to (2.1) and (2.2) is $\frac{3}{2}$, the minimum weight of a cover is 2, and the value of the optimal solution to (2.4) is $\frac{3}{2}$. This is a typical situation. Not having enough inequalities to define the desired polyhedron is equivalent to not having enough dual variables to obtain a min–max equation. And frequently we can obtain a better solution when we are not restricted to integral solutions. Two basic problems of polyhedral combinatorics are, for a given combinatorially defined polyhedron, to obtain enough inequalities, or equivalently, dual variables, for a min–max equality to hold and for an integer min–max equality to hold.

What we have discussed in this section is a special case of integer programming. Virtually all combinatorial optimization problems having linear objective functions can be formulated as integer linear programs, see Chapter 6 of this volume. For example, the incidence vectors of the matchings of any graph G are the feasible solutions to the following system:

$$0 \leqslant x_e \quad \text{for all } e \in E ,$$

$$x_e \text{ integer} ,$$

$$x(\delta(v)) \leqslant 1 \quad \text{for all } v \in V .$$

A standard approach to solving any integer programming problem is to add extra inequalities – cuts – which are satisfied by the integer solutions to the linear system (without integrality constraints) but violated by any fractional solutions which cannot be expressed as convex combinations of integral solutions. We have seen that if G is bipartite, then no extra inequalities need be added. If G is nonbipartite, then some must always be added.

One of the seductive aspects of polyhedral combinatorics is that for any integer linear program, there always exists a finite set of cuts, such that if they are added, the integrality constraints can be removed. Often, the necessary cuts have a very natural form. However a consequence of the developments in the field of complexity is that if a tractable such family of cuts exists for an NP-complete problem, then NP = co-NP. Consequently, most people do not believe they exist.

In closing this section, we note that all of the problems introduced in Section 1 have natural weighted generalizations, and it is these generalizations which are the topic of polyhedral combinatorics. We have already discussed the weighted matching problem.

Maximum weight spanning forest. Given a graph $G = (V, E)$, and a vector $(c_e : e \in E)$ of edge weights, find a spanning forest for which the sum of the edge weights is maximized. This is the prototype problem for the area of matroid optimization, one of the important branches of polyhedral combinatorics. The problem is solved by the obvious greedy algorithm – choose the edges in order of decreasing weight, as long as the edge does not complete a cycle with those already chosen. There are also attractive polyhedral theorems, which we discuss later.

Minimum weight node cover or maximum weight node packing. Given a graph $G = (V, F)$ and a vector $(c_v : v \in V)$ of node weights, find a node packing of maximum weight or a node cover of minimum weight. (These are equivalent because the complement of a node packing is a node cover.) These problems are NP-hard and only incomplete polyhedral descriptions are known.

Maximum weight cycle. Given a graph $G = (V, E)$ and a vector $c = (c_e : e \in E)$ of edge weights, find a simple cycle in G for which the sum of the weights is maximized. Setting $c_e = 1$ for all $e \in E$ or $c_e = -1$ for all $e \in E$ we obtain the longest and shortest cycle problems respectively. If we are given a vector $c' = (c'_e : e \in E)$ and define $c_e = M - c_e$ for M sufficiently large, then the optimal solution will be a minimum weight Hamilton cycle, i.e., the solution to the Travelling Salesman Problem. If all edge weights are negative, then we obtain the weighted girth problem – equivalently – given a set of positive weights, find a minimum weight simple cycle. This can be solved polynomially – just find, for each edge in turn, the weight of a shortest path joining its end nodes (not counting the edge itself) and add this to the weight of the edge. The minimum sum gives the optimal solution.

This is an example of a case where a problem is NP-hard for one class of objective functions, yet polynomially solvable for another class. In order to handle this situation polyhedrally, we will sometimes define polyhedra which appear less natural. For example, suppose P is the convex hull of the incidence vectors of the simple cycles of G. Since optimizing over P is NP-hard, we do not expect to obtain a complete linear description of P. However the *dominant* of any polyhedron P, denoted by dom(P), is the set of all x such that $x \geq y$ for some $y \in P$. If we minimize a positive objective function c over dom(P), we obtain an optimal solution which is a vertex of P, in this case, the incidence vector of a minimum weight cycle. If the objective function has a negative component c_j, then we can make the objective function arbitrarily negative by making x_j arbitrarily large. Thus we might expect to be able to obtain a polyhedral description of dom(P). See Section 6.

Minimum cost flow problems. Given a directed graph $G = (V, A)$, a vector $\alpha = (\alpha_j : j \in A)$ of positive integral arc capacities, a vector $c = (c_j : j \in A)$ of arc costs, designated nodes s, t and a positive integer k, we wish to find k directed paths from s to t such that each arc j appears in at most α_j of these paths and the sum of the costs of the paths is minimized where the cost of a path is the sum of the cost of the arcs in the path.

This is a fairly general example of a network flow problem. These form an important class of combinatorial optimization problems. They will only be discussed briefly here. The reader is referred to Chapter 4 of this volume.

3. Basic theory of polyhedra and linear systems

In this section we discuss the basic terminology and results of polyhedral theory which are used in later sections. The reader may wish to simply skim this section, and refer back to it as required. Good references are the recent books Schrijver (1986) and Nemhauser and Wolsey (1988) as well as the paper Bachem and Grötschel (1982). Throughout this section we illustrate the general theory by its application to the case of bipartite matching, introduced in the previous sections.

For any set S, recall that $\mathbb{R}^S$ denotes the set of real vectors indexed by S. Thus if I and J are finite sets, then $A \in \mathbb{R}^{I \times J}$ is a real matrix whose rows are indexed by the members of I and columns by the members of J. For $i \in I, j \in J$ we let A_{ij} denote the corresponding member of A and for $H \subseteq I$, we let $A[H]$ denote the submatrix $(A_{ij}: i \in H, j \in J)$ of A. Similarly, b_i is the element of $b \in \mathbb{R}^I$ indexed by i and $b[H] = (B_i: i \in H)$ for $H \subseteq I$. We denote the i-th row of A by $A[i]$ and the j-th column by A_j.

A polyhedron can be defined in two different ways, and it is this fact which is the basis for polyhedral combinatorics. First, a *polyhedron* is the solution set to a finite system of linear inequalities and equations. Let $a \in \mathbb{R}^J \setminus \{0\}$ and $\alpha \in \mathbb{R}$. The *halfspace* defined by the inequality $ax \le \alpha$ is the set of all $\hat{x} \in \mathbb{R}^J$ which satisfy $a\hat{x} \le \alpha$. The *hyperplane* defined by the inequality $ax \le \alpha$ is the set of all $\hat{x} \in \mathbb{R}^J$ satisfying $a\hat{x} = \alpha$. Thus our first definition of a polyhedron can be rephrased as:

a polyhedron is the intersection of a finite set of half spaces.

A *polytope* is a bounded polyhedron. That is, a polyhedron $P \subseteq \mathbb{R}^J$ is a polytope if and only if there exist $l, u \in \mathbb{R}^J$ such that $l \le x \le u$ for all $x \in P$.

Suppose we have a polyhedron P and wish to solve the optimization problem of maximizing cx for $x \in P$. The duality theory of linear programming provides us with a min–max theorem (see e.g., Nemhauser and Wolsey (1988) or Schrijver (1986)). Let

$$P = \{(x, u): A^1 x + B^1 u \le b^1, A^2 x + B^2 u = b^2, x \ge 0\}.$$

The *dual* linear program to maximizing $cx + du$, subject to $(x, u) \in P$ is

$$\text{minimize} \quad yb^1 + wb^2$$
$$\text{subject to} \quad yA^1 + wA^2 \ge c,$$
$$yB^1 + wB^2 = d, \tag{3.1}$$
$$y \ge 0.$$

Let P^* denote the set of feasible solutions to this dual linear program. The following basic results can be found in any text on linear programming or in Chapter 2 of this volume.

Theorem 3.1 (Weak duality). *If $(x, u) \in P$ and $(y, w) \in P^*$ then $cx + du \leqslant yb^1 + wb^2$.*

Corollary 3.2. *If $P^* \neq \emptyset$, then $cx + du$ cannot be made arbitrarily large, for $(x, u) \in P$.*

Theorem 3.3 (Strong duality). *If $\max\{cx + du: (x, u) \in P\}$ exists, then so too does $\min\{yb^1 + wb^2: (y, w) \in P^*\}$. Moreover*

$$\max\{cx + du: (x, u) \in P\} = \min\{yb^1 + wb^2: (y, w) \in P^*\} .$$

Theorem 3.4 (Complementary Slackness). *If $(\hat{x}, \hat{u}) \in P$ and $(\hat{y}, \hat{w}) \in P^*$ then they are both optimal solutions to the linear programs maximize$\{cx + du: (x, u) \in P\}$ and minimize$\{yb^1 + wb^2: (y, w) \in P^*\}$ respectively, if and only if*
(i) *$\hat{x}_j > 0$ implies $\hat{y}A^1_j + \hat{w}A^2_j = c_j$,*
(ii) *$\hat{y}_i > 0$ implies $A^1[i]x + B^1[i]u = b^1_i$.*

A particularly useful form of Theorem 3.3 is the following:

Lemma 3.5. *$P \neq \emptyset$ if and only if for every (y, w) satisfying*

$$yA^1 + wA^2 \geqslant 0 ,$$
$$yB^1 + wB^2 = 0 ,$$
$$y \geqslant 0 ,$$

we have $yb^1 + wb^2 \geqslant 0$.

This is a more general form of the well known Farkas Lemma (see, for example, Schrijver (1986)), obtained when only A^2, b^2, x and w are present. It is easy to deduce Lemma 3.5 from Farkas' Lemma.

Lemma 3.5 is essentially the case of Theorem 3.3, with $c = d = 0$. It can also be seen to imply Theorem 3.3. Moreover, one useful consequence is that it characterizes implied inequalities. We say that an inequality $ax \leqslant \alpha$ is *implied* by the system of inequalities $Ax \leqslant b$ if every x satisfying $Ax \leqslant b$ also satisfies $ax \leqslant \alpha$.

Corollary 3.6. *Suppose that the system $Ax \leqslant b$ has a solution. Then $ax \leqslant \alpha$ is implied if and only if there exists $\lambda \geqslant 0$ such that $a = \lambda A$ and $\alpha \geqslant \lambda b$.*

Proof. If such a λ exists, then the inequality $ax \leqslant (\lambda b)$ is a nonnegative combination of inequalities from $Ax \leqslant b$, so every solution to this system satisfies $ax \leqslant (\lambda b) \leqslant \alpha$, i.e., $ax \leqslant \alpha$ is implied. If no such λ exists, then by Lemma 3.5 there exists $\bar{x}$ and $\gamma \geqslant 0$ satisfying $A\bar{x} + \gamma b \geqslant 0$, $a\bar{x} + \gamma\alpha < 0$.

Suppose $\gamma = 0$. Let $\hat{x}$ satisfy $A\hat{x} \leq b$. Then for all $\rho \geq 0$, $A(\hat{x} - \rho\bar{x}) \leq A\hat{x} \leq b$, but $a(\hat{x} - \rho\bar{x}) = a\hat{x} - \rho a\bar{x}$. Since $a\bar{x} < 0$, by making ρ sufficiently large we can make $a(\hat{x} - \rho\bar{x})$ arbitrarily large, so the inequality $ax \leq \alpha$ is not implied, for any α. Finally, if $\gamma \neq 0$, then dividing by $-\gamma$, we obtain $A(\bar{x}/(-\gamma)) \leq b$, $a(\bar{x}/(-\gamma)) > \alpha$, so again, the inequality is not implied. $\square$

Before describing the second way of defining a polyhedron, we discuss the notions of linear and affine independence, as well as convex and affine hulls.

Let X be a finite subset of $\mathbb{R}^J$. Then X is *linearly independent* if whenever we have $\Sigma(\lambda_x x : x \in X) = 0$ for some $\lambda \in \mathbb{R}^X$, we have $\lambda = 0$. Similarly, X is said to be *affinely independent* if whenever $\Sigma(\lambda_x x : x \in X) = 0$ and $\Sigma(\lambda_x : x \in X) = 0$ for $\lambda \in \mathbb{R}^X$, we have $\lambda = 0$. That is, a set of vectors is affinely independent if and only if the set of vectors obtained by adding a new component having value one to each is linearly independent. For polyhedral combinatorics, affine independence is more important than linear independence because it is invariant under translations of the origin. For example, in $\mathbb{R}^2$ the vectors $\binom{0}{1}$ and $\binom{1}{2}$ are both linearly and affinely independent, but the vectors $\binom{1}{1}$, $\binom{2}{2}$ are affinely independent but linearly dependent. However the second vectors are obtained by adding $\binom{1}{0}$ to each of the first. In general we have:

Proposition 3.7. *For a finite set J, and a subset X of $\mathbb{R}^J$, the following are equivalent*:
  (i) *X is affinely independent.*
  (ii) *For any $w \in \mathbb{R}^J$, $\{x - w : x \in X\}$ is affinely independent.*
  (iii) *For any $\hat{x} \in X$, $\{x - \hat{x} : x \in X \setminus \{\hat{x}\}\}$ is linearly independent.*

Let X be a finite or infinite subset of $\mathbb{R}^J$. The *linear hull* of X or space generated by X is the set of all $\tilde{x} \in \mathbb{R}^J$ which can be expressed as $\tilde{x} = \Sigma(\lambda_x x : x \in \bar{X})$ for some finite $\bar{X} \subseteq X$. Such an $\tilde{x}$ is said to be a *linear combination* of X (or $\bar{X}$). If, in addition, $\Sigma(\lambda_x : x \in \bar{X}) = 1$, then $\tilde{x}$ is said to be an *affine combination* of X and the set of all such $\tilde{x}$ is called the *affine hull*. If we do not require $\Sigma(\lambda_x : x \in \bar{X})$ to be 1, but require $\lambda \geq 0$, then the set of all such $\tilde{x}$ is called the *conical hull* of X, or *cone generated* by X. If we require both $\Sigma(\lambda_x : x \in \bar{X}) = 1$ and $\lambda \geq 0$, then $\tilde{x}$ is said to be a *convex combination* of X and the set of all such $\tilde{x}$ is the *convex hull* of X. See Figure 3.1. We let cone(X) denote the cone generated by X and let conv(X) denote the convex hull of X.

The *linear* and *affine* ranks of $X \subseteq \mathbb{R}^J$ are the cardinalities of the largest linearly and affinely independent subsets of X, respectively, and are denoted by $r_l(X)$ and $r_a(X)$ respectively. We always have $r_l(X) \leq |J|$ and $r_a(X) \leq |J| + 1$. They are related as follows:

Proposition 3.8. *For any $S \subseteq \mathbb{R}^J$,*
  (i) *if 0 is in the affine hull of S, then $r_a(S) = r_l(S) + 1$;*
  (ii) *if 0 is not in the affine hull of S, then $r_a(S) = r_l(S)$.*

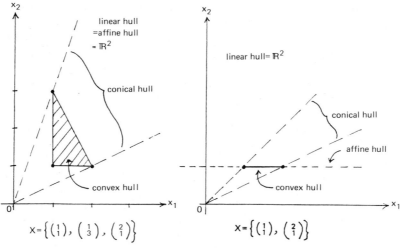

$$x = \left\{ \begin{pmatrix} 1 \\ 1 \end{pmatrix}, \begin{pmatrix} 1 \\ 3 \end{pmatrix}, \begin{pmatrix} 2 \\ 1 \end{pmatrix} \right\} \qquad x = \left\{ \begin{pmatrix} 1 \\ 1 \end{pmatrix}, \begin{pmatrix} 2 \\ 1 \end{pmatrix} \right\}$$

Fig. 3.1.

Now we apply these ideas to the case of bipartite matching. Let $G = (V, E)$ be a graph and for any $j \in E$, we let $\varepsilon^j \in \mathbb{R}^E$ be the edge's incidence vector, i.e.,

$$\varepsilon^j_k = \begin{cases} 1 & \text{if } k = j, \\ 0 & \text{if } k \in E \setminus \{j\}. \end{cases}$$

The matching polytope $M(G)$ is the convex hull of the incidence vectors of all matchings. The set $S = \{\varepsilon^j : j \in E\}$ is linearly independent, and $S \cup \{0\}$ is affinely independent, but not linearly independent. Since $S \cup \{0\} \subseteq M(G)$, $r_a(M(G)) = |E| + 1$ but $r_l(M(G)) = |E|$. The case for $PM(G)$ is more complicated and will be discussed later.

Now we can begin to describe the second way that polyhedra can be defined.

Theorem 3.9. *Let $P \subseteq \mathbb{R}^J$. Then P is a polytope, i.e., the solution set of a finite linear system $Ax \leq b$, $l \leq x \leq u$ if and only if there exists a finite set $X \subseteq \mathbb{R}^J$ such that P is the convex hull of X.*

Recall that in Theorem 2.3, we gave a finite linear system whose solution set in precisely $M(G)$ for a bipartite graph G.

Before we can describe the extension of Theorem 3.9 to (unbounded) polyhedra, we give the analogous but simpler result for cones. A *cone* is the solution set to a finite *homogeneous* linear system, i.e., a system of the form $Ax \geq 0$. A set X is a set of *generators* of a cone C if C is the conical hull of X.

Theorem 3.10 (Weyl (1935), Minkowski (1896)). *A set $C \subseteq \mathbb{R}^J$ is a cone, i.e., the solution set of a finite homogeneous linear system $Ax \geq 0$, if and only if there exists a finite set X of generators of C.*

Proof. First we show that the solution set C to any finite homogeneous system $Ax \geq 0$ has a finite set of generators. We use induction on the number of inequalities in this system; if there are none the set of unit vectors plus the vector all of whose components are -1 suffice. Now suppose we have a finite set X which generates $C = \{x: Ax \leq 0\}$ and we add a new inequality $ax \leq 0$ to our system. Partition X into sets $X^{>}, X^{0}, X^{<}$ depending on whether $ax > 0$, $ax = 0$ or $ax < 0$. For each pair (x, x') with $x \in X^{>}$, $x' \in X^{<}$, define

$$y(x, x') = (ax)x' - (ax')x . \tag{3.2}$$

Then $a \cdot y(x, x') = 0$ and $Ay(x, x') = (ax)Ax' - (ax')Ax \leq 0$. Therefore

$$X' = X^{<} \cup X^{0} \cup \{y(x, x'): x \in X^{>}, x' \in X^{<}\}$$
$$\subseteq C' = \{x: Ax \leq 0, ax \leq 0\} .$$

We claim that X' generates C'. For let $x^{*} \in C'$. Since $C' \subseteq C$, $x^{*} = \Sigma(\lambda_x x: x \in X)$ where $\lambda \geq 0$. This we can rewrite as

$$x^{*} = \sum_{X^{>}} \lambda_x x + \sum_{X^{0}} \lambda_x x + \sum_{X^{<}} \lambda_x x . \tag{3.3}$$

If $\lambda_x = 0$ for all $x \in X^{>}$, then x^{*} is a nonnegative linear combination of members of X', and we are done. If there exists $\hat{x} \in X^{>}$ such that $\lambda_{\hat{x}} > 0$, then there must exist $\tilde{x} \in X^{<}$ with $\lambda_{\tilde{x}} > 0$, for otherwise $ax^{*} > 0$. By (3.2) we have

$$(a\hat{x})\tilde{x} + (-a\tilde{x})\hat{x} - ay(\hat{x}, \tilde{x}) = 0 .$$

By subtracting a suitable multiple of this from (3.3), we can reduce one of $\lambda_{\hat{x}}, \lambda_{\tilde{x}}$ to zero, while giving $y(\hat{x}, \tilde{x})$ some positive coefficient. Repeating this process at most $|X^{>}| + |X^{<}|$ times results in an expression of x^{*} as a nonnegative combination of members of X', as required. Therefore X' generates C'.

Now suppose that C is the conical hull of a finite set $X \subseteq \mathbb{R}^{J}$. We wish to show that C is the solution set of a finite homogeneous system $Ax \leq 0$. Let $\bar{A} = \{a \in \mathbb{R}^{J}: ax \leq 0 \text{ for all } x \in X\}$. Then $\bar{A}$ is the solution set of a finite homogeneous linear system, so, by the first part of the proof, there is a finite set $A \subseteq \bar{A}$ such that every $a \in \bar{A}$ is a nonnegative linear combination of members of A. We claim that $C = \{x: Ax \leq 0\}$. Clearly $C \subseteq \{x: Ax \leq 0\}$. Suppose $\tilde{x} \not\in C$. That is, the linear system $\tilde{x} = \Sigma(\lambda_x x: x \in X)$, $\lambda \geq 0$ has no solution. By Lemma 3.5 (Farkas' Lemma), there exists $a \in \mathbb{R}^{J}$ satisfying $a\tilde{x} > 0$ but $ax \leq 0$ for all $x \in X$. Therefore $a \in \bar{A}$, but $\tilde{x}$ violates $a\tilde{x} \leq 0$. Therefore $\tilde{x} \not\in \{x: Ax \leq 0\}$, as required. $\square$

This result, called the Weyl–Minkowski Theorem, is one of the most fundamental results of polyhedral combinatorics. (Minkowski proved that the solution set to a finite homogeneous linear system is finitely generated. Weyl proved the converse.) The proof of the first part which we described could clearly be adopted to give an algorithm for constructing a finite set of generators. This is the so-called *double description method* of Motzkin et al. (1953). (It is developed significantly further in this reference.)

Now we are in a position to give a general representation theorem for polyhedra. This makes use of a natural relationship between polyhedra and cones, called *homogenization*. Let $P = \{x \in \mathbb{R}^J: Ax \leq b\}$ be a polyhedron. Define

$$\tilde{P} = \{(x, x_0) \in \mathbb{R}^{J \cup \{0\}}: Ax - bx_0 \leq 0, x_0 \geq 0\} .$$

Then $\tilde{P}$ is a cone in a space one dimension higher than that containing P. Moreover, P can be recovered from $\tilde{P}$ by requiring $x_0 = 1$, and then ignoring this component. This relationship allows us to obtain the following:

Theorem 3.11 (Motzkin (1936)). *For every polyhedron $P = \{x \in \mathbb{R}^J: Ax \leq b\}$ there exist finite sets $V, R \subseteq \mathbb{R}^J$ such that $P = \text{conv}(V) + \text{cone}(R)$. (That is, each $x \in P$ can be written as $x = y + z$, where $y \in \text{conv}(V)$, $z \in \text{cone}(R)$.) Conversely, for any finite sets $V, R \subseteq \mathbb{R}^J$, there exists a finite linear system $Ax \leq b$ such that $\text{conv}(V) + \text{cone}(R) = \{x \in \mathbb{R}^J: Ax \leq b\}$.*

Proof. Let P be a polyhedron and let $\tilde{P}$ be the result of homogenizing P. By Theorem 3.10, there is a finite set X of generators of $\tilde{P}$. Let R consist of all generators $x \in X$ for which $x_0 = 0$. Let V consist of all generators $x \in X$ for which $x_0 > 0$, scaled so that x_0 becomes 1. It is easy to see that for every $x \in P$, if we define a new coordinate equal to 1, then the resulting vector is a nonnegative combination of members of X, so that x is a convex combination of members of V plus a nonnegative combination of members of R. The converse is proved analogously. $\square$

Let P be a polyhedron. An inequality $ax \leq \alpha$ is called *valid* for P if $ax \leq \alpha$ for all $x \in P$; *supporting* if it is valid and there exists some $\hat{x} \in P$ satisfying $a\hat{x} = \alpha$. A *face* of a polyhedron is the set of all $x \in P$ satisfying $a\hat{x} = \alpha$, for some supporting inequality $ax \leq \alpha$. Also, by convention, the empty set and P itself are taken to be faces of P. Faces other than P are called *proper*.

Proposition 3.12. *Let F be a nonempty subset of $P = \{x \in \mathbb{R}^J: Ax \leq b\}$. Then F is a face of P if and only if there exists a subsystem $A'x \leq b'$ of $Ax \leq b$ such that $F = \{x \in P: A'x = b'\}$.*

Proof. Suppose F is a face of P. Then there exists a supporting inequality $ax \leq \alpha$ such that $F = \{x \in P: ax = \alpha\}$. Consider the linear program maximize $\{ax: x \in P\}$. The optimal solutions are precisely the members of F. Let $\hat{y}$ be an optimal dual solution and let $A'x \leq b'$ correspond to the positive coordinates of $\hat{y}$. By complementary slackness (Theorem 3.4), $F = \{x \in P: A'x = b'\}$ as required.

Conversely, if $F = \{x \in P: A'x = b'\}$ for some subsystem $A'x \leq b'$ of $Ax \leq b$, then add the inequalities of the system $A'x \leq b'$ to obtain an inequality $ax \leq \alpha$. Then every member x of F satisfies $ax = \alpha$, and every $x \in P \backslash F$ satisfies $ax < \alpha$, as required. $\square$

The nonempty faces of P are those subsets over which some linear objective function attains its maximum value. Note that we may define a polyhedron with two quite different appearing linear systems. However, since the faces are defined in terms of supporting inequalities, the set of faces is independent of the choice of defining system.

A *facet* of P is a maximal nonempty proper face. If $\{v\}$ is a face of P, for some $v \in P$, then v is called a *vertex*. Thus v is a vertex of P if and only if there is some linear objective function maximized over P only by v. Two vertices $u, v \in P$ are said to be *adjacent* if $\operatorname{conv}(\{u, v\})$ is a face of P. This face is called an *edge*.

Let $G = (V, E)$ be an arbitrary graph and consider the polyhedron defined by the system

$$x_e \geq 0 \quad \text{for all } x \in E \,,$$

$$x(\delta(v)) = 1 \quad \text{for all } v \in V \,.$$

This is called the *fractional matching polytope* of G, and denoted by $\mathrm{FM}(G)$. The incidence vector of every perfect matching is a vertex of this polytope but in general, for nonbipartite graphs, there are other nonintegral vertices as well.

Theorem 3.13. *Let $x \in \mathrm{FM}(G)$. Then x is a vertex if and only if $x_j \in \{0, \frac{1}{2}, 1\}$ for all $j \in E$ and the edges j for which $x_j = \frac{1}{2}$ form node disjoint odd cycles.*

Proof. The necessity of the condition follows from an easy adaptation of the proof of Theorem 2.1 and we omit the details. The sufficiency can be seen as follows. Let $\bar{x}$ satisfy the above properties, and define $c_j = -1$ if $\bar{x}_j = 0$, $c_j = 0$ if $\bar{x}_j > 0$. Then $\bar{x}$ is the unique member x of $\mathrm{FM}(G)$ for which $cx = 0$, since for all $x \in \mathrm{FM}(G) \backslash \{\bar{x}\}$, $cx < 0$. Therefore $\bar{x}$ is a vertex. $\square$

Note that this time we are starting with a linear system, and determining the form of the vertices. This is the reverse of the normal direction.

The *dimension of $S \subseteq \mathbb{R}^J$*, denoted by $\dim(S)$, is defined to be $r_a(S) - 1$. This corresponds to our intuitive notions. For example, a tetrahedron has dimension three, a triangle has dimension two, a line segment has dimension one and a point has dimension zero. Note that the empty set has dimension -1.

Let $A \in \mathbb{R}^{I \times J}$, $b \in \mathbb{R}^I$, let $I = I^= \cup I^\leq$ be a partition of I and let

$$P = \{x \in \mathbb{R}^J: A[I^=]x = b[I^=]; \ A[I^\leq]x \leq b[I^\leq]\} \,.$$

The *equality set I^** of P is the set of all $i \in I$ such that $A[i]x = b_i$, for all $x \in P$.

We call $A[I^*]x = b[I^*]$ the *equality subsystem*. We always have $I^= \subseteq I^*$, but there may be members of $I^\leqq$ which also belong to I^*. (By replacing each equation $ax = \alpha$ with inequalities $ax \leq \alpha$, $-ax \leq -\alpha$, we see that every polyhedron can be expressed with $I^= = \emptyset$.)

We call a point $\tilde{x}$ which satisfies $A[i]\tilde{x} < b_i$ for all $i \in I \backslash I^*$ an *interior point* of P. If $I^* = I$, then any member of P is an interior point. Suppose $I^* \subset I$. For each $i \in I \backslash I^*$, there must exist $x^i \in P$ satisfying $A[i]x^i < b_i$. If we define $\tilde{x} = \Sigma \, (x^i : i \in I \backslash I^*) / |I \backslash I^*|$, then $\tilde{x}$ is an interior point of P. Thus every non-empty polyhedron has interior points.

The following expression of the dimension of a polyhedron in terms of the rank of its equality set is fundamental.

Theorem 3.14. *Let $P = \{x \in \mathbb{R}^J : Ax \leq b\}$ be a polyhedron, where $A \in \mathbb{R}^{I \times J}$, and let I^* be the equality set. Then $\dim(P) = |J| - \rho$, where ρ is the linear rank of the matrix $A[I^*]$.*

Proof. Suppose that X is a set of $\dim(P) + 1$ affinely independent members of P. Then by Proposition 3.7 iii), for any $\hat{x} \in X$, $\{x - \hat{x} : x \in X \backslash \{\hat{x}\}\}$ is a set of linearly independent vectors satisfying $A[I^*]x = 0$. Therefore $r_l(A[I^*]) \leq |J| - (|X| - 1) = |J| - \dim(P)$, by basic linear algebra.

Conversely, let $\tilde{x}$ be an interior point of P. Again, by basic linear algebra, there exists a set X of $|J| - r_l(A[I^*])$ linearly independent solutions to $A[I^*]x = 0$. Then for $\varepsilon_x > 0$ sufficiently small, using Proposition 3.7 iii), the vectors $\tilde{x} + \varepsilon_x x$ for $x \in X$ are affinely independent members of P, so $\dim(P) \geq |J| - r_l(A[I^*])$, which gives the result. $\square$

A polyhedron $P \subseteq \mathbb{R}^J$ is said to be of *full dimension* if $\dim(P) = |J|$, or equivalently, no linear equation is satisfied by all members of P. Intuitively, it means that P cannot be embedded in a space having lower dimension than $\mathbb{R}^J$.

Let v be a vertex of $P = \{x \in \mathbb{R}^J : Ax \leq b\}$, where $A \in \mathbb{R}^{I \times J}$. Since $\{v\}$ has dimension zero, we must have $|J| = r_l(A[I^*])$. Inequalities not in the equality subsystem of $\{v\}$ play no part in the definition of v.

Let $G = (V, E)$ be a bipartite graph with matching polytope $M(G)$ and perfect matching polytope $PM(G)$. We have seen that $M(G) = \{x \in \mathbb{R}^E : Ax \leq 1, x \geq 0\}$ and $PM(G) = \{x \in \mathbb{R}^E : Ax = 1, x \geq 0\}$, where A is the node edge incidence matrix of G. By Proposition 3.12, $PM(G)$ is a face of $M(G)$. (Also, it consists of all $x \in M(G)$ satisfying the valid inequality $x(E) \leq |V|/2$ with equality.) We noted, following Proposition 3.8, that $r_a(M(G)) = |E| + 1$, so $\dim(M(G)) = |E|$, i.e., $M(G)$ is full dimensional. Let $\bar{E}$ be the set of edges of G which do not belong to any perfect matching. The equality subsystem of $PM(G)$ is $Ax = 1$, $x_j = 0$ for all $j \in \bar{E}$. The rank of this system is $|\bar{E}| + |V| - \kappa(G')$, where $G' = (V, E \backslash \bar{E})$. (Recall that $\kappa(G)$ denotes the number of components of G, for any graph G.) Therefore $\dim(PM(G)) = |E \backslash \bar{E}| - |V| + \kappa(G')$. If G is connected, and every edge belongs to a perfect matching, then $\dim(PM(G)) = |E| - |V| + 1$. (Note that this implies that such a graph has

$|E| - |V| + 1$ perfect matchings whose incidence vectors are linearly independent. It is a nontrivial exercise to construct such a set.)

From the point of view of finding defining linear systems for polyhedra specified as convex combinations of vectors, the facets (maximal nonempty proper faces) are the most important faces.

We say that an inequality $ax \le \alpha$ *induces* a face F of P if it is valid for P and $F = \{x \in P : ax = \alpha\}$. A system of inequalities and equations which define a polyhedron P is *minimal* if

(i) no inequality can be made into an equation without reducing the size of the solution set;

(ii) no inequality or equation can be omitted without enlarging the solution set.

Theorem 3.15. *Let* $P = \{x \in \mathbb{R}^J : A[I^*]x = b[I^*],\ A[I \backslash I^*]x \le b[I^*]\}$ *be a nonempty polyhedron, where* $A \in \mathbb{R}^{I \times J}$. *Then this defining system is minimal if and only if*

(i) *the rows of* $A[I^*]$ *are linearly independent and*

(ii) *for each* $i \in I \backslash I^*$, *the inequality* $A[i]x \le b_i$ *induces a distinct facet of P.*

Proof. Suppose that the system is minimal. If some row of $A[I^*]$ were a linear combination of other rows, then either the corresponding equation is redundant or else $P = \emptyset$, in either case a contradiction, so (i) holds.

Let $i \in I \backslash I^*$. Let P' be the solution set to the system obtained by removing the inequality $A[i]x \le b_i$. Then there exists $\tilde{x} \in P' \backslash P$, since our system is minimal. That is, we have

$$A[i]\tilde{x} > b_i, \qquad A[I^*]\tilde{x} = b[I^*],$$
$$A[I \backslash (I^* \cup \{i\})]\tilde{x} \le b[I \backslash (I^* \cup \{i\})].$$

P has an interior point x^0 which satisfies

$$A[I^*]x^0 = b[I^*], \qquad A[I \backslash I^*]x_0 < b[I \backslash I^*].$$

Therefore, for some $\varepsilon > 0$, the vector $z = \varepsilon x^0 + (1 - \varepsilon)\tilde{x}$ will satisfy

$$A[I^*]z = b[I^*], \qquad A[I \backslash (I^* \cup \{i\})]z < b[I \backslash (I^* \cup \{i\})],$$
$$A[i]z = b_i.$$

Therefore the inequality $A[i]x \le b_i$ induces a nonempty proper face F of P, having equality set $I^* \cup \{i\}$. Moreover, F must be a maximal proper face, since $\{i\}$ has no nonempty proper subset, and no other inequality could induce the same face. Thus (ii) is established.

Conversely, suppose that (i) and (ii) hold. It follows from (ii) that no inequality can be made into an equation without reducing the solution set.

Therefore I^* is the equality set and if any one of these equations were omitted, it follows from Theorem 3.14 that the dimension would increase, and therefore the solution set would be larger. Finally, let $i \in I \backslash I^*$ and let F be the facet of P induced by the inequality $A[i]x \leq b_i$. Let x^0 be an interior point of P and let $\tilde{x}$ be an interior point of F. Then for $\varepsilon > 0$ sufficiently small, the vector $z = (1 + \varepsilon)\tilde{x} - \varepsilon x^0$ will satisfy

$$A[I^*]z = b[I^*], \qquad A[I \backslash (I^* \cup \{i\})]z \leq b[I \backslash (I^* \cup \{i\})],$$
$$A[i]z > b_i.$$

Thus $z \notin P$, but the only inequality it violates is $A[i]x \leq b_i$. Hence our system is minimal. $\square$

We can now give two characterizations of facets, which are used extensively in polyhedral combinatorics.

Theorem 3.16. *Let F be a nonempty proper face of $P = \{x \in \mathbb{R}^J : Ax \leq b\}$ where $A \in \mathbb{R}^{I \times J}$ and let I^* be the equality set of P. Then the following are equivalent*:
(i) *F is a facet of P.*
(ii) *$\dim(F) = \dim(P) - 1$.*
(iii) *if $a, \bar{a} \in \mathbb{R}^J$ and $\alpha, \bar{\alpha} \in \mathbb{R}$ satisfy $F = \{x \in P: ax = \alpha\} = \{x \in P: \bar{a}x = \bar{\alpha}\}$ and both $ax \leq \alpha$ and $\bar{a}x \leq \bar{\alpha}$ are valid for P, then there exists $\lambda \in \mathbb{R}^{I^*}$ and positive $\gamma \in \mathbb{R}$ such that $\bar{a} = \gamma a + \lambda A[I^*]$ and $\bar{\alpha} = \gamma \alpha + \lambda b[I^*]$.*

Proof. We can assume that $A[I^*]x = b[I^*]$, $A[I \backslash I^*]x \leq b[I \backslash I^*]$ is a minimal defining system. Suppose that F is a facet. Then the equality set of F is $I^* \cup \{i\}$ for some $i \in I \backslash I^*$. Therefore, by Theorem 3.14, $\dim(F) \geq \dim(P) - 1$. But if $\dim(F) = \dim(P)$, then again by Theorem 3.14, there must exist λ such that $A[i] = \lambda A[I^*]$. If $b_i = \lambda b[I^*]$ then $F = P$ and if $b_i \neq \lambda b[I^*]$, then $F = \emptyset$, in either case a contradiction. Thus (i) implies (ii).

Now suppose that (ii) holds and let $ax \leq \alpha$ and $\bar{a}x \leq \bar{\alpha}$ be valid inequalities for P which induce F. By adding the equations $ax = \alpha$, $\bar{a}x = \bar{\alpha}$ to the defining system for P, we get a (redundant) defining system for F, and the equality subsystem $A'x = b'$ includes $A[I^*]x = b[I^*]$ and these two equations. If either a or $\bar{a}$ were a linear combination of rows of $A[I^*]$, then we would have $F = P$ or $F = \emptyset$, in either case a contradiction.

Since (ii) holds, $\dim(F) = \dim(P) - 1$ and so $r_l(A') = r_l(A[I^*]) + 1$. Therefore $\bar{a} = \gamma a + \lambda A[I^*]$ for $\gamma \in \mathbb{R}$, $\lambda \in \mathbb{R}^{I^*}$. If $\gamma = 0$, then $\bar{a}$ is a linear combination of rows of $A[I^*]$, which we already saw was impossible. If $\gamma < 0$ then a vector $x \in P$ satisfying $ax < \alpha$ would satisfy $\bar{a}x > \bar{\alpha}$, which would contradict the fact that P has an interior point. Therefore $\gamma > 0$ as required. Finally, if $\bar{\alpha} \neq \gamma \alpha + \lambda b[I^*]$, then $F = \emptyset$, a contradiction. Therefore (iii) holds.

Now we show that (iii) implies (i). Suppose that F is not a facet, i.e., not a maximal proper face. Let $H = \{i \in I \backslash I^*: A[i]x = b_i$, for all $x \in F\}$. By

Theorem 3.15, $|H| \geq 2$. Let $h, k \in H$. Since we assumed that our defining system is minimal there exists $\bar{x}$ which satisfies all inequalities and equations of our system except for the one indexed by k. Moreover, by taking an appropriate convex combination of $\bar{x}$ with an interior point of P, we can obtain $\hat{x}$ satisfying

$$A[I^*]\hat{x} = b[I^*],$$

$$A[i]\hat{x} < b[i] \quad \text{for all } i \in (I \setminus I^*) \setminus \{k\},$$

$$A[k]\hat{x} > b[\hat{x}].$$

For any strictly positive vector $\lambda \in \mathbb{R}^H$, if we let

$$a = \sum_{i \in H} \lambda_i A[i] \quad \text{and} \quad \alpha = \sum_{i \in H} \lambda_i b[i],$$

the inequality $ax \leq \alpha$ is valid for P and induces F. By choosing $\lambda_k > 0$ first sufficiently small and then sufficiently large, we can obtain such valid inequalities $a^1 x \leq \alpha^1$ and $a^2 x \leq \alpha^2$ such that $a^1 \hat{x} \leq \alpha^1$ and $a^2 \hat{x} > \alpha^2$. But this means that $a^2 x \leq \alpha^2$ cannot be obtained as a positive multiple of $a^1 x \leq \alpha^1$, plus a linear combination of equations $A[I^*]x = b[I^*]$. Hence (iii) does not hold, for $a^1 x \leq \alpha^1$ and $a^2 x \leq \alpha^2$, and we are done. $\square$

It follows from Theorems 3.15 and 3.16 that if P is of full dimension, then a minimal defining system has no equations and one inequality which induces each facet. Moreover, for each facet, the choice of inequality is unique, up to positive multiples. However when P is not of full dimension then although the bijection between facets and inequalities in a minimal system still holds, the 'near uniqueness' of facet inducing inequalities does not.

Consider again $M(G)$ and $PM(G)$ for a bipartite graph $G = (V, E)$. Let us suppose that G is connected. Now, $M(G) = \{x \in \mathbb{R}^E : Ax \leq 1, x \geq 0\}$, and it is of full dimension. For any $j \in E$, the inequality $x_j \geq 0$ is essential, for the vector $-\varepsilon^j$ (where ε^j is the incidence vector of edge j) satisfies all other inequalities, but is not in $M(G)$. Therefore $\{x \in M(G): x_j = 0\}$ is a facet for all $j \in E$. If node u is adjacent to a single node v, then the degree constraint $x(\delta(u)) \leq 1$ is implied by the constraint $x(\delta(v)) \leq 1$, and hence can be omitted unless these are identical. But this can only happen if v also has degree one, so since we assumed that G is connected, this would imply that G is K_2. Then $M(G)$ requires a single upper bound constraint $x_j \leq 1$ for the one edge, which can be viewed as $x(\delta(v)) \leq 1$ for either node. For any node v having degree two or more, the degree constraint $x(\delta(v)) \leq 1$ is facet inducing, for if j, k are distinct edges of $\delta(r)$, then $\hat{x} = \varepsilon^j + \varepsilon^k \notin M(G)$, but this is the only constraint it violates.

Recall that $\dim(PM(G)) = |E \setminus \bar{E}| - |V| + \kappa(G')$, where $\bar{E}$ is the set of edges in no perfect matching and $G' = G - \bar{E}$. A basis of the equality system consists of the equations $x_j = 0$ for all $j \in \bar{E}$, plus the degree constraints $x(\delta(v)) = 1$ for all nodes but one of each component of G'. The only candidates for facet inducing inequalities are the nonnegativity constraints $x_j \geq 0$ for $j \in E \backslash \bar{E}$. Let E^j consist of j, plus all edges of $G - j$ which belong to no perfect matching. Then $E^j \supset \bar{E}$, for all $j \in E \backslash \bar{E}$. The face of PM($G$) induced by $x_j \geq 0$ is the same as PM($G - j$). Therefore this face is a facet, i.e., has dimension one less than PM(G), if and only if $G - E^j$ has exactly $|E^j \backslash \bar{E}| - 1$ more components than $G - \bar{E}$. Further, for such a j, for all $k \in E^j \backslash \bar{E}$, the inequality $x_k \geq 0$ induces the same facet.

In closing, we mention a classical theorem which shows that a member of a polyhedron P can be expressed as a convex combination of a 'small' number of members of P.

Theorem 3.17 (Carathéodory (1911)). *Let $S \subseteq \mathbb{R}^J$ have dimension d and suppose $x \in \mathrm{conv}(S)$. Then there exists $\bar{S} \subseteq S$ such that S is affinely independent (and hence $|\bar{S}| \leq d + 1$) and $x \in \mathrm{conv}(\bar{S})$.*

Proof. Let $\bar{S}$ be a smallest subset of S for which there exists $\lambda > 0$ such that $x = \Sigma (\lambda_s s : s \in \bar{S})$ and $\Sigma (\lambda_s : s \in \bar{S}) = 1$. If $\bar{S}$ is affinely dependent, then there exists $S' \subseteq \bar{S}$ and $\mu = (\mu_s : s \in S')$ such that $\mu_s \neq 0$ for all $s \in S'$, $\Sigma (\mu_s s : s \in S') = 0$ and $\Sigma (\mu_s : s \in S) = 0$. Choose $t \in S'$ such that $\lambda_t / \mu_t = \min\{\lambda_s / \mu_s : s \in S'\}$. Let $\lambda_s' = \lambda_s - \lambda_t \mu_s / \mu_t$, for $s \in S'$, and $\lambda_s' = \lambda_s$ for $s \in \bar{S} \backslash S'$. Then $\lambda_s' \geq 0$ for all $s \in \bar{S}$; $\Sigma_{s \in \bar{S}} \lambda_s' = 1$, $x = \Sigma (\lambda_s' s : s \in \bar{S})$ and $\lambda_t' = 0$. This contradicts our choice of $\bar{S}$. $\square$

We note too that an analogous result holds for cones. If $x \in \mathrm{cone}(S)$, for $S \subseteq \mathbb{R}^J$, then there exists affinely independent $\bar{S} \subseteq S$ such that $x \in \mathrm{cone}(\bar{S})$.

4. Linear systems and combinatorial optimization

In this section we illustrate many of the techniques of polyhedral combinatorics, using the examples of the previous sections. Suppose we have a combinatorial optimization problem. Generally we have a finite ground set E, a weight c_e associated with each element of E and a family $\mathcal{F}$ of feasible subsets. We wish to find feasible $S \in \mathcal{F}$ for which $c(S) = \Sigma_{e \in S} c_e$ is maximized. We employ a five step process.

   (i) Represent the members of $\mathcal{F}$ by vectors; usually the 0–1 incidence vectors of the sets $S \in \mathcal{F}$ are used.
   (ii) Define the polyhedron P to be the convex hull of the vectors of part (i).
   (iii) Obtain a linear system sufficient to define P.
   (iv) Apply linear programming duality to obtain a min–max theorem.
   (v) Develop an algorithm using the above min–max theorem as a stopping criterion.

In fact, (iv) and (v) above are often combined, as is illustrated by the problem of finding a maximum weight forest in a graph. We are given a graph

$G = (V, E)$ and a vector $c = (c_e: e \in E)$ of edge weights and we wish to find a set $F \subseteq E$ such that F contains no cycles and $c(F)$ is maximized.

It is well known that the so-called greedy algorithm solves this problem. Sort the edges in order of decreasing weight. That is, $E = \{e_1, e_2, \ldots, e_m\}$ where $c_{e_1} \geq c_{e_2} \geq \cdots \geq c_{e_m}$. Construct F^* as follows: Initially $F^* = \emptyset$. For i going from 1 to m, if $F^* \cup \{e_i\}$ has no cycles and $c_{e_i} \geq 0$, then add e_i to F^*.

We represent a forest with edge set F by its 0–1 incidence vector $x^F \in \mathbb{R}^E$. We let $F(G)$, the *forest polytope*, denote the convex hull of these vectors.

Theorem 4.1. *For any graph $G = (V, E)$, the forest polytope $F(G)$ is the set of all $x \in \mathbb{R}^E$ satisfying*

$$x_e \geq 0 \quad \text{for all } e \in E, \tag{4.1}$$

$$x(E(S)) \leq |S| - 1 \quad \text{for all } S \subseteq V. \tag{4.2}$$

Edmonds (1971) showed that the greedy algorithm could also be used to construct a dual solution to the problem of maximizing cx subject to (4.1), (4.2). This provided the basis for his proof of Theorem 4.1.

Proof of Theorem 4.1. It is easy to see that inequalities (4.1) and (4.2) are valid for $F(G)$, and that every integer solution is the incidence vector of the edge set of a forest. What remains to show is that if we let $P = \{x \in \mathbb{R}^E: x \text{ satisfies (4.1) and (4.2)}\}$ then every vertex of P is integer valued.

Let $\hat{x}$ be a vertex of P. Then there is some linear objective function cx maximized over P only by $\hat{x}$. The dual linear program to maximizing cx subject to (4.1) and (4.2) is the following:

$$\text{minimize} \quad \sum_{S \subseteq V} y_S \cdot (|S| - 1)$$

$$\text{subject to} \quad y_S \geq 0 \quad \text{for all } S \subseteq E,$$

$$\sum (y_S: e \in E(S)) \geq c_e \quad \text{for all } e \in E.$$

The greedy algorithm as stated (essentially the form due to Kruskal (1956)) starts with a forest consisting of $|V|$ components, each a singleton. When edge e_i is considered, if it joins distinct components of the current forest, it is added to the forest, i.e., the components are combined. If not, the edge is ignored. For each $i \in \{1, 2, \ldots, m\}$ let $A(e_i)$ be the nodeset of the new component formed by adding e_i to F^*, if this occurs. We now compute a dual solution by considering the edges of F^* in the order reverse to that in which they were added to F^*. Let $F^* = \{f_1, f_2, \ldots, f_r\}$ where the edges were added in this order. We let $\hat{y}_{A(f_r)} = c_{f_r}$. For j going from $r - 1$ to 1 by steps of -1, we let

$$\hat{y}_{A(f_j)} = c_{f_j} - \sum (y_{A(f_i)}: j + 1 \leq i \leq r)$$

and both ends of f_j are in $A(f_i)$).

Let $\hat{y}_S = 0$ for all other sets S. (If $c_{e_1} \leq 0$, then we obtain $\hat{y} \equiv 0$.) It is easy to verify that $\hat{y}$ is a feasible solution to the dual. Moreover, if $\hat{y}_S > 0$, then the forest F^* contains $|S| - 1$ edges of $E(S)$. If $e \in F^*$, then $\Sigma (\hat{y}_S : e \in S) = c_e$. These last two properties are just the complementary slackness conditions for optimality of feasible solutions x^{F^*} and $\hat{y}$ to these two linear programs, so they are both optimal. In particular, since $\hat{x}$ was the unique member of P which maximized cx, we have $\hat{x} = x^{F^*}$, i.e., $\hat{x}$ is integer valued and in fact the incidence vector of F^*, as required. $\square$

Note the format of this proof. We showed that a proposed linear system which contained $F(G)$ was sufficient by showing that when we optimized an arbitrary objective function over this system, we always got an optimal solution which was in $F(G)$. We proved optimality by simultaneously constructing an optimal solution to the dual linear program. Admittedly, in this case there are easier ways to prove that the greedy algorithm works for this problem and also easier ways to prove Theorem 4.1. However many theorems of polyhedral combinatorics have been developed in this algorithmic context.

The above result was actually proved in the context of matroids. A *matroid* $M = (E, \mathcal{F})$ is an ordered pair consisting of a finite groundset E and a nonempty family $\mathcal{F}$ of so-called independent subsets of E which satisfy the following:

(M1) Every subset of an independent set is independent.
(M2) For every $A \subseteq E$, all maximal (with respect to set inclusion) members of $\{I \in \mathcal{F} : I \subseteq A\}$ have the same cardinality, called the *rank* of A, denoted by $r(A)$.

Thus $I \subseteq E$ belongs to $\mathcal{F}$ if and only if $|I| = r(I)$. A *basis of $A \subseteq E$* is a set $I \subseteq A$ satisfying $|I| = r(I) = r(A)$.

If E is the edgeset of a graph, and $\mathcal{F} = \{I \subseteq E : I$ contains no cycles$\}$ then $(E, \mathcal{F})$ is a matroid called the *forest matroid* of G. The rank of $A \subseteq E$ equals $|V(A)| - \kappa(G[A])$. Here $V(A)$ is the set of all nodes incident with members of A. Recall that $G(A)$ is the graph $(V(A), A)$ and $\kappa(G)$ is the number of components of G. If $G(A)$ is connected, then $r(A) = |V(A)| - 1$.

Whitney (1935) introduced matroids as an abstraction of the notion of linear independence of the sets of columns of a matrix. At the same time van der Waerden (1937) discovered these structures while axiomatizing algebraic independence. For background information, see Nemhauser and Wolsey (1988), Lawler (1976), Papadimitriou and Steiglitz (1982) or Welsh (1976).

The instance of matroids which motivated Whitney was the one obtained when we let the groundset be the set E of columns of a matrix A, and say that $S \subseteq E$ is independent if S is linearly independent over some field. If we let A be the node–edge incidence matrix of a graph G, and take linear independence over GF(2) (i.e., we take all operations modulo 2), then the independent sets of columns of A correspond to the edge sets of forests in G.

If $(E, \mathcal{F})$ satisfies (M1) but not necessarily (M2), then it is called an *independence system*. The greedy algorithm can be extended directly to independence systems: We are given a vector $c = (c_e : e \in E)$ of element weights and wish to find $I \in \mathcal{F}$ for which $c(I)$ is maximized. We start with $I = \emptyset$ and consider the elements in order of decreasing weight. If $I \cup \{e\} \in \mathcal{F}$, then we add e to I. Rado (1957) and independently Edmonds (1971), Gale (1968) and Welsh (1968) proved that if $(E, \mathcal{F})$ is a matroid, then for any c, the greedy algorithm correctly solves the problem. Edmonds (1971) also showed that if $(E, \mathcal{F})$ is not a matroid, then for some c, the greedy algorithm fails. (If $(E, \mathcal{F})$ violates (M2) then there are bases I_1, I_2 of $A \subseteq E$ such that $|I_1| < |I_2|$. Define

$$
c_e = \begin{cases} 1 & \text{for } e \in I_1, \\ 1 - \varepsilon & \text{for } e \in I_2 \backslash I_1, \\ -1 & e \in E \backslash (I_1 \cup I_2). \end{cases}
$$

For $\varepsilon > 0$ the greedy algorithm will return I_1, but for ε sufficiently small, the correct answer is I_2.)

Let $M = (E, \mathcal{F})$ be a matroid. Edmonds defined the independent set polytope $P(M)$ to be the convex hull of the incidence vectors of the independent sets of M.

Theorem 4.2 (Edmonds (1971)). *For any matroid $M = (E, \mathcal{F})$, $P(M)$ is the set of all $x \in \mathbb{R}^E$ satisfying*

$$x_e \geq 0 \quad \text{for all } e \in E, \tag{4.3}$$

$$x(A) \leq r(A) \quad \text{for all } A \subseteq E. \tag{4.4}$$

This generalizes Theorem 4.1, and it is a good exercise to deduce Theorem 4.1 from this. (See Theorem 7.2.) We give a separate non algorithmic proof of Theorem 4.2 due to M. Grötschel, which is a modification of an argument of Lovász (1979) for the matching polytope.

Proof of Theorem 4.2. We can assume that $\{e\} \in \mathcal{F}$, for all $e \in E$. Therefore the set of unit vectors plus the zero vector is a set of $|E| + 1$ affinely independent members of $P(M)$, so this polytope is of full dimension. Therefore an inequality $ax \leq \alpha$ is facet inducing if and only if, for any valid inequality $bx \leq \beta$ which is not a positive multiple of $ax \leq \alpha$, there is some $\hat{x} = P(M)$ such that $a\hat{x} = \alpha$ and $b\hat{x} < \beta$ (i.e., $ax \leq \alpha$ induces a maximal face). (See Theorem 3.16.) Suppose that $ax \leq \alpha$ is facet inducing, and let $\mathcal{W} = \{S \subseteq E : ax^S = \alpha\}$. Suppose for some e that $a_e < 0$. If there existed $S \in \mathcal{W}$ such that $e \in S$, then by (M1) $S' = S \backslash \{e\} \in \mathcal{F}$, but $ax^{S'} > \alpha$, contradicting the validity of $ax \leq \alpha$. Therefore for every $S \in \mathcal{W}$ we have $x_e^S = 0$, so $ax \leq \alpha$ must be a positive multiple of the valid inequality $-x_e \leq 0$, of the form (4.3).

Otherwise, $a_e \geq 0$ for all $e \in E$. Let $A = \{e \in E : a_e > 0\}$. Suppose $S \in \mathcal{W}$ satisfied $|S \cap A| < r(A)$. By (M2) we could find $e \in A \backslash S$ such that $S' = S \cup$

$\{e\} \in \mathcal{F}$. But since $a_e > 0$, we have $ax^{S'} > \alpha$, a contradiction. Therefore every $S \in \mathcal{W}$ satisfies $|S \cap A| = r(A)$. Therefore $ax \leq \alpha$ must be a positive multiple of the rank inequality (4.4) $x(A) \leq r(A)$. $\square$

Now let us consider the case of matchings in a nonbipartite graph. Edmonds (1965a) developed a polynomially bounded algorithm which found a maximum weight (perfect) matching in a graph. (See also Lawler (1976).) Just as in the proof of Theorem 4.1, it used linear programming duality and an explicit characterization of the convex hull of the feasible solutions to prove optimality. Here, however, we give a nonalgorithmic proof.

Theorem 4.3 (Edmonds (1965a)). *The convex hull of the incidence vectors of the perfect matchings of $G = (V, E)$ is the solution set of the system*

$$x \geq 0, \tag{4.5}$$

$$x(\delta(v)) = 1 \quad \text{for all } v \in V, \tag{4.6}$$

$$x(\delta(S)) \geq 1 \quad \text{for all } S \subseteq V \text{ such that } 3 \leq |S| \text{ and } |S| \text{ is odd.} \tag{4.7}$$

Recall that for any $S \subseteq V$, we let $E(S)$ denote the set of edges with both ends in S. The inequalities (4.7) assert that it is impossible to saturate all nodes of an odd cardinality subset S of the nodes using only edges of $E(S)$. At least one edge of $\delta(S)$ must be used. This is equivalent to requiring

$$x(E(S)) \leq \tfrac{1}{2}(|S| - 1) \quad \text{for all } S \subseteq V \text{ such that } 3 \leq |S| \text{ and } |S| \text{ odd.} \tag{4.8}$$

An inequality (4.8) is called a *blossom inequality*. We can deduce (4.7) from (4.8) for a set S by subtracting one half the constraints (4.6) for each node $v \in S$. Similarly we can deduce (4.8) from (4.7).

Proof of Theorem 4.3 (Schrijver (1983)). Let P be the solution set to (4.5)–(4.7). It is easy to see that the incidence vector x^M of every perfect matching of G satisfies (4.5)–(4.7), i.e. $P \subseteq \mathrm{PM}(G)$. What remains to show is the converse, i.e., every vertex of P is in $\mathrm{PM}(G)$.

Let $\hat{x}$ be a vertex of P. Then there exists $J \subseteq E$ and a family $\mathcal{W}$ of odd subsets of V such that $\hat{x}$ is the unique solution to (4.6), $x_j = 0$ for all $j \in J$ and $x(\delta(S)) = 1$ for all $S \in \mathcal{W}$.

Case 1. $\mathcal{W} = \emptyset$. Then $\hat{x}$ is a vector of the polyhedron defined by (4.5), (4.6) and so by Theorem 3.13, the only edges for which $\hat{x}_j$ is not integral are those belonging to the edge sets of disjoint odd cycles. Suppose such a cycle exists, having nodeset C. Then $\hat{x}(\delta(V(C))) = 0$, contradicting (4.7). So in this case, $\hat{x}$ is integral.

Case 2. $\mathcal{W} \neq \emptyset$. Choose $S \in \mathcal{W}$ and let G^1 and G^2 be the graphs obtained from G by shrinking S and $\bar{S} = V \setminus S$ respectively to pseudonodes. All inequalities (4.5)–(4.7) for G^1 and G^2 are satisfied by $\hat{x}$, so if we let $\hat{x}^1$ and $\hat{x}^2$ be the restrictions of $\hat{x}$ to the edges of G^1 and G^2 respectively, then by induction, $\hat{x}^1 \in \mathrm{PM}(G^1)$ and $\hat{x}^2 \in \mathrm{PM}(G^2)$. Therefore each can be expressed as a convex combination of incidence vectors of perfect matchings of the respective graphs. That is

$$\hat{x}^1 = \sum_{i\in I_1} \lambda_i^1 x^i, \quad \sum_{i\in I_1} \lambda_i^1 = 1 \text{ and } \lambda^1 \geq 0,$$

$$\hat{x}^2 = \sum_{j\in I_2} \lambda_j^2 \bar{x}^j, \quad \sum_{j\in I_2} \lambda_j^2 = 1 \text{ and } \lambda^2 \geq 0,$$

where each x^i is the incidence vector of a perfect matching of G^1 and each $\bar{x}^j$ is the incidence vector of a perfect matching of G^2. Now we show that these matchings can be 'spliced', to express $\hat{x}$ as a convex combination of incidence vectors of perfect matchings of G.

Let $e \in \delta(S)$ and let I_1^e and I_2^e be the indices of the vectors x^i and $\bar{x}^j$ respectively for which $x_e^i = 1$ and $\bar{x}_e^j = 1$. Then

$$\hat{x}_e = \sum_{i\in I_1^e} \lambda_i^1 = \sum_{j\in I_2^e} \lambda_j^2.$$

Choose $i \in I_1^e$ and $j \in I_2^e$ and suppose $\lambda_i^1 \geq \lambda_j^2$. The union of the matchings corresponding to x^i and $\bar{x}^j$ is a perfect matching in G (which contains e). Let x^{ij} be its incidence vector. Let $\lambda^{ij} = \lambda_j^2$ and let $\lambda_i^1 := \lambda_i^1 - \lambda^{ij}$, $\lambda_j^2 := 0$. Repeat this process. When we are done we will have a set $\{x^{ij}\}$ of incidence vectors of perfect matchings of G and nonnegative multipliers x_{ij} such that $\sum \lambda_{ij} x^{ij}$ suitably restricted equals both $\sum_{i\in I_1^e} \lambda_i^1 x^i$ and $\sum_{i\in I_2^e} \lambda_j^2 \bar{x}^j$.

Now repeat this process for all $e \in \delta(S)$. We thereby obtain an expression for $\hat{x}$ as a convex combination of incidence vectors of perfect matchings of G. Therefore $\hat{x} \in \mathrm{PM}(G)$.

Since all vertices of P are in $\mathrm{PM}(G)$, we must have $P = \mathrm{PM}(G)$, and we are done. $\square$

Other nonalgorithmic proofs of this theorem have been given by Balinksi (1972), Lovász (1979) and Seymour (1981). As we remarked, $\mathrm{PM}(G)$ could equally well be defined using (4.5), (4.6), (4.8). in this form a direct generalization gives a linear system sufficient to define $M(G)$, the convex hull of the incidence vectors of all matchings.

Theorem 4.4 (Edmonds (1965a)). *$M(G)$ is equal to the set of $x \in \mathbb{R}^E$ satisfying*

$$x \geq 0,$$

$$x(\delta(v)) \leq 1 \quad \text{for all } v \in V,$$

$$x(E(S)) \leq \tfrac{1}{2}(|S| - 1) \quad \text{for all } S \subseteq V \text{ such that } |S| \geq 3, \text{ odd}.$$

Note that the inequalities (4.7), while equivalent to (4.8) for perfect matchings, are not valid for matchings, but inequalities (4.8) are still valid.

This theorem can be deduced directly from Theorem 4.3. Construct two disjoint copies of G, then join corresponding nodes of the two copies. Every matching of G is contained in a perfect matching of the resulting graph, G^*. Conversely, every perfect matching of G^* induces a matching in the subgraph corresponding to G. We can now use Theorem 4.3 applied to G^* to derive Theorem 4.4 for G. See Schrijver (1983 or 1986).

Now suppose we wished to apply the five step process of this section to an NP-hard problem such as the maximum weight stable set problem or the travelling salesman problem. Karp and Papadimitriou (1982) showed that unless NP = co-NP, no complete, tractable formulation can be obtained for the polyhedron corresponding to an NP-hard problem. 'Tractable' means that for any inequality $ax \le \alpha$ in such a proposed system, it is possible to verify in polynomial time that it belongs. More simply, it should be possible to validate the value of α, i.e., to prove that no feasible solution $\hat{x}$ could ever have $a\hat{x} > \alpha$.

We illustrate why this is the case with the travelling salesman problem, formulated as the following decision problem: Given $G = (V, E)$, a vector c of edge costs and a bound β, does there exist a hamiltonian cycle of G having cost at most β? If the answer is 'YES', then a Hamiltonian cycle of cost at most β is a short certificate establishing this fact. Suppose the answer is 'NO', and we know a linear system $Ax \ge b$ such that $\text{TSP}(G) = \{x \in \mathbb{R}^E : Ax \ge b\}$. The dual linear program to minimizing cx subject to $Ax \ge b$ is to maximize yb subject to $yA \le c$, $y \ge 0$. Therefore there would exist a feasible dual solution $\hat{y}$ for which $\hat{y}b > \beta$. Moreover, by choosing $\hat{y}$ to be basic, we would be sure that $\hat{y}$ had at most $|E|$ nonzero components. Equivalently, there exists a subsystem $\bar{A}x \ge \bar{b}$ of $Ax \ge b$ having at most $|E|$ inequalities, and associated multipliers $\hat{y}$ such that $\hat{y}\bar{A} \le c$ and $\hat{y}\bar{b} > \beta$. This system, plus $\hat{y}$ will provide a certificate of a 'NO' answer, provided that we can verify polynomially (possibly with a polynomial amount of extra information) that each of the inequalities in the system $\bar{A}x \ge \bar{b}$ is valid for $\text{TSP}(G)$. (This would imply that the coefficients in the inequalities have length polynomially bounded in the size of G, which in turn implies this property for $\hat{y}$.) Thus we would have shown that a NP-complete problem belongs to co-NP which would imply that NP = co-NP. (See the Appendix.)

Note that it is easy to validate the inequalities in our defining systems for matchings, and also for matroids, provided that an efficient subroutine for computing $r(A)$, for $A \subseteq E$, is available.

A general, powerful method of proving the validity of an inequality was proposed by Chvátal (1973), and is essentially the same as the cut generation method of Gomory (1960, 1963). It is based upon the fact that it is often easy to obtain an *integer* programming formulation of combinatorial optimization problems, and, in principle, all valid inequalities for the desired convex hull of the integer solutions can be derived from this.

Suppose that the feasible solutions to a combinatorial optimization problem correspond to the *integer* solutions to the linear system $Ax \le b$. Let $\lambda \ge 0$. Then

$(\lambda A)x \leqslant \lambda b$ is a valid inequality, implied by $Ax \leqslant b$. (See Corollary 3.6.) If λA is integer valued, then since every integer solution x to $Ax \leqslant b$ will make $(\lambda A)x$ integer valued, the inequality $(\lambda A)x \leqslant \lfloor \lambda b \rfloor$ is valid. Such an inequality is called a *Chvátal–Gomory cut*.

Let $P = \{x : Ax \leqslant b\}$ be a polyhedron and let P_I be the convex hull of the integer members of P. A *truncation proof* of the validity (for P_I) of an inequality $ax \leqslant \alpha$ is a sequence $(a^i x \leqslant \alpha^i : i = 1, 2, \ldots, n)$ of inequalities, such that each $a^i x \leqslant \alpha^i$ is a Chvátal–Gomory cut with respect to the starting system $Ax \leqslant b$, plus previously generated inequalities $a^j x \leqslant \alpha^j$, for $j = 1, 2, \ldots, i - 1$; and $a^n = a$ and $\alpha^n \leqslant \alpha$. (Note that we do not exclude the possibility that both λA and λb are integer valued, for a Chvátal–Gomory cut.) We call n the *length* of the derivation.

Theorem 4.5 (Chvátal (1973) for polytopes, Schrijver (1980) for polyhedra). *The inequality $ax \leqslant \alpha$ is valid for the integer solutions to $Ax \leqslant b$ if and only if there exists a finite length derivation of $ax \leqslant \alpha$, starting with $Ax \leqslant b$.*

Let us illustrate this with respect to matchings in a nonbipartite graph $G = (V, E)$. The incidence vectors of matchings are precisely the integer solutions to

$$x_e \geqslant 0 \quad \text{for all } e \in E \tag{4.9}$$

$$x(\delta(v)) \leqslant 1 \quad \text{for all } v \in V . \tag{4.10}$$

Let $S \subseteq V$ be such that $|S| \geqslant 3$, odd. Adding $\frac{1}{2}$ of the inequality (4.10) for each $v \in V$, and $\frac{1}{2}$ of the inequality $-x_e \leqslant 0$ (4.9) for each $e \in \delta(S)$, we obtain the Chvátal–Gomory cut

$$x(E(S)) \leqslant \lfloor \tfrac{1}{2}|S| \rfloor$$

which is the required blossom inequality (4.8). Thus all blossom inequalities are valid and indeed have a truncation proof of length 1. (But this does *not* show that they are sufficient to define $M(G)$!)

Now we consider the travelling salesman polytope of a graph G, i.e., the convex hull of the *tours*, the incidence vectors of the Hamiltonian cycles. Dantzig et al. (1954) noted that the tours of G were precisely the integer solutions to the following system:

$$0 \leqslant x \leqslant 1 , \tag{4.11}$$

$$x(\delta(v)) = 2 \quad \text{for all } v \in V , \tag{4.12}$$

$$x(\delta(S)) \geqslant 2 \quad \text{for all } \emptyset \neq S \subset V . \tag{4.13}$$

The constraints (4.13) are called the *subtour elimination* constraints. They prohibit solutions consisting of some number of disjoint cycles, which would be permitted by (4.11) and (4.12). They are equivalent to

$$x(E(S)) \leqslant |S| - 1 \quad \text{for all } \emptyset \neq S \subseteq V . \tag{4.14}$$

A *comb* is a set of sets $H, T_1, T_2, \ldots, T_k \subseteq V$ such that

$$|H \cap T_i| \geqslant 1 \quad \text{for } i = 1, 2, \ldots, k ,$$

$$|T_i \backslash H| \geqslant 1 \quad \text{for } i = 1, 2, \ldots, k ,$$

$$T_i \cap T_j = \emptyset \quad \text{for } 1 \leqslant i < j \leqslant k ,$$

$$k \geqslant 3, \text{ odd} .$$

The set H is called the *handle* and the T_i are called the *teeth*. (See Figure 4.1.)

Theorem 4.6 (Chvátal (1973a); Grötschel and Padberg (1979, 1979a)). *For each comb in G, the comb inequality*

$$x(E(H)) + \sum_{i=1}^{k} x(E(T_i)) \leqslant |H| + \sum_{i=1}^{k} (|T_i| - 1) - \frac{k+1}{2} \tag{4.15}$$

is valid for TSP(G).

Proof. Add one half of each of the inequalities (4.12) for the nodes of H; (4.14) for T_i, $T_i \backslash H$ and $T_i \cap H$, for $i = 1, \ldots, k$ (for those sets having cardinality at least two), plus the inequalities $-x_e \leqslant 0$ (4.11) for edges $e \in \delta(H)$, but not in $E(T_i)$ for some $i \in \{1, 2, \ldots, k\}$. This gives

$$x(E(H)) + \sum_{i=1}^{k} x(E(T_i)) \leqslant |H| + \sum_{i=1}^{k} (|T_i| - 1) - \frac{k}{2} .$$

Since k is odd, the right hand side is fractional; truncating gives (4.15) and

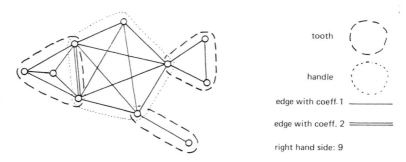

tooth

handle

edge with coeff. 1 ——————

edge with coeff. 2 ════════

right hand side: 9

Fig. 4.1.

shows that (4.15) is a Chvátal–Gomory cut, with respect to (4.11), (4.12) and (4.14). □

Chvátal (1973a) introduced comb inequalities, but required $|H \cap T_i| = 1$ for $i = 1, 2, \ldots, k$. We call such combs *simple*. The generalization above, which permits teeth to meet handles in more than one node, is due to Grötschel and Padberg (1979).

The combs for which $|T_i| = 2$ for all teeth T_i are of particular interest. A *2-factor* in a graph $G = (V, E)$ is a set of pairwise disjoint cycles which contain all nodes of G. Edmonds and Johnson (1970), see also Aráoz et al. (1983), gave the following characterization.

Theorem 4.7 (Edmonds and Johnson (1970)). *The convex hull of the incidence vectors of the 2-factors of G is the solution to the linear system* (4.11), (4.12) *and* (4.15) *for all (simple) combs of G for which all teeth are of cardinality two.*

Grötschel and Pulleyblank (1986) generalized combs to clique trees. A *clique tree* is a set $\{H_1, H_2, \ldots, H_s, T_1, T_2, \ldots, T_t\}$ of subsets of V which satisfy
 (i) $T_i \cap T_j = \emptyset$ for $1 \le i < j \le t$;
 (ii) $H_i \cap H_j = \emptyset$ for $1 \le i < j \le s$;
 (iii) for each $i \in \{1, 2, \ldots, t\}$, $2 \le |T_i| \le n - 2$ and some $v \in T_i$ belongs to no H_j, for $1 \le j \le s$;
 (iv) for each $j \in \{1, 2, \ldots, s\}$, the number of T_i having nonempty intersection with H_j is odd, and at least three;
 (v) for $i \in \{1, 2, \ldots, s\}$ and $j \in \{1, 2, \ldots, t\}$, if $H_i \cap T_j \ne \emptyset$, then $H_i \cap T_j$ is an articulation set of the subgraph C of G with nodeset $\bigcup_{i=1}^{s} H_i \cup \bigcup_{j=1}^{t} T_j$ and edge set $\bigcup_{i=1}^{s} E(H_i) \cup \bigcup_{j=1}^{t} E(T_j)$; moreover, C is connected.

See Figure 4.2. The sets H_i are called *handles* and the sets T_j are called *teeth*. For each $j \in \{1, 2, \ldots, t\}$, we let t_j be the number of handles intersecting T_j. The *clique tree inequality* is

$$\sum_{i=1}^{s} x(E(H_i)) + \sum_{j=1}^{t} x(E(T_j)) \le \sum_{i=1}^{s} |H_i| + \sum_{j=1}^{t} (|T_j| - t_j) - \frac{t+1}{2} . \tag{4.16}$$

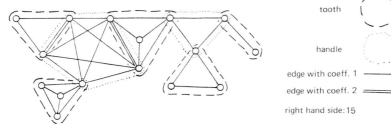

tooth

handle

edge with coeff. 1 ————

edge with coeff. 2 ════

right hand side: 15

Fig. 4.2.

The term 'clique tree' was given to these structures because the travelling salesman problem on an arbitrary graph can be reduced to the problem on a complete graph. (Add any missing edges, with prohibitively high costs.) In this case the graphs $G[H_i]$ and $G[T_j]$ are all cliques. However the inequalities (4.16) remain valid for all graphs.

Theorem 4.8 (Grötschel and Pulleyblank (1986)). *For each clique tree in G, the corresponding clique tree inequality* (4.16) *is valid for* TSP(G).

Note that a subtour elimination constraint is a clique tree inequality for a clique tree with a single tooth $T_1 = S$ and no handles. Also, combs are special cases of clique trees and Theorem 4.8 can be proved in a manner analogous to the way we proved Theorem 4.6. Each clique tree inequality is shown to be a Chvátal–Gomory cut obtained from (4.11)–(4.13), plus inequalities (4.16) corresponding to smaller clique trees. (See Grötschel and Pulleyblank (1986).) Therefore there is a truncation proof of the validity of every clique tree inequality. Chvátal et al. (1988) have shown that there exist clique tree inequalities for which the shortest truncation proofs have length which grows exponentially with the size of G.

We discuss these inequalities further in Section 7.

5. Separation and partial descriptions

The *separation* problem for a polyhedron is the following: Given a polyhedron $P \subseteq \mathbb{R}^J$ and a point $\hat{x} \in \mathbb{R}^J$, determine whether $\hat{x} \in P$. If not, find an inequality $ax \leq \alpha$ valid for P but for which $a\hat{x} > \alpha$. There are both practical and theoretical reasons for interest in this problem. First, the basic idea underlying the cutting plane approach to integer programming is to start with a 'simple' polyhedron P^0 which contains the polyhedron P^* over which we wish to optimize. We then maximize the desired objective function cx over P^0. Let x^0 be the optimum thereby obtained. Solve the separation problem for x^0 and P^*. If $x^0 \in P^*$ then it is the desired optimum. If not, add the separating inequality $a^0x \leq \alpha^0$ found to our system describing P^0 and repeat the process. In this way we obtain a sequence $P^0 \supset P^1 \supset \cdots \supset P^*$ of polyhedra. Our hope is that for some n, not too large, the maximum of cx over P^n will belong to P^*, and we will terminate. If we can guarantee that each separating inequality $a^ix \leq \alpha^i$ induces a facet of P^*, then we can at least be sure that the process will terminate in finite time. Since the number of distinct facets is finite, after a finite number n of iterations we are sure to have the optimal solution x^n to maximizing cx over P^n belonging to P^*. On the other hand, it is easy to construct examples which show that if we do not restrict our choice of separating inequalities, then we need never terminate. (Let $P^* = \{x \in \mathbb{R}: x \leq 0\}$, let $P^0 = \{x \in \mathbb{R}: x \leq 1\}$, let $c = (1)$, and let $ax^i \leq \alpha^i$ be the inequality $x \leq (2^{-(i+1)})$ for $i = 0, 1, 2, \ldots$.)

The famous ellipsoid algorithm for linear programming of Khachian (1979) established another important theoretical connection between separation and optimization. Namely, that if we could do the former polynomially, we could also do the latter polynomially. This is due to the following. It is well known that the problem of maximizing cx, subject to $Ax \leq b$ can be reduced to the problem of determining whether the linear system $Ax \leq b$, $cx \geq \gamma$ has a feasible solution. (Effectively, perform binary search to find the largest value of γ, for which this latter system has a feasible solution.) So suppose we wish to solve the problem of finding x^* satisfying $Ax^* \leq b$, if such an x^* exists. The ellipsoid method begins with an ellipsoid E^0 certain to contain any possible solution to $Ax \leq b$, then tries the center point x^0. If this is feasible, then it terminates. If not, it finds a violated inequality $A[i]x^0 > b_i$ and constructs a new ellipsoid E^1 containing $E^0 \cap \{x: A[i]x \leq b_i\}$. Any feasible solution to the original system must now lie in E^1, and the process repeats with the center point x^1 of E^1. In this way a sequence $E^0 \supset E^1 \supset E^2 \supset \cdots$ of ellipsoids is constructed, each containing all possible feasible solutions, as well as a sequence $x^0, x^1, x^2, \ldots$ of 'candidates'. It can be shown that if the E^i are constructed properly, then their volumes decrease geometrically, and each successive x^i can be computed in polynomial time. Moreover, it can be shown that if, after some polynomial number n of iterations, x^n is not feasible, then there is no feasible solution to $Ax \leq b$. (See Grötschel et al. (1981, 1988), Schrijver (1986), or Nemhauser and Wolsey (1988) for details.)

What is important for us is that we do not require the system $Ax \leq b$ to be given explicitly (although things are especially simple when it is.) All we require is to be able to solve the separation problem for each of the candidate x^i. Thus, whenever we can separate over a class of polyhedra in polynomial time, we can also optimize polynomially. This was shown independently by Grötschel, Lovász and Schrijver (1981), Karp and Papadimitriou (1982) and Padberg and Rao (1981). Note too that the above statement does hide certain technical difficulties, required to make the optimization-separation equivalence precise for certain classes of polyhedra. However if we restrict ourselves to polyhedra with integer or half-integer vertices, as is usually the case in polyhedral combinatorics, then no problems arise. (See Grötschel et al. (1981, 1988).) Also, in Grötschel et al. (1981) and Karp and Papadimitriou (1982) it was assumed that the solution set to $Ax \leq b$ was of full dimension. This assumption is not present in Padberg and Rao (1980) and Grötschel et al. (1988), although the former paper restricts attention to bounded polyhedra.

We note here that Grötschel et al. (1981) and Padberg and Rao (1981) also proved the converse – that if we can optimize polynomially we can separate polynomially. This will be discussed in Section 6, after we have introduced polarity.

Now we consider the polyhedra $M(G)$ and $PM(G)$. If G is bipartite, then the defining linear systems have only a polynomial number of inequalities, and the corresponding separation problems are trivial. If G is nonbipartite, then we must be able to separate over the odd sets, i.e., for a given $\hat{x}$ (which we can assume satisfies $\hat{x} \geq 0$, $\hat{x}(\delta(v)) = 1$ for all $v \in V$) we wish to determine whether there exists $S \subseteq V$ with $|S|$ odd such that $\hat{x}(\delta(S)) < 1$. This problem was solved by Padberg and Rao (1982), and is discussed later in this section.

For the case of a matroid polyhedron $P(M)$, and a given nonnegative $\hat{x} \in \mathbb{R}^E$, we wish to determine whether there exists $A \subseteq E$ such that $\hat{x}(A) > r(A)$. This problem was solved by Cunningham (1984) as a special case of minimization of a submodular set function. (A function $f: 2^E \to \mathbb{R}$ is *submodular* if $f(S) + f(T) \geqslant f(S \cup T) + f(S \cap T)$, for all $S, T \subseteq E$. The rank function of a matroid is submodular, as is $f(A) - \hat{x}(A)$, for any submodular function f and any fixed vector $\hat{x}$.) For it is equivalent to determine whether the minimum of the submodular function f defined by $f(A) = r(A) - \hat{x}(A)$ is nonnegative, for all $A \subseteq E$. (See Cunningham (1984, 1985) or Nemhauser and Wolsey (1988).)

Matroid intersection provides an additional example. Suppose that $M_1 = (E, \mathscr{F}_1)$ and $M_2 = (E, \mathscr{F}_2)$ are matroids defined on the same ground set. The *intersection* of M_1 and M_2, is the independence system on E consisting of all $S \in \mathscr{F}_1 \cap \mathscr{F}_2$. This is a very general structure which includes many combinatorial optimization problems as instances. For example, let $G = (V_1 \cup V_2, E)$ be a bipartite graph. If we let $\mathscr{F}_i = \{J \subseteq E : |J \cap \delta(v)| \leqslant 1 \text{ for all } v \in V_i\}$, then $M_i = (E, \mathscr{F}_i)$ is a matroid on E, called a *partition matroid*, for $i = 1, 2$. Now $\mathscr{F}_1 \cap \mathscr{F}_2$ is the set of all matchings of G. As a second example, let $G = (N, A)$ be a directed graph. Let $\mathscr{F}_1$ consist of all sets S of arcs such that S is the edge set of a forest in the underlying undirected graph. Let $\mathscr{F}_2 = \{S \subseteq A : |S \cap \delta^+(v)| \leqslant 1 \text{ for all } v \in N\}$, where $\delta^+(v)$ is the set of arcs with heads equal to v. Then again $M_1 = (A, \mathscr{F}_1)$ and $M_2 = (A, \mathscr{F}_2)$ are matroids and their intersection is the set of all *branchings* in G. That is, $S \in \mathscr{F}_1 \cap \mathscr{F}_2$ if and only if each component of the subgraph (V, S) is a tree, with all arcs directed away from some root node.

Edmonds showed that the convex hull of the incidence vectors of $\mathscr{F}_1 \cap \mathscr{F}_2$, for any matroids $M_1 = (E, \mathscr{F}_1)$ and $M_2 = (E, \mathscr{F}_2)$ is precisely the intersection of $P(M_1)$ and $P(M_2)$.

Theorem 5.1 (Edmonds (1979), see also Nemhauser and Wolsey (1988)). *Let $M_1 = (E, \mathscr{F}_2)$ and $M_2 = (E, \mathscr{F}_2)$ be matroids. Then the convex hull of the incidence vectors of $\mathscr{F}_1 \cap \mathscr{F}_2$ is given by*

$$x_e \geqslant 0 \quad \text{for all } e \in E ,$$

$$x(A) \leqslant \min\{r_1(A), r_2(A)\} \quad \text{for all } A \subseteq E ,$$

where $r_i(A)$ is the rank of A in M_i, for $i = 1, 2$.

Note that the separation problem for the intersection of M_1 and M_2 can be solved by first solving the problem for M_1, then solving it for M_2. So Cunningham's method actually solves the separation problem for a much larger class of problems than just matroids.

At the end of Section 8 we discuss a generalization of the matroid intersection problem, the so-called submodular flow problem.

Now suppose we have a situation, like the travelling salesman problem, for which we only know a partial defining system for the associated polyhedron. We can apply the separation based methodology just described, using the inequalities which we know. However, there now exists the possibility that we may terminate with an optimal solution x^n to P^n such that $x^n \not\in P^*$ and yet either no inequality of our system separates x^n from P^*, or else we are unable to find such an inequality which does exist. What is surprising is that for many problems, this approach, possibly combined with branch and bound, produces optimal solutions.

Let us illustrate with the travelling salesman problem. In this case we start with a very weak relaxation $P^0 = \{x \in \mathbb{R}^E : 0 \le x \le 1, x(\delta(v)) = 2 \text{ for all } v \in V\}$. Let x^0 be an optimal solution to the problem of minimizing cx over P^0. The first class of inequalities for which we wish to solve the separation problem is for the subtour elimination constraints (4.13). We wish to find whether there exists $\emptyset \ne S \subset V$ such that $x^0(\delta(S)) < 2$. Padberg and Hong (1980) showed that this can be done using the Gomory–Hu procedure for finding the maximum flow between all pairs of nodes in an undirected graph. For each edge $uv \in E$, we construct (directed) arcs (u, v) and (v, u), each having capacity x^0_{uv}. Then, for each pair s, t of nodes, we wish to compute the value of a maximum s–t-flow, subject to these capacities. By the max-flow–min-cut theorem (see Chapter 4 of this volume) this will equal the minimum capacity of a cut in G which separates s from t. The minimum over all pairs s, t will give the minimum value of $x^0(\delta(S))$, over all $\emptyset \ne S \subset V$. If this minimum is at least 2, then no constraint (4.13) is violated. If any cut has capacity less than 2, then the corresponding constraint will serve for $a^0 x \le \alpha^0$. Note that it is sufficient to choose some fixed $s \in V$ and then consider all $t \in V \setminus \{s\}$.

Gomory and Hu (1961) described a more sophisticated method than naively trying all such pairs s, t based on the notion of a *flow equivalent tree*. This is a tree T defined on the nodeset V for which each edge has a capacity α_j, and such that for all $s, t \in V$, the minimum of $x^0(\delta(S))$ for $s \in S$, $t \not\in S$ equals the minimum value of α_j for the edges on the path in T joining s and t. (See Figure 5.1.) Moreover, when we remove this minimum capacity edge from T, the nodes of T are partitioned into two connected components with nodesets S and $\bar{S}$. Then cut $\delta(S) = \delta(\bar{S})$ in G is a minimum capacity cut separating s and t. Note that the tree makes it easy for us to see that a minimum capacity cut in G

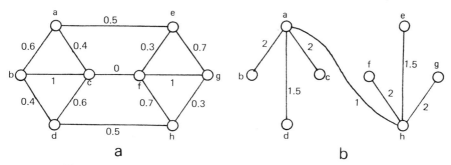

Fig. 5.1. A flow equivalent tree. (a) G; (b) a flow equivalent tree.

separating nodes d and g has capacity 1, and equals $\delta(S)$ where $S = \{a, b, c, d\}$.

It is not obvious that a flow equivalent tree exists. However, a flow equivalent tree can be constructed as follows. Suppose we have a partition of V into $V_1 \cup V_2 \cup \cdots \cup V_k$. Let $\bar{G}$ be obtained from G by shrinking each part V_i to form a single node v_i and suppose we know a flow equivalent tree T for $\bar{G}$. (Initially the partition consists of a single part V.) If each part is a singleton, then $\bar{G} = G$ and we are done. If not, suppose $|V_i| \geq 2$ for some i. Delete from T the node corresponding to V_i. For each component K of the resulting forest, shrink in G all nodes belonging to the sets V_j for which the corresponding v_j are in K to a pseudonode v_K. Let G' be the resulting graph. Choose $s, t \in V_i$ and find a minimum s–t-cut in G'. Let S and $\bar{S}$ be the shores of this cut. Split V_i into two new parts $V_i \cap S$ and $V_i \cap \bar{S}$. A new flow equivalent tree is constructed by joining the nodes corresponding to $V_i \cap S$ and $V_i \cap \bar{S}$ in the new $\bar{G}$, and giving this edge the same capacity as $\delta(S)$. Then we join any node v_j of T which was adjacent to v_i to one of the nodes corresponding to $V_i \cap S$ or $V_i \cap \bar{S}$, depending on whether the node v_K corresponding to the component K containing v_j was in S or $\bar{S}$. See Gomory and Hu (1961) or Ford and Fulkerson (1962) for more details.

Notice that this procedure constructs a flow equivalent tree in the time required to solve $|V| - 1$ max flow problems, which gives the same bound as if we fix some $s \in V$ and then consider all $t \in V \setminus \{s\}$.

By constructing a flow equivalent tree, we can find an inequality which violates (4.13), if one exists. Padberg and Rao (1982) showed that a flow equivalent tree T could also be used to solve the separation problems for the matching blossom constraints (4.7). Call an edge e of T odd if both components of $T \setminus \{e\}$ have an odd number of nodes. They showed that if we chose the odd edge of T having minimum capacity, then the corresponding cut in G is a minimum capacity cut $\delta(S)$ for which $|S|$ is odd.

They also described a method to solve the separation problem for the constraints of the 2-factor problem (see Theorem 4.7), i.e., for comb inequalities in which all teeth have cardinality two, by reducing it to this problem of separation over odd sets. Barahona and Conforti (1987) described how to solve the minimum cut problem for cuts of the form $\delta(S)$, with $|S| \geq 2$, even. As with the Gomory–Hu procedure, they require all capacities to be nonnegative.

At present, no polynomially bounded method is known for solving the separation problem for the class of clique trees or even combs. (See Padberg and Rinaldi (1987a) for a detailed discussion and analysis of both heuristic and exact methods for this problem.) Nevertheless, large 'real-world' travelling salesman problems have been solved to provable optimality using manual and automated separation heuristics. Grötschel (1980) solved a 120 city problem using this approach. He required thirteen LP runs and added a total of 36 subtour elimination constraints and 60 comb inequalities. Of the 60 combs, 21 were non simple. Crowder and Padberg (1980) solved a 318 'city' problem (introduced by Lin and Kernighan (1973) which arose in the routing of a digitally controlled laser drilling machine). More recently Padberg and Rinaldi

(1987) solved a 532 city problem, arising from American cities and reported the solution of problems of 1002 and 2392 nodes arising from circuit layout problems. Grötschel and Holland (1988) describe the solution of a number of real world problems, the largest consisting of 666 cities, distributed around the globe. Note though that in these last two instances, a limited amount of branch and bound was required to prove optimality. Grötschel and Holland (1988) is also recommended for a discussion of many of the issues involved in successfully implementing algorithms of this kind. See also Padberg and Rinaldi (1987b).

These methods have also been used successfully for linear ordering problems (Grötschel, Jünger and Reinelt (1984)), determining the gound state of spin glasses (Barahona and Maccioni (1982), Barahona et al. (1988)) and some partitioning problems (Grötschel and Wakabayashi (1987)).

6. Polarity, blocking and antiblocking

Suppose we know a finite set G of generators for a polyhedral cone $C = \{x \in \mathbb{R}^J: Ax \geq 0\}$. That is, $C = \{x \in \mathbb{R}^J: x = \Sigma \, (\lambda_g g: g \in G)$ where $\lambda_g \geq 0$ for all $g \in G\}$. There is a symmetry between A and G. On the one hand, a vector x is a nonnegative combination of members of G if and only if it satisfies $Ax \geq 0$. Conversely, a vector y is a nonnegative combination of rows of A, i.e., valid for C, if and only if it satisfies $yg \geq 0$ for each $g \in G$. The polyhedral cone $C' = \{y \in \mathbb{R}^J: yG \geq 0\}$ is called the *polar cone* of C. Note the relationships: defining inequalities of C' are generators of C and vice versa.

The following is an example. The *cycle cone* $C(G)$ of a graph $G = (V, E)$ is the cone generated by the incidence vectors of the cycles of G. The following gives a linear system sufficient to define $C(G)$.

Theorem 6.1 (Seymour (1979a)). *For any graph $G = (V, E)$, the cycle cone $C(G)$ is the set of all $x \in \mathbb{R}^E$ satisfying*

$$x \geq 0, \tag{6.1}$$

$$x(K \setminus \{j\}) - x_j \geq 0 \quad \text{for every cut } K \text{ of } G, \text{ for every } j \in K. \tag{6.2}$$

(The validity of (6.2) follows from the fact that any cycle which uses j must also use some other edge of K. Hence $x_j \leq x(K \setminus \{j\})$ for every cut K, for every $j \in K$.)

Now consider the cone $C'(G)$ defined by

$$C'(G) = \{x \in \mathbb{R}^E: x(C) \geq 0 \text{ for every cycle } C \text{ of } G\}.$$

This is just the polar cone of $C(G)$, so it is generated by the unit vectors (corresponding to (6.1)) plus the vectors $x^{K,j}$, defined for each cut K and $j \in K$ by

$$x_e^{K,j} = \begin{cases} 1 & \text{if } e \in K \setminus \{j\}, \\ -1 & \text{if } e = j, \\ 0 & \text{if } e \notin K. \end{cases}$$

For general polyhedra, we define polars as follows. Let $P \subseteq \mathbb{R}^J$ be a polyhedron. The *polar cone* of P is defined to be $\Pi = \{(\pi, \pi_0) \in \mathbb{R}^{J \cup \{0\}}: \pi x - \pi_0 \leq 0 \text{ for all } x \in P\}$. (That is Π consists of the homogenized form of the valid inequalities for P.)

Theorem 6.2 (see Nemhauser and Wolsey (1988)). *If P is of full dimension, and has vertices, then for any $\pi^* \neq 0$, (π^*, π_0^*) is an extreme ray of Π if and only if (π^*, π_0^*) induces a facet of P. Conversely, $ax^* - a_0 \leq 0$ induces a facet of Π if and only if x^* is a vertex of P and $ar^* \leq 0$ induces a facet of Π if and only if r^* is an extreme ray of P.*

(For more detail, see Schrijver (1986), Nemhauser and Wolsey (1988) and Rockafellar (1970).)

For polyhedral combinatorics, there are two useful variants, introduced by Fulkerson – blocking and anti-blocking pairs of polyhedra. Let $P \subseteq \mathbb{R}^J$ be any polyhedron. The *dominant* of P, denoted by $\text{dom}(P)$, is the unbounded polyhedron consisting of all those $x \in \mathbb{R}^J$ such that $x \geq x'$ for some $x' \in P$, i.e., $\text{dom}(P) = P + \mathbb{R}_+^J$. The dominant of P has the interesting algorithmic property that it distinguishes between nonnegative and arbitrary objective functions. If $P \neq \emptyset$ and $c \geq 0$, then $\min\{cx: x \in P\} = \min\{cx: x \in \text{dom}(P)\}$. If C has negative components, then $\min\{cx: x \in P\}$ may be finite, but $\min\{cx: x \in \text{dom}(P)\}$ will be unbounded.

Theorem 6.3 (Fulkerson (1971, 1972), see Schrijver (1986) or Nemhauser and Wolsey (1988)). *Let S be a finite set of vectors in $\mathbb{R}_+^J$ and let $P = \text{dom}(\text{conv}(S))$. Then $P = \{x \in \mathbb{R}_+^J: dx \geq 1 \text{ for all } d \in D \text{ (for some finite set } D \subseteq \mathbb{R}_+^J)\}$ if and only if $\text{dom}(\text{conv}(D)) = \{x \in \mathbb{R}_+^J: sx \geq 1 \text{ for all } s \in S\}$.*

For any $S \subseteq \mathbb{R}^J$, the *blocker* $B(S)$ is defined to be $\{x \in \mathbb{R}_+^J: sx \geq 1 \text{ for all } s \in S\}$. For any finite $S \subseteq \mathbb{R}_+^J$, if P is the polyhedron $\text{dom}(\text{conv}(S))$, then $B(P) = \{x \in \mathbb{R}_+^J: sx \geq 1 \text{ for all } s \in S\}$. Thus $B(P)$ is a polyhedron called the *blocking polyhedron* of P, and the pair $P, B(P)$ is called a *blocking pair*. It follows from Theorem 6.3 that $B(B(P)) = P$. Using linear programming duality, we obtain the following relation between min–max theorems.

Corollary 6.4. *Let S, D be finite subsets of $\mathbb{R}_+^J$. The following are equivalent:*

$$\text{for each } l \in \mathbb{R}_+^J, \quad \min\{ls: s \in S\} = \max\{1 \cdot x: x \geq 0, xd \leq l$$
$$\text{for all } d \in D\}; \quad (6.3)$$

$$\text{for all } w \in \mathbb{R}_+^J, \quad \min\{wd: d \in D\} = \max\{1 \cdot y: y \geq 0, ys \leq w$$
$$\text{for all } s \in S\}. \quad (6.4)$$

Another equivalent, but symmetric, form is due to Lehman (1979):

Theorem 6.5 (Lehman's length-width inequality). *Let S, D be finite subsets of* $\mathbb{R}_+^J$. *Then* (6.3) *and* (6.4) *are equivalent to*

$$s \cdot d \geq 1 \quad \text{for all } s \in D, \tag{6.5}$$

and

$$\min\{ls: s \in S\} \cdot \min\{wd: d \in D\} \leq lw \quad \text{for all } l, w \in \mathbb{R}_+^J . \tag{6.6}$$

An example of blocking polyhedra is given by *T*-joins and *T*-cuts. Let $G = (V, E)$ be a graph and let *T* be an even cardinality subset of *V*. A *T-join* is a set $F \subseteq E$ such that $|F \cap \delta(v)|$ is odd for $v \in T$ and even for $v \in V \setminus T$. Note that if $|V|$ is even, and $T = V$, then a minimum cardinality *T*-join is a perfect matching, if one exists. A *T-cut* is a cut $J = \delta(S)$ for $S \subseteq V$ such that $|T \cap S|$ is odd (and hence $|T \setminus S|$ is odd). Note that if *F* is a *T*-join and *J* is a *T*-cut, then $|J \cap F| \geq 1$.

Let *P* be the dominant of the convex hull of the incidence vectors of the *T*-joins.

Theorem 6.6 (Edmonds and Johnson (1973)). *P is equal to the set of* $x \in \mathbb{R}^E$ *satisfying*

$$x_e \geq 0 \quad \text{for all } e \in E$$

$$x(J) \geq 1 \quad \text{for every T-cut J} .$$

In other words, suppose we are given a nonnegative vector $c = (c_e: e \in E)$ of edge weights. Let $\mathcal{J}$ be the set of all *T*-cuts. Using linear programming duality, the minimum weight $c(F)$ of any *T*-join *F* equals the maximum of $\Sigma_{J \in J} \, y_J$, subject to the condition that $y_J \geq 0$ for all $J \in J$, and $\Sigma \, (y_J: e \in J \in \mathcal{J}) \leq c_e$ for all $e \in E$. (This is a 'fractional' packing of *T*-cuts.) (Seymour (1981) showed that if we restrict ourselves to integral *c*, and *G* is bipartite, then there is a maximum packing of *T*-cuts such that y_J is integral for all $J \in \mathcal{J}$. In general, there always exists an optimal solution *y* which is half-integral.)

Now apply Theorem 6.3 to Theorem 6.6. This yields immediately that if *Q* is the dominant of the set of incidence vectors of *T*-cuts in *G*, then

$$Q = \{x \in \mathbb{R}^J: x \geq 0 \text{ and } x(F) \geq 1 \text{ for every T-join } F\} .$$

Similarly, we obtain a min–max theorem asserting that the minimum of $c(J)$, over all *T* cuts *J* is equal to the maximum fractional packing of *T*-joins. (Note that the integrality results for these fractional packings do not follow from blocking theory.)

Let $P \subseteq \mathbb{R}_+^J$ be a polyhedron. The *submissive*, or *monotone completion* of *P*, denoted by sub(*P*), is the set of all vectors *x* satisfying $0 \leq x \leq \tilde{x}$ for some $\tilde{x} \in P$ (i.e., sub(*P*) = $(P - \mathbb{R}_+^J) \cap \mathbb{R}_+^J$). Suppose that we maximize an objective function cx for $x \in \mathrm{sub}(P)$. If $c \geq 0$, then this maximum will have the same value as when we maximize over p. However, if any component c_e is negative, we can be sure that $x_e^* = 0$ in an optimal solution x^* to $\max\{cx: x \in \mathrm{sub}(P)\}$. We can optimize cx over $\mathrm{sub}(P)$ by first setting all negative weights to zero, then optimizing over P, then setting to zero any components of the optimal solution corresponding to negative weights. (This is possible if we can optimize over P.)

Theorem 6.7 (Fulkerson (1971, 1972), see Schrijver (1986)). *Let S be a finite set of vectors in $\mathbb{R}_+^J$ and let $P = \mathrm{sub}(\mathrm{conv}(S))$. Then $P = \{x \in \mathbb{R}_+^J: dx \leq 1$ for all $d \in D$ (for some finite subset D of $\mathbb{R}_+^J$)\} if and only if $\mathrm{sub}(\mathrm{conv}(D)) = \{x \in \mathbb{R}_+^J: sx \leq 1$ for all $s \in S\}$.*

For any $S \subseteq \mathbb{R}^J$, the *antiblocker* $A(S)$ is defined to be $\{x \in \mathbb{R}_+^J: sx \leq 1\}$ for all $s \in S$. For finite $S \subseteq \mathbb{R}_+^J$, if P is the polyhedron $\mathrm{sub}(\mathrm{conv}(S))$, then $A(P) = \{x \in \mathbb{R}_+^J: sx \leq 1$ for all $s \in S\}$. Thus $A(P)$ is a polyhedron called the *antiblocking polyhedron of P* and the pair $P, B(P)$ is called an *antiblocking pair*. Theorem 6.7 implies that $A(A(P)) = P$, in this case.

Note the parallels between Theorems 6.3 and 6.7 and the definitions of blockers and antiblockers. Basically we reverse inequality signs.

We have the following analogues of Corollary 6.4 and Theorem 6.5.

Corollary 6.8. *Let $S, D \subseteq \mathbb{R}_+^J$. The following are equivalent:*

$$\text{for each } l \in \mathbb{R}_+^J, \quad \max\{ls: s \in S\} = \min\{1 \cdot x: x \geq 0, dx \geq l$$

$$\text{for all } d \in D\}; \qquad (6.7)$$

$$\text{for each } w \in \mathbb{R}_+^J, \quad \max\{wd: d \in D\} = \min\{1 \cdot y: y \geq 0, ys \geq w$$

$$\text{for all } s \in S\}. \qquad (6.8)$$

Theorem 6.9 (Lehman (1965)). *Let S, D be finite subsets of $\mathbb{R}_+^J$. Then (6.7) and (6.8) are equivalent to*

$$s \cdot d \leq 1 \text{ for all } s \in S, d \in D, \qquad (6.9)$$

and

$$\max\{ls: s \in S\} \cdot \max\{wd: d \in D\} \geq lw \text{ for all } lw \in \mathbb{R}_+^J. \qquad (6.10)$$

One of the best known applications of antiblocking theory is the relationship with perfect graphs. A graph $G = (V, E)$ is *perfect*, if for every node induced subgraph G', the size of the largest stable set or node packing, denoted by $\alpha(G')$, equals the minimum number of cliques required to contain all the nodes of G', denoted by $\bar{\chi}(G')$. These graphs were introduced by Berge (1960) (see Berge and Chvátal (1984) for a good survey), who made two conjectures.

the first of which has been proved and the second of which is still open. For any graph G, $\bar{G}$ denotes the complement of G. That is u, v are adjacent in $\bar{G}$ if and only if they are not adjacent in G.

Theorem 6.10 (Lovász (1972)). Perfect Graph Theorem. *G is perfect if and only if $\bar{G}$ is perfect.*

A *chord* of a cycle is an edge not in the cycle which has both ends in the cycle.

Conjecture 6.11. Perfect Graph Conjecture. *G is perfect if and only if neither G nor $\bar{G}$ contains an odd cycle having five or more nodes which has no chords.*

Chvátal (1975) noted that results of Lovász (1972) and Fulkerson (1970) combined to give the following.

Theorem 6.12. *$G = (V, E)$ is perfect if and only if the convex hull of the incidence vectors of the stable sets of G is given by*

$$x \geq 0 \,,$$

$$x(K) \leq 1 \quad \text{for every maximal clique } K \,.$$

It is not hard to prove Theorem 6.12 directly, see Grötschel et al. (1988), and then antiblocking theory provides the Perfect Graph Theorem 6.10. See Schrijver (1986) for details and another application of antiblocking.

We close this section by noting one important additional application of polarity. Grötschel et al. (1981) and Padberg and Rao (1981) showed that optimization for a polyhedron was equivalent to separation for a polar polyhedron, and conversely. Hence the fact that a polynomially bounded separation routine enabled us to optimize polynomially using the ellipsoid algorithm, when applied to this polar yielded the reverse implication. When we can polynomially optimize over a class of polyhedra, we can also solve the associated separation problem polynomially.

7. Strengthening min–max theorems I: Essential inequalities

Recall that our motivation for finding polyhedral descriptions of combinatorial optimization problems was so that we could use linear programming duality to obtain min–max theorems. In this section we discuss one way of strengthening these theorems: obtaining nonredundant polyhedral descriptions, or equivalently, reducing the set of dual objects necessary for a min–max equality to hold.

We saw (Theorem 3.15) that a defining linear system $A^= x = b^=$, $A^\leq x \leq b^\leq$ was minimal for $P = \{x : A^= x = b^=, A^\leq x \leq b^\leq\}$ if and only if no inequality from the system $A^\leqslant x \leqslant b^\leqslant$ is tight for all $x \in P$; each induces a distinct facet of P and the rows of $A^=$ are linearly independent. Let us see how these facts can be used to improve our linear description of $P(M)$, the convex hull of the incidence vectors of the independent sets of a matroid $M = (E, \mathscr{F})$. Since we assumed that every singleton plus $\emptyset$ belong to $\mathscr{F}$, $P(M)$ is of full dimension so there are no equations satisfied by all members of $P(M)$. We wish to determine which of the inequalities

$$x(A) \leqslant r(A) \quad \text{for } A \subseteq E \tag{7.1}$$

are essential (see Theorem 4.2).

The set $A \subseteq E$ is said to be *closed* if $r(A \cup \{e\}) > r(A)$ for every $e \in E \backslash A$. That is, it is maximal for its rank. The set $A \subseteq E$ is said to be *nonseparable* if whenever $S \subseteq A$ satisfies $r(S) + r(A \backslash S) = r(A)$, we have $S = \emptyset$ or $S = A$. Any inequality (7.1) for which A is not both closed and nonseparable can be dropped, for it is implied by others. We now show that the converse is true – all inequalities (7.1) for A closed and nonseparable are facet inducing.

Theorem 7.1 (Edmonds, see Giles (1975)). *For a matroid $M = (E, \mathscr{F})$, the inequality (7.1) is facet inducing for $P(M)$ if and only if A is closed and nonseparable.*

Proof. We show that if A is closed and nonseparable, then the inequality (7.1) is facet inducing. As we remarked, the other direction is easy. Let $\mathscr{W} = \{I \in \mathscr{F}: |I \cap A| = r(A)\}$. Suppose that $ax \leqslant \alpha$ is a valid inequality for $P(M)$ which is tight for the incidence vectors of all $I \in \mathscr{W}$ and $a \neq 0$.

First we show that $a_j = a_k$ for all $j, k \in A$. For suppose not. Let $A_1 = \{j \in A: a_j$ takes on the minimum value over $A\}$ and let $A_2 = A \backslash A_1$. Let I be a basis of A obtained by extending a basis I_2 of A_2. Let $I_1 = I \backslash I_1$. Since A is nonseparable and $A_1 \neq \emptyset \neq A_2$, $|I_1| < r(A_1)$. Therefore there exists $e \in A_1 \backslash I_1$ such that $I_1 \cup \{e\} \in \mathscr{F}$. Therefore there exists $e' \in I_2$ such that $I' = I \cup \{e\} \backslash \{e'\}$ is a basis of A. But this means that $I, I' \in \mathscr{W}$, and $a(I) = a \cdot x^I > a(I') = a \cdot x^{I'}$, a contradiction.

Now we show that $a_j = 0$ for all $j \in E \backslash A$. Let I be a basis of A. Since $I \in \mathscr{W}$, $a(I) = \alpha$. Since A is closed, $I \cup \{j\} \in \mathscr{F}$, i.e., $I \cup \{j\} \in \mathscr{W}$, so $a(I) + a_j = \alpha$. Therefore $a_j = 0$.

This means that the inequality is a positive multiple of (7.1), and so this inequality is facet inducing, see Theorem 3.16. $\square$

Let us apply this to the forest matroid of a graph $G = (V, E)$. The rank of A is $|A| - \kappa(G(A))$, where $\kappa(G(A))$ is the number of connected components of $G(A)$. Thus $A \subseteq E$ is closed if and only if every edge having both ends in the same component of $G(A)$ is already in A. Moreover, A is nonseparable if and only if $G(A)$ is nonseparable, in the graph theoretic sense. That is, $G(A)$ should be connected and contain no cutnodes. Thus we can obtain:

Theorem 7.2. *Let $G = (V, E)$ be a graph. The forest polytope $F(G)$ is the solution set to the following system:*

$$x_e \geqslant 0 \quad \text{for all } e \in E,$$

$$x(E(S)) \leqslant |S| - 1 \quad \text{for all } S \subseteq V \text{ such that } G[S] \text{ is nonseparable}.$$

Applying linear programming duality, we have the following min–max theorem.

Corollary 7.3. *Let $G = (V, E)$ be a graph and let $c = (c_e: e \in E)$ be a vector of edge costs. The maximum of $c(F)$, taken over all forests F is equal to the minimum of $\Sigma_{S \in \mathcal{S}}\, y_S(|S| - 1)$ subject to $y \geqslant 0$ and $\Sigma\,(y_S: u, v \in S \in \mathcal{S}) \geqslant c_{uv}$ for all $uv \in E$, where $\mathcal{S}$ is the set of all $S \subseteq V$ such that $G[S]$ is nonseparable.*

Note that if any sets were removed from $\mathcal{S}$, then there would be some cost vectors c for which Corollary 7.3 would no longer hold. So in this sense, we have a best possible min–max theorem.

The case of matroid intersections is surprisingly similar. Let $M_1 = (E, \mathcal{F}_1)$ and $M_2 = (E, \mathcal{F}_2)$ be matroids, with rank functions r_1 and r_2 respectively. The *rank* in $M_1 \cap M_2$ of $S \subseteq E$ is the size of the largest subset of S belonging to $\mathcal{F}_1 \cap \mathcal{F}_2$. We denote this by $r(S)$.

Note that in general $r(S) \leqslant \min\{r_1(S), r_2(S)\}$, and strict inequality may occur. However the strongest set of valid inequalities with 0–1 coefficients we can write down for the intersection of $P(M_1)$ and $P(M_2)$ is

$$
\begin{aligned}
&x \geqslant 0, \\
&x(S) \leqslant r(S) \quad \text{for all } S \subseteq E.
\end{aligned}
\tag{7.2}
$$

We can define *r-closed* and *r-nonseparable* with respect to this matroid intersection rank function just as we did for matroids.

Theorem 7.4 (Giles (1975)). *Let $M_1 = (E, \mathcal{F}_1)$ and $M_2 = (E, \mathcal{F}_2)$ be matroids and suppose that $\{e\} \in \mathcal{F}_1 \cap \mathcal{F}_2$ for all $e \in E$. Then an inequality (7.2) is facet inducing for $P(M_1) \cap P(M_2)$ if and only if S is r-closed and r-nonseparable.*

This theorem has many applications, for it, combined with Edmonds' matroid intersection theorem, enables us to deduce many combinatorial theorems. For example, let $G = (V_1 \cup V_2, E)$ be a bipartite graph. As in Section 5, we define partition matroids $M_1 = (E, \mathcal{F}_1)$ and $M_2 = (E, \mathcal{F}_2)$ as follows: For $i = 1, 2$, let $\mathcal{F}_i = \{J \subseteq E: |J \cap \delta(v)| \leqslant 1 \text{ for all } v \in V_i\}$. For any $S \subseteq E$, the rank $r_i(S)$ in M_i is just the number of nodes of V_i incident with edges of S. The matchings of G are precisely the members of $\mathcal{F}_1 \cap \mathcal{F}_2$. For any $S \subseteq E$, S is closed and nonseparable in M_i if and only if $S = \delta(v)$ for some $v \in V_i$. In this case, $r_i(S) = 1$. Therefore, it follows from Theorem 5.1 and 7.1 that $M(G)$ is the set of all $x \in \mathbb{R}^E$ satisfying

$$x \geq 0 \,, \tag{7.3}$$

$$x(\delta(v)) \leq 1 \quad \text{for all } v \in V_1 \,, \tag{7.4}$$

$$x(\delta(v)) \leq 1 \quad \text{for all } v \in V_2 \,. \tag{7.5}$$

Now consider the linear program of maximizing $x(E)$, for $x \in M(G)$, i.e., x satisfying (7.3)–(7.5). Since $M(G)$ is bounded and nonempty ($0 \in M(G)$), by linear programming duality, the dual has an optimal solution y. Assuming $E \neq \emptyset$, the maximum of $x(E)$ is positive so there is some $v \in V$ such that $y_v > 0$. By complementary slackness, every maximum matching M of G satisfies $|M \cap \delta(v)| = 1$. This observation enables us to characterize those sets $S \subseteq E$ which are r-closed and r-nonseparable, where r is the rank function of $M_1 \cap M_2$. That is, $r(S)$ is just the size of the largest matching contained in S. Let v be a node of $G(S)$ which meets every maximum matching. Then $r(\delta(v) \cap S) = 1$ and $r(S \backslash \delta(v)) = r(S) - 1$, so S can be nonseparable only if $S \backslash \delta(v) = \emptyset$. Moreover S can be closed only if it is a maximal subset of $\delta(v)$. Thus S is closed and nonseparable only if $S = \delta(v)$ for some node v. Therefore a minimal description of $M(G)$ is obtained by including the inequality $x(\delta(v)) \leq 1$ for all $v \in V$ such that $\delta(v)$ is maximal, plus some nonnegativity constraints (7.3). But all these are essential, for if any $x_e \geq 0$ were omitted, then the vector $x = -\varepsilon^e$ would satisfy all remaining constraints and it does not belong to $M(G)$. Thus we have the following.

Theorem 7.5. *Let $G = (V, E)$ be a bipartite graph. A minimal linear system sufficient to define $M(G)$ is*

$$x_e \geq 0 \quad \text{for all } e \in E \,,$$

$$x(\delta(v)) \leq 1 \quad \text{for all } v \in V \text{ such that } \delta(v) \text{ is maximal}.$$

Note too that since $M(G)$ is of full dimension, the minimal linear system of Theorem 7.5 is unique, up to positive multiples.

The case of a nonbipartite graph $G = (V, E)$ is more complex, because we have to consider the case of the blossom inequalities. We say that $S \subseteq V$ is *critical* (or *hypomatchable*) if $G[S] - v$ has a perfect matching, for all $v \in S$. Necessarily, a critical graph has an odd number of nodes, is connected, and unless it consists of a single node, is nonbipartite.

Theorem 7.6 (Pulleyblank and Edmonds (1974)). *For any graph $G = (V, E)$, the following is the unique (up to positive multiples) minimal linear system sufficient to define $M(G)$:*

$$x_j \geq 0 \quad \text{for all } j \in E \,, \tag{7.6}$$

$$x(\delta(v)) \leqslant 1 \quad \text{for all } v \in V \text{ such that } \delta(v) \text{ is maximal, and}$$
$$\text{not contained in a triangle of } G , \qquad (7.7)$$

$$x(E(S)) \leqslant \tfrac{1}{2}(|S| - 1) \quad \text{for all } S \subseteq V \text{ such that } |S| \geqslant 3,$$
$$G[S] \text{ is critical and non-separable.} \qquad (7.8)$$

This theorem enables us to illustrate three of the main techniques for proving that an inequality is essential, i.e., facet inducing. As we did for bipartite graphs, we can show the inequalities (7.6) are essential by showing that if any are omitted, then we get a solution to all others which does not belong in $M(G)$, namely a negative unit vector.

We can show that a valid inequality $ax \leqslant \alpha$ for P is facet inducing by showing that there are $\dim(P)$ affinely independent members of P which satisfy $ax = \alpha$, and that not all members of P satisfy $ax = \alpha$. Consider the case of a degree constraint (7.7). Since $0 \in M(G)$, and (7.,7) is not tight for the zero vector, each induces a proper face. Since $\dim(M(G)) = |E|$, we must construct $|E|$ independent members of $M(G)$. For each $j \in \delta(v)$ let $x^j = \varepsilon^j$. For each $j \not\in \delta(v)$, our maximality condition plus the fact that $\delta(v)$ is not contained in a triangle guarantees that we can find $k \in \delta(v)$ such that k and j are disjoint. Let $x^j = \varepsilon^j + \varepsilon^k$. Each of the vectors x^j, $j \in E$ satisfies $x(\delta(v)) = 1$, and the matrix of these vectors suitably ordered is triangular, so they are linearly, and hence affinely independent. Therefore $x(\delta(v)) \leqslant 1$ is facet inducing.

We can show that the inequalities (7.8) are facet inducing by an argument analogous to that used in proving Theorem 7.1 (Lovász (1979)). That is, we prove that the face induced by each inequality (7.8) is a maximal proper face. It can also be shown by constructing independent vectors, see Pulleyblank and Edmonds (1974). See Giles (1976) for another proof.

Giles (1975, 1976) characterized the facet inducing inequalities for the convex hull of the incidence vectors of the branchings of G. He also introduced a unification of branchings and matchings called branching forests (Giles (1982, 1982a, 1982b)).

The last example we consider is the travelling salesman polytope of the complete graph $K_n = (V, E)$, denoted by Q^n. This case is somewhat different, in that we do not know a complete description of Q^n and the polyhedron is not full dimensional; it has dimension $\binom{n}{2} - n$ (Grötschel and Padberg (1979)). This means that we may get inequalities $ax \leqslant \alpha$ and $bx \leqslant \beta$ which induce the same facet, and yet look quite different. (If $D = \{x \in \mathbb{R}^J : Ax \leqslant b\}$, where $A \in \mathbb{R}^{I \times J}$, and I^* is the equality set of P, then facet inducing inequalities $ax \leqslant \alpha$ and $a'x \leqslant \alpha'$ induce the same facet of P if and only if there exists $\lambda \in \mathbb{R}^{I^*}$ and positive $\gamma \in \mathbb{R}$ such that $a' = \gamma \cdot a + \lambda A[I^*]$, $\alpha' = \gamma \cdot \alpha + \lambda b[I^*]$. See Theorem 3.16(iii). Note that the second equation is actually implied by the first.) Hence if we wish to obtain a nonredundant set of valid inequalities, we must not only ensure that they are facet inducing, but also that no two induce the same facet.

Theorem 7.7 (Grötschel and Padberg (1979)). *For all* $n \geqslant 5$, *the inequalities* $x_j \geqslant 0$ *induce distinct facets of* Q^n.

Theorem 7.8 (Grötschel and Padberg (1979a)). *For all* $n \geqslant 4$ *and* $S \subseteq V$ *satisfying* $2 \leqslant |S| \leqslant \lfloor n/2 \rfloor$, *the subtour elimination constraints* $x(\delta(S)) \geqslant 1$ *induce distinct facets of* Q^n.

The constraints $x(\delta(S)) \geqslant 2$ and $x(\delta(\bar{S})) \geqslant 2$ are obviously identical. Moreover, no subtour elimination constraints induce trivial facets.

Theorem 7.9 (Grötschel and Padberg (1979a)). *Every comb inequality induces a facet of* Q^n.

If $\{H, T_1, T_2, \ldots, T_k\}$ is a comb, then so too is $\{V \setminus H, T_1, T_2, \ldots, T_k\}$ and these induce the same facet of Q_n. Grötschel (1977) showed that in all other cases, each comb induces a facet distinct from all other combs, subtour elimination constraints and nonnegativity constraints.

Theorems 7.8 and 7.9 are subsumed by the following:

Theorem 7.10 (Grötschel and Pulleyblank (1986)). *Each clique tree inequality is facet inducing for* Q^n. *Moreover, distinct clique trees induce distinct facets, with the exception of the comb and subtour elimination cases previously described.*

There are many further classes of facets known for Q^n. See Grötschel and Padberg (1985) for a comprehensive survey, and in particular Maurras (1975), Cornuéjols et al. (1985) and Fleischmann (1988). (The latter two references focus on a variation of the travelling salesman problem wherein each node must be visited at least once.)

Naddef and Rinaldi (1988) describe a composition procedure which enables new, very complicated, facets to be obtained from known classes of facets. All non-spanning clique trees are derivable from subtour elimination constraints using their methods.

Norman (1955) stated that the set of all comb, subtour elimination and nonnegativity constraints provided a complete description of Q^n, for $n = 6$ and 7 and conjectured that it also held for $n = 8$. Recently Fleischmann (1988), and independently, Boyd and Cunningham (1988) and Naddef (1987) found a facet inducing inequality for Q^7 which did not belong to any of these classes. Boyd and Cunningham (1988) did prove that the combs, subtour elimination and nonnegativity constraints are a complete system for Q^6, and these together with the new facets provide a complete system for Q^7. They also showed that for Q^8, the combs, subtour elimination and nonnegativity constraints are only a small fraction of the facet inducing inequalities.

8. Strengthening min–max theorems II: Dual integrality

A second way that we can strengthen min–max theorems obtained via linear programming duality is to show that, for integral objective functions, there exists an optimal dual solution which is integral, or half-integral, valued. Such theorems usually have a much more combinatorial flavor. However we will see that there are combinatiorial optimization polyhedra for which we cannot have both a minimal defining system ('naturally' scaled) and dual integrality. In some cases extra redundant inequalities must be added.

A matrix A is *totally unimodular* if every square submatrix has determinant $0, 1$ or -1. A well known case for which we can obtain integral optimal dual solutions, as well as primal solutions, is that of polyhedra having the form $P = \{x \in \mathbb{R}^J: Ax \leq b\}$ where b is integral valued, and A is totally unimodular.

Theorem 8.1 (Hoffman and Kruskal (1956)). *Let A be an integral matrix. Then A is totally unimodular if and only if, for every integral vector b, all vertices of the polyhedron $\{x: Ax \leq b, x \geq 0\}$ are integral.*

Suppose we have a polyhedron $P = \{x \in \mathbb{R}^J: Ax \leq b\}$ where A is totally unimodular and b is integral. Let $c \in \mathbb{R}^J$ be integer valued. The dual linear program to maximizing cx subject to $Ax \leq b$ is maximize yb, subject to $yA = c$, $y \geq 0$. Let $P^* = \{y: yA = c, y \geq 0\}$. Then $P^* = \{y: yA \leq c, y(-A) \leq -c$ and $y \geq 0\}$. It is easy to show that if A is totally unimodular, then so too is $\begin{bmatrix} A \\ -A \end{bmatrix}$, so if c is integral, it follows from Theorem 8.1 that all vertices of P^* are integer valued. That is, there exists an integral optimal dual solution.

Totally unimodular matrices arise frequently in polyhedral combinatorics. In fact, most development during the 1950's and early 1960's involved polyhedra defined by totally unimodular systems. If A is the node–edge incidence matrix of a bipartite or directed graph, then A is totally unimodular. (This follows easily by induction on the size of a square submatrix S. If some column of S is all zero, then $\det(S) = 0$. If some column contains a single nonzero, then $\det(S) = \pm \det(S')$, where S' is obtained from S by deleting the row and column corresponding to this element. If every column contains two nonzeros, then if A comes from a directed graph, then the sum of the rows of A is the zero vector. If A comes from a bipartite graph, then the sum of the rows of A corresponding to the nodes in one part minus the sum for the rows in the other part is the zero vector. Thus, in either case, $\det(S) = 0$.)

This fact easily gives König's Theorem 1.1 concerning the size of a largest matching in a bipartite graph. It is easy to see that the incidence vectors of matchings of bipartite $G = (V, E)$ are the *integral* solutions to

$$x \geq 0, \tag{8.1}$$

$$Ax \leq 1, \tag{8.2}$$

where A is the node edge incidence matrix of G. By Theorem 8.1, all vertices of the polyhedron defined by this system are integral, so it defines $M(G)$. (Note that we have reproved Theorem 2.3.) The dual linear program to maximizing $1 \cdot x$, subject to (8.1) and (8.2) is minimize $1 \cdot y$ subject to

$$y \geq 0 , \tag{8.3}$$

$$yA \geq 1 . \tag{8.4}$$

Since A is totally unimodular if and only if $-A$ is totally unimodular, we can write (8.4) as $y(-A) \leq -1$, and apply Theorem 8.1 to see that there is always an integer optimal solution y^*. Then clearly $y_v^* \in \{0, 1\}$ for all $v \in V$ so if we let $W = \{v \in V: y_v^* = 1\}$ then W is a node cover of G, and so by linear programming duality, the size of a largest matching equals the size of a smallest node cover.

Note too that the famous max-flow min-cut theorem of Ford and Fulkerson (1956) and Elias, Feinstein and Shannon (1956) also follows easily from Theorem 8.1. See Chapter 4 of this volume.

The property of A being totally unimodular is trivially in co-NP. We can prove that A is not totally unimodular by displaying a square submatrix S for which $\det(S) \not\in \{0, \pm1\}$. Seymour (1980) showed that this property is also in NP, by showing that every totally unimodular matrix could be constructed via three simple types of composition from so called network matrices, their transposes and two exceptions. Edmonds described how a decomposition procedure can be used to obtain a polynomial algorithm which will, given a $(0, \pm1)$-matrix A, either find a method of constructing it using Seymour's procedure, or else show that it is not totally unimodular. Thus testing a matrix for total unimodularity is in P. See Schrijver (1986), Chapters 19–21, for details.

Another class of matrices is formed by balanced matrices, introduced by Berge (1969, 1970). A $(0, 1)$-matrix M is *balanced* if it has no square submatrix of odd order in which each row and column contain exactly two 1's. The following theorem from Schrijver (1986) combines results of Berge and Las Vergnas (1970), Berge (1972) and Fulkerson, Hoffman and Oppenheim (1974).

Theorem 8.2. *Let M be a $\{0, 1\}$-matrix. Then the following are equivalent*:
  (i) *M is balanced*;
  (ii) *for every $(0, 1)$-vector b and every integral vector c, both sides of the linear programming duality equation*

$$\min\{cx: x \geq 0, Mx \geq b\} = \max\{yb: y \geq 0, yM \leq c\}$$

have integral optima, if the linear programs are feasible;
  (iii) *for each $(1, \infty)$-vector b and each integral vector c, both sides of the*

linear programming duality equation

$$\max\{cx: x \geqslant 0, Mx \leqslant b\} = \min\{yb: y \geqslant 0, yM \geqslant c\}$$

have integral optimal solutions, if the optima are finite.

See also Truemper and Chandrasekaran (1978).

We say that a linear system $Ax \leqslant b$ is *totally dual integral* or *TDI* if for every integer valued c such that $\max\{cx: Ax \leqslant b\}$ exists, the corresponding dual linear program has an integral optimal solution. Giles and Pulleyblank (1979) show that for any rational linear system $Ax \leqslant b$, there exists a positive rational α such that the equivalent system $(\alpha A)x \leqslant \alpha b$ is *TDI*. However, in general α is very small and αb is not integer valued. When it is integer valued, we obtain an important consequence.

Theorem 8.3 (Edmonds and Giles (1977)). *If P is the solution set of a TDI system $Ax \leqslant b$ with b integer valued, then every nonempty face of P contains an integer valued point. In particular, every vertex of P is integer valued.*

This was proved by Hoffman (1974), see also Hoffman (1982), for pointed polyhedra – polyhedra with vertices. This idea of establishing primal integrality by means of dual integrality was also used by Lehman (1979) and Fulkerson (1971). Let us note that this theorem follows from linear programming duality and the following 'primal' result.

Proposition 8.4. *Every nonempty face of a rational polyhedron $P \subseteq \mathbb{R}^J$ contains an integer point if and only if, for every integral $c \in \mathbb{R}^J$ such that $\max\{cx: x \in P\}$ exists, this maximum is integer valued.*

We saw in Section 3 that F is a nonempty proper face of P if and only if there is some objective function cx which is maximized over P precisely by the members of F. Hence every nonempty face of P contains an integral point if and only if every real objective function maximized over P attains its maximum for an integral point. Note the two ways in which this is strengthened by Proposition 8.4. First, we only consider integral c. But this is no restriction, since P is rational and the elements of P that maximize cx also maximize $(\alpha c)x$ for any $\alpha > 0$. Second, we do not consider the values of the optimal solution x^* but only the objective value cx^*. If the polyhedron has vertices, then it is easy to see that if P has a fractional vertex x^*, then there is some integer objective function c whose optimum is fractional. For let c^* be an integer objective function maximized over P only by x^*. Then for integer M sufficiently large, the vector c^j defined by

$$c_i^j = \begin{cases} M \cdot c_i^* & \text{if } i \neq j, \\ M \cdot c_i^* + 1 & \text{if } i = j. \end{cases}$$

is also maximized by x^*, and the difference between c^*x^* and c^jx^* is precisely x_j^*. Therefore, if x^* has a fractional component x_j^*, so too is at least one of c^jx^* and $(M \cdot c^*)x^*$. (This is the idea of the proof of Hoffman (1974), see also Giles (1975).)

For the general case, a more refined argument is required. Edmonds and Giles (1977) prove Proposition 8.4 by means of an integer form of Farkas' Lemma:

Lemma 8.5 (Kronecker (1884), see Schrijver (1986)). *Let A and b be rational. Then the system of equations $Ax = b$ has an integer solution if and only if λb is integer for every λ such that λA is integer.*

This lemma follows from the fact that an integer matrix can be put into Hermite normal form. (See Schrijver (1986) or Nemhauser and Wolsey (1988).) Note how this implies the sufficiency in Proposition 8.4. Let F be a minimal face of $P = \{x \in \mathbb{R} : Ax \leq b\}$ which contains no integral point. Then $F = \{x \in \mathbb{R}^J : \bar{A}x = \bar{b}\}$ where $\bar{A}x \leq \bar{b}$ is a subsystem of $Ax \leq b$. If F contains no integral point, then by Lemma 8.5, there exists λ such that $c = \lambda \bar{A}$ is integral, but $\gamma = \lambda \bar{b}$ is fractional. But $\max\{cx : x \in P\} = \gamma$, proving the result. (The necessity in Proposition 8.4 is trivial.)

We are particularly interested in the converse of Theorem 8.3.

Theorem 8.6 (Giles and Pulleyblank (1979)). *If $P = \{x : Ax \leq b\}$ is an integer polyhedron, i.e., a polyhedron for which every nonempty face contains an integral point, then there exists a TDI system $A'x \leq b'$ with b' integral such that $P = \{x : A'x \leq b'\}$.*

Schrijver showed that this could be strengthened as follows.

Theorem 8.7 (Schrijver (1981)). *Let P be a full dimensional polyhedron defined by a rational linear system. Then there is a unique minimal TDI system $Ax \leq b$ with A integral such that $P = \{x : Ax \leq b\}$. Moreover, every nonempty face of P will contain an integral point if and only if b is integral.*

The proofs of these theorems both depend on the following idea. The objective functions c which attain a maximum over P can be divided, based on the minimal face F over which the optimum is attained. For each minimal nomempty face F, the set of objective functions which attain their maximum over F form a rational cone (generated by the inequalities tight for F). For any rational cone C, there is a finite set B of integer valued members of C such that every integral member of C is an integral linear combination of members of B. (We call B a *Hilbert basis*; its existence was established by Hilbert (1890), see Schrijver (1986).) For each $c \in B$, we add the (possibly redundant) inequality $cd \leq \gamma$, where $\gamma = cx$ for any $x \in F$. The system is now TDI, and in view of Proposition 8.4, the polyhedron is integral if and only if the resulting right hand side is integral. Uniqueness follows from the fact that every pointed rational cone has a unique minimal Hilbert basis.

A minimal TDI defining system as in Theorem 8.7 will contain an inequality which induces each facet of *P*. However in general a complete set of facet inducing inequalities will not be TDI, and extra inequalities must be added to achieve this property. It is surprising though that for many combinatorial polyhedra, minimal defining systems are TDI, when they are scaled so that all entries are integral, and the coefficients of each constraint and right-hand side have no common divisor.

For example, consider a matroid polyhedron $P(M)$. Our generalized greedy algorithm actually constructed an integral dual solution whenever the cost function c was integer. This implies that the minimal defining system (see Theorem 7.1) is TDI. This has an interesting application to forests in a graph. Let $G = (V, E)$ be a graph and let $c = (c_j: j \in E)$ be a vector of integral edge costs. An *induced subgraph cover* $\mathcal{K}$ of G is a finite family of node induced nonseparable subgraphs of G which contain each edge j at least c_j times. The *size* of $\mathcal{K}$ is $\Sigma\,(|K| - 1: K \in \mathcal{K})$. Corollary 7.3 can be strengthened to: the maximum weight of a forest of G equals the minimum size of an induced subgraph cover of G.

Edmonds (1979) showed that the defining system (7.2) for the intersection of two matroids is TDI, from which it follows easily that the minimal such system is also TDI.

Cunningham and Marsh (1978) showed that the minimal defining system for $M(G)$, the matching polytope of G, described in Theorem 7.6 is TDI. This yields a number of combinatorial consequences.

Let $G = (V, E)$ and let $c \in \mathbb{R}^E$. A *critical cover* of c is a family $(C_i: i \in I)$ of subsets of V such that for all $i \in I$, $G[C_i]$ is critical and for each $j \in E$,

$$c_j \leq |\{i \in I: j \in \delta(C_i) \text{ and } |C_i| = 1\}|$$
$$+ |\{i \in I: j \in E(C_i) \text{ and } |C_i| \geq 3\}|\,.$$

The *weight* of the cover is

$$\tfrac{1}{2} \sum (|C_i| - 1: i \in I, |C_i| \geq 3) + |\{i \in I: |C_i| = 1\}|\,.$$

Corollary 8.8. *For any* $G = (V, E)$, *for any integer* $c \in \mathbb{R}^E$, *the maximum of* $c(M)$ *taken over all matchings* M *of* G *equals the minimum weight of a critical cover of* c.

In the case that G is bipartite, this specializes to Egerváry's Theorem (Theorem 2.6). If G is nonbipartite and $c_j = 1$ for all $j \in E$, we get Edmonds' Theorem (Theorem 1.2). If G is bipartite, and $c_j = 1$ for all $j \in E$, then we obtain again König's Theorem (Theorem 1.1).

The case of *b-matching* is an instance for which we know both a minimal defining linear system and a minimal TDI system and these two systems are different. Let $G = (V, E)$ be a graph and let $b = (b_v : v \in V)$ be a vector of positive integers. A *b-matching* is a nonnegative integral $x \in \mathbb{R}^E$ satisfying $x(\delta(v)) \le b_v$ for all $v \in V$. Edmonds (1965a) (see also Edmonds and Johnson (1970), Aráoz et al. (1983), and Pulleyblank (1973)) showed that $M(G, b)$, the convex hull of the *b*-matchings, is given by the following linear system:

$$x_j \ge 0 \quad \text{for all } j \in E \,,$$

$$x(\delta(v)) \le b_v \quad \text{for all } v \in V \,,$$

$$x(E(S)) \le \tfrac{1}{2}(b(S) - 1) \quad \text{for all } S \subseteq V \text{ such that } b(S) \text{ is odd} \,.$$

In general, this system is not minimal. For each $v \in V$, let b^v be the vector obtained by decreasing the value of b_v by one. We say that G is *b-critical* if G has no perfect *b*-matching, but G does have a perfect b^v-matching for all $v \in V$. For any $v \in V$, we let $N(v)$ be the set of nodes of $V \setminus \{v\}$ which are adjacent to v.

Theorem 8.9 (Pulleyblank (1973)). *The following is the unique, up to positive multiples, minimal linear system sufficient to define $M(G, b)$:*

$$x_j \ge 0 \quad \text{for all } j \in E \,; \tag{8.5}$$

$$x(\delta(v)) \le b_v \quad \text{for all } v \in V \text{ such that } b(N(v)) \ge b_v + 2$$

$$\text{or } b(N(v)) = b_v + 1 \text{ and } E(N(v)) = \emptyset$$

$$\text{or } v \text{ belongs to a two node component of } G, \text{ and}$$

$$b_v = b_w, \text{ where } w \text{ is the other node}; \tag{8.6}$$

$$x(E(S)) \le \tfrac{1}{2}(b(S) - 1) \quad \text{for all } S \subseteq V \text{ such that } |S| \ge 3, \, G[S] \text{ is}$$

$$b\text{-critical and contains no cutnode } i$$

$$\text{having } b_i = 1. \tag{8.7}$$

This theorem directly generalizes Theorem 7.6. But this linear system is not TDI. For suppose that G consists of a triangle having $b_v = 2$ for all $v \in V$. Then no inequalities (8.7) are present. If we take $c_j = 1$ for all $j \in E$, then the maximum value of cx for a *b*-matching x is 3, which cannot be achieved with an integral dual solution.

A graph $G = (V, E)$ is said to be *b-bicritical* if $b_v \ge 2$ for all $v \in V$ and if whenever a node i has its constraint b_i decreased by two, there exists a perfect *b*-matching. These *b*-bicritical graphs give the new inequalities which must be added, to obtain a TDI system.

Theorem 8.10 (Cook (1983), Pulleyblank (1981)). *The unique minimal TDI system for $M(G, b)$ is given by (8.5)–(8.7) plus*

$$x(E(S)) \leq \tfrac{1}{2}b(S) \quad \text{for every } S \subseteq V \text{ such that } G[S] \text{ is}$$
$$b\text{-bicritical, connected, and every node } v$$
$$\text{of } V \setminus S \text{ adjacent to a node of } S \text{ has } b_v \geq 2.$$
(8.8)

Informally, then, for b-matchings if an integer min–max theorem is desired, many more dual variables must be used than are required if a fractional one is acceptable. (Note that this implies Cunningham and Marsh's result which proved that the system of Theorem 7.6 is TDI.)

See Cook and Pulleyblank (1987) for extensions of these results to other versions of matching problems.

Let $P = \{x \in \mathbb{R}^J : Ax \leq b\}$, where $A \in \mathbb{R}^{I \times J}$. For each vertex v of P, let I^v be the index set of the inequalities which are tight for v. That is, v is the unique solution to $A[I^v]x = b[I^v]$, and for each $i \in I \setminus I^v$, $A[i]v < b_i$. Hoffman and Oppenheim (1978) defined the system $Ax \leq b$ to be *locally strongly unimodular* at vertex v if $A[I^v]$ has a full rank submatrix with determinant ± 1. Note that if A and b are integral, this implies that v is integer valued, using Cramer's rule. They also showed that the system (4.5), (4.6), (4.8) of Theorem 4.3 which defined the matching polytope $M(G)$ was locally strongly unimodular at each vertex, hence providing another proof of this theorem. Gerards and Sebö showed that this property is in fact implied by total dual integrality.

Theorem 8.11 (Gerards and Sebö (1987)). *Let $Ax \leq b$ be a TDI system of inequalities, with A integral, such that $P = \{x : Ax \leq b\}$ is full dimensional. Then $Ax \leq b$ is locally strongly unimodular at every vertex of P.*

Chandrasekaran (1981) showed that if $Ax \leq b$ is a TDI system with A integral, then for any integral vector c such that an optimum exists, an integral optimum can be found in polynomial time.

Consider the problems:

Given a rational system $Ax \leq b$ of linear inequalities,

does it determine an integral polyhedron?   (8.9)

Given a rational system $Ax \leq b$, is it TDI?   (8.10)

Both these problems are in co-NP (see Schrijver (1986), Ch. 22) and neither are known to be in NP. If we restrict A to being integral of fixed rank, then in fact these problems can both be solved polynomially (Cook, Lovász, Schrijver (1984)).

Edmonds and Giles (1977) introduce the following extension of the TDI property. They defined a system $Ax \leq b$ to be *box TDI* if the system $Ax \leq b$, $l \leq x \leq u$ is *TDI for all choices of l and u*. Although we have seen that every polyhedron is defined by a TDI system, it is not true that every polyhedron is defined by a box TDI system.

Theorem 8.12 (Edmonds and Giles (1977)). *If P is defined by a box TDI system, then there exists a $(0, \pm 1)$-matrix A and a vector b such that $P = \{x: Ax \leq b\}$.*

Cook showed that the property of being box TDI depends only on the polyhedron.

Theorem 8.13 (Cook (1986)). *Let P be a polyhedron defined by some box TDI system and let $Ax \leq b$ be any TDI system such that $P = \{x: Ax \leq b\}$. Then $Ax \leq b$ is a box TDI system.*

Edmonds and Giles (1977) also gave a very general extension of matroid intersection, which provided an example of a class of box TDI systems. Let N be a finite set. A family $\mathscr{F}$ of subsets of N is called a *crossing family* if for every $S, T \in \mathscr{F}$ such that $S \cap T \neq \emptyset$ and $S \cup T \neq N$, we have $S \cup T$ and $S \cap T$ in $\mathscr{F}$. Suppose we are given a directed graph $G = (N, E)$, a crossing family $\mathscr{F}$ of subsets of N, a submodular function f defined on $\mathscr{F}$, vectors $l, u \in \mathbb{R}^E$ and a vector $c \in \mathbb{R}^E$ of arc costs. The *submodular flow problem is*

$$\text{maximize} \quad cx$$
$$\text{subject to} \quad l \leq x \leq u, \tag{8.11}$$
$$x(\delta^-(S)) - x(\delta^+(S)) \leq f(S) \quad \text{for all } S \in \mathscr{F}.$$

(We let $\delta^+(S)$ and $\delta^-(S)$ respectively denote the sets of arcs with heads and tails in S.)

Theorem 8.14 (Edmonds and Giles (1977)). *If l, u and f are integral, then for any c such that the minimum exists, there is an integral optimal solution and an integral optimal dual solution.*

That is, they show that the above system is TDI, or equivalently, that the system (8.11) is box TDI.

The minimum cost network flow problem of Section 2 is obtained as follows: Let $\mathscr{F}_1 = \{\{v\}: v \in N\}$ and $\mathscr{F}_2 = \{N \backslash \{v\}: v \in N\}$. Let $\mathscr{F} = \mathscr{F}_1 \cup \mathscr{F}_2$. Define $f(\{s\}) = f(N \backslash \{s\}) = k$, $f(\{t\}) = f(N \backslash \{t\}) = -k$ and $f(\{v\}) = f(N \backslash \{v\}) = 0$ for all $v \in N \backslash \{s, t\}$. Let $l = 0$ and $u = \alpha$.

The problem of finding a minimum weight independent set in the intersection of matroids $M_1 = (E, \mathscr{F}_1)$ and $M_2 = (E, \mathscr{F}_2)$ having rank functions r_1 and r_2 respectively can be modeled as follows: Construct a directed graph $G = (N, E)$, in which all arcs are pairwise disjoint, i.e., each arc plus its two endnodes forms a separate component. For each set $S \subseteq E$ we construct two sets for our crossing family $\mathcal{F}$. We let S^t be the set of all tails of arcs in S and we let $\bar{S}^h$ be the set of all nodes which are *not* heads of arcs in S. Then $\mathcal{F} = \{S^t, \bar{S}^h : S \subseteq E\}$. We define $f(S^t) = \min\{r_1(S), k\}$ and $f(\bar{S}^h) = \min\{r_2(S), k\}$ for $S \subseteq E$, where $k = \min\{r_1(E), r_2(E)\}$.

If we now let $l = 0$ and $u = 1$, we obtain the minimum weight matroid intersection problem as a special case of the submodular flow problem. Edmonds and Giles (1977) actually develop the above construction in the more general situation of polymatroid intersection.

We mention one additional application of submodular flows. Let $G = (N, E)$ be an acyclic directed graph. Let $\mathcal{D}(G) = \{S \subset V : \emptyset \neq S \neq N$ and $\delta^+(S) = \emptyset\}$. That is, $\mathcal{D}(G)$ is the set of nonempty proper subsets of N which have no arcs directed in. Then $\mathcal{D}(G)$ is a crossing family and the set of arcs having exactly one end in S for $S \in \mathcal{D}(G)$ is a directed cut. A set T of arcs which meets every directed cut is called a *cut transversal*. The incidence vectors of the cut transversals are the integral solutions to the system

$$0 \leqslant x_e \leqslant 1 \quad \text{for all } e \in E ,$$

$$x(\delta^-(S)) \geqslant 1 \quad \text{for all } S \in \mathcal{F} = \mathcal{D}(G) .$$

Again, we can apply Theorem 8.14 plus total dual integrality to deduce that for any vector c of nonnegative integral arc costs, the minimum of $c(T)$, over all cut transversals T equals the maximum number of directed cuts we can pack, using each arc e at most c_e times. This result is due to Lucchesi and Younger (1978).

See Edmonds and Giles (1977) and Schrijver (1984) for more applications and extensions of these submodular flow results. See also Frank (1974) for a discussion of combinatorial methods for solving submodular flow problems. See Edmonds and Giles (1977), Cook, (1986) and Schrijver (1986) for further results on and applications of box TDI.

9. Dimension

Generally one of the first problems treated when studying the polyhedron of a combinatorial polyhedron is the calculation of its dimension. As our examples of the previous section show, when the polyhedron is of full dimension, the problem is usually trivial. However when it is not, the situation may become quite complicated. Edmonds et al. (1982) (see also Padberg and Rao (1980)) show that we can compute the dimension of any set $S \subseteq \mathbb{R}^J$ by solving $2(|J| + 1)$ linear optimization problems over S. The idea is to simultaneously construct a system $Ax = b$ of linearly independent equations satisfied by S and a set X of affinely independent members of S. If we have $|X| + r_l(A) = |J|$, we know that $\dim(S) = |X| - 1$. If $|X| + r_l(A) < |J|$, then we construct a vector a which is linearly independent of the rows of A and such that every $x \in X$

satisfies $ax = \alpha$ for some α. We then solve the problems of computing $\alpha_0 =$ $\max\{ax: x \in S\}$ and $\alpha_1 = \min\{ax: x \in S\}$. Let x^0 and x^1 be points which achieve this maximum and minimum. Suppose x^0 is affinely dependent on X. Then there exist $(\lambda_x: x \in X)$ such that $\lambda(X) = 1$ and $x^0 = \Sigma (\lambda_x x: x \in X)$. Then $\alpha_0 = ax^0 = \Sigma (\lambda_x(ax): x \in X) = \alpha$. Similarly, if x^1 is affinely dependent on X then $\alpha_1 = \alpha$. Therefore, if $\alpha_0 \neq \alpha_1$, at least one of x^0, x^1 can be added to X, and the set will remain affinely independent. If $\alpha_0 = \alpha_1$, then every member x of S satisfies $ax = \alpha$, and we add this equation to our system. Then repeat.

Let us consider the case of the perfect matching polytope $\mathrm{PM}(G)$ of an arbitrary graph $G = (V, E)$. If G is bipartite, and every edge belongs to some perfect matching, then $\dim(\mathrm{PM}(G)) = |E| - |V| + \kappa(G)$, where $\kappa(G)$ is the number of connected components. For none of the nonnegativity constraints $x_e \geq 0$ can be tight for $\mathrm{PM}(G)$, so the equality subsystem is just $Ax = 1$, where A is the node-edge incidence matrix. The rank of A is $|V| - \kappa(G)$ and the result follows from Theorem 3.14.

For the case of nonbipartite G, Naddef (1982) gave a good characterization of this value. Edmonds et al. (1982) showed how a decomposition process due to Lovász could be used to decompose G into bipartite graphs and graphs called 'bricks'. A graph $G = (V, E)$ is *bicritical* if $G - u - v$ has a perfect matching for every $u, v \in V$. A *brick* is a 3-connected bicritical graph. The key result in this paper was to show that if $G = (V, E)$ is a brick, then for any $S \subseteq V$ such that $3 \leq |S| \leq |V| - 3$, some perfect matching M satisfies $|M \cap \delta(S)| \geq 3$. Since bicritical graphs have perfect matchings containing every edge (for $uv \in E$, consider $G - u - v$), the equality subsystem of (4.5)–(4.7) is just $Ax = 1$, where A is the node–edge incidence matrix. Since bricks are non-bipartite, and connected (consider u, v belonging to the same part of the bipartition, or u, v belonging to different components), $r_l(A) = |V|$. Therefore, if G is a brick, $\dim(\mathrm{PM}(G)) = |E| - |V|$.

It is a trivial consequence of this that the minimum possible number of distinct perfect matchings of a brick is at least $|E| - |V| + 1$. This settled a conjecture of Lovász and Plummer (1975) on a lower bound on this number, for a bicritical graph. At present this is the best general bound, and it is actually a bound on the number of *affinely independent* incidence vectors of perfect matchings.

A closely related problem is computing the rank of the set of incidence vectors of perfect matchings of G, over $\mathrm{GF}(2)$. This is apparently more difficult and was only recently settled by Lovász (1987). He again uses the brick decomposition to build a basis of this set over $\mathrm{GF}(2)$.

10. Adjacency

The *graph* or *skeleton* $G(P)$ of a polyhedron P has a node for each vertex v of P, and nodes u, v of $G(P)$ are adjacent if and only if $\mathrm{conv}(\{u, v\})$ is an edge (face of dimension one) of P. Thus we have the following.

Theorem 10.1. *For vertices* u, v *of a polyhedron* P, *the following are equivalent*:

(i) u *and* v *are nonadjacent*,

(ii) *if* $x = \frac{1}{2}u + \frac{1}{2}v$, *then* x *is a convex combination of vertices of* P *other than* u *and* v,

(iii) *any supporting hyperplane of* P *which passes through both* u *and* v *must contain some point of* P *not on the line joining* u *and* v.

This theorem shows that the property of being adjacent is in co-NP. Also, if we know a defining system $Ax \leq b$ for $P \subseteq \mathbb{R}^J$, then we can show that distinct vertices u and v are adjacent by exhibiting a subsystem $A'x \leq b'$ satisfying $A'u = A'v = b'$ and such that $r_l(A') = |J| - 1$. See Theorem 3.14. Thus this property is also in NP.

It has been hoped that an adjacency criterion for a class of polytopes could provide the basis for an efficient algorithm which uses some sort of local search technique. This was motivated largely by the success of the simplex algorithm for linear programming which proceeds by a series of pivots from feasible basis to feasible basis until the optimum is obtained. When a linear program is nondegenerate, there is a bijection between feasible bases and vertices of the polyhedron of feasible solutions. Indeed, in any linear program, the nondegenerate simplex pivots correspond exactly to moving between adjacent vertices of the associated polyhedron. But combinatorial optimization problems are notoriously degenerate!

Trubin (1969) proved that two vertices of the convex hull of the incidence vectors of the node packings of a graph were adjacent if and only if the corresponding vertices were adjacent on the polyhedron defined by a certain linear relaxation. He then suggested using the simplex algorithm on the relaxation, only restricting oneself to pivots that yield new integral solutions. Balas and Padberg (1972) observed that the problem with the approach is the high degree of degeneracy of the problem. That is, to each vertex (basic feasible solution) there exists a large set of feasible bases and it is not true that arbitrary bases corresponding to adjacent vertices will differ by a single simplex pivot. Thus the problem is how to find a 'short' path through the set of feasible bases corresponding to a vertex to enable one to make a nondegenerate pivot. They also showed that there did exist a sequence of pivots from an arbitrary solution to the optimal solution for which the length was polynomially bounded, but it required knowing the optimum in advance. (See also Ikura and Nemhauser (1985).) Moreover, for network optimization problems, Cunningham (1979) showed that if a certain pivot rule was applied, then exponentially long sequences of degenerate pivots (called 'stalling') can be avoided.

Sometimes testing adjacency of vertices of combinatorial polyhedra can be easy. Let $S(G)$ denote the convex hull of the incidence vectors of the node packings, or stable sets, of G. We denote the symmetric difference of sets S and T by $S \triangle T$. Thus $S \triangle T = (S \cup T)\backslash(S \cap T)$.

Theorem 10.2 (Chvátal (1975)). *Let* S_1, S_2 *be node packing of* $G = (V, E)$. *The* *vertices corresponding to S_1 and S_2 are adjacent if and only if $G[S_1 \triangle S_2]$ is connected.*

Proof. Let x^1 and x^2 be the vertices corresponding to S_1 and S_2 respectively. Suppose $G[S_1 \triangle S_2]$ is not connected. Let K be the nodeset of one component. Let x^3 and x^4 be the vertices of $(S_1 \backslash K) \cup (S_2 \cap K)$ and $(S_2 \backslash K) \cup (S_1 \cap K)$ respectively. Then $\frac{1}{2}x^1 + \frac{1}{2}x^2 = \frac{1}{2}x^3 + \frac{1}{2}x^4$ and $x^3, x^4 \notin \{x^1, x^2\}$ so by (ii) of Theorem 10.1, x^1 and x^2 are not adjacent.

Suppose $G[S_1 \triangle S_2]$ is connected. Define $c = (c_v : v \in V)$ by

$$
c_v = \begin{cases} M & \text{for } v \in S_1 \cap S_2, \\ |\delta'(v)| & \text{for } v \in S_1 \triangle S_2, \\ -1 & \text{for } v \notin S_1 \cup S_2, \end{cases}
$$

where for each $v \in S_1 \triangle S_2$, $\delta'(v)$ is the set of edges of $G[S_1 \triangle S_2]$ incident with v and M is some large number. Then $cx^1 = cx^2 = M|S_1 \cap S_2| + |E(S_1 \triangle S_2)|$.

Let $\hat{S}$ be any stable set of G whose incidence vector $\hat{x}$ satisfies $c\hat{x} \geq M|S_1 \cap S_2| + |E(S_1 \triangle S_2)|$. Then $\hat{S}$ must contain all nodes of $S_1 \cap S_2$, and $c(\hat{S} \cap (S_1 \triangle S_2))$ must be at least $|E(S_1 \triangle S_2)|$. But $c(\hat{S} \cap (S_1 \triangle S_2))$ equals the number of edges of $E(S_1 \triangle S_2)$ incident with nodes of $\hat{S}$, and since $G[S_1 \triangle S_2]$ is connected and bipartite, the only possibilities for $\hat{S}$ are S_1 and S_2. So by (iii) of Theorem 10.1, x^1 and x^2 are adjacent. $\square$

A corollary of Theorem 10.2 is that the incidence vectors of matchings M_1 and M_2 of $G = (V, E)$ are adjacent on $M(G)$ if and only if $M_1 \triangle M_2$ consists of a single alternating path or a single alternating cycle. If M_1 and M_2 are perfect, then only the second possibility can occur. (This follows by applying Theorem 10.2 to the line graph of G.)

By contrast, it may be very difficult to test adjacency.

Theorem 10.3 (Papadimitriou (1978)). *It is NP-complete to decide whether two given vertices v_1, v_2 of Q^n ($=\mathrm{TSP}(K_n)$) are nonadjacent.*

(This also holds for the asymmetric travelling salesman polytope $\vec{Q}_n$, the convex hull of the incidence vectors of the directed Hamiltonian cycles on the complete directed graph $\vec{K}_n$.)

The *diameter* of a polyhedron P is the maximum length of a shortest path between any pair of nodes of $G(P)$. Padberg and Rao (1974) showed that the diameter of the asymmetric travelling salesman polytope is only two! Thus any tour is either adjacent to the optimal tour, or else there is a third tour adjacent to both. This makes local search look attractive, but in view of Theorem 10.3 (for the asymmetric case) just seeing whether two tours correspond to adjacent vertices is already as hard as the original problem.

An even more striking example of the irrelevance of adjacency to optimization was given by Barahona and Mahjoub (1986). The *cut polytope* of a graph

$G = (V, E)$ is the convex hull of the incidence vectors of the cuts of G. Given an arbitrary vector w of edge weights, it is an NP-hard problem to find a cut J for which $w(J)$ is maximized, even for a complete graph. Barahona and Mahjoub showed that the cut polytope of a complete graph has diameter one. That is, every vertex is adjacent to the optimal solution!

One of the most famous open problems concerning the combinatorics of polytopes is the *Hirsch conjecture*: If P is a polytope of dimension d with f facets, then the diameter of P is at most $f - d$. (See Klee and Kleinschmidt (1987) for a survey.) Recently Naddef (1988) proved that this holds for all polyhedra having 0–1 vertices which includes most of combinatorial interest.

Theorem 10.4 (Naddef (1988)). *Let P be a polytope of dimension d having f facets for which all vertices are 0–1 valued. Then the diameter of P is at most $f - d$.*

Proof. We proceed by induction on d. Let u and v be arbitrary vertices. It is shown in Naddef and Pulleyblank (1984) that there is a full dimensional 0–1 polytope $P' \subseteq \mathbb{R}^d$ such that $G(P') = G(P)$. (Basically, if all $x \in P$ satisfy an equation $ax \leq \alpha$, then drop any coordinate j for which $a_j \neq 0$. It is easy to verify that this does not affect adjacency.) Therefore there is a path in $G(P)$ joining u and v of length at most d. (Consider for example the sequence of nondegenerate pivots of the simplex algorithm going from u to v, for a suitable objective function.) Therefore the diameter of P is at most d. If $f \geq 2d$ then we are done. Suppose $f < 2d$. Since every vertex must belong to at least d facets, some facet F contains u and v. But F is a 0–1 polytope of dimension $d - 1$ and the result now follows by applying induction to F. $\square$

Several people have studied the Hamiltonicity properties of the graphs of combinatorial polyhedra. We say that a graph $G = (V, E)$ is *Hamiltonian-connected* if for every $u, v \in V$, there is a Hamiltonian path which joins u and v. Unless $G = K_2$, this implies that every edge of G belongs to a Hamiltonian cycle. A *hypercube* is the graph of the convex hull of all 0–1 vectors of a given dimension. Hypercubes are bipartite, and hence not Hamiltonian connected, but almost. For any nodes u, v belonging to opposite parts of the bipartition of a hypercube, there exists a Hamiltonian path joining u and v. The following is a very general Hamiltonicity property.

Theorem 10.5 (Naddef and Pulleyblank (1984)). *Let P be any polytope with 0–1 vertices. Then either $G(P)$ is a hypercube or else it is Hamiltonian-connected.*

Let us interpret this theorem in terms of $PM(G)$ for a graph $G = (V, E)$. We noted that it followed from Theorem 10.2 that the incidence vectors of perfect matchings M_1 and M_2 of G are adjacent vertices of $PM(G)$ if and only if $M_1 \triangle M_2$ is the edgeset of a single even cycle. Let $\bar{E}$ be the set of edges of G which belong to perfect matchings. It is easy to see that $G(PM(G))$ is a hypercube if and only $\bar{E}$ is the union of node disjoint even cycles. (In this case, the dimension of PM(G) is equal to the number of such cycles.) Therefore, for any graph G for which the edges belonging to perfect matchings do not just form a collection of disjoint even cycles, for any two distinct perfect matchings M and M', it is possible to order all perfect matchings of G into a sequence $M = M_1, M_2, \ldots, M_r = M'$ such that for each $i = 1, 2, \ldots, r - 1$, $M_i \triangle M_{i+1}$ is a single even cycle.

A comprehensive study of adjacency of combinatorial polyhedra, plus many examples, is in Hausmann (1980).

11. Extended formulations and projection

In this final section, we discuss some recent results concerning ways to effectively make use of extra variables when dealing with combinatorial optimization problems. Suppose we have a combinatorial optimization problem: maximize $\Sigma\,(c_e : e \in S)$, where S is a member of a family $\mathscr{S}$ of feasible subsets of a finite groundset E. Throughout this chapter we have been concerned with the convex hull of the incidence vectors of the members of $\mathscr{S}$, which forms a convex polyhedron in $\mathbb{R}^E$. We have attempted to find a linear system $Ax \leq b$ sufficient to define this polyhedron, for then our optimization problem can be formulated as the linear program: maximize cx subject to $Ax \leq b$. We call such a formulation, for which there exists one variable for each member of the groundset E, a *natural* formulation. (For more detail, see Liu (1988).)

In some cases it is advantageous to introduce extra variables to our formulation, i.e., variables which do not correspond to members of E. This not only may enable us to reduce the number of inequalities in the system, but also may lead to substantial simplification in the form of the inequalities. In this way our problem could become: maximize cx subject to $Ax + Bu \leq b$. We call such a formulation of our problem an *extended* formulation.

For example, consider the case of the submissive of the perfect matching polytope of a graph $G = (V, E)$ (see Section 6). This is the convex hull of the incidence vectors of the matchings of G which are subsets of perfect matchings. Since we know complete formulations of PM(G), we can easily obtain an extended formulation of sub(PM(G)), for

$$\text{sub(PM}(G)) = \{x \in \mathbb{R}^E : 0 \leq x \leq u \text{ for some } u \in \text{PM}(G)\}\,.$$

That is, we have $x \in \text{sub(PM}(G))$ if and only if x satisfies

$$0 \leq x \leq u\,, \tag{11.1}$$

$$u \geq 0\,, \tag{11.2}$$

$$u(\delta(v)) = 1 \quad \text{for all } v \in V\,, \tag{11.3}$$

$$u(\delta(S)) \geqslant 1 \quad \text{for all } S \subseteq V \text{ such that } |S| \geqslant 3, \text{ odd}. \tag{11.4}$$

If G is bipartite, then the inequalities (11.4) are redundant. In this case, our number of variables is $2|E|$ and our number of constraints is $2|E| + |V|$. We call such a formulation, for which both the number of variables and constraints are polynomial in the size of the input, a *compact* or *succinct* formulation.

Let $P = \{(x, u) \in \mathbb{R}^{J \cup K} : Ax + Bu \leqslant b\}$, where $A \in \mathbb{R}^{I \times J}$ and $B \in \mathbb{R}^{I \times K}$. The *projection* of P onto the x variables is defined by

$$P_x = \{x \in \mathbb{R}^J : \text{there exists } u \in \mathbb{R}^K \text{ such that } Ax + Bu \leqslant b\}.$$

Thus if we let P be the polyhedron defined by (11.1)–(11.4), then $\mathrm{sub}(\mathrm{PM}(G)) = P_x$. The projection of a polyhedron is itself a polyhedron and is generated by a set of generators of P from which the components corresponding to the variables being eliminated have been dropped. There are several questions we ask with respect to these ideas:

    (i) How do we obtain extended formulations of polyhedra for which we do not known natural formulations?

    (ii) If we have a natural formulation of a problem, for which the number of constraints is exponential in the size of the input, it is possible to find a compact (extended) formulation?

    (iii) Suppose we know an extended formulation of a problem. How do we obtain a natural formulation, i.e., how do we obtain a linear system sufficient to define the projection onto the variables of a natural formulation?

Often extended formulations come from algorithms for solving the underlying combinatorial optimization problem. If these algorithms are polynomially bounded, then we often obtain compact formulations. In Ball et al. (1987) it is shown how a very simple algorithm for solving the minimum cost single-source–double-sink Steiner tree problem in a directed graph can be used to obtain both a simple compact formulation and a very complex natural formulation. In Martin et al. (1987) it is shown how dynamic programming based algorithms can be used to obtain extended formulations. In Liu (1988) and Martin (1987) it is shown how a polynomially bounded separation routine can be used to produce compact formulations.

An interesting example of a successful solution to (ii) was provided by Maculan (1987). For a directed graph $G = (N, E)$ with designated root node r, an *arborescence* (or *spanning branching*, see Section 5) rooted at r is a spanning tree for which all arcs are directed away from r. Edmonds (1967) showed that the convex hull of the incidence vectors of the arborescences rooted at r is given by the system

$$x \geqslant 0,$$

$$x(\delta^+(v)) = 1 \quad \text{for all } v \in N \backslash \{r\},$$

$$x(E(S)) \leqslant |S| - 1 \quad \text{for all } S \subseteq N.$$

(Recall that $\delta^+(v)$ is the set of arcs directed into v and $E(S)$ is the set of arcs with both ends in S.) Giles (1976) showed that for general graphs, most of these constraints are essential, i.e., there will be an exponential number of constraints in any natural formulation.

Wong (1984) proposed defining $|N| - 1$ disjoint flow subproblems. For each $v \in N \setminus \{r\}$, we are required to ship one unit of flow from r to v. Let x^v be the vector of variables for this problem. Let b^v be a vector zero in all components except for those indexed by r and v and let $b^v_r = -1$ and $b^v_v = +1$. Then a set of constraints sufficient for the subproblem can be written as

$$x^v \geq 0 ,$$
$$Ax^v = b^v ,$$

where A is the node–arc incidence vector of G. He then introduced a vector $x \in \mathbb{R}^E$ of additional variables and required $x^v \leq x$ for all $v \in N \setminus \{r\}$ and $x \leq 1$. The idea is that if $x_j > 0$, for some $j \in E$, then this arc becomes available for use in all the subproblems. Maculan (1987) showed that if we minimize cx subject to all these constraints, then an optimal solution always exists for which the x variables will be the incidence vector of the minimum cost arborescence rooted at r. In other words, the arborescence polytope is a 'projection' of the solution set of this system, as described below. See also Liu (1988) and Nemhauser and Wolsey (1988).

Note that this extended formulation has $|N| \cdot |E|$ variables and $(2|E| + |N| - 2)|N|$ constraints. Thus this is a compact formulation.

There has been much interest recently in trying to determine whether there exists a compact formulation for the perfect matching polytope of an undirected graph. Barahona (1988) gave such a formulation for planar graphs. Yannakakis (1988) showed that there does not exist a *symmetric* extended formulation of $\text{PM}(K_{2n})$. An extended formulation is called symmetric if the set of constraints and extra variables is independent of the ordering of the nodes. Nevertheless, Barahona (1988a) has shown that a minimum weight perfect matching problem in an arbitrary graph can be solved by solving a polynomial number of minimum mean weight cycle problems. (The mean weight of a cycle is the sum of the edge weights, divided by the number of edges.) Moreover, finding a minimum mean weight cycle can be formulated as a polynomially sized linear program.

Now we consider the third question above. Suppose that we know a linear system $Ax + Bu \leq b$ which defines a polyhedron P and we wish to obtain a linear system sufficient to define P_x, the projection onto the x variables. A classical method is Fourier–Motzkin elimination. This is an analogue of Gaussian elimination, but which works for systems of inequalities. (See Nemhauser and Wolsey (1988) or Schrijver (1986).) However this method has seldom been successful in combinatorial situations, because we normally want to project away a set of variables and if we attempt to do this sequentially, the intermediate polyhedra encountered become extremely complex.

Balas and Pulleyblank (1983) proposed the following method, based upon the idea of Benders' decomposition.

Lemma 11.1. *Let* $P = \{(x, u) \in \mathbb{R}^{J \cup K}: Ax + Bu < b\}$. *Let* W *be the cone* $\{w \in \mathbb{R}^I: w \geq 0, wB = 0\}$, *where* $A \in \mathbb{R}^{I \times J}$ *and* $B \in \mathbb{R}^{I \times K}$, *and let* G *be any set of generators of* W. *Then*

$$P_x = \{x \in \mathbb{R}^J: (gA)x \leq gb \text{ for all } g \in G\} .$$

This can be proved quite easily using Farkas' Lemma (see Balas and Pulleyblank (1983)), and essentially reduces the problem of finding a linear system sufficient to define P_x to the problem of finding a finite set of generators for W. We call W the *projection cone*. (If $|K| = 1$, i.e., we are projecting away a single variable, then this is just Fourier–Motzkin elimination.)

Let us illustrate this for the case of sub(PM(G)) for a bipartite graph $G = (V, E)$. (See Liu (1988) and Liu and Pulleyblank (1989).) Suppose we create a second edge e' parallel to each edge e of G. Let E' be the set of new edges created, and let G' be the expanded graph. For any perfect matching M of G', the edges $M \cap E$ comprise a matching $\bar{M}$ of G which is contained in a perfect matching of G. Conversely, each such $\bar{M}$ is precisely the edgeset of $M \cap E$ in some perfect matching M of G. Therefore we obtain the following extended formulation:

$$x \geq 0, \quad u \geq 0,$$

$$Ax + Au = 1,$$

where A is the node edge incidence matrix of G, x and u are the vectors of variables corresponding to E and E' respectively.

The projection cone, required to project onto the x variables, is defined by

$$W = \{w \in \mathbb{R}^V: wA \geq 0\} .$$

That is, a vector $(w_v: v \in V)$ is in W if $w_u + w_v \geq 0$ for every edge uv. It is not hard to show that if G is bipartite then the extreme rays of W are generated by vectors having one of the following forms:

$$x = \varepsilon^v \quad \text{for some } v \in V , \tag{11.5}$$

$$x_v = \begin{cases} -1 & \text{for all } v \in S , \\ +1 & \text{for all } v \in N(S) , \\ 0 & \text{otherwise} , \end{cases} \tag{11.6}$$

for some $S \subseteq V_1$ or V_2, where $V = V_1 \cup V_2$ is the bipartition of V.

(See Balas and Pulleyblank (1983) or Liu and Pulleyblank (1988).) Therefore we apply Lemma 11.1 to obtain a natural formulation of sub(PM(G)) for a bipartite graph $G = (V_1 \cup V_2, E)$. For any $S \subseteq V_1$ or V_2, let $J_S = \delta(N(S)) \setminus \delta(S)$.

Theorem 11.2 (Weinberger (1976), Cunningham and Green-Krótki (1986)).
Let $G = (V_1 \cup V_2, E)$ be a bipartite graph. Then sub(PM(G)) *is defined by the
following system*:

$$x \geqslant 0, \tag{11.7}$$

$$Ax \leqslant 1, \tag{11.8}$$

$$x(J_S) \leqslant |N(S)| - |S| \quad \text{for all } S \subseteq V_1 \text{ or } V_2. \tag{11.9}$$

The constraints (11.8) come from the rays (11.5) and the constraints (11.9)
from the rays (11.6). Note that this is another case for which the extended
formulation has polynomial size, but the natural formulation has exponentially
many constraints, all of which may be facet inducing.

The edge doubling construction described above is still valid for nonbipartite
graphs, however in this case the projection cone W becomes considerably more
complicated. At present no explicit natural formulation of sub(PM(G)) for a
nonbipartite graph is known.

A closely related example is the case of the *perfectly matchable subgraph
polytope* of a graph $G = (V, E)$. In this case, we wish to determine the convex
hull of the incidence vectors of those $S \subseteq V$ such that $G[S]$ has a perfect
matching. We denote this by PMS(G). An extended formulation can be given
as follows:

$$\text{PMS}(G) = \{x \in \mathbb{R}^V \colon \text{there exists } u \in M(G) \text{ satisfying } Au = x\}$$

where A is the node edge incidence matrix.

When G is bipartite, we have the extended formulation

$$-Ix + Au = 0, \tag{11.10}$$

$$u \geqslant 0, \tag{11.11}$$

$$Au \leqslant 1. \tag{11.12}$$

(See Theorem 2.3.) Subtracting (11.10) from (11.12) gives the equivalent
formulation

$$\begin{aligned}
-Ix + Au &= 0, \\
u &\geqslant 0, \\
Ix &\leqslant 1.
\end{aligned}$$

The projection cone required to eliminate the u variables is therefore the same
as for the submissive of PM(G) previously discussed, so using Lemma 11.1 we
obtain the following:

Theorem 11.3 (Balas and Pulleyblank (1983)). *For a bipartite graph* $G = (V_1 \cup V_2, E)$ *the perfectly matchable subgraph polytope* PMS(G) *is defined by the following system*:

$$0 \leqslant x \leqslant 1, \tag{11.13}$$

$$x(S) - x(N(S)) \leqslant 0 \quad \text{for all } S \subseteq V_1 \text{ or } V_2. \tag{11.14}$$

In fact, the system (11.13), (11.14) can be reduced to the following:

$$0 \leqslant x \leqslant 1,$$

$$x(V_1) - x(V_2) = 0,$$

$$x(S) - x(N(S)) \leqslant 0 \quad \text{for all } S \subseteq V_1.$$

Balas and Pulleyblank (1987) use an extension of these methods to obtain PMS(G) for a nonbipartite graph G.

We close this section by noting that the two terminal Steiner tree example of Ball et al. (1987) provides an example of a problem which has a compact formulation, but for which the natural formulation has not only exponentially many facets, but also has facets whose coefficients grow exponentially with the size of the input. See also Nemhauser and Wolsey (1988) where projection is a tool used extensively.

Appendix: P, NP and co-NP

In this appendix, we describe briefly the classes P, NP and co-NP, as these are closely linked to the central themes of polyhedral combinatorics. Excellent general references are Garey and Johnson (1979) or Papadimitriou and Steiglitz (1982), and we limit ourselves here to a very brief summary.

An *instance* of a problem is a single occurrence of such a problem. An instance of a problem is specified by providing a certain *input*. For example, the input to graph optimization problems normally consists of a description of the particular graph, plus possibly some additional data. The *size of an instance* is the number of characters, or binary bits, required to represent the instance. For reasons of convenience, we often prefer problems to be phrased as *decision problems*, which can be answered with a 'yes' or 'no'. Thus, for example, instead of asking for a largest matching in G, we might give as input both G and an integer k and then ask whether G has a matching of cardinality at least k.

We can leave the notion of algorithm quite vague for present purposes. (It is made precise in the above references.) Suffice it to say that the execution of an algorithm on an instance of a problem consists of performing a sequence of *elementary steps*, the execution time of each of which is independent of the size of the particular instance. The total number of elementary steps performed will in general depend on the particular instance. For example, an elementary step might be checking whether a particular edge and node are incident, or comparing two integers. (We have to be careful with this however – if 'long' integers are permitted, then the time required to compare them may grow linearly with their length, and hence not be independent of the size of the input.)

The class P is the set of all decision problems which can be solved 'polynomially'. That is, for each problem $P \in P$, there must exist an algorithm and a polynomial $p(l)$ such that an instance of P whose encoding is of length l can be solved by the algorithm in at most $p(l)$ elementary steps.

Note that the definition of P makes it permissible for us to be imprecise in specifying both the size of an instance and what is meant by an elementary step. For most "reasonable" ways of specifying a problem instance, the lengths of the encodings will be polynomially related. For example, the length of an encoding of a graph is $O(|V|^2)$ if the adjacency matrix is given, $O(|V| + |E|)$ if a list of nodes and edges or adjacency lists are given. Similarly, whether the number of elementary steps taken to add two edges is '1' or linear in the length of the numbers will not affect whether an algorithm solves a particular problem with a polynomial number of steps, provided that the numbers produced and used by the algorithm have length which is polynomially bounded in the size of the input.

The most important class of problems for our purpose in the class NP. These are the problems for which a 'yes' answer can be verified in a polynomial amount of time, provided that some extra information is given. This extra information is called a *certificate* and for each instance, its length must be polynomially bounded in the length of the corresponding input. *Note however that time required to obtain the certificate in the first place is not counted.*

For example, consider the question of determining whether a graph G is Hamiltonian. The input is some encoding of G. No algorithm is known which will solve this problem in a polynomial number of elementary steps. But trivially the problem is in NP – a certificate consists of a list of the edges belonging to a Hamiltonian cycle. Given this extra information, it is indeed easy to verify that the graph is Hamiltonian.

Trivially $P \subseteq NP$ – for each problem in P, the empty set is a quite satisfactory certificate. A problem is NP-complete if it is in NP, and showing that it is in P would imply $P = NP$. More specifically, a problem is NP-complete if a polynomially bounded algorithm for solving it could be used once as a subroutine to obtain a polynomially bounded algorithm for every problem in NP. S.A. Cook (1971) showed that an NP-complete problem existed. Karp (1972) showed that many 'classical' hard problems of combinatorial optimization (including determining whether a graph is Hamiltonian) are NP-complete, and since then hundreds of problems have been shown to be NP-complete.

A problem is NP-*hard* if a polynomially bounded algorithm for it would result in a polynomially bounded algorithm for every problem in NP. The differences are that the problem itself need not lie in NP and we permit more than one call to the subroutine. (For a discussion of issues of reducibility, the interested reader should see Garey and Johnson (1979).) All NP-complete problems are NP-hard, but in addition, the optimization versions of many NP-complete problems are NP-hard, e.g., given a graph G and a vector c of edge costs, find a Hamilton cycle in G the sum of whose edge costs in minimized. (This is the Travelling Salesman Problem.)

We must introduce one additional class of problems. The class co-NP is roughly the class of decision problems for which a 'no' answer can be polynomially verified, given an appropriate certificate. (More precisely, suppose that for some problem P, P^* is the set of all inputs which are valid, and for which the answer is yes. The *complement* of P^* is the set of all other possible inputs. A problem is in co-NP if its complement is in NP. This means that an invalid input, or an input for which the answer is 'no' can be verified in time polynomial in the length of the input, given an appropriate certificate. Usually the problem of validation of the input is trivial, so the issue is the short certificate for the 'no' answer.) Again $P \subseteq$ co-NP, and although it is not known whether $P = NP \cap$ co-NP, polynomially bounded algorithms are known for virtually all problems belonging to $NP \cap$ co-NP.

For example, consider the problem: does a bipartite graph G have a matching containing k edges. The problem is certainly in NP – a 'yes' certificate could consist of a list of the set of edges belonging to such a matching. By virtue of the theorem of König, the problem is in co-NP – a 'no' certificate would consist of a node cover of fewer than k nodes. Moreover, the problem is in P.

Now consider the problem: given a graph G and an integer k, does G have a simple cycle with at least k edges? Again the problem is trivially in NP – if the answer is 'yes' a certificate could consist of the edge set of such a cycle. But at present it is not known whether the problem is in co-NP. How can one be convinced succinctly that no such cycle exists? Since this probem has been shown to be NP-complete, many people feel that it cannot lie in co-NP.

If any NP-complete problem is shown to be in co-NP, it then follows that NP = co-NP. Thus if any NP-complete problem is in co-NP, if follows that, in particular, there does exist a short proof that a graph has no long cycles.

In summary, three of the most important questions of algorithmic complexity are the following:

Is $P = NP$?

Is $NP =$ co-NP?

Is $P = NP \cap$ co-NP?

A 'yes' answer to the first would imply a 'yes' answer to the second and third, but not conversely. However we should note that recent algorithmic developments have given strong support to the argument that these questions are not very important from a point of view of solving 'real-world' problems. Polynomially bounded algorithms (cf. Kachian and Karmarkar) for linear programming perform far worse than the simplex method, which has no polynomial bound. (Note that the 'fast' versions of Karmarkar's algorithm, reported at various meetings, rely on settings of certain parameters and lose the polynomial bound.) Moreover, real instances of NP-complete problems are regularly solved to provable optimality or near optimality in practice, often using the methods of polyhedral combinatorics.

Acknowledgements

I am grateful to Francisco Barahona, Bill Cook, Donna Crystal Llewellyn, Bruce Gamble, Wei-guo Liu, George Nemhauser and Lex Schrijver for many helpful comments and suggestions.

References

J. Aráoz, W. Cunningham, J. Edmonds and J. Green-Krótki (1983), Reductions to 1-matching polyhedra, *Networks* **13**, 455–473.

A. Bachem and M. Grötschel (1982), New aspects of polyhedral theory, in: B. Korte (ed.), *Modern Applied Mathematics, Optimization and Operations Research* (North-Holland, Amsterdam) 51–106.

E. Balas and M. Padberg (1972), On the set covering problem, *Operations Research* **20**, 1152–1161.

E. Balas and W.R. Pulleyblank (1983), The perfectly matchable subgraph polytope of a bipartite graph, *Networks* **13**, 486–516.

E. Balas and W.R. Pulleyblank (1987), The perfectly matchable subgraph polytope of an arbitrary graph, Research Report 87470-OR, Inst. für Operations Research, Universität Bonn; to appear in *Combinatorica*.

M.L. Balinski (1972), Establishing the matching polytope, *Journal of Combinatorial Theory Series B* **13**, 1–13.

M.O. Ball, W.-G. Liu and W.R. Pulleyblank (1987), Two terminal Steiner tree polyhedra, Research Report CORR 87–33, Department of Combinatorics and Optimization, University of Waterloo; to appear in *Proceedings of C.O.R.E. XX Anniversary Conference* (MIT Press, Cambridge, MA)

F. Barahona (1988), On cuts and matchings in planar graphs, Research Report 88503-OR, Institut für Operations Research, Universität Bonn.

F. Barahona (1988a), Reducing matching to polynomial size linear programming, Research Report CORR 88-51, Department of Combinatorics and Optimization, University of Waterloo.

F. Barahona and M. Conforti (1987), A construction for binary matroids, *Discrete Mathematics* **66**, 213–218.

F. Barahona, M. Grötschel, M. Jünger and G. Reinelt (1988), An application of combinatorial optimization to statistical physics and circuit layout design, *Operations Research* **36**, 493–513.

F. Barahona and E. Maccioni (1982), On the exact ground states of three dimensional Ising spin glasses, *Journal of Physics (A)*, *Math. Gen.* **15**, L611–L615.

F. Barahona and A.R. Mahjoub (1986), On the cut polytope, *Mathematical Programming* **36**, 157–173.

C. Berge (1957), Two theorems in graph theory, *Proceedings of the National Academy of Science* **43**, 842–844.

C. Berge (1960), Problèmes de colorations en théorie des graphes, *Publication of the Institute of Statistics, University of Paris* **9**, 123–160.

C. Berge (1969), The rank of a family of sets and some applications to graph theory, in: W.T. Tutte (ed.), *Recent Progress in Combinatorics*, Proceedings of the Third Waterloo Conference on Combinatorics, Waterloo, Ontario, 1968 (Academic Press, New York) 49–57.

C. Berge (1970), Sur certains hypergraphes généralisant les graphes bipartites, in: P. Erdös, A. Rényi and V.T. Sós, (eds.), *Combinatorial Theory and Its Applications I*, Proceedings Colloquium on Combinatorial Theory and its Applications, Balatonfüred, Hungary, 1969 (North-Holland, Amsterdam) 119–133.

C. Berge (1972), Balanced matrices, *Mathematical Programming* **2**, 19–31.

C. Berge and M. Las Vergnas (1970), Sur un théorème du type König pour hypergraphes, in: A. Gewirtz and L.V. Quintas, (eds.), *International Conference on Combinatorial Mathematics*, New York, 1970; *Annals of the New York Academy of Sciences* **175** [Article 1], 32–40.

C. Berge and V. Chvátal (eds.) (1984), *Topics on Perfect Graphs*; *Annals of Discrete Mathematics* **21**.

G. Birkhoff (1946), Tres observaciones sobre el algebra lineal, *Revista Facultad de Ciencias Exactas, Puras y Aplicadas Universidad Nacional de Tucuman, Serie A* (*Mathematicas y Fisica Teorica*) **5**, 147–151.

J.-M. Bourjolly and W.R. Pulleyblank (1987), König-Egerváry graphs, 2-bicritical graphs and fractional matchings, Research Report CORR 87-38, Department of Combinatorics and Optimization, University of Waterloo; to appear in *Discrete Applied Mathematics*.

S.C. Boyd and W.H. Cunningham (1988), Small travelling saleman polytopes, Research Report 88540 OR, Institut für Operations Research, Universität Bonn.

C. Carathéodory (1911), Über den Variabilitätsbereich der Fourierschen Konstanten von positiven harmonischen Funktionen, *Rendiconto del Circolo Matematico di Palermo* **32**, 193–217.

R. Chandrasekaran (1981), Polynomial algorithms for totally dual integral systems and extensions, in: P. Hansen (ed.), *Studies on Graphs and Discrete Programming*; *Annals of Discrete Mathematics* **11**, 39–51.

V. Chvátal (1973), Edmonds polytopes and a hierarchy of combinatorial problems, *Discrete Mathematics* **4**, 305–337.

V. Chvátal (1973a), Edmonds polytopes and weakly Hamiltonian graphs, *Mathematical Programming* **5**, 29–40.

V. Chvátal (1975), On certain polytopes associated with graphs, *Journal of Combinatorial Theory Series B* **13**, 138–154.

V. Chvátal, W. Cook and M. Hartmann (1988), On cutting-plane proofs in combinatorial optimization, Rutcor Research Report 27-88, Rutgers University.

S.A. Cook (1971), The complexity of theorem-proving procedures, *Proceedings of 3rd Annual ACM Symposium on Theory of Computing* (A.C.M., New York) 151–158.

W. Cook (1983), A minimal totally dual integral defining system for the b-matching polyhedron, *SIAM Journal on Algebraic and Discrete Methods* **4**, 212–220.

W. Cook (1986), On box totally dual integral polyhedra, *Mathematical Programming* **34**, 48–61.

W. Cook, L. Lovász and A. Schrijver (1984), A polynomial-time test for total dual integrality in fixed dimension, *Mathematical Programming Study* **22**, 64–69.

W. Cook and W.R. Pulleyblank (1987), Linear systems for constrained matching problems, *Mathematics of Operations Research* **12**, 97–120.

G. Cornuéjols, J. Fonlupt and D. Naddef (1985), The travelling salesman problem on a graph and some related integer polyhedra, *Mathematical Programming* **33**, 1–27.

H.P. Crowder and M.W. Padberg (1980), Solving large-scale symmetric traveling salesman problems to optimality, *Management Science* **26**, 495–509.

W.H. Cunningham (1979), Theoretical properties of the network simplex method, *Mathematics of Operations Research* **4**, 196–208.

W.H. Cunningham (1984), Testing membership in matroid polyhedra, *Journal of Combinatorial Theory Series B* **36**, 161–188.

W.H. Cunningham (1985), On submodular function minimization, *Combinatorica* **5**, 185–192.

W.H. Cunningham and J. Green-Krótki (1986), Dominants and submissives of matching polyhedra, *Mathematical Programming* **36**, 228–237.

W.H. Cunningham and A.B. Marsh III (1978), A primal algorithm for optimum matching, *Mathematical Programming Study* **8**, 50–72.

G.B. Dantzig, D.R. Fulkerson and S.M. Johnson (1954), Solution of a large-scale traveling salesman problem, *Operations Research* **2**, 393–410.

J. Edmonds (1965), Path, trees and flowers, *Canadian Journal of Mathematics* **17**, 449–467.

J. Edmonds (1965a), Maximum matching and a polyhedron with 0–1 vertices, *Journal of Research of the National Bureau of Standards* **69B**, 125–130.

J. Edmonds (1967), Optimum branchings, *Journal of Research of the National Bureau of Standards* **71B**, 233–240.

J. Edmonds (1971), Matroids and the greedy algorithm, *Mathematical Programming* **1**, 127–136.

J. Edmonds (1979), Matroid intersection, *Annals of Discrete Mathematics* **4**, 39–49.

J. Edmonds and R. Giles (1977), A min–max relation for submodular functions on graphs, *Annals of Discrete Mathematics* **1**, 185–204.

J. Edmonds and E.L. Johnson (1970), Matching: A well-solved class of integer linear programs, in: R.K. Guy et al. (eds.), *Proceedings of the Calgary International Conference on Combinatorial Structures and their Applications* (Gordon and Breach, London) 89–92.

J. Edmonds and E.L. Johnson (1973), Matching, Euler tours and the Chinese postman, *Mathematical Programming* **5**, 88–124.

J. Edmonds, L. Lovász and W.R. Pulleyblank (1982), Brick decompositions and the matching rank of graphs, *Combinatorica* **2**, 247–274.

E. Egerváry (1931), Matrixok kombinatorius tulajdonságairol (Hungarian) [On combinatorial properties of matrices], *Matematikai és Fizikai Lapok* **38**, 16–28.

P. Elias, A. Feinstein and C.E. Shannon (1956), A note on the maximum flow through a network, *IRE Transactions on Information Theory* **2**, 117–119.

B. Fleischmann (1988), A new class of cutting planes for the symmetric travelling salesman problem, *Mathematical Programming* **40**, 225–246.

L.R. Ford, Jr. and D.R. Fulkerson (1956), Maximal flow through a network, *Canadian Journal of Mathematics* **8**, 399–404.

L.R. Ford, Jr. and D.R. Fulkerson (1962), *Flows in Networks*, Princeton University Press, Princeton, NJ.

A. Frank (1984), Submodular flows, in: W.R. Pulleyblank (1984), 147–165.

D.R. Fulkerson (1970), The perfect graph conjecture and pluperfect graph theorem, in: R.C. Bose et al. (eds.), *Proceedings of the Second Chapel Hill Conference on Combinatorial Mathematics and Its Applications* (University of North Carolina Press, Chapel Hill, NC) 171–175.

D.R. Fulkerson (1970a), Blocking polyhedra, in: B. Harris (ed.), *Graph Theory and Its Applications* (Academic Press, New York) 93–112.

D.R. Fulkerson (1971), Blocking and anti-blocking pairs of polyhedra, *Mathematical Programming* **1**, 168–194.

D.R. Fulkerson (1972), Anti-blocking polyhedra, *Journal of Combinatorial Theory Series B* **12**, 50–71.

D.R. Fulkerson, A.J. Hoffman and R. Oppenheim (1974), On balanced matrics, *Mathematical Programming Study* **1**, 120–132.

D. Gale (1968), Optimal assignments in an ordered set: An application of matroid theory, *Journal of Combinatorial Theory* **4**, 176–180.

M.R. Garey and D.S. Johnson (1979), *Computers and Intractibility: A Guide to the Theory of NP-Completeness* (Freeman, San Francisco, CA).

A.M.H. Gerards and A. Sebö (1987), Total dual integrality implies local strong unimodularity, *Mathematical Programming* **38**, 69–74.

R. Giles (1975), Submodular Functions, Graphs and Integer Polyhedra, Ph.D. Thesis, University of Waterloo.

R. Giles (1976), Facets and other faces of branching polyhedra, *Colloq. Math. Soc. János Bolyai* **18**, *Combinatorics*, 401–418.

R. Giles (1982), Optimum matching forests I: Special weights, *Mathematical Programming* **22**, 1–11.

R. Giles (1982a), Optimum matching forests II: General weights, *Mathematical Programming* **22**, 12–38.

R. Giles (1982b), Optimum matching forests III: Facets of matching forest polyhedra, *Mathematical Programming* **22**, 39–51.

R. Giles and W.R. Pulleyblank (1979), Total dual integrality and integer polyhedra, *Linear Algebra and Its Applications* **25**, 191–196.

R.E. Gomory (1960), Solving linear programming problems in integers, in: R.E. Bellman and M. Hall, Jr. (eds.), *Combinatorial Analysis* (American Mathematical Society, Providence, RI) 211–215.

R.E. Gomory (1963), An algorithm for integer solutions to linear programs, in: R. Graves and P. Wolfe (eds.), *Recent Advances in Mathematical Programming* (McGraw-Hill, New York) 269–302.

R.E. Gomory and T.C. Hu (1961), Multi-terminal network flows, *SIAM Journal* **9**, 551–570.

M. Grötschel (1977), *Polyedrische Charakterisierungen Kombinatorischer Optimierungsprobleme* (Verlag Anton Hain, Meisenheim am Glan).

M. Grötschel (1980), On the symmetric travelling salesman problem: Solution of a 120-city problem, *Mathematical Programming Study* **12**, 61–77.

M. Grötschel and O. Holland (1988), Solution of large-scale symmetric travelling salesman problems, Research Report 73, Institut für Mathematik, Universität Augsburg.

M. Grötschel, M. Jünger and G. Reinelt (1984), A cutting plane algorithm for the linear ordering problem, *Operations Research* **32**, 1195–1220.

M. Grötschel, L. Lovász and A. Schrijver (1981), The ellipsoid method and its consequences in combinatorial optimization, *Combinatorica* **1**, 169–197.

M. Grötschel, L. Lovász and A. Schrijver (1988), *Geometric Algorithms and Combinatorial Optimization* (Springer-Verlag, Berlin).

M. Grötschel and M.W. Padberg (1979), On the symmetric travelling salesman problem I: Inequalities, *Mathematical Programming* **16**, 265–280.

M. Grötschel and M.W. Padberg (1979a), On the symmetric travelling salesman problem II: Lifting theorems and facets, *Mathematical Programming* **16**, 281–302.

M. Grötschel and M.W. Padberg (1985), Polyhedral theory, in Lawler et al. (1985), 251–302.

M. Grötschel and W.R. Pulleyblank (1986), Clique tree inequalities and the symmetric travelling salesman problem, *Mathematics of Operations Research* **11**, 537–569.

M. Grötschel and Y. Wakabayashi (1987), A cutting plane algorithm for a clustering problem, Research Report 9, Institut fur Mathematik, Universität Augsburg; to appear in *Mathematical Programming Series B*.

D. Hausmann (1980), *Adjacency on Polytopes in Combinatorial Optimization* (Anton Hain, Meisenheim am Glan).

D. Hilbert (1890), Über die Theorie der algebraischen Formen, *Mathematische Annalen* **36**, 473–534.

A.J. Hoffman (1974), A generalization of max-flow min-cut, *Mathematical Programming* **6**, 352–359.

A.J. Hoffman (1982), Ordered sets and linear programming, in: I. Rival (ed.), *Ordered Sets* (D. Reidel, Dordrecht) 619–654.

A.J. Hoffman and J.B. Kruskal (1956), Integral boundary points of convex polyhedra, in: H.W. Kuhn and A.W. Tucker (eds.), *Linear Inequalities and Related Systems* (Princeton University Press, Princeton, NJ) 223–246.

A.J. Hoffman and R. Oppenheim (1978), Local unimodularity in the matching polytope, *Annals of Discrete Mathematics* **2**, 201–209.

Y. Ikura and G.L. Nemhauser (1985), Simplex pivots on the set packing polytope, *Mathematical Programming* **33**, 123–138.

R.M. Karp (1972), Reducibility among combinatorial problems, in: R.E. Miller and J.W. Thatcher (eds.), *Complexity of Computer Computations* (Plenum Press, New York) 85–103.

R.M. Karp and C.H. Papadimitriou (1982), On linear characterizations of combinatorial optimization problems, *SIAM Journal on Computing* **11**, 620–632.

L.G. Khachian (1979), A polynomial algorithm in linear programming, *Soviet Mathematics Doklady* **20**, 191–194.

V. Klee and P. Kleinschmidt (1987), The d-step conjecture and its relatives, *Mathematics of Operations Research* **12**, 718–755.

D. König (1916), Gráfok és alkalmazásuk a determinánsok és halmazok elméletében (Hungarian), *Mathematikai és Természettudományi Értesitö* **34**, 104–119. German translation: Über Graphen und ihre Anwendung auf Determinantentheorie und Mengenlehre, *Mathematische Annalen* **77**, 453–465.

L. Kronecker (1984), Näherungsweise ganzzahlige Auflösung linearer Gleichungen, *Monatsberichte der Königlich Preussischen Akademie der Wissenschaften zu Berlin*, 1179–1193, 1271–1299.

J.B. Kruskal Jr. (1956), On the shortest spanning subtree of a graph and the traveling salesman problem, *Proceedings of the American Mathematical Society* **7**, 48–50.

E.L. Lawler (1976), *Combinatorial Optimization: Networks and Matroids* (Holt, Rinehart and Winston, New York).

E.L. Lawler, J.K. Lenstra, A.H.G. Rinnooy Kan and D.B. Shmoys (eds.) (1985), *The Traveling Salesman Problem: A Guided Tour of Combinatorial Optimization* (Wiley, New York).

A. Lehman (1979), On the width-length inequality, *Mathematical Programming* **17**, 403–417.

S. Lin and B.W. Kernighan (1973), An effective heuristic algorithm for the traveling salesman problem, *Operations Research* **21**, 498–516.

W.-G. Liu (1988), Extended Formulations and Polyhedral Projection, Ph.D. Thesis, Department of Combinatorics and Optimization, University of Waterloo.

W.-G. Liu and W.R. Pulleyblank (1989), On the dominant and submissive of the perfect matching polytope, Research Report CORR 89-10, Department of Combinatorics and Optimization University of Waterloo.

L. Lovász (1972), Normal hypergraphs and the perfect graph conjecture, *Discrete Mathematics* **2**, 253–267.

L. Lovász (1979), Graph theory and integer programming, in: P.L. Hammer, E.L. Johnson and B:H. Korte (eds.), *Discrete Optimization I*; *Annals of Discrete Mathematics* **4**, 141–158.

L. Lovász (1987), Matching structure and the matching lattice, *Journal of Combinatorial Theory, Series B* **43**, 187–222.

L. Lovász and M.D. Plummer (1975), On bicritical graphs, in: A. Hajnal, R. Rado and V.T. Sós (eds.), *Infinite and Finite Sets*; Colloq. Math. Soc. János Bolyai 10 (North-Holland, Amsterdam) 1051–1079.

L. Lovász and M.D. Plummer (1986), *Matching Theory* (Akademiai Kiadó, Budapest and North-Holland, Amsterdam).

C.L. Lucchesi and D.H. Younger (1978), A minimax relation for directed graphs, *J. London Math. Society* **17**, 369–374.

N. Maculan (1987), The Steiner problem in graphs, *Annals of Discrete Mathematics* **31**, 185–122.

R.K. Martin (1987), Using separation algorithms to generate mixed integer model reformulations, Graduate School of Business, University of Chicago.

R.K. Martin, R.L. Rardin and B.A. Campbell (1987), Polyhedral characterizations of discrete dynamic programming, Research Report CC 87-24, School of Industrial Engineering, Purdue University.

J.F. Maurras (1975), Some results on the convex hull of Hamiltonian cycles of symmetric complete graphs, in: B. Roy (ed.), *Combinatorial Programming: Methods and Applications* (Reidel, Dordrecht) 179–190.

H. Minkowski (1896), *Geometrie der Zahlen (Erste Lieferung)* (Teubner, Leipzig).

T.S. Motzkin (1936), Beiträge zur Theorie der linearen Ungleichungen (Inaugural Dissertation

Basel) Azriel, Jerusalem [English translation: *Contributions to the Theory of Linear Inequalities*, RAND Corporation Translation 22 (RAND, Santa Monica, CA 1952)].

T.S. Motzkin, H. Raiffa, G.L. Thompson and R.M. Thrall (1953), The double description method, in: H.W. Kuhn and A.W. Tucker (eds.), *Contributions to the Theory of Games Vol. II* (Princeton University Press, Princeton, NJ) 51–73.

D.J. Naddef (1982), Rank of maximum matchings in a graph, *Mathematical Programming* **22**, 52–70.

D.J. Naddef (1987), Private communication.

D.J. Naddef (1988), The Hirsch conjecture is true for (0, 1)-polytopes, to appear in *Mathematical Programming Series B*.

D.J. Naddef and W.R. Pulleyblank (1984), Hamiltonicity in 0, 1 polyhedra, *Journal of Combinatorial Theory Series B* **37**, 41–52.

D. Naddef and G. Rinaldi (1988), The symmetric travelling salesman polytope and its graphical relaxation: Composition of valid inequalities, Report RR-719-M, ARTEMIS-IMAG (Grenoble), to appear in *Mathematical Programming*.

G.L. Nemhauser and L.A. Wolsey (1988), *Integer and Combinatorial Optimization* (Wiley-Interscience, New York).

J. von Neumann (1953), A certain zero-sum two-person game equivalent to the optimal assignment problem, in: H.W. Kuhn and A.W. Tucker (eds.), *Contributions to the Theory of Games II*; Annals of Mathematics Studies 28 (Princeton University Press, Princeton, NJ) 5–12.

R.Z. Norman (1955), On the convex polyhedra of the symmetric travelling salesman problem (abstract), *Bulletin of the American Mathematical Society* **61**, 559.

M.W. Padberg and S. Hong (1980), On the symmetric travelling salesman problem: A computational study, *Mathematical Programming Study* **12**, 78–107.

M.W. Padberg and M.R. Rao (1974), The travelling salesman problem and a class of polyhedra of diameter two, *Mathematical Programming* **7**, 32–45.

M.W. Padberg and M.R. Rao (1981), The Russian method for linear inequalities III: Bounded integer programming, GBA Working paper 81-39 New York University, New York.

M.W. Padberg and M.R. Rao (1982), Odd minimum cut-sets and *b*-matchings, *Mathematics of Operations Research* **7**, 67–80.

M.W. Padberg and G. Rinaldi (1987), Optimization of a 532-city traveling salesman problem by branch and cut, *Operations Research Letters* **6**, 1–8.

M.W. Padberg and G. Rinaldi (1987a), Facet identification for the symmetric traveling salesman polytope, Report R204 IASI-CNR (Rome), to appear in *Mathematical Programming*.

M.W. Padberg and G. Rinaldi (1987b), A branch-and-cut approach to a travelling salesman problem with side constraints, Report R.203 IASI-CNR (Rome), to appear in *Management Science*.

C. Papadimitriou (1978), The adjacency relation on the traveling salesman polytope is NP-complete, *Mathematical Programming* **14**, 312–324.

C.H. Papadimitriou and K. Steiglitz (1982), *Combinatorial Optimization: Algorithms and Complexity* (Prentice-Hall, Englewood Cliffs, NJ).

W.R. Pulleyblank (1973), Faces of Matching Polyhedra, Ph.D. Thesis, University of Waterloo.

W.R. Pulleyblank (1981), Total dual integrality and *b*-matchings, *Operations Research Letters* **1**, 28–30.

W.R. Pulleyblank (ed.) (1984), *Progress in Combinatorial Optimization* (Academic Press, Toronto).

W.R. Pulleyblank and J. Edmonds (1975), Facets of 1-matching polyhedra, in: C. Berge and D. Ray-Chaudhuri (eds.), *Hypergraph Seminar* (Springer, Berlin) 214–242.

R. Rado (1957), Note on independence functions, *Proceedings of the London Mathematical Society* **7**, 300–320.

T. Rockafellar (1970), *Convex Analysis* (Princeton University Press, Princeton, NJ).

A. Schrijver (1980), On cutting planes, in: M. Deza and I.G. Rosenberg (eds.) *Combinatorics* 79 *Part II*; *Annals of Discrete Mathematics* **9**, 291–296.

A. Schrijver (1981), On total dual integrality, *Linear Algebra and Its Applications* **38**, 27–32.

A. Schrijver (1983), Short proofs on the matching polytope, *Journal of Combinatorial Theory Series B* **34**, 104–108.

A. Schrijver (1984), Total dual integrality from directed graphs, crossing families, and sub- and supermodular functions, in: W.R. Pulleyblank (1984), 315–361.

A. Schrijver (1986), *Linear and Integer Programming* (Wiley, New York).

P.D. Seymour (1979), On multi-colourings of cubic graphs, and conjectures of Fulkerson and Tutte, *Proceedings of the London Mathematical Society* **38**, 423–460.

P.D. Seymour (1979a), Sums of circuits, in: J.A. Bondy and U.S.R. Murty (eds.), *Graph Theory and Related Topics* (Academic Press, New York) 341–355.

P.D. Seymour (1980), Decomposition of regular matroids, *Journal of Combinatorial Theory Series B* **28**, 305–359.

P.D. Seymour (1981), On odd cuts and plane multicommodity flows, *Proceedings of the London Mathematical Society Series* (3) **42**, 178–192.

V. Trubin (1969), On a method of solution of integer linear programming problems of a special kind, *Soviet Mathematics Doklady* **10**, 1544–1546.

K. Truemper and R. Chandrasekaran (1978), Local unimodularity of matrix-vector pairs, *Linear Algebra and Its Applications* **22**, 65–78.

B.L. van der Waerden (1937), *Moderne Algebra* (2nd ed.) (Springer-Verlag, Berlin).

D.B. Weinberger (1976), Network flows, minimum coverings, and the four-color conjecture, *Operations Research* **24**, 272–290.

D.J.A. Welsh (1968), Kruskal's theorem for matroids, *Proceedings of the Cambridge Philosophical Society* **64**, 3–4.

D.J.A. Welsh (1976), *Matroid Theory* (Academic Press, New York).

H. Weyl (1935), Elementare Theorie der konvexen Polyeder, *Commentarii Mathematici Helvetici* **7**, 290–206. English translation: The elementary theory of convex polyhedra, in: H.W. Kuhn and A.W. Tucker (eds.), *Contributions to the Theory of Games I* (Princeton University Press, Princeton, NJ, 1950) 3–18.

H. Whitney (1935), On the abstract properties of linear dependence, *American Journal of Mathematics* **57**, 509–533.

R.T. Wong (1984), A dual ascent approach for Steiner tree problems on directed graphs, *Mathematical Programming* **28**, 271–287.

M. Yannakakis (1988), Expressing combinatorial optimization problems by linear programs, Preprint, AT&T Bell Laboratories, Murray Hill, NJ.

G.L. Nemhauser et al., Eds., *Handbooks in OR & MS, Vol. 1*
© Elsevier Science Publishers B.V. (North-Holland) 1989

Chapter VI

Integer Programming

*George L. Nemhauser**

School of Industrial and Systems Engineering, Georgia Institute of Technology, Atlanta, GA 30332, USA

Laurence A. Wolsey

Center for Operations Research & Econometrics, Université Catholique de Louvain, 34, Voie du Roman Pays, 1348 Louvain-la-Neuve, Belgium

1. Introduction

Integer programming deals with problems of maximizing or minimizing a function of many variables subject to inequality and equality constraints, and integrality restrictions on some or all of the variables. A remarkably rich variety of problems can be represented by discrete optimization models.

An important and widespread area of application concerns the management and efficient use of scarce resources to increase productivity. These applications include operational problems such as the distribution of goods, production scheduling and machine sequencing. They also include planning problems such as capital budgeting, facility location and portfolio analysis, and design problems such as communication and transportation network design, VLSI circuit design and the design of automated production systems.

There are applications in mathematics to the subjects of combinatorics, graph theory and logic. Statistical applications include problems of data analysis and reliability. Recent scientific applications involve problems in molecular biology, high energy physics and x-ray crystallography. A political application concerns the division of a region into election districts.

Some of these discrete optimization models will be developed in the next section, but their number and variety is so great that we can only present a few of them. The main purpose of this article is to present the mathematical foundations of integer optimization models and the algorithms that can be used to solve them.

The material for this chapter is taken almost entirely from the book, *Integer and Combinatorial Optimization* by Nemhauser and Wolsey (1988) where the subject is covered in much greater breadth and depth.

* Research supported by National Science Foundation Grant ECS-8719128.

Throughout the paper, we assume that the function is to be maximized and the constraints are linear. It is also common to require the variables to be nonnegative. Hence, we write the *linear mixed integer programming problem as*

(MIP) $\max\{cx + hy : Ax + Gy \leqslant b, x \in Z_+^n, y \in R_+^p\}$

where Z_+^n is the set of nonnegative integral n-dimensional vectors, R_+^p is the set of nonnegative real p-dimensional vectors and $x = (x_1, \ldots, x_n)$ and $y = (y_1, \ldots, y_p)$ are the *variables* or *unknowns*. An *instance* of the problem is specified by the *data* (c, h, A, G, b), with c an n-vector, h a p-vector, A an $m \times n$ matrix, G an $m \times p$ matrix and b an m-vector. We do not distinguish between row and column vectors unless the clarity of the presentation makes it necessary to do so. This problem is called mixed because of the presence of both integer and continuous (real) variables.

We assume throughout that all of the data is rational, i.e. each of the individual numbers is rational. Although in making this assumption we sacrifice some theoretical generality, it is a natural assumption for solving problems on a digital computer.

The set $S = \{x \in Z_+^n, y \in R_+^p, Ax + Gy \leqslant b\}$ is called the *feasible region* and an $(x, y) \in S$ is called a *feasible solution*. An instance is said to be *feasible* if $S \neq \emptyset$. The function

$$z = cx + hy$$

is called the *objective function*. A feasible point (x^0, y^0) for which the objective function is as large as possible, i.e.

$$cx^0 + hy^0 \geqslant cx + hy \quad \text{for all } (x, y) \in S$$

is called an *optimal solution*. If (x^0, y^0) is an optimal solution, $cx^0 + hy^0$ is called the *optimal value* or *weight* of the solution.

A feasible instance of MIP may not have an optimal solution. We say that an instance is *unbounded* if for any $\omega \in R^1$ there is a point $(x, y) \in S$ such that $cx + hy > \omega$. We use the notation $z = \infty$ to denote an unbounded instance.

In Section 4 we will establish that every feasible instance of MIP either has an optimal solution or is unbounded. This result requires the assumption of rational data. Thus to solve an instance of MIP means either to produce an optimal solution, show that it is unbounded, or show that it is infeasible.

The *linear (pure) integer programming problem*

(IP) $\max\{cx : Ax \leqslant b, x \in Z_+^n\}$

is the special case of MIP in which there are no continuous variables. The *linear programming problem*

(LP) $\max\{hy: Gy \leq b, y \in R_+^p\}$

is the special case of MIP in which there are no integer variables.

In many models, the integer variables are used to represent logical relationships and therefore are constrained to equal 0 or 1. Thus, we obtain the 0–1 MIP (resp. 0–1 IP) in which $x \in Z_+^n$ is replaced by $x \in B^n$, where B^n is the set of n-dimensional binary vectors.

This paper is divided into ten sections. In Section 2 we formulate several classes of problems using integer programming models, and in Section 3 we discuss formulations that are "good" with respect to the efficiency of solving them. Section 4 introduces some important theoretical aspects of integer programming models, including fundamental relationships between integer and linear programs, and computational complexity. Sections 5 and 6 treat relaxation and duality, and lay the foundation for the algorithms to be presented in the following sections. Sections 7, 8 and 9 present, respectively, cutting plane, branch-and-bound and approximation algorithms. Section 10 gives a brief, historical review and some references.

2. Integer programming models

An important and very common use of 0–1 variables is to represent binary choice. Consider an event that may or may not occur and suppose that part of the problem is to decide between these two possibilities. To model such a dichotomy, we use a binary variable x and let

$$x = \begin{cases} 1 & \text{if the event occurs}, \\ 0 & \text{if the event does not occur}. \end{cases}$$

The event itself may be almost anything, depending on the specific situation being considered. Several examples follow.

The 0–1 knapsack problem

Suppose there are n projects. The j-th project, $j = 1, \ldots, n$, has a cost of a_j and a value of c_j. Each project is either done or not, i.e. it is not possible to do a fraction of any of the projects. Also there is a budget of b available to fund the projects. The problem of choosing a subset of the projects that maximize the sum of the values while not exceeding the budget constraint is the 0–1 *knapsack problem*

$$\max\left\{\sum_{j=1}^n c_j x_j : \sum_{j=1}^n a_j x_j \leq b, x \in B^n\right\}.$$

Here the j-th event is the j-th project. This problem is called the knapsack problem because of the analogy to the hiker's problem of deciding what should be put in a knapsack, given a weight limitation on how much can be carried. In general, a problem of this sort may have several constraints. We then refer to the problem as the *multi-dimensional knapsack problem*.

Set covering, packing and partitioning problems

Let $M = \{1, \ldots, m\}$ be a finite set and $\{M_j: j \in N\}$, where $N = \{1, \ldots, n\}$, be a given collection of subsets of M. For example, the collection might consist of all subsets of size k, for some $k \leq m$. We say that $F \subseteq N$ is a *cover* of M if $\cup_{j \in F} M_j = M$, and $F \subseteq N$ is a *packing* with respect to M if $M_j \cap M_k = \emptyset$ for all $j, k \in F, j \neq k$. If $F \subseteq N$ is both a covering and a packing, then F is said to be a *partition* of M. In the set cover problem, c_j is the cost of M_j and we seek a minimum cost cover, while in the set packing problem c_j is the weight or value of M_j and we seek a maximum weight packing.

These problems are readily formulated as 0–1 IPs. Let A be the $m \times n$ incidence matrix of the family $\{M_j: j \in N\}$, i.e. for $i \in M$ and $j \in N$

$$a_{ij} = \begin{cases} 1 & \text{if } i \in M_j, \\ 0 & \text{if } i \notin M_j, \end{cases}$$

and interpret $x \in B^n$ as the incidence vector of a subset of N, i.e., for $j \in N$,

$$x_j = \begin{cases} 1 & \text{if } j \in F, \\ 0 & \text{if } j \notin F. \end{cases}$$

Then F is a cover (resp. packing, partition) if and only if $x \in B^n$ satisfies $Ax \geq 1$ (resp. $Ax \leq 1$, $Ax = 1$) where 1 is the m-vector all of whose components equal one. We see, for example, that the set packing problem is the special case of the 0–1 IP with A a 0–1 matrix, i.e. a matrix all of whose elements equal 0 or 1, and $b = 1$.

Many practical problems can be formulated as set covering problems. A typical application concerns facility location. Suppose we are given a set of potential sites $N = \{1, \ldots, n\}$ for the location of fire stations. A station placed at j costs c_j. We are also given a set of communities $M = \{1, \ldots, m\}$ that have to be protected. The subset of communities that can be protected from a station located at j is M_j. For example, M_j might be the set of communities that can be reached from j within ten minutes. Then the problem of choosing a minimum cost set of locations for the fire stations such that each community can be reached from some fire station within ten minutes is a set covering problem. There are many other applications of this type, including assigning customers to delivery routes, airline crews to flights, and workers to shifts.

The above models illustrate how we can use linear constraints on binary variables to represent certain relationships among discrete events. Now we consider how to model some other constraints.

The relation that neither or both of events 1 and 2 must occur is represented by the linear equality $x_2 - x_1 = 0$ in the binary variables x_1 and x_2. Similarly, the relation that event 2 can occur only if event 1 occurs is represented by the linear inequality $x_2 - x_1 \leq 0$. More generally, consider an activity that can be operated at any level y, $0 \leq y \leq u$. Now suppose that the activity can be undertaken only if some event represented by the binary variable x occurs. This relation is represented by the linear inequality $y - ux \leq 0$ since $x = 0$ implies $y = 0$ and $x = 1$ yields the original constraint $y \leq u$. We now consider two models that use this relationship.

Facility location problems

These problems, as our illustration of the set covering model, concern the location of facilities to serve clients economically. We are given a set $N = \{1, \ldots, n\}$ of potential facility locations and a set of clients $I = \{1, \ldots, m\}$. A facility placed at j costs f_j for $j \in N$. This problem is more complicated than the set covering application because each client has a demand for a certain good, and the total profit from satisfying the demand of client i from a facility at j is c_{ij}. The optimization problem is to choose a subset of the locations at which to place facilities, and then to assign the clients to these facilities so as to maximize total profit. In the uncapacitated facility location problem, there is no restriction on the number of clients that a facility can serve.

In addition to the binary variable $x_j = 1$ if a facility is placed at j and $x_j = 0$ otherwise, we introduce the continuous variable y_{ij} which is the fraction of the demand of client i that is satisfied from a facility at j. The condition that each client's demand must be satisfied is given by

$$\sum_{j \in N} y_{ij} = 1 \quad \text{for } i \in I. \tag{2.1}$$

Moreover, since client i cannot be served from j unless a facility is placed at j, we have the constraints

$$y_{ij} - x_j \leq 0 \quad \text{for } i \in I \text{ and } j \in N. \tag{2.2}$$

Hence the *uncapacitated facility location problem*, denoted UFL, is the MIP

$$\max \sum_{i \in I} \sum_{j \in N} c_{ij} y_{ij} - \sum_{j \in N} f_j x_j$$

subject to the constraints (2.1), (2.2) and $x \in B^n$, $y \in R_+^{mn}$.

It may be unrealistic to assume that a facility can serve any number of clients. Suppose a facility located at j has a capacity of u_j and the i-th client has a demand of b_i. Now we let y_{ij} be the quantity of goods sent from facility j to client i and h_{ij} be the profit per unit shipped. To formulate the *capacitated facility location problem* as an MIP, we replace (2.1) by

$$\sum_{j \in N} y_{ij} = b_i \quad \text{for } i \in I, \tag{2.3}$$

(2.2) by

$$\sum_{i \in I} y_{ij} - u_j x_j \leq 0 \quad \text{for } j \in N , \tag{2.4}$$

and c_{ij} by h_{ij} in the objective function.

The fixed charge network flow problem

We are given a network (see Figure 2.1) with a set of nodes V (facilities) and a set of arcs $\mathcal{A}$. An arc $e = (i, j)$ that points from node i to node j indicates a direct shipping route from node i to node j. Associated with each node i, there is a number b_i. Node i is a demand, supply or transit point respectively, depending on whether b_i is positive, negative or zero. We assume that the net demand is zero, i.e. $\Sigma_{i \in V} b_i = 0$. Each arc (i, j) has a flow capacity u_{ij} and a unit flow cost h_{ij}.

Let y_{ij} be the flow on arc (i, j). A flow is feasible if and only if it satisfies

$$y \in R_+^{|\mathcal{A}|} , \tag{2.5}$$

$$y_{ij} \leq u_{ij} \quad \text{for } (i, j) \in \mathcal{A} , \tag{2.6}$$

$$\sum_{\{j:\, (j,i) \in \mathcal{A}\}} y_{ji} - \sum_{\{j:\, (i,j) \in \mathcal{A}\}} y_{ij} = b_i \quad \text{for } i \in V . \tag{2.7}$$

The constraints (2.7) are the *flow conservation* constraints. The problem

$$\min\left\{ \sum_{(i,j) \in \mathcal{A}} h_{ij} y_{ij} : y \text{ satisfies } (2.5),\, (2.6) \text{ and } (2.7) \right\} \tag{2.8}$$

is known as the *network flow problem*.

The *fixed charge network flow problem* is obtained by imposing a fixed cost of c_{ij} if there is positive flow on arc (i, j). Now we introduce a binary variable x_{ij} to indicate whether arc (i, j) is used. The relation $y_{ij} = 0$ if $x_{ij} = 0$ is

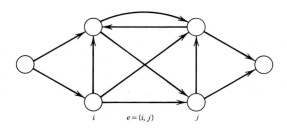

Fig. 2.1.

represented by

$$y_{ij} - u_{ij}x_{ij} \leqslant 0 \quad \text{for } (i, j) \in \mathcal{A} . \tag{2.9}$$

Hence we obtain the formulation

$$\min\left\{ \sum_{(i,j)\in\mathcal{A}} (c_{ij}x_{ij} + h_{ij}y_{ij}) \colon x \in B^{|\mathcal{A}|}, y \in R_+^{|\mathcal{A}|} \text{ satisfies } (2.7), (2.9) \right\} . \tag{2.10}$$

The fixed charge flow model is useful for a variety of design problems that involve material flows in networks. These include water supply systems, heating systems, and road networks.

The formulation of the traveling salesman problem given below provides another example of the use of binary variables to model logical relations. It also exhibits another important property of integer programming formulations; namely that it may be appropriate to use an extraordinarily large number of constraints in order to obtain a good formulation.

The traveling salesman problem

We are again given a set of nodes $V = \{1, \ldots, n\}$ and a set of arcs $\mathcal{A}$. The nodes represent cities and the arcs represent ordered pairs of cities between which direct travel is possible. For $(i, j) \in \mathcal{A}$, c_{ij} is the direct travel time from city i to city j. The problem is to find a tour, starting at city 1, that visits each other city exactly once and then returns to city 1, which takes the least total travel time. To formulate this problem, we introduce variables $x_{ij} = 1$ if j immediately follows i on the tour, $x_{ij} = 0$ otherwise. Hence if x is the incidence vector of a tour it must satisfy

$$x \in B^{|\mathcal{A}|} , \tag{2.11}$$

$$\sum_{\{i:\, (i,j)\in\mathcal{A}\}} x_{ij} = 1 \quad \text{for } j \in V , \tag{2.12}$$

$$\sum_{\{j:\, (i,j)\in\mathcal{A}\}} x_{ij} = 1 \quad \text{for } i \in V . \tag{2.13}$$

However, (2.11)–(2.13) are not sufficient to define the tours, since they are also satisfied by subtours; e.g. $x_{12} = x_{23} = x_{31} = x_{45} = x_{56} = x_{64} = 1$ satisfies (2.11)–(2.13) but does not correspond to a tour, see Figure 2.2.

One way to eliminate these subtours is to observe that in any tour there must be an arc that goes from $\{1, 2, 3\}$ to $\{4, 5, 6\}$ and an arc that goes from $\{4, 5, 6\}$ to $\{1, 2, 3\}$. In general for any $U \subset V$ with $2 \leqslant |U| \leqslant |V| - 2$, the constraints

$$\sum_{\{(i,j)\in\mathcal{A}\,:\, i\in U,\, j\in V\setminus U\}} x_{ij} \geqslant 1 \tag{2.14}$$

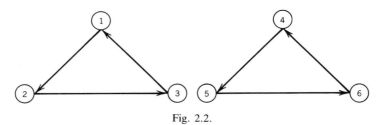

Fig. 2.2.

are satisfied by all tours, but a solution consisting of two or more subtours violates at least one of them. Hence the traveling salesman problem can be formulated as

$$\min\left\{ \sum_{(i,j)\in\mathcal{A}} c_{ij}x_{ij} : x \text{ satisfies } (2.11)\text{--}(2.14)\right\}. \tag{2.15}$$

An alternative to the set of constraints (2.14) is

$$\sum_{\{(i,j)\in\mathcal{A}\,:\,i\in U,\,j\in U\}} x_{ij} \leq |U| - 1 \quad \text{for } 2 \leq |U| \leq |V| - 2, \tag{2.16}$$

which also excludes all subtours but no tours.

However, regardless of whether we use (2.14) or (2.16), the number of these constraints is nearly $2^{|V|}$. This huge number of constraints might motivate us to seek a more compact formulation. Formulations involving more variables and fewer constraints exist, but the most well-known ones are weaker in a sense to be defined in Section 3.

Disjunctive constraints

In the usual statement of an optimization problem, it is assumed that all of the constraints must be satisfied. But in some applications, only one of a pair, or more generally k of m sets of constraints must hold. In this case, we say that the constraints are disjunctive.

An example with $k = 1$ and $m = 2$ is shown in Figure 2.3 where the feasible region is shaded.

Disjunctive constraints arise naturally in many models. A simple illustration is when we need to define a variable equal to the minimum of two other variables, i.e. $y = \min(u_1, u_2)$. This can be done with the two inequalities

$$y \leq u_1 \quad \text{and} \quad y \leq u_2$$

together with one of two inequalities

$$y \geq u_1 \quad \text{or} \quad y \geq u_2 .$$

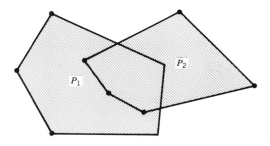

Fig. 2.3.

Suppose $P^i = \{y \in R_+^p: A^i y \leq b^i, y \leq d\}$ for $i = 1, \ldots, m$. Note that there is a vector ω such that for all i, $A^i y \leq b^i + \omega$ is satisfied for any y, $0 \leq y \leq d$. Hence there is a y contained in at least k of the sets P^i if and only if the set of points (x, y) satisfying

$$A^i y \leq b^i + \omega(1 - x_i) \quad \text{for } i = 1, \ldots, m \,,$$

$$\sum_{i=1}^m x_i \geq k \,,$$

$$y \leq d \,,$$

$$x \in B^m, \quad y \in R_+^p \,,$$

(2.17)

is not empty. This follows since $x_i = 1$ yields the constraint $A^i y \leq b^i$ while $x_i = 0$ yields the trivial constraint $A^i y \leq b^i + \omega$.

When $k = 1$, an alternative formulation is

$$A^i y^i \leq x_i b^i \quad \text{for } i = 1, \ldots, m \,,$$

$$y^i \leq x_i d \quad \text{for } i = 1, \ldots, m \,,$$

$$\sum_{i=1}^m x_i = 1 \,,$$

$$\sum_{i=1}^m y^i = y \,,$$

$$x \in B^m, y \in R_+^p, y^i \in R_+^p \quad \text{for } i = 1, \ldots, m \,.$$

(2.18)

Two natural applications for disjunctive constraints are scheduling problems in which either job i precedes job j or vice versa, and the representation of piecewise linear functions, see Figure 2.4, in which either y lies in $[a_1, a_2]$, or $[a_2, a_3]$, etc.

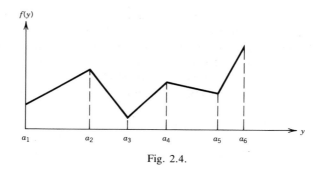

Fig. 2.4.

Good formulations are essential to solving integer programming problems efficiently. In the next section, we explain why some formulations may be better than others.

3. Choices in model formulation

We have formulated several integer optimization problems to motivate the richness and variety of applications. Although a formulation may give insight into the structure of the problem, our goal is to find an optimal or nearly optimal solution. As we have already suggested, many integer programming problems can be formulated in several ways. Moreover, in contrast to linear programming:

> *In integer programming, formulating a "good" model is of crucial importance to solving the model.*

Indirectly, the subject of "good" model formulation is a major topic of this article, and is closely related to the algorithms themselves.

A model is specified by the variables, objective function and constraints. Typically, defining the variables is the first question addressed in formulating a model. Often the variables are chosen simply from the definition of a solution, i.e. a solution specifies the values of certain unknowns and so we define a variable for each unknown. Once the variables and an objective function have been defined, say in an IP, we can speak of an implicit representation of the problem

$$\max\{cx: x \in S \subset Z^n_+\}$$

where S represents the set of feasible points in Z^n_+. Now we say that

$$\max\{cx: Ax \le b, x \in Z^n_+\}$$

is a *valid IP formulation* if $S = \{x \in Z^n_+: Ax \le b\}$.

In general, when there is a valid formulation, there are many choices of (A, b), and it is usually easy to find some (A, b) that yields a valid formulation. But an obvious choice may not be a good one when it comes to solving the problem. We believe that choosing a suitable (A, b) is a very important aspect of constructing integer programming models.

The following example illustrates different formulations of a set $S \subseteq Z^n_+$.

Example 3.1.

$$S = \{(0000), (1000), (0100), (0010), (0001), (0110), (0101), (0011)\}$$
$$\subseteq B^4 .$$

The reader can easily check that

(a) $\qquad S = \{x \in B^4 : 93x_1 + 49x_2 + 37x_3 + 29x_4 \leqslant 111\}$

gives a valid formulation. Two other formulations that are easily established to be valid are

(b) $\qquad S = \{x \in B^4 : 2x_1 + x_2 + x_3 + x_4 \leqslant 2\}$,

(c) $\qquad S = \{x \in B^4 : 2x_1 + x_2 + x_3 + x_4 \leqslant 2$
$$\begin{aligned} x_1 + x_2 \quad\quad &\leqslant 1 \\ x_1 \quad + x_3 \quad &\leqslant 1 \\ x_1 \quad\quad + x_4 &\leqslant 1\} . \end{aligned}$$

How should we compare different formulations? Later we will see that most integer programming algorithms require an upper bound on the value of the objective function, and the efficiency of the algorithm is very dependent on the sharpness of the bound. An upper bound is often determined by solving the linear program

$$z_{LP} = \{\max cx : Ax \leqslant b, x \in R^n_+\}$$

since $P = \{x \in R^n_+ : Ax \leqslant b\} \supseteq S$. Now given two formulations, $P^i = \{x \in R^n_+ : A^i x \leqslant b^i\}$ for $i = 1, 2$, let $z^i_{LP} = \max\{cx : x \in P^i\}$. Note that if $P^1 \subseteq P^2$, then $z^1_{LP} \leqslant z^2_{LP}$. Therefore, we say that $\{x \in Z^n_+ : A^1 x \leqslant b^1\}$ is a *stronger (better)* formulation than $\{x \in Z^n_+ : A^2 x \leqslant b^2\}$ if $P^1 \subset P^2$. We leave it to the reader to check that in Example 3.1, (c) is a better formulation than (b), which, in turn, is a better formulation than (a).

A striking example of one formulation being better than another, in the sense just described, is provided by the uncapacitated facility location problem. We obtain a formulation with fewer constraints than the one given in Section 2 by replacing (2.2) by

$$\sum_{i \in I} y_{ij} - mx_j \leqslant 0 \quad \text{for all } j \in N . \tag{3.1}$$

When $x_j = 0$, (3.1) says that no clients can be served from facility j, and when $x_j = 1$, there is no restriction on the number of clients that can be served from facility j. In fact, by summing (2.2) over $i \in I$ for each j, we obtain (3.1). Although with $x \in B^n$, (2.2) and (3.1) give the same set of feasible solutions, with $x \in R_+^n$, (2.2) gives a much smaller feasible set than (3.1). Our ability to solve the formulation with (2.2) is remarkably better than with the more compact formulation that uses (3.1).

We belabor this point because it is instinctive to believe that computation time increases and computational feasibility decreases as the number of constraints increases. But, trying to find a formulation with a small number of constraints is often a very bad strategy. In fact, one of the main algorithmic approaches involves the systematic addition of constraints, known as cutting planes, see Section 7.

The traveling salesman problem provides a nice illustration of the suitability of choosing a formulation with a very large number of rows. In Section 2 we gave two different sets of constraints, (2.14) and (2.16), for eliminating subtours. Both formulations contain a huge number of constraints, far too many to write down explicitly. Nevertheless, algorithms for the traveling salesman problem that solve these formulations have been successful on problems with more than 2000 cities (Padberg and Rinaldi 1987a, b).

So far we have emphasized the choice of constraints in obtaining a good formulation, given that the variables have already been defined, because for most problems this is the part of the formulation where there is the greatest freedom of choice. There are, however, problems in which the quality of the formulation depends on the choice of variables. For the traveling salesman problem it is possible just by introducing n additional variables to obtain a formulation with approximately n^2 constraints (Miller et al., 1960). However, this formulation is much weaker than that of Section 2. On the other hand, it is possible to obtain a formulation of equal strength to the one given in Section 2 with approximately n^3 constraints by introducing n^3 new variables (Wong, 1980).

In our formulation of a network flow problem, we defined the variables to be the arc flows. However, in certain situations it is more advantageous to define variables that represent the flow on each path between two given nodes. Such a formulation involves many more variables, but eliminates the need for some flow conservation constraints and can be preferable for finding integral solutions.

We now give two radically different formulations of a production lot-sizing problem that depend on the choice of variables. The object is to minimize the sum of the costs of production, storage and set-up, given that known demands in each of T periods must be satisfied. For $t = 1, \ldots, T$, let d_t be the demand in period t, and c_t, p_t and h_t be the set-up, unit production and unit storage costs respectively in period t.

One formulation is obtained by defining y_t, s_t, as the production and end storage in period t, and a binary variable x_t, indicating whether $y_t > 0$ or not. This leads to the model

$$\min \sum_{t=1}^{T} (p_t y_t + h_t s_t + c_t x_t),$$

$$y_1 = d_1 + s_1,$$

$$s_{t-1} + y_t = d_t + s_t \quad \text{for } t = 2, \ldots, T,$$

$$y_t \leq \omega_t x_t \quad \text{for } t = 1, \ldots, T,$$

$$s_T = 0,$$

$$s, y \in R_+^T, \quad x \in B^T,$$

(3.2)

where $\omega_t = \sum_{i=t}^{T} d_i$ is an upper bound on y_t for all t.

A second possibility is to define q_{it} as the quantity produced in period i to satisfy the demand in period $t \geq i$, and x_t as above. Now we obtain the model

$$\min \sum_{t=1}^{T} \sum_{i=1}^{t} (p_i + h_i + h_{i+1} + \cdots + h_{t-1}) q_{it} + \sum_{t=1}^{T} c_t x_t,$$

$$\sum_{i=1}^{t} q_{it} = d_t \quad \text{for } t = 1, \ldots, T,$$

$$q_{it} \leq d_t x_i \quad \text{for } i = 1, \ldots, T, \text{ and } t = i, \ldots, T,$$

$$q \in R_+^{T(T+1)/2}, \quad x \in B^T.$$

(3.3)

In (3.3) if we replace $x \in B^T$ by $0 \leq x_t \leq 1$ for all t, then the resulting linear programming problem has an optimal solution with $x \in B^T$ (Krarup and Bilde, 1977). But this is almost never the case for (3.2), which is the inferior formulation for solving the problem by certain integer programming techniques.

There is a similar result for the formulations (2.17) and (2.18) for finding a point that satisfies 1 of m sets of linear constraints. To solve $\max\{cy: y \in \bigcup_{k=1}^{m} P^k\}$, the obvious approach is to solve the problems $\max\{cy^i: y \in P^i\}$ for $i = 1, \ldots, m$ and take the best solution found. Alternatively, the linear program $\max\{cy: y \text{ satisfies } (2.18)\}$ always has an optimal solution with $x \in B^m$ (Balas, 1979). This is not the case using (2.17), which is therefore a weaker formulation.

4. Properties of integral polyhedra and computational complexity

The feasible set S of an integer program is described by the integral points in a polyhedron $P = \{x \in R_+^n: Ax \leq b\}$, i.e. $S = P \cap Z^n$. We note that any polyhedron P can also be represented by a convex combination of its extreme points plus a nonnegative linear combination of its extreme rays. A bounded polyhedron, called a *polytope*, is a polyhedron that is contained in some bounded region or, equivalently, has no extreme rays. The reader is referred to Chapter 5 for the definitions of polyhedron, extreme points and rays, facets, etc.

The *convex hull* of S, denoted by conv(S), is the set of points that can be written as a finite convex combination of points in S, i.e.

$$\text{conv}(S) = \left\{ x \in R^n : x = \sum_{i=1}^{t} \lambda_i x^i, \sum_{i=1}^{t} \lambda_i = 1, \lambda \in R_+^t , \right.$$

$$\left. \text{where } x^1, \dots, x^t \text{ is any finite set of points in } S \right\} .$$

Thus if S is finite, it is obvious that conv(S) is a polytope whose extreme points are some subset of S. Moreover, this result holds so long as $P = \{x \in R_+^n : Ax \leq b\}$ is a rational polyhedron.

Theorem 4.1. *If P is a rational polyhedron and $S = P \cap Z^n \neq \emptyset$, then* conv($S$) *is a rational polyhedron whose extreme points are a subset of S and whose extreme rays are the extreme rays of P.*

Theorem 4.1 extends straightforwardly to mixed integer sets with rational data.

Theorem 4.1 has several interesting consequences. First of all, it tells us that the integer program max$\{cx : x \in S\}$ where $S = P \cap Z^n$ can be formulated as the linear program

$$\max \{cx : x \in \text{conv}(S)\} . \tag{4.1}$$

However this observation, by itself, is not computationally helpful since to use it we would need to know a linear inequality description of conv(S), and generally the number of inequalities needed to describe conv(S) is extremely large. In the next section, we will address the problem of constructing conv(S), or more specifically, a polyhedron Q, conv(S) $\subseteq Q \subseteq P$, such that max$\{cx : x \in Q\}$ gives an optimal solution to (4.1).

Just knowing that an integer program can be reformulated as a linear program allows us to conclude that if an IP is neither infeasible nor unbounded, then it has an optimal solution, i.e. max cx is attained by a point in S, and more specifically, by an extreme point of conv(S).

There is an interesting proof of Theorem 4.1 (Giles and Pulleyblank, 1979) which shows that conv(S) is generated by nonnegative linear combinations of the extreme rays of P plus convex combinations of a subset of S, where the required subset of S consists of integral points that are convex combinations of the extreme points of P and "small" multiples of the extreme rays of P. This observation is important in addressing the question of the size of numbers that are needed to solve integer programming problems. In particular, it yields a bound on the magnitude of the size of the coefficients that can occur in an optimal solution to (4.1).

Given $P = \{x \in R^n_+ : Ax \le b\}$ where (A, b) is an integral $m \times (n + 1)$ matrix, let

$$\theta_A = \max_{i,j} |a_{ij}|, \quad \theta_b = \max_i |b_i| \quad \text{and} \quad \theta = \max(\theta_A, \theta_b).$$

Theorem 4.2. *Let* $S = P \cap Z^n$. *If* x *is an extreme point of* conv(S), *then* $x_j \le \omega = ((m + n)n\theta)^n$ *for* $j = 1, \dots, n$.

There is also an analogous theorem that gives a bound on the magnitude of the coefficients in the facet-defining inequalities of conv(S), see Karp and Papadimitriou (1982).

One consequence of Theorem 4.2 is that even when S is not finite, explicit upper bounds $x_j \le \omega$ for $j = 1, \dots, n$ can be added to the formulation of any integer programming problem whose objective function is bounded over the feasible region. This result, together with a scheme for recognizing unboundedness, see Section 5, shows that every integer (and mixed integer) programming problem can be solved finitely. In contrast, some nonlinear problems with integer variables are impossible to solve. For example, it is impossible to describe an algorithm that decides whether $\{x \in Z^n : f(x) = 0\}$ is feasible or not, when f can be any polynomial function (Jeroslow, 1972).

Theorem 4.2 is also important in analyzing the computational complexity of integer programs. An instance of

(IP) $\max\{cx : Ax \le b, x \in Z^n_+\}$

is described by the rational (or equivalently integer) matrices A, b, and c. Since integers are encoded by their binary expansion, the length of the input needed to encode the instance is approximately $L = mn\log(\theta)$ where here $\theta = \max\{\theta_A, \theta_b, \theta_c\}$ with $\theta_c = \max_j |c_j|$. Now in the theory of computational complexity, we measure the space and time required to solve a problem as a function of L; in particular one fundamental question is whether these parameters are polynomial functions of L. In this regard, Theorem 4.2 says that the answer to an integer programming problem, i.e. an optimal solution, if one exists, has length at most $n(\log(\omega) + 1)$, which is a polynomial function of L.

On the other hand, the number of points in S that are candidates for an optimal solution may be as large as $(\omega + 1)^n$, a number that is not polynomial in L even for $0, 1$ problems for which $\omega = 1$. This means that the brute force approach of enumerating all $(\omega + 1)^n$ possible solutions and then checking each one for feasibility by substitution requires an amount of work that cannot be bounded by a polynomial in L unless both ω and n are fixed. Indeed no algorithm is known for IP or even for deciding whether $S = \{x \in Z_+^n : Ax \le b\}$ is empty or not that is guaranteed to run in polynomial time. However, from Theorem 4.2, to verify that $S \ne \emptyset$ it suffices to be given a vector $x \in Z_+^n$ with $x_j \le \omega$ for $j = 1, \ldots, n$, and then to check that it is feasible.

Corollary 4.3. *If $S = \{x \in Z_+^n : Ax \le b\}$ is not empty, then there is a "short" (polynomial length) proof of this fact.*

Even for fixed n, $(\omega + 1)^n$ is not polynomial in L. Nevertheless, we have the following result.

Theorem 4.4 (Lenstra, 1983). *For fixed n, IP is solvable in polynomial time.*

This is a deep theorem that has a very technical proof. The approach is to restructure IP in a manner such that enumeration becomes polynomial. Unfortunately the degree of the polynomial is too large for the enumeration to be practical.

In the language of computational complexity, Corollary 4.3 says that the *nonnegative integer feasibility problem* of deciding that S is nonempty belongs to the class NP (*nondeterministic polynomial*). On the other hand, no short proof is known for showing that S is empty. That is, it is not known whether the *nonnegative integer infeasibility problem* belongs to NP. The reader should pause to think about the subtle difference between the feasibility and infeasibility problems. Note that short proofs for both the feasibility and infeasibility problems are necessary but not sufficient for showing that the feasibility, or equivalently the infeasibility, problem can be solved in polynomial time.

The above remarks on the feasibility problem can be extended to finding the optimal value of IP since IP can be transformed to a sequence of *lower bound feasibility* problems: given $c \in Z^n$ and an integer z, decide whether $S(z) = S \cap \{x : cx \ge z\}$ is not empty. In particular, if $S(z)$ is not empty and $S(z + 1)$ is empty, then the optimal value of IP equals z. To ensure that the number of lower bound feasibility problems that need to be solved is polynomially bounded in L, we determine lower and upper bounds on z from Theorem 4.2 and use binary search on z to specify the sequence of problems.

Almost all of the special cases of the general (mixed) integer programming problem that we introduced in Section 2, including knapsack, set packing, partitioning and covering, fixed charge network and traveling salesman are theoretically, in a well-defined way, equally as difficult as the general problem. In particular an optimization problem is called NP-hard if there exists a polynomial-time transformation of the general integer program to it. For example, IP can be transformed to a knapsack problem by multiplying each constraint by an appropriate positive integer weight and then summing the scaled constraints. The required weights are generally very large, but are polynomial in L. Garey and Johnson (1979) give an extensive list of NP-hard problems. The important attribute of an NP-hard problem is that it is solvable in polynomial-time if, and only if, the general integer program is solvable in polynomial-time.

Either all NP-hard problems or none of them can be solved in polynomial time. One should understand that the conjecture – no NP-hard problem can be solved in polynomial time – simply means that each of these problems has some very difficult instances. The relation of difficult instances to real and/or randomly generated data sets, and the efficiency of non-polynomial time algorithms may be quite different for any two NP-hard problems. This issue is poorly understood. However, many large instances of a variety of NP-hard problems can be solved rapidly, and even when we cannot find an optimal solution or prove that a good candidate solution is optimal, it is frequently possible to obtain a feasible solution that can be shown to be within a specified tolerance of being optimal. If this were not the case, one could not justify the widespread use of mathematical programming systems for solving mixed-integer programming problems. On the other hand, the limitations of these systems in terms of the size of problems that can be solved and the speed of solution make integer programming a very challenging area for research.

5. Relaxation and valid inequalities

This section and the following one focus on ways of obtaining upper bounds w on the optimal value z_{IP} of an integer program. The computation of upper bounds on z_{IP} is essential to integer programming algorithms since the primary way of establishing the optimality of a feasible solution x is to find a $w \geq z_{IP}$ such that $w = cx$. In more practical terms, when $w = cx + \varepsilon$, $\varepsilon > 0$, we have established that x is a solution whose value is within ε of the optimal value.

The idea of both relaxation and duality is to replace IP by an easier problem that can be used to obtain an upper bound. Frequently, it is necessary to refine these problems iteratively to obtain successively tighter bounds. As we will see, duality and relaxation are closely related and each has its advantages. For example, any feasible solution to a dual problem will yield an upper bound, but a relaxation must be solved to optimality to guarantee that its value is an upper bound on z_{IP}. On the other hand, if an optimal solution to a relaxation is a feasible solution to IP, then it is also an optimal solution to IP, while the dual problem is in an entirely different space.

A *relaxation* of

(IP) $z_{IP} = \max\{cx: x \in S\}$

is any maximization problem

(RP) $z_{RP} = \max\{z_{RP}(x): x \in S_{RP}\}$

with the following two properties:

(R1) $S_{RP} \supseteq S$,

(R2) $cx \leq z_{RP}(x)$ for $x \in S$.

We have chosen (R1) and (R2) so that

Proposition 5.1. *If* RP *is infeasible so is* IP, *and otherwise* $z_{IP} \leq z_{RP}$.

An obvious way to obtain a relaxation is to satisfy (R1) by dropping one or more of the constraints that define S and to satisfy (R2) by setting $z_{RP}(x) = cx$.

Linear programming relaxation

The *linear programming relaxation* of IP with $S = P \cap Z^n$ is obtained by deleting the integrality constraints from IP and thus is given by

(LP) $z_{LP} = \max\{cx: x \in P\}$

where $P = \{x \in R_+^n: Ax \leq b\}$. By Theorem 4.1, if $S \neq \emptyset$ then the extreme rays of P and conv(S) coincide. Thus, in addition to Proposition 5.1, we obtain

Proposition 5.2. *If* LP *unbounded, then* IP *is either infeasible or unbounded.*

We can actually associate an infinite family of linear programming relaxations with IP since for any polyhedron $Q \supseteq$ conv(S).

(LP(Q)) $z(Q) = \max\{cx: x \in Q\}$

is a relaxation of IP. However, to improve on the bound $z_{LP} = z(P)$, we need to chose $Q \subset P$. So to obtain improved linear programming relaxations, we now consider the problem of finding inequalities that are satisfied by all points in S but not all points in P.

Valid inequalities

An inequality $\pi x \leq \pi_0$ is *valid* for S, or equivalently conv(S), if $\pi x \leq \pi_0$ for all $x \in S$. Given two valid inequalities $\pi x \leq \pi_0$ and $\gamma x \leq \gamma_0$ that are not scalar multiples of each other, we say that $\pi x \leq \pi_0$ is *stronger* or *dominates* $\gamma x \leq \gamma_0$ if $\pi \geq \gamma$, $\pi_0 \leq \gamma_0$, and at least one of the inequalities is strict. A *maximal* valid inequality is one that is not dominated by any other valid inequality for S. The set of maximal valid inequalities contains all of those inequalities that define facets of conv(S), but not all maximal valid inequalities define facets.

We present three general methods for generating valid inequalities. First observe that any nonnegative linear combination of valid inequalities for S is also valid for S.

Integer rounding

For any real number a, let $\lfloor a \rfloor$ denote its round down or integer part.

Proposition 5.3. *If $\pi x \leq \pi_0$ is a valid inequality for $S \subseteq Z^n$ with π integral, then $\pi x \leq \lfloor \pi_0 \rfloor$ is a valid inequality for S.*

Proof. For all $x \in S$, πx is integral and therefore equal to or less than the largest integer equal to or less than π_0. $\square$

The rounding operation is shown in Figure 5.1. Suppose $\pi x \leq \pi_0$ is a linear combination of the constraints $A'x \leq b'$ with π integral, π_0 fractional, and the greatest common divisor of the coefficients of π equal to 1. Rounding down π_0 pushes the hyperplane $\pi x = \pi_0$ into the region $A'x \leq b'$ until it hits an integer point y. However, y need not be in the feasible region so the hyperplane $\pi x = \lfloor \pi_0 \rfloor$ need not contain a point of S.

Example 5.1.

$$S = \{x \in Z_+^n : Ax \leq b\},$$

$$A = \begin{bmatrix} -1 & 2 \\ 5 & 1 \\ -2 & -2 \end{bmatrix}, \quad b = \begin{bmatrix} 4 \\ 20 \\ -7 \end{bmatrix}.$$

Figure 5.2 shows the polytope defined by the constraints $Ax \leq b$ and $x \geq 0$ (the outer polytope), the feasible integral points (black dots) and conv(S) (the

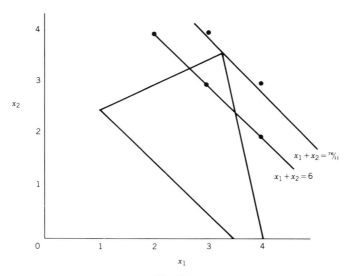

Fig. 5.1.

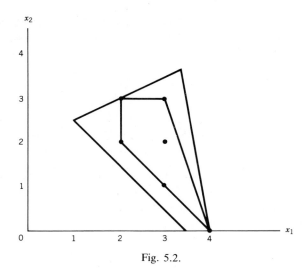

Fig. 5.2.

inner polytope). We have

$$S = \left\{ \binom{2}{2}, \binom{2}{3}, \binom{3}{1}, \binom{3}{2}, \binom{3}{3}, \binom{4}{0} \right\} = \{x^1, x^2, \ldots, x^6\}.$$

Combining the inequalities $Ax \le b$ with weights $(\frac{4}{11} \ \frac{3}{11} \ 0)$ yields the valid inequality $x_1 + x_2 \le \frac{76}{11}$ for S. As there are no points of Z^2 such that $x_1 + x_2 = \frac{76}{11}$, it is permissible to push the hyperplane inward until it meets a point of Z^2 giving the valid inequality $x_1 + x_2 \le 6$. It is fortuitous in the example that the line $x_1 + x_2 \le 6$ happens to contain a point of S.

Disjunctive inequalities

Here we combine two inequalities, each of which is valid for a part of S to obtain a weaker inequality that is valid over S.

Proposition 5.4. *Suppose* $S = S^1 \cup S^2$ *and* $\pi^i x \le \pi_0^i$ *is valid for* $S^i \subseteq R_+^n$ *for* $i = 1, 2$. *Then*

$$\sum_{j=1}^{n} \min(\pi_j^1, \pi_j^2) x_j \le \max(\pi_0^1, \pi_0^2)$$

is valid for S.

In particular, consider the two valid inequalities for S with $x_k \in Z^1$:

(a) $$\sum_{j=1}^{n} \pi_j x_j - \alpha(x_k - \delta) \le \pi_0,$$

(b) $$\sum_{j=1}^{n} \pi_j x_j + \beta(x_k - \delta - 1) \le \pi_0,$$

where $\alpha \geqslant 0$, $\beta \geqslant 0$ and δ is an integer. Note that (a) shows that

(c) $\qquad \sum_{j=1}^{n} \pi_j x_j \leqslant \pi_0$

is valid for $x \in S$ with $x_k \leqslant \delta$, and (b) shows that (c) is valid for $x \in S$ with $x_k \geqslant \delta + 1$. Hence (c) is valid for S since $x_k \in Z^1$ implies $x_k \leqslant \delta$ or $x_k \geqslant \delta + 1$.

Example 5.2. An example of a disjunctive inequality is shown in Figure 5.3 where $S = P \cap Z^2$ and

$$P = \{x \in R^2_+ : -x_1 + x_2 \leqslant \tfrac{1}{2}, \tfrac{1}{2}x_1 + x_2 \leqslant \tfrac{5}{4}, x_1 \leqslant 2\} .$$

The first two constraints can be rewritten as

$$-\tfrac{1}{4}x_1 + x_2 - \tfrac{3}{4}(x_1 - 0) \leqslant \tfrac{1}{2} ,$$

$$-\tfrac{1}{4}x_1 + x_2 + \tfrac{3}{4}(x_1 - 1) \leqslant \tfrac{1}{2} .$$

Hence $-\tfrac{1}{4}x_1 + x_2 \leqslant \tfrac{1}{2}$ is valid for $x \in S$.

Superadditive inequalities

A real-valued function F with domain $D \subseteq R^m$, $0 \in D$ and $F(0) = 0$, is called *superadditive* over D if $F(d_1) + F(d_2) \leqslant F(d_1 + d_2)$ for all $d_1, d_2, d_1 + d_2 \in D$, and *nondecreasing* over D if $d_1, d_2 \in D$ and $d_1 < d_2$ implies $F(d_1) \leqslant F(d_2)$.

Let a_j for $j = 1, \ldots, n$ be the columns of A. Now if F is superadditive and nondecreasing, and $x \in S = \{x \in Z^n_+ : Ax \leqslant b\}$, then

$$\sum_{j=1}^{n} F(a_j)x_j \leqslant \sum_{j=1}^{n} F(a_j x_j) \leqslant F\left(\sum_{j=1}^{n} a_j x_j\right) \leqslant F(b) .$$

Hence we obtain

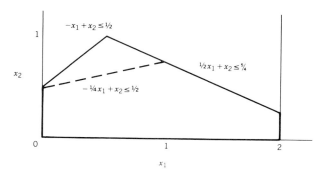

$-x_1 + x_2 \leqslant \tfrac{1}{2}$

$\tfrac{1}{2}x_1 + x_2 \leqslant \tfrac{5}{4}$

$-\tfrac{1}{4}x_1 + x_2 \leqslant \tfrac{1}{2}$

x_2

x_1

Fig. 5.3.

Proposition 5.5. *If F is superadditive and nondecreasing over R^m, then*

$$\sum_{j=1}^{n} F(a_j)x_j \leq F(b)$$

is a valid inequality for $S = \{x \in Z_+^n : Ax \leq b\}$.

Example 5.3. We give two families of functions that are readily shown to be superadditive and nondecreasing.

    (i) $F(d) = \lfloor ud \rfloor$ for $u \in R_+^m$. Figure 5.4 shows this function with $m = 1$ and $u = 1$. Note that F is the function that corresponds to the integer rounding procedure.

    (ii) $F_\alpha(d) = \lfloor d \rfloor + (f_d - \alpha)^+/(1 - \alpha)$ where $0 < \alpha < 1$, $f_d = d - \lfloor d \rfloor$, and $x^+ = \max(x, 0)$, see Figure 5.5. These functions are typically used to generate valid inequalities for mixed integer programs.

    The three approaches given above for generating valid inequalities are robust since

Theorem 5.6. *If $\pi x \leq \pi_0$ is a valid inequality for $S = \{x \in Z_+^n : Ax \leq b\} \neq \emptyset$, then:*

    1. *There exists a superadditive, nondecreasing function F such that $F(a_j) \geq \pi_j$ for $j = 1, \ldots, n$ and $F(b) \leq \pi_0$ (Jeroslow, 1979; Johnson, 1973).*

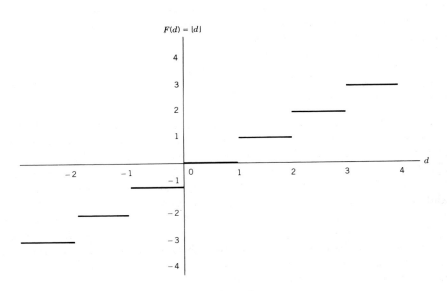

Fig. 5.4.

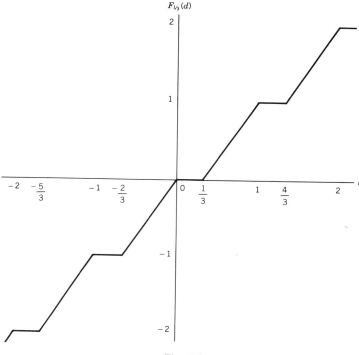

Fig. 5.5.

2. *The inequality $\pi x \leqslant \pi_0$ or a valid inequality that dominates it can be obtained by starting with the linear inequalities $Ax \leqslant b$ and $x \geqslant 0$, and then taking linear combinations and integer rounding a finite number of times* (Chvátal, 1973; Schrijver, 1980).

3. *If $x \in B^n$, the inequality $\pi x \leqslant \pi_0$ or a valid inequality that dominates it can be obtained by starting with the linear inequalities $Ax \leqslant b$, $0 \leqslant x \leqslant 1$ and then taking linear combinations and integer rounding a finite number of times* (Chvátal, 1973; Schrijver, 1980).

Statements 1, 2 and 3 can be made constructive and therefore can be turned into finite algorithms that produce successively tighter linear programming relaxations for solving IP. In particular, given the relaxation $Q = \{x \in R_+^n : A'x \leqslant b'\} \subseteq P$ and an optimal solution x^* to the linear programming relaxation LP(Q), if x^* is integral it is an optimal solution to IP; otherwise a valid inequality for S that is not satisfied by x^* can be constructed and added to Q to obtain a tighter linear programming relaxation. Unfortunately, finite usually means extremely large for these general procedures, so the algorithms are not practical. However, this basic idea does work well for some classes of integer programs where valid inequalities that define facets of conv(S) are known. This is the subject of Section 7.

We now consider some other relaxations of IP.

Modulo arithmetic and the shortest path relaxation

Suppose LP has an optimal solution and let x^0 be a basic or extreme point optimal solution to LP. If this solution is not degenerate, i.e. all of the basic variables are positive, and we assume that an optimal integer solution is near x^0, then it is plausible to think that these basic variables (some of them may be slack variables) will be positive in an optimal solution to IP. This provides part of the motivation for the *cone relaxation* in which we drop the nonnegativity restrictions on the basic variables in a basic optimal solution to LP. Assuming that the slack variables of the active constraints are nonbasic, the nonnegativity of these variables defines a cone, see Figure 5.6 whereas the inactive constraints are dropped as their slack variables become unrestricted. Another attractive feature is that the cone relaxation can be reduced to a problem in which the constraints are modular equations, and can be solved as a minimum weight path problem on a directed graph. The difficulty is that the graph can be very large.

To obtain the minimum weight path formulation, we consider a modular equation of the form

$$\sum_{j=1}^{n} a_j x_j = b \quad (\text{mod } \delta), \quad x \in Z_+^n, \tag{5.1}$$

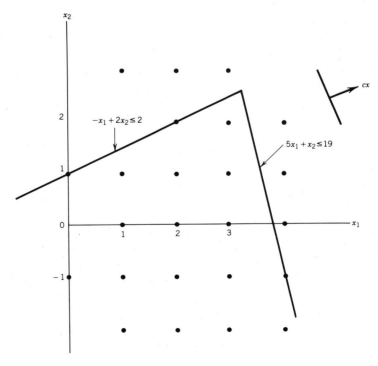

Fig. 5.6.

where the coefficients are integers and mod δ means that both sides of the equation must have the same remainder when divided by δ. Feasible solutions to (5.1) can be represented on a digraph with node set $\{0, 1, \ldots, \delta - 1\}$. From each node i, there are arcs $e_j(i) = (i, (i + a_j) \bmod \delta)$ for $j = 1, \ldots, n$. The arcs $e_j(i)$ for $i = 0, \ldots, \delta - 1$, are called *variable j arcs*.

For the modular equation

$$78x_1 - 68x_2 + 37x_3 + x_4 = 141 \quad (\bmod\, 6), \quad x \in Z_+^4, \qquad (5.2)$$

the digraph is shown in Figure 5.7, where we use the observation that $78 = 0$ mod 6, $-68 = 4$ mod 6, etc.

Now we observe that any path in the digraph from node 0 to node b mod δ corresponds to a feasible solution to (5.1) in which x_j equals the number of variable j arcs in the path. Therefore to solve the problem $\{\min cx$ subject to (5.1)$\}$, it suffices to find a minimum weight path from node 0 to node b mod δ. For (5.2) we obtain

$$\min\{cx: 0x_1 + 4x_2 + x_3 + x_4 = 3\, (\bmod\, 6), x \in Z_+^4\},$$

and it suffices to find a shortest path from node 0 to node 3.

This idea naturally extends to a multidimensional version of (5.1) in which there are m modular equations and the k-th equation, for $k = 1, \ldots, m$ must be satisfied mod δ_k.

Lagrangian relaxation

Frequently, the constraints $Ax \le b$ of IP can be partitioned into two sets of constraints $A^1x \le b^1$ and $A^2x \le b^2$, where A^1 has $m_1 < m$ rows, so that the relaxation

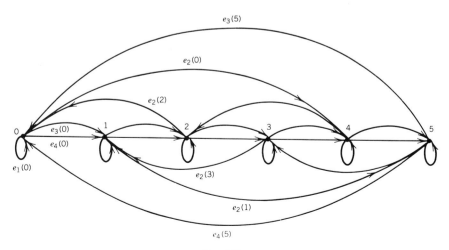

Fig. 5.7.

$$\max\{cx: x \in Q\} \text{ where } Q = \{x \in Z_+^n: A^2x \leqslant b^2\} \tag{5.3}$$

obtained by dropping the constraints $A^1x \leqslant b^1$ is easy to solve. A classical example of this situation occurs when $A^2x \leqslant b^2$ are the constraints of a network flow problem.

The idea of dropping constraints leads to a family of relaxations

$$\text{LR}(\lambda) \qquad z_{\text{LR}}(\lambda) = \max\{z(\lambda, x): x \in Q\}$$

where $z(\lambda, x) = cx + \lambda(b^1 - A^1x)$ and $\lambda \in R_+^{m_1}$. $\text{LR}(\lambda)$ is called a *Lagrangian relaxation* of IP with respect to the constraints $A^1x \leqslant b^1$. Note that $\lambda(b^1 - A^1x) \geqslant 0$ for all $x \in S$ since $\lambda \geqslant 0$, thus $z(\lambda, x) \geqslant cx$ for all $x \in S$. $\text{LR}(0)$ is the problem obtained by dropping the constraints $A^1x \leqslant b^1$. However, a smaller upper bound may be obtained by choosing $\lambda \neq 0$. The problem of choosing a λ that gives the least upper bound leads to a dual problem that will be studied in the next section.

Decomposition and cost splitting

There is another closely related relaxation that involves isolating sets of constraints by increasing the dimensions of the problem. Again suppose that the constraints have been partitioned into sets $A^1x \leqslant b^1$ and $A^2x \leqslant b^2$, and although the original problem is hard, the problem becomes easy if *either* set of constraints is omitted.

An example of this type of situation occurs in the traveling salesman problem (2.11)–(2.14) in which if the subtour elimination constraints are dropped we obtain a matching problem, and if the degree constraints are dropped we obtain a spanning tree problem.

To decompose the problem, we first observe that IP is equivalent to the problem in $2n$ dimensional space

$$\max\{c^1x^1 + c^2x^2: x^1 \in Q^1, x^2 \in Q^2, x^1 - x^2 = 0\}$$

where $Q^i = \{x^i \in Z_+^n: A^ix \leqslant b^i\}$ for $i = 1, 2$ and $c^1 + c^2 = c$. We take a Lagrangian relaxation with respect to the constraints $x^1 - x^2 = 0$ to obtain the decomposed problems

$$z^1(\lambda) = \max\{(c - \lambda)x^1: x \in Q^1\} \quad \text{and} \quad z^2(\lambda) = \max\{\lambda x^2: x \in Q^2\}$$

where $\lambda \in R^n$. The multiplier vector λ is unconstrained since $x^1 - x^2 = 0$ is a set of *equality* constraints. Now we obtain that $z_{\text{IP}} \leqslant z^1(\lambda) + z^2(\lambda)$ for all $\lambda \in R^n$.

Benders decomposition

Lagrangian relaxation can be viewed as a method for handling complicating constraints. We now consider the dual notion of complicating variables. In particular, in the mixed integer program

$$\text{(MIP)} \qquad z = \max cx + hy \, ,$$

$$Ax + Gy \leqslant b \, ,$$

$$x \in X \subseteq Z_+^n, \quad y \in R_+^p \, ,$$

we can view the integer variables x as complicating variables to what would otherwise be a linear program, and the continuous variables y as complicating variables to what would otherwise be a pure integer program. For example, in a fixed-charge network flow problem where the integer variables represent decisions about which arcs to use in a network, the problem in the y space is an ordinary network flow problem once x is specified.

The procedure, due to Benders (1962), described below shows how MIP can be reformulated as a problem in $Z_+^n \times R^1$, i.e. there is only one continuous variable. However, this formulation generally contains a huge number of linear constraints. Since one expects only a small subset of these constraints to be active in an optimal solution, a natural relaxation is obtained by dropping most of them temporarily.

As a first step, we suppose that the integer variables x have been fixed. The resulting linear program is

$$\text{LP}(x) \qquad z_{\text{LP}}(x) = \max hy \, ,$$

$$Gy \leqslant b - Ax \, ,$$

$$y \in R_+^p \, ,$$

and its dual is

$$\min\{u(b - Ax) : u \in Q\} \quad \text{where } Q = \{u \in R_+^m : uG \geqslant h\} \, .$$

An advantage in working with the dual here is that its constraint set Q is independent of x. If $Q = \emptyset$, then LP(x) is either unbounded or infeasible. The interesting case is when $Q \neq \emptyset$. Then LP(x) is either infeasible or has an optimal solution. In particular, LP(x) is infeasible if and only if Q has an extreme ray v such that $v(b - Ax) < 0$; otherwise the optimal value of LP(x) is given by $u(b - Ax)$ where u is an extreme point of Q.

Thus, if we let v^j for $j \in J$ be the extreme rays of Q and u^k for $k \in K$ be the extreme points of Q, it follows that when $Q \neq \emptyset$, MIP can be stated as

$$z = \max\{cx + \min_{k \in K} \{u^k(b - Ax)\}\,,$$

$$v^j(b - Ax) \geq 0 \quad \text{for } j \in J\,, \tag{5.4}$$

$$x \in X\,.$$

This yields the Benders representation of MIP given by

Theorem 5.7. MIP *can be reformulated as*

$$z = \max \eta\,,$$

$$\eta \leq cx + u^k(b - Ax) \quad \text{for } k \in K\,,$$

$$v^j(b - Ax) \geq 0 \quad \text{for } j \in J\,, \tag{MIP'}$$

$$x \in X, \quad \eta \in R^1\,.$$

Example 5.4 (*Uncapacitated facility location*). Here it is convenient to use a slightly different formulation of MIP' given by

$$z = \max cx + \eta'\,,$$

$$\eta' \leq u^k(b - Ax) \quad \text{for } k \in K\,,$$

$$v^j(b - Ax) \geq 0 \quad \text{for } j \in J\,,$$

$$x \in X, \quad \eta' \in R^1.$$

We consider the formulation of the uncapacitated facility location problem given in Section 2,

$$z = \max \sum_{i \in I} \sum_{j \in N} c_{ij} y_{ij} - \sum_{j \in N} f_j x_j\,,$$

$$\sum_{j \in N} y_{ij} = 1 \quad \text{for } i \in I\,,$$

$$y_{ij} - x_j \leq 0 \quad \text{for } i \in I, j \in N\,,$$

$$x \in B^n, \quad y \in R_+^{mn}\,,$$

where $N = \{1, \ldots, n\}$ and $I = \{1, \ldots, m\}$.

In this case LP(x) is

$$z_{LP}(x) = \max \sum_{i \in I} \sum_{j \in N} c_{ij} y_{ij}\,,$$

$$\sum_{j \in N} y_{ij} = 1 \quad \text{for } i \in I\,,$$

$$y_{ij} \leq x_j \quad \text{for } i \in I, j \in N\,,$$

$$y \in R_+^{mn}\,.$$

Now rather than applying the Benders reformulation directly, we will take advantage of the fact that $LP(x)$ can be decomposed into m subproblems. For $i \in I$, we consider the problem

$$LP^i(x) \qquad z_{LP}^i(x) = \max \sum_{j \in N} c_{ij} y_{ij} ,$$

$$\sum_{j \in N} y_{ij} = 1 ,$$

$$y_{ij} \leq x_j \quad \text{for } j \in N ,$$

$$y \in R_+^n .$$

Note that $z_{LP}(x) = \sum_{i \in I} z_{LP}^i(x)$.

Clearly, $LP^i(x)$ is feasible and bounded for $x \in B^n \setminus \{0\}$. Hence to describe $z_{LP}^i(x)$, it suffices to find the extreme points of

$$U^i(x) = \{u_i \in R^1, w_i \in R_+^n : u_i + w_{ij} \geq c_{ij} \text{ for } j \in N\}$$

where $w_i = (w_{i1}, \ldots, w_{in})$. It is easily seen that these extreme points are

$$u_i = c_{ik}, \quad w_i = ((c_{i1} - c_{ik})^+, \ldots, (c_{in} - c_{ik})^+) \qquad \text{for } k \in N .$$

Hence

$$z_{LP}^i(x) = \min_{k \in N} \left[c_{ik} + \sum_{j \in N} (c_{ij} - c_{ik})^+ x_j \right] .$$

As a result we can write the Benders reformulation

$$z = \max - \sum_{j \in N} f_j x_j + \sum_{i \in I} \eta_i ,$$

$$\eta_i \leq c_{ik} + \sum_{j \in N} (c_{ij} - c_{ik})^+ x_j \quad \text{for } i \in I \text{ and } k \in N ,$$

$$\sum_{j \in N} x_j \geq 1 ,$$

$$x \in B^n, \quad \eta \in R^m ,$$

which has at most $nm + 1$ constraints. The standard Benders reformulation, obtained directly from $LP(x)$ without decomposition, has an exponential number of constraints.

6. Duality

A weak dual of IP with $z_{IP} = \max\{cx: x \in S\}$ is any minimization problem

(DP) $z_D = \min\{z_D(u): u \in S_D\}$

that satisfies

(D1) $z_D(u) \geqslant cx$ for all $x \in S$ and $u \in S_D$.

Analogous to Proposition 5.1, we have

Proposition 6.1. *If* DP *is feasible then* $z_{IP} \leqslant z_D$. *If* DP *has an unbounded objective value, then* IP *is infeasible.*

By solving a weak dual, we can approximate z_{IP} from above. We call $\Delta_D = z_D - z_{IP}$ *the duality gap*. Weak duals are easy to construct. For example, by taking the dual of a linear programming relaxation of IP we obtain a weak dual

The general relationship between duality and relaxation is

Proposition 6.2. *If a problem is dual to a relaxation of* IP, *then it is also dual to* IP.

As with relaxations we may frequently consider a sequence of dual problems in order to iteratively refine the bounds.

We now consider the problem of constructing a dual to $\max\{cx: x \in S\}$ with $S = \{x \in Z_+^n: Ax \leqslant b\}$ for which the duality gap equals zero. Such a dual problem is called a *strong* dual. To motivate strong duality, we introduce the *value function* of an integer program given by

$$z(d) = \max\{cx: x \in S(d)\},$$

$$\text{with } S(d) = \{x \in Z_+^n: Ax \leqslant d\} \quad \text{for } d \in D, \tag{6.1}$$

where A and c are fixed and d is a parameter in $D \subseteq R^m$. Depending on our need we may take $D = R^m$ or $D = Z^m$ or $D = \{d \in R^m: S(d) \neq \emptyset\}$. We say that $z(d) = -\infty$ if $S(d) = \emptyset$ and $z(d) = \infty$ if the objective value is unbounded from above.

The following propositions give some elementary properties of the value function.

Proposition 6.3. $z(0) \in \{0, \infty\}$. *If* $z(0) = \infty$, *then* $z(d) = \pm\infty$ *for all* $d \in R^m$. *If* $z(0) = 0$, *then* $z(d) < \infty$ *for all* $d \in R^m$.

Problems with $z(d) = \pm \infty$ for all $d \in R^m$, e.g., $\max\{x_1: 2x_1 - x_2 \leqslant d, x \in Z_+^2\}$ reduce to feasibility problems. Thus, for simplicity of exposition, it is convenient to ignore them here. Hence, we assume $z(0) = 0$ so that $z(d) < \infty$ for all $d \in R^m$.

Proposition 6.4. *The value function of* IP *is superadditive over* $D = \{d \in R^m: S(d) \neq \emptyset\}$.

The problem of finding an upper bound on the optimal value of IP can be generalized to the problem of finding a function $g(d): R^m \to R^1$ such that $g(d) \geqslant z(d)$ for all $d \in R^m$. Thus a dual problem to IP can be formulated as

$$\min\{g(b): g(d) \geqslant z(d) \text{ for } d \in R^m, g: R^m \to R^1\} \tag{6.2}$$

or, equivalently, as

$$\min\{g(b): g(d) \geqslant cx \text{ for } x \in S(d) \text{ and } d \in R^m\}. \tag{6.3}$$

This dual is strong since there are feasible solutions with $g(b) = z(b)$, e.g., the function g where $g(d) = z(d)$ when $z(d) > -\infty$ and $g(d) = 0$ otherwise.

Some restrictions on g are needed to obtain a meaningful dual problem. Since $z(d)$ is nondecreasing, it is natural to assume that $g(d)$ is nondecreasing. Then g satisfies $g(d) \geqslant cx$ for $x \in S(d)$ if and only if $g(Ax) \geqslant cx$ for $x \in Z_+^n$. Thus when g is nondecreasing, (6.3) can be stated as

$$\min g(b),$$
$$g(Ax) \geqslant cx \quad \text{for } x \in Z_+^n, \tag{6.4}$$
$$g \text{ nondecreasing}.$$

Now suppose that we assume that g is linear, i.e. $g(d) = ud$ with $u \in R_+^m$. Thus we require $uAx \geqslant cx$ for all $x \in Z_+^n$. This last condition is equivalent to $uA \geqslant c$. Thus we obtain the weak dual

$$\min\{ub: uA \geqslant c, u \in R_+^m\},$$

which is the dual of the linear programming relaxation of IP. Linear functions are too restrictive to obtain strong duality but superadditive functions turn out to be just what we need.

Superadditive duality

There are two important reasons for restricting the function g to be superadditive in the dual problem (6.4).

a. The purpose of the dual problem is to estimate the value function from above and the value function is superadditive over the domain for which it is finite.

b. If g is superadditive, the condition $g(Ax) \geq cx$ for $x \in Z_+^n$ is equivalent to $g(a_j) \geq c_j$ for $j \in N$. This is true since $g(Ae_j) \geq ce_j$ is the same as $g(a_j) \geq c_j$ for $j \in N$, and if g is superadditive, then $g(a_j) \geq c_j$ for $j \in N$ implies

$$g(Ax) \geq \sum_{j \in N} g(a_j) x_j \geq \sum_{j \in N} c_j x_j = cx \quad \text{for } x \in Z_+^n .$$

Condition b. enables us to state a *superadditive dual problem* independent of x.

$$w = \min F(b) ,$$

(SDP)
$$F(a_j) \geq c_j \quad \text{for } j \in N ,$$

$$F(0) = 0 ,$$

$$F : R^m \to R^1, \quad \text{nondecreasing and superadditive.}$$

We can establish results analogous to linear programming duality for the primal problem IP and the dual problem SDP.

Proposition 6.5 (Weak duality). *If F is feasible to* SDP *and x is feasible to* IP, *then $cx \leq F(b)$.*

For the remainder of this section, we assume that $P = \{x \in R_+^n : Ax \leq b\}$ contains explicit bound constraints. The fact that conv(S) is a polyhedron whose facet defining inequalities can be represented by superadditive, nondecreasing functions leads to the following result.

Theorem 6.6 (Strong duality). 1. *If* IP *is feasible, then* SDP *is feasible and $w = z(b)$.*

2. *If* IP *is infeasible, then the dual objective function is unbounded from below $(w = -\infty)$.*

The familiar *complementary slackness* condition of linear programming duality carries over to superadditive integer programming duality. In particular if x^0 is an optimal solution to IP and F^0 is an optimal superadditive dual solution, then

$$(F^0(a_j) - c_j) x_j^0 = 0 \quad \text{for } j \in N .$$

Lagrangian duality

For any Lagrangian relaxation LR(λ) of IP, see Section 5, the problem of finding a λ that minimizes the upper bound $z_{LR}(\lambda)$ is

(LD) $z_{LD} = \min\limits_{\lambda \geqslant 0} z_{LR}(\lambda)$,   where $z_{LR}(\lambda) = \max\{z(\lambda, x): x \in Q\}$,

$z(\lambda, x) = cx + \lambda(b^1 - A^1 x)$ and $Q = \{x \in Z_+^n: A^2 x \leqslant b^2\}$.

Problem LD is called the *Lagrangian dual* of IP with respect to the constraints $A^1 x \leqslant b^1$. LD is obviously a weak dual to IP since $z_{LR}(\lambda) \geqslant cx$ for all $\lambda \geqslant 0$ and $x \in S$. Although we will see that LD is not generally a strong dual, we will give properties on Q that yield strong duality.

If for fixed λ the Lagrangian relaxation is relatively easy to solve, then the Lagrangian dual becomes a practical way of getting a good upper bound on z_{IP} since problem LD is then also relatively easy to solve, at least for a good approximate solution. To see this, observe that for fixed $x \in Q$, $z(\lambda, x)$ is an affine function of λ, see Figure 6.1. Thus, since it suffices to assume that Q is a finite set, $z_{LR}(\lambda)$ can be determined by solving the linear program

$$z_{LR}(\lambda) = \min\{w: w \geqslant z(\lambda, x) \text{ for } x \in Q\} .$$

Hence, as shown in Figure 6.1, $z_{LR}(\lambda)$ is the maximum of a finite number of affine functions and therefore is piecewise linear and convex. The minimization of piecewise linear, convex functions subject only to nonnegativity constraints is a well-studied problem. Subgradient optimization, see Chapter 7, is one way of determining z_{LD}.

We now study how the solution of the Lagrangian dual relates to the solution of IP and we also give a linear programming formulation for determining z_{LD}.

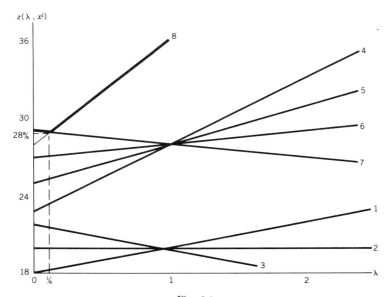

Fig. 6.1.

Here we fix λ and view

$$z(\lambda, x) = (c - \lambda A^1)x + \lambda b^1$$

as an affine function of x. It then follows that $z_{LR}(\lambda)$ can be determined by solving the linear program

$$z_{LR}(\lambda) = \max\{z(\lambda, x): x \in \mathrm{conv}(Q)\} .$$

Now using linear programming duality, we obtain

Theorem 6.7.

(a) $\quad z_{LD} = \min_{\eta, \lambda} \eta$

$$\begin{aligned}
\eta + \lambda(A^1 x^k - b^1) &\geq c x^k \quad \text{for } k \in K , \\
\lambda A^1 r^j &\geq c r^j \quad \text{for } j \in J , \\
\lambda &\geq 0 ;
\end{aligned} \tag{6.5}$$

(b) $\quad z_{LD} = \max c\left(\sum_{k \in K} \alpha_k x^k + \sum_{j \in J} \beta_j r^j \right),$

$$\begin{aligned}
\sum_{k \in K} \alpha_k &= 1 , \\
A^1\left(\sum_{k \in K} \alpha_k x^k + \sum_{j \in J} \beta_j r^j \right) &\leq b^1 , \\
\alpha \in R_+^{|K|}, \quad \beta \in R_+^{|J|} ;
\end{aligned} \tag{6.6}$$

(c) $\quad z_{LD} = \max\{cx: A^1 x \leq b^1, x \in \mathrm{conv}(Q)\}$

where $\{x^k \in R_+^n : k \in K\}$ and $\{r^j \in R_+^n : j \in J\}$ are the extreme points and extreme rays of $\mathrm{conv}(Q)$.

Theorem 6.7 shows that z_{LD} can be calculated from the linear program (6.5) or its dual.

The reader familiar with linear programming decomposition will recognize the dual of the linear program (6.5) as the reformulation obtained when Dantzig–Wolfe price decomposition is applied to $\max\{cx: A^1 x \leq b^1, A^2 x \leq b^2, x \in R_+^n\}$ where $\mathrm{conv}(Q) = \{x \in R_+^n : A^2 x \leq b^2\}$ and λ are the "dual prices" associated with the constraints $A^1 x \leq b^1$. It follows that (6.5) is the dual of the Dantzig–Wolfe reformulation. Alternatively, (6.5) is the reformulation obtained by applying Benders' decomposition to the dual linear program

$$\min\{\lambda b^1 + \mu b^2: \lambda A^1 + \mu A^2 \geq c, \lambda \in R_+^{m_1}, \mu \in R_+^{m_2}\} .$$

Corollary 6.8. 1. $z_{IP} = z_{LD}$ *for all c if and only if*

$$\text{conv}(Q \cap \{x \in R_+^n : A^1 x \leqslant b^1\}) = \text{conv}(Q) \cap \{x \in R_+^n : A^1 x \leqslant b^1\} \ .$$

2. $z_{LD} = z_{LP}$ *for all c if all the extreme points of* $\{x \in R_+^n : A^2 x \leqslant b^2\}$ *are integral.*

In summary,

$$\text{conv}(S) \subseteq \text{conv}(Q) \cap \{x \in R_+^n : A^1 x \leqslant b^1\} \subseteq \{x \in R_+^n : Ax \leqslant b\}$$

and thus $z_{IP} \leqslant z_{LD} \leqslant z_{LP}$. But because some faces of the respective polyhedra can coincide, we may obtain $z_{IP} = z_{LD}$ or $z_{LD} = z_{LP}$ for particular c even if the condition of Corollary 6.8 does not hold. Figure 6.2 illustrates this.

The inner polytope is $\text{conv}(S)$. The outer polytope is $\{x \in R_+^n : Ax \leqslant b\}$. The inner polytope together with the shaded region is $\text{conv}(Q) \cap \{x \in R_+^n : A^1 x \leqslant b^1\}$. Four different objective functions are indicated and the results are summarized below.

objective functions	objective values
c^1	$z_{IP} = z_{LD} = z_{LP}$
c^2	$z_{IP} < z_{LD} = z_{LP}$
c^3	$z_{IP} < z_{LD} < z_{LP}$
c^4	$z_{IP} = z_{LD} < z_{LP}$

It also is possible to characterize problems where $z_{IP} = z_{LD}$ in terms of a complementarity condition. We will obtain this result as a corollary to

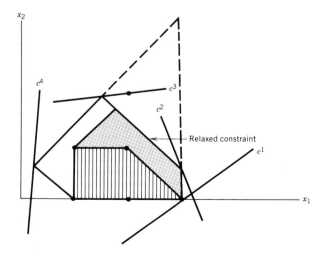

Fig. 6.2.

Theorem 6.9. $z_{IP} > z_{LD} - \varepsilon$ *if and only if there exists* $\lambda^* \geq 0$ *and* $x^* \in S$ *such that* $\lambda^*(b^1 - A^1x^*) \leq \delta_1$, $z(\lambda^*, x^*) \geq z_{LR}(\lambda^*) - \delta_2$ *and* $\delta_1 + \delta_2 \leq \varepsilon$.

Theorem 6.9 can also be helpful in identifying (nearly) optimal solutions to IP. For example in the process of solving $LR(\lambda)$, we may find an $x \in S$ that is nearly optimal in $LR(\lambda)$ and nearly satisfies complementary slackness.

By putting $\delta_1 = \delta_2 = \varepsilon = 0$ in Theorem 6.9, we obtain necessary and sufficient conditions for the duality gap to be zero.

Corollary 6.10. $z_{IP} = z_{LD}$ *if and only if there exists* $\lambda^* \geq 0$ *and* $x^* \in S$ *such that* $\lambda^*(b^1 - A^1x^*) = 0$ *and* $z_{LR}(\lambda^*) = z(\lambda^*, x^*)$.

The complementarity slackness conditions are also useful in right-hand side parametrics as shown in the following corollary to Theorem 6.9.

Corollary 6.11. *Let* x^* *be an optimal solution to* $LR(\lambda^*)$ *where* $\lambda^* \geq 0$, *and define* $d^* = A^1x^*$. *Then* x^* *is an optimal solution to*

$$\max\{cx: A^1x \leq d^1, x \in Q\}$$

for all $d^1 \in D = \{d \in R^{m_1}: d_i = d_i^* \text{ if } \lambda_i^* > 0, d_i \geq d_i^* \text{ if } \lambda_i^* = 0\}$.

Example 6.1 (*Flow problem with budget constraint*). Suppose there is a set of n jobs that may be assigned to a set of n workers where c_{ij} is the value of assigning worker i to job j and t_{ij} is the cost of training worker i to do job j. We have a training budget of b units. We wish to maximize the total value of the assignment subject to the budget constraint, i.e.

$$\max \sum_{i \in N} \sum_{j \in N} c_{ij}x_{ij},$$

(1) $$\sum_{j \in N} x_{ij} \leq 1 \quad \text{for } i \in N,$$

(2) $$\sum_{i \in N} x_{ij} \leq 1 \quad \text{for } j \in N,$$

(3) $$\sum_{i \in N} \sum_{j \in N} t_{ij}x_{ij} \leq b,$$

$$x \in B^{n^2},$$

where $N = \{1, \ldots, n\}$.

First we observe that the problem is NP-hard. If we then wish to choose a Lagrangian relaxation, there are four options to consider. Note that in each option the relaxed problem $LR(\lambda)$ is considerably easier to solve than the original problem.

1. Lagrangian relaxation with respect to (3). Then $LR_1(\lambda)$, $\lambda \in R^1_+$, is an assignment problem with objective function

$$\lambda b + \sum_{i \in N} \sum_{j \in N} (c_{ij} - \lambda t_{ij}) x_{ij} .$$

2. Lagrangian relaxation with respect to (1) and (2). Then $LR_2(u, v)$, $u \in R^n_+$, $v \in R^n_+$, is a knapsack problem with objective function

$$\sum_{i \in N} u_i + \sum_{j \in N} v_j + \sum_{i \in N} \sum_{j \in N} (c_{ij} - u_i - v_j) x_{ij} .$$

3. Lagrangian relaxation with respect to (1) or (2), say (1). Then $LR_3(u)$, $u \in R^n_+$, is a knapsack problem with generalized upper bound constraints (see Section 8) and objective function

$$\sum_{i \in N} u_i + \sum_{i \in N} \sum_{j \in N} (c_{ij} - u_i) x_{ij} .$$

4. Lagrangian relaxation with respect to (1) or (2), and (3), say (1) and (3). Only generalized upper bound constraints remain. Thus the Lagrangian $LR_4(u, \lambda)$, $u \in R^n_+$, $\lambda \in R^1_+$, with objective function

$$\lambda b + \sum_{i \in N} u_i + \sum_{i \in N} \sum_{j \in N} (c_{ij} - u_i - \lambda t_{ij}) x_{ij}$$

is trivial to solve. For each j, an i is chosen to maximize $c_{ij} - u_i - \lambda t_{ij}$ and the corresponding x_{ij} is set to one if $c_{ij} - u_i - \lambda t_{ij} > 0$.

In choosing a Lagrangian relaxation there are two major questions to consider: how strong is the bound z_{LD} and how difficult to solve is the dual (LD)?

When Q is a set of assignment constraints or a set of generalized upper bound constraints, Corollary 6.8 applies and $z^1_{LD} = z^4_{LD} = z_{LP}$. As

$$Q^3 = \left\{ x \in B^{n^2} : \sum_{i \in N} x_{ij} = 1 \text{ for } j \in N, \sum_{i \in N} \sum_{j \in N} t_{ij} x_{ij} \le b \right\}$$

$$\subsetneq Q^2 = \left\{ x \in B^{n^2} : \sum_{i \in N} \sum_{j \in N} t_{ij} x_{ij} \le b \right\} ,$$

and

$$\text{conv}(Q^2) \subsetneq \left\{ x \in R^{n^2}_+ : \sum_{i \in N} \sum_{j \in N} t_{ij} x_{ij} \le b, x_{ij} \le 1 \text{ for } i, j \in N \right\} ,$$

we have

$$z_{IP} \le z^3_{LD} \le z^2_{LD} \le z^1_{LD} = z^4_{LD} = z_{LP} ,$$

and each of the inequalities will be strict for some objective function.

We now consider two ways of strengthening the Lagrangian dual of problem IP.

Cost splitting duality

Here we use the relaxation $CS(\lambda)$ given in Section 5. Note that $CS(\lambda)$ can be restated as

$$(CS(c^1)) \quad z(c^1) = \max\{c^1 x^1: x^1 \in Q^1\} + \max\{(c - c^1)x^2: x^2 \in Q^2\}$$

where $Q^i = \{x^i \in Z^n_+: A^i x^i \leq b^i\}$ for $i = 1, 2$. Since $z(c^1) \geq cx$ for all $c^1 \in R^n$ and all $x \in S$, we obtain the *cost splitting dual*

$$z_{CSD} = \min\{z(c^1): c^1 \in R^n\}.$$

The following result is an immediate corollary of (c) of Theorem 6.7.

Theorem 6.12.

$$z_{CSD} = \max\{cx: x \in \operatorname{conv}(x \in Z^n_+: A^1 x \leq b^1)$$
$$\cap \operatorname{conv}(x \in Z^n_+: A^2 x \leq b^2)\}$$

and $z_{CSD} \leq z_{LD}$.

In Example 6.1, we might take $A^1 x \leq b^1$ to be constraint sets (1) and (3) and $A^2 x \leq b^2$ to be constraint sets (2) and (3). This yields $z_{CSD} \leq z^3_{LD}$ with the inequality strict for some objective functions.

Surrogate duality

Consider the problem

$$(SD(\lambda)) \quad z_{SD}(\lambda) = \max\{cx: \lambda A^1 x \leq \lambda b^1, x \in Q\}.$$

The problem $SD(\lambda)$ is called the *surrogate relaxation* of $IP(Q)$ with respect to $A^1 x \leq b^1$. $SD(\lambda)$ contains a single "complicating" constraint. For instance when $Q = Z^n_+$, the surrogate relaxation is a knapsack problem. The *surrogate dual* of $IP(Q)$ is the problem

$$(SD) \quad z_{SD} = \min_{\lambda \geq 0} z_{SD}(\lambda).$$

Proposition 6.13.
  (i) $LR(\lambda)$ *is a relaxation of* $SD(\lambda)$ *for* $\lambda \geq 0$.
  (ii) $z_{LD} \geq z_{SD}$.

Although the surrogate dual can be used computationally, it does not have such nice theoretical properties as the Lagrangian dual.

7. Cutting plane algorithms

Here we work with a sequence of successively tighter linear programming relaxations of IP until, hopefully, we produce one with an integral optimal solution. The basic idea is very simple and is illustrated in Figure 7.1. If the optimal solution x^* that we find to a linear programming relaxation is fractional, then we find a valid inequality for S that is not satisfied by x^*, or "cuts off x^*" from conv(S). Then we add the inequality or cut to the linear program to obtain a tighter relaxation, and we iterate this basic step.

In fact, if x^* is a basic optimal solution with at least one fractional basic variable, it is easy to find such a valid inequality. In particular, in any other solution to the LP relaxation, at least one of the nonbasic variables must be positive. But since these variables are nonnegative integers, at least one of them must be equal to or greater than one, or

$$\sum_{j \in J} x_j \geq 1 \tag{7.1}$$

where J is the index set of nonbasic variables.

Different cuts that use more detailed information from the optimal LP solution are the so-called *Gomory fractional cuts*. Consider a fractional basic variable in the optimal LP solution given by the equation

$$x_i + \sum_{j \in J} a_{ij} x_j = a_{i0} . \tag{7.2}$$

For $j \in J \cup \{0\}$, let f_{ij} be the fractional part of a_{ij}, i.e. $f_{ij} = a_{ij} - \lfloor a_{ij} \rfloor$. Thus for any solution to (7.2) with x_i integral, we have

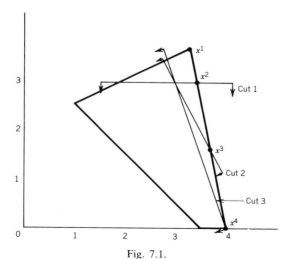

Fig. 7.1.

$$\sum_{j \in J} f_{ij} x_j = \text{integer} + f_{i0} \, .$$

But, since $f_{ij} \geqslant 0$ and $x_j \geqslant 0$ for all J and $0 < f_{i0} < 1$, it follows that

$$\sum_{j \in J} f_{ij} x_j \geqslant f_{i0} \tag{7.3}$$

is a valid inequality. The cut (7.3) also can be obtained from the integer rounding procedure given in Section 5. By systematically using these cuts in the cutting plane algorithm outlined above, we obtain a finite algorithm for solving general integer programs. Moreover, there is a related family of cuts which, under certain strong assumptions, yields a finite algorithm for general mixed integer programs. These results are not obvious since, for example, it is not possible to solve general IP's using the cuts (7.1). However, we will not pursue such algorithms in greater detail because they do not work well in practice. They fail because an extremely large number of these cuts frequently are required for convergence.

Strong cutting plane algorithms

Empirical evidence indicates that for a cutting plane algorithm to perform efficiently, it is necessary to use cuts that are strong in the sense that they define facets of conv(S), or at least faces of conv(S) of reasonably high dimension. Thus for particular classes of problems, we must study S to obtain a class or classes of strong valid inequalities that define or approximate at least part of conv(S), and then we must develop algorithms for producing inequalities from the class(es) that cuts off a fractional solution to the LP relaxation. Because this line of attack has recently proven to be very success-ful, we will develop it further.

First, we suppose knowledge of a family $\mathcal{F}$ of strong valid inequalities for IP and that our objective is to solve the linear program

LP($\mathcal{F}$)   max cx ,

$Ax \leq b$,

$\pi x \leq \pi_0$ for $(\pi, \pi_0) \in \mathcal{F}$,

$x \in R_+^n$.

In general, the class $\mathcal{F}$ may be far too large to write down all of the inequalities explicitly so we resort to a cutting plane algorithm with respect to these inequalities. That is we solve a linear program with only a small number (perhaps none) of the inequalities from $\mathcal{F}$ included. As above, if the solution x^* is integral, it is an optimal solution to LP($\mathcal{F}$). Otherwise, we must find one or more of the inequalities from $\mathcal{F}$ that cuts off x^*. In contrast with a cutting plane algorithm that uses the cuts (7.3), this may be a formidable task. What we are doing, is trading off the ease of cut generation, as is the case with the cuts (7.3), in order to produce strong cuts so that the algorithm may terminate after a reasonable number of cuts have been added.

The problem of finding a member of $\mathcal{F}$ that cuts off a point $x^* \notin \text{conv}(S)$ has been studied in Chapter 5. There it was shown that the *separation problem for the polyhedron defined by the family of inequalities $\mathcal{F}$*: "Does x^* satisfy all of the inequalities of $\mathcal{F}$? If not, find an equality from $\mathcal{F}$ that is not satisfied by x^*", can be solved in polynomial time if and only if the *optimization problem for the polyhedron defined by family $\mathcal{F}$*, i.e. $\max\{cx: \pi x \leq \pi_0 \text{ for } (\pi, \pi_0) \in \mathcal{F}\}$, can be solved in polynomial time. For most IPs, see Section 4, the optimization problem is NP-hard. Therefore, except possibly for some simple classes of inequalities, the separation problem is also NP-hard. Nevertheless, by using fast approximate methods or heuristics, it is frequently possible to solve the separation problem quickly. This will be illustrated below for 0–1 and mixed 0–1 integer programs.

Cover inequalities for 0–1 knapsack constraints
We consider the constraint set of a 0–1 knapsack problem

$$S = \left\{ x \in B^n : \sum_{j \in N} a_j x_j \leq b \right\} \tag{7.4}$$

where $N = \{1, \ldots, n\}$, $a_j \in Z_+^1$ for $j \in N$ and $b \in Z_+^1$. Since $a_j > b$ implies $x_j = 0$ for all $x \in S$, we assume $a_j \leq b$ for all $j \in N$. It is convenient to order the coefficients monotonically so that $a_1 \geq a_2 \geq \cdots \geq a_n$. We represent elements of B^n by characteristic vectors so that for $R \subseteq N$ the vector x^R has components $x_j^R = 1$ if $j \in R$ and $x_j^R = 0$ otherwise. If $x^C \in S$ we say that C is an *independent set*, otherwise C is a *dependent set*.

It is easy to see that the n constraints $x_j \geq 0$ give facets of $\text{conv}(S)$ and $x_j \leq 1$ gives a facet if $\{j, k\}$ is an independent set for all $k \in N \setminus \{j\}$.

We now begin to develop the cover inequalities. As $x^C \notin S$ when C is a dependent set, we obtain

Proposition 7.1. *If C is a dependent set then*

$$\sum_{j \in C} x_j \leq |C| - 1 \tag{7.5}$$

is a valid inequality for S.

A dependent set is *minimal* if all of its subsets are independent. Note that if a dependent set C is not minimal, then $\sum_{j \in C} x_j \leq |C| - 1$ is the sum of $\sum_{j \in C'} x_j \leq |C'| - 1$ and $x_j \leq 1$ for $j \in C \setminus C'$, where C' is a minimal dependent set. The *extension* $E(C)$ of a minimal dependent set C is the set $C \cup \{k \in N \setminus C: a_k \geq a_j \text{ for all } j \in C\}$. Note that if $R \subseteq E(C)$ and $|R| \geq |C|$, then $x^R \notin S$. Hence we obtain

Proposition 7.2. *If C is a minimal dependent set then*

$$\sum_{j \in E(C)} x_j \leq |C| - 1 \tag{7.6}$$

is a valid inequality for S.

In some instances the inequalities (7.6) give facets of conv(S).

Proposition 7.3. *Let $C = \{j_1, \ldots, j_r\}$ be a minimal dependent set with $j_1 < j_2 < \cdots < j_r$. If any of the following conditions holds, then (7.6) gives a facet of* conv(S).
   (a) $C = N$,
   (b) $E(C) = N$ and (i) $(C\backslash\{j_1, j_2\}) \cup \{1\}$ is independent,
   (c) $C = E(C)$ and (ii) $(C\backslash\{j_1\}) \cup \{p\}$ is independent where $p = \min\{j: j \in N\backslash E(C)\}$,
   (d) $C \subset E(C) \subset N$ and (i) and (ii).

A simple consequence of Proposition 7.3 is

Corollary 7.4. *If C is a minimal dependent set for S and (C_1, C_2) is any partition of C with $C_1 \neq \emptyset$, then $\Sigma_{j \in C_1} x_j \leq |C_1| - 1$ gives a facet of* conv($S(C_1, C_2)$)) *where $S(C_1, C_2) = S \cap \{x \in B^n: x_j = 0$ for $j \in N\backslash C$, $x_j = 1$ for $j \in C_2\}$.*

Using Corollary 7.4 and a "lifting procedure" given in the two following propositions, we can obtain inequalities that define facets of conv(S).

Proposition 7.5. *Suppose $S \subseteq B^n$, $S^\delta = S \cap \{x \in B^n: x_1 = \delta\}$ for $\delta \in \{0, 1\}$ and*

$$\sum_{j=2}^{n} \pi_j x_j \leq \pi_0 \tag{7.7}$$

is valid for S^0. If $S^1 = \emptyset$, then $x_1 \leq 0$ is valid for S. If $S^1 \neq \emptyset$, then

$$\alpha_1 x_1 + \sum_{j=2}^{n} \pi_j x_j \leq \pi_0 \tag{7.8}$$

is valid for S for any $\alpha_1 \leq \pi_0 - \zeta$ where

$$\zeta = \max\left\{\sum_{j=2}^{n} \pi_j x_j: x \in S^1\right\}.$$

Moreover if $\alpha_1 = \pi_0 - \xi$ and (7.7) gives a face of dimension k of conv(S^0), *then (7.8) gives a face of dimension $k + 1$ of* conv(S). *(If (7.7) gives a facet of* conv(S^0), *then (7.8) gives a facet of* conv(S).)

The lifting principle is also applicable to extending a valid inequality from S^1 to S. Using the same notation as in Proposition 7.5, we have the analogous result

Proposition 7.6. *Suppose* (7.7) *is valid for* S^1. *If* $S^0 = \emptyset$, *then* $x_1 \geq 1$ *is valid for* S. *If* $S^0 \neq \emptyset$, *then*

$$\gamma_1 x_1 + \sum_{j=2}^{n} \pi_j x_j \leq \pi_0 + \gamma_1 \qquad (7.9)$$

is valid for S *for any* $\gamma_1 \geq \zeta - \pi_0$ *where*

$$\zeta = \max\left\{\sum_{j=2}^{n} \pi_j x_j : x \in S^0\right\}.$$

Moreover, if $\gamma_1 = \zeta - \pi_0$ *and* (7.7) *gives a face of dimension* k *of* conv(S^1), *then* (7.9) *gives a face of dimension* $k + 1$ *of* conv(S).

When $\alpha_1 = \pi_0 - \zeta$ in Proposition 7.5 or when $\gamma_1 = \zeta - \pi_0$ in Proposition 7.6, we say that the *lifting is maximum*.

Propositions 7.5 and 7.6 are meant to be used sequentially. Combining them with Corollary 7.4, we can generate facets of conv(S), called *lifted cover inequalities*.

Proposition 7.7. *If* C *is a minimal dependent set for* S *and* (C_1, C_2) *is any partition of* C *with* $C_1 \neq \emptyset$, *then* conv(S) *has a facet represented by*

$$\sum_{j \in N \setminus C} \alpha_j x_j + \sum_{j \in C_2} \gamma_j x_j + \sum_{j \in C_1} x_j \leq |C_1| - 1 + \sum_{j \in C_2} \gamma_j \qquad (7.10)$$

where $\alpha_j \geq 0$ *for all* $j \in N \setminus C$ *and* $\gamma_j \geq 0$ *for all* $j \in C_2$.

The order of the variables in the lifting affects the coefficients. However, we should begin with a $j \in N \setminus C$, for beginning with $k \in C_2$ is equivalent to starting with $\sum_{j \in C_1 \cup \{k\}} x_j \leq |C_1|$.

Example 7.1. $S = \{x \in B^5 : 3x_1 + x_2 + x_3 + x_4 + x_5 \leq 4\}$.
   a. $C = \{1, 4, 5\}$ is a minimal dependent set and $E(C) = \{1, 4, 5\}$. By Proposition 7.3, $x_1 + x_4 + x_5 \leq 2$ gives a facet of conv(S).
   b. $C = \{1, 4, 5\}$, $C_1 = \{4, 5\}$, $C_2 = \{1\}$. By Corollary 7.4, $x_4 + x_5 \leq 1$ gives a facet of conv$\{(x_4, x_5) \in B^2 : x_4 + x_5 \leq 4 - 3 = 1\}$. First we lift with respect to the variable x_3 by applying Proposition 7.5. This yields

$$\alpha_3 = 1 - \max[x_4 + x_5 :$$
$$\{(x_4, x_5) \in B^2 : x_4 + x_5 \leq 4 - 3x_1 - x_3, x_1 = x_3 = 1\}].$$

Hence $\alpha_3 = 1$ and $x_3 + x_4 + x_5 \leqslant 1$ gives a facet of conv$\{x \in B^3: x_3 + x_4 + x_5 \leqslant 1\}$. Now we lift with respect to x_1 by applying Proposition 7.6. Hence

$$\gamma_1 = \max[x_3 + x_4 + x_5: \{x \in B^3: x_3 + x_4 + x_5 \leqslant 4\}] - 1 = 2.$$

Thus $2x_1 + x_3 + x_4 + x_5 \leqslant 3$ gives a facet of conv$\{x \in B^4: 3x_1 + x_3 + x_4 + x_5 \leqslant 4\}$. Finally, we lift with respect to x_2 by applying Proposition 7.5. Hence

$$\alpha_2 = 3 - \max[2x_1 + x_3 + x_4 + x_5: \{x \in B^4: 3x_1 + x_3 + x_4 + x_5 \leqslant 3\}].$$

Hence $\alpha_2 = 0$ and $2x_1 + x_3 + x_4 + x_5 \leqslant 3$ gives a facet of conv(S).

By symmetry, lifting in the order (x_2, x_1, x_3) yields the facet represented by $2x_1 + x_2 + x_4 + x_5 \leqslant 3$. The orders (x_2, x_3, x_1) or (x_3, x_2, x_1) show that the original inequality $3x_1 + x_2 + x_3 + x_4 + x_5 \leqslant 4$ also gives a facet of conv(S). We have not considered lifting x_1 first because, as explained before the example, this yields $x_1 + x_4 + x_5 \leqslant 2$ which we already know gives a facet.

When $C_2 = \emptyset$ in Proposition 7.7, there is a formula that nearly determines all of the lifting coefficients.

Proposition 7.8 (Balas, 1975). *Let* $C = \{j_1, \ldots, j_r\}$ *be a minimal dependent set with* $j_1 < j_2 < \cdots < j_r$. *Let* $\mu_h = \sum_{k=1}^{h} a_{j_k}$ *for* $h = 1, \ldots, r$, $\mu_0 = 0$ *and* $\lambda = \mu_r - b \geqslant 1$. *Every valid inequality of the form*

$$\sum_{j \in N \setminus C} \alpha_j x_j + \sum_{j \in C} x_j \leqslant |C| - 1$$

that represents a facet of conv(S) *satisfies*:
    (i) *if* $\mu_h \leqslant a_j \leqslant \mu_{h+1} - \lambda$, *then* $\alpha_j = h$,
    (ii) *if* $\mu_{h+1} - \lambda + 1 \leqslant a_j \leqslant \mu_{h+1} - 1$, *then* (a) $\alpha_j \in \{h, h+1\}$ *and* (b) *there is at least one facet of the form* (7.10) *with* $\alpha_j = h + 1$.

Example 7.2.

$$S = \{x \in B^{10}: 35x_1 + 27x_2 + 23x_3 + 19x_4 + 15x_5 + 15x_6 + 12x_7 + 8x_8$$
$$+ 6x_9 + 3x_{10} \leqslant 39\}.$$

Let $C = \{6, 7, 8, 9\}$. Then $\mu_0 = 0$, $\mu_1 = 15$, $\mu_2 = 27$, $\mu_3 = 35$, $\mu_4 = 41$ and $\lambda = 2$. Proposition 7.8 yields

$$
\alpha_j = \begin{cases}
0 & \text{if } 0 \le a_j \le 13 \,, \\
0 \text{ or } 1 & \text{if } a_j = 14 \,, \\
1 & \text{if } 15 \le a_j \le 25 \,, \\
1 \text{ or } 2 & \text{if } a_j = 26 \,, \\
2 & \text{if } 27 \le a_j \le 33 \,, \\
2 \text{ or } 3 & \text{if } a_j = 34 \,, \\
3 & \text{if } 35 \le a_j \le 39 \,.
\end{cases}
$$

Hence the only facet that can be obtained from lifting $x_6 + x_7 + x_8 + x_9 \le 3$ is represented by

$$
3x_1 + 2x_2 + x_3 + x_4 + x_5 + x_6 + x_7 + x_8 + x_9 \le 3 \,.
$$

A cutting plane algorithm for 0–1 integer programs

We now use the cover and lifted cover inequalities in a strong cutting plane algorithm for the general 0–1 integer programming problem

$$
\text{(BIP)} \qquad \max \sum_{j \in N} c_j x_j \,,
$$

$$
\sum_{j \in N} a_{ij} x_j \le b_i \quad \text{for } i = 1, \ldots, m \,,
$$

$$
x \in B^n \,.
$$

Observe that the ith constraint can be transformed into one with nonnegative coefficients, i.e. a knapsack inequality, by complementing variables. In particular we replace x_j by y_j if $a_{ij} \ge 0$ and x_j by $1 - y_j$ if $a_{ij} < 0$, which yields $\sum_{j \in N} a'_{ij} y_j \le b'_i$, where $a'_{ij} = a_{ij}$ if $a_{ij} \ge 0$, $a'_{ij} = -a_{ij}$ if $a_{ij} < 0$ and $b'_i = b_i - \sum_{\{i: a_{ij} < 0\}} a_{ij}$.

Thus when considered individually, which is what we do, the constraints of BIP can be viewed as knapsack inequalities. This motivates a cutting plane algorithm for BIP based on the extended cover inequalities (7.6) and the lifted cover inequalities (7.10) for constraints of the form (7.4).

We begin by considering the separation problem for the class of inequalities (7.5). Here C is an unknown subset of N and given a point $x^* \in R^n_+ \setminus B^n$ we want to find a C (assuming that one exists) with $\sum_{j \in C} a_j > b$ and $\sum_{j \in C} x_j^* > |C| - 1$. Introducing a vector $z \in B^n$ to represent the unknown set C, we attempt to choose z such that $\sum_{j \in N} a_j z_j > b$ and $\sum_{j \in N} x_j^* z_j > \sum_{j \in N} z_j - 1$. The second inequality is equivalent to $\sum_{j \in N} (1 - x_j^*) z_j < 1$.

Thus we obtain the *Separation Problem for Cover Inequalities*

$$
\zeta = \min \left\{ \sum_{j \in N} (1 - x_j^*) z_j \colon \sum_{j \in N} a_j z_j \ge b + 1, \, z \in B^n \right\}. \tag{7.11}
$$

Note that, since the constraint coefficients are integral, $\sum_{j \in N} a_j z_j > b$ is equivalent to $\sum_{j \in N} a_j z_j \ge b + 1$.

Proposition 7.9. *Let* (ζ, z^C) *be an optimal solution to* (7.11). *Then*

(a) *if* $\zeta \geqslant 1$, x^* *satisfies all the cover inequalities for* S,

(b) *if* $\zeta < 1$, $\sum_{j \in C} x_j \leqslant |C| - 1$ *is a most violated cover inequality for* S, *and it is violated by the amount* $1 - \zeta$.

It is now straightforward to implement a strong cutting plane algorithm for BIP. As the initial relaxation we take $\{x \in R^n_+ : Ax \leqslant b, x \leqslant 1\}$. The separation algorithm for BIP involves the solution of the knapsack separation problem (7.11) for each constraint $\sum_{j \in N} a_{ij} x_j \leqslant b_i$, restated as a knapsack inequality. We note that when A and b are nonnegative, the algorithm will terminate with an optimal solution to the problem

$$\max\Bigg\{cx: Ax \leqslant b, x \leqslant 1,$$
$$\sum_{j \in C} x_j \leqslant |C| - 1 \text{ for all } C \text{ with } \sum_{j \in C} a_j \nleqslant b, x \in R^n_+ \Bigg\}$$

where a_j is the j-th column of A.

Example 7.3. We apply a strong cutting plane algorithm to the BIP

$$\max 77x_1 + 6x_2 + 3x_3 + 6x_4 + 33x_5 + 13x_6 + 110x_7 + 21x_8 + 47x_9,$$
$$774x_1 + 76x_2 + 22x_3 + 42x_4 + 21x_5 + 760x_6$$
$$+ 818x_7 + 62x_8 + 785x_9 \leqslant 1500,$$
$$67x_1 + 27x_2 + 794x_3 + 53x_4 + 234x_5 + 32x_6$$
$$+ 797x_7 + 97x_8 + 435x_9 \leqslant 1500,$$
$$x \in B^9.$$

Iteration 1. Solution of the linear programming relaxation LP^1 of BIP yields $x_4^1 = x_5^1 = x_7^1 = x_8^1 = 1$, $x_1^1 = 0.71$, $x_3^1 = 0.35$, $x_j^1 = 0$ otherwise and $z_{LP}^1 = 225.7$. Solution of the separation problem (7.11) for row 1 yields $\zeta = 0.29$, $z_1 = z_7 = 1$, $z_j = 0$ otherwise, giving the violated cover inequality $x_1 + x_7 \leqslant 1$. Here $E(C) = C$.

Solution of the separation problem (7.11) for row 2 yields $\zeta = 0.65$, $z_3 = z_7 = 1$, $z_j = 0$ otherwise, giving the violated cover inequality $x_3 + x_7 \leqslant 1$. Again $E(C) = C$.

Iteration 2. Solution of the linear programming relaxation LP^2 of BIP with the two additional constraints $x_1 + x_7 \leqslant 1$, $x_3 + x_7 \leqslant 1$ yields $x_2^2 = x_4^2 = x_5^2 =$

$x_7^2 = x_8^2 = 1$, $x_9^2 = 0.61$, $x_j^2 = 0$ otherwise and $z_{LP}^2 = 204.8$. Solution of the separation problem (7.11) for row 1 gives the violated cover inequality $x_7 + x_9 \le 1$. Solution of the separation problem (7.11) for row 2 gives $\zeta \ge 1$ showing that x^2 satisfies all the cover inequalities for this row.

Iteration 3. Solution of the LP relaxation LP^3 obtained from LP^2 by addition of the constraint $x_7 + x_9 \le 1$ yields $x_2^3 = x_4^3 = x_5^3 = 1$, $x_1^3 = 0.63$, $x_7^3 = 0.37$, $x_9^3 = 0.63$, $x_j^3 = 0$ otherwise, and $z_{LP}^3 = 177.1$. Row 1 gives $C = \{1, 9\}$ and the extended cover cut $x_1 + x_7 + x_9 \le 1$. Row 2 gives no cut.

Iteration 4. Solution of LP^4 having a total of four additional constraints yields $x_2^4 = x_4^4 = x_5^4 = x_7^4 = x_9^4 = 1$, $x_j^4 = 0$ otherwise, and $z_{LP}^4 = 176$. As this solution is integer, it solves BIP.

This example raises two issues. Given that the separation problem (7.11) is a knapsack problem, which is an NP-hard problem, should we solve (7.11) exactly or use a fast heuristic algorithm? In practice, heuristics have been used very effectively. But this, of course, means that some cover inequalities may be missed by the separation procedure.

The second issue stems from the observation that the first two cuts generated from row 1 in the course of the algorithm are $x_1 + x_7 \le 1$, $x_7 + x_9 \le 1$, which are dominated by the third cut $x_1 + x_7 + x_9 \le 1$. Hence, we could speed up the algorithm if we could obtain this stronger cut from row 1 on the first iteration.

To obtain the stronger cut, remember from Proposition 7.7 that every minimal cover C gives rise to a family of *lifted cover inequalities* (7.10), where the coefficient $\{a_j\}$ and $\{\gamma_j\}$ can be chosen so that (7.10) defines a facet of the knapsack convex hull.

This suggests a heuristic separation algorithm for lifted cover inequalities based on the following ideas:

(a) Given x^*, for each row of (A, b) solve the knapsack problem (7.11) to obtain a cover C, giving a "most violated" inequality $\sum_{j \in C} x_j \le |C| - 1$. Note that x^* may satisfy this inequality.

(b) Order the elements of $N \setminus C$ in a "greedy" fashion, and using Proposition 7.5 obtain an inequality of the form

$$\sum_{j \in N \setminus C} \alpha_j x_j + \sum_{j \in C} x_j \le |C| - 1.$$

If this inequality is violated by x^*, take it as a cut and process the next row of (A, b).

(c) Otherwise choose a $K \subset C$ and find a "violated" cover inequality for

$$S^K = \left\{ x \in B^{n - |K|} : \sum_{j \in N \setminus K} a_j x_j \le b - \sum_{k \in K} a_k \right\}.$$

Then use Propositions 7.5 and 7.6 to obtain an inequality of the form

$$\sum_{j \in N \setminus C} \alpha_j x_j + \sum_{j \in C \setminus K} x_j + \sum_{j \in K} \beta_j x_j \leq \pi_0 .$$

(Note that (c) may be repeated for different choices of K until an inequality violated by x^* is found or an appropriate stopping criterion is reached.)

Given the heuristic nature of the above separation algorithm, we can no longer determine a priori what problem will be solved at the termination of the strong cutting plane algorithm. We can only assert that the cuts generated at least include all the cover inequalities. Even this assertion may be false if we use a heuristic algorithm for the knapsack problem (7.11). However computational experience shows that the use of the lifted cover inequalities in place of the extended cover inequalities leads to significant improvements in performance.

Example 7.3 (continued). We apply the strong cutting plane algorithm, where the separation algorithm for lifted cover inequalities is applied to each row of BIP.

Phase 1
Iteration 1
   Row 1. The cover inequality $x_1 + x_7 \leq 1$ is lifted to obtain the cut $x_1 + x_2 + x_7 + x_9 \leq 1$.
   Row 2. The cut $x_3 + x_7 \leq 1$ is generated.
Iteration 2
   Solution of the new relaxation yields $x_2^2 = x_4^2 = x_5^2 = x_7^2 = x_8^2 = 1$, $x_j^2 = 0$ otherwise, $z_{LP}^2 = 176$. As x^2 is integer, it is an optimal solution of BIP.

Other applications of strong cutting plane algorithms to BIPs
   Strong cutting plane algorithms have been developed for several combinatorial optimization problems including the traveling salesman problem, the bipartite subgraph problem, the max cut problem, the node packing problem, and matching and constrained matching problems. Some of these are discussed in Chapter 5. However, the most significant opportunities for practical applications lie in the solution of large-scale mixed 0–1 integer programs.

Fixed charge flow models
   Here we discuss only briefly some of the ideas developed for fixed charge flow problems since, as we have already seen for the cover inequalities for knapsack constraints, a detailed development requires considerable space. The fundamental constraints that are used to model fixed charge flow problems are of the form

$$y_j \leq a_j x_j \qquad\qquad (7.12)$$

where y_j is the flow on arc j, a_j is the capacity of arc j and $x_j \in \{0, 1\}$. The flow on arc j can be positive only if $x_j = 1$, in which case a fixed charge is incurred. The constraint (7.12) is known as a *variable upper bound constraint*.

Now consider a flow model with a single node with an exogenous supply of b and n outflow arcs, see Figure 7.2. For each $j \in N = \{1, \ldots, n\}$ the flow $y_j \in R_+^1$ on the j-th arc is bounded by the capacity a_j if arc j is open ($x_j = 1$) and equals 0 otherwise. Since the total outflow cannot exceed b, this model can be represented by the mixed integer region

$$T = \left\{ x \in B^n, \, y \in R_+^n : \sum_{j \in N} y_j \leqslant b, \, y_j \leqslant a_j x_j \text{ for } j \in N \right\}. \tag{7.13}$$

Our objective is to find strong valid inequalities for T. Note that if $y_j = a_j x_j$ for all $j \in N$, T is simply a knapsack set. Thus our approach is to generalize the cover inequalities previously developed for knapsack sets.

Let $\lambda = \sum_{j \in C} a_j - b$ be the excess capacity of the arcs in a dependent set C. For $k \in C$, the capacity of the set $C \setminus \{k\}$ is

$$\min \left\{ \sum_{j \in C \setminus \{k\}} a_j, \, b \right\} = b - (a_k - \lambda)^+$$

and for any $C' \subset C$, the capacity of the set $C \setminus C'$ is $b - (\sum_{j \in C'} a_j - \lambda)^+ \leqslant b - \sum_{j \in C'} (a_j - \lambda)^+$. Thus we have proved

Proposition 7.10. *If $C \subseteq N$ is a dependent set of S and $\lambda = \sum_{j \in C} a_j - b$, then*

$$\sum_{j \in C} y_j \leqslant b - \sum_{j \in C} (a_j - \lambda)^+ (1 - x_j) \tag{7.14}$$

is a valid inequality for T given by (7.13).

Moreover if $\max_{j \in C} a_j > \lambda$, it can be shown that the inequality (7.14) gives a facet of conv(T).

Now we consider a more general model that also includes inflow arcs. Let

$$T = \left\{ x \in B^n, \, y \in R_+^n : \sum_{j \in N^+} y_j - \sum_{j \in N^-} y_j \leqslant b, \, y_j \leqslant a_j x_j \text{ for } j \in N \right\} \tag{7.15}$$

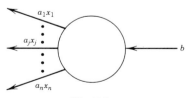

Fig. 7.2.

where $N^+ \cup N^- = N$, see Figure 7.3. Here $a_j \in R_+^1$ for $j \in N$ and $b \in R^1$, i.e. b can be negative. We say that $C \subseteq N^+$ is a *dependent set* if $\Sigma_{j\in C} a_j > b$. Note, for example, that if $b < 0$, every subset of N^+ is dependent.

We can now generalize Proposition 7.10.

Proposition 7.11. *If $C \subseteq N^+$ is a dependent set, $\lambda = \Sigma_{j\in C} a_j - b$ and $L \subseteq N^-$, then*

$$\sum_{j\in C} [y_j + (a_j - \lambda)^+(1 - x_j)] \leq b + \sum_{j\in L} \lambda x_j + \sum_{j\in N^-\setminus L} y_j \qquad (7.16)$$

is a valid inequality for T given by (7.15).

Moreover,

Theorem 7.12. *If $b > 0$, $\max_{j\in C} a_j > \lambda$ and $a_j > \lambda$ for $j \in L$, then (7.16) gives a facet of $\mathrm{conv}(T)$ where T is given by (7.15).*

Example 7.4. The feasible set T is given by

$$y_1 + y_2 + y_3 + y_4 \leq 9 + y_5 + y_6 ,$$
$$y_1 \leq 5x_1, \quad y_2 \leq 5x_2, \quad y_3 \leq x_3, \quad y_4 \leq 3x_4, \quad y_5 \leq 3x_5, \quad y_6 \leq x_6 ,$$
$$y \in R_+^6, \quad x \in B^6 .$$

Taking $C = \{1, 2, 3\}$ and $L = \{5\}$, we have $\lambda = 2$ and (7.16) yields

$$[y_1 + 3(1 - x_1)] + [y_2 + 3(1 - x_2)] + y_3 \leq 9 + 2x_5 + y_6 .$$

Theorem 7.12 establishes that this inequality defines a facet of $\mathrm{conv}(T)$.

The flow model with constraint set T given by (7.15) is much more general than it appears. With some additional simple constraints, it can be used to

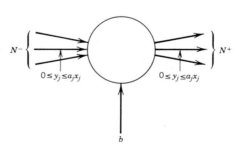

Fig. 7.3.

represent any linear inequality involving both continuous and 0–1 variables in which some of the continuous variables have simple upper bounds and the others variable upper bounds. We demonstrate its versatility with two simple examples:

Example 7.5 (*Facility location*).

$$T' = \left\{ x_0 \in B^1, \, y \in R^n_+ : \sum_{j \in N^+} y_j \le a_0 x_0, \, y_j \le a_j \text{ for } j \in N^+ \right\}$$

where $0 < a_j < a_0$ for all $j \in N^+$. Here a_0 is the capacity of a facility and $x_0 = 1$ if and only if the facility is open. The flow from the facility to client j is y_j and a_j is the maximum requirement of client j. This can be rewritten as

$$T = \Big\{ (y, y_0) \in R^{n+1}_+, \, x \in B^{n+1} :$$

$$\sum_{j \in N^+} y_j \le 0 + y_0, \, y_j \le a_j x_j, \, j \in N^+ \cup \{0\} \Big\}$$

with the additional constraints $x_j = 1$ for $j \in N^+$ and $y_0 = a_0 x_0$.
   Taking $C = \{j\}$ so that $\lambda = a_j$ and $L = N^- = \{0\}$, (7.16) yields

$$y_j \le a_j x_0 \quad \text{for } j \in N^+.$$

Example 7.6 (*Machine scheduling*). Suppose that two jobs must be executed on the same machine. The i-th job for $i = 1, 2$ has an earliest start time of l_i and a processing time of $p_i > 0$. The machine can only process one job at a time. Our objective is to model this restriction.
   Let $\delta = 1$ if job 1 is processed before job 2 and $\delta = 0$ otherwise, and for $i = 1, 2$ let t_i be the time at which the machine begins to process job i. Then we have the model

$$t_1 - t_2 \ge p_2 - \omega \delta ,$$

$$-t_1 + t_2 \ge p_1 - \omega(1 - \delta) ,$$

$$t_i \ge l_i \quad \text{for } i = 1, 2, \quad \delta \in B^1 ,$$

where ω is a suitably large number so that the first constraint is valid when $\delta = 1$ and the second is valid when $\delta = 0$.
   Suppose $l_2 + p_2 > l_1$. By substituting $y_i = t_i - l_i$ and $x_3 = \delta$, the first constraint becomes

$$y_2 \le (l_1 - l_2 - p_2) + y_1 + \omega x_3$$

with $y_1, y_2 \ge 0$ and $x_3 \in B^1$. As in the previous example, this is of the form T

with additional constraints $y_3 = \omega x_3$, etc. Here $N^+ = \{2\}$, $N^- = \{1, 3\}$ and $b = l_1 - l_2 - p_2 < 0$. Taking $C = \emptyset$ and $L = \{3\}$, (7.16) yields $0 \le -\lambda + \lambda x_3 + y_1$, or in terms of the original variables

$$t_1 \ge l_1 + (l_2 + p_2 - l_1)(1 - \delta).$$

8. Branch-and-bound

In this section we present a general scheme whereby, through the use of controlled enumeration and relaxation and/or duality, integer programming problems are solved by dividing the feasible set S into a set of subsets $\{S^i: 1 = 1, \ldots, k\}$ and then solving the problem over each of the subsets. We say that $\{S^i: i = 1, \ldots, k\}$ is a *division* of S if $\cup_{i=1}^{k} S^i = S$. A division is called a *partition* if $S^i \cap S^j = \emptyset$ for $i, j = 1, \ldots, k$, $i \ne j$.

Proposition 8.1. *Let*

$$(\text{IP}^i) \qquad z_{\text{IP}}^i = \max\{cx: x \in S^i\}$$

where $\{S^i\}_{i=1}^{k}$ is a division of S. Then $z_{\text{IP}} = \max_{i=1, \ldots, k} z_{\text{IP}}^i$.

Proposition 8.1 expresses the familiar idea of *divide and conquer*. In other words, if it is too difficult to optimize over S, perhaps the problem can be solved by optimizing over smaller sets and then putting the results together.

The division is frequently done recursively as shown in the tree of Figure 8.1.

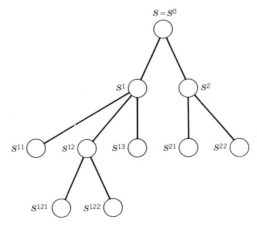

Fig. 8.1.

Here the sons of a given node, e.g. (S^{11}, S^{12}, S^{13}) are the sons of S^1, represent a division of the feasible region of their father.

When $S \subseteq B^n$, a simple way of doing the recursive division is shown in Figure 8.2. Here $S^{\delta_1 \cdots \delta_k} = S \cap \{x \in B^n : x_j = \delta_j \in \{0, 1\}$ for $j = 1, \ldots, k\}$ and the division is a partition of S.

Carried to the extreme, division can be viewed as total enumeration of the elements of S. Total enumeration is not viable for problems with more than a very small number of variables. To have any hope of working, the enumerative approach needs to avoid dividing the initial set into too many subsets.

Suppose S has been divided into subsets $\{S^1, \ldots, S^k\}$. If we can establish that no further division of S^i is necessary, we say that the enumeration tree can be *pruned* at the node corresponding to S^i or, for short, that S^i can be pruned.

Proposition 8.2. *The enumeration tree can be pruned at the node corresponding to S^i if any one of the following three conditions holds.*
1. *Infeasibility*: $S^i = \emptyset$.
2. *Optimality*: *An optimal solution of* IP^i *is known.*
3. *Value dominance*: $z_{IP}^i \le z_{IP}$.

We would like to be able to apply Proposition 8.2 without necessarily having to solve IP^i. To accomplish this, we use relaxation or duality. Let RP^i be a relaxation of IP^i with $S^i \subseteq S_R^i$ and $z_R^i(x) \ge cx$ for $x \in S^i$ and let DP^i be (weakly) dual to IP^i. From the properties of relaxation and duality, we obtain

Proposition 8.3. *The enumeration tree can be pruned at the node corresponding to S^i if any one of the following conditions holds.*

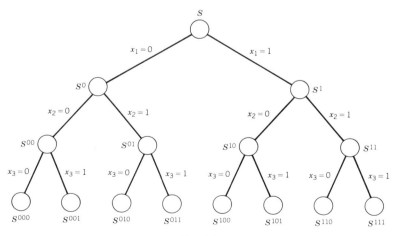

Fig. 8.2.

1. RP^i *is infeasible.*
2. *An optimal solution* x_R^i *to* RP^i *satisfies* $x_R^i \in S^i$ *and* $z_R^i = cx_R^i$.
3. $z_R^i \leq \underline{z}_{IP}$, *where* $\underline{z}_{IP}$ *is the value of some feasible solution of* IP.
4. *The objective value of* DP^i *is unbounded from below.*
5. DP^i *has a feasible solution of value equal to or less than* $\underline{z}_{IP}$.

Note that RP^i must be solved to optimality in order to apply value dominance, but when using duality to obtain bounds, value dominance may be applicable with respect to dual feasible solutions that are not optimal. On the other hand, RP^i may yield a feasible solution to IP that establishes or improves the lower bound $\underline{z}_{IP}$. Thus when upper bounds are found by solving a dual problem, other procedures may be needed to find feasible solutions and lower bounds, see Section 9.

An enumerative relaxation algorithm is frequently called *branch-and-bound* or *implicit enumeration*. We now give a general branch-and-bound algorithm for solving IP. In the description of the algorithm, L is a collection of integer programs $\{IP^i\}$, each of which is of the form $z_{IP}^i = \max\{cx: x \in S^i\}$ where $S^i \subseteq S$. Associated with each problem in L is an upper bound $\bar{z}^i \geq z_{IP}^i$.

General branch-and-bound algorithm.
1. *Initialization.* $L = \{IP\}$, $S^0 = S$, $\bar{z}^0 = \infty$ and $\underline{z}_{IP} = -\infty$.
2. *Termination test.* If $L = \emptyset$, then (a) if $\underline{z}_{IP} > -\infty$ the solution x^0 that yielded $\underline{z}_{IP} = cx^0$ is optimal, and (b) if $\underline{z}_{IP} = -\infty$, $S = \emptyset$.
3. *Problem selection and relaxation.* Section and delete a problem IP^i from L. Solve its relaxation RP^i. Let z_R^i be the optimal value of the relaxation and x_R^i be an optimal solution if one exists.
4. *Pruning.* a. If $z_R^i \leq \underline{z}_{IP}$, go to Step 2. (Note if the relaxation is solved by a dual algorithm, then the step is applicable as soon as the dual value reaches or falls below $\underline{z}_{IP}$.)
   b. If $x_R^i \notin S^i$, go to Step 5.
   c. If $x_R^i \in S^i$ and $cx_R^i > \underline{z}_{IP}$, let $\underline{z}_{IP} = cx_R^i$. Delete from L all problems with $\bar{z}^i \leq \underline{z}_{IP}$. If $cx_R^i = z_R^i$ go to Step 2, otherwise go to Step 5.
5. *Division.* Let $\{S^{ij}\}_{j=1}^k$ be a division of S^i. Add problems $\{IP^{ij}\}_{j=1}^k$ to L where $\bar{z}^{ij} = z_R^i$ for $j = 1, \ldots, k$. Go to Step 2.

Branch-and-bound using linear programming relaxations

Commercial codes for general mixed integer programs use linear programming relaxations. Here we discuss the strategies used by these codes. For simplicity, we confine the presentation to IP, however all of the ideas carry over straightforwardly to MIP's.

In the initial relaxation S is replaced by $S_{LP} = \{x \in R_+^n: Ax \leq b\}$. We also take $z_R(x) = cx$ in each relaxation.

Pruning criteria

When solving linear programming relaxations, the pruning criteria of in-feasibility, optimality and value dominance given in Proposition 8.3 are directly applicable. Suppose the linear programming relaxation at node i of the enumeration tree is

$$z^i_{LP} = \max\{cx: x \in S^i_{LP}\}, \text{ where } S^i_{LP} = \{x \in R^n_+: A^i x \le b^i\}.$$

If LP^i has an optimal solution, we denote the one found by x^i.

The pruning conditions are:

1. $S^i_{LP} = \emptyset$ (infeasibility)
2. $x^i \in Z^n_+$ (optimality)
3. $z^i_{LP} \le \underline{z}_{IP}$ where $\underline{z}_{IP}$ is the value of a known feasible solution to IP (value dominance). Note that if LP^i is solved by a dual algorithm, we may be able to prune before an optimal solution to LP^i is found. Also, we may wish to use the weaker condition $z^i_{LP} \le \underline{z}_{IP} + \varepsilon$ for some given tolerance $\varepsilon > 0$.

Division

Since we use a linear programming relaxation at each node, the division is done by adding linear constraints. An obvious way to do this is to take $S = S^1 \cup S^2$ with $S^1 = S \cap \{x \in R^n_+: dx \le d_0\}$ and $S^2 = S \cap \{x \in R^n_+: dx \ge d_0 + 1\}$ where $(d, d_0) \in Z^{n+1}$. If x^0 is the solution to the relaxation

(LP^0) $\quad z^0_{LP} = \max\{cx: x \in S^0_{LP}\}$ where $S^0_{LP} = \{x \in R^n_+: Ax \le b\}$

we can choose (d, d_0) so that $d_0 < dx^0 < d_0 + 1$. This is highly desirable since it yields $x^0 \notin S^1_{LP} \cup S^2_{LP}$ and therefore the possibility that, for $i = 1, 2$,

$$z^i_{LP} = \max\{cx: x \in S^i_{LP}\} < z^0_{LP}.$$

In practice, only very special choices of (d, d_0) are used.

Variable dichotomy: Here $d = e_j$ (the j-th unit vector) for some $j \in N$. Then x^0 will be infeasible in the resulting relaxations if $x^0_j \notin Z^1$ and $d_0 = \lfloor x^0_j \rfloor$. See Figure 8.3. Note that if $x_j \in B^1$, then the left branch yields $x_j = 0$ and the right branch yields $x_j = 1$.

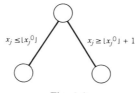

$x_j \le \lfloor x^0_j \rfloor \qquad \qquad x_j \ge \lfloor x^0_j \rfloor + 1$

Fig. 8.3.

An important practical advantage of this division is that only simple lower and upper bound constraints are added to the linear programming relaxation. Thus it is only necessary to keep track of the bounds and the size of the basis does not increase.

The size of the enumeration tree is obviously a function of the bounds on the variables. It is also very dependent on the quality of the bounds produced by the (linear programming) relaxation. In particular,

Proposition 8.4. *If node t of the enumeration tree with constraint set S^t is such that* $\max\{cx: x \in S_R^t\} > z_{IP}$, *then node t cannot be pruned.*

Proposition 8.4 indicates that, regardless of how we develop the tree, the bounds (quality of relaxations) are the primary factor in the efficiency of a branch-and-bound algorithm. Nevertheless, tree development strategies, such as which subproblem corresponding to an unpruned node should be considered next and which fractional variable should be selected for the dichotomous division, are also important. We now consider these problems.

Node Selection

Given a list L of active subproblems or, equivalently, a partial tree of unpruned or *active* nodes, the question is to decide which node should be examined in detail next. Here there are two basic options – *a priori rules* that determine in advance the order in which the tree will be developed, and *adaptive rules* that choose a node using information (bounds, etc.) about the status of the active nodes

A widely used (essentially) a priori rule is *depth first search* plus *backtracking* or *last in first out* (LIFO). In depth first search, if the current node is not pruned, the next node considered is one of its two sons. Backtracking means that when a node is pruned, we go back on the path from this node towards the root until we find the first node (if any) that has a son that has not yet been considered. Depth first search plus backtracking is a completely a priori rule if we fix a rule for choosing branching variables and specify that the left son is considered before the right son. An example of depth first search plus backtracking with left sons first is given in Figure 8.4. The nodes are numbered in the order in which they are considered. An underlined node is assumed to have been pruned.

Depth first search has two principle advantages:

1. The linear programming relaxation for a son is obtained from the linear programming relaxation of its father by the addition of a simple lower or upper bound constraint. Hence given the optimal solution for the father node, we can directly reoptimize by the dual simplex algorithm without a basis reinversion or a transfer of data.

2. Experience seems to indicate that feasible solutions are more likely to be found deep in the tree than at nodes near the root. The success of a branch-and-bound algorithm is very dependent on having a good lower bound z_{IP} for value dominance pruning.

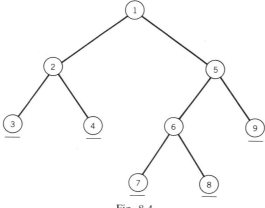

Fig. 8.4.

The default option in most commercial codes is depth first when the current node is not pruned. At least one son is considered immediately. Rules for choosing a son will be discussed later. However when a node is pruned, the next node is not generally determined by the backtracking strategy. Before explaining how this selection is done, we mention one other essentially a priori rule which is the opposite of depth first search. The level of a node in an enumeration tree is the number of edges in the unique path between it and the root. In *breadth first search*, all of the nodes at a given level are considered before any nodes at the next lower level. While this means of node selection is not practical for solving general integer programs using linear programming relaxations, it has some interesting properties, one of which is its use in heuristics.

Several reasonable criteria can be given for choosing an active node.

a. Choose a node that has to be considered in any case. By Proposition 8.4, if there is a unique node with the largest upper bound it must be considered. This argument mitigates for the rule *best upper bound*, i.e. when a node has been pruned, next select one from among the active nodes that has the largest upper bound. In other words, select an $i \in L$ that maximizes $\bar{z}^i$.

b. Choose a node that is most likely to contain an optimal solution. The reason for this is that once we have found an optimal solution, even if we are unable to prove immediately that it is optimal, we will have obtained the largest possible value of $\underline{z}_{IP}$. This is very important for subsequent pruning. Suppose $\hat{z}^i \leqslant \bar{z}^i$ is an estimate of z^i_{IP}. The rule *best estimate* is to choose an $i \in L$ that maximizes $\hat{z}^i$.

c. While trying to find an optimal solution is highly desirable, it may be more practical to try to find quickly a feasible solution $\hat{x}$ such that $c\hat{x} > \underline{z}_{IP}$. The criterion

$$\max_{i \in L} \frac{\bar{z}^i - \underline{z}_{IP}}{\bar{z}^i - \hat{z}^i},$$

which we call *quick improvement*, attempts to achieve this objective. Note that node i with $\hat{z}^i > \underline{z}_{IP}$ will be preferred to node j with $\hat{z}^j \leq \underline{z}_{IP}$. Moreover, preference will be given to nodes for which $\bar{z}^i - \hat{z}^i$ is small. One expects that such nodes will yield a feasible solution quickly. Quick improvement is used in some commercial codes as the default option once a feasible solution is known.

Branching variable selection

Suppose we have chosen an active node i. Associated with it is the linear programming solution x^i. Now we must choose a variable to define the division. We restrict it to the index set $N^i = \{j \in N: x_j^i \not\in Z^1\}$. Empirical evidence shows that the choice of a $j \in N^i$ can be very important to the running time of the algorithm. Frequently, there are a few variables that need to be fixed at integer values and then the rest turn out to be integer-valued in linear programming solutions. Because robust methods for identifying such variables have not been established, a common way of choosing a branching variable is by *user specified priorities*. This means that an ordering of the variables is specified as part of the input and that branching variables are selected from N^i according to this order. For example, a 0–1 variable corresponding to whether a project should be done would be given higher priority than 0–1 variables corresponding to detailed decisions within the project.

Other possibilities involve *degradations* or *penalties*. Degradation attempts to estimate the decrease in $\bar{z}^i$ that is caused by requiring x_j to be integral. Suppose $x_j = x_j^i = \lfloor x_j^i \rfloor + f_j^i$ and $f_j^i > 0$. Then by branching on x_j, we estimate a decrease of $D_j^{-i} = p_j^{-i} f_j^i$ for the left son and $D_j^{+i} = p_j^{+i}(1 - f_j^i)$ for the right son. The coefficients $\{p_j^{-i}, p_j^{+i}\}$ can be specified as part of the input or estimated in several different ways; e.g. by using dual information at the node or by using information on previous branchings involving x_j. Penalties involve more elaborate calculations to determine the coefficients $\{p_j^{-i}, p_j^{+i}\}$ and yield a lower bound on the decrease in $\bar{z}^i$. They were used in early commercial codes, but are not in favor now because they are too costly to compute relative to the value of the information they give.

Generalized upper bound constraints

Many integer programs with binary variables have *generalized upper bound constraints* of the form

$$\sum_{j \in Q_i} x_j = 1 \quad \text{for } i = 1, \ldots, p \tag{8.2}$$

where the Q_i's are disjoint subsets of N. Here we explore the branching scheme given in Figure 8.5, which has proved to be a very efficient way of handling these constraints and is widely used in mathematical programming systems.

Suppose in a solution of a linear programming relaxation, we have $0 < x_k < 1$ for some $k \in Q_i$. Conventional branching on x_k is equivalent to $x_k = 0$ or

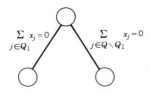

Fig. 8.5.

$\Sigma_{j \in Q_i \setminus \{k\}} x_j = 0$ since the latter equality is equivalent to $x_k = 1$. Now unless there is a good reason for singling out x_k as the variable that is likely to equal one, the $x_k = 1$ branch probably contains relatively few solutions as compared to the $x_k = 0$ branch. If this is the case, almost no progress will have been made since the node with $x_k = 0$ corresponds to nearly the same feasible region as its father.

It appears to be more desirable to try to divide the feasible region of the father roughly equally between the sons. To accomplish this, we consider the branching rule

$$\sum_{j \in Q_i'} x_j = 0 \quad \text{or} \quad \sum_{j \in Q_i \setminus Q_i'} x_j = 0 . \tag{8.3}$$

We can use (8.3) for any Q_i' such that $k \in Q_i'$ and $\Sigma_{j \in Q_i'} x_j < 1$. It seems reasonable to take Q_i' and $Q \setminus Q_i'$ of nearly equal cardinality.

A simple implementation of the branching rule (8.3) is obtained by indexing the variables in (8.2) as $x_{i_1}, x_{i_2}, \ldots, x_{i_t}$. The choice of Q_i' is then specified by an index j, $1 \le j \le t - 1$.

The optimization of piecewise-linear nonconvex functions can be done by branch-and-bound in a similar manner.

Branch-and bound using structure

Here we discuss briefly how branch-and-bound is combined with other bounding schemes, such as a Lagrangian dual, and with cutting plane algorithms.

When solving a structured problem for which the Lagrangian dual gives the upper bounds, it is natural to use the structure available in each subproblem to find good feasible solutions rapidly. Such solutions improve the lower bounds and hence help in pruning the tree. Heuristics for finding good feasible solutions will be presented in the next section. In addition, knowledge of the structure leads to special purpose branching rules.

As we have seen, strong cutting plane algorithms for structured problems require a separation routine for finding a violated valid inequality. If the separation routine fails, we can think of the cuts already added as giving a reformulation of the problem which can be solved by a standard branch-and-bound code. Again it is important to use special purpose branching rules, or priorities based on any special structure of the problem. In addition, it is desirable also to generate cuts at nodes of the branch-and-bound tree. Providing these are valid for the initial solution set S, this leads to a continuation of the reformulation during the enumeration with correspondingly tighter bounds. This approach has been used by Hoffman and Padberg (1985) among others, and is called *branch-and-cut*.

9. Heuristics

In this section we discuss ad hoc techniques for improving or simplifying the formulation of IP's, and some methods for finding and evaluating the quality of primal and dual feasible solutions.

Preprocessing

Given a formulation, preprocessing refers to elementary operations that can be performed to improve or simplify the formulation by tightening bounds on variables, fixing values, etc. Preprocessing can be thought of as a phase between formulation and solution. It can greatly enhance the speed of a sophisticated algorithm which might, for example, be unable to recognize the fact that some variable can be fixed and then eliminated from the model. Occasionally a small problem can be solved in the preprocessing phase or by combining preprocessing with some enumeration. Although this approach had been advocated as a solution technique in the early development of integer programming, under the name of implicit enumeration, this is not the important role of these simple techniques. Their main purpose is to prepare a formulation quickly and automatically for a more sophisticated algorithm. Unfortunately, it has taken a long time for researchers to recognize the fact that there is generally a need for both phases in the solution of practical problems.

Tightening bounds

We have seen that a common constraint in MIP's is $y_j \le u_j x_j$, where u_j is an upper bound on y_j and x_j is a binary variable. So long as $x_j \in \{0, 1\}$, the tightness of the upper bound does not matter. But if we consider a relaxation with $0 \le x_j \le 1$, it becomes important to have a tight bound. Suppose, for example, that the largest feasible value of y_j is $u'_j < u_j$, and there is a fixed cost $f_j > 0$ associated with x_j. If $y_j = u'_j$ in an optimal solution, and we use the constraint $y_j \le u_j x_j$, we will obtain $x_j = u'_j / u_j < 1$. On the other hand, if we use the constraint $y_j \le u'_j x_j$, we obtain $x_j = 1$.

In some cases, good bounds can be determined analytically. In general tight bounds can be determined by solving a linear program with the objective of maximizing y_j. Doing this for each variable with an upper bound constraint may be prohibitively time consuming, so a good compromise is to approximate the upper bounds heuristically.

Example 9.1. We show part of a fixed charge flow model in Figure 9.1 with the accompanying formulation:

$$y_1 + y_2 \qquad\qquad\qquad = 1.46\,,$$
$$y_3 + y_4 \qquad\qquad = 0.72\,,$$
$$-y_2 - y_3 \qquad + y_5 \qquad\qquad = 0\,,$$
$$y_6 \qquad = 0.32\,,$$
$$-y_5 - y_6 + y_7 = 0\,,$$
$$0 \leq y_i \leq \omega x_i\,, \quad x_i \in B^1 \quad \text{for } i = 1, \ldots, 7\,,$$

where ω is a large positive number since the arcs do not have capacity constraints.

It is easy to tighten the bounds giving $u_1 = u_2 = 1.46$, $u_3 = u_4 = 0.72$, $u_6 = 0.32$, $u_5 = u_2 + u_3 = 2.18$ and $u_7 = u_5 + u_6 = 2.50$. In addition, we can set $x_6 = x_7 = 1$ as the flow into node 7 must use these arcs.

Adding logical inequalities, fixing variables and removing redundant constraints

Preprocessing of this sort is most useful for binary IP's. Consider a single inequality in binary variables, i.e. $S = \{x \in B^n : \Sigma_{j \in N} a_j x_j \leq b\}$. Using the transformation given in Section 7 we can assume that $a_j > 0$ for $j \in N$. Now if $\Sigma_{j \in C} a_j > b$ for $C \subseteq N$, we obtain the cover inequality $\Sigma_{j \in C} x_j \leq |C| - 1$ derived earlier. Those for $|C| = 1$ or 2 are very easy to derive, and it may then be possible to combine some of them to fix variables. For example, $x_1 + x_2 \leq 1$ and $x_1 + (1 - x_2) \leq 1$ yield $x_1 = 0$.

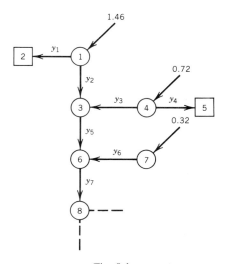

Fig. 9.1.

The application of these simple ideas is easy to see by considering an example.

Example 9.2. We use x_i' to denote $1 - x_i$.

$$-3x_2 - 2x_3 \leqslant -2 \quad (\qquad 3x_2' + 2x_3' \leqslant 3),$$
$$-4x_1 - 3x_2 - 3x_3 \leqslant -6 \quad (4x_1' + 3x_2' + 3x_3' \leqslant 4),$$
$$2x_1 - 2x_2 + 6x_3 \leqslant \quad 5 \quad (2x_1 + 2x_2' + 6x_3 \leqslant 7),$$
$$x \in B^3.$$

The first constraint yields $x_2' + x_3' \leqslant 1$ or $x_2 + x_3 \geqslant 1$. The third constraint yields $x_2' + x_3 \leqslant 1$ or $x_3 \leqslant x_2$. Combining these two yields $x_2 = 1$. Now the first constraint is redundant and the second and third reduce to $4x_1' + 3x_3' \leqslant 4$ and $2x_1 + 6x_3 \leqslant 7$. From these two, we obtain $x_1' + x_3' \leqslant 1$ and $x_1 + x_3 \leqslant 1$, or $x_1 + x_3 = 1$. Thus, by substitution, we can eliminate either x_1 or x_3.

A second stage of preprocessing can be carried out after an upper bound has been obtained by linear programming. In particular, variables can be fixed by using the reduced prices that are obtained from a linear programming solution. Let $\bar{c}_j$ be the reduced profit of nonbasic variable j in a basic optimal solution to the linear programming relaxation. Then a simple bounding argument gives

Proposition 9.1. *If x_j is nonbasic at its lower (upper) bound in the solution of LP, $x_j \in Z_+^1$ and $z_{LP} + \bar{c}_j \leqslant \underline{z}$ ($z_{LP} - \bar{c}_j \leqslant \underline{z}$), there exists an optimal solution to the integer program with x_j at its lower (upper) bound.*

Finding primal and dual feasible solutions

Heuristic or approximate algorithms are designed to find good, but not necessarily optimal, solutions quickly. For a variety of problems with structure, it is easy to devise heuristic algorithms to find primal and dual feasible solutions. It is particularly desirable to find both primal and dual feasible solutions since the dual solution provides an upper bound on the deviation from optimality of the primal solution. Depending on the quality of the solution required, an approximate solution can be the final answer to a problem or can be an input to an exact algorithm. The lower and upper bounds provided by approximate solutions can be of great help in decreasing the running time of branch-and-bound algorithms.

Though it is difficult to describe completely general heuristic algorithms, three ideas are applicable in a wide variety of cases. The first is that of a *greedy*, alternatively called a *steepest ascent/descent* or *myopic*, algorithm.

Greedy algorithms are frequently applied to the maximization of set functions. Let $v(Q)$ be a real-valued function defined on all subsets of $N = \{1, \ldots, n\}$ and consider the problem $\max\{v(Q): Q \subseteq N\}$.

A greedy (heuristic) algorithm for maximizing a set function.
Initialization. $Q^0 = \emptyset$, $t = 1$.
Iteration t. Let $j_t = \arg \max_{j \in N \setminus Q^{t-1}} v(Q^{t-1} \cup \{j\})$ with ties broken arbitrarily.
If $v(Q^{t-1} \cup \{j_t\}) \leq v(Q^{t-1})$, stop. Q^{t-1} is a greedy solution. If
$v(Q^{t-1} \cup \{j_t\}) > v(Q^{t-1})$, set $Q^t = Q^{t-1} \cup \{j_t\}$. If $Q^t = N$, stop. N
is a greedy solution. Otherwise, $t \leftarrow t + 1$.

The idea of this greedy algorithm is simple. Given a set Q^t, the next element
chosen is one that gives the greatest immediate increase in value, provided that
such an element exists. Moreover, once an element is chosen, it is kept
throughout the algorithm.

In the uncapacitated facility location (UFL) problem of Section 2, we can
maximize the function

$$v(Q) = \begin{cases} \sum_{i \in I} \max_{j \in Q} c_{ij} - \sum_{j \in Q} f_j & \text{for } \emptyset \subset Q \subseteq N, \\ -\infty & \text{for } Q = \emptyset \text{ (since } Q = \emptyset \text{ is infeasible)} . \end{cases}$$

Example 9.3. Consider the uncapacitated location problem with the following
data: $m = 6$, $n = 5$,

$$C = (c_{ij}) = \begin{pmatrix} 12 & 13 & 6 & 0 & 1 \\ 8 & 4 & 9 & 1 & 2 \\ 2 & 6 & 6 & 0 & 1 \\ 3 & 5 & 2 & 10 & 8 \\ 8 & 0 & 5 & 10 & 8 \\ 2 & 0 & 3 & 4 & 1 \end{pmatrix}, \quad f = (f_j) = (4\ 3\ 4\ 4\ 7) .$$

Applying the greedy heuristic described above, we obtain:
Iteration 1. $Q^0 = \emptyset$,

j	1	2	3	4	5
$v(Q^0 \cup \{j\})$	31	25	27	21	14

Iteration 2. $Q^1 = \{1\}$, $v(Q^1) = 31$,

j	–	2	3	4	5
$v(Q^1 \cup \{j\})$		35	33	38	29

Iteration 3. $Q^2 = \{1, 4\}$, $v(Q^2) = 38$,

j	–	2	3	–	5
$v(Q^2 \cup \{j\})$		40	39		31

Iteration 4. $Q^3 = \{1, 2, 4\}$, $v(Q^3) = 40$,

j	–	–	3	–	5
$v(Q^3 \cup \{j\})$			37		33

As $v(Q^3 \cup \{j\}) \leq v(Q^3)$ for all $j \notin Q^3$, $Q^3 = \{1, 2, 4\}$ is a greedy solution with value 40.

There are generally several greedy heuristics for a given problem and intuition must be used to convert the "greedy" idea into a reasonable greedy heuristic. An equally valid greedy approach for the uncapacitated facility location problem is to start with all facilities open, and one by one close a facility that yields the greatest increase in profit.

For the 0–1 packing problem $\max\{cx: Ax \leq 1, x \in B^n\}$ where A is a 0–1 matrix, one greedy approach is to recursively set that variable to one for which the resulting solution is still feasible and for which c_j is as large as possible. However, examination of one or two examples quickly leads to the idea that c_j should be divided by the number of 1's in the column a_j, i.e. the "improved" greedy criterion is to choose a column for which the average increase in profit per row covered $c_j / \sum_{i \in I} a_{ij}$ is maximum.

The second idea of importance is that of *local search* or *interchange* heuristics. As the name implies, a heuristic of this type takes a given feasible solution and, by making only limited changes, tries to find a better feasible solution.

A k-interchange heuristic for $\max\{c(x): x \in S \subseteq B^n\}$. Given a positive integer k, $k \leq n$, let

$$N_k(x) = \left\{ z \in B^n : \sum_{j \in N} |z_j - x_j| \leq k \right\} \quad \text{for } x \in B^n .$$

Initialization. Find a point $x^1 \in S$.

Iteration t. Given a point $x^t \in S$, look for a point $x' \in N_k(x^t) \cap S$ with $c(x') > c(x^t)$. If no such point exists, stop. x^t is a k-interchange solution. Otherwise set $x^{t+1} = x'$ and $t \leftarrow t + 1$.

Clearly the amount of work per iteration in this algorithm depends crucially on k, and for the heuristic to be fast we typically limit k to values of 1, 2 or 3. Observe that when $k = n$, the algorithm asks for an examination of all the points in B^n. Again, depending on the problem structure, it is usual to make variations in the definition of $N_k(x)$. For the uncapacitated facility location problem, one reasonable choice given a set Q of open facilities is to look at the neighborhood in which either one of the existing facilities is closed, or one new facility is opened, or both occur simultaneously, i.e.

$$N_2'(Q) = \{F \subseteq N : |F \setminus Q| \leq 1 \text{ and } |Q \setminus F| \leq 1\} .$$

The third general principle is that often primal and dual heuristic solutions can be found in pairs. The complementary slackness conditions of linear programming yield one way of pairing heuristic solutions. We use the 0–1 packing problem $\max\{cx: Ax \leqslant 1, x \in B^n\}$ also to illustrate this idea. The dual of its linear programming relaxation is $\min\{\sum_{i=1}^{m} u_i: uA \geqslant c, u \in R_+^m\}$. Given a heuristic solution u^* to this dual, let $N^* = \{j \in N: \sum_{i=1}^{m} u_i^* a_{ij} = c_j\}$. Then the choice of an associated primal heuristic solution is restricted to the vectors x with $x_j = 1$ only if $j \in N^*$. Moreover, if such a primal feasible vector x^* can be found that also satisfies $\sum_{j \in N} a_{ij} x_j^* = 1$ for all i with $u_i^* > 0$, then by complementary slackness x^* and u^* are optimal solutions.

The pairing of primal and dual heuristics is now demonstrated for the uncapacitated facility location problem. First we consider the dual of the linear programming relaxation of UFL (see Section 2):

$$z_{LP} = \min \sum_{i \in I} u_i + \sum_{j \in N} t_j ,$$

$$u_i + w_{ij} \geqslant c_{ij} \qquad \text{for } i \in I, j \in N .$$

$$-\sum_{i \in I} w_{ij} + t_j \geqslant -f_j \qquad \text{for } j \in N ,$$

$$w_{ij}, t_j \geqslant 0 \qquad \text{for } i \in I, j \in N .$$

We can eliminate constraints and variables from this formulation by observing that

(a) for given w_{ij}, the only constraints on t_j are nonnegativity and $t_j \geqslant \sum_{i \in I} w_{ij} - f_j$, and hence in any optimal solution $t_j = (\sum_{i \in I} w_{ij} - f_j)^+$;

(b) for given u_i, $\sum_{j \in N} (\sum_{i \in I} w_{ij} - f_j)^+$ is minimized by setting w_{ij} as small as possible, i.e. $w_{ij} = (c_{ij} - u_i)^+$.

Hence the dual can be rewritten as

$$z_{LP} = \min_{u \in R^m} w(u), \quad \text{where } w(u) = \sum_{i \in I} u_i + \sum_{j \in N} \left(\sum_{i \in I} (c_{ij} - u_i)^+ - f_j \right)^+ .$$

$$(9.1)$$

Now we consider the association of primal and dual solutions. Given a primal solution with $Q \subseteq N$ the set of open facilities, one way to associate a dual solution is to take u_i equal to the second largest c_{ij} over $j \in Q$. The motivation for this lies in the complementary slackness condition $(y_{ij} - x_j) w_{ij} = 0$. For $j \in Q$, $x_j = 1$ in the primal solution, and for each i there is one $y_{ij} = 1$ with $j \in Q$. Hence if the complementary slackness condition is to hold, at most one $w_{ij} > 0$ for each $i \in I$ and $j \in Q$. As $w_{ij} = (c_{ij} - u_i)^+$, this leads to the heuristic choice of u_i suggested above. Taking the greedy solution $Q = \{1, 2, 4\}$ obtained for Example 9.3, the associated dual solution is

$u(12\ 4\ 2\ 5\ 8\ 2)$. Using the formula in (9.1), we obtain $w(u) = 33 + (0 + 2 + 6 + 5 + 0) = 46$.

Now conversely, suppose we are given a dual solution u that satisfies $\sum_{i \in I} (c_{ij} - u_i)^+ \leq f_j$ for $j \in N$ and we wish to associate a primal feasible solution with it. The linear programming complementarity conditions suggest associating a primal solution in which $x_j = 0$ if $\sum_{i \in I} (c_{ij} - u_j)^+ < f_j$. Let

$$J(u) = \left\{ j \in N : \sum_{i \in I} (c_{ij} - u_j)^+ = f_j \right\}.$$

The best solution that satisfies complementarity is obtained by solving

$$\max_{Q \subseteq J(u)} \left\{ \sum_{i \in I} \max_{j \in Q} c_{ij} - \sum_{j \in Q} f_j \right\}.$$

However this problem may not be much easier to solve than the original problem UFL. Therefore we take as a primal heuristic solution $Q(u)$, any minimal set $Q(u) \subseteq J(u)$ satisfying

$$\max_{j \in Q(u)} c_{ij} = \max_{j \in J(u)} c_{ij} \quad \text{for all } i \in I. \tag{9.2}$$

The following proposition tells us when $(Q(u), u)$ are optimal to UFL and the dual of its linear programming relaxation respectively.

Proposition 9.2. *Given a u that satisfies $\sum_{i \in I} (c_{ij} - u_i)^+ \leq f_j$ for all j with $u_i \leq \max_{j \in J(u)} c_{ij}$ for $i \in I$, and a primal solution $Q(u)$ defined by (9.2), let $k_i = |\{ j \in Q(u) : c_{ij} > u_i \}|$. If $k_i \leq 1$ for all $i \in I$, then $Q(u)$ is an optimal set of open facilities.*

Now we present a heuristic algorithm for the dual problem (9.1) that uses the ideas of greedy and interchange. After finding a dual solution, the algorithm constructs a primal solution from (9.2) and then uses Proposition 9.2 to check optimality.

Dual descent (*A greedy algorithm for* (9.1)). Begin with $u_i^0 = \max_{j \in N} c_{ij}$ for $i \in I$. Cycle through the indices $i \in I$ one-by-one attempting to decrease u_i to the next smaller value of c_{ij}. If one of the constraints $\sum_{i \in I} (c_{ij} - u_i)^+ \leq f_j$ for $j \in N$ blocks the decrease of u_i to the next smaller c_{ij}, u_i is decreased to the minimum value allowed by the constraint. When all of the u_i's are blocked from further decreases, the procedure terminates.

A possible improvement of this greedy heuristic is obtained by modifying the order in which the u_i's are considered as candidates to decrease. The reasoning is the same as in the case of the 0–1 packing problem. Let $H(u_i) = \{ j \in N : c_{ij} - u_i \geq 0 \}$. Rather than just cycling through the u_i's, we choose u_s next if

$|H(u_s)| \leq |H(u_i)|$ for all $i \in I$, as this implies the smallest increase in $\Sigma_{j \in N} \Sigma_{i \in I} (c_{ij} - u_i)^+$ per unit decrease in $\Sigma_{i \in I} u_i$. This discussion also justifies decreasing u_i only to the next smaller c_{ij}, rather than to the smallest permissible value.

There is a branch-and-bound algorithm for the uncapacited facility location problem, called DUALOC (see Erlenkotter, 1978), which obtains primal and dual feasible solutions at each node of the branch-and-bound tree by using a dual greedy algorithm followed by interchange steps for problem (9.1) combined with the primal heuristic given by (9.2). If a node is not pruned by these heuristics, then branching is accomplished by taking a $j \in N$ and considering the two problems with $x_j = 0$ and $x_j = 1$.

Randomized heuristics

An interchange heuristic stops when it finds a "locally optimal" solution relative to the chosen neighborhood structure. As combinatorial optimization problems may have many local optima, it is typical to run an interchange heuristic many times with randomly chosen starting points.

A different approach for trying to obtain a global optimum using an interchange heuristic is called *simulated annealing*. Despite the fancy name, the idea is very simple. While an interchange heuristic produces a sequence of solutions with increasing objective value, here we allow the objective value to decrease occasionally to avoid getting stuck at a local optimum.

Consider the problem

$$\max_{Q \subseteq N} \{c(Q): Q \in \mathscr{F}\} . \tag{9.4}$$

Suppose Q^0 is the current solution and we find a point Q^1 in the neighborhood of Q^0. If $c(Q^1) > c(Q^0)$, we proceed as before by replacing Q^0 with Q^1. On the other hand if $c(Q^1) \leq c(Q^0)$, we replace Q^0 with Q^1 with probability p where p is a decreasing function of $c(Q^0) - c(Q^1)$.

The motivation for moving to a point with a smaller objective value is that if we are stuck in a shallow local optimum, there is a chance of escaping by moving to a neighboring point with a lower objective value.

The probability p can also be decreased as a function of the number of iterations. The reasons for doing this are to obtain convergence, and that as the global optimum is approached making steps away from the optimum becomes less attractive.

We now describe one version of the simulated annealing algorithm for (9.4). Let $N(Q)$ denote the neighbors of Q, let $\alpha_0 > 0$, $0 < \beta < 1$ and $i = 0$.

Iteration i.
    (1) Given Q^i, generate $Q' \subseteq N(Q^i)$.
    (2) (a) If $c(Q') > c(Q^i)$, then $Q^{i+1} = Q'$
        (b) If $c(Q') \leq c(Q^i)$, then $Q^{i+1} = Q'$ with probability $p = \exp((c(Q') - c(Q^i))/\alpha_i)$ and $Q^{i+1} = Q^i$ with probability $1 - p$.

(3) $\alpha_{i+1} = \alpha_i(1 - \beta)$.

Now provided that

(i) it is possible to move from any set $Q \in \mathcal{F}$ to any other set $Q' \in \mathcal{F}$ in a finite number of iterations,

(ii) each set in a neighborhood is chosen with equal probability,

(iii) the neighborhoods are symmetric in the sense that $Q \in N(Q')$ if and only if $Q' \in N(Q)$,

it can be shown that the algorithm converges to the global optimum. However, the provable rate of convergence is exponential.

The empirical efficiency of simulated annealing depends on the neighborhood structure and the function c. For some combinatorial optimization problems, such as the traveling salesman problem and a variety of problems related to circuit design, simulated annealing has found much better solutions than those obtained by random start interchange.

Analysis of heuristics

We have emphasized the importance of finding both primal and dual feasible solutions, particularly when a primal feasible solution is taken as an approximation to an optimal solution. The dual solution provides an upper bound on the deviation from optimality of the primal solution and thus gives an a posteriori evaluation of the quality of the primal solution.

In addition to this evaluation of an instance, it is sometimes possible to give an a priori evaluation of a heuristic algorithm over all instances. One way to obtain results of this type is by *worst-case analysis*, that is by basing the evaluation on the worst possible outcome. Such an evaluation is called a *performance guarantee*. Two typical results give a flavor of the types of performance guarantees that have been achieved. First consider the set-covering problem

$$(\text{SC}) \qquad z_{\text{SC}} = \min\left\{ \sum_{j\in N} c_j x_j : \sum_{j\in N} a_{ij} x_j \geq 1 \text{ for } i \in M, x \in B^n \right\}$$

where $a_{ij} \in \{0, 1\}$ for all i and j. We assume that $\sum_{j\in N} a_{ij} \geq 1$ for $i \in M$, which is necessary and sufficient for a feasible solution. Let $M_j = \{i: a_{ij} = 1\}$.

Greedy heuristic for set covering.

Initialization. $M^1 = M$, $N^1 = N$, $t = 1$.

Iteration t. Select $j^t \in N^t$ to min $c_j / |M_j \cap M^t|$. Let $N^{t+1} = N^t \setminus \{j^t\}$ and $M^{t+1} = M^t \setminus M_{j^t}$. If $M^{t+1} = \emptyset$, the greedy solution is given by $x_j = 1$ for $j \notin N^{t+1}$ and $x_j = 0$ otherwise. Its cost is $z_G = \sum_{j\notin N^{t+1}} c_j$. If $M^{t+1} \neq \emptyset$, then $t \leftarrow t + 1$ and return.

We see that at each step the greedy heuristic selects the column that meets the largest number of uncovered rows per unit cost and then stops when a feasible solution has been found.

For any positive integer k, let

$$H(k) = 1 + \frac{1}{2} + \cdots + \frac{1}{k} ;$$

also let

$$d = \max_{j \in N} \sum_{i \in M} a_{ij} \quad \text{and} \quad \theta^t = \frac{c_{j_t}}{|M_{j_t} \cap M^t|} \quad \text{(from iteration } t\text{)} .$$

It turns out that the vector u^* defined by $u_i^* = \theta^t / H(d)$ for $i \in M^t \setminus M^{t+1}$ for all t is feasible for the dual of the linear programming relaxation of SC. This leads to the following performance guarantee for the greedy heuristic for the set covering problem.

Theorem 9.3 (Chvátal, 1979). *For the set covering problem*, $z_{\text{SC}} / z_{\text{G}} \geqslant 1 / H(d)$.

Note that the bound is independent of n and the objective coefficients and decreases only logarithmically with $|M|$.

For the uncapacitated facility location problem with $f_j = 0$ for all j and the additional constraint that no more than p facilities can be open, which is called the *p-facility uncapacitated location problem*, the greedy heuristic yields the performance guarantee given by the following theorem.

Theorem 9.4 (Cornuéjols, Fisher and Nemhauser, 1977). *Let z_{G} be the value of a greedy solution and z_{UFL} be the value of an optimal solution to the p-facility uncapacitated location problem. Then*

$$\frac{z_{\text{G}}}{z_{\text{UFL}}} \geqslant 1 - \left(\frac{p-1}{p}\right)^p \geqslant \frac{e-1}{e} \cong 0.63 .$$

Worst-case analyses of the type given in Theorems 9.3 and 9.4 have been carried out for a large variety of integer programming problems, and the results are far too numerous to give details here. However, it is important to have an appreciation of the range of results.

There are some problems for which finding a polynomial-time heuristic (H) which guarantees any fraction of the optimal value is NP-hard. This class includes the traveling salesman problem, the node packing problem, a minimization version of the *p*-facility uncapacitated location problem and several others. For some other problems, polynomial-time heuristics with a positive performance guarantee are known, but there is a gap between the best available performance guarantee and the smallest performance guarantee for which the problem is known to be NP-hard. The p-facility uncapacitated facility location problem is in this category. Finding an optimal solution is known to be NP-hard. By Theorem 9.4, there is a fast algorithm for achieving a performance guarantee of $(e-1)/e$. But the status of the open interval $((e-1)/e, 1)$ is unresolved; i.e. neither is a polynomial-time algorithm known for achieving a performance guarantee greater than $(e-1)/e$ for an arbitrary value of p, nor is it known whether achieving a performance guarantee between $(e-1)/e$ and 1 is NP-hard.

At the positive end of the spectrum, there are NP-hard problems for which polynomial-time heuristics give a solution such that the heuristic value divided by the optimal value is at least $1 - \varepsilon$ for any $\varepsilon > 0$. These are called *polynomial-time approximation schemes*. Often the running time of the algorithm is a polynomial function of $1/\varepsilon$ as well as the usual parameters, in which case we speak of a *fully polynomial approximation scheme*. There are, for example fully polynomial approximation schemes for the integer and 0–1 knapsack problems (see Lawler, 1979).

Another approach to the analysis of heuristics is probabilistic analysis. Its significance depends on having a probability distribution of the instances that is both realistic and mathematically tractable. We illustrate with two examples. A random graph on n nodes is one in which the edges in the graph are selected at random. In the simplest of these models, the events of the graph containing any edge are identically and independently distributed random variables, i.e. the probability that $(i, j) \in E$ is q for all $i, j \in V$. When $q = \frac{1}{2}$ all possible graphs on n nodes are equally likely. Then the probability of some property Q occuring on such a random graph with n nodes is simply the fraction of n node graphs that possess property Q. We say that almost all graphs possess property Q if the probability approaches one as $n \to \infty$. For our purposes, property Q could be that a certain heuristic finds an optimal solution to a given problem whose instance is specified by an n-node graph.

To illustrate this idea, consider the *p-node edge covering problem* of choosing p nodes so that the number of edges incident to the chosen set is maximum. The greedy heuristic begins by choosing a node of maximum degree, deletes this node and all edges incident to it and then repeats the process until p nodes have been chosen.

Theorem 9.5 (Cornuéjols, Nemhauser and Wolsey, 1980). *For the p-node edge covering problem, if p does not grow too fast with n, then* (a) *the greedy heuristic finds an optimal solution for almost all graphs,* (b) *the greedy solution gives an optimal solution to the linear programming relaxation of the problem for almost all graphs.*

Another stochastic model deals with problems in which the data are points in the plane. For example, *the p-median problem in the plane* is the special case of the p-facility uncapacitated location problem in which C is an $n \times n$ matrix and c_{ij} is the euclidean distance between points i and j in the plane; the objective is to choose p facilities to minimize the total distance between the chosen p facilities and the others. Here it may be natural to assume that the points are placed randomly in a unit square using a two-dimensional uniform distribution.

For the p-median problem, very sharp estimates have been obtained on the asymptotic behavior of the optimal value of the objective function z_M (and its linear programming relaxation z_{LM}). By this we mean, as p and n approach infinity in a well defined way, $z_M(p, n)$ approaches a function that depends only on p and n with a probability that goes to one (almost surely). Results of this type also can be used to analyze the asymptotic performance of heuristics since, as we have already shown, it is frequently not hard to analyze the behavior of the objective values produced by simple heuristics.

Theorem 9.6 (Fisher and Hochbaum, 1980; Papadimitriou, 1981; Ahn, Cooper, Cornuejols and Frieze, 1985). *For the p-median problem,*
  (i) $z_M(p, n) \rightarrow 0.377(n/p)$ *almost surely;*
  (ii) $z_{LM}(p, n) \rightarrow 0.376(n/p)$ *almost surely;*
  (iii) *there exists a fast heuristic that almost surely finds a solution within a fraction ε of optimal for any $\varepsilon > 0$.*

Observe that, for this stochastic model of the p-median problem, the asymptotic value of the absolute value of the duality gap is very small.

A final comment on these models and results concerns what is deducible from $(z_M - z_{LM})/z_{LM}$ regarding the number of nodes L in a branch-and-bound algorithm that uses linear programming relaxation. It has been shown that $(z_M - z_{LM})/z_{LM}$ converges to 0.00284 almost surely. Nevertheless, it has also been shown that a branch-and-bound algorithm will almost surely explore a number of nodes that is exponential in p.

10. Notes

These notes are designed to give a brief, historical view and appropriate references. The material for this chapter is taken almost entirely from the book, *Integer and Combinatorial Optimization* by Nemhauser and Wolsey (1988) where the subject is covered in much greater breadth and depth.

Other recent and complementary books on integer programming include Papadimitriou and Steiglitz (1982), Gondran and Minoux (1984), Schrijver (1986), Parker and Rardin (1988) and Grötschel, Lovasz and Schrijver (1988). Developments in integer programming through the 1960's are covered in the book by Garfinkel and Nemhauser (1972). In addition, many journals contain articles on integer programming. Some of the most relevant ones are *Operations Research, Management Science, Mathematical Programming, The European Journal of Operational Research, AIIE Transactions, Annals of Discrete Mathematics, Operations Research Letters* and *Discrete Applied Mathematics*.

Four volumes of comprehensive bibliographies on integer programming have been prepared at Bonn University, see Kastning (1976), Hausmann (1978) and von Randow (1982, 1985). A much briefer, but annotated bibliography is the subject of ÓhÉigeartaigh, Lenstra and Rinnooy Kan (1988).

Section 2. The book of Williams (1978) contains twenty linear and integer programming problems that are formulated, solved and the solutions are discussed.

Section 3. The study of "good" model formulation is recent, although some of the basic ideas can be traced back to the seminal papers of Dantzig, Fulkerson and Johnson (1954, 1959) on the traveling salesman problem. This topic is intimately related to that of strong cutting plane algorithms treated in Section 7.

Reformulations of knapsack sets were studied by Bradley, Hammer and Wolsey (1974), Balas (1975a), Hammer et al. (1975), Wolsey (1975) and Balas and Zemel (1978). Crowder, Johnson and Padberg (1983) produced a successful algorithm for 0–1 problems based upon these results. The "good" formulation for the uncapacitated facility location problem is part of the folklore – however among the first papers to use it are those of Spielberg (1969a,b).

Held and Karp (1970, 1971) were among the first researchers to successfully use the traveling salesman formulation with the subtour constraints (2.16). Another formulation of current interest is that of Finke, Claus and Gunn (1984) which, by introducing additional flow variables, allows one to formulate important variants of the traveling salesman problem. The traveling salesman problem has motivated a fantastic amount of research throughout the years, culminating in a book edited by Lawler, Lenstra, Rinnooy Kan and Shmoys (1985), and most recently in the resolution of a 2392 city problem by Padberg and Rinaldi (1987a,b).

Reformulations using different variables is a subject of current interest, see Balas and Pulleyblank (1983), Barany, Van Roy and Wolsey (1984), Eppen and Martin (1987), Martin (1987a and 1987b), and Pochet and Wolsey (1988). The classical multi-commodity reformulation for fixed-charge network flows can already be found in Rardin and Choe (1979).

Section 4. The concept of NP-completeness of Cook (1971) and its developments due to Karp (1972, 1975) have had a profound influence on integer programming, see Garey and Johnson (1979). For the size of numbers of extreme points and facet-defining inequalities, see the papers by Karp and Papadimitriou (1982) and Grötschel, Lovasz and Schrijver (1984, 1988). For surveys see Lenstra and Rinnooy Kan (1979), Johnson and Papadimitriou (1985) and an annotated bibliography Papadimitriou (1985).

The important equivalence between "optimization and separation" has been discussed in Chapter 5, see Grötschel, Lovasz and Schrijver (1981).

Section 5. Geoffrion and Marsten (1972) were among the first to formalize the idea of relaxation in integer programming. Valid inequalities were used first in the papers of Dantzig, Fulkerson and Johnson (1954, 1959) cited above, but the approach was systematically developed by Gomory, and the integer rounding procedure appears in Gomory (1958, 1963). However, the viewpoint taken here is due to Chvátal (1973) and Schrijver (1980). Disjunctive inequalities are discussed in Balas (1975b, 1979), Blair (1976) and Jeroslow (1977). The connection between valid inequalities and superadditive functions originated with Gomory (1965, 1967, 1969) and was later developed by Jeroslow (1978) and Johnson (1974, 1980). Cook, Kannan and Schrijver (1987) contains recent developments.

The shortest path relaxation is due to Gomory (1965) and was developed further by Shapiro (1968a,b). Lagrange multipliers were used by Everett (1963) and Lorie and Savage (1955), and then systematically by Held and Karp (1971). Recently the idea of cost-splitting has attracted attention, see Jornsten and Nasburg (1986) and Guignard and Kim (1987) among others. For a related approach called surrogate duality, see Greenberg and Pierskalla (1970).

Benders (1962) algorithm is classical. One of the most interesting computational successes with the approach is that of Geoffrion and Graves (1974). Cross decomposition is a recent attempt to simultaneously use Benders' algorithm and Lagrangian relaxation, see Van Roy (1983, 1986).

Section 6. Superadditive duality in integer programming was explicitly developed in the seventies by Jeroslow (1979) and Johnson (1974, 1979, 1980a). See Wolsey for a survey (1981).

Lagrangian duality was motivated and explained in Geoffrion (1974). Surveys were presented by Fisher (1981) and Shapiro (1979). Some computational studies based on Lagrangian relaxation include papers on: the uncapacitated facility location problem, see Cornuejols, Fisher and Nemhauser (1977), Mulvey and Crowder (1979) and Neebe and Rao (1983); the capacitated facility location problem, see Geoffrion and McBride (1978); combinatorial scheduling problems, see Fisher (1973, 1976) and Potts (1985); power generator scheduling, see Muckstadt and Konig (1977); the generalized assignment problem, see Fisher, Jaikumar and Van Wassenhove (1986); production planning, see Graves (1982), Thizy and Van Wassenhove (1988) and Afentakis and Gavish (1986).

Section 7. The cuts (7.1) are due to Dantzig (1959), and the cuts (7.2) to Gomory (1958). Gomory developed a beautiful theory of cutting planes almost single-handedly in the 1960's. Gomory (1969) introduced the idea of lifting. However, the cutting plane approach was not successful computationally until the development of strong cutting plane algorithms in the late 70's. This is now one of the most active research topics in integer programming.

The first successes were with the traveling salesman problem, see Grötschel and Padberg (1976), Padberg and Hong (1980), Grötschel (1980), Crowder and Padberg (1980), and, most recently Padberg and Rinaldi (1987a,b).

Crowder, Johnson and Padberg (1983) developed a 0–1 integer programming cutting plane algorithm similar to the one described in this section.

Work on fixed-charged flow models started with Padberg, Van Roy and Wolsey (1985) and Van Roy and Wolsey (1985). Computational results are reported in Van Roy and Wolsey (1987) and Pochet and Wolsey (1988).

Numerous other problems have now been analyzed and tackled using this approach. A partial list follows: *lot sizing problems* see Eppen and Martin (1985), Pochet (1986), Goemans (1987), Wolsey (1988), and Leung and Magnanti (1986); *Steiner tree problems*, see Prodon, Liebling and Gröflin (1985); *generalized assignment*, see Gottlieb and Rao (1987); *machine scheduling*, see Balas (1985), Queyranne (1987) and Dyer and Wolsey (1987); *three index assignment problem*, see Balas and Saltzman (1986); *perfectly matchable subgraphs*, see Balas and Pulleyblank (1983); *set covering*, see Balas and Ho (1980), Balas and Ng (1985), and Cornuéjols and Sassano (1986); *node packing*, see Padberg (1973) and, Nemhauser and Trotter (1975); *facility location*, see Cornuejols and Thizy (1982b) Cho, Johnson et al., (1980) and Cho et al., (1983); *matching*, see Grötschel and Holland (1985); *max cut problem*, see Barahona, Grötschel and Mahjoub (1985), and Barahona and Mahjoub (1986); *mixed integer programming*, see Martin and Schrage (1985), and Van Roy and Wolsey (1986).

Section 8. See Beale (1979) and Land and Powell (1979) for descriptions of linear programming based algorithms and a survey of commercial mathematical programming systems. See Johnson and Suhl (1980) and Johnson et al. (1985) for two integer programming studies with such systems.

Nearly every algorithm for an NP-hard problem, which is not based on an LP based relaxation, is a special purpose branch-and-bound algorithm calling for the use of structure in all of the steps such as bounding, etc. Typically the bounds are computed very quickly and the branch and bound trees can be very large. Some typical computational studies and surveys are given in the following papers: *machine scheduling*, see Carlier (1982); *vehicle routing*, see Christofides (1985); set covering, see Baker and Fisher (1981) and Marsten and Shepardson (1981); *knapsack problem*, see Martello and Toth (1979, 1981) and Balas and Zemel (1980); *traveling salesman problem*, see Balas and Toth (1985); *fixed cost network problems and network design*, see Barr, Glover and Klingman (1981), Suhl (1985), Beasley (1984), and Magnanti and Wong (1984).

Parallel architectures can be used to speed up branch-and-bound searches; see, for example, Kindervater and Lestra (1986), Lai and Sprague (1985), Trienekens (1986) and Pruul et al. (1988).

Section 9. Preprocessing is part of most mathematical programming systems; see, for example, Brearley, Mitra and Williams (1975). Logical inequalities and their use in preprocessing have been studied by Guignard and Spielberg (1977, 1981) and Spielberg (1979).

The use of heuristics for problems with structure, in particular greedy and interchange heuristics, is classical. The importance of primal–dual heuristics is more recent. Baker and Fisher (1981) have developed an algorithm for the set covering problem based on primal–dual heuristics which is similar to the Erlenkotter (1978) approach to the uncapacitated facility location problem described in the text.

Randomized heuristics is a subject of current interest and research, see, Metropolis et al. (1953), Kirkpatrick, Gelatt and Vecchi (1983), Hajek (1985), Bonomi and Lutton (1984), Lundy and Mees (1986) and Maffioli (1986). Recently the idea of "tabu lists" yielded good results, see Glover (1985).

The analysis of heuristics flourished in the seventies, see Fisher (1980), Korte (1979), and Rinnooy Kan (1986) for surveys and Wolsey (1980) for an exposition of the significance of duality in analyzing heuristics.

Surveys of techniques and results in the field of probabilistic analysis can be found in Karp and Steele (1985). An annotated bibliography is given by Karp, Lenstra, McDiarmid and Rinnooy Kan (1985).

Interactive computational systems are important for the effective implementation of heuristics, see Fisher (1986).

References

R. Aboudi and G.L. Nemhauser (1987), A strong cutting plane algorithm for an assignment problem with side constraints, Report J-87-3, Industrial and Systems Engineering, Georgia Institute of Technology.

P. Afentakis and B. Gavish (1986), Optimal lot-sizing algorithms for complex product structures, *Operations Research* **34**, 237–249.

S. Ahn, C. Cooper, G. Cornuéjols and A.M. Frieze (1988), Probabilistic analysis of a relaxation for the *k*-median problem, *Mathematics of Operations Research* **13**, 1–31.

E.K. Baker and M.L. Fisher (1981), Computational results for very large air crew scheduling problems, *Omega* **9**, 613–618.

E. Balas (1975a), Facets of the knapsack polytope, *Mathematical Programming* 8, 146–164.

E. Balas (1975b), Disjunctive programming: Cutting planes from logical conditions, in: O.L. Mangasarian et al. (eds.), *Nonlinear Programming 2* (Academic Press, New York) 279–312.

E. Balas (1979), Disjunctive programming, *Annals of Discrete Mathematics* **5**, 3–51.

E. Balas (1985), On the facial structure of scheduling polyhedra, *Mathematical Programming Study* **24**, 197–218.

E. Balas and A. Ho (1980), Set covering algorithms using cutting planes, heuristics, and subgradient optimization: A computational study, *Mathematical Programming Study* 12, 37–60.

E. Balas and S.M. Ng (1989), On the set covering polytope I: All facets with coefficients in $\{0, 1, 2\}$, *Mathematical Programming* **43**, 57–70.

E. Balas and W.R. Pulleyblank (1983), The perfectly matchable subgraph polytope of a bipartite graph, *Networks* **13**, 486–516.

E. Balas and M.J. Saltzman (1986), Facets of the three-index assignment polytope, MSRR-529, Graduate School of Industrial Administration, Carnegie-Mellon University.

E. Balas and P. Toth (1985), Branch and bound methods, in: Lawler, Lenstra et al. (1985) 361–403.

E. Balas and E. Zemel (1978), Facets of the knapsack polytope from minimal covers, *SIAM Journal on Applied Mathematics* **34**, 119–148.

E. Balas and E. Zemel (1980), An algorithm for large zero–one knapsack problems, *Operations Research* **28**, 1130–1145.

F. Barahona, M. Grotschel and A.R. Mahjoub (1985), Facets of the bipartite subgraph polytope, *Mathematics of Operations Research* **10**, 340–358.

F. Barahona and A.R. Mahjoub (1986), On the cut polytope, *Mathematical Programming* **36**, 157–173.

I. Barany, T.J. Van Roy and L.A. Wolsey (1984), Uncapacitated lot-sizing: The convex hull of solutions, *Mathematical Programming Study* **22**, 32–43.

R.S. Barr, F. Glover and D. Klingman (1981), A new optimization method for large scale fixed charge transportation problems, *Operations Research* **29**, 448–463.

E.M.L. Beale (1979), Branch and bound methods for mathematical programming systems, *Annals of Discrete Mathematics* **5**, 201–219.

J.E. Beasley (1984), An algorithm for the Steiner problem in graphs, *Networks* **14**, 147–160.

J.F. Benders (1962), Partitioning procedures for solving mixed variables programming problems, *Numerische Mathematik* **4**, 238–252.

O. Bilde and J. Krarup, (1977), Sharp lower bounds and efficient algorithms for the simple plant location problem, *Annals of Discrete Mathematics* **1**, 79–97.

C.E. Blair (1976), Two rules for deducing valid inequalities for 0–1 problems, *SIAM Journal of Applied Mathematics* **31**, 614–617.

E. Bonomi and J.L. Lutton (1984), The *N*-city travelling salesman problem: Statistical mechanics and the metropolis algorithm, *SIAM Review* 26, 551–568.

G.H. Bradley, P.L. Hammer and L.A. Wolsey (1974), Coefficient reduction for inequalities in 0–1 variables, *Mathematical Programming* **7**, 263–282.

A.L. Brearley, G. Mitra and H.P. Williams (1975), An analysis of Mathematical programming problems prior to applying the simplex method, *Mathematical Programming* **8**, 54–83.

J. Carlier (1982), The one-machine sequencing problem, *European Journal of Operations Research* **11**, 42–47.

D.C. Cho, E.L. Johnson, M.W. Padberg and M.R. Rao (1983), On the uncapacitated plant location problem I: Valid inequalities and facets, *Mathematics of Operations Research* **8**, 579–589.

D.C. Cho, M.W. Padberg and M.R. Rao (1983), On the uncapacitated plant location problem II: Facets and lifting theorems, *Mathematics of Operations Research* **8**, 590–612.

N. Christofides (1985), Vehicle routing, in: Lawler, Lenstra et al. (1985) 431–448.

V. Chvátal (1973), Edmonds polytopes and a hierarchy of combinatorial problems, *Discrete Mathematics* **4**, 305–337.

V. Chvátal (1979), A greedy heuristic for the set covering problem, *Mathematics of Operations Research* **4**, 233–235.

S.A. Cook (1971), The complexity of theorem-proving procedures, in: *Proceedings of the 3rd Annual ACM Symposium on Theory of Computing Machinery*, ACM.

W. Cook, R. Kannan and A. Schrijver (1987), Chvátal closures for mixed integer programming problems, Report No. 86444-OR, Bonn University.

G. Cornuéjols, M.L. Fisher and G.L. Nemhauser (1977), Location of bank accounts to optimize float: An analytic study of exact and approximate algorithms, *Management Science* **23**, 789–810.

G. Cornuéjols, G.L. Nemhauser and L.A. Wolsey (1980), Worst case and probabilistic analysis of algorithms for a location problem, *Operations Research* **28**, 847–858.

G. Cornuéjols and A. Sassano (1989), On the 0, 1 facets of the set covering polytope, *Mathematical Programming* **43**, 45–56.

G. Cornuéjols and J.M. Thizy (1982), Some facets of the simple plant location polytope, *Mathematical Programming* **23**, 50–74.

H.P. Crowder, E.L. Johnson and M.W. Padberg (1983), Solving large-scale zero–one linear programming problems, *Operations Research* **31**, 803–834.

H.P. Crowder and M.W. Padberg (1980), Solving large-scale symmetric traveling salesman problems to optimality, *Management Science* **26**, 495–509.

G.B. Dantzig (1959), Note on solving linear programs in integers, *Naval Research Logistics Quarterly* **6**, 75–76.

G.B. Dantzig, D.R. Fulkerson and S.M. Johnson (1954), Solution of a large-scale traveling salesman problem, *Operations Research* **2**, 393–410.

G.B. Dantzig, D.R. Fulkerson and S.M. Johnson (1959), On a linear-programming, combinatorial approach to the traveling salesman problem, *Operations Research* **7**, 58–66.

M. Dyer and L.A. Wolsey (1987), Formulating the single machine sequencing problem with release dates as a mixed integer program, RO 870629, Département de Mathematiques, Ecole Polytechnique Fédérale de Lausanne.

G.D. Eppen and R.K. Martin (1987), Solving multi-item capacitated lot-sizing problems using variable redefinition, *Operations Research* **35**, 832–848.

D. Erlenkotter (1978), A dual-based procedure for uncapacitated facility location, *Operations Research* **26**, 992–1009.

H. Everett, III (1963), Generalized Lagrange multiplier method for solving problems of optimum allocation of resources, *Operations Research* **11**, 399–417.

G. Finke, A. Claus and E. Gunn (1984), A two commodity network flow approach to the travelling salesman problem, *Congressus Numerantium* **41**, 167–178.

M.L. Fisher (1973), Optimal solution of scheduling problems using Lagrange multipliers: Part I, *Operations Research* **21**, 1114–1127.

M.L. Fisher (1976), A dual algorithm for the one-machine scheduling problem, *Mathematical Programming* **11**, 229–251.

M.L. Fisher (1980), Worst-case analysis of heuristic algorithms, *Management Science* **26**, 1–18.

M.L. Fisher (1981), The Lagrangian relaxation method for solving integer programming problems, *Management Science* **27**, 1–18.

M.L. Fisher (1986), Interactive optimization, *Annals of Operations Research* **4**, 541–556.

M.L. Fisher and D.S. Hochbaum (1980), Probabilistic analysis of the planar K-median problem, *Mathematics of Operations Research* **5**, 27–34.

M.L. Fisher, R. Jaikumar and L.N. Van Wassenhove (1986), A multiplier adjustment method for the generalized assignment problem, *Management Science* **32**, 1095–1103.

M.R. Garey and D.S. Johnson (1979), *Computers and Intractibility: A Guide to the Theory of NP-Completeness* (Freeman, New York).

R.S. Garfinkel and G.L. Nemhauser (1972), *Integer Programming* (Wiley, New York).

A.M. Geoffrion (1974), Lagrangean relaxation for integer programming, *Mathematical Programming Study* **2**, 82–114.

A.M. Geoffrion and G. Graves (1974), Multicommodity distribution system design by Benders decomposition, *Management Science* **20**, 822–844.

A.M. Geoffrion and R.E. Marsten (1972), Integer programming algorithms: A framework and state-of-the-art survey, *Management Science* **18**, 465–491.

A.M. Geoffrion and R. McBride (1978), Lagrangian relaxation applied to capacitated facility location problems, *AIIE Transactions* **10**, 40–47.

R. Giles and W.R. Pulleyblank (1979), Total dual integrality and integral polyhedra, *Linear Algebra and Its Applications* **25**, 191–196.

F. Glover (1985), Future paths for integer programming and links to artificial intelligence, Report 85-8, Center for Applied Artificial Intelligence, University of Colorado.

M. Goemans, (1987), Generation Dynamique d'Inequalites Valables pour des Problemes de Planification de la Production comprenant des Temps de Lancement", Engineer's Thesis, Universite Catholique de Louvain.

R.E. Gomory (1958), Outline of an algorithm for integer solutions to linear programs, *Bulletin of the American Mathematical Society* **64**, 275–278.

R.E. Gomory (1963), An algorithm for integer solutions to linear programs, in: R. Graves and P. Wolfe (eds.), *Recent Advances in Mathematical Programming* (McGraw-Hill, New York, 269–302.

R.E. Gomory (1965), On the relation between integer and non-integer solutions to linear programs, *Proceedings of the National Academy of Science* **53**, 260–265.

R.E. Gomory (1967), Faces of an integer polyhedron, *Proceedings of the National Academy of Science* **57**, 16–18.

R.E. Gomory (1969), Some polyhedra related to combinatorial problems, *Linear Algebra and Its Applications* **2**, 451–558.

M. Gondran and M. Minoux (1984), *Graphs and Algorithms* (Wiley-Interscience, New York).

E.S. Gottleib and M.R. Rao (1986), The generalized assignment Problem I: Valid inequalities and facets, School of Business Administration, New York University.

S.C. Graves (1982), Using Lagrangean techniques to solve hierarchical production planning problems, *Management Science* **28**, 260–274.

H.J. Greenberg and W.P. Pierskalla (1970), Surrogate mathematical programming, *Operations Research* **18**, 924–939.

M. Grötschel (1980), On the symmetric travelling salesman problem: Solution of a 120-city problem, *Mathematical Programming Study* **12**, 61–77.

M. Grötschel and O. Holland (1985), Solving matching problems with linear programming, *Mathematical Programming* **33**, 243–259.

M. Grötschel, M. Junger and G. Reinelt (1984), A cutting plane algorithm for the linear ordering problem, *Operations Research* **32**, 1195–1220.

M. Grötschel, L. Lovasz and A. Schrijver (1981), The ellipsoid method and its consequences in combinatorial optimization, *Combinatorica* **1**, 169–197.

M. Grötschel, L. Lovasz and A. Schrijver (1984), Geometric methods in combinatorial optimization, in: W. Pulleyblank (ed.), *Progress in Combinatorial Optimization* (Academic Press, New York) 167–184.

M. Grötschel, L. Lovasz and A. Schrijver (1988), *Geometric Algorithms and Combinatorial Optimization* (Springer, Berlin).

M. Grötschel and M.W. Padberg (1979), On the symmetric travelling salesman problem 1: Inequalities, *Mathematical Programming* **16**, 265–280.

M. Guignard and S. Kim (1987), Lagrangian decomposition: A model yielding stronger Lagrangian bounds, *Mathematical Programming* **39**, 215–228.

M. Guignard and K. Spielberg (1977), Reduction methods for state enumeration integer programming, *Annals of Discrete Mathematics* **1**, 273–286.

M. Guignard and K. Spielberg (1981), Logical reduction methods in zero–one programming (Minimal preferred variables), *Operations Research* **29**, 49–74.

B. Hajek (1985), A tutorial survey of theory and applications of simulated annealing, *Proceedings of the 24th IEEE Conference on Decision and Control*, 755–760.

P.L. Hammer, E.L. Johnson and U.N. Peled (1975), Facets of regular 0–1 polytopes, *Mathematical Programming* **8**, 179–206.

D. Hausmann (1978) (ed.), *Integer Programming and Related Areas: A Classified Bibliography 1976–1978* (Springer, Berlin).

M. Held and R.M. Karp (1970), The traveling salesman problem and minimum spanning trees, *Operations Research* **18**, 1138–1162.

M. Held and R.M. Karp (1971), The traveling salesman problem and minimal spanning trees: Part II, *Mathematical Programming* **1**, 6–25.

K. Hoffman and M. Padberg (1985), LP-based combinatorial problem solving, *Annals of Operations Research* **4**, 145–194.

R.G. Jeroslow (1972), There cannot be any algorithm for integer programming with quadratic constraints, *Operations Research* **21**, 221–224.

R.G. Jeroslow (1977), Cutting plane theory: Disjunctive methods, *Annals of Discrete Mathematics* **1**, 293–330.

R.G. Jeroslow (1978), Cutting plane theory: Algebraic methods, *Discrete Mathematics* **23**, 121–150.

R.G. Jeroslow (1979), An introduction to the theory of cutting planes, *Annals of Discrete Mathematics* **5**, 71–95.

D.S. Johnson and C.H. Papadimitriou (1985), Computational Complexity, in: Lawler, Lenstra et al. (1985) 37–86.

E.L. Johnson (1973), Cyclic groups, cutting planes and shortest paths, in: T.C. Hu and S. Robinson (eds.), *Mathematical Programming* (Academic Press, New York) 195–211.

E.L. Johnson (1974), On the group problem for mixed integer programming, *Mathematical Programming Study* **2**, 137–179.

E.L. Johnson (1979), On the group problem and a subadditive approach to integer programming, *Annals of Discrete Mathematics* **5**, 97–112.

E.L. Johnson, (1980), *Integer Programming-Facets, Subadditivity, and Duality for Group and Semi-group Problems* (SIAM Publications, Philadelphia).

E.L. Johnson, M.M. Kostreva and U.H. Suhl (1985), Solving 0–1 Integer Programming Problems Arising from Large Scale Planning Models, *Operations Research* 33, 803–819.

E.L. Johnson and U.H. Suhl (1980), Experiments in integer programming, *Discrete Applied Mathematics* 2, 39–55.

K.O. Jornsten and M. Nasberg (1986), A new Lagrangian relaxation approach to the generalized assignment problem, *European Journal of Operations Research* 27, 313–323.

R.M. Karp (1972), Reducibility among combinatorial problems, in: R.E. Miller and J.W. Thatcher (eds.), *Complexity of Computer Computations* (Plenum Press, New York) 85–103.

R.M. Karp (1975), On the complexity of combinatorial problems, *Networks* 5, 45–68.

R.M. Karp, J.K. Lenstra, C.J.H. McDiarmid and A.H.G. Rinnooy Kan (1985), Probabilistic analysis, in: ÓhÉigeartaigh et al. (1985) 52–88.

R.M. Karp and C.H. Papadimitriou (1982), On linear characterizations of combinatorial optimization problems, *SIAM Journal on Computing* 11, 620–632.

R.M. Karp and J.M. Steele (1985), Probabilistic analysis of heuristics, in: Lawler, Lenstra et al. (1985) 207–250.

C. Kastning (1976) (ed.), *Integer Programming and Related Areas, A Classified Bibliography*, Lecture Notes in Economics and Mathematical Systems 128 (Springer, Berlin).

G.A.P. Kindervater and J.K. Lenstra (1986), An introduction to parallelism in combinatorial optimization, *Discrete Applied Mathematics* 14, 135–156.

S. Kirkpatrick, C.D. Gelatt Jr. and M.P. Vecchi (1983), Optimization by simulated annealing, *Science* 220, 671–680.

B. Korte (1979), Approximative algorithms for discrete optimization problems, *Annals of Discrete Mathematics* 4, 85–120.

J. Krarup and O. Bilde (1977), Plant location, set covering, and economic lot-size: An $O(mn)$ algorithm for structured problems, in: *Numerische Methoden bei Optimierungsaufgaben, Band 3: Optimierung bei Graphentheoretischen und Ganzzahlligen Problemen* (Birkhauser, Basel) 155–186.

T.-H. Lai and A. Sprague (1985), Performance of parallel branch-and-bound algorithms, *IEEE Transactions on Computers* 34, 962–964.

A.H. Land and S. Powell (1979), Computer codes for problems of integer programming, *Annals of Discrete Mathematics* 5, 221–269.

E.L. Lawler, J.K. Lenstra, A.H.G. Rinnooy Kan and D.B. Shmoys (1985) (eds.), *The Traveling Salesman Problem: A Guided Tour of Combinatorial Optimization* (Wiley, New York).

H.W. Lenstra, Jr. (1983), Integer programming with a fixed number of variables, *Mathematics of Operations Research* 8, 538–547.

J.K. Lenstra and A.H.G. Rinnooy Kan (1979), Computational Complexity of Discrete Optimization Problems, *Annals of Discrete Mathematics* 4, 121–140.

J. Leung and T.L. Magnanti (1986), Valid inequalities and facets of the capacitated plant location problem, Working Paper OR149-86, Operations Research Center, Massachusetts Institute of Technology.

J. Lorie and L.J. Savage (1955), Three problems in capital rationing, *Journal of Business* 28, 229–239.

M. Lundy and A. Mees (1986), Convergence of an annealing algorithm, *Mathematical Programming* 34, 111–124.

F. Maffioli (1986), Randomized algorithms in combinatorial optimization: A survey, *Discrete Applied Mathematics* 14, 157–170.

T.L. Magnanti and R.T. Wong (1984), Network design and transportation planning: Models and algorithms, *Transporation Science* 18, 1–55.

R.E. Marsten and F. Shepardson (1981), Exact solution of crew scheduling problems using the set partitioning model: Recent successful applications, *Networks* 11, 165–178.

S. Martello and P. Toth (1979), The 0–1 knapsack problem, in: N. Christofides, A. Mingozzi, P. Toth and M. Sandi (eds.), *Combinatorial Optimization* (Wiley, New York) 237–279.

S. Martello and P. Toth (1981), A branch and bound algorithm for the zero–one multiple knapsack problem, *Discrete Applied Mathematics* **3**, 275–288.

R.K. Martin (1987a), Generating alternative mixed-integer programming models using variable redefinition, *Operations Research* **35**, 820–831.

R.K. Martin (1987b), Using separation algorithms to generate mixed integer model reformulations, Graduate School of Business, University of Chicago.

R.K. Martin and L. Schrage (1985), Subset coefficient reduction cuts for 0–1 mixed integer programming, *Operations Research* **33**, 505–526.

N. Metropolis, A. Rosenbluth, M. Rosenbluth, A. Teller and E. Teller (1953), Equations of state calculations by fast computing machines, *Journal of Chemical Physics* **21**, 1087–1091.

C.E. Miller, A.W. Tucker and R.A. Zemlin (1960), Integer programming formulations and traveling salesman problems, *Journal of the Association for Computing Machinery* **7**, 326–329.

J.A. Muckstadt and S.A. Koenig (1977), An application of Lagrangian relaxation to scheduling in power generating systems, *Operations Research* **25**, 387–403.

J.M. Mulvey and H.M. Crowder (1979), Cluster analysis: An application of Lagrangian relaxation, *Management Science* **25**, 329–340.

A.W. Neebe and M.R. Rao (1983), An algorithm for the fixed charge assignment of users to sources problem, *Journal of the Operational Research Society* **34**, 1107–1115.

G.L. Nemhauser and L.E. Trotter (1975), Vertex packings: Structural properties and algorithms, *Mathematical Programming* **8**, 232–248.

G.L. Nemhauser and L.A. Wolsey (1984), A recursive procedure for generating all cuts for 0–1 mixed integer programs, Core DP 8439, Université Catholique du Louvain.

G.L. Nemhauser and L.A. Wolsey (1988), *Integer and Combinatorial Optimization* (Wiley, New York).

M. ÓhÉigeartaigh, J.K. Lenstra and A.H.G. Rinnooy Kan (1985) (eds.), *Combinatorial Optimization: Annotated Bibliographies* (Wiley, New York).

M.W. Padberg (1973), On the facial structure of set packing polyhedra, *Mathematical Programming* **5**, 199–215.

M.W. Padberg and S. Hong (1980), On the symmetric traveling salesman problem: A computational study, *Mathematical Programming Study* **12**, 78–107.

M.W. Padberg and G. Rinaldi (1987a), Optimization of a 532-city traveling salesman problem by branch and cut, *Operations Research Letters* **6**, 1–8.

M.W. Padberg and G. Rinaldi (1987b), Facet identification for the symmetric traveling salesman polytope, New York University.

M.W. Padberg, T.J. Van Roy and L.A. Wolsey (1985), Valid linear inequalities for fixed charge problems, *Operations Research* **33**, 842–861.

C.H. Papadimitriou (1981), Worst-case and probabilistic analysis of a geometric location problem, *SIAM Journal on Computing* **10**, 542–557.

C.H. Papadimitriou (1985), Computational complexity, in: ÓhÉigeartaigh et al. (1985) 39–51.

C.H. Papadimitriou and K. Steiglitz (1982), *Combinatoral Optimization: Algorithms and Complexity* (Prentice-Hall, Engelwood Cliffs.)

R.G. Parker and R.L. Rardin (1988), *Discrete Optimization* (Academic Press, New York).

Y. Pochet (1988), Valid inequalities and separation for capacitated economic lot sizing, *Operations Research Letters* **7**, 109–116.

Y. Pochet and L.A. Wolsey (1988), Lot-size models with backlogging: Strong formulations and cutting planes, *Mathematical Programming* **40**, 317–336.

C.N. Potts (1985), A Lagrangian based branch and bound algorithm for single machine scheduling with precedence constraints to minimize total weighted completion time, *Management Science* **31**, 1300–1311.

E. Pruul, G.L. Nemhauser and R. Rushmeier (1988), Branch-and-bound and parallel computation: An historical note, *Operations Research Letters* **7**, 65–69.

M. Queyranne (1987), Structure of a simple scheduling polyhedron, University of British Columbia.

R.L. Rardin and U. Choe (1979). Tighter relaxations of fixed charge network flow problem, Industrial and Systems Engineering Report J-79-18, Georgia Institute of Technology.

J.M. Thizy and L. Van Wassenhove (1988), Decomposition algorithm for the multi-product lot-sizing problem with capacity constraints, *AIIE Transactions*, to appear.

A.H.G. Rinnooy Kan (1986), An introduction to the analysis of approximation algorithms, *Discrete Applied Mathematics* **14**, 111–134.

A. Schrijver (1980), On cutting planes, *Annals of Discrete Mathematics* **9**, 291–296.

A. Schrijver (1986), *Linear and Integer Programming* (Wiley, Chichester).

J.F. Shapiro (1968a), Dynamic programming algorithms for the integer programming problem 1: The integer programming problem viewed as a knapsack type problem, *Operations Research* **16**, 103–121.

J.F. Shapiro (1968b) Group theoretic algorithms for the integer programming programming problem-II: Extensions to a general algorithm, *Operations Research* **18**, 103–121.

J.F. Shapiro (1979), A survey of Lagrangian techniques for discrete optimization, *Annals of Discrete Mathematics* **5**, 113–138.

K. Spielberg (1969a), Plant location with generalized search origin, *Management Science* **16**, 1965–1978.

K. Spielberg (1969b), Algorithms for the simple plant location problem with some side conditions, *Operations Research* **17**, 85–111.

K. Spielberg (1979), Enumerative methods in integer programing, *Annals of Discrete Mathematics* **5**, 139–183.

U. Suhl (1985), Solving large scale mixed integer programs with fixed charge variables, *Mathematical Programming* **32**, 165–182.

H.W.J.M. Trienekens (1986), Parallel branch and bound on an MIMD system, Report 8640/A, Econometric Institute, Erasmus University, Rotterdam.

T.J. Van Roy (1983), Cross decomposition for mixed integer programming, *Mathematical Programming* **25**, 46–63.

T.J. Van Roy (1986), A cross decomposition algorithm for capacitated facility location, *Operations Research* **34**, 145–163.

T.J. Van Roy and L.A. Wolsey (1985), Valid inequalities and separation for uncapacitated fixed charge networks, *Operations Research Letters* **4**, 105–112.

T.J. Van Roy and L.A. Wolsey (1986), Valid inequalities for mixed 0–1 programs, *Discrete Applied Mathematics* **14**, 199–213.

T.J. Van Roy and L.A. Wolsey (1987), Solving mixed 0–1 programs by automatic reformulation, *Operations Research* **35**, 45–57.

R. von Randow (1982) (ed.), *Integer Programming and Related areas, A Classified Bibliography 1978–1981*, Lecture Notes in Economics and Mathematical Systems 197 (Springer, Berlin).

R. von Randow (1985) (ed.), *Integer Programming and Related Areas, A Classified Bibliography 1981–1984*, Lecture Notes in Economics and Mathematical Systems 243 (Springer, Berlin).

H.P. Williams (1978), *Model Building in Mathematical Programming* (Wiley, New York).

L.A. Wolsey (1975), Faces for a linear inequality in 0–1 variables, *Mathematical Programming* **8**, 165–178.

L.A. Wolsey (1980), Heuristic analysis, linear programming and branch and bound, *Mathematical Programming Study* **13**, 121–134.

L.A. Wolsey (1981), Integer programming duality: Price functions and sensitivity analysis, *Mathematical Programming* **20**, 173–195.

L.A. Wolsey (1988), Uncapacitated lot sizing with start-up costs, CORE Discussion Paper 8801, Université Catholique de Louvain.

R.T. Wong (1980), Integer programming formulations of the traveling salesman problem, *Proceedings of the IEEE International Conference on Circuits and Computers*.

G.L. Nemhauser et al., Eds., *Handbooks in OR & MS, Vol. 1*
© Elsevier Science Publishers B.V. (North-Holland) 1989

Chapter VII

Nondifferentiable Optimization

Claude Lemaréchal

INRIA, Domaine de Voluceau, BP 105 – Rocquencourt, 78153 Le Chesnay, France

There are many situations in operations research where one has to optimize a function which fails to have derivatives for some values of the variables. This is what Nondifferentiable Optimization (NDO) or Nonsmooth Optimization (NSO) deals with. For this kind of situation, new tools are required to replace standard differential calculus, and these new tools come from convex analysis.

Section 1 contains the necessary concepts and the essential basic properties, while some examples of practical problems motivating the use of NSO are listed in Section 2. In Section 3, we show how and why classical methods fail. Section 4 is devoted to some possibilities that can be used when a special structure exists in the nonsmooth problem. The so-called subgradient methods, coming mainly from the Soviet Union (Kiev), are studied in Section 5, and more recent methods, mainly developed in the West (the bundle methods), in Section 6. Finally, we give in Section 7 some orientations for future research; the relevant literature is reviewed in Section 8 with its bibliography.

Our development is by no means original but is largely based on the previous Zowe (1985). See also the somewhat similar review of Lemaréchal (1980).

1. Introduction

We will consider as a prototype problem the unconstrained minimization of a real function f:

$$\text{minimize } f(x) \text{ on } \mathbb{R}^n \tag{1.1}$$

where, in contrast to the standard situation, we do not require f to have continuous derivatives. More precisely: we are content if the gradient of f exists almost everywhere and if, at every point x where the gradient is not defined, at least the *directional derivative*

$$f'(x; d) := \lim_{t \downarrow 0} \frac{1}{t} [f(x + td) - f(x)] \tag{1.2}$$

exists in every direction d.

To simplify the presentation, we restrict most of our development to the case when f is a *convex function* from R^n to R (it is known that (1.2) then automatically holds). It is in this framework that things are easiest to explain. However, the theory can be extended to more general f with only technical changes.

Typically, the function f in (1.1) will be "piecewise-C^1", i.e. R^n will be composed of regions inside which the gradient ∇f exists and is continuous, and at the boundary of which ∇f jumps (although f itself is continuous). Consider, e.g. the function in one dimension:

$$f(x) := \begin{cases} -x & \text{for } x < 0, \\ x^2 & \text{for } x \geq 0. \end{cases} \qquad (1.3)$$

Then $\nabla f(x) = -1$ for negative x and $\nabla f(x) = 2x$ for positive x. At $x = 0$ the gradient is not defined but, obviously, the two limits $\lim_{x \uparrow 0} \nabla f(x) = -1$ and $\lim_{x \downarrow 0} \nabla f(x) = 0$ taken together characterize the (first order) behaviour of f close to the kink $x = 0$. This leads us to the following substitution of the gradient: the *subdifferential* of f at x is (conv denotes the closed convex hull)

$$\partial f(x) := \text{conv}\{ g \in \mathbb{R}^n \mid g = \lim \nabla f(x_i),\ x_i \to x,$$
$$\nabla f(x_i) \text{ exists}, \nabla f(x_i) \text{ converges}\} . \qquad (1.4)$$

This definition makes sense since, for convex f, the gradient exists almost everywhere. The subdifferential is a non-empty convex compact set which reduces to the gradient in case f is differentiable at x; the elements of $\partial f(x)$ are called *subgradients*. For the above f of (1.3) one gets: for $x \neq 0$, $\partial f(x)$ is the singleton $\nabla f(x)$, namely

$$\partial f(x) = \{\nabla f(x)\} = \begin{cases} -1 & \text{for } x < 0, \\ 2x & \text{for } x > 0, \end{cases} \qquad (1.5)$$

while

$$\partial f(0) = [-1, 0] . \qquad (1.6)$$

As expected, there is a close relation between the subdifferential and the directional derivative. Actually the directional derivative $f'(x; \cdot)$ is the *support function* of $\partial f(x)$, i.e.

$$f'(x; d) = \max_{g \in \partial f(x)} g^T d . \qquad (1.7)$$

It is easily checked, for example, that (1.7) together with (1.5) gives back (1.6).

The definition (1.4) is not the most classical one, but it lends itself to generalizations for nonconvex f. On the other hand, if f is convex, the differential quotient in (1.2) is monotonic in t; $f(x + d) \geq f(x) + f'(x, d)$ and this, together with (1.7), gives another equivalent characterization:

$$\partial f(x) = \{g \in \mathbb{R}^n \mid g^T(z - x) \leq f(z) - f(x) \text{ for all } z \in \mathbb{R}^n\} . \qquad (1.8)$$

Finally, for fixed x, $f'(x, d)$ is convex in d. As such, it has a subdifferential at $d = 0$, which is precisely $\partial f(x)$.

It is important to understand what (1.8) says, in addition to (1.7): the latter is local and, loosely speaking, means

$$f(x + td) \geq f(x) + tg^T d + o(t) \quad \forall g \in \partial f(x)$$

while (1.8) is global and says that, for all $t \geq 0$, $o(t)$ in the above estimate is nonnegative.

Properties (1.7) and (1.8) immediately give the *necessary and sufficient optimality condition* for the convex problem (1.1):

$$x^* \text{ is optimal for (1.1) (i.e. } f(x^*) \leq f(x) \text{ for all } x)$$

$$\Leftrightarrow 0 \in \partial f(x^*) . \qquad (1.9)$$

Hence the set X^* of optimal points for (1.1) is characterized by

$$X^* = \{x^* \in \mathbb{R}^n \mid 0 \in \partial f(x^*)\} .$$

To exclude pathological situations we will often assume that X^* is nonempty and bounded.

For the following, we will make the general assumption:

$$\text{At every } x, \text{ we know } f(x) \text{ and one (arbitrary) } g \in \partial f(x) . \qquad (1.10)$$

This assumption is actually fairly natural and a subgradient can usually be computed using only standard differential calculus (see Section 2 and more precisely Proposition 2.1). Loosely speaking: even if $\nabla f(x)$ does not exist, it does exist at some x_i "infinitely close" to x (see (1.4)) and this $g_i = \nabla f(x_i)$ is "infinitely close" to some $g \in \partial f(x)$. In practice, there will be a black box (a computer subprogram, sometimes called an oracle) which, given $x \in R^n$, answers $f = f(x)$ and $g \in \partial f(x)$. The situation will thus be similar to that in ordinary, smooth optimization, except that g will not vary continuously with x. For example, with f of (1.3), the black box could be

$$g := \begin{cases} -1 & \text{for } x < 0 , \\ 2x & \text{for } x \geq 0 . \end{cases}$$

By contrast, Section 4 will be devoted to problems for which the black box is more informative, namely

$$\text{At every } x, \text{ we know } f(x) \text{ and the full set } \partial f(x). \quad (1.11)$$

To finish this section, we mention the lines along which the present theory is extended to the non-convex case: the basic tool is still definition (1.4) which, as already mentioned, makes sense when ∇f exists on a dense set. This is the case when f is *locally Lipschitzian* and, as such, has a gradient almost everywhere. Then $\partial f(x)$ is still a convex compact set, its support function still defines, through (1.7), a certain generalization of the directional derivative. In many applications the locally Lipschitzian f will be the result of some inner maximization, say $f(x) = \max_y h(x, y)$; in this special situation, the directional derivative (1.2) does exist and is given in terms of the subdifferential (1.4) by formula (1.7) (see Proposition 2.1); however, the global property (1.8) does not hold, then.

2. Examples of nonsmooth problems

Functions with discontinuous derivatives are frequent in operations research. Sometimes they arise already when modelling the problem itself, sometimes they are introduced artificially during the solution procedure. The latter appears as soon as one is concerned with any kind of *decomposition*.

2.1. Inherent nondifferentiability

Let x, a nonnegative variable, represent an income. In many economic systems, it induces a *tax* $T(x)$, which has discontinuous derivatives; a set of thresholds is given:

$$0 = a_0 < a_1 < \cdots < a_m = +\infty$$

together with rates $r_0, r_1, \ldots, r_{m-1}$, and T is given as follows:

$$\text{for } a_i \leq x < a_{i+1}, \quad T(x) := T_i + r_i x$$

with $T_0 := 0$, $T_i := T_{i-1} + a_i(r_{i-1} - r_i)$ (so T is continuous! it must even be a contraction, $|r_i| < 1$! it should also be increasing, $r_i \geq 0$! and even convex, $r_{i+1} > r_i$!). See Figure 2.1.

Remark 2.1. Convexity of T corresponds to the explicit expression

$$T(x) = \max\{T_i + r_i x \mid i = 0, \ldots, m-1\}, \quad (2.1)$$

which is easily checked. With relation to (1.1), convexity is a nice property in the present context since one usually wishes to minimize taxes; however, it is not the general rule in operations research: on the contrary, one often has to minimize concave functions (economies of scale).

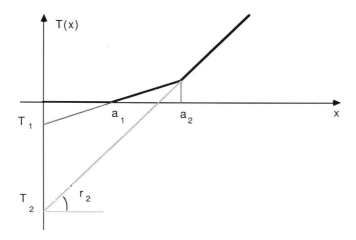

Fig. 2.1.

Expression (2.1) defines a class of functions which are frequently encountered in NSO, namely piecewise linear functions. More generally one can have functions like

$$f(x) = \max\{f_i(x) \mid i = 1, \ldots, m\} \tag{2.2}$$

where each f_i is smooth. Even more generally, one can have

$$f(x) = \max\{h(x, y) \mid y \in Y\} \tag{2.3}$$

where h is smooth with respect to x.

Minimizing a function given by (2.1), (2.2) or (2.3) is called the *minimax problem*. Note that computing f in (2.3) may be a time consuming task. These types of problems, however, are fully in the framework of assumption (1.10) thanks to the following result which states that g is available "for free" once f has been computed:

Proposition 2.1. *Let Y be a compact set, let $h(x, y)$ be a continuous function such that $\nabla_x h(x, y)$ is also continuous (jointly in x and y); then consider f defined by (2.3) and call*

$$M(x) := \{\nabla_x h(x, y) \mid y \text{ optimal at } x, \text{ i.e. } h(x, y) = f(x)\}$$

the set of "optimal gradients" at x. Then
  (i) conv $M(x) = \partial f(x)$ *of* (1.4)
  (ii) $f'(x, d) = \max\{g^T d \mid g \in M(x)\}$, *i.e.* (1.7) *holds.* □

Note, as a corollary, that f has a gradient whenever h is maximized at a single y, and differentiability usually fails when this y is no longer unique.

Functions of type (2.2) can be encountered in Tchebychef approximation, or also when the constraints of the optimization problem are treated through exact penalties. Note also, finally, that (2.3) is quasi equivalent to the so-called *semi-infinite programming* problem (T is an infinite set)

$$\min \ f(x) \quad \text{s.t.} \quad c(x, t) \leq 0 \ \forall t \in T$$

and both problems call for very similar methods.

2.2. Parametric decomposition

Suppose a given optimization problem has two (groups of) variables, x and y say, with the property that, for fixed x, minimizing with respect to y is very easy. An elementary instance of this situation is

$$\min c(x)^{\mathrm{T}} y, \tag{2.4a}$$

$$Ay = b, \tag{2.4b}$$

$$y \geq 0. \tag{2.4c}$$

Of course, it is then attractive to minimize with respect to y first, and then to minimize with respect to x the resulting function

$$f(x) := \min_y \{ c(x)^{\mathrm{T}} y \mid Ay = b, \ y \geq 0 \}. \tag{2.5}$$

Apply Proposition 2.1: at a given $\bar{x}$, call $y(\bar{x})$ the optimal polyhedron in (2.5). Provided $Y(\cdot)$ remains bounded in the neighborhood of $\bar{x}$, we have

$$\partial f(\bar{x}) = \{ C'(\bar{x})^{\mathrm{T}} y \mid y \in Y(\bar{x}) \},$$

where C' is the Jacobian matrix of $c(\cdot)$ (observe that $C'^{\mathrm{T}} Y(\bar{x})$ is its own closed convex hull). Thus, computing the full ∂f implies the knowledge of *all solutions* of the linear program, while (1.10) amounts to finding one (arbitrary) solution.

Let us illustrate this point. Suppose (2.5) has a unique solution $\bar{y}$ at $\bar{x}$. For x close enough to $\bar{x}$, $\bar{y}$ is still the unique solution (see Figure 2.2), so $f(x) = c(x) \cdot \bar{y}$ and the variation of c alone gives the variation of f:

$$\nabla f(\bar{x}) = C_x'(\bar{x})^{\mathrm{T}} \cdot \bar{y}.$$

On the other hand, suppose there are several optimal y's in (2.5), i.e. $\bar{x}$ is a *kink*, where $\bar{y}$ jumps between optimal extreme points, say $\bar{y}$ and $\bar{y}_1$ on Figure 2.2; then ∇f jumps between $C'^{\mathrm{T}}\bar{y}$ and $C'^{\mathrm{T}}\bar{y}_1$, each of these two vectors being a valid gradient in some region of the x-space. All this is just what Proposition 2.1 says.

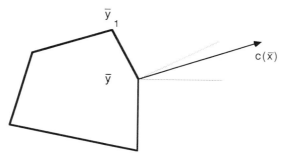

Fig. 2.2.

2.3. Decomposition by prices

Common optimization problems, in operations research, have the separable form

$$\min \sum_{i=1}^{n} f_i(x_i) , \qquad (2.6a)$$

$$\sum_{i=1}^{n} a_i(x_i) = 0 \qquad (2.6b)$$

where each $a_i(x) \in R^m$, say. Forming the Lagrangian function (with $u \in R^m$)

$$L(x, u) := \sum [f_i(x_i) + u^{\mathrm{T}} a_i(x_i)] \qquad (2.7)$$

and the dual function

$$q(u) := \min_x L(x, u) = \sum_i \min_{x_i} [f_i(x_i) + u^{\mathrm{T}} a_i(x_i)]$$

(obtainable via a minimization simpler than (2.6) because it is decomposed), the dual problem

$$\max \ q(u)$$

is sometimes useful for the solution of (2.6). Again, it is a problem of the form (1.1) and again, from Proposition 2.1, after computing $q(u)$ to obtain a primal variable $\bar{x}$, say, the constraint value $\sum a_i(\bar{x})$ gives either $\nabla q(u)$ (if $\bar{x}$ is the unique minimizer of $L(u, \cdot)$) or a subgradient in $\partial q(u)$ (in fact, q is concave, so (1.8) holds for $-q$).

Remark 2.2. These properties are totally independent of any smoothness in (2.6). An extreme case is integer programming problems, where x in (2.6) is further constrained by

$$x_i \in \{0, 1\}, \quad i = 1, \ldots, n .$$

Forming the Lagrangian function (2.7), we now define the dual function as

$$q(u) := \min L(x, u) , \quad x \in \{0, 1\}^n ,$$

which is trivial to compute, *no matter how complicated the functions f and a are* (it suffices to store the values $f_i(0)$, $a_i(0)$, $f_i(1)$, $a_i(1)$). Yet, the results of this section remain valid and q is as simple as possible, namely piecewise linear as in (2.1) (with $m = 2^n$, however). □

Iterating over u to solve (2.6) is sometimes called "Lagrangian relaxation" and we see that it fully belongs to the field of nondifferentiable optimization.

2.4. Decomposition by quotas (or allocation)

Another decomposition scheme can be used for (2.6). Take n vectors $y_i \in R^m$ and consider, for $i = 1, \ldots, n$,

$$v_i(y_i) := \min_z \{ f_i(z) \mid a_i(z) = y_i \} . \tag{2.8}$$

Clearly, solving (2.6) just amounts to solving

$$\min \sum v_i(y_i) ,$$

$$\sum y_i = 0$$

which is essentially an unconstrained problem, but again non-smooth; differential properties of v_i are quite a technical subject; let us just mention that the subdifferential of v_i is given by Lagrange multipliers in (2.8), whenever this makes sense.

2.5. Stiff problems

An intuitive way to think of our kind of non-C^1 functions is to interpret them as C^2 functions with, at some points, very large eigenvalues in the Hessian matrix (then the gradient varies very rapidly).

Thus, smooth but badly conditioned problems can also be viewed as candidates for nonsmooth optimization. Although the theory of Section 1 does not apply, this view is still fruitful, in that it may help make classical methods more robust against large condition numbers. Section 6 below shows that *bundle methods*, precisely, consist in extending the theory of Section 1, so as to make it meaningful even for smooth f.

Remark 2.3. A conclusion of this Section 2 is that nonsmoothness is not reflected by any practical difficulty in computing gradients. All the examples above show that a nonsmooth function may be difficult to compute but, once this is done, a subgradient is readily obtained by applying usual differential calculus (Proposition 2.1). In this respect, and in view of (1.10) and Proposition 2.1, nonsmooth optimization is neither more nor less complicated than classical, smooth, optimization. □

3. Failure of smooth methods

3.1. Failure of convergence

In a classical smooth method one replaces f at x by a *linear or a quadratic model*

$$\nabla f(x)^{\mathrm{T}} d \quad [\approx f(x + d) - f(x)], \tag{3.1}$$

$$\nabla f(x)^{\mathrm{T}} d + \tfrac{1}{2} d^{\mathrm{T}} \nabla^2 f(x) d \quad [\approx f(x + d) - f(x)], \tag{3.2}$$

and one minimizes these models. Minimization of (3.1) on the unit ball gives the steepest descent and minimization of (3.2) gives Newton's method; compare formula (5.1) and (5.2), respectively. Obviously the above models are no longer defined at a kink and, close to a kink, they no longer provide an efficient approximation of f. If the minimal x^* is a kink (and this is almost the rule for non-smooth f), the search directions coming from either (3.1) or (3.2) become of little use when x approaches x^*.

As a result, the inappropriate smooth model (3.1) or (3.2) may cause convergence to a nonoptimal kink. Constructing examples to illustrate this statement is quite instructive. In R^2, consider the simple function

$$f_1(\xi, \eta) := 3(\xi^2 + 2\eta^2)$$

and apply the steepest descent algorithm, starting from $x_0 := (2, 1)$ (see the chapter on unconstrained optimization in this volume). A bit of calculation shows that $x_1 = (2, -1)/3$ and $x_2 = x_0/9$. Thus, the sequence $\{x_k\}$ generated by the steepest algorithm alternates between the two half-lines

$$H_{\pm} := \{(\xi, \eta) \,|\, 2\eta = \pm\, \xi\}$$

as shown on Figure 3.1, and tends to the optimal $x^* = (0, 0)$, as expected.

Now consider $f_2 := f_1^{1/2}$. Because its gradient is proportional to that of f_1, the same steepest descent algorithm generates the same $\{x_k\}$, which converges to the same $x^* = 0$, again optimal. Observe the new fact, however, that the corresponding gradient sequence $\{\nabla f_2(x_k)\}$ no longer converges to 0 but oscillates between the two fixed values $2^{1/2}(1, \pm 1)$.

Finally, construct a domain D containing the whole sequence $\{x_k\}$, for example

$$D := \{(\xi, \eta) \,|\, 0 \le |\eta| \le 2\xi\}$$

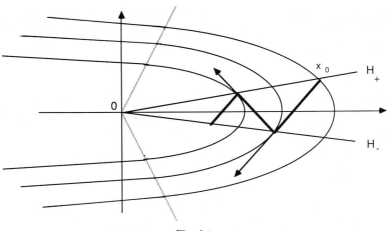

Fig. 3.1.

and modify f_2 out of D so that 0 is no longer optimal. For example extend the
contours of f_2 by half-lines outside D (see Figure 3.1). The following function

$$f(\xi, h) := \begin{cases} [3(\xi^2 + 2\eta^2)]^{1/2} & \text{if } 0 \leqslant |\eta| \leqslant 2\xi , \\ (\xi + 4|\eta|)3^{-1/2} & \text{otherwise} , \end{cases} \qquad (3.3)$$

does the job; it is convex, differentiable except on the left semi-axis, and
"minimal" at $\xi = -\infty$. Notwithstanding, $\{x_k\}$ still converges to 0, totally
ignoring the real behaviour of f.

Note that it is not difficult to perturb f_1 with a small non-quadratic term so
that the same disaster happens (faster) with Newton's method. We can also
make 0 the only kink in the space, or place the minimum of f where we want,
etc. . . At any rate, the lesson of this example is that it is unwise to use classical
Taylor models in nonsmooth optimization.

3.2. Failure of optimality test

Even without the pitfall of the above example, there remains a crucial
handicap for a smooth method in a nonsmooth context. This is the *lack* of an
implementable *stopping rule*. For a C^1-function the gradient will become small
in norm, say

$$|\nabla f(x_k)| \leqslant \varepsilon \quad (\varepsilon > 0 \text{ small}) , \qquad (3.4)$$

when x_k approaches some optimal x^*; this can be used to stop the iterations
automatically. However, for nonsmooth f a criterion like (3.4) does not make
sense, even if the gradient existed at all iterates. E.g., for the function
$f(x) := |x|$ we have $|\nabla f(x_k)| = 1$ in (3.4) at each $x_k \neq 0$, no matter how close x_k
is to the optimal kink $x^* = 0$.

Considering definition (1.4), a stopping rule based on the optimality condition (which is now (1.9)) implies an exploration of the whole space neighboring the limit x^* we are interested in. Section 6.2 will exploit this fact.

3.3. *Failure of gradient approximations*

Another nasty property of nonsmooth functions is that computing subgradients is compulsory and finite differences are dangerous. For $x = (\xi, \eta, \phi) \in R^3$, consider the example $f(x) := \max\{\xi, \eta, \phi\}$. Its subdifferential at the origin is the unit simplex (apply Proposition 2.1):

$$\partial f(0) = \text{conv}\{(1, 0, 0), (0, 1, 0), (0, 0, 1)\} .$$

On the other hand using forward, backward and central differences, we obtain respectively the points $(1, 1, 1)$, $(0, 0, 0)$ and $(\frac{1}{2}, \frac{1}{2}, \frac{1}{2})$ as candidates for an "approximate gradient"; none of them is close to $\partial f(0)$, i.e. none of them really represents the behaviour of f near x.

Actually, a mere finite differencing in nonsmooth optimization is a sin against mathematics. It is only because the differential $\delta f = \nabla f(x)^T \delta x$ varies linearly with the differential δx, in the smooth case, that it can be estimated by finite differences: a linear function is *uniquely determined* by its (finite set of) values on the canonical basis. No argument of that sort can be used in nonsmooth optimization, just because δf is *no longer linear* (see (1.7)): the differential δf must be estimated by $t^{-1}[f(x + td) - f(x)] = \delta f$ when $\delta x = td$ for all direction $d \in R^n$, and not only for a set of n directions.

Luckily, Remark 2.3 tells us that computing subgradients is usually not that difficult.

4. Special methods for special problems

In some problems, the nondifferentiability has a structure which makes them amenable to a classical, smooth, nonlinear programming problem. Basically, these problems are those where one *can construct* the full subdifferential $\partial f(x)$, and one *wishes to use* it numerically. Most of these problems have the form (2.2) (with m small). One can also encounter

$$f(x) = \sum_{i=1}^{m} |f_i(x)| . \tag{4.1}$$

A unified way to describe them all is to consider functions of the type

$$f(x) := h[C(x)] \tag{4.2}$$

where C maps R^n into R^m, each $C_i(x)$ is smooth while h maps R^m into R but is convex and nondifferentiable, like $|\cdot|_\infty$ or $|\cdot|_1$. For (4.2) to be amenable as above, one must assume that h itself is simple enough. The word "simple" roughly means: (4.2) would be easily solvable if C were linear. Of course, problems of this type are closer to nonlinear programming than to nonsmooth optimization; it is preferable to follow R. Fletcher in speaking of *composite problems*.

To solve problems of this class, one encounters first some *tricks*, generally aimed at smoothing f.

We give two examples:

For small $\varepsilon > 0$, one observes that

$$|f(x)| = (f^2(x))^{1/2} \simeq (f^2(x) + \varepsilon)^{1/2} \tag{4.3}$$

and this can help smoothing l_1-type functions. As for l_∞-type functions, one can observe that

$$\max\{f_1, \ldots, f_m(x)\} = \max_u \left\{ \sum u_i f_i(x) \mid u_i \geq 0, \sum u_i = 1 \right\}$$

$$\simeq \max_u \left\{ \sum u_i f_i(x) - \tfrac{1}{2}\varepsilon \sum u_i^2 \mid u_i \geq 0, \sum u_i = 1 \right\} =: f_\varepsilon(x) . \tag{4.4}$$

Computing the maximal u in (4.4) amounts to projecting the vector $\varepsilon^{-1}[f_1(x), \ldots, f_m(x)] \in R^m$ onto the unit-simplex. This maximal u is unique, call it $u_\varepsilon(x)$, so the function $f_\varepsilon(x)$ is differentiable, with gradient given by Proposition 2.1:

$$\nabla f_\varepsilon(x) = \sum u_{\varepsilon i}(x)\nabla f_i(x) .$$

Of course the resulting approximating function (4.3) or (4.4), although smooth, will suffer from the usual bad conditioning of penalty-type functions.

The real operation underlying these smoothing techniques is a transformation of the nonsmooth problem into an equivalent smooth problem in which constraints usually appear. Let us illustrate this point on the finite minimax problem. Here, we will use the material of the chapter on nonlinear optimization in this volume. We start with the remark that

$$\min \ f(x) \quad \text{where} \ f(x) := \max\{f_1(x), \ldots, f_m(x)\} \tag{4.5}$$

is equivalent to the problem with $n + 1$ variables and m constraints

$$\min \ v \tag{4.6a}$$
$$v \geq f_i(x), \quad i = 1, \ldots, m . \tag{4.6b}$$

Associated with (4.6) is the Lagrangian function

$$v + \sum u_i(f_i(x) - v) .$$

Among the optimality conditions, there appears immediately

$$u_i \geq 0, \qquad \sum u_i = 1 ; \tag{4.7}$$

therefore, it makes sense to consider the ad hoc Lagrangian function,

$$L(x, u) := \sum u_i f_i(x) \tag{4.8}$$

whose connection with (4.5) is clear (compare (4.4)).

Now, the usual first-order optimality conditions for (4.6) are as follows: if x^*, v^* solves (4.6), then clearly $v^* = f(x^*)$ and there exist u_i^* satisfying (4.7) together with

$$\sum u_i^* \nabla f_i(x^*) = 0 , \tag{4.9a}$$

$$u_i^* = 0 \quad \text{if } v^* > f_i(x^*) . \tag{4.9b}$$

This is nothing but the optimality condition (1.9) written for the problem (4.5), and using Proposition 2.1 to characterize $\partial f(x^*)$: setting

$$I(x) := \{i \mid f_i(x) = f(x)\} , \tag{4.10}$$

we have for optimal x^*

$$\exists u_i^*, \ i \in I(x^*) \quad \text{s.t. } u_i^* \geq 0, \ \sum u_i^* = 1, \ \sum u_i^* \nabla f_i(x^*) = 0 . \tag{4.11}$$

Remark 4.1. Note the following explanation of Proposition 2.1, in relation with (1.7): take x and d in R^n; we have

$$f_i(x + td) = f_i(x) + t\nabla f_i(x)^T d + o_i(t) ;$$

for $t > 0$ small enough, those i's not in $I(x)$ do not matter when computing $f(x + td)$, i.e.

$$f(x + td) = \max\{ f_i(x) + t\nabla f_i(x)^T d + o_i(t) \mid i \in I(x)\}$$
$$= f(x) + t \max\{\nabla f_i(x)^T d \mid i \in I(x)\} + o(t) \tag{4.12}$$

and formula (1.7) readily follows via convexification of the set

$$\{\nabla f_i(x) \mid i \in I(x)\} .$$

Second-order optimality conditions can also be derived for (4.6). First of all, to say that the gradients of the active constraints of (4.6)

$$\{\{-1, \nabla f_i(x^*)\} \mid i \in I(x^*)\}$$

are linearly independent is to say that the gradients of the active f_i's in (4.5)

$$\{\nabla f_i(x^*)\,|\,i\in I(x^*)\}$$

are affinely independent, i.e. u^* in (4.11) is unique. Now a vector orthogonal to the gradients of the active constraints at $\{v^*, x^*\}$ is a $\{w, d\}$ such that

$$\nabla f_i(x^*)^\mathrm{T} d = w \quad \forall i\in I(x^*)\,.$$

This implies $w = f'(x, d)$ (all the $\nabla f_i^\mathrm{T} d$ have the same, hence maximal, value); furthermore $w = 0$ (otherwise (4.11) could not hold) so such a d is characterized by

$$\nabla f_i(x^*)^\mathrm{T} d = f'(x^*, d)\ (=0) \quad \forall i\in I(x^*)\,. \tag{4.13}$$

As a result, the second-order optimality condition is: if the $\nabla f_i(x^*)$, $i\in I(x^*)$, are affinely independent, then, for d satisfying (4.13),

$$d^\mathrm{T} \sum u_i^* \nabla^2 f_i(x^*)d \geq 0\,. \tag{4.14}$$

Let us interpret this: for d satisfying (4.13) and z arbitrary in R^n,

$$f(x + td + t^2 z) - f(x)$$
$$\simeq t^2 \max\{\tfrac{1}{2}d^\mathrm{T}\nabla^2 f_i(x^*)d + \nabla f_i(x^*)^\mathrm{T} z\,|\,i\in I(x^*)\}\,.$$

Therefore we obtain, fixing d in (4.13),

$$\forall z\in R^n,\ \exists i\in I(x^*)\quad \text{s.t.}\ \tfrac{1}{2}\alpha_i(d) + \nabla f_i(x^*)^\mathrm{T} z \geq 0$$

(where we have set $\alpha_i(d) := d^\mathrm{T}\nabla^2 f_i(x^*)d$). By a theorem of the alternative, this implies that there exists $u_i^* = u_i^*(d)$ satisfying (4.11) and

$$0 \leq \sum u_i^*(d)\alpha_i(d) = d^\mathrm{T}\sum u_i^*(d)\nabla^2 f_i(x^*)d\,. \tag{4.15}$$

It is interesting to note that this second-order condition, together with the first-order condition (4.11), is valid without any qualification condition. Of course, if (4.11) has a unique solution u^*, then $u_i^*(d)$ do not depend on d in (4.15) and we get back (4.14).

Accordingly, for x close to x^*, it is a good idea to minimize the function

$$\tilde{f}(d) := f(x) + \max\{\nabla f_i(x)^\mathrm{T} d\,|\,i\in I(x)\} + \tfrac{1}{2}d^\mathrm{T} H d \tag{4.16}$$

(where H approximates the matrix in (4.14)) which can be viewed as a satisfactory approximation to $f(x + d)$: the d-space can be decomposed in two subspaces:

– one, tangent to the constraints, where (4.13) holds; there, f is smooth and $\tilde{f}$

agrees with the Lagrangian function (4.8) which, because of (4.11) and (4.14), must be minimal at x^*;
- its orthogonal complement, where the first-order approximation $\tilde{f}$ of f is good enough: no second-order term matters because the first-order term is already positive.

From this point, the way is open to algorithms specially tailored for solving (4.6), or more generally (4.2): linearize C and add to h a quadratic term coming from the second order Taylor development along the kinky surface of h (i.e. where the nonsmooth nature of h does not play a role). From example, in the spirit of sequential quadratic programing to solve (4.6), the best idea to solve (4.5) is to define the direction-finding problem (x, standing for the current iterate x_k, is fixed, d is the variable)

$$\min_d \max_i [f_i(x) + \nabla f_i(x)^T d] + \tfrac{1}{2} d^T H d \tag{4.17}$$

where H is some quasi-Newton update for the Hessian of the Lagrangian function (4.8) (considering that v is a linear variable in (4.6), there is no reason to introduce any curvature along the v-axis!).

Methods of this Section 4 do not treat the problem in its full generality (1.10) and they do not really differ from classical methods for smooth optimization. For example, they do not fit with Section 2.5. On the other hand, they are worth studying because they are open to generalizations; for example, it is fruitful to use (4.16) as a basis for constructing methods coping with (1.10), even if the explicit use of all the underlying f_i's must eventually be given up.

5. Subgradient methods

5.1. Rationale

Suppose for the moment that f is smooth, say C^1 or C^2, at the current iterate x_k. In a standard first order method one makes a positive step t_k along the negative gradient (compare 3.1):

$$x_{k+1} := x_k - t_k \nabla f(x_k), \tag{5.1a}$$

$$t_k > 0 \quad \text{(line search)}. \tag{5.1b}$$

The direction $-\nabla f(x_k)$ is a direction of descent; hence a line search along $x_k - t \nabla f(x_k)$, $t \geq 0$, will provide some $t_k > 0$ such that $f(x_{k+1}) < f(x_k)$. If we want to do better toward second-order, we may add some conditioner and multiply $\nabla f(x_k)$ by a matrix H_k (which is ideally close to the inverse of the Hessian of f at x_k, compare (3.2)), to obtain the scheme

$$\text{compute } H_k, \tag{5.2a}$$

$$x_{k+1} := x_k - t_k H_k \nabla f(x_k), \tag{5.2b}$$

$$t_k > 0 \quad \text{(line search)}. \tag{5.2c}$$

544 C. Lemaréchal

For nonsmooth f the gradient at x_k may not exist, but it is clear what to do. By assumption (1.10) we know at least one subgradient at x_k; hence we will replace the gradient in (5.1) and (5.2), respectively, by a subgradient g_k. Normalizing the search direction we obtain as generalization of (5.1)

$$x_{k+1} := x_k - t_k g_k/|g_k| \quad \text{where } g_k \in \partial f(x_k), \tag{5.3a}$$

$$t_k > 0 \quad \text{(suitable)}. \tag{5.3b}$$

The corresponding extension of (5.2) will be the subject of Sections 5.2 and 5.3.

How can we choose t_k in (5.3)?

Consider once more the function (3.3) at a point of nondifferentiability, say $x_k := (0,0)$. By definition (1.4) the vector $g_k := 2^{1/2}(1,1)$ is a subgradient at x_k. An inspection of the level lines in figure 3.1 tells us that this special $-g_k$ is *not a direction of descent*. There is no $t_k > 0$ such that $f(x_{k+1}) < f(x_k)$ with this g_k in (5.3). In contrast to (5.1), the steplength t_k cannot be determined via a line search. And note: even when the negative subgradient in (5.3) is a direction of descent, it is not advisable to make a line search, which could generate the disastrous steepest descent path of Figure 3.1. Nonsmoothness requires new ideas for the stepsize.

The following simple but basic observation shows us what to do: let x^* be optimal; from (1.8), the angle between $-g_k$ and $x^* - x_k$ is acute; hence, for $t > 0$ small enough $x_k - tg_k/|g_k|$ is closer to x^* than x_k. More precisely:

Lemma 5.1. *Suppose x_k is not optimal and let x^* be any optimal point. Then*

$$|x_{k+1} - x^*| < |x_k - x^*| \tag{5.4}$$

whenever

$$0 < t_k < 2[f(x_k) - f(x^*)]/|g_k|. \tag{5.5}$$

Proof. By definition (5.3), we have

$$|x^* - x_{k+1}|^2 = |x^* - x_k + t_k g_k/|g_k||^2$$
$$= |x^* - x_k|^2 + 2t_k(x^* - x_k)^T g_k/|g_k| + t_k^2 g_k^T g_k/|g_k|^2,$$

which we write as

$$|x^* - x_{k+1}|^2 = |x^* - x_k|^2 - 2t_k b_k + t_k^2 \tag{5.6}$$

with $b_k := (x_k - x^*)^T g_k/|g_k|$. Then, (5.4) holds for t_k between 0 and $2b_k$.

Using (1.8) with $x = x_k$, $g = g_k$ and $z = x^*$ gives

$$b_k \geq [f(x_k) - f(x^*)]/|g_k| > 0, \tag{5.7}$$

so (5.5) implies the required property. $\square$

Now let us choose the stepsize so that

$$t_k \downarrow 0 \quad \text{when } k \to +\infty .$$

This yields an argument for convergence to a true optimum: indeed, if (5.4) does not hold, then Lemma 5.1 implies that (5.5) does not hold, $f(x_k)$ is close to $f(x^*)$ (if k is large) and we are done.

There is still another item which has to be considered for choosing the sequence $\{t_k\}$, however: let x_0 be the starting point for iteration (5.3) and put $A := \sum_{j=0}^{\infty} t_j$. Then for each iteration index k,

$$|x_0 - x_k| \le |x_0 - x_1| + |x_1 - x_2| + \cdots + |x_{k-1} - x_k|$$
$$= t_0 + t_1 + \cdots + t_{k-1} \le A . \tag{5.8}$$

In other words: we stay all the time in a ball with radius A around the starting point x_0. To be on the safe side, we choose the small t_k such that, neverthelesss, the sum of the t_k is large, say $+\infty$. Then also some optimal x^*, even far away from the starting point x_0, will not be out of reach. In summary, we obtain the following specification for (5.3):

$$x_{k+1} := x_k - t_k g_k / |g_k| \quad \text{with } g_k \in \partial f(x_k) ,$$

$$t_k \text{ such that } t_k \downarrow 0 \text{ and } \sum_{k=0}^{\infty} t_k = \infty . \tag{5.9}$$

Then, everything is set for the following result.

Theorem 5.1. *Suppose the set X^* of optimal points is nonempty and bounded. Then, for arbitrary starting point x_0, the sequence x_k provided by (5.9) is bounded and all its limit points are in X^*.* $\square$

We omit the proof, which is rather technical.

Iteration (5.9) is of utmost simplicity; in particular, no line search is needed, of course. Unfortunately, one can expect only a poor convergence speed. Let us suppose for a moment that the x_k, given by (5.9), would tend to x^* *with geometric convergence rate* (also called *R-linear convergence*), i.e., there exists $M > 0$ and $0 < q < 1$ such that

$$|x_k - x^*| \le M q^k \quad \text{for all } k .$$

Then, for all k,

$$t_k = |x_{k+1} - x_k| \le |x_{k+1} - x^*| + |x^* - x_k| \le M(q+1)q^k .$$

Summing up over k we would obtain

$$\sum_{k=0}^{\infty} t_k \le M(q+1) \sum_{k=0}^{\infty} q^k = M(q+1)/(1-q) .$$

We get a contradiction since by choice of the t_k the left-hand side is $+\infty$. Consequently we have the disappointing supplement to the convergence result:

The convergence of the process (5.9) *is less than geometric.*

Geometric convergence does require $\{t_k\}$ to be a geometric sequence. Thus, an alternative to (5.9) is the following rule for the stepsize:

$$\text{choose } t_0 > 0, \ q \in \,]0, 1[\ \text{and take } t_k := t_0 q^k \ . \tag{5.10}$$

Then x_k converges geometrically to some limit $\bar{x}$ which, in view of (5.8), may not be optimal. It can be shown, however, that $\bar{x}$ is optimal when t_0 and q are larger than some (not computable) thresholds, respectively.

Finally, suppose we are in the following special situation:

the optimal value of f, say f^*, is known . $\tag{5.11}$

Then, instead of picking the stepsize blindly according to some *qualitative* rule (5.9) or (5.10), we can use Lemma 5.1 to control t_k in a *quantitative* way, namely:

$$\text{choose } \lambda \in \,]0, 2[\ \text{and take } t_k := \lambda [f(x_k) - f^*]/|g_k| \ . \tag{5.12}$$

This computable steplength, which incorporates the knowledge we have of f, x_k and X^*, guarantees a monotonic decrease of the distance from x_k to X^* (for all k) and actually the whole sequence $\{x_k\}$ does converge to some $x^* \in X^*$. As for the rate of convergence, various theorems can be proved, for example,

Theorem 5.2. *Suppose f has a minimizer x^*, the optimal value $f^* = f(x^*)$ is known and for some $l > 0$*

$$f(x) - f(x^*) \geq l|x - x^*| \quad \text{for all } x \ . \tag{5.13}$$

Then iteration (5.3) *with stepsize rule* (5.12) *provides a sequence converging to x^* with geometric convergence rate.* $\square$

Remark 5.1. The function

$$f(x) := \max\{f_1(x), \ldots, f_m(x), 0\} \ ,$$

whose minimization is equivalent to the solution of the (assumed feasible) inequality system

find x such that $f_i(x) \leq 0$ $(1 \leq i \leq m)$,

can serve as an example where one knows $f(x^*)$ $(=0)$ without knowing x^*. For linear f_i's, iteration (5.3) with stepsize rule (5.12) is known as the relaxation method for solving the above inequality system.

5.2. Acceleration along the gradient

In case we neither know the optimal function value f^*, nor do we want to risk convergence to a non-optimal $\bar{x}$, then there remains only one way to accelerate the convergence of the subgradient method: we have to give up the Markov nature of iteration (5.3) by adding information obtained in previous steps. Essentially two approaches are known, both due to N.Z. Shor, which we study in Sections 5.2 and 5.3.

The first approach (dilation along the gradient) is based on the following idea: suppose, starting from x_0, we have found x_1 by a move along $-g_0$ and we have selected g_1 as the new subgradient at x_1. Then it makes sense to shorten that part of $-g_1$ which is collinear to the just used direction $-g_0$. Even more can be said: since the gradient direction is so notoriously bad – even in the smooth case – it is worthless to look for x^* (*i.e. to place the subsequent x_k's*) out of a region roughly orthogonal to g_0. Therefore let us dilate the space by a linear operator H_1 whose only difference from the unit matrix is to multiply g_0 by a coefficient smaller than 1: the dilation coefficient. If we cumulate the dilations of each iteration and write $\{H_k\}$ in a condensed form, then we obtain the following formulae:

$$d_k := -H_k g_k / (g_k^T H_k g_k)^{1/2}, \qquad x_{k+1} := x_k + t_k d_k,$$
$$H_{k+1} := \alpha_k (H_k - \beta_k d_k d_k^T) \tag{5.14a}$$

where α_k, β_k, t_k are suitable positive parameters and the initial matrix H_0 is positive definite, for example $H_0 = \alpha I$. For $\alpha_k \equiv 1$ and $\beta_k \equiv 0$ we get back (5.3). The choice $\beta_k = 1$ corresponds to a projection: g_k becomes a null-vector of H_{k+1}, and of all subsequent H_{k+i} as well.

One parameter choice proves to be especially interesting. Let n be the dimension of the space and choose α_k, β_k and t_k in (5.14a) as constants:

$$\alpha_k := n^2/(n^2 - 1), \quad \beta_k := 2/(n + 1), \quad t_k := 1/(n + 1). \tag{5.14b}$$

Then the following convergence result holds without further assumption on the convex f.

Theorem 5.3. *Suppose the starting point x_0 and the starting matrix $H_0 = \alpha I$ are such that $|x_0 - x^*|^2 \leq \alpha$ for some optimal x^*. Then there exists $M > 0$ and $q < 1$ such that for the sequence generated by (5.14a,b):*

$$\min_{0 \leq j \leq k} [f(x_j) - f(x^*)] \leq M q^k \quad \text{for all } k. \quad \square \tag{5.15}$$

Thus, a subsequence of the function values $f(x_k)$ converges to $f(x^*)$ with R-linear convergence rate. A closer analysis shows that, for large n, $q \approx 1 - 1/(2n^2)$.

Hence, unfortunately, q is close to 1, tending to 1 as n increases.

The method (5.14a,b) is nothing but the so-called ellipsoid method, recently popularized in a different context (see the Chapter on linear programming, in this volume).

5.3. Dilation along the difference of gradients

Despite their simplicity and their convergence properties, methods of Section 5.2 have a very disappointing numerical behaviour; one can say that the situation is about the same as in Section 5.1; compare the simplicity of iteration 5.9, and the generality of Theorem 5.1.

Another dilation is motivated by Figure 5.1. When f is really stiff, ie. when the angle between g_k and g_{k+1} is wide open (although x_k and x_{k+1} are close together) both directions $-g_k$ and $-g_{k+1}$ are bad and zig-zags appear; furthermore, the optimal x^* is likely to lie near the hyperplane

$$g_{k+1}^T(x^* - x_{k+1}) = g_k^T(x^* - x_{k+1}),$$

in which f is apparently kinky. Hence, it might be a good idea to dilate the space along the unwished direction $g_{k+1} - g_k$. The iteration formulae take on the form

$$d_k := H_k g_k, \tag{5.16a}$$

$$x_{k+1} := x_k + t_k d_k, \tag{5.16b}$$

$$H_{k+1} := H_k - \beta_k p_k p_k^T / p_k^T (g_{k+1} - g_k)$$

$$\text{where } p_k := H_k(g_{k+1} - g_k), \tag{5.16c}$$

compare (5.14a); we have absorbed the parameter α_k in the stepsize t_k. Here again, $\beta_k \equiv 0$ gives back the original formula (5.3).

Observe that the choice $\beta_k \equiv 1$ corresponds again to a projection along $g_{k+1} - g_k$, and then $d_{k+1}^T(g_{k+1} - g_k) = 0$.

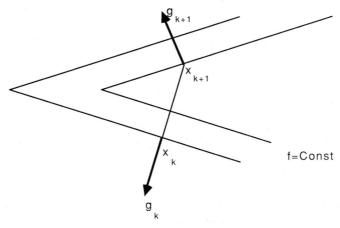

Fig. 5.1.

Here, however, no rule other than pure heuristics is known for controlling the dilatation parameter β_k and the stepsize t_k. It can be observed that, if f is quadratic (hence smooth) with minimum x^* and if t_k is optimal,

$$f(x_k + t_k d_k) \leq f(x_k + t d_k) \quad \forall t > 0$$

then $(x^* - x_{k+1})^{\mathrm{T}} (g_{k+1} - g_k) = 0$, i.e. $\beta_k = 1$ is the best choice. Of course, this is of little use in the general case: whenever $\beta_k = 1$, $g_{k+1} - g_k$ becomes a null-vector of H_{k+i}, $i \geq 1$. Note also the similarity with quasi-Newton methods; for example, the Davidon–Fletcher–Powell update takes $\beta_k \equiv 1$ and adds the matrix

$$(x_{k+1} - x_k)(x_{k+1} - x_k)^{\mathrm{T}} / (x_{k+1} - x_k)^{\mathrm{T}} (g_{k+1} - g_k)$$

to H_{k+1} of (5.16) (see the chapter of unconstrained optimization, in this volume).

Despite very bad theoretical properties, method (5.16) has potentially very good numerical qualities.

5.4. Cutting planes

Suppose that, at iteration k, some set D_k is known to contain an optimal point x^*. After having computed x_{k+1} and $g_{k+1} \in \partial f(x_{k+1})$, we know from (1.8) that

$$x^* \in D_k \cap \{x \mid g_{k+1}^{\mathrm{T}}(x - x_{k+1}) \leq 0\} . \tag{5.17}$$

With this point of view in mind, it remains to place x_{k+1} (in D_k!). The first idea has been to minimize the under-estimate

$$\hat{f}_k(x) := \max\{ f(x_i) + g_i^{\mathrm{T}}(x - x_i) \mid i = 0, \dots, k\} \leq f(x) , \tag{5.18}$$

giving x_{k+1} as solution of the linear program

$$\min v , \tag{5.19a}$$
$$v \geq f(x_i) + g_i^{\mathrm{T}}(x - x_i) , \quad i = 0, \dots, k . \tag{5.19b}$$

This is the original cutting plane algorithm (note that – at least for small k – we may have to add a constraint $x \in D$ for some bounded D to guarantee a finite optimum in (5.19)).

Then one can easily prove:

Theorem 5.4. *Suppose there is some K such that (5.19) has a bounded solution at iteration K. Then (5.19) has an optimal solution for all $k \geq K$ as well, f has an optimal solution x^*, $\hat{f}_k(x_{k+1}) \uparrow f(x^*)$ and $f(x_k) \to f(x^*)$.* □

Because $\hat{f}_k$ is a piecewise linear approximation of f, it is reasonable to expect good convegence when f itself looks piecewise linear around x^*, i.e. when an assumption like (5.13) holds. This property, however, is incompatible with a smooth f, for which the optimality condition tells us that, at least for x close to x^*,

$$l|x - x^*|^2 \leq f(x) - f(x^*) \leq L|x - x^*|^2 \tag{5.20}$$

with $l \geq 0$ and L finite. For this case, the following holds.

Theorem 5.5. *Suppose f is C^2 and strongly convex, i.e. (5.20) holds with $0 < l \leq L < +\infty$. Then the cutting plane algorithm (5.19) converges geometrically with a ratio equivalent to $1 - (l/L)^n$ when $n \to \infty$. (n is the dimension of the space).* □

Nonsmooth functions that are difficult to minimize rapidly are those for which the space neighbouring a given optimum x^* is divided in two regions, one where (5.13) holds, the other where it is (5.20). The following loose statement explains what we have in mind:

Claim 5.1.
  – It is easy to minimize rapidly a function resembling $f(\xi, \eta) = \xi^2 + \eta^2$: take Newton's method.
  – It is easy to minimize rapidly a function resembling $|\xi| + |\eta|$: use the algorithm given by (5.19).
  – It is difficult to minimize rapidly a function resembling $\xi^2 + \eta^4$ (singular Hessian at the optimum).
  – Exactly for the same reason, it is difficult to minimize rapidly a function resembling $|\xi| + \eta^2$ (general nonsmooth).

Considerations of this kind have given birth to a new school of optimization in which, instead of basing one's reasoning on local properties (like in Lemma 5.1., for example, or in all areas of smooth optimization) one uses global arguments (like in (5.17)). An optimization process is then considered as a *game* between the *algorithm* (which computes x_k) and the *black box* (1.10). For the algorithm, the game consists in obtaining good convergence properties against the worst possible black box. With this minimax point of view in mind, it is natural to place x_{k+1} with the sole help of "sure" information, like $x^* \in D_k$, ignoring any "dubious" information like (3.1), (3.2), or even $\hat{f}_k \approx f$ in (5.18).

Then the apparently best idea is to define x_{k+1} as

x_{k+1} is the center of gravity of D_k .

The resulting algorithm, obtained by defining D_{k+1} from (5.17), is known as the method of *center of gravity*. With this method, the volume of D_k is divided at each iteration by a non-negligible factor, which allows the following result:

Theorem 5.6. *The method of centers of gravity converges linearly and its ratio is equivalent to* $1 - 1/(e - 1)n$ *when* $n \to \infty$. $\square$

Now a major result in this theory of "global algorithms" is as follows:

Theorem 5.7. *For any minimization method using only the information from the black box* (1.10), *there exists a convex function for which the method converges at best linearly with ratio* $q = \exp(-Y/n)$. $\square$

In the above theorem, Y is a positive constant. Note that, when $n \to \infty$, the ratio q is thus equivalent to $1 - Y/n$.

As a result, if global algorithms are ranked according to the criterion "worst rate of convergence (independently of f) in the case of many variables", the conclusion is:
- the method of centers of gravity is qualitatively optimal, since its ratio behaves like $1 - 1/n$; unfortunately, one does not know an implementable way to compute the center of gravity of a polyhedron;
- the ellipsoid method (5.14a,b) is not bad, since its ratio behaves like $1 - 1/n^2$;
- the cutting plane method (5.19) is horrible: its ratio behaves like $1 - e^{-n}$, and depends on the function being minimized; furthermore, the complexity of an iteration k (the number of constraints in (5.19)) goes to infinity with k; for fairness, however, it must be said that the theoretical properties of this method have not been much studied; we add that the bundle methods of Section 6 are elaborated variants of (5.19).

Before closing this section, let us mention two more directions of present research, concerning the same theory.

First, observe that D_k is usually a polyhedron given by its faces:

$$D_k = \{x \mid g_i^T x \leq q_i, \ i = 0, \ldots, k\}. \tag{5.21}$$

For example, the optimal value of (5.19) can be shown to satisfy $v_{k+1} \leq f(x_k)$; therefore, if we set

$$q_i := f(x_k) - f(x_i) + g_i^T x_i, \quad i = 0, \ldots, k, \tag{5.22}$$

we see that any optimal x_{k+1} lies in the D_k thus defined by (5.21), (5.22).

Then, why not try to define "centers" which are easier to compute than the center of gravity? One example is the maximizer over D_k of the function

$$F_k(x) := \prod_{i \leq k} (q_i - g_i^T x) \tag{5.23}$$

or equivalently of $\text{Log } F_k$, which is concave. Of course, one cannot maximize F_k in a finite amount of time, but one can take x_{k+1} as the result of a limited number of Newton's iterations.

A function like F_k of (5.23) is sometimes called a *F-distance*, which is 0 on the boundary of D_k, positive inside. Note also that the cutting plane iterate solving (5.19) can also be called a center, maximizing the function

$$\min_{i \leq k} (q_i - g_i^T x)$$

instead of (5.23).

The second idea consists in defining the "safeguard-polyhedron" like D_k in the graph space R^{n+1} instead of R^n. Clearly enough, any minimum pair $(f(x^*), x^*)$ lies in (compare (5.19))

$$D_k' := \{(v, x) \mid v \geq f(x_i) + g_i^T(x - x_i), \ i \leq k; \ v \leq f(x_k)\} .$$

The x-part of a center (v_{k+1}, x_{k+1}) of D_k' is likely to be a better approximation of x^* than a center of D_k. In this respect, cutting plane is a clumsy idea, which places (v_{k+1}, x_{k+1}) on a *vertex* of D_k' (the lowest one).

6. Bundle methods

The rationale for methods in this Section is to force the decrease $f(x_{k+1}) < f(x_k)$ by all means, in contrast to the methods of Section 5.

6.1. A conceptual first order ε-descent method

Suppose for the moment that we know the whole subdifferential at the current iterate x_k; in Section 6.2 we will drop this assumption. Then, instead of performing a step in the direction of a randomly chosen subgradient (as in subgradient method), let us select that g_k in $\partial f(x_k)$ providing the steepest descent. The directional derivative $f'(x_k; d)$ being a measure for the descent we can expect (in a first order sense and for small t) along $x_k + td, t > 0$, we are led to the direction finding subproblem

$$\min_{|d| \leq 1} f'(x_k; d) . \tag{6.1}$$

The additional constraint $|d| \leq 1$ in (6.1) becomes necessary, since $f'(x_k; \cdot)$ is positively homogeneous. In case f is smooth one has $f'(x_k; d) = f'(x_k)d$, i.e., (6.1) is just the minimization of the classical *first order model* (3.1). We use (1.7) to rewrite (6.1) in the form

$$\min_{|d| \leq 1} \max_{g \in \partial f(x_k)} g^T d . \tag{6.2}$$

The unit ball and $\partial f(x_k)$ are nonempty convex compact sets. Hence, by a well-known Minimax Theorem, (6.2) is equivalent to

$$\max_{g \in \partial f(x_k)} \min_{|d| \le 1} g^T d . \tag{6.3}$$

For given g the minimizing d of length 1 is $-g/|g|$. In summary, for solving (6.1), we have to study the minimum-norm problem (which is uniquely solvable since $\partial f(x_k)$ is a nonempty closed convex set)

$$\min_{g \in \partial f(x_k)} |g| . \tag{6.4}$$

If and only if g_k is the subgradient at x_k closest to the origin, then $d_k := -g_k/|g_k|$ minimizes $f'(x_k; \cdot)$ and one has $f'(x_k; d_k) = -|g_k|$. Because of (1.9), $g_k \ne 0$ for nonoptimal x_k and thus $f'(x_k; d_k) < 0$, i.e. (6.1) does provide a descent direction as long as there is one. We are led to the iteration scheme

$$d_k := -g_k/|g_k| \quad \text{with } |g_k| = \min_{g \in \partial f(x_k)} |g| , \tag{6.5a}$$

$$x_{k+1} := x_k + t_k d_k \quad \text{with } f(x_k + t_k d_k) = \min_{t \ge 0} f(x_k + t d_k) . \tag{6.5b}$$

In case the gradient exists at x_k, the subdifferential is $\{\nabla f(x_k)\}$ and (6.5) reduces to the classical steepest descent method (with exact line search). Hence the example discussed in Section 3.1 warns us that for nonsmooth f the above iteration may collapse close to a kink. It is important to understand the reason for this failure and to develop a feeling of what could serve as safeguard in (6.5) against non-convergence in the nonsmooth situation. For this purpose consider once more the function (3.3) and the path shown in Figure 3.1. Going back to definition (1.4) we realize that the limits

$$2^{1/2}(1, 1) = \lim \nabla f(x_{2k}) \quad \text{and} \quad 2^{1/2}(1, -1) = \lim \nabla f(x_{2k+1})$$

belong to the subdifferential of f at the origin. A more detailed (but straightforward) analysis shows that $\partial f(0)$ is the part of the ellipsis displayed in Figure 6.1:

$$\partial f(0) = \{(\xi, \eta) \,|\, 2\xi^2 + \eta^2 \le 6; \ \xi \le 3^{-1/2}\} .$$

Consequently iteration (6.5) would use at $x_k := 0$ the excellent direction $d_k = -(1, 0)$.

Unfortunately, 0 is never reached: Figure 3.1 shows that we walk in shorter and shorter steps on a zigzagging path along the two directions

$$d' := d_{2k} = (-1, -1)2^{-1/2} , \tag{6.6a}$$

$$d'' := d_{2k+1} = (-1, 1)2^{-1/2} . \tag{6.6b}$$

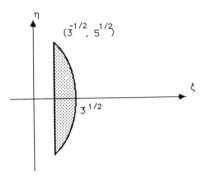

Fig. 6.1.

In a strictly local sense d' or d'' provides the steepest descent at x_k, whereas in a more global sense d' and d'' are less and less profitable. The more we approach 0, the poorer the (sub)gradient information becomes, due to the nondifferentiability at 0. This suggests enriching the information at x_k and replacing $\partial f(x_k)$ in (6.5) by $\cup_{y \in B} \partial f(y)$, where B is a suitable neighborhood of x_k. Then for x_k close to its limit 0, the enlarged set $\cup_{y \in B} \partial f(y)$ will contain $\partial f(0)$, i.e., the above ideal direction $(-1, 0)$ will be a candidate for the line search and we will escape. Luckily we have at hand an object in convex analysis which helps to realize what we have in mind. Fix some small $\varepsilon > 0$ and add this ε in the inequality defining the subdifferential (we attach ε as a subscript),

$$\partial_\varepsilon f(x) := \{ g \in \mathbb{R}^n \mid g^T(z - x) \leq f(z) - f(x) + \varepsilon \text{ for all } z \in \mathbb{R}^n \} .$$
$$(6.7)$$

This so-called ε-subdifferential, whose elements are called ε-subgradients, is again a nonempty convex compact set (same proof as for $\varepsilon = 0$), and the basic auxiliary result holds:

Lemma 6.1. *For every x and every $\varepsilon > 0$ there exists a neighborhood B of x such that*

$$\partial_\varepsilon f(x) \supset \bigcup_{y \in B} \partial f(y) .$$

Proof. Let x and $\varepsilon > 0$ be given. For $p \geq 0$, denote by B_p the ball of radius p around x. Let L be a Lipschitz constant of f on B_1; set

$$p := \min(1, \varepsilon/2L), \quad B := B_p ,$$

let $y \in B$ and $g \in \partial f(y)$ be given. We prove $g \in \partial_\varepsilon f(x)$. Indeed, from the subgradient inequality (1.8):

$$g^T(z - y) \leq f(z) - f(y) \quad \text{for all } z \in R^n ,$$

which we write

$$g^T(z - x) + g^T(x - y) \leqslant f(z) - f(x) + f(x) - f(y) ;$$

this implies

$$g^T(z - x) \leqslant f(z) - f(x) + |f(x) - f(y)| + |g| \cdot |x - y| .$$

Now observe that $y \in B \subset B_1$. Therefore we obtain, using the Lipschitz condition

$$g^T(z - x) \leqslant f(z) - f(x) + 2L|x - y| \leqslant f(z) - f(x) + 2Lp$$

$$\leqslant f(z) - f(x) + \varepsilon .$$

Thus, g satisfies the defining inequality (6.7) and the lemma is proved.   □

Lemma 6.1 shows that the set $\partial_\varepsilon f(x_k)$ contains in a condensed form the subgradient information from a whole neighbourhood of x_k. As we will see, this will help to overcome the shortcoming caused by nonsmoothness.

To become more precise, fix some small $\varepsilon > 0$ throughout the following and replace $\partial f(x)$ by $\partial_\varepsilon f(x)$. If we add the same ε in the definition of the directional derivative (for convex f the operation lim in (1.2) can be replaced by inf)

$$f'_\varepsilon(x; d) := \inf_{t > 0} \frac{1}{t} [f(x + td) - f(x) + \varepsilon] , \tag{6.8}$$

then this ε-directional derivative again is the support function of the ε-subdifferential (same proof as for $\varepsilon = 0$):

$$f'_\varepsilon(x; d) = \max_{g \in \partial_\varepsilon f(x)} g^T d$$

(compare (1.7)). The arguments used at the beginning of this Section 6.1 show that also the ε-modified problems

$$\min_{|d| \leqslant 1} f'_\varepsilon(x_k; d) \tag{6.9}$$

and

$$\min_{g \in \partial_\varepsilon f(x_k)} |g| \tag{6.10}$$

correspond to each other. In words: if g_k solves (6.10), then $d_k := -g_k/|g_k|$ minimizes $f'_\varepsilon(x_k; \cdot)$ and $f'_\varepsilon(x_k; d_k) = -|g_k|$. As long as $0 \notin \partial_\varepsilon f(x_k)$ the minimal g_k in (6.10) is nonzero and thus $f'_\varepsilon(x_k; d_k) < 0$. Definition (6.8) implies that a move along d_k guarantees a decrease of at least ε:

$$0 \not\in \partial_\varepsilon f(x_k) \quad \Rightarrow \quad f(x_k + td_k) < f(x_k) - \varepsilon \text{ for suitable } t > 0 .$$
$$(6.11)$$

Now suppose $0 \in \partial_\varepsilon f(x_k)$. Put $g = 0$ in definition (6.7) to realize that x_k is already "almost" optimal; more precisely:

$$0 \in \partial_\varepsilon f(x_k) \quad \Rightarrow \quad f(x_k) \leqslant f(x) + \varepsilon \text{ for all } x .$$
$$(6.12)$$

Taken together, (6.11), (6.12) motivate the following ε-modification of iteration (6.5):

$$d_k := -g_k / |g_k| \quad \text{with } |g_k| = \min_{g \in \partial_\varepsilon f(x_k)} |g| ,$$
$$(6.13a)$$

$$x_{k+1} := x_k + t_k d_k \quad \text{with } f(x_k + t_k d_k) = \min_{t \geqslant 0} f(x_k + td_k) .$$
$$(6.13b)$$

Obviously any pathological behaviour as in Figure 3.1 is now excluded. Indeed, if $\inf f(x) > -\infty$, then in finitely many steps one must reach some x_k such that $0 \in \partial_\varepsilon f(x_k)$, i.e., x_k is ε-optimal. Hence $0 \in \partial_\varepsilon f(x_k)$ serves as a stopping criterion. We summarize:

Theorem 6.1. *Let* $f^* := \inf f(x)$ *and let* $\{x_k\}$ *be the sequence generated by* (6.13) *for arbitrary starting point* x_0.
   (a) *If* $f^* = -\infty$ *then* $\lim_{k \to \infty} f(x_k) = -\infty$.
   (b) *If* $f^* > -\infty$ *then there exists* k *such that* $f(x_k) \leqslant f^* + \varepsilon$. $\square$

Before we discuss an implementation of the above idea let us give another explanation for the change caused in the convergence behaviour by the transition from (6.5) to (6.13). The disaster in Figure 3.1 stems from the discontinuity of the subproblem in (6.5):

$$x \to d(x) := -g(x) / |g(x)| \quad \text{where } |g(x)| = \min_{g \in \partial f(x)} |g| .$$

Although the x_k converge to 0, the directions (compare with (6.6))

$$d(x_{2k}) = d' \quad \text{and} \quad d(x_{2k+1}) = d''$$

do not converge to $d(0) = (-1, 0)$. Using a result about the Lipschitz continuity of the point-to-set mapping $x \to \partial_\varepsilon f(x)$, one can easily verify that the slightly modified mapping in (6.13)

$$x \to d_\varepsilon(x) := -g_\varepsilon(x) / |g_\varepsilon(x)| \quad \text{where } |g_\varepsilon(x)| = \min_{g \in \partial_\varepsilon f(x)} |g|$$

becomes continuous. Thus for x_k close to 0 the directions $d(x_k)$, used in (6.13), will be sufficiently close to the ideal direction $d(0) = (-1, 0)$ and we will make a move away from x_k, overtaking 0.

6.2. Implementation

Let us come back to the general situation (1.10) where at x_k we know but one subgradient g_k. Despite this minimal information, the bundle idea realizes (6.13) in a rather sophisticated way. The basic idea of a *bundle-type-algorithm* consists in replacing $\partial_\varepsilon f(x_k)$ by some inner approximating polytope P (*forming of the bundle*) and in solving (6.13) with $\partial_\varepsilon f(x_k)$ replaced by P. Provided P is a sufficiently good approximation, then we will find a direction along which a line search yields some x_{k+1} with a decrease of almost ε. In case P is a bad approximation (the line search will let us know this), then we stay at x_k and try to improve the approximating P by adding a further subgradient (so-called *nullstep*). These two items are the crucial ingredients of all bundle methods. We will try to describe in very short terms the two mentioned basic steps by avoiding all technical details (which, of course, are very important for an efficient implementation); in particular we will not specify what the above "almost ε" means.

Let $g_j \in \partial f(x_j)$, $j = k - 1, k - 2, \ldots$, be a collection of subgradients already computed. It is a trivial exercise to show that each g_j is a p_j-subgradient at x_k, where

$$p_j := f(x_k) - f(x_j) - g_j^{\mathrm{T}}(x_k - x_j) \tag{6.14}$$

(proceed as in the proof of Lemma 6.1). Then it is not difficult to choose P, for example

$$P := \left\{ \sum \lambda_j g_j \mid \lambda_j \geq 0, \; \sum \lambda_j = 1, \; \sum \lambda_j p_j \leq \varepsilon \right\} \tag{6.15}$$

which can be proved to be contained in $\partial_\varepsilon f(x_k)$. Note that $\varepsilon \geq 0$ is a free parameter that can be controlled, depending on one's optimism: a small ε hopefully gives a good approximation of $\partial_\varepsilon f(x_k)$ while a large ε corresponds to a large expected decrease in f.

Replacing $\partial_\varepsilon f(x_k)$ by P in (6.13), the determination of a search direction reduces to a quadratic programming problem:

$$d = -\mathrm{argmin}\{|g|^2/g \in P\} . \tag{6.16}$$

In case P provides a good approximation of $\partial_\varepsilon f(x_k)$, then the resulting direction yields a decrease of almost ε and we are done. Now suppose that, on the contrary, P is a bad approximation. Then it may happen that the substitute problem (6.16) provides a direction d which is not even a descent direction; recall that not every negative subgradient guarantees a decrease. Then we compute a further subgradient g_+ at $x_k + td$ for some small $t > 0$. By Lemma 6.1, g_+ is an ε-subgradient at x_k. On the other hand, because $g_+ \in \partial f(x_k + td)$ and because d is bad, we have essentially

$$g_+^{\mathrm{T}}[x - (x + td)] \leq f(x) - f(x + td) \leq 0 ,$$

i.e. $g_+^T d \geq 0$. As suggested by Figure 6.2, this implies that the polytope

$$P_+ := \text{conv}(P \cup \{g_+\}) \subset \partial_\varepsilon f(x_k)$$

is a definitely better approximation than P. Hence, it remains to solve (6.16) with this new P_+ and to do the next line-search starting from the same x_k. This is a *null-step*.

The key property of this mechanism, namely that P_+ is definitely larger than P, has an analytical formulation:

Theorem 6.2. *If infinitely many null-steps are performed, then the solution of* (6.16) *tends to* 0. □

The proof of this statement, not particularly interesting, can be replaced by a look at Figure 6.2. As a result, when $|d|$ and ε are small, then x_k is approximately optimal (see (6.12): the 0-vector is almost in $\partial_\varepsilon f(x_k)$); to say that $|d|$ does not become small, on the other hand, means that, at some stage, the process terminates with a downhill d. This is what happens when 0 is far from $\partial_\varepsilon f(x_k)$.

6.3. The bundle algorithms

Exploiting all these ideas, one obtains the following schematic algorithm: start from $x_1 \in R^n$, $g_1 \in \partial f(x_1)$, set $p_1 = 0$. At each iteration k:
  a. Compute the direction: $d_k = -\sum_{j=1}^k \lambda_j g_j$ where $\lambda \in R^k$ solves (compare (6.14), (6.15); ε is a control parameter)

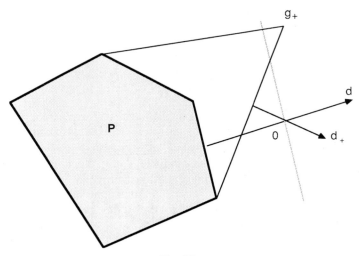

Fig. 6.2.

$$\min \ \frac{1}{2}\Big|\sum \lambda_j g_j\Big|^2 ,\tag{6.17a}$$

$$\lambda_j \geq 0 ,\tag{6.17b}$$

$$\sum \lambda_j = 1 ,\tag{6.17c}$$

$$\sum \lambda_j p_j \leq \varepsilon .\tag{6.17d}$$

b. Check for stopping: if $|d_k|$ is small then quit or [reduce ε and go to a].
c. Do the line-search: find $t > 0$, $g_{k+1} \in \partial f(x_k + t d_k)$ with $g_{k+1}^T d_k$ large enough, yielding

either a descent step: $f(x_k + t d_k)$ small enough; then $x_{k+1} = x_k + t d_k$;
or a null step: $p_{k+1} := f(x_k) - f(x_k + t d_k) + t g_{k+1}^T d_k \leq \varepsilon$; then $x_{k+1} = x_k$.

d. Update the weights: in case of a descent step set $p_{k+1} = 0$ and replace each p_j by

$$p_j + f(x_{k+1}) - f(x_k) - t g_j^T d_k ;$$

replace k by $k + 1$ and loop to a.

Two details (among others) have been neglected in the above description. One is that, despite the appearances to the contrary, the size of (6.17) needs not grow indefinitely with k: after solving (6.17) one can set $g_0 = -d_k$ and $p_0 = \sum_{j=1}^k \lambda_j p_j$ because g_0 is a p_0-subgradient at x_k; then this p_0 is updated at step d and all convergence proofs remain valid if the $(k+1)$st problem (6.17) contains just the two elements (p_0, g_0) and (p_{k+1}, g_{k+1}).

The second detail concerns the line-search: what does it mean to require "$g_{k+1}^T d_k$ large enough" and "$f(x_k + t d_k)$ small enough". After solving (6.17), let $s \geq 0$ be the multiplier associated with the last constraint, i.e. (6.17) is equivalent to (compare Section 2.3)

$$\min \ \frac{1}{2}\Big|\sum \lambda_j g_j\Big|^2 + s \sum \lambda_j p_j ,\tag{6.18a}$$

$$\lambda_j \geq 0 , \quad \sum \lambda_j = 1 .\tag{6.18b}$$

Examining the optimality conditions, one can see that

$$v_k := -|d_k|^2 - s\varepsilon \leq -|d_k|^2 < 0$$

can be considered as an estimate of $f'(x_k, d_k)$. Then, choosing $0 < m_1 < m_2 < 1$,

$$g_{k+1}^T d_k \text{ large enough means } g_{k+1}^T d_k \geq m_2 v_k ,$$

$$f(x_k + t d_k) \text{ small enough means } f(x_k + t d_k) \leq f(x_k) + m_1 t v_k ,$$

in the spirit of what is done in classical, smooth, optimization.

We mention that ε for step a. should not be thought of as a small parameter (which would give basically the steepest descent method, whose convergence is so bad, even in the smooth case; recall Section 2.5). Quite the contrary, the difficulty in this algorithm is that ε should be suitably chosen at each iteration, and this is crucial for fast convergence. Instead of choosing ε, one could choose s and solve (6.18); but, s is probably even more difficult to choose empirically than ε (at least, ε is homogeneous to f-values, but what about s?). However, (6.18) provides a link with Sections 4 and 5. We begin with the latter and consider again (5.18). To simplify notations, assume x_k is the best iterate: $f(x_k) \leq f(x_i)$, $i \leq k$. Minimizing $\hat{f}_k$ to find x_{k+1} makes sense only if $\hat{f}_k \approx f$ near x_k (i.e. where the optimum is likely to lie); but there are good reasons to think that this is not the case and that $\hat{f}_k$ is far too optimistic (although $\hat{f}_k(x_i) = f(x_i)$, $i \leq k$); one of these reasons is the so slow convergence observed for the cutting plane algorithm. Therefore, it may appear as a sensible idea to minimize $\hat{f}_k(x) + \frac{1}{2}s|x - x_k|^2$ (for some chosen s) which is less optimistic than $\hat{f}_k$. Furthermore, use (6.14) as a notation to write $\hat{f}_k$ as

$$\hat{f}_k(x_k + d) = f(x_k) + \max\{-p_j + g_j^T d \mid j \leq k\} . \qquad (6.19)$$

In summary we obtain

$$\min \ v + \tfrac{1}{2}s|d|^2 , \qquad (6.20a)$$
$$v \geq -p_j + g_j^T d , \qquad (6.20b)$$

which is just (5.19) when $s = 0$.

Applying duality theory to this problem (see Section 2.3) we obtain now

$$x_{k+1} = x_k - s^{-1} \sum \lambda_j g_j \quad \text{with } \lambda \text{ solving (6.18)} .$$

Thus, a bundle method appears as a stabilization of the cutting plane algorithm, and also as a method of centers in the graph space (see the very end of Section 5.4). Note, however, that this does not help in choosing s in (6.18) or ε in (6.17).

The link with Section 4, now, will give an interpretation for the additional term $s|d|^2$. To make this link more suggestive, consider instead of P of (6.15), the coarser

$$P' := \text{conv}\{g_j \mid p_j \leq \varepsilon\} \subset P .$$

Then the corresponding projection problem (6.17) or (6.18) becomes

$$\min \ \frac{1}{2} \left| \sum \lambda_j g_j \right|^2 , \quad \lambda_j \geq 0, \ \sum \lambda_j = 1 , \qquad (6.21)$$

which can be interpreted as: to compute the direction, take only those g_j that are close to $\partial f(x_k)$, and pretend that they are in $\partial f(x_k)$ (actually, the first bundle methods, known as *conjugate subgradient methods*, were based on this idea).

Now apply again duality theory to (4.16): $\tilde{f}$ is minimized at $d = -H^{-1}[\Sigma\ \lambda_i\nabla f_i(x_k)]$ where $\lambda \in R^{I(x)}$ solves

$$\min \frac{1}{2}\left[\sum \lambda_i\nabla f_i(x)\right]H^{-1}\left[\sum \lambda_i\nabla f_i(x)\right], \quad \lambda_i \geqslant 0, \ \sum \lambda_i = 1 \ ,$$

whose analogy with (6.21) is clear.

Thus, we obtain the further interpretation of bundle methods: at iteration k, we are (temporarily) faced with the minimax function $\hat{f}_k$ of (6.19). Of this function, only those pieces

$$f(x_k) - p_j + g_j^\mathrm{T}d \quad \text{with } p_j \text{ small}$$

are reliable (see above). Neglecting the small p_j, we can consider that those pieces are linear approximations of some functions f_j, which in turn induce a curvature in some Lagrangian function. In bundle methods, this Hessian is taken as $H = sI$, for want of a better approximation. Finally, going from P' to P, i.e. from (6.21) to (6.18), is the same as going from (4.16) to (4.17). It amounts to using the pieces neglected in (6.21) as further safeguards to help computing d.

Our final comment about bundle methods is that they can be extended to more general f without conceptual difficulty. The key idea is to take Lemma 6.1 as a *definition* of $\partial_\varepsilon f(x)$ for nonconvex f:

$$\partial_\varepsilon f(x) = \text{conv} \cup \{\partial f(y) | |y - x| \leqslant \varepsilon\} \ ,$$

which amounts to changing p_j in (6.14) to $p_j = |x_k - x_j|$.

7. Directions for future developments

For smooth f and $\varepsilon \to 0$ iteration (6.13) reduces to the classical steepest descent method which is not more than linearly convergent. To obtain faster convergence one has to replace the first order model (3.1) behind the steepest descent idea by the second order model (3.2). Minimization of (3.2) leads to (Quasi-) Newton methods of type (5.2) which are at least superlinearly convergent and consequently behave much better in practice. There arises the natural and challenging question in NSO: Can we develop a "second order" model for nonsmooth f, based on the ε-modifications of standard definitions from convex analysis introduced in Section 6, i.e., a model which for smooth f and $\varepsilon \to 0$ reduces to (3.2)? The minimization of such a model should lead to much better convergence behaviour.

We will mention two possible approaches toward this aim.

7.1. *Directional second order approximation of f*

We start with the following proposal for a *second directional derivative* at x in direction d (provided the limit exists)

$$f''(x; d) := \lim_{t \downarrow 0} \frac{1}{t} [f'(x + td; d) - f'(x; d)] . \tag{7.1}$$

For $C^2 f$ the Mean-Value Theorem implies

$$\frac{1}{t} [f'(x + td; d) - f'(x; d)] = \frac{1}{t} [\nabla^2 f(x + \theta td)td]^T d \quad \text{with } \theta \in (0, 1) ;$$

taking the limit we see that $f''(x; d)$ reproduces the Hessian:

$$f''(x; d) = d^T \nabla^2 f(x) d . \tag{7.2}$$

We remark that, contrary to $f'(x; d)$, the above limit does not exist for every convex f; the function $f(x) := |x|^\alpha$ with $\alpha \in (1, 2)$ and $x = 0$ may serve as a counter example.

Provided $f''(x; d)$ exists we can define the model

$$f'(x; d) + \tfrac{1}{2} f''(x; d) . \tag{7.3}$$

For $C^2 f$ (7.3) is identical with (3.2) and thus minimization of (7.3) leads to Newton's method. This looks rather promising. However, we still feel uneasy. Firstly, in view of Figure 3.1, an ε is missing somewhere in (7.3); as we know from Section 6.1, such ε helps to avoid shortcomings due to nonsmoothness. Secondly, we do not dispose of a max-expression of type (1.7) for $f''(x; d)$. Such a relation, however, is important for an eventual implementation of (7.3); compare Section 6.2. The following idea proves to be helpful. Consider another limit (provided it exists)

$$c(x; d) := \lim_{\varepsilon \downarrow 0} \frac{f'_\varepsilon(x; d) - f'(x; d)}{\varepsilon^{1/2}} . \tag{7.4}$$

A straightforward geometric argument shows that the infimum $f'_\varepsilon(x; d)$ is the slope of the line through $(x, f(x) - \varepsilon)$ which supports the graph of $f(x + \alpha d)$, $\alpha \geq 0$, from below. Hence in (7.4) we compare the difference between this slope and that of the tangent at $(x, f(x))$ to the *vertical* increment $\varepsilon^{1/2}$. In (7.1) the tangents in direction d at $x + td$ and x are compared to the *horizontal* increment t. At the first glance there is no relation between these two limits. A closer analysis shows however that, thanks to convexity, they are closely related.

Theorem 7.1. *Let x and d be given. Suppose one of the limits* (7.1) *and* (7.4), *respectively, exists. Then the other one exists as well and*

$$f''(x; d) = \tfrac{1}{2} c(x; d)^2 . \quad \Box$$

The proof of the above statement is very technical.

Provided $f''(x; d)$ exists, then, because of Theorem 7.1, we may write $c(x; d)^2/4$ instead of $f''(x; d)/2$ in (7.3). Further, we will not cause a disaster if we replace $c(x; d)$ by $[f'(x; d) - f'(x; d)]/\sigma^{1/2}$ for fixed small positive σ. This leads to the modification of (7.3):

$$M_\sigma(x; d) := f'(x; d) + \frac{1}{4\sigma} [f'_\sigma(x; d) - f'(x; d)]^2 . \tag{7.5}$$

This $M_\sigma(x; \cdot)$ is a model at x which can be minimized to obtain a direction d_σ, say (x, standing for x_k, is fixed, d is the variable).

To justify this approach, we first observe that, in contrast to (7.3), the model (7.5) is well-defined even if $f''(x, d)$ does not exist. Further, all quantities in M_σ can be computed via suitable max-terms. Finally, let us show that the direction d_σ is at least as good as the direction d_ε which we use in the corresponding first order iteration (6.13). We proceed in several steps from the smooth to the nonsmooth situation.

Consider a quadratic function $f(x) := \tfrac{1}{2} x^{\mathrm{T}} A x + b^{\mathrm{T}} x$ with symmetric positive definite matrix A. Straightforward computation of the inf in (6.8) gives

$$f'_\sigma(x; d) = f'(x; d) + (2\sigma d^{\mathrm{T}} A d)^{1/2} , \tag{7.6}$$

hence

$$M_\sigma(x; d) = x^{\mathrm{T}} A d + b^{\mathrm{T}} d + \tfrac{1}{2} d^{\mathrm{T}} A d \equiv f(x + d) - f(x)! \tag{7.7}$$

As a result, we obtain for every $\sigma > 0$ the Newton direction:

$$d_\sigma = - A^{-1}(Ax + b) = -(\nabla^2 f(x))^{-1} \nabla f(x) . \tag{7.8}$$

Obviously there is no reason for the d_ε of Section 6.1 to be close to the Newton direction.

In case f is C^2 then for small σ our model $M_\sigma(x; d)$ is close to the second order model (3.2). Hence we can expect that, at least for small σ, the direction d_σ will be close once more to the Newton direction, whereas for small ε the first order direction d_ε will be close to the steepest descent direction.

When f is C^1 a convergence result can be proved comparable to the one for the steepest descent method and smooth f; for the general case, finally, we observe that $M_\sigma(x, 0) = 0$; hence $M_\sigma(x, d_\sigma) < 0$, which obviously implies $f'(x, d_\sigma) < 0$, i.e. d_σ is at least a descent direction. It turns out that (at least if $0 \not\in \partial_\sigma f(x)!$) the optimal d_σ does satisfy $f'_\sigma(x, d_\sigma) < 0$, i.e. a move in the direction d_σ guarantees a decrease of at least σ. We summarize: the above model combines the advantage of Newton's model in the region where f is smooth with a guaranteed decrease of at least σ in every step.

The above model is still waiting for an implementation. Unfortunately, the building technique of Section 6.2 essentially results in the cutting plane algorithm (5.19). Hence, some new idea is still really needed.

7.2. First order approximation of the subdifferential

Let us come back to the approximate optimality condition (6.12). As already mentioned, the point-to-set mapping $x \to \partial_\varepsilon f(x)$ varies in a Lipschitzian way with x. Even more can be said: $f'_\varepsilon(x, p)$ which, for fixed $\varepsilon > 0$ and p, varies in a Lipschitzian way with x, does have directional derivatives

$$f''_\varepsilon(x, p; d) := \lim_{t \downarrow 0} \frac{1}{t} [f'_\varepsilon(x + td, p) - f'_\varepsilon(x, p)] . \tag{7.9}$$

Hence, our motivation is as follows: since we want to solve

$$f'_\varepsilon(x, p) \geq 0 \ \forall p \in R^n , \quad \text{i.e. } 0 \in \partial_\varepsilon f(x) , \tag{7.10}$$

what about applying the idea of Newton's method? In other words: let us replace f'_ε in (7.10) by its first order approximation coming from (7.9), to obtain the iteration:

$$\text{Let } d_k \text{ solve } f'_\varepsilon(x_k, p) + f''_\varepsilon(x_k, p; d) \geq 0 \ \forall p \in R^n , \tag{7.11a}$$

$$x_{k+1} := x_k + t_k d_k , \quad t_k > 0 \text{ suitable} . \tag{7.11b}$$

Several really intricate questions must be addressed before this approach can become practical. Among them are (i) how good is d_k coming from (7.11) in terms of minimizing f? (ii) when can be compute numerically a solution of (7.11)? or even: when does (7.11) have a solution? (iii) just as in (7.3) we do not have a nice expression like (1.7) for f''_ε of (7.9), and once again this will be critical for an eventual implementation. No practical answer to these questions is foreseen in the near future.

Nevertheless, the present approach poses an interesting, purely mathematical, question: just in the same way as f'_ε is related to $\partial_\varepsilon f$, can we relate the derivative in (7.9) to some derivative of the multi-valued mapping $\partial_\varepsilon f(x)$? Or, even more generally, it is possible to define a derivative of a multi-valued mapping?

Several proposals have been made in the past for such an object, each with its own motivation. For our purpose, what we need is a *first order approximation*, i.e.: let $F(t)$ be a subset of R^n depending on the parameter $t \in [0, 1]$ ($F(t)$ stands for $\partial_\varepsilon f(x + td)$), and denote by B the unit ball in R^n; we want to find another set $S(t)$, depending on the same parameter t, and such that

$$\forall \varepsilon > 0, \ \exists \delta > 0: \ t \in [0, \delta] \quad \Rightarrow$$

$$S(t) \subset F(t) + \varepsilon t B \ \text{ and } \ F(t) \subset S(t) + \varepsilon t B \ ; \tag{7.12}$$

and

$$\text{the mapping } S \text{ is simple, in a sense to be specified.} \tag{7.13}$$

We will henceforth assume that $F(t)$ is convex for each t, and therefore we will require also $S(t)$ to be convex for each t.

By analogy with the single-valued case, the simplest S would be defined via a set $F'(0) \subset R^n$ (the derivative of $F(t)$ at $t = 0$) by the equation

$$S(t) := F(0) + t F'(0) . \tag{7.13a}$$

Unfortunately, the existence of such an $F'(0)$ is ruled out even for mappings as simple as $F(t) := (1 - t) B$. Hence, we have to content ourselves with some more general mapping S and the next idea that comes to mind is to require

$$S(t) = (1 - t) S(0) + t S(1) \quad \forall t \in [0, 1] \tag{7.13b}$$

(assuming that $t = 1$ is in the domain of S), a property that resembles linearity, but restricted to $t \in [0, 1]$.

Even more generally, we may require only one inclusion in (7.13b) namely:

$$S(t) \supset (1 - t) S(0) + t S(1) , \tag{7.13c}$$

which means the more intrinsic property

$$S \text{ has a convex graph} . \tag{7.13d}$$

An advantage of (7.13d) is that it can be directly generalized to $t \in R^n$.

On the other hand, *canonicity* must also be taken into account when specifying (7.13): there should be only one S satisfying (7.12), (7.13). Indeed (7.13b) implies it, but (7.13d) does not; to recover it, a convenient supplement is maximality:

$$\text{The graph of } S \text{ contains the graph of all other mappings}$$
$$\text{satisfying (7.12), (7.13d)} . \tag{7.13d}'$$

Alternately, this maximal convex approximation can be defined as satisfying the property (compare (7.13a) and (7.13b)):

$$S(t) = \cap \left\{ y + t \frac{S(\tau) - y}{\tau} \,\middle|\, y \in F(0) \right\} \quad \forall \tau \in \,]0, t] . \tag{7.13e}$$

A mapping possessing the defining property (7.13e) has the following nice

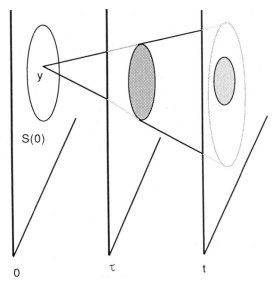

Fig. 7.1.

geometric interpretation, in 2 dimensions (see Figure 7.1): consider y as a luminous spot at $t = 0$, which illuminates the space at t; $S(\tau)$ is an opaque object in the space at τ; then there is a zone at t which is always dark, wherever y is in $F(0)$; this is just $S(t)$, and the property holds independently of the value of $\tau \leq t$.

8. Commented bibliography

As mentioned earlier, a constant reference throughout this paper is Zowe (1985), and also Lemaréchal (1980); see also the recent Kiwiel (1988).

For fairly extensive bibliographies, see Nurminskii (1982), Lemaréchal and Mifflin (1978), Kiwiel (1985).

Section 1. The reference book for all the necessary concepts from convex analysis is Rockafellar (1970). A minimal but easy to read introduction is Section 8 and the appendices of Lasdon (1970). For extensions to nonconvex situations, the basic material is in Clarke (1975, 1983). In practice, the Lipschitz assumption is too general and some additional hypotheses must be included. For convenient subclasses of Lipschitz functions see the review of Lemaréchal (1986).

Section 2. Genuinely nondifferentiable problems often appear in an infinite dimensional setting: shape optimization (Myslinski and Sokolowski (1985), Neittaanmaki and Tiba (1984)), optimal control (Outrata (1983), and more generally Clarke (1983)); operations research (Hanscom et al. (1985), Cullum et al. (1975), Chapter 9 of Grötschel et al. (1987)), Tchebychef approximation, for example in circuit design (Hald and Madsen (1981)). Another source of nonsmooth problems is in stochastic programming (Ruszczynski (1986)); we mention that, for these problems, methods of Section 5 (known there as stochastic gradient) are often most efficient (Goursat et al. (1986)).

Proposition 2.1 is due to Danskin (1966) for the case when h is maximized at a single y (i.e. when $\nabla f(x)$ exists); in its most general form, it can be found for example in Clarke (1975).

The approach in Section 2.2 is generally called Benders decomposition, see a review in Geoffrion (1972); an interesting case is when x and y are ordered in a hierarchical control system (Ruszczynski (1982)). Differential properties of the resulting f form one of the hard subjects in nonlinear analysis, with many papers devoted to it; see for example Fiacco (1984).

Section 2.3 represents an extremely important field of mathematical programming. Good treatments are in Lasdon (1970), Geoffrion (1971a,b). Even if the technique does not directly solve the problem via dual maximization (Bertsekas et al. (1983a)), duality often plays a central role – for example in integer programming (Fisher et al. (1975)). As for Section 2.4 see for example Geoffrion (1970), Hogan (1973), Silverman (1972). Here again, differential properties of $v(y)$ are a central issue, we again refer to Fiacco (1984). A combination of price- and quota-decomposition is considered in Mahey (1986). Finally, see several specific applications in operations research in Shor (1985).

Section 3. The example of non-convergence is inspired from Wolfe (1975); see also Demjanov and Malozemov (1974). An example involving only linear functions is given in Wolfe (1974). The example of Section 3.3 is due to M.J. Todd; for sophisticated use of finite differences, see Gupal (1977), p. 15 of Shor (1985) and also Theorem I.17.1 of Demjanov and Vasiliev (1986).

Section 4. The first instance of an algorithm for composite optimization was probably due to Demjanov (1968), giving what essentially is the steepest descent for (4.5) or equivalently the projected gradient method for (4.6). For penalty-type approaches, see Chapter 3 of Bertsekas (1982). For optimality conditions see Fletcher and Watson (1980), Ben Tal and Zowe (1982) (where condition (4.15) is derived); for methods based thereon, see Pschenichnyi and Danilin (1978) and Fletcher (1982).

Sometimes, methods for composite optimization can become quite sophisticated, like for minimizing the maximal eigenvalue of a varying matrix (Fletcher (1985), Overton (1988), Overton and Womersley (1988)). One would imagine that this problem has the form (4.5) but this is false; for example, the subdifferential is not a polyhedron, but an ellipsoid, see Kato (1976).

We mention also another approach for convex optimization, given in Kao and Meyer (1981); it is applicable to the *separable* case, when f is a sum of one-dimensional convex functions. The approach is original in that, rather than a lower-approximation of f based on its subgradients, it is an upper-approximation that is considered, based on convex combinations of f at iteratively computed sampling points.

Section 5. For a general description of subgradient methods, we refer to the monograph of Shor (1985). See for example Nurminskii and Zhelikhowski (1977) for various generalization.

The space dilation along the gradient was defined in Shor (1970) and its son the ellipsoid method in Judin and Nemirowski (1976). The second dilation (along the difference of gradients) dates from Shor and Zhurbenko (1971); it is much less known, though much more used in Soviet Union.

The cutting plane method is due independently to Cheney and Goldstein (1959) and Kelley (1960). The seminal works for the "school of global algorithms" were Judin and Nemirovsky (1976) where Theorems 5.6 and 5.7 were proved, while the method of centers of gravity is due to Levin (1965). Theorem 5.5 was proved in Wolfe (1970); see also p. 147 of Nemirovsky and Judin (1983); the latter book is a *must* concerning this global theory.

The idea of placing x_{k+1} at a "center" of a "safety set" exists also in the context of nonlinear programming, see Bui Trong Lieu and Huard (1966), where the terminology "*F*-distance" is introduced. The particular center of (5.21) is to be compared to those coming from projective geometry as in Karmarkar (1984), de Ghellinck and Vial (1988). Along these lines, we refer to various works such as Sonnevend (1985, 1986).

Section 6. Although the cutting plane method (5.19) itself can be considered as the very first instance of a bundle method, the ideas of Section 6 were consciously exploited in the first place by Lemaréchal (1974), and then independently by Lemaréchal (1975), Wolfe (1975). The algorithm of Section 6.3 was presented in Lemaréchal (1976) and formalized in Lemaréchal et al. (1981); its variant (6.18), defined in Lemaréchal (1978), was developed in Mifflin (1982), Kiwiel (1983); according to Kiwiel (1989), this latter variant might give definitely better results.

For the nonconvex case, Feuer (1974) realized that a mere Lipschitz assumption is not enough and adapted the bundling idea to max-functions. The minimal assumption is that of Bihain (1984) and the mathematically most satisfactory goes along semi-smoothness of Mifflin (1977).

Finally, all the above references are contained in the exhaustive monograph Kiwiel (1985), which is the best reference for a complete and detailed setting of all these methods, most refined proofs of convergence, extensions to nonconvex and constrained cases, some numerical illustrations and a fairly complete bibliography. Additional comparative results can be found in Lemaréchal (1982), Zowe (1985).

Section 7. Only few papers have been published yet, since these ideas are quite new. Concerning Section 7.1, there are only Lemaréchal and Zowe (1983) and Lemaréchal and Strodiot (1985); for Theorem 7.1 and related material, see Seeger (1986), and also Hiriart-Urruty (1986). The directional derivative (7.9) was obtained in Lemaréchal and Nurminskii (1980) and the views expressed in 7.2 come from Auslender (1982), Demjanov et al. (1986),

Lemaréchal and Zowe (1988); property (7.13b) is essentially due to Gautier (1978); a good review of differentiability problems for multi-valued mappings is Penot (1984).

Bibliography

S. Agmon (1954), The relaxation method for linear inequalities, *Canadian Journal of Mathematics* **6**, 382–392.

A. Auslender (1982), On the differential properties of the support function of the subdifferential of a convex function, *Mathematical Programming* **24**(3), 257–268.

A. Ben Tal and J. Zowe (1982), Necessary and sufficient optimality conditions for a class of nonsmooth minimization problems, *Mathematical Programming* **24**(1), 70–91.

D.P. Bertsekas (1982), *Constrained Optimization and Lagrange Multiplier Methods* (Academic Press, New York).

D.P. Bertsekas, G.S. Lauer, N.R. Sandell, T.A. Posbergh (1983), Optimal short-term scheduling of large-scale power systems, *IEEE Transactions on Automatic Control* **28**(1), 1–11.

A. Bihain (1984), Optimization of upper semi differentiable functions, *Journal of Optimization Theory and Applications* **4**, 545–568.

Bui Trong Lieu and P. Huard (1966), La méthode des centres dans un espace topologique, *Numerische Mathematik* **8**, 56–67.

E.W. Cheney and A.A. Goldstein (1959), Newton's method for convex programming and Tchebycheff approximation, *Numerische Mathematik* **1**, 253–268.

F.H. Clarke (1975), Generalized gradients and applications, *Transactions of the A.M.S.* **205**, 247–262.

F.H. Clarke (1983), *Optimization and Nonsmooth Analysis* (Wiley, New York).

J. Cullum, W.E. Donath and P. Wolfe (1975), The minimization of certain nondifferentiable sums of eigenvalues of symmetric matrices, in: M.L. Balinski and P. Wolfe (eds), *Nondifferentiable Optimization*, Mathematical Programming Study 3 (North-Holland, Amsterdam) 35–55.

J.M. Danskin (1966), The theory of max–min with applications, *SIAM Journal on Applied Mathematics* **14**(4), 641–655.

V.F. Demjanov (1968), Algorithms for some minimax problems, *Journal of Computer and System Science* **2**, 342–380.

V.F. Demjanov, C. Lemaréchal and J. Zowe (1986), Approximation to a set-valued mapping I: A proposal, *Applied Mathematics and Optimization* **14**(3), 203–214.

V.F. Demjanov and V.N. Malozemov (1974), *Introduction to Minimax* (Wiley, New York).

V.F. Demjanov and L.V. Vasiliev (1985), *Nondifferentiable Optimization* (Optimization Software, Inc./Springer-Verlag, Berlin).

A. Feuer (1974), An implementable mathematical programming algorithm for admissible fundamental functions, Ph.D. Thesis, Dept of Mathematics, Columbia Univ.

A.V. Fiacco (ed.) (1984), *Sensitivity, Stability and Parametric Analysis*. Mathematical Programming Study 21 (North-Holland, Amsterdam).

M.L. Fischer, W.D. Northup and J.F. Shapiro (1975), Using duality to solve discrete optimization problems: theory and computational experience, in: M.L. Balinski and P. Wolfe (eds.), *Nondifferentiable Optimization*, Mathematical Programming Study 3 (North-Holland, Amsterdam) 56–94.

R. Fletcher (1982), Second order corrections for nondifferentiable optimization, in: G.A. Watson (ed.), *Numerical Analysis*, Lectures Notes in Mathematics 912, (Springer-Verlag, Berlin) 85–114.

R. Fletcher (1985), Semi-definite matrix constraints in optimization, *SIAM Journal on Control and Optimization* **23**(4), 493–513.

R. Fletcher and G.A. Watson (1980), First and second order conditions for a class of nondifferentiable optimization problems. *Mathematical Programming* **18**(3), 291–307.

S. Gautier (1978), Différentiabilité des multi-applications, Working Paper, Dept. of Mathematics, Univ. of Pau.

A.M. Geoffrion (1970), Primal resource-directive approaches for optimizing nonlinear decomposable systems, *Operations Research* **18**(3), 375–403.

A.M. Geoffrion (1971a), Elements of large scale programming, *Management Science* **16**(11), 652–675.

A.M. Geoffrion (1971b), Duality in nonlinear programming: A simplified application-oriented development, *SIAM Review* **13**(11), 1–37.

A.M. Geoffrion (1972), Generalized Benders decomposition, *Journal of Optimization Theory and Applications* **10**(4), 237–260.

G. de Ghellinck and J.P. Vial (1986), A polynomial Newton method for linear programming, *Algorithmica* **1**(4), 425–453.

M. Goursat, J.P. Quadrat and M. Viot (1986), Stochastic gradient methods for optimizing electrical transportation networks, in: V.I. Arkin, A. Shiryaev, R. Wets (eds.), *Stochastic Optimization*. Lecture Notes in Control and Information Sciences 81 (Springer-Verlag, Berlin) 373–387.

M. Grötschel, L. Lovasz and A. Schrijver (1987), *The Ellipsoid Method and Combinatorial Optimization* (Springer-Verlag, Berlin).

A.M. Gupal (1977), A method for the minimization of almost-differentiable functions, *Cybernetics* **13**(1), 115–117.

J. Hald and K. Madsen (1981), Combined LP and quasi-Newton methods for minimax optimization, *Mathematical Programming* **20**(1), 49–62.

M.A. Hanscom, V.H. Nguyen and J.J. Strodiot (1985), A reduced subgradient algorithm for network problems with convex nondifferentiable costs, in: V.F. Demjanov and D. Pallaschke (eds.), *Nondifferentiable Optimization: Motivations and Applications*, Lecture Notes in Economics and Mathematical Systems 255 (Springer-Verlag, Berlin) 318–322.

J.B. Hiriart-Urruty (1986), A new set-valued second order derivative for convex functions, in: J.B. Hiriart-Urruty (ed.), *Fermat Days 85: Mathematics for Optimization* (North-Holland, Amsterdam) 157–182.

W. Hogan (1973), Directional derivatives for extremal-valued functions with applications to the completely convex case, *Operations Research* **20**(1), 188–209.

D.B. Judin and A.S. Nemirovskii (1976), Estimation of the informational complexity of mathematical programming problems, *Matekon* **13**, 2–45.

C.Y. Kao and R.R. Meyer (1981), Secant approximation methods for convex optimization, in: H. König, B. Korte, K. Ritter (eds.), *Mathematical Programming Study* 14 (North-Holland, Amsterdam) 143–162.

N. Karmarkar (1984), A new polynomial time algorithm for linear programming, *Combinatorica* **4**(4), 373–395.

T. Kato (1976), *Perturbation Theory for linear operators* (Springer-Verlag, Berlin).

J.E. Kelley (1960). The cutting plane method for solving convex programs, *Journal of the SIAM* 8, 703–712.

K.C. Kiwiel (1983), An aggregate subgradient method for nonsmooth convex minimization, *Mathematical Programming* **27**(3), 320–341.

K.C. Kiwiel (1985), *Methods of Descent for Nondifferentiable Optimization*. Lecture Notes in Mathematics 1133 (Springer-Verlag, Berlin).

K.C. Kiwiel (1988), A survey of bundle methods for nondifferentiable optimization, *Proceedings XIII International Symposium on Mathematical Programming* (Tokyo).

K.C. Kiwiel (1989), Proximity control in bundle methods for convex nondifferentiable minimization, *Mathematical Programming* (to appear).

L.S. Lasdon (1970), *Optimization Methods for Large Scale Problems* (MacMillan, New York).

C. Lemaréchal (1974), An algorithm for minimizing convex functions, in: J.L. Rosenfeld (ed.), *Proceedings IFIP'74 Congress* (North-Holland, Amsterdam) 552–556.

C. Lemaréchal (1975), An extension of Davidon methods to nondifferentiable problems, in: M.L. Balinski and P. Wolfe (eds.), *Mathematical Programming Study* 3 (North-Holland, Amsterdam) 95–109.

C. Lemaréchal (1976), Combining Kelley's and conjugate gradient methods, Abstracts, IX International Symposium on Mathematical Programming (Budapest), 158–159.

C. Lemaréchal (1978), Nonsmooth optimization and descent methods, Report RR 784, IIASA, 2361 Laxenburg (Austria).

C. Lemaréchal (1980), Nondifferentiable optimization, in: L.C.W. Dixon, E. Spedicato, G.P. Szegö (eds.), *Nonlinear Optimization* (Birkhäuser, Basel) 149–199.

C. Lemaréchal (1982), Numerical experiments in nonsmooth optimization, in: E. A. Nurminski (ed.), *Progress in nonsmooth optimization*, Proceedings CP 82.58, IIASA, 2361 Laxenburg (Austria), 61–84.

C. Lemaréchal (1986), Basic theory in nondifferentiable optimization, *Optimization* **17**(6) 827–858.

C. Lemaréchal and R. Mifflin (eds.) (1978), *Nonsmooth Optimization* (Pergamon Press, Oxford).

C. Lemaréchal and E.A. Nurminski (1980), Sur la différentiabilité de la fonction d'appui du sous-différentiel approché, *Comptes Rendus Académie des Sciences Paris* **290**(18), 855–858.

C. Lemaréchal and J.J. Strodiot (1985), Bundle methods, cutting-plane algorithms and σ-Newton directions, in: V.F. Demjanov and D. Pallaschke (eds.), *Nondifferentiable Optimization*, Lecture Notes in Economics and Mathematical Systems 255 (Springer-Verlag, Berlin) 25–33.

C. Lemaréchal, J.S. Strodiot and A. Bihain (1981), On a bundle algorithm for nonsmooth optimization, in: O.L. Mangasarian, G.L. Meyer, S.M. Robinson (eds.), *Nonlinear Programming 4* (Academic Press, New York) 245–282.

C. Lemaréchal and J. Zowe (1983), Some remarks on the construction of higher order algorithms for convex optimization, *Applied Mathematics and Optimization* **10**(1), 51–68.

C. Lemaréchal and J. Zowe (1987), Approximation to a set valued mapping II: Existence, uniqueness, characterization, Schwerpunktprogramm der Deutschen Forschungsgemeinschaft "Anwendungsbezogene Optimierung und Steuerung", Report No. 5.

A.Y. Levin (1965), On an algorithm for minimizing a convex function, *Soviet Mathematics Doklady* **6**(1), 286–290.

P. Mahey (1986), Méthodes de décomposition et décentralisation en programmation linéaire, *RAIRO Rech. Opér.* **20**(4), 287–306.

R. Mifflin (1977), Semi-smooth and semi-convex functions in constrained optimization, *SIAM Journal on Control and Optimization* **15**(6), 959–972.

R. Mifflin (1982), A modification and an extension of Lemaréchal's algorithm for nonsmooth minimization, in: D.C. Sorensen and R.J.B. Wets (eds.), *Mathematical Programming Study* 17, (North-Holland, Amsterdam) 77–90.

T. Motzkin and I. Schönberg (1954), The relaxation method for linear inequalities, *Canadian Journal of Mathematics* **6**, 393–404.

A. Myslinski and J. Sokolowski (1985), Nondifferentiable optimization problems for elliptic systems, *SIAM Journal on Control and Optimization* **23**(4), 632–648.

P. Neittaanmaki and D. Tiba (1984), On the finite element approximation of the boundary control for two-phase Stefan problems, in: A. Bensoussan J.L. Lions (eds.), *Analysis and Optimization of Systems*, Lecture Notes in Control and Information Sciences 62 (Springer-Verlag, Berlin) 356–370.

A.S. Nemirovsky and D.B. Yudin (1983), *Problem complexity and method efficiency in optimization* (Wiley, New York).

E.A. Nurminski (ed.) (1982), *Progress in Nondifferentiable Optimization*, Publication CP-82-58, IIASA, 2361 Laxenburg, Austria.

E.A. Nurminski and A.A. Zhelikhowskii (1977), ε-quasi-gradient method for solving nonsmooth extremal problems, *Cybernetics* **13**(1), 109–114.

J.V. Outrata (1983), On a class of nonsmooth optimal control problems, *Applied Mathematics and Optimization* **10**(4), 287–306.

M.L. Overton (1988), On minimizing the maximum eigenvalue of a symmetric matrix, *SIAM Journal on Matrix Analysis and Applications* **9**, 256–268.

M.L. Overton and R.S. Womersley (1988), On minimizing the spectral radius of a nonsymmetric matrix function – Optimality conditions and duality theory, *SIAM Journal on Matrix Analysis and Applications* **9**, 473–498.

J.P. Penot (1984), Differentiability of relations and differential stability of perturbed optimization problems, *SIAM Journal on Control and Optimization* **22**(4), 529–551.

B.T. Poljak (1977), Subgradient methods: A survey of Soviet research, in: C. Lemaréchal and R. Mifflin (eds.) *Nonsmooth Optimization* (Pergamon Press, Oxford) 5–30.

B.N. Pschenichny and Y.M. Danilin (1978), *Numerical Methods for Extremal Problems* (Mir, Moscow).

R.T. Rockafellar (1970), *Convex Analysis* (Princeton University Press, Princeton).

A. Ruszczynski (1982), Nondifferentiable functions in hierarchical control problems, in: E.A. Nurminski (ed.), *Progress in Nondifferentiable Optimization*, Publication CP-82-58, IIASA, 2361 Laxenburg, Austria, 145–172.

A. Ruszczynski (1986), A linearization method for nonsmooth stochastic programming problems, *Mathematics of Operations Research* **12**(1), 32–49.

A. Seeger (1986), Analyse du second ordre de problèmes non différentiables, Ph.D. Thesis, Dept. of Mathematics, Univ. of Toulouse.

N.Z. Shor (1970), Utilization of the operation of space dilatation in the minimization of convex functions, *Cybernetics* **6**(1), 7–15.

N.Z. Shor (1985), *Minimization Methods for Nondifferentiable Functions* (Springer-Verlag, Berlin).

N.Z. Shor and N.G. Zhurbenko (1971), A minimization method using the operation of extension of the space in the direction of the difference of two successive gradients, *Cybernetics* **7**(3), 450–459.

G.J. Silverman (1972), Primal decomposition of mathematical programs by resource allocation. I Basic theory and a direction finding procedure. II Computational algorithm with an application to the modular design programming, *Operation Research* **20**(1), 58–93.

G. Sonnevend (1985), A modified ellipsoid method for the minimization of convex functions with superlinear convergence [finite termination] for well-conditioned C^3 smooth [piecewise linear] functions, in: V.F. Demjanov and D. Pallaschke (eds.), *Nondifferentiable Optimization*. Lecture Notes in Economics and Mathematical Systems 255 (Springer-Verlag, Berlin) 264–277.

G. Sonnevend (1986), A new method for solving a set of linear (convex) inequalities and its applications, in: B. Martos (ed.), *Proceedings 5th IFAC-IFORS Symposium on Dynamic Modelling* (Pergamon Press, Oxford).

P. Wolfe (1970), Convergence theory in nonlinear programming, in: J. Abadie (ed.), *Integer and Nonlinear Programming* (North-Holland, Amsterdam) 1–36.

P. Wolfe (1974), A method of conjugate subgradients for minimizing nondifferentiable functions, Proceedings, 12th Annual Allerton Conference on Circuit and System Theory, University of Illinois at Urbana, Champaign 8–15.

P. Wolfe (1975), A method of conjugate subgradients for minimizing nondifferentiable functions, in: M.L. Balinski and P. Wolfe (eds.), *Nondifferentiable Optimization*, Mathematical Programming Study 3 (North-Holland, Amsterdam) 145–173.

J. Zowe (1985), Nondifferentiable optimization, in: K. Schittkowski (ed.), *Computational Mathematical Programming* (Springer-Verlag, Berlin) 323–356.

G.L. Nemhauser et al., Eds., *Handbooks in OR & MS, Vol. 1*
© Elsevier Science Publishers B.V. (North-Holland) 1989

Chapter VIII

Stochastic Programming

Roger J.-B. Wets

Department of Mathematics, University of California, Davis, CA, 95616, U.S.A.

1. Introduction: The model

It is difficult to find examples of systems to be controlled or simply analyzed, that do not include some level of uncertainty about the values to assign to some of the parameters or about the actual design of some of the components of the system. In a rather large number of cases not much is lost by assuming that these 'uncertain' quantities are actually known, either because the level of uncertainty is low, or because these quantities play an insignificant role in the process that we want to analyze or control. But then there are those cases when the parameters that are uncertain play a central role in the analysis of the decision making process, and the model builder cannot ignore the special character of these parameters, without running the risk of invalidating all possible implications that he may draw from his analysis.

As uncertainty is a broad concept, it is possible – and often useful – to approach it in many different ways. One rather general approach which has been successfully applied to a wide variety of problems is to assign explicitly or implicitly, a probability distribution to the various unknown parameters. There is *no* implication that there is necessarily a solid statistical basis to back up the choice of a particular distribution. In fact, in some cases there may be no statistical data available about the phenomenon that are to be modeled by random variables (and associated probability distribution). A typical example is when the model is used in the context of policy setting and there is no concrete evidence available about future events, that may include such imponderables as technological or social developments. In such cases, the 'probability space' may consist of a number of scenarios, and the associated probability measure could only be a subjective (or 'expert') measure of the reliability to attach to these various scenarios; a well done analysis would then certainly include a study of the sensitivity of the solution to perturbations of this 'probability measure'.

The *stochastic programming model* can be viewed as an extension of the linear and nonlinear programming models to *decision models where the coefficients that are not known with certainty have been given a probabilistic representation*. In the context of the mathematical programming models, some versions of this model were introduced in the late 1950's by Dantzig, Beale, Tintner, and Charnes and Cooper, but there had already been a number of simple stochastic programming models that had been formulated (and solved) in inventory theory, micro-economics and system maintenance, for example. There had also been studies of certain statistical problems that are related to stochastic programming, but there are however differences between the formulation of the stochastic optimization problems that come from statistics and those that are motivated by decision making under uncertainty. In mathematical statistics, it is mostly the analysis of 'wait-and-see' solutions that is of interest, i.e., when information is collected, and used 'during' the decision process. Stochastic programming is mostly concerned with problems that require a 'here-and-now' decision, without making further observations of the random variables (or, more precisely, of the quantities modeled as random variables). The solution must be found on the basis of the a *priori* information about these random quanties. Moreover, because of the underlying motivation, the search for efficient solution techniques occupies central stage. In this chapter of the Handbook we deal almost exclusively with results that have direct bearing on the design of solution procedures (and associated approximation schemes).

The following problem will serve as our general formulation of a *stochastic programming problem*:

$$\text{minimize} \quad E\{f_0(x, \boldsymbol{\xi})\}$$

$$\text{subject to} \quad E\{f_i(x, \boldsymbol{\xi})\} \leq 0, \; i = 1, \ldots, s, \qquad (1.1)$$

$$E\{f_i(x, \boldsymbol{\xi})\} = 0, \; i = s + 1, \ldots, m,$$

$$x \in X \subset R^n,$$

where
- $\boldsymbol{\xi}$ is a random vector with support $\boldsymbol{\Xi} \subset R^N$,
- P is a probability distribution function on R^N,
- $f_0 : R^n \times \boldsymbol{\Xi} \to R \cup \{+\infty\}$,
- $f_i : R^n \times \boldsymbol{\Xi} \to R$, $i = 1, \ldots, m$,
- X is closed,

for all $x \in X$, and $i = 0, 1, \ldots, m$, the *expectation functional*

$$(Ef_i)(x) := E\{f_i(x, \boldsymbol{\xi})\} = \int_{\boldsymbol{\Xi}} f_i(x, \xi) \, dP(\xi)$$

is finite unless $\{\xi \mid f_0(x, \xi) = \infty\}$ has positive probability, and then

$$(Ef_0)(x) := \int_{\boldsymbol{\Xi}} f_0(x, \xi) \, dP(\xi) = \infty,$$

and the feasibility set

$$S = X \cap \{x \mid Ef_i(x) \leq 0, \ i = 1, \ldots s; \ Ef_i(x) = 0, \ i = s + 1, \ldots, m\}$$
$$\cap \{x \mid (Ef_0)(x) < \infty\}$$

is assumed nonempty. We shall denote both the distribution function of ξ and the associated probability measure by P.

We allow f_0 and Ef_0 to take on the value $+\infty$. This, of course, suggests the presence of hidden constraints. We shall see later that we are naturally led to include this feature in the general formulation problem, to allow for '*induced constraints*' determined by future feasibility considerations.

The richness of the model allows for a wide range of applications (the reader could consult the general references, in particular the bibliography cited at the end of this chapter). Here we mention just a couple of examples to illustrate some of the features of the model.

Example 1.1. *Reservoir Management.* Reservoirs that supply water for irrigation and urban consumption usually have a hierarchical layout that allows for rather sophisticated water management. The difference between a well-managed and an optimally managed system may very well mean passing from a drought-like situation to one that is nearly 'normal'. The difficulty in choosing an 'optimal' control policy is that inflows, and to a lesser extent the demands, are stochastic. Many decisions (releases, storage locations, etc.) must be made before the values of these random quantities are observed. The problem is of the following type:

$$\text{minimize} \quad E\{f_0(x, \xi)\} = cx + x^{\mathrm{T}}Rx + E\left\{\sum_{k=1} \theta_k(T_k x - h_k)\right\}$$

$$\text{subject to} \quad E\{f_i(x, \xi)\} = -P\{g_i(x) \leq q_i\} + \alpha_i \leq 0, \ i = 1, \ldots, s,$$

$$f_i(x) = A_i x - b_i = 0, \ i = s + 1, \ldots, m,$$

$$x \in S = \{x \mid 0 \leq x_j \leq u_j, \ j = 1, \ldots, n\},$$

where $\xi = (T, h, q)$ are the random quantities of the problem, the functions θ_k are used to evaluate the deviations between the water made available $T_k x$ (resulting from decisions x_j and realizations t_{kj}) and the observed demand h_k in region k; the other terms in the objective function represent the operational costs. The first s constraints model the need to keep the water level in reservoir i above a certain specified level most of the time (with probability α_i), and the last $m - s$ constraints are the flow balance equations (inflow = outflow). The upper bounds on the x_j indicate that there are limitations on the amount of water that can be released or shifted from one reservoir to another in the given time period.

Example 1.2. *Assets and liability management.* Uncertainties about cash flow, cost of funds and return on investments are an intrinsic component in the management of assets and liabilities of any financial institution. The problem is to choose an investment strategy (x_{ij}^{kl}: asset k purchased in period i and sold in period j) that will maximize expected returns. The model takes on the following form:

$$\text{maximize} \quad E\{f_0(x, \xi)\} = g_{10}(x^1) + E_{\xi_1}\{\varphi_{10}(x^1; \xi^1)\}$$

$$\text{subject to} \quad f_{1i}(x^1) \le 0, \quad i = 1, \ldots, m_1,$$

and for $k = 2, \ldots, K$, $\varphi_{k-1,0}(x^1, \ldots, x^{k-1}; \xi^1, \ldots, \xi^{k-1})$ is the optimal value of the (stochastic) program

$$\text{maximize} \quad g_{k0}(x^k) + E_{\xi_k}\{\varphi_{k0}(x^1, \ldots, x^k; \xi^1, \ldots, \xi^{k-1}, \xi^k)\}$$

$$\text{subject to} \quad f_{ki}(x^1, \ldots, x^k, \xi^1, \ldots, \xi^{k-1}) \le 0, \quad i = 1, \ldots, m_k,$$

and $\varphi_{k+1,0} = 0$. This is a K-stage problem. The x^k represent the assets bought and sold in period k, the random quantities ξ_k come from returns on assets and deposits/withdrawals, the constraints come from legal restrictions, as well as budgetary, liquidity and policy limitations. The objective takes into account returns on investments, as well as penalties for early withdrawal (necessitated by the need to meet the constraints).

Returning to our basic model, it is even clearer from the following equivalent formulation of problem (1.1):

$$\text{minimize} \quad Ef_0(x)$$

$$\text{subject to} \quad Ef_i(x) \le 0, \quad i = 1, \ldots, s, \tag{1.2}$$

$$Ef_i(x) = 0, \quad i = s + 1, \ldots, m,$$

$$x \in X \subset R^n,$$

that we are just dealing with a nonlinear program. The only difference is that we explicitly allow for the possibility that the functions Ef_i, $i = 0, \ldots, m$, have an integral representation. It may seem that our only concern should be to identify the properties (linearity, convexity, differentiability) of the expectation functionals Ef_i, and leave the task of solving (1.2) to the appropriate nonlinear programming package. And in fact, the study of expectation functionals is a central theme of the theory of stochastic programming. But the research cannot stop at that point. To evaluate Ef_i just for one x, or the (sub)gradient at x, may be a much more onerous task than solving any reasonable nonlinear programming problem. If the functions $f_i(x, \cdot)$ are separable, so that

$$\int f_i(x, \xi) \, dP(\xi) = \sum_{j=1}^N \int f_{ij}(x, \xi_j) \, dP_j(\xi_j), \tag{1.3}$$

we known pretty well how to handle such cases; univariate calculus as well as one-dimensional numerical integration routines are well developed. It is when the evaluation of the expectation functionals relies on multi-dimensional integration that stochastic programming problems cannot be 'solved' by standard nonlinear programming techniques. Moreover, one cannot get away with blanket assumptions such as the integrands $\{f_i, i = 0, \ldots, m\}$ are differentiable or convex. There are some important models when the integrands are not even continuous.

The presence of uncertainty requires the decision to be prudent but at the same time it should take advantage of the unusual situations that may arise. These two factors play a significant role in the formulation of stochastic optimization problems, and they enter in various ways into the model. When reliability considerations are in the foreground, they are usually included in the form of constraints. In other models, they may enter in the form of penalties, and sometimes it may even be difficult to identify precisely the components of the objective function that come from reliability considerations. In one way or another, every stochastic optimization model must reflect an attitude toward risk. This is why it is often possible to pass from one type of formulation to an equivalent one, that in terms of the equation and functions involved may appear to be quite different. This is also why we shall avoid making the classical distinction between reliability models (stochastic programs with probabilistic constraints) and penalty models (that include stochastic programs with recourse).

Before we analyze, in Sections 3 and 4, the type of constraints and objective functions that arise in various stochastic programming, we review briefly in Section 2 the more useful properties of expectation functionals. Optimality conditions and duality results are mentioned in Section 5. Section 6 is concerned with approximation schemes, and serves as an introduction to the description of the major solution strategies in Sections 7. Finally, Section 8 is devoted to questions of sensitivity and stability of the solution with respect to perturbations of the underlying probability measure, and the implications of these results for stochastic programs with incomplete information.

Section 2 provides the theoretical background to much of what follows. It brings together and expands on a number of results that are widely scattered in the literature, and for those reasons we provide the technical details. After the defintion of an expectation function and the statement of Proposition 2.1, the first time reader may very well skip ahead to Section 3 (returning to Section 2 only as needed).

2. Expectation functionals

This section is mostly a grab-bag collection of results about expectation functionals and their subgradients. We proceed from generalities to the more specific cases. Let

$$g = R^n \times \Xi \to R \cup \{\infty\} = (-\infty, \infty]$$

denote the integrand, and as always, let P be a probability distribution function with support $\Xi \subset R^n$; the *support* of P is the smallest subset of Ξ of probability

1. We assume (i) that the expectation functional

$$Eg : R^n \to R \cup \{\infty\}$$

is well-defined for all x in R^n, which means here that for all x the function $g(x, \cdot)$ is measurable and that $E\{g(x, \xi) \mid g(x, \xi) \leq 0\} > -\infty$, and, (ii) that Eg not identically $+\infty$, i.e., Eg is a *proper* function. The *effective domain* of a function h, the set on which a function is not $+\infty$, is denoted by

$$\text{dom } h := \{x \mid h(x) < \infty\} .$$

Proposition 2.1. *If the function* $x \mapsto g(x, \xi)$ *is a.s. convex (resp. affine, linear or sublinear), then so is the expectation functional* Eg.

Proof. The assertions, linear and affine, simply follow from the linearity of the integral. Convexity follows from the fact that the operation $\int dP(\xi)$ can be viewed as taking a nonnegative linear combination of convex functions. The sublinearity assertion follows from convexity and linearity (restricted to a ray). $\square$

Proposition 2.2. *Suppose that the function* $x \mapsto g(x, \xi)$ *is a.s. l.s.c. (lower semicontinuous) and that either there exists a summable function* β *such that a.s.*

$$\beta(\xi) \leq g(x, \xi) \quad \text{for all } x \in R^n$$

or the function $x \mapsto g(x, \xi)$ *is a.s. convex. Then the expectation function is also lower semicontinuous.*

Proof. If g is integrably bounded below by an integrable function, we appeal to Fatou's Lemma.

In the convex case, since we already know that Eg is convex, to prove that it is also l.s.c. it suffices to show that it is continuous at the end point x^0 of any line segment $(x^0, x^1]$ contained in the relative interior of the convex set dom Eg. A.s. convexity and lower semicontinuity of $g(\cdot, \xi)$ imply that the function

$$\lambda \mapsto g((1 - \lambda)x^0 + \lambda x^1, \xi) := h(\lambda, \xi)$$

is a.s. continuous, convex on $[0, 1]$ and finite, except possible at $\lambda = 0$. Thus

$$h(\lambda, \xi) = 2(1 - \lambda)h(\tfrac{1}{2}, \xi) - (1 - 2\lambda)h(1, \xi) + \Delta(\lambda, \xi) ,$$

where $\Delta(\cdot, \xi)$ is a.s. continuous on $[0, 1]$ and finite, nonnegative and monotonically decreasing on $(0, \tfrac{1}{2}]$. By the Monotone Convergence Theorem $\int \Delta(\lambda, \xi) dP(\xi)$ is continuous at $\lambda = 0$. Since $Eg(x^{1/2})$ and $Eg(x^1)$ are finite and by integrating both sides of the above equation, we have

$$Eg(x^\lambda) = 2(1-\lambda)Eg(x^{1/2}) - (1-2\lambda)Eg(x^1) - \int \Delta(\lambda, \xi)\, dP(\xi),$$

from which it follows that Eg is continuous on $[x^0, x^1]$ at x^0. $\quad\square$

Since taking the expectation has a smoothing effect, the function Eg could easily have continuity or differentiability properties that are not shared by the individual functions $g(\cdot, \xi)$. To illustrate this, we give two continuity results.

Proposition 2.3. *Suppose* $x \mapsto g(x, \xi)$ *is uniformly continuous at* $\hat{x}$, *i.e. for all* $\xi > 0$ *there exists a neighborhood* V *of* $\hat{x}$ *such that for all* y *in* V, $|g(\hat{x}, \xi) - g(y, \xi)| < \varepsilon$ *almost surely. Then* Eg *is continuous at* $\hat{x}$.

Proof. For all y in V,

$$|Eg(\hat{x}) - Eg(y)| \leq \int |g(\hat{x}, \xi) - g(y, \xi)| P(d\xi) < \varepsilon. \quad\square$$

Proposition 2.4. *Suppose* $g(x, \xi) = \psi(\zeta(x, \xi))$ *where* $\zeta : R^n \times \Xi \to R^M$, *and* $\psi : R^M \to (-\infty, \infty]$, Q_x *is the distribution function of the random vector* $\zeta(x, \cdot)$, *and the map* $x \mapsto Q_x$ *is continuous at* $\hat{x}$ *in the following sense: for all* $\varepsilon > 0$, *there exists a neighborhood* V *of* $\hat{x}$ *such that for all* y *in* V

$$\int d|Q_{\hat{x}} - Q_y|(\xi) < \varepsilon. \tag{2.1}$$

Suppose moreover that there exists a neighborhood W *of* $\hat{x}$ *such that on* W, $g(\cdot, \xi)$ *is almost uniformly bounded. Then* Eg *is continuous at* $\hat{x}$.

Proof. Let β be the uniform bound, i.e., such that $|g(\cdot, \xi)| \leq \beta$ on W for almost all ξ in Ξ. Then, if we restrict ourselves to y in W,

$$|Eg(\hat{x}) - Eg(y)| = \left| \int \psi(\zeta)\, dQ_{\hat{x}}(\zeta) - \int \psi(\zeta)\, dQ_y(\zeta) \right|$$

$$\leq \beta \int d|Q_{\hat{x}} - Q_y|(\xi).$$

The result now follows directly from the assumed continuity of the distribution functions at $\hat{x}$ (with respect to x). $\quad\square$

A typical case where one would use this last proposition is when $\zeta = T(\xi)x + h(\xi)$ and the distributions of the random matrix T and random vector h are absolutely continuous. Continuity of Eg could be asserted without requiring that $x \mapsto g(x, \xi)$ be continuous (a.s.). This situation does occur in integer stochastic programming.

We usually need, at least locally, stronger continuity properties. If Eg is convex, then it is locally Lipschitz on int Eg, the interior of its effective domain. Local Lipschitz properties also follow from the next proposition.

Proposition 2.5. *The expectation functional Eg is locally Lipschitz relative to* dom Eg, *whenever to any bounded set V, open relative to* dom Eg, *there corresponds a summable function $\beta : \Xi \to R$ such that for any x^0, x^1 in V, one has*

$$|g(x^0, \xi) - g(x^1, \xi)| \le \beta(\xi)\|x^0 - x^1\| . \qquad (2.2)$$

It is Lipschitz on dom Eg *if (2.2) holds for any pair in* dom Eg.

Proof. From (2.2), one has

$$|Eg(x^0) - Eg(x^1)| \le \int |g(x^0, \xi) - g(x^1, \xi)| \, dP(\xi)$$

$$\le \int \beta(\xi)\|x^0 - x^1\| \, dP(\xi) ,$$

and this yields the assertions since β is summable. $\square$

A function $h : R^n \to R \cup \{\infty\}$ is *inf-compact* if it is lower semicontinuous and for all α in R, its (lower) *level sets* $\text{lev}_\alpha h$ are bounded, where

$$\text{lev}_\alpha h := \{x \mid h(x) \le \alpha\} .$$

If h is coercive, or if it is l.s.c. and its effective domain is compact, then it is inf-compact. Our interest in this concept comes from the fact that for h proper, proving inf-compactness is tantamount to establishing the existence of points that minimize h, since then

$$\text{argmin } h = \bigcap_{\{\alpha \mid \text{lev}_\alpha h \ne \emptyset\}} \text{lev}_\alpha h \qquad (2.3)$$

is compact.

To state the next proposition it is useful to introduce the following concepts. The *epigraph* of h is the set

$$\text{epi } h = \{(x, \alpha) \in R^n \times R \mid \alpha \ge f(x)\} .$$

By cl h (co h, resp.) we denote the function whose epigraph is the *closure* (*convex hull*, resp.) of epi h. Note that cl h is the l.s.c. regularization of h, i.e.,

$$\text{cl } h(x) := \inf_{\{x^\nu \to x\}} \liminf_{\nu \to \infty} h(x^\nu) . \qquad (2.4)$$

where the notation is intended to suggest that the infimum is taken with respect to all sequences $\{x^\nu\}_{\nu=1}^\infty$ converging to x. From Caratheodory's Theorem about convex hulls, we have that

$$\text{co } h(x) := \inf\left\{ \sum_{k=0}^n \lambda_k h(x^k) \,\middle|\, \sum_{k=0}^n x^k = x, \sum_{k=0}^n \lambda_k = 1, \lambda_k \geq 0 \right\}.$$

A proper l.s.c. function h is inf-compact, if cl co h is inf-compact, since the closed set $\text{lev}_\alpha h$ is contained in the bounded set $\text{lev}_\alpha(\text{cl co } h)$. A proper l.s.c. convex function h is inf-compact if and only if its *recession function* (where x is any point in $\text{dom}(h)$)

$$\text{rc } h(y) := \lim_{\lambda \to \infty} \frac{h(x + \lambda y) - h(x)}{\lambda} \tag{2.5}$$

is a sublinear function (follows from the definition), positive everywhere except at $y = 0$, where rc $h(0) = 0$.

Proposition 2.6. *Suppose Eg is l.s.c., $\xi \mapsto \text{cl co } g(\cdot, \xi)$ is measurable, $(E \text{ cl co } g)$ is proper, and a.s. cl co $g(\cdot, \xi)$ is inf-compact. Then Eg is inf-compact.*

Proof. Let $h(x, \xi) := \text{cl co } g(x, \xi)$. In view of the preceding remarks and earlier propositions, it will suffice to show that the proper, l.s.c, convex, expectational function Eh, defined by

$$Eh(x) := \int h(x, \xi) \, dP(\xi),$$

is inf-compact. And this will follow from the identity

$$\text{rc } Eh = \int \text{rc } h(\cdot, \xi) \, dP(\xi), \tag{2.6}$$

since by assumption rc $h(\cdot, \xi)$ is a.s. a positive (except at 0) sublinear function, and in view of Proposition 2.1 and the fact that $\int \beta \, dP > 0$ if β is a.s. positive, these properties are transmitted to rc Eh. To prove the identity, observe that Eh is proper, and thus there is x^0 such that a.s. $x^0 \in \text{dom } h(\cdot, \xi)$. Then, for every y,

$$\text{rc } h(y, \xi) = \lim_{\nu \to \infty} h_\nu(y, \xi)$$

with

$$h_\nu(y, \xi) = \lambda_\nu^{-1}[h(x^0 + \lambda_\nu y, \xi) - h(x^0, \xi)]$$

where $\{\lambda_\nu\}_{\nu=1}^\infty$ is a positive sequence that goes to $+\infty$. The collection $\{h_\nu(y,\cdot)\}_{\nu=1}^\infty$ is an increasing sequence of quasi-integrable functions $(E\{h_\nu(y, \xi)\le 0\} > -\infty)$ that converges to rc $h(y,\cdot)$, Applying Beppo Levi's Theorem yields (2.6). □

The second part of this section deals with the (sub)differentiability of expectation functionals. We can only present a sampling of the possible results. *Gradients and subgradients* of h (or Eh) with respect to x are denoted by $\nabla h(\nabla Eh)$ and $\partial h(\partial Eh)$. *Smooth* and continuously differentiable refer to the same property; a function $h: R^n \to R$ is *subsmooth on a neighborhood V* of x, if for all $y \in V$,

$$h(y) = \max_{t \in T} \theta_t(y)$$

where T is a compact topological space, each θ_t is smooth and both $\theta_t(y)$ and $\nabla_t\theta_t(y)$ are jointly continuous in t and y.

Proposition 2.7. *Suppose $g(\cdot, \xi)$ is a.s. smooth at x^0, and that there exists a neighborhood V of x^0 such that Eg is finite on V, and for all x in V, the function*

$$\xi \mapsto e(x, \xi) := \frac{g(x, \xi) - g(x^0, \xi) - \nabla g(x^0, \xi)(x - x^0)}{\|x - x^0\|}$$

is absolutely summable. Then Eg is smooth at x^0, and

$$\nabla Eg(x^0) = \int \nabla g(x^0, \xi)\, dP(\xi). \tag{2.7}$$

Proof. For all $x \in V$, we have

$$Eg(x) = Eg(x^0) + E\{\nabla g(x^0, \xi)\}(x - x^0) + E\{e(x, \xi)\}\|x - x_0\|.$$

Now, from a.s. smoothness at x^0, we know that $|e(x, \xi)|$ converges a.s. to 0 as x goes to x^0, and since $|e(x, \xi)|$ is summable it follows from Lebesgue's Dominated Convergence Theorem that $E\{e(x, \xi)\}$ converges to 0. This, and the fact that the preceding identity also implies that $E\{\nabla g(x^0, \xi)\}$ is well defined, shows that $E\{\nabla g(x^0, \xi)\}$ is the gradient of Eg at x^0. □

Proposition 2.5 is about all that can be done to guarantee smoothness. But not withstanding its limitations, it covers a number of interesting applications. For example, suppose that Eg is finite on a neighborhood of x^0, and

$$g(x, \xi) = \varphi(h(\xi) - T(\xi)x) \tag{2.8}$$

with h a random m-vector and T an $(m \times n)$-random matrix; we identify the components of ξ with the elements of h and T. If $\varphi : R^m \to (-\infty, \infty]$ is smooth a.e. (with respect to the Lebesgue measure), P is a continuous distribution function, then

$$\nabla Eg(x^0) = -E\{\nabla\varphi(h(\xi) - T(\xi)x^0)T(\xi)\}, \qquad (2.9)$$

provided that the summability condition of Proposition 2.5 is satisfied. This will always be the case if Ξ is bounded: the function $e(x, \xi)$, defined in Proposition 2.5, is then a.s. bounded on Ξ since in this setup $\xi \mapsto \nabla\varphi(h(\xi) - T(\xi)x^0)$ is a.s. continuous on Ξ. The identity (2.9) is also satisfied if φ is convex, since then Eg is convex and finite on V which with the convexity of φ yields the summability of the error function

$$e(x, \xi) = \frac{\varphi(h - Tx) - \varphi(h - Tx^0) - \nabla\varphi(h - Tx^0)T(x - x^0)}{\|x - x^0\|}$$

where $\xi = (h, T)$. We do not give a detailed proof, since in the convex case there is a much more general formula that completely characterizes the subgradients of expectation functionals, see Propositions 2.10 and 2.11.

In the subdifferential case, we are interested in the counterpart of (2.7), or at least in the inclusion

$$\partial Eg(x) \subset \int \partial g(x, \xi)\, dP(\xi). \qquad (2.10)$$

But first we need to know if the term on the right is well-defined. A set-valued map

$$\xi \mapsto \Gamma(\xi) : \Xi \rightrightarrows R^M$$

is a *random closed set*, if for all ξ, $\Gamma(\xi)$ is a closed set and for any open (or closed, or compact) set $G \subset R^M$,

$$\Gamma^{-1}(G) = \{\xi \in \Xi \mid \Gamma(\xi) \cap G \neq \emptyset\}$$

is measurable. A function $g : R^n \times \Xi \to (-\infty, \infty]$ is a *random l.s.c. function* if

$$\xi \mapsto \mathrm{epi}\, g(\cdot, \xi) : \Xi \rightrightarrows R^{n+1}$$

is a random closed set. It is not difficult to see that if g is a random l.s.c. function, so is $y \mapsto t^{-1}[h(x + ty) - h(x)]$ for any x and $t > 0$. Since the epi-limits inferior or superior of random l.s.c. functions are again random l.s.c. functions, it follows from the definitions (see the Appendix) that:

Proposition 2.8. *Suppose* $g: R^n \times \Xi \to (-\infty, \infty]$ *is a random lower semicontinuous function, then so are the contingent derivatives*

$$(y, \xi) \mapsto g'(x, \xi; y)$$

and (upper) epi-derivatives

$$(y, \xi) \mapsto g^{\uparrow}(x, \xi; y)$$

(where g' *and* $g^{\uparrow}$ *are* ∞ *for all* y, *if* $g(x, \xi) = \infty$). *Moreover the subdifferential map*

$$\xi \mapsto \partial g(x, \xi): \Xi \to R^n$$

is a random closed set.

Proof. From the remarks that precede the proposition we already know that for any x, $g^{\uparrow}(x, \cdot\,; \cdot)$ is a random l.s.c. function. Moreover, $y \mapsto g^{\uparrow}(x, \xi; y)$ is convex as follows from the properties of the epi-derivative. Now note that for any y, the map

$$\xi \mapsto \Gamma_y(\xi) := \{v \in R^n \mid v \cdot y \leq g^{\uparrow}(x, \xi; y)\}$$

is a random closed convex set, and that

$$\partial g(x, \xi) = \bigcap_{y \in R^n} \Gamma_y(\xi),$$

from which the last assertion follows. $\square$

The expectation of a random set Γ is the set

$$E\Gamma = \int \Gamma(\xi)\, dP(\xi) := \mathrm{cl}\left\{\int u(\xi)\, dP(\xi) \mid u \text{ and } L_1\text{-selection of } \Gamma\right\},$$

where cl stands for closure – without 'cl' this is the Aumann integral. This gives a precise meaning to the inclusion (2.9) and related formulas. We begin with a general inclusion that goes in the other direction.

Proposition 2.9. *Suppose* $g: R^n \times \Xi \to (-\infty, \infty]$ *is a random lower semicontinuous function with Eg finite, l.s.c. at x, and such that for almost all ξ, $g(\cdot, \xi)$ is subdifferentiably regular at x. Suppose also that for some scalar β, $t^{-1}[g(x + ty, \cdot) - g(x, \cdot)] \geq \beta$ a.s. for all y in a neighborhood of 0 and $0 < \bar{t} \leq t$. Then*

$$E\{\partial g(x, \cdot)\} \subset \partial(Eg)(x).$$

Proof. From Fatou's Lemma it follows that for any sequence $\{y^\nu\}$ converging to y, and $t_\nu \downarrow 0$,

$$\int \liminf_{\nu \to \infty} t_\nu^{-1}(g(x + t_\nu y^\nu, \xi) - g(x, \xi))P(d\xi)$$

$$\leq \liminf_{\nu \to \infty} \int t_\nu^{-1}(g(x + t_\nu y^\nu, \xi) - g(x, \xi))P(d\xi)$$

provided, as is the case under our assumptions, the difference quotients

$$t^{-1}[g(x + ty, \xi) - g(x, \xi)]$$

are (uniformly) bounded below on a neighborhood of y for all t sufficiently close to 0. Taking the infimum with respect to all sequences converging to y preserves the inequality and hence

$$\int g'(x, \xi; y)P(d\xi) \leq (Eg)'(x; y),$$

as follows from the definitions of epi-limit inferior (A.1), of contingent derivative (A.4), and of the expectation functional. Since

$$(Eg)'(x; \cdot) \leq (Eg)^\uparrow(x; \cdot),$$

(see (A.6)) from the preceding inequality and the a.s. subdifferential regularity of $g(\cdot, \xi)$ at x, we have

$$E\{g^\uparrow(x, \xi; \cdot)\} \leq (Eg)^\uparrow(x; \cdot).$$

These are sublinear functionals (Proposition 2.1), hence from the definition of subgradients, Proposition 2.8, and the defnition of the expectation of a random set, we obtain

$$E\{\partial g(x, \xi)\} \subset \partial Eg(x).$$

Both sets are nonempty since the (uniform) lower bound on the difference quotients implies that $g^\uparrow(x, \cdot; 0\} > 0$ almost surely. □

We can apply this proposition to the convex case, but sharper results are possible.

Proposition 2.10. *Suppose* $g: R^n \times \Xi \to (-\infty, \infty]$ *is a random l.s.c. convex function (i.e.,* $x \mapsto g(x, \cdot)$ *is a.s. convex), such that Eg is finite on a neighborhood of* x*. Then*

$$E\{\partial g(x, \cdot)\} = \partial Eg(x).$$

Proof. In the convex case, we know that the contingent and epi-derivatives coincide (Appendix) and can be expressed as

$$g'(x, \xi; y) = g^\uparrow(x, \xi; y) = \lim_{t \downarrow 0}[t^{-1}(g(x + ty; \xi) - g(x, \xi))] \,.$$

Since the difference quotients are monotone decreasing as t goes to 0, and the finiteness of Eg on a neighborhood of x implies that their expectation is finite for t sufficiently close to 0, we can rely on the Beppo Levi (monotone) convergence theorem to obtain the identity

$$\int g^\uparrow(x, y; \xi)P(d\xi) = \int g'(x, y; \xi)P(d\xi)$$
$$= (Eg)'(x; y) = (Eg)^\uparrow(x; y) \,,$$

that yields the asserted equality. □

If x belongs to the boundary of the effective domain of Eg, then even in the convex case we cannot guarantee equality. However one always has the following:

Proposition 2.11. *Suppose* $g: R^n \times \Xi \to (-\infty, \infty]$ *is a random l.s.c. convex function such that* $Eg > -\infty$ *and* $Eg(x)$ *is finite. Then*

$$\partial Eg(x) = E\{\partial g(x, \cdot)\} + \mathrm{rc}[\partial Eg(x)]$$

where rc *denotes the recession (or asymptotic) cone.*

Proof. As in the proof of Proposition 2.10, we have that whenever $Eg(x + ty)$ is finite for some $t > 0$, $E\{g^\uparrow(x, \cdot; y)\} = (Eg)^\uparrow(x; y)$; in the other directions $(Eg)^\uparrow(x; y) = \infty$. From this it follows that

$$(Eg)^\uparrow(x; y) = E\{g^\uparrow(x, \cdot; y)\} + \psi_{T(x)}(y)$$

where $\psi_{T(x)}$ is the indicator function of the tangent cone $T(x)$ of dom Eg at x; $T(x) = \{y \mid Eg(x + ty) < \infty \text{ for some } t > 0\}$, and $\psi_S(y) = 0$ if $y \in S$, $= \infty$ otherwise. The subgradient relation now follows from the definition of the subgradient-set (A.7), the fact that the sets involved are convex, and that for a convex set C, rc C is the largest closed convex cone such that $C + \mathrm{rc}\, C \subset C$. □

In general, i.e. without local convexity, we usually have to rely on the following proposition to obtain the desired inclusion, that becomes an equality in the subdifferentiable case.

Proposition 2.12. *Suppose* $g: R^n \times \Xi \to (-\infty, +\infty]$ *is a random l.s.c. function with Eg finite at x. Suppose also that for almost all ξ, $g(\cdot, \xi)$ is subsmooth on a neighborhood of x and that $\alpha: \Xi \to R$ is a summable function such that for all x_1, x_2 in a neighborhood of x,*

$$g(x_1, \xi) - g(x_2, \xi) \leqslant \alpha(\xi)|x_1 - x_2| .$$

Then

$$\partial Eg(x) \subset E\{\partial g(x, \cdot)\} .$$

If Eg is subdifferentiably regular at x, the inclusion is acutally an equality.

Proof. Since $g(\cdot, \xi)$ is a.s. subsmooth, we have that

$$g^\uparrow(x, \xi; y) = g'(x, \xi; y) = \limsup_{\substack{x' \to x \\ t \downarrow 0}} \frac{g(x' + ty, \xi) - g(x', \xi)}{t} .$$

Now, the assumptions imply that t sufficiently small,

$$t^{-1}[g(x' + ty, \xi) - g(x', \xi)] \leqslant \alpha(\xi)\|y\| ,$$

and from Fatou's Lemma it follows that

$$\int g^\uparrow(x, \xi; y) P(d\xi) \geqslant \limsup_{\substack{x' \to x \\ t \downarrow 0}} t^{-1}[Eg(x' + ty) - Eg(x')]$$

$$\geqslant (Eg)^\uparrow(x) .$$

Here again the inclusion follows from the definition of the subgradient set. If *Eg* is subdifferentiably regular at *x*, equality follows from Proposition 2.9. $\square$

Many special cases are of interest in the applications of these formulas in stochastic programming. For example:

Proposition 2.13. *Suppose that $g: R^n \times \Xi \to (-\infty, \infty]$ is a function of the following type:*

$$g(x, \xi) = g_0(x, \xi) + \psi_S(x)$$

where ψ_S is the indicator function of a closed nonempty set $S \subset R^n$, and g_0 is a finite valued function such that to any bounded open set V there corresponds a summable function α with

$$|g_0(x^1, \xi) - g_0(x^2, \xi)| \leqslant \alpha(\xi)|x^1 - x^2|$$

for any pair x^1, x^2 in V. Then

$$\partial Eg(x) \subset \partial Eg_0(x) + \partial \psi_S(x) ,$$

with equality if Eg_0 and ψ_S are subdifferentiably regular at x. In particular, this implies that if $v \in \partial Eg(x)$, there exist $v_S \in \partial \psi_S(x)$, i.e., a normal to S at x, and a measurable function $\xi \mapsto u_0(x, \xi): \Xi \to R^n$ such that

$$u_0(x, \cdot) \in \partial g_0(x, \cdot) \quad a.s. , \tag{2.11}$$

$$v = v_s + \int u_0(x, \xi) \, dP(\xi) . \tag{2.12}$$

The proof of this proposition follows directly from the earlier results. The last assertion is a consequence of the inclusion (2.9) and the definition of the expectation of a random set.

3. Anticipative models and adaptive models

The distinction between anticipative and adaptive models is more useful from a modeling, than a technical viewpoint. There are however certain formulations that are germane to anticipative models. Typically we are confronted with the following situation. A decision x must be made in an uncertain environment described by a parameter ξ. We have equipped Ξ, the space of possible realizations of ξ, with a probability structure that reflects either the actual probabilities or simply a subjective measure of the weight to be given to a single event or a class of events in the choice of an optimal decision. *Anticipative models* are those for which the decision does not depend in any way on future observations of the environment.

For such models, feasibility (when the constraints depend on ξ) is expressed either in terms of a *probabilistic (or chance) constraint* such as

$$P\{\xi \mid g_k(x, \xi) \leqslant 0, k = 1, \ldots, q\} \geqslant \alpha \tag{3.1}$$

with $\alpha \in (0, 1]$ the reliability level, or involves some of the moments of the constrained quantities such as

$$E\{g_k(x, \cdot)\} + \beta[\text{var } g_k(x, \cdot)]^{1/2} \leqslant 0 \tag{3.2}$$

for β a positive constant. To bring these constraints in concordance with the canonical form (1.1), we define f_i as follows:

$$f_i(x, \xi) = \begin{cases} \alpha - 1 & \text{if } g_k(x, \xi) \leqslant 0, \ k = 1, \ldots, q , \\ \alpha & \text{otherwise} , \end{cases} \tag{3.3}$$

in the case of probabilistic constraints. In the other case the constraints involve the sum of two functions that are both expectation functions, since

$$\text{var } g_k(x, \cdot) = E\{g_k(x, \cdot) - Eg_k(x)\}^2 .$$

Reliability considerations may lead to an objective function of the type

$$\text{minimize} \quad P[\xi \mid g_0(x, \xi) \le \gamma] \tag{3.4}$$

where γ is a constant. If the criterion is in terms of utilities or costs, the objective is as in (1.1) with f_0 continuous with respect to x.

Although it may sometimes be possible to deal with probabilistic constraints by relying on techniques that have been developed for smoother functions f_i, the intrinsic discontinuities introduced by probabilistic constaints, cf. (3.3), create a number of difficulties that are better dealt with separately.

We take (3.1) as our general prototype with g_k continuous in x and measurable in ξ; if $q \ge 2$ we speak of *joint probabilistic constraints*. We note that the functions g are then random lower semicontinuous functions. Let $S := \{x \text{ satisfying } (3.1)\}$. We define

$$\kappa(\xi) := \{x \mid g_k(x, \xi) \le 0, \ k = 1, \ldots, q\} , \tag{3.5}$$

and thus

$$\kappa^{-1}(x) := \{\xi \mid g_k(x, \xi) \le 0, \ k = 1, \ldots, q\} . \tag{3.6}$$

If $\alpha = 1$, the functions g_k are continuous with respect to ξ and the random set

$$(x, \xi) \mapsto \{y \in R^k \mid y \ge g_k(x, \xi), \ k = 1, \ldots, q\}$$

is upper semicontinuous (closed graph) then $S = \cap \kappa(\xi)$. Hence S is closed. It is convex if the functions $g_k(\cdot, \xi)$ are convex. One can even show that it is polyhedral under the following conditions: the g_k's are affine in x, and co Ξ (the convex hull of Ξ) is polyhedral.

It is much more difficult to characterize the set of feasible solutions when $\alpha < 1$, since there is usually no subset of Ξ that yields S as an intersection of the $\kappa(\xi)$. One must quickly resort to the study of special cases. Since

$$S = \bigcup_{\{\Sigma \subseteq \Xi \mid P(\Sigma) \ge \alpha\}} \bigcap_{\xi \in \Sigma} \kappa(\xi) ,$$

we see that if P has finite support, S will be closed (the sets $\kappa(\xi)$ are closed since the functions $g(\cdot, \xi)$ are continuous, and the union involves only a finite number of terms). But even if the sets $\kappa(\xi)$ are convex, S will usually not be convex. To obtain convexity one needs a certain type of unimodality. A probability measure P or R^N is *quasi-concave* if for any pair U, V of convex, measurable subsets of R^N and for any $\lambda \in [0, 1]$ one has

$$P[(1 - \lambda)U + \lambda V] \geq \min\{P(U), P(V)\} . \tag{3.7}$$

Proposition 3.1. *Let S denote the set of feasible solutions, i.e., those x that satisfy (3.1). Suppose that the functions*

$$(x, \xi) \mapsto g_k(x, \xi) : R^n \times \Xi \to R, \quad k = 1, \ldots, q ,$$

are convex, and the probability measure P is quasi-concave, then, for any α in $[0, 1]$, S is a closed convex set.

Proof. If S is empty, or $\alpha = 0$, there is nothing to prove. Suppose $x^0, x^1 \in S$; then with $x^\lambda = (1 - \lambda)x^0 + \lambda x^1$,

$$\kappa^{-1}(x^\lambda) \supset (1 - \lambda)\kappa^{-1}(x^0) + \lambda\kappa^{-1}(x^1) ,$$

since for $k = 1, \ldots, q$, $g_k(x^0, \xi^0) \leq 0$ and $g_k(x^1, \xi^1) \leq 0$ imply that for $\lambda \in [0, 1]$,

$$g_k(x^\lambda, \xi^\lambda) \leq (1 - \lambda)g_k(x^0, \xi^0) + \lambda g_k(x^1, \xi^1) \leq 0 .$$

The monotonicity and quasi-concavity of P yields

$$\begin{aligned} P[\kappa^{-1}(x^\lambda)] &\geq P[(1 - \lambda)\kappa^{-1}(x^0) + \lambda\kappa^{-1}(x^1)] \\ &\geq \min\{P[\kappa^{-1}(x^0)], P[\kappa^{-1}(x^1)]\} , \end{aligned}$$

which implies that $P(\kappa^{-1}(x^\lambda)) \geq \alpha$ since x^0, x^1 are in S. To see that S is closed, simply observe that the continuity (convexity plus finiteness) of the functions g implies that the multifunction κ^{-1} is upper semincontinuous, from which it follows that

$$P(\kappa^{-1}(x)) \geq \limsup_{k \to \infty} P(\kappa^{-1}(x^k))$$

where $\{x^k, k = 1, \ldots\}$ is any sequence converging to x. $\square$

A large class of quasi-concave probability measures can be identified by means of the following result.

Proposition 3.2. *Suppose h is a density function of a continuous distribution function defined on R^N and $h^{-1/N}$ is convex. Then the probability measure defined on the Borel subsets of R^N by $P(A) := \int_A h(s) \, ds$ is quasi-concave.*

A density of the form $h(s) = e^{-Q(s)}$ with Q convex corresponds to a quasi-concave measure, since $[e^{-Q(s)}]^{-1/N}$ is the composition of a convex with a nondecreasing convex function. Probability measures of this type are called *logarithmic concave*, they include the (nondegenerate normal), the multivariate Dirichlet and the Wishart distributions. The multivariate t and F density (as well as some multivariate Pareto Densities) are quasi-concave measures but not logarithmic concave.

The typical case covered by Proposition 3.1 is when the functions $g_k(x, \xi)$ are of the type

$$g_k(x, \xi) = a_k(x) + \xi_k ,$$

with the functions a_k convex and the joint distribution of the random variables ξ_k quasi-concave. The limitations in applying this result come mostly from the requirement of *joint* convexity in x and ξ. When the coefficients of the decision variables depend on ξ, we are mostly outside the domain of the application of Proposition 3.1. In such cases, one usually has no other recourse than to rely on approximations of the constraints as exemplified by the following result.

Proposition 3.3. *Let*

$$S := \left\{ x \in R^n \mid P\left[\sum_{j=1}^n a_j(\xi) x_j \geq \beta(\xi) \right] \geq \alpha \right\}$$

and

$$S' := \left\{ x \in R^n \mid (1-\alpha)^{-2} \left(\sum_{j=0}^n \sigma_{jk} x_j x_k \right)^{1/2} - \sum_{j=0}^n \mu_j x_j \leq 0, \, x_0 = 1 \right\},$$

where $a_0 = \beta$, μ_j is the expectation of a_j and σ_{jk} the covariance of $a_j(\cdot) a_k(\cdot)$. Then S' is closed and convex, and $S' \subset S$. The set S itself is convex if the random variables $\{a_j, j = 0, \ldots, n\}$ are jointly normal and $\alpha \geq \frac{1}{2}$.

Proof. With $a_0 = \beta$, the probabilistic constraint becomes

$$P[\zeta(x, \xi) \geq 0] \geq \alpha, \quad x_0 = 1 ,$$

where $\zeta(x, \xi) := \sum_{j=0}^n a_j(\xi) x_j$. By one side of Chebyshev's inequality, any x that satisfies these conditions must necessarily satisfy

$$\bar{\zeta}(x) - (1-\alpha)^{-2} \sigma_\zeta(x) \geq 0, \quad x_0 = 1 ,$$

where $\bar{\zeta}(x)$ is the expectation of $\zeta(x, \cdot)$ and $\sigma_\zeta^2(x)$ its covariance matrix. This shows that $S' \subset S$. The convexity of S' follows directly from the fact that $\sigma_\zeta^2(x)$ is a positive semidefinite quadratic form (in x).

If the random coefficients (including the constant term) are jointly normal, so is $\zeta(x, \cdot)$, the probabilistic constraint is equivalent to

$$\Phi^{-1}(\alpha)\sigma_\zeta(x) - \mu(x) \leq 0 ,$$

where Φ is the standard normal distribution function. Convexity follows from the fact that $\sigma_\phi z(x)$ is a covariance matrix, and that for $\alpha \geq \frac{1}{2}$, $\Phi^{-1}(\alpha) \geq 0$.   □

Consider now the situation when observations are allowed *before* choosing the decision x. This corresponds to optimization in a learning environment by opposition to anticipative models where the decision takes into account all possible future environments. We think in terms of *adaptive optimization*.

Typically, the observations will only provide partial information about the environment. Let $\mathscr{B}$ be the collection of all the relevant information that could become available after making an observation. Technically, $\mathscr{B}$ is a subset (a subfield) of the space of all possible events $\mathscr{A}$ (the σ-field generated by ξ). Since the decision can only depend on the events that could be observed, x must be $\mathscr{B}$-*adapted* or $\mathscr{B}$-*measurable*. We must now allow for a large class of solutions: $\mathscr{B}$-measurable functions instead of just points in R^n. The problem becomes:

$$\begin{aligned}
\text{minimize} \quad & z = E\{f_0(x(\xi), \xi)\mid\mathscr{B}\} \\
\text{subject to} \quad & E\{f_i(x(\xi), \xi)\mid\mathscr{B}\} \leq 0, \ i=1,\ldots,s , \\
& E\{f_i(x(\xi), \xi)\mid\mathscr{B}\} = 0, \ i=s+1,\ldots,m , \qquad (3.8) \\
& x(\xi) \in X \ \text{a.s.} , \\
& \xi \mapsto x(\xi) \ \text{is} \ \mathscr{B}\text{-measurable} ,
\end{aligned}$$

where $E\{\cdot\mid\mathscr{B}\}$ denotes *conditional expectation* with respect to $\mathscr{B}$. It is easy to see that under mild conditions, a solution can be found by solving for every ξ the deterministic (finite dimensional) program:

$$\begin{aligned}
\text{minimize} \quad & z(\xi) = E\{f_0(x, \cdot)\mid\mathscr{B}\} \\
\text{subject to} \quad & E\{f_i(x, \cdot)\mid\mathscr{B}\}(\xi) \leq 0, \ i=1,\ldots,s , \qquad (3.9) \\
& E\{f_i(x, \cdot)\mid\mathscr{B}\}(\xi) = 0, \ i=s+1,\ldots,m , \\
& x \in X .
\end{aligned}$$

Each problem is of the same type as (1.1). Note also, that all ξ that belong to the same atom (with respect to P) of $\mathscr{B}$ generate identical versions of problem (3.9).

In the case of complete information, i.e., when $\mathscr{B} = \mathscr{A}$, problem (3.8) is known as the *distribution problem*, the accent is then not so much on finding a solution as to derive the distribution function of the optimal value. On the other hand, the case of no information, i.e., $\mathcal{B} = \{\emptyset, \Xi\}$, brings us back full circle to the anticipative models.

Even if it was possible to find the optimal solution of (3.8), it usually yields a much too complicated function to allow for practical implementation, unless $\mathcal{B}$ is a very simple σ-field. To avoid this level of complexity, one specifies an admissible class of decision rules $\{x(\lambda, \cdot), \lambda \in \Lambda\}$ that depends on a finite number of parameters λ. The problem becomes one of choosing λ so as to optimize the response of the system to all situations that could arise. More specifically, assuming that the function $\xi \mapsto x(\lambda, \xi)$ are $\mathcal{B}$-measurable,

$$\begin{aligned}
\text{minimize} \quad & z = E\{f_0(x(\lambda, \xi), \xi)\} \\
\text{subject to} \quad & E\{f_i(x(\lambda, \xi), \xi)\} \le 0, \ i = 1, \ldots, s, \\
& E\{f_i(x(\lambda, \xi), \xi)\} = 0, \ i = s+1, \ldots, m, \\
& x(\lambda, \xi) \in X \text{ a.s.}
\end{aligned} \tag{3.10}$$

This again is a problem of the type (1.1), except that the minimization is with respect to λ. Some good examples are inventory models where the search for an optimal policy has been replaced by the search for an optimal (s, S)-policy, and stochastic programming models that have been studied in the context of policy setting in agricultural economics (under the label of the *active approach*).

4. Recourse problems

The *recourse model* incorporates both anticipation *and* adaptation in a single mathematical model. In other words, this model reflects a tradeoff between long-term anticipatory strategies and the associated short-term adaptive adjustments. For example, there is a tradeoff between capital investments and the cost of day-to-day operations, between the design and layout of an overall strategy and the adjustments necessary to respond to particular situations. The two-stage linear version of this model has been studied extensively:

$$\begin{aligned}
\text{minimize} \quad & z = cx + E\{Q(x, \xi)\} \\
\text{subject to} \quad & b_i - A_i x \le 0, \ i = 1, \ldots, m, \\
& x \ge 0,
\end{aligned} \tag{4.1}$$

where

$$Q(x, \xi) = \inf_{y \in R_+^{n'}} \{q(\xi)y \mid W(\xi)y = h(\xi) - T(\xi)x\}; \tag{4.2}$$

some or all the coefficients of the matrices and vectors q, W, h, and T could be random variables. The long term decision is made before the environment

$$\xi \sim [q(\xi), W(\xi), h(\xi), T(\xi)]$$

can be observed. Later, any discrepancies that may exist between $h(\xi)$ and $T(\xi)x$ are made up by corrective action, a *recourse decision*, that minimizes $q(\xi)y$ and satisfies $W(\xi) = h(\xi) - T(\xi)x$, $y \ge 0$. Immediate costs as well as future (recourse) costs are taken into account. Q is called the *recourse cost function*.

In terms of the canonical problem (1.1), f_0 is simply $cx + Q(x, \xi)$ and the f_i's are the linear constraints $b_i - A_i x \le 0$. A more general model when only partial information is available would take the following form. As in Section 3, let $\mathcal{B}$ again denote the σ-field of observable events, then the recourse cost function will be found by solving for each ξ,

$$\begin{aligned}
&\text{minimize} && z = E\{f_{20}(x, y, \cdot) | \mathcal{B}\}(\xi) \\
&\text{subject to} && E\{f_{2i}(x, y, \cdot) | \mathcal{B}\}(\xi) \le 0, \ i = 1, \ldots, s', \\
& && E\{f_{2i}(x, y, \cdot) | \mathcal{B}\}(\xi) = 0, \ i = s' + 1, \ldots, m', \\
& && y \in Y \subset R^n .
\end{aligned} \tag{4.3}$$

The functions f_2 are supposed to have the same properties as those of the canonical problem (1.1). In the 'linear case' (4.2), we have assumed that complete information will be available before selecting y, i.e., $\mathcal{B} = \mathcal{A}$. (A more complicated situation, is when $\mathcal{B}$ depends nonlinearly on x.) If we denote by $Q(x, \xi)$ the optimal value of (4.3), the recourse problem is still of the same type as (4.1), except that in the general case we may have nonlinearities in the deterministic constraints and cost functions, i.e.,

$$\begin{aligned}
&\text{minimize} && z = f_{10}(x) + E\{Q(x, \xi)\} \\
&\text{subject to} && f_{1i}(x) \le 0, \ i = 1, \ldots, s, \\
& && f_{1i}(x) = 0, \ i = s + 1, \ldots, m, \\
& && x \in X .
\end{aligned} \tag{4.4}$$

This again is a problem of the type (1.1), the function f_0 is defined as $f_{10} + Q$. Whenever problem (4.3) is infeasible, $Q(x, \xi) = \infty$, from which it follows that $E\{Q(x, \xi)\} < \infty$ if and only if problem (4.3) is feasible a.s. (ignoring extreme cases of no interest in practice). Let

$$K_2 := x \in R^n \,|\, E\{Q(x, \xi) < \infty\} = \text{dom } EQ ,$$

denote the set of *induced constraints*. Problem (4.4) is said to have *complete recourse* if $K_2 = R^n$, and *relatively complete recourse* if K_2 is contained in

$$K_1 := \{x \in X \mid f_{1i}(x) \leq 0, \ i = 1, \ldots, s;$$
$$f_{1i}(x) = 0, \ i = s + 1, \ldots, m\} \, ;$$

simple recourse refers to the case when the constraints of (4.3) determine uniquely the recourse decision for all x and ξ.

This is a very rich model that covers a wide range of possibilities. For example, when

$$f_{2i}(x, y, \xi) = \begin{cases} 1 - \alpha & \text{if } T(\xi)x + W(\xi)y - h(\xi) \geq 0 \, , \\ \alpha & \text{otherwise} \, , \end{cases}$$

we have a model with conditional probabilistic constraints on the choice of the recourse decision. Variants could also involve not just deterministic constraints on x, but also expectation constraints as in (1.1), or the recourse decision could be subject to various restrictions as in (3.10), etc.

It should be emphasized that the two stages do not necessarily refer to time units, they correspond to steps in the decision process. For instance, the x, y variables may each represent a sequence of control actions over a given time horizon, i.e.,

$$x = (x(0), x(1), \ldots, x(T)) \, , \qquad y = (y(0), y(1), \ldots, y(T)) \, ,$$

the recourse decision y being used to correct the basic trend set by the variables x. The decisions $y(t)$ are taken in different time periods, but for our purposes can be handled as *one* recourse action. Multistage stochastic programs with *block-separable recourse* fall naturally in such a mold. In other instances, this *two-stage dynamical* model provides an attractive alternative, that is numerically tractable, to a more detailed model that would include the full stochastic dynamics.

The multistage recourse problem allows for that possibility:

given $\quad \{\mathcal{B}_t, t = 1, \ldots, T\}$ with $\mathcal{B}_1 \subset \mathcal{B}_2 \ldots \subset \mathcal{B}_T \subset \mathcal{A}$

minimize $\quad z = E\{f_{10}(x^1(\xi), \xi) + Q_1(x^1(\xi), \xi) \mid \mathcal{B}_1\}$

subject to $\quad E\{f_{1i}(x^1(\xi), \xi) \mid \mathcal{B}_1\} \leq 0, \ i = 1, \ldots, s_1 \, ,$ $\qquad\qquad$ (4.5)

(a.s.) $\quad E\{f_{1i}(x^1(\xi), \xi) \mid \mathcal{B}_1\} = 0, \ i = s_{1+1}, \ldots, m_1 \, ,$

$\qquad\quad x^1(\xi) \in X_1 \subset R^{n_1} \, ,$

$\qquad\quad \xi \mapsto x^1(\xi)$ is $\mathcal{B}_1$ measurable ,

where for $t = 2, \ldots, T$, with $\bar{x}^t = (x^1, x^2, \ldots, x^{t-1})$,

$$Q_{t-1}(\vec{x}^t, \xi) = \inf E\{f_{t0}(\vec{x}^t, x^t(\xi), \xi) + Q_t(x^1, \vec{x}^t(\xi), \xi) | \mathcal{B}_t\} \qquad (4.6)$$

$$\text{subject to} \quad E\{f_{ti}(\vec{x}^t, x^t(\xi), \xi) | \mathcal{B}_t\} \le 0, \quad i = 1, \ldots, s_t,$$

$$\text{(a.s.)} \quad E\{f_{ti}(\vec{x}^t, x^t(\xi), \xi) | \mathcal{B}_t\} = 0, \quad i = s_{t+1}, \ldots, m_t,$$

$$(\vec{x}^t, x^t(\xi)) \in X_t \subset R^{n_t},$$

$$\xi \mapsto x^t(\xi) \text{ is } \mathcal{B}_t\text{-measurable},$$

$$Q_T \equiv 0.$$

The σ-field $\mathcal{B}_t$ represents the information available at time t. For $i = 0, \ldots, m_t$ and $t = 1, \ldots, T$ the functions

$$((\vec{x}^t, x^t), \xi) \mapsto f_{ti}((\vec{x}^t, x^t), \xi)$$

are $\mathcal{B}_t$-random l.s.c. functions. The sets X_t are closed. If no information can be collected before the first observation, then $\mathcal{B}_1 = \{\emptyset, \Xi\}$, and the decision x^1 is (totally) anticipative.

The properties of multistage problems are similar to those of two-stage problems, and can be obtained by repeated applications of the results of Section 2 about expectation functions. One further extension is to allow for *infinite horizon*. For such models one may be interested in a 'here and now' decision x^1, but also in finding stationary policies (in the Markov case), or designing finite horizon approximation schemes, etc.

As formulated, our multistage recourse model does not allow for the explicit dependence of the information fields on the decisions, however that does not mean that the observed quantities cannot depend on x. Suppose that at time t we can observe the state of the system s^t defined by

$$s^t := \sum_{k \le t} x^k - \sum_{k \le t} \xi^k$$

with $x^k \in R^n$ the decision at time k, and $\xi^k \in R^n$ the components of ξ that occur at stage k. The observations depend on the past decisions, but one can clearly re-express the information gained in terms of 'observed' ξ^k and thus have the problem fit in the mold of the multistage recourse problem. There are, however, problems that cannot be reduced to this situation, and then a more general model must be introduced.

5. Optimality conditions

Optimality conditions for stochastic programs can be obtained from the known optimality conditions for nonlinear programs of the type (1.2), and then relying on the subdifferential calculus for expectation functions (Section 2) to cast these conditions in an appropriate form. We begin with a very general result (not quite the sharpest possible):

Proposition 5.1. *Consider the stochastic program* (1.1) *and suppose that for* $i = 0, \ldots, m$, *the function* Ef_i *are locally Lipschitz and* $X = R^n$. *If* x^* *is a local optimal solution at which the Mangasarian–Fromovitz constraint qualifications are satisfied, i.e.,* $y = 0$ *is the only solution of the system*

$$y_i \geqslant 0 \quad and \quad y_i Ef_i(x^*) = 0 \quad for \ i = 1, \ldots, s \ ,$$

$$0 \in \sum_{i=1}^{m} y_i \partial Ef_i(x^*) \ ,$$

then there exists a multiplier y *that satisfies the optimality conditions*

$$y_i \geqslant 0 \quad and \quad y_i Ef_i(x^*) = 0 \quad for \ i = 1, \ldots, s \ , \tag{5.1}$$

$$0 \in \partial Ef_0(x^*) + \sum_{i=1}^{m} y_i \partial Ef_i(x^*) \ . \tag{5.2}$$

These conditions only involve the expectation functionals. However, to recognize optimality (and to use it in a numerical setting) we are mostly interested in *pointwise* conditions (with respect to every ξ in $\varXi$). To this effect one can appeal to the results of Section 2, in particular Proposition 2.13.

For example, if the functions f_i, $i = 0, \ldots, m$, are finite valued and locally Lipschitz at x^*, with summable Lipschitz constant, i.e. to any bounded neighborhood of x^* there corresponds a summable function α such that for any pair x^1, x^2 in V

$$|f_i(x^1, \xi) - f_i(x^2, \xi)| \leqslant \alpha(\xi)\|x^1 - x^2\| \ .$$

Assuming again that the Mangasarian–Fromovitz qualifications are satisfied at x^* (a local minimum), then there exist multipliers $(y_1, \ldots, y_s, y_{s+1}, \ldots, y_m)$ and measurable functions

$$\xi \mapsto u_i(x^*, \xi) : \varXi \to R^n \quad for \ i = 0, \ldots, m \ ,$$

such that for almost all ξ,

$$u_i(x^*, \xi) \in \partial f_i(x^*, \xi) \ ,$$

and

$$y_i \geqslant 0, \ y_i Ef_i(x^*) = 0 \quad for \ i = 1, \ldots, s \ , \tag{5.3}$$

$$0 = \int \left[u_0(x^*, \xi) + \sum_{i=1}^{m} y_i u_i(x^*, \xi) \right] dP(\xi) + v_X(x^*) \tag{5.4}$$

where $v_X(x^*)$ is a normal to X at x^*. If there are no inequality constraints, then the complementarity slackness conditions (5.3) disappear. With

$$p(x^*, \xi) = u_0(x^*, \xi) + \sum_{i=1}^{m} y_i u_i(x^*, \xi),$$

we can reexpress the optimality conditions as follows: for almost all $\xi \in \Xi$,

$$x^* \in \operatorname{argmin}[f_0(x, \xi) - p(x^*, \xi)x \mid f_i(x, \xi) = 0, \ i = 1, \ldots, m].$$
$$(5.5)$$

The interpretation to give the multipliers $p(x^*, \xi)$ can directly be surmised from the preceding relation. Indeed, if after making our decision x we were allowed to adjust this decision to take into account the actual outcome of the random coefficients ξ, and if the cost of making these adjustments is determined by the linear function $p(x^*, \xi) \cdot x$, there would be no advantage in having this option available since we would end up with the same solution x^*. Thus p is a price system that corresponds to the *nonanticipativity* condition imposed on x. These constraints can be introduced explicitly in the problem by a simple reformulation. To simplify the presentation, let us consider the following abstract version of (1.1):

$$\text{find } x \in S \text{ such that } x \text{ minimizes } Ef_0(x), \tag{5.6}$$

where the feasibility set is as defined in Section 1. Although, it is clear that x *cannot* depend on ξ, let us go one step further, and state the problem in form that allows us to introduce this constaint explicitly. To do so, let us replace the decision space R^n, by the space $\mathcal{M}(\Xi; R^n)$ of all measurable functions $\xi \mapsto x(\xi) : \Xi \to R^n$. Of course, we must now restrict ourselves to the constant functions. It is easy to see that as long as the set S is measurable, and that f_0 is a random lower semicontinuous function, our problem is equivalent to the following (infinite dimensional) optimization problem:

$$\text{find } x \in \mathcal{M}(\Xi; R^n) \text{ such that } x(\xi) = E\{x(\xi)\} \text{ a.s.,}$$
$$(5.7)$$
$$x(\xi) \in S \text{ a.s. and } x \text{ minimizes } \int f_0(x(\xi), \xi) \, dP(\xi).$$

We have just seen that under the appropriate conditions there exist multipliers $p(\xi)$ such that x^* is a minimum if for almost all ξ in Ξ,

$$x^* \in \operatorname{argmin}\{f_0(x, \xi) - p(\xi)x \mid x \in S\}.$$

Thus the multipliers $p(\cdot)$ are those associated with the ('constancy') nonanticipativity constraint $x(\cdot) = E\{x\}$ a.s. In fact, rather than starting our analysis of the optimality conditions as we have done, it is more logical (and rewarding) to first derive optimality conditions for problems where all but the nonanticipativity constraints have been relegated to an abstract set. Problem (5.7) has been cast in that form. However, to get the full flavor of these results and their implications, one must consider the multistage version.

Let us consider the following model that includes the multistage recourse problem (4.5):

$$\text{given } \{\mathcal{B}_t, t = 1, \ldots, T\} \text{ with } \mathcal{B}_1 \subset \mathcal{B}_2 \subset \cdots \subset \mathcal{B}_T \subset \mathcal{A} \qquad (5.8)$$

$$\text{minimize} \quad E\{f_0(x^1(\xi), x^2(\xi), \ldots, x^T(\xi))\}$$

$$\text{subject to} \quad x^t(\xi) \in S_t(\xi) \text{ a.s. and } \xi \mapsto x^t(\xi) \text{ is}$$

$$\mathcal{B}_t\text{-measurable, } 1 \leq t \leq T .$$

The nonanticipativity conditions can be expressed in terms of the following linear constraints

$$x^t(\xi) = E^t\{x(\xi) \mid \mathcal{B}_t\} \text{ a.s. } \text{ for } t = 1, \ldots, T .$$

The optimality conditions for this problem are of the same nature as those for problem (5.7), i.e., if we assume enough regularity,

$$x^* = (x^{1*}(\cdot), x^{2*}(\cdot), \ldots, x^{T*}(\cdot))$$

(locally) optimal implies the existence of multipliers

$$p_t(\cdot), \quad t = 1, \ldots, T ,$$

such that

$$E\{\boldsymbol{p}_t \mid \mathcal{B}_t\} = 0 \text{ a.s., } \quad t = 1, \ldots, T ,$$

and for almost all ξ and Ξ,

$$x^* \in \text{argmin}\{f_0(x, \xi) - \sum_t p_t(\xi)x^t \mid x^t \in S_t(\xi), 1 \leq t \leq T\} ,$$

provided f_0 is finite valued and the *constraints are nonanticipative*. This last condition is germane to dynamic stochastic optimization problems and can be viewed as an extra constraint qualification. What is required is that the multifunctions

$$\xi \mapsto S_t(\xi) : \Xi \to R^n \text{ are } \mathcal{B}_t\text{-measurable} .$$

If this is the case, there will be no constraints *induced* on the decisions to be taken at time t by constraints that only appear in the formulation of the problem at a subsequent time. As an example where this condition fails, consider

$$\mathcal{B}_1 = \{\emptyset, \Xi\}, \quad \mathcal{B}_2 = \mathcal{A} - \text{the Borel field on } [1, 2] = \Xi,$$

$$S_1 = R_+, \quad S_2(\xi) = \{(x^1, x^2) \mid x^1 + x^2(\xi) \leq \xi, x^2(\xi) \geq 0\}$$

(recall that Ξ is the support of the distribution). We take the liberty of simply writing x^1 instead of $x^1(\xi)$ since to be $\mathcal{B}_1$-measurable, the functions $x^1(\cdot)$ must be constant. The second stage constraints impose on x^1 the restriction $x^1 \leq 1$; which is an 'active' induced constraint, in that it restricts the choice of x^1 beyond the restrictions that explicitly appear in S_1. The theory of optimality conditions for problems that involve constraints that do not satisfy the nonanticipativity condition requires the introduction of 'singular' multipliers in order to attach a nonzero dual weights to the induced constraints. Proposition 2.11 hints at the way to approach this question in the convex case.

This discussion of the optimality conditions has been much too brief, but we have touched upon the two aspects that differentiate the theory for stochastic optimization problems from that for deterministic problems: the presence of the nonanticipativity constraint, and the special role played by induced constraints.

6. Approximations

If P is a discrete distribution, say $p_l = P\{\xi = \xi^l\}$ for $l = 1, \ldots, L$, with L relatively small, i.e.,

$$\int f_i(x, \xi) \, dP(\xi) = \sum_{l=1}^{L} p_l f_i(x, \xi^l), \tag{6.1}$$

or if the function $f_i(x, \cdot)$ are separable, cf. (1.3), it is not much more difficult to solve the stochastic programming problem (1.1) than solving a comparable deterministic optimization problem. The purpose of approximation schemes is to reduced finding a solution (or an approximate solution) of (1.1) to solving a problem involving only these simple expectation functionals. The form (6.1) ensues from discretization of the space Ξ of possible realizations of ξ, whereas one relies on separable approximations of the functions $f_i(x, \cdot)$ to be able to use (1.3). We begin with this latter possibility.

Let $D = (d^1, \ldots, d^N)$ be a linear basis for R^N, and for each $j = 1, \ldots, N$, define

$$f_{ij}(x, \eta) := f_i(x, \eta d^j).$$

Denoting by P_j the marginal distribution function of the random vairable $\zeta = d^j \xi$, we may hope that with an appropriate choice of the vectors d^j, $\varphi_{i,D}(x) := \sum_{j=1}^{N} \int f_{ij}(x, \zeta_j) \, dP_j(\zeta_j)$ approximates $\int f_i(x, \xi) \, dP(\xi)$. In general however, this is only a crude approximation, good enough maybe for deriving bounds but not sharp enough for use in a claim of near-optimality. This approximation can be somewhat improved by relying on a collection of such approximates, at least when $\xi \mapsto f_i(x, \xi)$ is convex. Indeed for given basis D, the definition of f_{ij} and the convexity imply that

$$\sum_{j=1}^{N} f_{ij}(x, d^j \zeta) \geq f_i(x, \xi) ,$$

and hence

$$\varphi_{i,D}(x) \geq Ef_i(x) .$$

Thus, for $\mathcal{D}$ any collection of bases, we have

$$\inf_{D \in \mathcal{D}} \varphi_{i,D}(x) \geq Ef_i(x) . \tag{6.2}$$

On the contrary, if $\xi \mapsto f_i(x, \xi)$ is concave, then for any $D \in \mathcal{D}$ the function $\varphi_{i,D}$ minorizes Ef_i, in which case

$$\sup_{d \in \mathcal{D}} \varphi_{i,D}(x) \leq Ef_i(x) . \tag{6.3}$$

The use we can make of these inequalities depends very much on the specific form of the stochastic program (1.1). For example, if $f_i(x, \cdot)$ is concave, and we replace the constraint $E\{f_i(x, \xi)\} \leq 0$ by the collection

$$\varphi_{i,D}(x) \leq 0 , \quad D \in \mathcal{D} ,$$

we obtain an outer approximation of the feasibility set S. Or still, if $f_0(x, \cdot)$ is convex, and we use

$$\varphi_0(x) := \inf_{D \in \mathcal{D}} \varphi_{0,D}(x) ,$$

as objective, the solution will yield an upper bound for the optimal value of the original problem.

It usually is difficult to obtain a simple expression for these approximating functions in terms of x. To remedy this, one may try to approximate the functions f_i, in both x and ξ. A good example is the use of sublinear approximates for linear recourse problems (4.1), (4.2). Let us consider the case when q and W are fixed. Then $Q(x, \xi) = \psi(h(\xi) - T(\xi)x)$ where

$$\psi(t) := \inf\{qy \mid Wy = t, \ y \geq 0\} .$$

The function $t \mapsto \psi(t)$ is sublinear. Assuming, without loss of generality, that W is of full row rank m', for any linear basis $D = \{d^1, \ldots, d^{m'}\}$,

$$\psi_D(t) := \inf\{q_D^+ y^+ + q_D^- y^- \mid Dy^+ - Dy^- = t, \ y^+ \ge 0, \ y^- \ge 0\}$$

is a separable sublinear function that majorizes ψ; here for $i = 1, \ldots, m'$,

$$(q_D^+)_i := \inf\{qy \mid Wy = d^i, \ y \ge 0\},$$

$$(q_D^-)_i := \inf\{qy \mid Wy = -d^i, \ y \ge 0\}.$$

For any collection of bases $\mathscr{D}$, $\psi(t) \le \inf_{D \in \mathscr{D}} \psi_D(T)$ and, of course,

$$E\{Q(x, \xi)\} \le \inf_{D \in \mathscr{D}} \int \psi_D(h(\xi) - T(\xi)x) \, dP(\xi).$$

Again, we obtain an upper bound that can be improved by making the collection $\mathscr{D}$ rich enough. Because the functions ψ_D are so easy to handle – they are simple recourse cost functions (see Section 7.4) – this approach can be used advantageously in the calculation of upper bounds when other schemes, to be mentioned below, become too onerous. One should also note that this decomposition of ψ suggests the potential use of parallel processors, since each function ψ_D could be assigned to a separate processor.

Let us now turn to approximations by *discretization*, or more generally, by approximations of the probability distribution. Because of the different nature of the expectation functionals that appear in the constraints and the objective functions, it pays off to treat them separately. In both cases, we want to obtain conditions that allow us to assert the convergence of optimal solutions, more precisely to assert the epi-convergence of the essential objective functions of the approximating stochastic programs, and then be able to rely on Theorems A.1 and A.2. For the essential objective function of (1.1), we write

$$F(x) := \begin{cases} Ef_0(x) & \text{if } x \in S, \\ \infty & \text{otherwise}, \end{cases} \tag{6.4}$$

and for the approximating problems

$$F^\nu(x) := \begin{cases} E^\nu f_0(x) & \text{if } x \in S^\nu, \\ \infty & \text{otherwise}, \end{cases} \tag{6.5}$$

where

$$E^\nu f_i(x) = \int f_i(x, \xi) \, dP^\nu(\xi), \quad i = 0, \ldots, m, \tag{6.6}$$

$$S^\nu = X \cap \{x \mid E^\nu f_i(x) \le 0, \ i = 1, \ldots, s\}$$
$$\cap \{x \mid E^\nu f_i(x) = 0, \ i = s+1, \ldots, m\} \cap \{x \mid E^\nu f_0(x) < \infty\} \tag{6.7}$$

and P^ν is a probability measure approximating P. In applications, P^ν will usually be discrete.

If just the constraints involve expectation functionals, we can rely in a wide variety of cases on either Corollary 6.2 when the constraints are of type (3.2) or Proposition 6.3 for probabilistic constraints.

Proposition 6.1. *Suppose* $\{P^\nu, \nu = 1, \ldots\}$ *is a sequence of probability measures converging in distribution to* $P^\infty := P$, f *is a random lower semicontinuous function on* $R^n \times \Xi$ *such that, for a fixed* x, $\xi \mapsto f(x, \xi)$ *is continuous on* Ξ *and, for all* $\varepsilon > 0$,
  (i) *there exists a neighborhood* V *of* x *such that*

$$|f(y, \xi) - f(x, \xi)| < \varepsilon \quad \text{for all } y \in V .$$

  (ii) *there exists a compact subset* $K_\varepsilon \subset \Xi$ *such that*

$$\int_{\Xi \setminus K_\varepsilon} |f(x, \xi)| P^\nu(\mathrm{d}\xi) < \varepsilon \quad \text{for all } \nu = 1, \ldots, \infty .$$

Then, the expectation functionals $E^\nu f = \int f(\cdot, \xi) \, \mathrm{d}P^\nu(\xi)$ *converge continuously to* $Ef = \int f(\cdot, \xi) \, \mathrm{d}P(\xi)$ *at* x, *i.e., for any sequence* $(x^\nu, \nu = 1, \ldots)$ *converging to* x, *we have*

$$Ef(x) = \lim_{\nu \to \infty} E^\nu f(x^\nu) .$$

Proof. For any sequence $\{x^\nu, \nu = 1, \ldots\}$ converging to x,

$$E^\nu f(x^\nu) - Ef(x) = \int (f(x^\nu, \xi) - f(x, \xi)) P^\nu(\mathrm{d}\xi) + (E^\nu f(x) - Ef(x)) .$$

The first term in the sum on the right is $\leq \varepsilon$ as follows from (i) and $P^\nu(\Xi) = 1$. For ν sufficiently large, the second term is $\leq 3\varepsilon$, since

$$E^\nu f(x) - Ef(x) = \left(\int_{K_\varepsilon} f(x, \xi) \, \mathrm{d}P^\nu(\xi) - \int_{K_\varepsilon} f(x, \xi) \, \mathrm{d}P(\xi) \right)$$

$$+ \int_{\Omega \setminus K_\varepsilon} f(x, \xi) \, \mathrm{d}P^\nu(\xi) - \int_{\Omega \setminus K_\varepsilon} f(x, \xi) \, \mathrm{d}P(\xi) ,$$

where the two last terms are $\leq \varepsilon$ by condition (ii), and the first one is $\leq \varepsilon$ for ν sufficiently large since on K_ε, $f(x, \cdot)$ is bounded and the P^ν converge in distribution to P. $\square$

Corollary 6.2. *Consider the stochastic program* (1.1) *with essential objective function* (6.4). *Suppose that*

(i) $f_0(\cdot, \xi)$ *does not depend on* ξ,
(ii) $x \mapsto Ef_0 = f_0(\cdot, \xi)$ *is continuous*,
(iii) *no equality constraints*: $X = R^n$, $s = m$,
(iv) *for* $i = 1, \ldots, m$, *the expectation functionals* Ef_i *are lower semicontinuous, and satisfy for all* x *the conditions imposed on* f *in Proposition 6.1*,
(v) *the feasibility set* $\emptyset \neq S = \mathrm{cl}\{x \mid Ef_i(x) < 0, i = 1, \ldots, m\}$,
(vi) *the sequence of probability distribution functions*, $\{P^\nu, \nu = 1, \ldots\}$ *converge in distribution to* P.

Then, the essential objective functions F^ν *of the approximating problems epi-converge to* F. *Hence, for any subsequence* $\{\nu_k, k = 1, \ldots\}$ *with* $x^k \in$ argmin F^{ν_k} (x^k *solves the problem* (1.1) *with* P *replaced by* P^{ν_k}), *and* $\{x^k, k = 1, \ldots\}$ *converging to* x, *we have that* x *is an optimal solution of* (1.1).

Proof. From the Proposition it follows that for $i = 1, \ldots, m$, the $E^\nu f_i$ continuously converge to Ef_i. In particular, this implies that for any sequence $\{x^\nu, \nu = 1, \ldots\}$ converging to x,

$$0 \geqslant Ef_i(x) = \lim_{\nu \to \infty} E^\nu f_i(x^\nu), \quad i = 1, \ldots, m,$$

if for ν sufficiently large $E^\nu f_i(x^\nu) \leqslant 0$. This means that if for ν sufficiently large, $x^\nu \in S^\nu$, then $x \in S$, and thus

$$\liminf_{\nu \to \infty} F^\nu(x^\nu) = \lim_{\nu \to \infty} f_0(x^\nu) + \liminf_{\nu \to \infty} \delta_{S^\nu}(x^\nu) \geqslant f_0(x) + \delta_S(x) = F(x)$$

where δ_C is the indicator function of the set C. This is condition (A.1). To obtain the second condition (A.2), let $x \in \mathrm{int}\, S$, i.e. $Ef_i(x) < 0$ for $i = 1, \ldots, m$. This means that for any sequencxe $\{x^\nu, \nu = 1, \ldots\}$ converging to x, $E^\nu f_i(x^\nu) < 0$, for $i = 1, \ldots, m$ for ν sufficiently large, i.e. $x^\nu \in S^\nu$ and hence, by continuity of f_0.

$$F(x) = \lim_{\nu \to \infty} F^\nu(x^\nu) = \lim_{\nu \to \infty} f_0(x^\nu).$$

In fact, the same holds if $x \in \mathrm{cl}\{x \mid Ef_i(x) < 0, i = 1, \ldots, m\}$, take a sequence $\{x^k, k = 1, \ldots\}$ converging to x such that $Ef_i(x^k) < 0$, $i = 1, \ldots, m$. For every k, and all $\nu \geqslant \nu_k$ we have that $E^\nu f_i(x^k) < 0$, $i = 1, \ldots, m$, as follows from the above. A diagonalization argument (set $x^\nu = x^k$ if $\nu_k \leqslant \nu < \nu_{k+1}$) allows us to exhibit the desired sequence.

The remaining assertion is just a consequence of the epi-convergence of the essential objectives, cf. Theorem A.2. □

This Corollary is just an example of the type of results one may be able to obtain, and it is easy to see how to modify the assumptions so that it would also apply to the case when there are also equality constraints. Although the conditions may not be too restrictive when the functions f_i are continuous, they cannot be used to handle the case of probabilistic constraints, cf. (3.3). For these we need to rely on conditions of a somewhat different type.

Proposition 6.3. *Consider the stochastic program*

$$\text{minimize } f_0(x)$$
$$\text{subject to } Ef_1(x) \leqslant 0 ,$$

(6.8)

where $f_0: R^n \to R$ is continuous, and $f_1: R^n \times \Xi \to R$ is given by (3.3), i.e.,

$$f_1(x, \xi) = \begin{cases} \alpha - 1 & \text{if } g_i(x, \xi) \leqslant 0, \ k = 1, \ldots, q , \\ \alpha & \text{otherwise} , \end{cases}$$

(6.9)

with the g_k continuous on $R^n \times \Xi$. We assume that Ef_1 is continuous and that $S = \mathrm{cl}\{x \mid Ef_1(x) < \infty\} \neq \emptyset$. Suppose that the probability measures $\{P^\nu, \nu = 1, \ldots\}$ converge to P in distribution, and that the sequence $\{\alpha_\nu, \nu = 1, \ldots\}$ converges to α. Then, the essential objectives of the approximating problems

$$F^\nu(x) = \begin{cases} f_0(x) & \text{if } E^\nu f_1(x) \leqslant (\alpha - \alpha_\nu) , \\ \infty & \text{otherwise} , \end{cases}$$

epi-converge to the essential objective function of (6.8),

$$F(x) = \begin{cases} f_0(x) & \text{if } Ef_1(x) \leqslant 0 , \\ \infty & \text{otherwise} . \end{cases}$$

In particular, this implies that if $x^\nu \in \mathrm{argmin} \, F^\nu$, and if x^∞ is any cluster point of the sequence $\{x^\nu, \nu = 1, \ldots\}$, then $x^\infty \in \mathrm{argmin} \, F$.

Proof. Let $\{x^\nu, \nu = 1, \ldots\}$ a sequence with x^∞ as limit point. Set

$$\kappa^{-1}(x) := \{\xi \mid g_k(x, \xi) \leqslant 0, \ k = 1, \ldots, q\} ,$$

see Section 3. From the continuity of the g_k, it follows that

$$\kappa^{-1}(x^\infty) \supset \limsup_{\nu \to \infty} \kappa^{-1}(x^\nu) .$$

And from the convergence in distribution, in particular Lemma B1, this implies that $\limsup_{\nu \to \infty} P^\nu(\kappa^{-1}(x^\nu)) \leqslant P(\kappa^{-1}(x^\infty))$. Since $Ef_1(x) = \alpha - P(\kappa^{-1}(x))$,

$$\liminf E^\nu f_1(x^\nu) \geqslant Ef_1(x^\infty) ,$$

whenever for some subsequence of the $\{x^\nu, \nu = 1, \ldots\}$ the condition $E^\nu f_1(x^\nu) \leqslant (\alpha - \alpha^\nu)$ is satisfied, it follows that $Ef_1(x^\infty) \leqslant 0$. Thus

$$\liminf_{\nu \to \infty} F^{\nu}(x^{\nu}) = \lim_{\nu \to \infty} f_0(x^{\nu}) + \liminf_{\nu \to \infty} \delta_{\{x \mid E^{\nu}f_1(x) \leqslant (\alpha - \alpha_{\nu})\}}(x^{\nu})$$

$$\geqslant f_0(x^{\infty}) + \delta_S(x^{\infty}) = F(x^{\infty}),$$

where δ_Q is the indicator function of the set Q. This proves condition (A.1) of epiconvergence.

Next, choose x in $\{x' \mid Ef_1(x') < \infty\}$. Because the convergence of the P^{ν} implies convergence in distribution, and the continuity of Ef_1 at x implies that $\kappa^{-1}(x)$ is a P-continuity set, it follows that

$$P(\kappa^{-1}(x)) = \lim_{\nu \to \infty} P^{\nu}(\kappa^{-1}(x))$$

and hence, for ν sufficiently large,

$$E^{\nu}f_1(x) < \alpha - \alpha^{\nu}.$$

In which case, it is obvious that

$$F(x) = \lim_{\nu \to \infty} [f_0(x) + \delta_{\{x' \mid E^{\nu}f_1(x') \leqslant \alpha - \alpha_{\nu}\}}(x)] = \lim_{\nu \to \infty} F^{\nu}(x).$$

Now consider any x that belongs to S, and pick a sequence $\{x^k, k = 1, \ldots\}$ that converges to x, with $Ef_1(x^k) < 0$. From the above, it follows that for every k there exists ν_k such that for all $\nu \geqslant \nu_k$, $E^{\nu}f_1(x^k) < \alpha - \alpha^{\nu}$. If we set $x^{\nu} := x^k$ for $\nu'_k \leqslant k < \nu'_{k+1}$ (where ν'_k is defined recursively by $\nu'_k = \max\{\nu'_{k-1} + 1, \nu_k\}$), we obtain (A.2), since then also $F(x) = \lim_{\nu \to \infty} F^{\nu}(x^{\nu})$. □

The case of the expectation functional appearing in the objective forces us to allow for the possibility that f_0 takes on the value ∞. Consider the example of a stochastic program with recourse (4.4) with less than complete recourse, i.e., $Q(x, \xi) = \infty$ for any pair (x, ξ) for which (4.3) is not feasible.

Proposition 6.4. *Consider the stochastic program*

$$minimize \quad Ef_0(x)$$

$$subject\ to \quad f_i(x) \leqslant 0, \ i = 1, \ldots, s,$$

$$f_i(x) = 0, \ i = s + 1, \ldots, m, \qquad (6.10)$$

$$x \in X \subset R^n,$$

where $f_0 : R^n \times \Xi \to R \cup \{\infty\}$ *is a random l.s.c. function, the feasibility set*

$$S := \{x \in X \mid f_i(x) \leqslant 0, \ i = 1, \ldots, s; \ f_i(x) = 0, \ i = s + 1, \ldots, m\}$$

$$\cap \{x \mid Ef_0(x) < \infty\}$$

is nonempty and closed. Suppose that

$$\text{dom } f_0 := \{(x, \xi) \mid f_0(x, \xi) < \infty\} = \{x \mid Ef_0(x) < \infty\} \times \Xi \ ,$$

for all x in S,

$$\xi \mapsto f_0(x, \xi) \text{ is continuous on } \Xi \ ,$$

and for all ξ in Ξ,

$$x \mapsto f_0(x, \xi) \text{ is locally lower Lipschitzian on } S \ ,$$

in the following sense: to any x in S, there corresponds a neighborhood V of x and a bounded continuous function $\beta : \Xi \to R$ such that for all $x' \in V$ and $\xi \in \Xi$,

$$f_0(x, \xi) - f_0(x', \xi') \leq \beta(\xi) \cdot \|x - x'\| \ .$$

Suppose moreover that the sequence $\{P^\nu, \nu = 1, \ldots\}$ converges in distribution to P^∞ such that for all x in S, the sequence $\{P^\nu, \nu = 1, \ldots, \infty\}$ is $f_0(x, \cdot)$-tight, i.e., to every $x \in S$ and $\varepsilon > 0$ there corresponds a compact set $K_\varepsilon \subset \Xi$ such that for all $\nu = 1, \ldots, \infty$,

$$\int_{\Xi \setminus K_\varepsilon} |f_0(x, \xi) \, dP^\nu(\xi)| < \varepsilon \ ,$$

and

$$\int_\Xi \inf_{x \in R^n} f_0(x, \xi) \, dP^\nu(\xi) > -\infty \ .$$

Then any cluster point x^* of any sequence

$$\left\{ x^\nu \in \underset{x \in S}{\text{argmin}} \left(E^\nu f_0(x) = \int f_0(x, \xi) P^\nu(d\xi) \right); \nu = 1, \ldots \right\}$$

solves the stochastic optimization problem (6.10).

Although the convergence results provide us with a lot of flexibility in the design of the approximating measures, to obtain acceptable error bounds for the approximating solutions in terms of some measure of the distance between P^ν and P, usually requires a finer discretization of P than is practical. To fix the ideas, just consider the case when ξ is a 10-dimensional random vector whose components are independent and are continuously distributed. Then a crude discretization involving 10 mass points for each one of the components of ξ would involve 10 billion points, i.e. each evaluation of the integral in (6.1) would require 10^{10} additions.

One alternative is to replace P in (1.1) by P^l (or P^u resp.) to obtain a lower (upper resp.) bound and bracket the optimal value. To improve the error estimate, the approximating distributions are refined by introducing as few additional points as possible but still 'maximize' the potential improvement. To guarantee that the given distributions will provide upper or lower bounds, one relies on the convexity properties of the integrands $f(x, \cdot)$ or $f_0(x, \cdot)$.

If g is a random l.s.c. function defined on $R \times \Xi$ and $\xi \mapsto g(x, \xi)$ is convex, then for any partition $\mathcal{S} = \{S^k, k = 1, \ldots, \nu\}$ of Ξ, we have

$$Eg(x) \leq \sum_{k=1}^{\nu} p_k(x, \xi^k) \tag{6.11}$$

where

$$\xi^k = E\{\xi \mid S^k\} \quad \text{and} \quad p_k = P[\xi \in S^k].$$

This results from the repeated application of Jensen's inequality; if $\xi \mapsto g(x, \xi)$ is concave the reverse inequality holds. As application consider the linear recourse model (4.1) with only q and T stochastic. Then $Q(x, \cdot)$ is convex, and solving (4.1) with P replaced by P^l that assigns probability p_k to ξ^k, will provide a lower bound. It can be refined by splitting one or more cells in the partitioning, for example the one with p_k maximum. Other partitioning strategies, that in some instances are much better than splitting the cell of maximum probability, have been proposed. The choice of the best partitioning scheme very much depends on the problem at hand.

To obtain an upper bound in this situation, one could rely on the following observation: let ext Ξ and rext Ξ be two collection points in R^n such that

$$\text{co ext } \Xi + \text{pos rext } \Xi \supset \Xi ,$$

where co Q [pos resp.] is the convex [positive resp.] hull of Q. If $\xi \mapsto g(x, \xi)$ is a proper, lower semicontinuous, extended real-valued function, we have that

$$Eg(x) \leq \sup_{(\lambda, \mu)} \int_{\text{ext } \Xi} g(x, e)\lambda(\mathrm{d}e) + \int_{\text{rext } \Xi} \text{rc } g(x, r)\mu(\mathrm{d}r) , \tag{6.12}$$

where rc $g(x, \cdot)$ is the recession function of $g(x, \cdot)$, λ is a probability measure on ext Ξ, and μ is a nonnegative measure on rext Ξ such that

$$\int_{\text{ext } \Xi} e\lambda(\mathrm{d}e) + \int_{\text{rext } \Xi} r\mu(\mathrm{d}r) = \bar{\xi} .$$

When Ξ is compact, then this upper bound can be improved by relying on the following: let $\nu(\xi, \cdot)$ and λ be probability measures defined on ext Ξ, such that

$$\int_{\text{ext } \Xi} e\nu(\xi, de) = \xi, \qquad \lambda(A) := \int_{\Xi} \nu(\xi, A) \, dP(\xi),$$

where A ranges over the measurable subsets of ext Ξ, then

$$Eg(x) \leqslant \int_{\text{ext } \Xi} g(x, e)\lambda(de).\tag{6.13}$$

When $\Xi = [\alpha, \beta]$ is an interval, then $\xi = (1-p)\alpha + p\beta$ for some $p \in [0, 1]$. In this case λ assigns a mass $(1-\theta)$ to α and θ to β with $\theta = (E\{\xi\} - \alpha)/(\beta - \alpha)$. The preceding inequality becomes

$$Eg(x) \leqslant (1-\theta)g(x, \alpha) + \theta g(x, \beta).\tag{6.14}$$

This is the *Edmundson–Madansky* inequality. A similar type of calculation can be carried out when $\Xi \subset R^n$ is a bounded rectangle and the random variables are independent, or when Ξ is a simplex. In the dependent case when Ξ is contained in the bounded rectangle $S := \times_{j=1}^N [\alpha_j, \beta_j]$, its generalization is given by the following inequality:

$$Eg(x) \leqslant \sum_{e \in \text{ext } S} g(x, e)p_e\tag{6.15}$$

where

$$e := (e_1, \ldots, e_N) \quad \text{and} \quad e_j = \alpha_j \text{ or } \beta_j,$$

$$\bar{e} := (\bar{e}_1, \ldots, \bar{e}_N), \quad e\text{'s kitty-corner vertex}$$
$$(\bar{e}_j = \alpha_j \text{ if } e_j = \beta_j \text{ and vice-versa}),$$

$$p_e := \left(\prod_{j=1}^N (-1)^{d[e_j]}(\bar{e}_j - \hat{m}_j) + \gamma_e \right) \Big/ \prod_{j=1}^N (\beta_j - \alpha_j),$$

$$\gamma_e := \sum_{\Lambda \subset \{1, \ldots, N\}} \left(\iota(\bar{\Lambda}, \bar{e}) \prod_{j \in \Lambda} \bar{e}_j \right) \iota(\Lambda, e)\rho_\Lambda,$$

$$\iota(\Lambda, e) := \prod_{j \in \Lambda} (-1)^{d[\bar{e}_j]}, \qquad \bar{\Lambda} = \{1, \ldots, N\} \setminus \Lambda,$$

$$\rho_\Lambda := \int_{\Xi} \left(\prod_{j \in \Lambda} \xi_j \right) dP(\xi) - \prod_{j \in J} \hat{m}_j,$$

$$\hat{m}_j := \int_{\Xi} \xi_j \, dP(\xi),$$

$$d[e_j] = \begin{bmatrix} 0 & \text{if } e_j = \alpha_j, \\ 1 & \text{if } e_j = \beta_j. \end{bmatrix}$$

As in (6.11), to obtain a sharper bound, we can use partitioning and calculate for each cell the bound derived from (6.15) and combine them. Any refinement of the partition will improve lower and upper bounds. The challenge is to split as few cells as possible – so as to minimize the increase in size of the approximating problem and keep its structure as close as possible to that of the problem just solved – and still guarantee a substantial improvement in the resulting bound. There are a few cases when an optimal split can be easily identified, but, because of the work that would be required for calculating an optimal split, the practical procedures rely mostly on heuristics that measure differences in values or slopes in order to 'maximize' the gain in nonlinearity in the approximating function $E^\nu g = \int g(x, \xi) \, dP^\nu(\xi)$ in the neighborhood of the point of interest. Moreover, since most of the time the same partition is used for calculating upper and lower bounds, the split is made so as to balance the potential gains in the upper and lower bound.

Another important technique for obtaining bounds on Ef is to identify the class $\mathcal{P}$ of distributions that contains P and define

$$ P^l \in \operatorname*{argmin}_{Q \in \mathcal{P}} \int_\Xi f(x, \xi) \, dQ(\xi), \qquad P^\mu \in \operatorname*{argmax}_{Q \in \mathcal{P}} \int_\Xi f(x, \xi) \, dQ(\xi). $$

The measures P^l and P^μ are *extremal* in that they minimize or maximize a linear form on the set $\mathcal{P}$. The choice of the class depends very much on the characteristics of P that are considered to be important and how good of an approximation is really called for. One possibility, about the only one that has been seriously studied, is to define $\mathcal{P}$ as the set of distributions with support Ξ whose first moments match those of P. The extremal measure is then obtained as the solution of a moment or generalized moment problem. All the upper and lower bounds mentioned earlier can be shown to be the solutions of appropriately defined moment problems that involve only first moments or conditional first moments. But there is room here for much more creativity, and classes $\mathcal{P}$ that involve restriction on type, as well as on higher moments, are also being investigated. Another possibility is to define $\mathcal{P}$ in terms of bounding measures (not necessarily probability measures).

$$ \mathcal{P} = \{Q \text{ probability measures on } (\Xi, \mathcal{A}): $$
$$ P^-(A) \leqslant Q(A) \leqslant P^+(A) \text{ for all } A \in \mathcal{A} \}, $$

in which case P^l and P^μ consist of 'pasted' pieces of P^+ and P^-.

There are many other possibilities to design approximations (e.g., by majorizing or minorizing the given distribution function P), and for particular classes of problems much can be done to sharpen the preceding bounds (e.g., for stochastic programs with simple or network recourse). For these however, we must refer to the literature. All these approximation schemes can be applied equally well to expectation functionals that appear in the constraints.

However, if the integrand is discontinuous, which is the case when the model involves probabilistic constraints, then special discretization procedures are more appropriate (for these also we must refer to the literature).

7. Solution procedures

Because of the richness of the models covered under the heading 'stochastic programming', one cannot expect a universal algorithm. At this point it will be useful to consider subclasses of problems and methods. We begin, however, with a couple of methods that can be applied to rather wide classes of problems. Please consult the references for a more complete discussion of the algorithms and their numerical performance.

7.1. Stochastic quasi-gradient methods

These methods, whose roots lie in the theory of stochastic approximation, are in theory only applicable to problems of type (1.1) that satisfy convexity assumptions. However, in a number of instances stochastic quasi-gradient methods have been used for nonconvex problems and their performance has been quite satisfactory. It is a 'general' method for solving nonlinear (convex) stochastic optimization of the type (1.1). The price to pay is that it does not provide error estimates for the solution obtained, the convergence is only guaranteed in a probabilistic sense, and numerical instabilities could be introduced as a result of the transformations needed to bring the original problem in the form required for the application of the method.

Let us consider the following version of the canonical stochastic optimization problem (1.1):

$$\text{minimize} \quad E\{f_0(x, \boldsymbol{\xi})\}$$
$$\text{subject to} \quad x \in S \subset R^n \,,$$

where f_0 and S are as defined in Section 1. The stochastic quasi-gradient algorithm generates a sequence $\{x^1, x^2, \ldots\}$ of points in S through the recursive formula:

$$x^{\nu+1} := \text{prj}_S[x^\nu - \rho_\nu \zeta^\nu] \,,$$

where prj_S denotes projection on S, ρ_ν is a sequence of scalars that tend to 0 and ζ^ν is a stochastic quasi-gradient of Ef at x^ν. More precisely, ζ^ν is a random vector that satisfies

$$Ef_0(x^*) - Ef_0(x^\nu) \geq E\{\zeta^\nu \mid x^0, \ldots, x^\nu\}(x^* - x^\nu) + \gamma_\nu$$

with γ_ν a sequence that goes to 0 as ν goes to ∞ and x^* an optimal solution (assuming one exists). The idea is that, at least asymptotically,

$$E\{\zeta^{\nu}|x^0, \ldots, x^n\} \in \partial Ef(x^{\nu}).$$

The method converges with probability 1 to the optimal solution under the following conditions:
   (i) Ef_0 is a convex finite-valued function,
  (ii) S is convex and compact,
 (iii) the parameters ρ and γ satisfy with probability 1 the conditions

$$\rho_{\nu} \geq 0, \quad \sum_{\nu=0}^{\infty} \rho_{\nu} = \infty, \quad \sum_{\nu=0}^{\infty} E\{\rho_{\nu}|\gamma_{\nu}| + \rho_{\nu}^2\|\zeta^{\nu}\|^2\} < \infty.$$

For example $\rho_{\nu} = 1/\nu$ is such a sequence when $\gamma_{\nu} \equiv 0$ and $\|\zeta^{\nu}\|$ is bounded. The convergence proof is derived from a modified super-martingale convergence argument. Note that only the convexity of Ef_0 is required, not that of $f_0(\cdot, \xi)$. This observation is important when applying the method to stochastic programs with probabilistic constraints, for example.

Typically, ζ^{ν} is obtained as a subgradient of $f_0(x^{\nu}, \xi^{\nu})$ where ξ^{ν} is a sample of the random variable $\boldsymbol{\xi}$, or more generally $\zeta^{\nu} = (1/L)\Sigma_{l=1}^{L} v^l$, where each $v^l \in \partial f(x^{\nu}, \xi^l)$ and the ξ^l are L independent samples of the random variable $\boldsymbol{\xi}$. However, these are not the only possibilities, and many variants can be used to overcome various obstacles. These may come from the lack of differentiability of the function $f_0(\cdot, \xi)$ or from the difficulty to compute its gradient, even when it is known to be differentiable (for multiperiod stochastic programs, for example).

To illustrate the problems that need to be faced in the implementation of the method, we consider its application to the linear recourse problem (4.1). It works essentially as follows. Let x^{ν} belong to the domain of finiteness of EQ and satisfy the linear constraints $b - Ax \leq 0, x \geq 0$. We draw a sample $(q^{\nu}, h^{\nu}, t^{\nu}, W^{\nu})$ of the random quantities in problem (4.2) and find

$$\pi^{\nu} \in \text{argmax}\{\pi(h^{\nu} - T^{\nu}x^{\nu}) \mid \pi W^{\nu} \leq q^{\nu}\}.$$

The vector $c - \pi^{\nu}T^{\nu}$ is then a stochastic quasi-gradient of $Ef_0 = c + EQ$ at x^{ν}. The next operation to be carried out is the projection of $x^{\nu} + \rho_{\nu}(c - \pi^{\nu}T^{\nu})$ on the set $S = \{x: Ax \geq 0, x \geq 0\} \cap \{x: EQ(x) < \infty\}$. This may or may not be easy. In general, it requires the solution of an optimization problem with quadratic objective and possibly nonlinear constraints. Thus, each iteration could conceivable be very expensive. And that is not in keeping with the strategy of the method. By its nature, the method has to come to terms with the fact that many (small) steps will be required, but each step should then involve only a modicum of calculations.

Thus, one of the possible stumbling blocks is the *projection* on S. There are a number of tricks that can be used to simplify this operation, but generally, it can easily be carried out only if S is the result of the intersection of a bounded or unbounded rectangle with a linear (or separable convex) inequality constraints or if S is a ball. The additional constraints must be removed. This can be done by including them in the objective after appropriate penalization, or casting the procedure in the framework of the Augmented Lagrangian Method. However, as is well known, such reformulation could introduce numerical instabilities, and one must then find a way to cope with these.

Another potential stumbling block is the choice of the *step sizes* ρ_ν. In theory, any sequence that satisfies the convergence conditions will do. But in the implementation of the method we are interested in the properties of *finite* sequence of x^ν. Because of this, letting ρ_ν go too fast to zero could have undesired consequences, i.e., the tail of the series we are looking at may appear to cluster around some point that could be very far away from the optimal solution. To overcome this, adaptive procedures for the choice of the step size have been developed. The information that is usually used to increase or decrease the step size, comes from estimates of the variance of the stochastic quasi-gradient.

This type of information can also be used in the choice of a *stopping criterion*. The most common stopping criterion, however, is based on a comparison of the values of the objective at successive iterates. Since a precise evaluation of the objective is one of the operations that we are trying to avoid by resorting to quasi-gradient methods, the following quantity

$$(1/(M+1)) \sum_{h=\nu-M}^{\nu} f(x^h, \xi^h)$$

is used as an estimate for $Ef_0(x^\nu)$, where M could be relatively large. The search for a better solution is terminated when these estimates record no noticeable improvement.

7.2. Scenario aggregation

This class of methods is aimed at solving conceivably large, multiperiod stochastic optimization problems when only a limited number of realizations of the random quantities need to be considered. This could be the case because the random variables describe physical phenomena with only a small number of possible realizations, or because the realizations correspond to a few scenarios that need to be taken into account in the search for a 'hedging' solution in an optimization under uncertainty problem (i.e., when no statistical information may be available about the unknown parameters). Let $\{\xi^1, \ldots, \xi^L\} = \Xi$ be the support of the random vector ξ, and $p_l = P\{\xi = \xi^l\}$. The canonical problem (1.1), assumed to be solvable, becomes

$$\text{minimize} \quad \sum_{l=1}^{L} p_l f_0(x, \xi^l)$$

$$\text{subject to} \quad \sum_{l=1}^{L} p_l f_i(x, \xi^l) \leq 0, \quad i = 1, \ldots, s, \tag{7.1}$$

$$\sum_{l=1}^{L} p_l f_i(x, \xi^l) = 0, \quad i = s+1, \ldots, m,$$

$$x \in X \subset R^n.$$

Suppose that for $l = 1, \ldots, L$,

$$x^l \in \operatorname{argmin}\{ f_0(x, \xi^l) \mid x \in S_l \} \tag{7.2}$$

where

$$S_l = \{ x \in X \mid f_i(x, \xi^l) \leq 0, \ i = 1, \ldots, s;$$
$$f_i(x, \xi^l) = 0, \ i = s+1, \ldots, m \}.$$

Then

$$\hat{x} = \sum_{l=1}^{L} p_l x^l$$

could be a reasonable estimate of the optimal solution of (7.1). Although in general $\hat{x}$ is not the optimal solution, it may not even be feasible since $S = \cap_l S_l$, it was obtained by solving only deterministic versions of (1.1). The idea is to modify the objective of (7.2) so as to generate a sequence of estimates $\hat{x}^\nu$ that will converge to the optimal solution of (7.1), where

$$\hat{x}^\nu = \sum_{l=1}^{L} p_l \hat{x}^{l\nu}$$

with

$$x^{l\nu} \in \operatorname{argmin}\{ f_0^\nu(x, \xi^l) \mid x \in S_l \}. \tag{7.3}$$

The general principle that allows us to proceed in this manner is called the *principle of scenario aggregation*. A particular implementation goes as follows: for a fixed $\theta > 0$,

$$\nu = 0: \quad f_0^0 := f_0, \ w^0(\xi) = 0;$$
$$\nu > 0: \quad f_0^\nu l(x, \xi) := f_0(x, \xi) + w^{\nu-1}(\xi)x + \tfrac{1}{2}\theta |x - \hat{x}^{\nu-1}|,$$
$$w^\nu(\xi) = w^{\nu-1}(\xi) + \theta[x^\nu(\xi) - \hat{x}^\nu].$$

Provided that we are in the convex case, or mildly nonconvex, the sequence $\{\hat{x}^\nu, \nu = 1, \ldots\}$ converges to the optimal solution, with strict improvement at each step. The convergence rate (known to be linear) may be relatively slow. However, the process of blending the decision $x^{l\nu}$ iteratively, is likely to identify fairly early the activities $(x_j^{l\nu} > 0)$ that will be part of the optimal solution.

There is also a version of the updating mechanism for multistage problems that calculates $\hat{x}$ by taking into account the fact that if ξ and ξ' are two realizations that agree up to time t, then the corresponding decisions x and x' must also agree up to time t (nonanticipativity).

7.3. *Recourse problems*: *Large scale linear programming techniques*

We consider only linear recourse problems (4.1) whose random elements have a discrete distribution (finite support). This means that for some finite L,

$$EQ(x) = E\{Q(x, \xi)\} = \sum_{l=1}^{L} p_l Q(x, \xi^l) \, .$$

Our discussion here is limited to the case when only h and T are random (i.e., with fixed recourse), and the problem at hand exhibits no further structural properties. Problems with simple recourse will be discussed in the next subsection; for other special recourse structure (transportation, network flow, etc.), the main steps of the solutions procedures are similar to those to be described below, but in the derivation of the 'cuts' much is gained by taking advantage of the special structure to speed up the calculations. Also, we shall pay no attention to particular 'structures' of the random quantities, although that may justify tailoring the algorithms to fit the particular situation. For example, if ξ has a representation of the form

$$\xi = \zeta^0 + \eta_1 \zeta^1 + \cdots + \eta_K \zeta^K \, ,$$

where the $\zeta^k \in R^N$, the η^k and 1-dimensional random variables, and K is relatively small (compared to N), we may want to work in this K-dimensional space to carry out discretizations (cf. Section 6) as well as the bunching operations mentioned below.

We shall also not be concerned here to know if the problem was originally formulated in this form, or if it did arise through discretization, or if the ξ^l come from a (stratified or not) sample of ξ, or if the ξ^l are no more than the available data (P is then the empirical distribution), or even if the problem comes up as a 'linking' problem in scenario analysis, cf. the previous subsection. The methods to be discussed, however, presuppose that L is not too large (typically less than 10 000), otherwise we would again resort to approximations in order to reduce the problem to a more manageable size.

It is easy to see that the problem at hand has a dual block angular structure, and that one should be able to take advantage of this structure. The *L-shaped algorithm* to be described next, based on the Benders decomposition method, takes advantage of the properties of the linear recourse problem to (dramatically) reduce the work required to generate feasibility (induced constraints) and optimality cuts (that engender a piecewise linear approximation of EQ on its domain of finiteness).

Step 0. Initialize: $\nu = r = s = 0$.

Step 1. Set $\nu = \nu + 1$ and solve the linear program

$$
\begin{aligned}
\text{minimize} \quad & cx + \theta \\
\text{subject to} \quad & Ax \geq 0, \\
& D_k x \geq d_k, \quad k = 1, \ldots, r, \\
& E_k x + \theta \geq e_k, \quad k = 1, \ldots, t, \\
& x \geq 0.
\end{aligned}
$$

Let (x^ν, θ^ν) be an optimal solution.

Step 2. For $\zeta^\nu := (h^{*\nu} - T^{*n} x^\nu)$, a lower bound of the possible values of the random vector $h - Tx^\nu$ with respect to a cone contained in pos W (for example, an orthant), solve the linear program ($e := (1, 1, \ldots, 1)$):

$$
\begin{aligned}
\text{minimize} \quad & v = ev^+ + ev^- \\
\text{subject to} \quad & Wy + Iv^+ - Iv^- = \zeta^\nu, \\
& y \geq 0, \ v^+ \geq 0, \ v^- \geq 0.
\end{aligned}
$$

if the optimal value $v^\nu = 0$, go to Step 3; otherwise use the optimal simplex multipliers σ^ν to generate a feasibility cut: set $r = r + 1$, and define

$$
D_r = \sigma^\nu T^{*\nu}, \qquad d_r = \sigma^\nu h^{*\nu}.
$$

Step 3. For every $l = 1, \ldots, L$, solve the linear program

$$
\text{minimize} \quad [q^l y : Wy = h^l - T^l x^\nu, \ y \geq 0].
$$

Let $\pi^{l\nu}$ be the optimal multipliers associated with the optimal solution of the l-th problem. Set $t = t + 1$ and define

$$
E_t = \sum_{l=1}^{L} p_l \pi^{l\nu} T^l, \qquad e_t = \sum_{l=1}^{L} p_l \pi^{l\nu} h^l.
$$

If $\theta^\nu \geq e_t - E_t x^\nu$, stop; x^ν is an optimal solution. Otherwise return to Step 1, adding the optimality cut determined by (E_t, e_t).

In Step 2 we have implicity assumed the existence of a lower bound that can be identified with some point (h, T) in the support of the random vector $(\boldsymbol{h}, \boldsymbol{T})$. This is not always possible, but the feasibility criteria that have been developed for linear recourse problems always allow us to reduce checking for feasibility (and generating the associated cut) to solving in Step 2 a few linear programs (by opposition to L).

Large computational gains can be made by relying in Step 3 on *bunching procedures*. The basic idea is that if B is an optimal basis for some $\xi^l = (q^l, h^l, T^l)$, it is also optimal for all $\xi = (q, h, T)$ such that

$$B^{-1}(h - Tx^v) \geq 0, \qquad q - (q_B B^{-1})W \geq 0$$

where q_B is the subvector of q that corresponds to the columns of W that are in B. There are different strategies for organizing the bunching procedures, all aimed at minimizing the number of operations. The trickling down procedure with Schur complement updates of the bases is apparently the most efficient. Other possibilities are being explored such as relying on QR factorizations of the bases, and parallel processing.

A nesting procedure (solutions being passed down the stage-ladder and cuts being pushed up) extends this method to multistage problems.

A more advance version of this algorithm, which relies on subdifferential-type techniques, requires the following modifications:

(i) in Step 3 we do not aggregate the π^{lv} to generate a piecewise linear approximation of EQ, but use them to construct piecewise linear approximations of the $Q(\cdot, \xi^l)$, with

$$E_{tl} := \pi^{lv} T^l, \qquad e_{tl} = \pi^{lv} h^l.$$

(ii) In Step 1, the (master) program is replaced by the following:

$$\text{minimize} \quad cx + \sum_{l=1}^{L} p_l \theta_l + \tfrac{1}{2}\|x - x^{v-1}\|^2$$

$$\text{subject to} \quad Ax \geq 0,$$

$$D_i x \geq d_k, \quad k = 1, \ldots, r,$$

$$E_{kl} x + \theta_l \geq e_{kl}, \quad k = 1, \ldots, t, \, l = 1, \ldots L,$$

$$x \geq 0.$$

The convergence is much aided by the introduction of the proximal point term $\tfrac{1}{2}\|x - x^{v-1}\|^2$, and the disaggregation of the feasibility cuts improves the approximation. Unless L is large, the performance of this algorithm is better than that of the (straight) L-shaped method.

7.4. *Recourse problems*: *Nonlinear programming techniques*

Since stochastic programming problems are, in some sense, just nonlinear optimization problems, almost any nonlinear programming technique could be used to solve them. However, they possess some rather marked characteristics, generally, function and gradient evaluations are very difficult and time consuming. This means that the methods that require numerous function evaluations will usually perform rather poorly. Because of this, decomposition-type methods are again favored, although sometimes in disguised form.

The methods that we sketch out here have been developed first for simple recourse problems, to be later extended to problems with linear recourse. By *simple recourse* we mean that the 'decision' is completely determined by the decision x and the observation ξ. In the linear case, when only h is random, the problem takes the form:

$$\text{minimize} \quad cx + E\{\psi(y) \,|\, y = h - Tx\}$$

$$\text{subject to} \quad Ax \geq b, \; x \geq 0,$$

where ψ is a convex piecewise linear function. A common case is when

$$\psi(y) := \sum_{i=1}^{m'} \psi_i(y_i); \; \psi_i(y_i) := q_i^+ y_i \; \text{if} \; y_i \geq 0,$$

$$:= q_i^- y_i \; \text{if} \; y_i \leq 0.$$

The *SupPORT package* relies on multi-point linearization of the function $\Psi := E\psi$, to replace the problem by

$$\text{minimize} \quad cx + \sum_{k=1}^{K} \lambda \Psi(\chi^k)$$

$$\text{subject to} \quad \sigma^K \colon \; Ax \geq b,$$

$$\pi^K \colon \; Tx - \sum_{k=1}^{K} \lambda \chi^k = 0,$$

$$\theta^K \colon \; \sum_{k=1}^{K} \lambda_k = 1,$$

$$x \geq 0, \; \lambda_k \geq 0,$$

where $(\sigma^K, \pi^K, \theta^K)$ are the multipliers associated with the optimal solution of this problem. The vectors χ^k, generated by solving the (Lagrangian) sub-problems

$$\text{minimize} \quad \Psi(\chi) + \pi^k \chi,$$

can be viewed as *tenders* to be measured against the possible outcomes of the random vector $h - Tx$.

Also the *Lagrangian finite generation* technique, was originally developed for simple recourse problems, but of the following more general form:

$$\text{minimize} \quad \rho(x) + E\{\psi(y, q) \mid y = h - Tx\}$$

$$\text{subject to} \quad Ax \geq b, \; 0 \leq x \leq r,$$

where ρ and ψ are linear-quadratic functions of the type:

$$\rho(x) := cx + \sum_{j=1}^{n} (d_j/2r_j)x_j^2,$$

$$\psi(y, q) := \sum_{i=1}^{m'} \psi(y_i, q_i), \quad \psi(y_i, q_i) := q_i e_i \theta(e_i^{-1} y_i),$$

$$\theta(\tau) := 0 \text{ if } \tau \leq 0, \quad := \tau^2/2 \text{ if } 0 \leq \tau \leq 1, \quad := \tau - \tfrac{1}{2} \text{ if } \tau \geq 1.$$

The quantities e_i, d_j and the random variables q_i are positive. The method is based on showing that the following problem

$$\text{minimize} \quad yb + E\left\{zh + \sum_{i=1}^{m'} (e_i/2q_i)z_i^2\right\} + \sum_{j=1}^{n} r_j d_j \theta(d_j^{-1} w_j)$$

$$\text{subject to} \quad w = c - yA - E\{zT\},$$

$$0 \leq z \leq q, \; y \geq 0,$$

is dual to the linear-quadratic recourse problem. It then relies on a finite element representation of the functions $z : \Xi \to R^{m'}$ to approximate this dual problem (which is barely stochastic) by a deterministic quadratic programming problem. The approximation is refined by enriching appropriately the collection of finite elements.

7.5. Stochastic programs with probabilistic constraints

The major numerical obstacle is still the need to calculate values and gradients of the expectation functionals, i.e., of the probabilistic constraints. Some of the approximations results of Section 6 may be of help here, but those possibilities have not yet been fully investigated.

One interesting possibility is the use of penalty functions to recast the problem in the form:

$$\text{minimize} \quad f_0(x)$$

$$\text{subject to} \quad Ef_1(x) \leq 0, \; f_i(x) \leq 0, \; i = 2, \ldots, m,$$

where for $i = 2, \ldots, m$, the functions f_i are convex. The function f_1 is defined by (3.3) for some $\alpha \in (0, 1)$, P is log-concave, and the functions g_k jointly convex in x and ξ. From Propositions 3.1 and 3.2, it follows that Ef_1 is then log-convex, and the approximating problem

$$\text{minimize} \quad f_\sigma(x)$$
$$\text{subject to} \quad f_i(x) \leq 0, \ i = 2, \ldots, m ,$$

is a convex optimization problem. Here σ is a parameter that will tend to ∞ and f_σ is the penalized objective

$$f_\sigma(x) := f_0(x) - \sigma \ln(M^{-1} Ef_1(x))$$

with $M < 0$ a lower bound for Ef_1 on the fesibility set S.

Again, in theory any technique could be used for solving this convex optimization problem. However, as for stochastic programs with recourse, the major difficulty comes from the need to compute values and gradients of the expectational functions Ef_1 or of its logarithm. Because of this, decomposition-type techniques are again among the favorite ones, either in the form of cutting hyperplane algorithms or descent directions calculated by relying on an appropriate dual problem.

In connection with this class of problems, much research has been devoted to speed up the calculation of multidimensional integerals for various multivariate distributions, refining *quasi-Monte Carlo* techniques for multidimensional integration, and developing the use of Boole–Bonferroni inequalities to approximate probabilistic constraints.

Since the difficulty of evaluating Ef_1 may depend to a large extent on the distribution of ξ, one can in some instances simplify the calculations by modeling the random phenomena by distribution functions of a given type, such as the sum of lower dimensional multivariate gamma (or normals) or by polynomial distribution (in this latter case the problem to be solved is of a geometric program).

8. Stability and incomplete information

Because all statistical information is by its essence finite, the passage from statistical data to a probabilistic model always entails a certain level of approximation. In this sense, all stochastic optimization models are with 'incomplete information', and this underscores the importance of studying the dependence of the solution on the probability measure. The convergence results of Section 6 can be used in certain situations, more generally one has the following:

Proposition 8.1. *Let us consider*

$$Eg(x; u, P) = g_1(x; u) + \int_\Xi g_2(x, \xi; u) \, dP(\xi)$$

as a function on $R^n \times U \times \mathscr{P}$ where U is a topological space (of parameters) and $\mathscr{P}$ a set of probability measures. Let G be an open bounded subset of R^n. Suppose that

(i) *g_2 is continuous on* cl $G \times \Xi \times U$ *(with Ξ viewed as a subset of R^n);*

(ii) *the collection*

$$\{g_2(x, \, \cdot \, ; u); \, x \in \text{cl } G, \, u \in U\}$$

is uniformly integrable with respect to $\mathscr{P}$, i.e. for each $\varepsilon > 0$ there is a compact set $K \subset R^N$ such that for each $x \in$ cl G, $u \in U$ and $P \in \mathscr{P}$

$$\int_{\Xi \setminus K} |g_2(x, \, \xi; u)| \, \mathrm{d}P(\xi) < \varepsilon \, ;$$

(iii) *g_1 is a proper extended real-valued l.s.c. function on* cl $G \times U$, *and at some point $x_0 \in$ argmin $Eg(\, \cdot \, ; u^0, P^0)$:*

$$g_1(x_0; u_0) \geqslant \inf_{V \in \mathcal{N}(x^0)} \limsup_{u \to u_0} \inf_{x \in V} g_1(x; y) \, ,$$

where $\mathcal{N}(x^0)$ denotes the neighborhood system at x^0;

(iv) argmin $Eg(\, \cdot \, ; u^0, P^0) \subset G$.

Then, if $\mathscr{P}$ is given the narrow topology (weak convergence of probability measures), we have

(a) *$(u, P) \mapsto \inf Eg(\, \cdot \, ; u, P)$ is continuous at (u^0, P^0);*

(b) *$(u, P) \mapsto$ argmin $Eg(\, \cdot \, ; u, P) : U \times \mathscr{P} \rightrightarrows R^n$ is semicontinuous at (u^0, P^0) in the following sense: to each $\varepsilon > 0$, there corresponds a neighborhood $V_\varepsilon \times Q_\varepsilon$ of (u^0, P^0) such that, for all $(u', P') \in V_\varepsilon \times Q_\varepsilon$,*

$$\text{argmin } Eg(\, \cdot \, ; u', P') \subset \text{argmin } Eg(\, \cdot \, ; u^0, P^0) + \varepsilon B \, ,$$

with εB the ball of radius ε in R^n.

When argmin $Eg(\, \cdot \, ; u^0, P^0)$ is single-valued, the last assertion simply means that the argmin multifunction is continuous on a neighborhood of (u^0, P^0).

This proposition helps alleviate, to some extent, our worries about the choice of the probability measure in those models when only very limited information, or no information, about the distribution of the uncertain parameters is available. One question it does not resolve, is that of knowing if the solution obtained by using an approximating probability measure, can be considered as a *consistent* estimate of the (true) optimal solution. This has been studied in the following framework: let $(Z, \mathscr{F}, \mu)$ be a sample space and $(\mathscr{F}^\nu)_{\nu=1}^\infty$ an increasing sequence of sigma-fields contained in $\mathscr{F}$ that model the increase in information, obtained after each sampling of ξ, or model generally, after each sampling of given function of ξ. A sample ζ – e.g., $\zeta = \{\xi^1, \xi^2, \ldots\}$, independent samples of ξ – leads to a sequence of probability measures

$\{P^\nu(\,\cdot\,;\zeta)\}_{\nu=1}^{\infty}$ defined on $(\Xi,\mathscr{A})$. Since only information collected up to stage ν can be used in the choice of P^ν, we must have that for all $A\in\mathscr{A}$, $\zeta\mapsto P^\nu(A;\zeta)$ is $\mathscr{F}^\nu$-measurable. A typical case is when the $\{P^\nu\}_{\nu=1}^{\infty}$ are the empirical measures. Since the P^ν depend on ζ, the solutions of the approximating problems

$$x^\nu(\zeta)\in\operatorname*{argmin}\left\{\int f_0(x,\xi)\,dP^\nu(\xi;\zeta)\,\middle|\,x\in S\right\}$$

are functions of ζ. Here, f_0 is a random lower semicontinuous function and S is the closed set defined in Section 1. Consistency demands the convergence with probability 1 of the $\{x^\nu(\,\cdot\,)\}_{\nu=1}^{\infty}$ to x^* the optimal solution of (1.1), as the $P^\nu(\,\cdot\,;\zeta)$ μ-almost surely (narrowly) converge to P. The result follows from the general theory of epi-convergence, once it has been shown that the expectation functionals

$$E^\nu f(x,\zeta)=\int f_0(x,\xi)\,dP^\nu(\xi;\zeta)\quad\text{if }x\in S\,,$$

$$=\infty\qquad\qquad\qquad\text{otherwise}\,,$$

are random lower semicontinuous functions that epi-converge μ-almost surely to

$$Ef(x)=\int f_0(x,\xi)\,dP(\xi)\quad\text{if }x\in S\,,$$

$$=\infty\qquad\qquad\qquad\text{otherwise}\,.$$

A related question is to estimate the 'rate' of convergence. In this context, this means to derive the asymptotic properties of the distribution of the random quantity (that measures the error in the solution):

$$\lim_{\nu\to\infty}(x^*-x^\nu(\,\cdot\,))$$

or an appropriately scaled version of that vector, say $\sqrt{\nu}\|x^*-x^\nu(\,\cdot\,)\|$. Probabilistic error bounds can be obtained by means of the Central Limit Theorem which can be applied whenever the active constraints (at the minimum) determine a differentiable manifold. In more general situations, the limit law of the random vector $\sqrt{\nu}\|x^*-x^\nu(\,\cdot\,)\|$ is known to have a distribution that is composed of the sums of truncated normals restricted to lower dimensional subspaces of R^n.

9. References

1. General references dealing with modeling, approximations schemes and solutions techniques, are:

Y. Ermoliev and R.J.-B. Wets (eds.) (1987), *Numerical Procedures for Stochastic Optimization* (Springer-Verlag, Berlin).
A. Prekopa and R. J.-B. Wets (eds.) (1986), *Stochastic Programming 84: I & II* (North-Holland, Amsterdam). (Also: *Mathematical Programming Study* **27** and **28**.)

For more about relationship between stochastic programming models and other stochastic optimization problems,

M.A.H. Dempster (1980), *Stochastic Programming* (Academic Press, London).
Y. Ermoliev (1976), *Stochastic Programming Methods* (Nauka, Moscow).

and for a bibliography (up to 1975) that includes many papers dealing with applications:

I.M. Stancu-Minasian and M.J. Wets (1977), A research bibliography in stochastic programming: 1955–1975, *Operations Research* **24**, 1078–1119.

2. For expectation functionals, convexity and lower semicontinuity results as well as some subdifferentiability results appear in

R.J.-B. Wets (1974), Stochastic programs with fixed recourse: The equivalent deterministic problem, *SIAM Review* **16**, 309–339.

Pure continuity is first considered in

L. Stougie (1985), Design and analysis of algorithms for stochastic integer programming, Thesis, Centrum for Wiskunde en Informatica, Amsterdam,

whereas Lipschitz continuity in the nonconvex case was studied in

J.B. Hiriart-Urruty (1978), Conditions nécessaires d'optimalité pour un programme stochastique avec recours, *SIAM J. Control and Optimization* **16**, 317–329.

Subdifferentiability results, as stated, are new although there are many specialized results that can be found in the articles mentioned above. In the convex case, there is an important formula that applies to the multistage case:

R.T. Rockafellar and R.J.-B. Wets (1982), On the interchange of subdifferentiation and conditional expectation for convex functionals, *Stochastics* **7**, 173–182.

3. The first formulation of stochastic programs with probabilistic constraints is attributed to A. Charnes, W. Cooper and G. Symond. The general quasi-concavity and log-concavity results for stochastic programs with probabilistic constraints are due to

A. Prékopa (1973), Logarithmic concave measures with applications to stochastic programming, *Acta. Sci. Math. (Szeged)* **32**, 301–316.

4. The formulation of stochastic programs with recourse is credited to G. Dantzig and M. Beale. However, like for stochastic programs with probabilistic

constraints, one can find in the literature (inventory theory, statistical hypotheses testing, and reliability) many examples of problems that can be formulated as (simple) stochastic programs with recourse, at a much earlier date.

5. For the duality theory for convex stochastic programs, consult

R.T. Rockafellar and R.J.-B. Wets (1976), Nonanticipativity and $\mathscr{L}^1$-martingales in stochastic optimization problems, *Mathematical Programming Study* **6**, 170–187 (also in: R. Wets (ed.), *Stochastic Systems, Modeling, Identification and Optimization* (North-Holland, Amsterdam)).
R.T. Rockafellar and R.J.-B. Wets (1978), The optimal recourse problem in discrete time: $\mathscr{L}^1$-multipliers for inequality constraints, *SIAM J. Control and Optimization* **16**, 16–36.

and the references given therein. Optimality conditions for recourse problems (non-convex case) have first been given by J.-B. Hiriart-Urruty, *op cit.* A review (including more recent results) appears in

M. Dempster (1986), On stochastic programming: II. Dynamic problems under risk, Research report DAL TR 86-5, Dalhousie University, June 1986.

6. In addition to the general references, the following articles report about the sharper results mentioned at the end of the section:

P. Kall (1987), Stochastic programs with recourse: an upper bound and the related moment problem, *Zeitschrift fur Operations Research* **31**, A 119–A 141.
A. Gaivoronski (1986), Stochastic optimization techniques for finding optimal submeasures, in: V. Arkin, A. Shiraev and R. Wets (eds.), *Stochastic Optimization*, Lecture Notes in Control and Information Sciences 81 (Springer-Verlag, Berlin) 351–363.
W. Klein Haneveld (1986), *Duality in Stochastic Linear and Dynamic Programming*, Lecture Notes in Economics and Mathematical Systems 274 (Springer-Verlag, Berlin)

and examples of bounds for specialized structures, can be found in

S. Wallace (1987), A piecewise linear upper bound on the network recourse function, *Mathematical Programming* **38**, 133–146.
J.R. Birge and R.J.-B. Wets (1988), Sublinear upper bounds for stochastic programs with recourse, *Mathematical Programming* **43**, 131–149.

For convergence consult the references given for Section 1, and for the problem with probabilistic constraints:

J. Wang, Continuity of feasible solution sets of probabilistic constrained programs, to appear in *J. Optimization Theory and Applications*.

7. For algorithmic solution procedures, refer to 'Numerical Procedures for Stochastic Optimization', *op cit.*; also for multidimensional integration techniques. For more recent developments,

R.T. Rockafellar and R.J.-B. Wets (1987), The principle of scenario aggregation in optimization under uncertainty, Manuscript, University of Washington, May 1987,

describes the scenario aggregation method,

A. Ruszczynski (1987), A linearization method for nonsmooth stochastic programming, *Mathematics of Operations Research* **12**, 32–49.

A. Ruszczynski, Regularized decomposition of stochastic programs: algorithmic techniques and numerical results, Techn. Report, Instytut Automatyki Politechnika Warszawska, May 1987,

give the 'regularized' version of the L-shaped method,

K. Ariyawansa, D.C. Sorensen and R.J.-B. Wets (1987), Parallel schemes to approximate values and subgradients of the recourse function in certain stochastic programs, Manuscript, Argonne National Labs., September 1987.
S. Robinson (1986), Bundle-based decomposition: Description and preliminary results, in: A. Prékopa, J. Szelezsan and B. Strazicky (eds.), *System Modelling and Optimization*, Lecture Notes in Control and Information Sciences 84 (Springer-Verlag, Berlin) 751–756.
D. Medhi, Decomposition of structured large-scale optimization problems and parallel optimization, Techn. Report No. 718, Computer Sciences Department, University of Wisconsin-Madison, 1987.

are methods adapted to multi-processing, and

A. Prékopa (1988), Boole–Bonferroni inequalities and linear programming, *Operations Research* **36**, 145–162.

introduces the use of the Boole–Bonferroni inequalities to evaluate probabilistic constraints.

8. For an overview of the stability results:

J. Dupačova (1986), Stochastic programming with incomplete information: A survey of results on postoptimization and sensitivity analysis, *Optimization* **18**, 507–532.

The general result (Proposition 8.1) comes from

P. Kall (1987), On approximations and stability in stochastic programming, in: J. Guddat, H.Th. Jongen, B. Kummer, and F. Nozicka (eds.), *Parametric Optimization and Related Topics* (Akademie-Verlag, Berlin) 387–407.
S.M. Robinson and R.J.-B. Wets (1987), Stability in two-stage stochastic programming, *SIAM J. Control and Optimization* **25**, 1409–1416.

A description of the statistical framework for stochastic programs with incomplete information can be found in

J. Dupačova and R.J.-B. Wets (1988), Asymptotic behavior of statistical estimators and of optimal solutions for stochastic optimization problems, *The Annals of Statistics* **16**, 1517–1549.
W. Roemisch and R. Schultz (1989), Distribution sensitivity in stochastic programming, *Mathematical Programming*, to appear.

and the sharpest asymptotic results are in

A.J. King (1986), Asymptotic behaviour of solutions in stochastic optimization: non-smooth analysis and the derivation of non-normal limit distributions, Doctoral Thesis, University of Washington, December 1986.

Appendix A. Epi-convergence and subdifferentiability

Let $\{g; g^\nu, \nu = 1, \ldots\}$ be a collection of extended real-valued functions defined on R^n. We say that

$$g = \underset{\nu \to \infty}{\text{epi-lim}}\ g^{\nu}$$

if for all $x \in R^{n}$,

$$\underset{\{x^{\nu} \to x\}}{\inf}\ \underset{\nu \to \infty}{\lim\inf}\ g^{\nu}(x^{\nu}) := (\text{epi-li}\ g^{\nu})(x) \geqslant g(x)\ , \qquad (\text{A.1})$$

$$\underset{\{x^{\nu} \to x\}}{\inf}\ \underset{\nu \to \infty}{\lim\sup}\ g^{\nu}(x^{\nu}) := (\text{epi-ls}\ g^{\nu})(x) \leqslant g(x)\ , \qquad (\text{A.2})$$

the infima are with respect to all subsequences converging to x; the functions g^{ν} *epiconverge to g* (which is necessarily lower semicontinuous). The terminology comes from the fact that this convergence corresponds to the set convergence of the epigraphs. Although epi-convergence appears to be related to pointwise convergence, it is neither implied, nor does it imply pointwise convergence. To see this simply observe that pointwise convergence only requires that $\lim\inf g^{\nu}(x^{\nu}) \geqslant g(x)$ for the sequence $\{x^{\nu} = x\}_{\nu=1}^{\infty}$, but only allows for the use of that specific sequence to satisfy $\lim\sup g^{\nu}(x^{\nu}) \leqslant g(x)$. The two convergence notions coincide if the collection of functions is *equi-lower semicontinuous*, i.e., if to any x there corresponds $\varepsilon_{x} > 0$ such that for every $0 < \varepsilon < \varepsilon_{x}$, there exists $\delta_{\varepsilon} > 0$ and ν_{ε} such that for all $\nu \geqslant \nu_{\varepsilon}$,

$$\underset{\|y-x\| < \delta_{\varepsilon}}{\inf}\ g^{\nu}(y) \geqslant \min[\,g^{\nu}(x) - \varepsilon,\ \varepsilon^{-1}\,]\ . \qquad (\text{A.3})$$

It is easy to verify that monotone collections of lower semicontinuous functions are equi-lower semicontinuous. This means that outer or inner approximations of g that pointwise converge, also epi-converge.

Our interest in epi-convergence in optimization theory comes mostly from the following results.

Theorem A.1. *Suppose $g = \text{epi-lim}_{\nu \to \infty}\ g^{\nu}$, where $\{g;\ g^{\nu},\ \nu = 1, \ldots\}$ is a collection of extended real-valued lower semicontinuous functions defined on R^{n}. Then*

$$\underset{\nu \to \infty}{\lim\sup}(\inf g^{\nu}) \leqslant \inf g\ .$$

Moreover, if for all $\varepsilon > 0$, there exists ν_{ε} and a compact set K such that for all $\nu \geqslant \nu_{\varepsilon}$

$$\underset{K}{\inf}\ g^{\nu} \leqslant \inf g^{\nu} + \varepsilon\ ,$$

then

$$\underset{\nu \to \infty}{\lim}(\inf g^{\nu}) = \inf g\ .$$

For $h : R^{n} \to [-\infty, \infty]$, define

$$\text{argmin}\ h := \{x \in R^{n}\,|\,h(x) \leqslant \inf h\}\ ,$$

and for $\varepsilon > 0$,

$$\varepsilon\text{-argmin } h := \{x \in R^n \mid h(x) \leq \varepsilon + (\inf h)\} \ .$$

Theorem A.2. *Suppose $g = $ epi-lim$_{\nu \to \infty}$ g^ν where $\{g; g^\nu, \nu = 1, \ldots\}$ is a collection of extended real-valued lower semicontinuous functions on R^n, and $\bar{x} = $ lim$_{k \to \infty}$ x^k where for all k, $x^k \in $ argmin g^{ν_k}, and the $\{\nu_k\}$ determine a subsequence. Then*

$$\bar{x} \in \text{argmin } g \quad and \quad \inf g = \lim_{k \to \infty} (\inf g^{\nu_k}) \ .$$

Moreover, if lim$_{\nu \to \infty}$(inf g^ν) $= $ inf g, *then* $x \in $ argmin g *implies the existence of sequences $\{\varepsilon_\nu\} \downarrow 0$ and $\{x^\nu\}$ such that for all ν, $x^\nu \in \varepsilon_\nu$-argmin g^ν.*

It can be shown that epi-convergence is the weakest type of convergence for lower semicontinuous functions that guarantees the convergence of infima and optimal solutions (in terms of the conditions made explicit in Theorems A.1 and A.2). One can also localize the theory: observe that if $g = $ epi-lim$_{\nu \to \infty}$ g^ν, then also

$$(g + \psi_G) = \text{epi-lim}_{\nu \to \infty}(g^\nu + \psi_G) \ ,$$

where G is an open set and ψ_G is the (indicator) function of G, taking the value 0 on G, and $+\infty$ outside G.

Although what precedes is very brief, it should however be clear that when approximating functions (globally or locally) in a variational context, epi-limits will play an important role, in particular in the definition of subderivatives and subgradients. The *contingent derivative* of an l.s.c. function $h : R^n \to (-\infty, \infty]$ at a point x (at which h finite) can be defined by

$$h'(x; \, \cdot \,) := \text{epi-li}_{t \downarrow 0} \frac{h(x + t \cdot) - h(x)}{t} \tag{A.4}$$

where epi-li is the epi-limit inferior as defined by (A.1). This function $h'(x; \, \cdot \,)$ is lower semicontinuous, positively homogeneous with $h'(x; 0) < \infty$. The (*upper*) *epi-derivative* of an l.s.c. function $h : R^n \to (-\infty, \infty]$ at x (at which h is finite) is

$$h^\uparrow(x; \, \cdot \,) := \text{epi-ls}_{x' \to x} h'(x'; \, \cdot \,) \tag{A.5}$$

where epi-ls is the epi-limit superior as defined by (A.2). It is lower semicontinuous and sublinear (convex, positively homogeneous and $h(x, 0) < \infty$). In view of the definition (A.2) of epi-ls, we always have that

$$h'(x; \, \cdot \,) \leq h^\uparrow(x; \, \cdot \,) \ . \tag{A.6}$$

If equality holds, the function h is *subdifferentiably regular*. Whenever h is convex on a neighborhood of x, or subsmooth around x, it is subdifferentiably regular at x.

The *subgradients* of h (a lower semicontinuous function defined on R^n with values in $(-\infty, \infty]$) at a point x at which h is finite are the elements of:

$$\partial h(x) := \{v \in R^n \mid vy \leqslant h^{\uparrow}(x; y) \text{ for all } y \in R^n\} . \tag{A.7}$$

From the properties of $h^{\uparrow}(x; \cdot)$ it follows that ∂h is a closed convex set. It is nonempty if and only if $h^{\uparrow}(x; 0) > -\infty$. When h is convex, then

$$\partial h(x) = \{v \mid h(x + y) - h(x) \geqslant vy, \text{ for all } y \in R^n\} . \tag{A.8}$$

This follows from the subdifferentiable regularity of convex functions and the fact that for convex function

$$h'(x; y) = \inf_{t>0}[t^{-1}(h(x + ty) - h(x))] .$$

If h is subsmooth on a neighborhood V of x (i.e., if for all $y \in V$, $h(y) = \max_{t \in T_x} \theta_t(y)$, where T_x is a compact topological space, each θ_t is smooth, and both $\theta_t(y)$ and $\nabla \theta_t(y)$ are jointly continuous in t and y), one has

$$\partial h(x) := \mathrm{co}\{\nabla \theta_t(x) \mid t \in T_x\} \tag{A.9}$$

where 'co' stands for convex hull. In particular in the smooth case

$$\partial h(x) = \nabla h(x) . \tag{A.10}$$

If h is locally Lipschitzian at x, and assuming that $\partial h(x)$ is nonempty, it can be shown that

$$\partial h(x) = \mathrm{co}\{\lim_{x^i \to x} \nabla h(x^i) \mid h \text{ is differentiable at } x^i\} . \tag{A.11}$$

Appendix B. Convergence or probability measures

The lemma generalizes conditions (iii) and (iv) of Billingsley's Portemanteau Theorem. It is used here to obtain the upper semicontinuity of the feasibility set of stochastic programs with probabilistic constraints, cf. Proposition 6.3.

Lemma B.1. *Suppose* $\{P; P_\nu, \nu = 1, \ldots\}$ *are probability measures on* $(R^N, \mathcal{B})$. *Then the following conditions are equivalent*
   (i) *the* P^ν *weak*-converge to* P;
   (ii) *for any sequence* $\{F^\nu, \nu = 1, \ldots\}$ *of closed sets, and any closed set* F *such that* $\limsup_{\nu \to \infty} F^\nu \subset F$,

$$\limsup_{\nu \to \infty} P_\nu(F^\nu) \leqslant P(F) ;$$

(iii) *for any sequence* $\{G^\nu, \nu = 1, \ldots\}$ *of open sets, and any open set G such that* $G \subset \mathcal{O} - \liminf_{\nu \to \infty} G^\nu$

$$\limsup_{\nu \to \infty} P_\nu(G^\nu) \geqslant P(G) .$$

(*For a sequence of sets* $\{S^\nu, \nu = 1, \ldots\}$, $\limsup_{\nu \to \infty} S^\nu \subset S$ *if epi-li* $\delta_{S^\nu} \geqslant \delta_S$, *where* δ_D *is the indicator function of the set* D, *and* $S \subset \mathcal{O} - \liminf_{\nu \to \infty} S^\nu$ *if* $(R^N \backslash S) \supset \limsup_{\nu \to \infty} (R^N \backslash S^\nu)$.)

Proof. Clearly it suffices to prove that (i) implies (ii) since (ii) and (iii) are essentially identical, and a special case of (ii):

$$\limsup_{\nu \to \infty} P_\nu(F) \leqslant P(F) \quad \text{for all closed sets } F , \tag{B.1}$$

already implies (i), cf. the Portemanteau Theorem.

Let us begin by considering the (special) case when $\{S^\nu\}$ is any sequence of measurable sets converging to $\emptyset = F$. Since the P_ν weak*-converge to F, from Prohorov's Theorem it follows that to any $\varepsilon > 0$, there corresponds a compact set $K_\varepsilon \subset R^N$, such that for all ν, $P_\nu(R^N \backslash K_\varepsilon) < \varepsilon$. Convergence of the $\{S^\nu\}$ to $\emptyset$, implies that for all ν sufficiently large $S^\nu \subset R^N \backslash K_\varepsilon$ and hence $P_\nu(S^\nu) < \varepsilon$. Since this holds for all $\varepsilon > 0$, it implies that $\lim P_\nu(S^\nu) = 0$.

Now let us consider an arbitrary sequence $\{F^\nu\}$. For $\varepsilon > 0$, let us use the notations

$$\varepsilon^0 Q := \{x \in R^N \,|\, \mathrm{dist}(x, Q) < \varepsilon\}$$

if the set Q is nonempty, and $\varepsilon Q := \mathrm{cl}\, \varepsilon^0 Q$ for its closure. If $Q = \emptyset$, then $\varepsilon^0 Q := \{x \in R^N \,|\, \mathrm{dist}(x, 0) > \varepsilon^{-1}\}$ and similarly $\varepsilon Q = \mathrm{cl}\, \varepsilon^0 Q$. Because the F^ν converge to F, we have that for all $\varepsilon > 0$, $\lim(F^\nu \backslash \varepsilon^0 F) = \emptyset$, and this tells us that

$$\limsup_{\nu \to \infty} P_\nu(F^\nu) \leqslant \limsup_{\nu \to \infty} [P_\nu(F^\nu \backslash \varepsilon^0 F) + P_\nu(\varepsilon F)]$$

$$\leqslant \limsup_{\nu \to \infty} P_\nu(F^\nu \backslash \varepsilon^0 F) + \limsup_{\nu \to \infty} P_\nu(\varepsilon F)$$

$$\leqslant 0 + P(\varepsilon F)$$

where the last inequality follows from the above ($\{S^\nu = F^\nu \backslash \varepsilon^0 F, \nu = 1, \ldots\}$ is a sequence that converges to $\emptyset$) and the Portemanteau Theorem. From this the asserted inequality follows, since the above holds for all $\varepsilon > 0$, and the uppersemicontinuity ('right continuity') of probability measure implies that

$$P(F) = \lim_{\varepsilon \downarrow 0} P(\varepsilon F) . \qquad \square$$

G.L. Nemhauser et al., Eds., *Handbooks in OR & MS, Vol. 1*
© Elsevier Science Publishers B.V. (North-Holland) 1989

Chapter IX

Global Optimization

A.H.G. Rinnooy Kan

Econometric Institute, Erasmus University, Rotterdam, The Netherlands

G.T. Timmer

Econometric Institute, Erasmus University, Rotterdam, and ORTEC Consultants, Rotterdam, The Netherlands

1. Introduction

Many problems can be posed as *mathematical programming* problems, i.e. problems in which an *objective function*, that depends on a number of *decision variables*, has to be optimized subject to a set of *constraints*. This has been appreciated since the second World War and, together with the introduction of high speed computers, it has led to major research activities in many countries. The aim of these activities has been to develop efficient methods to solve subclasses of the above mentioned problem. Many criteria according to which subclasses can be defined have been proposed, e.g. are there any stochastic elements in the problem formulation or not, are the decision variables allowed to take on any real value or are they constrained to be, say, integers, do the decision variables appear in a linear or in a nonlinear way in the problem formulation, etc., etc. Here, we will restrict our discussion to *nonlinear programming* problems in which both the objective function and the constraints, formulated in terms of functions of the decision variables that have to be equal to or smaller than some constant, depend on the decision variables in a continuous but possibly nonlinear way.

Let $f : \mathbb{R}^n \to \mathbb{R}$ be a continuous real valued objective function and let $G \subset \mathbb{R}^n$ be the *feasible region*, i.e. the region in which none of the constraints is violated. Our starting point is the observation that most of the many nonlinear programming methods that have been developed aim for a *local optimum* (say local minimum), i.e. a point $x^* \in G$ such that there exists a neighbourhood B of x^* with

$$f(x^*) \leq f(x) \quad \forall x \in B \cap G . \tag{1.1}$$

In general, however, several local optima may exist and the corresponding function values may differ substantially. The problem of designing algorithms that distinguish between these local optima and locate the best possible one is known as the *global optimization* problem, and forms the subject of this chapter.

In the absence of reliable codes for the global optimization problem most problems are not modelled as such. Many problems, however, are of a global nature. This is especially true for many *technical design* problems (Dixon & Szegö 1978b; Archetti & Frontini 1978). *Economic applications*, where multimodal cost functions have to be minimized, have also been reported (Archetti & Frontini 1978). Another global optimization problem often encountered in econometrics is that of locating the global maximum of a likelihood function. Thus, there is no need to dwell on the practical usefulness of quick and reliable methods to solve the global optimization problem.

In the case where there are no constraints, the global optimization problem is to find the *global optimum* (say global minimum) x_* of a real valued objective function $f: \mathbb{R}^n \to \mathbb{R}$, i.e. to find a point $x_* \in \mathbb{R}^n$ such that

$$f(x_*) \leq f(x) \quad \forall x \in \mathbb{R}^n . \tag{1.2}$$

Unless stated otherwise, we will assume f to be twice continuously differentiable. For obvious computational reasons, one usually assumes that a set $S \subset \mathbb{R}^n$, which is convex, compact and contains the global minimum as an interior point, is specified in advance. None the less, the problem to find

$$y_* = \min_{x \in S} f(x) \tag{1.3}$$

remains essentially one of *unconstrained* optimization.

Any method for global optimization has to account for the fact that a numerical procedure can never produce more than approximate answers. Thus, the global optimization problem might be considered solved if, for some $\varepsilon > 0$, an element of one of the following sets has been identified (Dixon 1978):

$$A_x(\varepsilon) = \{x \in S \,|\, \|x - x_*\| \leq \varepsilon\} , \tag{1.4}$$

$$A_f(\varepsilon) = \{x \in S \,|\, |f(x) - f(x_*)| \leq \varepsilon\} . \tag{1.5}$$

A disadvantage of the first mentioned possibility (1.4) is that small perturbations in the problem data may have major effects on the location of x_* (Archetti & Betro 1978a). (The problem is not *well posed*.) A third possibility (Betro 1981) is obtained by defining

$$\phi(y) = \frac{m(\{z \in S \,|\, f(z) \leq y\})}{m(S)} , \tag{1.6}$$

where $M(.)$ is the *Lebesgue measure* and taking

$$A_\phi(\varepsilon) = \{x \in S \mid \phi(f(x)) \le \varepsilon\} \, . \tag{1.7}$$

We note, however, that this set may contain points whose function values differ considerably from y_*.

So far only few solution methods for the global optimization problem have been developed, certainly in comparison with the multitude of methods that aim for a local optimum. The relative difficulty of global optimization as compared to local optimization is easy to understand. If we assume that f is twice continuously differentiable, then all that is required to test if a point is a local minimum is knowledge of the first and second order derivatives at this point. If the test does not yield a positive result, the continuous differentiability of the function ensures that a neighbouring point can be found with a lower function value. Thus, a sequence of points converging to a local optimum can be constructed.

Such local tests are obviously not sufficient to verify global optimality. Indeed, in some sense the global optimization problem as stated in (1.3) is inherently unsolvable in a finite number of steps. For any continuously differentiable function f, any point $\bar{x}$ and any neighbourhood B of $\bar{x}$, there exists a function f' such that $f + f'$ is continuously differentiable, $f + f'$ equals f for all points outside B and the global minimum of $f + f'$ is $\bar{x}$. (($f + f'$) is an *indentation* of f.) Thus, for any point $\bar{x}$, one cannot guarantee that it is not the global minimum without evaluating the function in at least one point in every neighbourhood B of $\bar{x}$. As B can be chosen arbitrarily small, it follows that any method designed to solve the global optimization problem would require an unbounded number of steps (Dixon 1978).

Of course, this argument does not directly apply to the case where one is satisfied with an approximation of the global minimum. In particular, if an element of $A_x(\varepsilon)$ is sought, then enumerative strategies that only require a finite number of function evaluations can be easily shown to exist. These strategies, however, are of limited practical use, and it appears that the above observation does prohibit the construction of practical methods for the global optimization problem. Hence, either a further restriction of the class of objective functions or a further relaxation of what is required of an algorithm will be inevitable in what follows.

Subject to this first conclusion, the methods developed to solve the global optimization problem can be divided into two classes, depending on whether or not they incorporate any stochastic elements (Dixon & Szegö 1975, 1978a; Fedorov 1985).

Deterministic methods do not involve any stochastic concepts. To provide a rigid guarantee of success, such methods unavoidably involve additional assumptions on f.

Most *stochastic methods* involve the evaluation of f in a random sample of points from S and subsequent manipulations of the sample. As a result, we do sacrifice the possibility of an *absolute guarantee* of success. However, under very mild conditions on the sampling distribution and on f, the probability that an element of $A_x(\varepsilon)$, $A_f(\varepsilon)$ or $A_\phi(\varepsilon)$ is sampled can be shown to approach 1 as the sample size increases (Solis & Wets 1981).

Irrespective of whether a global optimization method is deterministic or stochastic, it always aims for an appropriate *convergence guarantee*. In some cases, all that can be asserted is that the method performs well in an empirical sense. This is far from satisfactory. Ideally, one would like to be assured that the method will find an element of $A_x(\varepsilon)$, $A_f(\varepsilon)$ or $A_\phi(\varepsilon)$ in a *finite* number of steps, and under appropriate conditions some deterministic methods provide such a guarantee. Frequently, that best that one can do is to establish an *asymptotic* guarantee, which ensures convergence to the global minimum as the computational effort goes to infinity. As we have seen, stochastic methods usually provide a stochastic version of such a guarantee, i.e. *convergence in probability* or *with probability 1* (*almost surely*, *almost everywhere*).

The existence of any type of asymptotic guarantee immediately raises the issue of an appropriate *stopping rule* for the algorithm. This is already an important question in regular nonlinear programming (where it is usually dealt with in an ad hoc fashion), but acquires additional significance in global optimization where the *trade-off* between *reliability* and *effort* is at heart of every computational experiment. The design of an appropriate stopping rule which weighs costs and benefits of continued computation against each other, forms a problem of great inherent difficulty, and we shall be able to report only partial success in solving it satisfactorily.

Rather than reviewing global optimization methods according to the distinction between deterministic and stochastic methods, we prefer to use a different classification, based on what might be called the underlying *philosophy* of the method. From the literature, five such philosophies can be identified:

(a) *Partition and search.* Here, S is partitioned into successively smaller subregions among which the global minimum is sought, much in the spirit of branch-and-bound methods for combinatorial optimization. A few of these deterministic methods are reviewed in Section 2.

(b) *Approximation and search.* In this approach, f is replaced by an increasingly better approximation that is easier from a computational point of view. Some methods of this type are reviewed in Section 3.

(c) *Global decrease.* These methods aim for a permanent improvement in f-values, culminating in arrival at the global minimum. A few of them will be reviewed in Section 4.

(d) *Improvement of local minima.* Exploiting the availability of an efficient local search routine, these methods seek to generate a sequence of local minima of decreasing value. Clearly, the global minimum is the last one encountered in this sequence. Some examples are given in Section 5.

(e) *Enumeration of local minima.* Complete enumeration of local minima (or at least of a promising subset of them) is clearly a way to solve the global optimization problem. Some methods developed for that purpose are discussed in Section 6.

It would have been appropriate to conclude the chapter by a discussion of the empirial performance of the methods discussed in the various sections. Unfortunately, the computational evidence is far from complete. To the extent that experiments have been carried out at all, it is often not clear under what conditions this has been done, in particular with respect to the stopping rule involved. Certainly, none of these experiments capture the full trade-off between reliability and effort that was alluded to above and will be a crucial factor in choosing an appropriate global optimization technique. What little can be said on this issue, will be said in Section 7.

Apart from some special classes (Pardalos & Rosen 1985), no attention will be given to the constrained global optimization problem. Only very little work has been done in this field. It is still very unclear what line of approach could be successful. Some initial attempts using penalty functions are described in (Timmer 1984).

2. Partition and search

A natural approach to solve the global optimization problem is through an appropriate generalization of *branch and bound methods*, a solution technique that is well known from the area of combinatorial optimization.

At any stage of such a procedure, we have a *partition* of S in subsets S_α ($\alpha \in A$), a *lower bound* $\text{LB}(S_\alpha)$ on $\min_{x \in S_\alpha} \{f(x)\}$ for all $\alpha \in A$, and an *upper bound* $UB = f(\tilde{x})$ ($\tilde{x} \in S$) representing the smallest feasible solution value found so far.

Clearly, subsets S_α for which $\text{LB}(S_\alpha) \geq UB$ can never contain the global minimum x_* and can be eliminated. If after possible further improvement of UB any subset is left for which $UB - \text{LB}(S_\alpha) > 0$, then the partition is further refined – most naturally by dividing the subset $S_{\alpha'}$ with $\text{LB}(S_\alpha) = \min_{\alpha \in A} \{\text{LB}(S_\alpha)\}$ into smaller subsets – and the next stage is initiated.

There are many variations on this theme, each of which yields convergence to the global minimum under many different conditions (Horst 1986; Horst & Tuy 1987; Pinter 1983, 1986a, 1988; Strongin 1978; Tuy 1987). Typically, such conditions ensure that the lower bounding procedure is *asymptotically accurate*, in that $\text{LB}(S_\alpha)$ approaches the global minimum of f over S_α when the volume of S_α becomes sufficiently small. Of course, for arbitrary functions f, finding a lower bound on the global minimum value y_* is of the same inherent difficulty as finding y_* itself. Thus, all procedures in this category involve additional assumptions of f.

We propose to discuss two typical examples, each of which is attractive in that the inevitable additional assumptions on f are reasonable in themselves, and are in addition cleverly exploited to speed up the procedure.

In the first example (McCormick 1983), S is assumed to be a *hyperrectangle* $\{x \in \mathbb{R}^n \mid a \leq x \leq b\}$ and f is supposed to be a *factorable function*, i.e., f is the last in a sequence of functions $f^{(1)}, f^{(2)}, \ldots$, where this *factorization sequence* is built up as follows:

$$f^{(j)}(x_1, \ldots, x_n) = x_j \quad (j = 1, \ldots, n) \tag{2.1}$$

and for all $k > n$, one of the following holds:

$$f^{(k)}(x) = f^{(g)}(x) + f^{(h)}(x) \quad \text{for some } g, h < k , \tag{2.2}$$

$$f^{(k)}(x) = f^{(g)}(x) \cdot f^{(h)}(x) \quad \text{for some } g, h < k, \quad \text{or} \tag{2.3}$$

$$f^{(k)}(x) = F(f^{(g)}(x)) \quad \text{for some } g < k , \tag{2.4}$$

where F belongs to a given class C of simple functions $\mathbb{R} \rightarrow \mathbb{R}$ (e.g., $F(t) = t^l$, $F(t) = e^t$, $F(t) = \sin t, \ldots$).

The reader can easily verify that this is a natural way to view complicated objective functions that are given in explicit algebraic form. Indeed, the order in which the $f^{(j)}$ appear usually corresponds to the order in which $f(x_1, \ldots, x_n)$ would be computed for given values of the arguments x_j ($j = 1, \ldots, n$).

In the context of a branch-and-bound procedure, the idea is now to have the S_α correspond to appropriate hyperrectangles $\{x \in \mathbb{R}^n \mid a(\alpha) \leqslant x \leqslant b(a)\}$, and to use the factorization sequence $(f^{(k)} \mid k = 1, 2, \ldots)$ to compute lower bounds for $k = 1, 2, \ldots$ by computing *convex lower bounding functions* $l_\alpha^{(k)}$ and *concave upper bounding functions* $u_\alpha^{(k)}$ with the property that

$$l_\alpha^{(k)}(x) \leqslant f^{(k)}(x) \leqslant u_\alpha^{(k)}(x) \quad \forall x \in S_\alpha \ (\alpha \in A) . \tag{2.5}$$

In doing so, we ultimately arrive at a convex lower bounding function for f over S_α, whose minimum value over S_α provides an appropriate lower bound $LB(S_\alpha)$. If the minimum value is achieved at $x = x(\alpha)$, then $f(x(\alpha))$ provides an upper bound on y_* and a possible improvement on UB.

Any convex function $l_\alpha^{(k)}$ and concave function $u_\alpha^{(k)}$, for which (2.5) holds and for which asymptotic accuracy can be demonstrated, yields a correct branch-and-bound procedure. There is clear trade-off between the accuracy of the bounds and the effort required for their computation. One extreme possibility is to use the tools of *interval analysis* (Ratschek 1985; Walster et al. 1985) which quickly yields constants $L_\alpha^{(k)}$ and $U_\alpha^{(k)}$ so that (2.5) holds with $l_\alpha^{(k)}(x) = L_\alpha^{(k)}$, $u_\alpha^{(k)}(x) = U_\alpha^{(k)}$. At the other end of the spectrum, one would strive to find the best possible bounding functions, i.e., to take $l_\alpha^{(k)}$ equal to the *convex lower envelope* of $f^{(k)}$ on S_α and $u_\alpha^{(k)}$ equal to the *concave upper envelope*. Generally, given $l_\alpha^{(j)}$ and $u_\alpha^{(j)}$ for all $j < k$ (note that these functions can be taken equal to $f^{(j)}$ for $j = 1, \ldots, n$) relatively tight convex respectively concave bounds $l_\alpha^{(k)}$ and $u_\alpha^{(k)}$ can be computed by exploiting relation (2.2), (2.3) or (2.4) in the following way (McCormick 1983). If (2.2) holds, then clearly we may take

$$l_\alpha^{(k)}(x) = l_\alpha^{(g)}(x) + l_\alpha^{(h)}(x) , \tag{2.6}$$

$$u_\alpha^{(k)}(x) = u_\alpha^{(g)}(x) + u_\alpha^{(h)}(x) . \tag{2.7}$$

If (2.3) holds, then we have to presuppose (quite reasonably) that lower bounds $L_\alpha^{(g)}$, $L_\alpha^{(h)}$ and upper bounds $U_\alpha^{(g)}$, $U_\alpha^{(h)}$ over S_α are provided for $f^{(g)}(x)$ and $f^{(h)}(x)$ respectively. Assuming the lower bounds to be non-positive and the upper bounds to be nonnegative (analogous results hold for the other cases), we may take

$$\begin{aligned} l_\alpha^{(k)}(x) = \max\{ &U_\alpha^{(h)} l_\alpha^{(g)}(x) + U_\alpha^{(g)} l_\alpha^{(h)}(x) - U_\alpha^{(g)} U_\alpha^{(h)} , \\ &L_\alpha^{(h)} l_\alpha^{(g)}(x) + L_\alpha^{(g)} l_\alpha^{(h)}(x) - L_\alpha^{(g)} L_\alpha^{(h)} \} , \end{aligned} \tag{2.8}$$

$$\begin{aligned} u_\alpha^{(k)}(x) = \min\{ &L_\alpha^{(g)} u_\alpha^{(h)}(x) + U_\alpha^{(h)} u_\alpha^{(g)}(x) - L_\alpha^{(g)} U_\alpha^{(h)} , \\ &L_\alpha^{(h)} u_\alpha^{(g)}(x) + U_\alpha^{(g)} u_\alpha^{(h)}(x) - L_\alpha^{(h)} U_\alpha^{(g)} \} . \end{aligned} \tag{2.9}$$

Finally, if (2.4) holds, we presuppose (again quite reasonably) that we are given convex lower and concave upper bounding functions (L and U respectively) for F over the interval $[L_\alpha^{(g)}, U_\alpha^{(g)}]$, and that F attains its minimum and maximum on this interval in $y_{\min}$ and $y_{\max}$ respectively. We then may take

$$l_\alpha^{(k)}(x) = L(\mathrm{mid}\{l_\alpha^{(g)}(x), u_\alpha^{(g)}(x), y_{\min}\}) , \tag{2.10}$$

$$u_\alpha^{(k)}(x) = U(\mathrm{mid}\{l_\alpha^{(g)}(x), u_\alpha^{(g)}(x), y_{\max}\}) , \tag{2.11}$$

where the mid operator selects the middle value.

Clearly, there is a lot of room in this approach for clever ad hoc ideas, whose ultimate value can only be established in computational experiments (Mentzer 1985).

The second example to be discussed now is a special case of *concave minimization subject to convex constraints*: $f(x)$ is concave, and $S' = \{x \in \mathbb{R}^n \mid Ax = b, x \geq 0\}$. It is well known that the global minimum of f occurs at one of the extreme points of S'.

There is an extensive literature on this type of problem (see (Pardalos & Rosen 1986)). For a good example of a branch-and-bound approach that truly explores special structure, we assume that $f(x)$ is quadratic: $f(x) = p^\mathrm{T}x - \frac{1}{2}x^\mathrm{T}Qx$ (Q positive semi-definite) (Rosen 1983). This problem is more general than it appears to be at first glance: both 0–1 programming and the general linear complementarity problem are special cases.

Prior to partitioning S', we first compute lower and upper bounds on y_*. For an upper bound, f is maximized subject to $x \in S'$. This easy calculation yields a point $\bar{x}$ and n eigenvectors of the Hessian at $\bar{x}$, say, $u_1, \ldots, u_n$. In an effort to move as far away as possible from $\bar{x}$, we then solve $2n$ linear programs of the form: $\max\{\pm u_i^\mathrm{T}x \mid x \in S'\}$ and find at most $2n$ different extreme points v_i of S'.

The one for which $f(x)$ is minimal produces the required *upper bound* UB on y_*.

Now, each v_i defines a halfspace $\{x \in \mathbb{R}^n \mid w_i^{\mathrm{T}}(x - \bar{x}) \le w_i^{\mathrm{T}}(v_i - \bar{x})\}$ ($w_i \in \{u_i, -u_i\}$) of which the intersection is a hyperrectangle containing S'. Obviously f achieves its minimum over this hyperrectangle at one of its 2^n vertices; it is easy to find out which one, and this yields a *lower bound* on y_*.

In addition, we also construct a hyperrectangle inscribing the ellipsoid $\{x \in \mathbb{R}^n \mid f(x) = \mathrm{UB}\}$, again of the form $\cap_i \{x \in \mathbb{R}^n \mid w_i^{\mathrm{T}}(x - \bar{x}) \le d_i\}$ with appropriate constants d_i that can easily be computed. Clearly, x_* cannot be contained in the interior of this hyperrectangle, and the intersection of its exterior with S' defines an appropriate family of subsets in which to look for x_*. Each of these at most $2n$ polytopes can be embedded in a surplex rooted at the corresponding v_i, and a suitable procedure (in particular, the original one in a recursive fashion) can be called upon to solve these subproblems.

Several variations on this theme have been proposed (Zilverberg 1983; Kalantari 1984), each of which fully exploits the extreme point property of the problem. Generalizations of the problem, up to the case where f is the difference of two convex functions and S' is arbitrary convex, in which some form of Benders decomposition is clearly called for, have also been attacked. There is no doubt that if a problem exhibits special structure of the above kind, then specialized algorithms of this nature are the ones to turn to. Obviously, this will not always be the case.

3. Approximation and search

If the global optimum of f is difficult to find, it may be attractive to deal with an approximation $\tilde{f}$ of f instead. Whatever the form of this approximation, it should of course yield a computational advantage over the original objective function. In each iteration, one will then typically start by computing the global minimum $\tilde{x}$ of the current approximation $\tilde{f}$. If the approximation is found to be good enough, the algorithm stops. If not, $\tilde{f}$ is updated, usually so as to satisfy the equality $\tilde{f}(\tilde{x}) = f(\tilde{x})$.

Several well known global optimization techniques, both deterministic and stochastic ones, can be viewed as belonging in this category.

It is appropriate at this point to mention that several of the techniques described in this section combine characteristics of both the approximation and search and the partition and search philosophy. Based on the current approximation $\tilde{f}$ of f these methods focus on subsets of S in which the global minimum is known to be located. However, since the partition of S is implicit and based on the approximation $\tilde{f}$ of f, these methods are described in the current section.

In view of our discussion in the previous section, we start with a deterministic approach which is based on the observation that $\tilde{f}$ can be taken equal to any asymptotically accurate *lower bounding function* of f, chosen in such a way that the computation of its global minimum can be carried out efficiently.

A popular example of such a method (Shubert 1972) is based on the assumption that a *Lipschitz constant L* is given so that

$$|f(x_1) - f(x_2)| \leq L\|x_1 - x_2\| \tag{3.1}$$

for all $x_1, x_2 \in S$. In the case that $n = 1$, the method essentially consists of iterative updates of a piecewise linear function with directional derivatives equal to L or $-L$, which forms an adaptive Lipschitzian minorant function of f.

Initially, f is evaluated at some arbitrary point x_1. A piecewise linear function ψ_1 is defined by

$$\psi_1(x) = f(x_1) - L\|x - x_1\| . \tag{3.2}$$

Now an iterative procedure starts, where in iteration k $(k \geq 2)$ a global minimum of ψ_{k-1} on S is chosen as the point $\tilde{x}_k$ where f is next evaluated. A new piecewise linear function ψ_k is constructed by a modification of ψ_{k-1}:

$$\psi_k(x) = \max\{f(x) - L\|x - \tilde{x}_k\|, \psi_{k-1}(x)\}, \quad k = 2, 3, \ldots . \tag{3.3}$$

Hence

$$\psi_{k-1}(x) \leq \psi_k(x) \leq f(x) \quad \forall x \in S , \tag{3.4}$$

$$\psi_k(\tilde{x}_i) = f(\tilde{x}_i) \quad (i = 1, \ldots k) . \tag{3.5}$$

In each iteration, the piecewise linear approximation for f will improve. The method is stopped when the difference between the global minimum of ψ_k, which is a lower bound on the global minimum of f, and the best function value found is smaller than ε, indicating that a member of $A_f(\varepsilon)$ has been found. To conclude the description, note that ψ_k is completely determined by the location and the value of its minima. If ψ_k is described in terms of these parameters it is no problem to find one of its global minima.

The above method can be generalized to n dimensions in at least two different ways. In the first approach (Mladineo 1986) ψ_k is defined as in (3.3). The graph of ψ_k in $\mathbb{R}^{n+1}$ is then defined by a set of intersecting *cones* in $\mathbb{R}^{n+1}$, whose axes of symmetry are all parallel to the $(n + 1)$-th unit vector. To find the global minimum of ψ_k now amounts to intersecting the cone corresponding to $\tilde{x}_k$ with the previous ones, which turns out to be equivalent to solving a set of linear equations and a single quadratic one.

In the second generalization (Wood 1985), cones are replaced by inner approximating *simplices*. In each iteration, we have a collection of such simplices in $\mathbb{R}^{n+1}$ that bound parts of the graph of f from below, always including the part containing the global minimum point (x_*, y_*). The function evaluation at $\tilde{x}$ allows one to intersect the current collection with the complement of a simplex whose zenith is at $(\tilde{x}, f(\tilde{x}))$ as well as with the halfspace defined by $y \leq f(\tilde{x})$: what remains outside the simplex and below the hyperplane defines the new set of simplices.

Finally, we mention (Pinter 1986b) which describes a general framework for generalizing Lipschitz-type methods to higher dimensions.

It is appropriate in the context of approaches such as the above to refer briefly to the literature on *minimax optimality of algorithms*. The one-dimensional method and its n-dimensional cone generalization can be shown to minimize the *worst case error* $f(\tilde{x}) - y_*$, after a fixed number of steps over all *sequential sampling rules* that search for the global minimum of functions satisfying (3.1) for given L (Shubert 1972; Mladineo 1986). There are other results of this nature, obtained with respect to different criteria of optimality and different classes of algorithms (see (Basso 1985)). For a fundamental comparison between deterministic and stochastic methods along these lines we refer to (Sukharev 1971; Anderssen & Bloomfield 1975; Archetti & Betro 1978b; Sobol 1982).

It is also appropriate at this point to discuss briefly a related deterministic approach to the global minimization of functions with given Lipschitz constant, which was originally proposed in (Evtushenko 1971). The theoretical background of this method is very simple. Suppose that the function has been evaluated at k points $x_1, \ldots, x_k$ and that $M_k = \min\{f(x_1), \ldots, f(x_k)\}$ is the smallest function value found so far. For $i = 1, 2, \ldots, k$, let V_i be the sphere $\{x \in \mathbb{R}^n \mid \|x - x_i\| \le r_i\}$, where

$$r_i = (f(x_i) - M_k + \varepsilon)/L .\tag{3.6}$$

Then, for any $x \in V_i$,

$$f(x) \ge f(x_i) - Lr_i = M_k - \varepsilon .\tag{3.7}$$

Hence, if the spheres V_i $(i = 1, \ldots, k)$ cover the whole set S, then the point $\tilde{x}_i$ for which $f(\tilde{x}_i) = M_k$ is an element of $A_f(\varepsilon)$. Thus, this result converts the global minimization problem to the problem of covering S with spheres. In the simpled case of one-dimensional global optimization where S is an interval $\{x \in \mathbb{R} \mid a \le x \le b\}$, this covering problem is solved by choosing x_1 to be equal to $a + \varepsilon/L$ and

$$x_k = x_{k-1} + \frac{2\varepsilon + f(x_k) - M_k}{L} \quad (k = 2, 3, \ldots) .\tag{3.8}$$

The method is stopped if $x_k \ge b$.

A generalization of this algorithm for n-dimensional problems $(n > 1)$ consists of systematically covering S with hypercubes whose edgelength is $2r_i/\sqrt{n}$, where r_i is given by (3.6), i.e. cubes inscribed in the spheres V_i.

All the deterministic techniques based on (3.1) have a major drawback: the number of function evaluations required is very large. To analyse this number, let S be a hypersphere with radius r, so that

$$m(S) = \frac{r^n \pi^{n/2}}{\Gamma(1 + \frac{1}{2}n)}, \tag{3.9}$$

where Γ denotes the gamma function. Furthermore, let c be the maximum of f over S and suppose that f has been evaluated in k points $x_1, \ldots, x_k$. The function value in a point x can only be known to be a greater than the global minimum value y_* if the function has been evaluated in a point x_i within distance $(f(x_i) - y_*)/L$ of x. Hence, the hyperspheres with radii $(f(x_i) - y_*)/L$ centered at the points x_i, $i = 1, \ldots, k$, must cover S to be sure that the global minimum has been found. The joint volume of these k hyperspheres is smaller than

$$\frac{k\left(\frac{c - y_*}{L}\right)^n \pi^{n/2}}{\Gamma(1 + \frac{1}{2}n)}. \tag{3.10}$$

Thus, for the k hyperspheres to cover S we require

$$k > \left(\frac{r}{c - y_*}\right)^n L^n. \tag{3.11}$$

Unless the derivative of f in the direction of the global minimum equals $-L$ everywhere, L is greater than $r/(c - y^*)$, and the computational effort required increases exponentially with n. Thus, the price paid for a finite deterministic guarantee of convergence to $A_f(\varepsilon)$ appears to be very high.

We now turn to stochastic methods that can be viewed as operating on a suitable approximation of f. The underlying assumption here is that f is produced by a certain *random mechanism*. Information on the particular realization of the mechanism is obtained by evaluating f at a suitably chosen set of points. In each iteration, $\tilde{f}$ can then be taken equal to the *expected outcome* of the random mechanism, *conditioned* on the function evaluations that have occurred so far.

An appropriate random mechanism is provided by the notion of a *stochastic process*, i.e., a finite and real valued function $f(x, \omega)$, which for fixed x is a random variable defined on an appropriate probability space and for fixed ω a deterministic real valued function on S. Thus, as desired, there corresponds an objective function f to every realization of the random variable ω (Kushner 1964).

With each stochastic process, we associate a *family of finite dimensional distributions*

$$\Pr\{f(x_1) \leq y_1, \ldots, f(x_k) \leq y_k\} \quad (x_1, \ldots, x_k \in S; k = 1, 2, \ldots). \tag{3.12}$$

Two processes sharing the same family (3.12) are called *equivalent*. The process is called *Gaussian* if each distribution (3.12) is normal. It can be shown

(Cramer & Leadbetter 1967) that the specification of such a process amounts to the specification of an appropriate *covariance function* $R: S \times S \to \mathbb{R}$, defined by

$$R(x_1, x_2) = \text{cov}(f(x_1), f(x_2)), \qquad (3.13)$$

which has to be symmetric and nonnegative definite.

A particularly attractive choice within the class of Gaussian distributions is obtained if we take $R(x_1, x_2) = \sigma^2 \min\{x_1, x_2\}$, where σ^2 is a given constant. This is the celebrated *Wiener process*, which combines the advantage of unusual analytical tractability with the disadvantage of having nowhere differentiable (albeit continuous) realizations with probability 1. Though less than an ideal choice in view of the latter property, this model does yield an attractive global optimization technique for the case that $n = 1$. This technique (Woerlee 1984), which improves on some earlier work in (Archetti & Betro 1979a, 1979b) is based on a result from the theory of Wiener processes (Shepp 1979) which allows us to compute the expectation of the minimum value y_{min} of the Wiener process in an interval $[x, \bar{x}]$, conditioned on given function values $f(x)$ and $f(\bar{x})$:

$$E(y_{min} \mid x, f(x), \bar{x}, f(\bar{x}))$$
$$= \min\{f(x), f(\bar{x})\}$$
$$+ C(x, f(x), \bar{x}, f(\bar{x})) \int_{-\infty}^{0} N(\min\{f(x), f(\bar{x})\}$$
$$- \max\{f(x), f(\bar{x})\}, \sigma^{-2}(x - x)) \, dt, \qquad (3.14)$$

where

$$C(x, f(x), \bar{x}, f(\bar{x})) = - \left(\frac{\pi(\bar{x} - x)\sigma}{2} \right)^{1/2} \exp\left(\frac{(f(\bar{x}) - f(x))^2}{2\sigma^2(\bar{x} - x)} \right) \qquad (3.15)$$

and $N(\mu, \sigma^2)$ is the normal density function with mean μ and variance σ^2.

Thus, given a set of points $x_1 < x_2 < \cdots < x_k$ at which f has been evaluated so far, we can compute the posterior expectation (3.14) of the minimum value y_i^* for every interval (x_i, x_{i+1}) $(i = 1, \ldots, k - 1)$, and select the interval (x_j, x_{j+1}) for which the value y_j^* is minimal. As a next point at which to evaluate f, we can choose the expected location of the minimum given by

$$\int_{x_j}^{x_{j+1}} t p(t \mid y_j^*, x_j, f(x_j), x_{j+1}, f(x_{j+1})) \, dt \qquad (3.16)$$

with

$$p(t \mid y_j^*, x_j, f(x_j), x_{j+1}, f(x_{j+1}))$$

$$= \overline{C}(t, y_j^*, x_j, f(x_j), x_{j+1}, f(x_{j+1}))$$

$$\times \exp\left(- \frac{(y_j^* - f(x_j))^2}{2t} - \frac{(y_j^* - f(x_{j+1}))^2}{2(\sigma^2(x_{j+1} + x_j) - t)} \right.$$

$$\left. + \frac{(y_j^* - f(x_j) - f(x_{j+1}))^2}{2\sigma^2(x_j + x_{j+1})} \right), \tag{3.17}$$

where

$$\overline{C}(t, y_j^*, x_j, f(x_j), x_{j+1}, f(x_{j+1}))$$

$$= \frac{(y_j^* - f(x_j))(y_j^* - f(x_{j+1}))\sigma^3(x_{j+1} - x_j)^{3/2}}{\sqrt{2\pi}(y_j^* - f(x_j) - f(x_{j+1}))t^{3/2}(\sigma^2(x_{j+1} - x_j) - t)^{3/2}}. \tag{3.18}$$

The method can be initiated by using a set of equidistant points $\bar{x}_1, \ldots, \bar{x}_m$ in S to estimate σ by the maximum likelihood estimator

$$\hat{\sigma}^2 = \frac{1}{m} \sum_{i=2}^{m} \frac{(f(\bar{x}_i) - f(\bar{x}_{i-1}))^2}{(\bar{x}_i - \bar{x}_{i-1})}. \tag{3.19}$$

To develop an appropriate stopping rule, we could, for example, drop an interval $[x_i, x_{i+1}]$ if the probability of finding a function value better than the currently lowest one $\tilde{y}$,

$$\Pr\{ \min_{x \in [x_i, x_{i+1}]} \{f(x)\} < \tilde{y} \mid f(x_i), f(x_{i+1})\}$$

$$= \exp\left(-2 \frac{(\tilde{y} - f(x_i))(\tilde{y} - f(x_{i+1}))}{\sigma^2(x_{i+1} - x_i)} \right), \tag{3.20}$$

is sufficiently small, and terminate the algorithm if all intervals except the one containing $\tilde{y}$ are eliminated.

The above description demonstrates that the simple 1-dimensional Wiener approach already leads to fairly cumbersome computations. Moreover, its generalization to the case $n > 1$ is not obvious – many attractive properties of the one-dimensional process do not generalize to higher dimensions. And as remarked already, the almost everywhere nondifferentiability of its realizations continues to be unfortunate.

Let us describe briefly a possible way to overcome these imperfections. It is based on a different Gaussian process, for which

$$R(x_i, x_2) = \frac{\sigma^2}{1 + \|x_1 - x_2\|^2}.$$ (3.21)

Such a process is known to be equivalent with one whose realizations are continuously differentiable with probability 1. Its conditional expectation $Ef(x)$ subject to evaluations $f(x_1), \ldots, f(x_k)$ is given by

$$(f(x_1), \ldots, f(x_k))^{\mathrm{T}} V_k^{-1}(R(x, x_1), \ldots, R(x, x_k))$$ (3.22)

where $V = (v_{ij}) = (R(x_i, x_j))$. For the particular case given by (3.21), (3.22) is equal to $\sum_{i=1}^k (\alpha_i/(1 + \|x - x_i\|^2))$ for appropriate constants α_i, so that the stationary points of $Ef(x)$ can be found by finding all roots of a set of polynomial equations. This can be done, for example, by the method from (Garcia & Zangwill 1979) discussed in Section 6, and hence we may take the approximation $\tilde f$ equal to $Ef(x)$ to arrive at another example of an algorithm in the current category.

Both stochastic approaches described above can be viewed as special cases of a more general *axiomatic approach* (Zilinskas 1982). There, uncertainty about the values of $f(x)$ other than those observed at $x_1, \ldots, x_k$, is assumed to be representable by a binary relation $\leqslant_x$, where $(a, a') \geqslant_x (b, b')$ signifies that the event $\{f(x) \in (a, a')\}$ is at least as likely as the event $\{f(x) \in (b, b')\}$. Under some reasonable assumptions on this binary relation (e.g., transitivity and completeness), there exists a unique density function p_x that is compatible with the relation in that for every pair of countable unions of intervals (A, A'), one has that $A \geqslant_x A'$ if and only if

$$\int_A p_x(t)\, dt \geqslant \int_{A'} p_x(t)\, dt.$$

For the special case that all densities are Gaussian and hence characterized by their means μ_x and variances σ_x^2, it is then tempting to approach the question of where f should be evaluated next in the axiomatic framework of utility maximization. For this, one has to presuppose that a preference relation is defined on the set of all pairs (m_x, s_x). Subject again to some reasonable assumptions about this preference relation and the utility function involved, the surprising result is that the uniquely rational choice for a next point of evaluation is the one for which the probability of finding a function value smaller that $\tilde y - \varepsilon$ is maximal. In the case of the Wiener process, this amounts to the selection of the interval which maximizes (3.20) with $\tilde y$ replaced by $\tilde y - \varepsilon$, say (x_j, x_{j+1}), and to take

$$x_{k+1} = x_j + \frac{(\tilde y - \varepsilon - f(x_j))(x_{j+1} - x_j)}{2\tilde y - f(x_j) - f(x_{j+1}) - 2\varepsilon}.$$ (3.23)

This, by the way, is not necessarily the same choice as dictated by (3.16).

The brief description of the above stochastic approximation and search methods confirms our earlier impression that this class of methods combines strong theoretical properties with cumbersome computational requirements. A deterministic approach can be shown to be optimal in the worst case sense, a stochastic approach can be shown to be optimal in the expected utility sense, but neither method can be recommended unless evaluations of the original function f are outrageously expensive, in which case a Gaussian stochastic model may be appropriate.

4. Global decrease

A natural technique to find the global minimum is to generate a sequence of points with decreasing function values that converges to x_*. Such a sequence can be initiated by starting out in any direction of local decrease. The difficulty, obviously, is to continue the sequence properly without getting stuck at a local minimum from which the sequence cannot escape.

An interesting and much investigated way to achieve global reliability is to use *random directions*. In the k-th iteration of such a method, having arrived at $x_k \in S$, one generates a point $\xi_k \in S$ from a distribution G_k and chooses x_k as a function D of x_{k-1} and ξ_k in such way that

$$f(x_k) = f(D(x_{k-1}, \xi_k)) \leq \min\{f(x_{k-1}), f(\xi_k)\} . \tag{4.1}$$

If the distributions G_k satisfy

$$\prod_{k=1}^{\infty} (1 - G_k[A]) = 0 , \tag{4.2}$$

for every $A \subset S$ with positive volume $m(A)$, then it is easy to show that

$$\lim_{k \to \infty} \Pr\{x_k \in A_f(\varepsilon)\} = 1 , \tag{4.3}$$

i.e., we have convergence to $A_f(\varepsilon)$ in probability. To prove (4.3), all that has to be observed is that the probability in question is equal to

$$1 - \lim_{k \to \infty} \prod_{i=1}^{k} (1 - G_i(A_f(\varepsilon))) \tag{4.4}$$

which converges to 1 because of (4.2) (Solis & Wets 1981).

The function D can be interpreted in many ways. For instance, it may correspond to minimization of $f(\alpha x_{k-1} + (1 - \alpha)\xi_k)$ over all $\alpha \in [0, 1]$ (Gavioni 1975), or to minimization of some polynomial approximating f on this interval (Bremmerman 1970), or even to just taking the minimum of $f(x_{k-1})$ and $f(\xi_k)$ (Rastrigin 1963). The range of α can be extended to $[0, 2]$,

introducing the notion of *reversals* (Lawrence & Steiglitz 1972) with generally
better computational results (Schrack & Choit 1976). Hundreds of further
references can be found in (Devroye 1979).

The correctness of these methods is easily understood: condition (4.2)
guarantees that there is no systematic bias against any subset of S with positive
volume, and in particular no such bias against $A_f(\varepsilon)$. Only sporadic results are
available on the rate of convergence (Rastrigin 1963), and the issue of a
stopping rule has not been resolved at all. Experiments confirm that these
methods are fast but rather unreliable in practice.

A deterministic global descent approach is hard to imagine, unless one is
prepared to impose stringent conditions on f. There is, none the less, an
interesting class of approaches, both deterministic and stochastic, that is based
on appropriate perturbations of the *steepest descent trajectory*

$$\frac{dx(t)}{dt} = -g(x(t)) , \tag{4.5}$$

where $g(x)$ is the gradient of f at x.

Deterministically, one tries to perturb (4.5) in such a way that the method
cannot converge to local minima outside $A_f(\varepsilon)$, i.e.

$$\frac{d^2x(t)}{dt^2} = -s(f(x(t)))g(x(t)) , \tag{4.6}$$

where the function s has to be small if $f(x(t)) > y_* + \varepsilon$ and goes to infinity as
$x(t)$ approaches $A_f(\varepsilon)$ so as not to restrict the curvature of the trajectory in
that region. In (Griewank 1981), $s(f(x(t)))$ is taken equal to $\alpha/(f(x(t)) - y_* -
\varepsilon)$ which leads to the differential equation

$$\frac{d^2x(t)}{dt^2} = -\alpha\left(I - \frac{dx(t)}{dt}\frac{dx(t)^{\mathrm{T}}}{dt}\right)\frac{g(x(t))}{f(x(t)) - y_* - \varepsilon} . \tag{4.7}$$

We omit a detailed motivation of (4.7), since it suffers from several weaknesses. Obviously, an appropriate target level $y_* + \varepsilon$ is not easily specified. In
addition, convergence can only be verified empirically and not established
analytically for any significant class of objective functions.

A stochastic analogue of (4.7) offers better possibilities. Here, one considers
the *stochastic differential equation*

$$\frac{dx(t)}{dt} = -g(x(t)) + \varepsilon(t)\frac{dw(t)}{dt} , \tag{4.8}$$

where $w(t)$ is an n-dimensional Wiener process. (If $\varepsilon(t) = \varepsilon_0$ for all t, this is
known among physicists as the Smoluchovski–Kramers equation.) The solution
to (4.8) is a stochastic process $x(t)$ that has the following useful property
(Schuss 1980): if $\varepsilon(t) = \varepsilon_0$ for all t, then the probability density function $p(z)$ of

$x(t)$ becomes proportional to $\exp(-2f(z)/\varepsilon_0^2)$ as t goes to infinity. If we now let ε_0 go to 0, this implies that (Aluffi-Pentini et al. 1985) $p(z)$ converges to a Dirac delta function concentrated on x_* (provided that the global minimum is unique). Thus, if t and ε_0 would jointly go to ∞ and 0 respectively, at an appropriate rate, then the trajectory converges to the global minimum in the above probabilistic sense.

Though attractive from a theoretical point of view, the above procedure has been found wanting computationally, since it requires a costly numerical integration. The reader may have noticed the similarities between this approach and the *simulated annealing* method (Kirkpatrick et al. 1983), which also involves a suitably perturbed local search procedure.

A continuous version of simulated annealing is close in spirit to the random direction method. Having arrived at some point x, a method of this type will generate a random neighbouring point $\bar{x}$ and continue the procedure from $\bar{x}$ if $\Delta f = f(\bar{x}) - f(x) \leq 0$ or, with probability $\exp(-\Delta f/\beta)$, if $\Delta f > 0$. Here, β is the *cooling parameter* which has to be decreased at an appropriate rate as the process continues.

Experiments with variations on this approach suggest that it is the method's willingness to accept an occasional decrease in quality that is responsible for its success, rather than a metaphysical resemblance between optimization and the annealing behaviour of physical systems. A continuous version of the approach could exploit this idea in various ways.

The main problem to cope with in such an extension is an appropriate selection mechanism for a random neighbour. One promising approach (Al-Khayyal et al. 1985) is to intersect a line going through x in a random direction with the boundaries of S, calculate the distance between the intersection points and travel a certain fraction γ of that distance from x (allowing reflection at the boundary) where γ is decreased as the method progresses.

The theoretical properties of this type of approach are very similar to those obtained for the stochastic differential equation approach: convergence with probability one to the global minimum for sufficiently smooth functions and sufficiently slowly decreasing cooling parameter. However, convergence can be very slow, and the asymptotic result does not really provide a useful stopping rule. This remains a vexing open question.

5. Improvement of local minima

The global descent techniques discussed in the previous section were partially inspired by steepest descent, but did not really exploit the full power of such a local search procedure in spite of the fact that the global minimum can obviously be found among the local ones. Hence, a logical next step is to investigate the possibility of generating a sequence of local minima with decreasing function values. Ideally, the last local minimum in the sequence generated by such an algorithm should demonstrably be the global one.

A well known deterministic method belonging to this class that has great intuitive appeal is the *tunneling method* (Levy & Gomez 1980). Actually, this method can be viewed as a generalization of the *deflation technique* (Goldstein & Price 1971) to find the global minimum of a one dimensional polynomial. This latter method works as follows.

Consider a local minimum x^* of a one dimensional polynomial f, and define

$$f_1(x) = \frac{f(x) - f(x^*)}{(x - x^*)^2} \, . \tag{5.1}$$

If f is a polynomial of degree m, then f_1 is a polynomial of degree $m - 2$. If, in addition, it can be shown that the global minimum of $f_1(x)$ is positive, then x^* is the global minimum of f. In case there is a point $\bar{x}$ for which $f_1(x)$ is negative, then $f(\bar{x}) < f(x^*)$ and x^* is not the global minimum. In the latter case one can continue from a new local minimum which can be found by starting a local search in $\bar{x}$. To determine whether the global minimum is positive, we proceed iteratively considering $f_1(x)$ as the new basic function.

This method converges rapidly in a finite number of iterations if f is a one-dimensional polynomial, but there is no reason to expect such attractive behaviour if we seek to generalize it to arbitrary objective functions and higher dimensions. Yet, this is precisely what the tunneling method sets out to do.

The tunneling method consists of two phases. In the first phase (minimization phase) the local search procedure is applied to a given point x_0 in order to find a local minimum x^*. The purpose of the second phase (tunneling phase) is to find a point x different from x^*, but with the same function value as x^*, which is used as a starting point for the next minimization phase. This point is obtained by finding a zero of the *tunneling function*

$$T(x) = \frac{f(x) - f(x^*)}{\|x - x_m\|^{\lambda_0} \Pi_{i=1}^{k} \|x - x_i^*\|^{\lambda_i}} \, , \tag{5.2}$$

where $x_i^*, \ldots, x_k^*$ are all local minima with function value equal to $f(x^*)$ found in previous iterations, and λ_0, λ_i are positive parameters of the method. Subtracting $f(x^*)$ from $f(x)$ eliminates all points satisfying $f(x) > f(x^*)$ as a possible solution. The term $\Pi_{i=1}^{k} \|x - x_i^*\|^{\lambda_i}$ is introduced to prevent the algorithm from choosing the previously found minima as a solution. To prevent the zero finding algorithm to converge to a stationary point of

$$\frac{f(x) - f(x^*)}{\Pi_{i=1}^{k} \|x - x_i^*\|^{\lambda_i}} \, , \tag{5.3}$$

which is not a zero of (5.2), the term $\|x - x_m\|^{\lambda_0}$ is added, with x_m chosen appropriately.

If the global minimum has been found, then (5.2) will become positive for all x. Therefore the method stops if no zero of (5.2) can be found.

The tunneling method has the advantage that, provided that the local search procedure is of the descent type, a local minimum with smaller function value is located in each iteration. Hence, it is likely that a point with small function value will be found relatively quickly. However, a major drawback of the method is that it is difficult to be certain that the search for the global minimum has been sufficiently thorough. In essence, the tunneling method only reformulates the problem: rather than solving the original minimization problem, one now must prove that the tunneling function does not have a zero. This, however, is once again a global problem which is strongly related to the original one. The information gained during the foregoing iterations is of no obvious use in solving this new global problem, which therefore appears to be as hard to solve as the original one. Thus, lacking any sort of guarantee, the method is at best of some heuristic value. A decent stopping rule is hard to find and even harder to justify.

A final method in this category can be criticized on similar grounds. It is the method of *filled functions*, developed in (Ge Renpu 1983, 1984). In its simplest form, for a given sequence of local minima $x_1^*, \ldots, x_k^*$, the method considers the auxiliary function $\bar{f}(x) = \exp(-\|x_k^*\|^2/\rho^2)/(r + f(x))$. For an appropriate choice of parameters r and ρ, it can be shown that a method of local descent applied to $\bar{f}$ will lead to a point x_{k+1} starting from which a decent procedure applied to f will arrive at a better local minimum x_{k+1}^* (i.e., with $f(x_{k+1}^*) < f(x_k^*)$), if such an improved local minimum exists. Unfortunately, appropriate values for the parameters have to be based on information about f that is not readily available. As in the case of the tunneling method, it seems to be difficult to identify a significant class of objective functions for which convergence to the global minimum can be guaranteed.

6. Enumeration of local minima

The final class of methods that we shall consider is superficially the most naive one: it is based on the observation that enumeration of all local minima will certainly lead to the detection of the global one. Of course, it is easy to conceive of testfunctions where the number of local minima is so large as to render such an approach inherently useless. Barring such examples, however, this class contains some of the computationally most successful global optimization techniques.

We start with a discussion of deterministic approaches based on this idea. As in (Branin 1972), we consider the differential equation

$$\frac{dg(x(t))}{dt} = \mu g(x(t)), \quad \text{where } \mu \in \{-1, +1\}. \tag{6.1}$$

The exact solution of (6.1) in terms of the gradient vector is

$$g(x(t)) = g(x(0))e^{\mu t}. \tag{6.2}$$

Clearly, if $\mu = -1$, then the points $x(t)$ satisfying (6.2) will tend to a stationary point with increasing t. If $\mu = +1$, then the points will move away from that stationary point.

In the region of x space where the Hessian H of f is nonsingular, (6.1) is identical to the *Newton equation*

$$\frac{dx(t)}{dt} = \mu H^{-1}(x(t)) \cdot g(x(t)) . \tag{6.3}$$

The differential equation (6.3) has the disadvantage that it is not defined in regions where the *determinant* det $H(.)$ is zero. To overcome this problem let the *adjoint matrix* Adj H be defined by H^{-1} det H. A transformation of the parameter t enables (6.3) to be written as

$$\frac{dx(t)}{dt} = \mu \text{Adj } H(x(t)) \cdot g(x(t)) . \tag{6.4}$$

Equation (6.4) has several nice features. It defines a sequence of points on the curve $x(t)$, where the step from the k-th to the $(k+1)$-th point of this sequence is equivalent to a *Newton step* with variable stepsize and alternating sign, i.e. $\mu \alpha_k H^{-1}(x(t)) \cdot g(x(t))$ (Branin 1972; Hardy 1975). This sequence of points on the curve $x(t)$ solving (6.4) has to terminate in a stationary point of f (Branin calls this an *essential singularity*), or in a point where Adj $H(x(t)) \cdot g(x(t)) = 0$ although $g(x(t)) \neq 0$ (an *extraneous singularity*).

A global optimization method would now be to follow the curve $x(t)$ solving (6.4) in the above way for a given sign from any starting point, until a singularity is reached. Here, some extrapolation device is adopted to pass this singularity. If necessary, the sign of (6.4) is then changed, after which the process of generating points on the curve solving (6.4) is continued. The trajectory followed in this way depends, of course, on the starting point and on $g(x(0))$. It can be shown that the trajectories either lead to the boundary of S or return to the starting point along a closed curve (Gomulka 1975, 1978).

It has been conjectured that in the absence of extraneous singularities all trajectories pass through all stationary points. The truth of this conjecture has not yet been determined, nor is it known what conditions on f are necessary to avoid extraneous singularities. An example of a function of simple geometrical shape that has an extraneous singularity is described in (Treccani 1975).

To arrive at a better understanding of this method, we note again that in each point on a trajectory the gradient is proportional to a fixed vector $g(x(0))$ (cf. (6.2)). Hence, for a particular choice of $x(0)$ the trajectory points are a subset of the set $C(x(0)) = \{x \in S \mid g(x) = \lambda g(x(0)), \lambda \in \mathbb{R}\}$, which of course contains all stationary points (take $\lambda = 0$). Unfortunately, $C(x(0))$ can consist of several components, only one of which coincides with the trajectory that will be followed. All stationary points could be found if it would be possible to start the method once in each component of $C(x(0))$, but it is not known how such starting points could be obtained.

Recently, it has been suggested (Diener 1986) that the components of $C(x(0))$ could be connected by, e.g., lines $\{x \in S \mid g(x(0))^{\mathrm{T}} x = g(x(0))^{\mathrm{T}} x_\alpha\}$, for an appropriate finite set $\{x_\alpha \mid \alpha \in A\}$. Such a finite set can be shown to exist under very general conditions, but to construct it in such a way that the trajectory connecting all stationary points can be found by using local information only is not easy. Of course, one could never expect this type of method to be immune to an indentation argument, but it may be possible to identify non-trivial classes of objective functions for which finite convergence can be guaranteed.

The relation between the trajectories of (6.1) and the set $C(x(0))$ can be exploited in a different way as well. Rather than keeping λ fixed and tracing the solution to the differential equation, we can allow λ to decrease from 1 (where $x = x(0)$ is a solution) to 0 (where a solution corresponds to a stationary point) and trace a solution x as a function of λ. Thus, we interpret the set $\{x \in S \mid g(x) = \lambda g(x(0)), \lambda \in [0, 1]\}$ as giving rise to a *homotopy*, and may use *simplicial approximation* techniques to compute the path $x(\lambda)$ (Garcia & Gould 1980). By allowing λ to vary beyond the interval $[0, 1]$, we could hope to generate all stationary points, but of course run into the same problem as above when $C(x(0))$ contains several components.

There are, however, better ways to use homotopies in the current context (Garcia & Zangwill 1979). Let us assume that the equalities $g(x) = 0$ can be rewritten as

$$\psi_j(z) = 0 \quad (j = 1, \ldots, n) \tag{6.5}$$

where ψ_j is a *polynomial* function. We can view this as a set of equations over $\mathbb{C}^n$ and ask for a procedure to compute all the roots of (6.5), i.e., all stationary points of f.

To initiate such a procedure (Garcia & Zangwill 1979), we choose integers $q(j)$ $(j = 1, \ldots, n)$ with the property that, for every sequence of complex vectors with $\|z\| \to \infty$, there exists an $l \in \{1, \ldots, n\}$ and a corresponding infinite subsequence for which $\lim \psi_l(z)/(z_l^{q(l)} - 1)$ does not converge to a negative real number. Intuitively, this means that $z_l^{q(l)} - 1$ dominates $\psi_l(z)$. Such integers $q(j)$ can always be found.

Now, let us consider the system

$$(1 - \lambda)(z_j^{q(j)} - 1) + \lambda \psi_j(z) = 0 \quad (j = 1, \ldots, n). \tag{6.6}$$

For $\lambda = 0$, we obtain a trivial system with $Q = \prod_{j=1}^n q(j)$ solutions $z^{(h)}$. For $\lambda = 1$, we recover the original set of equations. The idea is to increase λ from 0 to 1 and trace the solution paths $z^{(h)}(\lambda)$. Standard techniques from homotopy theory can be used to show that some of these paths may diverge to infinity as $\lambda \to 1$ (the choice of $q(i)$ precludes such behaviour for any $\lambda \in (0, 1)$, as can easily be seen), but the paths cannot cycle back and every root of (6.5) must occur as the endpoint of some path. *Simplicial pivoting* techniques offer the possibility to trace these paths to any degree of accuracy required.

We now turn to stochastic methods that enumerate all local minima. In most methods of this type, a descent local search procedure P is initiated in some or all points of a random sample drawn from S, in an effort to identify all the local minima that are potentially global.

The simplest way to make use of the local search procedure P occurs in a folklore method known as *multistart*. Here, P is applied to every point in a sample, drawn from a uniform distribution over S, and the local minimum with the lowest function value found in this way is the candidate value for y_*.

It is easy to see that this candidate value (or, indeed, already the smallest function value in the sample prior to application of P) converges to y_* with probability 1 under very weak smoothness assumptions on f (Rubinstein 1981). At the same time, it is obvious that this method is very wasteful from a computational point of view, in that the same local minimum is discovered again and again. Before discussing possible improvements, we first consider the question of an appropriate stopping rule.

An interesting analysis of multistart was initiated in (Zielinski 1981) and extended in (Boender & Zielinski 1982; Boender & Rinnooy Kan 1983; Boender 1984). It is based on a *Bayesian* estimate of the *number of local minima* W and of the *relative size* of each region of attraction $\theta_l = m(R(x^*))/m(S)$, $l = 1, \ldots, W$, where a *region of attraction* $R(x^*)$ is defined to be the set of all points in S starting from which P will arrive at x^*.

Why are the above parameters W and θ_l important? It suffices to observe that, if their values are given, the outcome of an application of Multistart is easy to analyze. We can view the procedure as a series of experiments in which a sample from a *multinomial* distribution is taken. Each *cell* of the distribution corresponds to a minimum x^*; the *cell probability* is equal to the probability that a uniformly sampled point will be allocated to $R(x^*)$ by P, i.e. equal to the corresponding θ_l. Thus, the probability that the l-th local minimum is found b_l times ($l = 1, \ldots, W$) in N trials is

$$\frac{N!}{\Pi_{l=1}^{W} b_l!} \cdot \prod_{l=1}^{W} \theta_l^{b_l} . \tag{6.7}$$

It is impossible, however, to distinguish between outcomes that are identical up to a relabeling of the minima. Thus, we have to restrict ourselves to *distinguishable aggregates* of the random events that appear in (6.7). To calculate the probability that w different local minima are found during N local searches and that the i-th minimum is found a_i times ($a_i > 0$, $\Sigma_{i=1}^{w} a_i = N$), let c_j be the number of a_i's equal to j and let $S_W(w)$ denote the set of all permutations of w different elements of $\{1, 2, \ldots, W\}$. The required probability is then given by (Boender 1984)

$$\frac{1}{\Pi_{i=1}^{N} c_i!} \cdot \frac{N!}{\Pi_{i=1}^{w} a_i!} \cdot \sum_{(\pi_1, \ldots, \pi_w) \in S_W(w)} \prod_{i=1}^{w} \theta_{\pi_i}^{a_i} . \tag{6.8}$$

One could use (6.8) to obtain a *maximum likelihood estimate* of the unknown number of local optima *W*. Unfortunately, (6.8) appears to attain a (possibly non-unique) global minimum in infinity for all possible outcomes a_i ($i = 1, \ldots, w$) (Boender 1984).

Formula (6.8) can be used, however, in a *Bayesian* approach in which the unknowns $W, \theta_1, \ldots, \theta_W$ are assumed to be themselves random variables for which a *prior distribution* can be specified. Given the outcome of an application of multistart, Bayes's rule is used to compute the *posterior distribution*, which incorporates both the prior beliefs and the sample information.

In (Boender & Rinnooy Kan 1983), it is assumed that a priori each number of local minima between 1 and ∞ is equally probable, and that the relative sizes of the regions of attraction $\theta_1, \ldots, \theta_W$ follow a uniform distribution on the ($W - 1$)-dimensional simplex.

After lengthy calculations, surprisingly simple expressions emerge for the posterior expectation of several interesting parameters. For instance, the posterior probability that there are *K* local minima is equal to

$$\frac{(K-1)!K!(N-1)!(N-2)!}{(N+K-1)!(K-w)!w!(w-1)!(N-w-2)!} \tag{6.9}$$

and the posterior expectation of the number of local minima is

$$\frac{w(N-1)}{N-w-2}. \tag{6.10}$$

This theoretical framework is quite an attractive one, the more so since it can be easily extended to yield *optimal Bayesian stopping rules*. Such rules incorporate assumptions about the costs and potential benefits of further experiments and weigh these against each other probabilistically to calculate the optimal stopping point. Several loss structures and corresponding stopping rules are described in (Boender & Rinnooy Kan 1987). They provide a completely satisfactory solution to the stopping problem for multistart.

Another Bayesian stopping rule which can be used for methods based on a uniform sample such as Multistart has been proposed in (Betro 1981, Betro and Schoen 1987). Here, for each set $C \subset R$, the probability that $f(x) \in C$ for a uniformly sampled point *x* is specified in a prior distribution and updated as a result of the sample. In this way a posterior distribution is obtained for $\phi(y)$ (see (1.6)) for every possible *y*. The test whether or not a point *x* (which may depend on the sample) is an element of $A_\phi(\varepsilon)$, i.e. $\phi(f(x)) \leqslant \varepsilon$, can now be formulated as a Bayesian decision problem. A Bayesian stopping rule based on the optimal solution of this decision problem can be used to decide if additional sampling is advisable or not.

We now return to the issue of computational efficiency. To avoid useless local searches, the local search procedure should be initiated no more than once, or better still exactly once, in every region of attraction. Clustering analysis is a natural tool to consider next.

The basic idea behind clustering methods is to start from a uniform sample from S, to create groups of mutually close points that correspond to the relevant regions of attractions, and to start P no more than once in every such region. Two ways to create such groups from the initial sample have been proposed. The first, called *reduction* (Becker & Lago 1970), removes a certain fraction, say $1 - \gamma$, of the sample points with the highest function values. The second, called *concentration* (Törn 1978), transforms the sample by allowing one or at most a few steepest descent steps from every point.

Note that these transformations do not necessarily yield groups of points that correspond to regions of attraction of f. For instance, if we define the *level set* $L(y)$ to be $\{x \in S \mid f(x) \leq y\}$, then the groups created by sample reduction correspond to the *connected components* of a level set, and these do not necessarily correspond to regions of attraction. We return to this problem later.

Several ways have been proposed to identify the clusters of points that result from either sample reduction or concentration. The basic framework, however, is always the same. Clusters are formed in a *stepwise fashion*, starting from a *seed point*, which may be the unclustered point with lowest function value or the local minimum found by applying P to this point. Points are added to the cluster through application of a *clustering rule* until a *termination criterion* is satisfied. Where the methods differ, is in their choice of the clustering rule and of the corresponding termination criterion.

As elsewhere in geometrical cluster analysis, the two most popular clustering rules are based on recognizing clusters by means of either the *density* (Törn 1976) or the *distances* among the points. In the former case, the termination criterion will refer to the fact that the number of points per unit volume within the cluster should not drop below a certain level. In the latter case, it will express that a certain *critical distance* between pairs of closest points within the cluster should not be exceeded.

Unlike the usual clustering problem we know here that the points originally come from a uniform distribution. Can this be exploited in the analysis? If the clusters are based on concentration of the sample, the original distribution can no longer be recognized. However, if the clusters have been formed by reduction of the sample, then within each cluster the original uniform distribution still holds. Moreover, as pointed out above, the clusters correspond to connected components of a level set of a continuously differentiable function. These two observations provide a powerful tool in obtaining statistically correct termination criteria.

Since the connected components of a level set can be of any geometrical shape, the clustering procedure should be able to produce clusters of widely varying geometrical shape. Such a procedure, *single linkage* clustering, was described in (Boender et al. 1982; Timmer 1984). In this method, clusters are formed by adding the closest unclustered point to the current cluster until the distance of this point to the cluster exceeds the *critical distance*. (The distance between a point and a cluster is defined as the distance of this point to the closest point in the cluster.) If no more points can be added to the cluster, the cluster is terminated. Provided that there are still points to be clustered, P is then applied to the unclustered sample point with smallest function value, and a new cluster is formed around the resulting local minimum.

Actually, the method is implemented in an *iterative* fashion, where points are sampled in groups of fixed size, say N, and the expanded sample is clustered (after reduction) from scratch in every iteration. If X^* denotes the set of local minima that have been found in previous iterations, then the elements of X^* are used as the seed points for the first clusters. If, for some $\sigma > 0$, the critical distance in iteration k is chosen to be

$$r_k = \pi^{-1/2}\left[\Gamma(1 + \tfrac{1}{2}n)m(S)\sigma\,\frac{\log kN}{kN}\right]^{1/n}, \tag{6.11}$$

then the resulting method has strong theoretical properties.

For instance, if $\sigma > 4$, then even if the sampling continues forever, the total number of local searches ever started by single linkage can be proved to be finite with probability 1. Furthermore, if we define y_γ such that

$$\frac{m(\{x \in S \mid f(x) \le y_\gamma\})}{m(S)} = \gamma, \tag{6.12}$$

then for any $\sigma > 0$ a local minimum will be found by single linkage in every connected component of $L(y_\gamma)$ in which a point has been sampled, within a finite number of iterations with probability 1 (Timmer 1984; Rinnooy Kan & Timmer 1987a).

In order to assign a point to a cluster in single linkage, it suffices that this point is close to one point already in the cluster. In principle it should be possible to design superior methods by using information of more than two sample points simultaneously. In (Timmer 1984) an approach is suggested in which S is partitioned into small *hypercubes* or *cells*. If there are kN sample points, a cell A is said to be *full* if it contains more than $\tfrac{1}{2}m(A)kN/m(S)$ reduced sample points, i.e. more than half the expected number of sample points in A. If a cell is not full, it is called *empty*. Intuitively, one would think that if the cells get smaller with increasing sample size, then each component of $L(y_\gamma)$ can be approximated by a set of full cells, and different components of $L(y_\gamma)$ will be separated by a set of empty cells. Hence, we could let a cluster correspond to a connected subset of S which coincides with a number of full cells. These clusters can be found by applying a single linkage type algorithm to the full cells, such that if two cells are neighbours, then they are assigned to the same cluster. Note that in this approach a cluster corresponds to a set of cells instead of a set of reduced sample points.

The *mode analysis* method, based on this idea and originally proposed in (Timmer 1984), is again iterative. In iteration k, for some $\sigma > 0$, S is divided into cells of measure $(m(S)\sigma \log kN)/(kN)$. After sample reduction, it is determined which cells are full. Sequentially, a seed cell is chosen and a cluster is grown around this seed cell such that each full cell which is a neighbour of a

cell already in the cluster is added to the cluster until there are no more such
cells.

Initially, the cells that contain local minima previously found are chosen as
seed cells. If this is no longer possible, P is applied to the point $\bar{x}$ which has the
smallest function value among the reduced sample points which are in unclustered full cells. The cell containing $\bar{x}$ is then chosen as the next seed cell.

The properties of this mode analysis method are comparable to the properties of single linkage. In (Timmer 1984; Rinnooy Kan & Timmer 1987a) it is
shown that if $\sigma > 20$ (this is not the sharpest possible bound), then, even if the
sampling continues forever, the total number of local searches ever applied in
Mode Analysis is finite with probability 1. If $\sigma > 0$, then in every connected
component of $L(y_\gamma)$ in which a point has been sampled, a local minimum will
be found by mode analysis in a finite number of iterations with probability 1.

Both single linkage and mode analysis share one major deficiency. The
clusters formed by these methods will (at best) correspond to the connected
components of a level set instead of regions of attraction. Although a region of
attraction cannot intersect with several components of a level set, it is
obviously possible that a component contains more than one region of attraction. Since only one local search is started in every cluster, it is therefore
possible that a local minimum will not be found although its region of
attraction contains a (reduced) sample point.

We conclude that both single linkage and mode analysis lack an important
guarantee that multistart was offering, namely that if a point is sampled in
$R(x^*)$, then the local minimum x^* will be found.

We conclude this section by discussing methods that combine the computational efficiency of clustering methods with the theoretical virtues of multistart.
These multi-level methods exploit the function values in the sample points to
derive additional information about the structure of f. These methods are again
applied iteratively to an expanding sample. In the *multi-level single linkage
method*, the local search procedure P is applied to every sample point, except if
there is another sample point within the critical distance which has a smaller
function value. Formulated in this way, the method does not even produce
clusters and it can indeed be applied to the entire sample without reduction or
concentration. Of course, it is still possible to use the reduced sample points
only, if one believes that it is unlikely that the global minimum will be found by
applying P to a sample point which does not belong to the reduced sample. If
desired, clusters can be constructed by associating a point to a local minimum if
there exists a chain of points linking it to that minimum, such that the distance
between each successive pair is at most equal to the critical distance and the
function value is decreasing along the chain. Clearly a point could in this way
be assigned to more than one minimum. This is perfectly acceptable.

In spite of its simplicity, the theoretical properties of multi-level single
linkage are quite strong. If the critical distance is chosen as in (6.11) and if
$\sigma > 4$, then even if sampling continues forever, the total number of local
searches ever started by multi-level single linkage is finite with probability 1

(Timmer 1984; Rinnooy Kan & Timmer 1987b). At the same time we can prove, however, for every $\sigma > 0$ that all local minima (including the global one) will be located in the long run. More precisely, consider the connected component of the level set $L(y)$ containing a local minimum x^* and define the *basin* $Q(x^*)$ as the connected component corresponding to the largest value for y for which this component contains x^* as its only stationary point. It is then possible to show that in the limit, if a point is sampled in $Q(x^*)$, then the local minimum x^* will be found by the procedure. As a result, if $\sigma > 0$, then any local minimum x^* will be found by multi level single linkage within a finite number of iterations with probability 1.

We finally mention a method which is called *multi-level mode analysis*. This method is a generalization of mode analysis in a similar way and for the same reasons as multi-level single linkage is a generalization of single linkage. As in mode analysis, S is partitioned into cells of measure $(m(S)\sigma \log kN)/(kN)$. After sample reduction, it is determined which cells contain more than $\frac{1}{2}\sigma \log kN$ reduced sample points; these are labeled to be full. For each full cell the function value of the cell is defined to be equal to the smallest function value of any of the sample points in the cell. Finally, for every full cell, P is applied to a point in the cell except if the cell has a neighbouring cell which is full and has a smaller function value. Note that we still reduce the sample. Although this is not longer strictly necessary, it creates the extra possibility that two regions of attraction are recognized as such only because a cell on the boundary of both regions is empty.

For multi-level mode analysis essentially the same results hold as for multi-level single linkage.

Since the methods described in this section and multistart result in the same set of minima with a probability that tends to 1 with increasing sample size, we can easily modify and use the stopping rules which were designed for multistart (Boender & Rinnooy Kan 1987).

The limited computational experience available (cf. the next section) confirms that this final class of stochastic methods does offer an attractive mix of reliability and speed.

7. Concluding remarks

As mentioned earlier, it is not easy to design a representative and fair computational experiment in which the performance of various global optimization methods is compared, if only because the inevitable trade off between reliability and effort is rarely discussed explicitly, let alone captured by an appropriate stopping rule. The choice of test functions is also crucial, in that each method can easily be fooled by some test functions and will perform uncommonly well on appropriately chosen other ones.

An effort is currently under way to arrive at a suitable set of text problems and to set up guidelines for a proper test which at least provides explicit

Table 7.1
Test functions (Dixon & Szegö 1978b)

GP	Goldstein and Price
BR	Branin (RCOS)
H3	Hartman 3
H6	Hartman 6
S5	Shekel 5
S7	Shekel 7
S10	Shekel 10

information on implementational details. Here, we can do little better than to summarize the experiments carried out on a limited set of test functions that was proposed in (Dixon & Szegö 1978b). The test functions are listed in Table 7.1.

Initial experiments have revealed that the results of multi-level single linkage were the most promising and therefore this method has been compared with a few leading contenders whose computational behaviour is described in (Dixon & Szegö 1978). In this reference methods are compared on the basis of two criteria: the number of function evaluations and the running time required to solve each of the seven test problems. To eliminate the influence of the different computer systems used, the running time required is measured in *units of standard time*, where one unit corresponds to the running time needed for 1000 evaluations of the S5 test function in the point (4, 4, 4, 4).

In Table 7.3 and Table 7.4, we summarize the computational results of the methods listed in Table 7.2.

The computational results bear out that a stochastic global optimization method such as multi-level single linkage provides an attractive combination of theoretical accuracy and computational efficiency. As such, the method can be recommended for use in situations where little is known about the objective function, for instance, if f is given in the form of a *black box* subroutine. It may

Table 7.2
Methods tested

Description	References	Computational results
A Trajectory	(Branin & Hoo 1972)	(Gomulka 1978)
B Density clustering (concentration)	(Törn 1976)	(Törn 1978)
C Density clustering	(de Biase & Frontini 1978)	(de Biase & Frontini 1978)
D Multi-level single linkage	(Timmer 1984)	(Timmer 1984)
E Random direction	(Bremmerman 1970)	(Dixon & Szegö 1978b)
F Controlled random search	(Price 1978)	(Price 1978)

Table 7.3
Number of function evaluations

Function Method	GP	BR	H3	H6	S5	S7	S10
A	–	–	–	–	5500	5020	4860
B	2499	1558	2584	3447	3649	3606	3874
C	378	597	732	807	620	788	1160
D	148	206	197	487	404	432*	564
E	300	160	420L	515	375L	405L	336L
F	2500	1800	2400	7600	3800	4900	4400

L: The method did not find the global minimum.
*: The global minimum was not found in one of the four runs.

Table 7.4
Number of units standard time

Function Method	GP	BR	H3	H6	S5	S7	S10
A	–	–	–	–	9	8.5	9.5
B	4	4	8	16	10	13	15
C	15	14	16	21	23	20	30
D	0.15	0.25	0.5	2	1	1*	2
E	0.7	0.5	2L	3	1.5L	1.5L	2L
F	3	4	8	46	14	20	20

L: The method did not find the global minimum.
*: The method did not find the global minimum in one of the four runs.

be possible to improve it even further by developing an appropriate rule to modify the sampling distribution as the procedure continues. This, however, would seem to presuppose a specific *global model* of the function, as would any attempt to involve function values directly in the stopping rule.

At the end of this chapter, it is appropriate to conclude that global optimization as a research area is still on its way to maturity. The variety of techniques proposed is impressive, but their relative merits have neither been analyzed in a systematic manner nor properly investigated in computational experiments. In view of the significance of the global optimization problem, it is to be hoped that this challenge will meet with an appropriate response in the near future.

References

Al-Khayyal, F., R. Kertz, and G.A. Tovey (1985), Algorithms and diffusion approximations for nonlinear programming with simulated annealing, to appear.

Aluffi-Pentini, F., V. Parisi and F. Zirilli (1985), Global optimization and stochastic differential equations, *Journal of Optimization Theory and Applications* **47**, 1–17.

Anderssen, R.S. and P. Bloomfield (1975), Properties of the random search in global optimization, *Journal of Optimization Theory and Applications* **16**, 383–398.

Archetti, F. and B. Betro (1978a), A priori analysis of deterministic strategies for global optimization, in (Dixon & Szegö 1978a).

Archetti, F. and B. Betro (1978b), On the effectiveness of uniform random sampling in global optimization problems, Technical Report, University of Pisa, Pisa, Italy.

Archetti, F. and B. Betro (1979a), Stochastic models in optimization, *Bolletino Mathematica Italiana*.

Archetti, F. and B. Betro (1979b), A probabilistic algorithm for global optimization, *Calcolo* **16**, 335–343.

Archetti, F. and F. Frontini (1978), The application of a global optimization method to some technological problems, in (Dixon & Szegö 1978a).

Basso, P. (1985), Optimal search for the global maximum of functions with bounded seminorm, *SIAM Journal of Numerical Analysis* **22**, 888–903.

Becker, R.W. and G.V. Lago (1970), A global optimization algorithm, in: *Proceedings of the 8th Allerton Conference on Circuits and Systems Theory*.

Betro, B. (1981), Bayesian testing of nonparametric hypotheses and its application to global optimization, Technical Report, CNR-IAMI, Italy.

Betro, B. and F. Schoen (1987), Sequential stopping rules for the multistart algorithm in global optimization, *Mathematical Programming* **38**, 271–280.

Boender, C.G.E. and R. Zielinski (1982), A sequential Bayesian approach to estimating the dimension of a multinomial distribution, Technical Report, The Institute of Mathematics of the Polish Academy of Sciences.

Boender, C.G.E., A.H.G. Rinnooy Kan, L. Stougie and G.T. Timmer (1982), A stochastic method for global optimization, *Mathematical Programming* **22**, 125–140.

Boender, C.G.E. and A.H.G. Rinnooy Kan (1983), A Bayesian analysis of the number of cells of a multinomial distribution, *The Statistician* **32**, 240–248.

Boender, C.G.E. and A.H.G. Rinnooy Kan (1987), Bayesian stopping rules for multistart global optimization methods, *Mathematical Programming* **37**, 59–80.

Boender, C.G.E. (1984), The generalized multinomial distribution: A Bayesian analysis and applications, Ph.D. Dissertation, Erasmus Universiteit Rotterdam (Centrum voor Wiskunde en Informatica, Amsterdam).

Branin, F.H. (1972), Widely convergent methods for finding multiple solutions of simultaneous nonlinear equations, *IBM Journal of Research Developments*, 504–522.

Branin, F.H. and S.K. Hoo (1972), A method for finding multiple extrema of a function of n variables, in: F.A. Lootsma (ed.), *Numerical Methods of Nonlinear Optimization* (Academic Press, London).

Bremmerman, H. (1970), A method of unconstrained global optimization, *Mathematical Biosciences* **9**, 1–15.

Cramer, H. and M.R. Leadbetter (1967), *Stationary and Related Stochastic Processes* (Wiley, New York).

De Biase, L. and F. Frontini (1978), A stochastic method for global optimization: its structure and numerical performance, in (Dixon & Szegö 1978a).

Devroye, L. (1979), A bibliography on random search, Technical Report SOCS, McGill University, Montreal.

Diener, I. (1986), Trajectory nets connecting all critical points of a smooth function, *Mathematical Programming* **36**, 340–352.

Dixon, L.C.W. (1978), Global optima without convexity, Technical report, Numerical Optimization Centre, Hatfield Polytechnic, Hatfield, England.

Dixon, L.C.W. and G.P. Szegö (eds.) (1975), *Towards Global Optimization* (North-Holland, Amsterdam).

Dixon, L.C.W. and G.P. Szegö (eds.) (1978a), *Towards Global Optimization 2* (North-Holland, Amsterdam).

Dixon, L.C.W. and G.P. Szegö (1978b), The global optimization problem, in (Dixon & Szegö 1978a).

Evtushenko, Y.P. (1971), Numerical methods for finding global extrema of a nonuniform mesh, *U.S.S.R. Computing Machines and Mathematical Physics* **11**, 1390–1403.

Fedorov, V.V. (ed.) (1985), *Problems of Cybernetics, Models and Methods in Global Optimization.* (USSR Academy of Sciences, Council of Cybernetics, Moscow).

Garcia, C.B. and W.I. Zangwill (1978), Determining all solutions to certain systems of nonlinear equations, *Mathematics of Operations Research* **4**, 1–14.

Garcia, C.B. and F.J. Gould (1980), Relations between several path following algorithms and local global Newton methods, *SIAM Review* **22**, 263–274.

Gaviani, M. (1975), Necessary and sufficient conditions for the convergence of an algorithm in unconstrained minimization. In (Dixon & Szegö 1975).

Ge Renpu (1983), A filled function method for finding a global minimizer of a function of several variables, *Dundee Biennial Conference on Numerical Analysis.*

Ge Renpu (1984), The theory of the filled function method for finding a global minimizer of a nonlinearly constrained minimization problem, *SIAM Conference on Numerical Optimization*, Boulder, CO.

Goldstein, A.A. and J.F. Price (1971), On descent from local minima. *Mathematics of Computation* **25**, 569–574.

Gomulka, J. (1975), Remarks on Branin's method for solving nonlinear equations, in (Dixon & Szegö 1975).

Gomulka, J. (1978), Two implementations of Branin's method: numerical experiences, in (Dixon & Szegö 1978a).

Griewank, A.O. (1981), Generalized descent for global optimization, *Journal of Optimization Theory and Applications* **34**, 11–39.

Hardy, J.W. (1975), An implemented extension of Branin's method, in (Dixon & Szegö 1975).

Horst, R. (1986), A general class of branch-and-bound methods in global optimization with some new approaches for concave minimization, *Journal of Optimization Theory and Applications* **51**, 271–291.

Horst, R. and H. Tuy (1987), On the convergence of global methods in multiextremal optimization, *Journal of Optimization Theory and Applications* **54**, 253–271.

Kalantari, B. (1984), Large scale global minimization of linearly constrained concave quadratic functions and related problems, Ph.D. Thesis, Computer Science Department, University of Minnesota.

Kirkpatric, S., C.D. Crelatt Jr., and M.P. Vecchi (1983), Optimization by simulated annealing, *Science* **220**, 671–680.

Kushner, M.J. (1964), A new method for locating the maximum point of an arbitrary multipeak curve in presence of noise, *Journal of Basic Engineering* **86**, 97–106.

Lawrence, J.P. and K. Steiglitz (1972), Randomized pattern search, *IEEE Transactions on Computers* **21**, 382–385.

Levy, A. and S. Gomez (1980), The tunneling algorithm for the global optimization problem of constrained functions, Technical Report, Universidad National Autonoma de Mexico.

McCormick, G.P. (1983), *Nonlinear Programming: Theory, Algorithms and Applications* (John Wiley and Sons, New York).

Mentzer, S.G. (1985), Private communication.

Mladineo, R.H. (1986), An algorithm for finding the global maximum of a multimodal, multivatiate function, *Mathematical Programming* **34**, 188–200.

Pardalos, P.M., and J.B. Rosen (1986), Methods for global concave minimization: A bibliographic survey, *SIAM Review* **28**, 367–379.

Pinter, J. (1983), A unified approach to globally convergent one-dimensional optimization algorithms, Technical report, CNR-IAMI, Italy.

Pinter, J. (1986a), Globally convergent methods for n-dimensional multi-extremal optimization, *Optimization* **17**, 187–202.

Pinter, J. (1986b), Extended univariate algorithms for n-dimensional global optimization, *Computing* **36**, 91–103.

Pinter, J. (1988), Branch and Bound algorithms for solving global optimization problems with Lipschitzian structure, *Optimization* **19**, 101–110.

Price, W.L. (1978), A controlled random search procedure for global optimization, in (Dixon & Szegö 1978a).

Rastrigin, L.A. (1963), The convergence of the random search method in the extremal control of a many-parameter system, *Automation and Remote Control* **24**, 1337–1342.

Ratschek, H. (1985), Inclusion functions and global optimization, *Mathematical Programming* **33**, 300–317.

Rinnooy Kan, A.H.G. and G.T. Timmer (1987a), Stochastic global optimization methods. Part I: Clustering methods, *Mathematical Programming* **39**, 27–56.

Rinnooy Kan, A.H.G. and G.T. Timmer (1987b), Stochastic global optimization methods. Part II: Multi-level methods, *Mathematical Programming* **39**, 57–78.

Rosen, J.B. (1983), Global minization of a linearly constrained concave function by partion of feasible domain, *Mathematics of Operations Research* **8**, 215–230.

Rubinstein, R.Y. (1981), *Simulation and the Monte Carlo Method* (John Wiley & Sons, New York).

Schrack, G. and M. Choit (1976), Optimized relative step size random searches, *Mathematical Programming* **16**, 230–244.

Schuss, Z. (1980), *Theory and Applications of Stochastic Differential Equations* (John Wiley and Sons, New York).

Shepp, L.A. (1979), The joint density of the maximum and its location for a Wiener process with drift, *Journal of Applied Probability* **16**, 423–427.

Shubert, B.O. (1972), A sequential method seeking the global maximum of a function, *SIAM Journal on Numerical Analysis* **9**, 379–388.

Sobol, I.M. (1982), On an estimate of the accuracy of a simple multidimensional search, *Soviet Math. Dokl.* **26**, 398–401.

Solis, F.J. and R.J.E. Wets (1981), Minimization by random search techniques, *Mathematics of Operations Research* **6**, 19–30.

Strongin, R.G. (1978), *Numerical Methods for Multiextremal Problems* (Nauka, Moscow).

Sukharev, A.G. (1971), Optimal strategies of the search for an extremum, *Computational Mathematics and Mathematical Physics* **11**, 119–137.

Timmer, G.T. (1984), Global optimization: A stochastic approach, Ph.D. Dissertation, Erasmus University Rotterdam.

Törn, A.A. (1976), Cluster analysis using seed points and density determined hyperspheres with an application to global optimization, in: *Proceeding of the third International Conference on Pattern Recognition*, Coronado, CA.

Törn, A.A. (1978), A search clustering approach to global optimization, in (Dixon & Szegö 1978a).

Treccani, G. (1975), On the critical points of continuously differentiable functions, in (Dixon & Szegö 1975).

Tuy, H. (1987), Global optimization of a difference of two convex functions, *Mathematical Programming Study* **30**, 150–182.

Walster, G.W., E.R. Hansen and S. Sengupta (1985), Test results for a global optimization algorithm, in: P.T. Boggs and R.B. Schnabel (eds.), *Numerical Optimization 1984* (SIAM, Philadelphia, PA).

Woerlee, A. (1984), A Bayesian global optimization method, Masters Thesis, Erasmus University Rotterdam.

Wood, G.R. (1985), Multidimensional bisection and global minimization, Technical report, University of Canterbury.

Zielinski, R. (1981), A stochastic estimate of the structure of multi-extremal problems, *Mathematical Programming* **21**, 348–356.

Zilinskas, A. (1982), Axiomatic approach to statistical models and their use in multimodel optimization theory, *Mathematical Programming* **22**, 104–116.

Zilverberg, N.D. (1983), Global minimization for large scale linear constrained systems, Ph.D. Thesis, Computer Science Dept., University of Minnesota.

G.L. Nemhauser et al., Eds., *Handbooks in OR & MS, Vol. 1*
© Elsevier Science Publishers B.V. (North-Holland) 1989

Chapter X

Multiple Criteria Decision Making: Five Basic Concepts

P.L. Yu

School of Business University of Kansas Lawrence, KS 66045, U.S.A.

1. Introduction

Ever since Adam, human beings have been confronted with multiple criteria decision making problems (MCDM). Our food should taste good, smell good, look good and be nutritious. We want to have a good life, which may mean more wealth, more power, more respect and more time for ourselves, together with good health and a good second generation, etc. Indeed, in the records of human culture, all important political, economical and cultural events have involved multiple criteria in their evolutions.

Although analysis of multicriteria problems has been scattered in our human history, putting this analysis into a formal mathematical setting is fairly new. Although there are a number of scholars and scientists who have made contributions in this mathematical analysis of MCDM, Pareto [30] is perhaps one of the most recognized pioneers in this analysis. Interested readers are referred to [38, 39] for some historical notes.

The purpose of this article is not to report all significant events of who did what in the history, because that would almost surely be impossible. Rather, we shall sketch some important aspects of MCDM so that the reader can have a general picture of MCDM and be able to find the related literature for their further study.

We start with preferences as binary relations (Section 2) in which the reader can learn how mathematical functional relations are extended to binary relations to represent revealed preferences and learn some solution concepts of MCDM. Then we will present a class of MCDM methods which model human goal seeking behaviors (Section 3). Satisficing solutions, compromise solutions and goal programming will be sketched in this section. Numerical ordering is one of our great human inventions. There is a great interest in representing the preferences in terms of real valued functions or numerical orderings. This will be sketched in Section 4. Certainly, not all revealed preferences can be represented by numerical orderings. We use Section 5 to introduce domination structures and their related solutions to tackle the problems of representing such revealed preferences and locating good solutions. As linear functions are the best and simplest functions in mathematical analysis, linear cases always yield special results. We treat linear cases and their related topics including the MC and MC^2 simplex method in Section 6. Finally, we offer some further comments in Section 7 as a summary and conclusion.

2. Preference structures and classes of nondominated solutions

2.1. *Preference as a binary relation*

Let us consider possible outcomes of the decision *one pair at a time*. For any pair, say y^1 and y^2, one and only one of the following can occur:

(i) we are convinced that y^1 is better than or preferred to y^2, denoted by $y^1 > y^2$;

(ii) we are convinced that y^1 is worse than or less preferred to y^2 denoted by $y^1 < y^2$;

(iii) we are convinced that y^1 is equivalent or equally preferred to y^2, denoted by $y^1 \sim y^2$; or

(iv) we have no sufficient evidence to say either (i), (ii) or (iii), denoted by $y^1 ? y^2$, thus, the preference relation between y^1 and y^2 is *indefinite* or not yet clarified.

Note that each of the above statements involves *a comparison or relation* between a pair of outcomes. The symbols '>', '<', '~' and '?' are *operators* defining the comparison and relations. Specifying whether '>', '<', '~' or '?' is defined for each pair of Y. Any revealed preference information, accumulated or not, can then be represented by a subset of the Cartesian Product $Y \times Y$ as follows:

Definition 2.1. (i) A preference based on $>$ (respectively $<$, '~', or ?) is a subset of $Y \times Y$, denoted by $\{>\}$ (respectively $\{<\}$, $\{\sim\}$, or $\{?\}$), so that whenever $(y^1, y^2) \in \{>\}$ (respectively $\{<\}$, $\{\sim\}$, or $\{?\}$) $y^1 > y^2$ (respectively $y^1 < y^2$, $y^1 \sim y^2$, or $y^1 ? y^2$).

(ii) For convenience, we also define $\{\gtrsim\} = \{>\} \cup \{\sim\}$; $\{>?\} = \{>\} \cup \{?\}$; $\{\gtrsim?\} = \{\gtrsim\} \cup \{?\}$, etc.

(iii) By a preference (or revealed preference) structure we mean the collection of all the above preferences. As such structures are uniquely determined by $\{>\}$, $\{\sim\}$, $\{?\}$) (see Remark 2.1(iii)), a preference structure will be denoted by $\mathscr{P}(\{>\}, \{\sim\}, \{?\})$ or simply by $\mathscr{P}$.

Remark 2.1. (i) Note that $>$, $<$, $\sim$ and ? are operators, while $\{>\}$, $\{<\}$, $\{\sim\}$ and $\{?\}$ are sets of revealed preference information.

(ii) The sets $\{>\}$ and $\{<\}$ are *symmetric*. That is, $(y^1, y^2) \in \{>\}$ iff $(y^2, y^1) \in \{<\}$. Thus, if $\{>\}$ is known, then $\{<\}$ is also known and vice versa.

(iii) $\{>\}$, $\{<\}$, $\{\sim\}$ and $\{?\}$ form a partition of $Y \times Y$. In view of (ii), knowning $\{<\}$ and one of $\{\sim\}$ or $\{?\}$, we could derive the remaining preferences.

(iv) Observe that the larger is $\{?\}$, the less clarified is the revealed preference, which usually may cloud the decision process. Sometimes, it may take discipline and/or new information for the decision maker to clarify his/her preference in order to reach the final solution. Dr. B. Roy and his associates have introduced the interesting concepts of *pseudo-orders* to help resolve part of the problems. The interested reader is referred to [33] and the citations therein.

Example 2.1. Consider the following preference over three candidates for a junior management position. Assume that each candidate is evaluated according to three criteria: ability, cooperation, and enthusiasm. Let the score of each criterion range from 0 to 9, the higher the better. Let y_i^j be the score on criterion i for candidae j. Since the score for each candidate is difficult to specify precisely, let the preference be given by $y^1 > y^2$ if and only if (*iff*) there is at least one criterion i so that $y_i^1 - y_i^2 \geq 2$, and $y_k^2 - y_k^1 < 2$ for the remaining criteria $(k \neq i)$. Consider the scores given in Table 2.1.

Table 2.1
Candidate scores

Criteria	y^1	y^2	y^3
Ability	7	8	9
Cooperation	8	9	7
Enthusiasm	9	7	8

We obtain the following:

$$\{>\} = \{(y^1, y^2), (y^2, y^3), (y^3, y^1)\},$$
$$\{<\} = \{(y^2, y^1), (y^3, y^2), (y^1, y^3)\},$$
$$\{\sim\} = \{(y^1, y^1), (y^2, y^2), (y^3, y^3)\},$$
$$\{?\} = \emptyset.$$

Example 2.2 (Value function). Let $v(y)$ be a value function defined on Y such that $v(y^1) > v(y^2)$ iff $y^1 > y^2$ and $v(y^1) = v(y^2)$ iff $y^1 \sim y^2$. Then

$$\{>\} = \{(y^1, y^2) \in Y^2 \mid v(y^1) > v(y^2)\},$$
$$\{\sim\} = \{(y^1, y^2) \in Y^2 \mid v(y^1) = v(y^2)\},$$
$$\{?\} = \emptyset.$$

Example 2.3 (A lexicographic ordering). Let $y = (y_1, y_2, \ldots, y_q)$ be indexed so that the k-th component is overwhelmingly more important than the $(k+1)$-th component for $k = 1, \ldots, q-1$. A lexicographic ordering preference is defined as follows: the outcome $y^1 = (y_1^1, \ldots, y_q^1)$ is preferred to $y^2 = (y_1^2, \ldots, y_q^2)$ iff $y_1^1 > y_1^2$ or there is some $k \in \{2, \ldots, q\}$ so that $y_k^1 > y_k^2$ and $y_j^1 = y_j^2$ for $j = 1, \ldots, k-1$. In locating the lexicographical maximum point over Y, one can first find the maximum points with respect to y_1 on Y. If the solution set, denoted by Y_1, contains only a single point, then stop; otherwise, find the maximum points with respect to y_2 on Y_1. If the solution set, denoted by Y_2, contains only a single point, then stop; otherwise find the maximum point with respect to y_3 on Y_2, etc. This process continues until a *unique* 'solution' or no 'solution' is found. Note that no two distinct points can be lexicographically 'equal'. We have:

$$\{>\} = \{(y^1, y^2) \mid y^1 \text{ is lexicographically preferred to } y^2\},$$

$$\{\sim\} = \{(y, y) \mid y \in Y\},$$

$$\{?\} = \emptyset.$$

Example 2.4 (Pareto preference). For each component y_i let greater values be more preferred, and assume that no other information on the preference is available or established. Then Pareto preference is defined by $y^1 > y^2$ iff $y^1 \geq y^2$, i.e., component-wise $y_i^1 \geq y_i^2$, $i = 1, \ldots, q$, and $y^1 \neq y^2$. Observe that $y^1 \geq y^2$ may include equality while $y^1 \geqq y^2$ does not. Note that

$$\{\sim\} = \{(y, y) \mid y \in Y\},$$

$$\{>\} = \{(y^1, y^2) \mid y^1 \geq y^2\} \quad \text{and}$$

$$\{?\} = \{F(y^1, y^2) \mid \text{neither } y^1 \geq y^2 \text{ nor } y^2 \geq y^1\}.$$

Similar to the lower and upper level sets (supports) of a real valued function, one can define *better, worse, equivalent* or *indefinite* sets of a given preference as follows:

Definition 2.2. Given a preference and a point $y^0 \in Y$, we define the *better, worse, equivalent* or *indefinite* sets with respect to (w.r.t.) y^0 as:
    (i) $\{y^0 <\} = \{y \in Y \mid y^0 < y\}$ (the better set w.r.t. y^0),
    (ii) $\{y^0 >\} = \{y \in Y \mid y^0 > y\}$ (the worse set w.r.t. y^0),
    (iii) $\{y^0 \sim \} = \{y \in Y \mid y^0 \sim y\}$ (the equivalent set w.r.t. y^0),
    (iv) $\{y^0 ?\} = \{y \in Y \mid y^0 ? y\}$ (the indefinite set w.r.t. y^0),
    (v) $\{y^0 \gtrsim\} = \{y \in Y \mid y^0 \gtrsim y\}$,
    (vi) $\{y^0 > ?\} = \{y^0 >\} \cup \{y^0 ?\}$,
    (vii) $\{y^0 \gtrsim ?\} = \{y^0 \gtrsim\} \cup \{y^0 ?\}$.

It would be instructional for the reader to specify those sets defined in Definition 2.2 for Example 2.1–2.4.

2.2. Characteristics of preferences

To study the characteristics of preference information, one may start with the general concept of binary relations on Y, which are defined to be subsets of

$Y \times Y$. Denote this subset by R. Note that preferences defined by $>$, $<$, $\sim$ or ? are binary relations.

Definition 2.3. The binary relation R on Y is:
  (i) *reflexive* if $(y, y) \in R$ for every $y \in Y$; otherwise, it is *irreflexive*;
  (ii) *symmetric* if $(y^1, y^2) \in R$ implies that $(y^2, y^1) \in R$ for every y^1, y^2 of Y; otherwise, it is *asymmetric*;
  (iii) *transitive* if $(y^1, y^2) \in R$ and $(y^2, y^3) \in R$ implies that $(y^1, y^3) \in R$, for every $y^1, y^2, y^3 \in Y$; otherwise, it is *nontransitive*;
  (iv) *complete or connected* if $(y^1, y^2) \in R$ or $(y^2, y^1) \in R$ for every $y^1, y^2 \in Y$ and $y^1 \neq y^2$.
  (v) an *equivalence* if R is reflective, symmetric and transitive.

Example 2.5. let Y be the students currently enrolled at a university.
  (i) Let R_1 be defined by 'being a classmate in at least one class'. Thus, $(y^1, y^2) \in R_1$ iff y^1 and y^2 are classmates in at least one class. Broadly speaking, one can be a classmate to himself or herself. Note that R_1 so defined is reflexive, symmetric, nontransitive (why?) and not complete.
  (ii) Let R_2 be defined by 'being older than'. Thus, $(y^1, y^2) \in R_2$ iff y^1 is older than y^2. Assume that no two students were born at the very same instant. We see that R_2 is irreflexive, asymmetric, transitive, and complete.
  (iii) Let R_3 be defined by 'being of the same sex'. Thus, $(y^1, y^2) \in R_3$ iff y^1 is of the same sex as y^2. Assume that each student is either male or female (not both as in the pathological case). We see that R_3 is reflexive, symmetric, and transitive; and therefore, is an *equivalence*. Note also that R_3 is not complete (why?).

Remark 2.2. From Definition 2.1, regarding $\{>\}$, $\{<\}$, $\{\sim\}$ and $\{?\}$ as binary relations, in order to be consistent with logic and linguistic usage, we require and assume throughout this paper that $\{>\}$ and $\{<\}$ are *both irreflexive and asymmetric*, that $\{\sim\}$ is *reflexive and symmetric* and that $\{?\}$ is *symmetric*.

To appreciate the meaning of completeness, let

$$'Y^2 = \{(y^1, y^2) \mid y^1 \neq y^2; \ y^1 \in Y, \ y^2 \in Y\} \,.$$

we see that
  (i) $\{>\}$ is complete iff $\{>\} \cup \{<\} = 'Y^2$,
  (ii) $\{\gtrsim\}$ is complete iff $\{\gtrsim\} \cup \{\lesssim\} \supset 'Y^2$,
  (iii) $\{>?\}$ is complete iff $\{>?\} \cup \{<?\} = 'Y^2$.

Remark 2.3. Due to Remark 2.1 and Definition 2.1, we immediately have:
  (i) $\{\gtrsim?\}$ is complete.
  (ii) $\{>\}$ is complete implies that $\{\gtrsim\}$ and $\{>?\}$ are complete. (The converse is not true.)

Example 2.6. (i) In Example 2.1, $\{>\}$ is complete, but not transitive. (ii) In Example 2.2, $\{>\}$ is transitive, but in general not complete; $\{\gtrsim\}$ is both transitive and complete. (iii) In Example 2.3, $\{>\}$ is complete and transitive, so is $\{\gtrsim\}$. (iv) In Example 2.4, $\{>\}$ is transitive but not complete, while $\{>?\}$ is complete but not transitive.

Remark 2.4. Transitivity is used for obvious logic consistency while completeness is used for indicating how complete is the revealed preference. Both of them are needed when we want to express our preference in a numerical value function as to be discussed in Section 4. For further exploration on transitivity and completeness see [12, 46].

Suppose that Y is convex. Then the concept of quasi-convexity in real valued function can be extended to that of preferences as follows:

Definition 2.4. let Y be a convex set.
(i) $\{\gtrsim\}$ is *quasi-convex* iff $y^1 \gtrsim y^2$ implies that $y^1 \gtrsim (1-\lambda)y^1 + \lambda y^2$ for any $\lambda \in]0, 1[$, the open interval from 0 to 1.
(ii) $\{\gtrsim\}$ is *quasi-concave* iff $y^1 \lesssim y^2$ implies that $y^1 \lesssim (1-\lambda)y^1 + \lambda y^2$ for any $\lambda \in]0, 1[$.

One can show (see [46]):

Theorem 2.1. *Suppose that* $\{\gtrsim\}$ *are transitive and complete over a convex set* Y. *Then*
(i) $\{\gtrsim\}$ *is quasi-convex iff* $\{y\gtrsim\}$ *is a convex set for all* $y \in Y$;
(ii) $\{\gtrsim\}$ *is quasi-concave iff* $\{y\lesssim\}$ *is a convex set for all* $y \in Y$.

2.3. Classes of Nondominated Solutions

An optimal solution is the one that we cannot do better. That is, no other alternative can be better than the optimal solution. This observation leads to a number of nondominated solution concepts.

Definition 2.5. Given a preference structure $\mathscr{P}(\{>\}, \{\sim\}, \{?\})$ defined on the outcome space Y, we define:
(i) $y^0 \in Y$ is an $N[<]$-solution (point) iff $\{y^0<\} \cap Y = \emptyset$, the collection of all such solutions is denoted by $N[<]$;
(ii) $y^0 \in Y$ is an $N[\lesssim]$-solution iff $\{y^0\lesssim\} \cap Y = \{y^0\}$, the collection of all such solutions is denoted by $N[\lesssim]$;
(iii) $y^0 \in Y$ is an $N[<?]$-solution iff $\{y^0 <?\} \cap Y = \emptyset$, the collection of all such solutions is denoted by $N[<?]$;
(iv) $y^0 \in Y$ is an $N[\lesssim?]$-solution iff $\{y^0\lesssim?\} \cap Y = \{y^0\}$, the collection of all such solutions is denoted by $N[\lesssim?]$.

Remark 2.5. If we have only one criterion, then (i) $N[<] = N[\lesssim]$, which is an ordinary optimal solution set; (ii) $N[\lesssim]$, if nonempty, contains at most one point; and (iii) as $\{?\} = \emptyset$ in this case, $N[<?] = N[<]$ and $N[\lesssim?] = N[\lesssim]$. Thus, $N[<] = N[\lesssim] = N[<?] = N[\lesssim?]$. These properties usually do not hold for multiple criteria problems.

The following can be easily established.

Theorem 2.2. (i) $N[\lesssim?] \subset N[<?] \subset N[<]$;
 (ii) $N[\lesssim?] \subset N[\lesssim] \subset N[<]$;
 (iii) $N[\lesssim?]$ *contains at most one point.*

Remark 2.6. By definition, (i) $N[<]$ may contain y^1 and y^2 so that $y^1 \sim y^2$ or $y^1 ? y^2$; (ii) $N[\lesssim]$ may contain y^1 and y^2 so that $y^1 ? y^2$; (iii) $N[<?]$ may contain y^1 and y^2 so that $y^1 \sim y^2$; and (iv) $N[\lesssim?]$, if nonempty, will contain only one 'clear' superium solution, and no ambiguity or hesitation on alternative optimals would occur.

Remark 2.7. In application, we may first try to locate $N[<]$, then $N[\lesssim]$ or $N[<?]$, and, finally, $N[\lesssim?]$. In this paper, unless otherwise specified, we shall focus on $N[<]$.

3. Goal setting and compromise solutions

3.1. Introduction

It has been recognized that each human being has a set of ideal goals to achieve and maintain (see Ch. 9 of [46] and the citations therein). When a perceived state (or value) has deviated from its targeted or ideal state (or value), a charge (tension or pressure) will be produced to prompt an action to reduce or eliminate the deviation. The behavior of taking actions, including adjustment of the ideal values, to move the perceived states to the targeted ideal states is called *goal-seeking behavior*.

This goal-seeking behavior, which has been well documented in psychological literature (for instance, see [46] and the citations therein), has an important and pervasive impact on human decision making. In this section, we shall focus on two concepts that define human goal-seeking behavior. This first one is related to satisficing models, which are treated in Section 3.2, the other is related to compromise models including goal programming, which are treated in Section 3.3. All of these are static models. For the dynamic version of goal-seeking behaviors we refer to Chapter 9 of [46].

3.2. Satisficing models

3.2.1. Goal Setting

Definition 3.1. Goal setting for satisficing models is defined as the procedure of identifying a satisficing set S such that, whenever the decision outcome is an element of S, the decision maker will be happy and satisfied and is assumed to have reached the optimal solution.

Let our MCDM problem be specified by the criteria $f = (f_1, \ldots, f_q)$ and the feasible set is $X = \{x \in R^n \mid g(x) \leqq 0\}$, where $g = (g_1, \ldots, g_m)$. Note that the outcome of a decision x is specified by $y(x) = f(x)$.

In specifying S one can start with each individual f_k and find its satisficing or acceptable intervals. He then can consider two or more criteria simultaneously for their corresponding tradeoff. In a general form, the final satisficing set S can be defined as the union of

$$S_k = \{f \mid G_k(f) \geqq 0\}, \quad k = 1, \ldots, r, \tag{3.1}$$

where f is a point in R_k and G_k is a vector function which reflects the tradeoff over f (see Chapters 5 and 6 of [46] for further discussion). Note that when the union contains a single set (i.e., $r = 1$), $S = S_1$ and S is defined by a system of inequalities.

Example 3.1. Let us consider a problem of selecting an athlete for a basketball team. Assume quickness, f_1, and accuracy of shooting, f_2, of the player are essential. Let both f_1 and f_2 be indexed from 0 to 10, where the higher the index, the better the player. Assume that a player, x, will be selected with satisfaction if $f_1(x) \geqq 9$ or $f_2(x) \geqq 9$, or $f_1(x) + f_2(x) \geqq 15$. Now set $G_1(f) = f_1(x) - 9$, $G_2(f) = f_2(x) - 9$, and $G_3(f) = f_1(x) + f_2(x) - 15$. We see that each $S_i = \{f \mid G_i(f) \geqq 0\}$, $i = 1, 2, 3$, specifies a satisficing set and $S = S_1 \cup S_2 \cup S_3$ is not convex.

3.2.2. Satisficing models and their interactive methods

Once S, the satisficing set, has been determined, finding a satisficing solution x^0, such that $f(x^0) \in S$, is a mathematical programming problem.

Since $S = \bigcup_{k=1}^r S_k$, $Y \cap S \neq \emptyset$ iff there is an S_k such that $Y \cap S_k \neq \emptyset$. As we need only one point of $Y \cap S$ when it is nonempty, we could verify individually if $S_k \cap Y \neq \emptyset$, $k = 1, \ldots, r$, and find one point from the nonempty intersections.

Note that to verify whether or not $S_k \cap Y$ is empty and to find a point in $S_k \cap Y$, if it is nonempty, we can use the following mathematical program.

Rewrite each set in (3.1) as

$$S_k = \{f(x) \mid G_{kj}(f(x)) \geqq 0, j = 1, \ldots, J_k\}, \tag{3.2}$$

where G_{kj}, $j = 1, \ldots, J_k$, are components of G_k, and J_k is the number of components of G_k.

Program 3.1.

$$V_k = \min \sum_{j=1}^{J_k} d_j,$$

s.t. $G_{kj}(f(x)) + d_j \geqq 0, \quad j = 1, \ldots, J_k,$

$x \in X, \quad d_j \geqq 0,$

$j = 1, \ldots, J_k.$

It is readily verified that $S_k \cap Y \neq \emptyset$ iff $V_k = 0$. We thus have:

Theorem 3.1. *Let* $S = \bigcup_{k=1}^r S_k$. *Then a satisficing solution exists iff there is at least one* $k \in \{1, \ldots, r\}$ *such that the corresponding program 3.1 yields* $V_k = 0$.

Remark 3.1. Observe that when one satisficing solution is found the decision problem is solved, at least temporarily. Otherwise the decision maker can activate either a *positive problem solving* or *negative problem avoidance* to restructure the problem. The former will enable careful restudy and restructuring of the problem so as to find a solution, perhaps a new one, which lies in the satisficing set. The latter will try to reduce the aspiration levels or play down the importance of making a good decision, thus, 'lowering' the satisficing set to have a nonempty intersection with Y. While the psychological attitude in problem solving and in problem avoidance may be different (see Chapter 9 of [46] for further discussion), the final consequence is the same. That is, eventually, the newly structured problem enables the decision maker to have $S \cap Y \neq \emptyset$. Here we will not discuss the restructuring of a problem to obtain a satisficing solution. Instead we will examine helpful information to aid the decision maker in restructuring his satisficing set S and feasible set Y. The following provides some helpful information.

(i) Depending on the formation of S, if Program 3.1 is used to identify a satisficing solution, one can produce x^k, $k = 1, \ldots, r$, which solves Program 3.1 with S_k as the satisficing set. One then can compute $f(x^k)$, $G_k(f(x^k))$, the distance from $f(x^k)$ to S_k, and tradeoff among the $G_{kj}(f(x))$, $j = 1, \ldots, J_k$, at x^k. All of these can be helpful for the dicision maker to reframe S_k.

(ii) Suppose that it has been revealed or established that '*more is better*' for each criterion. Then the revealed preference contains at least the Pareto preference (see Example 2.4). One can then generate: (A) all or some representatives of the $N[<]$-points, the corresponding $f(x)$, and optimal weights $\Lambda^*(x)$ for the $N[<]$-points (see Section 5 for further discussion); (B) the value $f_k^* = \max\{f_k(x) \mid x \in X\}$, $k = 1, \ldots, q$, which gives the best value of $f_k(x)$ over X. This information can help the decision maker to restructure his S. Relaxing of the target goal with reference to the *ideal point* $(f_1^*, \ldots, f_q^*)$ sequentially and iteratively with the decision maker, until a satisficing solution is obtained, is certainly an art. It is especially useful when X and f are fairly fixed and not subject to change.

(iii) If possible (for instance, in bicriteria cases), displaying Y and S, even if only partially, can help the decision maker conceptualize where Y and S are, to make it easier to restructure the problem.

One must keep in mind that with X, $f(x)$ and S, one can generate as much information as one wishes, just as one can generate as many statistics from sample values as he wants. However, relevant information (e.g., useful statistics) which can positively affect the problem solving may not be too much. Irrelevant information can become a burden for decision analysis and decision making.

3.3. Compromise models

In this section, mathematical formulation of goal seeking behavior in terms of a distance function will be described. Because it is simple to understand and compute, the concept has much general appeal to many scholars. We shall start with the most simple form and then gradually extend the concept to more complex cases. In Section 3.3.1, the basic concept and preference structure of compromise models are introduced. Section 3.3.2 is devoted to computational aspects including goal programming and *maximin* programming and Section 3.3.3 to a discussion on dynamic adjustment of ideal points for a final optimal solution.

3.3.1. Regret functions and compromise solutions

Let the satisficing set S of Section 3.2.2 be a set of only one point y^*. That is, y^* is a unique target. Typically, when each criterion $f_i, i = 1, \ldots, q$, is characterized by 'more is better', one can set $y^* = (y_1^*, \ldots, y_q^*)$ where $y_i^* = \sup\{f_i(x) \mid x \in X\}$. In this case, y^* is called an *ideal (or utopia) point* because usually y^* is not attainable. Note that, individually, the y_i^* may be attainable. But to find a point y^* which can simultaneously maximize each $f_i, i = 1, \ldots, q$, is usually very difficult.

In group decision problems, if each criterion represents a player's payoff, then y^*, if obtainable, would make each player happy because it would simultaneously maximize each player's payoff. Even if one is a dictator, he cannot do better tha y^* for himself. As y^* is usually not attainable, a compromise is needed, if no other alternative is available to dissolve the group conflict. This offers a natural explanation of why the solution to be introduced is called a *compromise solution*. (See [44].) The reader can extend this explanation easily to multiple criteria problems.

Now, given $y \in Y$, the *regret* of using y instead of obtaining the *ideal* point y^* may be approximated by the distance between y and y^*. Thus, we define the (group) regret of using y by

$$r(y) = \| y - y^* \|, \tag{3.3}$$

where $\| y - y^* \|$ is the distance from y to y^* according to some specified norm. Typically, the ℓ_p-norm will be used in our discussion because of its ease in understanding, unless otherwise specified. To make this more specific, define for $p \geq 1$,

$$r(y; p) = \| y - y^* \|_p = \left[\sum_i |y_i - y_i^*|^p \right]^{1/p} \tag{3.4}$$

and

$$r(y; \infty) = \max\{|y_i - y_i^*|, i = 1, \ldots, q\}. \tag{3.5}$$

Then $r(y; p)$ is a measurement of regret from y to y^* according to the ℓ_p-norm.

Definition 3.2. The compromise solution with respect to the ℓ_p-norm is $y^p \in Y$, which minimizes $r(y; p)$ over Y; *or* is $x^p \in X$, which minimizes $r(f(x); p)$ over X.

Remark 3.2. In group decision problems, $r(y; p)$ may be interpreted as group regret and the compromise solution y^p is the one which minimizes the group regret in order to maintain a 'cooperative group spirit'. As the parameter p varies, the solution y^p can change.

Note that $r(y; p)$ treats each $|y_i^* - y_i|$ as having the same importance in forming the group regret. In multiple criteria problems, if the criteria have different degrees of importance, then a weight vector $w = (w_1, w_2, \ldots, w_q)$, $w \geq 0$, may be assigned to signal the different degrees of importance. In this case, we define

$$r(y; p, w) = \|y - y^*\|_{p,w}$$

$$= \left[\sum_i w_i^p |y_i - y_i^*|^p\right]^{1/p}$$

$$= \left[\sum_i |w_i y_i - w_i y_i^*|^p\right]^{1/p}. \tag{3.6}$$

The concept of compromise solutions can then naturally be extended to include the regret function of (3.6).

Definition 3.3. The compromise solution with respect to $r(y; p, w)$ of (3.6) is $y^{pw} \in Y$, which minimizes $r(y; p, w)$ over Y; or is $x^{pw} \in X$, which minimizes $r(f(x); p, w)$ over X.

Remark 3.3. Observe that the weight vector w as in (3.6) has the effect of changing the scale of each criterion. Once the scale is adjusted (i.e., by $w_i y_i = w_i f_i(x)$ for all $i = 1, \ldots, q$), the regret function is reduced to that of equal weight. Thus, in studying the properties of compromise solutions, without loss of generality, one may focus on the equal weight case. We shall assume the equal weight case from now on, unless specified otherwise.

Remark 3.4. Observe that the compromise solution is *not scale independent*. Scale independence, an important criterion in group decision problems, can prevent players from artificially changing the scale to obtain a better arbitration for themselves. Note that when the scale of $f_i(x)$ or y_i is changed and the weight of importance of each criterion is changed, so is the compromise solution.

Remark 3.5. Compromise solutions with proper assumptions enjoy a number of properties such as feasibility, least group regret, no dictatorship, Pareto optimality, uniqueness, symmetry, independence of irrelevant alternatives, continuity, monotonicity and boundedness. In terms of parameter p (associated with p-norms), we may say that when $p = 1$, the sum of the group utility is most emphasized and when $p = \infty$, the individual regret of the group is most emphasized. Being limited by space, we refer the reader to [13, 44, 46] for the details and further exploration.

Remark 3.6. The concept of compromise solutions implicitly has assumed a very strong preference assumption. Because of the numerical ordering by regret function, there is no ambiguity in preference comparison. For any two points y^1 and y^2, either y^1 is better, worse or equivalent to y^2. Exactly one of the three case must happen (see Example 2.2). There are no such things as 'indefinite' sets in the preference of compromise solutions. Before we finally use this assumption, precaution is needed to verify that it is fulfilled; otherwise, a misleading solution may result.

3.3.2. Computing compromise solutions

3.3.2.1. The ideal point as the target point. To find a compromise solution when the ideal point is the target point, we have to solve $q + 1$ mathematical programming problems. The first q problems are to find the utopia or ideal point, $y^* = (y_1^*, \ldots, y_q^*)$ where $y_i^* = \max\{f_i(x) \mid x \in X\}$. The last one is to find the compromise solution y^p. Suppose that X contains only countable points. We will have $q + 1$ integer programming problems. Otherwise, if X is a region, we will have $q + 1$ nonlinear programming problems.

Suppose X and $f_i(x)$, $i = 1, \ldots, q$, have some special structure. More efficient computational techniques are available. For instance, if X is a convex set and each $f_i(x)$ is concave, then we have first q concave programming and then a convex programming (because $r(f(x); p)$ is convex under the assumptions). If X is a polyhedron defined by a system of linear inequalities and each $f_i(x)$ is linear, then the ideal points y^* can be found by q simple linear programming problems. Furthermore, the compromise solutions of y^1 and y^∞ can be found by a linear programming problem (the other compromise solution y^p, $1 < p < \infty$, can be found by convex programming). See [46] for details.

3.3.3.2. General target points and goal programming. The computation for the compromise solution with general target point can be slightly more complicated. This is due to the possibility that $y_i^* \geq y_i$ for all $y \in Y$ and $i = 1, \ldots, q$ may no longer hold. The following method of changing variables can be of help.

Lemma 3.1. *Let*

$$d_i^+ = \begin{cases} y_i - y_i^* & \text{if } y_i > y_i^* , \\ 0 & \text{otherwise} ; \end{cases}$$

$$d_i^- = \begin{cases} y_i^* - y_i & \text{if } y_i < y_i^* , \\ 0 & \text{otherwise} . \end{cases}$$

Then:
  (i) $y_i^* - y_i = d_i^- - d_i^+$,
  (ii) $|y_i^* - y_i| = d_i^- + d_i^+$,
  (iii) $d_i^+, d_i^- \geq 0$.

Note that d_i^+ is the value of y_i exceeding y_i^* (like a surplus variable) and d_i^- is the value of y_i below y_i^* (like a slack variable). The proof of the lemma is straightforward.

Lemma 3.2. *The definition of d_i^+ and d_i^- in Lemma 3.1 is satisfied if and only if d_i^+ and d_i^- are nonnegative and satisfy*:

$$y_i^* - y_i = d_i^- - d_i^+ , \qquad d_i^+ \cdot d_i^- = 0 .$$

Now given a target point y^* the compromise solution with ℓ_p-distance can be found by solving:

Program 3.2.

$$\min \sum_i |y_i^* - f_i(x)|^p = \min[r(f(x); p)]^p \tag{3.7}$$

$$\text{s.t.} \quad g(x) \leq 0 .$$

Note that since $[r(f(x); p)]^p$ is a strictly increasing function of $r(f(x); p)$, x^0 minimizes $[r(f(x); p)]^p$ if and only if it minimizes $r(f(x); p)$. The form of (3.7) makes it easier to find the compromise solution.

We now can apply Lemma 3.1 and 3.2 to remove the sign of the absolute values in (3.7) and get:

Program 3.3.

$$\min \sum_{i=1}^{q} (d_i^- + d_i^+)^p$$

$$\text{s.t.} \quad y_i^* - f_i(x) = d_i^- - d_i^+ , \quad i = 1, 2, \ldots, q ,$$

$$d_i^+, d_i^- \geq 0, \quad i = 1, 2, \ldots, q ,$$

$$g(x) \leq 0 .$$

Note that because of redundancy, the constraints of $d_i^+ \cdot d_i^- = 0$, $i = 1, \ldots, q$, are dropped.

Theorem 3.2. *Given a target point* y^*, x^0 *is the compromise solution with respect to the* ℓ_p*-distance if and only if* x^0 *solves Program 3.3.*

Remark 3.7. (i) Suppose that all $f_i(x)$, $i = 1, \ldots, q$, and $g(x)$ are linear. Then Program 3.3 for ℓ_1-compromise solutions reduces to a linear program typically known as (linear) *goal programming*. By adding weights to or imposing lexicographical ordering on the criteria one can generalize the concept discussed here to a variety of goal programming formats. One notes that goal programming is a special class in the domain of compromise solutions. The major advantages of goal programming and ℓ_1-compromise solutions are that they are easily understood and that they can be easily computed by linear programs.

(ii) When all $f_i(x)$, $i = 1, \ldots, q$, and $g(x)$ are linear, Program 3.3 for ℓ_2-compromise solutions becomes a quadratic program. The program can be solved without major difficulty.

(iii) When all $f_i(x)$, $i = 1, \ldots, q$, and $g(x)$ are linear, Program 3.3 for ℓ_∞-compromise solutions becomes a linear program.

3.3.3. Interactive methods of compromise models

For nontrivial decision problems, an optimal decision usually cannot be reached by applying the compromise solution only once. The following interactive method, according to Figure 3.1, may be helpful.

Box (1): Identifying X, f and y^* is an art that requires careful observation and conversation with the decision maker. (See Chapter 9 of [46] for further discussion.) The target point y^*, weight vector w and p for ℓ_p-distance may be more difficult to specify precisely. However, one can use the ideal point as the first step of approximation for y^*, select some representative weights for w and let $p = 1, 2, \infty$ to begin.

Box (2): One can locate compromise solutions according to Program 3.3 for the specified values of y^*, w and p.

Box (3): All relevant information obtained in Box (1) and (2) can be presented to the decision maker. These include X, f, Y, ideal points y_i^*, $i = 1, \ldots, q$, the optimal vector value which maximizes the i-th criterion, and the compromise solutions y^1, y^2, y^∞ with their weights and norms.

Box (4) and (6): If an optimal solution is reached in Box (3) and the decision maker is satisfied, the process is terminated at Box (6); otherwise, we go to Box (5) to obtain more information.

Box (5): Through conversation, we may obtain new information on X, f, y^*, weight vector w and norm parameter p. Note that each of these five elements may change with time. To help the decision maker locate or change the target point, one may use the 'one at a time method'. That is, only one value of f_i or

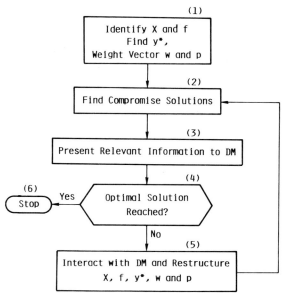

Fig. 3.1.

y_i, $i = 1, \ldots, q$, is to be changed and the rest are to remain unchanged. One may ask the decision maker: "Since no satisfactory solution is obtained with the current target point y^*, would it be possible to decrease (or increase) the value of y_i^*? And, if so, by how much?" This kind of suggestive question may help the decision maker think hard and carefully of possible changes in the target points. The other method is called the 'pairwise trade-off method'. We first select two criteria, say f_i and f_j, and then ask: "To maintain the same degree of satisfaction for the target point, everything else being equal, how many units of f_j must be increased in order to compensate a one-unit decrease in f_i?" Again, this kind of suggestive question can help the decision maker think hard and carefully of the possible changes in the target points. Finally, we recall that the target point may be regarded as the satisficing set containing a single satisficing solution. Thus, by locating the satsificing set, we may locate the target point.

Remark 3.8. Comparing Section 3.2 with Section 3.3, we know that satisficing models are more general and flexible in applications, while compromise models are more specific and rigid. The former is loose while the latter makes sense only when strong assumptions are satisfied. However, with flexible interpretation and artful applications in interaction with the decision maker, the two methods can complement each other. After all, both concepts stem from the goal seeking assumption and try to minimize the distance from the criteria space Y to a set of satisficing points or a target point. In a broader perspective, both models are the same.

3.4. Further comments

Utilizing human goal-seeking behavior, we have described the main concepts of satisficing and compromise solutions. In a real world, although specifying the satisficing set or the target point is not trivial, we can always start with the ideal point and then interact with the decision maker as to gradually reach the final decision. For more details see Chapter 4 of [46]. There is a rich literature related to satisficing and compromise models. For instance, for goal programming see [3, 25, 28] and those quoted therein; for different kinds of norms or penalty functions and modifications see [15, 24, 31] and the citations therein; for restructuring ideal points see [49].

4. Value functions

Numerical systems, as a great invention of human beings, have a prevailing impact on our culture and thinking. It is natural and important for us to ask: is it possible to express our preference over the outcomes in terms of numbers so that the larger the number the stronger the preference, and if it is, how do we do it?

In contrast to the concept of minimizing the distance from the ideal point or satisficing concept as discussed in Section 3, there is a school of thought that each outcome has 'utility' to the decision maker and the decision maker tends to or should choose the one which maximizes his/her 'utility'. The following are some immediate questions: under what conditions can we represent a preference structure by the ordering of a value function? Can we use additive or monotonic value functions to represent the preference structure? How do we construct such value functions? To avoid confusion, we use *value functions* instead of utility functions in our discussion because utility functions are usually reserved for the discussion when uncertainty in the outcomes is involved.

To facilitate our presentation and understanding we shall start with what can be said about preference if a value function exists (Section 4.1). We then discuss what would be the minimum requirement for a value function to exist (Section 4.2). As the additive and monotonic value functions play an important role in applications, we shall devote Section 4.3 to the discussion of the conditions for additive and monotonic value functions to exist. Some brief accounts of existing methods of constructing value functions will be discussed in Section 4.4.

4.1. Revealed preference from a value function

Suppose that our preference structure $\mathcal{P}$ can be presented by a value function $v: Y \to R^1$ so that $y^1 > y^2$ iff $v(y^1) > v(y^2)$ and $y^1 \sim y^2$ iff $v(y^1) = v(y^2)$ and that Y is convex and v is continuous on Y. We immediately can obtain the following properties for $\mathcal{P}$. (See Example 2.2.)

(i) $\{?\} = \emptyset$.

(ii) $\{>\}$ and $\{\gtrsim\}$ are transitive.

(iii) Let $\{\tilde{Y}\}$ be the collection of all isovalued curves (or surfaces) of v in Y. Note that different isovalued curves never interset. Since Y is convex and v is continuous, $V = v[Y]$ is an interval which contains dense countable rational numbers. Their corresponding isovalued curves are thus countable and dense in $\{\tilde{Y}\}$.

(iv) $\{y<\}$ and $\{y>\}$ are open sets in Y for every $y \in Y$.

Remark 4.1. (i) The property (i) is essential. If $\{?\} \neq \emptyset$ then value function representation cannot offer meaningful numerical ordering. We shall assume that $\{?\} = \emptyset$ throughout this section. (ii) Properties (i)–(ii) together means that $\mathscr{P}$ is a weak order in literature. (iii) Properties (i)–(iii) conversely assure the existence of value function representation (Theorem 4.1). (iv) Properties (i)–(ii) and (iv) conversely assure the existence of *continuous* value function representation (Theorem 4.3).

4.2. Existence of value functions

Recall (Remark 4.1) that throughout this section we assume $\{?\} = \emptyset$ and that $\mathscr{P}$ is a weak order iff $\{?\} = \emptyset$ and both $\{>\}$ and $\{\gtrsim\}$ are transitive. If $\mathscr{P}$ is a weak order then $\{\sim\}$ is an equivalent relation. If we define $\tilde{Y} = \{\tilde{y}\}$ as the *collection of all indifference classes $\tilde{y}$ in Y*, we can define $>'$ over $\tilde{Y}$ as the preference on the equivalence classes:

Definition 4.1. Define $>'$ *over $\tilde{Y}$* such that $\tilde{y}^1 >' \tilde{y}^2$ iff for any $y^1 \in \tilde{y}^1$, $y^2 \in \tilde{y}^2$, we have $y^1 > y^2$, where $\tilde{y}^i \in \tilde{Y}$ is the set of points indifferent to y^i.

Throughout this section Y will be assumed to be convex. We define a value function as follows:

Definition 4.2. $v : Y \to R^1$ is called a *value function* for $\mathscr{P}$ on Y if for every $y^1, y^2 \in Y$, we have $y^1 > y^2$ iff $v(y^1) > v(y^2)$, and $y^1 \sim y^2$ iff $v(y^1) = v(y^2)$.

Definition 4.3. A subset $A \subseteq Y$ is said to be $>$-*dense in Y iff* $y^1 > y^2$, $y^1, y^2 \in Y$, but $y^1, y^2 \notin A$ implies that there exists $z \in A$ such that $y^1 > z$ and $z > y^2$.

For instance, the rational numbers are '$<$'-dense in R^1, since tor any $r_1 < r_2, r_1, r_2$ not rational, there exists a rational number $r_3 \in R^1$ such that $r_1 < r_3 < r_2$. The following is a well-known result (see [12]; review Remark 4.1(iii)).

Theorem 4.1. *There exists a value function v for $\mathscr{P}$ on Y iff* (i) *on Y is a weak order, and* (ii) *there is a countable subset of $\tilde{Y}$ which is $>'$-dense in $\tilde{Y}$.*

Note that the Pareto preference (Example 2.4) on R^q, $q \geq 2$, is not a weak order (because $\{?\} \neq \emptyset$). Therefore, it cannot be represented by a value function. The lexicographic ordering preference on R^q, $q \geqq 2$, cannot be represented by a value function either, even though it is a weak order, because $\{y^0 \sim\} = \{y^0\}$, implying that there exists no countable subset of $\tilde{Y}$ which is $>'$-dense in Y.

In practice it may be very tedious if not impossible to verify the countability condition of Theorem 4.1. The following theorem of [12] is helpful.

Theorem 4.2. *Let Y be a rectangular subset of R^q, such that on Y: (i) $\mathscr{P}$ is a weak order; (ii) $y^1 \geqslant y^2$ implies $y^1 > y^2$; and (iii) $y^1 > y^2$, $y^2 > y^3$ implies that there exist $a \in]0, 1[$, $b \in]0, 1[$ such that $ay^1 + (1 - a)y^3 > y^2$ and $y^2 > by^1 + (1 - b)y^3$. Then there exists a value function v for $\mathscr{P}$ on Y.*

We shall now proceed with some interesting results from topology. Let $\mathscr{T}$ be the topology on Y so that $(Y, \mathscr{T})$ is a topological space. Note that Y is separable *iff* Y contains a countable subset, and the closure of the subset is Y. Corresponding to Remark 4.1(iv), the following is well known (see [8]).

Theorem 4.3. *There exists a continuous value function v for $\mathscr{P}$ on Y in the topology $\mathscr{T}$ if: (i) $\mathscr{P}$ on Y is a weak order; (ii) $(Y, \mathscr{T})$ is connected and separable; and (iii) $\{y<\}$, $\{y>\} \in \mathscr{T}$, for every $y \in Y$.*

4.3. Additive and monotonic value functions and preference separability

Assume that there are q different criteria (or attributes), the outcome space Y is the Cartesian product $Y = \Pi_{i=1}^{q} Y_i$, where each Y_i is a connected interval in R^1 and let the index set of criteria be $Q = \{1, 2, \ldots, q\}$. Given a partition of Q, $\{I_1, \ldots, I_m\}$, $I_j \neq Q$ ($m \leqq q$), (i.e., $\bigcup_{k=1}^{m} I_k = Q$ and $I_i \cap I_j = \emptyset$ if $i \neq j$), we denote the complement of I_j by $\bar{I}_j = Q \backslash I_j$.

We introduce the following notation:
  (i) $z_k = y_{I_k}$ is the vector with $\{y_i \mid i \in I_k\}$ as its components, $k = 1, \ldots, m$,
  (ii) $Y_{I_k} = \Pi_{i \in I_k} Y_i$,
  (iii) $y = (y_{I_1}, \ldots, y_{I_m}) = (z_1, \ldots, z_m)$.
Note that $y_{I_k} \in Y_{I_k}$.
The existence of an additive and monotonic value function for $\mathscr{P}$ depends primarily on preference separability:

Definition 4.4. Given that $I \subset Q$, $I \neq Q$, $z \in Y_I$ and $w \in Y_{\bar{I}}$, we say that z (or I) is *preference separable*, or $>$-*separable*, iff $(z^0, w^0) > (z^1, w^0)$ for any $z^0, z^1 \in Y_I$ and some $w^0 \in Y_{\bar{I}}$ implies that $(z^0, w) > (z^1, w)$ for all $w \in Y_{\bar{I}}$.

Some authors use a different terminology. Keeney and Raiffa (see [26]) for instance use the term preferential independence for preference separability.

Observe that Pareto preference, lexicographic ordering and preference of compromise solutions are all preference separable with respect to each subset of Q.

Definition 4.4 implies that whenever z is $>$-separable, and w is fixed, z^0 is preferred to z^1 no matter where w is fixed, because $(z^0, w^0) > (z^1, w^0)$ for any $w^0 \in Y_{\bar{I}}$. This means that if z (or I) is $>$-separable we can separate it from the remaining variables in the process of constructing the value function v. However, I being $>$-separable does not imply that $\bar{I}$ is $>$-separable, even if $\mathcal{P}$ does have a value function representation.

Example 4.1. Let $\mathcal{P}$ be represented by $v(y) = y_2 \exp(y_1)$, $y_1, y_2 \in R^1$. We see, that y_2 or $I_2 = \{2\}$ is $>$-separable, since $\exp(y_1) > 0$. However, y_2 can be negative, so that y_1 or $\bar{I}_2 = I_1 = \{1\}$ are *not* $>$-separable.

Definition 4.5. A value function $v(y)$ is *additive iff* there are $v_i(y_i): Y_i \to R^1$, $i = 1, \ldots, q$, such that $v(y) = \sum_{i=1}^q v_i(y_i)$.

Definition 4.6. If $\{I_1, \ldots, I_m\}$ and $z = (z_1, \ldots, z_m)$ are a partition of Q and y respectively, and if $v(z) = (v_1(z_1), \ldots, v_m(z_m))$, then v is said to be *strictly increasing in v_i*, $i \in \{1, \ldots, m\}$, *iff* v is strictly increasing in v_i, with v_k $(k = 1, \ldots, m; k \neq i)$ fixed.

We shall write $v(z) = v(v_k(z_k), \bar{v}_k(\bar{z}_k))$, where $\bar{v}_k(\bar{z}_k)$ denotes the functions of the variables z_j other than z_k (i.e., $j \neq k$), whenever we wish to emphasize z_k. Note that if $v_k(z_k^0) > v_k(z_k^1)$, z_k^0 and $z_k^1 \in Y_{I_k}$, then $(z_k^0, \bar{z}_k) > (z_k^1, \bar{z}_k)$ for any fixed $\bar{z}_k$, because of the monotonicity.
The following theorems of [46] link additive and monotonic value functions to $>$-separability in an obvious way.

Theorem 4.4. *If $v(y)$ is additive then $\mathcal{P}$ enjoys $>$-separability for any subset of Q.*

Theorem 4.5. *If $v(y)$ as defined in Definition 4.6 is strictly increasing in v_i, $i \in \{1, \ldots, m\}$, then z_i and I_i are $>$-separable.*

The (partial) converse of the above theorem will be the focus of the remaining discussion of this section.

Definition 4.7. Let $I \subset Q$, $I \neq Q$. I is said to be *essential* if there exists some $y_{\bar{I}} \in Y_{\bar{I}}$ such that not all elements of Y_I are indifferent at $y_{\bar{I}}$. I is *strictly essential* if *for each* $y_{\bar{I}} \in Y_{\bar{I}}$ not all elements of Y_I are indiffeent at $y_{\bar{I}}$. If I is not essential it is called *inessential*.

Obviously, to be essential, Y_I must consist of a least two points. If I is inessential then it does not need to be considered when the value function is constructed. It is therefore innocent to assume that each $i \in Q$ is essential.
We shall now provide several theorems, most of which are due to [9] and [17]. These theorems partially reverse Theorem 4.5. We first introduce:

Assumption 4.1. (i) Each topological space $(Y_i, \mathcal{T}_i)$, $i = 1, \ldots, q$, and thus $(Y, \mathcal{T})$, with $Y = \Pi_{i=1}^q Y_i$, $\mathcal{T} = \Pi_{i=1}^q \mathcal{T}_i$ is topologically separable and connected;

(ii) $\mathcal{P}$ on Y is a weak order, and for each $y \in Y$, $\{y>\} \in \mathcal{T}$ and $\{y<\} \in \mathcal{T}$.

If Assumption 4.1 holds, then the existence of a continuous value function v is guaranteed by Theorem 4.3. Theorems 4.6–4.9 will give us a more precise specification of the form of v. First, we shall consider special cases (Theorems 4.6 and 4.7) of [9] which we shall subsequently present in a generalized form (Theorems 4.8 and 4.9), as proposed by Gorman [17].

Theorem 4.6. *Assume that Assumption 4.1 holds.* $v(y)$ *can be written as* $v(y) = F(v_1(y_1), \ldots, v_q(y_q))$, *where* F *is continuous and strictly increasing in* v_i $(i = 1, \ldots, q)$ *which are all continuous, iff each* $\{i\}$, $i = 1, \ldots, q$, *is* $>$-*separable.*

Theorem 4.7. *Assume that Assumption 4.1 holds. If there are at least three components of Q that are essential, then we can write* $v(y) = \Sigma_{i=1}^q v_i(y_i)$, *where each v_i is continuous, iff each possible subset $I \subset Q$ is $>$-separable.*

Theorem 4.8. *Let $\{I_0, I_1, \ldots, I_m\}$ and $(z_0, z_1, \ldots, z_m)$ be a partition of Q and y respectively. Assume that Assumption 4.1 holds. Then*

$$v(y) = F(z_0, v_1(z_1), \ldots, v_m(z_m)),$$

where $F(z_0, \cdot)$ is continuous and strictly increasing in v_i $(i = 1, \ldots, m)$, iff each I_i, $i = 1, \ldots, m$, is $>$-separable.

Note that if $I_0 = \emptyset$, and each z_i contains only one y_i and $q = m$, then Theorem 4.8 reduces to Theorem 4.6.

Theorem 4.9. *Let $\mathcal{I}^* = \{I_1, \ldots, I_m\}$ and $(z_1, \ldots, z_m)$ be a partition of Q and y respectively. Assume that Assumption 4.1 holds, $m \geq 3$, and let $\{i\}$ be strictly essential for each $i \in Q$. Then we can write*

$$v(y) = \sum_{i=1}^m v_i(z_i)$$

iff $\bigcup_{k \in S} I_k$, $S \subset M = \{1, \ldots, m\}$ (i.e., the union of any subsets of $\mathcal{I}^*$) is $>$-separable.

Observe that if $\mathcal{I}^* = \{\{i\} | i \in Q\}$, Theorem 4.9 reduces to Theorem 4.7.

Additive value functions play an important role in applications. Theorem 4.7 and 4.9 are useful but very tedious to verify. Note that there are $2q - 2$ subsets of Q. Hence, it is almost technically inhibitive to verify $>$-separability for each subset of Q, especially when Q is large. The following new results of Yu and Takeda [48] offer a relief.

Definition 4.8. (i) Two subsets I_1 and I_2 of Q are said to *overlap* iff none of the following: $I_1 \cap I_2$, $I_1 \backslash I_2$, $I_2 \backslash I_1$ are empty.

(ii) Let $\mathscr{I}$ be a collection of subsets of Q. Then: (1) $\mathscr{I}$ is said to be *connected* if for any A, B of $\mathscr{I}$ there is a sequence $\{I_1, I_2, \ldots, I_s\}$ of $\mathscr{I}$ such that I_{k-1} overlaps with I_k ($k = 2, \ldots, s$), and $I_1 = A$ and $I_s = B$; and (2) $\mathscr{I}$ is $>$-*separable* if each element of $\mathscr{I}$ is $>$-separable.

Definition 4.9. A collection of nonempty subsets of Q, $\mathscr{I} = \{I_1, \ldots, I_r\}$, $r \geq 2$, is an *additive covering* of Q if (i) $\mathscr{I}$ is connected, (ii) Q is contained by the union of the elements of $\mathscr{I}$ and (iii) each element of Q is contained by no more than two elements of $\mathscr{I}$.

Note that additive coverings of Q can be meaningfully defined only when Q has $q \geq 3$ elements. That $q \geq 3$ will be assumed from now on.

Example 4.2. Let $Q = \{1, 2, 3, 4, 5\}$. Then $\mathscr{I}_1 = \{\{1, 2\}, \{2, 3\}, \{3, 4\}, \{4, 5\}\}$ and $\mathscr{I}_2 = \{\{1, 2, 3\}, \{3, 4\}, \{1, 5\}\}$ are two additive coverings of Q. But $\mathscr{I}_3 = \{\{1, 2, 3\}, \{2, 3, 5\}, \{3, 4\}\}$ is *not* an additive covering of Q because 3 is contained by three elements of $\mathscr{I}_3$.

Given an additive covering $\mathscr{I} = \{I_1, \ldots, I_r\}$, we define:

$$A_{ij} = I_i \cap I_j, \tag{4.1}$$

$$\hat{I}_k = I_k \backslash (\bigcup \{I_i \in \mathscr{I} \mid i \neq k\}) \tag{4.2}$$

where $i, j, k = 1, \ldots, r$.

Note, $\hat{I}_k$ is the collection of elements in I_k which are not contained by other I_i, $i \neq k$. By definition, all elements of $\{A_{ij} \mid i > j\}$ and $\{\hat{I}_k \mid k = 1, \ldots, r\}$ are *mutually disjoint* and each element of Q must be in some I_i and so must be in some A_{ij} or $\hat{I}_k$. Thus, the totality of all nonempty A_{ij} and $\hat{I}_k$ forms a partition of Q. For convenience, such collection of $\{A_{ij} \mid i > j\}$ and $\hat{I}_k$, $k = 1, \ldots, r$, will be denoted by

$$\mathscr{D}(\mathscr{I}) = \{J_t \mid t = 1, \ldots, m\} \tag{4.3}$$

where $J_t \neq \emptyset$ is either an element of $\{A_{ij}\}$ or an element of $\{\hat{I}_k\}$.

Since $\mathscr{D}(\mathscr{I})$ is a partition of Q, $\mathscr{D}(\mathscr{I})$ must have $m \geq 3$ elements. In order to see this point, we first observe that if $m = 1$, then the single element of $\mathscr{D}(\mathscr{I})$ is either of the type of A_{ij} or that of $\hat{I}_k$ defined by (4.1) and (4.2) respectively. In either case $\mathscr{D}(\mathscr{I})$ cannot be a partition of Q. When $m = 2$, there are three possible kinds of combinations for $\mathscr{D}(\mathscr{I})$: $\{A_{ij}, A_{kl}\}$, $\{A_{ij}, \hat{I}_k\}$ and $\{\hat{I}_k, \hat{I}_j\}$.

Again, none of these three kinds can be a partition of Q without contradiction. We summarize the above into:

Lemma 4.1. *For each additive covering $\mathscr{I}$ of Q, there is a unique partition $\mathscr{D}(\mathscr{I})$ of Q which is derived by (4.1)–(4.3). $\mathscr{D}(\mathscr{I})$ contains $m \geq 3$ elements.*

The following is a main result.

Theorem 4.10. *Suppose that the preference structure $\mathscr{P}$ on Y can be represented by a continuous value function and enjoys the following properties:*
(i) each $\{i\}$ of Q is strictly essential; and
(ii) there is an additive covering $\mathscr{I} = \{I_1, \ldots, I_r\}$, $r \geq 2$, of Q such that $\mathscr{I}$ is $\succ$-separable.
Then the preference can be additively represented by

$$v(y) = v(z_1, \ldots, z_m) = \sum_{t=1}^{m} v_t(z_t) \tag{4.4}$$

where $(z_1, \ldots, z_m)$ is the partition of y corresponding to $\mathscr{D}(\mathscr{I})$ defined in (4.3).

Example 4.3. Let $Q = \{1, 2, \ldots, 9\}$ and $\mathscr{I}_1 = \{\{1, 2, 3\}, \{4, 5, 6\}, \{7, 8, 9\}, \{1, 4, 7\}\}$. (See Figure 4.1.)

Then $\mathscr{D}(\mathscr{I}_1) = \{\{1\}, \{4\}, \{7\}, \{2, 3\}, \{5, 6\}, \{8, 9\}\}$ is the corresponding partition of Q. If the assumptions of Theorem 4.10 hold, we can write

$$v(y) = v_1(y_1) + v_4(y_4) + v_7(y_7) + v_{23}(y_2, y_3)$$
$$+ v_{56}(y_5, y_6) + v_{89}(y_8, y_9).$$

Now if we add $I_5 = \{2, 5, 8\}$ to $\mathscr{I}_1$, we obtain

$$\mathscr{I}_2 = \{\{1, 2, 3\}, \{4, 5, 6\}, \{7, 8, 9\}, \{1, 4, 7\}, \{2, 5, 8\}\}.$$

and the corresponding partition (see Figure 4.1),

$$\mathscr{D}(\mathscr{I}_2) = \{\{1\}, \{2\}, \{3\}, \{4\}, \{5\}, \{6\}, \{7\}, \{8\}, \{9\}\}.$$

Now suppose that the assumptions of Theorem 4.10 holds. Then we can write

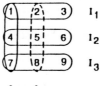

Fig. 4.1.

the corresponding value function as $v(y) = \Sigma_{i=1}^{9} v_i(y_i)$. Note that there are only five subsets of Q in $\mathscr{I}_2$ to be verified for $\succ$-separability.

For further applications such as orthogonal square designs and progressive decomposition of the form of value function the reader is referred to [48].

4.4. Elicitation techniques for constructing value functions

Although space limitations prevent us from discussing elicitation methods in detail, it is still useful to give a brief summary of frequently used general classes of methods to construct value functions to represent preference information. All methods mentioned below are discussed in detail in Chapter 6 of [46].

One large class of techniques is a direct application of calculus. These methods are usually based on the construction of approximate indifference curves. This class includes methods using trade-off ratios, tangent planes, gradients and line integrals. Some of these methods are also discussed in [46].

A second class has specifically been developed for the case of additive value functions. A well-known method in this class is the Midvalue Method [26], which is based on pairwise information on $\{\sim\}$ and $\{\succ\}$.

A third class takes into account the fact that usually the revealed preference contains conflicting information, making it a virtually impossible task to construct a consistent value function. The conflicting nature of the information may be due to an unclear perception on the part of the DM of his true preference structure, or imperfect and/or incorrectly used interaction techniques. The objective of these methods is to find a value function and/or ideal point which minimizes the inconsistencies. Some of the techniques, such as regression analysis, are based on statistical theory, others on mathematical programming models, such as least distance and minimal inconsistency methods (using some appropriate ℓ_p-norm). Included are methods based on weight ratios, pairwise preference information, or the distance from a (perhaps unknown) ideal/target point (see Section 6.3.4 of [46] and the citations therein). Another group of methods in this class is that of eigen weight vectors (see e.g., [34], [4], and Section 6.3.3 of [46]). Yet another group uses holistic assessment. An example is the orthogonal design of experiment (see Section 6.3.3.2 of [46] and citations therein).

Each method has its strengths and weaknesses. The selection of the best/correct method is truly an art and poses a challenge for analyst and the decision maker.

5. Nondominated solutions and cone domination structures

5.1. Introduction

In the previous two sections, we focus on preference structures which implicitly or explicitly assume that $\{?\} = \emptyset$. No ambiguity exists in preference.

Once the proper regret function or value function is determined, MCDM becomes a one-dimensional comparison or a mathematical programming problem. In this section we shall tackle the problems with $\{?\} \neq \emptyset$.

Recall (Definition 2.2) that $\{y^0<\}$; $\{y^0>\}$, $\{y^0\sim\}$ and $\{y^0?\}$ are the sets of points in Y which are better (preferred), worse (less preferred), equivalent and indefinite to y^0.

For simplicity, we shall rewrite

$$\{y^0<\} = y^0 + P(y^0)$$

with $P(y^0)$ as the set of *preferred* factors,

$$\{y^0>\} = y^0 + D(y^0)$$

with $D(y^0)$ as the set of *dominated* factors,

$$\{y^0\sim\} = y^0 + I(y^0)$$

with $I(y^0)$ as the set of *indifferent* or *equivalent* factors, and

$$\{y^0?\} = y^0 + U(y^0)$$

with $U(y^0)$ as the set of *unclarified* or *indefinite* factors.

Example 5.1. (i) In Pareto preference (Example 2.4), for each y, $P(y) = \Lambda^{\geq} = \{d \in R^q \,|\, d \geq 0\}$, $D(y) = \Lambda^{\leq}$, $P(y) = -D(y)$, $I(y) = \{0\}$, $U(y) = R^q \backslash (\Lambda^{\leq} \cup \Lambda^{\geq})$. Note that $\Lambda^{\leq}$ and $\Lambda^{\geq}$ are only $(\frac{1}{2})^q$ of R^q which shrink very rapidly as q is increased. Consequently $U(y)$ increases very rapidly as q is increased.

(ii) If the preference is represented by a concave differentiable value function $v(y)$, then $D(y)$ contains $\{d \,|\, \nabla v(y) \cdot d < 0\}$ which is a 'half' space, no matter what is the dimensionality of Y. Except linear $v(y)$, $D(y)$ is a function of y and in general $D(y) \neq -P(y)$. Note that in general $D(y)$ and $P(y)$ are not convex cones. Nevertheless, if we use the *tangent cones* of $\{y>\}$ and $\{y<\}$ at y to represent the *local* sets of preferred and dominated factors, denoted by $LD(y)$ and $LP(y)$, respectively, then $LD(y)$ and $LP(y)$ can be convex cones and $LD(y) = -LP(y)$. For a detail of such treatment, see Chapter 7 of [46].

In order to simplify our presentation, we shall assume the following throughout this section.

Assumption 5.1. For each $y \in Y$, $D(y)$ and $P(y)$ are convex cones. Furthermore, $D(y) = -P(y)$.

Remark 5.1. Pareto preference (Example 5.1(i)) satisfies Assumption 5.1, so the preference represented by a linear value function. As indicated in Example 5.1(ii), one can use $LD(y)$ and $LP(y)$ to replace $D(y)$ and $P(y)$ respectively when the assumption does not hold. If we do so, our results stated in this section are still valid, but only on local sense (local optimal vs. global optimal). For the details of such treatment and conditions for the local results also to be valid as the global results refer to Chapter 7 of [46].

The following can be easily derived.

Lemma 5.1. (i) *If Assumption 5.1 holds, then* $y^0 \in N[<]$ *iff there is no* $y \in Y$ *such that* $y^0 \in y + D(y)$.

(ii) *If in addition,* $I(y) = \{0\}$ *for all* $y \in Y$ *(as in Pareto preference), then* $N[\lesssim?] = N[<?] \neq \emptyset$ *iff* $N[<]$ *is singleton and* $N[\lesssim?] = N[<]$.

From Lemma 5.1(ii), we see that when $I(y) = \{0\}$ for all $y \in Y$, $N[\lesssim?]$ or $N[<?]$ become an extreme concept, and $N[<]$ become a focus of study. To simplify our presentation, without confusion, from now on (including Section 6) we adopt the following:

Definition 5.1. A point $y^0 \in Y$ is a nondominated point or N-points iff $y^0 \in N[<]$.

In the next subsection, 5.2, we discuss some basic properties of N-points when $D(y)$ is constant. In Section 5.3 we explore the case when $D(y)$ varies with y. Further comments will be offered in Section 5.4.

5.2. Constant cone domination structures and solutions

For simplicity, when $D(y) = \Lambda$ for all y, we shall call Λ the *dominated cone* and denote the set of all nondominated points or 'N-points' by $N(Y, \Lambda)$. The following can be easily verified (for instance, see [45, 46]).

Theorem 5.1. *If* $\Lambda_1 \subset \Lambda_2$ *then* $N(Y, \Lambda_2) \subset N(Y, \Lambda_1)$.

Intuitively, the theorem says that if Λ is larger (thus the unclarified set $U(y)$ is smaller) then the resulting set of N-points will be smaller. That is, if one can have a 'clearer' idea of the preference by having a larger dominated set Λ, then one shall have 'less fuzziness' in the final solution by having a smaller set of N-points. As an extreme, when Λ becomes a half-space, the resulting N-point may likely become unique and the decision problem can be solved with clarity. Maximizing an additive function over Y has a close relation with finding N-points. Toward this end, let us introduce the following concepts:

Definition 5.2. (i) Y is Λ-convex if $Y + \Lambda$ is a convex set;

(ii) the polar cone of Λ is defined by $\Lambda^* = \{\lambda \mid \lambda \cdot d \leq 0 \text{ for all } d \in \Lambda\}$; its interior is denoted by int Λ^*; and

(iii) given $\lambda \in \Lambda^*$, $\lambda \neq 0$, the set of all maximum points in Y with respect to $\lambda \cdot y$ is denoted by $Y^0(\lambda)$.

For further details on cone-convexity see [45, 46].

Theorem 5.2. (i) $\bigcup \{Y^0(\lambda)|\lambda \in \text{int } \lambda^*\} \subset N(Y, \Lambda)$.
(ii) *If Y is Λ-convex and Λ is pointed (that is, $\Lambda \cap (-\Lambda) = \{0\}$), then*

$$N(Y, \Lambda) \subset \cup \{Y^0(\lambda)|\lambda \in \Lambda^*, \lambda \neq 0\} .$$

Note that the theorem states conditions for N-points to be found by maximizing a linear function over Y; (i) is a sufficient condition and (ii) a necessary condition. If one is interested in the entire set of N-points, then the theorem serves as an approximation for the set; (i) is the 'inner' approximation and (ii) the 'outer' approximation for $N(Y, \Lambda)$. The results are derived in [45, 46]; their further refinement can be found in [21]. Note that cone convexity plays a vital role in the derivation. Without it, (ii) can be failed. In Figure 5.1, $Y = Y' \cup \{A, B, C\}$ $\{A, B, C\} = N(Y, \Lambda^{\leqq})$. But $C \not\subset Y^0(\lambda)$ for any $\lambda \in \Lambda^{\geqq}$; $\lambda \neq 0$. Note, $\Lambda^{\geqq}$ is the polar cone of $\Lambda^{\leqq}$. That is to say, C, which may be the final solution, can never be located by maximizing a linear function over Y. In order to overcome this difficulty, let us introduce the following notion.

A cone which is closed polyhedron (for instance, $\Lambda^{\leqq}$) is called a polyhedral cone. If Λ is a polyhedral cone, so is Λ^*. In this case, there are a finite number of vectors $\{H^1, \ldots, H^p\}$ so that Λ^* is the cone generated by $\{H^1, \ldots, H^p\}$. That is,

$$\Lambda^* = \left\{ \sum_{i=1}^{p} a_i H^i \, \middle| \, a_i \in R^1, a_i \geqq 0 \right\} .$$

$\{H^1, \ldots, H^p\}$ will be called a *generator* of Λ^*. As an example, $\Lambda^{\geqq} = (\Lambda^{\leqq})^*$ and $\{(1, 0), (0, 1)\}$ is a generator of $\Lambda^{\geqq}$.

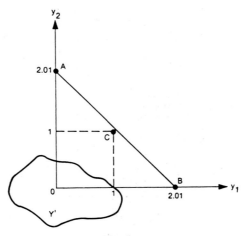

Fig. 5.1.

From now on, unless otherwise specified, whenever Λ is a polyhedral cone we shall assume that $\{H^1, \ldots, H^p\}$ is a generator for Λ^*.

Let $r(j)$ be a vector in R^{p-1} representing $\{r_k \in R^1 | k \neq j, \; k = 1, \ldots, p\}$. Define $Y(r(j)) = \{y \in Y | H^k \cdot y \geq t_k, \; k \neq j, \; k = 1, \ldots, p\}$.

Note that r_k may be regarded as an aspiration level or satisfying level for $H^k \cdot y$.

Theorem 5.3 (Theorem 4.3 of [45]). *Let $\Lambda' = \Lambda \cup \{0\}$ be a polyhedral cone. Then $y^0 \in N(Y, \Lambda)$ if and only if for any arbitrary $j = 1, \ldots, p$, there is $r(j)$ such that y^0 uniquely maximizes $H^j \cdot y$ over $Y(r(j))$.*

Note that the above theorem is very general. No cone convexity is assumed and Y can be any form or any shape. The theorem essentially says that in search of $N(Y, \Lambda)$ by mathematical programming, constraints and objective functions are interchangeable. In Figure 5.1, C, an N-point, can be located by maximizing y_2 over $Y(r(2)) = \{y \in Y | y_1 \geq 0.1\}$ or by maximizing y_1 over $Y(r(1)) = \{y \in Y | y_2 \geq 0.1\}$. In Figure 5.2 we see that y^1 never satisfies the condition in Theorem 5.3 and this is not an N-point; while y^0 satisfies the condition and is an N-point.

Observe that when Λ is not a polyhedral cone, one can always select such a cone that is contained by Λ. In view of Theorem 5.1 we will not miss any N-points if we use a smaller dominated cone to locate them.

5.3. Variable cone domination structures and methods for seeking good solutions

In this subsection we describe a convergent method and a heuristic method to locate $N(Y, D(\cdot))$. To begin, let us assume that each $D(y)$ contains $\Lambda^{\leq}$. Define $\Lambda^0 = \cap \{D(y) | y \in Y\}$ and set $Y^0 = Y$. Note that $\Lambda^0 \supset \Lambda^{\leq}$. Recursively

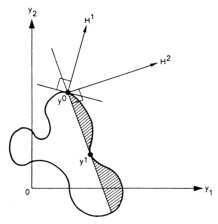

Fig. 5.2.

let us define, for $n = 0, 1, 2, \ldots$.

$$\Lambda^n = \cap \{D(y) \mid y \in Y^n\} \quad \text{and} \quad Y^{n+1} = N(Y^n, \Lambda^n).$$

Then

$$Y^{n+1} \subset Y^n \quad \text{and} \quad \Lambda^{n+1} \supset \Lambda^n.$$

It follows that the sequences converge, say $Y^n \to \tilde{Y}$, $\Lambda^n \to \tilde{\Lambda}$ as $n \to \infty$. Furthermore, it can be shown (see [46]) that for each n, $Y^n \supset N(Y, D(\cdot))$ and $\tilde{Y} \supset N(Y, D(\cdot))$.

The above observation allows us to locate $N(Y, D(\cdot))$ according to Flow Chart 1 ('method 1').

Flow Chart 1 is self-explanatory. Although the method guarantees a convergent set containing the N-points, it may not be effective and efficient. The following heuristic method according to Flow Chart 2 ('method 2') can be more efficient in reaching the final decision at the risk of missing some N-points.

Let us explain method 2 according to Flow Chart 2.

Box (0): We first explore the relationship among the criteria and locate some plausible aspiration levels and trade-offs among the criteria. Then we use Theorem 5.2 or 5.3 to locate a set of initial 'good' alternatives corresponding to

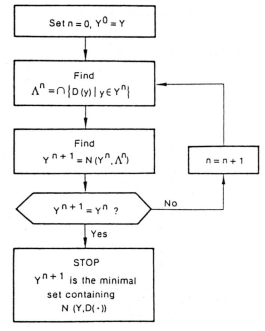

Flow Chart 1.

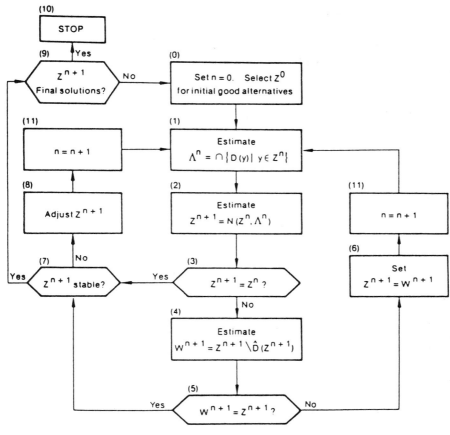

Flow Chart 2.

different aspiration levels and trade-offs, using mathematical programming if necessary. One can also start with the points which respectively maximize the individual criteria. This initial set is denoted by Z^0. It need not contain too many points, but it should be fairly representative as to avoid missing possible N-points.

Box (1): We should first estimate $D(y)$ for some representative points in Z^n and find their intersection for Λ^n. The more representative points considered, the smaller is Λ^n and the less chance there is to miss N-points; but it may take longer to find the final solutions. In estimating $D(y)$, we can use the definition to locate it directly, or we can use the bounds of trade-off ratios to locate it indirectly [46].

Box (2): Here we can use Theorem 5.2 or 5.3 to locate the entire set of Z^{n+1} or to locate a representative set for Z^{n+1}, depending on how much we want to avoid missing some N-points.

Boxes (3) *and* (4): Box (3) is a comparison to see if the process has reached a steady state. If not, the process will continue to Box (4), which is to eliminate those dominated points in Z^{n+1}. Here $\hat{D}(Z^{n+1})$ denotes estimated dominated points in Z^{n+1}, and W^{n+1} be the remaining 'good' alternatives after the elimination.

Boxes (5) *and* (6): Box (5) is a comparison to see if the elimination in Box (4) is effective. If $W^{n+1} = Z^{n+1}$, then Z^{n+1} can be a set of N-points and the process can reach its steady state. Box (6) is to replace Z^{n+1} by W^{n+1} for the next iteration.

Boxes (7)–(10): Z^{n+1} is *stable* if no element in Z^{n+1} is dominated by any other element in Z^{n+1}, and every element outside of Z^{n+1} is dominated by some element in $Z^{n+1} = N(Z^{n+1}, D(\cdot))$. If this condition is fulfilled, Z^{n+1} probably can be the set of all N-points. In Box (9), nondominance is verified either by Theorem 5.2 or 5.3. If Z^{n+1} is the set of all N-points, the process is stopped at Box (10) with Z^{n+1} as the set for the final decision. Otherwise, the process should be repeated again from Box (0). If Z^{n+1} is not stable, then Z^{n+1} contains some dominated points or there are N-points not contained in Z^{n+1}. We shall accordingly either eliminate the dominated points from Z^{n+1} or add new N-points into Z^{n+1}. This adjustment on Z^{n+1} is performed at Box (8).

Box (11): This step is obvious for changing the step variable in the process.

Example 5.2. Consider Y and $D(\cdot)$ given in Figure 5.3. Using the first method, we start with $\Lambda^0 = \Lambda^\leq$ and find $Y^1 = \{y^0, y^1, y^2\}$. Taking $\Lambda^1 = \bigcap \{D(y^j) | j = 1, 2, 3\}$, we have $Y^1 = N(Y^1, \Lambda^1)$. Thus, the process of method 1 converges with $\hat{Y} = Y^1$.

We now use method 2 and start with $Z^0 = \{y^0, y^1, y^2, y^3\}$ and $\Lambda^0 = \Lambda^\leq$ in boxes (1) and (2), respectively. Then Box (2) will produce $Z^1 = \{y^0, y^1, y^2\}$ ($= Y^1$ in method 1). Note that $Z^1 \neq Z^0$. Boxes (3) and (4) will make $W^1 =$

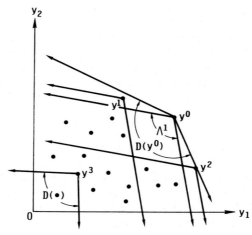

Fig. 5.3.

$\{y^0\} \neq Z^1$. The process then goes through Boxes (5), (6), (11), (1), (2) with $Z^2 = \{y^0\}$. Since $Z^2 = W^2$, the process goes through Boxes (4), (5) and (7). At Boxes (7) and (9) we verify that indeed Z^2 is stable and contains the only N-point. The process ends with $Z^2 = \{y^0\}$ as the final solution.

Observe that method 1 and 2 can be made interactive processes by involving the DM in each of some of the steps. The DM's inputs in estimating Λ^n, Z^n, $D(\cdot)$ and W^n can greatly simplify the process, not to mention that it is a learning process which, when properly executed, can be very interesting and convincing to both the researchers and the DM. The process will, in a practical sense, terminate in a finite number of steps: At the end, either final solutions are obtained, or a time limitation is reached, or no further useful conclusion can be derived to justify the continuation.

5.4. Further comments

Being limited by space, we could not explore those questions raised in Remark 5.1, such as under what conditions Y is Λ-convex, and under what conditions local N-points are indeed global N-points? How do we extend the concept of concave functions to concave preference, etc.? The interested reader is referred to Chapter 7 of [46] and the citations therein. Further topics that are related to nondominated solutions can also be found in [1, 22, 36, 41, 42]. Finally, we notice that when $N[\leq?] \neq \emptyset$, it contains only a unique point and the ambiguity of MCDM problems would thus be resolved. How do we restructure MCDM problems as to assure $N[\leq?] \neq \emptyset$? We shall report these explorations in the near future.

6. Linear cases and MC^2 simplex method

6.1. Introduction

When the objective functions and the constraints are defined by linear functions, finding the N-points or final solutions becomes mathematically manageable. In this section we describe the multicriteria (MC) simplex method and the multicriteria multiconstraint-level (MC^2) simplex method to help resolve the difficulty of decision problems.

In algebraic form, the MC^2-simplex method can be represented by

$$\text{`max'} \quad Cx$$

$$\text{s.t.} \quad Ax \leqq D, \quad x \geqq 0, \tag{6.1}$$

where $C = C_{q \times n}$, $A = A_{m \times n}$, and $D = D_{m \times k}$ are matrices. Note that if $k = 1$, D is a vector, and (6.1) becomes the MC simplex problem; and if also $q = 1$, then C is a vector, and (6.1) becomes the ordinary simplex problem.

The MC^2 simplex formulation can arise in many ways. Recall that theorem 5.3 implies that to find N-points, the constraints and the objective functions in mathematical programming formulation are interchangeable. One may put some criteria in constraints with multiple levels and thus result in a MC^2 simplex form. Another case is in the design of optimal systems, in which one wishes to design a system which is optimal over all contingencies rather than finding an optimal point within a given system (see [37] and Chapter 8 of [46] for further discussion). Alternatively, one may view the constraint level as occurring according to a random rule or influenced by some uncertain factor but contained within a set. In multiple person decision-making, the resource levels may reflect the views of different coalitions of the players.

6.2. Nondominated solutions

The following result (see [47]) connects the relationship between N-points and the MC simplex method.

Theorem 6.1. *When D is a column vector, x^0 is an N-point in X with respect to $D(y) = \Lambda^\leqq$ (i.e., $Cx^0 \in N(Y, \Lambda^\leqq)$) iff there exists some $\lambda > 0$ such that x_0 solves*

$$\max \quad \lambda Cx$$
$$\text{s.t.} \quad Ax \leqq D_{m \times 1}, \quad x \geqq 0. \tag{6.2}$$

Thus, by varying λ over $\Lambda^> = \{\lambda \mid \lambda > 0\}$, we can locate all possible nondominated extreme points (N_{ex}-points) of X. Indeed, there are only a finite number of N_{ex}-points) of X. Indeed, there are only a finite number of N_{ex}-points in X and they are connected. (That is to say, by simplex pivoting, one can always arrive at any N_{ex}-point from other N_{ex}-point without leaving the bases of N_{ex}-points.) Locating all N_{ex}-points is in fact computationally feasible. Once all N_{ex}-points are located, they can be used to locate the entire N-points. (See [46, 47] for further discussion.)

Now suppose $\Lambda' = \Lambda \cup \{0\}$ is a general pointed polyhedral cone with $\{H^1, \ldots, H^p\}$ as a generator for Λ^*. One can define $C' = HC$, where H is the matrix with H^j as its j-th row. Then $Cx^0 \in N(Y, \Lambda)$ iff there is $\lambda_{1 \times p} > 0$ so that x^0 is a solution of (6.2) with C' replacing C. (See [46, 47] for further discussion.) This result suggests that in locating N_{ex}-points for a general polyhedral dominated cone Λ, one can first convert the objective coefficient C into C' and then it becomes a problem of locating N_{ex}-points with dominated cone $\Lambda^\leqq$. Thus, unless otherwise specified, we shall assume $D(y) = \Lambda^\leqq$ for all y throughout the remainder of this subsection.

6.3. Potential solutions and MC^2 simplex method

Returning to (6.1), we generalize the concept of nondominated solutions into that of a potential solution by defining: *A basis J is a potential basis* (without confusion we also call J a *potential solution*) for the MC^2 problem (6.1) iff there exist $\lambda > 0$ and $\sigma > 0$ such that J is an optimal basis for

$$\max \quad \lambda C x$$

$$\text{s.t.} \quad A x \leqq D\sigma, \quad x \geqq 0. \tag{6.3}$$

Note that if D is a vector, then $\sigma \in R^1$. By normalization, we can set $\sigma = 1$ and (6.3) reduces to (6.2). Then Theorem 6.1 ensures that a potential solution with D being a vector is indeed an N_{ex}-point. Thus, the concept of potential solutions is a generalization of that of non-dominated solutions.

Note that the simplex tableau of (6.3) can be written as:

A	I	$D\sigma$	
$-\lambda C$	0	0	(6.5)

(6.4) is to the right of the first row; (6.5) to the right of the second row.

Let B be the basis matrix associated with J. Since each set of basic vectors j is uniquely associated with a column index set, we shall, without confusion, let J be this set of indices and J' the set of non-basic columns. The simplex tableau associated with J is

$B^{-1}A$	B^{-1}	$B^{-1}D\sigma$	(6.6)
$\lambda C_B B^{-1}A - \lambda C$	$\lambda C_B B^{-1}$	$\lambda C_B B^{-1}D\sigma$	(6.7)

where $(6.6) = B^{-1} \cdot (6.4)$ (i.e., premultiply (6.4) by B^{-1} on both sides of the equation), $(6.7) = \lambda C_B \cdot (6.6) + (6.5)$, and C_B is the submatrix of criteria columns associated with the basis vectors.

Dropping σ and λ, we obtain the MC^2 simplex tableau associated with basis J:

$B^{-1}A$	B^{-1}	$B^{-1}D$	(6.8)
$C_B B^{-1}A - C$	$C_B B^{-1}$	$C_B B^{-1}D$	(6.9)

which we write as

Y	W
Z	V

where $Y = [B^{-1}A, B^{-1}]$, $W = B^{-1}D$, $Z = [C_B B^{-1}A - C, C_B B^{-1}]$ and $V = C_B B^{-1}D$.

It is immediately obvious that the MC^2 tableau is a symmetric extension of the MC tableau. In fact, for a particular value of σ, the MC^2 problem reduces to the MC problem.

Let $W(J)$ and $Z(J)$ be the submatrices of the tableau associated with basis J.

Define

$$\Gamma(J) = \{\sigma > 0 \,|\, W(J)\sigma \geqq 0\}\,, \qquad \Lambda(J) = \{\lambda > 0 \,|\, \lambda Z(J) \geqq 0\}\,.$$

Note that, because of (6.6) and (6.8), the system is feasible for all $\sigma \in \Gamma(J)$; and because of (6.7) and (6.9), the system is also optimal for all $\lambda \in \Lambda(J)$. Immediately, we have [37, 46]:

Theorem 6.2. *J is a potential solution iff*

$$\Lambda(J) \times \Gamma(J) \neq \emptyset\,.$$

The following can be proved [37, 46], the results of which can be used as effective subroutines for verifying if $\Gamma(J) \neq \emptyset$ and $\Lambda(J) \neq \emptyset$.

Theorem 6.3. *Given a basis J:*
(i) $\Lambda(J) \neq \emptyset$ iff $w_{max} = 0$ for

$$\max \quad w = \sum_{j=1}^{q} e_j$$

$$\text{s.t.} \quad Z(J)x + e = 0\,,$$

$$x \geqq 0\,, \quad e \geqq 0 \quad \text{where } e \in R^q\,;$$

(ii) $\Gamma(J) \neq \emptyset$, iff $w'_{max} = 0$ for

$$\max \quad w' = \sum_{i=1}^{k} d_i$$

$$\text{s.t.} \quad yW(J) + d = 0\,,$$

$$y \geqq 0\,, \quad d \geqq 0 \quad \text{where } d \in R^k\,.$$

There are practical ways to verify whether a basis is a potential solution, and practical ways to determine which constraints are 'effective' or 'redundant' is defining $\Gamma(J)$ and $\Lambda(J)$. It can be shown [37, 46] that the set of all potential bases is connected (that is, using pivoting, one can arrive at any potential solution from any other potential solution without leaving potential bases). This result makes locating all potential solutions feasible. We indeed have a simple PC computer program [6] for locating all potential solutions.

Given a potential basis, its corresponding sets of weights $\Lambda(J)$ and $\Gamma(J)$ on criteria and constraint levels can be specified. Even if we do not know the precise weights λ and σ, as long as $\lambda \in \Lambda(J)$ and $\sigma \in \Gamma(J)$ we know that J is the optimal solution and the decision process terminates at J for the solution. Since there are only a finite number of potential bases, locating them and identifying their corresponding weight sets can greatly simplify the difficulty in finding the 'final' solution. For general domination structures $D(\cdot)$, we may want to apply the second method described in Section 5.3. We first obtain all relevant information concerning the weights among the criteria and the constraint levels and locate some initial set of potential solutions. Then we interact with the DM and iteratively seek the final solution.

6.4. Further comments

MC^2 simplex method is a natural extension of the simplex method. Most results of the simplex method, including duality theory, can be easily extended to that of MC^2 simplex method. Many interesting and related concepts can be found in Chapter 8 of [46] and the citations therein.

7. Conclusion

We have sketched five important topics of MCDM problems. Many more topics such as interactive method including adapted gradient search method [16], surrogate worth tradeoff method [19], Zionts–Wallenius method [51], preference over uncertain outcomes, multicriteria dynamic optimization problems, and second order games can be found in Chapter 10 of [46] and the citations therein. The following books [2, 11, 14, 18, 20, 23, 24, 27, 29, 35, 36, 40, 43, 50] can also be of interest to readers for further exploration. The reader who is interested in decision aid and MCDM in abstract spaces is referred to [32] and to [7] respectively and the citations therein.

Finally, let us observe that with creative thinking and processing, two numbers (0 and 1) can generate infinitely many numbers in complex numerical systems; three primary colors (red, yellow and blue) can produce an infinite spectrum of colors; and seven basic notes of sound (do, ra, mi, . . .) can compose an infinite number of songs. Undoubtedly, with creative thinking and practicing, the five basic concepts of MCDM can generate infinitely many more concepts and be applied to infinite many nontrivial problems. Rigid habitual ways of thinking usually are the stumbling blocks to creativity. In solving nontrivial decision problems, we need not only the mastery of the mathematical tools but also a good understanding of human behavior and common wisdom (see Chapter 9 of [46] for a detailed discussion). At least, we should not become overenthusiastic with one particular concept or method as to cut our 'feet' to fit the already made 'shoes'.

References

[1] Benson, H.P. and Morin, T.L., The vector maximization problem: Proper efficiency and stability, *SIAM J. Applied Mathematics* **32** (1977) 64–72.
[2] Changkong, V. and Haimes, Y.Y., *Multiobjective Decision Making: Theory and Methodology* (North-Holland, New York, 1983).

[3] Charnes, A. and Cooper, W.W., Goal programming and constrained regression–A comment, *Omega* **3** (1975) 403–409.

[4] Cogger, K.O. and Yu, P.L., Eigen weight vectors and least distance approximation for revealed preference in pairwise weight ratios, *J. Optim. Theory Appl.* **46**(4) (1985) 483–491.

[5] Chien, I.S., Restructuring and Computer Support in Multiple Criteria Decision Making, Ph.D. Dissertation, School of Business, University of Kansas, Lawrence, KS (1987).

[6] Chien, I.S. and Yu, P.L., MC2, PC program for MC^2-simplex method. Interested readers, please send \$9 (handling fee) for a diskette.

[7] Dauer, J.P. and Stadler, W., A survey of vector optimization in infinite-dimensional space, Part 2, *J. Optim. Theory Appl.* **51**(2) (1986) 205–241.

[8] Debreu, G., Representation of a Preference Ordering by a Numerical Function, in: R.M. Thrall, C.H. Coombs, and R.L. Davis (eds.), *Decision Processes* (Wiley, New York, 1954).

[9] Debreu, G., Topological methods in cardinal utility theory, in: K.J. Arrow, S. Karlin, and P. Suppes (eds.), *Mathematical Methods in Social Sciences* (Stanford University Press, Stanford, CA, 1960).

[10] Dyer, J.S., Interactive goal programming, *Management Science* **19** (1970) 62–70.

[11] Fandel, G., Grauer, M., Kurzhanski, A. and Wierzbicki, A.P. (eds.), *Large-Scale Modelling and Interactive Decision Analysis*, Proceedings, *Eisenach, GRD, 1985*, Lecture Notes in Economics and Mathematical Systems No. 273 (Springer-Verlag, New York, 1986).

[12] Fishburn, P.C., *Utility Theory for Decision Making* (Wiley, New York, 1970).

[13] Freimer M. and Yu, P.L., Some new results on compromise solutions for group decision problems, *Management Science* **22** (1976) 688–693.

[14] Gal, T., *Postoptimal Analyses, Parametric Programming and Related Topics* (McGraw-Hill, New York, 1979).

[15] Gearhart, W.B., Compromise solutions and estimation of the noninferior set, *J. Optim. Theory Appl.* **28** (1979) 29–47.

[16] Geoffrion, A.M., Dyer, J.S. and Feinberg, A., An interactive approach for multicriteria optimization with an application to operation of an academic department, *Management Science* **19** (1972) 357–368.

[17] Gorman, W.M., The structure of utility functions, *Rev. Econ. Stud.* **35** (1968) 367–390.

[18] Haimes, Y.Y., and Changkong, V. (eds.), *Decision Making with Multiple Objectives*, Proceedings, *Cleveland, OH, 1984*, Lecture Notes in Economics and Mathematical Systems No. 242 (Springer-Verlag, New York, 1985).

[19] Haimes, Y.Y. and Hall, W.A., Multiobjectives in water resources systems analysis: The surrogate worth trade off method, *Water Resource Research* **10** (1974) 615–623.

[20] Hansen, P. (ed.), *Essays and Surveys on Multiple Criteria Decision Making*, Proceedings, *Mons, 1982*, Lecture Notes in Economics and Mathematical Systems No. 209 (Springer-Verlag, New York, 1983).

[21] Hartley, R., On cone-efficiency, cone-convexity and cone-compactness, *SIAM J. Applied Mathematics* **34** (1978) 211–222.

[22] Hazen, G.B., and Morin, T.L., Optimality conditions for non-conical multiple-objective programming, *J. Optim. Theory Appl.* **40** (1983) 25–59.

[23] Hwang, C.L. and Masud, A.S.M., *Multiple Objective Decision Making – Methods and Applications: A State-of-the-Art Survey* (Springer-Verlag, New York, 1979).

[24] Hwang, C.L. and Yoon, K., *Multiple Attribute Decision Making – Methods and Applications: A State-of-the-Art Survey* (Springer-Verlag, New York, 1981).

[25] Ignizio, J.P., *Goal Programming and Extensions* (D.C. Heath, Lexington, MA, 1976).

[26] Keeney, R.L. and Raiffa, H., *Decisions with Multiple Objectives: Preferences and Value Tradeoffs* (Wiley, New York, 1976).

[27] Krantz, D.H., Luce, R.D., Suppes, P. and Tversky, A., *Foundations of Measurement* Vol. I (Academic Press, New York, 1971).

[28] Lee, S.M., *Goal Programming for Decision Analysis* (Auerbach, Philadelphia, PA, 1972).

[29] Morse, J.N. (ed.), *Organizations: Multiple Agents with Multiple Criteria*, Proceedings, *University of Delaware, Newark, 1980*, Lecture Notes in Economics and Mathematical Systems No. 190 (Springer-Verlag, New York, 1981).

[30] Pareto, V., *Manuale di Economica Politica*, Societa Editrice Libraria, Milano, Italy, 1906; Piccola Biblioteca Scientifica No. 13 (Societa Editrice Libraria, Milano, Italy, 1919). Translated into English by A.S. Schwier, as *Manual of Political Economy* (MacMillan, New York, 1971).

[31] Pascoletti, A. and Serafini, P., Scalarizing vector optimization problems, *J. Optim. Theory Appl.* **42** (1984) 499–524.

[32] Roy, B. A conceptual framework for a prescriptive theory of decision-aid, in: M.K. Starr and M. Zeleny (eds.), *Multiple Criteria Decision Making*, TIMS Studies in Management Sciences, Vol. 6 (North-Holland, Amsterdam, 1977).

[33] Roy, B. and Vincke, Ph., Pseudo-orders: Definition, properties and numerical representation, *Mathematical Social Sciences* **14** (1987) 263–274.

[34] Saaty, T.L., *The Analytic Hierarchy Process* (McGraw-Hill, New York, 1980).

[35] Sawaragi, Y., Inoue, K. and Nakayama, H. (eds.), *Toward Interactive and Intelligent Decision Support Systems – Volume 1 and 2, Proceedings, Kyoto, Japan, 1986*, Lecture Notes in Economics and Mathematical Systems No. 285 (Springer-Verlag, New York, 1987).

[36] Sawaragi, Y., Nakayama, H. and Tanino, T., *Theory of Multiobjective Optimization* (Academic Press, Orlando, FL, 1985).

[37] Seiford, L. and Yu, P.L., Potential solutions of linear systems: The multi-criteria multiple constraint levels program, *J. Math. Anal. Appl.* **69** (1979) 283–303.

[38] Stadler, W., A survey of multicriteria optimization or the vector maximization problem, Part I: 1776–1960, *J. Optim. Theory Appl.* **69** (1979) 1–52.

[39] Stadler, W., A Comprehensive Bibliography on Multicriteria Decision Making and Related Areas, University of California, Working Paper, Berkeley, CA (1981).

[40] Steuer, R.E., *Multiple Criteria Optimization* (Wiley, New York, 1985).

[41] Takeda, F. and Nishida, T., Multiple criteria decision problems with fuzzy domination structures, *Fuzzy Sets and Systems* **3** (1980) 123–136.

[42] Tanino, T. and Sawaragi, Y., Stability of Nondominated Solutions in Multicriteria Decision Making, *J. Optim. Theory Appl.* **30** (1980) 229–253.

[43] White, D.J., *Optimality and Efficiency* (Wiley, New York, 1982).

[44] Yu, P.L., A class of solutions for group decision problems, *Management Science* **19** (1973) 936–946.

[45] Yu, P.L., Cone convexity, cone extreme points and nondominated solutions in decision problems with multiobjectives, *J. Optim. Theory Appl.* **14** (1974) 319–377.

[46] Yu, P.L., *Multiple Criteria Decision Making: Concepts, Techniques and Extensions* (Plenum Press, New York, 1985).

[47] Yu, P.L. and Zeleny, M., The set of all nondominated solutions in the linear case and a multicriteria simplex method, *J. Math. Anal. Appl.* **49** (1974) 430–468.

[48] Yu, P.L. and Takeda, E., A verification theorem of preference separability for additive value functions, *J. Math. Anal. Appl.* **126**(2) (1987) 382–396.

[49] Zeleny, M., The theory of the displaced ideal, in: M. Zeleny (ed.), *Multiple Criteria Decision Making: Kyoto 1975* (Springer-Verlag, New York, 1975) 151–205.

[50] Zeleny M., *Multiple Criteria Decision Making* (McGraw-Hill, New York, 1982).

[51] Zionts, S. and Wallenius, J., An interactive programming method for solving the multiple criteria problem, *Management Science* **22** (1976) 652–663.

Subject Index